Mandarin Chinese
Concise Dictionary

Chinese – English
English – Chinese

Berlitz Publishing
New York · Munich · Singapore

Edited by the Langenscheidt editorial staff

Based on a dictionary compiled by LEXUS

Activity section by Jenny Ying Lu

Book in cover photo: © Punchstock/Medioimages

© 2007 Berlitz Publishing/APA Publications GmbH & Co. Verlag KG
Singapore Branch, Singapore

Berlitz Publishing
193 Morris Avenue
Springfield, NJ 07081
USA

Printed in Germany
ISBN 978-981-268-019-8

07 08 09 10 11 5. 4. 3. 2. 1.

Preface

This new dictionary of English and Chinese is a tool with more than 40,000 references for learners of the Chinese language at beginner's or intermediate level.

The Chinese in this dictionary is mainland Chinese, written in simplified characters, with pinyin pronunciation. A short appendix of important Taiwanese equivalents in traditional characters has also been included.

The two sides of this dictionary, the English-Chinese and the Chinese-English, are quite different in structure and purpose. The English-Chinese is designed for productive usage, for self-expression in Chinese. The Chinese-English, which can also be accessed through a specially compiled radical index, is a decoding dictionary to enable the native speaker of English to understand Chinese.

Clarity of presentation has been a major objective. Is the *mouse* you need for your computer, for example, the same in Chinese as the *mouse* you don't want in the house? The English-Chinese dictionary is rich in sense distinctions like this – and in translation options tied to specific, identified senses. The user-friendly layout with all headwords in blue allows the user to have quick access to all the words, expressions and their translations.

The additional activity section provides the user with an opportunity to develop language skills with a selection of engaging word puzzles. The games are designed specifically to improve vocabulary, spelling, grammar and comprehension in an enjoyable style.

Designed for a wide variety of uses, this dictionary will be of great value to those who wish to learn Chinese and have fun at the same time.

Contents

How to use the dictionary

To get the most out of your dictionary you should understand how and where to find the information you need. Whether you are writing a text in Chinese or want to understand a text in Chinese, the following pages should help.

1. How and where do I find a word?

1.1 English headwords. The English word list is arranged in alphabetical order.

Sometimes you might want to look up terms made up of two separate words, for example **antivirus program**, or hyphenated words, for example **absent-minded**. These words are treated as though they were a single word and their alphabetical ordering reflects this. Compound words like **bookseller**, **bookstall**, **bookstore** are also listed in alphabetical order.

The only exception to this strict alphabetical ordering is made for English phrasal verbs – words like ♦**go off**, ♦**go out**, ♦**go up**. These are positioned directly after their main verb (in this case **go**), rather than being scattered around in alphabetical positions.

1.2 Chinese headwords. The Chinese word list is arranged in English alphabetical order by being sorted on the romanization system, pinyin. So if you know how a word is pronounced, or how it is written in pinyin, you can look it up straightforwardly.

If, however, you are decoding a Chinese character, and have no idea how it is pronounced or written in pinyin, then you will have to make use of the Radical Index in order to find out the pinyin for the character in question. An explanation of the Radical Index is given on page 14.

1.3 Running heads

If you are looking for an English or a Chinese word you can use the **running heads** printed in bold in the top corner of each page. The running head on the left tells you the *first* headword or compound on the left-hand page and the one on the right tells you the *last* headword or compound on the right-hand page.

2. Swung dashes

2.1 A swung dash (~) replaces the entire headword when the headword is repeated within an entry:

> **sly** jiǎohuá 狡猾; *on the* ~ mìmì 秘密

Here *on the* ~ means *on the sly*.

2.2 When a headword changes form in an entry, for example if it is put in the past tense or in the plural, then the past tense or plural ending is added to the swung dash - but only if the rest of the word doesn't change:

> **fluster** *v/t* shǐ jǐnzhāng 使紧张; *get ~ed* jǐnzhāng 紧张

> **fore**: *come to the* ~ tuō yǐng ér chū 脱颖而出

But:

> **horrify**: *I was horrified* wǒ bèi xiàhuàile 我被吓坏了

> ***come back** huílái 回来; *it came back to me* wǒ xiǎng qǐláile 我想起来了

2.3 Double or treble headwords are replaced by a single swung dash:

> ♦ **hold on** *(wait,* TELEC*)* děngyíxià 等一下; *now ~ a minute!* biézháojí! 别着急!

> ♦ **measure up to**: *~X* dádào X de biāozhǔn 达到X的标准

3. What do the different typefaces mean?

3.1 All Chinese and English headwords and the Arabic numerals differentiating between English parts of speech appear in **bold**:

> **alcoholic 1** *n* xùjiǔ zhě 酗酒者 **2** *adj* hán jiǔjīng 含酒精

3.2 *italics* are used for:

a) abbreviated grammatical labels: *adj, adv, v/i, v/t* etc
b) all the indicating words which are the signposts pointing to the correct translation for your needs
c) explanations

> **mailbox** *(in street)* yóutǒng 邮筒; *(for house, e-mail)* xìnxiāng 信箱

Thai 1 *adj* Tàiguó 泰国 **2** *n* (*person*) Tàiguó rén 泰国人; (*language*) Tàiguó yǔ 泰国语

serve 1 *n* (*in tennis*) fāqiú 发球 **2** *v/t food, meal* duānshang 端上; *customer in store* zhāodài 招待; *one's country, the people* fúwù 服务

水面 **shuǐmiàn** surface (*of water*)

伤感情 **shānggǎnqíng** hurt (*emotionally*)

把 **bǎ** *measure word for knives and chairs*; 一把刀 *yìbǎ dāo* a knife; 一把钳子 *yìbǎ qiánzi* a pair of pliers/pincers ◊ (*marking an object moved for emphasis to the start of a sentence*): 我要把车修了 *wǒ yào bǎ chē xiūle* I'll have the car repaired

3.3 All phrases (examples and idioms) are given in **secondary bold italics**:

剩 **shèng** remain, be left over; 没剩什么 *méishèng shénme* there is nothing left

vent *n* (*for air*) tōngfēng kǒng 通风孔; *give ~ to feelings, emotions* fàxiè 发泄

3.4 The normal typeface is used for the translations.

3.5 If a translation is given in italics, and not in the normal typeface, this means that the translation is more of an *explanation* in the other language and that an explanation has to be given because there is no real equivalent:

stag party *hūnqián nánzi jùhuì* 婚前男子聚会

阿姨 **āyí** auntie (*used also to address a woman of an age similar to one's parents*)

4. What do the various symbols and abbreviations tell you?

4.1 A solid black lozenge is used to indicate a phrasal verb:

♦**auction off** *v/t* pāimài diào 拍卖掉

4.2 A white lozenge is used to divide up longer entries into more easily digested chunks of related bits of text:

a, an ◊ (*no translation*): *~ bus* gōnggòng qìchē 公共汽车; *I'm ~ student* wǒ shì xuésheng 我是学生 ◊ (*with a measure word*) yī 一; *can I have ~ cup of coffee?* qǐng

gěi wǒ yìbēi kāfēi? 请给我一杯咖啡?; *five men and ~ woman* wǔge nánde yíge nǔde 五个男的一个女的
◊ (*per*): *$50 ~ time* yícì wǔshí měiyuán 一次五十美元

It is also used, in the Chinese-English dictionary, to split different translations when the part of speech of each translation is different:

白 **bái** white ◊ in vain ◊ family name

冷冻 **lěngdòng** freeze ◊ frozen

4.3 The abbreviation F tells you that the word or phrase is used colloquially rather than in formal contexts. The abbreviation V warns you that a word or phrase is vulgar or taboo. Be careful how you use these words.

4.4 The symbol ⇩ means that a Taiwanese equivalent translation is given in the Taiwanese appendix on pages 669-671.

4.5 A colon before an English or Chinese word or phrase means that usage is restricted to this specific example (at least as far as this dictionary's choice of vocabulary is concerned):

accord *of one's own ~* zìyuàn 自愿

通缉 **tōngjī** 被通缉 **bèi tōngjī** wanted

4.6 The letters X and Y are used to indicate insertion points for other words if you are building a complete sentence in Chinese, for example:

grateful gǎnjī 感激; *be ~ to X* duì X xīncún gǎnjī 对 X 心存感激

pelt 1 *v/t*: *~ X with Y* jiāng Y tóuxiàng X 将 Y 投向 X

Suspension points (...) are used in a similar way:

below 1 *prep* zài … de xiàmian 在 … 的下面

5. Does the dictionary deal with grammar too?

5.1 All English headwords are given a part of speech label, unless, in normal modern English, the headword is only used as one part of speech and so no confusion or ambiguity is likely. In these cases no part of speech label is needed.

abolish fèichú 废除

lastly zuìhòu 最后

glory *n* róngyù 荣誉

own[1] *v/t* yōngyǒu 拥有

5.2 Chinese headwords are not given part of speech labels. Where their English translations can be of more than one part of speech, then these are separated by a white lozenge. For example:

> 统 计 **tǒngjì** statistics ◊ statistical

> 挖 掘 **wājué** excavate ◊ excavation

5.3 Where a Chinese word has a grammatical function, this is illustrated:

> 被 **bèi** quilt ◊ (*passive indicator*): 被 炒 鱿 鱼 了 ***bèi chǎo yóuyú le*** be fired; 被 淘 汰 ***bèi táotài*** be eliminated

> 了 **le** (*particle indicating completed action*): 雨 停 了 ***yǔtíngle*** it has stopped raining ◊ (*particle indicating change of state*): 头 发 白 了 ***tóufa báile*** his hair is going gray; 我 买 了 ***wǒ mǎi le*** I'll take it ◊ (*for emphasis*): 你 太 好 了 ***nǐ tài hǎo le*** that's very kind

6. de 的 with adjectives.

In translations of adjectives the word **de** 的 has been omitted. This should be added if you are using a Chinese adjective (especially one of more than one syllable) attributively before a noun. Usually the noun would also have to have more than one syllable:

> **faded** *color*, *jeans* tuìsè 退色

> **faded jeans** tuìsède niúzǎikù 退色 的 牛仔裤

The pronunciation of Chinese

All Chinese characters in this dictionary are accompanied by a romanized script known as pinyin. Not all pinyin letters, or groups of letters, are pronounced as you would normally expect them to be in English. The following is a guide to the pronunciation of pinyin.

Initial consonants

b	more abrupt than English, like p in s*p*are
c	like ts in be*ts*
ch	like ch in *ch*urch, pronounced with the tip of the tongue curled back
d	more abrupt than English, like t in s*t*are
g	more abrupt than English, like c in s*c*are; always hard as in *g*o or *g*irl
h	like the Scottish pronunciation of lo*ch*, with a little friction in the throat
j	like j in *j*eep, pronounced with the lips spread as in a smile
k	pronounced with a slight puff of air as in *c*op
p	pronounced with a slight puff of air as in *p*op
q	like ch in *ch*eap, pronounced with the lips spread as in a smile
r	like r in *r*ung, pronounced with the tip of the tongue curled back
sh	like sh in *sh*irt, pronounced with the tip of the tongue curled back
t	pronounced with a slight puff of air as in *t*op
x	like sh in *sh*eep, pronounced with the lips spread as in a smile
z	like ds in be*ds*
zh	like j in *j*udge, pronounced with the tip of the tongue curled back

Finals

a	as in f*a*ther
ai	as in *ai*sle
an	as in r*an* (with the *a* slightly longer as in *ah*); but: yan as in *yen*
ang	as in r*ang* (with the *a* slightly longer as in *ah*)
ao	like ow in h*ow*
e	as in h*er*
ei	as in *ei*ght
en	as in op*en*
eng	like *en* in op*en* and g

er   like *err* – but with the tongue curled back and the sound coming from the back of the throat

i   (1) as in maga*zi*ne
      (2) after c, ch, r, s, sh, z and zh like the i in b*i*rd

ia   like ya in *y*ard

ian   similar to *yen*

iang *i* (as in maga*zi*ne) merged with *ang* (above) – but without lengthening the *a*

iao   as in *yow*l

ie   like ye in *ye*s

in   as in th*in*

ing   as in th*ing*

iong *i* (as in maga*zi*ne) merged with *ong* (below)

iu   like yo in *yo*ga

o   as in m*o*re

ou   as in d*ou*gh

ong   oong with oo as in s*oo*n

u   (1) as in r*u*le
      (2) after j, q and x like the 'u' sound in French t*u* or German *ü*ber

ua   w followed by *a* (above)

uai   similar to *why*

uan   w followed by *an* (above)

uang w followed by *ang* (above)

ue   u (above) followed by e as in l*e*t

ui   similar to *way*

un   like uan in tr*uan*t

uo   similar to *war*

ü   as in French t*u* or German *ü*ber

üe   ü followed by e as in g*e*t

Tones

First tone, as in 鸡 **jī** (chicken): a high, level tone with the volume held constant.

Second tone, as in 极 **jí** (extreme, extremely): rises sharply from middle register and increasing in volume, shorter than the first tone; like a surprised 'what?'

Third tone, as in 脊 **jǐ** (ridge): starts low, then falls lower before rising again to a point slightly higher than the starting point; louder at the beginning and end than in the middle; slightly longer than the first tone.

Fourth tone, as in 季 **jì** (season): starts high then drops sharply in pitch and volume; like saying 'right' when agreeing to an instruction.

Abbreviations

adj	adjective	NAUT	nautical
adv	adverb	*pej*	pejorative
ANAT	anatomy	PHOT	photography
BIO	biology	PHYS	physics
BOT	botany	POL	politics
Br	British English	*prep*	preposition
CHEM	chemistry	*pron*	pronoun
COM	commerce, business	*prov*	proverbial
		PSYCH	psychology
COMPUT	computers, IT term	RAD	radio
		RAIL	railroad
conj	conjunction	REL	religion
EDU	education	s.o.	someone
ELEC	electricity, electronics	SP	sports
		sth	something
F	familiar, colloquial	TECH	technology
fig	figurative	TELEC	telecommunications
FIN	financial	THEA	theatre
fml	formal usage	TV	television
GRAM	grammar	V	vulgar
hum	humorous	*v/i*	intransitive verb
interj	interjection	*v/t*	transitive verb
LAW	law	→	see
MATH	mathematics	®	registered trademark
MED	medicine		
MIL	military	⇩	Taiwanese equivalent given in the appendix
MOT	motoring		
MUS	music		

How to find Chinese characters in the Chinese-English dictionary using the Radical Index

How can I look up the meaning of a Chinese character if I don't know how to pronounce it? This is a problem that the Radical Index solves.

There are two sets of tables to be used: the Radical Chart and the Radical Index. The Radical Chart is a means for leading you into the Radical Index; and the Radical Index is a means for leading you to the entry in the Chinese-English dictionary.

1. First you have to identify the radical in the Chinese character which you want to look up. Then look for this radical in the Radical Chart on pages 14-15 and find its radical number.

2. Go to the Radical Index and find the section starting with the number allocated to the radical you have just looked up. This number is printed as a heading.

3. If this is a shortish section, you will be able to see the Chinese character you want without any difficulty. If this is a long section, you can use another device to home in on the character you are looking for.

4. Count the number of strokes in the character you are looking for (not including the strokes in the radical itself). The Chinese characters are listed according to their stroke count. The number to the left of the characters gives you the stroke count (minus the radical strokes) in each block of characters. This narrows down the list of characters you will have to scan through.

5. When you have found the character you are looking for in the Radical Index, you will see its pinyin pronunciation given. You can then go to the Chinese-English dictionary - which is ordered in English alphabetical order according to the pinyin pronunciation - and use this like an ordinary dictionary.

6. Some Chinese characters can be analyzed as having more than one possible radical. When this happens, we have used the radical which has the smallest number of strokes.

7. Some radicals have variants. These are listed after the main radical in both the Radical Chart and the Radical Index.

Radical Chart

1 stroke

#	Radical
1	丶
2	一
3	丨
4	丿
5	乙,乛,亅,乚

2 strokes

#	Radical
6	亠
7	冫
8	冖
9	讠
10	二
11	十
12	厂
13	匚
14	卜
15	刂
16	冂
17	八,丷
18	人,入
19	亻
20	勹
21	几,凡
22	厶
23	又,㕛
24	廴
25	辶
26	卩,㔾
27	阝 (left)
28	阝 (right)
29	凵
30	刀,ク
31	力

3 strokes

#	Radical
32	氵
33	忄,小
34	宀
35	丬
36	广
37	门
38	辶
39	工
40	土
41	士
42	艹
43	大
44	廾
45	尢
46	寸
47	扌
48	小,⺌
49	口
50	囗
51	巾
52	山
53	彳
54	彡
55	夕
56	夂
57	犭
58	饣
59	彐,彑
60	彐,彑

4 strokes

#	Radical
61	尸
62	己,巳
63	弓
64	女
65	幺
66	子
67	纟
68	马
69	巛
70	灬
71	斗
72	文
73	方
74	火
75	心
76	户
77	衤
78	王
79	韦
80	木
81	犬
82	歹
83	车
84	戈
85	比
86	瓦
87	止
88	支
89	日
90	曰
91	贝

15

92 见	129 疋,疋	163 采
93 父	130 皮	164 身
94 牛,牛,牛		165 角
95 手	**6 strokes**	
96 毛		**8 strokes**
97 气	131 衣	
98 攵	132 羊,⺶,⺷	166 青
99 片	133 米	167 其
100 斤	134 耒	168 雨
101 爪,爫	135 老	169 齿
102 月	136 耳	170 金
103 欠	137 西,襾	171 隹
104 风	138 页	172 鱼
105 殳	139 庀	
106 聿,⺕,⺻	140 虫	**9 strokes**
107 毌	141 缶	
108 水,氺	142 舌	173 音
	143 竹,⺮	174 革
5 strokes	144 臼	175 骨
	145 自	176 食
109 穴	146 血	177 鬼
110 立	147 舟	
111 疒	148 羽	**10 strokes**
112 衤	149 艮,阝	
113 示	150 糸	178 髟
114 石		
115 龙	**7 strokes**	**11 strokes**
116 业		
117 目	151 辛	179 鹿
118 田	152 言	
119 罒	153 麦	**12 strokes**
120 皿	154 走	
121 钅	155 赤	180 黑
122 矢	156 豆	181 鼠
123 禾	157 酉	
124 白	158 辰	**14 strokes**
125 瓜	159 里	
126 鸟	160 足	182 鼻
127 用	161 豸	
128 矛	162 谷	

Radical Index

甲 jiǎ
申 shēn
且 qiě
史 shǐ
央 yāng
凹 āo
出 chū
归 guī
5 师 shī
曳 yè
6 串 chuàn
7 非 fēi
畅 chàng
8 临 lín

4 丿

1 九 jiǔ
乃 nǎi
匕 bǐ
2 千 qiān
川 chuān
么 me
久 jiǔ
及 jí
3 乏 fá
午 wǔ
升 shēng
长 zhǎng, cháng
币 bì
反 fǎn
丹 dān
氏 shì

乌 wū
4 乎 hū
生 shēng
失 shī
乐 lè, yuè
丘 qiū
5 丢 diū
年 nián
乒 pāng
杀 shā
后 hòu
向 xiàng
兆 zhào
6 卵 luǎn
希 xī
囱 cōng
系 xì, jì
7 乖 guāi
8 拜 bài
垂 chuí
重 zhòng, chóng
9 乘 chéng
11 甥 shēng
13 孵 fū
舞 wǔ
睾 gāo
14 靠 kào

5 乙, 乛, 亅, 乚

乙 yǐ
1 刁 diāo

了 le, liǎo
2 飞 fēi
乞 qǐ
习 xí
也 yě
3 书 shū
以 yǐ
予 yǔ
孔 kǒng
4 电 diàn
民 mín
司 sī
5 买 mǎi
6 乱 luàn
7 乳 rǔ
承 chéng
14 豫 yù

6 亠

1 亡 wáng
2 六 liù
3 市 shì
4 亥 hài
交 jiāo
亦 yì
5 亩 mǔ
弃 qì
6 变 biàn
卒 zú
京 jīng
氓 máng
享 xiǎng
夜 yè

7 哀 āi	14 凝 níng	5 词 cí
亮 liàng		评 píng
亭 tíng	**8 冖**	识 shí
8 高 gāo		诉 sù
离 lí	2 冗 rǒng	译 yì
衰 shuāi	3 写 xiě	诈 zhà
衷 zhōng	4 军 jūn	诊 zhěn
9 毫 háo	5 罕 hǎn	证 zhèng
率 shuài	7 冠 guàn,	诅 zǔ
烹 pēng	guān	诋 dǐ
10 就 jiù		6 诧 chà
亵 xiè	**9 讠**	诚 chéng
12 膏 gāo		该 gāi
裹 guǒ	2 订 dìng	诡 guǐ
豪 háo	讣 fù	话 huà
15 赢 yíng	讥 jī	诗 shī
	计 jì	试 shì
7 冫	认 rèn	详 xiáng
	3 记 jì	询 xún
4 冰 bīng	让 ràng	诘 jié
冲 chōng	讨 tǎo	诙 huī
次 cì	训 xùn	7 诞 dàn
决 jué	讯 xùn	诲 huì
5 冻 dòng	议 yì	说 shuō,
况 kuàng	4 访 fǎng	shuì
冷 lěng	讽 fěng	诵 sòng
冶 yě	讳 huì	诬 wū
6 净 jìng	讲 jiǎng	误 wù
8 准 zhǔn	诀 jué	诱 yòu
凋 diāo	论 lùn	语 yǔ
凉 liáng	设 shè	8 调 diào,
凌 líng	讼 sòng	tiáo
9 凑 còu	许 xǔ	读 dú
减 jiǎn	讶 yà	诽 fěi

课 kè
谅 liàng
诺 nuò
请 qǐng
谁 shuí
谈 tán
谊 yì
诿 wěi
9 谍 dié
谎 huǎng
谜 mí
谋 móu
谓 wèi
谐 xié
谚 yàn
10 谦 qiān
谤 bàng
谢 xiè
谣 yáo
11 谨 jǐn
谬 miù
12 谱 pǔ
13 遣 qiǎn
谵 zhān

10 二

二 èr
1 亏 kuī
2 云 yún
6 些 xiē

11 十

十 shí
2 支 zhī
3 古 gǔ
4 华 huá
协 xié
5 克 kè
6 卓 zhuó
卑 bēi
卖 mài
丧 sāng,
   sàng
直 zhí
卒 zú
7 南 nán
8 真 zhēn
索 suǒ
9 啬 sè
10 博 bó
韩 hán
辜 gū

12 厂

厂 chǎng
2 厄 è
历 lì
厅 tīng
3 厉 lì
4 厌 yàn
压 yā
6 厕 cè
7 厚 hòu

厘 lí
8 原 yuán
9 厩 jiù
厢 xiāng
10 厨 chú
厦 xià,
   shà
厥 jué
12 厮 sī
14 赝 yàn

13 匚

2 区 qū
巨 jù
匹 pǐ
4 匠 jiàng
5 匣 xiá
医 yī
8 匪 fěi
匿 nì

14 卜

卜 bǔ
3 卡 kǎ, qiǎ
外 wài
处 chù,
   chǔ
占 zhàn
4 贞 zhēn
6 卧 wò
卓 zhuó

15 刂

3	刊	kān
4	创	chuàng
	刚	gāng
	划	huá, huà
	列	liè
	刑	xíng
	则	zé
	刘	liú
5	别	bié
	利	lì
	判	pàn
	刨	bào
	删	shān
6	刺	cì
	到	dào
	刮	guā
	刽	guì
	剂	jì
	刻	kè
	刹	chà, shā
	刷	shuā
	制	zhì
7	剑	jiàn
	剃	tì
	削	xiāo, xuē
8	剥	bō, bāo
	剧	jù
	剖	pōu
	剔	tī
9	副	fù
10	割	gē
	剩	shèng

16 冂

2	内	nèi
4	肉	ròu
	同	tóng
	网	wǎng
6	周	zhōu

17 八，丷

	八	bā
2	分	fēn
	公	gōng
3	兰	lán
	只	zhǐ, zhī
4	并	bìng
	共	gòng
	关	guān
	兴	xīng, xìng
5	兑	duì
	兵	bīng
	弟	dì
6	单	dān, chán
	典	diǎn
	具	jù
	卷	juǎn, juàn
7	兹	zī
	前	qián

	首	shǒu
	差	chà, cī, chā, chāi
8	兼	jiān
9	黄	huáng
	兽	shòu
10	尊	zūn

18 人，入

	人	rén
	入	rù
1	个	gè
2	仓	cāng
	从	cóng
	介	jiè
	今	jīn
3	丛	cóng
	令	lìng
4	合	hé
	会	huì
	企	qǐ
	全	quán
	伞	sǎn
	众	zhòng
	尬	gà
5	含	hán
	余	yú
6	命	mìng
	舍	shě, shè
10	禽	qín
	舒	shū

19 亻

1 亿 yì
2 仇 chóu
  化 huà
  仅 jǐn
  仆 pū, pú
  仁 rén
  仍 réng
  什 shí,
     shén
3 代 dài
  付 fù
  们 men
  他 tā
  仙 xiān
  仪 yí
  仗 zhàng
  仔 zǎi, zǐ
4 传 chuán
  伐 fá
  仿 fǎng
  份 fèn
  伏 fú
  伙 huǒ
  价 jià
  件 jiàn
  伦 lún
  任 rèn
  伤 shāng
  似 sì, shì
  伟 wěi
  伪 wěi
  伍 wǔ

  休 xiū
  仰 yǎng
  伊 yī
  优 yōu
  仲 zhòng
5 伴 bàn
  伯 bó
  但 dàn
  低 dī
  佛 fó
  估 gū
  何 hé
  伶 líng
  你 nǐ
  伸 shēn
  伺 cì
  体 tǐ
  位 wèi
  佣 yòng,
     yōng
  佑 yòu
  住 zhù
  作 zuò,
     zuō
6 侧 cè
  侈 chǐ
  供 gōng,
     gòng
  佳 jiā
  侥 jiǎo,
     yáo
  佬 lǎo
  例 lì
  侣 lyǔ

  佩 pèi
  侨 qiáo
  使 shǐ
  侍 shì
  侠 xiá
  依 yī
  侦 zhēn
  侄 zhí
  侏 zhū
7 保 bǎo
  便 biàn
  促 cù
  俄 é
  俘 fú
  侯 hóu
  俭 jiǎn
  俊 jùn
  俐 lì
  俩 liǎ,
     liǎng
  俏 qiào
  侵 qīn
  俗 sú
  侮 wǔ
  信 xìn
  修 xiū
  俚 lǐ
  俑 yǒng
8 倍 bèi
  倡 chàng
  倒 dǎo,
     dào
  俯 fǔ
  候 hòu

健 jiàn
借 jiè
俱 jù
倦 juàn
倾 qīng
倚 yǐ
债 zhài
值 zhí
倌 guān
9 偿 cháng
假 jiǎ,
    jià
傀 kuǐ
偶 ǒu
偏 piān
停 tíng
偷 tōu
做 zuò
10 傲 ào
傍 bàng
储 chǔ
傅 fù
傧 bīn
11 催 cuī
傻 shǎ
12 僚 liáo
像 xiàng
13 僵 jiāng
僻 pì
14 儒 rú
15 儡 lěi

20 勹

1 勺 sháo
2 勾 gōu
勿 wù
匀 yún
3 包 bāo
匆 cōng
句 jù
4 匈 xiōng
5 甸 diàn
7 匍 pú
9 够 gòu
匐 fú

21 儿

儿 ér
2 允 yǔn
3 兄 xiōng
4 先 xiān
充 chōng
光 guāng
5 克 kè
兑 duì
9 兜 dōu

22 几, 几

几 jǐ
1 凡 fán
2 凤 fèng
5 壳 ké, qiào
秃 tū

6 凯 kǎi
凭 píng
9 凰 huáng
12 凳 dèng

23 厶

2 允 yǔn
3 台 tái
去 qù
5 县 xiàn
6 参 cān
7 垒 lěi
8 能 néng

24 又, ㄨ

又 yòu
1 叉 chā
2 双 shuāng
友 yǒu
劝 quàn
支 zhī
3 对 duì
发 fā, fà
圣 shèng
4 观 guān
欢 huān
戏 xì
6 艰 jiān
取 qǔ
受 shòu
叔 shū
7 叙 xù

8 难 nán,
　　 nàn
11 叠 dié

25 廴

4 廷 tíng
　 延 yán
6 建 jiàn

26 卩 , 㔾

2 卫 wèi
3 印 yìn
　 叩 kòu
5 即 jí
　 却 què
7 卸 xiè
8 卿 qīng

27 阝 L

2 队 duì
4 防 fáng
　 阶 jiē
　 阳 yáng
　 阴 yīn
　 阵 zhèn
　 阱 jǐng
5 阿 ā, ē
　 陈 chén
　 附 fù
　 际 jì
　 陆 lù

陀 tuó
阻 zǔ
6 降 jiàng,
　　 xiáng
　 陋 lòu
　 陌 mò
　 限 xiàn
7 除 chú
　 陡 dǒu
　 险 xiǎn
　 院 yuàn
　 陨 yǔn
8 陵 líng
　 陪 péi
　 陶 táo
　 陷 xiàn
9 隆 lóng
　 随 suí
　 隐 yǐn
10 隘 ài
　 隔 gé
　 隙 xì
11 障 zhàng
12 隧 suì

28 阝 R

2 邓 dèng
4 邦 bāng
　 那 nà,
　　 nèi
　 邪 xié
5 邻 lín
　 邮 yóu

6 郊 jiāo
　 郎 láng
　 耶 yé, yē
　 郁 yù
　 郑 zhèng
7 郡 jùn
8 部 bù
　 都 dū, dōu
11 鄙 bǐ

29 凵

2 凶 xiōng
6 函 hán
　 画 huà

30 刀, 刂

　 刀 dāo
2 切 qiē
3 召 zhāo,
　　 zhào
4 负 fù
　 色 sè,
　　 shǎi
　 危 wēi
　 争 zhēng
5 龟 guī
　 免 miǎn
6 券 quàn
　 兔 tù
9 剪 jiǎn
　 象 xiàng
13 劈 pī

31 力

力 lì
2 办 bàn
劝 quàn
3 加 jiā
务 wù
幼 yòu
4 动 dòng
劣 liè
5 劫 jié
励 lì
男 nán
助 zhù
6 劲 jìn
努 nǔ
势 shì
7 勃 bó
勉 miǎn
勋 xūn
勇 yǒng
9 勘 kān
11 勤 qín

32 氵

2 汉 hàn
汇 huì
汁 zhī
3 池 chí
汗 hàn
江 jiāng
汤 tāng
污 wū

4 沧 cāng
沉 chén
泛 fàn
沟 gōu
沥 lì
没 méi,
   mò
沛 pèi
汽 qì
沙 shā
汰 tài
汪 wāng
沃 wò
汩 gǔ
5 波 bō
泊 bó, pō
法 fǎ
沸 fèi
河 hé
沮 jǔ
泪 lèi
泌 mì
沫 mò
泥 ní
泞 níng
泡 pào
泼 pō
泣 qì
浅 qiǎn
泄 xiè
泻 xiè
沿 yán
泳 yǒng
油 yóu

泽 zé
沾 zhān
沼 zhǎo
治 zhì
注 zhù
沱 tuó
6 洛 luò
测 cè
洞 dòng
洪 hóng
浑 hún
活 huó
济 jǐ, jì
浇 jiāo
洁 jié
津 jīn
浓 nóng
派 pài
洽 qià
洒 sǎ
洼 wā
洗 xǐ
洋 yáng
洲 zhōu
浊 zhuó
浏 liú
7 涤 dí
浮 fú
海 hǎi
浩 hào
涣 huàn
渐 jiàn
浸 jìn
酒 jiǔ

浚 jùn
浪 làng
流 liú
润 rùn
涩 sè
涉 shè
涛 tāo
涕 tì
涂 tú
涡 wō
涎 xián
消 xiāo
涌 yǒng
浴 yù
涨 zhàng, zhǎng
浣 huàn

8 淡 dàn
淀 diàn
涵 hán
涸 hé
混 hún, hùn
淋 lín
清 qīng
深 shēn
渗 shèn
淌 tǎng
淘 táo
添 tiān
淆 xiáo
涯 yá
淹 yān
液 yè

淫 yín
淤 yū
渔 yú
渊 yuān
淇 qí
渎 dú

9 渤 bó
渡 dù
溉 gài
港 gǎng
湖 hú
滑 huá
溅 jiàn
渴 kě
溃 kuì
湿 shī
湍 tuān
湾 wān
温 wēn
游 yóu
渝 yú
渣 zhā
滞 zhì
滋 zī
渲 xuàn
湄 méi

10 滨 bīn
滚 gǔn
滥 làn
漓 lí
溜 liū, liù
滤 lù
满 mǎn
漠 mò

溺 nì, niào
溶 róng
溯 sù
滩 tān
滔 tāo
溪 xī
溢 yì
源 yuán
滓 zǐ
滂 pāng

11 滴 dī
漏 lòu
漫 màn
漂 piāo
漆 qī
漱 shù
演 yǎn
潢 huáng

12 澳 ào
潮 cháo
澈 chè
澄 chéng
潦 liǎo
潜 qián

13 濒 bīn
激 jī
澡 zǎo

15 瀑 bào, pù

17 灌 guàn

33 忄, 小

1 忆 yì
3 忙 máng

3	忏 chàn	惯 guàn		**34** 宀	
4	忱 chén	悸 jì			
	怀 huái	惊 jīng	*2*	宁 níng	
	快 kuài	惧 jù		它 tā	
	忧 yōu	情 qíng	*3*	安 ān	
	忡 chōng	惕 tì		守 shǒu	
	松 sōng	惋 wǎn		宇 yǔ	
	忸 niǔ	惜 xī		宅 zhái	
5	怖 bù	惘 wǎng		字 zì	
	怪 guài	惚 hū	*4*	宏 hóng	
	怜 lián	悴 cuì		牢 láo	
	怕 pà	*9* 惰 duò		宋 sòng	
	怯 qiè	愤 fèn		完 wán	
	性 xìng	慌 huāng		灾 zāi	
	怩 ní	惶 huáng	*5*	宝 bǎo	
6	恫 dòng,	慨 kǎi		宠 chǒng	
	tōng	愧 kuì		定 dìng	
	恨 hèn	惺 xīng		官 guān	
	恒 héng	愉 yú		审 shěn	
	恍 huǎng	愕 è		实 shí	
	恢 huī	*10* 慑 shè		宜 yí	
	恼 nǎo	慎 shèn		宙 zhòu	
	恰 qià	*11* 慷 kāng		宗 zōng	
	恸 tòng	慢 màn	*6*	宫 gōng	
7	悔 huǐ	*12* 懊 ào		客 kè	
	悯 mǐn	懂 dǒng		室 shì	
	悄 qiāo	憎 zēng		宪 xiàn	
	悟 wù	憔 qiáo		宣 xuān	
	悦 yuè	*13* 憾 hàn	*7*	宾 bīn	
	悚 sǒng	懒 lǎn		害 hài	
8	惭 cán	懈 xiè		家 jiā	
	惨 cǎn	*14* 懦 nuò		宽 kuān	
	悼 dào			宵 xiāo	
	惦 diàn			宴 yàn	

宰 zǎi
8 密 mì
寄 jì
寂 jì
宿 sù, xiǔ, xiù
9 富 fù
寒 hán
寓 yù
10 寞 mò
寝 qǐn
塞 sāi, sài, sè
11 察 chá
寡 guǎ
蜜 mì
赛 sài
寨 zhài

35 丬

3 壮 zhuàng
妆 zhuāng
4 状 zhuàng
6 将 jiāng

36 广

广 guǎng
3 庆 qìng
庄 zhuāng
4 庇 bì
床 chuáng
库 kù

序 xù
应 yìng, yīng
5 底 dǐ
店 diàn
废 fèi
府 fǔ
庙 miào
庞 páng
6 庭 tíng
度 dù
7 唐 táng
席 xí
座 zuò
8 康 kāng
廊 láng
麻 má
庸 yōng
10 廓 kuò
廉 lián
11 腐 fǔ
15 鹰 yīng
16 靡 mí, mǐ

37 门

门 mén
1 闩 shuān
2 闪 shǎn
3 闭 bì
闯 chuǎng
问 wèn
4 间 jiān, jiàn

闷 mēn, mèn
闰 rùn
闲 xián
5 闹 nào
闸 zhá
6 阀 fá
阁 gé
闻 wén
7 阅 yuè
阄 jiū
8 阐 chǎn
阉 yān
9 阔 kuò
阑 lán

38 辶

2 边 biān
3 达 dá
过 guò
迈 mài
迄 qì
迁 qiān
巡 xún
迅 xùn
迂 yū
4 迟 chí
返 fǎn
还 huán
进 jìn
近 jìn
连 lián
违 wéi

	迎 yíng	8	逮 dǎi		**40 土**	
	远 yuǎn		逻 luó			
	运 yùn	9	游 yóu		土 tǔ	
	这 zhè,		逼 bī	3	场 chǎng	
	zhèi		遍 biàn		地 dì	
5	迪 dí		道 dào		圾 jī	
	迭 dié		遏 è		在 zài	
	迫 pò		遗 yí		寺 sì	
	述 shù		遇 yù		尘 chén	
6	迸 bèng,	10	遣 qiǎn		至 zhì	
	bìng		遥 yáo		考 kǎo	
	迹 jì		遢 ta	4	坝 bà	
	迷 mí		遛 liū		坊 fāng,	
	逆 nì	11	遭 zāo		fáng	
	适 shì	12	遮 zhē		坟 fén	
	送 sòng	12	遵 zūn		坏 huài	
	逃 táo	13	避 bì		坚 jiān	
	退 tuì		邀 yāo		均 jūn	
	选 xuǎn		邂 xiè		坑 kēng	
	逊 xùn	15	邋 lā		块 kuài	
	追 zhuī				坍 tān	
	逅 hòu		**39 工**		坛 tán	
7	递 dì				址 zhǐ	
	逗 dòu		工 gōng		坠 zhuì	
	逢 féng	2	功 gōng		坐 zuò	
	逛 guàng		巧 qiǎo	5	垃 lā	
	逝 shì		左 zuǒ		坯 pī	
	速 sù	4	攻 gōng		坪 píng	
	通 tōng		巫 wū		坡 pō	
	透 tòu		贡 gòng		坦 tǎn	
	途 tú	6	项 xiàng		坞 wù	
	造 zào				幸 xìng	
	逐 zhú				垄 lǒng	
	逍 xiāo			6	城 chéng	

垫 diàn
垢 gòu
垮 kuǎ
型 xíng
7 埃 āi
埋 mái
埔 pǔ
8 堵 dǔ
堆 duī
堕 duò
基 jī
培 péi
域 yù
9 堡 bǎo
堤 dī
堪 kān
塔 tǎ
堰 yàn
10 塑 sù
塌 tā
塘 táng
填 tián
11 境 jìng
墙 qiáng
墅 shù
墟 xū
12 增 zēng
13 壁 bì
17 壤 rǎng

41 士

士 shì
3 吉 jí

4 声 shēng
志 zhì
7 壶 hú
9 喜 xǐ
10 鼓 gǔ
11 嘉 jiā
17 馨 xīn

42 艹

1 艺 yì
2 艾 ài, yì
节 jié
3 芒 máng
芝 zhī
4 芭 bā
苍 cāng
芳 fāng
芬 fēn
花 huā
芥 jiè
劳 láo
芦 lú
芹 qín
苏 sū
苇 wěi
芯 xīn
芽 yá
5 茄 qié, jiā
苯 bèn
范 fàn
苟 gǒu
茎 jīng
苛 kē

苦 kǔ
茅 máo
茂 mào
苗 miáo
苹 píng
若 ruò
苔 tái
英 yīng
茁 zhuó
茉 mò
6 草 cǎo
茬 chá
茶 chá
荡 dàng
荒 huāng
荤 hūn
茧 jiǎn
荐 jiàn
荔 lì
茫 máng
荣 róng
药 yào
荫 yīn
荨 xún
7 荷 hé
获 huò
莱 lái
莉 lì
莲 lián
莽 mǎng
莫 mò
莓 méi
莺 yīng
8 堇 jǐn

菠 bō	
菜 cài	
菲 fēi	
菇 gū	
菊 jú	
菌 jūn, jùn	
菱 líng	
萝 luó	
萌 méng	
菩 pú	
萨 sà	
萄 táo	
萎 wěi	
萧 xiāo	
营 yíng	
著 zhù	
萦 yíng	
9 葱 cōng	
蒂 dì	
董 dǒng	
葛 gě	
蒋 jiǎng	
葵 kuí	
落 luò, là	
募 mù	
葡 pú	
惹 rě	
葬 zàng	
10 蓝 lán	
蒙 méng	
墓 mù	
幕 mù	
蓬 péng	
蒜 suàn	

蓄 xù	
蒸 zhēng	
蓓 bèi	
11 蔼 ǎi	
蔽 bì	
蔓 mán,	
màn,	
wàn	
蔑 miè	
摹 mó	
慕 mù	
蔗 zhè	
12 蕉 jiāo	
蔬 shū	
蕨 jué	
蕃 fān	
13 薄 bó, bò,	
báo	
蕾 lěi	
薯 shǔ	
薪 xīn	
14 藏 cáng,	
zàng	
藉 jí	
15 藕 ǒu	
藤 téng	
16 蘑 mó	
藻 zǎo	

	43 大	
	大	dà
1	太	tài
3	夺	duó

	尖	jiān
	夸	kuā
5	奔	bēn,
		bèn
	奋	fèn
	奈	nài
	奇	qí
6	奖	jiǎng
	美	měi
	契	qì
	牵	qiān
7	套	tào
8	奢	shē
	爽	shuǎng
9	奥	ào

	44 廾	
3	异	yì
4	弄	lòng,
		nòng
11	弊	bì

	45 尢	
	尤	yóu

	46 寸	
	寸	cùn
3	寻	xún
	导	dǎo
	寺	sì
4	寿	shòu

6 封 fēng

7 耐 nài

7 辱 rǔ

射 shè

8 尉 wèi

47 弋

式 shì

48 扌

1 扎 zā, zhā, zhá

2 扒 bā, pá

打 dǎ

扑 pū

扔 rēng

3 扬 yáng

执 zhí

扣 kòu

扩 kuò

扫 sǎo

托 tuō

4 抑 yì

找 zhǎo

折 zhé

抓 zhuā

把 bǎ

扳 bān

扮 bàn

报 bào

抄 chāo

扯 chě

抖 dǒu

扼 è

扶 fú

抚 fǔ

护 hù

技 jì

拒 jù

抗 kàng

抠 kōu

拟 nǐ

扭 niǔ

抛 pāo

批 pī

抢 qiǎng

扰 rǎo

抒 shū

投 tóu

5 押 yā

拥 yōng

择 zé

招 zhāo

拙 zhuō

拗 niù, ǎo, ào

拔 bá

拌 bàn

抱 bào

拨 bō

拆 chāi

抽 chōu

担 dān, dàn

抵 dǐ

拐 guǎi

拣 jiǎn

拘 jū

拉 lā

拢 lǒng

抹 mǒ

拇 mǔ

拧 nǐng

拍 pāi

抨 pēng

披 pī

抬 tái

拖 tuō

拓 tuò

6 挣 zhēng

拯 zhěng

指 zhǐ

拽 zhuài, yè

按 àn

持 chí

挡 dǎng

拱 gǒng

挂 guà

挥 huī

挤 jǐ

括 kuò

挪 nuó

拼 pīn

拾 shí

拴 shuān

挑 tiāo

挺 tǐng

挖 wā

挝 wō

7	振 zhèn		推 tuī	12	撰 zhuàn
	捉 zhuō	9	握 wò		撞 zhuàng
	挨 āi, ái		援 yuán		播 bō
	捕 bǔ		揍 zòu		撤 chè
	挫 cuò		插 chā		撑 chēng
	捣 dǎo		搽 chá		撮 cuō
	捍 hàn		搀 chān		撅 juē
	换 huàn		搓 cuō		捻 niǎn
	捡 jiǎn		搭 dā		撬 qiào
	捐 juān		搁 gē		撒 sā, sǎ
	捆 kǔn		搅 jiǎo		撕 sī
	捏 niē		揭 jiē	13	擀 gǎn
	损 sǔn		揩 kāi		操 cāo
	捅 tǒng		揽 lǎn		撼 hàn
	挽 wǎn		搂 lǒu		擂 léi, lèi
8	掩 yǎn		揉 róu		擅 shàn
	掷 zhì		搔 sāo	14	擤 xǐng
	捺 nà		搜 sōu		擦 cā
	措 cuò		提 tí	16	攒 zǎn
	掉 diào	10	携 xié	17	攘 rǎng
	接 jiē		摇 yáo		
	捷 jié		摆 bǎi		**49** 小, 丷
	据 jù		搬 bān		
	掘 jué		搏 bó		小 xiǎo
	控 kòng		搐 chù	1	少 shǎo,
	掠 lüè		搞 gǎo		shào
	描 miáo		摸 mō	2	尔 ěr
	捻 niǎn		摄 shè	3	当 dāng,
	排 pái		摊 tān		dàng
	捧 pěng		搪 táng	3	尘 chén
	掐 qiā	11	摘 zhāi		尖 jiān
	授 shòu		摧 cuī	4	肖 xiāo,
	探 tàn		撇 piē, piě		xiào
	掏 tāo		摔 shuāi	5	尚 shàng

6	尝 cháng		吹 chuī			呦 yōu
7	党 dǎng		呆 dāi			呸 pēi
8	常 cháng		吨 dūn			和 hé, hè,
	堂 táng		吠 fèi			huò, hú
9	辉 huī		否 fǒu			呜 wū
	掌 zhǎng		告 gào			知 zhī
			吼 hǒu	6		哆 duō

50 口

	口 kǒu		君 jūn			哈 hā
2	叭 bā		吭 kēng			哄 hǒng
	叮 dīng		呕 ǒu			咯 gē
	号 háo,		启 qǐ			咳 ké, hāi
	hào		吮 shǔn			哪 nǎ, něi
	叫 jiào		听 tīng			品 pǐn
	可 kě		吞 tūn			哇 wā
	另 lìng		吻 wěn			响 xiǎng
	叹 tàn		呀 ya			哑 yǎ
	叶 yè		吟 yín			咽 yān,
	右 yòu		员 yuán			yàn
	叨 dāo		吱 zhī			咬 yǎo
3	吃 chī		吝 lìn			哟 yōu
	吊 diào	5	哎 āi			咱 zán
	各 gè		咕 gū			咨 zī
	吗 ma		呵 hē			咧 liē, liě
	名 míng		呼 hū			咪 mī
	吐 tǔ		咀 jǔ			哝 nóng
	吸 xī		咖 kā, gā			虽 suī
	吓 xià, hè		咙 lóng	7		啊 ā, á, a
	吁 yù, xū		鸣 míng			唉 āi, ài
	吉 jí		呢 ne, ní			哺 bǔ
4	吧 ba		咆 páo			唇 chún
	吵 chǎo		呻 shēn			哥 gē
	呈 chéng		味 wèi			哼 hēng
			咒 zhòu			唤 huàn
			呱 guā			哨 shào

7 唆 suō
哮 xiào
唁 yàn
哲 zhé
唠 lào
唧 jī
哦 ó, ò, é

8 唱 chàng
啡 fēi
唬 hǔ
哗 huā, huá
啃 kěn
啦 la
啮 niè
啪 pā
啤 pí
商 shāng
售 shòu
唾 tuò
唯 wéi
啸 xiào
啄 zhuó
喵 miāo
唿 hū
喋 dié

9 喘 chuǎn
喊 hǎn
喝 hē, hè
喉 hóu
喀 kā
喇 lǎ
喷 pēn
喂 wèi

喧 xuān
喻 yù
嗒 dā
喱 lí
喙 huì
喔 ō, wol
喜 xǐ

10 嗓 sǎng
嗜 shì
嗡 wēng
嗅 xiù
嘟 dū
嗦 suo
嗝 gé
嗳 ài, āi
嗨 hāi, hēi
嗬 hē
嗯 ńg, ňg

11 嘎 gā
嘛 má
嗽 sòu
嘘 xū
嘈 cáo

12 嘲 cháo
嘶 sī
嘱 zhǔ
噜 lū
嘿 hēi
噢 ō

13 器 qì
噪 zào
嘴 zuǐ
噱 xué, jué

14 嚎 háo
嚏 tì
嚓 cā

15 嚣 xiāo, āo

17 嚼 jiáo, jiào, jué
嚷 rǎng

51 囗

2 囚 qiú
四 sì
3 回 huí
团 tuán
因 yīn
4 囤 dún
困 kùn
围 wéi
园 yuán
5 固 gù
国 guó
图 tú
7 圃 pǔ
圆 yuán
8 圈 quān

52 巾

巾 jīn
2 布 bù
帅 shuài
3 帆 fān

吊 diào
4 帐 zhàng
5 帚 zhǒu
　帖 tiē
6 帮 bāng
　带 dài
　帝 dì
8 帷 wéi
9 幅 fú
　帽 mào
10 幌 huǎng
12 幢 zhuàng

53 山

山 shān
3 岁 suì
　屿 yǔ
4 岔 chà
　岛 dǎo
　岗 gāng
　岖 qū
5 岸 àn
　岭 lǐng
　岩 yán
　岳 yuè
6 炭 tàn
　峡 xiá
　峋 xún
7 峨 é
　峰 fēng
　峻 jùn
8 崩 bēng
　崇 chóng

崎 qí
　崖 yá
　崭 zhǎn
9 嵌 qiàn
12 嶙 lín
18 巍 wēi

54 彳

3 行 xíng,
　　háng
4 彻 chè
　役 yì
5 彼 bǐ
　径 jìng
　往 wǎng,
　　wàng
　征 zhēng
6 待 dài
　很 hěn
　律 lǜ
　衍 yǎn
7 徒 tú
8 得 dé, de,
　　děi
　衔 xián
9 街 jiē
　循 xún
　御 yù
10 微 wēi
12 德 dé
13 衡 héng
14 徽 huī

55 彡

4 形 xíng
　杉 shān
5 衫 shān
6 须 xū
8 彩 cǎi
　彬 bīn
12 影 yǐng

56 夕

夕 xī
3 多 duō
　岁 suì
8 梦 mèng

57 夂

2 冬 dōng
3 各 gè
4 条 tiáo
5 备 bèi
6 复 fù
7 夏 xià
9 惫 bèi

58 犭

2 犯 fàn
4 狂 kuáng
　犹 yóu
5 狗 gǒu
　狐 hú

狙 jū
狒 fèi
6 狠 hěn
狡 jiǎo
狮 shī
狭 xiá
狱 yù
独 dú
狩 shòu
7 狼 láng
狸 lí
8 猜 cāi
猎 liè
猫 māo
猛 měng
猪 zhū
猕 mí
9 猴 hóu
猾 huá
猩 xīng
猥 wěi
猬 wèi
13 獭 tà

59 饣

2 饥 jī
4 饭 fàn
饮 yǐn
饨 tún
饪 rèn
5 饱 bǎo
饯 jiàn
饰 shì

饲 sì
6 饼 bǐng
饵 ěr
饺 jiǎo
饶 ráo
蚀 shí
7 饿 è
馁 něi
8 馆 guǎn
馄 hún
馅 xiàn
9 馈 kuì
馊 sōu
11 馒 mán

60 彐, 彑, 彐

3 寻 xún
4 灵 líng
5 录 lù
帚 zhǒu
8 彗 huì

61 尸

尸 shī
1 尺 chǐ
2 尼 ní
3 尽 jìn
4 层 céng
局 jú
尿 niào
屁 pì
尾 wěi

5 届 jiè
居 jū
屈 qū
屉 tì
6 屏 bǐng,
píng
屎 shǐ
屋 wū
7 屑 xiè
展 zhǎn
8 屠 tú
9 屡 lǚ
属 shǔ
犀 xī
12 履 lǚ

62 己, 巳

己 jǐ
巳 yǐ
1 巴 bā
3 异 yì
导 dǎo
6 巷 xiàng

63 弓

弓 gōng
1 引 yǐn
3 弛 chí
4 张 zhāng
5 弧 hú
弥 mí
弦 xián

6	弯 wān
7	弱 ruò
8	弹 tán,
	dàn
9	强 qiáng
	粥 zhōu
16	疆 jiāng

64 女

	女 nǚ
2	奶 nǎi
	奴 nú
3	妇 fù
	好 hǎo,
	hào
	奸 jiān
	妈 mā
	如 rú
	她 tā
	妄 wàng
	妃 fēi
4	妒 dù
	妨 fáng
	妓 jì
	妙 miào
	妥 tuǒ
	妖 yāo
	姊 zǐ
	妞 niū
5	妹 mèi
	姑 gū
	姐 jiě
	姆 mǔ

	妻 qī
	始 shǐ
	委 wěi
	姓 xìng
	妾 qiè
6	姜 jiāng
	娇 jiāo
	姥 lǎo
	耍 shuǎ
	娃 wá
	姨 yí
	姻 yīn
	姿 zī
	要 yāo
7	娩 miǎn
	娘 niáng
	娱 yú
	娴 xián
8	婚 hūn
	婪 lán
	婆 pó
	婉 wǎn
	婴 yīng
	婊 biǎo
9	媒 méi
	嫂 sǎo
	婿 xù
10	嫉 jí
	嫁 jià
	媳 xí
	嫌 xián
11	嫩 nèn
12	嬉 xī
17	孀 shuāng

65 幺

	乡 xiāng
	幺 yāo
1	幻 huàn
6	幽 yōu

66 子

	子 zǐ
2	孕 yùn
3	存 cún
	孙 sūn
4	孝 xiào
	孜 zī
5	孤 gū
	学 xué
	孟 mèng
6	孩 hái

67 纟

2	纠 jiū
3	红 hóng
	级 jí
	纪 jì
	纫 rèn
	纤 xiān,
	qiàn
	约 yuē
4	纯 chún
	纺 fǎng
	纷 fēn
	纲 gāng

	纳 nà		绩 jì		驱 qū
	纽 niǔ		绿 lǜ	5	驾 jià
	纱 shā		绵 mián		驹 jū
	纬 wěi		绳 shéng		驶 shǐ
	纹 wén		维 wéi		驼 tuó
	纸 zhǐ		绪 xù		驻 zhù
	纵 zòng		续 xù	6	骇 hài
5	绊 bàn		缀 zhuì		骄 jiāo
	经 jīng		综 zōng		骆 luò
	练 liàn	9	编 biān		骂 mà
	绍 shào		缔 dì	7	验 yàn
	绅 shēn		缎 duàn	8	骑 qí
	细 xì		缓 huǎn	9	骗 piàn
	线 xiàn		缉 jī		骚 sāo
	织 zhī		缆 lǎn	11	骡 luó
	终 zhōng		缕 lǚ	14	骤 zhòu
	组 zǔ		缅 miǎn		
	绉 zhòu		缘 yuán	**69 巛**	
6	绑 bǎng	10	缠 chán		
	给 gěi, jǐ		缝 féng,		巢 cháo
	绘 huì		fèng		
	结 jiē		缚 fù	**70 灬**	
	绝 jué		缤 bīn		
	络 luò	11	缩 suō	4	杰 jié
	绕 rào	12	缮 shàn	5	点 diǎn
	绒 róng	13	缰 jiāng	6	羔 gāo
	统 tǒng				烈 liè
7	继 jì	**68 马**			热 rè
	绢 juàn			7	焉 yān
	绦 tāo		马 mǎ	8	焦 jiāo
	绣 xiù	3	驰 chí		然 rán
8	绷 bēng		驯 xùn		煮 zhǔ
	绸 chóu	4	驳 bó	9	煎 jiān
	绰 chuò		驴 lú		照 zhào

10	熬 áo
	熙 xī
	熊 xióng
	熏 xūn
11	熟 shú,
	shóu
12	燕 yàn

71 斗

	斗 dòu,
	dǒu
7	斜 xié

72 文

	文 wén
2	齐 qí
6	斋 zhāi
	紊 wěn

73 方

	方 fāng
4	房 fáng
	放 fàng
5	施 shī
6	旅 lǚ
	旁 páng
7	旋 xuán,
	xuàn
	族 zú
10	旗 qí

74 火

	火 huǒ
1	灭 miè
2	灯 dēng
	灰 huī
3	灿 càn
	灸 jiǔ
	灶 zào
	灼 zhuó
4	炒 chǎo
	炬 jù
	炉 lú
	炎 yán
	炖 dùn
5	烂 làn
	炼 liàn
	炮 pào
	烁 shuò
	烃 tīng
	炸 zhà,
	zhá
	炫 xuàn
6	烦 fán
	烘 hōng
	烬 jìn
	烤 kǎo
	烧 shāo
	烫 tàng
	烟 yān
	烛 zhú
7	焊 hàn
	焕 huàn
	烯 xī

8	焚 fén
	焰 yàn
9	煌 huáng
	煤 méi
	煳 hú
	煨 wēi,
	wèi
	煸 biān
10	熔 róng
	煽 shān,
	shàn
	熄 xī
11	熨 yùn
12	燃 rán
13	燥 zào
15	爆 bào

75 心

	心 xīn
1	必 bì
3	忌 jì
	忍 rěn
	忘 wàng
4	忽 hū
	念 niàn
	怂 sǒng
	态 tài
	忠 zhōng
5	怠 dài
	急 jí
	怒 nù
	思 sī
	怨 yuàn

怎	zěn	**76 户**			玫	méi	
总	zǒng				玩	wán	
6 恶	è, wù, ě	户	hù		现	xiàn	
恩	ēn	4 房	fáng	5	玻	bō	
恳	kěn	所	suǒ		珐	fà	
恐	kǒng	肩	jiān		珊	shān	
恋	liàn	戾	lì		珍	zhēn	
恕	shù	5 扁	biǎn		玷	diàn	
息	xī	6 扇	shàn	6	班	bān	
恙	yàng	8 雇	gù		珠	zhū	
恣	zì			7	琅	láng	
7 患	huàn	**77 礻**			理	lǐ	
您	nín				球	qiú	
悉	xī	1 礼	lǐ		琐	suǒ	
悬	xuán	3 社	shè		望	wàng	
恿	yǒng	祀	sì	8	斑	bān	
悠	yōu	4 视	shì		琴	qín	
8 悲	bēi	祈	qí		琢	zhuó	
惩	chéng	5 神	shén	9	瑰	guī	
惠	huì	祝	zhù		瑚	hú	
惑	huò	祖	zǔ		瑞	ruì	
9 愁	chóu	祠	cí		瑜	yú	
慈	cí	6 祥	xiáng		瑕	xiá	
感	gǎn	7 祷	dǎo	10	璃	lí	
想	xiǎng	祸	huò	11	璜	huáng	
意	yì	8 禅	chán				
愚	yú	9 福	fú	**79 韦**			
愈	yù						
10 愿	yuàn	**78 王**		韧	rèn		
11 慧	huì						
慰	wèi	王	wáng	**80 木**			
		1 玉	yù				
		3 玛	mǎ	木	mù		
		4 环	huán	1 本	běn		

术 shù

2 朵 duǒ
机 jī
朴 pǔ
权 quán
朽 xiǔ
杂 zá

3 材 cái
村 cūn
杜 dù
杆 gǎn,
   gān
杠 gàng
极 jí
李 lǐ
杏 xìng
杨 yáng
杖 zhàng

4 杰 jié
采 cǎi
板 bǎn
杯 bēi
枫 fēng
构 gòu
柜 guì
果 guǒ
林 lín
枪 qiāng
枢 shū
松 sōng
析 xī
枕 zhěn
枝 zhī

5 柏 bǎi, bó

标 biāo
柄 bǐng
查 chá
栋 dòng
柑 gān
架 jià
枯 kū
栏 lán
柳 liǔ
某 mǒu
柠 níng
染 rǎn
柔 róu
柿 shì
树 shù
相 xiāng
栅 shān,
   zhà
柱 zhù
柚 yòu,
   yóu
栎 yuè, lì

6 柴 chái
档 dàng
格 gé
根 gēn
桂 guì
核 hé
桨 jiǎng
桔 jú
框 kuàng
栖 xī, qil
桥 qiáo
桑 sāng

栓 shuān
桃 táo
桅 wéi
校 xiào,
   jiào
样 yàng
案 àn
桩 zhuāng
桌 zhuō
桦 huà

7 梗 gěng
检 jiǎn
梨 lí
梁 liáng
梅 méi
渠 qú
梢 shāo
梳 shū
梯 tī
桶 tǒng
梧 wú
械 xiè

8 棒 bàng
棺 guān
棍 gùn
集 jí
椒 jiāo
棵 kē
椰 liáng
棱 léng,
   líng
棉 mián
棚 péng
棋 qí

森 sēn
椭 tuǒ
椰 yē
椅 yǐ
植 zhí
椎 zhuī, chuí
棕 zōng
椋 liáng
9 椽 chuán
概 gài
槐 huái
楞 lèng
楼 lóu
楔 xiē
榆 yú
楂 zhā
榄 lǎn
槌 chuí
榈 lú
榉 jǔ
10 榜 bǎng
槛 jiàn, kǎn
榴 liú
模 mó, mú
榨 zhà
榛 zhēn
槟 bīng
11 槽 cáo
横 héng
樱 yīng
樟 zhāng
橄 gǎn

12 橙 chéng
橱 chú
橇 qiāo
橡 xiàng
橹 lǔ
橘 jú
13 檬 méng
檐 yán

81 犬

犬 quǎn
6 臭 chòu, xiù
哭 kū
9 献 xiàn

82 歹

歹 dǎi
2 死 sǐ
5 残 cán
6 殊 shū
殉 xùn
8 殖 zhí
10 殡 bìn

83 车

车 chē
1 轧 yà, zhá
2 轨 guǐ
3 轩 xuān
4 轰 hōng

轮 lún
软 ruǎn
转 zhuàn, zhuǎn
5 轻 qīng
轴 zhóu
6 轿 jiào
较 jiào, jiǎo
7 辅 fǔ
辆 liàng
8 辈 bèi
辊 gǔn
9 毂 gū, gǔ
辐 fú
辑 jí
输 shū
10 辗 zhǎn
12 辙 zhé

84 戈

戈 gē
2 成 chéng
戍 shù
3 戒 jiè
我 wǒ
4 或 huò
5 威 wēi
咸 xián
栽 zali
战 zhàn
6 载 zǎi, zài
7 戚 qī

8 裁 cái	**89 日**	晚 wǎn
10 截 jié		晤 wù
11 戮 lù	日 rì	*8* 晷 guǐ
13 戴 dài	*1* 旦 dàn	晶 jīng
14 戳 chuō	*2* 早 zǎo	景 jǐng
	3 旱 hàn	量 liàng
85 比	旷 kuàng	晾 liàng
	时 shí	普 pǔ
比 bǐ	*4* 昂 áng	晴 qíng
2 毕 bì	昌 chāng	暑 shǔ
6 毙 bì	昏 hūn	晰 xī
	昆 kūn	暂 zàn
86 瓦	明 míng	智 zhì
	旺 wàng	晳 xī
瓦 wǎ	易 yì	*9* 暗 àn
6 瓷 cí	*5* 春 chūn	暖 nuǎn
瓶 píng	昧 mèi	暇 xiá
	是 shì	*10* 暧 ài
87 止	显 xiǎn	*11* 暴 bào
	星 xīng	*14* 曝 bào
止 zhǐ	映 yìng	*16* 曦 xī
2 此 cǐ	昭 zhāo	
3 步 bù	昨 zuó	**90 曰**
4 歧 qí	昵 nì	
武 wǔ	*6* 晃 huàng,	*2* 曲 qū
肯 kěn	huǎng	*4* 者 zhě
5 歪 wāi	晋 jìn	*5* 冒 mào
6 耻 chǐ	晒 shài	*8* 替 tì
11 整 zhěng	晓 xiǎo	曾 céng,
	晕 yūn,	zēng
88 支	yùn	最 zuì
	7 晨 chén	
敲 qiāo	匙 chí,	
	shi	

91 贝

贝 bèi
3 财 cái
4 败 bài
　贯 guàn
　贬 biǎn
　贩 fàn
　购 gòu
　货 huò
　贫 pín
　贪 tān
　责 zé
　账 zhàng
　质 zhì
　贮 zhù
5 贷 dài
　费 fèi
　贵 guì
　贺 hè
　贱 jiàn
　贸 mào
　贴 tiē
　贻 yí
6 贿 huì
　赂 lù
　赃 zāng
　资 zī
7 赊 shē
　赈 zhèn
8 赐 cì
　赌 dǔ
　赋 fù
　赔 péi

　赏 shǎng
　赎 shú
9 赖 lài
10 赚 zuàn
11 赘 zhuì
12 赞 zàn
　赠 zèng
13 赡 shàn

92 见

见 jiàn
4 规 guī
　视 shì
5 觉 jué, jiào
　览 lǎn

93 父

父 fù
2 爷 yé
4 斧 fǔ
　爸 bà
6 爹 diē

94 牛, 牜, ⺧

牛 niú
3 牡 mǔ
4 牧 mù
　物 wù
　牦 máo
5 牲 shēng
　牯 gǔ

6 特 tè
　牺 xī
7 犁 lí
8 犊 dú

95 手

手 shǒu
6 拿 ná
　挛 luán
　拳 quán
　挚 zhì
8 掰 bāi
11 摩 mó
12 擎 qíng
15 攀 pān

96 毛

毛 máo
5 毡 zhān
8 毯 tǎn

97 气

气 qì
4 氛 fēn
5 氟 fú
　氢 qīng
6 氧 yǎng
8 氮 dàn
　氯 lǜ

98 攵

2 收 shōu
3 改 gǎi
4 放 fàng
5 故 gù
　政 zhèng
6 敌 dí
　效 xiào
　致 zhì
7 敢 gǎn
　教 jiào,
　　jiāo
　救 jiù
　敏 mǐn
　赦 shè
8 敞 chǎng
　敦 duì,
　　dūn
　敬 jìng
　散 sǎn, sàn
9 数 shù,
　　shǔ,
　　shuò
11 敷 fū
　整 zhěng

99 片

　片 piān
4 版 bǎn
8 牌 pái
　牒 dié

100 斤

　斤 jīn
1 斥 chì
4 所 suǒ
　欣 xīn
7 断 duàn
8 斯 sī
9 新 xīn

101 爪, 爫

　爪 zhuǎ,
　　zhǎo
4 爬 pá
　采 cǎi
　斧 fǔ
6 奚 xī
　爱 ài
　舀 yǎo
13 爵 jué

102 月

　月 yuè
2 肌 jī
　肋 lèi
　有 yǒu
3 肠 cháng
　肚 dǔ, dù
　肝 gān
　肛 gāng
　肘 zhǒu
4 肮 āng

肪 fáng
肥 féi
肺 fèi
肤 fū
服 fú
股 gǔ
朋 péng
肾 shèn
胁 xié
育 yù
胀 zhàng
肢 zhī
肿 zhǒng
肩 jiān
肯 kěn
5 胞 bāo
背 bèi
胆 dǎn
胡 hú
脉 mò
胖 pàng
胚 péi
胜 shèng
胎 tāi
胃 wèi
胧 lóng
胛 jiǎ
胫 jìng
6 脆 cuì
胳 gē
脊 jǐ
胶 jiāo
胯 kuà
朗 lǎng

脑 nǎo
脓 nóng
脐 qí
胸 xiōng
胰 yí
脏 zàng, zāng
脂 zhī
胱 guāng
胭 yān
7 脖 bó
脯 fǔ
脚 jiǎo
脸 liǎn
脱 tuō
豚 tún
8 朝 cháo, zhāo
腊 là
脾 pí
腔 qiāng
腆 tiǎn
腕 wàn
腋 yè
腌 yān
腱 jiàn
期 qī
9 腹 fù
腻 nì
腮 sāi
腾 téng
腿 tuǐ
腺 xiàn
腰 yāo

腭 è
10 膀 bǎng
膊 bó
膜 mó
11 膝 xī
12 膨 péng
膳 shàn
13 臂 bì
臀 tún
臊 sāo

103 欠

欠 qiàn
4 欧 ōu
欣 xīn
7 欲 yù
8 款 kuǎn
欺 qī
9 歇 xiē
10 歌 gē
歉 qiàn

104 风

风 fēng
8 飓 jù
11 飘 piāo

105 殳

4 殴 ōu
5 段 duàn
6 殷 yīn

9 彀 gū, gǔ
毁 huǐ
殿 diàn

106 聿, 肀, 聿

4 肃 sù
7 肆 sì

107 母

母 mǔ
2 每 měi
4 贯 guàn
毒 dú

108 水, 氺

水 shuǐ
1 永 yǒng
5 泵 bèng
泰 tài
泉 quán
6 浆 jiāng
10 黎 lí

109 穴

穴 xuè
2 究 jiū
穷 qióng
3 空 kōng, kòng
帘 lián

4	穿 chuān	3	疙 gē		痱 fèi
	窃 qiè		疚 jiù		瘀 yū
	突 tū		疟 nüè	9	瘩 dá, da
5	窍 qiào		疡 yáng		瘦 shòu
	容 róng		疝 shàn		瘟 wēn
	窄 zhǎi	4	疤 bā	10	瘪 biě, biē
6	窑 yáo		疮 chuāng		瘤 liú
	窒 zhì		疯 fēng		瘫 tān
7	窗 chuāng		疫 yì		瘠 jí
	窖 jiào		疣 yóu	11	瘸 qué
	窘 jiǒng	5	病 bìng		瘾 yǐn
	窝 wō		疾 jí	12	癌 ái
8	窟 kū		痉 jìng	13	癞 lài
	窥 kuī		疲 pí		癖 pǐ
	窦 dòu		疼 téng	16	癫 diān

	立 lì		疹 zhěn		
1	产 chǎn		症 zhèng		
4	亲 qīn		疸 da, dǎn		
	竖 shù		疱 pào		
5	竞 jìng		痂 jiā	2	补 bǔ
	站 zhàn	6	疵 cī		初 chū
6	竟 jìng		痕 hén	3	衬 chèn
	章 zhāng		痊 quán		衩 chǎ
7	童 tóng		痒 yǎng	5	被 bèi
9	端 duān		痔 zhì		袍 páo
	竭 jié	7	痘 dòu		袒 tǎn
			痪 huàn		袜 wà
			痢 lì		袖 xiù
			痛 tòng	7	裤 kù
			痣 zhì		裙 qún
			痫 xián		裕 yù
2	疗 liáo	8	痹 bì	8	褂 guà
	疖 jiē		痴 chī		裸 luǒ
			痰 tán		裱 biǎo
				9	褐 hè

褪 tuì
褛 lǚ
10 褥 rù
襤 lán
11 褶 zhě
13 襟 jīn

113 示

示 shì
5 祟 suì
6 祭 jì
票 piào
8 禁 jìn, jīn

114 石

石 shí
3 矿 kuàng
码 mǎ
4 砍 kǎn
砂 shā
研 yán
砚 yàn
砖 zhuān
5 础 chǔ
砾 lì
砰 pēng
破 pò
砸 zá
6 硅 guī
硕 shuò
7 硫 liú
确 què

硬 yìng
8 碍 ài
碑 bēi
碘 diǎn
碉 diāo
碌 lù
碰 pèng
碎 suì
碗 wǎn
9 磁 cí
磋 cuō
碟 dié
碳 tàn
10 磅 bàng
磕 kē
碾 niǎn
11 磺 huáng
磨 mó
12 礁 jiāo

115 龙

龙 lóng
6 聋 lóng
龛 kān
袭 xí

116 业

业 yè
7 凿 záo

117 目

目 mù
2 盯 dīng
3 盲 máng
4 盾 dùn
看 kàn,
kān
眉 méi
盼 pàn
省 shěng,
xǐng
眨 zhǎ
盹 dǔn
5 眠 mián
眩 xuàn
6 眼 yǎn
7 睑 jiǎn
8 督 dū
睫 jié
睛 jīng
瞄 miáo
睦 mù
睡 shuì
10 瞒 mán
瞎 xiā
瞌 kē
11 瞥 piē
12 瞪 dèng
瞧 qiáo
瞬 shùn
瞳 tóng

118 田

	田	tián
	由	yóu
4	界	jiè
	畏	wèi
5	留	liú
	畜	xù, chù
6	累	lèi, lěi
	略	lüè
7	畴	chóu
	番	fān
8	畸	jī

119 罒

3	罗	luó
4	罚	fá
5	罢	bà
8	署	shǔ
	罩	zhào
	置	zhì
	罪	zuì

120 皿

	皿	mǐn
4	盆	pén
	盈	yíng
5	盎	àng
	监	jiān
	盐	yán
	益	yì
6	盗	dào

	盒	hé
	盔	kuī
	盘	pán
	盛	shèng, chéng
	盖	gài
7	尴	gān
8	盟	méng
11	盥	guàn

121 钅

2	钉	dìng
	针	zhēn
3	钓	diào
4	钞	chāo
	钝	dùn
	钙	gài
	钢	gāng
	钩	gōu
	钮	niǔ
	钦	qīn
	钥	yào
	钟	zhōng
5	铂	bó
	铃	líng
	铆	mǎo
	铅	qiān
	钱	qián
	钳	qián
	铁	tiě
	铀	yóu
	钻	zuān, zuàn

6	铲	chǎn
	铬	gè
	铰	jiǎo
	铝	lǚ
	铭	míng
	铜	tóng
	银	yín
	铐	kǎo
7	锄	chú
	锋	fēng
	锅	guō
	链	liàn
	铺	pù
	锐	ruì
	锁	suǒ
	销	xiāo
	锌	xīn
	锈	xiù
	铸	zhù
	锉	cuò
8	锤	chuí
	错	cuò
	锭	dìng
	键	jiàn
	锦	jǐn
	锯	jù
	锣	luó
	锚	máo
	锡	xī
	锥	zhuī
9	镀	dù
	锻	duàn
	锹	qiāo
10	镑	bàng

镊 niè
镍 niè
镇 zhèn
11 镜 jìng
13 镰 lián
镯 zhuó
15 镳 biāo
17 镶 xiāng

122 矢

4 矩 jǔ
6 矫 jiǎo
7 短 duǎn
8 矮 ǎi
9 疑 yí

123 禾

2 私 sī
秀 xiù
3 秆 gǎn
季 jì
4 科 kē
秒 miǎo
秋 qiū
香 xiāng
种 zhòng,
zhǒng
5 称 chēng,
chèng,
chèn
秤 chèng
积 jī

秘 mì, bì
秦 qín
秩 zhì
租 zū
6 秽 huì
移 yí
7 程 chéng
稍 shāo
税 shuì
稀 xī
8 稠 chóu
稚 zhì
9 稳 wěn
10 稻 dào
稿 gǎo
稽 jī
稼 jià
11 穆 mù
12 黏 nián
穗 suì

124 白

白 bái
2 皂 zào
3 的 de, dì,
dí
4 皇 huáng

125 瓜

瓜 guā
11 瓢 piáo

126 鸟

鸟 niǎo
2 鸡 jī
3 鸢 yuān
4 鸥 ōu
鸦 yā
5 鸵 tuó
鸭 yā
鸫 dōng
6 鸽 gē
7 鹅 é
8 鹊 què
鹉 wǔ
11 鹦 yīng
12 鹫 jiù
13 鹭 lù
17 鹳 guàn

127 用

用 yòng
甩 shuǎi

128 矛

矛 máo

129 疋, 疋

6 蛋 dàn
7 疏 shū
8 楚 chǔ
9 疑 yí

130 皮

皮 pí
5 皱 zhòu

131 衣

衣 yī
5 袋 dài
6 裂 liè
装 zhuāng
7 裔 yì

132 羊, 𦍌, 𦍋

羊 yáng
3 养 yǎng
4 羞 xiū
5 着 zháo,
zhe,
zhāo,
zhuó
6 善 shàn
羡 xiàn
7 群 qún
11 羹 gēng

133 米

米 mǐ
3 类 lèi
4 粉 fěn
料 liào
5 粗 cū

粒 lì
粘 zhān,
nián
6 粪 fèn
7 粮 liáng
8 粹 cuì
精 jīng
9 糊 hú, hù,
hū
10 糙 cāo
糕 gāo
糖 táng
11 糟 zāo
12 糨 jiàng
14 糯 nuò

134 耒

4 耙 pá
耕 gēng
耗 hào

135 老

老 lǎo

136 耳

耳 ěr
4 耽 dān
耸 sǒng
5 聊 liáo
职 zhí
6 联 lián

7 聘 pìn
8 聚 jù
9 聪 cōng

137 西, 覀

西 xī
4 栗 lì
6 粟 sù
12 覆 fù

138 页

页 yè
2 顶 dǐng
顷 qǐng
3 顺 shùn
4 顿 dùn
顾 gù
颂 sòng
顽 wán
预 yù
5 颈 gěng,
jǐng
领 lǐng
颅 lú
6 颊 jiá
颌 hé
7 频 pín
颓 tuí
颐 yí
颖 yǐng
8 颗 kē
9 额 é

题 tí
颜 yán
10 颠 diān
13 颤 chàn,
   zhàn
17 颧 quán

139 庀

2 虎 hǔ
  虏 lǔ
3 虐 nüè
4 虑 lù
  虔 qián
5 虚 xū

140 虫

  虫 chóng
2 虱 shī
3 虹 hóng
  蚂 mǎ
  虾 xiā
  蚁 yǐ
  蚤 zǎo
4 蚕 cán
  蚊 wén
  蚋 ruì
  蚝 háo
  蚪 dǒu
  蚓 yǐn
5 蛆 qū
  蛇 shé
  蚱 zhà

蚯 qiū
6 蛤 gé, há
  蛮 mán
  蛙 wā
  蜒 yán
  蛛 zhū
  蜓 yán
  蛞 kuò
  蛴 qí
7 蜂 fēng
  蜕 tuì
  蜗 wō
  蜃 shèn
  蜇 zhē
  蜊 li
8 蝉 chán
  蜡 là
  蝇 yíng
  蜘 zhī
  蜻 qīng
  蜥 xī
  蜚 fēi
  蜴 yì
  蜷 quán
  蜿 wān
  螂 láng
  蜢 měng
9 蝶 dié
  蝴 hú
  蝗 huáng
  蝠 fú
  蝌 kē
  蝓 yú
  蝙 biān

10 融 róng
  螯 áo
  蟆 ma
  螃 páng
11 螺 luó
  螫 shì, zhē
  螬 cáo
  蟑 zhāng
  蟀 shuài
13 蟹 xiè
  蠓 měng
14 蠕 rú
15 蠢 chǔn

141 缶

3 缸 gāng
4 缺 quē
8 罂 yīng
17 罐 guàn

142 舌

  舌 shé
5 甜 tián
7 辞 cí
8 舔 tiǎn

143 竹, ⺮

  竹 zhú
3 竿 gān
4 笆 bā
  笔 bǐ

笋 sǔn

笑 xiào

5 笨 bèn

笛 dí

第 dì

符 fú

笺 jiān

笼 lǒng

笤 tiáo

6 策 cè

答 dá

等 děng

筏 fá

筋 jīn

筐 kuāng

筛 shāi

筒 tǒng

筑 zhù

筝 zhēng

7 筹 chóu

简 jiǎn

筷 kuài

签 qiān

8 箔 bó

箍 gū

管 guǎn

箕 jī

算 suàn

9 箭 jiàn

篓 lǒu

篇 piān

箱 xiāng

10 篡 cuàn

篮 lán

篱 lí

篷 péng

篝 golu

11 簇 cù

簧 huáng

12 簿 bù

13 簸 bó, bò

14 籍 jí

144 臼

臼 jiù

7 舅 jiù

145 自

自 zì

146 血

血 xuè,
　 xiě

5 衅 xìn

147 舟

舟 zhōu

4 般 bān

舱 cāng

航 háng

舰 jiàn

5 舶 bó

船 chuán

舵 duò

舷 xián

6 艇 tǐng

148 羽

羽 yǔ

4 翅 chì

翁 wēng

6 翘 qiào

翔 xiáng

10 翱 áo

11 翼 yì

12 翻 fān

14 耀 yào

149 艮, 艮

既 jì

150 糸

4 紧 jǐn

素 sù

6 絮 xù

紫 zǐ

11 繁 fán

151 辛

辛 xīn

6 辟 pì

7 辣 là

9 辨 biàn

辩 biàn

10 辡 biàn	*8* 豌 wān	**160** 足
12 瓣 bàn		
	157 酉	足 zú
152 言		*2* 趴 pā
	3 配 pèi	*4* 距 jù
言 yán	酌 zhuó	跄 qiàng
6 誉 yù	*4* 酗 xù	跃 yuè
7 誓 shì	酝 yùn	趾 zhǐ
12 警 jǐng	*5* 酣 hān	*5* 跋 bá
	酥 sū	跌 diē
153 麦	*6* 酬 chóu	践 jiàn
	酱 jiàng	跑 pǎo
麦 mài	酷 kù	跚 shān
	酪 lào	跛 bǒ
154 走	酯 zhǐ	*6* 跺 duò
	7 酸 suān	跟 gēn
走 zǒu	酵 xiào,	跪 guì
3 赶 gǎn	jiào	跨 kuà
起 qǐ	酿 niàng	路 lù
5 超 chāo	*8* 醇 chún	跳 tiào
趋 qū	醋 cù	跷 qiāo
越 yuè	醉 zuì	跤 jiāo
8 趣 qù	*9* 醒 xǐng	*7* 踉 liàng
趟 tāng		*8* 踩 cǎi
	158 辰	踏 tà
155 赤		踢 tī
	辰 chén	踪 zōng
赤 chì		踝 huái
7 赫 hè	**159** 里	*9* 蹄 tí
		踱 duó
156 豆	里 lǐ	*10* 蹈 dǎo
	4 野 yě	蹋 tà
豆 dòu		蹒 pán
5 登 dēng		*11* 蹦 bèng

12 蹲 dūn
蹼 pǔ
13 躁 zào

161 豸

3 豹 bào
5 貂 diāo
7 貌 mào

162 谷

谷 gǔ

163 釆

释 shì

164 身

身 shēn
3 躬 gōng
4 躯 qū
6 躲 duǒ
8 躺 tǎng

165 角

角 jiǎo,
　　jué
6 触 chù
解 jiě,
　　xiè

166 青

青 qīng
6 静 jìng

167 其

其 qí

168 雨

雨 yǔ
3 雪 xuě
4 雳 lì
5 雾 wù
雹 báo
雷 léi
零 líng
6 需 xū
霆 tíng
7 霉 méi
震 zhèn
8 霍 huò
霓 ní
9 霜 shuāng
霞 xiá
13 霸 bà
露 lù, lòu
霹 pī

169 齿

齿 chǐ
5 龄 líng

6 龈 yín
9 龋 qǔ

170 金

金 jīn
5 鉴 jiàn

171 隹

2 隼 sǔn
3 雀 què
4 雄 xióng
雅 yǎ
5 雏 chú
6 雌 cí
8 雕 diāo

172 鱼

鱼 yú
4 鲁 lǔ
鱿 yóu
5 稣 sū
6 鲜 xiān
7 鲤 lǐ
鲨 shā
8 鲸 jīng
鲱 fēi
9 鳄 è
10 鳍 qí
鳏 guān
11 鳕 xuě
鳗 mán

12 鳞 lín
鳟 zūn

173 音

音 yīn
4 韵 yùn

174 革

革 gé
2 勒 lè
4 靶 bǎ
靴 xuē
6 鞍 ān
鞋 xié
鞑 dá
7 鞘 qiào
8 鞠 jū
9 鞭 biān

175 骨

骨 gū
4 骰 tóu
5 骷 kū
6 骸 hái
9 髅 lóu
12 髓 suǐ

176 食

食 shí
7 餐 cān

177 鬼

鬼 guǐ
4 魂 hún
魁 kuí
5 魅 mèi
11 魔 mó

178 髟

4 髦 máo
6 髻 jì
8 鬃 zōng
鬈 quán
10 鬓 bìn

179 鹿

鹿 lù
2 麂 jǐ
8 麓 lù

180 黑

黑 hēi
3 墨 mò
4 默 mò
5 黝 yǒu

181 鼠

鼠 shǔ

182 鼻

鼻 bí
3 鼾 hān

Chinese - English

A

啊 ā (*surprise, wonderment*) oh

啊 à (*realization*) ah

阿尔巴尼亚 Ā'ěrbāníyà Albania ◊ Albanian

阿富汗 Āfùhàn Afghanistan ◊ Afghan

阿根廷 Āgēntíng Argentina ◊ Argentinian

哀 āi sorrow; mourning

唉 āi alas

挨 āi be next to

唉 āi (*when someone calls your name*): 小王？- 唉，什么事儿？ *xiǎo Wáng? – āi, shénme shìr?* Wang? – yes, what's up?

哎 āi (*dissatisfaction*): 哎，你怎么没告诉我呢？ *āi, nǐ zěnme méi gàosù wǒ ne?* well, why didn't you tell me then?

挨 ái undergo, suffer; endure

癌 ái cancer

矮 ǎi short *person*; low

嗳 ǎi (*disagreement*): 嗳，说哪儿去了 *ǎi, shuō nǎr qù le* hey, don't be silly

爱 ài love; like; be in the habit of; 做爱 *zuò'ài* make love; 有爱心 *yǒu àixīn* caring; 爱发脾气 *ài fā píqì* short-tempered

嗳 ài (*annoyance*): 嗳，我怎就忘不了她呢？ *ài, wǒ zěn jiù wàngbùliǎo tā ne?* why can't I just forget her?

碍 ài block; hinder; obstruct

爱称 àichēng diminutive, short form of a name

挨打 āidǎ get a beating

哀悼 āidào mourn; grieve

哀悼者 āidào zhě mourner

挨饿 ái'è starve

爱尔兰 Ài'ěrlán Ireland ◊ Irish

爱抚 àifǔ caress; fondle; pet

爱管事 ài guǎnshì bossy

爱国 àiguó patriotic

爱国者 àiguó zhě patriot

爱国主义 àiguó zhǔyì patriotism

哀号 āiháo howl

爱好 àihào enjoy ◊ hobby

爱护 àihù cherish; take care of

埃及 Āijí Egypt ◊ Egyptian

挨脚 áijiāo get caught in the rain

挨近 āijìn approach

暧昧 àimèi ambiguous; dubious; 和 … 有暧昧关系 *hé … yǒu àimèi guānxī* have an affair with …

埃面子 àimiànzi be determined to save face

爱慕 àimù affection; worship ◊ be attached to; be attracted to

矮胖 ǎipàng tubby

爱情 àiqíng love

爱情生活 àiqíng shēnghuó lovelife

哀求 āiqiú implore

爱人 àirén husband; wife

哀伤 āishāng plaintive

爱上 àishàng fall in love with

唉声叹气 āishēng-tànqì sigh

哎呀 āiya! wow!; 哎呀，我的天啊！ *āiya, wǒde tiān'a!* good heavens!; 哎呀，糟了！ *āiya, zāole!* oh, no!

唉哟！ āiyō! ouch!

哀乐 āiyuè lament MUS

挨着 āizhe be next to

挨着 áizhe linger; put off; procrastinate

癌症 áizhèng cancer

矮壮 ǎizhuàng stocky, thickset

矮子 ǎizi short person; dwarf

艾滋病 àizībìng Aids

阿拉伯 Ālābó Arabia ◊ Arab(ic)

阿弥陀佛 Āmítuófó Amitabha Buddha

安 ān peace ◊ peaceful ◊ fit; install, set up ◊ how (*rhetorical questions*)

鞍 ān saddle

按 àn press, push; click on ◊

according to

岸 **àn** shore

案 **àn** (legal) case; record; file

暗 **àn** dark; dim; secret

案板 **ànbǎn** worktop; workbench

暗淡 **àndàn** dim, gloomy; bleak; black; 使暗淡 **shǐ àndàn** dim the headlights

安定 **āndìng** calm ◊ secure

安放 **ānfàng** position

安抚 **ānfǔ** conciliatory ◊ pacify

昂贵 **ángguì** expensive

盎司 **àngsī** ounce

肮脏 **āngzāng** dirty; filthy

安好 **ānhǎo** be installed, be up

安家 **ānjiā** settle down; set up home

案件 **ànjiàn** case LAW

暗礁 **ànjiāo** reef; hidden danger

按揭贷款 **ànjiē dàikuǎn** mortgage

安静 **ānjìng** calm ◊ peacefully ◊ calm down; shut up ◊ silent, quiet; placid ◊ in silence

按扣 **ànkòu** snap fastener, press stud

按喇叭 **àn lǎba** honk the horn

安乐死 **ānlèsǐ** euthanasia

安乐椅 **ānlèyǐ** easy chair

按铃 **ànlíng** ring (the bell)

安眠药 **ānmiányào** sleeping pill

按摩 **ànmó** massage

按摩技师 **ànmójìshī** chiropractor

按摩小姐 **ànmó xiǎojie** masseuse

按摩院 **ànmóyuàn** massage parlor

按摩浴缸 **ànmó yùgāng** whirlpool, jacuzzi

按钮 **ànniǔ** button (on machine)

安排 **ānpái** arrange, fix; arrange for; lay out; allocate; order ◊ arrangement

安全 **ānquán** safe ◊ safely ◊ safety; security; 处于安全状态 **chǔyú ānquán zhuàngtài** be safe

安全出口 **ānquán chūkǒu** fire escape

安全带 **ānquándài** seat belt

安全岛 **ānquándǎo** traffic island

安全感 **ānquángǎn** sense of security

安全检查 **ānquán jiǎnchá**

security check

安全装置 **ānquán zhuāngzhì** safeguard

暗杀 **ànshā** assassinate ◊ assassination

岸上 **ànshang** on shore

暗杀者 **ànshā zhě** assassin

按时 **ànshí** on time

暗示 **ànshì** hint; implication ◊ imply, insinuate; point to, indicate

安慰 **ānwèi** comfort; console; soothe ◊ comfort; compensation; consolation

安心 **ānxīn** reassured

安葬 **ānzàng** bury the dead

按照 **ànzhào** according to

暗指 **ànzhǐ** imply

按住 **ànzhù** pin; hold down

安装 **ānzhuāng** fit, install ◊ installation

鞍子 **ānzi** saddle

案子 **ànzi** case

凹 **āo** concave; sunken

鳌 **áo** pincers

熬 **áo** endure; boil

傲 **ào** arrogant; obstinate

凹处 **āochù** dent; recess (in wall)

澳大利西亚 **Àodàlāxīyà** Australasia ◊ Australasian

澳大利亚 **Àodàlìyà** Australia ◊ Australian

奥地利 **Àodìlì** Austria ◊ Austrian

懊悔 **àohuǐ** remorse; regret

奥林匹克运动会 **Àolínpǐkè Yùndònghuì** Olympic Games

傲慢 **àomàn** arrogance ◊ arrogant, haughty

澳门 **Àomén** Macao ◊ Macanese

奥秘 **àomì** great mystery

懊丧 **àosàng** depressed; morose

凹凸不平 **āotū bùpíng** lumpy

鳌虾 **áoxiā** lobster

凹陷 **āoxiàn** dip; hollow ◊ sunken cheeks ◊ cave in

翱翔 **áoxiáng** hover; soar

熬夜 **áoyè** stay up late; burn the midnight oil

奥运会 **Àoyùnhuì** Olympics

阿司匹林 **āsīpǐlín** aspirin

阿姨 **āyí** auntie (used also to address a woman of one's parents' age)

B

八 **bā** eight

疤 **bā** scar

拔 **bá** pull out, extract

靶 **bǎ** target

把 **bǎ** *measure word for knives and chairs*; 一把刀 **yìbǎ dāo** a knife; 一把钳子 **yìbǎ qiánzi** a pair of pliers/pincers ◊ (*marking an object moved for emphasis to the start of a sentence*): 我要把车修了 **wǒ yào bǎ chē xiūle** I'll have the car repaired

爸 **bà** dad, pop

霸 **bà** tyrant, despot

坝 **bà** dam

罢 **bà** stop, cease

把 **bà** handle

吧 **ba** (*to make suggestions*): 走吧 **zǒu ba** let's go ◊ (*in tag questions*) is he?; isn't he?; are you?; aren't you? etc; 你很忙吧 **nǐ hěn máng ba** you're very busy, aren't you?

爸爸 **bàba** dad, pop

靶场 **bǎchǎng** shooting range

拔出 **báchū** extract, pull out ◊ extraction

拔出插头 **báchū chātóu** unplug

霸道 **bàdào** domineering

罢工 **bàgōng** strike (*of workers*)

罢工者 **bàgōng zhě** striker

拔河 **báhé** tug of war

白 **bái** white ◊ in vain ◊ family name

百 **bǎi** hundred

柏 **bǎi** cypress

摆 **bǎi** place; lay

败 **bài** be defeated; defeat; fail

拜 **bài** congratulate

拜拜 **bāibāi** bye-bye

白班儿 **báibānr** day shift

百倍 **bǎibèi** hundredfold

摆布 **bǎibù** manipulate ◊ manipulation; 任由 X 摆布 **rènyóu X bǎibù** be at X's mercy

白菜 **báicài** Chinese cabbage

白痴 **báichī** idiot

摆翅 **bǎichì** flutter (*of wings*)

摆动 **bǎidòng** swing; wag; wiggle

白饭 **báifàn** boiled rice

摆放 **bǎifàng** set out *goods*

拜访 **bàifǎng** call on, visit ◊ visit

白费力 **bái fèilì** waste one's time, go to a lot of trouble for nothing

百分比 **bǎifēnbǐ** percentage

百分之 **bǎifēnzhī** percent; 百分之百 **bǎifēnzhī bǎi** one hundred percent

白宫 **Báigōng** White House

百和花 **bǎihéhuā** lily

白喉 **báihóu** diphtheria

白桦 **báihuà** birch

败坏 **bàihuài** spoil

百花齐放 **Bǎihuāqífàng** Hundred Flowers Movement

白灰 **báihuī** lime

百货商店 **bǎihuò shāngdiàn** department store

摆架子 **bǎi jiàzi** put on airs; behave snobbishly

白酒 **báijiǔ** clear grain spirit

白开水 **báikāishuǐ** boiled water

百科词典 **bǎikē cídiǎn** encyclopedia; dictionary

百科全书 **bǎikēquán shū** encyclopedia

白兰地 **báilándì** brandy; cognac

白领工人 **báilǐng gōngrén** white-collar worker

败露 **bàilù** emerge

拜年 **bàinián** pay a New Year's visit; wish a happy New Year; 给李先生拜年 **gěi Lǐ xiānsheng bàinián** wish Mr Li a happy New Year

摆弄 **bǎinòng** fiddle with; fool around with; toy with; twiddle

白葡萄酒 **bái pútaojiǔ** white wine

白人 **báirén** white *person*

百日咳 **bǎirìké** whooping cough

白日梦 **báirì mèng** daydream

白肉 **báiròu** white meat; boiled pork fat

白色 **báisè** white

白手起家的人 **báishǒuqǐjiāde rén** self-made man

白糖 **báitáng** white sugar

白天 **báitiān** daytime, day ◊ in the daytime

白涂料 **bái túliào** whitewash

摆脱 **bǎituō** get rid of; free oneself from

拜托 **bàituō** request; 拜托！ **bàituō!** do me a favor!

百万 **bǎiwàn** million

百万富翁 **bǎiwànfùwēng** millionaire

摆碗筷 **bǎi wǎnkuài** set the table

白皙 **báixī** fair *complexion*

掰下 **bāixià** break off

败兴者 **bàixìng zhě** spoilsport

白血病 **báixuě bìng** leukemia

百叶帘 **bǎiyè lián** venetian blind

白银 **báiyín** silver

柏油 **bǎiyóu** asphalt, tar

白字 **báizì** typo in Chinese characters

拔尖儿 **bájiānr** excellent

八角 **bājiǎo** star anise

巴基斯坦 **Bājīsītǎn** Pakistan ◊ Pakistani

芭蕾舞 **bāléiwǔ** ballet

芭蕾舞演员 **bāléiwǔ yǎnyuán** ballet dancer

拔毛 **bámáo** pluck

把门人 **bǎmén rén** bouncer, doorman

班 **bān** class; shift (*at work*) ◊ *measure word for bus, train etc*; 下一班飞机 **xià yì bān fēijī** the next flight

搬 **bān** move; shove; dislodge

斑 **bān** stain; spot; stripe ◊ striped

扳 **bān** turn; pull

板 **bǎn** board; sheet (*of metal, glass*)

版 **bǎn** edition; page (*of newspaper*)

半 **bàn** half; 十点半 **shídiǎnbàn** half past ten

瓣 **bàn** petal; segment

拌 **bàn** stir; mix; 拌色拉 **bàn sèlā** dress a salad

绊 **bàn** stumble, trip

扮 **bàn** get dressed up as; play the role of

办 **bàn** do; manage; deal with; 办签证 **bàn qiānzhèng** apply for a visa

版本 **bǎnběn** edition; version

半场 **bànchǎng** half time

伴唱 **bànchàng** backing (*singers*)

伴唱组 **bànchàng zǔ** backing group

搬出 **bānchū** move out

班船 **bānchuán** liner (*ship*)

版次 **bǎncì** impression (*of a book*)

绊倒 **bàndǎo** knock over; trip; stumble

半岛 **bàndǎo** peninsula

办到 **bàndào** manage to do

半导体 **bàndǎotǐ** semiconductor

板凳 **bǎndèng** stool

斑点 **bāndiǎn** spot

办法 **bànfǎ** method; means; way; way out; solution

邦 **bāng** nation; state

帮 **bāng** help ◊ gang; 帮 X 个忙 **bāng X ge máng** do X a favor

绑 **bǎng** bind

磅 **bàng** pound (*weight, sterling*)

棒 **bàng** stick; club ◊ great; excellent

榜 **bǎng** official announcement

棒棒冰 **bàngbàngbīng** Popsicle®

棒棒糖 **bàngbàng táng** sucker, lollipop

绑绷带 **bǎng bēngdài** bandage

半个小时 **bànge xiǎoshí** half an hour

半个月 **bàngeyuè** two weeks

绑架 **bǎngjià** kidnap ◊ kidnaping

邦交 **bāngjiāo** diplomatic relations

绑架者 **bǎngjià zhě** kidnaper

棒极了 **bàngjíle** fantastic, superb

帮忙 **bāngmáng** help

办公楼 **bàngōnglóu** office (*building*)

办公室 **bàngōngshì** office (*room*)

办公时间 **bàngōng shíjiān** office hours

绑票 **bǎngpiào** hold to ransom

棒球 **bàngqiú** baseball

棒球场 **bàngqiú chǎng** ballpark

棒球棍 **bàngqiú gùn** baseball bat

棒球帽 **bàngqiú mào** baseball cap

棒球运动员 **bàngqiú yùndòngyuán** baseball player

帮手 **bāngshǒu** helper

帮头 **bāngtóu** godfather (*in mafia*)

傍晚 **bàngwǎn** toward evening ◊ dusk

绑鞋带 **bǎng xiédài** do up one's shoelaces

帮凶 **bāngxiōng** accessory; accomplice

榜样 **bǎngyàng** role model; 树立好榜样 **shùlì hǎo bǎngyàng** set a good example

帮助 **bāngzhù** help, assist ◊ help, assistance

绑住 **bǎngzhù** lash down; tie up

棒子 **bàngzi** stick; pole

版画 **bǎnhuà** engraving; print

扳机 **bānjī** trigger

班级 **bānjí** school class; grade

搬家 **bānjiā** move, move house

绊脚 **bànjiǎo** stumble

绊脚石 **bànjiǎoshí** obstacle

搬进 **bānjìn** move in

半径 **bànjìng** radius

半决赛 **bànjuésài** semifinal

板栗 **bǎnlì** Chinese chestnut

办理 **bànlǐ** handle, take care of

伴侣 **bànlǚ** companion; company

斑马 **bānmǎ** zebra

伴娘 **bànniáng** bridesmaid

般配 **bānpèi** complement; 他们很般配 **tāmén hěn bānpèi** they complement each other

半票 **bànpiào** half-price ticket

搬迁 **bānqiān** relocate

搬迁公司 **bānqiān gōngsī** movers

半球 **bànqiú** hemisphere

版权 **bǎnquán** copyright

伴儿 **bànr** companionship

办事处 **bànshì chù** office, bureau

扳手 **bānshǒu** wrench (*tool*)

伴随 **bànsuí** pursue; accompany; follow

半天 **bàntiān** half a day; a long time

版图 **bǎntú** territory

半途 **bàntú** halfway

板岩 **bǎnyán** slate

扮演 **bànyǎn** play, portray ◊ portrayal; 扮演哈姆莱特 **bànyǎn Hāmǔláitè** as Hamlet

半夜 **bànyè** midnight; 半夜三更 **bànyè sāngēng** in the middle of the night

半圆形 **bànyuánxíng** semicircle ◊ semicircular

搬运 **bānyùn** carry; handle

拌匀 **bànyún** toss; mix

搬运工(人) **bānyùn gōng(rén)** porter; stevedore; laborer

斑疹伤寒 **bānzhěn shānghán** typhus

板子 **bǎnzi** board; plate

搬走 **bānzǒu** move away

伴奏 **bànzòu** accompaniment, backing ◊ accompany MUS

伴奏组 **bànzòu zǔ** backing group

包 **bāo** bag; pack ◊ bundle; wrap; assure; hire; 包春卷 **bāo chūnjuǎn** wrap a spring roll; 一包香烟 **yībāo xiāngyān** a pack of cigarettes; 把 ... 包起来 **bǎ ... bāo qǐlái** bundle up

剥 **bāo** peel

雹 **báo** hail

薄 **báo** thin

宝 **bǎo** treasure ◊ precious

保 **bǎo** protect; keep; guarantee

饱 **bǎo** full

堡 **bǎo** castle

豹 **bào** leopard

报 **bào** newspaper; report

暴 **bào** sudden; violent

爆 **bào** explode; blow up

抱 **bào** take in one's arms, hug

刨 **bào** plane (*tool*)

保安 **bǎo'ān** ensure public safety

报案 **bào'àn** report a case

保安部 **bǎo'ānbù** security

保安部队 **bǎo'ān bùduì** security forces

保安人员 **bǎo'ān rényuán** security guard

包办 **bāobàn** cater for

包办旅行 **bāobàn lǚxíng**
package deal, package tour

雹暴 **báobào** hailstorm

宝贝 **bǎobèi** treasure; darling

包庇 **bāobì** harbor

保镖 **bǎobiāo** bodyguard

保持 **bǎochí** hold, maintain; keep,
stay ◊ preservation; 保持沉默
bǎochí chénmò stay silent; 保持
距离 **bǎochí jùlí** keep one's
distance; 保持冷静 **bǎochí
lěngjìng** keep one's cool; 与 X 保
持联络 **yǔ X bǎochí liánluò** keep
in contact with X

报仇 **bàochóu** take revenge

报酬 **bàochóu** reward;
remuneration

保存 **bǎocún** conserve, preserve;
embalm

报答 **bàodá** repay

保单 **bǎodān** warranty (card)

报道 **bàodào** cover; report, report
on; present oneself ◊ coverage;
report, story

暴跌 **bàodiē** drop; crash

暴动 **bàodòng** outbreak of
violence

爆发 **bàofā** break out; erupt ◊
outbreak; eruption

暴发户 **bàofāhù** nouveau riche

报贩 **bàofàn** newsvendor

报废 **bàofèi** scrap

暴风雪 **bàofēngxuě** snowstorm

暴风雨 **bàofēngyǔ** rainstorm

报复 **bàofù** pay back *fig*; retaliate
◊ retaliation; revenge ◊ vindictive;
报复 X **bàofù X** get even with X

报告 **bàogào** break *news*; report,
account ◊ presentation

饱嗝儿 **bǎogér** belch

保管 **bǎoguǎn** take care of ◊
storeman ◊ certainly

报关 **bàoguān** customs
declaration

曝光 **bàoguāng** exposure; 曝光
不足 **bàoguāng bù zú**
underexposed

宝贵 **bǎoguì** precious; valuable

包裹 **bāoguǒ** package; parcel

包含 **bāohán** comprise;
incorporate; include

饱和 **bǎohé** saturation

保护 **bǎohù** conservation;
protection ◊ preserve; protect;
safeguard; shelter; shield

保护地区 **bǎohù dìqū**
reservation (*special area*)

保护费 **bǎohùfèi** protection
money

包机 **bāoji** charter flight

报价 **bàojià** quotation ◊ quote
price

保健 **bǎojiàn** health care

报警 **bàojǐng** raise the alarm

饱经沧桑 **bǎo jīng cāngsāng**
checkered *career*

饱经风霜 **bǎo jīng fēngshuāng**
weather-beaten

报警器 **bàojǐngqì** siren

暴君 **bàojūn** despot, tyrant

剥壳 **bāoké** shell

包括 **bāokuò** consist of; count,
include; take in ◊ including

暴力 **bàolì** violence ◊ violent

爆裂 **bàoliè** burst

保龄球 **bǎolíng qiú** bowling;
bowl; 打保龄球 **dǎ bǎolíng qiú**
bowl; go bowling

保龄球道 **bǎolíng qiú dào**
bowling alley

保留 **bǎoliú** keep, hang on to;
hold; reserve ◊ reservation

暴露 **bàolù** reveal; expose ◊
skimpy

暴乱 **bàoluàn** disorder, unrest,
riot

暴露自己 **bàolù zìjǐ** give oneself
away

保密 **bǎomì** keep secret; conceal ◊
secrecy ◊ secret

爆米花 **bàomǐhuā** puffed rice;
popcorn

暴民 **bàomín** mob

报名 **bàomíng** register; enrol; sign
up

报名参军 **bàomíng cānjūn** enlist

保姆 **bǎomǔ** nanny; housekeeper

报幕 **bàomù** announce a program

暴怒 **bàonù** fury

暴虐 **bàonüè** oppressive,
tyrannical ◊ tyranny

爆破 **bàopò** blow up; pop, burst

抱歉 **bàoqiàn** be sorry, regret

宝石 **bǎoshí** precious stone, jewel

保释 **bǎoshì** bail ◊ bail out LAW

报失 **bàoshī** report a loss

保释金 **bǎoshì jīn** bail

保守 **bǎoshǒu** conservative; straight

保守承诺 **bǎoshǒu chéngnuò** keep a promise

报税 **bàoshuì** make a tax declaration

宝塔 **bǎotǎ** pagoda

报摊儿 **bàotānr** newsstand

暴跳如雷 **bàotiào rúléi** go on the rampage

包围 **bāowéi** encircle; mob; lay siege to; surround; 被 X 包围 **bèi X bāowéi** be surrounded by X

保卫 **bǎowèi** defend ◊ defense

保温瓶 **bǎowēn píng** vacuum flask, thermos flask

保险 **bǎoxiǎn** insurance; safety ◊ safe ◊ be bound to

保险单 **bǎoxiǎndān** insurance policy

保险费 **bǎoxiǎnfèi** premium

保险杠 **bǎoxiǎn gàng** bumper

保险公司 **bǎoxiǎn gōngsī** insurance company

保险柜 **bǎoxiǎnguì** safe (for valuables)

保险金额 **bǎoxiǎn jīn'é** sum insured

保险丝 **bǎoxiǎnsī** fuse

保险丝盒 **bǎoxiǎnsī hé** fusebox

保险丝线 **bǎoxiǎnsī xiàn** fuse wire

保鲜纸 **bǎoxiān zhǐ** clingfilm

报销 **bàoxiāo** claim expenses

报销帐户 **bàoxiāo zhànghù** expense account

暴行 **bàoxíng** atrocity; brutality; outrage

保修期 **bǎoxiūqī** warranty period

保养 **bǎoyǎng** maintain ◊ maintenance

报应 **bàoyìng** just deserts; 他会得到报应 **tā huì dédào bàoyìng** he'll get his comeuppance

保佑 **bǎoyòu** bless

暴雨 **bàoyǔ** torrential rain

抱怨 **bàoyuàn** grumble, moan

暴躁 **bàozào** cranky, bad-tempered; fiery; hot-headed

爆炸 **bàozhà** blast, explosion ◊ explode, go off; blow (of tire); detonate

保障 **bǎozhàng** guarantee; security

保证 **bǎozhèng** assurance; security, guarantee ◊ ensure, guarantee; pledge; promise; 我向你保证 **wǒ xiàng nǐ bǎozhèng** you have my word

暴政 **bàozhèng** tyranny

保证期 **bǎozhèngqī** guarantee period

报纸 **bàozhǐ** newspaper

保质 **bǎozhì** keep (of food)

保重 **bǎozhòng** look after oneself; 保重! **bǎozhòng!** take care (of yourself)!

保住 **bǎozhù** keep

包装 **bāozhuāng** pack; package ◊ packaging

包装材料 **bāozhuāng cáiliào** packaging

包装纸 **bāozhuāngzhǐ** wrapping paper

刨子 **bàozi** plane (tool)

包租 **bāozū** charter

拔起 **báqǐ** pull up

跋涉 **báshè** trudge; wade

八十 **bāshí** eighty

巴士 **bāshì** bus

把手 **bǎshou** handle

把握 **bǎwò** grasp; seize; certainty

巴西 **Bāxī** Brazil ◊ Brazilian

靶心 **bǎxīn** bull's-eye

八月 **bāyuè** August ◊ in August

巴掌 **bāzhang** palm of the hand

八字胡 **bāzì hú** mustache

BB机 **BB jī** bleeper, pager

杯 **bēi** cup; glass; 一杯茶 **yìbēi chá** a cup of tea

悲 **bēi** sad; mournful

背 **bēi** carry on one's back

卑 **bēi** low; inferior; humble

碑 **bēi** monument; gravestone

北 **běi** north ◊ northern; northerly

倍 **bèi** -fold; 价格长三倍 **jiàgé zhǎng sānbèi** treble the price; X

比 Y 大 … 倍 **X bǐ Y dà … bèi** X outnumbers Y by … times

辈 **bèi** generation; lifetime

背 **bèi** back ◊ recite; memorize

贝 **bèi** shellfish

备 **bèi** have; be equipped with; prepare

被 **bèi** quilt ◊ (*passive indicator*) 被炒鱿鱼了 **bèi chǎo yóuyú le** be fired; 被淘汰 **bèi táotài** be eliminated

悲哀 **bēi'āi** mournful; sad; distressed

背包 **bēibāo** pack; backpack, rucksack

卑鄙 **bēibǐ** cowardly; mean, nasty; sordid

卑鄙交易 **bēibǐ jiāoyì** sharp practice

卑鄙行为 **bēibǐ xíngwéi** dirty trick

北部 **běibù** north; X 北部 **X běibù** north of X

被捕 **bèibǔ** be under arrest

悲惨 **bēicǎn** tragic; miserable ◊ misery

北朝鲜 **Běi Cháoxiān** North Korea ◊ North Korean

被单 **bèidān** sheet

被动 **bèidòng** passive; 被动形式 **bèidòng xíngshì** in the passive

被动语态 **bèidòng yǔtài** passive

北方 **běifāng** north ◊ northern

北方人 **běifāng rén** northerner

被告 **bèigào** accused, defendant; defense

被告席 **bèigào xí** dock (*in court*)

卑躬屈膝 **bēigōng qūqī** slimy

悲观 **bēiguān** pessimistic; dim ◊ pessimism

悲观者 **bēiguān zhě** pessimist

悲后 **bèihòu** behind ◊ behind one's back

北极 **Běijí** Arctic; North Pole

卑贱 **bēijiàn** humble, lowly

备件 **bèijiàn** spare part

北京 **Běijīng** Beijing, Peking

背景 **bèijǐng** setting, background; 以 … 为背景 **yǐ … wéi bèijǐng** set in, located in

北京烤鸭 **Běijīng kǎoyā** Peking duck

背景音乐 **bèijǐng yīnyuè** piped music

背景资料 **bèijǐng zīliào** background information

北极熊 **běijíxióng** polar bear

悲剧 **bēijù** tragedy

贝壳 **bèiké** shell

蓓蕾 **bèilěi** bud

贝类 **bèilèi** shellfish

卑劣 **bēiliè** contemptible; shoddy

北美洲 **Běi Měizhōu** North America ◊ North American

背面 **bèimiàn** back

背叛 **bèipàn** betray; break away ◊ betrayal

被迫 **bèipò** forced

被褥 **bèirù** quilt

悲伤 **bēishāng** sad ◊ grief

背书 **bèishū** endorse

背诵 **bèisòng** recite

被套 **bèitào** quilt cover

悲痛 **bēitòng** grief; mourning ◊ grieve

悲痛欲绝 **bēitòngyùjué** be prostrate with grief

备忘录 **bèiwànglù** memo

碑文 **bēiwén** inscription

背向 **bèixiàng** back onto

背心 **bèixīn** undershirt; vest; T-shirt

背阴 **bèiyīn** in the shade

备用 **bèiyòng** spare

备用车轮 **bèiyòng chēlún** spare wheel

备用磁盘 **bèiyòng cípán** backup disk

备用轮胎 **bèiyòng lúntāi** spare tire

备有 **bèiyǒu** stock

北约 **Běiyuē** NATO

北越 **Běiyuè** North Vietnam ◊ North Vietnamese

倍增 **bèizēng** double

背着 **bēizhe** carry, hump

备注 **bèizhù** remarks; notes

杯子 **bēizi** cup; glass

被子 **bèizi** cover; quilt

奔 **bēn** run fast

本 **běn** copy ◊ root, origin ◊ originally ◊ this ◊ *measure word for* *books*; 四本书 *sìběn shū* four books

笨 **bèn** stupid, dumb; clumsy

奔波 **bēnbō** rush around; juggle *fig*

奔驰 **bēnchí** dash, speed

笨蛋 **bèndàn** idiot; ass(hole)

本地 **běndì** local; native

本地人 **běndì rén** local (person)

绷 **bēng** tack; tighten; bounce

崩 **bēng** collapse; burst

泵 **bèng** pump

蹦 **bèng** leap; skip; jump

蹦蹦车 **bèngbèngchē** motor rickshaw

绷床 **bēngchuáng** trampoline

绷带 **bēngdài** bandage

迸发 **bèngfā** outburst

绷紧 **bēngjǐn** tense up

崩溃 **bēngkuì** breakdown, collapse ◊ crumble; give way

绷绳 **bēngshéng** string

绷索 **bēngsuǒ** tightrope

崩塌 **bēngtā** collapse

本国 **běnguó** native

本国语 **běnguó yǔ** native language

本来 **běnlái** actual ◊ actually; to begin with, originally

本领 **běnlǐng** ability

本能 **běnnéng** instinct ◊ instinctive

奔跑 **bēnpǎo** sprint

本钱 **běnqián** capital

本人 **běnrén** personal ◊ personally, oneself

本身 **běnshēn** itself; in itself

笨手笨脚 **bènshǒu bènjiǎo** clumsy

本性 **běnxìng** nature, character

本质 **běnzhì** nature ◊ fundamental

笨重 **bènzhòng** cumbersome

笨拙 **bènzhuō** clumsy; awkward ◊ clumsiness

逼 **bī** force

鼻 **bí** nose

比 **bǐ** compare; compete with; 我比不过 *wǒ bǐ bú guò* I can't rival that; X 比 Y 好 *X bǐ Y hǎo* X is better than Y; 他比我高 *tā bǐ wǒ gāo* he's taller than me

鄙 **bǐ** lowly; mean; my humble

笔 **bǐ** writing implement ◊ *measure word for sums of money*; 一大笔钱 *yí dà bǐ qián* a large sum of money

必 **bì** must

毕 **bì** finish

币 **bì** money; currency

避 **bì** avoid; prevent

壁 **bì** wall

臂 **bì** arm

闭 **bì** close; shut

边 **biān** side; rim

边 ... 边 ... **biān ... biān ...**: 我们边喝/吃边谈 *wǒmén biānhē / chī biān tán* let's talk over a drink / meal; 边听边写 *biān tīng biān xiě* listen and take notes

编 **biān** weave; organize; edit; write; make up 编辫子 *biān biànzi* plait

鞭 **biān** whip

扁 **biǎn** flat

贬 **biǎn** devalue

变 **biàn** change; change into, become; 变老 *biànlǎo* get old

辨 **biàn** differentiate

辩 **biàn** discuss; argue

辫 **biàn** plait

便 **biàn** convenient ◊ defecate; shit; urinate; piss ◊ then

便秘 **biànbì** constipation

辨别 **biànbié** differentiate; distinguish

辩驳 **biànbó** dispute; refute

遍布 **biànbù** widespread

变成 **biànchéng** become

编程序 **biān chéngxù** program

辨出 **biànchū** discern

鞭打 **biāndǎ** whip, flog, lash ◊ whipping

扁担 **biǎndan** yoke, shoulder pole

便当 **biàndāng** lunch box

变得 **biànde** become, go

贬低 **biǎndī** belittle, run down

变动 **biàndòng** alteration; swing, upheaval

扁豆 **biǎndòu** scarlet runner

编队 **biānduì** formation

蝙蝠 **biānfú** bat

便服 **biànfú** casual wear; civilian clothes

编号 **biānhào** number ◊ serial number

辩护 **biànhù** plead; defend ◊ defense; 为 X 辩护 **wèi X biànhù** defend X LAW; stick up for X

变化 **biànhuà** change, switch; variation ◊ vary

变化无常 **biànhuà wúcháng** fickle, volatile

辩护律师 **biànhù lǜshī** defense lawyer

辩护人 **biànhù rén** defense lawyer

辩护证人 **biànhù zhèngrén** defense witness

编辑 **biānjí** edit ◊ editor ◊ editorial; 体育 / 政治栏编辑 **tǐyù / zhèngzhì lán biānjí** sports / political editor

便笺 **biànjiān** pad (*for writing*)

边疆 **biānjiāng** frontier

编辑部 **biānjíbù** editorial department

边界 **biānjiè** border; boundary

边境 **biānjìng** border; frontier

遍及世界 **biànjí shìjiè** worldwide

便利 **biànlì** convenient

变量 **biànliàng** variable

编列 **biānliè** list

辩论 **biànlùn** debate

便秘 **biànmì** constipated ◊ constipation

鞭炮 **biānpào** firework; firecracker

便盆 **biànpén** chamber pot; potty (*for baby*)

变迁 **biànqiān** change

辨认 **biànrèn** make out, spot

辨认出 **biànrèn chū** recognize

变速杆 **biànsùgǎnr** gear lever, gear shift

变速器 **biànsùqì** gearbox; transmission

变态 **biàntài** abnormal; kinky ◊ metamorphosis

变态心理 **biàntài xīnlǐ** perversion

扁桃腺 **biǎntáoxiàn** tonsil

扁桃腺炎 **biǎntáoxiàn yán** tonsillitis

便条 **biàntiáo** note; compliments slip

便条本 **biàntiáo běn** notepad

便条纸 **biàntiáo zhǐ** notepaper

变通 **biàntōng** flexible

编舞 **biān wǔ** choreography; choreographer

边线 **biānxiàn** touchline; sideline; foul line

边线外 **biānxiàn wài** touch

便鞋 **biànxié** cloth shoes; slippers

变形 **biànxíng** buckle (*change shape*)

变压器 **biànyāqì** transformer

贬义 **biǎnyì** derogatory, disparaging

贬抑 **biǎnyì** pejorative

便衣 **biànyī** plain clothes; civilian clothes

变音 **biànyīn** inflection

边缘 **biānyuán** edge, border; brim; fringe; periphery; surround ◊ outlying

编造 **biānzào** make up, concoct

编织 **biānzhī** knit; weave ◊ knitting; weaving

编制 **biānzhì** compile

贬值 **biǎnzhí** depreciate; devalue ◊ depreciation; devaluation

变质 **biànzhì** spoil; deteriorate

编织物 **biānzhīwù** knitting

便装 **biànzhuāng** civilian dress

鞭子 **biānzi** whip

辫子 **biànzi** braid, plait

标 **biāo** mark, sign

表 **biǎo** table; form; meter; watch; surface; outside ◊ show, express

表达 **biǎodá** convey, express; formulate; show; 表达能力强 **biǎodá nénglì qiáng** articulate; 表达意见 **biǎodá yìjiàn** have one's say

表达法 **biǎodáfǎ** expression

表带 **biǎodài** watch strap

表弟 **biǎodì** cousin (*younger male on mother's side*)

标点 **biāodiǎn** punctuation

标点符号 **biāodiǎn fúhào** punctuation mark

表哥 **biǎogē** cousin (*elder male*)

表格 **biǎogé** form; table;

spreadsheet

裱糊 **biǎohú** paper

标记 **biāojì** sign; symbol

表姐 **biǎojiě** cousin (*elder female on mother's side*)

表决 **biǎojué** decide by vote

表决通过 **biǎojué tōngguò** pass, approve

表露 **biǎolù** show, display

表妹 **biǎomèi** cousin (*younger female on mother's side*)

表面 **biǎomiàn** surface; 表面上 **biǎomiàn shang** on the surface

标明 **biāomíng** mark

表明 **biǎomíng** indicate

表皮 **biǎopí** cuticle ◊ superficial

标签 **biāoqiān** label; nametag; sticker

标枪 **biāoqiāng** javelin

表情 **biǎoqíng** expression

表示 **biǎoshì** give, convey; show; express; mean ◊ display; expression; gesture

标题 **biāotí** heading; headline

标题点 **biāotídiǎn** bullet point

表现 **biǎoxiàn** show; behave ◊ performance; behavior

表兄 **biǎoxiōng** cousin (*elder male on mother's side*)

表演 **biǎoyǎn** act; perform; play; stage ◊ acting; performance; exhibition

表扬 **biǎoyáng** praise; pay a compliment

表演者 **biǎoyǎn zhě** entertainer; performer

标语 **biāoyǔ** slogan

标语牌 **biāoyǔpái** placard

标志 **biāozhì** mark; logo

标准 **biāozhǔn** standard; criterion

标准杆数 **biāozhǔn gānshù** par

婊子 **biǎozi** prostitute, whore

臂膀 **bìbǎng** arm

必备 **bìbèi** precondition, prerequisite

弊病 **bìbìng** disadvantage; mistake; defect

必不可少 **bìbù kěshǎo** necessary; vital

壁橱 **bìchú** cabinet

彼此 **bǐcǐ** each other

必定 **bìdìng** must; be sure to ◊ for sure; definitely

弊端 **bìduān** corrupt practices

别 **bié** other ◊ don't ◊ leave; part; 还要别的吗？**hái yào biéde ma?** anything else?; 别的东西 **biéde dōngxi** something else; 别动！**biédòng!** don't move!

瘪 **biě** shriveled; shrunken; flat *tire*

别处 **biéchù** elsewhere

别具一格 **biéjùyìgé** unique

别离 **biélí** leave; part from

别人 **biérén** someone else; other people; 别人都去 **biérén dōu qù** everyone else is going

别墅 **biéshù** villa

别针 **biézhēn** safety pin

比分 **bǐfēn** score; goal; 比分是多少？**bǐfēn shì duōshǎo?** what's the score?

庇护 **bìhù** asylum; refuge; shelter

笔画 **bǐhuà** stroke (*in writing*)

壁画 **bìhuà** fresco; mural

避讳 **bìhuì** taboo

笔迹 **bǐjì** handwriting

笔记 **bǐjì** write down ◊ notes

比价 **bǐjià** price ratio ◊ compare prices

比较 **bǐjiào** compare ◊ comparison ◊ comparative ◊ comparatively; relatively; rather; 比较便宜 **bǐjiào piányi** cheaper ◊ it costs less

比较级 **bǐjiào jí** comparative (form)

笔记本 **bǐjìběn** notebook; notebook computer

毕竟 **bìjìng** after all

比基尼 **bǐjīní** bikini

避开 **bìkāi** dodge, evade; ward off; keep out; make oneself scarce

鼻孔 **bíkǒng** nostril

壁垒 **bìlěi** rampart

避雷导线 **bìléi dǎoxiàn** lightning conductor

比例 **bǐlì** proportion; scale

鼻梁 **bíliáng** bridge (*of nose*)

比例绘图 **bǐlì huìtú** scale drawing

比利时 **Bǐlìshí** Belgium ◊ Belgian

壁炉台 **bìlútái** mantelpiece, mantelshelf

壁炉 **bìlú** fireplace; hearth

比率 bǐlǜ rate

闭路电视 bìlù diànshì closed-circuit television

笔帽 bǐmào cap (of pen)

避免 bìmiǎn avoid, avert; keep off

笔名 bǐmíng pen name

闭幕式 bìmùshì closing ceremony

宾 bīn guest

避难所 bìnànsuǒ haven; sanctuary; refuge

彬彬有礼 bīnbīn yǒu lǐ well-mannered

冰 bīng ice

兵 bīng soldier

柄 bǐng stem

饼 bǐng round, flat cake; pancake

病 bìng illness ◊ sick

并 bìng combine; merge ◊ and ◊ (negative intensifier): 我并不在意 wǒ bìng bú zàiyì I really don't mind

冰雹 bīngbáo hail

冰场 bīngchǎng ice rink

冰川 bīngchuān glacier

冰灯 bīngdēng ice-lantern

冰点 bīngdiǎn freezing point

冰冻 bīngdòng freeze

病毒 bìngdú virus, bug ◊ viral

病房 bìngfáng hospital room

并发症 bìngfā zhèng complications MED

冰封 bīngfēng frozen

饼干 bǐnggān cookie; cracker

冰糕 bīnggāo ice cream

冰棍儿 bīnggùnr Popsicle®

病假 bìngjià sick leave

并肩 bìngjiān side by side

病菌 bìngjūn germ

冰咖啡 bīngkāfēi iced coffee

冰块 bīngkuài ice cube

冰冷 bīnglěng ice-cold

兵力 bīnglì troops; armed forces; military strength

病例 bìnglì case MED

冰凉 bīngliáng frozen

病理学 bìnglǐxué pathology

病理学家 bìnglǐxuéjiā pathologist

兵马俑 bīngmǎyǒng terracotta army

并排 bìngpái side by side

并且 bìngqiě and; besides

冰淇淋 bīngqílín ice cream

冰淇淋店 bīngqílín diàn ice cream parlor

冰球 bīngqiú (ice) hockey

病人 bìngrén patient; sick person

病弱 bìngruò invalid ◊ sickly

冰山 bīngshān iceberg

病史 bìngshǐ case history, medical history

病态 bìngtài morbid; pathological; sick society

冰糖 bīngtáng candy sugar

病痛 bìngtòng pain; ailment

宾馆 bīnguǎn hotel; guest house

冰箱 bīngxiāng refrigerator, icebox; freezer

冰鞋 bīngxié ice-skate

兵役义务 bīngyì yìwù military service

病友 bìngyǒu friend made in the hospital; fellow patient

冰镇 bīngzhèn chilled

病症晚期 bìngzhèng wǎnqī terminally ill

冰柱 bīngzhù icicle

屏住呼吸 bǐngzhù hūxī hold one's breath

滨海区 bīnhǎiqū coastal region

殡仪馆 bìnyíguǎn funeral home

濒于 bīnyú be on the verge of

逼迫 bīpò push, pressure

壁球 bìqiú squash (game)

必然 bìrán inevitable ◊ inevitably

必然性 bìrán xìng certainty, inevitability

比如 bǐrú for example

比萨 bǐsà pizza

比赛 bǐsài competition; contest; match; 我和你比赛 wǒ hé nǐ bǐsài I'll race you; 与 X 比赛 yǔ X bǐsài compete against X

比赛场地 bǐsài chǎngdì arena

比赛项目 bǐsài xiàngmù event

闭上 bìshàng close ◊ closed

毕生 bìshēng lifetime ◊ all one's life

鄙视 bǐshì despise; scorn

匕首 bǐshǒu dagger

必死 bìsǐ mortal

壁毯 bìtǎn tapestry

鼻涕 bítì snot

笔芯 bǐxīn pencil lead; pen refill

必修 bìxiū compulsory *course*

必须 bìxū must, have (got) to ◊ obligatory

必需 bìxū necessary

必需品 bìxū pǐn necessity

必须要 bìxū yào call for

必要 bìyào essential, necessary

必要时 bìyàoshí if necessary, at a pinch

必要性 bìyào xìng necessity ◊ must

毕业 bìyè graduate ◊ graduation

毕业生 bìyèshēng graduate

鼻音 bíyīn twang

笔友 bǐyǒu penfriend, penpal

比喻 bǐyù analogy ◊ figurative

避孕 bìyùn birth control; contraception

避孕器 bìyùn qì contraceptive

避孕套 bìyùn tào condom

避孕药 bìyùn yào contraceptive (pill), the pill

逼真 bīzhēn true to life

笔直 bǐzhí straight; upright

币值 bìzhí currency value

壁纸 bìzhǐ (wall)paper

币制 bìzhì monetary system

鼻子 bízi nose

闭嘴 bìzuǐ be quiet; 闭嘴! *bìzuǐ!* be quiet!, shut up!

拨 bō dial *telephone number*

播 bō sow seed; broadcast

波 bō wave

剥 bō peel

铂 bó platinum

伯 bó uncle (*father's elder brother*)

脖 bó neck

博 bó extensive; broad

驳 bó refute

跛 bǒ lame

博爱 bó'ài universal love; fraternity

薄饼 bóbǐng pancake

伯伯 bóbó uncle (*father's elder brother*); *used to address a man older than one's father*

菠菜 bōcài spinach

波长 bōcháng wavelength

驳斥 bóchì refute; disprove

拨出 bōchū set aside, earmark

驳船 bóchuán barge

驳倒 bódǎo refute; outargue

波动 bōdòng fluctuate ◊ fluctuation

搏动 bódòng pulsate

搏斗 bódòu fight, battle

波段 bōduàn frequency RAD

剥夺 X 的 Y bōduó Xde Y strip X of Y

播放 bōfàng transmission ◊ transmit

波状 bōfú wavy

伯父 bófù uncle (*father's elder brother*)

脖颈儿 bógěngr (nape of) neck

剥光衣服 bōguāng yīfu strip, undress

渤海湾 Bóhǎi Wān Bohai Gulf

拨号 bōhào dial

拨号盘 bōhào pán dial

拨号音 bōhàoyīn dial tone

薄荷 bòhe mint; peppermint

薄荷糖 bòhetáng peppermint candy

簸箕 bòji dustpan

拨款 bōkuǎn fund ◊ grant

波兰 Bōlán Poland ◊ Polish

波浪 bōlàng wave

拨浪鼓 bōlànggǔ rattle (*toy*)

博览会 bólǎnhuì trade fair

玻璃 bōli glass

玻璃杯 bōlibēi glass (*for drinking*)

玻璃纤维 bōli xiānwéi fiberglass

玻璃纸 bōlizhǐ cellophane

菠萝 bōluó pineapple

剥落 bōluò flake off, peel

勃鲁斯歌手 bólǔsī gēshǒu blues singer

勃鲁斯音乐 bólǔsī yīnyuè blues

勃起 bóqǐ erection ◊ erect

勃然大怒 bórán dànù fly into a rage

薄弱 bóruò weak; vulnerable

薄纱 bóshā gauze

博士 bóshì doctor; doctorate, PhD

播送 bōsòng on the air

波涛 bōtāo wave

薄雾 bówù haze, mist

博物馆 bówùguǎn museum

薄雾笼罩 bówù lǒngzhào misty

博物学家 **bówù xuéjiā** naturalist

跛行 **bǒxíng** limp

剥削 **bōxuē** exploit ◊ exploitation; rip-off

博学 **bóxué** well-read

播音 **bōyīn** broadcast ◊ broadcasting

播音员 **bōyīn yuán** radio announcer; broadcaster

播种 **bōzhǒng** sow *seeds*

驳船 **bózhuán** barge (*boat*)

脖子 **bózi** neck

补 **bǔ** darn; patch up; 补车票 **bǔ chēpiào** buy a ticket after boarding

捕 **bǔ** catch

部 **bù** department, ministry; unit

不 **bù** no; non …, un …, in …; not ◊ won't ◊ (*in questions*): 疼不疼？ **téng bùténg?** does it hurt?; 疼不？ **téng bù?** does it hurt?

步 **bù** pace, step

部 **bù** unit

布 **bù** material, cloth

簿 **bù** book; exercise book; notebook

不安 **bù'ān** uneasy ◊ disquiet; 令人不安 **lìngrén bù'ān** disturbing, worrying; uneasy

不安分 **bù ānfèn** restless

不安全 **bù ānquán** insecure; unsafe

不安全感 **bù ānquángǎn** insecurity

不必 **búbì** unnecessary ◊ needn't

不变 **búbiàn** always, invariably ◊ unswerving

不便 **búbiàn** inconvenient

步兵 **bùbīng** infantry; infantry soldier

不必要 **bú bìyào** unnecessary

不测事件 **bùcè shìjiàn** contingency

补偿 **bǔcháng** compensate for; make up for; reimburse ◊ recompense

不超过 **bù chāoguò** within; no more than

不成比例 **bù chéng bǐlì** disproportionate

不称职 **bú chènzhí** incompetent ◊ incompetence

补充 **bǔchōng** add to ◊ additional; incidental ◊ addition

不纯 **bùchún** impure

不辞辛苦 **bùcí xīnkǔ** spare no effort

不错 **búcuò** not bad; excellent

不大 **búdà** small

不大可能 **bú dà kěnéng** improbable, unlikely

不丹 **Bùdān** Bhutan ◊ Bhutanese

不当 **búdàng** unsuitable

不到 **bú dào** under, less than

捕到 **bǔdào** catch

布道 **bùdào** preach; preach a sermon

不道德 **bú dàodé** immoral ◊ immorality

布道坛 **bùdàotán** pulpit

不得不 **bùdébù** have to, be compelled to

不得了 **bùdéliǎo** fantastic ◊ extremely ◊ no way out; 好得不得了 **hǎo dé bùdéliǎo** absolutely fantastic, out of this world; 多得不得了 **duōde bùdéliǎo** a hell of a lot

不得人心 **bùdé rénxīn** unpopular

不得入内 **bùdé rùnèi** no trespassing

补丁 **bǔdīng** darn; patch

布丁 **bùdīng** pudding

不定冠词 **búdìng guàncí** indefinite article

不定式 **búdìngshì** infinitive

不动 **búdòng** motionless

不动产 **bùdòngchǎn** real estate

不动产商 **bùdòngchǎn shāng** developer; real estate agent

不动产中间商 **búdòng chǎn zhōngjiān shāng** real estate agent

不断 **bùduàn** constant, continual

不对 **bú duì** be wrong ◊ incorrect

部队 **bùduì** corps, unit; forces

不对劲儿 **bú duì jìnr** shifty; strange

步伐 **bùfá** step

不方便 **bù fāngbiàn** inconvenient ◊ inconvenience

部分 **bùfen** part, bit; component;

piece, section; patch; proportion ◊ partly

补付 **bǔfù** pay extra; pay later

不服 **bùfú** disobey

不符 **bùfú** not agree with; not comply with

不服从 **bù fúcóng** disobedience ◊ insubordinate

不服管 **bù fúguǎn** rebellious

不负责任 **búfùzérèn** irresponsible

不干涉 **bùgānshè** hands-off ◊ non-intervention

不干预 **bù gānyù** noninterference, nonintervention

布告 **bùgào** bulletin; announcement

布告板 **bǔgào bǎn** bulletin board

不给 **bù gěi** withhold

不共戴天 **búgòng dàitiān** mortal *enemy*

不够 **búgòu** insufficient; 不够好 **búgòuhǎo** not good enough

不顾 **búgù** regardless of, irrespective of

不关你的事! **bùguān nǐde shì!** mind your own business!

不管 **bùguǎn**: 我才不管呢! **wǒ cái bùguǎn ne!** I don't give a damn!; for all I care; 不管什么 **bùguǎn shénme** no matter what, whatever; 不管他们多大 **bùguǎn tāmen duō dà** however big they are; 不管她说什么 **bùguǎn tā shuō shénme** no matter what she says

不顾后果 **búgù hòuguǒ** reckless

不规范 **bùguīfàn** irregular

不规矩 **bù guīju** unruly

不规律 **bùguīlǜ** irregular

不规则 **bùguīzé** irregular

补过 **bǔguò** make amends

不过 **búguò** however

不寒而栗 **bùhán'érlì** shake with fear

不含铅 **bù hán qiān** lead-free

不好 **bùhǎo** bad ◊ badly

不合法 **bù héfǎ** illegal, wrongful

不合格 **bù hégé** unqualified

不合逻辑 **bù hé luójí** illogical

不合群 **bù héqún** unsociable

不合适 **bù héshì** unsuitable

不和谐 **bù héxié** discord

步话机 **bùhuàjī** walkie-talkie

捕获 **bǔhuò** capture; catch

捕获物 **bǔhuò wù** catch (*of fish*)

不活跃 **bù huóyuè** inactive

簿记 **bùjì** bookkeeping

部件 **bùjiàn** unit

不间断 **bù jiānduàn** uninterrupted

不讲道德 **bù jiǎng dàodé** unscrupulous

不坚固 **bù jiāngù** unstable

不健康 **bú jiànkāng** unfit; unhealthy; sickly

不结盟 **bù jiéméng** nonaligned

不结实 **bù jiēshí** flimsy

不及格 **bù jígé** flunk

不仅 **bùjǐn** not only

捕鲸 **bǔjīng** whaling

布景 **bùjǐng** scenes, set THEA

不景气 **bù jǐngqì** recession; depression ◊ unhealthy *economy*

不经心 **bù jīngxīn** inattentive

补救 **bǔjiù** remedy

不久 **bùjiǔ** before long, soon

不久之后 **bùjiǔ zhīhòu** soon after

布局 **bùjú** layout

不拘礼节 **bùjū lǐjié** offhand

不拘束 **bùjūshù** irrepressible

不拘形式 **bùjū xíngshì** free and easy

不可避免 **bùkě bìmiǎn** inevitable, unavoidable ◊ inevitably

不可分割 **bùkě fēngē** indivisible; inseparable

不可否认 **bùkě fǒurèn** undeniable

不可救药 **bùkě jiùyào** incorrigible

不可靠 **bù kěkào** unreliable

不可理解 **bùkě lǐjiě** incomprehensible

不可能 **bù kěnéng** impossible ◊ that can't be right; that's out of the question

不客气 **bú kèqi** impolite ◊ you're welcome

不可饶恕 **bùkě ráoshù**

unforgivable

不可思议 **bùkě sīyì** unthinkable; uncanny ◊ mysteriously

不可挽回 **bùkě wǎnhuí** irretrievable

不可信 **bù kěxìn** questionable

不可原谅 **bùkě yuánliàng** inexcusable

不可战胜 **bùkě zhànshèng** unbeatable

不快 **búkuài** unhappy; 令人不快 **lìngrén búkuài** miserable; unsavory; disagreeable

不愧于 **bú kuìyú** live up to; be worthy of

不老实 **bù lǎoshi** deceitful

布雷区 **bùléiqū** minefield

不理 **bùlǐ** brush aside; ignore

不利 **búlì** detrimental; disadvantageous; unfavorable; 对 … 不利 **duì … búlì** to the detriment of

不连贯 **bù liánguàn** incoherent

布料 **bùliào** cloth, fabric, material

不了解 **bù liáojiě** be out of touch

不礼貌 **bù lǐmào** impolite, disrespectful

不领情 **bù lǐngqíng** ungrateful

不利之处 **búlì zhīchù** disadvantage

不漏水 **búlòushuǐ** watertight

不论 **búlùn** no matter

部落 **bùluò** tribe

不落俗套 **búluò sútào** unconventional

布满 **bùmǎn** be full of; be bristling with

不满 **bùmǎn** discontent, dissatisfied; disgruntled; resentful ◊ displeasure; dissatisfaction; resentment ◊ resent

不满意 **bù mǎnyì** discontented; dissatisfied

部门 **bùmén** department; division; sector

不免 **bùmiǎn** unavoidable

不免一死 **bùmiǎnyìsǐ** mortal ◊ mortality

不明朗 **bù mínglǎng** noncommittal, vague ◊ vaguely

不能 **bùnéng** not be able to; be

unable; can't; mustn't; shouldn't; cannot be …

不能消化 **bùnéng xiāohuà** indigestible

不能抑制 **bùnéng yìzhì** irrepressible

不偏不倚 **bù piānbùyǐ** detachment, objectivity

不偏袒 **bù piāntǎn** unbiased

不偏心 **bù piānxīn** dispassionate

补票 **bǔpiào** buy a ticket after boarding

补票费 **bǔpiàofèi** excess fare

不平常 **bù píngcháng** extraordinary; unusual

不平等 **bù píngděng** unequal ◊ inequality

不平衡 **bū pínghéng** unbalanced, lop-sided

不恰当 **bú qiàdàng** improper; undeserved; unfortunate

不清楚 **bù qīngchu** unclear

不请自到 **bùqǐngzìdào** come uninvited, gatecrash

不确定 **bú quèdìng** indefinite; uncertain ◊ uncertainty

不然 **bùrán** otherwise; not so

不然的话 **bùrán dehuà** otherwise

不让步 **bú ràngbù** uncompromising

不容置疑 **bùróng zhìyí** indisputable ◊ indisputably

哺乳 **bǔrǔ** breastfeed

不如 **bùrú** not as good as … ◊ be better to …

哺乳动物 **bǔrǔ dòngwù** mammal

不少 **bùshǎo** quite a lot (of)

不慎 **búshèn** careless

不是 **búshì** not; no

捕食 **bǔshí** prey on

不适当 **búshì dàng** unduly ◊ inappropriate; inadequate

不适合 **bú shìhé** unfit; unsuitable; inappropriate

不实际 **bù shíjì** impractical

不适用 **bú shìyòng** inapplicable

部首 **bùshǒu** radical (*of Chinese character*)

不受欢迎 **bú shòu huānyíng** unpopular; undesirable

捕兽机关 **bǔshòu jīguān** trap

不守秩序 **bù shǒu zhìxù** disorderly

不受重视 **bú shòu zhòngshì** neglected

不舒服 **bùshūfu** unwell, poorly; uncomfortable

不熟练 **bù shúliàn** inept; unskilled

不顺眼 **bú shùnyǎn** eyesore

不舒适 **bù shūshì** uncomfortable

不熟悉 **bù shúxī** unfamiliar; 不熟悉 X **bù shúxī X** be unfamiliar with X

不太可能 **bú tài kěnéng** unlikely

补贴 **bǔtiē** allowance, grant

不通 **bùtōng** impassable

不同 **bùtóng** different; distinct; varied; various ◊ differ ◊ otherwise, differently

不同寻常 **bùtóng xúncháng** unusual

不同意 **bù tóngyì** disagree

不同意见 **bùtóng yìjiàn** disagreement

不透明 **bù tòumíng** opaque

不褪色 **bú tuìsè** colorfast

不完美 **bù wánměi** imperfect

不完全 **bù wánquán** partial

不完整 **bù wánzhěng** incomplete

部位 **bùwèi** position

不卫生 **bú wèishēng** unhygienic, insanitary

不像 **búxiàng** unlike

不祥 **búxiáng** ominous

不相符 **bù xiāngfù** incompatible ◊ incompatibility

不相干 **bù xiānggān** irrelevant

不相关 **bù xiāngguān** unrelated

不现实 **bú xiànshí** impractical; unrealistic

不显眼 **bù xiǎnyǎn** inconspicuous

不显著 **bù xiǎnzhù** dim

不小心 **bùxiǎoxīn** careless ◊ by accident

不懈 **búxiè** relentless

不谢 **búxiè** that's alright (*when somebody says thank you*)

不协调 **bùxiétiáo** clash; discord ◊ incongruous

不幸 **búxìng** poor; ill-fated;

unfortunate, unlucky; tragic; regrettable ◊ regrettably ◊ misfortune

不行 **bùxíng** it's not allowed; that's out ◊ impossible

步行 **bùxíng** walk; hike ◊ on foot

不幸的是 **búxìng de shì** unfortunately

不醒人事 **bù xǐng rénshì** unconscious; 打得 X 不醒人事 **dǎde X bù xǐng rénshì** knock X unconscious

不幸事故 **búxìng shìgù** mishap

不信任 **búxìnrèn** mistrust

不朽 **bùxiǔ** immortal ◊ immortality

不锈钢 **búxiùgāng** stainless steel

不炫耀 **bú xuànyào** unpretentious

不许 **bùxǔ** not allowed; 不许动！ **bùxǔdòng!** don't make a move!

不寻常 **bù xúncháng** uncommon

补牙 **bǔyá** filling (*in tooth*)

不言而喻 **bù yán ér yù** self-evident

不厌其烦 **búyànqífán** thorough

不要 **bùyào** not want; don't; 我不要，谢谢 **wǒ bùyào, xièxiè** not for me, thanks

不要脸 **bú yào liǎn** shameless

不宜食用/饮用 **bùyí shíyòng/yǐnyòng** be unfit to eat/drink

不一样 **bù yíyàng** it varies

不遗余力 **búyíyúlì** be unstinting in one's efforts

不一致 **bù yízhì** inconsistent; uneven, patchy ◊ clash

不用 **búyòng**: 不用，我来吧 **búyòng, wǒ lái ba** no, I'll do it; 不用，谢谢 **búyòng, xièxie** no thank you; 不用客气 **búyòngkèqì** don't mention it; 不用了！ **búyòngle!** don't bother!

不由自主 **bùyóu zìzhǔ** compulsive; stray

捕鱼 **bǔyú** fish; fishing

哺育 **bǔyù** feed; bring up

不育 **búyù** sterile

不愿 **búyuàn** be unwilling

不愿意 **bú yuànyì** disinclined

不在 **búzài** be away; be out

不赞成 **bú zànchéng** disapprove (of)

不早了 **bù zǎo le** get on ◊ it's getting late

不怎么样 **bù zěnme** not very, not particularly

不怎么样 **bù zěnme yàng** lousy ◊ not really; not much

不粘 **bùzhān** nonstick

部长 **bùzhǎng** minister POL; secretary ◊ ministerial

不扎实 **bù zhāshí** shaky

不真诚 **bù zhēnchéng** insincere

不正常 **bú zhèngcháng** abnormal

不整洁 **bù zhěngjié** unkempt

不整齐 **bù zhěngqí** disheveled

不正确 **bú zhèngquè** incorrect ◊ incorrectly

不真实 **bù zhēnshí** unreal; untrue

不只 **bùzhǐ** not only

布置 **bùzhì** arrange; fit out ◊ arrangement

不知害臊 **bùzhī hàisào** it's a disgrace

不知所措 **bù zhī suǒ cuò** in a daze, dazed ◊ overwhelm; paralyze *fig*; be at a loss

不值一读 **bùzhí yìdú** unreadable

不值一顾 **bùzhí yígù** beneath contempt

不知怎的 **bùzhī zěnde** somehow

不忠 **bù zhōng** disloyal; unfaithful; treacherous ◊ disloyalty; infidelity

不重要 **bú zhòngyào** unimportant

不中意 **bù zhōngyì** not appealing

不中用 **bù zhōngyòng** useless

步骤 **bùzhòu** procedure

补助 **bǔzhù** subsidy

不准 **bùzhǔn** forbid ◊ not allowed; not accurate

不准停车 **bùzhǔn tíngchē** no stopping

捕捉 **bǔzhuō** catch

簿子 **bùzi** notebook

不自然 **bú zìrán** labored, stilted; self-conscious

不自在 **bú zìzài** discomfort; 我跟他在一起感到不自在 **wǒ gēn tā zài yìqǐ gǎndào bú zìzài** I feel uncomfortable with him

不足 **bùzú** inadequate; unsatisfactory

不尊重 **bù zūnzhòng** disrespect

不足为奇 **bùzú wéiqí** unsurprising

不足信 **bù zúxìn** flimsy *excuse*

C

搽 **cā** dab

擦 **cā** mop, wipe

擦掉 **cādiào** erase; rub off; wipe away; wipe off

擦干 **cāgān** (wipe) dry

擦光剂 **cāguāngjì** polish

猜 **cāi** guess

才 **cái** talent ◊ only; only if; 他昨天才到 **tā zuótiān cái dào** he only arrived yesterday; 你说了他们才能做 **nǐ shuōle tāmen cáinéngzuò** they won't do anything until you say so

裁 **cái** cut *paper, cloth*

材 **cái** timber; material

财 **cái** assets; wealth

采 **cǎi** pick; mine

踩 **cǎi** step; trample on; tread on; 踩刹车 **cǎi shāchē** apply the brake(s)

彩 **cǎi** color

菜 **cài** dish; vegetable; (non-staple) food

彩笔 **cǎibǐ** highlighter; marker

猜测 **cāicè** guess; conjecture; speculation ◊ speculate

彩色照片 **cǎicè zhàopiàn** color photograph

财产 **cáichǎn** possession; property

菜单 **càidān** menu

菜刀 **càidāo** kitchen knife

彩电 **cǎidiàn** color TV

裁定 **cáidìng** convict ◊ conviction; sentencing; 裁定X无罪/有罪 **cáidìng X wúzuì/yǒuzuì** find X innocent/guilty

采访 **cǎifǎng** interview

采访者 **cǎifǎng zhě** interviewer

裁缝 **cáifeng** dressmaker; tailor

财富 **cáifù** treasure; wealth

采购 **cǎigòu** purchase ◊ purchaser ◊ purchasing

采购员 **cǎigòu yuán** buyer, purchaser

彩虹 **cǎihóng** rainbow

才华 **cáihuá** brilliance; intelligence

菜花 **càihuā** cauliflower

采集 **cǎijí** collect

裁减 **cáijiǎn** reduce

裁决 **cáijué** judgment; ruling; verdict

裁军 **cáijūn** disarm ◊ disarmament

采矿 **cǎikuàng** mining

材料 **cáiliào** materials

采纳 **cǎinà** adopt ◊ adoption

才能 **cáinéng** ability

菜农 **càinóng** truck farmer

彩排 **cǎipái** dress rehearsal

裁判（员）**cáipàn (yuán)** umpire; referee; judge

裁判院 **cáipàn yuàn** tribunal

彩票 **cǎipiào** lottery ticket; raffle ticket

菜谱 **càipǔ** recipe

彩色 **cǎisè** color

彩色电视 **cǎisè diànshì** color television

彩色胶卷 **cǎisè jiāojuǎn** color film

采石场 **cǎishíchǎng** quarry (*for mining*)

踩踏板 **cǎi tàbǎn** pedal

财务 **cáiwù** finance ◊ financial

财务部 **Cáiwù Bù** Treasury Department

财务处 **cáiwùchù** accounts (department)

财务软件 **cáiwù ruǎnjiàn** accounting software

猜想 **cāixiǎng** guess

采用 **cǎiyòng** use

菜油 **càiyóu** rapeseed oil; vegetable oil

踩油门儿 **cǎi yóuménr** put one's foot down, accelerate; rev up

裁员 **cáiyuán** cut back, downsize ◊ layoff

财源 cáiyuán means
菜园 càiyuán vegetable garden
财政 cáizhèng finance ◊ fiscal
财政年度 cáizhèng niándù fiscal year
才智 cáizhì wisdom
擦净 cājìng mop up
擦亮 cāliàng polish
餐 cān meal
惭 cán ashamed
蚕 cán silkworm
惨 cǎn tragic; brutal; disastrous
惨案 cǎn'àn massacre
惨败 cǎnbài massacre; thrashing
残暴 cánbào cruel
餐车 cānchē restaurant car
蚕豆 cándòu broad bean
残废 cánfèi disabled, crippled
残废者 cánfèi zhě disabled person
舱 cāng ship's cabin; aircraft cabin; module
仓 cāng storehouse
苍 cāng dark green; blue; grey
藏 cáng hide
苍白 cāngbái pale; wan
仓促 cāngcù hasty
舱口 cāngkǒu hatch (on ship)
仓库 cāngkù depot, warehouse; storehouse; stockroom, store
苍鹭 cānglù heron
藏匿 cángnì hide ◊ secretion
仓鼠 cāngshǔ hamster
参观 cānguān tour
餐馆 cānguǎn restaurant
参观者 cānguān zhě visitor
苍蝇 cāngying fly (insect)
残骸 cánhái remains; wreck; wreckage; debris
残迹 cánjì remnant
残疾 cánjí disabled, handicapped ◊ disability, physical handicap
参加 cānjiā attend; compete; enter, go in for, take part in; sit exam; participate; join; join in ◊ participation; 参加考试 **cānjiā kǎoshì** sit an exam
蚕茧 cánjiǎn silk cocoon
参加者 cānjiā zhě entrant, participant; entry; turnout
餐巾 cānjīn napkin

残疾人士 cánjí rénshì disabled person, cripple
餐具 cānjù tableware
餐具垫 cānjù diàn place mat
餐具柜 cānjùguì sideboard
参军 cānjūn enlist
参考 cānkǎo refer to ◊ reference
参考书 cānkǎo shū reference book
参考书目 cānkǎo shūmù bibliography
残酷 cánkù cut-throat competition; savage; sick sense of humor; cruel
惭愧 cánkuì ashamed
灿烂 cànlàn radiant; brilliant; magnificent
残缺 cánquē incomplete
残忍 cánrěn brutal, cruel, ferocious ◊ brutally; in cold blood ◊ cruelty
参赛 cānsài play SP; participate (in match, contest)
参赛表 cānsàibiǎo entry form
参赛者 cānsài zhě participant; contestant
餐室 cānshì dining room
餐厅 cāntīng dining hall; restaurant
惨痛 cǎntòng painful
参议员 cānyìyuán senator
参议院 cānyìyuàn senate
参与 cānyù participate in; be a party to
残余 cányú remainder; remains
残渣 cánzhā residue
餐桌 cānzhuō dining table
餐座 cānzuò booth
操 cāo hold, grasp; do; speak
槽 cáo trough; tank; groove
草 cǎo grass; straw
操 cào ∨ fuck
草地 cǎodì lawn
草稿 cǎogǎo (rough) draft
操劳 cāoláo work hard; struggle
操练 cāoliàn drill MIL
草帽 cǎomào straw hat
草莓 cǎoméi strawberry
草皮 cǎopí turf
草坪 cǎopíng lawn; meadow; green space
草率 cǎoshuài careless, sloppy;

hasty

草图 **cǎotú** outline; sketch

操心 **cāoxīn** worry

槽牙 **cáoyá** molar

草药 **cǎoyào** herbal medicine

草原 **cǎoyuán** grasslands

嘈杂 **cáozá** noisy

操纵 **cāozòng** operate; control; manipulate; rig

操纵装置 **cāozòng zhuāngzhì** controls

操作 **cāozuò** operate ◊ operation

操作方法 **cāozuò fāngfǎ** mode

操作手则 **cāozuò shǒuzé** operating instructions

操作系统 **cāozuò xìtǒng** operating system

操作者 **cāozuò zhě** operator

擦伤 **cāshāng** graze, scrape

擦洗 **cāxǐ** scrub

擦油 **cāyóu** put cream on

擦子 **cāzi** grater

册 **cè** volume; (exercise) book

测 **cè** measure

侧 **cè** lateral, side

策 **cè** strategy

测定 **cèdìng** gauge

测航 **cèháng** navigate

策划 **cèhuà** intrigue

测量 **cèliáng** measure ◊ measurement

策略 **cèlüè** tactics; strategy

侧面 **cèmiàn** side; profile

策谋 **cèmóu** contrive

参差不齐 **cēncī bùqí** jagged

层 **céng** coat, layer; coating; story (*of building*); tier

曾 **céng** ever; once; formerly; 我曾喜欢过他 **wǒ céng xǐhuānguò tā** I used to like him

曾经 **céngjīng** ever; once; formerly

厕所 **cèsuǒ** toilet, bathroom

测验 **cèyàn** test

侧翼 **cèyì** flank

插 **chā** insert; stick in

差 **chā** difference MATH

叉 **chā** fork

茶 **chá** tea

搽 **chá** rub in

查 **chá** check; test; 查地图 **chá dìtú** consult a map

察 **chá** inspect; examine

差 **chà** bad; poor *quality*; inferior ◊ badly ◊ lack; be short of; 差五分九点 **chà wǔfēn jiǔdiǎn** five (minutes) of nine; 差一刻五点 **chà yíkè wǔdiǎn** a quarter of 5

茶包 **chábāo** teabag

茶杯 **chábēi** teacup

茶杯碟 **chábēidié** saucer

差别 **chābié** difference; 没什么差别 **méi shénme chābié** it doesn't make any difference, it doesn't change anything

查查 **cháchá** check

叉车 **chāchē** forklift (truck)

茶匙 **cháchí** teaspoon

查出 **cháchū** dig up

差错 **chācuò** mistake; discrepancy

茶袋 **chádài** teabag

茶点 **chádiǎn** refreshments, tea and snacks

差额 **chā'é** balance, remainder

搽粉 **cháfěn** powder

茶馆 **cháguǎn** tea house

查号台 **cháhàotái** information TELEC

茶壶 **cháhú** teapot

插花 **chāhuā** arrangement

插话 **chāhuà** interrupt; 我插不上话 **wǒ chābúshàng huà** I couldn't get a word in edgewise

拆 **chāi** tear open; take apart; dismantle; demolish

柴 **chái** firewood

拆除 **chāichú** demolish

拆掉 **chāidiào** tear down

拆毁 **chāihuǐ** demolish ◊ demolition

拆开 **chāikāi** take to pieces; unravel; dismantle

差使 **chāishǐ** errand

拆下 **chāixià** unfix

拆卸 **chāixiè** dismantle

柴油 **cháiyóu** diesel

茶几 **chájī** coffee table

茶巾 **chájīn** tea cloth

差劲 **chàjìn** disappointing; bad; useless

差距 **chājù** gap; difference; distance

茶具 **chájù** tea service, tea set
察觉 **chájué** detect, discern
岔开 **chàkāi** diverge; sidetrack
察看 **chákàn** check on; look up
查明 **cháming** determine; make sure
禅 **Chán** Zen
缠 **chán** wind round; bind; wrap; 硬缠着 X **yìng chánzhe X** impose oneself on X
蝉 **chán** cicada
产 **chǎn** give birth to; produce ◊ product; property
阐 **chǎn** explain
铲 **chǎn** shovel
颤 **chàn** tremble
颤动 **chàndòng** pulsate
颤抖 **chàndǒu** quaver; shake; shiver
产房 **chǎnfáng** labor ward
长 **cháng** long ◊ length
尝 **cháng** taste; 尝一尝 **chángyīcháng** have a taste
偿 **cháng** repay; compensate for; fulfil
常 **cháng** frequent
肠 **cháng** intestines
场 **cháng** place; space; course; court SP; field SP; round; scene; meeting place
厂 **chǎng** factory; plant
敞 **chǎng** spacious; open
唱 **chàng** sing
畅 **chàng** smooth; unimpeded
长白山 **Chángbáishān** Changbai mountain
长柄勺 **cháng bǐngsháo** ladle
常常 **chángcháng** frequently, often
长城 **Chángchéng** the Great Wall
长处 **chángchu** advantage; strength
常春藤 **chángchūnténg** ivy
长笛 **chángdí** flute
场地 **chǎngdì** site
长度 **chángdù** length
长短 **chángduǎn** length
唱反调 **chàng fǎndiào** dissent from
长方形 **chángfāng xíng** rectangle ◊ rectangular

偿付 **chángfù** settlement, payment
唱歌 **chànggē** sing (a song)
常规 **chángguī** customary; standard; routine ◊ custom, practice; rut; 常规上 … **chángguī shàng …** it is customary to …
长号 **chánghào** trombone
偿还 **chánghuán** pay back; settle
唱机 **chàngjī** record player
长江 **Chángjiāng** Yangtze River
场景 **chǎngjǐng** scene
长颈鹿 **chángjǐnglù** giraffe
长久 **chángjiǔ** long; long-time ◊ forever, always
敞开 **chǎngkāi** open
敞开天窗说亮话 **chǎngkāi tiānchuāng shuō liànghuà** get down to basics
常客 **chángkè** regular
厂矿企业 **chǎngkuàng qǐyè** industrial enterprises
场面 **chǎngmiàn** scene
长年 **chángnián** all year round
长袍 **chángpáo** gown
长跑 **chángpǎo** long-distance running
敞篷货车 **chǎngpéng huòchē** wagon
唱片 **chàngpiān** album, record
长篇大论 **chángpiān dàlùn** monolog
唱片架 **chàngpiān jià** record rack
长波 **chángpō** long wave
长期 **chángqī** the long term ◊ long-term ◊ permanently
常青 **chángqīng** evergreen
偿清 **chángqīng** pay off
长沙发 **cháng shāfā** couch
厂商 **chǎngshāng** commercial and industrial enterprises; factories and stores; manufacturer
长舌 **chángshé** gossip
昌盛 **chāngshèng** flourish; do well ◊ flourishing
常识 **chángshí** general knowledge
尝试 **chángshì** attempt; try; taste
常识 **chángshì** common sense
长寿 **chángshòu** long life
场所 **chǎngsuǒ** place

畅所欲言 **chàngsuǒyùyán** vocal

长条 **chángtiáo** strip

畅通 **chàngtōng** unobstructed

长统袜 **chángtǒngwà** stocking

长途 **chángtú** long distance

长途电话 **chángtú diànhuà** long-distance call

长途汽车 **chángtú qìchē** (long-distance) bus

肠胃 **chángwèi** intestines and stomach; guts

畅销 **chàngxiāo** in demand; selling well

畅销书 **chàngxiāo shū** best-seller

长袖 **chángxiù** long-sleeved

长袖运动服 **chángxiù yùndòngfú** tracksuit

肠炎 **chángyán** enteritis

长椅 **chángyǐ** bench

常用 **chángyòng** in common use; everyday

长于 **chángyú** be good at

长远 **chángyuǎn** long-range; long-term

厂长 **chǎngzhǎng** director of a factory

长征 **Chángzhēng** Long March

肠子 **chángzi** intestine

产后 **chǎnhòu** postnatal

忏悔 **chànhuǐ** repent; confess ◊ confession; penitence

搀假 **chānjiǎ** adulterate

产假 **chǎnjià** maternity leave

缠结 **chánjié** snarl

产科病房 **chǎnkē bìngfáng** maternity ward

产科医师 **chǎnkē yīshī** obstetrician

产量 **chǎnliàng** production; capacity; output; yield; turnover ◊ turn over

阐明 **chǎnmíng** explain; interpret

产品 **chǎnpǐn** produce ◊ product

铲平 **chǎnpíng** bulldoze, demolish

产前 **chǎnqián** antenatal

缠绕 **chánrào** wrap; wind; curl

缠人 **chánrén** clingy

产生 **chǎnshēng** produce; emerge; generate; give rise to

阐述 **chǎnshù** explain

铲子 **chǎnzi** shovel; spade

禅宗佛教 **Chánzōng Fójiào** Zen Buddhism

抄 **chāo** copy; transcribe; plagiarize

钞 **chāo** bank bill

超 **chāo** exceed; surpass; transcend ◊ super; ultra; extra

巢 **cháo** nest

潮 **cháo** tide ◊ damp

嘲 **cháo** ridicule; mock

朝 **cháo** toward; facing ◊ court; dynasty

炒 **chǎo** cook; stir-fry

吵 **chǎo** make a noise; quarrel

炒菜 **chǎo cài** cook ◊ stir-fried dish

炒菜锅 **chǎocàiguō** wok

超车 **chāochē** pass, overtake

超出 **chāochū** exceed ◊ beyond; 超出我的能力范围 *chāochū wǒde nénglì fànwéi* it's beyond me

朝代 **cháodài** dynasty

超短裙 **chāoduǎnqún** mini, miniskirt

炒饭 **chǎofàn** fried rice ◊ fry rice

超过 **chāoguò** exceed; outgrow; overtake, pass ◊ over

吵架 **chǎojià** argue ◊ argument

超级大国 **chāojí dàguó** superpower

超级市场 **chāojí shìchǎng** supermarket

潮流 **cháoliú** trend

炒面 **chǎomiàn** fried noodles ◊ fry noodles

吵闹 **chǎonào** carry on, make a fuss ◊ noise; scene

嘲弄 **cháonòng** jeer; mockery

钞票 **chāopiào** bank bill

超声波 **chāoshēngbō** ultrasound

朝圣者 **cháoshèng zhě** pilgrim

朝圣之行 **cháoshèng zhī xíng** pilgrimage

超时 **chāoshí** overrun

潮湿 **cháoshī** moist; damp

潮水 **cháoshuǐ** tide

超速 **chāosù** overdrive ◊ speed ◊ speeding

超文本 **chāowénběn** hypertext

抄袭 **chāoxí** copy

朝鲜 **Cháoxiān** Korea

朝向 **cháoxiàng** look onto, face

嘲笑 **cháoxiào** laugh at, poke fun at; taunt ◊ taunt

抄写 **chāoxiě** copy; transcribe

巢穴 **cháoxué** den; lair

超音速 **chāoyīnsù** supersonic

炒鱿鱼 **chǎo yóuyú** dismiss, fire; 被炒鱿鱼了 **bèi chǎo yóuyú le** be fired

超载 **chāozài** overload

超支 **chāozhī** overdraft ◊ overdraw; overspend; 超支八百美元 **chāozhī bābǎi měiyuán** be $800 overdrawn

超重 **chāozhòng** overload ◊ overweight

超重的行李 **chāozhòngde xíngli** excess baggage

超自然 **cháozìrán** supernatural

吵嘴 **chǎozuǐ** quarrel

查票员 **chápiào yuán** (ticket) inspector

插入 **chārù** insert; slot in ◊ insertion; 把 X 插入 Y **bǎ X chārù Y** insert X into Y

茶室 **cháshì** tearoom

插手 **chāshǒu** involvement

插头 **chātóu** pin; plug ELEC

插图 **chātú** illustration

查问 **cháwèn** questioning

插销 **chāxiāo** bolt

查询 **cháxún** enquire

茶叶 **cháyè** tea; tea leaves

差异 **chāyì** gap

诧异 **chàyì** amazed

搽用 **cháyòng** put on

查阅 **cháyuè** look up; consult

叉子 **chāzi** cross; fork

查字典 **chá zìdiǎn** look up; consult a dictionary

插嘴 **chāzuǐ** butt in, chip in

插座 **chāzuò** socket

车 **chē** vehicle; car; bus

扯 **chě** pull; bear; tell lies; talk nonsense

撤 **chè** pull back; withdraw

彻 **chè** thorough; penetrating

车把 **chēbǎ** handlebars

车床 **chēchuáng** lathe

车次 **chēcì** train number; bus number

扯蛋 **chědàn** talk nonsense

彻底 **chèdǐ** exhaustive, thorough; outright; resounding; radical; solid *support* ◊ radically; right, completely; soundly

彻底变革 **chèdǐ biàngé** revolutionize

彻底击垮 **chèdǐ jīkuǎ** undermine

车顶架 **chēdǐng jià** roof rack

车队 **chēduì** convoy, fleet (of vehicles)

撤回 **chèhuí** withdraw

车祸 **chēhuò** traffic accident

车架横梁 **chējià héngliáng** crossbar

车间 **chējiān** workshop

车库 **chēkù** garage

撤离 **chèlí** evacuate; move out; pull out

车辆 **chēliàng** vehicle

车龙 **chēlóng** traffic jam

车轮 **chēlún** wheel

沉 **chén** sink

晨 **chén** morning

陈 **chén** old; stale ◊ lay out; display

衬 **chèn** line *coat etc*

陈词滥调 **chéncí làndiào** platitude

衬垫 **chèndiàn** lining

沉淀物 **chéndiànwù** sediment

陈腐 **chénfǔ** conventional; hackneyed

撑 **chēng** support, hold up

称 **chēng** call; say; weigh; 称 … 的 重量 **chēng … de zhòngliàng** weigh

乘 **chéng** by ◊ multiply; 二乘四 **èr chéng sì** 2 by 4

橙 **chéng** orange (*color*, *fruit*)

成 **chéng** achieve; become; succeed; mature

诚 **chéng** honest; sincere

城 **chéng** city; wall

呈 **chéng** submit

程 **chéng** rule; pattern

惩 **chéng** punish

澄 **chéng** clear

承 **chéng** hold; carry; undertake

秤 **chèng** scales

承包 **chéngbāo** commission;

contract

城堡 **chéngbǎo** castle; fortress

呈报 **chéngbào** declare

承包人 **chéngbāo rén** contractor

成本 **chéngběn** cost

成本加运费 **chéngběn jiā yùnfèi** cost and freight

成本价格 **chéngběn jiàgé** cost price

成比例 **chéng bǐlì** proportional

乘车 **chèngchē** ride

惩处 **chéngchǔ** punish; penalize

承担 **chéngdān** bear; undertake; 承担责任 *chéngdān zérèn* be held responsible; take responsibility

成单行 **chéngdānháng** in single file

呈递 **chéngdì** submit; hand in; hand over

程度 **chéngdù** degree, extent; measure; 在一定程度上 *zài yídìng chéngdùshang* to a certain extent; in a way

成堆 **chéngduī** in piles; loads of

承兑 **chéngduì** cash; accept *check*

惩罚 **chéngfá** discipline; penalty; punishment ◊ punish

成分 **chéngfèn** component; ingredient

撑杆跳 **chēnggān tiào** vault

撑竿跳高 **chēnggān tiàogāo** polevault

成功 **chénggōng** do well, succeed, prosper ◊ success ◊ successful; fruitful ◊ successfully; 取得成功 *qǔdé chénggōng* work out, succeed

成果 **chéngguǒ** achievement; success

称号 **chēnghào** title; designation

称呼 **chēnghu** form of address ◊ address

乘机 **chéngjī** fly (*in plane*)

成绩 **chéngjì** achievement; results

成见 **chéngjiàn** prejudice; stereotype

呈交 **chéngjiāo** put in, submit

成交！ **chéngjiāo!** it's a deal!

成吉思汗 **Chéngjísīhàn** Genghis Khan

成就 **chéngjiù** achievement

撑开 **chēngkāi** open *umbrella*

乘客 **chéngkè** passenger

诚恳 **chéngkěn** sincere

乘客座位 **chéngkè zuòwèi** passenger seat

成立 **chénglì** establish, set up ◊ foundation

成名 **chéngmíng** make a name for oneself

成年 **chéngnián** come of age ◊ adult ◊ F all year

承诺 **chéngnuò** promise; commit; pledge

尘垢 **chéngòu** grime

澄清 **chéngqīng** clarify; acquit, clear; unravel; settle (*of liquid*)

成人 **chéngrén** adult

承认 **chéngrèn** acknowledge, recognize; admit, confess; concede ◊ admission; recognition

成人片 **chéngrén piān** adult film

橙色 **chéngsè** orange (*color*)

诚实 **chéngshí** honest, truthful ◊ honesty; integrity

城市 **chéngshì** city ◊ civic

城市化 **chéngshìhuà** urbanization

成熟 **chéngshóu** ripen

承受 **chéngshòu** bear, carry; 承受压力 *chéngshòu yālì* be under pressure

成熟 **chéngshú** full-grown; grown-up; ripe; mature ◊ maturity ◊ mature; ripen

成套 **chéngtào** complete set; 成套用品 *chéngtào yòngpǐn* complete set of equipment

成为 **chéngwéi** become; turn into

呈文 **chéngwén** submission; petition

乘务员 **chéngwùyuán** conductor; ticket collector; steward; stewardess

呈现 **chéngxiàn** arise; materialize

成效 **chéngxiào** effect

称心如意 **chèngxīn rúyì** desirable

程序 **chéngxù** program; procedure; system; order

程序表 **chéngxùbiǎo** schedule

程序员 **chéngxùyuán** programmer

诚意 **chéngyì** honesty; sincerity

成瘾者 **chéngyǐn zhě** addict

盛有 **chéngyǒu** hold

乘游艇 **chéng yóutǐng** yachting

成员 **chéngyuán** member

成员人数 **chéngyuán rénshù** membership

成员证 **chéngyuánzhèng** membership card

成员资格 **chéngyuán zīgé** membership

称赞 **chēngzàn** praise

成长 **chéngzhǎng** grow ◊ growth

诚挚 **chéngzhì** sincere ◊ sincerely

称职 **chèngzhí** competent

橙汁 **chéngzhī** orange juice; orangeade

称重量 **chēng zhòngliàng** weigh

撑柱 **chēngzhù** stilts (*under house*)

沉着冷静 **chéngzhuó lěngjìng** imperturbable

橙子 **chéngzi** orange (*fruit*)

橙子酱 **chéngzijiàng** marmalade

沉积 **chénjī** deposit

沉浸 **chénjìn** immerse oneself in

陈旧 **chénjiù** outmoded

衬里 **chènlǐ** lining; 安衬里 **ān chènlǐ** line (*with material*)

衬料 **chènliào** lining; padding

陈列 **chénliè** display ◊ be on display

陈列柜 **chénlièguì** display cabinet

沉闷 **chénmèn** dreary; close, oppressive *weather*; dejected; reserved *character*

沉没 **chénmò** sink, go under

沉默 **chénmò** silent ◊ silence

沉默寡言 **chénmò guǎyán** silent; taciturn

沉溺 **chénnì** addiction

衬裙 **chènqún** underskirt

衬衫 **chènshān** shirt; blouse

陈述 **chénshù** set out

沉思 **chénsī** thoughtful, pensive ◊ muse

沉痛 **chéntòng** deeply distressed

尘土 **chéntǔ** dust

晨曦 **chénxī** daybreak

称心 **chènxīn** be satisfied with

沉重 **chénzhòng** heavy; serious; oppressive *weather*

沉着 **chénzhuó** level-headed, composed; self-possessed

车子 **chēzi** bicycle; car

车牌 **chēpái** license plate

车牌号码 **chēpái hàomǎ** license number

车皮 **chēpí** freight car

车票 **chēpiào** ticket

车身 **chēshēn** bodywork

车胎 **chētāi** tire

车胎爆炸 **chētāi bàozhà** blowout

车条 **chētiáo** spoke

撤退 **chètuì** retreat; withdraw ◊ withdrawal

车厢 **chēxiāng** car (*of train*)

撤销 **chèxiāo** undo COMPUT; withdraw; cancel; get rid of ◊ withdrawal

车站 **chēzhàn** bus stop; bus station; station

车辙 **chēzhé** rut

吃 **chī** eat; take; live on; absorb; suffer; bear; 吃点儿饭怎么样？ **chī diǎnr fàn zěnmeyàng?** what about some dinner?; 吃早餐 **chī zǎocān** have breakfast

池 **chí** pool; pond

迟 **chí** late

持 **chí** hold; grasp; keep; maintain; manage

匙 **chí** spoon

尺 **chǐ** Chinese foot; rule; ruler

耻 **chǐ** shame; disgrace

齿 **chǐ** tooth

赤 **chì** red; bare

翅 **chì** wing; shark's fin

斥 **chì** scold

翅膀 **chìbǎng** wing

吃饱了 **chī bǎo le** full up

持不同政见者 **chí bùtóng zhèngjiàn zhě** dissident

吃不消 **chībùxiāo** unbearable

吃草 **chīcǎo** graze

吃醋 **chīcù** be jealous

尺寸 **chǐcùn** dimension; measurement

迟到 **chídào** be late

赤道 **chìdào** equator

吃的 **chīde** food

尺度 **chǐdù** measure; standard; rule

迟钝 **chídùn** clumsy, awkward; stupid; backward; numb

吃饭 **chīfàn** eat, have a meal

吃个饱 **chīgebǎo** eat one's fill

齿冠 **chǐguàn** crown (*on tooth*)

吃光 **chīguāng** eat up; scoff

吃好 **chīhǎo** enjoy!

迟缓 **chíhuǎn** slow; hesitant

持家 **chíjiā** keep house, run a home

赤脚 **chìjiǎo** barefoot

赤脚医生 **chìjiǎo yīshēng** barefoot doctor

吃惊 **chījīng** be amazed; be surprised; 令人吃惊 **lìngrén chījīng** staggering

持久 **chíjiǔ** enduring

吃苦 **chīkǔ** bear hardships; suffer

吃亏 **chīkuī** be at a disadvantage ◊ disadvantaged

吃力 **chīlì** with difficulty ◊ punishing

齿轮 **chǐlún** gear

赤裸裸 **chì luǒluo** in the nude

持枪歹徒 **chíqiāng dǎitú** gunman

耻辱 **chǐrǔ** dishonor; disgrace; shame

池塘 **chítáng** pond

赤陶 **chìtáo** terracotta

持械抢劫 **chíxiè qiǎngjié** armed robbery

持续 **chíxù** continue; last; endure

持续不断 **chíxù búduàn** persistent

持续观察 **chíxù guānchá** monitor

吃药 **chīyào** take medicine

齿龈 **chǐyín** gum

持异议 **chí yìyì** dissent

持有 **chíyǒu** possess, hold ◊ possession

迟于 **chíyú** past; later than

迟早 **chízǎo** sooner or later

斥责 **chìzé** rebuke, reprimand

吃住 **chīzhù** board and lodging

尺子 **chǐzi** ruler (*for measuring*)

赤子 **chìzǐ** newborn child

赤字 **chìzì** shortfall, deficit

充 **chōng** full

冲 **chōng** push forward; charge; attack; flush; rinse

虫 **chóng** insect

重 **chóng** repeat; double ◊ again ◊ layer

宠爱 **chǒng'ài** dote on

崇拜 **chóngbài** worship

崇拜者 **chóngbài zhě** admirer; worshipper

重播 **chóngbō** repeat (broadcast)

冲刺 **chōngcì** spurt (*in race*)

充当 **chōngdāng** serve as

充电 **chōngdiàn** charge; recharge

冲掉 **chōngdiào** flush away

重迭 **chóngdié** overlap

冲动 **chōngdòng** impulse; 凭一时的冲动 **píng yìshíde chōngdòng** on the spur of the moment

宠儿 **chǒng'ér** pet, favorite

重放 **chóngfàng** replay

充分 **chōngfèn** full; ample; sufficient

冲锋 **chōngfēng** charge (*of troops*)

重逢 **chóngféng** meet again

冲锋枪 **chōngfēngqiāng** submachine gun

重复 **chóngfù** repetition; duplicate; action replay ◊ repeat; echo ◊ repetitive; 我是不是重复了？ **wǒ shìbúshì chóngfù le?** am I repeating myself?

崇高 **chónggāo** lofty; exalted

虫害 **chónghài** plague of insects

宠坏 **chǒnghuài** spoil ◊ spoilt

重婚 **chónghūn** bigamy

冲昏了头 **chōnghūn le tóu** get carried away

重获 **chónghuò** regain

冲击 **chōngjī** lunge at; lash; charge

重建 **chóngjiàn** rebuild

崇敬 **chóngjìng** revere

冲浪板 **chōnglàngbǎn** surfboard

冲浪运动 **chōnglàng yùndòng** surfing

冲浪者 **chōnglàng zhě** surfer

充满 **chōngmǎn** fill up ◊ be full of

充满怨恨 **chōngmǎn yuànhèn** bitter

充气 **chōngqì** inflate ◊ pneumatic
充任 **chōngrèn** occupy; hold the post of
重赛 **chóngsài** replay
重申 **chóngshēn** echo *views*; reiterate
重审 **chóngshěn** reopen
充实 **chōngshí** beef up ◊ full *life*
冲突 **chōngtú** clash; conflict
重温 **chóngwēn** brush up
宠物 **chǒngwù** pet (*animal*)
冲洗 **chōngxǐ** develop *photograph*; flush ◊ development
重现 **chóngxiàn** reappear
重写 **chóngxiě** rewrite
重新 **chóngxīn** again
重新安排 **chóngxīn ānpái** reorganize, rearrange ◊ reorganization
重新出现 **chóngxīn chūxiàn** resurface
重新发展 **chóngxīn fāzhǎn** redevelop
重新开始 **chóngxīn kāishǐ** go back to the drawing board; renew ◊ renewal; fresh start
重新开张 **chóngxīn kāizhāng** reopen
重新考虑 **chóngxīn kǎolǜ** reconsider
重新命名 **chóngxīn mìngmíng** rename
重新评价 **chóngxīn píngjià** revaluation
重新武装 **chóngxīn wǔzhuāng** rearm
重新装修 **chóngxīn zhuāngxiū** redecorate
充血 **chōngxuè** congestion; MED hyperemia
虫牙 **chóngyá** decayed tooth
重阳节 **Chóngyángjié** Double Ninth Festival
重印 **chóngyìn** reprint
重影 **chóngyǐng** double
充裕 **chōngyù** abundant
虫子 **chóngzi** insect; worm
充足 **chōngzú** ample; sufficient ◊ sufficiently
重组 **chóngzǔ** shake-up ◊ reshuffle; reorganize

抽 **chōu** pull out; draw
稠 **chóu** thick; dense
筹 **chóu** plan; prepare
酬 **chóu** reward; remuneration
愁 **chóu** worry
仇 **chóu** enemy; hatred
丑 **chǒu** ugly
臭 **chòu** stinking
酬报 **chóubào** reward; payment
筹备 **chóubèi** arrange
抽不开身 **chōu bù kāi shēn** tied up, busy
抽出 **chōuchū** pull out, draw
抽搐 **chōuchù** convulsion; twitch
仇敌 **chóudí** enemy
丑恶 **chǒu'è** repulsive, revolting
仇恨 **chóuhèn** hatred; enmity
筹划 **chóuhuà** map out
筹集 **chóují** raise *money*
抽奖 **chōujiǎng** raffle
丑角 **chǒujiǎo** comedian; clown
抽筋 **chōujīn** cramp
酬金 **chóujīn** fee
丑角 **chǒujué** clown
抽开 **chōukāi** pull away
抽空 **chōukòng** take time; devote time
丑陋 **chǒulòu** ugly, hideous
筹码 **chóumǎ** chip, counter
臭骂一顿 **chòumà yídùn** bawl out
愁闷 **chóumèn** worried; down
稠密 **chóumì** thick; dense
稠密度 **chóumì dù** density
臭名远扬 **chòumíng yuǎnyáng** infamous
臭名昭著 **chòumíng zhāozhù** infamous
抽泣 **chōuqì** sob
臭气 **chòuqì** stink
抽税 **chōushuì** tax; levy a tax
抽丝 **chōusī** run (*in pantyhose*)
抽屉 **chōuti** drawer
臭味儿 **chòuwèir** stink
丑闻 **chǒuwén** scandal
抽吸 **chōuxī** suction
抽象 **chōuxiàng** abstract
抽烟 **chōuyān** smoke
抽样 **chōuyàng** sampling
臭氧 **chòuyǎng** ozone
臭氧层 **chòuyǎng céng** ozone

layer

抽油烟机 **chōuyóu yānjī** hood (*over cooker*)

出 **chū** out ◊ go out; come out; give out; publish; produce; happen

初 **chū** beginning ◊ first

橱 **chú** cupboard

除 **chú** eliminate; remove; except; divide MATH; 除 ... 外 **chú ... wài** apart from ...

锄 **chú** hoe

雏 **chú** young *bird*

储 **chǔ** store up

处 **chǔ** get along with; manage; be situated in

穿 **chuān** wear; pierce; penetrate; 穿衣服 **chuān yīfu** get dressed, dress; 穿黄色衣服 **chuān huángsè yīfu** dressed in yellow; 我穿不上裤子 **wǒ chuān bú shàng kùzī** I can't get these pants on

传 **chuán** pass on; spread; infect; transmit; call

船 **chuán** boat, ship, vessel; 在船上 **zài chuánshàng** be aboard

喘 **chuǎn** breathe heavily; 喘不过气来 **chuǎn bū guò qì lái** breathless, out of breath

串 **chuàn** string together ◊ bunch; kebab ◊ *measure word for strings, bunches of things*; 一串项链 **yíchuàn xiàngliàn** a necklace

传播 **chuánbō** spread

船舶 **chuánbó** shipping

喘不过气 **chuǎn bū guò qì** breathlessness

船舱 **chuáncāng** cabin

船厂 **chuánchǎng** dockyard

传达 **chuándá** pass on; transmit ◊ janitor; 请传达给我 **qǐng chuándá gěi wǒ** please keep me informed

穿戴 **chuāndài** wear; dress

传单 **chuándān** flyer (*leaflet*)

传导 **chuándǎo** conduct ELEC

传道 **chuándào** preach

传道人 **chuándào rén** preacher

传达器 **chuándáqì** transmitter

传递 **chuándì** pass on; convey

传动 **chuándòng** transmission

船队 **chuánduì** convoy

疮 **chuāng** sore

窗 **chuāng** window

床 **chuáng** bed

创 **chuàng** start; initiate

窗板 **chuāngbǎn** shutter

创办 **chuàngbàn** found, start

创办人 **chuàngbàn rén** promoter

窗玻璃 **chuāng bōlí** windowpane

床单 **chuángdān** sheet

床垫 **chuángdiàn** mattress

窗户 **chuānghu** window

创建 **chuàngjiàn** found, establish

创建人 **chuàngjiàn rén** founder

创可贴 **chuàngkětiē** adhesive plaster

窗口 **chuāngkǒu** hatch; window; contact

创立 **chuànglì** found, establish

窗帘 **chuānglián** curtain; drapes

床铺 **chuángpù** bunk

闯入 **chuǎngrù** burst into a room

创伤性 **chuàngshāng xìng** traumatic

床上用品 **chuángshàng yòngpǐn** bedclothes, linen

创始人 **chuàngshǐ rén** founder; originator

窗台 **chuāngtái** windowsill

床头 **chuángtóu** bedstead

穿过 **chuānguò** cross ◊ through

创新 **chuàngxīn** create ◊ revolutionary *new ideas*

创业 **chuàngyè** enterprise; 有创业才能 **yǒu chuàngyè cáinéng** entrepreneurial

创业园 **chuàngyèyuán** venture park

创造 **chuàngzào** create

创造者 **chuàngzào zhě** creator

床罩 **chuángzhào** bedspread

创作 **chuàngzuò** create; compose ◊ creation

传呼 **chuánhū** page

传唤 **chuánhuàn** subpoena; summon to court

传话 **chuánhuà** pass on a message

传呼机 **chuánhūjī** pager

传教 **chuánjiào** do missionary work

传教士 **chuánjiàoshì** missionary

穿孔 **chuān kǒng** puncture
窗框 **chuānkuàng** sash
船篷 **chuánpéng** awning
传票 **chuánpiào** subpoena; summons
船票 **chuánpiào** ticket (*for ship*)
传奇 **chuánqí** legend
喘气 **chuǎnqì** gasp (for breath); pant
传球 **chuánqiú** pass (the ball)
传染 **chuánrǎn** infect ◊ contagious
传染性 **chúanrǎn xìng** catching; infectious
船首 **chuánshǒu** prow
传授 **chuánshòu** teach
传说 **chuánshuō** legend ◊ legend has it; it is said
传送 **chuánsòng** carry (*of sound*)
传送带 **chuánsòng dài** conveyor belt
穿梭 **chuānsuō** shuttle
穿梭业务 **chuānsuō yèwù** shuttle service
穿梭营运 **chuānsuō yíngyùn** shuttlebus
船台 **chuántái** berth
传统 **chuántǒng** tradition ◊ traditional ◊ traditionally
穿透 **chuāntòu** penetrate
船头 **chuántóu** bow (*of ship*)
船桅 **chuánwéi** mast
船尾电动机 **chuánwěi diàndòngjī** outboard motor
传闻 **chuánwén** hearsay; rumor ◊ it is said
船屋 **chuánwū** houseboat
船坞 **chuánwù** dock
喘息 **chuǎnxī** gasp, pant; puff
传下来 **chuánxiàlái** hand down
船舷 **chuánxián** side of a ship
传销 **chuánxiāo** pyramid selling
传下去 **chuánxiàqù** hand on
传讯 **chuánxùn** summons
船员 **chuányuán** sailor
传阅 **chuányuè** circulate
船长 **chuánzhǎng** captain, skipper
传真 **chuánzhēn** fax; 用传真传 **yòng chuánzhēn chuán** fax, send by fax; 把 X 传真给 Y **bǎ X chuánzhēn gěi Y** fax X to Y

传真机 **chuánzhēnjī** fax machine
船主 **chuánzhǔ** shipowner
穿着 **chuānzhuó** clothing; 穿着单薄 *chuānzhuó dānbó* scantily clad
椽子 **chuánzi** rafter
出版 **chūbǎn** publish; come out
出版公司 **chūbǎn gōngsī** publishing company
出版社 **chūbǎnshè** publisher
出版物 **chūbǎnwù** publication
出版业 **chūbǎnyè** publishing
储备 **chǔbèi** store; reserve ◊ stock up on; stockpile
储备金 **chǔbèi jīn** reserves FIN
储备物资 **chǔbèi wùzī** stockpile
除冰 **chúbīng** de-ice
除冰器 **chúbīng qì** de-icer
储藏 **chǔcáng** store; deposit
除草剂 **chúcǎojì** weedkiller
出差错 **chū chācuò** slip up
出差 **chūchāi** go on a business trip
出产 **chūchǎn** yield; produce
出场 **chūchǎng** entrance
出丑 **chūchǒu** make a spectacle of oneself; 别当众让我出丑 *bié dāngzhòng ràng wǒ chūchǒu* don't show me up in public
橱窗 **chúchuāng** display window; store window ◊ in the window
初次 **chūcì** the first time
储存 **chǔcún** put aside, put by; save; bank ◊ stock; store; reserves
出错 **chūcuò** make a mistake; stumble over
处得来 **chùdelái** get on, be friendly
触电 **chùdiàn** shock
除掉 **chúdiào** eliminate
出尔反尔 **chū'ěr fǎněr** backpedal; contradict oneself
出发 **chūfā** departure ◊ leave; set off
除法 **chúfǎ** division
触发 **chùfā** trigger off
出发点 **chūfā diǎn** starting point
厨房 **chúfáng** kitchen
处方 **chǔfāng** prescribe ◊ prescription
除非 **chúfēi** only if; unless
橱柜 **chúguì** compartment

出国 chūguó go abroad
出汗 chūhàn sweat, perspire
出航 chūháng outgoing *flight*
储户 chǔhù depositor
出乎意料 chūhū yìliào
  unexpected ◊ strangely enough
吹 chuī blow
垂 chuí hang down; droop
锤 chuí hammer
吹风器 chuīfēngqì hairdrier
吹干 chuīgān blow-dry
吹鼓手 chuīgǔshǒu *band that
  plays at weddings and funerals*
吹口 chuīkǒu mouthpiece
吹口哨 chuī kǒushào whistle
垂柳 chuíliǔ weeping willow
吹灭 chuīmiè blow out *candle*
吹牛 chuīniú boast, talk big
吹牛拍马 chuīniú pāimǎ suck
  up; brown nose; be obsequious
吹气 chuīqì blow
吹哨 chuīshào blow
垂死 chuísǐ dying
垂下 chuíxià hang
垂涎 chuíxián lick one's lips; 令人
  垂涎 **lìngrén chuíxiàn**
  mouthwatering
吹嘘 chuīxū show off, brag
垂直 chuízhí perpendicular;
  vertical
垂直上移 chuízhí shàngyí scroll
  up
垂直下移 chuízhí xiàyí scroll
  down
锤子 chuízi hammer
初级 chūjí elementary
雏鸡 chújī baby chicken
出家 chūjiā become a monk / nun
出价 chūjià bid
触角 chùjiǎo antenna, feeler
出家人 Chūjiā rén Buddhist
  monk / nun
出借 chūjiè lend; loan
初级阶段 chūjí jiēduàn infancy
出境 chūjìng leave the country
处境 chǔjìng position
初级小学 chūjí xiǎoxué lower
  elementary school
处决 chǔjué execute, put to death
触觉 chùjué touch
出口 chūkǒu exit; export; outlet ◊

export
出口处 chūkǒuchù exit
出口商 chūkǒushāng exporter
出口物 chūkǒuwù exports
出来 chūlái come out; get out; be
  out ◊ out
畜栏 chùlán corral
除了 chúle apart from, aside from,
  except; all but; besides; excluding;
  除了 X 以外 **chúle X yǐwài** except
  for X; 除了 X 之外 **chúle X
  zhīwài** in addition to X
处理 chǔlǐ attend to; take care of;
  deal with; process *data*; treat ◊
  disposal (*of waste*); treatment,
  processing
处理不当 chǔlǐ búdàng
  mishandle
处理器 chǔlǐqì processor
出路 chūlù exit, way out
出卖 chūmài sell; betray, sell out
出毛病 chū máobìng break down
  ◊ broken
除毛剂 chúmáojì hair remover
出名 chūmíng well-known ◊
  become famous
触摸 chùmō feel; touch
春 chūn spring
纯 chún pure; neat, straight *drink*;
  net *price*; solid *gold*
唇 chún lip
蠢 chǔn stupid
处男 chù'nán virgin (*male*)
出纳员 chū'nàyuán cashier; teller
蠢材 chǔncái clown
纯粹 chúncuì pure; unspoilt
唇读 chúndú lipread
纯度 chúndù purity
春分 Chūnfēn Spring equinox
唇膏 chúngāo lipstick
春季 chūnjì spring, springtime
春节 Chūnjié Chinese New Year,
  Spring Festival
纯洁 chúnjié innocent; pure;
  honest
纯净 chúnjìng clean
春卷 chūnjuǎn spring roll
纯利润 chún lìrùn net profit
纯巧克力 chún qiǎokèlì plain
  chocolate
蠢人 chǔnrén fool

纯熟 **chúnshú** proficient; skillful

春天 **chūntiān** spring

处女 **chǔnǚ** virgin (*female*)

纯正 **chúnzhèng** pure

纯种 **chúnzhǒng** pedigree, thoroughbred

戳 **chuō** jab; prick

绰号 **chuòhào** nickname

出钱 **chūqián** chip in; fork out

出勤 **chūqín** attendance

出去 **chūqù** go out; 出去! **chūqù!** get out!

除去 **chúqù** drop; remove; obliterate; strip

出去吃 **chūqù chī** eat out

出去一会儿 **chūqù yíhuìr** step out, go out

出让 **chūràng** part with; sell; lease out

出人意外 **chūrényìwài** surprisingly

出入境口 **chūrùjìng kǒu** terminal

出身 **chūshēn** family background

出神 **chūshén** fascinated ◊ space out

出生 **chūshēng** be born; 孩子什么时候出生 **háizi shénme shíhòu chūshēng?** when is the baby due?

畜生 **chùshēng** beast; brute

出声 **chūshēng** aloud; 别出声! **bié chūshēng!** just be quiet!, hush!

出生地 **chūshēng dì** birthplace

出生率 **chūshēng lǜ** birthrate

出生年份 **chūshēng niánfèn** year of birth

出生日期 **chūshēng rìqī** date of birth

出生证 **chūshēng zhèng** birth certificate

出神儿 **chūshénr** go into a trance; space out

出示 **chūshì** show

出事 **chūshì** go wrong; have an accident

厨师 **chúshī** chef; cook

出事故 **chū shìgù** crash COMPUT

出售 **chūshòu** put up for sale

触手 **chùshǒu** tentacle

储水池 **chǔshuǐ chí** tank (*for water etc*)

出庭 **chūtíng** appearance (*in court*)

锄头 **chútou** pickaxe; hoe

出席 **chūxí** be present; attend

除夕 **Chúxī** Chinese New Year's Eve

出现 **chūxiàn** appear; emerge

出血 **chūxiě** hemorrhage

除臭剂 **chúxiù jì** deodorant

除锈剂 **chúxiùjì** rust remover

储蓄 **chǔxù** save; deposit ◊ savings

初选 **chūxuǎn** primary

出血 **chūxuè** bleed

初学者 **chūxué zhě** beginner

储蓄银行 **chǔxū yínháng** savings bank

储蓄帐户 **chǔxù zhànghù** savings account

初一 **Chūyī** (Chinese) New Year's Day; Grade 1 in Junior High

出游 **chūyóu** outing, trip

出狱 **chūyù** get out of prison

处于 **chǔyú** be (*in a situation*); 处于困境 **chǔyú kùnjìng** be stranded

出院 **chūyuàn** discharge

出证 **chūzhèng** give evidence

出众 **chūzhòng** excel, shine

初中 **chūzhōng** junior high school

出皱褶 **chū zhòuzhě** wrinkle

出租 **chūzū** rent ◊ for rent

出租车 **chūzūchē** taxi, cab

出租车司机 **chūzūchē sījī** taxidriver, cab driver

出租车停车处 **chūzūchē tíngchēchù** taxi rank, cab stand

出租车站 **chūzūchē zhàn** taxi rank, cab stand

出租汽车 **chūzū qìchē** cab, taxi

出租汽车司机 **chūzū qìchē sījī** cab driver, taxi driver

磁 **cí** magnetism; china; ceramic

瓷 **cí** porcelain; china

词 **cí** term; word

慈 **cí** kind

雌 **cí** female

辞 **cí** word

祠 **cí** ancestral temple

此 **cǐ** this

刺 **cì** prick (*pain*); prickle, spine;

thorn; splinter ◊ stab

次 cì time

刺鼻 cìbí pungent

辞别 cíbié say goodbye ◊ farewell

磁带 cídài cassette; tape

磁带驱动器 cídài qūdòngqì tape drive

词典 cídiǎn dictionary

刺耳 cì'ěr ear-piercing; shrill; grating

词根 cígēn root (of word)

刺骨 cìgǔ piercing

此后 cǐhòu after this; henceforth

伺候 cìhou attend to; wait on; serve

词汇 cíhuì vocabulary

词汇表 cíhuì biǎo vocabulary; glossary

刺激 cìjī stimulate; irritate

此刻 cǐkè at present, right now

此路不通 cǐ lù bù tōng dead end

磁盘 cípán disk

磁盘带机 cípán dàijī disk drive

瓷漆 cíqī enamel

瓷器 cíqì porcelain; china

瓷器厂 cíqìchǎng porcelain factory

慈善 císhàn benevolent; charitable

慈善机构 císhàng jīgòu charity (organization)

慈善家 císhànjiā philanthropist

磁石 císhí magnet

次数 cìshù number of times; frequency

刺探 cìtàn pry into

祠堂 cítáng ancestral temple

刺痛 cìtòng smart

刺透 cìtòu pierce

辞退 cítuì dismiss, fire

此外 cǐwài besides; also

词尾 cíwěi ending (of word)

刺猬 cìwei hedgehog

慈祥 cíxiáng kind; loving

雌性 cíxìng female

词性 cíxìng part of speech

磁性 cíxìng magnetism ◊ magnetic

雌性动植物 cíxìng dòngzhíwù female

刺绣 cìxiù embroider ◊ embroidery

刺绣品 cìxiùpǐn embroidery

次序 cìxù order

次序颠倒 cìxù diāndǎo out of order

次要 cìyào minor, secondary; peripheral

赐予 cìyǔ bestow

词藻华丽 cízǎo huálì flowery

辞职 cízhí quit; resign ◊ resignation

此致 cǐzhì yours truly; best regards

瓷砖 cízhuān tile

葱 cōng scallion; green onion; Chinese onion

匆 cōng hasty; urgent

丛 cóng bushes

从 cóng from; 从十八世纪起 **cóng shíbā shìjì qǐ** from the 18th century; 从他来中国以后 … **cóng tā lái Zhōngguó yǐhòu …** ever since he came to China … ; 我从没去过北京 **wǒ cóng méi qùguò Běijīng** I've never been to Beijing; 从 … 以来 **cóng … yǐlái** since …; 从明天开始 **cóng míngtiān kāishǐ** (starting) from tomorrow; 从五月一日起生效 **cóng wǔyùe yīrì qǐ shēngxiào** effective May 1; 从现在开始 **cóng xiànzài kāishǐ** from now on; 从星期一到星期三 **cóng xīngqīyī dào xīngqīsān** from Monday to Wednesday; 从 Y 中减去 X **cóng Y zhōng jiǎnqù X** deduct X from Y

从不 cóng bù never

从 … 下来 cóng … xiàlái get off

从此 cóngcǐ from now on; henceforth

匆匆 cōngcōng hurried

从句 cóngjù clause

从来 cónglái ever

从来不 cónglái bù never; 她从来不工作 **tā cónglái bù gōngzuò** she never does a stroke

从来没 cónglái méi (has) never; 他从来没去过那儿 **tā cónglái méi qùguò nàr** he has never been there

丛林 cónglín jungle

匆忙 **cōngmáng** hasty ◊ in a hurry; 匆忙做 ... **cōngmáng zuò** ... do ... in a rush; 匆忙写 **cōngmáng xiě** dash off

聪敏 **cōngmǐn** smart

聪明 **cōngmíng** intelligent, bright, clever ◊ intelligence

从前 **cóngqián** earlier; in the past; once upon a time

从容 **cóngróng** calm; leisurely

从事 **cóngshì** engage in; deal with

从事间谍活动 **cóngshì jiàndié huódòng** spy

从头到尾 **cóngtóu dàowěi** from beginning to end; from top to toe; through

从头至尾 **cóngtóu zhìwěi** overall

从中 **cóngzhōng** from among; between; out of

从中获利 **cóngzhōng huòlì** cash in on

凑合 **còuhe** rough it; make the best of ◊ so-so, average

凑巧 **còuqiǎo** luckily; by chance

粗 **cū** thick; coarse; rough

醋 **cù** vinegar

促 **cù** urge

篡改 **cuàngǎi** fiddle, falsify

粗暴 **cūbào** rough; gruff; 粗暴地 对待 **cūbàode duìdài** manhandle

粗笨 **cūbèn** crude; awkward

粗糙 **cūcāo** coarse; rough

促成 **cùchéng** contribute to; shape

促动 **cùdòng** motivate

粗话 **cūhuà** bad language

催 **cuī** rush; drive; urge

摧 **cuī** break; destroy

脆 **cuì** fragile; brittle; crisp

催促 **cuīcù** hurry up; press for

催化转化器 **cuīhuà zhuǎnhuà qì** catalytic converter

摧毁 **cuīhuǐ** destroy; devastate

摧毁性 **cuīhuǐ xìng** devastating

催泪气 **cuīlèi qì** tear gas

催眠疗法 **cuīmián liáofǎ** hypnotherapy

催眠曲 **cuīmián qǔ** lullaby

催眠术 **cuīmiánshù** hypnosis

脆弱 **cuìruò** weak; frail

催账单 **cuīzhàng dān** reminder

促进 **cùjìn** advance, further; stimulate ◊ boost

醋栗 **cùlì** gooseberry

粗鲁 **cūlǔ** crude, vulgar; ignorant; fresh, impertinent; rude; 他待她 很粗鲁 **tā dài tā hěn cūlǔ** he was very unpleasant to her

粗略 **cūlüè** rough; cursory

粗面 **cūmiàn** matt

村 **cūn** village

存 **cún** exist; survive; store; save

寸 **cùn** Chinese inch

存储 **cúnchǔ** deposit

存储力 **cúnchǔlì** memory COMPUT

存储器 **cúnchǔqì** memory chip

存储容量 **cúnchǔ róngliàng** storage capacity COMPUT

存放 **cúnfàng** keep, store; check (*in checkroom*)

存放行李处 **cúnfàng xíngli chù** baggage check

存根 **cúngēn** stub

存活 **cúnhuó** survive

存货 **cúnhuò** stock

存款 **cúnkuǎn** savings ◊ deposit

村里人 **cūnlǐ rén** villager

存盘 **cúnpán** save; saving

存入 **cúnrù** pay in; deposit; 存入 帐户 **cúnrù zhànghù** credit an amount to an account

村舍 **cūnshè** cottage

存为 **cúnwéi** save as COMPUT

存在 **cúnzài** exist ◊ existence

存折 **cúnzhé** bank book

村庄 **cūnzhuāng** village

错 **cuò** wrong ◊ mistake; fault; 是 你的／我的错 **nǐde／wǒde cuò** it's your/my fault; 不错 **bú cuò** not bad; excellent; 错了 **cuòle** that's wrong; you're wrong

撮 **cuō** group, clump

搓 **cuō** rub; twist

挫 **cuò** foil, thwart

锉 **cuò** file

挫败 **cuòbài** foil, thwart

措词 **cuòcí** phrase ◊ wording

锉刀 **cuòdāo** file (*for wood, nails*)

错过 **cuòguò** miss

错觉 **cuòjué** misconception; illusion

错开 **cuòkāi** stagger

磋商 **cuōshāng** consult

挫伤 **cuòshāng** bruise

措施 **cuòshī** step, measure

错视 **cuòshì** optical illusion

错误 **cuòwù** error, mistake ◊ wrong; false ◊ wrongly; 犯错误 **fàn cuòwù** make a mistake; go wrong; 使 ... 犯错误 **shǐ ... fàn cuòwù** trip up; 错误地 **cuòwùde** by mistake

错印 **cuòyìn** misprint

挫折 **cuòzhé** setback; failure; rebuff

错综复杂 **cuòzōng-fùzá** complicated

粗砂 **cūshā** grit

粗石 **cūshí** rubble

促使 **cùshǐ** impel; spur; cause to happen

粗饲料 **cū sìliào** roughage

粗俗 **cūsú** coarse, vulgar; gross; tasteless

粗体 **cūtǐ** bold

粗心 **cūxīn** careless, slipshod; thoughtless

粗心大意 **cūxīn dàyì** negligent

簇叶丛生 **cùyè cóngshēng** overgrown

粗硬 **cūyìng** coarse

促孕药 **cùyùnyào** fertility drug

粗壮 **cūzhuàng** stocky

D

答 dā reply, answer

搭 dā pitch; put up; take

打 dá dozen

达 dá arrive at, reach

答 dá reply, answer

打 dǎ hit, beat; play; make; do; get ◊ beating

大 dà big, large; great

答案 dá'àn answer

打败 dǎbài thrash; defeat ◊ thrashing; defeat; 被打败 **bèi dǎbài** get a thrashing

大白菜 dàbáicài Chinese cabbage

打扮 dǎbàn dress up; put on make-up; get dolled up ◊ style; dress; make-up

打包 dǎbāo package; pack; bale

大杯 dàbēi mug

大便 dàbiàn defecate; shit F ◊ feces; shit F

搭便车 dā biànchē ride, lift ◊ hitch a ride; get a lift

大鼻子 dà bízi pej Westerner; Caucasian (literally: big nose)

大伯子 dàbózi brother-in-law (husband's older brother)

大步 dàbù stride

打补丁 dǎ bǔdīng patch

大不列颠 Dà Bùlièdiān Great Britain ◊ British

打不碎 dǎ bú suì unbreakable

大步走 dàbù zǒu stride

打草图 dǎ cǎotú outline

大草原 dàcǎoyuán prairie

大吵大闹 dàchǎo dà'nào make a scene

搭车 dāchē thumb a ride; take a cab

搭乘 dāchéng fly

达成交易 dáchéng jiāoyì clinch a deal

达成协议 dáchéng xiéyì reach agreement on

大吃 dàchī big eater; food freak ◊ tuck away; gorge oneself

大吃大喝 dàchīdàhē eat, drink and be merry

大吃一惊 dàchīyìjīng stun; be flabbergasted

大锤 dàchuí sledge hammer

大吹大擂 dàchuī dàléi hype

大葱 dàcōngī leek; Chinese onion

大错 dàcuò blunder; big mistake

大胆 dàdǎn bold, daring

大胆地说 dàdǎn de shuō speak out

搭档 dādàng partner

搭档关系 dādàng guānxi partnership

达到 dádào come to; reach, attain; accomplish

大道 dàdào avenue; main road

达到顶峰 dádào dǐngfēng peak

打电话 dǎ diànhuà call, phone; make a call ◊ (tele)phone; 给X打电话 **gěi X dǎ diànhuà** give X a call

打电话给 dǎ diànhuà gěi call

打电话来 dǎ diànhuà laí call in

大调 dàdiào major MUS

大跌 dàdiē plummet

打动 dǎdòng touch, move

大豆 dàdòu soybean

打赌 dǎdǔ bet

打断 dǎduàn interrupt

打盹儿 dǎdǔnr doze; have a nap

大多数 dà duōshù bulk, majority; most

大都市 dà dūshì metropolis ◊ metropolitan

大肚子 dà dùzi paunch ◊ pregnant

打发 dǎfa idle away

大发雷霆 dà fā léitíng fly off the handle

大方 dàfang generous; liberal ◊ generosity

大方的举动 dàfang de jùdòng

sporting gesture

大发脾气 **dàfā píqì** blow up, get really angry

大风 **dàfēng** gale

答复 **dáfù** answer; respond ◊ answer; response

大概 **dàgài** about, roughly ◊ rough, approximate

大纲 **dàgāng** syllabus

大钢琴 **dàgāngqín** grand piano

打嗝 **dǎgé** belch, burp

大哥 **dàgē** eldest brother; *a term of address for a man of similar age to oneself*

大哥大 **dàgēdà** cell phone

嗝儿 **dǎgér** hiccup ◊ have the hiccups

大公无私 **dàgōng wúsī** selfless

搭钩 **dāgōu** buckle

打勾 **dǎgōu** check ◊ check (mark), tick

打鼓 **dǎgǔ** beat a drum; play drums

大褂 **dàguà** gown

达观 **dáguān** resilient

达官贵人 **dáguān guìrén** dignitary

打官司 **dǎ guānsī** sue; 和 X 打官司 **hé X dǎ guānsī** take X to court

大规模 **dàguīmó** wholesale, indiscriminate; large-scale

大姑姐 **dàgūjiě** sister-in-law (*husband's elder sister*)

大海 **dàhǎi** sea

打鼾 **dǎ hān** snore

大喊 **dàhǎn** call, call out; shout, shout out

大汗淋漓 **dàhàn línlí** covered in sweat

打哈欠 **dǎ hāqian** yawn

打呵欠 **dǎ hēqian** yawn

打滑 **dǎhuá** skid

大黄蜂 **dàhuángfēng** hornet

大会 **dàhuì** convention

打昏 **dǎhūn** stun

打火机 **dǎhuǒjī** (cigarette) lighter

打火钥匙 **dǎhuǒ yàoshi** ignition key

呆 **dāi** slow-witted; dull; blank ◊ F stay

待 **dāi** wait

带 **dài** bring; take ◊ belt; area; 我能带个朋友来吗? **wǒ néng dàige péngyǒu láima?** can I bring a friend?

代 **dài** replace ◊ era; generation

袋 **dài** bag; pack

戴 **dài** put on; wear

贷 **dài** loan ◊ borrow, lend

待 **dài** await, wait for

呆板 **dāibǎn** mechanical ◊ mechanically

代表 **dàibiǎo** represent ◊ representative

代表大会 **dàibiǎo dàhuì** congress

代表人 **dàibiǎo rén** representative

代表团 **dàibiǎotuán** delegation

代表我／他 **dàibiǎo wǒ／tā** on my／his behalf

逮捕 **dàibǔ** arrest

代词 **dàicí** pronoun

贷方 **dàifāng** credit

大夫 **dàifu** doctor, physician

急工 **dàigōng** go-slow

代沟 **dàigōu** generation gap

待会 X **dāihuǐr** in a minute

代价 **dàijià** cost

代价惨重 **dàijià cǎnzhòng** costly

带菌者 **dàijùn zhě** carrier (*of disease*)

贷款 **dàikuǎn** loan

带来 **dàilái** bring; bring about

代理 **dàilǐ** represent; act for

代理处 **dàilǐ chù** agency

带领 **dàilǐng** lead; guide

代理权 **dàilǐ quán** proxy

代理人 **dàilǐ rén** agent; representative

代理商 **dàilǐ shāng** rep, representative; agent

急慢 **dàimàn** snub

代母 **dàimǔ** surrogate mother; godmother

带球 **dàiqiú** dribble SP

戴上帽子 **dàishang màozi** put one's hat on

待售 **dàishòu** for sale

代替 **dàitì** stand in for; substitute

代替人 **dàitìrén** replacement

歹徒 **dǎitú** mobster, gangster

带血 **dàixuè** bloody, blood-stained

呆一会儿 **dāi yíhuìr** stick around

代用品 **dàiyòngpǐn** makeshift

待遇 **dàiyù** perk; package; treatment

呆在 **dāizài** stay, remain; 呆在家里 **dāi zài jiālǐ** stay at home; 呆在一起 **dāi zài yìqǐ** stay together, stick together

带着 **dàizhe** carry; leave on

呆滞 **dāizhì** glazed *expression*

带状疱疹 **dàizhuàng pàozhěn** shingles

带子 **dàizi** belt; tape; strip

袋子 **dàizi** bag

打击 **dǎjī** blow ◊ hit; deal a blow to

打架 **dǎjià** fight

大家 **dàjiā** everyone; all of us

大剪刀 **dàjiǎndāo** shears

打搅 **dǎjiǎo** bother, disturb; 请勿打搅 **qǐngwù dǎjiǎo** please do not disturb

大叫 **dàjiào** shout, bawl, yell

打交道 **dǎ jiāodào** have dealings with

大教堂 **dà jiàotáng** cathedral

打结 **dǎjié** knot, tie

大姐 **dàjiě** eldest sister

大惊小怪 **dàjīng xiǎoguài** fuss

大祭司 **dà jìsī** high priest

搭救 **dājiù** save, rescue

打击乐 **dǎjīyuè** percussion

打击乐器 **dǎjī yuèqì** percussion instrument

大咀大嚼 **dàjǔdàjué** munch

打开 **dǎkāi** open; turn on; switch on ◊ wide-open

打开包裹 **dǎkāi bāoguǒ** unpack

打瞌睡 **dǎ kēshuì** doze off; snooze

打孔 **dǎ kǒng** punch *hole* ◊ perforated

打孔机 **dǎkǒngjī** punch (*tool*)

大口袋 **dà kǒudài** sack

大块 **dàkuài** chunk

打烂 **dǎlàn** break down

打雷 **dǎléi** thunder

打量 **dǎliang** look over; size up

大梁 **dàliáng** girder

大量 **dàliàng** generous; great; heavy; plentiful ◊ wealth of; loads of

大量买进 **dàliàng mǎijìn** buy up

大量生产 **dàliàng shēngchǎn** mass-produce ◊ mass-production

打猎 **dǎliè** hunt

打临时工 **dǎ línshígōng** (work as a) temp

大理石 **dàlǐshí** marble

大陆 **dàlù** continent, mainland; mainland China

大路 **dàlù** main road

打乱 **dǎluàn** disrupt; screw up

大麻 **dàmá** hemp; marijuana

大马哈鱼 **dàmǎhāyú** salmon

大麦 **dàmài** barley

大门 **dàmén** (entrance) door; gate

打磨机 **dǎmójī** sander

大模型 **dàmóxíng** mock-up

大牧场 **dà mùchǎng** ranch

单 **dān** simple; only; single; odd *number* ◊ list; sheet; bill

担 **dān** carry on one's shoulder; undertake

丹 **dān** red

胆 **dǎn** gall bladder; courage, guts

蛋 **dàn** egg

氮 **dàn** nitrogen

淡 **dàn** faint; weak; bland *taste*; pale *color*; light; 淡粉 **dànfěn** pale pink

诞 **dàn** birth

但 **dàn** but; only

旦 **dàn** dawn

担 **dàn** burden

弹 **dàn** bullet; bomb; pellet

大男人主义者 **dà nánrén zhǔyì zhě** chauvinist

大男子气 **dànánziqì** macho

大闹一场 **dànào yìchǎng** kick up a stink

蛋白 **dànbái** white (*of egg*)

蛋白质 **dànbáizhì** protein

担保 **dānbǎo** guarantee; vouch for; sponsor ◊ sponsorship

担保人 **dānbǎo rén** guarantor; sponsor

单薄 **dānbó** scanty

蛋炒饭 **dànchǎofàn** egg fried rice

诞辰 **dànchén** birthday

单程 **dānchéng** one-way

单程票 **dānchéng piào** one-way ticket

单纯 **dānchún** simple; pure; alone

单词 **dāncí** word

单打 **dāndǎ** singles (*in tennis*)

弹道导弹 **dàndào dǎodàn** ballistic missile

单调 **dāndiào** monotonous; dull; drab

单调乏味 **dāndiào fáwèi** monotonous

单独 **dāndú** alone; independently of; in isolation

单方面 **dān fāngmiàn** unilateral

当 **dāng** work as; equal; should ◊ in front of ◊ when; just at; 当 ... 的时候 **dāng ... de shíhòu** when ...; 把 X 当成 Y **bǎ X dāngchéng Y** confuse X with Y

党 **dǎng** party

挡 **dǎng** block, obstruct ◊ gear

档 **dàng** shelf; file

荡 **dàng** shake; swing

当 **dàng** right; proper ◊ pawn; equal; treat as; think

胆敢 **dǎngǎn** dare

档案 **dàng'àn** file; records; archives

档案室 **dàng'ànshì** archives

档案箱 **dàng'ànxiāng** file cabinet

蛋糕 **dàngāo** cake

当场 **dāngchǎng** immediately, on the spot; 当场抓获 **dāngchǎng zhuāhuò** caught in the very act

当代 **dāngdài** contemporary ◊ the present era

党代会 **dǎngdàihuì** party conference

当地 **dāngdì** local

当地人 **dāngdì rén** native; local

当地时间 **dāngdì shíjiān** local time

当地特产 **dāngdì tèchǎn** local produce

耽搁 **dāngē** detain, hold up

挡风玻璃 **dǎngfēng bōli** windshield

当今 **dāngjīn** nowadays

当局 **dāngjú** the authorities

挡路 **dǎnglù** be in the way

当铺 **dàngpù** pawnshop

当前 **dāngqián** present

荡秋千 **dàng qiūqiān** swing; rock

当权 **dāngquán** ruling

当权派 **dāngquánpài** the Establishment

当权者 **dāngquán zhě** the authorities; decision-maker

当然 **dāngrán** of course, naturally; 当然可以 **dāngrán kěyǐ** by all means

当时 **dāngshí** at that time; then

当天 **dàngtiān** on the same day

胆固醇 **dǎngùchún** cholesterol

党委 **dǎngwěi** party committee

当心 **dāngxīn** be careful

当演员 **dāng yǎnyuán** go on the stage

党员 **dǎngyuán** party member

当中 **dāngzhōng** in the middle

当众 **dāngzhòng** in public, publicly

党中央 **Dǎng-Zhōngyāng** Communist Party Central Committee

挡住 **dǎngzhù** block out

淡化 **dànhuà** play down

蛋黄 **dànhuáng** yolk

单簧管 **dānhuángguǎn** clarinet

淡季 **dànjì** low season, off-season

担架 **dānjià** stretcher

单价 **dānjià** unit cost; unit price

单脚跳 **dānjiǎotiào** hop

胆结石 **dǎnjiéshí** gallstone

蛋壳 **dànké** eggshell

胆量 **dǎnliàng** guts, nerve

丹麦 **Dānmài** Denmark ◊ Danish

胆囊 **dǎnnáng** gall bladder

单排扣 **dānpáikòu** single-breasted

单枪匹马 **dānqiāng pīmǎ** single-handed

胆怯 **dǎnqiè** cowardly

单亲 **dānqīn** single parent

单亲家庭 **dānqīn jiātíng** single parent family

单曲唱片 **dānqǔ chàngpiàn** single (*record*)

单人 **dānrén** solo

担任 **dānrèn** take on; act as

单人床 **dānrénchuáng** single bed

单人房间 **dānrén fángjiān** single room

单人沙发 **dānrén shāfā** armchair

单色 **dānsè** plain, self-colored

淡色 **dànsè** tint

单身 **dānshēn** single, unmarried

诞生 **dànshēng** be born ◊ birth

单身汉 **dānshēn hàn** bachelor

单身母亲 **dānshēn mǔqīn** single mother

单身女子 **dānshēn nǚzi** single woman

但是 **dànshì** but; nevertheless

单数 **dānshù** singular

淡水 **dànshuǐ** fresh water

单体 **dāntǐ** module

单体设计 **dāntǐ shèjì** modular

弹头 **dàntóu** warhead

大怒 **dànù** be fuming

淡忘 **dànwàng** gradually forget

单位 **dānwèi** unit; work unit

耽误 **dānwù** delay, hold up

胆小 **dǎnxiǎo** cowardice ◊ cowardly

胆小鬼 **dǎnxiǎo guǐ** coward

担心 **dānxīn** be afraid of; worry ◊ apprehensive; worried; 令人担心 **lìngrén dānxīn** worrying

单行道 **dānxíng dào** one-way street

弹药 **dànyào** ammunition

单一 **dānyī** isolated

担忧 **dānyōu** worry, concern; disturb, trouble ◊ worried ◊ worry

单元 **dānyuán** unit

但愿 **dànyuàn** hopefully

单张 **dānzhāng** leaflet

胆汁 **dǎnzhī** bile

胆子 **dǎnzi** courage

担子 **dànzi** burden

胆子大 **dǎnzi dà** brave

胆子小 **dǎnzi xiǎo** cowardly

刀 **dāo** knife

岛 **dǎo** island

捣 **dǎo** pound; thresh; attack

导 **dǎo** guide; lead; conduct

倒 **dǎo** fall; fall down; trip over; close down ◊ change; exchange

道 **dào** way; road; path; Tao ◊ say

倒 **dào** empty; pour; tip over; rewind; reverse ◊ upside-down ◊ however; actually; maybe

到 **dào** arrive; reach ◊ to; up to; 到时间了 **dào shíjiān le** time is up;

到我那儿去 **dào wǒ nàr qù** go to my place

盗 **dào** steal ◊ thief

悼 **dào** mourn

稻 **dào** paddy; rice

盗版 **dàobǎn** pirate ◊ pirate copy

倒闭 **dǎobì** go bankrupt, go bust

倒彩 **dàocǎi** catcall; boo

稻草人 **dàocǎorén** scarecrow

到场 **dàochǎng** appear

倒车 **dàochē** back, reverse *car*

倒出 **dàochū** pour out

到处 **dàochù** everywhere

悼词 **dàocí** lament

到此为止 **dàocǐ wéizhǐ** as yet

到达 **dàodá** arrival; arrivals ◊ arrive; come in; come to; get in; get to, reach ◊ in, arrived

导弹 **dǎodàn** (guided) missile

捣蛋 **dǎodàn** get up to mischief

倒档 **dàodǎng** reverse gear

道德 **dàodé** morals, ethics

道德高尚 **dàodé gāoshàng** virtuous

道德经 **Dàodéjīng** Tao Te Ching

到底 **dàodǐ** ever; at last; after all; to the end

祷告 **dǎogào** prayer; 道高一尺，魔高一丈 **dàogāo yìchǐ, mógāo yízhàng** *prov* magic works better than doctrine

稻谷 **dàogǔ** rice (*as crop*)

倒光 **dàoguāng** drain

导火线 **dǎohuǒ xiàn** fuse; catalyst

到家 **dàojiā** get in; get home

道家 **Dàojiā** Taoism, Taoist philosophy

道教 **Dàojiào** Taoism, Taoist religion

倒酒 **dàojiǔ** pour wine

道具 **dàojù** prop

倒空 **dàokōng** empty

到来 **dàolái** arrive, show up ◊ appearance

道理 **dàolǐ** sense; reason; principle; truth

道路 **dàolù** road

捣乱 **dǎoluàn** cause trouble; create unrest

捣乱分子 **dǎoluàn fènzǐ**

undesirable element

捣乱者 **dǎoluàn zhě** troublemaker

倒霉 **dǎoméi** have bad luck ◊ unfortunate

悼念 **dàoniàn** mourn

到期 **dàoqī** become due; mature; expire; be up

道歉 **dàoqiàn** apologize ◊ apology

盗窃 **dàoqiè** steal; burglarize ◊ break-in, burglary

道士 **Dàoshì** Taoist priest

倒数第二 **dàoshǔ dì'er** penultimate

倒数数 **dào shǔshù** countdown

倒塌 **dǎotā** collapse, cave in

倒台 **dǎotái** fall

稻田 **dàotián** paddy field, ricefield

倒下 **dǎoxià** fall down; collapse

导线 **dǎoxiàn** (electrical) wire; cable

倒叙 **dǎoxù** flashback

导演 **dǎoyǎn** direct *play*, *movie* ◊ direction ◊ director

盗用 **dàoyòng** embezzle ◊ embezzlement

导游 **dǎoyóu** courier; guide

导游旅游 **dǎoyóu lǚyóu** guided tour

岛屿 **dǎoyǔ** island

岛屿人 **dǎoyǔ rén** islander

导致 **dǎozhì** result in; set off

倒置 **dàozhì** invert

稻子 **dàozi** paddy

大炮 **dàpào** artillery; cannon

打喷嚏 **dǎ pēntì** sneeze

打屁股 **dǎ pìgǔ** spank

打平局 **dǎ píngjú** draw (*in match*)

大皮箱 **dà píxiāng** trunk

打破 **dǎpò** break; 打破沉默 **dǎpò chénmò** break the ice

打破纪录 **dǎpò jìlù** record-breaking

大气 **dàqì** atmosphere

大气外层 **dàqì wàicéng** upper atmosphere

大气污染 **dàqì wūrǎn** atmospheric pollution

打圈 **dǎquān** circle

大群 **dàqún** swarm; crowd

打扰 **dǎrǎo** disturb; trespass on

打入 **dǎrù** infiltrate; penetrate

打扫 **dǎsǎo** sweep; clean

大扫除 **dà sǎochú** spring-cleaning

打扫干净 **dǎsǎo gānjìng** clean out

大厦 **dàshà** high-rise building

打闪 **dǎshǎn** flash (*of lightning*)

打伤 **dǎshāng** wound

大赦 **dàshè** amnesty

大声 **dàshēng** in a loud voice

大声点 **dàshēng diǎn** speak up

大声呼喊 **dàshēng hūhǎn** give a cry; shout

大声说出 **dàshēng shuōchū** cry out

大声笑 **dàshēng xiào** roar with laughter

大使 **dàshǐ** ambassador

大使馆 **dàshǐguǎn** embassy

大手大脚的人 **dàshǒu dàjiǎo** wasteful; extravagant; 大手大脚地花钱 **dàshǒu dàjiǎo di huāqián** splash out

打手势 **dǎ shǒushì** gesticulate

打算 **dǎsuàn** intend; plan

大蒜 **dàsuàn** garlic

打碎 **dǎsuì** shatter; break ◊ broken, bust

大体来说 **dàtǐ láishuō** broadly speaking

打听 **dǎtīng** pry; inquire about; make enquiries; 向 X 打听 Y *xiàng X dǎtīng Y* ask X about Y

大厅 **dàtīng** hall

大提琴 **dà tíqín** cello

大体上 **dàtǐshang** in general

打通 **dǎtōng** (*on telephone*) get through

大头针 **dàtóuzhēn** pin

大腿 **dàtuǐ** thigh

打退堂鼓 **dǎ tuìtánggǔ** back off; get cold feet, chicken out

大屠杀 **dà túshā** carnage; massacre

大为 **dàwéi** great achievement ◊ greatly; 使大为吃惊 *shǐ dàwéi chījīng* amaze; 大为惊讶 *dàwéi jīngyà* marvel at

大乌鸦 **dà wūyā** raven

大虾 **dàxiā** shrimp

大象 **dàxiàng** elephant

大小 **dàxiǎo** size

打消疑虑 **dǎxiāo yílǜ** reassure

大写 **dàxiě** print (in block letters) ◊ capitalization; full form of Chinese numeral

大写字母 **dàxiě zìmǔ** capital letter(s)

)大型 **dàxíng** large-scale

大猩猩 **dàxīngxing** gorilla

大型衣柜 **dàxíng yīguì** walk-in closet

大型游艇 **dàxíng yóutǐng** cruise liner

大修 **dàxiū** overhaul

大西洋 **Dàxīyáng** Atlantic

大学 **dàxué** university

大学毕业后 **dàxué bìyèhòu** postgraduate

大削减 **dà xuējiǎn** slash, cut

大学生 **dàxué shēng** (college) student; undergraduate

大烟囱 **dà yāncōng** stack

打哑语 **dǎ yǎyǔ** mime

大衣 **dàyī** overcoat

大意 **dàyì** gist

大意 **dàyi** careless

打印 **dǎyìn** print, run off

答应 **dāyīng** reply; agree

打印机 **dǎyìnjī** printer

打印文本 **dǎyìn wénběn** hard copy

大雨 **dàyǔ** deluge; 大雨倾盆 **dàyǔ qīngpén** it's pouring (with rain)

大约 **dàyuē** approximate ◊ approximately, around, in the region of ◊ thereabouts

大跃进 **Dàyuèjìn** Great Leap Forward

大运河 **Dàyùnhé** Grand Canal

大斋节 **Dàzhāijié** Lent

打颤 **dǎzhàn** chatter

大帐篷 **dàzhàngpéng** marquee

打招呼 **dǎ zhāohu** greet

打折扣 **dǎ zhékòu** discount

大致 **dàzhì** more or less

大致说来 **dàzhì shuōlái** basically

打中 **dǎzhòng** hit *target*

大众 **dàzhòng** the masses

大众传媒 **dàzhòng chuánméi** mass media

大众化 **dàzhònghuà** popularize

打字 **dǎzì** type

大字标题 **dàzì biāotí** headline

打字机 **dǎzì jī** typewriter

打字员 **dǎzìyuán** typist

大宗 **dàzōng** block

大走财运 **dàzǒucáiyùn** make a killing

打坐 **dǎzuò** meditate ◊ meditation

大作 **dàzuò** great work, masterpiece

的 **de** of; 书的名字 **shūde míngzi** the title of the book ◊ (*makes adjectives attributive*): 漂亮的姑娘 **piàoliangde gūniang** a beautiful girl ◊ (*introducing relative clause*): 我喜欢的宾馆 **wǒ xǐhuande bīnguǎn** the hotel which I prefer

得 **de** (*before a qualifying word*): 好得多 / 容易得多 **hǎo de duō / róngyì de duō** a lot better / a lot easier ◊ (*when result of an action is expressed*): 看得见 **kàn de jiàn** be able to see

地 **de** (*to form adverbs*): 高兴地 **gāoxìngde** happily

得 **dé** get, obtain

德 **dé** morals; virtue

得不偿失 **dé bùchángshī** the loss outweighs the gain; 做 X 得不偿失 **zuò X dé bùchángshī** it doesn't pay to do X

得到 **dédào** get, obtain; reach *decision*

得到 ... 的风声 **dédào ... de fēngshēng** get wind of ...

得到消息 **dédào xiāoxi** hear from; get news of

得分 **défēn** score

得分运动员 **défēn yùndòngyuán** scorer

得感冒 **dé gǎnmaò** catch (a) cold

德国 **Déguó** Germany ◊ German

得过且过 **déguòqiěguò** muddle along

得啦, 得啦 **déla, déla** now, now!

得了 **déle** alright, that's enough!; 得了吧! **déleba!** will you stop that!

得了 ... 病 **déle ... bìng** be sickening for

得力助手 **délì zhùshǒu** righthand man

灯 **dēng** light; lamp

登 **dēng** climb

等 **děng** wait; grade, class; 你等着吧! **nǐ děngzhe ba!** just you wait!; 让 X 等 **ràng X děng** keep X waiting; 我们等他准备好 **wǒmen děng tā zhǔnbèihǎo** we'll wait until he's ready

凳 **dèng** stool

登场 **dēngchǎng** appear ◊ appearance (*in movie*)

等待 **děngdài** wait; wait for ◊ waiting

等等 **děngděng** and so on, etc ◊ hang on

登高 **dēnggāo** climb a mountain

登广告 **dēng guǎnggào** advertise

登广告者 **dēng guǎnggào zhě** advertiser

等候 **děnghòu** wait

等候室 **děnghòushì** waiting room

等候者名单 **děnghòuzhě míngdān** waiting list

登记 **dēngjì** check in; register; book ◊ registration

等级 **děngjí** class; classification; grade; rank

等价 **děngjià** of equivalent value

登记簿 **dēngjì bù** register

登机卡 **dēngjī kǎ** boarding card

登机口 **dēngjī kǒu** gate (*at airport*)

登记人 **dēngjì rén** registrar

等级制度 **děngjí zhìdù** hierarchy

灯笼 **dēnglong** lantern

灯泡 **dēngpào** light bulb

登山 **dēngshān** mountaineering

登山者 **dēngshān zhě** mountaineer, climber

等式 **děngshì** equation

灯塔 **dēngtǎ** lighthouse

等同 **děngtóng** equal

等退票 **děng tuìpiào** on standby

等退票旅客 **děng tuìpiào lǚkè** standby passenger

邓小平 **Dèng Xiǎopíng** Deng Xiaoping

邓小平理论 **Dèng Xiǎopíng lǐlùn** Deng Xiaoping theory

灯芯绒 **dēngxīnróng** corduroy

灯芯绒裤 **dēngxīnróng kù** cords

等一下 **děngyíxià** hold on; wait a moment

等于 **děngyú** equal; correspond to

灯罩 **dēngzhào** (lamp)shade

凳子 **dèngzi** stool

得体 **détǐ** proper; tactful

得知 **dézhī** become aware of

得罪 **dézuì** insult; offend

滴 **dī** drop; blob ◊ drip; trickle

堤 **dī** dike

低 **dī** low; junior

笛 **dí** bamboo flute

敌 **dí** enemy

底 **dǐ** bottom

递 **dì** pass

帝 **dì** emperor

弟 **dì** younger brother

第 **dì** *used to create ordinal numbers*

递 **dì** hand over, deliver

地 **dì** the earth; land; ground

堤岸 **dī'àn** embankment

点 **diǎn** dot; (decimal) point; point; drop; spot ◊ dip; dunk ◊ a little, some ◊ o'clock 好 / 容易点儿了吗? **hǎo / róngyì diǎnr le ma?** is that any better / easier?; 几点了? **jǐdiǎnle?** what's the time?

碘 **diǎn** iodine

电 **diàn** electric(al) ◊ electricity

垫 **diàn** cushion; mat

店 **diàn** store; shop

电报 **diànbào** telegram

颠簸 **diānbō** jolt ◊ bumpy

点菜 **diǎncài** order (*in restaurant*)

电唱机 **diànchàngjī** record player

电唱盘 **diànchàng pán** turntable

电车 **diànchē** streetcar

垫衬 **diànchèn** pad

电池 **diànchí** battery

典当 **diǎndàng** pawn

颠倒 **diāndǎo** reverse; 把 X 上下颠倒过来 **bǎ X shàngxià diāndǎo guòlái** turn X upside down

颠倒黑白 **diāndǎo hēibái** topsy-turvy

电灯 **diàndēng** electric light

电灯泡 **diàndēng pào** light bulb

点滴 **diǎndī** drip MED

电动机 **diàndòng jī** dynamo

典范 **diǎnfàn** characterize ◊ example; model

电饭锅 **diànfànguō** rice cooker

淀粉 **diànfěn** starch; cornstarch

颠覆分子 **diānfù fènzǐ** subversive

电工 **diàngōng** electrician

佃户 **diànhù** tenant

电话 **diànhuà** telephone; 打个电 话 **dǎ ge diànhuà** make a telephone call

电话簿 **diànhuà bù** phone book

电话磁卡 **diànhuà cíkǎ** phonecard

电话费 **diànhuà fèi** toll TELEC

电话号码 **diànhuà hàomǎ** telephone number

电话机 **diànhuàjī** telephone

电话交换台 **diànhuà jiāohuàntái** switchboard

电话亭 **diànhuà tíng** phone booth

电话线 **diànhuà xiàn** telephone line

点火 **diǎnhuǒ** light *fire*

点击 **diǎnjī** click COMPUT

电级 **diànjí** electrode

电缆 **diànlǎn** electricity cable

电缆塔 **diànlǎntǎ** pylon

典礼 **diǎnlǐ** ceremony ◊ ceremonial

垫料 **diànliào** pad; padding; upholstery

电流 **diànliú** electric current

电炉 **diànlú** hotplate; electric stove

点名 **diǎnmíng** roll call

电脑 **diànnǎo** computer

电脑化 **diànnǎo huà** computerize

电脑空间 **diànnǎo kōngjiān** cyberspace

电脑控制 **diànnǎo kòngzhì** computer-controlled

电脑使用 **diànnǎo shǐyòng** computing

惦念 **diànniàn** worry; worry about

电脑站 **diànnǎo zhàn** computer terminal

垫片 **diànpiàn** gasket; washer

电气 **diànqì** electricity

电器 **diànqì** electrical appliance

点燃 **diǎnrán** ignite

电热水器 **diàn rèshuǐqì** immersion heater

电热毯 **diànrètǎn** electric blanket

电扇 **diànshàn** electric fan

电视 **diànshì** television; 电视上 **diànshì shang** on TV

电视会议 **diànshì huìyì** video conference

电视机 **diànshì jī** television set

电视节目 **diànshì jiémù** television program

电视摄影室 **diànshì shèyǐng shì** television studio

电视游戏 **diànshì yóuxì** video game

电死 **diànsǐ** electrocute

电台 **diàntái** station RAD, TV

电梯 **diàntī** elevator

电筒 **diàntǒng** flashlight

点头 **diǎntóu** nod

玷污 **diànwū** taint; cast a slur on

癫痫 **diānxián** epileptic

点线 **diǎnxiàn** dotted line

电线 **diànxiàn** cable; wire; power line

癫痫发作 **diānxián fāzuò** epileptic fit

电线杆 **diànxiàn gān** telegraph pole

癫痫症 **diānxiánzhèng** epilepsy

点心 **diǎnxin** dim sum

电信 **diànxìn** telecommunications

典型 **diǎnxíng** characteristic; classic; representative; typical ◊ typically; 典型美国人 **diǎnxíng měiguórén** typically American

电压 **diànyā** voltage

点烟 **diǎnyān** light up *cigarette*

电椅 **diànyǐ** electric chair

电影 **diànyǐng** movie, motion picture

电影剧本 **diànyǐng jùběn** screenplay

电影迷 **diànyǐng mí** movie buff

电影明星 **diànyǐng míngxīng** movie star

电影院 **diànyǐng yuàn** movie theater

电影预告片 **diànyǐng yùgào piān** trailer

店员 **diànyuán** sales clerk

电源电缆 **diànyuán diànlǎn** power cable

点钟 **diǎnzhōng** o'clock; 五点钟 **wǔdiǎnzhōng** five o'clock

店主 **diànzhǔ** landlord; shopkeeper

点缀 **diǎnzhuì** decorate; jazz up

点子 **diǎnzi** pointer; 出点子 **chū diǎnzi** give advice

电子 **diànzǐ** electron ◊ electronic

垫子 **diànzi** cushion; padding

电子表 **diànzǐbiǎo** quartz watch

电子数据处理 **diànzǐ shùjù chǔlǐ** electronic data processing, EDP

电子信箱 **diànzǐ xìnxiāng** e-mail address

电子学 **diànzǐxué** electronics

电子邮件 **diànzǐ yóujiàn** e-mail; 打电子邮件 **dǎ diànzǐ yóujiàn** e-mail, send an e-mail

电子游戏 **diànzǐ yóuxì** computer game

凋 **diāo** wither

雕 **diāo** carve; engrave

刁 **diāo** wily

调 **diào** move, transfer

吊 **diào** hang; suspend

钓 **diào** fish with hook and line

掉 **diào** come out (of stain) ◊ (getting rid of): 吃掉 **chī diào** eat up; 擦掉 **cā diào** wipe off; 卖掉 **mài diào** sell off; 掉了 **diàole** come away (of button etc)

碉堡 **diāobǎo** fortress

调查 **diàochá** look into, check out; investigate; poll; survey ◊ investigation

调查方法 **diàochá fāngfǎ** line of inquiry

吊床 **diàochuáng** hammock

钓到 **diàodào** catch fish

吊灯 **diàodēng** chandelier

调动 **diàodòng** transfer

钓竿 **diàogān** fishing rod

调换 **diàohuàn** exchange

吊架 **diàojià** trapeze

雕刻 **diāokè** carve; engrave

雕刻（塑）**diāokè (sù)** sculpture

雕刻（塑）家 **diáokè (sù) jiā** sculptor

吊裤带 **diàokùdài** suspenders

掉落 **diàoluò** fall out

刁难 **diāonàn** give a hard time; create difficulties; be obstructive

貂皮 **diāopí** mink

貂皮大衣 **diāopí dàyī** mink (coat)

吊桥 **diàoqiáo** suspension bridge

掉色 **diàoshǎi** fade

吊死 **diàosǐ** hang

雕塑 **diāosù** sculpture

吊索运输车 **diàosuǒ yùnshūchē** ski lift

调头 **diàotóu** turn around

吊袜带 **diàowàdài** garter

凋谢 **diāoxiè** wither

吊唁 **diàoyàn** offer condolences

钓鱼 **diàoyú** go fishing

钓鱼杆 **diàoyúgān** fishing rod

掉转 **diàozhuǎn** steer; turn

第八 **dì bā** eighth

地板 **dìbǎn** floor; floorboard

第八十 **dì bāshí** eightieth

底部 **dǐbù** base; bottom

地产 **dìchǎn** estate

低潮 **dīcháo** low tide

底朝上 **dǐ cháo shàng** upside down

低沉 **dīchén** low; deep; oppressive

滴答 **dīdā** tick (of clock)

抵达 **dǐdá** arrive at

地带 **dìdài** zone; area

抵挡 **dǐdǎng** resist; repel

地道 **dìdào** authentic; idiomatic

低地 **dīdì** lowlands

弟弟 **dìdi** younger brother

地点 **dìdiǎn** place; spot; location

低调 **dī diào** low key

敌对 **díduì** hostile

跌 **diē** fall; stumble

爹 **diē** dad, pop

叠 **dié** stack, pile

蝶 **dié** butterfly

跌倒 **diēdǎo** fall over

爹爹 **diēdie** dad, pop

喋喋不休 **diédié bùxiū** chatter

跌跌撞撞 **diēdie zhuàngzhuàng** stagger

跌价 **diējià** price drop

跌落 **diēluò** drop

第二 **dì'èr** second; 第二大 ***dì'èr dà*** second biggest; 第二好 ***dì'èr hǎo*** second best

第二点 **dì'èrdiǎn** secondly

第二十 **dì'èrshí** twentieth

第二天 **dì'èr tiān** the day after

蝶泳 **diéyǒng** butterfly stroke

碟子 **diézi** dish

提防 **dīfáng** be on one's guard against

地方 **dìfāng** place ◊ local

地方政府 **dìfāng zhèngfǔ** local government

低峰时间 **dīfēng shíjiān** off-peak

滴干 **dīgān** drip-dry

低估 **dīgū** underestimate; undervalue

帝国 **dìguó** empire

帝国主义 **dìguó zhǔyì** imperialism

诋毁 **dǐhuǐ** slur

低级 **dījí** low; crude

地基 **dìjī** foundations

地极 **dìjí** pole ◊ polar

递交 **dìjiāo** hand over; deliver

地窖 **dìjiào** cellar; vaults

缔结 **dìjié** conclude *contract*

第九 **dì jiǔ** ninth

第九十 **dì jiǔshí** ninetieth

低卡路里 **dī kǎlùlǐ** low-calorie

抵抗 **dǐkàng** resist ◊ resistance

地雷 **dìléi** (land) mine

地理 **dìlǐ** geography

低廉 **dīlián** knockdown price

低领口 **dī lǐngkǒu** low-cut

第六 **dì liù** sixth

第六十 **dì liùshí** sixtieth

地理学 **dìlǐxué** geography

低落 **dīluò** subdued

弟妹 **dìmèi** sister-in-law (*younger brother's wife*); younger brothers and sisters

地面 **dìmiàn** ground; bottom

地面控制 **dìmiàn kòngzhì** ground control

低能 **dīnéng** ineffectual; mentally handicapped

低能儿 **dīnéng'ér** imbecile

叮 **dīng** sting; stab

钉 **dīng** nail; staple

丁 **dīng** cube

盯 **dīng** stare

顶 **dǐng** top; crest ◊ replace; cope with; push up ◊ very ◊ *measure word for hats*: 一顶草帽 ***yìdǐng cǎomào*** a straw hat

锭 **dìng** ingot

定 **dìng** set, fix; 那就定了! ***nà jiù dìng le!*** that settles it!

订 **dìng** order; subscribe

钉 **dìng** nail

定菜单 **dìng càidān** order (*in restaurant*)

定餐 **dìngcān** set meal

顶层公寓 **dǐngcéng gōngyù** penthouse

顶层楼座 **dǐngcéng lóuzuò** gallery

订单 **dìngdān** order (*for goods*); order form

叮当声 **dīngdāng shēng** tinkle; clink

顶点 **dǐngdiǎn** summit; culmination

定额 **dìng'é** quota; target

定发胶 **dìng fàjiāo** lacquer

顶峰 **dǐngfēng** high point, peak

顶风 **dǐngfēng** against the wind ◊ headwind

定购 **dìnggòu** order

定冠词 **dìngguàncí** definite article

订户 **dìnghù** customer; subscriber

订婚 **dìnghūn** engaged ◊ get engaged ◊ engagement

订婚戒指 **dìnghūn jièzhǐ** engagement ring

订货 **dìnghuò** order goods

定价 **dìngjià** price *goods*; set a price

订计划 **dìng jìhuà** plan

定金 **dìngjīn** deposit; down payment

订机票 **dìng jīpiào** book a flight

定居 **dìngjū** settle (down)

钉牢 **dìngláo** fix

定量 **dìngliàng** quota

定量供应 **dìngliàng gōngyìng** ration

顶楼 **dǐnglóu** garret

定论 **dìnglùn** verdict

钉帽 **dīngmào** head (*of nail*)

定名 **dìngmíng** entitled *book*

定期 **dìngqī** regular ◊ periodically ◊ set a date

定期航班 **dìngqī hángbān** scheduled flight

盯梢 **dīngshāo** tail, shadow

定时器 **dìngshíqì** timer; time switch

定时炸弹 **dìngshí zhàdàn** time bomb

订书钉 **dìngshūdīng** staple

订书机 **dìngshūjī** stapler

定位 **dìngwèi** location

丁香 **dīngxiāng** lilac

定向发射 **dìngxiàng fāshè** beam

丁香花 **dīngxiāng huā** lilac

定义 **dìngyì** definition

订阅 **dìngyuè** subscribe to *publication*

订阅者 **dìngyuè zhě** subscriber (*to publication*)

盯着 **dīngzhe** stare at; 盯着 X 的 眼睛 **dīngzhe X de yǎnjīng** look X straight in the eye

顶针 **dīngzhēn** thimble

顶住 **dǐngzhù** resist

订桌 **dìngzhuō** book a table

钉子 **dīngzi** brush-off; snub; nail; 钉钉子 ***dìng dīngzi*** hammer in a nail

定罪 **dìngzuì** conviction (*criminal*) ◊ convict

定做 **dìngzuò** made-to-measure; tailor-made

底盘 **dǐpán** chassis

地皮 **dìpí** plot of land to build on

底片 **dǐpiàn** negative (*photographic*)

地平线 **dìpíngxiàn** horizon

第七 **dì qī** seventh

地勤人员 **dìqín rényuán** ground crew, ground staff

第七十 **dì qīshí** seventieth

地球 **dìqiú** earth; world; globe

地球居民 **dìqiú jūmín** terrestrial

地球仪 **dìqiúyí** globe

低气压区 **dī qìyā qū** low (*in weather*)

地区 **dìqū** area; neighborhood; region ◊ regional

的确 **díquè** indeed; undeniably

敌人 **dírén** enemy

第三 **dìsān** third ◊ thirdly

第三方保险 **dìsān fāng bǎoxiǎn** third-party *or* liability insurance

第三个 **dìsān gè** third

第三十 **dìsānshí** thirtieth

第三世界 **Dìsān Shìjiè** Third World

第三者 **dìsānzhě** third party

低声 **dīshēng** softly

低声说 **dīshēng shuō** whisper; mutter

第十 **dìshí** tenth

地势 **dìshì** terrain

第十八 **dì shíbā** eighteenth

第十二 **dì shí'èr** twelfth

第十六 **dì shíliù** sixteenth

第十七 **dìshíqī** seventeenth

第十三 **dìshísān** thirteenth

第十四 **dìshísì** fourteenth

第十五 **dì shíwǔ** fifteenth

第十一 **dì shíyī** eleventh

滴水 **dīshuǐ** drain

第四 **dìsì** fourth

迪斯科 **dísīkē** disco

第四十 **dìsìshí** fortieth

递送 **dìsòng** deliver

地毯 **dìtǎn** carpet

地铁 **dìtiě** subway

迪厅 **dítīng** disco

低头 **dītóu** bow; duck *head*

地图 **dìtú** map

地图册 **dìtúcè** atlas

丢 **diū** lose; throw away

丢掉 **diūdiào** throw away

丢脸 **diūliǎn** lose face ◊ humiliating

丢弃 **diūqì** dump

丢失 **diūshī** lose

丢下 X 不管 **diūxià X bùguǎn** leave X unattended

低微 **dīwēi** humble

地位 **dìwèi** position, standing, status

地位低 **dìwèi dī** junior

地位低下 **dìwèi dīxià** underprivileged

第五 **dìwǔ** fifth

第五十 **dì wǔshí** fiftieth

低下 **dīxià** menial
地下 **dìxià** underground
地线 **dìxiàn** ground ELEC
抵消 **dǐxiāo** offset
地下室 **dìxiàshì** basement
地下通道 **dìxià tōngdào** underpass
地形 **dìxíng** geography; terrain
抵押 **dǐyā** mortgage
低压地区 **dīyā dìqū** low-pressure area
低压区 **dīyā qū** depression (*meteorological*)
敌意 **díyì** animosity, antagonism, hostility
第一 **dìyī** first; leading
第一百 **dì yìbǎi** hundredth
第一次 **dìyícì** the first time
第一个 **dìyígè** first
第一流 **dìyīliú** ace; first-class
低音提琴 **dīyīn tíqín** double-bass
低音乐器 **dīyīn yuèqì** bass
第一千个 **dì yì qiān gè** thousandth
第一手 **dìyīshǒu** at first hand
低于 **dīyú** below, beneath
低语 **dīyǔ** murmur
地狱 **dìyù** hell
低噪音 **dī zàoyīn** quiet
地震 **dìzhèn** earthquake
地震学 **dìzhènxué** seismology
地支 **dìzhī** earthly branches (*in Chinese calendar*)
抵制 **dǐzhì** resist; boycott
地址 **dìzhǐ** address
地质 **dìzhì** geology ◊ geological
低脂肪 **dīzhīfáng** low-fat
地质学 **dìzhìxué** geology
地质学者 **dìzhìxué zhě** geologist
地主 **dìzhǔ** land owner
笛子 **dízi** flute
底座 **dǐzuò** base
东 **dōng** east
鸫 **dōng** robin
冬 **dōng** winter
懂 **dǒng** understand; know
洞 **dòng** hole; cave
动 **dòng** move; 别动来动去！**bié dònglái dòngqù!** keep still!
冻 **dòng** freeze; 我冻坏了 **wǒ dònghuài le** I'm frozen

栋 **dòng** *measure word for houses*; 一栋房屋 **yídòng fángwū** a house
东北 **dōngběi** northeast
东部 **dōngbù** eastern
洞察 **dòngchá** insight
洞察力 **dòngchálì** perception
动产 **dòngchǎn** moveable assets
冻疮 **dòngchuāng** chilblain
动词 **dòngcí** verb
动荡不定 **dòngdàng búdìng** unstable
东道主 **dōngdàozhǔ** host
东方 **dōngfāng** east; the East; Orient ◊ eastern; oriental; Oriental
东方人 **dōngfāng rén** Oriental
冬菇 **dōnggū** dried winter mushroom
东海 **Dōnghǎi** East China Sea
懂行 **dǒngháng** expert
恫吓 **dònghè** threaten; intimidate
动画片 **dònghuà piān** animated cartoon
动画片摄制 **dònghuà piān shèzhì** animation
动机 **dòngjī** motive
冻僵 **dòngjiāng** numb with cold, frozen stiff
冻结 **dòngjié** freeze
冬季运动 **dōngjì yùndòng** winter sports
东拉西扯 **dōnglā xīchě** ramble (*in speaking*) ◊ rambling
动力 **dònglì** driving force; dynamism; momentum; incentive; stimulus; motivation
动乱 **dòngluàn** turmoil; unrest; upheaval
动脉 **dòngmài** artery
冬眠 **dōngmián** hibernation ◊ hibernate
东南 **dōngnán** southeast, southeastern
东南部 **dōngnán bù** southeast
东南亚 **Dōngnán Yà** Southeast Asia ◊ Southeast Asian
鸫鸟 **dōngniǎo** thrush
冬青 **dōngqīng** holly
动人 **dòngrén** moving
冻伤 **dòngshāng** frostbite ◊ frostbitten

东山再起 **dōngshān zàiqǐ** make a comeback

动身 **dòngshēn** set off

懂事 **dǒngshì** understanding; sensible

董事 **dǒngshì** board member; director

董事会 **dǒngshì huì** board of directors

董事会会议 **dǒngshìhuì huìyì** board meeting

董事长 **dǒngshìzhǎng** chairman of the board

动手 **dòngshǒu** get to work

动手动脚 **dòngshǒu dòngjiǎo** touch up; make a pass; get fresh

动手术 **dòng shǒushù** operate MED

冻死 **dòngsǐ** freeze to death; 我冻死了 **wǒ dòngsǐle** I'm freezing

冬天 **dōngtiān** winter

动物 **dòngwù** animal

动物学 **dòngwù xué** zoology ◊ zoological

动物园 **dòngwù yuán** zoo

东西 **dōngxi** thing

洞穴 **dòngxuè** cave

动摇 **dòngyáo** waver

动作 **dòngzuò** movement

都 **dōu** all; both ◊ even

陡 **dǒu** steep ◊ suddenly

抖 **dǒu** tremble; shake

豆 **dòu** bean

斗 **dòu** fight; struggle

逗 **dòu** tease; amuse ◊ funny

豆瓣酱 **dòubànjiàng** black bean sauce

兜捕 **dōubǔ** round up ◊ round-up

斗橱 **dǒuchú** bureau; chest of drawers

逗点 **dòudiǎn** comma

抖动 **dǒudòng** shake

兜风 **dōufēng** drive

豆腐 **dòufu** tofu, bean curd

逗号 **dòuhào** comma

豆浆 **dòujiāng** soy milk

逗留 **dòuliú** stay; stop over; linger

抖落 **dǒuluò** shake off

逗弄 **dòunòng** tease

斗殴 **dòu ōu** brawl

斗篷 **dǒupeng** cape

豆芽 **dòuyá** beansprouts

窦炎 **dòuyán** sinusitis

豆油 **dòuyóu** soy bean oil

斗争 **dòuzhēng** battle; struggle; fight for

都 **dū** city; capital

督 **dū** supervise

读 **dú** read; 他在读大学 **tā zài dú dàxué** he is at university

毒 **dú** poison; narcotics ◊ poisonous; toxic

独 **dú** only; alone

肚 **dǔ** tripe

堵 **dǔ** block

赌 **dǔ** gamble

肚 **dù** belly; stomach

度 **dù** degree ◊ spend, pass *time*

渡 **dù** cross *water*; ferry

妒 **dù** envy

端 **duān** end; extremity ◊ carry

短 **duǎn** short

段 **duàn** section; paragraph

缎 **duàn** satin

断 **duàn** break

短波 **duǎnbō** short wave

短处 **duǎnchù** shortcoming

断定 **duàndìng** conclude; decide

短棍 **duǎngùn** baton

断绝 **duànjué** break off

断绝关系 **duànjué guānxi** drop; 与X断绝关系 **yǔ X duànjué guānxi** finish with X, drop X

端口 **duānkǒu** port COMPUT

短裤 **duǎnkù** shorts

锻炼 **duànliàn** exercise ◊ gymnastics; workout

断裂 **duànliè** snap, break

短路 **duǎnlù** short circuit

断路开关 **duànlù kāiguān** circuit breaker

段落 **duànluò** paragraph

短跑 **duànpǎo** sprint

短跑运动员 **duǎnpǎo yùndòng yuán** sprinter

短篇小说 **duǎnpiān xiǎoshuō** short story

短期 **duǎnqī** short term

短缺 **duǎnquē** shortage

断然 **duànrán** point blank

端上 **duānshang** serve

断头 **duàntóu** break

短袜 **duǎnwà** sock

短文 **duǎnwén** essay

端午节 **Duānwǔjié** Dragon Boat Festival

断线 **duànxiàn** cut off *telephone*

短袖 **duǎnxiù** short-sleeved

断言 **duànyán** maintain, argue; affirm

短暂 **duǎnzàn** momentary, fleeting, short-lived

锻造 **duànzào** forge

缎子 **duànzi** satin

赌博 **dǔbó** bet; gamble ◊ gambling

独裁 **dúcái** dictatorial

独裁者 **dúcái zhě** dictator

赌场 **dǔchǎng** casino

独唱曲 **dúchàng qǔ** solo

独唱演员 **dúchàng yǎnyuán** soloist

堵车 **dǔchē** traffic jam

都城 **dūchéng** capital

渡船 **dùchuán** ferry

独创力 **dúchuànglì** originality

督促 **dūcù** urge; press

读错 **dúcuò** misread

嘟嘟声 **dūdu shēng** beep

读给 X 听 **dúgěi X tīng** read to X

度过 **dùguò** pass, spend *time*

毒害 **dúhài** poison

堆 **duī** heap, pile, mound ◊ pile up, stack

兑 **duì** exchange

对 **duì** correct; right ◊ against; toward; facing; opposite; with regard to; for; to ◊ pair ◊ face; 对啊！ **duì a!** that's right!; 对了！ **duìle!** that's it!, that's right!; X 对 Y **X duì Y** X against Y; X versus Y

队 **duì** team; line

对半 **duìbàn** fifty-fifty

对比 **duìbǐ** compare

对不起 **duìbùqǐ** sorry; I'm sorry; pardon me

对称 **duìchèn** symmetrical ◊ symmetry

堆成堆 **duīchéngduī** pile up

对待 **duìdài** treat ◊ treatment; 认真对待 X **rènzhēn duìdài X** take X seriously

对等 **duìděng** corresponding

对方 **duìfāng** opposite side

对付 **duìfu** handle; 对付 X **duìfu X** have X to reckon with

对话 **duìhuà** dialog

兑换 **duìhuàn** exchange

兑换率 **duìhuànlǜ** exchange rate

堆积 **duījī** pile up, heap up

对讲机 **duìjiǎngjī** intercom

对接处 **duì jiē chù** dock (*of spaceship*)

对抗 **duìkàng** opposite ◊ defiance

对立 **duìlì** oppose ◊ opposite; contrast ◊ contrary; 与 X 对立 **yǔ X duìlì** be at odds with X

对面 **duìmiàn** opposite; 邮局在银行的对面 **yóujú zài yínháng de duìmiàn** the post office is opposite the bank

对手 **duìshǒu** opponent, adversary

对外贸易 **duìwài màoyì** foreign trade

队伍 **duìwǔ** troops; ranks

兑现 **duìxiàn** cash *check*

对象 **duìxiàng** target; boyfriend; girlfriend

对象市场 **duìxiàng shìchǎng** target market

对象组 **duìxiàng zǔ** target group

队长 **duìzhǎng** captain (*of team*)

对照 **duìzhào** contrast

对折 **duìzhé** double

对质 **duìzhì** confront

对准 **duìzhǔn** point

妒忌 **dùjì** jealous ◊ jealousy; envy; 妒忌 ... **dùjì ...** be jealous of ...

独家 **dújiā** exclusive

度假 **dùjià** spend one's vacation

度假胜地 **dùjià shèngdì** resort

镀金材料 **dùjīn cáiliào** gilt

赌纪人 **dǔjì rén** bookmaker, bookie

独立 **dúlì** independence ◊ independent ◊ independently

度量衡 **dùliánghéng** system of measurement

独立日 **Dúlìrì** Independence Day

独立生活 **dúlì shēnghuó** fend for oneself

独轮车 **dúlún chē** barrow

独木舟 **dúmù zhōu** canoe

蹲 **dūn** squat, crouch

吨 **dūn** ton

钝 **dùn** blunt; dull

炖 **dùn** braise; simmer; stew

盾 **dùn** shield

顿 **dùn** *measure word for meals*; 一顿饭 **yīdùn fàn** a meal

敦促 **dūncù** call on, urge; press

独女 **dúnǚ** only daughter

钝吻鳄 **dùnwěn'è** alligator

多 **duō** a lot of; many; much; more ◊ how; however; 比 …多 **bǐ … duō** above, more than; 好得多 **hǎo dé duō** much better; 好／容易多了 **hǎo／róngyì duōle** so much better／easier; 多滑稽／悲哀！ **duō huáji／bēiāi!** how funny／sad!; 你／他多大年纪了？ **nǐ／tā duōdà niánji le?** how old are you／is he?; 要多长时间？ **yào duōcháng shíjiān?** how long does it take?; 多经常？ **duō jīngcháng?** how often?

夺 **duó** take by force

朵 **duǒ** *measure word for flowers, clouds*; 一朵花 **yīduǒ huā** a flower

躲 **duǒ** hide; dodge

跺 **duò** chop

舵 **duò** helm; rudder

堕 **duò** fall; sink

跺 **duò** stamp *foot*

多半儿 **duōbànr** in all likelihood ◊ the majority

躲避 **duǒbì** dodge; elude

多变 **duōbiàn** variable

多病 **duōbìng** sickly

踱步 **duóbù** pace up and down

多才多艺 **duōcái duōyì** versatile ◊ versatility

躲藏 **duǒcáng** hide; 躲藏起来 **duǒcáng qǐlái** go into hiding; 躲藏着 **duǒcángzhe** be in hiding

躲藏处 **duǒcángchù** hiding place

多草 **duōcǎo** grassy

多产 **duōchǎn** productive; prolific

多尘土 **duō chéntǔ** dusty

多愁善感 **duōchóu shàngǎn** corny

多刺 **duōcì** prickly

多次 **duōcì** time and again

夺得 **duódé** snatch

多风 **duōfēng** windy

多个 **duōgè** multiple

多功能 **duō gōngnéng** versatile ◊ versatility

多关系户 **duō guànxì hù** be well-connected

多国 **duōguó** multinational

多花 **duōhuā** flowery

夺回 **duóhuí** recapture

跺脚 **duòjiǎo** stamp one's feet

多久 **duōjiǔ** how long; 多久之前？ **duōjiǔ zhīqián?** how long ago?

多亏 **duōkuī** fortunately

堕落 **duòluò** degenerate; 使堕落 **shǐ duòluò** corrupt

多毛 **duōmáo** hairy

多么 **duōme** how; what; 多么蓝的天啊！ **duōme lán de tiān a!** what a blue sky!

多媒体 **duōméitǐ** multimedia

夺取 **duóqǔ** conquer; overcome

堕入 **duòrù** sink into

多沙 **duōshā** sandy

多山 **duōshān** mountainous

多少 **duōshǎo** much; many ◊ how much; how many; 你需要多少？ **nǐ xūyào duōshao?** how many do you need?; 多少钱？ **duōshao qián?** how much is it?

多石 **duōshí** stony

多数 **duōshù** majority ◊ most; 占多数 **zhàn duōshù** be in the majority

多水 **duōshuǐ** watery

哆嗦 **duōsuo** quake

堕胎 **duòtāi** abortion ◊ have an abortion

多雾 **duōwù** foggy

多险 **duōxiǎn** perilous

多香料 **duō xiāngliào** spicy

多谢 **duōxiè** thanks very much

多雪 **duōxuě** snowy

多烟 **duōyān** smoky

多样化 **duōyàng huà** diverse ◊ diversity; variety

多岩石 **duō yánshí** rocky

多疑 **duōyí** paranoid

多用途 **duō yòngtú** all-purpose

多于 **duōyú** excess ◊ in excess of, more than

多余 duōyú spare; redundant, superfluous

多雨 duōyǔ rainy

多云 duōyún overcast

多汁 duōzhī juicy

多种经营 duōzhǒng jīngyíng diversification ◊ diversify

多皱纹 duō zhòuwén rugged

毒品 dúpǐn drugs, narcotics

毒品贩子 dúpǐn fànzi pusher

肚脐 dùqí navel

堵塞 dǔsāi block, block up ◊ blockage; congestion ◊ congested

堵塞 dǔsè block; jam ◊ blocked

独身 dúshēn single

都市 dūshì metropolis

读数 dúshù reading

毒死 dúsǐ poison

杜松子酒 dùsōngzǐjiǔ gin

独特 dútè unique

独特性 dútèxìng peculiarity

赌徒 dǔtú gambler

读物 dúwù reading material

妒羡 dùxiàn envy

毒药 dúyào poison

毒液 dúyè venom

镀银 dùyín silver-plated

独一无二 dúyīwú'èr unique

独有 dúyǒu exclusive

独占 dúzhàn monopoly

读者 dúzhě reader

赌咒 dǔzhòu swear; take an oath

赌注 dǔzhù bet; stake

堵住 dǔzhù block in; clog up; 堵住了 **dǔzhùle** stuck fast

杜撰 dùzhuàn make up; invent

独自 dúzì alone; by itself; by myself; single-handed; 她独自 **tā dúzì** by herself

肚子 dùzi stomach; abdomen; belly

独子 dúzǐ only son

肚子疼 dùzi téng stomach-ache

独自一人 dúzì yīrén solitude

独奏曲 dúzòu qǔ solo

独奏演员 dúzòu yǎnyuán soloist

E

额 é forehead; volume (*of business*)
鹅 é goose
蛾 é moth
恶 è evil
腭 è palate
饿 è hunger ◊ hungry; 我饿了 **wǒ è le** I'm hungry
恶霸 èbà bully; despot
恶臭 èchòu stench
恶毒 èdú malevolent; savage; vicious
恶棍 ègùn gangster; ruffian
恶化 èhuà deteriorate
饿坏了 èhuàile ravenous
恶劣 èluè foul, nasty; vile
俄罗斯 Éluósī Russia ◊ Russian
恶梦 èmèng nightmare
恶魔 èmó devil; demon
恩 ēn favor; kindness
而 ér and; but
儿 ér child; son
耳 ěr ear
二 èr two
耳背 ěrbèi hard of hearing
而不是 ér búshì instead of
二冲程 èrchōngchéng two-stroke
二档 èrdǎng second gear
二等 èrděng second class
耳朵 ěrduǒ ear
儿歌 érgē nursery rhyme
耳垢 ěrgòu (ear)wax
耳光 ěrguāng clip around the ear
而后 érhòu then
耳环 ěrhuán earring
耳机 ěrjī headphones, earphones
二进制 èrjìn zhì binary
二进制位 èrjìn zhì wèi bit COMPUT

儿科学 érkēxué pediatrics
儿科学家 érkēxuéjiā pediatrician
二流 èrliú second-rate
二年级 èrniánjí sophomore
而且 érqiě moreover; plus
二十 èrshí twenty
二十分之一 èrshífēnzhīyī twentieth
二手 èrshǒu secondhand
儿童 értóng children
耳痛 ěrtòng earache
儿童节 Értóng Jié Children's Day
二头肌 èrtóu jī biceps
儿媳妇 érxífu daughter-in-law
耳语 ěryǔ whisper
二月 èryuè February
儿子 érzi son
扼杀 èshā strangle, throttle
饿死 èsǐ starve to death; 我饿死了 **wǒ èsǐ le** I'm starving
扼死 èsǐ strangle
额外 éwài additional, extra
额外品 éwài pǐn bonus
恶习 èxí vice
恶心 ěxin nausea ◊ revolting ◊ feel nauseous; 我感到恶心 **wǒ gǎndào ěxīn** I feel nauseous; 使恶心 **shǐ ěxīn** nauseate
恶性 èxìng malignant; virulent
恶意 èyì ill will; malice, spite ◊ malicious, spiteful
俄语 Éyǔ Russian (*language*)
鳄鱼 èyú crocodile
恶运，厄运 èyùn jinx
遏制 èzhì bottle up
蛾子 ézi moth
恶作剧 èzuòjù mischief; practical joke, prank

F

发 fā send out; give out; issue; emit

阀 fá valve

罚 fá punish

乏 fá lack ◊ exhausted

筏 fá raft

法 fǎ law; method

发 fà hair

发表 fābiǎo publish; issue

发表意见 fābiǎo yìjiàn comment; express an opinion

发财 fācái make a fortune; get rich

发愁 fāchóu worry; be anxious

发出 fāchū send off, dispatch; give off; issue

发错 fācuò mispronounce

发达 fādá developed ◊ develop

发大财 fā dàcái hit the jackpot

发达国家 fādá guójiā developed country

发呆 fādāi be in a daze

发电 fādiàn generate electricity

法典 fǎdiǎn code; statutes

发电机 fādiànjī generator

发电站 fādiànzhàn power station

法定 fǎdìng legal; statutory; 未到法定年龄 wèidào fǎdìng niánlíng below the legal age

发动 fādòng start; launch; mobilize

发动机 fādòngjī motor

发抖 fādǒu shake; shudder; tremble

发奋 fāfèn make an effort

发疯 fāfēng go crazy; 使 X 发疯 shǐ X fāfēng drive X mad

法官 fǎguān judge; 法官判定 … fǎguān pàndìng … the judge ruled that …

发光 fāguāng glow; shine

发光二极管 fāguāng èrjí guǎn LED, light-emitting diode

法规 fǎguī law; act; legislation

法国 Fǎguó France ◊ French

发慌 fāhuāng feel nervous

发挥 fāhuī summon up

发昏 fāhūn dazed

发火 fāhuǒ erupt; get angry

发货 fāhuò send goods

法家 fǎjiā legalism (philosophy)

法家 fǎjiā legalist

发夹 fàjiá hairpin

发奖 fājiǎng award prizes

发酵 fājiào ferment ◊ fermentation

罚金 fájīn fine

发掘 fājué find, uncover, unearth

罚款 fákuǎn fine

发狂 fākuáng go crazy

发困 fākùn drowsy

珐琅质 fàlángzhì enamel

法兰绒 fǎlánróng washcloth

发牢骚 fā láosāo grumble, complain, bitch; 爱发牢骚的人 ài fā láosao de rén grumbler

乏力 fálì weak

发亮 fāliàng shiny

法令 fǎlìng law; statute; court order

法律 fǎlǜ law ◊ legal

法轮功 fǎlúngōng Falungong sect

发麻 fāmá pins and needles ◊ get pins and needles; go numb

发霉 fāméi go moldy

发明 fāmíng invent ◊ invention

发明者 fāmíng zhě inventor

翻 fān overturn; roll over

帆 fān sail

烦 fán annoyed

反 fǎn anti-; counter- ◊ reverse; inside-out; 穿反了 chuānfǎnle back to front

返 fǎn return

饭 fàn (cooked) rice; food; meal

犯 fàn commit crime, blunder

帆板 fānbǎn sailboard; windsurfer

翻版 fānbǎn reprint

帆板运动 fānbǎn yùndòng

windsurfing
帆板运动员 **fānbǎn yùndòngyuán** windsurfer
反驳 **fǎnbó** contradict; counter; retort
帆布 **fānbù** canvas
帆布篷 **fānbùpéng** tarpaulin; awning
帆布鞋 **fānbùxié** sneakers
饭菜 **fàncài** food
反常 **fǎncháng** unnatural; warped;
反常现象 **fǎncháng xiànxiàng** freak
范畴 **fànchóu** category
翻船 **fānchuán** capsize
帆船 **fānchuán** junk; sailboat
饭店 **fàndiàn** hotel; restaurant
贩毒 **fàndú** drug dealing; drug trafficking ◊ push
反对 **fǎnduì** oppose; be against; take exception to; object; protest ◊ opposition; objection; 我抽烟你不反对吗? **wǒ chōuyān nǐ bù fǎnduì ma?** do you mind if I smoke?
反毒警 **fǎndú jǐng** narcotics agent
贩毒者 **fàndú zhě** drug dealer
犯法 **fànfǎ** break the law
反复 **fǎnfù** repeated
反复无常 **fǎnfù wúcháng** unpredictable; unstable; volatile
方 **fāng** square; to the power of MATH
房 **fáng** house; room
防 **fáng** prevent
妨 **fáng** hinder; obstruct
纺 **fǎng** spin
访 **fǎng** visit
仿 **fǎng** copy; imitate
放 **fàng** place, put, set; put on; release; 放在一边 **fàngzài yìbiān** put aside; 放风筝 **fàng fēngzhēng** fly a kite
犯病 **fànbìng** relapse MED
妨碍 **fáng'ai** hinder; obstruct
反感 **fǎngǎn** aversion; antipathy; dislike; revulsion; 使反感 **shǐ fǎngǎn** disgust
方案 **fāng'àn** plan; program
方便 **fāngbiàn** convenience ◊ convenient; 在你方便的时候

zài nǐ fāngbiàn de shíhòu at your convenience
方便面 **fāngbiànmiàn** instant noodles
方便食品 **fāngbiàn shípǐn** convenience food
防波堤 **fángbōdī** jetty
放长 **fàngcháng** let down *pants etc*
防虫药 **fángchóngyào** insect repellent
放大 **fàngdà** amplify; enlarge; magnify
放大镜 **fàngdàjìng** magnifying glass
防弹 **fángdàn** bullet-proof
放荡 **fàngdàng** debauchery ◊ debauched, dissolute; loose
放荡女子 **fàngdàng nǚzǐ** slut
放大器 **fàngdàqì** amplifier
房地产 **fángdìchǎn** property; real estate
房地产开发人 **fángdìchǎn kāifārén** property developer
房东 **fángdōng** landlord; landlady
方法 **fāngfǎ** method, means, way
防腐剂 **fángfǔjì** preservative
方格 **fānggé** check (*pattern*); box (*on form*)
放过 **fàngguò** let off; pass up
防护 **fánghù** protect
防滑 **fánghuá** nonskid
防滑链 **fáng huá liàn** snow chains
放回 **fànghuí** put back; return; replace
放回原处 **fànghuí yuánchù** put back
防火 **fánghuǒ** fire prevention
放火 **fànghuǒ** set fire to
放假 **fàngjià** be on leave; have a day off; have a vacation; 放假一星期 **fàngjià yìxīngqī** take a week off
房间 **fángjiān** room
放进去 **fàngjìnqù** put in; get in
放开 **fàngkāi** open up; let go of
房客 **fángkè** lodger; tenant
方块儿 **fāngkuàir** diamond
放慢 **fàngmàn** slacken off
方面 **fāngmiàn** aspect; side; 在这方面 **zài zhè fāngmiàn** in this respect

防抹舌 **fángmǒshé** tab

放屁 **fàngpì** fart; break wind

放弃 **fàngqì** abandon; give up; jettison

防窃警报器 **fángqiè jǐngbào qì** burglar alarm

放晴 **fàngqíng** clear up (*of weather*)

防热 **fángré** heat-resistant

放任 **fàngrèn** permissive

防晒膏 **fángshàigāo** sun block

放哨 **fàngshào** keep watch

放射 **fàngshè** radiate

放射尘 **fàngshèchén** fallout

放射疗法 **fàngshè liáofǎ** radiotherapy

放声大哭 **fàngshēng dàkū** burst into tears

放射性 **fàngshè xìng** radioactive ◊ radioactivity

方式 **fāngshì** way; manner; mode; approach; pattern

防守 **fángshǒu** defense

防水 **fángshuǐ** waterproof

放肆 **fàngsì** impertinent; audacious; presumptuous

放松 **fàngsōng** ease; relieve; lighten up; relax, unwind ◊ relaxed, easy ◊ relaxation

方糖 **fāngtáng** sugar cubes

反光 **fǎn'guāng** reflect

泛光灯 **fàn'guāngdēng** floodlight

反光镜 **fǎn'guāngjìng** mirror

犯规 **fàn'guī** break the rules; foul SP

翻滚 **fān'gǔn** roll

翻过来 **fān guòlái** turn over; overturn

方位 **fāng'wèi** directions

防卫 **fángwèi** defend; protect

访问 **fǎngwèn** pay a visit

放下 **fàngxià** put down, lay down; lower

芳香 **fāngxiāng** bouquet; fragrance

方向 **fāngxiàng** direction

方向盘 **fāngxiàng pán** steering wheel

方向指示器 **fāngxiàng zhǐshìqì** indicator

仿效者 **fǎngxiào zhě** imitator

放心 **fàngxīn** put one's mind at rest; rest assured

防锈 **fángxiù** rustproof

方言 **fāngyán** dialect

放映 **fàngyìng** screen *movie*

放映机 **fàngyìngjī** projector

防雨 **fángyǔ** showerproof

防御 **fángyù** defend ◊ defensive ◊ defense

仿造 **fǎngzào** copy ◊ imitation

放债者 **fàngzhài zhě** money-lender

仿照 **fǎngzhào** copy; imitate

方针 **fāngzhēn** policy; guideline

防止 **fángzhǐ** guard against; prevent

纺织 **fǎngzhī** textile

仿制 **fǎngzhì** fake

纺织品 **fǎngzhīpǐn** textiles

防撞头盔 **fángzhuàng tóukuī** crash helmet

房子 **fángzi** house; building

放纵 **fàngzòng** indulgence ◊ indulge; pamper

房租 **fángzū** rent

返回 **fǎnhuí** return; turn back; 顺原路返回 **shùn yuánlù fǎnhuí** retrace

反击 **fǎnjī** counter; hit back ◊ counter-attack

反间谍活动 **fǎn jiàndié huódòng** counterespionage

烦交 **fánjiāo** c/o, care of

反诘问 **fǎn jiéwèn** cross-examine

翻筋斗 **fān jīndǒu** somersault

反抗 **fǎnkàng** revolt

饭筐 **fànkuāng** hamper

反馈信息 **fǎnkuì xìnxī** feedback

泛滥 **fànlàn** overflow; flood

烦劳 ... **fánláo** ... would you mind ...?

翻了三番 **fānle sān fān** treble

翻领 **fānlǐng** lapel

贩卖 **fànmài** traffic in; peddle

繁忙 **fánmáng** busy

反面 **fǎnmiàn** reverse (side); opposite

烦恼 **fánnǎo** annoyance ◊ vexed; 令人烦恼 **lìngrén fánnǎo** annoying

反叛 **fǎnpàn** rebellion; mutiny

反叛军队 **fǎnpàn jūnduì** rebel troops

反叛者 **fǎnpàn zhě** rebel

翻篇儿 **fān piānr** turn over *page*; turn the page

翻起 **fānqǐ** turn up; turn over

蕃茄 **fānqié** tomato

番茄酱 **fānqiéjiàng** tomato ketchup

烦扰 **fánrǎo** bother, plague

烦人 **fánrén** irritating; troublesome ◊ nuisance

繁荣 **fánróng** boom ◊ flourishing, thriving; prosperous ◊ promote; develop

反射 **fǎnshè** reflect, mirror ◊ reflection

翻身 **fānshēn** turn over, roll over; toss and turn

反手击球 **fǎnshǒu jīqiú** backhand SP

繁体字 **fántǐzì** traditional Chinese characters

发怒 **fānù** flare up; be in a rage; get angry

饭碗 **fànwǎn** rice bowl

范围 **fànwéi** range; scope; 在一定范围内 **zài yídìng fànwéi nèi** within specific limits

反问 **fǎnwèn** rhetorical question

翻下 **fānxià** turn down

反响 **fǎnxiǎng** echo; repercussion

反省 **fǎnxǐng** reflect, think ◊ reflection, consideration

翻寻 **fānxún** rummage around

翻译 **fānyì** translate; interpret ◊ translation; interpretation; translator; interpreter; 翻译成英语 **fānyì chéng Yīngyǔ** translate into English

翻一番 **fānyìfān** double

反应 **fǎnyìng** react ◊ reaction

反应堆 **fǎnyìng duī** reactor

反应能力 **fǎnyìng nénglì** reflex

反右运动 **Fǎnyòu Yùndòng** Anti-rightists Campaign

犯有罪恶 **fànyǒu zuì'è** sin, commit a sin

繁育 **fányù** fertility ◊ breed; reproduce

翻阅 **fānyuè** leaf through

烦躁 **fánzào** fret ◊ irritable ◊ irritation

烦躁不安 **fánzào bù'ān** fidget

反证 **fǎnzhèng** disprove

反正 **fǎnzhèng** in any case; anyway

繁殖 **fánzhí** breed; reproduce ◊ reproduction ◊ reproductive

反之亦然 **fǎnzhī yìrán** vice versa

翻转 **fānzhuàn** overturn

犯罪 **fànzuì** commit a crime

犯罪率 **fànzuì lǜ** crime rate

反作用 **fǎnzuòyòng** reaction; counteraction

发牌 **fāpái** deal; deal the cards

发牌者 **fāpái zhě** dealer (*cards*)

发胖 **fāpàng** put on weight

发票 **fāpiào** receipt; invoice

发脾气 **fā píqì** huff; tantrum ◊ be in a huff; be in a temper; lose one's temper, get angry 爱发脾气 **ài fā píqì** short-tempered

发起 **fāqǐ** mount *campaign*; originate; initiate; launch; sponsor

发卡 **fàqiǎ** barrette; hairpin

发起人 **fāqǐ rén** creator; originator; sponsor

发球 **fāqiú** serve SP

罚球 **fáqiú** penalty SP

发球得分 **fāqiú défēn** ace (*in tennis*)

罚球区 **fáqiúqū** penalty area

发球人 **fāqiúrén** server (*in tennis*)

法人 **fǎrén** legal person; legal entity

发热器 **fārèqì** heater

发烧 **fāshāo** have a fever

发射 **fāshè** launch; blast off

发生 **fāshēng** happen, occur; take place

发生冲突 **fāshēng chōngtū** clash

发生的事情 **fāshēng de shìqíng** goings-on

发生关系 **fāshēng guānxi** have a relationship (*sexual*)

发生故障 **fāshēng gùzhàng** malfunction

发射上天 **fāshè shàngtiān** blast off

发射台 **fāshè tái** launch pad

发誓 **fāshì** swear; vow; pledge

发式 **fàshì** hairdo

发条 **fātiáo** clockwork

法庭 **fǎtíng** (law) court

乏味 **fáwèi** tasteless; bland; boring

发微光 **fāwēiguāng** glimmer

发现 **fāxiàn** discover; find; realize; notice ◊ discovery

发泄 **fāxiè** give vent to; release

发薪 **fāxīn** pay wages; pay salary

发信 **fāxìn** send off a letter

发行 **fāxíng** issue; publish; launch; release; distribute; put on sale

发型 **fàxíng** hairstyle

发薪日 **fāxīnrì** payday

法西斯 **fǎxīsī** fascist

法西斯主义 **fǎxīsī zhǔyì** fascism

法西斯主义者 **fǎxīsī zhǔyì zhě** fascist

法学 **fǎxué** law

发芽 **fāyá** sprout; germinate

发言 **fāyán** speak

发炎 **fāyán** inflammation ◊ become inflamed

发痒 **fāyǎng** itch; tickle; 使发痒 **shǐ fāyǎng** tickle

发扬 **fāyáng** develop; make the most of

发炎膏 **fāyángāo** inflammation

发言人 **fāyán rén** spokesman; spokeswoman; spokesperson

法衣 **fǎyī** robe

发音 **fāyīn** pronounce ◊ pronunciation

发音错误 **fāyīn cuòwù** mispronunciation

发育 **fāyù** grow ◊ growth

法语 **Fǎyǔ** French (*language*)

发源 **fāyuán** spring; rise; originate

法院 **fǎyuàn** court; courthouse

发展 **fāzhǎn** develop, build up; grow ◊ development; growth

发展中国家 **fāzhǎn zhōng guójiā** developing country

发作 **fāzuò** bout; seizure

非本意 **fēběnyì** involuntary

飞 **fēi** fly

非 **fēi** not

肥 **féi** fat; fatty; fertile ◊ fertilizer

费 **fèi** cost; fee ◊ cost; spend; expend

肺 **fèi** lung

吠 **fèi** bark (*of dog*)

废 **fèi** useless

沸 **fèi** boil

非 ... 非 ... **fēi ... fēi ...** neither ... nor ...

非 ... 即 ... **fēi ... jí ...** either ... or ...

肺癌 **fèi'ái** lung cancer

诽谤 **fěibàng** libel; slander ◊ defamation ◊ defamatory

诽谤活动 **fěibàng huódòng** smear campaign

非暴力 **fēi bàolì** nonviolence ◊ nonviolent

飞奔 **fēibēn** dash; run quickly

非常 **fēicháng** extraordinary ◊ extremely, very; 非常感谢 **fēicháng gǎnxiè** thanks very much

非常规 **fēi chángguī** nonstandard

废除 **fèichú** abolish, do away with; repeal, revoke; undo

肥大 **féidà** bulky

飞到 **fēidào** fly in; fly to

废掉 **fèidiào** scrap

飞碟 **fēidié** flying saucer

非法 **fēifǎ** illegal; 非法麻醉品 **fēifǎ mázuì pǐn** illegal drugs

非凡 **fēifán** remarkable, phenomenal ◊ remarkably

非法侵入 **fēifǎ qīnrù** trespass (on)

非法侵入者 **fēifǎ qīnrù zhě** trespasser

狒狒 **fèifei** baboon

飞过 **fēiguò** whizz by

废话 **fèihuà** nonsense; gibberish

飞回 **fēihuí** fly back

飞机 **fēijī** airplane

飞溅 **fēijiàn** splash

飞机场 **fēijīchǎng** airport

费解 **fèijiě** inexplicable; puzzling

飞机库 **fēijīkù** hangar

费劲 **fèijìn** strenuous

废金属 **fèijīnshǔ** scrap metal

飞机失事 **fēijī shīshì** plane crash

飞快 **fēikuài** lightning fast; quick as a flash

费力 **fèilì** effort; exertion; hard work ◊ laborious; strenuous; exhausting

肥料 **féiliào** fertilizer; manure

废料堆 **fèiliàoduī** scrap heap

菲律宾 **Fēilǜbīn** the Philippines

肥胖 **féipàng** plump; chubby; stout

肥胖症 **féipàngzhèng** obesity

飞跑 **fēipǎo** rush, fly; gallop

废品 **fèipǐn** trash, junk; waste product

废品站 **fèipǐnzhàn** junkyard

废气 **fèiqì** exhaust; fumes

废弃 **fèiqì** abandon ◊ disused; waste

非人造 **fēi rénzào** natural, non-artificial

飞逝 **fēishì** fly past (*of time*)

费事 **fèishì** painful

飞速 **fēisù** very fast; meteoric

沸腾 **fèiténg** boil

飞脱 **fēituō** fly off (*of hat etc*)

肥沃 **féiwò** fertile ◊ fertility

废物 **fèiwù** waste

飞行 **fēixíng** flight; flying ◊ fly

飞行甲板 **fēixíng jiǎbǎn** flight deck

飞行记录仪 **fēixíng jìlùyí** flight recorder

飞行路线 **fēixíng lùxiàn** flight path

飞行时间 **fēixíng shíjiān** flight time

飞行员 **fēixíngyuán** pilot

飞行中 **fēixíngzhōng** in-flight

废墟 **fèixū** ruins; wasteland

肺炎 **fèiyán** pneumonia

沸溢 **fèiyì** boil over

费用 **fèiyong** charge; fee; costs; expenses

鲱鱼 **fēiyú** herring

飞跃 **fēiyuè** leap; become popular; take off

肥皂 **féizào** soap

肥皂剧 **féizào jù** soap opera

非正式 **fēi zhèngshì** informal; unofficial ◊ unofficially

非正义 **fēizhèngyì** injustice ◊ unjust

废纸 **fèizhǐ** wastepaper; scrap paper

废纸篓 **fèizhǐlǒu** wastepaper basket

非洲 **Fēizhōu** Africa ◊ African

痱子 **fèizi** prickly heat

飞走 **fēizǒu** fly away

分 **fēn** divide; split; share ◊ cent; minute fraction ◊ *measure word for time, money, length*

坟 **fén** grave

焚 **fén** burn

粉 **fěn** powder ◊ pink

份 **fèn** portion; share; part; copy ◊ *measure word for newspapers, documents*; 一份报纸 **yífèn bàozhǐ** a newspaper; 一份饭 **yífèn fàn** a helping of food

粪 **fèn** excrement; dung

分包合同 **fēnbāo hétong** subcontract

分包人 **fēnbāo rén** subcontractor

分贝 **fēnbèi** decibel

粉笔 **fěnbǐ** chalk

粪便 **fènbiàn** dung

分别 **fēnbié** separate ◊ separately; respectively

分不开 **fēnbùkāi** inseparable

分岔 **fēnchà** branch off

分岔处 **fēnchàchù** fork

分成两半 **fēnchéng liǎngbàn** halve

分成四份 **fēnchéng sìfèn** quarter

粉刺 **fěncì** acne; pimples

分店 **fēndiàn** branch

奋斗 **fèndòu** strive, struggle

份额 **fèn'é** share

分发 **fēnfā** give out; distribute ◊ distribution

分房 **fēnfáng** allocate accommodation

粪肥 **fènféi** manure

封 **fēng** seal; board up ◊ *measure word for letters*; 三封信 **sānfēng xìn** three letters

锋 **fēng** edge; front (*weather*)

疯 **fēng** mad

枫 **fēng** maple

风 **fēng** wind; style; tendency

丰 **fēng** abundant

蜂 **fēng** bee

峰 **fēng** summit; peak

缝 **féng** sew; stitch

缝 **fèng** crack; seam; part (*in hair*)

凤 **fèng** phoenix

风暴 **fēngbào** storm

风暴警报 **fēngbào jǐngbào** storm warning

封闭 **fēngbì** seal; close up

风车 **fēngchē** windmill

奉承 **fèngchéng** flatter; suck up to ◊ flattery

讽刺 **fěngcì** mock, deride, ridicule ◊ ironic(al); satirical ◊ irony; satire

讽刺画 **fěngcì huà** cartoon; caricature

讽刺者 **fěngcì zhě** satirist

分割 **fēn'gē** division; split

分隔 **fēn'gé** isolate

分给 **fēn'gěi** distribute

蜂房 **fēngfáng** hive

丰富 **fēngfù** abundance ◊ abundant ◊ enrich; 丰富多彩的活动 **fēngfù duōcǎi de huódòng** a variety of things to do

风干 **fēnggān** seasoned *wood*

风格 **fēnggé** method; style; format

风寒 **fēnghán** cold

缝合 **fénghé** sew up

风和日丽 **fēnghé rìlì** *a gentle breeze and glorious sunshine*

凤凰 **fènghuáng** phoenix

风景 **fēngjǐng** view; landscape

风景画 **fēngjǐng huà** landscape (*painting*)

疯狂 **fēngkuáng** insane, crazy ◊ insanity ◊ insanely

锋利 **fēnglì** sharp

风凉话 **fēngliánghuà** wisecrack

风流 **fēngliú** romantic; unrestrained; admirable

风流人物 **fēngliú rénwù** influential person; moldbreaker; romantic hero; great man

风流韵事 **fēngliú yùnshì** love affair; romance

丰满 **fēngmǎn** busty; plump; rounded

风帽 **fēngmào** hood

蜂蜜 **fēngmì** honey

封面 **fēngmiàn** (front) cover

蜂鸣器 **fēngmíng qì** buzzer

分公司 **fēn gōngsī** branch (*of company*)

奉陪 **fèngpéi** *fml* accompany; 我有急事, 不能奉陪 **wǒ yǒu jíshì, bù néng fèngpéi** I'm sorry, I can't make it due to a prior engagement

风琴 **fēngqín** organ MUS

奉劝 **fèngquàn** *fml* advise

疯人 **fēngrén** madman

缝纫 **féngrèn** sew ◊ sewing

缝纫机 **féngrènjī** sewing machine

缝上 **féngshang** sew on

风扇皮带 **fēngshàn pídài** fan belt

丰盛 **fēngshèng** rich; copious; 丰盛可口 **fēngshèng kěkǒu** magnificent *meal*

风湿 **fēngshī** rheumatism

丰收 **fēngshōu** good harvest

封锁 **fēngsuǒ** blockade ◊ cordon off; seal off

风俗习惯 **fēngsú xíguàn** traditions, customs

风头主义者 **fēngtóu zhǔyì zhě** exhibitionist

蜂王 **fēngwáng** queen bee

风味 **fēngwèi** savor

缝隙 **fèngxì** crack

风险 **fēngxiǎn** risk; 有风险 **yǒu fēngxiǎn** adventurous; risky

蜂箱 **fēngxiāng** beehive

风行一时 **fēngxíng yìshí** all the rage

风信子 **fēngxìnzǐ** hyacinth

风雪大衣 **fēngxuě dàyī** parka

蜂拥 **fēngyōng** swarm

缝针 **féngzhēn** stitches

风筝 **fēngzheng** kite

疯子 **fēngzi** lunatic

风钻 **fēngzuàn** pneumatic drill

分行 **fēnháng** branch (*of bank, company*)

分号 **fēnhào** semicolon

粉红 **fěnhóng** pink

焚化炉 **fénhuàlú** incinerator

分机 **fēnjī** extension

分解 **fēnjiě** break up

分居 **fēnjū** separate; live apart

分开 **fēnkāi** break; part; separate; detach; 把 X 与 Y 分开 **bǎ X yǔ Y fēnkāi** separate X from Y

愤慨 **fènkǎi** indignant ◊ indignation

芬兰 **Fēnlán** Finland ◊ Finnish

分类 **fēnlèi** break down; classify;

group ◊ breakdown; classification; 给 ... 分类 **gěi ... fēnlèi** grade

分类广告 **fēnlèi guǎnggào** classified advertisement

分离 **fēnlí** separate ◊ separation

分裂 **fēnliè** division; partition; breach; rift; split ◊ divide; splinter

分裂人格 **fēnliè réngé** split personality

分流术 **fēnliú shù** bypass

分泌 **fēnmì** secrete ◊ secretion

分娩 **fēnmiǎn** childbirth; labor; delivery; 在分娩中 **zài fēnmiǎn zhōng** in labor

分泌物 **fēnmìwù** secretion

粉末 **fěnmò** powder

坟墓 **fénmù** grave; tomb

愤怒 **fènnù** anger ◊ angry

分配 **fēnpèi** allot; assign; allocate; distribute ◊ distribution

分批 **fēnpī** in groups; partially

分歧 **fēnqí** difference; gulf

分期付款 **fēnqī fùkuǎn** pay in installments ◊ installment plan

分散 **fēnsàn** scattered

分散注意力 **fēnsàn zhìyì lì** distract

焚烧 **fénshāo** burn

粉饰 **fěnshì** gloss over

愤世嫉俗 **fènshì jísú** cynical ◊ cynicism

愤世嫉俗者 **fènshì jísú zhě** cynic

分手 **fēnshǒu** split up; break up ◊ breakup; separation ◊ separated

分数 **fēnshù** fraction; mark

粉刷 **fěnshuā** paintwork ◊ whitewash

粉刷工 **fěnshuāgōng** painter

粉丝 **fěnsī** Chinese vermicelli, rice noodles

粉碎 **fěnsuì** shatter; pulverize

分析 **fēnxì** analysis ◊ analyze

分享 **fēnxiǎng** share

分心 **fēnxīn** distract; 使 X 分心 **shǐ X fēnxīn** drive X to distraction

分着 **fēnzhe** separately

分钟 **fēnzhōng** minute

分子 **fēnzǐ** numerator MATH; molecule ◊ molecular

分组 **fēnzǔ** divide into groups

佛 **Fó** Buddha

佛教 **Fójiào** Buddhism ◊ Buddhist

佛教徒 **Fójiào tú** Buddhist

否 **fǒu** no; not

否定 **fǒudìng** negative ◊ negate; deny; repudiate; 给予否定的回答 **jǐyǔ fǒudìngde huídá** answer in the negative

否决 **fǒujué** overrule; throw out; veto

否决权 **fǒujué quán** veto

否认 **fǒurèn** denial ◊ deny; disclaim; 否认自己和 X 有关系 **fǒurén zìjǐ hé X yǒu guānxi** dissociate oneself from X

否则 **fǒuzé** or else; otherwise

佛爷 **Fóye** Buddha

夫 **fū** husband; man

敷 **fū** apply

孵 **fū** hatch; incubate

肤 **fū** skin

扶 **fú** hold up; support

福 **fú** luck; happiness; fortune

辐 **fú** spoke

幅 **fú** *measure word for paintings, cloth*; 一幅画 **yìfú huà** a picture

浮 **fú** float

服 **fú** take *medicine*

斧 **fǔ** ax

腐 **fǔ** rotten; stale

抚 **fǔ** stroke

附 **fù** attach; enclose

副 **fù** vice-; deputy; assistant ◊ pack (*of cards*)

付 **fù** pay

父 **fù** father

富 **fù** rich, wealthy

复 **fù** again ◊ duplicate ◊ reply

腹 **fù** abdomen; stomach

负 **fù** negative; minus ◊ bear

妇 **fù** wife; woman

腐败 **fǔbài** corrupt

副本 **fùběn** copy

辅币 **fǔbì** token

浮标 **fúbiāo** buoy

副标题 **fùbiāotí** subheading

服兵役 **fú bīngyì** do military service

敷布 **fūbù** compress

腹部 **fùbù** stomach ◊ abdominal

复查 **fùchá** doublecheck

副产品 **fù chǎnpǐn** by-product

扶车 **fúchē** walker

俯冲 **fǔchōng** dive

孵出 **fūchū** hatch out

付出 **fùchū** pay out; stump up; put in *time*; donate ◊ donation; 付出的款项 **fùchūde kuǎnxiàng** payment

副词 **fùcí** adverb

服从 **fúcóng** obey; comply ◊ obedience ◊ obedient; 服从命令 **fúcóng mìnglìng** obey orders

附带 **fùdài** incidental; supplementary ◊ incidentally

附带条件 **fùdài tiáojiàn** proviso

负担 **fùdān** load; burden

辅导 **fǔdǎo** counsel; tutor ◊ counseling; tuition

辅导课 **fǔdǎokè** tutorial

副导演 **fù dǎoyǎn** assistant director

辅导员 **fǔdǎo yuán** counselor; tutor

负电 **fùdiàn** negative ELEC

浮雕 **fúdiāo** relief (*in sculpture*)

浮动 **fúdòng** float

复发 **fùfā** relapse

复方药 **fùfāngyào** mixture (*medicine made from a combination of compounds*)

夫妇 **fūfù** (married) couple

覆盖 **fùgài** cover

讣告 **fùgào** obituary

副歌 **fùgē** refrain MUS

浮垢 **fúgòu** scum

腹股沟 **fùgǔgōu** groin

敷裹 **fūguǒ** dress

符号 **fúhào** symbol

符合 **fúhé** agreement ◊ accordingly ◊ tally (with); conform (to) ◊ compatible; 符合标准 **fúhé biāozhǔn** be up to standard

复合 **fùhé** overlap

负荷 **fùhé** load; 负荷过重 **fùhé guòzhòng** overload

符合性 **fúhé xìng** compatibility

孵化器 **fūhuàqì** incubator

付回款 **fùhuíkuǎn** repayment

复活 **fùhuó** resurrection

复活节 **Fùhuójié** Easter

伏击 **fújī** ambush

附加 **fùjiā** add ◊ additional

附加费 **fùjiāfèi** extra charge; supplement; surcharge

附件 **fùjiàn** accessory; add-on; enclosure; attachment (*to e-mail*) ◊ enclose (*in letter*); attach

复件 **fùjiàn** duplicate

副教授 **fù jiàoshòu** associate professor

副驾驶员 **fù jiàshǐ yuán** co-pilot

附加物 **fùjiāwù** frill; extra; insert

附近 **fùjìn** close by ◊ neighboring; 他住在附近 **tā zhù zài fùjìn** he lives around here

副经理 **fù jīnglǐ** assistant manager

妇科医生 **fùkē yīshēng** gynecologist

付款 **fùkuǎn** pay ◊ payment

付款人 **fùkuǎn rén** payer

付款台 **fùkuǎn taí** cash desk

腐烂 **fǔlàn** decay; perish; rot ◊ rotten

富丽 **fùlì** palatial

敷料 **fūliào** dressing MED

福利 **fúlì** welfare

福利工作 **fúlì gōngzuò** welfare work

福利国家 **fúlì guójiā** welfare state

福利救济 **fúlì jiùjì** welfare

俘虏 **fúlǔ** capture ◊ prisoner; captive; 俘虏 X **fúlǔ X** take X prisoner

附录 **fùlù** appendix

负面 **fùmiàn** unfavorable, negative

覆灭 **fùmiè** demise; downfall

抚摸 **fǔmō** stroke; caress

抚摩 **fǔmó** stroke; caress

父母 **fùmǔ** parents ◊ parental

妇女 **fùnǚ** woman

夫妻 **fūqī** married couple

福气 **fúqi** luck; happiness

肤浅 **fūqiǎn** superficial; sketchy

付钱 **fùqián** pay

父亲 **fùqin** father

付清 **fùqīng** pay off *debt*

父亲身分 **fùqīn shēnfèn** paternity

夫人 **fūrén** Mrs; wife

富人 **fùrén** the rich; rich person

附入 **fùrù** enclose; add

服丧 **fúsāng** mourning; 在服丧 **zài fúsāng** in mourning

肤色 **fūsè** skin color

负伤 **fùshāng** injured

敷设 **fūshè** lay *cable*

辐射 **fúshè** radiate ◊ radiation

服侍 **fúshì** attend to

服饰 **fúshì** clothes and accessories; get-up

腐蚀 **fǔshí** corrode ◊ corrosion

俯视 **fǔshì** overlook

扶手 **fúshǒu** armrest; handrail; banister; balustrade

副手 **fùshǒu** mate

扶手椅 **fúshǒu yǐ** armchair

复数 **fùshù** plural

复述 **fùshù** relate; repeat

负数 **fùshù** negative (number)

附属公司 **fùshǔ gōngsī** subsidiary (company)

复数形式 **fùshù xíngshì** plural

伏特 **fútè** volt

伏特加 **fútèjiā** vodka

伏天 **fútiān** dog days

服贴 **fútiē** obedient; manageable

斧头 **fǔtou** ax

浮凸 **fútū** emboss

富翁 **fùwēng** rich man

俯卧撑 **fǔ wòchēng** push-up

服务 **fúwù** serve ◊ service

服务费 **fúwùfèi** service charge

服务行业 **fúwù hángyè** service industry; service sector

服务器 **fúwùqì** server COMPUT

服务区 **fúwùqū** service area

服务台 **fúwùtái** reception

服务员 **fúwù yuán** attendant; maid; clerk; waiter; waitress

复习 **fùxí** review; revise

父系 **fùxì** paternal

复写 **fùxiě** copy; duplicate

腹泻 **fùxiè** diarrhea

复习课程 **fùxí kèchéng** refresher course

附信 **fùxìn** covering letter

复兴 **fùxīng** revival ◊ revive

敷衍 **fūyǎn** stall; hold off ◊ perfunctory

抚养 **fǔyǎng** raise

抚养费 **fúyǎngfèi** maintenance (*money*)

扶养权 **fúyǎng quán** custody

副业 **fùyè** sideline

附议 **fùyì** second *motion*

福音 **fúyīn** gospel

辅音 **fǔyīn** consonant

复印 **fùyìn** copy; photocopy; duplicate

复映 **fùyìng** rerun

复印机 **fùyìn jī** copier

复印件 **fùyìn jiàn** copy

浮油 **fúyóu** (oil) slick

富有 **fùyǒu** wealthy; rich in; with a lot of ◊ be rich in; have plenty of

富有表情 **fùyǒu biǎoqíng** expressive

富裕 **fùyù** affluent, well-off

赋予权利 **fùyù quánlì** entitled; empowered

复杂 **fùzá** complex, complicated; intricate; involved; mixed *feelings*

负载 **fùzài** load ELEC

负责 **fùzé** answer for; take care of; be in charge of; accept responsibility for ◊ responsible; liable; conscientious

负责人 **fùzé ren** person in charge

负责任 **fù zérèn** be held accountable ◊ responsible

付账 **fùzhàng** pay the bill

复职 **fùzhí** be reinstated

复制 **fùzhì** copy; duplicate; clone; 复制一份档案 **fùzhì yífèn dǎng'an** make a copy of a file

复制品 **fùzhì pǐn** copy; replica; reproduction

复制钥匙 **fùzhì yàoshi** duplicate key

负重 **fùzhòng** burden

符咒 **fúzhòu** magic spell

辅助 **fǔzhù** auxiliary

服装 **fúzhuāng** dress; clothing; garment; costume; uniform

副主管 **fù zhǔguǎn** assistant director

副总管 **fù zǒngguǎn** deputy leader

副总统 **fù zǒngtǒng** vice president

富足 **fùzú** plenty

服罪 **fúzuì** plead guilty

副作用 **fùzuòyòng** side effect

G

嘎嘎声 **gāga shēng** rattle

该 **gāi** be supposed to; should; be next; 我该做什么？ **wǒ gāi zuò shēnme?** what should I do?; 该你了 **gāi nǐ le** it's your turn; over to you

改 **gǎi** change; correct

盖 **gài** cover ◊ top; lid; 盖好被子 **gàihǎo bèizi** tuck in

钙 **gài** calcium

改编 **gǎibiān** adapt; arrange; reorganize ◊ adaptation; arrangement

改变 **gǎibiàn** change, alter; transform; vary ◊ shift; transformation; change; 改变话题 **gǎibiàn huàtí** change the subject

改编本 **gǎibiān běn** version; adaptation

改革 **gǎigé** reform

改换 **gǎihuàn** switch; change

改建 **gǎijiàn** convert

改进 **gǎijìn** improve; upgrade ◊ development; improvement

概况 **gàikuàng** survey; overview

概括 **gàikuò** generalization ◊ generalize; sum up; summarize

概括性 **gàikuò xìng** broad; general

盖了帽了 **gàilemàole** terrific, awesome

概念 **gàiniàn** concept

改期 **gǎiqī** be postponed; be rescheduled

改日 **gǎirì** sometime; another day

改善 **gǎishàn** improve

概述 **gàishù** sum up ◊ summary

该死 **gāisǐ** damn

改天 **gǎitiān** another day; another time

改线 **gǎixiàn** diversion ◊ divert

改小 **gǎixiǎo** take in, make narrower

改写 **gǎixiě** rewrite; transliterate; paraphrase

改邪归正 **gǎixiéguīzhèng** rehabilitate; go straight

概要 **gàiyào** outline; overview

改用 **gǎiyòng** adapt

盖章 **gàizhāng** stamp; seal

改正 **gǎizhèng** amend; correct

盖住 **gàizhù** cover up

改装 **gǎizhuāng** do up; make over

盖子 **gàizi** lid; cap

改组 **gǎizǔ** reorganization ◊ reorganize

咖喱 **gālí** curry

干 **gān** dry; dried; empty ◊ dry; empty ◊ in vain

肝 **gān** liver

杆 **gān** pole

竿 **gān** rod

甘 **gān** sweet

敢 **gǎn** dare; 你敢！**nǐgǎn!** how dare you!

赶 **gǎn** drive out; banish; rush; catch up with; hurry; 赶时髦 **gǎn shímáo** keep up with the latest fashions

秆 **gǎn** stalk; straw

擀 **gǎn** roll out

感 **gǎn** feel; sense

干 **gàn** do ◊ stem; trunk; 你今晚干什么？ **nǐ jīnwǎn gàn shénme?** what are you doing tonight?; 干吧 **gàn ba** go ahead

干爸 **gānbà** godfather

干杯 **gānbēi** cheers!; 为 ... 干杯 **wèi ... gānbēi** toast; propose a toast to

干部 **gànbu** cadre; official

干草 **gāncǎo** hay

甘草 **gāncǎo** licorice

甘草栗子 **gāncǎo lìzi** water chestnut

赶超 **gǎnchāo** emulate; surpass

赶出 **gǎnchū** drive out; flush out

感到 **gǎndào** feel; 感到无聊 **gǎndào wúliáo** feel bored

赶掉 **gǎndiào** chase away

干掉 **gàndiào** kill, eliminate ◊ murder, elimination

感动 **gǎndòng** affect; move, touch ◊ moved, touched

干豆腐 **gāndòufu** dried bean curd

干儿子 **gān érzi** godson

感恩 **gǎn'ēn** gratitude

感恩节 **Gǎn'ēn Jié** Thanksgiving Day

钢 **gāng** steel

缸 **gāng** earthenware vessel; vat; jar

刚 **gāng** just

港 **gǎng** harbor, port

杠 **gàng** lever

尴尬 **gān'gà** embarrassed; awkward ◊ feel awkward ◊ embarrassment; 令人尴尬 **lìngrén gāngà** embarrassing

钢笔 **gāngbǐ** fountain pen

港币 **gǎngbì** Hong Kong dollar

刚才 **gāngcái** just now

杠杆 **gànggǎn** lever

刚刚 **gānggang** (only) just; 我刚刚看到她 **wǒ gānggang kàndào tā** I've just seen her

杠杆力量 **gànggǎn lìliàng** leverage

刚好 **gānghǎo** just right; exact ◊ exactly

钢筋混凝土 **gāngjīn hùnníng tǔ** reinforced concrete

港口 **gǎngkǒu** port, harbor

肛门 **gāngmén** anus

钢琴 **gāngqín** piano

钢琴家 **gāngqínjiā** pianist

岗哨 **gǎngshào** guard; lookout

港市 **gǎngshì** port (city)

钢丝绳 **gāngsī shéng** cable; high wire; tight-rope

钢铁厂 **gāngtiěchǎng** ironworks

港湾 **gǎngwān** harbor; bay

岗位 **gǎngwèi** guard

港务局 **gǎngwùjú** port authorities

缸子 **gāngzi** beaker; mug; bowl

干旱 **gānhàn** drought

干涸 **gānhé** dry out; dry up

感激 **gǎnjī** appreciation ◊ appreciate; feel grateful; be thankful ◊ thankfully

赶集 **gǎnjí** go to market

赶紧 **gǎnjǐn** hurry

干净 **gānjìng** clean

柑桔 **gānjú** tangerine

感觉 **gǎnjué** feeling; sensation; sense ◊ feel; experience; 我感觉累了 **wǒ gǎnjué lèi le** I feel tired

干枯 **gānkū** dry up ◊ dried up

甘苦 **gānkǔ** ups and downs

赶快 **gǎnkuài** hurry ◊ quickly

橄榄 **gǎnlǎn** olive

橄榄球 **gǎnlǎn qiú** rugby; football

橄榄油 **gǎnlǎn yóu** olive oil

干酪 **gānlào** cheese

干裂 **gānliè** dry and cracked; chapped

赶拢 **gǎnlǒng** round up

干妈 **gānmā** godmother

感冒 **gǎnmào** cold; flu ◊ catch a cold; 我感冒了 **wǒ gǎnmàole** I have a cold

甘美 **gānměi** luscious

擀面杖 **gǎnmiànzhàng** rolling pin

干女儿 **gān nǚ'er** goddaughter

赶跑 **gǎnpǎo** chase off; see off

感情 **gǎnqíng** expression; feeling; emotion; 我对他有很矛盾的感情 **wǒ duì tā yǒu hěn máodùnde gǎnqíng** I have mixed feelings about him

感染 **gǎnrǎn** contract, pick up; infect; influence; affect; become infected ◊ infected; infectious; septic

干扰 **gānrǎo** disturbance; interference ◊ interfere with; jam

感人 **gǎnrén** moving, touching

赶上 **gǎnshàng** catch; catch up

干涉 **gànshè** interfere; intervene; meddle ◊ interference

感叹 **gǎntàn** exclamation

感叹号 **gǎntànhào** exclamation point

干洗 **gānxǐ** dryclean ◊ drycleaning

干线 **gànxiàn** arterial road

干洗店 **gānxǐ diàn** dry cleaner

感谢 **gǎnxiè** thanks ◊ thank; say

thanks; be grateful

甘心 **gānxīn** willingly ◊ resign oneself to

感性 **gǎnxìng** sensory

感兴趣 **gǎn xìngqù** be interested

甘心情愿 **gānxīn qíngyuàn** willingly

甘心于 **gānxīn yú** reconcile oneself to

干洗衣物 **gānxǐ yīwù** drycleaning

肝炎 **gānyán** hepatitis

干预 **gānyù** poke one's nose into

敢于 **gǎnyú** dare

肝藏 **gānzàng** liver

干燥 **gānzào** dry

甘蔗 **gānzhe** sugar cane

感知 **gǎnzhī** feel

赶制 **gǎnzhì** run up *clothes*

感知能力 **gǎnzhī nénglì** perception

杆子 **gānzi** post (*wooden*)

赶走 **gǎnzǒu** chase away; banish ◊ family name

高 **gāo** big; tall; high ◊ top (*gear*); 比高 **bǐ ... gāo** above; higher/taller than

膏 **gāo** ointment; cream

糕 **gāo** cake

搞 **gǎo** do; make

高傲 **gāo'ào** lofty

高保真电器 **gāo bǎozhēn diànqì** hi-fi

告别 **gàobié** say goodbye; 向死者告别 **xiàng sǐzhě gàobié** pay one's last respects

告别会 **gàobié huì** leaving party

高超 **gāochāo** masterly

高潮 **gāocháo** climax; high tide

高大 **gāodà** enormous; massive

高等 **gāoděng** higher; advanced; elite

高等教育 **gāoděng jiàoyù** higher education

糕点 **gāodiǎn** bread; cakes and pastries

高调 **gāodiào** highbrow

高顶帽 **gāodǐngmào** top hat

高度 **gāodù** height; altitude

高尔夫俱乐部 **gāo'ěrfū jùlèbù** golf club (*organization*)

高尔夫(球) **gāo'ěrfū(qiú)** golf

高尔夫球场 **gāo'ěrfū qiúchǎng** golf course

高尔夫球棍 **gāo'ěrfū qiúgùn** golf club (*stick*)

告发 **gàofā** inform; inform on; 向警方告发 X **xiàng jǐngfāng gàofā X** report X to the police

告发人 **gàofā rén** informer

高峰 **gāofēng** peak; summit

高峰时间 **gāofēng shíjiān** peak hours; rush hour

高跟 **gāogēn** high-heeled

高跟鞋 **gāogēn xié** high heels; high-heeled shoes

高贵 **gāoguì** noble

搞鬼 **gǎoguǐ** cheat; play tricks; cause trouble

高呼 **gāohū** chant

搞坏 **gǎohuài** mess up, ruin

高级 **gāojí** high-class; high-level; select; upmarket; senior; top

稿件 **gǎojiàn** manuscript; article

高脚椅 **gāojiǎoyǐ** highchair

高架铁路 **gāojià tiělù** elevated railroad

高阶层 **gāo jiēcéng** high-level

高级法庭 **gāojí fǎtíng** Supreme Court

高空跳水 **gāokōng tiàoshuǐ** high diving

高粱 **gāoliáng** sorghum

高楼大厦 **gāolóu dàshà** high-rise buildings

高炉 **gāolú** blast furnace

搞乱 **gǎoluàn** confuse; mix up; mess up

告密 **gàomì** sneak; inform on

高明 **gāomíng** masterly

高能 **gāonéng** high-energy; high-power

高能汽车 **gāonéng qìchē** performance car

高能转向 **gāonéng zhuǎnxiàng** power steering

高频 **gāopín** high-frequency

高人一等 **gāorén yìděng** patronizing; superior; 他觉得自己高人一等 **tā juéde zìjǐ gāorén** he feels superior to others

高尚 **gāoshàng** noble

高烧 **gāoshāo** high fever

高耸于 **gāosǒng yú** dominate

高速 **gāosù** high-speed

告诉 **gàosu** tell; say; 别告诉妈妈 **bié gàosu māma** don't tell Mom

高速公路 **gāosù gōnglù** freeway; expressway

高速缓存 **gāosù huǎncún** cache COMPUT

高速火车 **gāosù huǒchē** high-speed train

睾丸 **gāowán** testicles

高效率 **gāo xiàolǜ** efficient; streamlined

高效益 **gāo xiàoyì** businesslike; highly efficient

高兴 **gāoxìng** happy; pleased, glad, delighted ◊ happily; 见到你真高兴! **jiàndào nǐ zhēn gāoxìng!** great to see you!

高新技术 **gāoxīn jìshù** high tech

高血压 **gāoxuèyā** hypertension, high blood pressure

高压 **gāoyā** high pressure; high-tension

高雅 **gāoyǎ** elegance ◊ elegant

羔羊 **gāoyáng** lamb

膏药 **gāoyao** plaster MED

高要求 **gāo yāoqiú** demanding ◊ tall order

高音 **gāoyīn** soprano

高音调 **gāoyīndiào** high-pitched

高原 **gāoyuán** plateau

搞运动 **gǎo yùndòng** campaign

搞糟 **gǎozāo** bungle; mess up

高涨 **gāozhǎng** upturn

告知 **gàozhī** inform

告终 **gàozhōng** culminate

稿子 **gǎozi** copy

嘎吱作声 **gāzhī zuòshēng** crunch

搁 **gē** put; add; put aside; deposit; 搁在...上 **gē zài ... shàng** rest on, lean on

割 **gē** cut; mow

哥 **gē** elder brother

歌 **gē** song

鸽 **gē** dove; pigeon

格 **gé** grid; grating; square (in board game)

革 **gé** leather

嗝 **gé** hiccups

隔 **gé** cut off; separate

铬 **gè** chrome, chromium

个 **gè** general purpose measure word; 两个问题 **liǎnggè wèntí** two questions; 一个人 **yīgè rén** a person

各 **gè** each; every; various

隔壁 **gébì** adjoining ◊ next door ◊ next-door neighbor

个别 **gèbié** individual

戈壁滩 **Gēbìtān** Gobi Desert

胳膊 **gēbo** arm

胳膊肘儿 **gēbozhǒur** elbow

割草机 **gécǎo jī** lawn mower

歌唱家 **gēchàng jiā** vocalist

歌唱团 **gēchàng tuán** vocal group

各处 **gèchù** everywhere

歌词 **gēcí** lyrics

疙瘩 **gēda** boil; pimple; lump; knot

格调 **gédiào** style

格斗 **gédòu** struggle

隔断 **géduàn** separate

哥哥 **gēge** elder brother

格格不入 **gégébùrù** go against the grain

咯咯地笑 **gēgē de xiào** giggle; gurgle; chuckle

给 **gěi** give; administer ◊ for; to; for the attention of

给以荣誉 **gěiyǐ róngyù** honor

歌剧 **gējù** opera

隔绝 **géjué** cut off; isolate

歌剧院 **gējù yuàn** opera house

隔开 **gékāi** partition off

蛤蜊 **gélí** clam

隔离 **gélí** isolate; segregate ◊ isolation; segregation; quarantine

隔帘 **gélián** screen

隔离间 **gélíjiān** isolation ward

格林威治标准时间 **Gélínwēizhì Biāozhǔn Shíjiān** Greenwich Mean Time

阁楼 **gélóu** attic; loft

哥们儿 **gēmenr** pal, buddy

革命 **gémìng** revolution ◊ revolutionary

革命家 **gémìng jiā** revolutionary

隔膜 **gémó** diaphragm

根 **gēn** root

跟 **gēn** follow ◊ with ◊ and ◊ heel

根本 **gēnběn** ultimate; underlying ◊ at all; fundamentally ◊ base; foundation; 他们根本不像 **tāmen gēnběn búxiàng** they're not at all alike

根除 **gēnchú** eradicate

耕 **gēng** plow

更 **gēng** change ◊ watch (*2 hour period*)

梗 **gěng** stalk

更 **gèng** more; even more; 更好 **gèng hǎo** better; 我更喜欢她了 **wǒ gèng xǐhuān tā le** I like her better

耕地 **gēngdì** plow ◊ arable land

更多 **gèngduō** more

更改 **gēnggǎi** alter ◊ alteration; 更改线路 **gēnggǎi xiànlù** reroute

更坏 **gènghuài** worse

更换 **gēnghuàn** exchange

耕牛 **gēngniú** (draft) ox

更新 **gēngxīn** renew; replace; upgrade

更衣室 **gēngyī shì** cubicle

耕种 **gēngzhòng** till; cultivate

耕作 **gēngzuò** cultivate ◊ cultivation

根基 **gēnjī** roots

根据 **gēnjù** basis ◊ according to; 根据具体环境来考虑X **gēnjù jùtǐ huánjìng lái kǎolǜ X** look at X in context

根据地 **gēnjùdì** stronghold

跟上 **gēnshàng** keep up

根深蒂固 **gēnshēndìgù** entrenched

跟随 **gēnsuí** follow; string along

根源 **gēnyuán** origin; source ◊ originate

跟着 **gēnzhe** follow

跟踪 **gēnzōng** stalk; trace; trail

跟踪会议 **gēnzōng huìyì** follow-up meeting

跟踪者 **gēnzōng zhě** stalker

跟踪追捕 **gēnzōng zhuībǔ** track down

歌曲 **gēqǔ** song

个儿 **gèr** height

隔热 **gérè** insulate ◊ insulation

隔热垫 **gérèdiàn** mat

个人 **gèrén** individual ◊ personal ◊ privately

个人电脑 **gèrén diànnǎo** personal computer

个人卫生 **gèrén wèishēng** personal hygiene

个人主义者 **gèrénzhǔyǐ zhě** individualist

哥儿们 **gērmen** buddy, pal

各色各样 **gèsè gèyàng** all kinds; a choice

格式 **géshì** layout

各式各样 **gèshì gèyàng** assortment

格式设定 **géshì shèdìng** format

歌手 **gēshǒu** singer

个体 **gètǐ** freelance; self-employed

个体户 **gètǐhù** privately owned small business; freelancer

个体遗传性征 **gètǐ yíchuán xìngzhēng** genetic fingerprint

格外 **géwài** particularly; extra

割腕 **gēwàn** slash one's wrists

歌舞表演 **gēwǔ biǎoyǎn** song and dance performance; cabaret

歌舞剧 **gēwǔjù** musical

革新 **géxīn** innovation ◊ innovative

个性 **gèxìng** personality; character; 他很有个性 **tā hěn yǒu gèxìng** he's a real character

革新者 **géxīn zhě** innovator

隔音 **géyīn** soundproof

胳肢 **gézhi** tickle

革制品 **gézhìpǐn** leather goods

各种各样 **gèzhǒng gèyàng** mixed, varied; miscellaneous; 各种各样的人 **gèzhǒng gèyàngde rén** all kinds of people

鸽子 **gēzi** dove; pigeon

格子 **gézi** checked ◊ grille

各自 **gèzì** respective ◊ individually; each; 各自付款 **gèzì fùkuǎn** go Dutch

弓 **gōng** bow

工 **gōng** work; worker

攻 **gōng** attack

功 **gōng** merit; service

供 **gōng** supply; provide

恭 **gōng** respectful

公 **gōng** public; male
宫 **gōng** palace
拱 **gǒng** arch
共 **gòng** common; joint; mutual ◊ together; altogether
公安局 **Gōng'ān jú** Public Security Bureau
公布 **gōngbù** announce; declare; release
共产党 **Gòngchǎndǎng** Communist Party
共产党员 **Gòngchǎndǎng yuán** Communist Party member
工厂 **gōngchǎng** factory
共产主义 **gòngchǎn zhǔyì** communism ◊ communist
工程 **gōngchéng** construction; engineering
工程师 **gōngchéngshī** engineer
共处 **gòngchǔ** coexist ◊ coexistence
供词 **gòngcí** confession
共存 **gòngcún** coexist ◊ coexistence
公道 **gōngdào** justice
工地 **gōngdì** building site
宫殿 **gōngdiàn** palace
拱顶 **gǒngdǐng** vault
攻读 **gōngdú** study
公愤 **gōngfèn** outrage
功夫 **gōngfu** kung-fu
公告牌 **gōnggào pái** bulletin board
公共 **gōnggòng** public
公共汽车 **gōnggòng qìchē** bus
公共汽车总站 **gōnggòng qìchē zǒngzhàn** bus station
公关 **gōngguān** public relations
公害 **gōnghài** environmental damage
公函 **gōnghán** official letter
恭贺 **gōnghè** congratulate
共和国 **gònghé guó** republic
共和主义 **gònghé zhǔyì** republicanism ◊ republican
共和主义者 **gònghé zhǔyì zhě** republican
工会 **gōnghuì** labor union
工会发言人 **gōnghuì fāyánrén** shop steward
公鸡 **gōngjī** rooster

攻击 **gōngjí** attack, assault; go for ◊ offensive
供给 **gōngjǐ** supply
弓箭 **gōngjiàn** bow and arrow
弓箭手 **gōngjiàn shǒu** archer
共计 **gòngjì** amount to, add up to
公斤 **gōngjīn** kilogram
恭敬 **gōngjìng** respect
工具 **gōngjù** tool; implement
公爵 **gōngjué** duke
工具格 **gōngjùgé** toolbar COMPUT
公开 **gōngkāi** public; open
功劳 **gōngláo** merit; service
公里 **gōnglǐ** kilometer
公路 **gōnglù** highway; road
公路赛车 **gōnglù sàichē** rally MOT
公路支线 **gōnglù zhīxiàn** access road
公猫 **gōngmāo** tomcat
拱门 **gǒngmén** archway
公民 **gōngmín** citizen ◊ civic; civil
公民权 **gōngmín quán** civil rights
公民投票 **gōngmín tóupiào** referendum
公墓 **gōngmù** graveyard, cemetery
功能 **gōngnéng** function
公鸟 **gōngniǎo** cock (*male bird*)
公牛 **gōngniú** bull
供暖 **gōngnuǎn** heating
公公 **gōnggōng** father-in-law (*husband's father*)
贡品 **gòngpǐn** tribute
公平 **gōngpíng** fair, just; balanced ◊ justice
公婆 **gōngpó** in-laws (*husband's parents*)
供求 **gōngqiú** supply and demand
公顷 **gōngqǐng** hectare
工人 **gōngrén** worker; workman
供认 **gòngrèn** confess ◊ confession
工人阶级 **gōngrén jiējí** working class
工伤 **gōngshāng** industrial accident
工商管理学硕士 **gōngshāng guǎnlǐxué shuòshì** MBA, master of business administration
公社 **gōngshè** commune

公升 **gōngshēng** liter
公式 **gōngshì** formula
供水 **gōngshuǐ** water supply
公司 **gōngsī** company; business; firm ◊ incorporated
公司车 **gōngsī chē** company car
公司法 **gōngsī fǎ** company law
公司形象 **gōngsī xíngxiàng** corporate image
公诉人 **gōngsùrén** (public) prosecutor
共同 **gòngtóng** collective; common; joint; shared; 和 X 有共同之处 *hé X yǒu gòngtóng zhīchù* have something in common with X
共同体 **gòngtóngtǐ** community
恭维 **gōngwei** compliment; flatter
公文 **gōngwén** document
公文包 **gōngwén bāo** briefcase
公物 **gōngwù** public property
公务员 **gōngwùyuán** civil servant
攻下 **gōngxià** capture
贡献 **gòngxiàn** contribute; devote ◊ contribution
恭喜 **gōngxǐ** congratulations
恭喜发财 **gōngxǐ fācái** wishing you prosperity (*a New Year greeting*)
公学 **gōngxué** public school
公羊 **gōngyáng** ram (*male sheep*)
供养 **gōngyǎng** keep, maintain, provide for
工业 **gōngyè** industry ◊ industrial
工业废料 **gōngyè fèiliào** industrial waste
工业化 **gōngyèhuà** industrialize
工业行动 **gōngyè xíngdòng** industrial action
工艺 **gōngyì** craft; technology
工艺美术 **gōngyì měishù** arts and crafts
供应 **gōngyìng** supply, provide ◊ provision
供应品 **gōngyìngpǐn** supplies
供应商 **gōngyìngshāng** supplier
供应与需求 **gōngyìng yǔ xūqiú** supply and demand
公用 **gōngyòng** communal; public
公用电话 **gōngyòng diànhuà** pay phone
公用实业 **gōngyòng shíyè** public utilities
共有者 **gòngyǒu zhě** part owner
公寓 **gōngyù** apartment
公园 **gōngyuán** park
公寓大厦 **gōngyù dàshà** apartment block
公约 **gōngyuē** pact; convention
公正 **gōngzhèng** fair, just; impartial ◊ fairly, justly ◊ fairness
公证 **gōngzhèng** authenticate; witness
公证人 **gōngzhèng rén** notary
公制 **gōngzhì** metric system
供职 **gòngzhí** serve; hold office
公职人员 **gōngzhí rényuán** official
公众 **gōngzhòng** public
公众交通运输工具 **gōngzhòng jiāotōng yùnshū gōngjù** public transportation
公主 **gōngzhǔ** princess
工资 **gōngzī** wage; salary
工资袋 **gōngzīdài** pay envelope
工作 **gōngzuò** work; job; business; employment ◊ work; 她很会工作 *tā hěn huì gōngzuò* she's a good worker; 工作的满足感 *gōngzuò de mǎnzúgǎn* job satisfaction
工作狂 **gōngzuòkuáng** workaholic
工作量 **gōngzuòliàng** workload
工作期间 **gōngzuò qījiān** work hours
工作日 **gòngzuòrì** work day
工作室 **gōngzuòshì** studio
工作台 **gōngzuò tái** workbench
工作许可 **gōngzuò xǔkě** work permit
工作站 **gōngzuòzhàn** work station
沟 **gōu** trench; ditch; channel
钩 **gōu** hook; jack(*playing cards*) ◊ crochet
狗 **gǒu** dog
购 **gòu** buy
够 **gòu** sufficient; enough; 够朋友 *gòu péngyǒu* true friend; 够大 *gòudà* quite big; big enough; 够

了 **gòule** that's enough; stop that!; 我 受 够 了 **wǒ shòugòu le** I've had enough; 五 十 美 元 够 了 吗 ？ **wǔshí měiyuán gòule ma?** will $50 be enough?

构 成 **gòuchéng** comprise, constitute

狗 狗 **gǒugǒu** doggie

篝 火 **gōuhuǒ** fire

构 架 **gòujià** structure ◊ structural

勾 结 **gōujié** collaborate

勾 结 者 **gōujié zhě** collaborator

购 买 **gòumǎi** purchase

狗 屁 **gǒu pì!** ∨ bullshit!

狗 屎 不 如 **gǒushǐ bùrú** ∨ dirtier than dog shit; lowest of the low

沟 通 **gōutōng** communicate ◊ communication

狗 窝 **gǒuwō** kennel

购 物 **gòuwù** shopping ◊ do one's shopping

购 物 人 **gòuwùrén** shopper

购 物 中 心 **gòuwù zhōngxīn** (shopping) mall

勾 销 **gōuxiāo** write off *debt*

勾 引 **gōuyǐn** pick up; seduce

构 造 **gòuzào** construction; design

钩 针 **gōuzhēn** crochet hook

钩 子 **gōuzi** hook

姑 **gū** aunt (*father's sister*); sister-in-law (*husband's sister*)

箍 **gū** hoop

估 **gū** estimate

孤 **gū** orphaned; lonely

鼓 **gǔ** drum

股 **gǔ** share, stock ◊ *measure word for smells, wind*; 一 股 风 **yīgǔ fēng** a gust of wind; 一 股 味 **yīgǔ wèi** a smell

古 **gǔ** ancient; antiquated

骨 **gǔ** bone

谷 **gǔ** valley; grain

雇 **gù** take on; employ; 他 被 雇 作 … **tā bèi gù zuò …** he's employed as a

顾 **gù** look around

故 **gù** therefore

固 **gù** solid; firm

瓜 **guā** melon

刮 **guā** scrape; shave

挂 **guà** hang; drape

刮 擦 **guācā** scrape

刮 掉 **guādiào** shave off; scrape off

挂 断 **guàduàn** hang up TELEC

刮 风 **guāfēng** blow

寡 妇 **guǎfù** widow

挂 钩 **guàgōu** hook, peg

呱 呱 叫 **guāguājiào** great

呱 呱 叫 声 **guāguā jiàoshēng** croak; quack

挂 号 **guàhào** register

挂 号 信 **guàhào xìn** registered letter; 寄 挂 号 信 **jì guàhào xìn** send a letter registered

乖 **guāi** good; well-behaved

拐 **guǎi** turn; 向 右 拐 **xiàng yòu guǎi** turn to the right

怪 **guài** strange

拐 棍 **guǎigùn** crook; walking stick

拐 角 **guǎijiǎo** turning

乖 戾 **guāilì** surly

乖 僻 **guāipǐ** morose

拐 骗 **guǎipiàn** kidnap

怪 人 **guàirén** freak, weirdo; crank; nerd

拐 弯 **guǎiwān** turn off; turn; corner; twist

拐 弯 抹 角 **guǎiwān mòjiǎo** beat around the bush

怪 物 **guàiwu** monster

怪 相 **guàixiàng** grimace

怪 异 **guàiyì** weird ◊ peculiarity

拐 杖 **guǎizhàng** walking stick

呱 啦 呱 啦 **guālā guālā** yap, yak

刮 脸 **guāliǎn** shave, have a shave

关 **guān** close, shut; turn off; 他 们 已 经 关 了 **tāmen yǐjīng guānle** they were shut

官 **guān** official

棺 **guān** casket, coffin

鳏 **guān** widower ◊ widowed

观 **guān** look at; observe

管 **guǎn** manage; control; concern oneself with; bother ◊ tube; pipe; 不 要 管 **bùyào** guǎn take no notice of

罐 **guàn** jar; pitcher

冠 **guàn** hat; crown

灌 **guàn** pour into

鹳 **guàn** stork

惯 **guàn** used to; accustomed

关 隘 **guān'ài** pass

关闭 **guānbì** close (down), shut (down); wind up ◊ closure ◊ closed

棺材 **gūancai** casket, coffin

观测 **guāncè** observe

观察 **guānchá** keep an eye on; monitor ◊ observation

惯常 **guàncháng** habitual

观察员 **guānchá yuán** observer

罐车 **guànchē** tanker (*truck*)

贯彻 **guànchè** implement; carry out

贯穿 **guànchuān** throughout

冠词 **guàncí** article

管道 **guǎndào** pipeline; tube; pipe

管道装置 **guǎndào zhuāngzhì** plumbing

观点 **guāndiǎn** point; point of view; view; slant

关掉 **guāndiào** turn off; be off

官方 **guānfāng** formal; official ◊ officially

鳏夫 **guānfū** widower

官服 **guānfú** robe

光 **guāng** light; brightness; glory ◊ finished; gone; bare; naked ◊ only

广 **guǎng** wide; broad; extensive

逛 **guàng** wander; stroll; 逛商店 **guàng shāngdiàn** walk around the stores

灌溉 **guàngài** irrigate ◊ irrigation

灌溉渠 **guàngài qú** irrigation canal

光笔 **guāngbǐ** light pen

光标 **guāngbiāo** cursor

广播 **guǎngbō** broadcast

广播电台 **guǎngbō diàntái** radio station

光彩 **guāngcǎi** brilliance

广场 **guǎngchǎng** square; place

光导纤维 **guāngdǎo xiānwéi** fiber optics

光点 **guāngdiǎn** blip

光碟 **guāngdié** disc

广东 **Guǎngdōng** Canton ◊ Cantonese

广东话 **Guǎngdōnghuà** Cantonese

广度 **guǎngdù** width; breadth

广而言之 **guǎng ér yán zhī** in general

广泛 **guǎngfàn** wide, extensive ◊ widely

广告 **guǎnggào** advertisement

广告公司 **guǎnggào gōngsī** advertising agency

广告牌 **guǎnggào pái** billboard

广告业 **guǎnggào yè** advertising (industry)

光顾 **guānggù** patronize

光滑 **guānghuá** smooth; glossy

光滑面 **guānghuámiàn** glaze

光环 **guānghuán** halo

光辉 **guānghuī** glow

光辉灿烂 **guānghuī cànlàn** splendor

光脚 **guāngjiǎo** be barefoot

光洁 **guāngjié** clear

广阔 **guǎngkuò** wide; great; enormous

光芒四射 **guāngmáng sìshè** radiate

光面 **guāngmiàn** glossy

光明 **guāngmíng** bright; rosy

光年 **guāngnián** light year

光盘 **guāngpán** CD-ROM; CD

光驱 **guāngqū** CD-ROM drive

光圈 **guāngquān** aperture

光荣 **guāngróng** honor; glory ◊ honorable; glorious

光天化日 **guāngtiān huàrì** in broad daylight

光秃秃 **guāng tūtū** bare; bald

观光 **guānguāng** look around; go sightseeing

观光客 **guānguāngkè** sightseer; tourist

观光旅游 **guānguāng lǚyóu** sightseeing tour

光纤 **guāng xiān** fiber optics

光线 **guāngxiàn** light; ray

光学 **guāngxué** optics

光泽 **guāngzé** shine; luster

光着头 **guāngzhe tóu** bareheaded

关怀 **guānhuái** show sympathy for; show concern for

关机 **guānjī** shut down COMPUT

管家 **guǎnjiā** housekeeper; butler ◊ run a household

关键 **guānjiàn** key, crucial, vital ◊ key; crux; bolt (*of door*)

关键钮 **guān jiànniǔ** off switch

关节 **guānjié** joint

关节炎 **guānjié yán** arthritis

关进 **guānjìn** put away

冠军 **guànjūn** champion; championship

观看 **guānkàn** watch

官吏 **guānlì** mandarin

管理 **guǎnlǐ** control; manage; administer; operate; run ◊ administration; management

关联 **guānlián** relevance

官僚 **guānliáo** bureaucrat ◊ bureaucratic

官僚程序 **guānliáo chéngxù** red tape

官僚制度 **guānliáo zhìdù** bureaucracy

官僚主义 **guānliáo zhǔyì** bureaucracy

惯例 **guànlì** custom; habit

管理人员 **guǎnlǐ rényuán** administrator; management team

管理学 **guǎnlǐxué** management studies

管理员 **guǎnlǐyuán** superintendent

关门 **guānmén** close *store etc*; close down; close the door ◊ closed

关门时间 **guānmén shíjiān** closing time

灌木 **guànmù** bush; shrub

灌木丛 **guànmùcóng** shrubbery; undergrowth

官能 **guānnéng** sense

关卡 **guānqiǎ** checkpoint

灌输 **guànshū** indoctrinate

关税 **guānshuì** customs duty, tariff

罐头 **guàntou** can (*for drinks etc*)

观望点 **guānwàng diǎn** vantage point

关系 **guānxi** connection, relation; relationship; 没关系 **méi guānxi** it doesn't matter; 外交关系 **wàijiāo guānxì** diplomatic relations; 与 X 关系好 **yǔ X guānxì hǎo** be on good terms with X

管弦乐 **guǎnxiányuè** orchestral music

管弦乐队 **guǎnxián yuèduì** orchestra

关小 **guānxiǎo** turn down *volume*

关系到 **guānxì dào** apply to, affect

关心 **guānxīn** concern; care; consideration ◊ be concerned about; care about

冠心病 **guànxīnbìng** coronary disease

惯性 **guànxìng** inertia

盥洗室 **guànxǐshì** washroom

关押 **guānyā** lock up

惯用 **guànyòng** commonly use; 惯用法 **guànyòngfǎ** common usage; habitual; 惯用左手 **guànyòng zuǒshǒu** left-handed

关于 **guānyú** with reference to, regarding; about

官员 **guānyuán** official

管乐器 **guǎnyuèqì** wind instrument

馆长 **guǎnzhǎng** curator

管制措施 **guǎnzhì cuòshī** controls, restrictions

观众 **guānzhòng** audience; crowd; spectators; viewers

罐装 **guànzhuāng** can ◊ canned

冠状动脉 **guànzhuàng dòngmài** coronary artery

冠状动脉血栓 **guànzhuàng dòngmài xuèshuān** coronary thrombosis

管子 **guǎnzi** pipe; tube

馆子 **guǎnzi** restaurant

管嘴 **guǎnzuǐ** jet

刮水器 **guāshuǐqì** windshield wiper

挂锁 **guàsuǒ** padlock

挂毯 **guàtǎn** tapestry; wall hanging

挂衣钩 **guàyīgōu** coat hook

瓜子 **guāzǐ** melon seed

古巴 **Gǔbā** Cuba ◊ Cuban

古板 **gǔbǎn** straitlaced, stuffy

鼓吹 **gǔchuī** advocate

鼓槌 **gǔchuí** drumstick

古代 **gǔdài** antiquity; ancient times; ancient China ◊ ancient

孤单 **gūdān** alone; solitary

古典 **gǔdiǎn** classic; classical

古典音乐 **gǔdiǎn yīnyuè** classical music

固定 **gùdìng** fasten; fix ◊ fixed; 把 X 固定在 Y 上 *bǎ X gùdìng zài Y shang* fasten X onto Y; 用针固定 *yòng zhēn gùdìng* pin

固定装置 **gùdìng zhuāngzhì** fixture

股东 **gǔdōng** stockholder, shareholder

古董 **gǔdǒng** antique

股东公司 **gǔdōng gōngsī** holding company

古董商 **gǔdǒng shāng** antique dealer

孤独 **gūdú** lonely; solitary

孤独感 **gūdú gǎn** loneliness

孤儿 **gū'ér** orphan

孤儿院 **gū'er yuàn** orphanage

股份 **gǔfèn** stock, share

股份公司 **gǔfèn gōngsī** joint-stock company

股份有限公司 **gǔfèn yǒuxiàn gōngsī** corporation

姑父 **gūfu** uncle (*father's sister's husband*)

辜负 **gūfù** disappoint

毂盖 **gǔgài** hubcap

故宫 **Gùgōng** *the former imperial palace in Beijing*; the Forbidden City

姑姑 **gūgu** auntie (*father's sister*)

古怪 **gǔguài** funny, odd; eccentric; 古怪的人 *gǔguài de rén* eccentric; weirdo

汩汩地流 **gǔgǔ de liú** gurgle

鼓鼓囊囊 **gǔgu nāngnang** bulging

固化 **gùhuā** solidify

骨灰 **gǔhuī** ashes (*after cremation*)

骨灰盒 **gǔhuīhé** urn (*for ashes*)

硅 **guī** silicon

归 **guī** return; belong to

龟 **guī** turtle; tortoise

鬼 **guǐ** ghost

轨 **guǐ** rail; track

贵 **guì** expensive; noble

桂 **guì** cassia; laurel; osmanthus

柜 **guì** cupboard

跪 **guì** kneel

鬼把戏 **guǐbǎxì** gimmick

贵宾 **guìbīn** guest of honor

归并 **guībìng** merge; 把 … 归并在一起 *bǎ … guībìng zài yìqǐ* lump together

轨道 **guǐdào** track; orbit; 绕轨道运行 *rào guǐdào yùnxíng* orbit

鬼地方 **guǐdìfāng** horrible place; dump

规定 **guīdìng** stipulate ◊ stipulation; regulation; rule; 违约罚款的规定 *wéiyuē fákuǎn de guīdìng* penalty clause; 规定的任期 *guīdìng de rènqī* stint; period of office

规范 **guīfàn** rules; standard

归附者 **guīfù zhě** convert

规格 **guīgé** specifications

归根结底 **guīgēn jiédǐ** boil down to

归功 **guīgōng** owing to; thanks to

鬼鬼祟祟 **guǐgui suìsui** shifty-looking; sneaky

规划 **guīhuà** plan ◊ planning

归还 **guīhuán** give back; return

归家 **guījiā** homecoming

诡计多端 **guǐjì duōduān** scheming

规矩点！**guījǔ diǎn!** behave (yourself)!

归类 **guīlèi** classify

规模 **guīmó** scale

桂皮 **guìpí** cinnamon

硅片 **guīpiàn** silicon chip

归属 **guīshǔ** belong to

柜台 **guìtái** counter, bar

归途 **guītú** way back

跪下 **guìxià** kneel

规则 **guīzé** rule; regulations

诡诈 **guǐzhà** underhand

规章 **guīzhāng** regulation

贵重 **guìzhòng** valuable

贵重物品 **guìzhòng wùpǐn** valuables

柜子 **guìzi** cabinet; cupboard

刽子手 **guìzishǒu** executioner

贵族 **guìzú** nobility

估计 **gūjì** calculate; estimate; assess; put the cost at ◊ estimate; valuation

古迹 **gǔjì** antiquities; historical

sites

顾及 **gùjí** take into account; consider

估价 **gūjià** appraise; value

骨节嶙峋 **gǔjié línxún** gnarled

故居 **gùjū** former residence

顾客 **gùkè** client, customer; consumer

顾客关系 **gùkè guānxi** customer relations

古老 **gǔlǎo** ancient

谷类 **gǔlèi** cereal

孤立 **gūlì** isolate; separate ◊ isolated

鼓励 **gǔlì** encourage; urge on ◊ encouragement; 鼓励的话 **gǔlìde huà** pep talk

谷粒 **gǔlì** grain

估量 **gūliáng** size up, weigh up; assess; estimate

孤零零 **gū línglíng** solitary; all alone

孤立无援 **gūlì wúyuán** defenseless

顾虑 **gùlǜ** misgivings, scruples

鼓膜 **gǔmó** eardrum

滚 **gǔn** roll ◊ get lost!

棍 **gùn** rod

滚出去! **gǔnchūqù!** get out!

滚蛋! **gǔndàn!** get lost!

滚动 **gǔndòng** roll

姑娘 **gūniang** girl

牯牛 **gǔníu** bull

滚开! **gǔnkāi!** ∨ fuck off!

咕哝 **gūnong** mumble, mutter

滚烫 **gǔntàng** piping hot

滚珠轴承 **gǔnzhū zhóuchéng** ball bearing

棍子 **gùnzi** stick; rod

锅 **guō** pot, pan; wok

国 **guó** state; country

果 **guǒ** fruit; result

裹 **guǒ** wrap

过 **guò** across; over ◊ pass; cross; spend; 走过 **zǒuguò** walk past ◊ (*past indicator*): 我去过中国 **wǒ qùguo Zhōngguó** I've been to China; 我吃过了 **wǒ chīguò le** I have eaten

锅铲 **guōchǎn** spatula

过程 **guòchéng** process

过错 **guòcuò** error; mistake

过道 **guòdào** corridor

过得快乐 **guòde kuàilè** enjoy oneself

过得去 **guòdequ** tolerable; acceptable ◊ be able to get by; be able to get through

过低评价 **guòdī píngjià** underrate

果冻 **guǒdòng** jelly

过度 **guòdù** excess ◊ excessive; undue; 过度感光 **guòdù gǎnguāng** overexpose

过渡 **guòdù** transition ◊ transitional

果断 **guǒduàn** decisive

过度紧张 **guòdù jǐnzhāng** hypertension

国防部 **Guófáng Bù** Department of Defense

国防部长 **Guófáng Bùzhǎng** Defense Secretary

国防开支 **guófáng kāizhī** defense budget

过分 **guòfèn** excessive; unreasonable ◊ unduly; 他太过分了 **tā tài guòfènle** he's gone too far; he's too much

果脯 **guǒfǔ** candied fruit

过高 **guògāo** exorbitant; extortionate; too high

过高估计 **guògāo gūjì** overestimate ◊ overrated

过高要价 **guògāo yàojià** overcharge

国歌 **guógē** national anthem

国会 **guóhuì** Congress ◊ Congressional

国会议员 **guóhuì yìyuán** Congressman, member of Congress

过火 **guòhuǒ** exaggerated; overdone ◊ exaggerate

国籍 **guójí** citizenship; nationality

国际 **guójì** international ◊ internationally

国家 **guójiā** country; nation; state ◊ national

国家队 **guójiāduì** national team

国家公园 **guójiā gōngyuán** national park

果酱 **guǒjiàng** jam; conserve

国际比赛 **guójì bǐsài** international (match)

过节 **guòjié** celebrate a festival

国际法庭 **Guójì Fǎtíng** International Court of Justice

国际货币基金 **Guójì Huòbì Jījīn** International Monetary Fund

国际劳动节 **Guójì Laódòngjié** International Labor Day

过境 **guòjìng** be in transit (*between countries*)

过境签证 **guòjìng qiānzhèng** transit visa

国际收支差额 **guójì shōuzhī chā'é** (international) balance of payments

过来 **guòlái** step in; come over ◊ across

国立 **guólì** national; state-run

过量 **guòliàng** overdose

锅炉 **guōlú** boiler

过滤 **guòlǜ** filter; strain; 过滤式咖啡壶 **guòlǜshì kāfēihú** percolator

过滤器 **guòlǜ qì** filter; strainer

过路人 **guòlùrén** passer-by

过滤嘴香烟 **guòlǜzuǐ xiāngyān** filter-tipped cigarette

国民 **guómín** national

过敏 **guòmǐn** allergy ◊ hypersensitive

国民党 **Guómíndǎng** Kuomintang, KMT, Nationalist Party

国民生产总值 **guómín shēngchǎn zǒngzhí** GNP, gross national product

国内 **guónèi** domestic; internal; 在国内 **zài guónèi** at home (*in country*)

国内航班 **guónèi hángbān** domestic flight

国内贸易 **guónèi màoyì** internal trade

国内生产总值 **guónèi shēngchǎn zǒngzhí** GDP, gross domestic product

国内外 **guónèiwài** at home and abroad

过年 **guònián** celebrate Chinese New Year

果皮 **guǒpí** peel (*of fruit*)

国旗 **guóqí** national flag

过期 **guòqī** out of date

国庆节 **Guóqìngjié** National Day

过去 **guòqù** past ◊ go by; 那都已经过去了 **nà dōu yǐjīng guòqù le** that's all past now; 在过去 **zài guòqù** in the past

过去分词 **guòqù fēncí** past participle

过去时 **guòqùshí** past tense

果然如此 **guǒrán rúcǐ** sure enough

果肉 **guǒròu** flesh (*of fruit*); pulp

过山车 **guò shān chē** roller coaster

过剩 **guòshèng** surplus

果实 **guǒshí** fruit

过时 **guòshí** out of date; dated; old-fashioned; out of fashion; stale *news*

果树 **guǒshù** fruit tree

过堂风 **guòtáng fēng** draft

国外 **guówài** abroad ◊ foreign

国王 **guówáng** king

国务访问 **guówù fǎngwèn** state visit

国务卿 **Guówùqīng** Secretary of State

国务院 **Guówùyuàn** Department of State, State Department

果馅饼 **guǒxiànbǐng** flan

果馅儿饼 **guǒxiànr bǐng** tart

国宴 **guóyàn** state banquet

过夜 **guòyè** stay the night, spend the night

过一会儿 **guò yíhuìr** by and by, soon

国营 **guóyíng** state-owned; state-run

国有化 **guóyǒu huà** nationalize

过于 **guòyú** excessively; too

果园 **guǒyuán** orchard

过早 **guòzǎo** untimely

国债 **guózhài** national debt

果汁 **guǒzhī** fruit juice

骨盆 **gǔpén** pelvis

孤僻 **gūpì** withdrawn; autistic

股票 **gǔpiào** stock, share

股票交易所 **gǔpiào jiāoyìsuǒ**

stock exchange

股票经纪人 **gǔpiào jīngjì rén** stockbroker

股票市场 **gǔpiào shìchǎng** stock market; 股票市场暴跌 *gǔpiào shìchǎng bàodiē* stockmarket crash

鼓起 **gǔqǐ** drum up; rouse

鼓起劲儿来！ **gǔ qǐ jìnr lái!** cheer up!

鼓起勇气 **gǔqǐ yǒngqì** pluck up courage

故事 **gùshi** story; tale; narrative; joke

鼓手 **gǔshǒu** drummer

固守 **gùshǒu** cling to

骨髓 **gǔsuǐ** bone marrow

固体 **gùtǐ** solid

骨头 **gǔtou** bone

顾问 **gùwèn** adviser; consultant

鼓舞 **gǔwǔ** encourage; 令人鼓舞 *lìngrén* **gǔwǔ** encouraging

股息 **gǔxī** dividend

故乡 **gùxiāng** home town; homeland

古雅小巧 **gǔyǎ xiǎoqiǎo** quaint

故意 **gùyì** deliberate; willful ◊ deliberately, on purpose

雇佣 **gùyōng** employ

雇佣兵 **gùyōngbīng** mercenary

固有 **gùyǒu** inherent

雇员 **gùyuán** employee; staff

鼓掌 **gǔzhǎng** applaud ◊ applause

故障 **gùzhàng** breakdown; defect; bug COMPUT

骨折 **gǔzhé** break, fracture ◊ broken

固执 **gùzhí** persistent, dogged; inflexible; stubborn; willful

雇主 **gùzhǔ** employer

孤注一掷 **gūzhù yízhì** desperate ◊ desperation; 孤注一掷之举 *gūzhù yízhì zhījǔ* an act of desperation

故作姿态 **gùzuò zītài** put on an act, put on airs

H

哈 **hā** exhale ◊ ha-ha

嗨，咳 **hāi** (*regret*): 嗨，我怎么给忘了呢？ *hāi, wǒ zěnme gěi wàng le?* oh no, how come I forgot it?

还 **hái** still; as well as; yet; quite; even more; also; 还有什么？ *háiyǒu shénme?* anything else?; 你还要吗？ *ní háiyào ma?* do you still want it?

海 **hǎi** sea

害 **hài** harm

海岸 **hǎi'àn** coast

海岸线 **hǎi'àn xiàn** coastline

海拔 **hǎibá** altitude; elevation; height above sea level

海报 **hǎibào** poster, bill

海豹 **hǎibào** seal (*animal*)

海边 **hǎibiān** seaside

海滨 **hǎibīn** seaside

海滨砂石 **hǎibīn shāshí** shingle

海滨胜地 **hǎibīn shèngdì** seaside resort

害虫 **hàichóng** pest; vermin

害处 **hàichu** damage; harm

海带 **hǎidài** kelp, (edible) seaweed

海胆 **hǎidǎn** sea urchin

海港 **hǎigǎng** seaport

海关 **hǎiguān** customs

海关官员 **hǎiguān guānyuán** customs officer

还好 **háihǎo** alright, not bad

海军 **hǎijūn** navy ◊ naval

海军基地 **hǎijūn jīdì** naval base

海军兰 **hǎijūn lán** navy blue

海军强国 **hǎijūn qiángguó** sea power

海军上将 **hǎijūn shàngjiàng** admiral

海里 **hǎilǐ** nautical mile

海陆兵 **hǎilùbīng** marine MIL

海洛因 **hǎiluòyīn** heroin

海绵 **hǎimián** sponge; foam rubber

海南岛 **Hǎinán Dǎo** Hainan Island

害鸟 **hàiniǎo** pest (*bird*)

海鸥 **hǎi'ōu** seagull

害怕 **hàipà** be afraid, be frightened; be afraid of, dread

海平面 **hǎipíngmiàn** sea level

骇人听闻 **hài rén tīngwén** hideous; shocking

海上 **hǎishàng** maritime; seafaring

还是 **háishi** or

海市蜃楼 **hǎishì shènlóu** mirage

害兽 **hàishòu** pest

海难 **hǎinàn** shipwreck; 遇海难 *yù hǎinàn* be shipwrecked

海损 **hǎisǔn** maritime damage

海滩 **hǎitān** beach

海豚 **hǎitún** dolphin

海外 **hǎiwài** overseas

海湾 **hǎiwān** gulf; inlet

海味 **hǎiwèi** seafood

海峡 **hǎixiá** channel; strait

海星 **hǎixīng** starfish

害羞 **hàixiū** shy

海洋 **hǎiyáng** ocean ◊ marine

海员 **hǎiyuán** sailor

海运 **hǎiyùn** ship; shipping

海蜇 **hǎizhé** jellyfish

孩子 **háizi** child

孩子气 **háiziqì** infantile

哈喇 **hāla** rancid

蛤蟆 **háma** toad

寒 **hán** cold

含 **hán** contain; suck

函 **hán** letter

喊 **hǎn** shout

汉 **Hàn** Han

汗 **hàn** sweat

旱 **hàn** dryness

焊 **hàn** weld

汉堡包 **hànbǎobāo** hamburger, beefburger

旱冰鞋 **hànbīng xié** roller skate;

四轮旱冰鞋 **sìlún hànbīng xié** in-line skate, rollerblade®

汉朝 **Hàncháo** Han Dynasty

行 **háng** line; row; trade; profession

航班 **hángbān** flight

航班号 **hángbān hào** flight number

航标 **hángbiāo** buoy

航程 **hángchéng** voyage

行道 **hángdào** lane (*on freeway*)

航海 **hánghǎi** voyage ◊ nautical ◊ navigate

航海家 **hánghǎi jiā** navigator

航海图 **hánghǎi tú** chart

行话 **hánghuà** jargon, slang

行家 **hángjia** expert; connoisseur

航空 **hángkōng** aviation ◊ aeronautical ◊ by air

航空公司 **hángkōng gōngsī** airline

航空母舰 **hángkōng mǔjiàn** aircraft carrier

航空摄影 **hángkōng shèyǐng** aerial photography

航空图 **hángkōng tú** chart

航空信件 **hángkōng xìnjiàn** air letter, airmail

航空邮件 **hángkōng yóujiàn** air letter, airmail

行列 **hángliè** procession

航天 **hángtiān** space flight

航天飞机 **hángtiān fēijī** space shuttle

航线 **hángxiàn** airline; flight route

航向 **hángxiàng** course

航行 **hángxíng** cruise

航行学 **hángxíng xué** navigation

行业 **hángyè** trade; profession

含糊 **hánhú** ambiguous

含糊不清 **hánhu bùqīng** unclear; 含糊地说 **hánhude shuō** mumble

含糊其辞 **hánhu qící** oblique; coy

旱季 **hànjì** dry season

罕见 **hǎnjiàn** rare

喊叫 **hǎnjiào** call; cry; cry out ◊ shouting

喊叫声 **hǎnjiào shēng** yell; scream

焊接 **hànjiē** weld; solder

焊接工人 **hànjiē gōngrén** welder

含酒精 **hán jiǔjīng** alcoholic

寒冷（刺骨）**hánlěng（cìgǔ）**icy cold, bitterly cold

含量 **hánliàng** content

汗淋淋 **hànlínlín** sweaty

寒流 **hánliú** stream of cold air

含氯氟烃 **hánlù fútīng** chlorofluorocarbon, CFC

汗沫儿 **hànmòr** sweat; lather

汗衫 **hànshān** T-shirt

鼾声 **hānshēng** snoring

喊声 **hǎnshēng** shout

函授 **hánshòu** correspondence course

寒暑表 **hánshǔbiǎo** thermometer

酣睡 **hānshuì** sound sleep

汗水 **hànshuǐ** sweat, perspiration

寒酸 **hánsuān** shabby

捍卫 **hànwèi** defend ◊ defense

捍卫者 **hànwèi zhě** champion

含蓄 **hánxù** reserve ◊ implicit

汉学 **hànxué** sinology

汉学家 **hànxuéjiā** sinologist

含药物 **hán yàowù** medicated

含义 **hányì** meaning

汉语 **Hànyǔ** Chinese

旱灾 **hànzāi** drought

汉藏 **Hànzàng** Sino-Tibetan

汉字 **Hànzì** Chinese character

汉族 **Hànzú** the Han people

蚝 **háo** oyster

毫 **háo** milli- ◊ in the least

好 **hǎo** good; fine ◊ well; quite; very; 比 … 好 **bǐ … hǎo** better than; 太好了！**tàihǎole!** great!

耗 **hào** use; consume

号 **hào** number

好 **hào** like

好吧 **hǎoba** very well, ok

毫不犹豫 **háobù yóuyù** like a shot, without the least hesitation

好吵闹 **hào chǎonào** rowdy

号称 **hàochēng** be called

好吃 **hǎochī** delicious; good to eat

好处 **hǎochù** advantage, benefit; compensation; 对你有好处 **duì nǐ yǒu hǎochù** it's to your advantage; it's good for you

耗费 **hàofèi** spend; use

好感 **hǎogǎn** fondness; affection

好管闲事 **hàoguǎn xiánshì** nosy

豪华 **háohuá** luxury ◊ luxurious; de luxe; plush; 豪华的生活方式 **háohuáde shēnghuó fāngshì** high life

嚎叫 **háojiào** howl

浩劫 **hàojié** havoc

好极了 **hǎojíle** excellent, very good

耗尽 **hàojìn** run down; use up; run out

好竞争 **hào jìngzhēng** competitive

好看 **hǎokàn** good-looking

毫克 **háokè** milligram

好客 **hàokè** hospitable; 好客的主人 **hàoké de zhǔrén** a congenial host

好了, 好了! **hǎole, hǎole!** there, there!

号码 **hàomǎ** number; size

毫米 **háomǐ** millimeter

好奇 **hàoqí** curious, inquisitive ◊ curiously

好强 **hàoqiáng** ambitious

好球 **hǎoqiú** strike (in baseball)

好奇心 **hàoqí xīn** curiosity; 引起好奇心 **yǐnqǐ hàoqí xīn** intrigue

好听 **hǎotīng** melodious; nice-sounding

好哇 **hǎowa** hurray

毫无 **háowú** not in the least; 毫无用处 **háowú yòngchù** no use at all

毫无顾忌 **háowú gùjì** regardless

好象 **hǎoxiàng** seem; resemble; look like ◊ apparently ◊ as if, as though

好笑 **hǎoxiào** amusing, funny; jovial

好心 **hǎoxīn** kind-hearted, sweet

好学 **hàoxué** academic, studious

好意 **hǎoyì** kindness

耗用 **hàoyòng** consume, use

蚝油 **háoyóu** oyster sauce

号召 **hàozhào** call; call on

豪猪 **háozhū** porcupine

好转 **hǎozhuǎn** get better, improve ◊ improvement, upturn

哈萨克斯坦 **Hāsàkèsītǎn** Kazakhstan ◊ Kazahk

哈腰 **hāyāo** stoop; bow

喝 **hē** drink

和 **hé** and; along with ◊ harmonious; mild ◊ sum; peace; 和 … 一起 **hé … yìqǐ** with

盒 **hé** case; box; container

颌 **hé** jaw

何 **hé** who; what; which; why; how

核 **hé** core, center; pip, pit

河 **hé** river

荷 **hé** lotus

合 **hé** join; fit; suit; 合你口味儿 **hé nǐ kǒuwèir** to your liking

褐 **hè** brown

贺 **hè** congratulate

和蔼可亲 **hé'ǎi kěqīn** amiable

河岸 **hé'àn** river bank

荷包蛋 **hébao dàn** fried egg

合抱双臂 **hébào shuāngbì** fold one's arms

河边 **hébiān** riverside

合并 **hébìng** merge, amalgamate ◊ merger

合不来 **hébùlái** not get on; be incompatible

喝采 **hècǎi** applaud; cheer; cheer on

合唱 **héchàng** sing in chorus ◊ choir

合成 **héchéng** synthesis

合成代谢激素 **héchéng dàixiè jīsù** anabolic steroid

河床 **héchuáng** riverbed

喝倒彩 **hè dàocǎi** boo

合得来 **hédelái** get on well; be compatible

合调 **hédiào** in tune

核对 **héduì** check

荷尔蒙 **hé'ěrméng** hormone

合法 **héfǎ** legal; legitimate; lawful

核反应堆 **hé fǎnyìng duī** nuclear reactor

合法性 **héfǎ xìng** legality

核废物 **hé fèiwù** nuclear waste

和服 **héfú** kimono

合格 **hégé** qualified; eligible; competent

合格会计师 **hégé kuàijì shī** certified public accountant

喝光 **hēguāng** drink up

和好 **héhǎo** make it up; be reconciled

和平 **héhu** conform with; 和乎语法 **héhu yǔfǎ** grammatical

荷花 **héhuā** lotus (flower)

和缓 **héhuǎn** gentle, mild

合伙 **héhuǒ** team up; form a partnership; 合伙攻击 **héhuǒ gōngjī** gang up on; 合伙经营 **héhuǒ jīngyíng** partnership COM

合伙人 **héhuǒ rén** partner

嘿 **hēi** (appreciation): 嘿，这可不错 **hēi, zhè kě búcuò** hey, this isn't bad at all

黑 **hēi** black; dark

黑暗 **hēi'àn** blackness; dark, darkness

黑白片 **hēibái piàn** black and white movie

黑板 **hēibǎn** blackboard

黑板擦 **hēibǎncā** blackboard eraser

黑板架 **hēibǎnjià** (blackboard) easel

黑客 **hēikè** hacker

黑麦 **hēimài** rye

黑莓 **hēiméi** blackberry

黑名单 **hēi míngdān** blacklist

黑啤酒 **hēi píjiǔ** dark beer

黑钱 **hēiqián** slush fund

黑人 **hēirén** black (person)

黑色 **hēisè** black (color)

黑社会 **hēi shèhuì** underworld

黑市 **hēishì** black market

黑市经济 **hēishì jīngjì** black economy

黑手党 **Hēishǒudǎng** Mafia

黑桃 **hēitáo** spades (in cards)

黑线鳕 **hēixiàn xuě** haddock

黑匣子 **hēi xiázi** black box

黑猩猩 **hēi xīngxing** chimpanzee

黑眼镜 **hēi yǎnjìng** dark glasses

核计 **héjì** calculate

合计 **héjì** add up

和解 **héjiě** make up

合金 **héjīn** alloy

喝酒 **hējiǔ** drink; drinking; 我不喝酒 **wǒ bù hējiǔ** I don't drink

河口 **hékǒu** rivermouth

河口湾 **hékǒu wān** estuary

荷兰 **Hélán** Holland, the Netherlands ◊ Dutch

合礼 **hélǐ** kosher

合理 **hélǐ** rational, reasonable; sensible, sound ◊ reasonably, rationally

核裂变 **hé lièbiàn** nuclear fission

合理化 **hélǐ huà** rationalize ◊ rationalization

河流 **héliú** river

合理性 **hélǐ xìng** rationality

河马 **hémǎ** hippopotamus

褐煤 **hèméi** brown coal

和睦 **hémù** harmony

痕 **hén** mark; trace; scar

很 **hěn** very; quite

狠 **hěn** hard-hearted

恨 **hèn** hate ◊ hatred

很棒 **hěnbàng** great

狠毒 **hěndú** malicious; venomous

核能 **hénéng** nuclear power, nuclear energy

核能站 **hénéng zhàn** nuclear power station

横 **héng** horizontal

哼唱 **hēngchàng** hum

横冲直撞 **héngchōng zhízhuàng** rampage

横渡 **héngdù** crossing NAUT

横幅 **héngfú** banner, streamer

横杆 **hénggān** crossbar (of high jump)

横贯 **héngguàn** cross

横跨 **héngkuà** span

横跨大西洋 **héngkuà Dàxīyáng** transatlantic

横梁 **héngliáng** beam

衡量 **héngliáng** consider; weigh up

衡量标准 **héngliáng biāozhǔ** yardstick

横木 **héngmù** crossbar (of goal)

横排 **héngpái** landscape print

恒温器 **héngwēn qì** thermostat

恒温育婴箱 **héngwēn yùyīng xiāng** incubator

横向 **héngxiàng** thwart

恒心 **héngxīn** stamina; persistence

痕迹 **hénjì** evidence; trail; traces

狠揍 **hěnzòu** beat up

和平 **hépíng** peace

和平队 **Hépíngduì** Peace Corps

和平主义 **hépíng zhǔyì** pacifism

和平主义者 **hépíng zhǔyì zhě** pacifist

和气 **héqi** polite; friendly; peaceable

呵欠 **hēqiàn** yawn

合群 **héqún** sociable ◊ fit in

和善 **héshàn** friendly

和尚 **héshàng** Buddhist monk

合身 **héshēn** fit

和声 **héshēng** harmony

核实 **héshí** verification ◊ verify

合适 **héshì** suitable, appropriate; right; convenient ◊ fit; 合适的位置 *héshìde wèizhi* niche

合算 **hésuàn** profitable

喝汤 **hētāng** drink soup

核桃 **hétáo** walnut

合同 **hétóng** contract ◊ contractual

合为一体 **hé wéi yītǐ** merge

核武器 **hé wǔqì** nuclear weapons

贺喜 **hèxǐ** congratulate

和谐 **héxié** harmonious

核心 **héxīn** core; kernel

贺信 **hèxìn** letter of congratulation

合意 **héyì** please; appeal to

合意男士 **héyì nánshì** eligible bachelor

合影 **héyǐng** group photo

合用 **héyòng** double up, share

和约 **héyuē** peace treaty

盒子 **hézi** box

合资企业 **hézī qǐyè** joint venture

合组 **hézǔ** consortium

喝醉 **hēzuì** get drunk

喝醉了 **hēzuìle** drunk; drunken

合作 **hézuò** cooperate, collaborate ◊ cooperation, collaboration ◊ cooperative

合作社 **hézuò shè** cooperative

合作者 **hézuò zhě** collaborator

轰 **hōng** chuck out, drive away

红 **hóng** red

虹 **hóng** rainbow

洪 **hóng** big ◊ flood

哄 **hǒng** coax

红宝石 **hóng bǎoshí** ruby

红茶 **hóngchá** black tea

红肠面包 **hóngcháng miànbāo** hot dog

宏大 **hóngdà** great

红灯 **hóngdēng** red light

红灯区 **hóngdēng qū** red light district

轰的一声 **hōngde yīshēng** bang

轰动 **hōngdòng** cause a sensation ◊ sensation ◊ sensational

红光满面 **hóngguāng mǎnmiàn** radiant

轰击 **hōngjī** shoot at; bombard

红军 **Hóngjūn** Red Army

烘烤 **hōngkǎo** toast

洪亮 **hóngliàng** sonorous

红绿灯 **hónglǜdēng** traffic light

轰鸣 **hōngmíng** roar

轰鸣声 **hōngmíng shēng** roar

虹膜 **hóngmó** iris (*of eye*)

哄骗 **hǒngpiàn** deceive; swindle

红润 **hóngrùn** glow ◊ rosy; ruddy

红色 **hóngsè** red

红色中国 **Hóngsè Zhōngguó** Red China

红十字 **Hóngshízì** Red Cross

红薯 **hóngshǔ** sweet potato

洪水 **hóngshuǐ** flood

洪水泛滥 **hóngshuǐ fànlàn** flooding

红桃 **hóngtáo** hearts (*in cards*)

红外线 **hóngwàixiàn** infra-red rays

宏伟 **hóngwěi** grandiose

红卫兵 **Hóngwèibīng** Red Guard

轰炸 **hōngzhà** bomb

轰炸机 **hōngzhà jī** bomber (*plane*)

轰炸警告 **hōngzhà jǐnggào** bomb scare

猴 **hóu** monkey

喉 **hóu** throat

吼 **hǒu** roar

后 **hòu** back; rear; behind

厚 **hòu** thick

候 **hòu** wait

厚板 **hòubǎn** slab

后背 **hòubèi** back

后备 **hòubèi** back up ◊ backup

后部 **hòubù** back

候车场 **hòuchē chǎng** cab rank, cab stand

候车室 **hòuchē shì** waiting room

后代 **hòudài** offspring; posterity

后跟 **hòugēn** heel
后果 **hòuguǒ** consequence; effect
后花园 **hòu huāyuán** backyard
后悔 **hòuhuǐ** regret; repent; be sorry
吼叫 **hǒujiào** bellow
吼叫声 **hǒujiào shēng** bellow
喉结 **hóujié** Adam's apple
候机室 **hòujī shì** departure lounge
后来 **hòulái** after; afterward; later, later on; subsequently
喉咙 **hóulóng** throat
后门 **hòumén** backdoor
后面 **hòumian** behind, in back
候鸟 **hòuniǎo** bird of passage
后勤学 **hòuqín xué** logistics
喉舌 **hóushé** mouthpiece, spokesperson
吼声 **hǒushēng** bellow
后视镜 **hòushì jìng** rear-view mirror
后天 **hòutiān** the day after tomorrow
后退 **hòutuì** back away; back off; back up (*in car*); stand back ◊ retrograde
后卫 **hòuwèi** back SP
候选人 **hòuxuǎn rén** candidate
后续 **hòuxù** follow up
喉炎 **hóuyán** laryngitis
厚颜无耻 **hòuyán wúchǐ** outrageous; impertinent
后腰 **hòuyāo** small of the back
后裔 **hòuyì** descendant
后院 **hòuyuàn** backyard
后者 **hòuzhě** latter
猴子 **hóuzi** monkey
呼 **hū** beep
忽 **hū** overlook ◊ suddenly
壶 **hú** jug; kettle; pot
湖 **hú** lake
核 **hú** pit (*in fruit*)
胡 **hú** mustache; beard
糊 **hú** stick
煳 **hú** burnt
虎 **hǔ** tiger
糊 **hù** mush
户 **hù** door; household; bank account
护 **hù** protect

互 **hù** mutual
花 **huā** flower; blossom ◊ spend; cost; 他们花了五百美金 **tāmen huāle wǔbǎi měijīn** it cost them $500
划 **huá** row; paddle; strike *match*
滑 **huá** slide; slip ◊ slippery, icy
华 **huá** glory; China
画 **huà** draw; paint; portray ◊ drawing; painting
话 **huà** talk; words; remark
化 **huà** change; melt; dissolve ◊ (*to make adjectives and nouns into verbs*) -ize; 大众化 **dàzhònghuà** popularize; 简化 **jiǎnhuà** simplify
画 **huà** stroke (*in character*); picture ◊ paint
花瓣 **huābàn** petal
滑板 **huábǎn** skateboard
画报 **huàbào** magazine
画笔 **huàbǐ** paintbrush
花边 **huābiān** lace
哗变 **huábiàn** mutiny
滑冰 **huábīng** skate ◊ skating
化冰 **huàbīng** defrost
滑冰场 **huábīng chǎng** ice rink
滑冰人 **huábīng rén** skater
划船 **huáchuán** row; paddle
花点 **huādiǎn** spotted
划掉 **huádiào** delete; strike out
化冻 **huà dòng** thaw
花朵 **huāduǒ** bloom
华而不实 **huá ér bùshí** ornate
华尔街 **Huá'ěrjiē** Wall Street
华尔兹 **huá'ěrzī** waltz
花费 **huāfèi** spend ◊ expenditure
化肥 **huàféi** artificial fertilizer
花粉 **huāfěn** pollen
划分 **huàfēn** divide; 划分轻重缓急 **huàfēn qīngzhòng huǎnjí** prioritize
花粉计数 **huāfěn jìshù** pollen count
花粉热 **huāfěn rè** hay fever
花岗石 **huāgǎng shí** granite
花岗岩 **huāgǎng yán** granite
化工 **huàgōng** chemical industry
滑旱冰 **huá hànbīng** skate
化合 **huàhé** combine
划痕 **huáhén** cut; score ◊ scratch

化合物 **huàhé wù** compound CHEM

画画 **huàhua** draw

花花公子 **huāhuā gōngzǐ** playboy

花环 **huāhuán** garland

怀 **huái** bosom ◊ cherish; 怀好意 **huái hǎoyì** mean well

踝 **huái** ankle

坏 **huài** bad

坏处 **huàichu** disadvantage

坏蛋 **huàidàn** gangster; villain

怀旧 **huáijiù** nostalgia ◊ nostalgic ◊ reminisce

怀念 **huáiniàn** long for

坏人 **huàirén** rogue

坏事 **huàishì** evil; evil thing

槐树 **huáishù** scholar tree

怀疑 **huáiyí** doubt; suspect; question ◊ suspicion ◊ skeptical

怀疑论者 **huáiyílùn zhě** skeptic

怀疑态度 **huáiyí tàidù** skepticism

怀有 **huáiyǒu** harbor *grudge etc*; 怀有恶意 **huáiyǒu èyì** spiteful; 怀有希望 **huáiyǒu xīwàng** expectant

怀孕 **huáiyùn** conceive; expect ◊ pregnant ◊ pregnancy; conception

怀着 **huáizhe** carry (*of pregnant woman*)

滑稽 **huájī** comical ◊ funnily; 滑稽的模仿 **huájī de mófǎng** (comic) impression; 滑稽短剧 **huájī duǎnjù** (comedy) sketch

画家 **huàjiā** artist, painter

花椒 **huājiāo** Sichuan pepper

花轿 **huājiào** bridal palanquin

滑稽可笑 **huájī kěxiào** very funny, hysterical

哗啦 **huālā** crash; clatter; crackle

滑来滑去 **huálái huáqù** slither

画廊 **huàláng** art gallery

哗啦声 **huālā shēng** crash; clatter; crackle

花蕾 **huālěi** bud

华丽的词藻 **huálìde cízǎo** rhetoric

滑轮 **huálún** pulley

画面 **huàmiàn** image

化名 **huàmíng** pseudonym

欢 **huān** happy

还 **huán** return, give back; 将X还给Y **jiāng X huángeǐ Y** give X back to Y

环 **huán** ring; circle

缓 **huǎn** slow; leisurely ◊ postpone, put off

换 **huàn** change; swap; switch; 换衣服 **huàn yīfu** change clothes; 用X换Y **yòng X huàn Y** exchange X for Y

患 **huàn** worry; catch *disease*

唤 **huàn** shout

幻 **huàn** unreal; magic

换班 **huànbān** change shifts

环保 **huánbǎo** environmental protection

患病 **huànbìng** be ill

欢畅 **huānchàng** cheerful

缓冲器 **huǎnchōng qì** buffer COMPUT

换档键 **huàndǎng jiàn** shift key

幻灯 **huàndēng** slide show

幻灯片 **huàndēng piàn** slide; transparency

荒 **huāng** desolate

慌 **huāng** nervous; 别慌 **biéhuāng** don't panic

黄 **huáng** yellow

皇 **huáng** emperor ◊ imperial

晃 **huǎng** dazzle

谎 **huǎng** lie

晃 **huàng** swing; wave

蝗虫 **huángchóng** locust

荒诞 **huāngdàn** absurd; grotesque

黄疸 **huángdǎn** jaundice

黄道带 **huángdào dài** zodiac

黄道十二宫图 **huángdào shí'èr gōngtú** signs of the zodiac

荒地 **huāngdì** wasteland; heath

皇帝 **huángdì** emperor ◊ imperial

黄帝 **Huángdì** Yellow Emperor

晃动 **huàngdòng** shake; waggle

黄豆 **huángdòu** soybean

荒废 **huāngfèi** lie fallow

黄蜂 **huángfēng** wasp

皇宫 **huánggōng** imperial palace

黄瓜 **huángguā** cucumber

黄海 **Huánghǎi** Yellow Sea

黄河 **Huánghé** Yellow River

皇后 **huánghòu** empress; queen

恍惚 **huǎnghū** trance

谎话 **huǎnghuà** lie

黄昏 **huánghūn** dusk, twilight

皇家 **huángjiā** royal family ◊ royal

黄金 **huángjīn** gold

黄金时间 **huángjīn shíjiān** prime time

荒凉 **huāngliáng** bleak; deserted; desolate; stark

慌忙 **huāngmáng** hurried

荒谬 **huāngmiù** preposterous, ridiculous ◊ ridiculously

荒漠 **huāngmò** barren

荒僻 **huāngpì** remote, out-of-the-way

黄色 **huángsè** yellow ◊ pornographic

黄色电影 **huángsè diànyǐng** blue movie

黄色杂志 **huángsè zázhì** pornographic magazine

黄色作品 **huángsè zuòpǐn** pornography

荒疏 **huāngshū** lose the knack

荒唐 **huāngtáng** ludicrous, absurd ◊ absurdity

黄铜 **huángtóng** brass

环顾 **huángù** look around

荒无人烟 **huāng wú rényān** uninhabited

荒野 **huāngyě** the bush; the wilds

黄油 **huángyóu** butter

荒原 **huāngyuán** wilderness

慌张 **huāngzhāng** nervous

幌子 **huǎngzi** front

皇族 **huángzú** royalty

缓和 **huǎnhé** lighten; soften; tone down ◊ détente; respite

欢呼 **huānhū** cheer ◊ cheering

还击 **huánjī** hit back

环礁湖 **huánjiāo hú** lagoon

缓解 **huǎnjiě** relax; alleviate; ease off; smooth over

环境 **huánjìng** environment; surroundings; setting

环境保护 **huánjìng bǎohù** environmental protection

环境保护论者 **huánjìng bǎohùlùn zhě** environmentalist

环境卫生部门 **huánjìng wèishēng bùmén** sanitation department

环境污染 **huánjìng wūrǎn** environmental pollution

欢聚 **huānjù** social gathering, get-together

欢快 **huānkuài** bright ◊ brightness

欢乐 **huānlè** happy; cheerful; convivial ◊ merriment

还礼 **huánlǐ** return the salute, salute back

缓慢 **huǎnmàn** slow; leisurely; tardy; 缓慢进行 **huǎnmàn jìnxíng** plod along, plod on

幻灭 **huànmiè** disillusionment

化脓 **huànóng** fester

唤起 **huànqǐ** evoke; arouse; call up

还钱 **huánqián** pay back

换钱 **huànqián** change money

欢庆 **huānqìng** festivities

还清 **huánqīng** pay off

换取 **huànqǔ** exchange; 用来换取 **yònglái huànqǔ** in exchange for

焕然一新 **huànrán yìxīn** renew; take on a new look

环绕 **huánrǎo** surround, encircle

涣散 **huànsàn** loose; limp

换算 **huànsuàn** convert

换算表 **huànsuàn biǎo** conversion table

欢喜 **huānxǐ** rapturous

幻想 **huànxiǎng** illusion; fantasy

幻象 **huànxiàng** illusion; 使幻想破灭 **shǐ huànxiǎng pòmiè** disillusion

欢笑 **huānxiào** mirth

欢欣 **huānxīn** jubilation

缓刑 **huǎnxíng** reprieve ◊ probation

唤醒 **huànxǐng** wake; rouse

唤醒电话 **huànxǐng diànhuà** wake-up call

缓刑监督官 **huǎnxíng jiāndūguān** probation officer

浣熊 **huànxióng** raccoon

还押 **huányā** be on remand

欢迎 **huānyíng** welcome ◊ reception; 受欢迎 **shòu huānyíng** be popular; go down well

患有 **huànyǒu** be suffering from

花盆 **huāpén** flowerpot

花瓶 **huāpíng** vase
花钱 **huāqián** spend
华侨 **Huáqiáo** overseas Chinese
划清界线 **huàqīng jièxiàn** delimit
花圈 **huāquān** wreath
花色俱全 **huāsè jùquán** assortment
花色牌 **huāsè pái** suit (*in cards*)
花商 **huāshāng** florist
花哨 **huāshao** flashy, gaudy
化身 **huàshēn** embodiment
花生 **huāshēng** peanut
华盛顿 **Huáshèngdùn** Washington
花生酱 **huāshēng jiàng** peanut butter
华氏 **huáshì** Fahrenheit
化石 **huàshí** fossil
划时代 **huàshídài** epoch-making
花时间 **huā shíjiān** time-consuming
花束 **huāshù** bouquet
滑水 **huáshuǐ** waterskiing
划算 **huásuàn** pay off; be worthwhile ◊ cost-effective
花坛 **huātán** flowerbed
滑梯 **huátī** slide
话题 **huàtí** topic of conversation
划艇 **huátǐng** rowboat
话务员 **huàwù yuán** telephonist; switchboard operator
化纤 **huàxiān** synthetic fiber
划线标出 **huàxiàn biāochū** mark out
滑翔 **huáxiáng** glide
滑翔机 **huáxiáng jī** glider
滑翔运动 **huáxiáng yùndòng** gliding
滑翔者 **huáxiáng zhě** glider (*person*)
滑行 **huáxíng** glide; slide; coast; taxi (*of airplane*)
滑行运动 **huáxíng yùndòng** gliding; sliding; coasting; taxiing
滑雪 **huáxuě** ski ◊ skiing
化学 **huàxué** chemistry ◊ chemical
滑雪道 **huáxuě dào** ski run
化学家 **huàxué jiā** chemist
化学疗法 **huàxué liáofǎ** chemotherapy

化学战 **huàxué zhàn** chemical warfare
滑雪杖 **huáxuě zhàng** ski pole
滑雪者 **huáxuě zhě** skier
化学制品 **huàxué zhìpǐn** chemical
花样滑冰 **huāyàng huábīng** figure skating
化验室 **huàyàn shì** laboratory
华裔 **Huáyì** person of Chinese descent
花园 **huāyuán** garden
画展 **huàzhǎn** exhibition of paintings
花招 **huāzhāo** trick
化妆 **huàzhuāng** put on make-up
化妆品 **huàzhuāng pǐn** make-up; cosmetics
化装室 **huàzhuāng shì** dressing room
化妆晚会 **huàzhuāng wǎnhuì** fancy-dress party
划子 **huázi** rowboat
护板 **hùbǎn** shield
湖滨 **húbīn** shore, lakeside
胡茬子 **húcházi** stubble
胡扯 **húchě** rave
呼出 **hūchū** breathe; breathe out
护创膏 **hùchuàng gāo** sticking plaster
蝴蝶 **húdié** butterfly
蝴蝶结 **húdié jié** bow (*knot*)
忽动忽停 **hūdòng hūtíng** jerky
护发剂 **hùfà jì** conditioner
煳饭 **húfàn** burnt rice
胡蜂 **húfēng** wasp
护封 **hùfēng** jacket (*of book*)
呼喊 **hūhǎn** call
呼唤 **hūhuàn** call; bleep
互换 **hùhuàn** exchange
互惠 **hùhuì** bilateral; reciprocal
灰 **huī** ash; dust
挥 **huī** wave
回 **huí** return; go back
悔 **huǐ** regret
毁 **huǐ** damage
会 **huì** be able to; meet ◊ meeting; 你会说法语吗？*nǐ huì shuō Fǎyǔ ma?* can you speak French?; 我说过我会去 *wǒ shuōguò wǒ huì qù* I said that I could go; 会用

电脑 **huìyòng diànnǎo** computer literate

喙 **huì** beak; snout

汇 **huì** converge

绘 **huì** paint; draw

灰暗 **huī'àn** dark; somber

回报 **huíbào** return *favor, invitation*

汇报 **huìbào** report card

回避 **huíbì** evade; duck

会场 **huìchǎng** meeting place

回车健 **huīchē jiàn** return key COMPUT

灰尘 **huīchén** dust

回程 **huíchéng** return journey

回程飞机 **huíchéng fēijī** return flight

回答 **huídá** answer, reply

回荡 **huídàng** echo

回到 **huídào** return, get back

回电话 **huí diànhuà** call back; 他能给我回电话吗? **tā néng gěi wǒ huí diànhuà ma?** can he call me back?

挥动 **huīdòng** swing; wield, brandish

汇兑 **huìduì** transfer *money*

挥发 **huīfā** evaporate

回放 **huífàng** playback

会费 **huìfèi** membership fee

恢复 **huīfù** recover; restore; return; bring back; resume ◊ recovery; 他恢复得很好 **tā huīfù de hěnhǎo** he has made a good recovery

恢复元气 **huīfù yuánqì** recuperate

恢复知觉 **huīfù zhījué** regain consciousness

回顾 **huígù** look back ◊ retrospective

惠顾 **huìgù** custom, patronage

回归线 **huíguī xiàn** tropic

回国 **huíguó** go home (*to one's own country*)

回合 **huíhé** round (*in boxing*)

汇合 **huìhé** join

会合 **huìhé** meet; convene; link up

悔恨 **huǐhèn** regret

绘画 **huìhuà** paint ◊ painting; picture

毁坏 **huǐhuài** destroy; ruin, wreck; mangle

辉煌 **huīhuáng** brilliant; glorious

挥霍 **huīhuò** wasteful; extravagant; lavish ◊ squander

回家 **huíjiā** go home

会见 **huìjiàn** meeting

灰浆 **huījiāng** mortar

回教 **Huíjiào** Islam

灰烬 **huījìn** ash

回扣 **huíkòu** bribe, kickback

汇款单 **huìkuǎn dān** money order

回来 **huílái** come back

贿赂 **huìlù** bribe ◊ bribery

汇率 **huìlǜ** exchange rate

会面 **huìmiàn** meet

毁灭 **huǐmiè** wreck; obliterate

灰泥 **huīní** plaster

汇票 **huìpiào** bill of exchange

会签 **huìqiān** countersign

回球 **huíqiú** return (*in tennis*)

回去 **huíqù** go back, return

毁容 **huǐróng** disfigure

灰色 **huīsè** gray

灰色跑犬 **huīsè pǎoquǎn** grayhound

回声 **huíshēng** echo

挥手 **huīshǒu** wave

回收 **huíshōu** recycle ◊ recycling

会谈 **huìtán** have a conversation

回头 **huítóu** turn back

回头生意 **huítóu shēngyì** repeat business

绘图 **huìtú** drawing

绘图人 **huìtú rén** illustrator

绘图仪 **huìtú yí** plotter COMPUT

绘图员 **huìtú yuán** draftsman

挥舞 **huīwǔ** wave

污物 **huìwù** filth

会晤 **huìwù** meet with

回响 **huíxiǎng** reverberate

回想 **huíxiǎng** think back

诙谐 **huīxié** humorous

灰心 **huīxīn** discouraged; frustrated; frustrating ◊ frustratingly

回信 **huíxìn** reply, write back ◊ (letter of) reply

彗星 **huìxīng** comet

回形针 **huíxíngzhēn** paper clip

会演 **huìyǎn** festival

回忆 **huíyì** recollect ◊ recollection; 引起 X 的回忆 **yǐnqǐ X de huíyì** jog X's memory

会议 **huìyì** convention, conference; congress; meeting

回忆录 **huíyìlù** memoirs

会议室 **huìyì shì** board room; meeting room

会议中心 **huìyì zhōngxīn** convention center

徽章 **huīzhāng** button, badge, pin

绘制 **huìzhì** draw

回转 **huízhuǎn** turn around

回嘴 **huízuǐ** answer back

护甲 **hùjiǎ** armor

胡椒 **hújiāo** pepper

胡椒薄荷 **hújiāo bòhé** peppermint

胡椒粉 **hújiāofěn** (ground) pepper

呼叫机 **hūjiào jī** bleeper

呼救 **hūjiù** emergency call

户口 **hùkǒu** household registration

狐狸 **húli** fox

护理 **hùlǐ** nurse ◊ nursing

护林员 **hùlínyuán** forest ranger

护理人员 **hùlǐ rényuán** nursing staff

胡乱 **húluàn** carelessly; 胡乱摆弄 **húluàn bǎinòng** fiddle around with

忽略 **hūlüè** neglect ◊ overlook, ignore

胡萝卜 **húluóbo** carrot

呼噜声 **hūlushēng** grunt; purr

护目镜 **hùmùjìng** goggles

荤 **hūn** meat or fish

昏 **hūn** dark ◊ swoon

婚 **hūn** marriage ◊ marry

混 **hùn** mix

昏暗 **hūn'an** dark; dim; obscure; dingy

胡闹 **húnào** make trouble; fool around

混蛋 **húndàn** bastard; pig

昏倒 **hūndǎo** faint

混合 **hùnhé** mix; combine; mingle; blend

混合物 **hùnhéwù** mix; mixture

昏厥 **hūnjué** fit MED ◊ pass out

婚礼 **hūnlǐ** marriage; wedding

婚礼蛋糕 **hūnlǐ dàngāo** wedding cake

婚礼日 **hūnlǐrì** wedding day

混乱 **hùnluàn** chaos; muddle ◊ chaotic; turbulent; 我的思维一片混乱 **wǒde sīwei yípiàn hùnluàn** my mind is in a whirl

昏迷 **hūnmí** black out ◊ blackout; coma ◊ unconscious

混凝土 **hùnníngtǔ** concrete

糊弄 **hùnong** mess around

婚前 **hūnqián** premarital

婚纱 **hūnshā** wedding dress

浑身 **húnshēn** the entire body ◊ all over; 我浑身都疼 **wǒ húnshēn dōu téng** it hurts all over

馄饨 **húntun** won ton (type of dumpling)

婚外 **hūnwài** extramarital

混淆 **hùnxiáo** confuse ◊ confusion

混血儿 **hùnxuè'ér** half-caste

婚姻 **hūnyīn** marriage ◊ marital

婚姻顾问 **hūnyīn gùwèn** marriage counselor

婚约 **hūnyuē** engagement

浑浊 **húnzhuó** cloudy; muddy

或 **huò** or

活 **huó** live ◊ alive ◊ work; 你有活儿干了 **nǐ yǒu huór gànle** you'll have a job, it won't be easy

伙 **huǒ** partner; bunch (of people)

火 **huǒ** fire

货 **huò** stock; goods

祸 **huò** accident

获 **huò** achieve

火把 **huǒbǎ** torch

伙伴 **huǒbàn** buddy

货板 **huòbǎn** pallet

活板门 **huóbǎnmén** trapdoor

货币 **huòbì** currency ◊ monetary

货舱 **huòcāng** hold

火柴 **huǒchái** match

火柴盒 **huǒcháihé** matchbox

货车 **huòchē** truck; freight car

火车 **huǒchē** train;

火车头 **huǒchētóu** locomotive

货车厢 **huòchēxiāng** freight car

火车站 **huǒchē zhàn** train station

货船 **huòchuán** freighter

货到付款 huòdào fùkuǎn collect on delivery

获得 huòdé acquire, get; achieve; capture; 获得成功 huòdé chénggōng achieve success; make it

活动 huódòng activity; pastime; pursuit ◊ move ◊ mobile

活动扳手 huódòng bānshǒu monkey wrench

活动边 huódòngbiān flap (of table)

活动过度 huódòng guòdù hyperactive

活动家 huódòngjiā campaigner

活动住房 huódòng zhùfáng mobile home

火锅 huǒguō hot pot

火红 huǒhóng lurid; fiery

火花 huǒhuā spark

火化 huǒhuà cremate ◊ cremation

火化场 huǒhuà chǎng crematorium

火花塞 huǒhuāsāi spark plug

火鸡 huǒjī turkey

货价 huòjià cost (of goods)

火箭 huǒjiàn rocket

获奖 huòjiǎng prizewinning ◊ win a prize

获奖者 huòjiǎng zhě prizewinner

火警 huǒjǐng fire alarm

火炬 huǒjù torch

活力 huólì vigor; vitality; spirit

霍乱 huòluàn cholera

货品 huòpǐn merchandise

活泼 huópo animated; brisk; lively; sprightly; vivacious

活泼有力 huópo yǒulì frisky

获取 huòqǔ extract

活塞 huósāi piston

火山 huǒshān volcano

火山口 huǒshān kǒu crater

获胜 huòshèng win ◊ winning ◊ winner

祸首 huòshǒu instigator; culprit; ringleader

货摊 huòtān booth

火腿 huǒtuǐ ham

货物 huòwù goods; cargo, freight; consignment, shipment

获悉 huòxī discover

火星 huǒxīng spark

活性洗涤剂 huóxìng xǐdí jì biological detergent

或许 huòxǔ perhaps

火焰 huǒyàn flame

活页夹 huóyè jiá binder (for papers)

活跃 huóyuè active; effervescent; vivid

货运列车 huòyùn lièchē freight train

货运站 huòyùnzhàn freight depot

活着 huózhe alive; living ◊ live

或者 huòzhě or; alternatively; 或者 … 或者 huòzhě … huòzhě either … or

获知 huòzhī find out

虎皮鹦鹉 hǔpí yīngwǔ budgerigar

糊墙纸 húqiángzhǐ wallpaper

忽然 hūrán suddenly

呼声 hūshēng clamor

忽视 hūshì neglect; disregard

护士 hùshì nurse

胡刷 húshuā shaving brush

胡说 húshuō nonsense

胡说八道 húshuō bādào nonsense

胡同 hútòng alley, lane

户头 hùtóu account

糊涂 hútu confused; 令人糊涂 lìngrén hútú confusing

护卫 hùwèi escort

互为补充 hùwéi bǔchōng complementary

呼吸 hūxī breath; breathing ◊ breathe

互相 hùxiāng reciprocal; mutual ◊ mutually; each other; one another

互相传 hùxiāng chuán pass around

弧形 húxíng arched

呼吁 hūyù appeal

护照 hùzhào passport

护照检查处 hùzhào jiǎncháchù passport control

互撞 hùzhuàng collision

胡子 húzi beard; mustache; whiskers; sideburns

胡子楂 húzi chá bristles

J

击 jī attack; strike; knock ◊ blow
鸡 jī chicken
基 jī base; foundation
机 jī machine; airplane; opportunity
奇 jī odd *number*
即 jí namely; promptly
吉 jí lucky; auspicious
集 jí collect ◊ episode
及 jí and ◊ reach
极 jí extreme ◊ extremely
级 jí level; grade; 我们是同级的 **wǒmen shì tóngjí de** we were in the same year
急 jí impatient; in a hurry; urgent
脊 jí ridge
几 jǐ some; a few; several; how many?; 几百美元 **jǐbǎi měiyuán** a few hundred dollars; 几张票 **jǐzhāng piào** a few tickets
系 jì fasten; tie; buckle
迹 jì mark; trace
计 jì calculate; count
技 jì skill
妓 jì prostitute
寄 jì send; mail
季 jì season
既 jì already ◊ since
记 jì remember; 记笔记 **jì bǐjì** take notes; 记不得 **jìbudé** I don't remember; 记不住 **jìbuzhù** I can't remember
忌 jì envy
纪 jì record
继 jì continue
系 jì button up; tie up
既 … 又 … **jì … yòu …** both … and …
加 jiā add ◊ plus
夹 jiā clip ◊ squeeze
家 jiā home; family; 在家 **zài jiā** at home
痂 jiā scab
佳 jiā very good; fine; beautiful
颊 jiá cheek

假 jiǎ false, fake; bogus; 假钞票 **jiǎchāopiào** counterfeit bill
甲 jiǎ first; armor; nail; A; *unspecified person or thing in lists etc*
架 jià shelf; rack; frame
价 jià price
假 jià vacation
驾 jià drive
加班 jiābān work overtime
甲板 jiǎbǎn deck
假扮 jiǎbàn impersonate
夹板夹 jiábǎn jiá splint
加倍 jiābèi double
加标点 jiā biāodiǎn punctuate
加冰 jiābīng iced
夹层 jiácéng compartment
家常闲话 jiācháng xiánhuà chitchat; gossip
甲虫 jiǎchóng beetle
家畜 jiāchù domestic animal
假定 jiǎdìng assume
加法 jiāfǎ addition MATH
假发 jiǎfà wig
价格 jiàgé price; cost
价格战 jiàgézhàn price war
加工 jiāgōng process; embellish
加固 jiāgù fasten; secure
加号 jiāhào plus sign
家伙 jiāhuo guy, fellow
嘉奖 jiājiǎng praise
佳节 jiājié celebration; festival
嫁接 jiàjiē graft BOT
夹紧 jiájǐn clamp
家具 jiājù furniture; 一件家具 **yíjiàn jiājù** a piece of furniture; 一套家具 **yítào jiājù** suite
加剧 jiājù intensify
家具罩 jiājù zhào dust cover
家具装饰材料 jiājù zhuāngshì cáiliào upholstery
茄克 jiākè jacket; coat
架空 jiàkōng overhead
加快 jiākuài accelerate, speed up
加宽 jiākuān widen

假面具 **jiǎ miànjù** disguise

价目表 **jiàmùbiǎo** tariff

煎 **jiān** shallow fry

尖 **jiān** tip, point ◊ pointed; sharp; acute

肩 **jiān** shoulder

监 **jiān** prison ◊ supervise

坚 **jiān** solid; firm

艰 **jiān** difficult

奸 **jiān** traitor; adultery ◊ wicked, evil; cunning

剪 **jiǎn** cut; clip; 把头发剪了 **bǎ tóufa jiǎn le** get one's hair cut

减 **jiǎn** reduce, take away, subtract ◊ minus

简 **jiǎn** uncomplicated, straightforward, simple

检 **jiǎn** inspect, check

捡 **jiǎn** collect, pick up

键 **jiàn** key

见 **jiàn** see; meet

溅 **jiàn** splash; splatter

剑 **jiàn** sword

腱 **jiàn** tendon

渐 **jiàn** gradually

舰 **jiàn** warship

箭 **jiàn** arrow

件 **jiàn** *measure word for items, matters, clothing, furniture;* 三件行李 **sānjiàn xíngli** three pieces of baggage; 一件 **yíjiàn** an article, an item; 一件短上衣 **yíjiàn duǎnshàngyī** a jacket

建 **jiàn** build; put up

健 **jiàn** healthy

加拿大 **Jiānádà** Canada ◊ Canadian

肩膀 **jiānbǎng** shoulder

简报 **jiǎnbào** briefing; clipping

简便机场 **jiǎnbiàn jīchǎng** landing strip

鉴别 **jiànbié** identify; differentiate

兼并 **jiānbìng** take over ◊ takeover

剑柄 **jiànbǐng** hilt

兼并投标 **jiānbìng tóubiāo** takeover bid

剪裁 **jiǎncái** cut to size; cut out

剪草钳 **jiǎncǎo qián** clippers

检测 **jiàncè** detect ◊ detection

检查 **jiǎnchá** check; examine; inspect ◊ examination; inspection;

检查…的拼写 **jiǎnchá … de pīnxiě** do a spellcheck on …

检察 **jiǎnchá** prosecute

检察官 **jiǎncháguān** prosecuting attorney

减产 **jiǎnchǎn** wind down production

检查员 **jiǎncháyuán** inspector

简称 **jiǎnchēng** abbreviation

建成 **jiànchéng** construct; be up; be built

坚持 **jiānchí** maintain; insist; hold; adhere; stand by, stick to ◊ insistent; 坚持自己的立场 **jiānchí zìjǐ de lìchǎng** stand one's ground; assert oneself

坚持不懈 **jiānchí búxiè** persistence, perseverance

剪出 **jiǎnchū** cut out

肩带 **jiāndài** shoulder strap; sash

煎蛋 **jiāndàn** fried egg

简单 **jiǎndān** simple; straightforward; humble ◊ briefly; simply ◊ simplicity

煎蛋卷 **jiān dànjuǎn** omelet

剪刀 **jiǎndāo** scissors

剪掉 **jiǎndiào** cut off

间谍 **jiàndié** spy

间谍活动 **jiàndié huódòng** espionage

坚定 **jiāndìng** firm; determined; confirmed; stalwart, staunch ◊ be firm, put one's foot down

鉴定 **jiàndìng** survey; assess

鉴定人 **jiàndìng rén** surveyor

监督 **jiāndū** supervise; monitor

尖端 **jiānduān** point (*of knife etc*)

简短 **jiǎnduǎn** brief

尖端产品 **jiānduān chǎnpǐn** top-quality product

舰队 **jiànduì** fleet

简而言之 **jiǎn ér yánzhī** in short

减肥 **jiǎnféi** slim, diet; lose weight

减肥食品 **jiǎnféi shípǐn** diet

姜 **jiāng** ginger (*spice*)

将 **jiāng** take; will; 将东西装入 **jiāng dōngxi zhuāngrù** pack; 将头发分开 **jiāng tóufa fēnkāi** part one's hair; 将…归档 **jiāng … guīdàng** file away; 他将去旅行 **tā jiāng qù lǚxíng** he's going to travel around

僵 **jiāng** stiff

缰 **jiāng** rein

桨 **jiāng** paddle; oar

讲 **jiāng** speak; talk; tell; 讲电话 **jiāng diànhuà** be on the telephone

奖 **jiǎng** award; prize

降 **jiàng** lower; sink

酱 **jiàng** paste; sauce

奖杯 **jiǎngbēi** trophy

讲道 **jiǎngdào** sermon

讲道德 **jiǎngdàodé** moral

降低 **jiàngdī** decline; die down; lower; reduce; 使降低 **shǐ jiàngdī** bring down

降低标价 **jiàngdī biāojià** mark down

降低等级 **jiàngdī děngjí** downgrade

间隔 **jiàngé** interval; distance

浆果 **jiāngguǒ** berry

糨糊 **jiànghú** paste

讲话 **jiǎnghuà** speak; deliver a speech

姜黄色 **jiānghuángsè** red; ginger

讲价 **jiǎngjià** haggle; bargain

降价 **jiàngjià** get cheaper, drop in price; drop (its) prices

讲解 **jiǎngjiě** explain

蒋介石 **Jiǎng Jièshí** Chiang Kai-shek

将近 **jiāngjìn** almost

奖金 **jiǎngjīn** bonus

将就 **jiāngjiù** make do with

讲究 **jiǎngjiu** fussy, particular ◊ be particular about

讲究细节 **jiǎngjiu xìjié** finicky

僵局 **jiāngjú** deadlock, impasse; stalemate

将军 **jiāngjūn** general ◊ check (in chess)

讲课 **jiǎngkè** give a lecture

将来 **jiānglái** in the future; 不远的将来 **bùyuǎnde jiānglái** in the near future

将来时 **jiāngláishí** future tense

讲理 **jiǎnglǐ** reason with ◊ reasonable

奖励 **jiǎnglì** award; reward

降临 **jiànglín** onset ◊ strike

降落 **jiàngluò** land

降落伞 **jiàngluòsǎn** parachute

奖品 **jiǎngpǐn** prize

奖赏 **jiǎngshǎng** prize

缰绳 **jiāngsheng** lead, leash; rein

讲师 **jiǎngshī** lecturer

讲实际 **jiǎng shíjì** hardheaded

讲述 **jiǎngshù** tell

将死 **jiāngsǐ** checkmate

讲台 **jiǎngtái** rostrum

坚固 **jiāngù** strong, solid; resistant; robust

兼顾 **jiāngù** combine; do both ... and ...; 兼顾 X 和 Y **jiāngù X hé Y** combine X with Y

见怪 **jiànguài** take badly; mind; take offense

监管人 **jiānguǎn rén** prison guard

坚果 **jiānguǒ** nut

坚果钳 **jiānguǒ qián** nutcrackers

坚果味儿 **jiānguǒ wèir** nutty *taste*

降温 **jiàngwēn** drop in temperature

讲习班 **jiǎngxíbān** workshop, seminar

奖学金 **jiǎngxuéjīn** scholarship

讲演 **jiǎngyǎn** lecture

讲演厅 **jiǎngyǎn tīng** lecture hall

将要 **jiāngyào** about to

僵硬 **jiāngyìng** stiff

酱油 **jiàngyóu** soy sauce

疆域 **jiāngyù** territory

降雨量 **jiàngyǔ liàng** rainfall

奖章 **jiǎngzhāng** medal

奖章获得者 **jiǎngzhang huòdé zhě** medalist

降职 **jiàngzhí** downgrade

讲座 **jiǎngzuò** course; lecture

减号 **jiǎnhào** minus sign

简化 **jiǎnhuà** simplify

减缓 **jiǎnhuǎn** drop; ease off; slacken off

监护人 **jiānhùrén** guardian

剪辑 **jiǎnjí** clip; cutting; editing ◊ edit ◊

减价 **jiǎnjià** reduce the price; 减价二十美元 **jiǎnjià èrshí měiyuán** knock $20 off

肩胛骨 **jiānjiǎgǔ** shoulder blade

渐渐 **jiànjiàn** gradually

尖叫 **jiānjiào** scream, shriek; yelp

建交 **jiànjiāo** establish diplomatic

relations

尖叫声 **jiānjiàoshēng** scream, screech

剪接 **jiǎnjiē** edit

简洁 **jiǎnjié** concise; lean

简介 **jiǎnjiè** blurb

间接 **jiànjiē** indirect ◊ indirectly

监禁 **jiānjìn** imprison; confine ◊ imprisonment; confinement

坚决 **jiānjué** determined, resolute; decided; strong; 坚决要求 *jiānjué yāoqiú* insist on

键卡 **jiànkǎ** keycard

健康 **jiànkāng** fit; healthy ◊ fitness; health; well-being, welfare ◊ be well

健康保险 **jiànkāng bǎoxiǎn** health insurance

健康检查 **jiànkāng jiǎnchá** checkup

健康食品 **jiànkāng shípǐn** health food

健康食品店 **jiànkāng shípǐndiàn** health food store

健康证书 **jiànkāng zhèngshū** medical certificate

尖刻 **jiānkè** cutting; bitter; harsh

艰苦 **jiānkǔ** difficult; strenuous

尖利 **jiānlì** sharp; piercing

建立 **jiànlì** establish, set up, found

建立桥梁 **jiànlì qiáoliáng** bridge *gap*

尖利声 **jiānlìshēng** screech

简陋 **jiǎnlòu** primitive, crude; humble

溅落 **jiànluò** splash down

减慢 **jiǎnmàn** slow down

健美锻炼 **jiànměi duànliàn** bodybuilding

见面 **jiànmiàn** meet

简明 **jiǎnmíng** concise

艰难 **jiānnán** difficult ◊ difficulty; hardship

艰难行走 **jiānnán xíngzǒu** plod

键盘 **jiànpán** keyboard

剪票 **jiǎnpiào** punch a ticket

简朴 **jiǎnpǔ** austere

柬埔寨 **Jiǎnpǔzhài** Cambodia ◊ Cambodian

拣起 **jiǎnqǐ** pick up

坚强 **jiānqiáng** strong; tough;

forceful

剪切 **jiǎnqiē** cut

减轻 **jiǎnqīng** alleviate; relieve; lighten; ease; soften; 减轻的情节 *jiǎnqīngde qíngjié* mitigating circumstances

减去 **jiǎnqù** minus ◊ subtract

尖儿 **jiānr** ace (*in cards*)

坚韧 **jiānrèn** tough; tenacious

键入 **jiànrù** key in, enter COMPUT

尖锐 **jiānruì** incisive; penetrating; pointed; sharp; shrill

尖锐刺耳 **jiānruì cì'ěr** strident

尖锐而深刻 **jiānruì ér shēnkè** searching

减弱 **jiǎnruò** die down; subside; moderate; shrink; wane ◊ muted

减色 **jiǎnsè** detract from

减少 **jiǎnshǎo** reduce; cut down; decline; dwindle ◊ reduction; 使减少 *shǐ jiǎnshǎo* diminish; deaden

建设 **jiànshè** build; construct; develop ◊ construction; development

健身 **jiànshēn** keep fit

尖声说出 **jiānshēng shuōchū** shriek

健身俱乐部 **jiànshēn jùlèbù** health club

健身中心 **jiànshēn zhōngxīn** fitness center

建设性 **jiànshè xìng** constructive

坚实 **jiānshí** solid

监视 **jiānshì** oversee; watch

见识 **jiànshí** experience; common sense

监视器 **jiānshìqì** monitor COMPUT

减速 **jiǎnsù** decelerate, slow down

尖酸刻薄 **jiānsuān kèbó** sour

尖塔 **jiāntǎ** spire, steeple

健谈 **jiàntán** talkative, chatty

剪贴板 **jiǎntiē bǎn** clipboard COMPUT

剪贴簿 **jiǎntiēbù** scrapbook

监听 **jiāntīng** listen to; listen in on; tap; bug

坚挺 **jiāntǐng** strong *currency*

简体字 **jiǎntǐzì** simplified characters

箭头 **jiàntóu** arrow; arrowhead

健忘 **jiànwàng** forgetful;

scatterbrained

奸污 **jiānwū** rape

见习 **jiànxí** become familiar with one's work; train

间隙 **jiànxì** gap

尖笑 **jiānxiào** smirk

尖啸 **jiānxiào** wail

减小 **jiǎnxiǎo** taper

见效 **jiànxiào** effective

尖啸声 **jiānxiàoshēng** wail

间歇 **jiànxiē** interval; lull

艰辛 **jiānxīn** suffering; hardship

减刑 **jiǎnxíng** commute a sentence

饯行 **jiànxíng** have a farewell meal

尖牙 **jiānyá** fang

检验 **jiǎnyàn** test

简要 **jiǎnyào** succinct

检疫 **jiǎnyì** quarantine

建议 **jiànyì** suggest, propose ◊ suggestion, proposition; 一项建议 **yíxiàng jiànyì** a piece of advice; a proposal

坚硬 **jiānyìng** rigid; hard

监狱 **jiānyù** prison, jail; penitentiary

鉴于 **jiànyú** in view of

检阅 **jiǎnyuè** review *troops*

建造 **jiànzào** build, construct ◊ building, construction (*activity*); 在建造中 **zài jiànzào zhōng** under construction

见证人 **jiànzhèng rén** witness

减震器 **jiǎnzhènqì** shock absorber

减震装置 **jiǎnzhèn zhuāngzhì** suspension

兼职 **jiānzhí** moonlight

简直 **jiǎnzhí** simply; utterly; 简直是最好的 **jiǎnzhí shì zuìhǎode** it is simply the best; 简直了 **jiǎnzhí le!** amazing!

剪纸 **jiǎnzhǐ** paper cut

建筑 **jiànzhù** building; construction; architecture

健壮 **jiànzhuàng** robust

建筑工地 **jiànzhù gōngdì** construction site

建筑工人 **jiànzhù gōngrén** construction worker

建筑公司 **jiànzhù gōngsī** construction company

建筑区 **jiànzhù qū** built-up area

建筑师 **jiànzhù shī** architect

建筑物 **jiànzhùwù** structure

建筑学 **jiànzhù xué** architecture

建筑业 **jiànzhù yè** construction industry

尖子 **jiānzi** top

剪子 **jiǎnzi** scissors

胶 **jiāo** glue

教 **jiāo** teach

礁 **jiāo** reef

浇 **jiāo** pour; water

交 **jiāo** hand over; cross; 把 X 交给 Y **bǎ X jiāogěi Y** send X to Y; 交朋友 **jiāo péngyǒu** make friends; 与 X 交朋友 **yǔ X jiāo péngyǒu** make friends with X

郊 **jiāo** suburbs

焦 **jiāo** burnt

嚼 **jiáo** chew

脚 **jiǎo** foot; bottom

角 **jiǎo** corner; horn; jiao (*Chinese money*)

搅 **jiǎo** stir

叫 **jiào** call; be called; summon; ask; draw, lead; 叫 X 帮忙 **jiào X bāngmáng** enlist the help of X; 叫 X 进去 **jià X jìnqù** send in X

较 **jiào** relatively

教 **jiào** teach ◊ religion

轿 **jiào** palanquin, sedan chair

校 **jiào** check; proofread

骄傲 **jiāo'ào** proud

骄傲自大 **jiāo'ào zìdà** arrogant

搅拌 **jiǎobàn** stir; whisk

搅拌器 **jiǎobànqì** mixer

脚背 **jiǎobèi** instep

脚本 **jiǎoběn** script

教鞭 **jiàobiān** pointer

胶布 **jiāobù** adhesive tape

脚步 **jiǎobù** footstep

叫菜 **jiàocài** order *food*

窖藏 **jiàocáng** hoard

交叉 **jiāochā** cross, intersect

交叉道 **jiāochādào** interchange

交叉路口 **jiāochā lùkǒu** junction

交叉双腿 **jiāochā shuāngtuǐ** cross one's legs

轿车 **jiàochē** car

交出 **jiāochū** give in, hand in, surrender

搅打 **jiǎodǎ** whip

胶带 **jiāodài** adhesive tape

搅蛋器 **jiǎodànqì** egg whisk

教导 **jiàodǎo** civilize; educate; instruct ◊ instruction

脚灯 **jiǎodēng** footlights

焦点 **jiāodiǎn** focus; 在焦点上 **zài jiāodiǎn shang** be in focus

脚底板 **jiǎodǐ bǎn** sole

搅动 **jiǎodòng** stir; move

角度 **jiǎodù** angle

交锋 **jiāofēng** cross swords; fight

焦干 **jiāogān** parched; very dry

娇惯 **jiāoguàn** spoil (indulge)

叫喊 **jiàohǎn** shout, yell

搅和 **jiǎohe** blend in

胶合板 **jiāohébǎn** plywood

搅和机 **jiǎohéjī** blender

脚后跟 **jiǎohòugēn** heel

狡猾 **jiǎohuá** crafty; cunning; devious; sly

交换 **jiāohuàn** exchange, swap; barter; trade; 交换意见 **jiāohuàn yìjiàn** confer

教皇 **jiàohuáng** pope

教诲 **jiàohuì** explain; instruct ◊ explanation; instruction

交货 **jiāohuò** deliver goods

搅和 **jiǎohuo** mix

交货付款 **jiāohuò fùkuǎn** collect on delivery

交互式 **jiāohùshì** interactive

焦急 **jiāojí** anxious ◊ anxiety; 焦急等待 **jiāojí děngdài** be anxious for

交际 **jiāojì** communication; contact

交界 **jiāojiè** border (on)

铰接车 **jiǎojiēchē** semi trailer

绞尽脑汁 **jiǎojìn nǎozhī** rack one's brains

焦距 **jiāojù** focal length

教具 **jiàojù** teaching aid

胶卷 **jiāojuǎn** film (for camera)

教科书 **jiàokē shū** textbook

交口称赞 **jiāokǒu chēngzàn** rave review

教练 **jiàoliàn** coach

较量 **jiàoliàng** compete; compare

教练员 **jiàoliàn yuán** trainer

交流 **jiāoliú** exchange; flow

交流电 **jiāoliúdiàn** alternating current

交流量 **jiāoliú liàng** traffic

角楼 **jiǎolóu** turret

焦虑 **jiāolǜ** agitation

焦虑不安 **jiāolǜ bù'ān** agitated

脚轮 **jiǎolún** caster

角落 **jiǎoluò** corner

角膜 **jiǎomó** cornea

酵母 **jiàomǔ** yeast

胶囊 **jiāonáng** capsule (of medicine)

娇嫩 **jiāonèn** tender; sensitive

教派 **jiàopài** denomination REL

交配 **jiāopèi** mate

脚蹼 **jiǎopǔ** flipper

娇气 **jiāoqì** squeamish; fragile

娇气包 **jiāoqìbāo** wimp

角球 **jiǎoqiú** corner (kick)

郊区 **jiāoqū** suburbs; outskirts ◊ suburban

教区牧师 **jiàoqū mùshī** vicar

教区牧师住所 **jiàoqū mùshī zhùsuǒ** vicarage

绞肉机 **jiǎoròujī** meat grinder

矫揉造作 **jiǎoróu zàozuò** affected

娇生惯养 **jiāoshēng guànyǎng** coddle

礁石 **jiāoshí** reef

教师 **jiàoshī** teacher

教室 **jiàoshì** classroom

教师培训 **jiàoshī péixùn** teacher training

教授 **jiàoshòu** professor

脚手架 **jiǎoshǒujià** scaffolding

教授职位 **jiàoshòu zhíwèi** chair (at university)

教书 **jiāoshū** teach

浇水筒 **jiāoshuǐtǒng** watering can

教唆 **jiàosuō** instigate

脚踏车 **jiǎotàchē** bicycle

交谈 **jiāotán** talk, converse

焦炭 **jiāotàn** coke

教堂 **jiàotáng** church

教堂集会 **jiàotáng jíhuì** congregation

脚踏实地 **jiǎotà shídì** down-to-earth

交替 **jiāotì** alternate

教条 **jiàotiáo** doctrine; dogma

教条主义 **jiàotiáo zhǔyì** dogmatism ◊ dogmatic

交通 **jiāotōng** traffic

绞痛 **jiǎotòng** colic

交通标志 **jiāotōng biāozhì** traffic sign

交通部 **Jiāotōng Bù** Department of Transportation

交通岛 **jiāotōng dǎo** traffic island

交通堵塞 **jiāotōng dǔsè** traffic jam; gridlock

交通费用 **jiāotōng fèiyòng** travel expenses

交通工具 **jiāotōng gōngjù** means of transportation

交通警 **jiāotōng jǐng** traffic cop; traffic police

焦头烂额 **jiāotóulàn'é** stressed out

脚腕 **jiǎowàn** ankle

交往 **jiāowǎng** mingle; mix with; contact ◊ dealings; contract; association

交响乐 **jiāoxiǎngyuè** symphony

娇小 **jiāoxiǎo** petite

胶鞋 **jiāoxié** sneakers

矫形 **jiǎoxíng** orthopedic ◊ orthopedics

侥幸 **jiǎoxìng** lucky; 他侥幸得以逃生 **tā jiǎoxìng déyǐ táoshēng** he's lucky to be alive

叫醒 **jiàoxǐng** wake

绞刑架 **jiǎoxíngjià** gallows

矫形外科 **jiǎoxíng wàikē** orthopedics; orthopedic surgery

教学 **jiāoxué** teaching

教训 **jiàoxun** lesson; moral; 教训 X **jiàoxun X** teach X a lesson

教养 **jiàoyǎng** upbringing; manners; breeding ◊ bring up; train

校样 **jiàoyàng** proof (of book)

交易 **jiāoyì** deal; transaction ◊ transact

交易会 **jiāoyìhuì** trade fair

脚印 **jiǎoyìn** footprint

交易所 **jiāoyìsuǒ** exchange

郊游 **jiāoyóu** excursion

教育 **jiàoyù** education ◊ educational ◊ educate

教员 **jiàoyuán** teacher

教员室 **jiàoyuán shì** staffroom

教育学 **jiàoyùxué** (the study of) education

焦躁 **jiāozào** harassed

交战 **jiāozhàn** (military) engagement ◊ fight ◊ belligerent

矫正 **jiǎozhèng** correct; adjust

校正 **jiàozhèng** correct ◊ correction

脚指 **jiǎozhǐ** toe

浇铸 **jiāozhù** cast; mold

脚注 **jiǎozhù** footer; footnote

骄子 **jiāozǐ** very talented person; whizzkid

饺子 **jiǎozi** Chinese dumpling

叫做 **jiàozuò** be called

家谱 **jiāpǔ** family tree

假期 **jiàqī** vacation; leave

加强 **jiāqiáng** intensify; reinforce; strengthen

家禽 **jiāqín** poultry (birds)

家禽肉 **jiāqínròu** poultry (meat)

加燃料 **jiā ránliào** refuel

加热 **jiārè** heat up

家人 **jiārén** family members

加热器 **jiārè qì** stove

假日 **jiàrì** (public) holiday

加入 **jiārù** add; join; 加入国籍 **jiārù guójí** become naturalized; 加入交易 **jiārù jiāoyì** come in on a deal

加上 **jiāshàng** add on ◊ plus; 加上一层 **jiāshàng yìcéng** cover, coat

假设 **jiǎshè** suppose ◊ assuming ◊ hypothesis ◊ hypothetical

加深 **jiāshēn** deepen

夹生 **jiāshēng** half-done

假释 **jiǎshì** parole; 获得假释 **huòdé jiǎshì** be on parole

驾驶 **jiàshǐ** drive; steer; fly; sail ◊ driving; driver; 左/右座驾驶 **zuǒ/yòu zuò jiàshǐ** left-/right-hand drive

驾驶船 **jiàshǐchuán** sail a boat

驾驶教练 **jiàshǐ jiàoliàn** driving instructor

驾驶机构 **jiàshǐ jīgòu** steering

驾驶室 **jiàshǐ shì** cab (of truck)

驾驶台 **jiàshǐ tái** bridge

驾驶学校 **jiàshǐ xuéxiào** driving school

驾驶学员 **jiàshǐ xuéyuán** beginner driver

驾驶员 **jiàshǐ yuán** driver

驾驶执照 jiàshǐ zhízhào driver's license

家属 jiāshǔ family members; household

加速 jiāsù accelerate; speed up ◊ acceleration

家庭 jiātíng family ◊ domestic

家庭妇女 jiātíng fùnǚ housewife

家庭录像 jiātíng lùxiàng home movie

家庭医生 jiātíng yīshēng family doctor

家庭主妇 jiātíng zhǔfù housewife

家庭作业 jiātíng zuòyè homework

家兔 jiātù rabbit

家务 jiāwù housework; chores

家务管理 jiāwù guǎnlǐ housekeeping

家务开消 jiāwù kāixiāo housekeeping (money)

家乡 jiāxiāng home; home town

假想 jiǎxiǎng imaginary, make-believe

加楔儿 jiāxiēr shove in

假惺惺 jiǎxīngxīng hypocritical ◊ hypocritically

假牙 jiǎyá dentures, false teeth

家用电脑 jiāyòng diànnǎo home computer

家用器械 jiāyòng qìxiè (household) appliance

加油 jiāyóu fill up; refuel; oil; come on!; go!

加油站 jiāyóuzhàn gas station

家喻户晓 jiāyù hùxiǎo household name

加载 jiāzài upload COMPUT

家长 jiāzhǎng head of household; parent

家长主义 jiāzhǎng zhǔyì paternalism

家长作风 jiāzhǎng zuòfēng paternalistic

假正经 jiǎzhèngjing prude ◊ prudish

假肢 jiǎzhī artificial limb

价值 jiàzhí value; worth; 价值上升/下降 jiàzhí shàngshēng / xiàjiàng rise / fall in value

jiàzhí kǎoshì driving test 驾驶考试

加重 jiāzhòng become heavier; deepen

假装 jiǎzhuāng pretend; (play)act; make believe; put on ◊ masquerade

甲状腺 jiǎzhuàngxiàn thyroid gland

假珠宝 jiǎ zhūbǎo costume jewelry

夹竹桃 jiāzhútáo oleander

夹子 jiāzi clip; clamp; clasp

架子 jiàzi stand; frame; shelf; airs

家族 jiāzú clan

鸡巴 jībā ∨ prick

击败 jībài beat, defeat; overpower

基本 jīběn basic, fundamental; main; essential ◊ foundation ◊ basically

急奔 jí bēn dash; race

基本利率 jīběn lìlǜ base rate

基本上 jīběnshang basically; essentially

基本原理 jīběn yuánlǐ basic principles

基本知识 jīběn zhīshí basic knowledge

级别 jíbié rank; level

级别条纹 jíbié tiáowén stripe (indicating rank)

疾病 jíbìng disease; illness; sickness

既不…也不… jìbù … yěbù … neither … nor …

机场 jīchǎng airport; airfield

继承 jìchéng inherit; 剥夺继承权 bōduó jìchéng quán disinherit

计程表 jìchéngbiǎo meter; taxi meter

计程车 jìchéngchē taxi

计程车司机 jìchéngchē sījī taxi driver

集成电路 jíchéng diànlù integrated circuit

继承人 jìchéngrén heir

急冲 jíchōng dash

基础 jīchǔ basis; foundation; 以…为基础 yǐ … wéi jīchǔ base on; be based on

挤出 jǐchū squeeze out

基础工作 jīchǔ gōngzuò

groundwork

基础结构 **jīchǔ jiégòu** infrastructure

击打 **jīdǎ** beat; hit; punch

即达 **jídá** incoming

极大 **jídà** enormous

鸡蛋 **jīdàn** egg

鸡蛋杯 **jīdànbēi** eggcup

击倒 **jīdǎo** knock out; flatten ◊ knockout

记得 **jìde** remember

基地 **jīdì** base

激动 **jīdòng** excite; inflame ◊ feverish; impassioned

机动 **jīdòng** flexible

机动车 **jīdòngchē** motor vehicle

激动人心 **jīdòng rénxīn** stirring

基督 **Jīdū** Christ ◊ Christian

嫉妒 **jídù** jealousy ◊ be jealous; envy; be envious

极度 **jídù** extreme; utmost ◊ extremely

忌妒 **jìdu** envy ◊ envious

季度 **jìdù** quarter ◊ quarterly

极端 **jíduān** drastic; extreme; unbelievable ◊ exceedingly

极端主义者 **jíduānzhǔyì zhě** extremist

基督教 **Jīdūjiào** Christianity ◊ Christian

基督徒 **Jīdū tú** Christian

饥饿 **jī'è** starvation; hunger ◊ hungry

街 **jiē** street

接 **jiē** contact; join; call for, collect; pick up; fetch; catch

结 **jiē** bear *fruit*

揭 **jiē** take off *lid*

阶 **jiē** steps; stairs

结 **jié** knot

节 **jié** festival; knot; verse ◊ *measure word for sections*, *lengths*; 一节竹子 **yìjié zhúzi** a length of bamboo

解 **jiě** untie

姐 **jiě** older sister

借 **jiè** borrow; lend ◊ loan; 借个手，行吗？ **jiè gè shǒu, xíng ma?** can you lend me a hand?; 借给 X Y **jiègěi X Y** lend X to Y

戒 **jiè** cut out; give up

界 **jiè** border; limit

结巴 **jiēba** stammer; stutter

接班人 **jiēbān rén** successor

戒备 **jièbèi** vigilance ◊ vigilant

结冰 **jiébīng** freeze; ice up

阶层 **jiēcéng** (social) class

截查 **jiéchá** intercept

结肠 **jiécháng** bowels; colon

劫车 **jiéchē** hijack a car

劫车者 **jiéchē zhě** carjacker

劫持 **jiéchí** hijack; abduct

接触 **jiēchù** contact ◊ touch

杰出 **jiéchū** brilliant, outstanding; eminent

解除 **jiěchú** take away

戒除 **jièchú** remove; get rid off; kick *habit*; 解除武装 **jiěchú wǔzhuāng** disarm ◊ disarmament

揭穿 **jiēchuān** expose ◊ exposure

介词 **jiècí** preposition

结存 **jiécún** balance FIN

解答 **jiědá** solution; answer; reply

接待 **jiēdài** greet; receive

接待处 **jiēdài chù** reception (area)

接待员 **jiēdài yuán** receptionist; desk clerk

街道 **jiēdào** street

街灯 **jiēdēng** streetlight

解冻 **jiědòng** defrost; thaw

戒毒 **jièdú** withdrawal (*from drugs*)

街段 **jiēduàn** block

阶段 **jiēduàn** phase, stage

截短 **jiéduǎn** cut short, curtail

解毒药 **jiědúyào** antidote

揭发 **jiēfā** uncover; discover

解放 **jiěfàng** liberate ◊ emancipated ◊ liberation; emancipation; the 1949 Communist victory in China

借方 **jièfāng** debit ◊ debtor

解放军 **Jiěfàngjūn** People's Liberation Army, PLA; PLA soldier

姐夫 **jiěfu** brother-in-law (*elder sister's husband*)

结构 **jiégòu** structure

解雇 **jiěgù** dismiss, sack; lay off ◊ dismissal

接管 **jiēguǎn** take charge, take over

结果 **jiéguǒ** result, outcome ◊ end

结核病 **jiéhé bìng** tuberculosis, TB

接合器 **jiēhé qì** adapter

结婚 **jiéhūn** marry; get married; 跟 X 结婚 **gēn X jiéhūn** get married to X

结婚公告 **jiéhūn gōnggào** banns

结婚戒指 **jiéhūn jièzhǐ** wedding ring

结婚礼服 **jiéhūn lǐfú** wedding gown

结婚证书 **jiéhūn zhèngshū** marriage certificate

结婚周年 **jiéhūn zhōunián** wedding anniversary

劫机 **jiéjī** hijack a plane

阶级 **jiējí** (social) class; 阶级斗争 **jiējí dòuzhēng** class warfare

截击 **jiéjī** intercept *missile*

节俭 **jiéjiǎn** economic ◊ economically

街角 **jiējiǎo** street corner

结交 **jiéjiāo** associate with

姐姐 **jiějie** older sister

结结巴巴 **jiējie bābā** broken *English etc*

接近 **jiējìn** near ◊ access ◊ verge on

竭尽 **jiéjìn** exhaust; use up; 竭尽所能 **jiéjìn suǒnéng** do one's utmost

洁净 **jiéjìng** clean; pure

捷径 **jiéjìng** short cut

解救 **jiějiù** extricate

戒酒 **jièjiǔ** give up alcohol; be on the wagon

劫机者 **jiéjī zhě** hijacker

结局 **jiéjú** outcome; ending

借据 **jièjù** IOU

解决 **jiějué** solve; settle *dispute*; sort out *problem* ◊ fix; settlement

解开 **jiěkāi** undo; loosen; unfasten; untie; 解开纽扣 **jiěkāi niǔkòu** unbutton

捷克 **Jiékè** Czech

捷克共和国 **Jiékè Gònghéguó** Czech Republic

借口 **jièkǒu** excuse; pretext

结块 **jiékuài** clot (*of blood*)

解缆 **jiělǎn** cast off

接连不断 **jiēlián búduàn** successive; 接连五天 **jiēlián wǔ tiān** 5 days in a row

接力赛 **jiēlì sài** relay (race)

节流阀 **jiéliú fá** throttle (*on motorbike etc*)

揭露 **jiēlù** expose; reveal

节录 **jiélù** excerpt

结论 **jiélùn** conclusion

睫毛 **jiémáo** eyelash

睫毛膏 **jiémáogāo** mascara

姐妹 **jiěmèi** sisters; 同父异母姐妹 **tóngfù yìmǔ jiěmèi,** 同母异父姐妹 **tóngmǔ yìfù jiěmèi** stepsister

界面 **jièmiàn** interface

解密码 **jiě mìmǎ** decipher

芥末 **jièmò** mustard

结膜炎 **jiémó yán** conjunctivitis

揭幕 **jiēmù** unveil

节目 **jiémù** program; show; 今晚有什么节目？ **jīnwǎn yǒu shénme jiémù?** what's on tonight?

节目表 **jiémù biǎo** listings magazine

节目单 **jiémùdān** program

接纳 **jiēnà** admit

节能 **jiénéng** save energy ◊ energy-saving

节拍 **jiépāi** rhythm; beat

解剖 **jiěpōu** dissect ◊ dissection; anatomy

揭起 **jiēqǐ** take up

截球 **jiéqiú** tackle SP

接球者 **jiēqiú zhě** receiver SP

接壤 **jiērǎng** border (on)

截然相反 **jiérán xiāngfǎn** contrasting; diametrically opposed

节日 **jiérì** festival; (public) holiday

吉尔吉斯 **Jíěrjísī** Kyrgyzstan ◊ Kirg(h)iz

介入 **jièrù** intervene ◊ intervention; 他不想介入 **tā bùxiǎng jièrù** he won't have anything to do with it

街上 **jiēshang** in the street

介绍 **jièshào** introduce ◊ introduction; profile; 我来介绍一下 … **wǒ lái jièshào yíxià …** may I introduce …?; 向 X 介绍 Y **xiàng X jièshào Y** brief X on Y

介绍信 **jièshào xìn** testimonial

节省 **jiéshěng** economize on;

save; stint on ◊ economy; saving ◊ economical

节省时间 **jiéshěng shíjiān** timesaving

结实 **jiēshi** sturdy; firm

解释 **jiěshì** explain; account for; interpret; rationalize ◊ explanation

接收 **jiēshōu** receive

接手 **jiēshǒu** take over ◊ catcher SP

接受 **jiēshòu** accept; take; receive; admit ◊ acceptance; 接受手术治疗 **jiēshòu shǒushù zhìliáo** undergo surgery; 我接受你的提议 **wǒ jiēshòu nǐde tíyì** I'll take you up on your offer; 接受 X 的意见 **jiēshòu X de yìjiàn** take X's advice

接收力 **jiēshōu lì** reception (*for TV etc*)

接收人 **jiēshōu rén** recipient

结束 **jiéshù** end, finish, conclude; put an end to

结算 **jiésuàn** balance the books; settle *bill*

结算单 **jiésuàn dān** (bank) statement

阶梯 **jiētī** step; stairs

接替 **jiētì** replace; relieve

解体 **jiětǐ** disintegrate

接通 **jiētōng** connect; put through

接通电源 **jiētōng diànyuán** plug in

解脱开 **jiětuō kāi** disentangle

结网 **jiéwǎng** spin *web*

结尾 **jiéwěi** conclusion, end

接吻 **jiēwěn** kiss

接下来 **jiēxiàlái** succeeding

界限 **jièxiàn** border; parameter

接线生 **jiēxiàn shēng** operator

戒严令 **jièyánlìng** martial law

解压缩 **jiě yāsuō** unzip COMPUT

介意 **jièyì** mind, object; object to; 我抽烟你介意吗? **wǒ chōuyān nǐ jièyì ma?** would you mind if I smoked?

解疑屏幕 **jiěyí píngmù** help screen

借用 **jièyòng** borrow ◊ on loan

节育 **jiéyù** birth control

节约 **jiéyuē** economize; save ◊

thrift ◊ thrifty; cost-conscious

解约 **jiěyuē** cancel a contract

节约行动 **jiéyuē xíngdòng** economy drive

结扎 **jiézā** sterilize

结账 **jiézhàng** checkout ◊ check out; settle an account; pay the bill

结账时间 **jiézhàng shíjiān** checkout time

接着 **jiēzhe** following

节肢 **jiézhī** amputate

节制 **jiézhì** moderation, restraint

戒指 **jièzhi** ring (*on finger*)

接种 **jiēzhòng** vaccinate; inoculate ◊ vaccination; inoculation; 接种 X 疫苗 **jiēzhòng X yìmiáo** be vaccinated against X

接种疫苗 **jiēzhòng yìmiáo** vaccinate

接住 **jiēzhù** catch

疖子 **jiēzi** boil

节奏 **jiézòu** rhythm; beat

杰作 **jiézuò** masterpiece

激发 **jīfā** arouse; work up

记分 **jìfēn** (keep the) score

讥讽 **jīfěng** sarcasm ◊ sarcastic

季风 **jìfēng** monsoon

季风雨季 **jìfēng yǔjì** monsoon season

记分员 **jìfēnyuán** scorer

继父 **jìfù** stepfather

挤干 **jǐgān** squeeze dry

及格 **jígé** pass (*in exam*)

几个 **jǐgè** a few, several; how many?

及格分 **jígéfēn** pass mark

技工 **jìgōng** mechanic; skilled worker

机构 **jīgòu** organization; institution; structure; mechanism

籍贯 **jíguàn** home; birthplace

激光 **jīguāng** laser

激光唱片 **jīguāng chàngpiān** compact disc

激光打印机 **jīguāng dǎyìn jī** laser printer

激光光束 **jīguāng guāngshù** laser beam

极好 **jí hǎo** fabulous, swell, marvelous

记号 **jìhao** mark, sign

集合 **jíhé** meet; assemble;

combine; pool ◊ set MATH

记恨 jìhèn bear a grudge

几何学 jǐhéxué geometric ◊ geometrical

几乎 jīhū almost

激化 jīhuà intensify; increase

计划 jìhuà plan; project; figure on; structure ◊ planning; program; project

计划表 jìhuàbiǎo schedule

极坏 jíhuài rotten

饥荒 jīhuāng famine

计划生育 jìhuà shēngyù family planning; birth control; one child policy

击毁 jīhuǐ destroy

机会 jīhuì opportunity, chance

集会 jíhuì meeting; assembly; rally; function

积极 jījí active; dynamic; positive; energetic

击剑 jījiàn fencing

即将 jíjiāng about to; on the brink of ◊ soon

即将来临 jíjiāng láilín upcoming

计件工作 jìjiàn gōngzuò piecework

寄件人 jìjiànrén sender

集结 jíjié mass

季节 jìjié season

积极分子 jījí fènzi activist; militant

唧唧叫 jīji jiào chirp

基金 jījīn fund

激进 jījìn radical

挤紧 jǐjǐn squeeze up

挤进 jǐjìn jam, squeeze

机警 jījǐng on the ball; alert

寂静 jìjìng quiet

基金会 jījīnhuì foundation

激进主义 jījìn zhǔyì radicalism

激进主义者 jījìn zhǔyì zhě radical

急救 jíjiù first aid

急救箱 jíjiùxiāng first-aid box, first-aid kit

积极性 jījíxìng initiative; dynamism; activity

积聚 jījù build-up ◊ build up, mount up

急剧 jíjù rapid; abrupt

即刻 jíkè immediate, instantaneous ◊ immediately, instantly; momentarily

疾苦 jíkǔ suffering

系牢 jìláo do up

积累 jīlěi accumulate; pile up

激励 jīlì boost; spur; stimulation; 激励 ... 前进 jīlì ... qiánjìn spur on

吉利 jílì fortunate; favorable; lucky

剂量 jìliàng dose

脊梁骨 jíliáng gǔ backbone; spine

计量器 jìliángqì gauge

激烈 jīliè intense; fierce; heated

机灵 jīling smart; sharp; nimble

急流 jíliú rapids; torrent

纪录 jìlù record; note ◊ minutes; log; 纪录保持者 jìlù bǎochí zhě record holder

纪律 jìlǜ discipline

击落 jīluò shoot down

纪录片 jìlù piān documentary

记录 X jìlù X keep track of X

挤满 jǐmǎn be full of

急忙 jímáng hurried; in a hurry

机密 jīmì classified; confidential; top secret

机敏 jīmǐn quickwitted

寂寞 jìmò lonely

计谋 jìmóu trick

继母 jìmǔ stepmother

金 jīn gold ◊ golden

津 jīn ford; ferry crossing

巾 jīn cloth

今 jīn now; today; the present

筋 jīn tendon

斤 jīn jin (500 grams)

紧 jǐn tight; tense; taut

锦 jǐn brocade

仅 jǐn only

尽 jǐn furthest; 尽里面 jǐn lǐmiàn back; very back; furthest back

尽 jìn exhaust; try one's best ◊ exhausted; finished ◊ to the limit

近 jìn close, near

进 jìn go in; enter; 请进! qǐngjìn! come in!

禁 jìn prohibit

劲 jìn strength; energy

浸 jìn soak

缉拿 jīná manhunt

挤奶 jǐnǎi milk

金边儿股票 **jīnbiānr gǔpiào** gilts

锦标旗 **jǐnbiāoqí** pennant

锦标赛 **jǐnbiāo sài** championship; tournament

进步 **jìnbù** advance; progress ◊ progressive

禁不住 **jīnbúzhù** can't help; 我禁不住笑了 *wǒ jīnbúzhù xiàole* I couldn't help laughing

进餐时间 **jìncān shíjiān** mealtime

进程 **jìnchéng** proceedings; course; process

紧凑 **jǐncòu** tight *timing*; compact; terse

禁得住 **jīndezhù** withstand

禁地 **jìndì** restricted area

筋斗 **jīndǒu** somersault

金额 **jīn'é** amount

技能 **jìnéng** technique; skills; knowhow

金发 **jīnfà** blond hair

谨防 **jǐnfáng** be wary of

劲风 **jìnfēng** high wind

茎 **jīng** stem

鲸 **jīng** whale

京 **jīng** capital city

惊 **jīng** alarm; surprise

精 **jīng** essence; spirit; seed; semen ◊ refined; excellent

晶 **jīng** crystal

经 **jīng** warp; longitude ◊ experience

井 **jǐng** well (*for water*)

警 **jǐng** warn ◊ alarm; police

景 **jǐng** landscape; scenery

颈 **jǐng** neck; throat

净 **jìng** clean; net

境 **jìng** border

镜 **jìng** mirror

静 **jìng** quiet

敬 **jìng** respect ◊ respectful

径 **jìng** path; diameter

紧盖器 **jǐn'gàiqi** fastener

金刚石 **jīngāngshí** diamond

警报 **jǐngbào** alarm; alert

胫部 **jìngbù** shin

精彩 **jīngcǎi** wonderful

警察 **jǐngchá** police; police oficer

警察国家 **jǐngchá guójiā** police state

警察纠捕队 **jǐngchá jiūbǔ duì** vice squad

警察局 **jǐngchájú** police station, station house

经常 **jīngcháng** often ◊ frequent; habitual

惊呆 **jīngdāi** bowl over, amaze

精打细算 **jīngdǎ xìsuàn** be on a budget

境地 **jìngdì** situation; position

静电 **jìngdiàn** static electricity

经典作品 **jīngdiǎn zuòpǐn** classic

经度 **jīngdù** longitude

精读课 **jīngdúkè** intensive course

惊愕 **jīng'è** stupefied

警方 **jǐngfāng** police

警告 **jǐnggào** warn ◊ warning

胫骨 **jìnggǔ** shin; shinbone

警官 **jǐngguān** police officer

警棍 **jǐnggùn** nightstick

经过 **jīngguò** pass by; pass ◊ past; by; via; through

精华 **jīnghuá** essence; goodness

净化 **jìnghuà** purify

惊慌 **jīnghuāng** alarmed ◊ get alarmed

惊惶失措 **jīnghuāng shīcuò** panic-stricken

静火山 **jìng huǒshān** dormant volcano

经济 **jīngjì** economy ◊ economic; economical

竞技 **jìngjì** athletics; sports

精简 **jīngjiǎn** abridge

惊叫 **jīngjiào** exclaim

经济舱 **jīngjìcāng** economy class

警戒 **jǐngjiè** warn

警戒线 **jǐngjiè xiàn** cordon

经济紧缩 **jīngjì jǐnsuō** austerity

井井有条 **jǐngjǐng yǒutiáo** in good trim; in order

经济气候 **jīngjì qìhòu** economic climate

经济情况 **jīngjì qíngkuàng** economics; financial circumstances

经纪人 **jīngjì rén** broker; middleman

经济上 **jīngjì shang** economically; in financial terms

经济特区 **jīngjì tèqū** special economic zone, SEZ

经济学 **jīngjìxué** economics

(*subject*)

经济学家 **jīngjìxuéjiā** economist

京剧 **Jīngjù** Peking Opera

警觉 **jǐngjué** alert

惊恐 **jīngkǒng** consternation; scare

净空高度 **jìngkōng gāodù** headroom

镜框 **jìngkuàng** frame (*of picture, glasses*)

境况 **jìngkuàng** circumstances

经理 **jīnglǐ** manager

经历 **jīnglì** experience; background ◊ go through

精力 **jīnglì** energy; drive

敬礼 **jìnglǐ** salute

精力充沛 **jīnglì chōngpèi** dynamic; vigorous; inexhaustible ◊ nervous energy

痉挛 **jìngluán** cramp

静脉 **jìngmài** vein

静脉内 **jìngmàinèi** intravenous

静脉曲张 **jìngmài qūzhāng** varicose vein

精美 **jīngměi** exquisite, beautiful

精密 **jīngmì** precise; accurate; sophisticated, complex

精明 **jīngmíng** clever; ingenious; calculating; shrewd ◊ ingenuity

进攻 **jìngōng** advance MIL; charge

惊跑 **jīngpǎo** stampede

敬佩 **jìngpèi** respect

精辟 **jīngpì** profound

惊奇 **jīngqí** amazement, surprise; wonder ◊ be amazed

精确 **jīngquè** precise; rigorous ◊ precisely ◊ precision

井然 **jǐngrán** neat; proper

惊人 **jīngrén** amazing, mind-boggling, breathtaking ◊ phenomenally

竞赛 **jìngsài** race; racing ◊ run

径赛 **jìngsài** track event; athletics meeting

景色 **jǐngsè** scenery

精神 **jīngshen** vigor; energy ◊ lively; vigorous; smart

精神 **jīngshén** soul; spirit; mind; essence ◊ mental; 精神好 / 坏 **jīngshén hǎo** / **huài** be in good / poor spirits

精神崩溃 **jīngshén bēngkuì** nervous breakdown

精神变态者 **jīngshén biàntài zhě** psychopath

精神病 **jīngshénbìng** mental illness ◊ psychiatric

精神病学 **jīngshénbìngxué** psychiatry

精神病院 **jīngshénbìngyuàn** mental hospital

精神错乱 **jīngshén cuòluàn** demented

精神分裂 **jīngshén fēnliè** schizophrenic

精神分裂症 **jīngshén fēnlièzhèng** schizophrenia

精神分裂症患者 **jīngshén fēnlièzhèng huàn zhě** schizophrenic

精神分析 **jīngshén fēnxī** psychoanalysis

精神分析学家 **jīngshén fēnxīxuéjiā** psychoanalyst

精神恍惚 **jīngshén huǎnghū** dreamy

精神科医生 **jīngshénkē yīshēng** psychiatrist

精神虐待 **jīngshén nüèdài** mental cruelty

精神失常 **jīngshén shīcháng** madness ◊ mentally disturbed

紧身套衫 **jǐngshēn tàoshān** sweater

经受 **jīngshòu** undergo; suffer

景泰蓝 **jǐngtàilán** cloisonné

惊叹 **jīngtàn** exclaim; admire; marvel at; 令人惊叹 **lìngrén jīngtàn** amazing; shattering

晶体 **jīngtǐ** crystal

警惕 **jǐngtì** alert ◊ watchful ◊ warily

惊跳 **jīngtiào** jump

晶体管 **jīngtǐguǎn** transistor

晶体管收音机 **jīngtǐguǎn shōuyīnjī** transistor radio

精通 **jīngtōng** be expert at; master ◊ impeccable; proficient ◊ mastery

精通世故 **jīngtōng shìgù** sophisticated

镜头 **jìngtóu** shot; scene;

photograph; lens

镜头盖 jìngtóu gài lens cover

尽管 jǐnguǎn although; despite, in spite of

尽管如此 jǐnguǎn rúcǐ all the same, nevertheless

警卫 jǐngwèi guard

紧握 jǐnwò clasp

精细 jīngxì meticulous; refined

惊吓 jīngxià fright ◊ frighten, scare; startle

惊险电影 jīngxiǎn diànyǐng thriller (*movie*)

惊险小说 jīngxiǎn xiǎoshuō thriller (*novel*)

经销 jīngxiāo distribute ◊ distribution

经销商 jīngxiāo shāng distributor

精心 jīngxīn carefully; nicely

精心制作 jīngxīn zhìzuò elaborate

精选 jīngxuǎn choice

竞选 jìngxuǎn run (for election)

竞选活动 jìngxuǎn huódòng election campaign

竞选人 jìngxuǎn rén contender

竞选总统 jìngxuǎn zǒngtǒng run for President

惊讶 jīngyà astonishment ◊ be astonished

经验 jīngyàn experience

敬仰 jìngyǎng admire; worship

精液 jīngyè sperm; semen

惊异 jīngyì stunned, amazed

敬意 jìngyì respect; deference; 表示敬意 biǎoshì jìngyì deferential; 令人惊异 lìngrén jīngyì stunning

精英 jīngyīng elite

经营 jīngyíng manage; operate; run ◊ running; trade; operations ◊ managerial

经营顾问 jīngyíng gùwèn management consultant

经由 jīngyóu by way of

鲸鱼 jīngyú whale

竞争 jìngzhēng compete; contend for ◊ competition; contest; rivalry

竞争对手 jìngzhēng duìshǒu competitor

竞争力很强 jìngzhēnglì

很强 hěnqiáng competitive

竞争者 jìngzhēng zhě contender; rival; contestant

精致 jīngzhì delicate; fancy; exquisite ◊ delicacy

径直 jìngzhí straight

晶质玻璃 jīngzhì bōlí crystal

警钟 jǐngzhōng alarm

净重 jìngzhòng net weight

精子 jīngzǐ sperm

镜子 jìngzi mirror; glasses, specs

精子库 jīngzǐ kù sperm bank

今后 jīnhòu in future

进化 jìnhuà evolve ◊ evolution

金婚纪念 jīnhūn jìniàn golden wedding anniversary

纪念 jìniàn commemorate, mark ◊ memorial; 作为对 X 的纪念 zuòwéi duì X de jìniàn in memory of X

纪念碑 jìniànbēi memorial; monument

纪念品 jìniàn pǐn souvenir; memento

紧急 jǐnjí urgent; imperative ◊ urgency

晋级 jìnjí promotion

近郊 jìnjiāo environs

紧急出口 jǐnjí chūkǒu emergency exit

紧接着 jǐnjiēzhe in the wake of

仅仅 jǐnjǐn only; merely; barely; solely

紧急情况 jǐnjí qíngkuàng emergency

近几天 jìnjǐtiān the past few days

禁酒 jìnjiǔ dry

紧急着落 jǐnjí zháoluò emergency landing

紧急状态 jǐnjí zhuàngtài state of emergency

尽可能 jìn kěnéng as far as possible; 尽可能最好 … jìn kěnéng zuìhǎo … the best possible …

进口 jìnkǒu import

进口商 jìnkǒushāng importer

金库 Jīnkù National Treasury

尽快 jǐnkuài as soon as possible

近况如何？ jìnkuàng rúhé? how are things?

近来 jìnlái recent ◊ recently

尽力 jìnlì endeavor

尽量 jĭnliàng as well as one can

尽量利用 jĭnliàng lìyòng make the most of

尽力而为 jìnlì érwéi do one's best

尽力解决 jìnlì jiějué grapple with

紧邻 jĭnlín the immediate neighborhood

禁令 jìnlìng ban

浸满水 jìnmǎnshuĭ waterlogged

今年 jīnnián this year

金牌 jīnpái gold medal

浸泡 jìnpào soak; immerse ◊ infusion

筋疲力尽 jīnpí lìjìn exhaust; drain ◊ exhausted; shattered

紧迫 jĭnpò extremely urgent

谨启 jĭnqĭ yours sincerely

金枪鱼 jīnqiāng yú tuna

近亲繁殖 jìnqīn fánzhí inbreeding

进去 jìnqu go in

禁区 jìnqū no-go area

进取心 jìnqŭ xīn enterprise, initiative

金融 jīnróng finance ◊ financial

金融家 jīnróng jiā financier

金融市场 jīnróng shìchǎng money market

进入 jìnrù enter; get in ◊ entrance; entry

金色 jīnsè golden

紧身 jĭnshēn tight-fitting; skin-tight

谨慎 jĭnshèn careful, cautious; discreet ◊ caution; tact, delicacy

晋升 jìnshēng promote

紧身套衫 jĭnshēn tàoshān sweater; sweatshirt

紧身胸衣 jĭnshēn xiōngyī bodice

紧身衣 jĭnshēn yī body suit; leotard

近视 jìnshi shortsighted ◊ myopia

浸湿 jìnshī soak

禁食 jìnshí fast (not eating)

近视眼 jìnshiyǎn shortsighted ◊ myopia

金首饰商 jīnshŏushìshāng goldsmith

金属 jīnshǔ metal

金属器具 jīnshǔ qìjù hardware

金属丝 jīnshǔsī wire

金属网 jīnshǔwǎng wire netting

近似 jìnsì almost; roughly ◊ border on

金丝雀 jīnsīquè canary

紧缩开支 jĭnsuō kāizhī economize

今天 jīntiān today; 今天几号? jīntiān jĭhào? what's the date today?; 今天上午 jīntiān shàngwǔ this morning; 今天晚上 jīntiān wǎnshang this evening; 今天下午 jīntiān xiàwǔ this afternoon; 今天星期几? jīntiān xīngqī jĭ? what day is it today?; 今天早晨 jīntiān zǎochén this morning

津贴 jīntiē subsidy; allowance

尽头 jìntóu end

劲头 jìntóu enthusiasm

浸透 jìntòu soak (through), saturate

进退两难 jìntuì liǎngnán dilemma

激怒 jīnù incense, infuriate; provoke ◊ enraged

妓女 jìnǚ prostitute

继女 jìnǚ stepdaughter

今晚 jīnwǎn tonight

紧握 jĭnwò clutch; grip

进行 jìnxíng carry out; execute; progress, move on; 在进行中 zài jìnxíngzhōng be under way

进修 jìnxiū continue one's education

紧要 jĭnyào critical

紧要关头 jĭnyào guāntóu tension

襟翼 jīnyì flap

进一步 jìnyíbù a step further; further

金银丝 jīnyín sī tinsel

禁用 jìnyòng heavy-duty; long-lasting; hard-wearing

金鱼 jīnyú goldfish

禁运 jìnyùn embargo

尽早 jĭnzǎo as early as possible

进站 jìn zhàn pull in, arrive

进展 jìnzhǎn proceed, progress

紧张 jĭnzhāng nervous; tense; uptight; stressed ◊ get nervous;

get flustered; tense up ◊ nervousness; tension; 别紧张 **bié jǐnzhāng** take it easy!

紧张感 **jǐnzhānggǎn** suspense

紧张慌乱 **jǐnzhāng huāngluàn** be in a flap

禁止 **jìnzhǐ** ban, forbid, prohibit ◊ ban, prohibition; 禁止 X 做 Y **jìnzhǐ X zuò Y** forbid X to do Y

禁止入内 **jìnzhǐ rùnèi** no admittance; off limits

禁止停车 **jìnzhǐ tíngchē** no parking

禁止吸烟 **jìnzhǐ xīyān** no smoking

窘况 **jiǒngkuàng** predicament

窘迫 **jiǒngpò** poverty-stricken; in a predicament

麂皮 **jǐpí** chamois (leather)

鸡皮疙瘩 **jīpí gēda** gooseflesh; 他使我浑身起鸡皮疙瘩 **tā shǐwǒ húnshēn qǐ jīpí gēda** he gives me the creeps

祭品 **jìpǐn** sacrifice

击破 **jīpò** strike down; fell

急迫 **jípò** urgent

吉普车 **jípǔchē** jeep

吉普赛人 **jípǔsài rén** gipsy

激起 **jīqǐ** prompt; cause; excite; work up

机器 **jīqì** machine; machinery

极其 **jíqí** extremely

记起 **jìqǐ** recall; remember

机枪 **jīqiāng** machine gun

技巧 **jìqiǎo** skill; knack

急切 **jíqiè** eager

激情 **jīqíng** passion

机器人 **jīqìrén** robot

击球 **jīqiú** bat; strike *ball* ◊ batting

击球员 **jīqiú yuán** batter

寄去 **jìqù** send in, mail in

极权主义 **jíquán zhǔyì** totalitarian

既然 **jìrán** since

既然这样 **jìrán zhèyàng** in that case

急人 **jírén** frightening; worrying

继任 **jìrèn** succeed (*to office etc*)

继任人 **jìrènrén** successor

鸡肉 **jīròu** chicken (*meat*)

肌肉 **jīròu** muscle

肌肉发达 **jīròu fādá** muscular

机身 **jīshēn** fuselage

寄生虫 **jìshēngchóng** parasite; sponger, freeloader

及时 **jíshí** prompt; timely ◊ promptly; in time

即时 **jíshí** immediately

即使 **jíshí** even if

疾驶 **jíshí** speed

集市 **jíshì** market

几时 **jǐshí** when; what time

集市广场 **jíshì guǎngchǎng** market place

计时钟 **jìshízhōng** time clock (*in factory*)

棘手 **jíshǒu** tricky

奇数 **jīshù** odd number

技术 **jìshù** skill; technique; technology ◊ technological

计数 **jìshù** count

技术娴熟 **jìshù xiánshú** workmanlike

技术性 **jìshù xìng** technical

技术员 **jìshùyuán** technician

祭祀 **jìsì** sacrifice

激素 **jīsù** steroids

计算 **jìsuàn** calculate; count; budget for; allow

计算出 **jìsuànchù** figure out

计算机 **jìsuànjī** computer; calculator

计算结果 **jìsuàn jiēguǒ** calculation

计算机科学 **jìsuànjī kēxué** computer science

计算机科学家 **jìsuànjī kēxué jiā** computer scientist

计算器 **jìsuàn qì** calculator

寄宿生 **jìsù shēng** boarder (*at school*)

急速行驶 **jísù xíngshǐ** zoom, race

寄宿学校 **jìsù xuéxiào** boarding school

吉他 **jítā** guitar

祭坛 **jìtán** altar

集体 **jítǐ** collective

几天 **jǐtiān** a few days, a couple of days

集体精神 **jítǐ jīngshén** team spirit

集体抛售 **jítǐ pāoshòu** raid FIN

集体协定 **jítǐ xiédìng** collective

bargaining

集团 **jítuán** group; bloc ◊ corporate

鸡腿 **jītuǐ** drumstick (*chicken leg*)

击退 **jītuì** repel

阄 jiū: 抓阄儿 **zhuājiūr** draw lots

酒 **jiǔ** alcoholic drink; liquor

九 **jiǔ** nine

久 **jiǔ** a long time

舅 **jiù** uncle (*mother's brother*); brother-in-law (*wife's brother*)

旧 **jiù** old; obsolete; former; threadbare

就 **jiù** right; directly; just; only; regarding; 就我而言 **jiù wǒ ér yán** as far as I'm concerned

救 **jiù** save; rescue

酒吧 **jiǔbā** bar

旧病复发 **jiùbìng fùfā** relapse ◊ have a relapse

韭菜 **jiǔcài** Chinese chives

纠察 **jiūchá** picket

纠察队 **jiūcháduì** picket

纠缠 **jiūchán** badger, pester

纠察线 **jiūcháxiàn** picket line

旧城区 **jiùchéngqū** inner city

臼齿 **jiùchǐ** molar

韭葱 **jiǔcōng** leek

酒店 **jiǔdiàn** bar; wineshop; restaurant

酒店伙计 **jiǔdiàn huǒjì** bartender

纠纷 **jiūfēn** dispute; quarrel

纠葛 **jiūgé** dispute; involvement

酒鬼 **jiǔguǐ** drunk; alcoholic

酒后开车 **jiǔhòu kāichē** drunk driving

救护车 **jiùhùchē** ambulance

旧货 **jiùhuò** second-hand goods

救急 **jiùjí** urgent

究竟 **jiūjìng** actually; at the end of the day; 你究竟在干什么? **nǐ jiūjìng zài gàn shénme?** what the hell are you doing?

酒精 **jiǔjīng** alcohol

酒精饮料 **jiǔjīng yǐnliào** liquor

舅舅 **jiùjiu** uncle (*mother's brother*)

救济院 **jiùjìyuàn** hospice

旧历 **jiùlì** Chinese lunar calendar

九龙 **Jiǔlóng** Kowloon

救命 **jiùmìng** save s.o.'s life ◊ help!

就寝 **jiùqǐn** go to bed

救球 **jiùqiú** save SP

救生 **jiùshēng** life-saving

救生圈 **jiùshēng quān** life belt

救生艇 **jiùshēng tǐng** lifeboat

救生衣 **jiùshēng yī** life jacket

救生员 **jiùshēng yuán** lifeguard

九十 **jiǔshí** ninety

就是 **jiùshi** exactly!

就事论事 **jiùshìlùnshì** *prov* call a spade a spade

就是说 **jiùshìshuō** that is to say

救世主 **jiùshìzhǔ** savior

灸术 **jiǔshù** moxibustion

九死一生 **jiǔsǐyìshēng** have a narrow escape

酒窝 **jiǔwō** dimple

酒席 **jiǔxí** banquet

就医 **jiùyī** go to the doctor

久远 **jiǔyuǎn** remote *ancestor*

九月 **jiǔyuè** September

纠正 **jiūzhèng** correct

纠正错误 **jiūzhèng cuòwù** put things right

就职 **jiùzhí** inauguration ◊ inaugural

就职仪式 **jiùzhí yíshì** induction ceremony

酒钻 **jiǔzuàn** corkscrew

就座 **jiùzuò** take a seat

就座勿动 **jiùzuò wùdòng** please remain seated

极为 **jíwéi** extremely

即位 **jíwèi** succeed ◊ succession

鸡尾酒 **jīwěijiǔ** cocktail

极微小 **jíwēixiǎo** microscopic

极限 **jíxiàn** limit; frontier

吉祥 **jíxiáng** lucky

挤向 **jǐxiàng** crowd

迹象 **jìxiàng** mark; pointer, sign

集线器 **jíxiànqì** hub COMPUT

讥笑 **jīxiào** scoff; laugh at

极小 **jíxiǎo** tiny; remote *possibility*

机械 **jīxiè** machinery; mechanism ◊ mechanical ◊ mechanically

机械化 **jīxièhuà** mechanize

机械装置 **jīxiè zhuāngzhì** mechanism

畸形 **jīxíng** freak; monstrosity ◊ misshapen; monstrous

疾行 **jíxíng** race; run

即兴 **jíxìng** improvise

急性 jíxìng acute *illness*

记性 jìxìng memory

鸡心领 jīxīn lǐng V-neck

继兄弟 jìxiōngdì stepbrother

积蓄 jīxù save up; keep ◊ savings

急需 jíxū be in urgent need of

继续 jìxù continue; go on; keep on; carry on; conduct

积雪 jíxuě snowy

积压 jīyā backlog

挤压 jǐyā press

鸡眼 jīyǎn corn (*on foot*)

给养 jǐyǎng provisions

技艺 jìyì skill; art; craft; workmanship

记忆 jìyì remember ◊ memory; recollection

记忆力 jìyìlì memory; 记忆力好／坏 **jìyìlì hǎo**／**huài** have a good／bad memory

基因 jīyīn gene

集邮 jíyóu stamp collecting

极右主义 jíyòu zhǔyì right-wing extremism

给予 jǐyǔ render; provide; give *answer*

基于 jīyú because of; on the basis of

机遇 jīyù chance; stroke of luck

积怨 jīyuàn rancor

纪元 jìyuán era, epoch

妓院 jìyuàn brothel

给予优先 jǐyǔ yōuxiān prioritize

记载 jìzǎi record

及早 jízǎo early; premature

急躁 jízào on edge

激增 jīzēng sudden increase; surge; explosion (*in population*)

机长 jīzhǎng captain (*of aircraft*)

记账 jìzhàng bookkeeping ◊ do the books; charge

记账人 jìzhàng rén bookkeeper

记者 jìzhě reporter; journalist

急诊医生 jízhěn yīshēng emergency doctor

记者招待会 jìzhě zhāodàihuì press conference

机制 jīzhì machine

机智 jīzhì tact; wit ◊ witty; resourceful

机智幽默 jīzhì yōumò wit

集中 jízhōng assemble; collect; centralize; concentrate ◊ cluster; focus (*of attention*)

集中精力 jízhōng jīnglì concentrate

脊柱 jǐzhù spine; spinal column ◊ spinal

记住 jìzhù remember; memorize; 记住锁门 **jìzhù suǒmén** remember to lock the door

系住 jìzhù tie up

集装箱 jízhuāng xiāng container

集装箱船 jízhuāng xiāng chuán container ship

急转弯 jízhuǎnwān hairpin curve

脊椎 jǐzhuī vertebra; 有脊椎 **yǒu jǐzhuī** vertebrate

基准 jīzhǔn benchmark

髻子 jìzi bun (*in hair*)

继子 jìzǐ stepson

机组 jīzǔ air crew

基座 jīzuò pedestal

拘 jū restrict

驹 jū foal

居 jū live; reside; occupy ◊ house; residence; 居要位 **jū yàowèi** have priority

局 jú department; office; game; set; situation

举 jǔ raise; hold up; elect ◊ act; deed

剧 jù drama; play; theater

锯 jù saw

聚 jù assemble; get together

巨 jù giant, huge

具 jù tool, utensil

句 jù sentence

据 jù according to; 据我所知 **jù wǒ suǒzhī** as far as I know, to the best of my knowledge

捐 juān donate; contribute

卷 juǎn roll; reel; coil ◊ curly, frizzy; 把 X 卷成球 **bǎ X juǎn chéngqiú** roll X into a ball

卷 juàn volume

圈 juàn pen; enclosure

卷尺 juǎnchǐ tape measure

卷发 juǎnfà curly hair

卷发卷 juǎnfà juǎn roller; tongs (*for hair*)

绢纺 juànfǎng silk spinning

卷角 juǎnjiǎo dog-eared

捐款 juānkuǎn donation;

contribution

捐款人 **juānkuǎn rén** contributor; donor

卷盘 **juǎnpán** spool

卷起来 **juǎn qǐlái** roll up; coil up

卷入 **juǎnrù** involvement; 卷入 X **juǎnrù X** get involved with X

捐献 **juānxiàn** contribute; donate ◊ contribution; donation

捐献者 **juānxiàn zhě** donor

卷心菜 **juǎnxīn cài** cabbage

捐赠 **juānzèng** donate; contribute

举办 **jǔbàn** organize; hold

剧本 **jùběn** (stage) play

聚苯乙烯 **jùběnyǐxī** polystyrene

剧变 **jùbiàn** upheaval

局部 **júbù** partial ◊ partially

剧场 **jùchǎng** theater

局促不安 **júcù bù'ān** feel ill at ease; squirm

举措 **jǔcuò** move

巨大 **jùdà** enormous, immense, vast; astronomical

锯掉 **jùdiào** saw off

蕨 **jué** fern

觉 **jué** sense; feel ◊ feeling

角 **jué** role

决 **jué** decide

掘 **jué** dig

绝 **jué** cut off ◊ absolute

绝版 **juébǎn** out of print

决不 **juébù** on no account, under no circumstances

决策者 **juécè zhě** mastermind; decision maker

觉察 **juéchá** perceive

觉得 **juéde** feel; think; 我觉得很冷 **wǒ juéde hěnlěng** I feel cold; 你觉得怎么样？ **nǐ juéde zěnmeyàng?** what do you make of it?

决定 **juédìng** decide, make up one's mind ◊ decision; resolution; 你来决定 **nǐ lái juédìng** you decide, it's up to you

决定性 **juédìng xìng** decisive, conclusive ◊ decidedly

决断力 **juéduànlì** judgment

绝对 **juéduì** absolute; total ◊ definitely, absolutely; 绝对不行！ **juéduì bùxíng!** no way!,

certainly not!

倔强 **juéjiàng** disobedient

绝交 **juéjiāo** sever relations; 我与 X 绝交 **wǒ yǔ X juéjiāo** I'm through with X

绝经期 **juéjīngqī** menopause

绝密 **juémì** top secret

绝妙 **juémiào** sensational, tremendous; magic

掘起 **juéqǐ** dig up

诀窍 **juéqiào** knack

决赛 **juésài** decider; final SP; 参加决赛者 **cānjiā juésài zhě** finalist

角色 **juésè** part, role

绝食 **juéshí** hunger strike

爵士音乐 **juéshì yīnyuè** jazz

爵士乐队 **juéshì yuèduì** jazz band

决算 **juésuàn** balance (sheet)

掘土机 **juétǔjī** excavator

绝望 **juéwàng** despair

决心 **juéxīn** determination, resolution

决选 **juéxuǎn** shortlist

决议 **juéyì** decision; resolution

绝缘 **juéyuán** insulation

绝缘材料 **juéyuán cáiliào** insulation

绝缘胶布 **juéyuán jiāobù** friction tape

绝种 **juézhǒng** extinct ◊ extinction

撅嘴 **juēzuǐ** pout

句法 **jùfǎ** syntax

飓风 **jùfēng** hurricane

拒服兵役者 **jù fú bīngyì zhě** conscientious objector

鞠躬 **jūgōng** bow

聚光灯 **jùguāng dēng** spotlight

句号 **jùhào** period, full stop

聚合 **jùhé** meet (of committee)

菊花 **júhuā** chrysanthemum

聚会 **jùhuì** gathering; get-together

聚集 **jùjí** assemble; gather; congregate

聚焦于 **jùjiāo yú** focus on

拘谨 **jūjǐn** stiff; uptight; reserved

拘禁 **jūjìn** lock up

狙击手 **jūjīshǒu** sniper

拒绝 **jùjué** refusal; denial; rejection ◊ refuse; deny; reject; 拒绝参加 **jùjué cānjiā** boycott; refuse to take part in

锯开 **jùkāi** saw

俱乐部 **jùlèbù** club

距离 **jùlí** distance ◊ apart

剧烈 **jùliè** fierce; energetic; 剧烈的头痛 **jùliè de tóutòng** splitting headache

拘留 **jūliú** detain; intern ◊ detention; 被拘留 **bèi jūliú** in custody

居留 **jūliú** stay; reside

居留证 **jūliúzhèng** residence permit

聚氯乙烯 **jùlǜyǐxī** PVC

局面 **júmiàn** situation

居民 **jūmín** inhabitant; resident

锯末 **jùmò** sawdust

军 **jūn** army

均 **jūn** same; equal ◊ all; both

君 **jūn** king; gentleman ◊ you *fml*

郡 **jùn** county; prefecture (*in old China*)

军备 **jūnbèi** armament

均等 **jūnděng** equal ◊ equality

军队 **jūnduì** army; the military; the services; troops

军阀 **jūnfá** warlord

军官 **jūnguān** officer MIL

均衡 **jūnhéng** balance; equalize (*pressure etc*)

均衡饮食 **jūnhéng yǐnshí** balanced diet

军火 **jūnhuǒ** ammunition

军舰 **jūnjiàn** warship

军警 **jūnjǐng** military police

峻岭 **jùnlǐng** high mountains

军旗 **jūnqí** colors MIL

军人 **jūnrén** serviceman; soldier

军事 **jūnshì** military

军事法庭 **jūnshì fǎtíng** court martial

军事学院 **jūnshì xuéyuàn** military academy

军事装备 **jūnshì zhuāngbèi** military installation

军衔 **jūnxián** rank

均匀 **jūnyún** even, regular ◊ evenly

君主 **jūnzhǔ** monarch

君子 **jūnzǐ** gentleman

举起 **jǔqǐ** lift; put up; 举起手来! **jǔqǐshǒulái!** hands up!

巨人 **jùrén** giant

沮丧 **jǔsàng** dejected; depressed; downcast; frustrated; 令人沮丧 **lìngrén jǔsàng** dismal

居士 **jūshì** hermit

居首位 **jū shǒuwèi** take the lead

拘束 **jūshù** awkward; constrained; unnatural; 别拘束 **bié jūshù** make yourself at home

据说 … **jùshuō** … it is said that …; they say …; be supposed to …; 据说他在香港 **jù shuō tā zài Xiānggǎng** he is reported to be in Hong Kong; 据说这首诗是 … 所作 **jùshuō zhèi shǒu shī shì … suǒzuò** the poem has been attributed to …

具体 **jùtǐ** concrete; specific

具体细致 **jùtǐ xìzhì** in minute detail

巨头 **jùtóu** tycoon

据为己有 **jùwéi jǐyǒu** pocket

据悉 … **jùxī** … it has emerged that …

局限 **júxiàn** limit; confine ◊ limitation

举行 **jǔxíng** stage; organize; hold

句型 **jùxíng** sentence pattern

举行罢工 **jǔxíng bàgōng** go on strike

聚乙烯 **jùyǐxī** polyethylene

具有 **jùyǒu** own; have; 具有想象力 **jùyǒu xiǎngxiànglì** imaginative

剧院 **jùyuàn** theater; opera house

剧增 **jùzēng** increase suddenly

举止 **jǔzhǐ** conduct, behavior

举止不当 **jǔzhǐbúdàng** misbehave

举止粗鲁 **jǔzhǐ cūlǔ** ill-mannered

聚酯纤维 **jùzhǐxiānwéi** polyester

举重 **jǔzhòng** weightlifting

举重运动员 **jǔzhòng yùndòngyuán** weightlifter

居住 **jūzhù** live

居住者 **jūzhù zhě** occupant

橘子 **júzi** mandarin orange

句子 **jùzi** sentence GRAM

锯子 **jùzi** saw

剧作家 **jùzuò jiā** dramatist, playwright

K

卡 **kǎ** card
喀嚓声 **kāchāshēng** snap, click
卡车 **kǎchē** truck
卡车司机 **kǎchē sījī** truck driver, teamster
咖啡 **kāfēi** coffee
咖啡店 **kāfēi diàn** coffee shop
咖啡馆 **kāfēiguǎn** café
咖啡壶 **kāfēi hú** coffee pot
咖啡机 **kāfēi jī** coffee maker
咖啡因 **kāfēiyīn** caffeine
开 **kāi** open; turn on; start; drive; boil; write *check* ◊ (*away*): 离开 *líkāi* leave; 走开 *zǒukāi* go away; 开户 *kāi hù* open a bank account
揩 **kāi** wipe
开本 **kāiběn** format
开采 **kāicǎi** mine; mine for
开叉 **kāichà** slit
开车 **kāichē** drive (a car)
开除 **kāichú** expel; discharge ◊ expulsion
开创 **kāichuàng** initiate ◊ initiation
开大 **kāidà** turn up *volume*
开刀 **kāidāo** operate; perform surgery
开灯 **kāidēng** turn the light on
开动 **kāidòng** work (*of machine*)
开端 **kāiduān** start, beginning
开发 **kāifā** develop
开放政策 **kāifàng zhèngcè** open-door policy
开发区 **kāifāqū** development area
开关 **kāiguān** switch
揩汗 **kāihàn** wipe away perspiration
开花 **kāihuā** bloom, blossom
开会 **kāihuì** hold a meeting; 他在开会 *tā zài kāihuì* he's in a meeting
开机 **kāijī** boot up
开奖 **kāijiǎng** draw; lottery result
开襟毛衣 **kāijīn máoyī** cardigan

开扣 **kāikòu** fly (*on pants*)
开阔 **kāikuò** extensive
开朗 **kāilǎng** open; clear; outgoing; cheerful
开门 **kāimén** open the door
开明 **kāimíng** enlighten ◊ progressive; enlightened
开幕 **kāimù** open; inaugurate; raise the curtain
开枪 **kāiqiāng** fire a gun
开球 **kāiqiú** kickoff ◊ kick off
开始 **kāishǐ** begin, start ◊ beginning ◊ initially
开始曲 **kāishǐqǔ** signature tune
开水 **kāishuǐ** boiled water
开庭 **kāitíng** sitting; hearing
开头 **kāitóu** start
开拓 **kāituò** pioneering; 开拓殖民地 *kāituò zhímíndì* colonize
开玩笑 **kāi wánxiào** joke; kid ◊ joking; 别开玩笑了! *bié kāi wánxiào le!* you can't be serious!, you must be joking!
开胃 **kāiwèi** appetizing
开胃酒 **kāiwèi jiǔ** aperitif
开胃品 **kāiwèi pǐn** appetizer
开小差 **kāi xiǎochāi** desert ◊ desertion
开心 **kāixīn** have a good time; 玩儿得很开心 *wánr de hěn kāixīn* it was great fun
凯旋 **kǎixuán** triumph
开演 **kāiyǎn** be on (*of program*)
开药方 **kāi yàofāng** prescribe
开业 **kāiyè** start a business
开账单 **kāi zhàngdān** bill, invoice
开着 **kāizhe** open
开支 **kāizhī** budget; expenditure; expenses
开走 **kāizǒu** drive
卡拉 OK **kǎlā OK** karaoke
卡路里 **kǎlùlǐ** calorie
刊 **kān** publication
砍 **kǎn** chop

看 **kàn** look at; see; watch; read; visit ◊ look, glance; 看电视 **kàn diànshì** watch television; 看天气吧 **kàn tiānqì ba** it depends on the weather; 我看是这样 **wǒ kàn shì zhèyàng** I suppose so; 我能看一下吗? **wǒ néng kàn yíxià ma?** can I have a look?

看病 **kànbìng** see a doctor

看不起 **kànbùqǐ** look down on, despise

刊出 **kānchū** publish

看穿 **kànchuān** see through

看待 **kàndài** view

砍刀 **kǎndāo** chopper

砍倒 **kǎndǎo** chop down

看得见 **kàndejiàn** be visible; show

砍掉 **kǎndiào** lop off

砍伐 **kǎnfá** fell *trees*

看法 **kànfǎ** view; belief; idea

康 **kāng** healthy

抗 **kàng** resist; fight

抗病毒程序 **kàng bìngdú chéngxù** antivirus program

康采恩 **kāngcǎi'ēn** group (of *companies*); concern

康复 **kāngfù** get well again; recuperate

抗菌 **kàngjūn** antiseptic

抗菌剂 **kàngjūnjì** antiseptic

抗菌素 **kàngjūnsù** antibiotic

慷慨 **kāngkǎi** generous; liberal; magnanimous

康乃馨 **kāngnǎixīn** carnation

抗热 **kàngrè** heatproof, heat-resistant

抗日战争 **Kàngrì Zhànzhēng** Anti-Japanese War

抗体 **kàngtǐ** antibody

看管 **kānguǎn** guard; look after

看管人 **kānguǎn rén** caretaker

抗议 **kàngyì** protest

看护 **kānhù** look after; nurse

看见 **kànjiàn** see; catch sight of, catch a glimpse of

看来 **kànlái** seemingly, it appears that ...; 在我看来 **zài wǒ kànlái** in my opinion

看门人 **kānmén rén** doorman; janitor

看起来 **kànqǐlái** seem, appear to be

看上去 **kànshàngqu** seemingly

看守 **kānshǒu** guard, lookout

勘探 **kāntàn** prospect for

看望 **kànwang** visit

刊物 **kānwù** publication; periodical

看作 **kànzuò** regard as, look on as; 把 X 看作 Y **bǎ X kànzuò Y** regard X as Y

烤 **kǎo** barbecue; broil; roast; bake ◊ barbecued; broiled; roast; baked; 烤牛肉 **kǎo niúròu** roast beef; barbecued beef; 烤猪肉 **kǎo zhūròu** roast pork; barbecued pork

考 **kǎo** examine, test *student*; take *exam*; 考驾照 **kǎo jiàzhào** take one's driving test

靠 **kào** lean against; be near; rely on; 靠 ... 生活 **kào ... shēnghuó** live on, subsist on

靠岸 **kào'àn** dock

靠背 **kàobèi** back (*of chair*)

靠不住 **kàobuzhù** unreliable; deceptive; dubious, shady

考察 **kǎochá** inspect; explore

考查 **kǎochá** examine

靠窗座位 **kàochuāng zuòwei** window seat

考垫 **kàodiàn** cushion

考古学 **kǎogǔ xué** archeology

考古学家 **kǎogǔ xué jiā** archeologist

靠近 **kàojìn** by, near

靠拢 **kàolǒng** move closer; close up

烤炉 **kǎolú** oven

考虑 **kǎolǜ** consider; think over ◊ consideration, thought

考虑不周 **kǎolǜ bùzhōu** inconsiderate

考虑到 **kǎolǜ dào** allow for, take account of; make allowances

考虑周到 **kǎolǜ zhōudào** discreet

烤面包 **kǎo miànbāo** toast

烤肉 **kǎoròu** roast; barbecue

考试 **kǎoshì** exam

考试卷 **kǎoshìjuàn** exam paper

烤土豆 **kǎo tǔdòu** baked potato
烤箱 **kǎoxiāng** oven
考验 **kǎoyàn** test
靠着 **kàozhe** lean on; rely on
卡片 **kǎpiàn** card
卡片目录 **kǎpiàn mùlù** card index
卡片钥匙 **kǎpiàn yàoshí** card key
卡通片 **kǎtōng piàn** cartoon
棵 **kē** *measure word for trees*; 一棵树 **yīkē shù** a tree
颗 **kē** *measure word for small round things*; 三颗米 **sānkē mǐ** three grains of rice
科 **kē** department
咳 **ké** cough
壳 **ké** shell
渴 **kě** thirst ◊ thirsty
可 **kě** can; may ◊ -able; 可变 **kěbiàn** changeable; variable
刻 **kè** carve ◊ quarter of an hour; 五点一刻 **wǔdiǎn yíkè** quarter after 5
课 **kè** class; lesson; subject
克 **kè** gram
客 **kè** guest
可爱 **kě'ài** delightful; lovable; cute
刻板 **kèbǎn** rigid
可悲 **kěbēi** pathetic
课本 **kèběn** textbook
可鄙 **kěbǐ** pitiful
可变 **kěbiàn** changeable; variable
可辨认出 **kě biànrén chū** discernible
刻薄 **kèbó** scathing; unkind, hurtful
客车 **kèchē** passenger train
课程 **kèchéng** course; curriculum
课程表 **kèchéngbiǎo** schedule
可耻 **kěchǐ** dishonorable
可充气 **kě chōngqì** inflatable
可除尽 **kě chú jìn** divisible
客店 **kèdiàn** guest house; inn
可调换 **kě diàohuàn** transferable
蝌蚪 **kēdǒu** tadpole
刻度 **kèdù** scale
客房 **kèfáng** guest room; spare room
克服 **kèfú** overcome, surmount
可观 **kěguān** substantial

客观 **kèguān** objective
可贵 **kěguì** valuable; praiseworthy
刻痕 **kèhén** nick; cut
科幻 **kēhuàn** science fiction
科技 **kējì** science and technology
可敬 **kějìng** worthy; venerable
可靠 **kěkào** reliable; responsible; trustworthy
可靠性 **kěkào xìng** reliability
可卡因 **kěkǎyīn** cocaine
苛刻 **kēkè** demanding; severe
可可 **kěkě** cocoa
可口 **kěkǒu** tasty
可口可乐 **Kěkǒu Kělè** Coca Cola®
刻苦 **kèkǔ** hard-working
克拉 **kèlā** carat
可怜 **kělián** pitiful; pitiable
客满 **kèmǎn** fully booked ◊ no vacancies
科目 **kēmù** subject
啃 **kěn** chew; gnaw; nibble
肯 **kěn** be willing to
肯定 **kěndìng** confirm; be sure about ◊ sure, certain, definite; positive GRAM ◊ certainly, definitely; 你能不能肯定？ **nǐ néngbùnéng kěndìng?** are you definite about that?; 他们现在肯定到了 **tāmen xiànzài kěndìng dàole** they must have arrived by now
可能 **kěnéng** possibility; chance ◊ possible; likely, probable ◊ possibly; maybe; 可能会下雨 **kěnéng huì xiàyǔ** it may rain
可能性 **kěnéng xìng** possibility; liability; likelihood; probability; prospect ◊ must
坑 **kēng** ditch; pit
坑道 **kēngdào** gallery; tunnel
坑害 **kēnghài** set up; frame
坑洼 **kēngwā** pothole
恳切请求 **kěnqiè qǐngqiú** appeal for
恳求 **kěnqiú** implore; plead for ◊ plea
可怕 **kěpà** terrible; terrifying; horrifying; formidable
客气 **kèqi** polite; friendly; 别客气 **biékèqì** you're welcome

苛求 **kèqiú** pushy

可取 **kěqǔ** advisable

客人 **kèrén** visitor; guest

可溶 **kěróng** soluble

可食用 **kě shíyòng** edible

瞌睡 **kēshuì** sleepy ◊ snooze

咳嗽 **késou** cough

可塑 **kěsù** pliable

课堂 **kètáng** classroom; lecture room

课题 **kètí** subject, topic

客厅 **kètīng** living room

磕头 **kētóu** kowtow

渴望 **kěwàng** crave; yearn for, long for ◊ craving; longing ◊ eager; wistful

可恶 **kěwù** horrible, repulsive

可惜 **kěxī** what a shame ◊ unfortunately

可笑 **kěxiào** funny, amusing; ridiculous

可信 **kěxìn** trusted; credible; reliable

可行 **kěxíng** workable; feasible

可行性研究 **kěxíngxing yánjiū** feasibility study

可信性 **kěxìn xìng** credibility

科学 **kēxué** science ◊ scientific

科学家 **kēxuéjiā** scientist

可疑 **kěyí** suspicious

可以 **kěyǐ** can; may ◊ OK ◊ -able ◊ not bad; 可以吗? – 可以 **kěyǐma? – kěyǐ** can I / he? – ok, you / he can; 可以喝 **kěyǐ hē** drinkable; 还可以 **hái kěyǐ** not bad; 我觉得可以 **wǒ juédé kěyǐ** that's OK or fine by me

可以忍受 **kěyǐ rěnshòu** tolerable, bearable

可以容忍 **kěyǐ róngrěn** acceptable

可以想象 **kěyǐ xiǎngxiàng** imaginable, conceivable

可再用 **kě zài yòng** reusable, recyclable

可争论 **kě zhēnglùn** debatable ◊ arguably

克制 **kèzhì** control oneself

空 **kōng** empty; bare; vacant ◊ sky; air

恐 **kǒng** be afraid; fear

孔 **kǒng** hole

空 **kòng** spare time; leisure time

控 **kòng** control

空白 **kòngbái** gap; hole; empty space; margin ◊ blank

恐怖 **kǒngbù** terror; horror ◊ scary

恐怖电影 **kǒngbù diànyǐng** horror movie

恐怖分子 **kǒngbù fènzi** terrorist

恐怖机构 **kǒngbù jīgòu** terrorist organization

恐怖症 **kǒngbùzhèng** phobia

恐怖主义 **kǒngbù zhǔyì** terrorism

空档 **kōngdǎng** neutral

空洞 **kōngdòng** empty; meaningless

空洞无物 **kōngdòng wúwù** wishy-washy

空额 **kòng'é** opening (*at work*)

空腹 **kōngfù** empty stomach

控告 **kònggào** indict; charge; sue ◊ charge; 被控告… **bèi kònggào**… be accused of…

空隔键 **kònggé jiàn** space-bar

控股权益 **kònggǔ quányì** controlling interest

恐吓 **kǒnghè** terrify; terrorize

恐慌 **kǒnghuāng** panic

空间 **kōngjiān** space; room; void

空姐 **kōngjiě** air hostess

恐惧 **kǒngjù** fear; terror

空军 **kōngjūn** air force

空军基地 **kōngjūn jīdì** airbase

空旷 **kōngkuàng** open *countryside*

恐龙 **kǒnglóng** dinosaur

空落落 **kōng luòluo** stark *decor, room*

恐怕 **kǒngpà** I'm afraid (*regret*)

空气 **kōngqì** air

空前 **kōngqián** unprecedented

空气动力 **kōngqì dònglì** aerodynamic

空气污染 **kōngqì wūrǎn** air pollution

孔雀 **kǒngquè** peacock

空缺 **kòngquē** opening

空儿 **kòngr** parking space

空手道 **kōngshǒudào** karate

控诉 **kòngsù** bring charges

空谈 **kōngtán** empty talk; 他只是空谈 **tā zhǐshì kōngtán** he's all talk

空调 **kōngtiáo** air-conditioning

空头支票 **kōngtóu zhīpiào** blank check

空位 **kòngwèi** blank; space

空隙 **kòngxì** opening; gap

空闲 **kòngxián** leisure; leisure time ◊ unoccupied; at a loose end

空想 **kōngxiǎng** daydream; utopian fantasy

空心 **kōngxīn** hollow

空虚 **kōngxū** empty; meaningless ◊ emptiness; void

空域 **kōngyù** airspace

空余 **kòngyú** free *room, table*

空运 **kōngyùn** air transport

空晕病 **kōngyūnbìng** airsickness

空余时间 **kòngyú shíjiān** leisure time

空着 **kōngzhe** empty; unoccupied *room*

控制 **kòngzhì** control; regulate; dominate ◊ control; domination; 我们无法控制的因素 **wǒmén wúfǎ kòngzhì de yīnsù** circumstances beyond our control

控制键 **kòngzhìjiàn** control key

控制盘 **kòngzhì pán** control panel

控制中心 **kòngzhì zhōngxīn** control center

空中交通 **kōngzhōng jiāotōng** air traffic

空中交通控制 **kōngzhōng jiāotōng kòngzhì** air-traffic control

空中交通控制人员 **kōngzhōng jiāotōng kòngzhì rényuán** air-traffic controller

空中小姐 **kōngzhōng xiǎojie** air hostess

空转 **kōngzhuàn** idling; in neutral

孔子 **Kǒngzǐ** Confucius

口 **kǒu** mouth

扣 **kòu** button up

口才 **kǒucái** eloquence

口吃 **kǒuchī** stutter; speech impediment

口齿不清 **kǒuchǐ bùqīng** inarticulate

扣除 **kòuchú** deduct; subtract ◊ deduction

口袋 **kǒudài** pocket

口服避孕药 **kǒufú bìyùnyào** contraceptive pill

口供 **kǒugōng** statement (*to police*)

口号 **kǒuhào** slogan

口红 **kǒuhóng** lipstick

叩击 **kòujī** rap; knock on

口径 **kǒujìng** caliber (*of gun*)

叩击声 **kòujī shēng** rap; knock

口技艺人 **kǒujì yìrén** ventriloquist

口渴 **kǒukě** thirsty

扣扣子 **kòu kòuzi** button up

口令 **kǒulìng** password

抠门儿 **kōuménr** stingy; tight-fisted

口腔卫生 **kǒuqiāng** oral hygiene

口琴 **kǒuqín** mouth organ

扣球 **kòuqiú** smash (*in tennis*)

扣人心弦 **kòu rén xīnxián** gripping

口哨声 **kǒushàoshēng** whistle (*sound*)

口授 **kǒushòu** dictate ◊ dictation

口水 **kǒushuǐ** saliva

口试 **kǒutóu** oral exam

口头 **kǒutóu** oral

口吐狂言 **kǒutù kuángyán** rant and rave

口香糖 **kǒuxiāng táng** chewing gum

扣押 **kòuyā** seize; impound ◊ seizure

扣眼儿 **kòuyǎnr** buttonhole

口译 **kǒuyì** interpret ◊ interpretation

口音 **kǒuyīn** accent

口淫 **kǒuyín** oral sex; blow job

口译者 **kǒuyì zhě** interpreter

口语 **kǒuyǔ** colloquial language ◊ colloquial; conversational

口子 **kǒuzi** tear; slit

扣子 **kòuzi** button

哭 **kū** cry

枯 **kū** dried up; parched

苦 **kǔ** bitter ◊ bitterness

酷 **kù** cool, great

库 **kù** storehouse; warehouse

裤 **kù** pants

夸 **kuā** praise; exaggerate

跨 **kuà** step; step across

胯 **kuà** hip

夸大 **kuādà** exaggerate

垮掉 **kuǎdiào** crack up; have a breakdown

酷爱 **kù'ài** go in for; enjoy

块 **kuài** piece; block; dollar; yuan; lump (*of sugar*); pane (*of glass*) ◊ *measure word for money, pieces*; 五块钱 *wǔkuài qián* five yuan; 一块派／面包 *yíkuài pài／miànbāo* a piece of pie／bread

快 **kuài** quick; rapid; sharp ◊ quickly; soon; 他快五十了 *tā kuài wǔshí le* he's getting on for 50

酷爱 **kù'ài** be in love with *job, hobby*

快餐 **kuàicān** fast food; quick snack

快餐店 **kuàicāndiàn** fast food restaurant

快车 **kuàichē** fast train

快吃 **kuàichī** eat quickly; bolt

快点儿! **kuàidiǎnr!** hurry up!; come on!

快感 **kuàigǎn** pleasurable feeling; thrill

快活 **kuàihuó** cheerful

会计 **kuàijì** accounting ◊ accountant; bookkeeper

快捷键 **kuàijiéjiàn** hot key

快进 **kuàijìn** fast forward

快乐 **kuàilè** joy; pleasure; bliss ◊ happy; 使人快乐 *shǐrén kuàilè* entertain

快门儿 **kuàiménr** shutter PHOT

快速 **kuàisù** fast; rapid; express ◊ velocity; rapidity

快艇 **kuàitǐng** speedboat

筷子 **kuàizi** chopsticks

快走 **kuàizǒu** hurry

夸奖 **kuājiǎng** praise

垮了 **kuǎle** break down; have a breakdown; be exhausted

宽 **kuān** broad; 十米宽 *shímǐkuān* 10m across

款 **kuǎn** sum of money; article (*of law, act*)

宽敞 **kuānchang** spacious

宽大 **kuāndà** spacious; lenient

款待 **kuǎndài** treat; 用 Y 款待 X *yòng Y kuǎndài X* treat X to Y

宽度 **kuāndù** width

筐 **kuāng** basket

狂 **kuáng** crazy

框 **kuàng** frame

矿 **kuàng** mine

旷 **kuàng** spacious

狂暴 **kuángbào** turbulent; ferocious ◊ turbulence; ferocity ◊ rage

矿藏 **kuàngcáng** mineral resources

矿层 **kuàngcéng** seam (*of ore*)

旷工 **kuànggōng** skip work ◊ absence (from work) ◊ absent

矿工 **kuànggōng** miner

狂欢 **kuánghuān** live it up

狂欢节 **kuánghuānjié** carnival

框架 **kuàngjià** outline; framework

矿井 **kuàngjǐng** mine shaft

旷课 **kuàngkè** play hookey ◊ absence (from school) ◊ absent

矿坑 **kuàngkēng** mine; pit

况且 **kuàngqiě** furthermore

狂犬病 **kuángquǎn bìng** rabies

矿泉水 **kuàngquánshuǐ** mineral water

狂热 **kuángrè** craze, fad ◊ fanatical; feverish

狂人 **kuángrén** madman, maniac

狂热者 **kuángrè zhě** fanatic

矿山 **kuàngshān** mine

矿石 **kuàngshí** ore

狂妄 **kuángwàng** arrogant; presumptuous

矿物 **kuàngwù** mineral

狂喜 **kuángxǐ** joy; rejoicing ◊ exult; rejoice ◊ overjoyed

狂笑 **kuángxiào** guffaw; howl with laughter ◊ guffaw, howl; hysterics

矿业 **kuàngyè** mining

狂饮 **kuángyǐn** bender (*drinking*)

宽宏大量 **kuānhóng dàliàng** generous

宽厚 **kuānhòu** lenient; soft

宽阔 **kuānkuò** wide *street, field*

宽容 **kuānróng** tolerant; lenient;

forbearing; broad *smile* ◊
tolerance ◊ condone
宽容度 **kuānróng dù** freedom;
latitude
款式 **kuǎnshì** cut (*of clothes, hair*)
宽恕 **kuānshù** forgive
宽松 **kuānsōng** loose; baggy
宽松裤 **kuānsōng kù** slacks
宽慰 **kuānwèi** relief ◊ be relieved
垮台 **kuǎtái** downfall; fall; 使 … 垮
台 **shǐ … kuǎtái** bring down
夸脱 **kuātuō** quart
夸耀 **kuāyào** showy; ostentatious
跨越 **kuàyuè** cross; pass; exceed
夸张 **kuāzhāng** exaggerate;
overdo ◊ ostentatious
裤衩 **kùchǎ** underpants; panties
库存 **kùcún** stock
裤兜 **kùdōu** pants pocket
苦干 **kǔgàn** toil
亏 **kuī** lose
盔 **kuī** helmet
窥察 **kuīchá** snoop around
葵花 **kuíhuā** sunflower
窥孔 **kuīkǒng** peephole
傀儡 **kuǐlěi** puppet
傀儡政府 **kuǐlěi zhèngfǔ** puppet
government
亏损 **kuīsǔn** deficit; loss ◊ make a
loss
魁梧 **kuíwú** burly ◊ great hunk
溃疡 **kuìyáng** ulcer
骷髅 **kūlóu** skeleton
捆 **kǔn** bundle
困 **kùn** tired
苦难 **kǔnàn** difficulty; suffering
苦难的经历 **kǔnànde jīnglì**
ordeal
苦恼 **kǔnǎng** distress; mental
suffering
苦恼 **kǔnǎo** vexed; worried ◊

worry; trouble; grief
哭闹纠缠 **kūnào jiūchán** whine
昆虫 **kūnchóng** insect; bug
困乏 **kùnfá** weary; 使人困乏
shǐrén kùnfá wearing
困惑 **kùnhuò** confused; perplexed
◊ perplexity; 使 … 困惑 **shǐ …
kùnhuò** puzzle, perplex
困境 **kùnjìng** mess, jam; plight
困倦 **kùnjuàn** sleepy
困难 **kùnnan** difficulty; trouble;
complication
困扰 **kùnrǎo** nagging; niggling
捆住 **kǔnzhù** tie down; make fast
扩 **kuò** expand
阔 **kuò** wide; rich
括 **kuò** include
扩充 **kuòchōng** branch out
扩大 **kuòda** expand; enlarge;
extend ◊ expansion; enlargement;
extension
括号 **kuòhào** brackets;
parentheses
扩建 **kuòjiàn** extension (*on house*)
扩军 **kuòjūn** arm; build up the
army
阔气 **kuòqi** wealthy
蛞蝓 **kuòyú** slug (*animal*)
扩张 **kuòzhāng** dilate (*of pupils*)
哭泣 **kūqì** weep
酷热 **kùrè** sweltering, very hot
哭诉 **kūsù** moan
枯萎 **kūwěi** droop; wilt ◊ wilting;
drooping
裤线 **kùxiàn** crease (*in pants*)
苦笑 **kǔxiào** wry smile
苦心 **kǔxīn** pains; 费苦心 **fèi
kǔxīn** take pains
枯燥 **kūzào** boring
枯燥无味 **kūzào wúwèi** bland
裤子 **kùzi** pants

L

拉 **lā** pull; draw; drag

辣 **là** hot, spicy

蜡 **là** wax

喇叭 **lǎba** trumpet; horn; loudspeaker; 按喇叭 **àn lǎba** hoot; sound one's horn

喇叭状 **lǎbazhuàng** flare (*in dress*)

拉丁美洲 **Lādīng Měizhōu** Latin America

拉丁字母 **Lādīng zìmǔ** Roman alphabet

拉肚子 **lādùzi** diarrhea

拉关系 **lā guānxi** pull strings

拉过来 **lā guòlái** draw up *chair*

拉环 **lāhuán** ring-pull

来 **lái** come ◊ (*toward speaker*): 拿进来 **nájìn lai** bring in; 过来 **guòlai** come over

来迟 **láichí** belated

来到 **láidào** come along, turn up, arrive

癞蛤蟆 **làiháma** toad

来回 **láihuí** back and forth; there and back; to and fro

来回票 **láihuí piào** round trip ticket

来历 **láilì** origin

来临 **láilín** approach; come; fall (*of night*)

来世 **láishì** afterlife

来往 **láiwǎng** contact; dealings

来由 **láiyóu** reason; cause

来源 **láiyuán** source

来自 **láizì** come from; originate in, stem from

垃圾 **lājī** garbage, trash; litter

辣椒 **làjiāo** chili pepper

拉紧 **lājǐn** pull tight

拉近 **lājìn** zoom in on

垃圾桶 **lājītǒng** trashcan

垃圾箱 **lājīxiāng** garbage can

垃圾站 **lājī zhàn** garbage dump

拉开 **lākāi** draw back, pull back; pull apart, separate

拉开拉链 **lākāi lāliàn** unzip

啦啦队 **lālā duì** cheerleaders

拉力 **lālì** tension

拉链 **lāliàn** fastener, zipper; 拉拉链 **lā lāliàn** zip up

喇嘛 **lǎma** lama

拉门 **lāmén** sliding door

拉面 **lāmiàn** hand-pulled noodles

栏 **lán** railing; hurdle; column (*of text*)

兰 **lán** orchid

拦 **lán** block; obstruct

蓝 **lán** blue

篮 **lán** basket

懒 **lǎn** lazy

缆 **lǎn** cable; rope

烂 **làn** decayed; rotten

滥 **làn** excessive

蓝宝石 **lánbǎoshí** sapphire

缆车 **lǎnchē** cable car

蓝调 **lándiào** blues

懒惰 **lǎnduò** laziness, indolence ◊ lazy, indolent

狼 **láng** wolf

浪 **làng** wave

栏杆 **lángān** barrier; railings

浪潮 **làngcháo** tide; wave

朗读 **lǎngdú** read aloud

浪费 **làngfèi** waste

浪花 **lànghuā** seaspray; foam

浪漫 **làngmàn** romantic ◊ romance

朗诵 **lǎngsòng** read out

榔头 **lángtou** hammer

浪头 **làngtóu** trend; wave; 赶浪头 **gǎn làngtóu** jump on the bandwagon

狼吞虎咽 **lángtūn hǔyàn** devour, wolf down ◊ voracious

懒鬼 **lǎnguǐ** idle, lazy

懒汉 **lǎnhàn** bum; hobo

拦河坝 **lánhébà** dam

兰花 **lánhuā** orchid

拦截 **lánjié** intercept *ball*

蓝领工人 **lánlǐng gōngrén** blue-collar worker

褴褛 **lánlǚ** ragged

烂泥 **lànní** mud

篮球 **lánqiú** basketball

懒散 **lǎnsǎn** laze around ◊ lethargic

蓝色 **lánsè** blue

蓝图 **lántú** blueprint

阑尾 **lánwěi** appendix

阑尾炎 **lánwěiyán** appendicitis

懒洋洋 **lǎnyāngyāng** unenthusiastic; listless

蓝眼睛 **lányǎnjing** blue eyes ◊ blue-eyed

滥用 **lànyòng** misuse; abuse

拦住 **lánzhù** hold back; stop; accost

篮子 **lánzi** basket

牢 **láo** pen; prison ◊ solid; sturdy

劳 **láo** work

老 **lǎo** old ◊ F very, dead; always; 他老迟到 **tā lǎo chídào** he's always late; 老了 **lǎo le** get on, grow old; pass away

老板 **lǎobǎn** owner (of a business); proprietor; boss; landlord

老板娘 **lǎobǎnniáng** landlady; proprietress

老成练达 **lǎochéng liàndá** worldly; sophisticated

唠叨 **láodao** go on; go on at

唠叨不停 **láodao bùtíng** nag

劳动 **láodòng** work; labor

劳动节 **Láodòngjié** Labor Day

劳动力 **láodònglì** manpower, workers; workforce

劳动日 **láodòngrì** working day

劳动者 **láodòng zhě** laborer

牢房 **láofáng** prison cell

牢固 **láogù** solid; sturdy; durable

老虎 **lǎohǔ** tiger

老虎机 **lǎohǔjī** slot machine; gambling machine

老虎钳 **lǎohǔqián** pliers; pincers

劳驾 **láojià** excuse me; would you mind; 劳驾帮帮忙 **láojià bāngbang máng** could you help me?

老家 **lǎojiā** home

姥姥 **lǎolao** grandma

劳累 **láolèi** tire ◊ tired

老练 **lǎoliàn** diplomacy, tact ◊ diplomatic; veteran

老年 **lǎonián** geriatric ◊ old age

老年病学 **lǎonián bìngxué** geriatrics

老气 **lǎoqì** old-fashioned *clothes*

老前辈 **lǎoqiánbèi** senior citizen; senior

老人 **lǎorén** old person; senior citizen

老人院 **lǎorényuàn** old people's home, nursing home

牢骚 **láosao** complaint

老实 **lǎoshi** honest

老师 **lǎoshī** teacher

老式 **lǎoshì** old-fashioned *equipment*

老是 **lǎoshì** always

老鼠 **lǎoshǔ** rat; mouse

劳损 **láosǔn** strain

老外 **lǎowài** foreigner; layman

老挝 **Lǎowō** Laos ◊ Laotian

老兄 **lǎoxiōng** pal, buddy

老早 **láozǎo** long ago

老子 **Lǎozǐ** Lao-tzu (*Taoist sage*)

劳资纠纷 **láozī jiūfēn** industrial dispute

拉票 **lāpiào** canvass POL

拉平 **lāpíng** even out; smooth out; 拉平比分 **lāpíng bǐfēn** even the score; 和 ... 拉平 **hé ... lāpíng** draw level with

拉萨 **Lāsà** Lhasa

拉伤 **lāshāng** pull, strain

拉舌 **lāshé** tab

拉屎 **lāshǐ** shit

拉手 **lāshǒu** doorknob

邋遢 **lāta** messy *person*; scruffy; slovenly

拉下 **lāxià** pull down; lower

蜡烛 **làzhú** candle

了 **le** (*particle indicating completed action*): 雨停了 **yǔtíngle** it has stopped raining ◊ (*particle indicating change of state*): 头发白了 **tóufa báile** his hair is going gray; 我买了 **wǒ mǎi le** I'll take it ◊ (*for emphasis*): 你太好了 **nǐ**

tài hǎo le that's very kind

勒 **lè** rein in; check

乐 **lè** joy; happiness

乐观 **lèguān** optimistic; hopeful; positive ◊ optimism

乐观者 **lèguān zhě** optimist

雷 **léi** thunder

累 **léi** accumulate

泪 **lèi** tear

累 **lèi** tired

类 **lèi** sort, type, kind

肋 **lèi** side (of body)

肋部 **lèibù** flank; side (of body)

雷达 **léidá** radar

雷锋叔叔 **Léi Fēng shūshu** do-gooder

肋骨 **lèigǔ** rib

累积 **lěijī** accumulate

雷鸣 **léimíng** thunder

类似 **lèisì** similar; comparable ◊ likeness

累死了 **lèi sǐ le** dead tired

类型 **lèixíng** type

雷雨 **léiyǔ** thunderstorm

雷阵雨 **léizhènyǔ** thundery shower

累赘 **léizhuì** cumbersome

勒令停职 **lèlìng tíngzhí** suspend

冷 **lěng** cold

棱 **léng** edge

冷冰冰 **lěng bīngbing** cold; icy

冷藏 **lěngcáng** chill; refrigerate ◊ refrigeration

冷淡 **lěngdàn** chilly; indifferent; impassive; frigid

冷冻 **lěngdòng** freeze ◊ frozen

冷冻室 **lěngdòngshì** freezer

冷冻食品 **lěngdòng shípǐn** frozen food

冷静 **lěngjìng** calm, collected

冷酷 **lěngkù** in cold blood ◊ cold-blooded; heartless

冷气 **lěngqì** chill (in air)

冷门 **lěngmén** outsider

冷面 **lěngmiàn** cold noodles

冷漠 **lěngmò** cool; remote, unfriendly; unconcerned; apathetic

冷凝 **lěngníng** condense ◊ condensation

冷盘 **lěngpán** cold cuts

冷却 **lěngquè** cool ◊ cooling

冷杉 **lěngshān** fir

冷烫 **lěngtàng** cold wave (in hairdressing)

冷笑 **lěngxiào** sneer

冷血 **lěngxuè** cold-blooded

冷饮 **lěngyǐn** cold drinks

棱锥体 **léngzhuītǐ** pyramid

乐趣 **lèqù** amusement; enjoyment; fun; pleasure

勒索 **lèsuǒ** extort; blackmail ◊ extortion; blackmail

乐意 **lèyì** with pleasure; willingly

乐于 **lèyú** willing; 乐于助人 **lèyú zhùrén** obliging

乐园 **lèyuán** paradise; amusement park

狸 **lí** beaver

梨 **lí** pear

犁 **lí** plow

离 **lí** leave ◊ from; 离这儿很远 **lí zhèr hěn yuǎn** it's far from here; 离圣诞节还有六星期 **lí Shèngdànjié háiyǒu liù xīngqī** Christmas is still six weeks away

礼 **lǐ** rite; ritual; etiquette

李 **lǐ** plum

里 **lǐ** in; inside ◊ neighborhood; measure of distance, approx. one third of a mile

理 **lǐ** reason ◊ pay attention to; put in order, sort

粒 **lì** grain, speck; particle

力 **lì** strength; power

立 **lì** stand

利 **lì** sharp ◊ profit; benefit

例 **lì** example

历 **lì** experience; calendar

俩 **liǎ** both; two; 他们俩儿 **tāmén liǎ** the two of them, both of them

帘 **lián** curtain; blind

联 **lián** join; unite with

连 **lián** link; connect ◊ even; 连 … 也不 **lián … yěbù** not even

莲 **lián** lotus

脸 **liǎn** face

恋 **liàn** love

炼 **liàn** refine

练 **liàn** practise; train

链 **liàn** chain

恋爱 **liàn'ài** love

联邦 **liánbāng** federation; union

联邦调查局 **Liánbāng Diàochájú** FBI, Federal Bureau of Investigation

联邦制 **liánbāngzhì** federal

连播 **liánbō** serialize

脸蛋儿 **liǎndànr** face

镰刀 **liándāo** sickle

凉 **liáng** cool; cold

良 **liáng** good

粮 **liáng** grain

量 **liáng** measure; 量体温 **liáng tǐwēn** take sb's temperature

两 **liǎng** two; 两盘磁带 **liǎngpán cídài** two cassettes

量 **liàng** capacity; quantity; volume

谅 **liàng** forgive

亮 **liàng** bright; light; clear

辆 **liàng** *measure word for vehicles*; 一辆小汽车 **yīliàng xiǎoqìchē** a car

炼钢厂 **liàngāngchǎng** steelworks

两倍 **liǎngbèi** double

两边 **liángbiān** bilateral

粮仓 **liángcāng** barn

两重 **liǎngchóng** double; dual

量出 **liángchū** measure out

两次 **liǎngcì** twice

亮度 **liàngdù** lightness; brightness

晾干 **liànggān** air-dry

谅解 **liàngjiě** understand; forgive

两极分化 **liǎngjí fēnhuà** polarize; split

量具 **liángjù** measuring instrument

凉开水 **liáng kāishuǐ** cold boiled water

凉快 **liángkuai** pleasantly cool

两面派 **liǎngmiànpài** two-faced

椋鸟 **liángniǎo** starling

两栖 **liǎngqī** amphibious

踉跄 **liàngqiàng** stagger; sway

俩儿 **liǎngr** two; both

粮食 **liángshi** grain; cereal

良师益友 **liángshī yìyǒu** mentor

凉爽 **liángshuǎng** cool; crisp; fresh ◊ freshness

凉台 **liángtái** balcony

连贯 **liánguàn** coherent; lucid

连贯性 **liánguàn xìng** continuity

两位数 **liǎngwèi shù** double figures

凉鞋 **liángxié** sandal

良心 **liángxīn** conscience

良性 **liángxìng** benign

联合 **liánhé** unite; form an alliance ◊ alliance; union ◊ concerted

联合国 **Liánhéguó** United Nations

联合企业 **liánhé qǐyè** cartel

联合收割机 **liánhé shōugējī** combine harvester

联合王国 **Liánhé Wángguó** United Kingdom

脸红 **liǎnhóng** blush

连环漫画 **liánhuán mànhuà** comic strip

连环碰撞 **liánhuán pèngzhuàng** pile-up, crash

恋家 **liànjiā** homeloving

廉价出售 **liánjià chūshòu** be on sale

离岸价格 **lí'àn jiàgé** FOB, free on board

连接 **liánjiē** join, connect; link

联接 **liánjiē** link; connect

联结 **liánjié** bond

连接处 **liánjiēchù** joint

联结处 **liánjiéchù** join

连接词 **liánjiēcí** conjunction GRAM

连接器 **liánjiē qì** connector COMPUT

连襟儿 **liánjīnr** brother-in-law

连裤袜 **liánkùwà** pantyhose

连累 **liánlěi** get ... involved

联络 **liánluò** contact, get in touch with ◊ liaison

联络网 **liánluò wǎng** network

联盟 **liánméng** coalition; league; union; alliance

连绵 **liánmián** continuous; 连绵一百英里 **liánmián yìbǎi yīnglǐ** it stretches for 100 miles

怜悯 **liánmǐn** sympathize with

脸盆 **liǎnpén** washbasin

莲蓬头 **liánpengtóu** shower head

脸皮厚 **liǎnpí hòu** thick-skinned; insensitive; shameless

连日 **liánrì** lasting for days

炼乳 **liànrǔ** condensed milk

联赛 **liánsài** league SP

脸色 **liǎnsè** color (*in cheeks*)

脸色苍白 **liǎnsè cāngbái** pallor

连锁店 **liánsuǒ diàn** chain store

连锁反应 **liánsuǒ fǎnyìng** chain reaction

链条 **liàntiáo** chain

连体双胞胎 **liántǐ shuāngbāotāi** Siamese twins

连同 **liántóng** in conjunction with

联系 **liánxì** contact; connect ◊ connection; 将 X 与 Y 联系起来 **jiāng X yǔ Y liánxì qǐlái** relate X to Y; 我们保持联系 **wǒmén bǎochí liánxì** we keep in touch

练习 **liànxí** practice; training; exercise

练习本 **liànxíběn** exercise book

联系电话 **liánxì diànhuà** contact number

连续 **liánxù** continuous; uninterrupted; consecutive; 连续两天 **liánxù liǎngtiān** for two days running

连续不断 **liánxù búduàn** continuous ◊ persistently

连衣裤 **liányīkù** dungarees

连衣裙 **liányīqún** dress

联运 **liányùn** connection (*train etc*)

帘子 **liánzi** curtain

连字号 **liánzìhào** hyphen

聊 **liáo** chat

疗 **liáo** treat ◊ treatment

了 **liǎo** finish, end ◊ understand; 对 X 了如指掌 **duì X liǎo rú zhǐzhǎng** have X at one's fingertips ◊ (*completed action*): 吃了 **chī liǎo** eat up ◊ (*ability*): 我去不了 **wǒ qù bu liǎo** I can't go; 我办得了 **wǒ bàn de liǎo** I can manage it

料 **liào** material, fabric

了不起 **liǎobùqǐ** terrific, fantastic

潦草 **liáocǎo** careless; messy; 潦草的字迹 **liáocǎode zìjī** scrawl, scribble

疗程 **liáochéng** course of treatment

疗法 **liáofǎ** cure; remedy; therapy

了结 **liǎojié** deal with; settle

了解 **liǎojiě** understand; 据了解

他们在加拿大 **jù liáojiě tāmén zài Jiānádà** they are understood to be in Canada

料理 **liàolǐ** take care of

聊天 **liáotiān** chat

料想 **liàoxiǎng** suppose

疗养 **liáoyǎng** convalesce

疗养地 **liáoyǎngdì** health resort

疗养期 **liáoyǎng qī** convalescence

疗养院 **liáoyǎngyuàn** sanatorium

篱笆 **líba** fence

离别 **líbié** separation ◊ separate; part from (*of people*)

利比亚 **Lìbǐyà** Libya ◊ Libyan

立场 **lìchǎng** standpoint; point of view

里程 **lǐchéng** mileage

里程碑 **lǐchéngbēi** milestone

里程表 **lǐchéng biǎo** odometer

里道 **lǐdào** inside lane (*of road*)

列 **liè** list ◊ column, row ◊ *measure word for trains*; 一列火车 **yīliè huǒchē** a train

裂 **liè** crack; split

烈 **liè** intense

劣 **liè** inferior; poor

猎 **liè** hunt

列车 **lièchē** train

列车长 **lièchē zhǎng** conductor (*on train*)

裂缝 **lièfèng** crack; crevice; gap; slit, opening

裂痕 **lièhén** crack

烈酒 **lièjiǔ** hard liquor

列举 **lièjǔ** enumerate

裂开 **lièkāi** disintegrate; split; damage; gape ◊ gaping *hole*

裂口 **lièkǒu** tear (*in cloth, paper*); burst; chip (*in cup*); split

列宁 **Lièníng** Lenin

猎枪 **lièqiāng** shotgun

猎区 **lièqū** hunting ground

猎取 **lièqǔ** hunt; prey on

猎犬 **lièquǎn** hunting dog; retriever

猎人 **lièrén** hunter

列入计划 **lièrù jìhuà** schedule

烈士 **lièshì** martyr

猎手 **lièshǒu** hunter

猎物 **lièwù** prey

烈性 **lièxìng** strong *drink*

劣质 **lièzhì** inferior; shoddy; trashy

咧嘴 **liězuǐ** grin

理发 **lǐfà** haircut; hairdressing ◊ style hair

立法 **lìfǎ** legislate ◊ legislation ◊ legislative

立法过程 **lìfǎ guòchéng** legislation

立法机构 **lìfǎ jīgòu** legislature

立方 **lìfāng** cubic

立方米 **lìfāngmǐ** cubic meter

立方形 **lìfāng xíng** cube

理发师 **lǐfàshī** hairdresser

理发厅 **lǐfàtīng** hairdressing salon; barber shop

礼服 **lǐfú** formal wear; tuxedo

利害 **lìhai** severe; tough; formidable

离合器 **líhéqì** clutch

离婚 **líhūn** divorce; get divorced ◊ divorced

里脊 **lǐjǐ** fillet

痢疾 **lìji** dysentery

立即 **lìjí** immediate ◊ immediately

理解 **lǐjiě** understand; view, perceive ◊ comprehension; understanding

离开 **líkāi** leave, depart; go away; quit; 我们明天离开 **wǒmén míngtiān líkāi** we're off tomorrow

立刻 **lìkè** immediately; in no time

力量 **lìliàng** power; strength; force; might

理疗 **lǐliáo** physiotherapy

理疗医生 **lǐliáo yīshēng** physiotherapist

利率 **lìlǜ** interest rate

理论 **lǐlùn** theory ◊ theoretical

利落 **lìluò** clear and concise; snappy

礼貌 **lǐmào** courtesy; politeness ◊ courteously; 有／没有礼貌 **yǒu／méiyǒu lǐmào** have good/bad manners

厘米 **límǐ** centimeter

里面 **lǐmiàn** inside

黎明 **límíng** daybreak

林 **lín** wood; forest

淋 **lín** drip; soak

临 **lín** overlook ◊ be about to

邻 **lín** neighbor; neighborhood

淋巴结 **línbājié** lymph gland

临床 **línchuáng** clinical

铃 **líng** bell

零 **líng** zero; nil; 零下十度 **língxià shídù** 10 degrees below zero; 从零开始 **cóng líng kāishǐ** start from scratch

陵 **líng** mound; tomb

灵 **líng** spirit; soul

领 **lǐng** neck; collar ◊ claim; withdraw *money*

另 **lìng** other; in addition

令 **lìng** order

领班 **lǐngbān** foreman

灵车 **língchē** hearse

凌晨 **língchén** early morning

领带 **lǐngdài** necktie

领导 **lǐngdǎo** leader; head; boss ◊ lead; 在他的领导下 **zài tāde lǐngdǎo xià** under his leadership

领导技巧 **lǐngdǎo jìqiǎo** leadership skills

领导人 **lǐngdǎo rén** leader; manager

零度 **língdù** zero degrees

领队 **lǐngduì** bandleader

灵感 **línggǎn** inspiration; brainwave

领海 **lǐnghǎi** territorial waters

领会 **lǐnghuì** grasp; comprehend; digest *information*

灵魂 **línghún** soul; spirit; 灵魂转世 **línghún zhuǎnshì** reincarnation

灵活 **línghuó** flexible; agile

零下 **língxià** below zero

灵机 **língjī** inspiration; 灵机一动 **língjīyídòng** have a flash of inspiration

零件 **língjiàn** (spare) part

领结 **lǐngjié** bow tie

领口 **lǐngkǒu** neckline

铃兰 **línglán** lily of the valley

伶俐 **línglì** quick; nimble; apt

领路 **lǐnglù** navigation

凌乱 **língluàn** untidy; messy

灵敏 **língmǐn** sharp; quick *mind*

陵墓 **língmù** mausoleum

零钱 **língqián** loose change, coins

灵巧 **língqiǎo** deft; quick

令人 **lìngrén** (*causing a person to*

feel something): 令人恶心 **lìngrén ěxin** disgusting, revolting; 令人愉快 **lìngrén yúkuài** enjoyable; 令人失望 **lìngrén shīwàng** disappointing

零散 **língsǎn** sporadic

零食 **língshí** snacks; nibbles; candy

领事 **lǐngshì** consul

领事馆 **lǐngshì guǎn** consulate

零售 **língshòu** retail

零售价 **língshòu jià** retail price

零售商 **língshòu shāng** retailer

零碎 **língsuì** incomplete; fragmented

领头 **lǐngtóu** lead race, procession

领土 **lǐngtǔ** territory ◊ territorial

另外 **lìngwài** other ◊ in addition; apart from that

另外收费 **lìngwài shōufèi** be extra

领先 **lǐngxiān** be in the lead; be ahead of ◊ in front; leading ◊ lead (in race)

零星 **língxīng** scattered

菱形 **língxíng** diamond; lozenge

另行通知 **lìngxíng tōngzhī** until further notice

领袖 **lǐngxiù** leader

领养 **lǐngyǎng** adopt ◊ adoption

另一个 **lìng yígè** another

另一件事 **lìng yījiàn shì** another matter; a different ball game

零用钱 **língyòng qián** allowance

零用现金 **língyòng xiànjīn** petty cash

领域 **lǐngyù** territory; field; preserve; sphere; 戏剧领域 **xìjù lǐngyù** the world of the theater

领子 **lǐngzi** collar

临海 **línhǎi** coastal

林火 **línhuǒ** forest fire

临街店铺 **línjiē diànpù** storefront

邻近 **línjìn** adjacent

临近 **línjìn** approach ◊ proximity

邻居 **línjū** neighbor

鳞片 **línpiàn** scale (on fish)

吝啬 **lìnsè** miserly, tight-fisted

吝啬鬼 **lìnsèguǐ** miser

临时 **línshí** provisional; temporary; casual

临时担任 **línshí dānrèn** act as, fill in as

临时工 **línshígōng** temp

林荫道 **línyīndào** avenue

淋浴 **línyù** take a shower ◊ shower

淋浴帘 **línyùlián** shower curtain

礼炮 **lǐpào** salute

礼品 **lǐpǐn** gift, present

离奇 **líqí** strange; uncanny

离弃 **líqì** abandon

力气 **lìqi** strength (physical)

沥青 **lìqīng** asphalt

里圈跑道 **lǐquān pǎodào** inside lane SP

例如 **lìrú** for instance, e.g.

利润 **lìrùn** profit

利润率 **lìrùnlǜ** profit margin

理事 **lǐshì** director; trustee

砾石 **lìshí** gravel

历史 **lìshǐ** history

历史性 **lìshǐxìng** historic; historical

历史学家 **lìshǐ xuéjiā** historian

理所当然 **lǐsuǒ dāngrán** naturally; of course

礼堂 **lǐtáng** (ceremonial) hall; church

离题 **lítí** beside the point

立体声装置 **lìtǐshēng zhuāngzhì** stereo system

留 **liú** stay; keep; let grow hair; 你留着吧 **nǐ liúzhe ba** please keep it, I insist

流 **liú** flow, run

硫 **liú** sulfur

柳 **liǔ** willow

六 **liù** six

遛 **liù** walk; 遛狗 **liùgǒu** walk the dog

遛冰场 **liūbīng chǎng** ice rink

流鼻涕 **liú bítì** runny nose

流鼻血 **liú bíxuè** nosebleed

流产 **liúchǎn** miscarriage

流畅 **liúchàng** smooth; fluent

流程图 **liúchéngtú** flowchart

流传 **liúchuán** spread; circulate

溜出去 **liūchūqù** slip out

流弹 **liúdàn** stray bullet

流荡 **liúdàng** drift

流动 **liúdòng** flow

流动工人 **liúdòng gōngrén** migrant worker

流动基金 **liúdòng jījīn** cash flow

流放 **liúfàng** exile

流感 **liúgǎn** flu

刘海 **liúhǎi** bangs; fringe

留话 **liúhuà** leave a message

硫磺 **liúhuáng** sulfur

流口水 **liú kǒushuǐ** dribble; slobber

浏览 **liúlǎn** skim; browse; flick through

流浪汉 **liúlànghàn** drifter; hobo

浏览器 **liúlǎn qì** browser COMPUT

流泪 **liúlèi** shed tears

流利 **liúlì** fluent ◊ fluency; 他讲一口流利的汉语 **tā jiǎng yìkǒu liúlìde Hànyǔ** he speaks fluent Chinese

流氓 **liúmáng** hoodlum; hooligan

留念 **liúniàn** keep as a memento

流沙 **liúshā** quicksand

留神 **liúshén** look out; pay attention

流逝 **liúshì** slip away; elapse; pass

六十 **liùshí** sixty

柳树 **liǔshù** willow

流水 **liúshuǐ** running water

六四 **Liùsì** Tiananmen Square (*incident*)

流苏 **liúsū** tassel

流体 **liútǐ** fluid

流亡 **liúwáng** exile

留下 **liúxià** bequeath; leave

流线型 **liúxiànxíng** streamlined

留心 **liúxīn** be alert, be observant; listen to, heed

流星 **liúxīng** meteor; falling star

流行 **liúxíng** in fashion, fashionable; popular; pop

流行病 **liúxíngbìng** epidemic

流行歌曲 **liúxíng gēqǔ** pop song; hit

流行款式 **liúxíng kuǎnshì** style, fashion

流行性 **liúxíngxìng** epidemic

流行性感冒 **liūxíngxìng gǎnmào** influenza

流行音乐 **liúxíng yīnyuè** pop music

留学 **liúxué** study abroad

流血 **liúxuè** bleed ◊ bleeding; bloodshed

留言 **liúyán** leave a message

流言蜚语 **liúyán fēiyǔ** gossip; scandal

六月 **liùyuè** June

流走 **liúzǒu** drain, flow away

例外 **lìwài** exception

礼物 **lǐwù** gift

利息 **lìxī** interest

离线 **líxiàn** go off-line

理想 **lǐxiǎng** ideal

理想化 **lǐxiǎnghuà** idealistic

理性 **lǐxìng** reason; sense

利息率 **lìxīlǜ** interest rate

力学 **lìxué** mechanics

离异 **líyì** break up (*of couple*)

礼仪 **lǐyí** protocol; etiquette; ceremony

利益 **lìyì** interest; advantage; benefit

利用 **lìyòng** use; exploit; take advantage of

理由 **lǐyóu** reason; cause; grounds

鲤鱼 **lǐyú** carp

俚语 **lǐyǔ** slang

力争 **lìzhēng** strive for

例证 **lìzhèng** illustration; example

理智 **lǐzhì** reason (*faculty*)

荔枝 **lìzhī** lychee

李子 **lǐzi** plum

里子 **lǐzi** lining

例子 **lìzi** example; case; instance

栗子 **lìzi** chestnut

粒子 **lìzǐ** particle PHYS

栗子树 **lìzi shù** chestnut tree

笼 **lóng** cage

聋 **lóng** deaf ◊ deafness

龙 **lóng** dragon

隆冬季节 **lóngdōng jìjié** in the depths of winter

垄断 **lǒngduàn** monopolize ◊ monopoly

龙骨 **lónggǔ** keel

龙卷风 **lóngjuǎn fēng** tornado; whirlwind

隆隆声 **lónglong shēng** boom; peal (*of thunder*)

笼统 **lóngtǒng** sweeping *statement*

龙头 **lóngtóu** faucet

龙虾 **lóngxiā** lobster

聋哑 **lóngyǎ** deaf-and-dumb

笼罩 **lǒngzhào** descend (*of mood,*

darkness)

隆重 **lóngzhòng** festive
笼子 **lóngzi** cage
楼 **lóu** building; story, floor
搂 **lǒu** hug, embrace
漏 **lòu** seep; drip; leak ◊ leaky
楼层 **lóucéng** floor, story
漏出 **lòuchū** escape, leak; seep
漏洞 **lòudòng** leak; loophole
漏斗 **lòudǒu** funnel
楼房 **lóufáng** building
露面 **lòumiàn** turn up; put in an
  appearance
漏气 **lòuqì** leak out (*of air, gas*)
楼上 **lóushàng** upstairs
楼梯 **lóutī** stairs, staircase
楼厅 **lóutīng** balcony
楼下 **lóuxià** downstairs
炉 **lú** oven
橹 **lǔ** paddle
鹿 **lù** deer
路 **lù** road; way; possibility; 五路
  有轨电车 **wǔlù yǒuguǐdiànchē**
  streetcar line 5
露 **lù** dew ◊ reveal
录 **lù** record
驴 **lǘ** donkey
铝 **lǚ** aluminum
缕 **lǚ** strand, lock
氯 **lǜ** chlorine
滤 **lǜ** filter, strain
率 **lǜ** level, amount, rate (*of pay*)
绿 **lǜ** green
卵 **luǎn** (human) egg
乱 **luàn** chaotic, in a mess ◊ chaos
卵巢 **luǎncháo** ovary
乱砍 **luànkǎn** slash
乱伦 **luànlún** incest
乱蓬蓬 **luàn péngpeng** ragged
乱七八糟 **luànqī bāzāo** in a
  mess, in confusion, topsy-turvy
卵石 **luǎnshí** pebble
乱弹 **luàntán** strum
乱涂 **luàntú** daub
乱写 **luànxiě** scrawl, scribble
绿宝石 **lǜbǎoshí** emerald
路边 **lùbiān** roadside
路标 **lùbiāo** roadsign; signpost;
  landmark
铝箔 **lǚbó** aluminum foil
绿茶 **lǜchá** green tea

旅程 **lǚchéng** itinerary
露出 **lùchū** expose, reveal
屡次 **lǚcì** over and over again
路堤 **lùdī** embankment
陆地 **lùdì** land, shore, dry land;
  mainland ◊ terrestrial
旅店 **lǚdiàn** hostel; inn
掠夺 **lüèduó** loot
掠夺者 **lüèduó zhě** looter
掠过 **lüèguò** skim *surface*
略过 **lüèguò** skip, omit
略微 **lüèwēi** hint, trace
滤干 **lǜgān** strain; drain
路过 **lùguò** pass by
绿化 **lǜhuà** put plants/trees in,
  plant up
鹿角 **lùjiǎo** antlers
路径 **lùjìng** path
旅客 **lǚkè** passenger
履历 **lǚlì** résumé
陆路 **lùlù** track; overland route
鲁莽 **lǔmǎng** rash, impetuous
路面 **lùmiàn** pavement, road
  surface
轮 **lún** wheel; round (*of drinks*)
论 **lùn** discuss
轮齿 **lúnchǐ** cog
轮船 **lúnchuán** steamer; ship
论点 **lùndiǎn** thesis
伦敦 **Lúndūn** London
轮毂 **lúngǔ** hub (*of wheel*)
轮换 **lúnhuàn** alternate
论据 **lùnjù** argument; reasoning
轮廓 **lúnkuò** contour, outline;
  silhouette
轮流 **lúnliú** alternate ◊ alternately;
  轮流做 **lúnliú zuò** do in rotation,
  take turns in doing
伦理学 **lúnlǐxué** ethics
轮盘赌 **lúnpán dǔ** roulette
轮胎 **lúntāi** tire
论文 **lùnwén** thesis, dissertation,
  treatise; paper
轮椅 **lúnyǐ** wheelchair
论语 **Lúnyǔ** Analects of Confucius
轮缘 **lúnyuán** rim (*of wheel*)
轮值表 **lúnzhí biǎo** rota
轮轴 **lúnzhóu** axle
轮子 **lúnzi** wheel
落 **luò** fall; sink; land (*of ball etc*);
  set (*of sun*)

锣 **luó** gong
骡 **luó** mule
裸 **luǒ** naked, bare
萝卜 **luóbo** turnip; radish
落地窗 **luòdìchuāng** French doors
落地灯 **luòdìdēng** floor lamp
落后 **luòhòu** backward ◊ be behind, trail; lose the lead; 在 X 方面落后 **zài X fāngmiàn luòhòu** be behind with X
落花生 **luòhuāshēng** groundnut
逻辑 **luójì** logic ◊ logical
落空 **luòkōng** fall through, fail
罗马数字 **Luómǎ shùzì** Roman numerals
螺母 **luómǔ** nut (*for bolt*)
罗盘仪 **luópán yí** compass
落泊 **luòpò** comedown
罗圈腿 **luóquān tuǐ** bandy
络腮胡子 **luòsāi húzi** full beard
螺栓 **luóshuān** bolt
落水 **luòshuǐ** fall into the water; 有人落水! **yǒurén luòshuǐ!** man overboard!
螺丝 **luósī** screw
螺丝刀 **luósīdāo** screwdriver
螺丝钉 **luósīdīng** screw
裸体 **luǒtǐ** naked, nude
裸体画 **luǒtǐ huà** nude
裸体主义者 **luǒtǐ zhǔyì zhě** nudist
骆驼 **luòtuo** camel
螺纹 **luówén** thread (*of screw*)
落下 **luòxià** go down, sink
裸胸 **luǒxiōng** topless
螺旋 **luóxuán** spiral
螺旋桨 **luóxuánjiǎng** propeller
录取 **lùqǔ** admit, take in
鹿肉 **lùròu** venison
绿色 **lǜsè** green
律师 **lǜshī** attorney, lawyer
露水 **lùshuǐ** dew
露宿街头 **lùsù jiētóu** sleep rough
芦笋 **lúsǔn** asparagus

露天 **lùtiān** open-air ◊ in the open air
旅途 **lǚtú** ride, drive; travels
芦苇 **lúwěi** reed
路线 **lùxiàn** route; way
录像 **lùxiàng** video; video recording
录像带 **lùxiàng dài** video cassette; videotape
录像机 **lùxiàng jī** video recorder, VCR
履行 **lǚxíng** fulfill ◊ fulfillment
旅行 **lǚxíng** travel; get around ◊ journey, trip; traveling
旅行包 **lǚxíngbāo** travel bag
旅行保险 **lǚxíng bǎoxiǎn** travel insurance
旅行袋 **lǚxíng dài** travel bag
旅行社 **lǚxíng shè** travel agency
旅行推销员 **lǚxíng tuīxiāo yuán** commercial traveler
旅行者 **lǚxíng zhě** traveler
旅行支票 **lǚxíng zhīpiào** traveler's check
陆续 **lùxù** one after the other
录音 **lùyīn** (tape) recording ◊ (tape) record ◊ audio
录音电话 **lùyīn diànhuà** answerphone
露营 **lùyíng** camp ◊ camping
录音机 **lùyīnjī** cassette player; cassette recorder; tape recorder
录音室 **lùyīn shì** recording studio
录音座 **lùyīnzuò** tape deck
旅游 **lǚyóu** tour ◊ tourism; tour
旅游公司 **lǚyóu gōngsī** tour operator
旅游业 **lǚyóu yè** tourism
旅游者 **lǚyóu zhě** tourist
旅游指南 **lǚyóu zhǐnán** guidebook
路障 **lùzhàng** barricade; roadblock
绿洲 **lǜzhōu** oasis
炉子 **lúzi** stove; furnace

M

妈 **mā** mom, ma

抹 **mā** wipe

麻 **má** hemp

马 **mǎ** horse; 老马识途 *lǎo mǎ shí tú prov* the old horse knows the way

码 **mǎ** yard

骂 **mà** curse, swear

吗 **ma** (*question indicator*): 你认识他吗？*nǐ rènshi tā ma?* do you know him?

马表 **mǎbiǎo** stopwatch

抹布 **mābù** cloth; dish cloth

马车 **mǎchē** cart

马达 **mǎdá** motor, engine

马大哈 **mǎdàhā** disaster area *fig*

妈的！**māde!** ∨ shit!

麻烦 **máfán** bother, trouble; 太麻烦你了 *tài máfán nǐle* you needn't have bothered

吗啡 **mǎfēi** morphine

马夫 **mǎfū** groom (*for horse*)

马虎 **mǎhū** careless, sloppy

埋 **mái** bury; 埋头于工作 *máitóu yú gōngzuò* bury oneself in work

买 **mǎi** buy

麦 **mài** wheat

迈 **mài** step

脉 **mài** blood vessel

卖 **mài** sell

脉搏 **màibó** pulse

迈步 **màibù** stride

买不到 **mǎi bú dào** unobtainable

埋藏 **máicáng** bury

买单 **mǎidān** pay the bill

买东西 **mǎi dōngxi** shop

卖方 **màifāng** seller

埋伏 **máifú** ambush

卖高价票 **mài gāojià piào** scalper

买家 **mǎijiā** buyer

麦克风 **màikèfēng** microphone

买卖 **mǎimài** buying and selling; business; 做 X 的买卖 *zuò X de*

买卖 **mǎimài** trade in X

麦片 **màipiàn** rolled oats

卖俏 **màiqiào** flirt

卖肉的 **màiròu de** butcher

麦乳精 **màirǔjīng** malted milk

卖艺 **màiyì** work as a performer

卖淫 **màiyín** prostitute onself

埋葬 **máizàng** bury

买主 **mǎizhǔ** purchaser; customer

卖主 **màizhǔ** seller, vendor

麦子 **màizi** wheat

麻将 **májiàng** mah-jong

马厩 **mǎjiù** stable

马克 **mǎkè** mark (*currency*)

马克思 **Mǎkèsī** Marx

马克思主义 **Mǎkèsīzhǔyì** Marxism ◊ Marxist

马克思主义者 **Mǎkèsīzhǔyì zhě** Marxist

马来西亚 **Mǎláixīyà** Malaysia ◊ Malaysian

马来语 **Mǎlái yǔ** Malay (*language*)

马拉松 **mǎlāsōng** marathon

马力 **mǎlì** horsepower

马列主义 **Mǎlièzhǔyì** Marxism-Leninism

马列主义者 **Mǎlièzhǔyì zhě** Marxist-Leninist

马笼头 **mǎ lóngtóu** bridle

马路 **mǎlù** street

妈妈 **māma** mom, ma

马马虎虎 **mǎma hǔhū** so-so, average, mediocre

麻木 **mámù** numb

蛮 **mán** quite; very

鳗 **mán** eel

瞒 **mán** conceal; keep secret

满 **mǎn** full

慢 **màn** slow

漫 **màn** overflow

漫步 **mànbù** ramble; saunter; wander ◊ rambling

满不在乎 **mǎn bù zàihu** not care at all

漫步者 **mànbù zhě** rambler

漫长 **màncháng** lengthy

慢动作 **màndòngzuò** slow motion

盲 **máng** blind

忙 **máng** busy ◊ be in a rush; 忙什么? **máng shénme?** what's the big rush?

盲点 **mángdiǎn** blind spot

芒果 **mángguǒ** mango

忙碌 **mánglù** busy; hectic; on the go ◊ bustle around; be busy; rush, scramble

盲目 **mángmù** blind; wild, crazy *scheme*

茫然 **mángrán** blank, vacant *look*

盲人 **mángrén** blind person; the blind

盲文 **mángwén** braille

蛮横 **mánhèng** harden *attitude* ◊ insolent

漫画 **mànhuà** comic

漫画书 **mànhuà shū** comic book

慢跑 **mànpǎo** jog ◊ jogging

满身 **mǎn shēn** the whole body; all over

蔓生植物 **mànshēng zhíwù** climbing plant

漫谈 **màntán** ramble ◊ rambling, incoherent

馒头 **mántou** steamed bun

漫无目的 **màn wú mùdì** aimless

慢性 **mànxìng** chronic

蔓延 **mànyán** spread (*of fire, disease, belief*); sprawl (*of city*); be overrun with ◊ contagious *fear, laughter*; sprawling; 四处蔓延 **sìchù mànyán** run wild

满意 **mǎnyì** satisfied; 令人满意 **lìngrén mǎnyì** fulfilling; satisfactory

漫游 **mànyóu** roam, wander around

满员 **mǎnyuán** full; booked up; packed

满月 **mǎnyuè** full moon

满洲 **Mǎnzhōu** Manchuria

慢走 **mànzǒu** goodbye, so long

满足 **mǎnzú** satisfy *needs, desires* ◊ satisfied, content, contented ◊ contentment; fulfillment; satisfaction

满族 **Mǎnzú** Manchu

猫 **māo** cat

锚 **máo** anchor

毛 **máo** hair; bristles; wool; mao (*Chinese money*)

矛 **máo** spear; javelin

铆 **mǎo** rivet

冒 **mào** emit, give off

毛笔 **máobǐ** writing brush

毛病 **máobìng** fault, defect; 车有点毛病 **chē yǒu diǎn máobìng** there is something wrong with the car

毛虫 **máochóng** caterpillar

冒充 **màochōng** impersonate, pose as

铆钉 **mǎodīng** rivet

矛盾 **máodùn** contradiction ◊ contradictory

冒犯 **màofàn** offend, insult

毛纺厂 **máofǎngchǎng** textile mill

毛骨悚然 **máogǔ sǒngrán** terrifying, hair-raising

冒号 **màohào** colon GRAM

铆接 **mǎojiē** rivet

毛巾 **máojīn** towel; washcloth

毛巾架 **máojīn jià** towel rail

毛孔 **máokǒng** pore

毛毛雨 **máomao yǔ** drizzle

猫咪 **māomī** puss, pussycat

牦牛 **máoniú** yak

毛皮 **máopí** coat, fur

茅舍 **máoshè** hovel

帽舌 **màoshé** visor

茂盛 **màoshèng** rampant; flourishing; luxuriant

冒失 **màoshī** presumptuous

毛毯 **máotǎn** blanket

猫头鹰 **māotóuyīng** owl

毛线 **máoxiàn** knitting wool

冒险 **màoxiǎn** adventure; venture, undertaking ◊ take a risk; venture into ◊ dangerous, risky; bold, audacious

冒险家 **màoxiǎnjiā** adventurer

帽檐 **màoyán** brim (*of hat*)

毛衣 **máoyī** sweater

贸易 **màoyì** trade, commerce

贸易差额 **màoyì chā'é** balance

of trade

贸易关系 **màoyì guānxi** trade relations

毛泽东 **Máo Zédōng** Mao Tsetung, Mao Zedong

毛泽东思想 **Máo Zédōng sīxiǎng** Mao Zedong thought

毛毡 **máozhān** felt

毛主席 **Máo Zhǔxí** Chairman Mao

毛主席像章 **Máo Zhǔxí xiàngzhāng** Mao badge

毛主席语录 **Máo Zhǔxí Yǔlù** Little Red Book

帽子 **màozi** cap; hat

麻雀 **máquè** sparrow

骂人 **màrén** curse, swear

骂人话 **màrénhuà** swearword

马赛克 **mǎsàikè** mosaic

马上 **mǎshàng** immediately, right now, straight away

马蹄 **mǎtí** hoof

马蹄铁 **mǎtítiě** horseshoe

马桶 **mǎtǒng** lavatory

码头 **mǎtóu** dock; wharf; port

马尾辫 **mǎwěibiàn** pigtail

马尾发 **mǎwěifà** ponytail

马戏团 **mǎxìtuán** circus

蚂蚁 **mǎyǐ** ant

麻油 **máyóu** sesame oil

马掌 **mǎzhǎng** horseshoe

麻疹 **mázhěn** measles

麻醉 **mázuì** anesthetize; drug ◊ anesthesia; anesthetic; drug ◊ high, stoned

麻醉剂 **mázuìjì** anesthetic; narcotic

麻醉品 **mázuìpǐn** narcotic; drug

麻醉师 **mázuì shī** anesthetist

煤 **méi** coal

霉 **méi** mold, mildew

没 **méi** not ◊ have not; 我没钱 **wǒ méi qián** I've got no money; 我没看过这本书 **wǒ méi kànguo zhè běn shū** I haven't read this book; 没多少 **méi duōshǎo** nothing much ◊ (in questions): 你去没去？ **nǐ qù méi qù?** did you go or not?

梅 **méi** plum

眉 **méi** eyebrow

每 **měi** every; each; per

美 **měi** beautiful, pretty, lovely

妹 **mèi** younger sister

美餐 **měicān** good meal

每次 **měicì** each time

美德 **měidé** morality

没的比 **méidebǐ** there's no comparison

梅毒 **méidú** syphilis

妹夫 **mèifū** brother-in-law (younger sister's husband)

没赶上 **méigǎnshàng** miss

每隔 **měigé** alternate

每个 **měigè** each

每个人 **měigè rén** everyone

每隔一天 **měigéyìtiān** every other day

湄公河 **Méigōnghé** Mekong River

没工作 **méi gōngzuò** jobless

美观 **měiguān** esthetic

没关系 **méi guānxi** it doesn't matter, never mind; it's a pleasure, you're welcome

玫瑰 **méigui** rose

美国 **Měiguó** America, USA ◊ American

美国人 **Měiguó rén** American

没骨气 **méi gǔqì** spineless

美好 **měihǎo** wonderful; good

美化 **měihuà** make more attractive; brighten up

没化妆 **méi huàzhuāng** unmade-up, without make-up

媒介 **méijiè** medium; means

没经验 **méi jīngyàn** inexperienced

没开 **méikāi** be off (of TV, machine, light)

煤矿 **méikuàng** coal-mine

美丽 **měilì** beautiful, lovely ◊ beauty

魅力 **mèilì** attraction, magnetism; charm; glamor

美利坚合众国 **Měilìjiān Hézhòngguó** United States of America

没礼貌 **méilǐmào** have no manners

眉毛 **méimao** eyebrow

美貌 **měimào** looks

妹妹 **mèimèi** younger sister

没门儿！**méiménr!** no way!

美妙 **měimiào** wonderful

每年 **měinián** yearly ◊ per annum

美女 **měinǚ** pin-up; pretty girl

煤气 **méiqì** coal gas

没前途 **méi qiántú** have no future ◊ hopeless, useless; 没前途的工作 **méi qiántú de gōngzuò** dead-end job

煤气灶 **méiqìzào** gas stove

没人 **méirén** nobody

每日 **měirì** daily

美容 **měiróng** cosmetic

美容家 **měiróng jiā** beautician

美容洗液 **měiróng xǐyè** face lotion

美容院 **měiróng yuàn** beauty parlor

美食 **měishí** delicacy

没事儿 **méi shìr** it's alright; 我没事儿 **wǒ méi shìr** I'm alright

美术片 **měishùpiàn** animation

每天 **měitiān** daily, everyday ◊ every day

媒体渲染 **méitǐ xuànrǎn** media hype

没完 **méiwán** never-ending

每晚 **měiwǎn** every evening

没完没了 **méiwán méiliǎo** on and on, endlessly; 没完没了地要X去做Y **méiwán méiliǎo de yào X qù zuò Y** go on and on at X to do Y

没完全准备好 **méi wánquán zhǔnbèi hǎo** not quite ready

美味 **měiwèi** delicacy

没味儿 **méiwèir** tasteless

没问题 **méi wèntí** certainly, no problem

每小时 **měi xiǎoshí** hourly; 每小时一百五十公里 **měi xiǎoshí yībǎi wǔshí gōnglǐ** at 150 km/h

没兴趣 **méi xìngqu** uninterested; uninteresting

没修面 **méi xiūmiàn** unshaven

美学 **měixué** esthetics

没牙 **méiyá** toothless

没一个 **méi yīgè** none

没用 **méiyòng** useless ◊ it's no use; 试也没用 **shì yě méiyòng** it's useless trying

没用的东西 **méiyòng de dōngxi** bum

没用的人 **méiyòng de rén** good-for-nothing

煤油 **méiyóu** paraffin; kerosene

没有 **méiyǒu** without ◊ no ◊ not ◊there is / are not; 没有多少 **méiyǒu duōshao** not much; not many; 没有咖啡／茶了 **méiyǒu kāfēi / chá le** there's no coffee / tea left; 没有钱 **méiyǒu qián** have no money ◊ (in questions): 你去了没有？**nǐ qùle méiyou?** did you go or not?

没有结果 **méiyǒu jiéguǒ** unproductive

没有察觉到 **méiyǒu juéchádào** be unaware of

没有什么 **méiyǒu shénme** nothing

没有时间 **méiyǒu shíjiān** have no time; be booked up

没有图案 **méiyǒu tú'àn** plain, unadorned

没有问题 **méiyǒu wèntí** no problem; without a hitch

没有希望 **méiyǒu xīwàng** hopeless

没有音乐天赋 **méiyǒu yīnyuè tiānfù** unmusical

美元 **měiyuán** US dollar

每月 **měiyuè** monthly

没粘住 **méi zhānzhù** come unstuck

没治了 **méizhìle** amazing

美洲 **Měizhōu** (continent of) America

美洲鹫 **měizhōu jiù** vulture

美洲山核桃 **měizhōu shānhétáo** pecan

每周一次 **měizhōu yīcì** weekly

闷 **mēn** stuffy, airless

门 **mén** door

闷 **mèn** bored; 闷死了 **mènsǐle** be bored to death

门把手 **mén bǎshǒu** doorknob

门垫 **méndiàn** doormat

蒙 **méng** cover

猛 **měng** fierce

梦 **mèng** dream

蒙蔽 **méngbì** deceive ◊ deception, deceit

蠓虫 **měngchóng** midge, gnat

蒙古 **Měnggǔ** Mongolia ◊ Mongolian

猛击 **měngjī** bang; blow ◊ blaze away

孟加拉 **Mèngjiālā** Bangladesh ◊ Bangladeshi

梦见 **mèngjian** dream about

猛拉 **měnglā** jerk, wrench

猛烈 **měngliè** fierce, violent; passionate ◊ with a vengeance

朦朦胧胧 **méngméng lónglóng** misty *color*

蒙蒙细雨 **méngméng xìyǔ** drizzle

蒙骗 **méngpiàn** cheat, deceive

猛扑 **měngpū** pounce, swoop

猛抬物价 **měngtái wùjià** bump up *prices*

猛推 **měngtuī** thrust, force

梦想 **mèngxiǎng** dream, fantasize

梦想家 **mèngxiǎng jiā** dreamer

萌芽 **méngyá** shoot, sprout

梦游者 **mèngyóu zhě** sleep walker

猛增 **měngzēng** jump, soar

猛掷 **měngzhì** hurl

蒙住眼睛 **méngzhù yǎnjīng** blindfold

孟子 **Mèngzǐ** Mencius

门阶 **ménjiē** doorstep

门槛 **ménkǎn** threshold

门口 **ménkǒu** gateway

门廊 **ménláng** porch, stoop

门铃 **ménlíng** doorbell

闷闷不乐 **mènmèn búlè** sullen

门牌号 **ménpáihào** house number

门票 **ménpiào** entrance ticket

闷热 **mēnrè** clammy, sultry

闷人 **mènrén** bore

门闩 **ménshuān** bolt; latch

闷死 **mēnsǐ** suffocate

门厅 **méntīng** lobby

门卫 **ménwèi** porter, doorman

门诊部 **ménzhěnbù** outpatient department

门诊治疗 **ménzhěn zhìliáo** outpatient treatment

闷住 **mēnzhù** smother

门柱 **ménzhù** goalpost

迷 **mí** lost ◊ fan; 足球迷 *zúqiúmí* soccer fan

谜 **mí** mystery; riddle

米 **mǐ** rice; meter

密 **mì** thick; close

秘 **mì** secret

蜜 **mì** honey

棉 **mián** cotton

眠 **mián** sleep

免 **miǎn** avoid; prohibit

面 **miàn** face; side; flour; noodle

面包 **miànbāo** bread

面包店 **miànbāo diàn** bakery

面包渣 **miànbāo zhā** breadcrumbs

棉布 **miánbù** cotton

面部 **miànbù** face; 面部拉皮手术 *miànbù lāpí shǒushù* facelift

免除 **miǎnchú** immune ◊ be exempt from; 免除 X 的 Y *miǎnchú X de Y* excuse X from Y

面的 **miàndī** cab, taxi

缅甸 **Miǎndiàn** Burma ◊ Burmese

面的司机 **miàndī sījī** cab driver

面对 **miànduì** confront, stand up to; face (toward)

面对面 **miàn duì miàn** face to face

面额 **miàn'é** denomination (*of money*)

免费 **miǎnfèi** free, free of charge; 免费入场 *miǎnfèi rùchǎng* admission free

免费样品 **miànfèi yàngpǐn** free sample

面粉 **miànfěn** (wheat) flour

面糊 **miànhú** batter

棉花 **miánhua** cotton

棉花糖 **miánhuā táng** cotton candy; marshmallow

面积 **miànjī** area; proportions

面颊 **miànjiá** cheek

面具 **miànjù** mask

面孔 **miànkǒng** face

勉励 **miǎnlì** encourage

面貌 **miànmào** face; appearance

面前 **miànqián** in front of; 在 X 面前 *zài X miànqián* in the presence of X

勉强 **miǎnqiǎng** manage with difficulty ◊ reluctant, grudging, forced ◊ reluctantly; 勉强及格 *miǎnqiǎng jígé* scrape through; 勉强维持生活 *miǎnqiǎng wéichí shēnghuó* scrape a living

面色 **miànsè** complexion

面纱 **miànshā** veil

面食 **miànshi** pasta; pastry

面试 **miànshì** (job) interview

面熟 **miànshú** seem familiar

免税 **miǎnshuì** tax-free; duty-free

免税商店 **miǎnshuì shāngdiàn** duty-free store

免税物品 **miǎnshuì wùpǐn** duty-free goods

缅腆 **miǎntiǎn** shy; timid; retiring ◊ shyness; timidity

面条 **miàntiáo** noodle

面团 **miàntuán** dough

绵羊 **miányáng** sheep

免疫 **miǎnyì** immune ◊ immunity

免疫性 **miǎnyìxìng** immune ◊ immunity

免疫系统 **miǎnyì xìtǒng** immune system

免职 **miǎnzhí** oust

免租 **miǎnzū** rent-free

免罪 **miǎnzuì** redeem *sinner*

喵 **miāo** miaow

苗 **miáo** young plant

秒 **miǎo** second

庙 **miào** temple; temple market

妙 **miào** wonderful; 妙极了！ *miàojíle!* fantastic!

秒表 **miǎobiǎo** stopwatch

妙不可言 **miàobùkěyán** magical, enchanting

描绘 **miáohuì** portray, represent; describe

庙会 **miàohuì** carnival

苗圃 **miáopǔ** nursery (*for plants*)

描述 **miáoshù** describe; depict, portray ◊ description; portrayal

苗条 **miáotiáo** slim, slight; trim

描写 **miáoxiě** describe ◊ description; portrayal

妙语 **miàoyǔ** punch line

庙宇 **miàoyǔ** temple

妙语 **miàoyǔ** witticism

秒针 **miǎozhēn** second hand

瞄准 **miáozhǔn** aim ◊ be aimed at

弥补 **míbǔ** catch up on; make up for; recoup; rectify ◊ compensation

灭 **miè** extinguish, put out

灭火 **mièhuǒ** put out a fire

灭火器 **mièhuǒqì** fire extinguisher

灭绝 **mièjué** die out; wipe out, eradicate, exterminate

灭亡 **mièwáng** decline, disappearance ◊ go under, be ruined

米粉 **mǐfěn** rice noodles; vermicelli

密封 **mìfēng** airtight ◊ seal

蜜蜂 **mìfēng** bee

迷宫 **mígōng** maze

猕猴桃 **míhóutáo** kiwi fruit

迷惑 **míhuo** mystify; mislead; confuse ◊ disoriented

密集 **mìjí** dense *crowd* ◊ swarm

米酒 **mǐjiǔ** rice wine

秘诀 **mìjué** formula

迷恋 **míliàn** be infatuated with, be nuts about

迷路 **mílù** lose one's way; 我迷路了 *wǒ mílù le* I'm lost

密码 **mìmǎ** code; combination; PIN; 通路密码 *tōnglù mìmǎ* access code

秘密 **mìmì** secret ◊ covert, under-cover

靡靡之音 **mǐmǐ zhī yīn** schmaltzy music; schmaltzy song

密谋 **mìmóu** conspire, plot

民 **mín** people; folk

民兵 **mínbīng** militia

名 **míng** name

鸣 **míng** ring, chime; toll; cry (*of birds, animals*)

明 **míng** bright; light

命 **mìng** life

敏感 **mǐngǎn** sensitive; touchy; acute *sense* ◊ sensitivity; 对冷/热敏感 *duì lěng / rè mǐngǎn* be sensitive to the cold / heat

敏感性 **mǐngǎnxìng** sensitivity

明白 **míngbái** understand ◊ clear

名册 **míngcè** roll, list

明朝 **Míngcháo** Ming Dynasty

明晨 **míngchén** tomorrow morning

名称 **míngchēng** name; designation

名词 **míngcí** noun

名次 **míngcì** place, position

民歌 **míngē** folk song

民歌手 **míngēshǒu** folk singer

明亮 **míngliàng** bright; light, brilliant ◊ brightness

明了 **míngliǎo** lucid

命令 **mìnglìng** command, order

命令式 **mìnglìng shì** dictatorial

鸣锣令 **míngluó lìng** gong; bell

命名 **mìngmíng** name

明年 **míngnián** next year

名牌 **míngpái** well-known brand

名牌服装 **míngpái fúzhuāng** designer clothes

名牌商品 **míngpái shāngpǐn** brand name

名片 **míngpiàn** business card, visiting card

明确 **míngquè** define ◊ definite; pronounced; explicit

明确指出 **míngquè zhǐchū** pinpoint

名人 **míngrén** prominent figure; celebrity

名声 **míngshēng** reputation; 有好 / 坏名声 **yǒuhǎo** / **huài míngshēng** have a good / bad reputation

名胜 **míngshèng** scenic spot

明天 **míngtiān** tomorrow; 明天上午 **míngtiān shàngwǔ** tomorrow morning (*between 10am and noon*); 明天早晨 **míngtiān zǎochén** tomorrow morning (*before 10am*)

铭文 **míngwén** inscription

明显 **míngxiǎn** clear, obvious; transparent

明星 **míngxīng** star

明信片 **míngxìnpiàn** postcard

名义上 **míngyì shàng** nominal

名誉 **míngyù** fame; reputation

命运 **mìngyùn** fate

明智 **míngzhì** wise; sensible

名字 **míngzi** name; given name; 你叫什么名字? **nǐ jiào shénme míngzi?** what's your name?

民航 **mínháng** civil aviation

民间 **mínjiān** civil; folk

民间舞 **mínjiānwǔ** folk dance

敏捷 **mǐnjié** quick, rapid; nimble; sharp, smart

民谣 **mínyáo** ballad

民意测验 **mínyì cèyàn** poll, survey

民意调查 **mínyì diàochá** poll, survey

民营企业 **mínyíng qǐyè** private sector

民乐 **mínyuè** folk music

民众 **mínzhòng** the people; the public

民主 **mínzhǔ** democracy ◊ democratic

民主党 **Mínzhǔ Dǎng** Democratic Party

民主主义者 **mínzhǔ zhǔyì zhě** democrat

民族 **mínzú** people; ethnic group; race; nation; nationality

民族主义 **mínzú zhǔyì** nationalism

密切 **mìqiè** intimate, close

迷人 **mírén** fascinating; charming, enchanting

弥撒 **mísa** mass REL

米色 **mǐsè** cream (*color*)

秘书 **mìshū** secretary ◊ secretarial

迷途知返 **mítú zhīfǎn** straighten out

迷惘 **míwǎng** be mixed up

迷信 **míxìn** superstition ◊ superstitious

密友 **mìyǒu** crony, pal

谜语 **míyǔ** riddle

蜜月 **mìyuè** honeymoon

迷住 **mízhù** enthrall, bewitch; 被 X 迷住 **bèi X mízhù** be hooked on X

摸 **mō** touch, feel; grope

膜 **mó** membrane

磨 **mó** grind; sharpen

魔 **mó** demon

抹 **mǒ** spread *butter etc*

磨 **mò** grind (down)

末 **mò** end

墨 **mò** ink

没 **mò** sink

殁 **mò** perish, meet one's end

末班车 **mòbānchē** last bus; last train

漠不关心 **mò bù guānxīn** indifference ◊ indifferent; nonchalant

摸不着头脑 **mōbùzháo tóunǎo** be baffled

摩擦 **mócā** friction ◊ rub

末代皇帝 **Mòdài Huángdì** Last Emperor

磨掉 **módiào** rub off (of paint etc)

抹掉 **mǒdiào** erase, wipe

魔法 **mófǎ** magic ◊ magical

模范 **mófàn** example, model ◊ exemplary

模仿 **mófǎng** imitate, mimic; forge ◊ imitation, impersonation

磨坊 **mòfáng** mill

蘑菇 **mógū** mushroom

磨光 **móguāng** polish

魔鬼 **móguǐ** devil; demon

模糊 **móhu** vague; indistinct; fuzzy, hazy; misty ◊ blur ◊ mist over

墨家 **Mòjiā** Mohism ◊ Mohist

墨镜 **mòjìng** sunglasses

魔力 **mólì** magic

茉莉 **mòli** jasmine

茉莉花茶 **mòlihuāchá** jasmine tea

莫名其妙 **mò míng qí miào** mysterious

模拟 **mónǐ** analog

摹拟 **mónǐ** mock, simulated, imitation ◊ simulate

末期 **mòqī** final stage; 十九／二十世纪末期 **shíjiǔ／èrshí shìjì mòqī** the late 19th／20th century

默契 **mòqì** chemistry (between people)

磨砂玻璃 **móshā bōlí** frosted glass

陌生 **mòshēng** strange, unfamiliar; alien

陌生人 **mòshēng rén** stranger

模式 **móshì** model, pattern

没收 **mòshōu** confiscate

墨守成规者 **mòshǒu chéngguī zhě** stick-in-the-mud

魔术 **móshù** conjuring tricks, magic

墨水 **mòshuǐ** ink

魔术师 **móshùshī** magician, conjurer

莫斯科 **Mòsīkē** Moscow

磨碎 **mósuì** grate

磨损 **mósǔn** wear; abrasion ◊ wear away, wear out ◊ worn

摸索 **mōsuǒ** grope

模特儿 **mótèr** (fashion) model

摩天大楼 **mótiān dàlóu** skyscraper

摩托 **mótuō** motor, engine

摩托车 **mótuōchē** motorcycle

谋 **móu** scheme

某 **mǒu** certain; some; 某处 **mǒuchù** somewhere; 某人 **mǒurén** a certain person, someone

谋杀 **móushā** murder

谋生 **móushēng** living ◊ earn one's living

末尾 **mòwěi** end

墨西哥 **Mòxīgē** Mexico ◊ Mexican

模型 **móxíng** model; prototype; cast, mold

磨牙 **móyá** molar

墨鱼 **mòyú** cuttlefish

某种 **mǒzhǒng** certain, particular

母 **mǔ** mother; female (of animal or bird)

幕 **mù** curtain; act (of play)

木 **mù** wood

墓 **mù** grave

目 **mù** eye

牧 **mù** tend livestock

母爱 **mǔ'ài** motherly love

母斑 **mǔbān** birthmark

母板 **mǔbǎn** motherboard

木板 **mùbǎn** plank

墓碑 **mùbēi** tombstone, gravestone

目标 **mùbiāo** aim, objective; goal; target

木材 **mùcái** lumber, wood

牧草 **mùcǎo** graze

木柴 **mùchái** firewood

牧场 **mùchǎng** pasture

牧场主 **mùchǎng zhǔ** rancher

牡丹 **mǔdān** peony

目瞪口呆 **mùdèng kǒudāi** stupefied, astonished

墓地 **mùdì** graveyard, cemetery

目的 **mùdì** purpose, aim, end

目的地 **mùdìdì** destination

木耳 **mù'ěr** wood-ear mushroom

木筏 **mùfá** raft

木工 **mùgōng** carpenter; joiner

木工活 **mùgōnghuó** woodwork (*activity*)

母狗 **mǔgǒu** bitch (*dog*)

目光 **mùguāng** look

木棍 **mùgùn** stick; club

幕后 **mùhòu** behind the scenes

幕后策划 **mùhòu cèhuà** mastermind, organize

母鸡 **mǔjī** hen

目击 **mùjī** witness

幕间 **mùjiān** interlude

木匠 **mùjiàng** carpenter

幕间休息 **mùjiān xiúxī** intermission

目击者 **mùjīzhě** eyewitness

募捐 **mùjuān** collect donations

募捐者 **mùjuān zhě** fundraiser

木刻 **mùkè** wood carving

母鹿 **mǔlù** doe

目录 **mùlù** catalog; directory; list; table of contents

暮 **mù** evening

母马 **mǔmǎ** mare

牡马 **mǔmǎ** stallion

牧民 **mùmín** herdsman

母牛 **mǔniú** cow

木偶 **mù'ǒu** puppet

木偶戏 **mù'ǒuxì** puppet show

木排 **mùpái** raft

目前 **mùqián** at present, currently

母亲 **mǔqīn** mother

母亲节 **Mǔqīnjié** Mother's Day

暮色降临 **mùsè jiànglín** get dark

牧师 **mùshī** priest, minister, clergyman, pastor

穆斯林 **Mùsīlín** Muslim

木炭 **mùtàn** charcoal

木纹 **mùwén** grain

木屋 **mùwū** log cabin

木屑 **mùxiè** chip (*of wood*)

母性 **mǔxìng** maternity ◊ motherly

母羊 **mǔyáng** ewe

牧羊犬 **mùyángquǎn** sheepdog

牧羊人 **mùyáng rén** shepherd

母语 **mǔyǔ** mother tongue

拇指 **mǔzhǐ** thumb

木制 **mùzhì** wooden

木制管乐器 **mùzhì guānyuèqì** woodwind instrument

墓志铭 **mùzhìmíng** epitaph

木制品 **mùzhìpǐn** woodwork (*object*)

目中无人 **mùzhōng wúrén** snooty

母猪 **mǔzhū** sow (*pig*)

木柱 **mùzhù** pin, skittle

模子 **múzi** mold

N

拿 **ná** carry (*in hand*); hold; fetch; collect; take, remove

哪 **nǎ** which; 哪一个？ **nǎ yīgè?** which one?

那 **nà** that; those ◊ then; 那不行 **nà bùxíng** that's not right, that's not allowed; 那两人 **nà liǎngrén** those two people; 那是什么？ **nà shì shénme?** what is that?; 那又怎么样？ **nà yòu zěnmeyàng?** so what?

拿不准 **ná bùzhǔn** be doubtful

拿出 **náchū** produce, take out

纳粹 **Nàcuì** Nazi

拿掉 **nádiào** get off, remove

拿动 **nádòng** manage

哪个 **nǎge** which; which one; who; 哪个是你的？ **nǎge shì nǐde?** which one is yours?; 哪个都行 **nǎge dōuxíng** either

那个 **nàge** that, that one

奶 **nǎi** milk

耐穿 **nàichuān** sturdy, hardwearing

耐久 **nàijiǔ** durable

奶酪 **nǎilào** cheese

耐力 **nàilì** stamina, endurance

奶奶 **nǎinai** grandma (*paternal*)

奶瓶 **nǎipíng** baby's bottle

耐心 **nàixīn** patience; 耐心点儿！ **nàixīn diǎnr!** just be patient!

耐用 **nàiyòng** hardwearing ◊ wear, last

奶油 **nǎiyóu** cream

奶子 **nǎizi** tit, boob

奶嘴 **nǎizuǐ** pacifier; nipple

拿来 **nálái** bring

哪里 **nǎli** where, whereabouts

那里 **nàli** there

那么 **nàme** such a ◊ (so) that ◊ then, therefore; 那么大／贵 **nàme dà／guì** that big／expensive; 那么多？ **nàme duō?** as much as that?

南 **nán** south ◊ southern; southerly

难 **nán** difficult, hard

男 **nán** man ◊ male

难 **nàn** disaster

男扮女装 **nánbàn nǚzhuāng** in drag ◊ transvestite

南边 **nánbiān** south; the south side; 在 X 的南边 **zài X de nánbiān** to the south of X

男傧相 **nán bīnxiàng** best man

南部 **nánbù** south

男厕 **náncè** men's room, washroom

难道 …？ **nándào …?** can it be that …?; 你难道没看见？ **nǐ nándào méi kànjiàn?** can't you see?

男低音 **nán dīyīn** bass

难度 **nándù** difficulty, hardness

南方 **nánfāng** south

南非 **Nánfēi** South Africa ◊ South African

南风 **nánfēng** southerly wind

男服务员 **nán fúwùyuán** waiter

男高音 **nán gāoyīn** tenor

南瓜 **nánguā** squash, pumpkin

难怪！ **nánguài!** no wonder!

难过 **nánguò** upset; sad, unhappy; sorry; 令人难过 **lìngrén nánguò** upsetting

囊肿 **nángzhǒng** cyst

男孩 **nánhái** boy

南海 **Nánhǎi** South China Sea

南韩 **Nánhán** South Korea ◊ South Korean

男护士 **nán hùshì** male nurse

南极 **Nánjí** South Pole ◊ Antarctic

男妓 **nánjì** male prostitute

难解 **nánjiě** obscure, difficult

难接近 **nán jiējìn** inaccessible

难堪 **nánkān** embarrassed; 使 X 难堪 **shǐ X nánkān** embarrass X, put X on the spot

难看 **nánkàn** ugly

难理解 **nán lǐjiě** unintelligible

南美 **Nánměi** South America ◊ South American

难免 **nánmiǎn** inevitable; inescapable

难民 **nànmín** refugee

男模特儿 **nán mótèr** male model

男朋友 **nán péngyou** boyfriend

男仆从 **nán púcóng** valet

男人 **nánrén** man, male

南沙群岛 **Nánshā Qúndǎo** Spratley Islands

男士护肤液 **nánshì hùfū yè** aftershave

难受 **nánshòu** feel ill-at-ease

难忘 **nánwàng** unforgettable

难为情 **nánwéiqíng** ashamed, embarrassed

难闻 **nánwén** foul-smelling

男性 **nánxìng** masculine, male

南亚 **Nányà** South Asia ◊ South Asian

难以 **nányǐ** *difficult to*

难以表述 **nányǐ biǎoshù** inexpressible

难以察觉 **nányǐ chájué** imperceptible

难以对付 **nányǐ duìfù** awkward, obstreperous

难以估量 **nányǐ gūliàng** inestimable

难以解答 **nányǐ jiědá** baffling

难以接近 **nányǐ jiējìn** unapproachable

难以描述 **nányǐ miáoshù** indefinable

难以扑捉 **nányǐ pūzhuō** elusive

难以确定 **nányǐ quèdìng** be in doubt

难以忍受 **nányǐ rěnshòu** unbearable

难以容忍 **nányǐ róngrěn** trying

难以想象 **nányǐ xiǎngxiàng** unimaginable

难以形容 **nányǐ xíngróng** indescribable

难以预料 **nányǐ yùliào** it is doubtful whether

难以置信 **nányǐ zhìxìn** unbelievable

男用卫生间 **nányòng wèishēngjiān** washroom, men's room

难住 **nánzhù** baffle, stump

男子汉气 **nánzǐhànqì** manhood, manliness

男子气 **nánzǐqì** masculine

男子气概 **nánzi qìgài** virility; machismo

脑 **nǎo** brain

闹 **nào** noisy ◊ make a noise; beef, bellyache

闹别扭 **nào bièniu** fall out, argue

闹鬼 **nàoguǐ** haunted

恼火 **nǎohuǒ** mad, sore ◊ be mad, be sore

闹剧 **nàojù** farce

脑门儿 **nǎoménr** forehead, brow

脑膜炎 **nǎomóyán** meningitis

恼怒 **nǎonù** annoyed, pissed

恼人 **nǎorén** annoying

闹事 **nàoshì** make a scene; riot

闹事者 **nàoshì zhě** rioter

脑髓 **nǎosuǐ** brain

脑外科医生 **nǎo wàikē yīshēng** brain surgeon

脑震荡 **nǎozhèndàng** concussion

闹着玩儿 **nàozhe wánr** playful; joking; 不是闹着玩儿的 **búshì nàozhe wánr de** it's no joke

闹钟 **nàozhōng** alarm clock

脑子 **nǎozi** brains, intelligence

拿起 **náqǐ** pick up

哪儿 **nǎr** where; 我哪儿都找不着 **wǒ nǎr dōu zhǎobùzháo** I can't find it anywhere

那儿 **nàr** there; 他在那儿！ **tā zài nàr!** there he is!

拿上去 **ná shàngqù** take up, fetch up

那时 **nàshí** then

那时候 **nàshíhòu** in those days

拿手好菜 **náshǒu hǎocài** specialty

纳税人 **nàshuì rén** taxpayer

那天 **nàtiān** the other day

哪些 **nǎxiē** which; which ones; who

那些 **nàxiē** those

捺着性子 **nàzhè xìngzi** keep one's temper

拿走 **názǒu** take away, remove

呢 **ne** (*in questions*):你呢？ *nǐ ne?* and you？ ◊ (*emphasis*): 他还没来呢！ *ta hái méi lái ne!* he still hasn't come!

哪 **něi** which

内 **nèi** inside ◊ inner; internal

那 **nèi** that; those

内部 **nèibù** inside, interior ◊ internal; inward; inner ◊ internally

内部人 **nèibùrén** insider

内部消息 **nèibù xiāoxi** inside information

内部装修 **nèibù zhuāngxiū** interior decoration

内存 **nèicún** RAM, random access memory

内弟 **nèidì** brother-in-law (*wife's younger brother*)

内地 **nèidì** interior; inland

内阁 **nèigé** cabinet POL

内含 **nèihán** built-in

内涵 **nèihán** hidden

内疚 **nèijiù** guilt; guilty conscience ◊ guilty; 我一直感到内疚 *wǒ yìzhí gǎndào nèijiù* it has been on my conscience

内科医生 **nèikē yīshēng** internist

内裤 **nèikù** underpants, panties

内陆 **nèilù** interior, inland

内蒙古 **Nèiménggǔ** Inner Mongolia ◊ Inner Mongolian

内蒙古大草原 **Nèiménggǔ Dà Cǎo Yuán** Inner Mongolian Grasslands

内幕交易 **nèimù jiāoyì** insider trading

内燃机 **nèiránjī** internal combustion engine

内容 **nèiróng** content; contents

内胎 **nèitāi** inner tube

内向 **nèixiàng** reserved; introverted

内斜视 **nèi xiéshì** cross-eyed

内心 **nèixīn** privately, inwardly

内兄 **nèixiōng** brother-in-law (*wife's older brother*)

内衣 **nèiyī** underwear

内脏 **nèizàng** guts; giblets

内战 **nèizhàn** civil war

内政 **nèizhèng** domestic policy; domestic affairs

内政部 **Nèizhèng Bù** Department of the Interior

内装 **nèizhuāng** built-in

嫩 **nèn** tender

能 **néng** can, be able to ◊ energy; 你能帮我吗？ *nǐ néng bāng wǒ ma?* can you help me?

能干 **nénggàn** capable

能够 **nénggòu** be able to

能见度 **néngjiàn dù** visibility

能力 **nénglì** ability, capacity; competence; faculty (*hearing, vision etc*)

能量 **néngliàng** power, energy; 能量爆发 *néngliàng bàofā* in a burst of energy

能量单位 **néngliàng dānwèi** power unit

能耐梗 **néngnàigěng** wise guy

能胜任 **néngshèngrèn** be equal to

能生育 **néng shēngyù** fertile

能手 **néngshǒu** expert

能养活 **néng yǎnghuó** viable *life form*

能源 **néngyuán** energy (*gas etc*)

嫩鸡 **nènjī** broiler (*chicken*)

嫩芽 **nènyá** shoot BOT

嗯 **ńg** (*questioning*): 嗯，你说什么？ *ńg, ni shud shénme?* huh?, what did you say?

嗯 **ǹg** (*promising*): 嗯！就这么办吧 *ǹg! jiù zhème bàn ba* ok, it's a deal!

泥 **ní** mud

你 **nǐ** you *sg* ◊ your *sg*

拟 **nǐ** draft, draw up

溺爱 **nì'ài** mollycoddle

年 **nián** year ◊ annual

粘 **nián** sticky ◊ stick

念 **niàn** think of; read (out loud); study

黏稠度 **niánchóu dù** consistency, texture

年初 **niánchū** start of the year

年底 **niándǐ** end of the year

年度 **niándù** year ◊ annual

粘附 **niánfù** adhere to

娘 **niáng** mother; woman

酿 **niàng** ferment; brew

娘家姓 **niángjiāxìng** maiden name

酿酒厂 **niàngjiǔchǎng** distillery; winery

娘儿们 **niángrmen** broad, chick

酿造 **niàngzào** brew

酿造厂 **niàngzào chǎng** brewery

酿造者 **niàngzào zhě** brewer

黏糊糊 **nián hūhu** sticky, clammy

年级 **niánjí** grade, class EDU

年纪 **niánjì** age

粘结 **niánjié** bond, stick

年龄 **niánlíng** age; 年龄为 **niánlíng wéi** at the age of

碾灭 **niǎnmiè** stub out

粘膜 **niánmó** mucous membrane

年青 **niánqīng** young

碾碎 **niǎnsuì** grind

捻碎 **niǎnsuì** scrunch up

念头 **niàntou** thought, idea

粘土 **niántǔ** clay

粘液 **niányè** mucus

年长 **niánzhǎng** senior; elder; eldest

年长者 **niánzhǎngzhě** elder

粘住 **niánzhù** stick, glue, adhere

撵走 **niǎnzǒu** throw out, expel

鸟 **niǎo** bird

尿 **niào** urine, piss

尿布 **niàobù** diaper

鸟类保护区 **niǎo lèibǎohù qū** bird sanctuary

鸟笼 **niǎolóng** birdcage

尿片 **niàopiàn** diaper

鸟嘴 **niǎozuǐ** bill, beak

尼泊尔 **Níbó'ěr** Nepal ◊ Nepalese

昵称 **nìchēng** pet name

你的 **nǐde** your sg ◊ yours sg; 你的朋友 **nǐde péngyǒu** a friend of yours

拟订 **nǐdìng** draft, draw up

捏 **niē** pinch; 一捏 **yìniē** a pinch (of salt etc)

镍 **niè** nickel

啮合 **nièhé** engage, become operative

捏造 **niēzào** invent

镊子 **nièzi** tweezers

逆风 **nìfēng** headwind

尼姑 **nígū** Buddhist nun

你好 **nǐ hǎo** hello, hi; 你好吗？**nǐ hǎo ma?** how do you do?; how are you?

霓虹灯 **níhóng dēng** neon light

霓虹灯管 **níhóng dēngguǎn** neon strip

泥浆 **níjiāng** slime

尼龙 **nílóng** nylon

你们 **nǐmen** you pl ◊ your pl

你们的 **nǐmende** your pl ◊ yours pl

你们自己 **nǐmén zìjǐ** yourselves ◊ by yourselves

匿名 **nìmíng** anonymous

您 **nín** you polite ◊ your polite

您的 **nínde** your polite ◊ yours polite

宁 **níng** peaceful

拧 **níng** twist; pinch

凝 **níng** condense; congeal

拧出 **níngchū** wring out

拧干 **nínggān** wring dry

凝固 **nínggù** freeze; congeal

凝结 **níngjié** set; coagulate; curdle

宁静 **níngjìng** peace, tranquility ◊ serene; tranquil, quiet, peaceful

拧开 **níngkāi** unscrew lid

柠檬 **níngméng** lemon

柠檬茶 **níngméng chá** lemon tea

柠檬汽水 **níngméng qìshuǐ** carbonated lemonade

柠檬水 **níngméng shuǐ** lemonade

柠檬汁儿 **níngméng zhīr** lemon juice

凝视 **níngshì** gaze; peer; gaze at ◊ stare; gaze

宁愿 **nìngyuàn** would rather

泥泞 **nínìng** muddy

泥石流 **níshí liú** landslide

逆时针 **nì shízhēn** counterclockwise

妞 **niū** chick, babe

牛 **niú** cattle; cow; bull; ox

扭 **niǔ** twist

扭打 **niǔdǎ** scuffle; fight

扭动 **niǔdòng** squirm, wriggle, writhe; wiggle

牛犊 **niúdú** calf

牛奶 **niúnǎi** (cow's) milk

牛奶场 **niúnǎichǎng** dairy

牛奶加工 **niúnǎi jiāgōng** dairy

忸怩 **niǔní** bashful
牛排 **niúpái** steak
牛皮纸 **niúpí zhǐ** brown paper
扭曲 **niǔqū** screw up, contort ◊ gnarled
牛肉 **niúròu** beef
牛肉面 **niúròumiàn** beef noodles
扭伤 **niǔshāng** sprain, wrench
纽约 **Niǔyuē** New York
牛仔 **niúzǎi** cowboy
牛仔布 **niúzǎi bù** denim
牛仔裤 **niúzǎikù** jeans
扭转 **niǔzhuǎn** deflect; turn around
扭转方向 **niǔzhuǎn fāngxiàng** deflect
泥瓦工 **níwǎgōng** bricklayer
泥瓦匠 **níwǎ jiàng** bricklayer; mason
你自己 **nǐ zìjǐ** yourself
脓 **nóng** pus
浓 **nóng** thick; strong *tea etc*
农 **nóng** agriculture, farming; farmer; peasant ◊ agricultural
弄 **nòng** do; make; obtain
脓包 **nóngbāo** pimple
农场 **nóngchǎng** farm
农场工人 **nóngchǎng gōngrén** farmworker
弄出 **nòngchū** get out, extract
农村 **nóngcūn** village; countryside ◊ rural
弄错 **nòngcuò** be mistaken
弄掉 **nòngdiào** shift, get rid of
浓度 **nóngdù** depth (*of color*); level
弄短 **nòngduǎn** shorten
弄翻 **nòngfān** upset, spill
农夫 **nóngfū** farmer
浓厚 **nónghòu** dense, thick; strong
农户 **nónghù** farm
弄坏 **nònghuài** break; wear out; spoil
弄糊涂 **nòng hútu** muddle
浓烈 **nóngliè** strong
弄乱 **nòngluàn** mess up; be in a mess; ruffle *hair*
浓密 **nóngmì** bushy
农民 **nóngmín** farmer; peasant
弄明白 **nòng míngbái** work out
弄清 **nòngqīng** make clear

农舍 **nóngshè** farmhouse
弄湿 **nòng shī** dampen, moisten
弄死 **nòngsǐ** kill
弄碎 **nòngsuì** crumble *stock cube*
浓缩 **nóngsuō** concentrated
农田 **nóngtián** field
浓烟 **nóngyān** smoke
农业 **nóngyè** agriculture ◊ agricultural
弄脏 **nòngzāng** dirty, soil; smudge
弄糟 **nòngzāo** screw up; spoil
弄直 **nòngzhí** straighten
脓肿 **nóngzhǒng** abscess
奴 **nú** slave
怒 **nù** anger; rage
女 **nǚ** female; feminine
暖 **nuǎn** warm
暖房 **nuǎnfáng** hothouse; greenhouse; conservatory
暖和 **nuǎnhuo** warm, snug
暖瓶 **nuǎnpíng** flask
暖气 **nuǎnqì** heating; central heating; radiator
女厕 **nǚcè** ladies room
女厕所 **nǚcèsuǒ** ladies room, powder room
女店主 **nǚ diànzhǔ** landlady
虐待 **nüèdài** ill-treat, abuse ◊ ill-treatment, abuse
疟疾 **nüèji** malaria
女儿 **nǚ'ér** daughter
女服务员 **nǚ fúwùyuán** waitress; (chamber)maid
女孩 **nǚhái** girl
怒号 **nùháo** howl; roar
怒吼 **nùhǒu** howl; roar; bellow
女皇 **nǚhuáng** empress
女继承人 **nǚ jìchéng rén** heiress
女警察 **nǚ jǐngchá** policewoman
奴隶 **núlì** slave
努力 **nǔlì** effort, attempt; endeavor ◊ laborious ◊ struggle; work hard
努力不懈 **nǔlì búxiè** plug away, persevere
怒目而视 **nùmù ér shì** glare at
女牧师 **nǚ mùshī** woman priest
挪 **nuó** slide
挪动 **nuódòng** move, shift; stir (*in sleep*)
懦夫 **nuòfū** coward ◊ cowardly
糯米 **nuòmì** glutinous rice

挪威 **Nuówēi** Norway ◊ Norwegian

诺言 **nuòyán** promise, word

女朋友 **nǚ péngyou** girlfriend (*of boy*)

女仆 **nǚpú** maid

女权 **nǚquán** women's rights

女权主义 **nǚquán zhǔyì** feminism

女权主义者 **nǚquán zhǔyì zhě** feminist

女人 **nǚrén** woman; female

女人气 **nǚrénqì** effeminate

怒容 **nùróng** scowl

女神 **nǚshén** goddess

女生 **nǚshēng** female student

怒视 **nùshì** scowl

女士 **nǚshì** lady ◊ ma'am ◊ Ms; Miss

女同性恋者 **nǚtóng xìngliàn zhě** lesbian

女王 **nǚwáng** queen

女巫 **nǚwū** witch

女性 **nǚxìng** female

女性朋友 **nǚxìng péngyou** girlfriend (*of girl*)

女婿 **nǚxù** son-in-law

女招待 **nǚzhāodài** hostess (*in bar*)

女主人 **nǚzhǔ rén** mistress (*employer, owner*); hostess

O

噢，喔 **ō** (*understanding*): 噢，我明白了 **ō, wǒ míngbái le** oh, I see

哦 **ó** (*doubt*): 哦，你确定吗？**ó, nǐ quèdìng ma?** really? are you sure?

鸥 **ōu** gull

偶 **ǒu** mate

藕 **ǒu** lotus root

殴打 **ōudǎ** assault, attack

偶尔 **ǒu'ěr** every now and then, occasionally ◊ occasional

欧化 **ōuhuà** westernize

偶然 **ǒurán** chance ◊ by chance; occasionally; 偶然发现 **ǒurán fāxiàn** happen across

偶然性 **ǒuránxìng** haphazard

偶数 **ǒushù** even *number*

呕吐 **ǒutù** bring up, throw up ◊ vomiting; vomit

偶像 **ǒuxiàng** heart throb, idol

欧元 **ōuyuán** euro

欧洲 **Ōuzhōu** Europe ◊ European

P

趴 **pā** lie on one's stomach
爬 **pá** climb; crawl
耙 **pá** rake
怕 **pà** fear
啪嗒声 **pādāshēng** patter
拍 **pāi** take *photograph*; shoot *film*; beat, pound; clap; pat
牌 **pái** plate; board; brand; card
排 **pái** line, row; tier; cluster; platoon ◊ rank (*in order*); discharge, expel; 排成长龙 **páichéng chánglóng** be backed up (*of traffic*)
派 **pài** group; pie
排版 **páibǎn** typeset
陪伴 **péibàn** companionship
派别 **pàibié** group; faction; sect
排斥 **páichì** exclude, bar; push away
排出 **páichū** discharge
排出的废气 **páichūde fèiqì** exhaust fumes
排除 **páichú** eliminate; cut out; exclude; rule out ◊ removal
排除故障 **páichú gùzhàng** troubleshooting
派出所 **pàichūsuǒ** police station
排除在外 **páichú zàiwài** exclude; ignore
拍打 **pāidǎ** buffet; patter; smack
排队 **páiduì** stand in line
排房 **páifáng** row house
排放 **páifàng** emission
排干 **páigān** drain *liquid*
排骨 **páigǔ** chop; spare ribs
排挤 **páijǐ** displace
迫击炮 **pǎijīpào** mortar
排练 **páiliàn** rehearse ◊ rehearsal
排列 **páiliè** sort COMPUT
拍卖 **pāimài** auction
拍卖掉 **pāimài diào** auction off
拍马屁 **pāi mǎpì** brown-nose
排尿 **páiniào** urinate, pass water
拍拍 **pāipāi** pat *dog etc*

派遣 **pàiqiǎn** send
排气管 **páiqìguǎn** exhaust (pipe)
排球 **páiqiú** volleyball
排去 **páiqù** drain away; drain off
派人去找 **pàirén qùzhǎo** send for
拍摄 **pāishè** film, shoot; photograph
拍摄场地 **pāishè chǎngdì** (film) set
派生 **pàishēng** derivative
拍手 **pāishǒu** clap, applaud
排水 **páishuǐ** drainage
排水工程 **páishuǐ gōngchéng** sewerage
排水沟 **páishuǐgōu** gutter
排水管 **páishuǐ guǎn** drainpipe
派往 **pàiwǎng** post; transfer
排演 **páiyǎn** rehearse ◊ rehearsal
拍照 **pāizhào** photograph
牌照 **páizhào** vehicle registration
拍子 **pāizi** bat; racket; club; stick
牌子 **páizi** sign; nameplate; brand, make
攀 **pān** climb
盘 **pán** dish; plate; set (*in tennis*) ◊ *measure word for cassettes, CDs*
判 **pàn** judge
叛 **pàn** betray
盼 **pàn** hope for; expect
攀登 **pāndēng** climb; scramble
盘点 **pándiǎn** take stock ◊ stocktaking
判断 **pànduàn** judge; make a judgment
判断能力 **pànduàn nénglì** discretion, judgment
旁 **páng** side
胖 **pàng** fat
旁边 **pángbiān** side; 在 X 的旁边 **zài X de pángbiān** next to X, beside X
庞大 **pángdà** enormous
判给 **pàngěi** award
旁观 **pángguān** look on, watch

膀胱 **pángguāng** bladder

旁观者 **pángguān zhě** bystander, onlooker

胖乎乎 **pànghūhū** plump

庞然大物 **pángrán dàwù** monster

旁听 **pángtīng** listen in; audit *course*

滂沱 **pāngtuó** pouring; 大雨滂沱 **dàyǔ pāngtuó** pouring with rain

叛国罪 **pànguó zuì** treason

螃蟹 **pángxiè** crab

胖子 **pàngzi** fat person, fatso

判决 **pànjué** pass judgment ◊ judgment, verdict

叛乱 **pànluàn** mutiny

叛逆 **pànnì** rebel

蹒跚 **pánshān** hobble; lurch; totter

叛徒 **pàntú** traitor

盼望 **pànwàng** long for

盘问 **pánwèn** question, quiz

判刑 **pànxíng** sentence; pass sentence; 判死刑 **pàn sǐxíng** condemn to death

盘旋 **pánxuán** twist, wind; circle

攀缘 **pānyuán** climb

盘子 **pánzi** plate

抛 **pāo** throw

跑 **pǎo** run; run away

泡 **pào** bubble ◊ soak, steep; brew, infuse (*of tea*)

炮 **pào** cannon; gun

炮兵 **pàobīng** artillery

跑步 **pǎobù** run, jog

泡菜 **pàocài** pickles

泡茶 **pàochá** make tea

跑车 **pǎochē** sports car

刨出 **páochū** dig out; dig up

炮弹 **pàodàn** shell MIL

跑道 **pǎodào** runway; racetrack; lane

跑掉 **pǎodiào** run off; run away

炮火 **pàohuǒ** gunfire; shelling

炮击 **pàojī** shell MIL

跑马 **pǎomǎ** the races

跑马道 **pǎomǎ dào** racecourse

抛锚 **pāomáo** break down; stall (*of vehicle*); anchor (*of ship*)

泡沫 **pàomò** foam, froth; suds; lather

泡沫橡胶 **pàomò xiàngjiāo** foam rubber

泡泡糖 **pàopao táng** bubble gum

抛起 **pāoqǐ** throw up *ball*

抛弃 **pāoqì** abandon; leave; discard; ditch ◊ desertion

跑气 **pǎoqì** flat *beer*

跑腿 **pǎotuǐ** run errands

咆哮 **páoxiào** growl; roar

疱疹 **pàozhěn** herpes; 嘴边疱疹 **zuǐbiān pàozhěn** cold sore

扒手 **páshǒu** pickpocket

爬行 **páxíng** creep; crawl

爬行动物 **páxíng dòngwù** reptile

耙子 **pázi** rake

呸 **pēi** (*scorn*): 呸！谁要你的臭钱！ *pēi! shéi yào nǐde chòuqián!* bah!, who needs your damn money!

陪 **péi** accompany, go with; escort

赔 **péi** pay compensation

配 **pèi** match, go together; 配钥匙 *pèi yàoshi* copy a key

陪伴 **péibàn** accompany

赔本 **péiběn** make a loss

赔偿 **péicháng** compensate ◊ compensation; damages

佩服 **pèifu** admire

配合 **pèihé** cooperate ◊ teamwork

配给 **pèijǐ** ration; 少量配给 *shǎoliàng pèijǐ* dole out

配给量 **pèijǐ liàng** ration

赔礼 **péilǐ** apologize

配偶 **pèi'ǒu** spouse

赔钱 **péiqián** be out of pocket

陪审团 **péishěntuán** jury

陪审员 **péishěnyuán** juror

胚胎 **pēitāi** embryo

陪同 **péitóng** escort; accompany

陪同者 **péitóngzhě** escort; companion; accompanist

培训 **péixùn** train; groom, prepare ◊ training

培训课程 **péixùn kèchéng** training course

培养 **péiyǎng** raise; develop; train; cultivate *plants*

配音 **pèiyīn** dub *movie*

配乐 **pèiyuè** soundtrack, score

培植 **péizhí** breeding ◊ cultivate *plants*

喷 pēn spray; spurt

盆 pén bowl; plant pot; 一盆花 **yīpén huā** a potted plant

喷出 pēnchū spout, spurt

盆地 péndì basin (*geographical*)

喷发胶 pēnfà jiāo hair spray

砰 pēng thump

烹 pēng cook

棚 péng shed; stall, pen

碰 pèng touch; knock; push; bump into; meet; 别碰! **bié pèng!** hands off!

碰杯 pèngbēi clink glasses

篷车 péngchē trailer

碰钉子 pèng dīngzi get the brushoff

捧腹大笑 pěngfù dàxiào crack up, laugh

抨击 pēngjī hit out at, criticize, attack

碰见 pèngjiàn bump into, meet

蓬乱 péngluàn unkempt, dishevelled; tousled

碰碰车 pèngpèngchē bumper car, dodgem®

捧起 pěngqǐ scoop up

碰巧 pèngqiǎo by chance, coincidentally; 如果你碰巧见到他 **rúguǒ nǐ pèngqiǎo jiàndào tā** if you happen to see him

烹饪书 pēngrèn shū cookbook

碰伤 pèngshāng bruise (*of fruit*)

蓬松 péngsōng fluffy

烹调 pēngtiáo cook ◊ cookery ◊ culinary

碰头 pèngtóu meet

棚屋 péngwū hut

朋友 péngyou friend

膨胀 péngzhàng expand; bulge; inflate *economy* ◊ expansion ◊ swollen; puffy

碰撞 pèngzhuàng collide

棚子 péngzi shack

喷壶 pēnhú watering can

盆景 pénjǐng bonsai

喷沫 pēnmò aerosol

喷墨(打印机) pēnmò (dǎyìnjī) inkjet (printer)

喷漆 pēnqī spray paint

喷枪 pēnqiāng spraygun

喷气发动机 pēnqì fādòngjī jet engine

喷气式 pēnqìshì jet

喷气式飞机 pēnqìshì fēijī jet plane

喷泉 pēnquán fountain

喷射 pēnshè squirt; spurt

喷嚏 pēntì sneeze

喷雾器 pēnwù qì spray

喷嘴 pēnzuǐ nozzle

劈 pī split *logs etc*

批 pī batch

披 pī put on; drape

脾 pí spleen

皮 pí skin; hide; leather; shell

癖 pǐ addiction; obsession

匹 pǐ *measure word for horses*; 四匹马 **sìpǐ mǎ** four horses

屁 pì fart; ass, butt

偏 piān leaning to one side; partial; 偏大 / 小 **piāndà / xiǎo** on the big / small side

篇 piān piece of writing ◊ *measure word for paper*, *books etc*; 一篇文章 **yìpiān wénzhāng** an article

骗 piàn cheat, deceive, con

片 piàn slice (*of bread etc*); stretch (*of land etc*) ◊ *measure word for slices*, *flat things*; 两片安眠药 **liǎngpiàn ānmiányào** two sleeping pills

偏爱 piān'ài favorite ◊ be partial to; have a soft spot for ◊ preference

偏差 piānchā difference; deviation

偏高 piāngāo sharp MUS

偏激 piānjī extreme *views*

骗计 piànjì swindle

偏见 piānjiàn prejudice; bias

骗局 piànjú deception; fraud; con; racket

片刻 piànkè moment

偏离 piānlí deviate; differ ◊ departure

片面 piànmiàn biased

篇名 piānmíng title (*of novel etc*)

偏僻 piānpì remote

偏偏 piānpiān of all people; just; 他偏偏不做 **tā piānpiān bú zuò** he just won't do it

骗取 piànqǔ defraud

偏袒 **piāntǎn** bias (*in favor of*) ◊ biased

偏头痛 **piāntóutòng** migraine

偏向 **piānxiàng** take sides

偏心 **piānxīn** prejudiced

便宜 **piányi** cheap; inexpensive

便宜货 **piányí huò** buy; bargain

片语 **piànyǔ** phrase

篇章 **piānzhāng** chapter

骗子 **piànzi** cheat; fraud; crook; con man

飘 **piāo** drift

瓢 **piáo** ladle

票 **piào** ticket

漂白剂 **piǎobái jì** bleach

漂泊 **piāobó** drift

瓢虫 **piáochóng** ladybug

飘荡 **piāodàng** drift; float

飘动 **piāodòng** flutter (*of flag*)

票贩子 **piàofànzi** scalper

漂浮 **piāofú** float; drift ◊ afloat

票价 **piàojià** fare

漂亮 **piàoliang** pretty, beautiful, lovely

漂亮的一举 **piàoliàng de yījǔ** coup, feat

票面价值 **piàomiàn jiàzhí** face value

瓢泼大雨 **piáopō dàyǔ** cloudburst

票券 **piàoquàn** voucher

漂洗 **piǎoxǐ** rinse

飘扬 **piāoyáng** flutter; flap; blow; fly (*of flag*)

皮包骨 **píbāogǔ** skinny

疲惫 **píbèi** exhausted

皮带 **pídài** leather belt

皮蛋 **pídàn** preserved egg

匹敌 **pǐdí** equal; evenly matched; 与 X 匹敌 **yǔ X pǐdí** match X

屁兜儿 **pìdōur** hip pocket

撇号 **piěhào** apostrophe

瞥见 **piējiàn** glimpse; catch a glimpse of; peek

撇去 **piēqù** skim *milk*

批发 **pīfā** wholesale

疲乏 **pífá** tired

批发商 **pīfāshāng** wholesaler

皮肤 **pífū** skin

批改 **pīgǎi** mark EDU

皮革 **pígé** leather

皮革制品 **pígé zhìpǐn** leather goods

屁股 **pìgu** bottom, butt

癖好 **pǐhào** mania, passion

披肩 **pījiān** shawl

僻静处 **pìjìngchù** hideaway

否极泰来 **pǐjítàilái** *prov* good luck comes after a lot of misfortune

啤酒 **píjiǔ** beer

啤酒厂 **píjiǔchǎng** brewery

啤酒花 **píjiǔhuā** hops

疲倦 **píjuàn** tire ◊ tiredness; fatigue ◊ tired; run-down; 令人疲倦 **lìngrén píjuàn** exhausting; 使 … 疲倦 **shǐ … píjuàn** wear out

劈开 **pīkāi** split

疲劳 **píláo** exhausted; 疲劳不堪 **píláo bùkān** totally exhausted

劈雳 **pīlì** crash (*of thunder*)

皮毛 **pímáo** fur, coat; skin; fleece

拼 **pīn** put together; spell

频 **pín** frequency

贫 **pín** poor

品 **pǐn** item, article

品尝 **pǐncháng** savor; taste, sample

拼凑 **pīncòu** piece together; pad *speech etc*

频道 **píndào** channel (*TV etc*)

品德 **pǐndé** virtue

频繁 **pínfán** frequently

瓶 **píng** bottle; jar

平 **píng** even, level; peaceful; safe; 二平 **èrpíng** two all

评 **píng** criticize

凭 **píng** rely on; lean on

平安 **píng'ān** safe ◊ safely; 平安到达 **píng'ān dàodá** arrive safe and sound; 平安无恙 **píng'ān wúyàng** unharmed

平常 **píngcháng** usually, normally ◊ common; conventional

平淡 **píngdàn** bland; tame; uneventful; flat *tone of voice*

平等 **píngděng** equal ◊ equality

平等主义 **píngděngzhǔyì** egalitarian

平底 **píngdǐ** flat *shoes*

平底锅 **píngdǐguō** frying pan; pan

平底雪橇 **píngdǐ xuěqiāo** toboggan

平凡 **píngfán** usual; normal

平方 **píngfāng** square MATH

平方根 **píngfāng gēn** square root

平放着 **píng fàngzhe** lie (*of object*)

平分 **píngfēn** share out

屏风 **píngfēng** partition, screen

平分球 **píngfēnqiú** equalizer SP

评估 **pínggū** evaluate, assess; take stock ◊ evaluation

苹果 **píngguǒ** apple

苹果酒 **píngguǒ jiǔ** cider

苹果派 **píngguǒ pài** apple pie

苹果汁儿 **píngguǒ zhīr** apple sauce

平衡 **pínghéng** balance; equilibrium ◊ balance; stabilize ◊ balanced

平衡力 **pínghéng lì** counterbalance

评价 **píngjià** assess, evaluate

平静 **píngjìng** quiet; calm; peaceful

平静下来 **píngjìng xiàlái** calm down

平局 **píngjú** draw, tie; deuce (*in tennis*)

凭据 **píngjù** evidence

平均 **píngjūn** average; 平均来说 *píngjūn láishuō* on average

平均水准 **píngjūn shuǐzhǔn** average; 高于/低于平均水准 *gāoyú / dīyú píngjūn shuǐzhǔn* above / below average

凭空 **píngkōng** unfounded, baseless

凭空想出 **píngkōng xiǎngchū** dream up

平乱警察 **píngluàn jǐngchá** riot police

评论 **pínglùn** review, write-up; commentary ◊ review; remark, comment

评论家 **pínglùn jiā** critic; commentator; reviewer

平面 **píngmiàn** plane ◊ level; graphic

平面交叉 **píngmiàn jiāochā** grade crossing

平面图 **píngmiàntú** ground plan

平民 **píngmín** civilian

屏幕 **píngmù** screen COMPUT

屏幕保护器 **píngmù bǎohùqì** screen saver

乒乓球 **pīngpāngqiú** table tennis; ping-pong

瓶塞 **píngsāi** cork; stopper

平时 **píngshí** ordinarily; usually

平台 **píngtái** patio

平坦 **píngtǎn** flat, level

平头 **píngtóu** crew cut

评委 **píngwěi** judge (*in competition*)

平稳 **píngwěn** smooth; steady

平息 **píngxī** cool down; die down; subside; appease

平行 **píngxíng** parallel

平行线 **píngxíngxiàn** parallel line

平胸 **píngxiōng** flat-chested

平易近人 **píngyì jìnrén** approachable

平庸 **píngyōng** commonplace; mediocre ◊ mediocrity

平庸的人 **píngyōngde rén** mediocrity

评语 **píngyǔ** comment; assessment

平原 **píngyuán** plain, prairie

平直 **píngzhí** straight; lank

平装书 **píngzhuāng shū** paperback, pocketbook

瓶装水 **píngzhuāng shuǐ** bottled water

瓶子 **píngzi** bottle

贫瘠 **pínjí** barren

聘金 **pìnjīn** retainer

贫困 **pínkùn** poor, deprived; destitute; impoverished ◊ poverty

贫困不堪 **pínkùn bùkān** poverty-stricken

频率 **pínlǜ** frequency

拼命 **pīnmìng** all out, like mad

贫民窟 **pínmínkū** slum

品牌 **pǐnpái** kind, variety; brand

拼盘 **pīnpán** cold platter

贫穷 **pínqióng** poor

品脱 **pǐntuō** pint

拼图游戏 **pīntú yóuxì** jigsaw (puzzle)

品位 **pǐnwèi** taste

拼写 **pīnxiě** spell

品行 **pǐnxíng** conduct, behavior

贫血 **pínxuè** anemia ◊ anemic

拼音 **pīnyīn** pinyin
聘用 **pìnyòng** hire, take on
品种 **pǐnzhǒng** breed
批评 **pīpíng** criticize ◊ criticism
脾气 **píqi** temperament; temper;
脾气好 **píqì hǎo** good-natured;
脾气坏 **píqì huài** bad-tempered,
ill-natured
皮箱 **píxiāng** suitcase
皮鞋 **píxié** leather shoes
癖性 **pǐxìng** idiosyncrasy
屁眼儿 **pìyǎnr** asshole
皮衣 **pīyī** leather garment; leather
clothing
皮疹 **pízhěn** rash MED
批准 **pīzhǔn** approve, pass ◊
approval, sanction
坡 **pō** slope
泼 **pō** splash
婆 **pó** old woman
破 **pò** break ◊ broken
迫 **pò** force; press ◊ pressing
破冰船 **pòbīngchuán** icebreaker
迫不及待 **pòbù jídài** pressing,
urgent ◊ can't wait
破产 **pòchǎn** bankrupt ◊ go
bankrupt; go into liquidation; be
in receivership ◊ bankruptcy
坡道 **pōdào** ramp
坡顶 **pōdǐng** brow (of hill)
泼妇 **pōfù** bitch; dragon (woman)
迫害 **pòhài** persecute ◊
persecution
破坏 **pòhuài** ruin; destroy;
sabotage; corrupt COMPUT ◊
destruction; disruption; sabotage
破坏公共财产行为 **pòhuài
gōnggòng cáichǎn xíngwéi**
vandalism
破坏公共财产者 **pòhuài
gōnggòng cáichǎn zhě** vandal
破坏性 **pòhuài xìng** destructive;
disruptive
迫降 **pòjiàng** forced landing
迫近 **pòjìn** close in; be imminent ◊
imminent
破旧 **pòjiù** beat-up; worn-out; run-
down; seedy
破烂 **pòlàn** ragged, tattered ◊
trash, crap
破牢 **pòláo** break out, escape

破裂 **pòliè** rupture; burst ◊
rupture; bust-up ◊ broken; in
ruins; cracked
破门而入 **pòmén ér rù** break in
破灭 **pòmiè** dash, shatter *hopes*
婆婆 **pópó** mother-in-law (of
woman)
破破烂烂 **pòpo lànlan** in tatters
迫切 **pòqiè** pressing
迫切需要 **pòqiè xūyào** cry out
for
破伤风 **pòshāngfēng** tetanus
迫使 **pòshǐ** force
破碎 **pòsuì** break, smash ◊ broken
剖 **pōu** cut open; dissect; analyze
剖腹产 **pōufùchǎn** cesarean
剖面 **pōumiàn** profile; section
破晓 **pòxiǎo** daybreak, dawn
破译 **pòyì** crack, solve
迫在眉睫 **pò zài méijié**
impending
破折号 **pòzhé hào** dash (in
punctuation)
铺 **pū** spread; unfold; pave
谱 **pǔ** musical notation
普遍 **pǔbiàn** general, widespread;
universal
普遍存在 **pǔbiàn cúnzài**
pervasive
瀑布 **pùbù** waterfall
铺床 **pūchuáng** make the bed
仆从 **púcóng** henchman
扑动 **pūdòng** flutter (of heart)
扑粉 **pūfěn** powder
匍匐植物 **púfú zhíwù** creeper
曝光 **pùguāng** expose ◊ exposure
普及 **pǔjí** generalize; popularize ◊
widespread; universal
扑克 **pūkè** poker; playing cards
扑克牌 **pūkèpái** playing cards
铺路石板 **pūlù shíbǎn** paving
stone
扑灭 **pūmiè** extinguish
谱曲 **pǔqǔ** compose
仆人 **púrén** servant
菩萨 **Púsà** Bodhisattva; Buddha
铺设 **pūshè** pave; lay
朴素 **pǔsù** modest; plain, simple ◊
modesty
葡萄 **pútao** grape; vine
葡萄干 **pútao gān** raisin

葡萄酒 **pútaojiǔ** wine

葡萄糖 **pútaotáng** glucose

葡萄牙 **Pútaoyá** Portugal ◊ Portuguese

葡萄柚 **pútaoyòu** grapefruit

葡萄柚汁 **pútaoyòu zhī** grapefruit juice

葡萄园 **pútáo yuán** vineyard

扑通 **pūtōng** splash (*noise*)

普通 **pǔtōng** ordinary; common, standard; plain *features etc*

普通股 **pǔtōnggǔ** equity

普通话 **Pǔtōnghuà** Mandarin, Putonghua

普通邮件 **pǔtōng yóujiàn** surface mail

铺位 **pùwèi** berth

普选 **pǔxuǎn** general election

溥仪 **Pǔ Yí** Pu Yi (*last Emperor of China*)

Q

漆 **qī** paint

妻 **qī** wife

七 **qī** seven

期 **qī** period; issue, edition

欺 **qī** cheat, deceive

鳍 **qí** fin

旗 **qí** flag

骑 **qí** ride; pedal

齐 **qí** even; neat

其 **qí** his; her; its

启 **qǐ** open; start; enlighten

起 **qǐ** get up; 起风了 **qǐ fēng le** it's getting windy ◊ (*ability*): 买得起 **mǎi de qǐ** be able to afford

器 **qì** device; utensil; meter

汽 **qì** vapor; steam

气 **qì** air; gas; 胃肠中的气 **wèicháng zhōng de qì** wind, flatulence

迄 **qì** until; by

掐 **qiā** nip

卡 **qiǎ** jam; choke

恰当 **qiàdàng** proper, correct; appropriate; applicable

恰到好处 **qiàdào hǎochù** to perfection

恰好 **qiàhǎo** just; in the nick of time

亲爱 **qī'ài** darling

千 **qiān** thousand

铅 **qiān** lead (*metal*)

牵 **qiān** pull; lead

签 **qiān** sign

迁 **qiān** move

前 **qián** before; in front of; ex-, former; 两天前 **liǎngtiān qián** 2 days ago; 前一个星期 **qián yīgè xīngqī** the week before

潜 **qián** dive; submerge ◊ hidden

钱 **qián** money; 我欠你多少？ **wǒ qiàn nǐ duōshǎo?** how much do I owe you?

浅 **qiǎn** shallow; light

欠 **qiàn** owe ◊ due, owed

钱包 **qiánbāo** wallet, billfold; purse

谦卑 **qiānbēi** humble

前辈 **qiánbèi** senior; elder

铅笔 **qiānbǐ** pencil

前臂 **qiánbì** forearm

浅薄 **qiǎnbó** shallow, superficial

前部 **qiánbù** foreground; 在 X 的前部 **zài X de qiánbù** at the front of X

潜藏 **qiáncáng** lurk

浅尝 **qiǎncháng** foretaste

虔诚 **qiánchéng** devout; pious; ardent

嵌齿轮 **qiàn chǐlún** cogwheel

前灯 **qiándēng** headlight

签订 **qiāndìng** sign; conclude *contract*

前额 **qián'é** forehead, brow

签发 **qiānfā** issue

前锋 **qiánfēng** forward SP

千分之一 **qiānfēnzhīyī** thousandth

前夫 **qiánfū** ex(-husband)

潜伏 **qiánfú** latent; potential

枪 **qiāng** gun

强 **qiáng** strong

墙 **qiáng** wall

抢 **qiǎng** rob; snatch, nab

强暴 **qiángbào** violent ◊ violently ◊ rape

墙报 **qiángbào** wall news-sheet

枪毙 **qiāngbì** shoot dead

墙壁 **qiángbì** wall

强大 **qiángdà** powerful

强盗 **qiángdào** robber; bandit

强调 **qiángdiào** emphasize, stress; accentuate

强度 **qiángdù** strength, force

抢购 **qiǎnggòu** snap up, buy

强化 **qiánghuà** intensive

强奸 **qiángjiān** rape

强奸犯 **qiángjiān fàn** rapist

抢劫 **qiǎngjié** rob; hold up ◊

robbery; holdup; raid; 我被抢劫
了 **wǒ bèi qiǎngjié le** I've been
robbed

抢劫犯 **qiǎngjié fàn** robber;
raider

强劲 **qiángjìn** strong; virile

抢救 **qiǎngjiù** rescue; recover;
save; salvage

跄踉 **qiàngliàng** stumble

强烈 **qiángliè** strong; fierce; keen
◊ intensity

谦恭 **qiāngōng** humility

钳工 **qiángōng** fitter

强迫 **qiǎngpò** coerce; compel; put
pressure on

枪伤 **qiāngshāng** gunshot wound

牵挂 **qiānguà** worry about

抢先报道 **qiǎngxiān bàodào**
scoop

强硬路线者 **qiángyìng lùxiàn
zhě** hardliner

强有力 **qiángyǒulì** powerful

枪支 **qiāngzhī** firearm

墙纸 **qiángzhǐ** wallpaper

强制 **qiángzhì** force ◊ mandatory

强壮 **qiángzhuàng** strong; sound;
hardy

前后颠倒 **qiánhòu diāndǎo** back
to front

千斤顶 **qiānjīndǐng** jack MOT

前景 **qiánjǐng** view; prospects

迁就 **qiānjiù** accommodate

迁居 **qiānjū** move house ◊ move;
migration

千克 **qiānkè** kilogram

潜力 **qiánlì** potential

牵连 **qiānlián** involve; 与 X 有牵
连 **yǔ X yǒu qiānlián** be mixed up
in X

前门 **qiánmén** front door

千米 **qiānmǐ** kilometer

前面 **qiánmian** front; in front;
ahead; 在 X 的前面 **zài X de
qiánmian** in front of X

签名 **qiānmíng** sign ◊ signature

前排 **qiánpái** front row

前妻 **qiánqī** ex(-wife)

牵强 **qiānqiáng** farfetched

欠缺 **qiànquē** go without; lack

前任者 **qiánrèn zhě** predecessor

潜入 **qiánrù** submerge

遣散 **qiǎnsàn** discharge

浅色 **qiǎnsè** light-colored; fair *hair*

牵涉 **qiānshè** entail

歉收 **qiànshōu** crop failure

签署 **qiānshǔ** sign

潜水 **qiánshuǐ** dive ◊ diving

潜水艇 **qiánshuǐtǐng** submarine

潜水员 **qiánshuǐyuán** diver

前所未闻 **qián suǒ wèi wén**
unheard-of

潜逃车 **qiántáochē** getaway car

前提 **qiántí** prerequisite; condition

前天 **qiántiān** the day before
yesterday

潜艇 **qiántǐng** submarine

前途 **qiántú** future; prospects

欠妥 **qiàntuǒ** inappropriate

前途未卜 **qiántú wèibǔ** journey
into the unknown

前夕 **qiánxī** eve

前线 **qiánxiàn** front, frontline

前行 **qiánxíng** proceed

潜行 **qiánxíng** prowl

谦虚 **qiānxū** modest, unassuming

谦逊 **qiānxùn** modest, unassuming
◊ modesty

前言 **qiányán** foreword; preface

迁移 **qiānyí** move; migrate;
transfer

潜意识 **qiányìshí** subconscious

签约方 **qiānyuēfāng** signatory

潜在 **qiánzài** potential

谴责 **qiǎnzé** condemn; accuse ◊
condemnation; accusation

欠债 **qiànzhài** be in debt; 欠 X 债
qiàn X zhài be indebted to X

千兆字节 **qiānzhào zìjié**
gigabyte

前者 **qiánzhě** the former

签证 **qiānzhèng** visa

牵制 **qiānzhì** diversion

钳制 **qiánzhì** clamp down on; 钳
制 **qiánzhì xīnwén** muzzle the
press

前缀 **qiánzhuì** prefix

签字 **qiānzì** sign *check etc*

钳子 **qiánzi** forceps; pliers; tongs

千字节 **qiānzìjié** kilobyte

前奏 **qiánzòu** overture; prelude

敲 **qiāo** knock

锹 **qiāo** spade

桥 qiáo bridge
瞧 qiáo look
巧 qiǎo skillful; coincidental
鞘 qiào sheath (*for knife*)
瞧不起 qiáobuqǐ look down on
憔悴 qiáocuì gaunt, haggard
敲打 qiāodǎ beat; drum
巧合 qiǎohé coincide ◊ coincidence
侨居 qiáojū live abroad
撬开 qiàokāi lever open
巧克力 qiǎokèlì chocolate
巧克力蛋糕 qiǎokèlì dàngāo chocolate cake
翘棱 qiáoleng warp
巧妙 qiǎomiào clever; neat; subtle
巧妙地安排 qiǎomiàode ānpái engineer, arrange
巧妙的手法 qiǎomiàode shǒufǎ sleight of hand
桥牌 qiáopái bridge (*cards*)
俏皮话 qiàopí huà quip
悄悄 qiāoqiao stealthy
跷跷板 qiāoqiāobǎn seesaw
悄然去逝 qiāorán qùshì slip away
敲响 qiāoxiǎng strike
敲诈 qiāozhà blackmail
敲钟 qiāozhōng ring
敲竹杠 qiāo zhúgàng cheat, rip off
恰恰 qiàqià exactly
恰如其分 qiàrú qífèn apt; applicable; accurate
洽商 qiàshāng negotiate
洽谈 qiàtán discuss; negotiate
卡住 qiǎzhù jam; lodge; be jammed; seize up
起博器 qǐbóqì pacemaker MED
器材 qìcái equipment
蛴螬 qícáo grub (*of insect*)
起草 qǐcǎo draw up
起草稿 qǐ cǎogǎo draft
起草人 qǐcǎo rén draftsman
汽车 qìchē automobile
汽车道 qìchē dào driveway
汽车旅馆 qìchē lǚguǎn motel
汽车喇叭 qìchē lǎba (car) horn
启程 qǐchéng leave
启程时间 qǐchéng shíjiān departure time

汽车棚 qìchēpéng car port
汽车修理站 qìchē xiūlǐzhàn garage
汽车业 qìchē yè automobile industry
汽车站 qìchē zhàn depot, bus station
气冲冲 qìchōngchōng furious
起初 qǐchū at first
汽船 qìchuán motorboat
气喘 qìchuǎn gasp ◊ asthma; 气喘嘘嘘 **qìchuǎn xūxū** be out of breath
起床 qǐchuáng get up; get out of bed; 起床走动 **qǐchuáng zǒudòng** be up and about
其次 qícì secondly
期待 qīdài expect; look forward to
脐带 qídài umbilical cord
期待以久 qīdài yǐjiǔ overdue; long-awaited
祈祷 qídǎo pray; wish for
启迪 qǐdí enlighten
起点 qǐdiǎn starting point
气垫船 qìdiànchuán hovercraft
启动 qǐdòng boot up
起动装置 qǐdòng zhuāngzhì starter motor; trigger; record button
切 qiē cut; carve *meat*
妾 qiè concubine
窃 qiè steal
企鹅 qǐ'é penguin
怯场 qièchǎng stage fright
切成薄片 qiēchéng báopiàn slice
切成丁 qiēchéng dīng dice
切成小条 qiēchéng xiǎotiáo shred
切除 qiēchú remove; cut out
切断 qiēduàn cut off, disconnect; sever
切合实际 qièhé shíjì realistic
切开 qiēkāi incision
切口 qiēkǒu cut
切片面包 qiēpiàn miànbāo sliced bread
窃窃私语 qièqiè sīyǔ whisper
切实可行 qièshí kěxíng viable, feasible
切碎 qiēsuì chop, mince

切碎机 **qiēsuìjī** (document) shredder

窃听 **qiètīng** eavesdrop; tap

窃听器 **qiètīng qì** bug; 装窃听器 **zhuāng qiètīng qì** bug; tap; wire up

茄子 **qiézi** eggplant

起反作用 **qǐ fǎn zuòyòng** counterproductive

启发性 **qǐfāxìng** illuminating

起飞 **qǐfēi** take off ◊ takeoff

起飞时间 **qǐfēi shíjiān** flight time

气氛 **qìfēn** atmosphere, mood; tone

气愤 **qìfèn** outraged

欺负 **qīfu** bully, pick on

起伏 **qǐfú** swell (of sea)

乞丐 **qǐgài** beggar

汽缸 **qìgāng** cylinder (of engine)

漆革 **qīgé** patent leather

气功 **qìgōng** qigong (Chinese system of breath control)

奇怪 **qíguài** strange, odd

器官 **qìguān** organ

妻管严 **qīguǎnyán** henpecked

气管炎 **qìguǎn yán** bronchitis

旗鼓相当 **qígǔ xiāngdāng** meet one's match

启航 **qǐháng** sail, depart

漆黑 **qīhēi** pitch black

起哄 **qǐhòng** jeer

气候 **qìhòu** climate

汽化 **qìhuà** vaporize

汽化器 **qìhuàqì** carburetor

期货 **qīhuò** futures

期货市场 **qīhuò shìchǎng** futures market

奇迹 **qíjī** miracle ◊ miraculous

期间 **qījiān** duration; 夏季期间 **xiàjì qījiān** through the summer; 在 X 期间 **zài X qījiān** during X

奇迹般 **qíjìbān** miraculous

迄今 **qìjīn** yet, so far

骑警 **qíjǐng** mounted police

汽酒 **qìjiǔ** sparkling wine

器具 **qìjù** device, gadget

起居室 **qǐjū shì** lounge

期刊 **qīkān** periodical; magazine

起来 **qǐlái** rise, stand up ◊ (start of action): 唱起来 **chàng qǐlai** start singing

起立 **qǐlì** stand, rise

气轮机 **qìlún jī** turbine

起落架 **qǐluòjià** undercarriage

起落装置 **qǐluò zhuāngzhì** landing gear

骑马 **qímǎ** ride (a horse) ◊ riding ◊ on horseback

起码 **qǐmǎ** at least

期满 **qīmǎn** expire ◊ expiry

起锚 **qǐmáo** weigh anchor

骑马人 **qímǎ rén** rider

妻妹 **qīmèi** sister-in-law (wife's younger sister)

奇妙 **qímiào** wonderful

器皿 **qìmǐn** vessel; container

起名 **qǐmíng** name, call

骑摩托车的人 **qí mótuōchē de rén** motorcyclist

亲 **qīn** kiss ◊ intimate ◊ relatives

侵 **qīn** invade

禽 **qín** bird; fowl

勤 **qín** hardworking

亲爱 **qīn'ài** dear; darling; 亲爱的王丽 **qīn'àide Wáng Lì** Dear Wang Li

亲爱的 **qīn'àide** darling, honey

亲笔签名 **qīnbǐ qiānmíng** autograph

芹菜 **qíncài** celery

秦朝 **Qín Cháo** Qin Dynasty

气馁 **qìněi** demoralized; 令人气馁 **lìngrén qìněi** unnerving; 使 ... 气馁 **shǐ ... qìněi** daunt

侵犯 **qīnfàn** encroach; breach; intrude ◊ intrusion

侵犯行为 **qīnfàn xíngwéi** aggression

侵犯者 **qīnfàn zhě** intruder

勤奋 **qínfèn** diligent, hard-working, industrious

氢 **qīng** hydrogen

轻 **qīng** light ◊ lightness

青 **qīng** green; blue; black; young

清 **qīng** clear; pure

倾 **qīng** incline

情 **qíng** feeling

晴 **qíng** sunny; clear

请 **qǐng** please ◊ ask; invite; 我可以请你吃顿饭吗? **wǒ kěyǐ qǐng nǐ chī dùn fàn ma?** can I invite you for a meal?; 请勿吸

烟! **qǐng wù xīyān!** no smoking, please!; 请勿打扰 **qǐngwù dǎjiǎo** please do not disturb

庆 **qìng** celebrate

清白 **qīngbái** pure; clear; flawless

情报 **qíngbào** intelligence; information; news

情报局 **qíngbàojú** intelligence service

轻便 **qīngbiàn** handy

请便 **qǐngbiàn** please yourself

轻搽 **qīngcā** dab

清仓大拍卖 **qīngcāng dà pāimài** clearance sale

清偿 **qīngcháng** settle; pay off ◊ settlement

清朝 **Qīng Chao** Qing Dynasty

清澈 **qīngché** clear *water, eyes*

清晨 **qīngchén** early morning

清楚 **qīngchu** clear ◊ understand (clearly); 我没讲清楚 **wǒ méi jiǎng qīngchu** I didn't make myself clear

清除 **qīngchú** clear *road, table*; clean up, purge

轻触 **qīngchù** brush, touch

清除堵塞 **qīngchú dǔsè** unblock

青春 **qīngchūn** youth

青春年代 **qīngchūn niándài** youth

青春期 **qīngchūn qī** adolescent ◊ adolescence; puberty

清单 **qīngdān** checklist

氢弹 **qīngdàn** hydrogen bomb

清淡 **qīngdàn** mild; weak; plain, simple; slack *period*

清淡色 **qīngdànsè** pastel

倾倒 **qīngdǎo** tip over; overturn

倾倒 **qīngdào** dump

轻而薄 **qīng'érbó** flimsy

轻浮 **qīngfú** flighty

情妇 **qíngfù** mistress (*lover*)

情感 **qínggǎn** emotion; passion ◊ emotional

请假 **qǐngjià** ask for leave

请教 **qǐngjiào** ask for advice

清教徒 **qīngjiàotú** puritan

清教徒式 **qīngjiàotúshì** puritanical

清洁 **qīngjié** cleanse ◊ clean, sanitary

情节 **qíngjié** plot

清洁工 **qīngjié gōng** cleaner

清洁剂 **qīngjié jì** cleanser

清洁女工 **qīngjié nǚgōng** cleaning woman

情景 **qíngjǐng** scene, sight

情景喜剧 **qíngjǐng xǐjù** sitcom

请客 **qǐngkè** invite guests; pay

轻快 **qīngkuài** brisk; springy

情况 **qíngkuàng** circumstances, situation; scenario; 在这种情况下 **zài zhèzhǒng qíngkuàng xià** under the circumstances

晴朗 **qínglǎng** bright, fine, sunny; clear

清理 **qīnglǐ** clear out

清凉 **qīngliáng** refreshing

轻量级 **qīngliàng jí** lightweight

情侣 **qínglǚ** couple

青绿色 **qīnglǜsè** turquoise

青霉素 **qīngméisù** penicillin

轻描淡写 **qīngmiáo dànxiě** downplay

轻蔑 **qīngmiè** contempt ◊ contemptuous; 用轻蔑的口吻谈 X **yòng qīngmiède kǒuwěn tán X** pour scorn on X

清明节 **Qīngmíngjié** Tomb Sweeping Day

青年 **qīngnián** youth

青年旅社 **qīngnián lǚshè** youth hostel

青年人 **qīngnián rén** young people; young person

青年招待所 **qīngnián zhāodài suǒ** youth hostel

轻拍 **qīngpāi** pat

倾盆大雨 **qīngpén dàyǔ** downpour, cloudburst ◊ be pouring

清漆 **qīngqī** varnish

轻敲 **qīngqiāo** tap

轻轻 **qīngqīng** lightly

轻轻移动 **qīngqīng yídòng** prowl

轻轻走 **qīngqīng zǒu** pad

请求 **qǐngqiú** ask; plead

情人 **qíngrén** lover

情人节 **Qíngrénjié** Valentine's Day

清嗓子 **qīng sǎngzi** clear one's throat

青少年 **qīngshàonián** teenager; youngster; young people ◊ teenage

轻视 **qīngshì** despise; scorn; put down, belittle

情书 **qíngshū** love letter

轻率 **qīngshuài** impetuous; indiscreet ◊ indiscretion

清爽 **qīngshuǎng** refreshing

轻松 **qīngsōng** relaxed

倾诉 **qīngsù** pour out

清算 **qīngsuàn** liquidation

青苔 **qīngtái** moss

轻弹 **qīngtán** flick

晴天霹雳 **qíngtiān pīlì** like a bolt from the blue

请帖 **qǐngtiě** invitation (*card*)

倾听 **qīngtīng** listen

蜻蜓 **qīngtíng** dragonfly

青铜 **qīngtóng** bronze

轻推 **qīngtuī** nudge

青蛙 **qīngwā** frog

请问 **qǐngwèn** excuse me; may I ask?; 请问几点了? **qǐngwèn jǐdiǎnle?** excuse me, what time is it?; 请问贵姓? **qǐngwèn guìxìng?** may I ask your name?

清晰 **qīngxī** vivid

清洗 **qīngxǐ** rinse; flush

倾向 **qīngxiàng** tendency; trend; current; disposition; 有 X 的倾向 **yǒu X de qīngxiàng** be subject to X

倾向于 **qīngxiàng yú** incline toward; tend toward

轻笑 **qīngxiào** chuckle

清晰度 **qīngxīdù** clarity; resolution

倾斜 **qīngxié** slope; tilt; lurch; dip ◊ slanting

轻信 **qīngxìn** credulous

清醒 **qīngxǐng** awake; conscious; sober

轻型小货车 **qīngxíng xiǎohuòchē** pick-up (truck)

清新悦目 **qīngxīn yuèmù** refreshing

轻信者 **qīngxìn zhě** sucker

情绪 **qíngxù** mood; spirits ◊ sentimental; 情绪低落 **qíngxù dīluò** be down; 情绪好 / 坏 **qíngxù hǎo / huài** be in a good / bad mood; 情绪稳定 **qíngxù wěndìng** well-balanced

轻摇 **qīngyáo** rock

轻音乐 **qīngyīnyuè** light music

情愿 **qíngyuàn** prefer; 我情愿在这儿住 **wǒ qíngyuàn zài zhèr zhù** I'd prefer to stay here

请愿书 **qǐngyuàn shū** petition

晴雨表 **qíngyǔ biǎo** barometer; indicator

青藏高原 **Qīngzàng Gāoyuán** Tibetan Plateau

请找 …? **qǐngzhǎo …?** can I talk to …?

清真寺 **qīngzhēnsì** mosque

庆祝 **qìngzhù** celebrate

庆祝会 **qìngzhù huì** celebration, party

庆祝活动 **qìngzhù huódòng** celebration, party

亲自动手 **qīngzì dòngshǒu** hands-on

轻罪 **qīngzuì** misdemeanor

亲和性 **qīnhéxìng** friendly

亲近 **qīnjìn** familiar ◊ affinity; 和 X 亲近 **hé X qīnjìn** be close to X

寝具 **qīnjù** bedding

勤快 **qínkuai** hardworking

勤劳 **qínláo** hardworking

侵略 **qīnlüè** invade ◊ invasion; aggression

亲密 **qīnmì** close; intimate ◊ intimacy

勤勉 **qínmiǎn** hard-working

亲昵 **qīnnì** (sexually) intimate ◊ intimacy

钦佩 **qīnpèi** admire ◊ admiration; 令人钦佩 **lìngrén qīnpèi** admirable

亲戚 **qīnqi** relatives

亲切 **qīnqiè** kind; familiar; genial

侵入 **qīnrù** intrude

亲身 **qīnshēn** bodily; firsthand

亲生父母 **qīnshēng fùmǔ** biological parents

侵蚀 **qīnshí** erode ◊ erosion

秦始皇 **Qínshǐhuáng** First Emperor of China

亲手 **qīnshǒu** in person; with one's own hands

亲属 **qīnshǔ** relation

侵吞 **qīntūn** embezzle; misappropriate

亲吻 **qīnwěn** kiss

侵袭 **qīnxí** affect MED; strike

勤杂工 **qínzá gōng** (hospital) orderly

侵占 **qīnzhàn** encroach on; overrun

亲自 **qīnzì** in person; personally

穷 **qióng** poor

穷困潦倒 **qióngkùn liáodǎo** down-and-out

穷人 **qióngrén** the poor; poor person

穷乡僻壤 **qióngxiāng pìrǎng** hick town ◊ out in the boonies

穷凶极恶 **qióngxiōng jí'è** enormity

棋盘 **qípán** board; chessboard

旗袍 **qípáo** qipao, cheongsam (*high-necked Chinese dress with side slits*)

起泡 **qǐpào** carbonated

气泡 **qìpào** bubble

起泡沫 **qǐ pàomò** frothy

漆皮 **qīpí** patent leather

欺骗 **qīpiàn** deceive; delude; doublecross; trick ◊ deceit; deception; fraud; hoax; trickery

欺骗性 **qīpiànxìng** fraudulent

漆器 **qīqì** lacquerware

乞求 **qǐqiú** bum; cadge; 跟 Y 乞求 X **gēn Y qǐqiú X** cadge X from Y

气球 **qìqiú** balloon

崎岖 **qíqū** rugged

齐全 **qíquán** complete

弃权 **qìquán** abstain ◊ abstention

骑上 **qíshàng** mount

祈神赐福 **qíshén cìfú** blessing

七十 **qīshí** seventy

骑师 **qíshī** jockey

祈使 **qíshǐ** imperative

歧视 **qíshì** discriminate against ◊ discrimination

启示 **qǐshì** message

漆刷 **qīshuā** paintbrush

汽水 **qìshuǐ** carbonated mineral water; carbonated drink

起水疱 **qǐ shuǐpào** blister

起诉 **qǐsù** sue; bring an action against, prosecute ◊ prosecution

其他 **qítā** other (*of people*)

其它 **qítā** other (*of things*)

其他的 **qítāde** the others (*people*)

其它的 **qítāde** the others (*things*)

奇谈 **qítán** yarn, story

乞讨 **qǐtǎo** beg

奇特 **qítè** original; unique; strange; curious

奇特服装 **qítè fúzhuāng** fancy dress

气体 **qìtǐ** gas

汽艇 **qìtǐng** motor boat

企图 **qǐtú** try, attempt

起推进作用 **qǐ tuījìn zuòyòng** propellant

秋 **qiū** fall, autumn

球 **qiú** ball

求 **qiú** implore, beseech

囚 **qiú** imprison ◊ prisoner

囚车 **qiúchē** patrol wagon

球队 **qiúduì** team (*for ball game*)

囚犯 **qiúfàn** prisoner; convict

秋分 **qiūfēn** autumn equinox

球杆 **qiúgān** cue (*for pool*); club (*for golf*)

球棍 **qiúgùn** bat

求婚 **qiúhūn** propose ◊ proposal

球茎 **qiújīng** bulb

求救 **qiújiù** call for help

求救信号 **qiújiù xìnhào** distress signal

丘陵 **qiūlíng** hill

球拍 **qiúpāi** bat; racket

秋千 **qiūqiān** swing

球体 **qiútǐ** sphere

秋天 **qiútiān** fall, autumn

蚯蚓 **qiūyǐn** earthworm

球员 **qiúyuán** soccer player; player

丘疹 **qiūzhěn** spot

球座 **qiúzuò** tee

期望 **qīwàng** hope for; expect ◊ prospect; expectation

气味 **qìwèi** smell, odor

气温 **qìwēn** temperature

栖息 **qīxī** perch

期限 **qīxiàn** deadline; time limit

气象 **qìxiàng** weather

气象学 **qìxiàngxué** meteorology ◊ meteorological

气象学家 **qìxiàngxuéjiā** meteorologist

气象预报员 **qìxiàng yùbàoyuán** weatherman

栖息处 **qīxīchù** perch

栖息地 **qīxīdì** habitat

器械 **qìxiè** apparatus; appliance

气压 **qìyā** air pressure

气压表 **qìyā biǎo** barometer

企业 **qǐyè** enterprise

企业家 **qǐyèjiā** entrepreneur

起义 **qǐyì** uprising

奇异的事物 **qíyìde shìwù** marvel

汽油 **qìyóu** gasoline, gas

汽油泵 **qìyóubèng** gas pump

其余 **qíyú** the remainder, the rest

起于 **qǐyú** result from

起源 **qǐyuán** be derived from; stem from ◊ origin, beginning

七月 **qīyuè** July

契约 **qìyuē** contract; deed

气质 **qìzhí** charisma

其中 **qízhōng** among; among which; of which

起重机 **qǐzhòng jī** crane; hoist

妻子 **qīzi** wife

妻姊 **qīzǐ** sister-in-law (*wife's elder sister*)

旗子 **qízi** flag

棋子 **qízǐ** man, piece (*in chess etc*)

骑自行车 **qí zìxíngchē** cycle, ride ◊ cycling

骑自行车的人 **qí zìxíngchē de rén** cyclist

区 **qū** district; zone

蛆 **qū** maggot

曲 **qū** curved

取 **qǔ** take; fetch; get

曲 **qǔ** tune; song; music

去 **qù** go; 去 X 的火车 **qù X de huǒchē** a train for X; 到 X 去有多远 **dào X qù yǒu duōyuǎn?** how far is it to X?; 去你的！**qùnǐde!** go to hell!

圈 **quān** ring, circle; lap, circuit; loop

拳 **quán** fist ◊ punch

泉 **quán** spring; stream

权 **quán** right; power; authority

全 **quán** whole; entire

犬 **quǎn** dog

劝 **quàn** persuade

全部 **quánbù** all; entire

全部付清 **quánbù fùqīng** pay up; pay in full

全部湿透 **quánbù shītòu** dripping (wet)

全长 **quáncháng** full-length

劝导 **quàndǎo** teach; advise; instruct

鬈发 **quánfà** curl; curly hair

蜷伏 **quánfú** snuggle down

劝告 **quàngào** advise, counsel

颧骨 **quángǔ** cheekbone

全国人大 **Quánguó Réndà** National People's Congress, NPC

权衡 **quánhéng** weigh up

拳击 **quánjī** box ◊ boxing; fight

全集 **quánjí** collected

拳击比赛 **quánjī bǐsài** boxing match

拳击场 **quánjī chǎng** ring

全景 **quánjǐng** panorama ◊ panoramic

拳击手 **quánjī shǒu** boxer, fighter

权力 **quánlì** power, authority

权利 **quánlì** right

全面 **quánmiàn** comprehensive; overall; all-round

全民所有制 **quánmín suǒyǒuzhì** national property; property of the people

全能者 **Quánnéng zhě** the Almighty

全球 **quánqiú** global

全球经济 **quánqiú jīngjì** global economy

全球气温升高 **quánqiú qìwēn shēnggāo** global warming

全球市场 **quánqiú shìchǎng** global market

拳曲 **quánqū** curl (up) ◊ curly

全权 **quánquán** power of attorney; full powers

全权代表 **quánquán dàibiǎo** authorized representative

全人类 **quánrénlèi** all humankind

全日 **quánrì** full-time

全日制 **quánrìzhì** full-time

全盛期 **quánshèngqī** heyday

全神贯注于 quánshén guànzhù yú engrossed in

全世界 quánshìjiè worldwide

全食宿 quán shísù full board

泉水 quánshuǐ spring water

劝说 quànshuō persuade ◊ persuasion

蜷缩 quánsuō writhe; double up; curl up; cower; 蜷缩在一起 quánsuō zài yìqǐ huddle together

圈套 quāntào trap; snare; noose; 设圈套 shè quāntào trap; set up

全体 quántǐ all; whole ◊ totality; 全体选民 quántǐ xuǎnmín electorate

拳头 quántou fist

权威 quánwēi authority

权威性 quánwēi xìng classic; definitive; authoritative

全心全意 quánxīn quányì whole-hearted

全息图 quánxītú hologram

痊愈 quányù recuperate; convalesce

劝止 quànzhǐ dissuade

圈子 quānzi circle

劝阻 quànzǔ advise against; 劝阻 X 不要去做 Y quànzǔ X bùyào qù zuò Y dissuade X from doing Y

区别 qūbié distinguish, discriminate between ◊ distinction; 区别好坏 qūbié hǎohuài know right from wrong

驱车离开 qūchē líkāi drive away; drive off

龋齿 qǔchǐ cavity

驱虫剂 qūchóng jì repellent

驱除 qūchú remove; drive out; boot out

取出 qǔchū take out, extract

驱除出境 qūchú chūjìng deport ◊ deportation

驱除舰 qūchú jiàn destroyer

驱除令 qūchú lìng deportation order

取代 qǔdài substitution; 用 X 取代 Y yòng X qǔdài Y substitute X for Y

渠道 qúdào drain

取得 qǔdé gain; achieve; acquire, obtain

曲调 qǔdiào tune

去掉 qùdiào remove; get rid of

驱动 qūdòng drive; 四轮驱动 sìlún qūdòng all-wheel drive

驱动器 qūdòngqì disk drive

缺 quē lack; miss

瘸 qué lame

雀 què sparrow

雀斑 quèbān freckle

缺点 quēdiǎn disadvantage; weakness, shortcoming

确定 quèdìng confirm, make certain; be sure

确定不变 quèdìng búbiàn fixed

缺乏 quēfá absence; deficiency; shortage ◊ lack; be short of

缺口 quēkǒu niche

缺钱 quēqián hard up

确切 quèqiè exact

确认 quèrèn confirm

缺少 quēshǎo lack

确实 quèshí really; actually

缺席 quēxí absent ◊ absence

缺陷 quēxiàn defect; downside

确信 quèxìn be convinced ◊ certainty, conviction; 使 … 确信 shǐ … quèxìn assure

确证 quèzhèng validate

瘸子 quézi cripple

区分 qūfēn differentiate between; tell the difference between; 区分 X 和 Y qūfēn X hé Y distinguish between X and Y

屈服 qūfú give in; succumb; knuckle under

驱赶 qūgǎn repel; chase away; dispel

躯干 qūgàn trunk

去骨 qùgǔ bone

去国者 qùguó zhě exile

区号 qūhào area code

取回 qǔhuí pick up

曲解 qūjiě misinterpret ◊ misinterpretation

曲径 qūjìng maze

取景器 qǔjǐng qì viewfinder

取决于 qǔjuéyú depend on

取款机 qǔkuǎn jī ATM, cash machine

取乐 qǔlè have fun

群 **qún** group; crowd; flock; cluster; 一群人 **yīqún rén** a crowd of people

裙 **qún** skirt

区内电话 **qūnèi diànhuà** local call

去年 **qùnián** last year

取暖 **qǔnuǎn** warm up

取暖器 **qǔnuǎn qì** radiator

群众 **qúnzhòng** the masses

裙子 **qúnzi** skirt

去皮 **qùpí** skin

曲奇 **qǔqí** cookie

驱散 **qūsàn** break up; disperse

趋势 **qūshì** tendency, trend

去世 **qùshì** pass away, die ◊ demise

躯体 **qūtǐ** body

去污剂 **qùwū jì** stain remover

取下 **qǔxià** take down; take off

曲线 **qūxiàn** curve

趋向 **qūxiàng** trend

取消 **qǔxiāo** cancel; revoke ◊ cancellation

取笑 **qǔxiào** deride; mock, send up ◊ derision; banter

区域 **qūyù** region, area

取悦 **qǔyuè** ingratiate oneself with

曲折 **qūzhé** twist

曲折行进 **qūzhé xíngjìn** zigzag

取之不尽 **qǔ zhī bù jìn** inexhaustible

曲轴 **qǔzhóu** crankshaft

驱逐 **qūzhú** expel; deport; kick out ◊ expulsion

屈尊 **qūzūn** deign to

R

燃 **rán** burn; ignite

染 **rǎn** color; dye

然而 **rán'ér** but, however; nonetheless; though

染发 **rǎnfà** dye one's hair

让 **ràng** let, allow; give way; make, cause; 让他进来 **ràng tā jìnlái** let him come in; 让我走! **ràng wǒ zǒu!** let me go!; 让人听懂 **ràng ren tīng dǒng** get through, make oneself understood; 让 X 等 **ràng X děng** keep X waiting

让步 **ràngbù** give way, capitulate; relent ◊ concession

让路 **rànglù** yield, give way

嚷嚷 **rāngrang** yell

让位 **ràngwèi** step down

然后 **ránhòu** then; next; afterward

燃料 **ránliào** fuel

染料 **rǎnliào** dye

染色 **rǎnsè** color; dye; stain; tint

染色剂 **rǎnsè jì** (wood) stain

染上 **rǎnshàng** catch

燃烧 **ránshāo** burn ◊ combustion

燃烧弹 **ránshāodàn** incendiary device

绕 **rào** around

绕道 **ráodào** go around; detour

绕道行驶 **ràodào xíngshǐ** detour

绕杆 **ràogān** turnstile

绕过 **ràoguò** bypass

扰乱 **rǎoluàn** disrupt ◊ disruption

扰频 **rǎopín** scramble

饶舌者 **ráoshé zhě** chatterbox

绕行 **ràoxíng** round

惹 **rě** start; cause; provoke; 惹麻烦 **rě máfan** cause trouble; play up; 惹人喜爱 **rě rén xǐ'ài** sweet, cute

热 **rè** hot; warm ◊ heat ◊ warm up

热爱 **rè'ài** love passionately

热忱 **rèchén** enthusiastic; hearty

热诚 **rèchéng** fervent

热带 **rèdài** tropics ◊ tropical

热带地区 **rèdài dìqū** tropics

热带雨林 **rèdài yǔlín** tropical rain forest

热点 **rèdiǎn** hot spot

热浪 **rèlàng** heatwave

热恋 **rèliàn** have a crush on ◊ madly in love; passionate

热烈 **rèliè** enthusiastic; heated *discussion*; wild *applause*

热门 **rèmén** popular; sought-after; blue chip

人 **rén** person; human being; people; man ◊ *used to form nationality words*: 法国人 **Fǎguó rén** Frenchman; Frenchwoman; the French

忍 **rěn** endure

认 **rèn** recognize; 认不出来了 **rèn bū chūlái le** beyond recognition

刃 **rèn** blade

任 **rèn** task; mission; term ◊ take responsibility

惹恼 **rěnǎo** exasperate

热闹 **rènao** exciting; lively ◊ hustle and bustle

忍不住 **rěnbúzhù**: 我忍不住 **wǒ rěnbúzhù** I can't help it

人称代词 **rénchēng dàicí** personal pronoun

认出 **rènchū** recognize, know; pick out

仁慈 **réncí** clemency; humanity; mercy; philanthropy ◊ kind; merciful; philanthropic

韧带 **rèndài** ligament

人道 **réndào** humane ◊ humanity

人道主义者 **réndào zhǔyì zhě** humanitarian

认得 **rènde** recognize

认定 **rèndìng** be sure of; identify

扔 **rēng** throw; throw away; drop; dump

仍 **réng** still, yet

扔掉 **rēngdiào** get rid of, dispose of; throw away ◊ disposal

人格 **réngé** personality

人工 **réngōng** man-made, artificial

人工呼吸器 **réngōng hūxī qì** respirator

人工流产 **réngōng liúchǎn** abortion

人工智能 **réngōng zhìnéng** artificial intelligence

仍然 **réngrán** still; 她可能仍然会来 **tā kěnéng réngrán huìlái** she might still come

扔下 **rēngxià** leave behind; 扔下 X 不管 **rēngxià X bùguǎn** turn one's back on X

任何 **rènhé** any; whatever; whichever

任何东西 **rènhé dōngxi** anything

任何人 **rènhé rén** anybody

人际罕至 **rénjì hǎnzhì** secluded

认可 **rènkě** acknowledgement

人口 **rénkǒu** population; 人口密集 **rénkǒu mìjí** densely populated

人类 **rénlèi** human race, man, mankind ◊ human

人类丧失免疫力病毒 **rénlèi sàngshī miǎnyìlì bìngdú** HIV

人类资源 **rénlèi zīyuán** human resources

人力 **rénlì** labor; manpower

人力车 **rénlìchē** rickshaw

人们 **rénmen** people, folk

人民 **rénmín** the people

人民币 **rénmínbì** renminbi, RMB

人民大会堂 **Rénmín Dàhuìtáng** Great Hall of the People

人民代表大会 **Rénmín Dàibiǎo Dàhuì** People's Congress

任命 **rènmìng** appointment; nomination ◊ appoint; designate

人民公社 **Rénmín Gōngshè** People's Commune

人民解放军 **Rénmín Jiěfàngjūn** People's Liberation Army

人民日报 **Rénmín Rìbào** People's Daily

忍耐 **rěnnài** endure

忍耐力 **rěnnàilì** endurance

任期 **rènqī** term of office

人权 **rénquán** human rights

人群 **rénqún** crowd, throng

人参 **rénshēn** ginseng

人生 **rénshēng** (human) life

认生 **rènshēng** be afraid of strangers

认识 **rènshi** know; get to know; recognize; 很高兴认识你 **hěn gāoxìng rènshí nǐ** pleased to meet you; 她认识汉字 **tā rènshí Hànzì** she can read Chinese characters

人事部 **rénshìbù** personnel (department)

人事部主任 **rénshìbù zhǔrèn** personnel manager

人世间 **rénshìjiān** the world ◊ earthly

忍受 **rěnshòu** accept; put up with, bear

人寿保险 **rénshòu bǎoxiǎn** life insurance

人体模型 **réntǐ móxíng** mannequin, dummy (for clothes)

认同 **rèntóng** approve of

惹怒 **rěnù** irritate

认为 **rènwéi** consider; believe, think; feel; 我不认为如此 **wǒ bú rènwéi rúcǐ** I don't think so; 认为有能力做 **rènwéi yǒu nénglì zuò** feel up to

人物 **rénwù** figure, personality; character (in book)

任务 **rènwù** assignment, mission; job, task

任务钮 **rènwùniǔ** task button

人性 **rénxìng** human ◊ humanity

任性 **rènxìng** headstrong

人行道 **rénxíngdào** sidewalk

人行横道 **rénxíng héngdào** (pedestrian) crosswalk

人烟稀少 **rényān xīshǎo** sparsely populated

任意 **rènyì** arbitrary

任意而为 **rènyì ér wéi** indiscriminate

任一个 **rèn yígè** either; any

任意球 **rènyì qiú** free kick

人员 **rényuán** personnel, staff

人造 **rénzào** artificial, man-made, synthetic

人造黄油 **rénzào huángyóu** margarine

人造卫星 **rénzào wèixīng** satellite

忍着 **rěnzhe** stifle, repress

认真 **rènzhēn** serious; earnest; conscientious ◊ in earnest; religiously

人质 **rénzhì** hostage; 被扣作人质 **bèi kòuzuò rénzhì** be taken hostage

人种 **rénzhǒng** race

认罪书 **rènzuì shū** confession

热切 **rèqiè** eager

热起来 **rèqǐlái** warm up

热情 **rèqíng** enthusiastic; warm; passionate ◊ warmth; enthusiasm; zest; passion

热气球 **rè qìqiú** balloon

热水袋 **rèshuǐdài** hot-water bottle

热水瓶 **rèshuǐpíng** vacuum flask

热死了 **rèsǐle** scorching hot

热腾腾 **rè téngteng** red-hot

热心 **rèxīn** enthusiastic; warm-hearted ◊ eagerness; zeal

热心肠 **rèxīncháng** warmhearted

热衷于 **rèzhōng yú** be wild about; 热衷于做 X **rèzhōng yú zuò X** be eager to do X

热中者 **rèzhōngzhě** enthusiast

日 **rì** sun; day

日报 **rìbào** daily paper

日本 **Rìběn** Japan ◊ Japanese

日本人 **Rìběn rén** Japanese

日常 **rìcháng** everyday; daily

日出 **rìchū** sunrise

日光 **rìguāng** daylight

日光灯 **rìguāngdēng** fluorescent light

日晷 **rìguī** sundial

日记 **rìjì** diary; journal

日间服 **rìjiānfú** day wear

日历 **rìlì** calendar

日落 **rìluò** sunset

日期 **rìqī** date

日晒肤色 **rì shài fūsè** tan

日蚀 **rìshí** eclipse

日语 **Rìyǔ** Japanese (*language*)

日元 **rìyuán** yen FIN

日志 **rìzhì** logbook

绒 **róng** down (*feathers*)

容 **róng** contain; tolerate ◊ face

溶 **róng** dissolve

荣 **róng** honor

融 **róng** melt; meld; merge; 融为一体 **róng wéi yìtǐ** integrate

冗长 **rǒngcháng** lengthy

融和 **rónghé** blend in

熔合 **rónghé** fusion

融化 **rónghuà** melt; thaw ◊ molten

熔化 **rónghuà** smelt

熔毁 **rónghuǐ** melt down

容积 **róngjī** volume

溶解 **róngjiě** dissolve

容积量 **róngjī liàng** cubic capacity

容量 **róngliàng** volume; capacity

熔流 **róngliú** torrent

熔炉 **rónglú** melting pot

绒毛 **róngmáo** down (*on bird*)

容貌 **róngmào** feature

绒面革 **róngmiàngé** suede

容纳 **róngnà** hold, contain

容器 **róngqì** container

融洽 **róngqià** peaceable; 与 X 关系融洽 **yǔ X guānxi róngqià** be friendly with X

容忍 **róngrěn** tolerate, stand for

荣幸 **róngxìng** privilege ◊ privileged

容许 **róngxǔ** permit, allow; tolerate

溶液 **róngyè** solution

容易 **róngyì** easy; effortless ◊ ease

容易饱人 **róngyì bǎorén** filling

容易上口 **róngyì shàngkǒu** catchy

荣誉 **róngyù** glory; honor; kudos

柔 **róu** soft; gentle

揉 **róu** knead; rub

鞣 **róu** tan

肉 **ròu** meat

柔道 **róudào** judo

肉店 **ròudiàn** butcher shop

肉冠 **ròuguàn** crest

肉桂 **ròuguì** cinnamon

柔和 **róuhé** soft; mild; subdued; mellow

肉麻 **ròumá** nauseating

肉末 **ròumò** ground meat

柔懦情调 **róunuò qíngdiào**

sentimentality

柔懦情感 **róunuò qínggǎn** sentiment

柔软 **róuruǎn** soft; supple

肉体 **ròutǐ** flesh

肉丸子 **ròuwánzi** meatball

肉馅 **ròuxiàn** mincemeat

肉眼 **ròuyǎn** naked eye

肉欲 **ròuyù** lust; sensuality

肉汁 **ròuzhī** gravy

如 **rú** like; as; if

乳 **rǔ** breast; milk; gel

辱 **rǔ** disgrace

入 **rù** enter

乳癌 **rǔ'ái** breast cancer

软 **ruǎn** soft; tender ◊ tenderness

软磁盘 **ruǎn cípán** diskette

软膏 **ruǎngāo** ointment; balm

软骨 **ruǎngǔ** gristle

软管 **ruǎnguǎn** hose

软件 **ruǎnjiàn** software

软木 **ruǎnmù** cork (*wood*)

软木塞 **ruǎnmùsāi** cork (*stopper*)

软盘 **ruǎnpán** floppy disk

软驱 **ruǎnqū** floppy drive

软弱 **ruǎnruò** weak

软卧 **ruǎnwò** soft sleeper (*on train*); first-class sleeping car

软性饮料 **ruǎnxìng yǐnliào** soft drink

软座 **ruǎnzuò** soft seat

入场费 **rùchǎngfèi** entrance fee

如此 **rúcǐ** thus, in this way; 我希望如此 **wǒ xīwàng rúcǐ** I hope so

入店行窃 **rùdiàn xíngqiè** shoplifter

蠕动 **rúdòng** squirm, writhe

乳房 **rǔfáng** breast

如果 **rúguǒ** if

如画 **rúhuà** picturesque

蚋 **ruì** gnat

锐 **ruì** sharp

锐不可当 **ruì bù kě dāng** inexorable; irresistible

瑞典 **Ruìdiǎn** Sweden ◊ Swedish

锐利 **ruìlì** piercing

瑞士 **Ruìshì** Switzerland ◊ Swiss

儒家 **Rújiā** Confucianism

如今 **rújīn** nowadays; at present, currently

入境 **rùjìng** enter *country*

入境签证 **rùjìng qiānzhèng** entry visa

入口 **rùkǒu** way in, entrance; inlet

辱骂 **rǔmà** abuse

入迷 **rùmí** be fascinated; be spellbound

润 **rùn** moist ◊ profit

润肤膏 **rùnfūgāo** moisturizer

润肤霜 **rùnfūshuāng** moisturizer

润喉糖 **rùnhóu táng** throat lozenges

润滑 **rùnhuá** lubricate ◊ lubrication

润滑剂 **rùnhuá jì** lubricant

润滑油箱 **rùnhuá yóuxiāng** sump

闰年 **rùnnián** leap year

润色 **rùnsè** polish

弱 **ruò** weak

若 **ruò** if ◊ like

弱点 **ruòdiǎn** weakness

若干 **ruògān** some; a number

弱小 **ruòxiǎo** puny

弱者 **ruòzhě** weakling

入神 **rùshén** be engrossed; be entranced

入室抢劫 **rùshì qiǎngjié** housebreaking

乳霜 **rǔshuāng** cream

入睡 **rùshuì** fall asleep

如同 **rútóng** just like; 如同往常 **rútóng wǎngcháng** as usual

乳头 **rǔtóu** nipple; teat

如下 **rúxià** the following ◊ as follows; see below

入乡随俗 **rùxiāngsuísú** *prov* when in Rome …

乳牙 **rǔyá** milk tooth

如意 **rúyì** hunky-dory

如愿 **rúyuàn** as planned; as hoped

乳罩 **rǔzhào** brassière

乳制品 **rǔzhì pǐn** dairy products

乳猪 **rǔzhū** sucking pig

S

撒 **sǎ** scatter; sprinkle
洒 **sǎ** sprinkle; spill
撒旦 **Sādàn** Satan
撒谎 **sāhuǎng** fib, lie
塞 **sāi** cram; jam; plug; squeeze in; stick in; 把 X 塞入 Y 手中 **bǎ X sāirù Y shǒu zhōng** thrust X into Y's hands
腮 **sāi** cheek
赛 **sài** competition; race
赛车 **sàichē** racing car
赛车运动员 **sàichē yùndòngyuán** racing driver
塞进 **sāijìn** tuck
赛马 **sàimǎ** horse race
赛跑 **sàipǎo** race (*on foot*)
赛跑者 **sàipǎo zhě** runner
腮腺炎 **sāixiànyán** mumps
塞住 **sāizhù** clog up; 塞住 … 的嘴 **sāizhù … de zuǐ** gag
塞子 **sāizi** plug, stopper
萨克斯管 **sàkèsīguǎn** saxophone
三 **sān** three
伞 **sǎn** umbrella
散 **sǎn** scattered; loose
散 **sàn** spread; distribute; disseminate
三八妇女节 **Sānbā Fùnǚjié** Women's Day
三胞胎 **sānbāotāi** triplets
三倍 **sānbèi** treble
伞兵 **sǎnbīng** paratrooper
散步 **sànbù** stroll ◊ take a stroll
散布 **sànbù** spread
三重唱 **sān chóng chàng** trio
三等仓 **sānděngcāng** third-class cabin
散发 **sànfā** distribute
丧 **sāng** mourning; 穿丧服 **chuān sāngfú** wear mourning
桑 **sāng** mulberry
丧 **sàng** lose
丧礼 **sānglǐ** funeral service
丧命 **sàngmìng** die

桑拿浴 **sāngnáyù** sauna
丧失 **sàngshī** loss ◊ forfeit; 使丧失名誉 **shǐ sàngshī míngyù** discredit
丧失志气 **sàngshī zhìqì** demoralized
桑树 **sāngshù** mulberry tree
三国 **Sānguó** Three Kingdoms
嗓音 **sǎngyīn** voice ◊ vocal
嗓子 **sǎngzi** throat
撒尿 **sāniào** pee, piss
三脚架 **sānjiǎojià** tripod
三角裤 **sānjiǎo kù** briefs
三角形 **sānjiǎo xíng** triangle ◊ triangular
伞菌 **sǎnjūn** toadstool
散开 **sànkāi** scatter
三轮车 **sānlúnchē** tricycle; pedicab
三明治 **sānmíngzhì** sandwich
三色堇 **sānsèjǐn** pansy
三十 **sānshí** thirty
散文 **sǎnwén** prose
三峡 **Sānxiá** Three Gorges
三心二意 **sānxīn èryì** half-hearted
三月 **sānyuè** March
搔 **sāo** scratch
扫 **sǎo** sweep; drag
扫除 **sǎochú** root out
搔动 **sāodòng** commotion
扫雷艇 **sǎoléi tǐng** minesweeper
扫拢 **sǎolǒng** sweep up
骚乱 **sāoluàn** commotion; turmoil; trouble; disturbances
扫描 **sǎomiáo** scan
扫描器 **sǎomiáoqì** scanner MED
扫描仪 **sǎomiáoyí** scanner COMPUT
扫灭 **sǎomiè** mow down
骚扰 **sāorǎo** harass; molest ◊ harassment
扫射 **sǎoshè** burst (of gunfire)
扫视 **sǎoshì** glance; glance at; scan

扫兴 **săoxìng** be disappointed

搔痒 **sāoyăng** scratch, have a scratch

扫帚 **sàozhou** broom

嫂子 **săozi** sister-in-law (*older brother's wife*)

撒手 **sāshŏu** release one's grip, let go; back out

撒种 **săzhŏng** sow *seeds*

涩 **sè** sharp, tart; tight

色 **sè** color

色彩 **sècăi** color, tone

色彩设计 **sècăi shèjì** color scheme

色度 **sèdù** shade

色鬼 **sèguĭ** womanizer

色拉 **sèlā** salad

色狼 **sèláng** wolf, womanizer

色盲 **sèmáng** color-blind

森林 **sēnlín** forest

森林学 **sēnlínxué** forestry

色情 **sèqíng** pornographic; erotic

色情作品 **sèqíng zuòpĭn** pornography

刹 **shā** brake

沙 **shā** sand

鲨 **shā** shark

杀 **shā** kill, slay

砂 **shā** sand

纱 **shā** thread, yarn

傻 **shă** dumb, dim; brainless; silly

纱布 **shābù** gauze

刹车 **shāchē** brake; skid ◊ brakes

刹车灯 **shāchē dēng** stoplight

刹车踏板 **shāchē tàbăn** brake pedal

杀虫剂 **shāchóngjì** pesticide; insecticide

沙袋 **shādài** sandbag

沙丁鱼 **shādĭngyú** sardine

沙发 **shāfā** sofa

沙发床 **shāfā chuáng** sofa bed

傻瓜 **shăguā** idiot, moron

杀害 **shāhài** kill; murder

筛 **shāi** sift

晒 **shài** put out in the sun ◊ too sunny

晒斑 **shàibān** sunburn

晒黑 **shài hēi** tan ◊ tanned

晒伤 **shàishāng** burn ◊ sunburnt

晒太阳 **shài tàiyáng** sunbathe; bask

筛子 **shāizi** sieve

色子 **shăizi** dice

砂浆 **shājiāng** mortar

沙坑 **shākēng** sandpit

砂砾 **shālì** grit

沙龙 **shālóng** salon

杀戮 **shālù** slaughter

沙漠 **shāmò** desert

山 **shān** mountain; mount

闪 **shăn** flash

疝 **shàn** hernia

扇 **shàn** fan ◊ *measure word for doors and windows*; 两扇窗 **liăngshàn chuāng** two windows; 给自己扇风 **gěi zìjĭ shānfēng** fan oneself

善 **shàn** good; kind-hearted

刹那 **shànà** instant

擅长 **shàncháng** be good at, excel at

删除 **shānchú** delete; erase; take out ◊ deletion

闪电 **shăndiàn** lightning; flash of lightning

闪电般 **shăndiànbān** in a flash

山地车 **shāndìchē** mountain bike

山顶 **shāndĭng** peak, summit

煽动 **shāndòng** incite; rouse; stir up; 煽动 X 做 Y **shāndòng X zuò Y** incite X to do Y

闪动 **shăndòng** flicker

山东半岛 **Shāndōng Bàndăo** Shandong Peninsula

煽动者 **shàndòng zhě** agitator

山峰 **shānfēng** peak, summit

伤 **shāng** hurt; strain ◊ wound

商 **shāng** business; quotient ◊ commercial

赏 **shăng** reward

上 **shàng** on; at the top; up ◊ get on, board; 上车 **shàng chē** get on the bus/train; 在屋顶上 **zài wūdĭng shang** up on the roof

删改 **shāngăi** censor

上岸 **shàng'àn** go ashore

伤疤 **shāngbā** scar

上班 **shàngbān** go to work; be at work; 我坐公车去上班 **wŏ zuò gōngchē qù shàngbān** I go to work by bus

上臂 **shàngbì** upper arm

商标 **shāngbiāo** brand name; trademark

商标概念 **shāngbiāo gàiniàn** brand image

上部 **shàngbù** top part, upper part

上菜 **shàng cài** serve (the food)

上层 **shàngcéng** upper

上层社会 **shàngcéng shèhuì** upper class

商场 **shāngchǎng** department store; bazaar

上场 **shàngchǎng** enter (of actors)

上车 **shàngchē** get on a train / bus / bicycle

上船 **shàngchuán** go aboard (a ship)

上床 **shàngchuáng** go to bed, turn in; 和 … 上床 **hé … shàngchuáng** go to bed with …

上等货 **shàngděnghuò** top-quality goods

上等阶层 **shàngděng jiēcéng** upper classes

上帝 **Shàngdì** God

商店 **shāngdiàn** shop; store

上吊 **shàngdiào** hang oneself

商定 **shāngdìng** agree; arrange

上发条 **shàng fātiáo** wind up

上飞机 **shàng fēijī** board a plane

伤风 **shāngfēng** catch a cold

伤感情 **shānggǎnqíng** hurt (emotionally)

伤害 **shānghài** wound; injury; bruise ◊ injure

上海 **Shànghǎi** Shanghai

伤寒 **shānghán** typhoid (fever)

商会 **shānghuì** chamber of commerce

上火车 **shàng huǒchē** board a train

上机 **shàngjī** log on

上级 **shàngjí** boss; superior

上交 **shàngjiāo** hand over

伤口 **shāngkǒu** wound; injury; cut

上来 **shànglái** board

商量 **shāngliang** discuss

上流 **shàngliú** high-class

上流社会 **shàngliú shèhuì** high society

上面 **shàngmian** top ◊ at the top ◊ up ◊ upper

伤脑筋 **shāng nǎojīn** annoying; frustrating

上年纪 **shàng niánjì** elderly, getting on in years; 他上了年纪 **tā shàngle niánjì** he's getting on

上牌 **shàngpái** register

商品 **shāngpǐn** commodity; goods

商品陈列室 **shāngpǐn chénlièshì** showroom

商品券 **shāngpǐn quàn** token

商品特色 **shāngpǐn tèsè** selling point

上坡 **shàngpō** uphill

上去 **shàngqù** come up; go up ◊ up

商人 **shāngrén** businessman; dealer; merchant; trader

伤人感情 **shāngrén gǎnqíng** cutting

上色 **shàngshǎi** brown (in cooking)

上身 **shàngshēn** upper body

上升 **shàngshēng** rise; climb

赏识 **shǎngshí** have great respect for

上市 **shàngshì** on the market ◊ launch

上述 **shàngshù** above-mentioned

上水 **shàngshuǐ** upstream

上司 **shàngsi** boss, chief

上诉 **shàngsù** appeal

商谈 **shāngtán** discuss, kick around

商讨 **shāngtǎo** discuss

上调 **shàngtiáo** push up

山谷 **shāngǔ** valley

闪光 **shǎnguāng** glisten

闪光灯 **shǎnguāngdēng** flash; flashlight

闪光指示灯 **shǎnguāng zhǐshìdēng** flasher MOT

闪光装置 **shǎnguāng zhuāngzhì** flare

上网 **shàngwǎng** log on; go on-line ◊ on-line

伤亡人士 **shāngwáng rénshì** casualties

上午 **shàngwǔ** morning ◊ in the morning; 上午好 **shàngwǔ hǎo** good morning

商务舱 **shāngwù cāng** business class

上相 **shàngxiàng** photogenic

上校 **shàngxiào** colonel

上下文 **shàngxià wén** context

伤心 **shāngxīn** sad; broken-hearted; heartrending ◊ distress; 令人伤心 *lìngrén shāngxīn* upsetting; depressing; disheartening

伤心事 **shāngxīn shì** sorrow

上学 **shàngxué** go to school

上演 **shàngyǎn** perform, put on

商业 **shāngyè** business; commerce ◊ commercial

上夜班 **shàng yèbān** work nights

商业化 **shāngyè huà** commercialize

商业会议 **shāngyè huìyì** business meeting

商业秘密 **shāngyè mìmì** trade secret

商业午餐 **shāngyè wǔcān** business lunch

商业信用书 **shāngyè xìnyòng shū** letter of credit

商业学 **shāngyè xué** business studies

商业学校 **shāngyè xuéxiào** business school

上衣 **shàngyī** top (*clothing*)

上一次 **shàng yīcì** last ◊ last time

上瘾 **shàngyǐn** be addicted to

上映 **shàngyìng** show

上游 **shàngyóu** upper reaches of a river

伤员 **shāngyuán** casualty

上闸 **shàngzhá** put the brakes on

上涨 **shàngzhǎng** rise; go up

珊瑚 **shānhú** coral

闪回 **shǎnhuí** flashback

山脊 **shānjí** ridge

闪开 **shǎnkāi** dodge

闪亮 **shǎnliàng** flash

善良 **shànliáng** generous; kind

山麓小丘 **shānlù xiǎoqiū** foothills

山脉 **shānmài** mountain range

山猫 **shānmāo** lynx

山毛榉 **shānmáo jǔ** beech

山坡 **shānpō** hill; hillside

山穷水尽 **shānqióng shuǐjìn** be at the end of one's tether

山区 **shānqū** mountainous area

删去 **shānqù** delete

山雀 **shānquè** tit (*bird*)

闪闪发光 **shǎnshǎn fāguāng** glitter

闪烁 **shǎnshuò** flash; glint; blink ◊ gleam

膳宿 **shànsù** board with

山头 **shāntóu** mountain top

善行 **shànxíng** goodness

山羊 **shānyáng** goat

赡养 **shànyǎng** support

赡养费 **shànyǎng fèi** alimony

闪耀 **shǎnyào** sparkle; twinkle; glare

善意 **shànyì** goodwill

善于 **shànyú** be good at

山楂 **shānzhā** haw (*berry*)

擅自 **shànzì** unauthorized

扇子 **shànzi** fan

擅自占地者 **shànzì zhàndì zhě** squatter

擅自占用 **shànzì zhànyòng** squat

烧 **shāo** burn; fry

稍 **shāo** slightly; 稍醉 *shāo zuì* slightly drunk, tipsy

勺 **sháo** spoon; 两勺糖 *liǎng sháo táng* two spoonfuls of sugar

少 **shǎo** few; less ◊ lack, be without; 少吃 / 说 *shǎo chī / shuō* eat / talk less

哨 **shào** whistle

少 **shào** young

哨兵 **shàobīng** sentry

少不得 **shǎobude** essential, indispensable

烧断 **shāoduàn** blow (*of fuse*)

烧毁 **shāohuǐ** burn down

烧焦 **shāojiāo** burn; singe ◊ charred

烧开 **shāokāi** boil

少量 **shǎoliàng** small amount ◊ meager

少男 **shàonán** teenage boy

少年 **shàonián** young person (*in early teens*)

少年犯 **shàoniánfàn** juvenile

delinquent

少年犯罪 **shàonián fànzuì** juvenile delinquency

少女 **shàonǚ** teenage girl

烧伤 **shāoshāng** burn

少数 **shǎoshù** few ◊ minority

少数几个 **shǎoshù jǐge** few

少数民族 **shǎoshù mínzú** ethnic minority

稍微 **shāowēi** a little; some ◊ slightly; marginally

少校 **shàoxiào** major MIL

稍许 **shāoxǔ** a little

少许 **shǎoxǔ** a little

少有 **shǎoyǒu** infrequent

少于 … **shǎoyú** … fewer than …

烧着 **shāozhe** burn; catch fire

哨子 **shàozi** whistle

杀气腾腾 **shāqì téngténg** murderous

沙丘 **shāqiū** (sand) dune

杀人犯 **shārénfàn** murderer

沙色 **shāsè** sandy color

沙沙声 **shāshashēng** rustle

杀死 **shāsǐ** kill

沙滩 **shātān** sandy beach

砂糖 **shātáng** granulated sugar

沙特阿拉伯 **Shātè'Ālābó** Saudi (Arabia) ◊ Saudi

纱线 **shāxiàn** yarn, thread

傻笑 **shǎxiào** giggle; titter

沙哑 **shāyǎ** rough; husky *voice*

沙岩 **shāyán** sandstone

鲨鱼 **shāyú** shark

砂纸 **shāzhǐ** sandpaper

砂质土壤 **shāzhì tǔrǎng** sandy soil

傻子 **shǎzi** dope, idiot

蛇 **shé** snake

舌 **shé** tongue

社 **shè** society

设 **shè** set up, establish

射 **shè** shoot

设备 **shèbèi** equipment

设备齐全 **shèbèi qíquán** self-contained

射程 **shèchéng** range

奢侈 **shēchǐ** extravagant; luxurious; magnificent ◊ extravagance

社工 **shègōng** social worker

社会 **shèhuì** society ◊ social

社会工作 **shèhuì gōngzuò** social work

社会习俗 **shèhuì xísú** convention

社会学 **shèhuì xué** sociology

社会渣滓 **shèhuì zhāzǐ** the dregs of society

社会主义 **shèhuì zhǔyì** socialism ◊ socialist

社会主义者 **shèhuì zhǔyì zhě** socialist

谁 **shéi** who; 谁是第一个？ *shéi shì dìyīgè?* who's first please?

谁的 **shéide** whose

射击 **shèjī** fire, shoot ◊ gunshot

涉及 **shèjí** involve; concern ◊ reference

设计 **shèjì** design; plan; create

社交 **shèjiāo** social interaction ◊ socialize

社交礼节 **shèjiāo lǐjié** social niceties

射击声 **shèjīshēng** shot

设计师 **shèjì shī** designer

设计失误 **shèjì shīwù** design fault

设计图 **shèjìtú** plan; design

设计学院 **shèjì xuéyuàn** design school

设计者 **shèjì zhě** creator

设立 **shèlì** set up, establish

社论 **shèlùn** editorial

射落 **shèluò** bring down

蛇麻草 **shémácǎo** hop (*plant*)

赦免 **shèmiǎn** pardon; amnesty ◊ absolve

深 **shēn** deep ◊ dearly *love*; 深绿 / 蓝 *shēn lǜ / lán* dark green / blue

身 **shēn** body

伸 **shēn** stretch; 伸长脖子 *shēncháng bózi* crane one's neck

神 **shén** god; deity ◊ divine; spiritual

肾 **shèn** kidney

渗 **shèn** seep; leak

深奥 **shēn'ào** deep; mysterious; baffling

申辩 **shēnbiàn** defend oneself

身材 **shēncái** build; figure

审查 **shěnchá** check; examine;

review

审查制度 **shěnchá zhìdù** censorship

深沉 **shēnchén** deep

申斥 **shēnchì** reprimand

伸出 **shēnchū** jut out, stick out; hold out

渗出 **shènchū** ooze

深度 **shēndù** depth

身分 **shēnfen** identity; status

身份的象征 **shēnfènde xiàngzhēng** status symbol

身分证 **shēnfenzhèng** identity card

身分证明 **shēnfen zhèngmíng** identification

生 **shēng** give birth to; grow; live ◊ raw; unripe; ... 有点儿生了 ... **yǒudiǎnr shēng le** ... is a little rusty

升 **shēng** rise; hoist ◊ liter

声 **shēng** sound

绳 **shéng** cord; rope

省 **shěng** province ◊ provincial

盛 **shèng** height ◊ flourishing, prosperous

剩 **shèng** remain, be left over; 没剩什么 **méishèng shénme** there is nothing left

胜 **shèng** win ◊ victory

圣 **shèng** saint; sage

身高 **shēngāo** height

声辩 **shēngbiàn** protest

生病 **shēngbìng** fall ill, be taken ill ◊ sick

声部 **shēngbù** part

生菜叶 **shēngcài yè** lettuce

生产 **shēngchǎn** produce; output ◊ childbirth; production

生产耗资 **shēngchǎn chéngběn** production costs

生产力 **shēngchǎnlì** productivity

生产能力 **shēngchǎn nénglì** production capacity

生产线 **shēngchǎn xiàn** production line

生产者 **shēngchǎn zhě** manufacturer

声称 **shēngchēng** claim; profess

生成 **shēngchéng** generate

牲畜 **shēngchù** stock; livestock

生存 **shēngcún** exist; live ◊ existence; being

声带 **shēngdài** vocal cords

圣诞节 **Shèngdàn Jié** Christmas; Christmas Day

圣诞卡 **Shèngdàn kǎ** Christmas card

圣诞快乐！ **Shèngdàn kuàilè!** Merry Christmas!

圣诞老人 **Shèngdàn Lǎorén** Santa Claus

圣诞礼物 **Shèngdàn lǐwù** Christmas present

圣诞树 **Shèngdàn shù** Christmas tree

圣诞夜 **Shèngdàn Yè** Christmas Eve

圣地 **shèngdì** sanctuary

声调 **shēngdiào** tone of voice; ring

省掉 **shěngdiào** spare

生动 **shēngdòng** vivid; graphic; lifelike

升高 **shēnggāo** raise

胜过 **shèngguò** outdo; eclipse

生孩子 **shēng háizi** give birth

省会 **shěnghuì** provincial capital

生活 **shēnghuó** live ◊ life

生活水平 **shēnghuó shuǐpíng** standard of living

生活方式 **shēnghuò fāngshì** way of life

生活费用 **shēnghuó fèiyòng** cost of living

生活史 **shēnghuó shǐ** life history

生活水准 **shēnghuó shuǐzhǔn** standard of living

升级 **shēngjí** escalation

生计 **shēngjì** livelihood; keep

圣经 **Shèngjīng** the Bible

声卡 **shēngkǎ** sound card

盛开 **shèngkāi** in full bloom

牲口 **shēngkou** livestock

生来 **shēnglái** genetically ◊ inborn; 他生来如此 **tā shēnglái rúcǐ** it's in his genes

胜利 **shènglì** victory, win ◊ victorious; 胜利的喜悦 **shènglì de xǐyuè** triumph

圣灵 **Shènglíng** Holy Spirit

胜利者 **shènglì zhě** victor

省略 **shěnglüè** leave out, omit

生闷气 **shēng mènqì** sulk; brood ◊ sulky

生面团 **shēngmiàn tuán** dough

声明 **shēngmíng** declare; state ◊ declaration; statement

生命 **shēngmìng** life

声名 **shēngmíng** reputation

声名败坏 **shēngmíng bàihuài** disreputable

声名狼籍 **shēngmíng lángjí** notorious

申明缘由 **shēnmíng yuányóu** justify *text*

盛年 **shèngnián** prime of one's life

生啤酒 **shēng píjiǔ** draft (beer)

举起 **shēngqǐ** hoist

升起 **shēngqǐ** rise; be up (*of sun*)

生气 **shēngqì** annoy; be annoyed; get worked up; 令人生气 **lìngrén shēngqì** infuriating; 使 X 生气 **shǐ X shēngqì** make X angry; 跟 X 生气 **gēn X shēngqì** be angry with X

生气勃勃 **shēngqì bóbo** spirited; energetic

升起来 **shēng qǐlái** come up

省却 **shěngquè** dispense with

圣人 **shèngrén** saint; sage

胜任 **shèngrèn** be equal to, be able to manage; 我觉得自己不能胜任 **wǒ juédé zìjǐ bùnéng shèngrèn** I don't feel up to it

生日 **shēngri** birthday; 生日快乐！ **shēngri kuàilè!** happy birthday!

升入 **shēngrù** soar (*of rocket*)

生手 **shēngshǒu** greenhorn

生疏 **shēngshū** rusty *subject*

声嘶力竭 **shēngsī lìjié** strident

生态 **shēngtài** ecology ◊ ecological

生态平衡 **shēngtài pínghéng** ecological balance

生态系统 **shēngtài xìtǒng** ecosystem

生态学 **shēngtàixué** ecology

生态学家 **shēngtài xuéjiā** ecologist

圣坛 **shèngtán** altar

生铁 **shēngtiě** cast iron

圣徒 **shèngtú** saint

深谷 **shēngǔ** ravine

声望 **shēngwàng** popularity; reputation; standing

生物 **shēngwù** being; organism ◊ biological

生物工艺学 **shēngwù gōngyì xué** biotechnology

生物学 **shēngwù xué** biology

生息 **shēngxī** yield

剩下 **shèngxia** be left, remain; 有五个剩下 **yǒu wǔgè shèngxià** there were five to spare

盛夏 **shèngxià** height of summer

声响 **shēngxiǎng** sound

圣像 **shèngxiàng** icon

生效 **shēngxiào** take effect; come into force; 使 … 生效 **shǐ … shēngxiào** validate

生肖 **shēngxiào** *the twelve animals of the Chinese horoscope*

盛行 **shèngxíng** prevailing

生锈 **shēngxiù** rust ◊ rusty

生涯 **shēngyá** career

盛宴 **shèngyàn** feast; spread

生意 **shēngyi** business; trade

声音 **shēngyīn** sound; noise; voice

生硬 **shēngyìng** abrupt, brusque; brisk

生意兴隆 **shēngyi xīnglóng** busy

生育 **shēngyù** bear *child*

声誉 **shēngyù** reputation; renown, fame

剩余 **shèngyú** surplus; remainder, rest ◊ be over, be left

声誉不好 **shēngyù bùhǎo** disreputable

剩余收入 **shèngyú shōurù** disposable income

生长 **shēngzhǎng** grow

升值 **shēngzhí** revalue

生殖 **shēngzhí** reproduce

生殖器 **shēngzhíqì** genitals

绳子 **shéngzi** cord

审核 **shěnhé** audit

深红色 **shēnhóng sè** dark red; crimson

深厚 **shēnhòu** deep, profound

神话 **shénhuà** myth

神话故事 **shénhuà gùshì** fairy tale

神话学 **shénhuà xué** mythology

深呼吸 **shēn hūxī** breathe deeply

审计 **shěnjì** audit

伸脚空间 **shēnjiǎo kōngjiān** leg room

肾结石 **shènjiéshí** kidney stone

神经 **shénjīng** nerve ◊ screwed up

神经崩溃 **shénjīng bēngkuì** nervous breakdown

神经病 **shénjīng bìng** mental illness ◊ crazy

神经病学家 **shénjīngbìng xuéjiā** neurologist

神经过敏 **shénjīng guòmǐn** neurotic

神经机能病 **shénjīng jīnéng bìng** neurosis

神经性 **shénjīng xìng** nervous

神经质 **shénjīng zhì** neurotic

审计师 **shěnjì shī** auditor

伸开四肢 **shēnkāi sìzhī** sprawl

神龛 **shénkān** shrine

深刻 **shēnkè** deep; 给人以深刻印象 **gěi rén yǐ shēnkè yìnxiàng** impressive, which makes a deep impression

伸懒腰 **shēn lǎnyāo** stretch

渗漏 **shènlòu** leak; drip; seep out

什么 **shénme** what ◊ anything; 什么事？ **shénme shì?** what is it?; 那是什么？ **nà shì shénme?** what is that?; 我没听见什么 **wǒ méi tīngjiàn shénme** I didn't hear anything; 什么时候还给我？ **shénme shíhou huángěi wǒ?** when can I have it back?; 什么也不缺 **shénme yě bùquē** want for nothing

神秘 **shénmì** mysterious; occult

申明 **shēnmíng** declare, profess; protest

深明真相 **shēnmíng zhēnxiàng** penetrating

审判 **shěnpàn** try ◊ trial

审判室 **shěnpàn shì** courtroom

神奇 **shénqí** supernatural

深切 **shēnqiè** profound

申请 **shēnqǐng** apply for; put in for ◊ application

申请表格 **shēnqǐng biǎogé** application form

申请人 **shēnqǐng rén** applicant; claimant

深入 **shēnrù** deep ◊ in depth

渗入 **shènrù** sink in

深深 **shēnshēn** profoundly; head over heels; 深深地爱上 X **shēnshen de àishàng X** fall madly in love with X

审慎 **shěnshèn** prudent; scrupulous ◊ prudence

神圣 **shénshèng** holy, sacred ◊ sanctity

绅士 **shēnshì** gentleman

审视 **shěnshì** survey

身势语 **shēnshì yǔ** body language

伸手 **shēnshǒu** stretch

深思 **shēnsī** ponder

申诉 **shēnsù** lodge a complaint ◊ complaint

伸缩 **shēnsuō** flexible; stretchy

身体 **shēntǐ** body ◊ physical; 身体不好 **shēntǐ bùhǎo** be in poor health

身体上 **shēntǐ shang** physically

神童 **shéntóng** (infant) prodigy

身为人父 **shēnwéi rénfù** fatherhood

审问 **shěnwèn** question

审问者 **shěnwèn zhě** interrogator

身陷困境 **shēnxiàn kùnjìng** deep trouble

神学 **shénxué** theology

审讯 **shěnxùn** examine; hear ◊ hearing; inquest

深夜 **shēnyè** in the dead of night

呻吟 **shēnyín** groan; moan

深渊 **shēnyuān** abyss

深远 **shēnyuǎn** far-reaching

深造 **shēnzào** continue one's education

伸展 **shēnzhǎn** stretch; extend; spread

伸展四肢 **shēnzhǎn sìzhī** stretch

甚至 **shènzhì** even; to the extent that

神志不清 **shénzhì bùqīng** stupor ◊ in a stupor

神志清醒 **shénzhì qīngxǐng** lucid ◊ lucidity

神职人员 **shénzhí rényuán** clergy

神志正常 **shénzhì zhèngcháng** sane ◊ sanity

慎重 **shènzhòng** careful

舍弃 **shěqì** abandon

赊欠 **shēqiàn** credit FIN

社区 **shèqū** community

设施 **shèshī** facilities

摄氏 **shèshì** Celsius; centigrade; 摄氏十度 **shèshì shídù** 10 degrees centigrade

射手 **shèshǒu** marksman

舌舔 **shétiǎn** lick

舌头 **shétóu** tongue

社团 **shètuán** society, organization

设想 **shèxiǎng** conceive of; visualize ◊ assumption

摄像机 **shèxiàng jī** video camera; camcorder

摄影 **shèyǐng** photography

摄影棚 **shèyǐng péng** studio

摄影师 **shèyǐng shī** photographer; cameraman

摄远镜头 **shèyuǎn jìngtóu** telephoto lens

设置 **shèzhì** locate

射中 **shèzhòng** shoot

诗 **shī** poem; verse; poetry

湿 **shī** wet; damp

师 **shī** master

狮 **shī** lion

失 **shī** lose

施 **shī** carry out

尸 **shī** corpse

十 **shí** ten

实 **shí** real; solid

识 **shí** know; recognize

石 **shí** stone

时 **shí** time; hour; 十八岁时 **shíbāsuì shí** at the age of 18; 午夜时 **wǔyèshí** at midnight

食 **shí** food ◊ eat

屎 **shǐ** feces, shit

史 **shǐ** history

使 **shǐ** cause; make; 使 … 吃亏 **shǐ … chīkuī** put at a disadvantage; 使 … 不高兴 **shǐ … bù gāoxìng** displease; 使 … 尴尬 **shǐ … gāngà** embarrass

始 **shǐ** begin, start

事 **shì** matter, affair

是 **shì** be ◊ yes; 是，我知道 **shì, wǒ zhīdào** yes, I know

室 **shì** room

市 **shì** city; market

式 **shì** type; style

试 **shì** try; 试做 X **shì zuò X** have a try at X

示 **shì** show; indicate

视 **shì** see; watch; 视 … 而定 **shì … érdìng** conditional on …

誓 **shì** vow

势 **shì** power

氏 **shì** family name

十八 **shíbā** eighteen

失败 **shībài** fail; lose ◊ failure; defeat

失败者 **shībài zhě** loser

失败主义 **shībài zhǔyì** defeatism ◊ defeatist

饰板 **shìbǎn** plaque

施暴虐 **shī bàonüè** tyrannize

饰边 **shìbiān** frill; fringe

事变 **shìbiàn** incident

识别 **shíbié** recognize; distinguish

士兵 **shìbīng** soldier; private; the ranks

时差 **shíchā** time difference

视察 **shìchá** inspect ◊ inspection

时差反应 **shíchā fǎnyìng** jetlag

失常 **shīcháng** unbalanced; abnormal

时常 **shícháng** frequently, often

市场 **shìchǎng** market; marketplace

市场调查 **shìchǎng diàochá** market survey

市场经济 **shìchǎng jīngjì** market economy

市场力量 **shìchǎng lìliàng** market forces

市场占有率 **shìchǎng zhànyǒulǜ** market share

市场主导 **shìchǎng zhǔdǎo** market leader

试车 **shìchē** test drive; trial run

世仇 **shìchóu** feud

驶出 **shìchū** pull out (of train, ship)

试穿 **shìchuān** try on

视窗 **shíchuāng** window

时代 **shídài** age, era; generation

实弹 **shídàn** live ammunition

适当 **shìdàng** proper, appropriate, suitable ◊ properly; duly

食道 **shídào** gullet

使得 **shǐde** so; so that ◊ make; cause

是的 **shìde** yes; that's right

实得工资 **shídé gōngzī** take-home pay

湿度 **shīdù** humidity

适度 **shìdù** moderate ◊ mildly; moderately; in moderation

十二 **shí'èr** twelve, dozen

视而不见 **shì'ér būjiàn** blind to

十二分之一 **shí'èr fēn zhīyī** twelfth

十二月 **shí'èryuè** December

示范 **shìfàn** demonstrate ◊ demonstration, demo

示范碟 **shìfàn dié** demo disk

释放 **shìfàng** release, free

施肥 **shīféi** fertilize

是否 **shìfǒu** whether or not

师傅 **shīfu** master

石膏 **shígāo** plaster

石膏绷带 **shígāo bēngdài** plaster cast

诗歌 **shīgē** poem; poetry

施工工地 **shīgōng gōngdì** construction site

石工技巧 **shígōng jìqiǎo** masonry (*skill*)

尸骨 **shīgǔ** skeleton

事故 **shìgù** accident; crash; 在事故中丧生 **zài shìgù zhōng sàngshēng** be killed in an accident

使馆 **shǐguǎn** embassy

试管 **shìguǎn** test tube

试管婴儿 **shìguǎn yīng'ér** test-tube baby

嗜好 **shìhào** hobby; addiction; 有吸毒嗜好 **yǒu xīdú shìhào** be on drugs

适合 **shìhé** suit; fit; be in accordance with; 适合于 X **shìhé yú X** be cut out for X

事后 **shìhòu** subsequent ◊ subsequently, afterward

石灰 **shíhuī** lime

失火 **shīhuǒ** fire ◊ catch fire

实际 **shíjì** real, actual; practical; substantive

世纪 **shìjì** century

时间 **shíjiān** time; while; interlude; 请再给我一些时间? **qǐng zài gěi wǒ yìxiē shíjiān?** can I have more time?; 时间自会定论 **shíjiān zì huì dìnglùn** time will tell

实践 **shíjiàn** practice

事件 **shìjiàn** event, happening; incident; business

时间安排 **shíjiān ānpái** timing

时间表 **shíjiān biǎo** timetable

时刻表 **shíkè biǎo** schedule

时间段 **shíjiānduàn** sitting

时间范围 **shíjiān fànwéi** timescale

时间间隔 **shíjiān jiàngé** time-lag

时间顺序 **shíjiān shùnxù** chronological

市郊 **shìjiāo** suburbs

施加压力 **shījiā yālì** put pressure on

世界 **shìjiè** world

世界大战 **shìjiè dàzhàn** world war

世界地图 **shìjiè dìtú** map of the world; atlas

世界观 **shìjièguān** world view

世界冠军 **shìjiè guànjūn** world champion

世界记录 **shìjiè jìlù** world record

世界强国 **shìjiè qiángguó** world power

世界性 **shìjiè xìng** cosmopolitan

世界著名 **shìjiè zhùmíng** world-famous

什锦 **shíjǐn** mixed; miscellaneous

试镜 **shìjìng** screen test

实际上 **shíjì shàng** actually, in fact; in practice

十几岁 **shíjǐ suì** be in one's teens

十九 **shíjiǔ** nineteen

诗句 **shījù** verse

视觉 **shìjué** vision ◊ visual; 视觉上来说 **shìjué shàng láishuō** visually

势均力敌 **shìjūn lìdí** evenly matched

时刻 **shíkè** moment ◊ constantly

时刻表 **shíkèbiǎo** schedule

蚀刻术 **shíkèshù** etching

石窟 **shíkū** grotto

实况 **shíkuàng** live

实况转播 **shíkuàng zhuǎnbō** live transmission

湿冷 **shīlěng** cold and damp

失利 **shīlì** lose out

实力 **shílì** strength

势力 **shìlì** strength, power

视力 **shìlì** sight, eyesight, vision

势利 **shìlì** snobbish

失恋 **shīliàn** be jilted

势力范围 **shìlì fànwéi** sphere of influence

失灵 **shīlíng** out of order; dead ◊ malfunction; jam ◊ be down

石榴 **shíliu** pomegranate

十六 **shíliù** sixteen

势利眼 **shìlìyǎn** snob

时髦 **shímáo** fashionable

失眠 **shīmián** insomnia

市民 **shìmín** city dweller

失明 **shīmíng** go blind

使命 **shǐmìng** mission; vocation

室内 **shìnèi** indoors; inside

室内设计 **shìnèi shèjì** interior design

室内设计者 **shìnèi shèjì zhě** interior designer

十年 **shínián** decade

施虐狂 **shīnüèkuáng** sadism

失陪 **shīpéi** please excuse me

食品 **shípǐn** food

视频 **shìpín** video COMPUT

食品杂货业 **shípǐn záhuò yè** grocery business

识破 **shípò** see through

食谱 **shípǔ** recipe; cookbook

十七 **shíqī** seventeen

时期 **shíqī** term; period

拾起 **shíqǐ** lift, pick up

士气 **shìqì** morale

史前 **shǐqián** prehistoric

事情 **shìqing** issue; matter

失去 **shīqù** lose; 失去控制 **shīqù kòngzhì** lose control; 失去知觉 **shīqù zhījué** lose consciousness

时区 **shíqū** time zone

拾取 **shíqǔ** pick up

市区 **shìqū** city area

湿热 **shīrè** humid

诗人 **shīrén** poet; 抒情诗人 **shūqíng shīrén** lyric poet

使人 **shǐrén** causative: 使人困乏 **shǐrén kùnfá** wearing, tiring; 使人兴奋 **shǐrén xīngfèn** exciting

食肉动物 **shíròu dòngwù** carnivore; predator

湿软 **shīruǎn** swampy

湿润 **shīrùn** moisture ◊ moist; soggy

失散 **shīsàn** stray

十三 **shísān** thirteen

时尚 **shíshàng** fashion

失身 **shīshēn** lose one's virginity

失声 **shīshēng** let out a cry

失势 **shīshì** fall from power

失事 **shīshì** have an accident

实施 **shíshī** implement; execute ◊ execution

实时 **shíshí** real time

时事 **shíshì** current affairs, current events

史诗 **shǐshī** epic

试试 **shìshi** try; 让我试试 **ràng wǒ shìshi** can I have a try?

事实 **shìshí** fact; truth

适时 **shìshí** well-timed

逝世 **shìshì** pass away

实事求是 **shíshì qiúshì** practical; down-to-earth

事实上 **shìshí shang** indeed, as a matter of fact

时事讨论节目 **shíshì tǎolùn jiémù** current affairs program

尸首分离 **shīshǒu fēnlí** decapitate

十四 **shísì** fourteen

时速 **shísù** speed

世俗 **shìsú** worldly; secular

失算 **shīsuàn** miscalculate

时态 **shítài** tense

食堂 **shítáng** cafeteria; canteen

食糖 **shítáng** sugar

尸体 **shītǐ** corpse, cadaver

失调 **shītiáo** disorder

视听 **shìtīng** audiovisual

湿透 **shītòu** soaked ◊ be wet through

石头 **shítou** stone

试图 **shìtú** attempt

室外 **shìwài** outdoors; outside ◊ outdoor

世外桃源 **shìwài táoyuán** oasis *fig*

失望 **shīwàng** be disappointed ◊ disappointment ◊ disappointed; 令人失望 **lìngrén shīwàng** disappointing ◊ dismay; 使 ... 失望 *shǐ ... shīwàng* disappoint; 让 X 失望 *ràng X shīwàng* let X down

视网膜 **shìwǎngmó** retina

示威 **shìwēi** demonstration, protest ◊ demonstrate

示威游行 **shìwēi yóuxíng** demonstration

示威者 **shìwēi zhě** demonstrator, protester

失误 **shīwù** mistake, error

十五 **shíwǔ** fifteen

食物 **shíwù** food; diet

事务 **shìwù** concern; affair

食物搅拌器 **shíwù jiǎobànqì** food mixer

史无前例 **shǐ wú qiánlì** unprecedented

事物 **shìwù** thing

失物招领处 **shīwù zhāolǐng chù** lost-and-found (office)

食物中毒 **shíwù zhòngdù** food poisoning

实习 **shíxí** work as an intern ◊ internship

世袭 **shìxí** hereditary; inherited

实现 **shíxiàn** fulfill; realize; come true ◊ realization

事先 **shìxiān** beforehand ◊ prior

事先形成 **shìxiān xíngchéng** preconceived

实习护士 **shíxí hùshì** student nurse

实习教师 **shíxí jiàoshī** student teacher

时新 **shíxīn** fashionable, stylish

实行 **shíxíng** implement, carry out

失信 **shīxìn** go back on one's word, break one's promise

实习期 **shíxí qī** trial period

实习生 **shíxí shēng** trainee

失修 **shīxiū** in a state of disrepair; run-down; derelict

世袭遗产 **shìxí yíchǎn** heritage

实验 **shíyàn** experiment

誓言 **shìyán** oath, vow

试演 **shìyǎn** audition

试验 **shìyàn** test; experiment; trial; 试验 X *shìyàn X* have X on trial; test X

试验方案 **shìyàn fāng'àn** pilot scheme

试样 **shìyàng** sample

式样 **shìyàng** style; type

试验期 **shìyàn qī** trial period

试验区 **shìyàn qū** pilot plant

使眼色 **shǐ yǎnsè** wink

实验室 **shíyàn shì** lab, laboratory

实验室技师 **shíyàn shì jìshī** laboratory technician

失业 **shīyè** unemployed, out of work ◊ unemployment

视野 **shìyě** vision; outlook; 使视野开阔 *shǐ shìyě kāikuò* broaden one's mind; 在 X 视野之内 *zài X shìyě zhī nèi* within sight of X

事业 **shìyè** undertaking; career

实业家 **shíyèjiā** industrialist

失业者 **shīyè zhě** the unemployed

诗意 **shīyì** poetic

十一 **shíyī** eleven

十亿 **shíyì** billion

适宜 **shìyí** appropriate, suitable

释义 **shìyì** paraphrase

示意 **shìyì** sign, signal; 他示意我前行 *tā shìyì wǒ qiánxíng* he motioned me forward

石英 **shíyīng** quartz

适应 **shìyìng** adapt; acclimate, acclimatize; adjust

侍应生 **shìyìng shēng** busboy

石英钟 **shíyīng zhōng** quartz clock

十一月 **shíyīyuè** November

食用 **shíyòng** consume

实用 **shíyòng** practical; useful

使用 **shǐyòng** apply, use, employ; access

适用 **shìyòng** applicable ◊ apply

试用 **shìyòng** probation ◊ try out

试用期 **shìyòng qī** probation period

使用时间 **shǐyòng shíjiān** access time

使用说明书 **shǐyòng shuōmíng shū** instruction manual

实用主义 **shíyòng zhǔyì** pragmatism

石油 **shíyóu** oil; petroleum

食油 **shíyóu** cooking oil

石油公司 **shíyóu gōngsī** oil company

石油化学产品 **shíyóu huàxué chǎnpǐn** petrochemical

石油输出国组织 **Shíyóu Shūchūguó Zǔzhī** OPEC, Organization of Petroleum Exporting Countries

食欲 **shíyù** appetite

十月 **shíyuè** October

誓约 **shìyuē** vow

适于 **shìyú**: 适于居住 **shìyú jūzhù** habitable, inhabitable; 适于青年 **shìyú qīngnián** youthful *fashion, music*; 适于远航 **shìyú yuǎnháng** seagoing

实在 **shízài** real ◊ really

施展 **shīzhǎn** unfold, develop; display

市长 **shìzhǎng** mayor

使者 **shìzhě** envoy

侍者 **shìzhě** bellhop

湿疹 **shīzhěn** eczema

市镇 **shìzhèn** urban

实证 **shízhèng** testament

市政 **shìzhèng** municipal

市政厅 **shìzhèng tīng** city hall

食指 **shízhǐ** forefinger, index finger

实质 **shízhì** essence; substance

实质上 **shízhì shang** substantially

始终 **shǐzhōng** from start to finish

始终不渝 **shǐzhōng bù yú** consistent ◊ consistently

市中心 **shì zhōngxīn** down-town ◊ city center

施主 **shīzhǔ** benefactor

时装 **shízhuāng** fashion

时装表演 **shízhuāng biǎoyǎn** fashion show

时装商店 **shízhuāng shāngdiàn** boutique

时装设计师 **shízhuāng shèjìshī** fashion designer

时装展览 **shízhuāng zhǎnlǎn** collection

狮子 **shīzi** lion

虱子 **shīzi** louse

师资 **shīzī** teachers

柿子 **shìzi** persimmon

十字架 **shízìjià** cross, crucifix

十字路口 **shízì lùkǒu** crossroads; intersection

狮子舞 **shīziwǔ** lion dance

失踪 **shīzōng** missing ◊ disappearance

十足 **shízú** absolute, complete; downright

氏族 **shìzú** family, kin; clan

失足跌倒 **shīzú diēdǎo** lose one's footing

收 **shōu** receive; accept

熟 **shóu** ripe; cooked; familiar ◊ ripeness ◊ soundly

手 **shǒu** hand

守 **shǒu** keep watch; guard; abide by

首 **shǒu** head ◊ first

瘦 **shòu** thin; lean

兽 **shòu** beast; animal

受 **shòu** receive; accept; 不受诱惑 **búshòu yòuhuò** resist temptation; 受感染 **shòu gǎnrǎn** go septic

授 **shòu** give; teach

售 **shòu** sell

售报亭 **shòubào tíng** newsstand

手臂 **shǒubì** arm

手边 **shǒubiān** within reach

手表 **shǒubiǎo** wristwatch

守财奴 **shǒucái nú** miser

收藏 **shōucáng** tuck away

收藏家 **shōucáng jiā** collector

收藏品 **shōucáng pǐn** collection

手册 **shǒucè** handbook

首倡 **shǒuchàng** pioneer

收成 **shōucheng** crop, harvest

首次公演 **shǒucì gōngyǎn** première

手袋 **shǒudài** purse

收到 **shōudào** receive, get

手电筒 **shǒudiàntǒng** flashlight

首都 **shǒudū** capital

收短 **shōuduǎn** take up *dress etc*

手段 **shǒuduàn** means

守法 **shǒufǎ** comply with the law

收费 **shōufèi** charge

收费处 **shōufèi chù** toll booth

收费公路 **shōufèi gōnglù** toll road

手风琴 **shǒufēng qín** accordion

手稿 **shǒugǎo** manuscript

收割 **shōugē** reap

手工 **shǒugōng** manual ◊ handiwork

手工业 **shǒugōngyè** craft; handicraft

手工业者 **shǒugōngyè zhě** craftsman

手工艺 **shǒugōngyì** handicraft

手工艺者 **shǒugōngyì zhě** craftsman

手工制作 **shǒugōng zhìzuò** handmade

收购 **shōugòu** purchase ◊ purchasing

守规矩 **shǒu guījǔ** behave (oneself)

受过教育 **shòuguò jiàoyù** educated

受害 **shòuhài** sustain damage; suffer an injury

受害者 **shòuhài zhě** victim

首航 **shǒuháng** maiden voyage

守候 **shǒuhòu** watch for

售后服务 **shòuhòu fúwù** after-sales service

守护 **shǒuhù** look after, watch

受欢迎 **shòu huānyíng** popular; welcome; well-received

收回 **shōuhuí** repossess; reclaim; retract

受贿 **shòuhuì** corruption

收获 **shōuhuò** harvest

售货亭 **shòuhuò tíng** kiosk

售货员 **shòuhuò yuán** sales clerk

收集 **shōují** collect

售价 **shòujià** retail price

收件人 **shōujiàn rén** addressee

手巾 **shǒujīn** towel

受惊 **shòujīng** panic

受精 **shòujīng** be fertilized; 使 … 受精 **shǐ … shòujīng** fertilize

受惊吓 **shòujīngxià** petrified

守旧 **shǒujiù** provincial

熟记 **shóujì** know by heart

收据 **shōujù** receipt

手绢 **shǒujuàn** handkerchief

收看 **shōukàn** view; tune in; tune in to

手铐 **shǒukào** handcuffs

受苦 **shòukǔ** suffer

收款人 **shōukuǎn rén** recipient; payee

收款台 **shōukuǎn tái** till, cash register

受冷遇 **shòu lěngyù** get the cold shoulder; be in the doghouse

受连累 **shòu liánlèi** incriminate oneself

狩猎 **shòuliè** hunt

首领 **shǒulǐng** leader

收留 **shōuliú** take in

手榴弹 **shǒuliúdàn** grenade

收买 **shōumǎi** purchase; buy off, bribe

守门人 **shǒumén rén** doorman; super

守门员 **shǒumén yuán** goalkeeper

寿命 **shòumìng** life, lifetime

受虐狂 **shòunüèkuáng** masochism

受虐狂者 **shòunüèkuáng zhě** masochist

受骗 **shòupiàn** be deceived; 易受骗 **yì shòupiàn** gullible

售票处 **shòupiào chù** box office, ticket office

售票机 **shòupiào jī** ticket machine

收票员 **shòupiào yuán** ticket collector

售票员 **shòupiào yuán** booking clerk, ticket seller

收瓶处 **shōupíng chù** bottle bank

手枪 **shǒuqiāng** handgun; pistol

收起来 **shōuqǐlái** put away

授权 **shòuquán** authorize; warrant; delegate ◊ mandate; power of attorney

兽群 **shòuqún** herd

熟人 **shóurén** acquaintance; friend

收入 **shōurù** income; revenue

受伤 **shòu shāng** wounded; 腿受

伤 **tuǐ shòu shāng** wounded in the leg

受伤害 **shòu shānghài** injured

受伤者 **shòu shāng zhě** the injured

受伤至残 **shòu shāng zhì cán** cripple

受审 **shòushěn** on trial

收拾 **shōushi** clear away; clear up, tidy up; pack up

首饰 **shǒushi** jewelry

守时 **shǒushí** be punctual ◊ punctuality

手势 **shǒushì** gesture

熟食店 **shóushí diàn** delicatessen, deli

收拾干净 **shōushí gānjìng** clean up

手势语言 **shǒushì yǔyán** sign language

手术 **shǒushù** surgery; operation; 做手术 **zuò shǒushù** have an operation

手术刀 **shǒushù dāo** scalpel

手术室 **shǒushù shì** operating room

收缩 **shōusuō** contract, shrink

手套 **shǒutào** glove

手提包 **shǒutí bāo** bag; purse

手提电话 **shǒutí diànhuà** cell phone

收听 **shōutīng** tune in; tune in to

手提式 **shǒutíshì** portable

手提行李 **shǒutí xíngli** hand baggage

手提衣箱 **shǒutí yīxiāng** suitcase

手推车 **shǒutuīchē** wheelbarrow

受托集团 **shòutuō jítuán** trust FIN

手腕 **shǒuwàn** wrist

售完为止 **shòuwán wéizhǐ** subject to availability

守卫 **shǒuwèi** guard

守卫队员 **shǒuwèi duìyuán** defense player

守卫者 **shǒuwèi zhě** guard, watchman

首先 **shǒuxiān** firstly, to begin with, in the first place

首相 **shǒuxiàng** prime minister

受限制 **shòu xiànzhì** restricted

手写 **shǒuxiě** handwritten ◊ write by hand

收信人 **shōuxìn rén** addressee; receiver

首席小提琴演奏者 **shǒuxí xiǎo tíqín yǎnzòu zhě** concertmaster

手续 **shǒuxù** formality; procedure

授勋 **shòuxūn** decorate

首演 **shǒuyǎn** début

收养 **shōuyǎng** adopt

手摇风琴 **shǒuyáo fēngqín** barrel organ

收益 **shōuyì** return, yield

兽医 **shòuyī** veterinary surgeon

受益 **shòuyì** benefit

手淫 **shǒuyín** masturbate

手印 **shǒuyìn** fingerprint

收音机 **shōuyīnjī** radio; 收音机里 **shōuyīnjī lǐ** on the radio

手艺人 **shǒuyì rén** craftsman; artisan

授予 **shòuyǔ** grant; present; confer

受约束 **shòu yuēshù** be bound, be committed; 受约束去做 X **shòu yuēshù qùzuò X** be bound to do X

受灾地区 **shòuzāi dìqū** disaster area

守则 **shǒuzé** rules

手轧 **shǒuzhá** parking brake

手掌 **shǒuzhǎng** palm

手杖 **shǒuzhàng** walking stick

手指 **shǒuzhǐ** finger

手指甲 **shǒuzhǐjiǎ** fingernail

收支平衡 **shōuzhī pínghéng** balance ◊ break even

受重伤 **shòu zhòngshāng** seriously injured

手爪子 **shǒuzhuǎzi** paw

手镯 **shǒuzhuó** bracelet

手足之情 **shǒuzú zhī qíng** fraternal love

书 **shū** book

梳 **shū** comb

输 **shū** lose

叔 **shū** uncle

熟 **shú** cooked; ripe; familiar ◊ ripeness ◊ soundly

赎 **shú** redeem

数 **shǔ** count

鼠 shǔ mouse; rat

暑 shǔ summer heat

属 shǔ belong to; 我属龙 **wǒ shǔ lóng** I was born in the year of the dragon

数 shù number

树 shù tree

竖 shù vertical

术 shù skill; art

述 shù tell, narrate

束 shù bundle, bunch, sheaf; 一束玫瑰 **yīshù méigui** a bunch of roses

刷 shuā clean ◊ brush

刷掉 shuādiào brush off

耍滑头 shuǎ huátóu try to be clever; 跟 X 耍滑头 **gēn X shuǎ huátóu** get smart with X

摔 shuāi fall; drop; throw down

帅 shuài handsome; snazzy

衰败 shuāibài go to seed

摔倒 shuāidǎo fall, fall down

甩干 shuǎigān spin-dry

甩干机 shuǎigān jī (spin-)dryer, (tumble-)dryer

摔跤 shuāijiāo fall; slip; wrestle

摔跤比赛 shuāijiāo bǐsài wrestling match

摔跤运动 shuāijiāo yùndòng wrestling

摔跤运动员 shuāijiāo yùndòng yuán wrestler

衰老 shuāilǎo senile

衰老状态 shuāilǎo zhuàngtài senility

衰落 shuāiluò go downhill, deteriorate

衰弱 shuāiruò weak ◊ waste away

衰退 shuāituì decay; decline

率直 shuàizhí plain; blunt

刷净 shuājìng scour

刷卡 shuākǎ smartcard

闩 shuān bolt ◊ catch (on door)

拴 shuān tie up, tether; 把 X 拴在 Y 上 **bǎ X shuān zài Y shàng** hitch X to Y; chain X to Y

双 shuāng both; even; double; dual; twin ◊ measure word for pairs; 一双袜子 **yīshuāng wàzi** a pair of socks

霜 shuāng frost

双胞胎 shuāng bāo tāi twins

双倍 shuāngbèi double

双边 shuāngbiān bilateral

双层玻璃 shuāngcéng bōli double glazing

双层床 shuāngcéng chuáng bunk beds

双重 shuāngchóng double

双打 shuāngdǎ doubles SP

霜冻 shuāngdòng frost

双方 shuāngfāng both sides

媚妇 shuāngfù widow

双关语 shuāngguānyǔ pun

双击 shuāngjī double click

爽快 shuǎngkuài refreshed; invigorating

双排扣式 shuāngpái kòushì double-breasted

双人床 shuāngrén chuáng double bed

双人房 shuāngrén fáng double (room)

爽身粉 shuāngshēnfěn talcum powder

双数 shuāngshù even number

双下巴 shuāngxiàba double chin

双向交通 shuāngxiàng jiāotōng two-way traffic

双性 shuāngxìng bisexual

双语 shuāngyǔ bilingual

栓剂 shuānjì suppository

栓牢 shuānláo attach

耍弄 shuǎnòng kick around

栓塞 shuānsè embolism

栓住 shuānzhù bolt; hitch

耍小聪明 shuǎ xiǎo cōngmíng smart, cute

刷牙 shuāyá brush one's teeth

刷子 shuāzi brush

书包 shūbāo schoolbag

鼠标 shǔbiāo mouse COMPUT

鼠标垫 shǔbiāodiàn mouse mat

数不清 shǔbuqīng innumerable; incalculable, countless

蔬菜 shūcài vegetable

蔬菜农场 shūcài nóngchǎng truck farm

蔬菜水果商 shūcài shuǐguǒ shāng greengrocer

输出 shūchū output; export

书呆子 shūdāizi bookworm;

pedant

竖笛 shùdí recorder MUS

书店 shūdiàn bookstore

输掉 shūdiào lose

数额 shù'é amount, sum

书法 shūfǎ calligraphy

书房 shūfáng study, den

竖放 shùfàng stand

舒服 shūfu comfortable ◊ well

束缚 shùfù tie; bind

树干 shùgàn trunk

疏忽 shūhū oversight

谁 shuí who

水 shuǐ water

睡 shuì sleep; 我睡不着 **wǒ shuìbùzháo** I couldn't get to sleep; 睡个懒觉 **shuìgè lǎnjiào** sleep late

税 shuì tax; duty; tariff

水坝 shuǐbà dam

水边 shuǐbiān waterside

水彩 shuǐcǎi watercolor

水彩画 shuǐcǎihuà watercolor (painting)

水池 shuǐchí pond; basin

睡袋 shuìdài sleeping bag

水电站 shuǐdiànzhàn hydroelectric power plant

水痘 shuǐdòu chicken pox

睡房 shuìfáng bedroom

水肺 shuǐfèi air tank, aqualung

水管 shuǐguǎn water pipe

水果 shuǐguǒ fruit

水果色拉 shuǐguǒ sèlā fruit salad

睡过头 shuì guòtóu oversleep

水花 shuǐhuā spray

睡觉 shuìjiào sleep; go to bed; 我需要好好睡一觉 **wǒ xūyào hǎohǎo shuìyíjiào** I need a good sleep; 和 … 睡觉 **hé … shuìjiào** sleep with …

水晶 shuǐjīng crystal

水坑 shuǐkēng puddle

水库 shuǐkù reservoir

睡裤 shuìkù pajama pants

睡懒觉 shuì lǎnjiào sleep late

水冷却 shuǐlěngquè water-cooling

水力发电 shuǐlì fādiàn hydroelectric

水龙头 shuǐlóngtóu faucet

水路 shuǐlù waterway

水面 shuǐmiàn surface (of water)

睡眠 shuìmián sleep

水墨画 shuǐmòhuà ink wash painting

水泥 shuǐní cement

水牛 shuǐniú water buffalo

水暖工 shuǐnuǎngōng plumber

水疱 shuǐpào blister

水平 shuǐpíng standard, level; horizontal

水平面 shuǐpíngmiàn water level; level surface

水栖 shuǐqī aquatic, water-dwelling

水上运动 shuǐshàng yùndòng watersports

水手 shuǐshǒu sailor, seaman

税收 shuìshōu tax revenue

水手领 shuǐshǒu lǐng crew neck

水獭 shuǐtǎ otter

水桶 shuǐtǒng pail, bucket

水位 shuǐwèi water level

税务调查员 shuìwù diàocháyuán tax inspector

税务局 shuìwùjú tax office

水箱 shuǐxiāng cistern

睡醒 shuìxǐng wake up

睡眼惺忪 shuìyǎn xīngsōng bleary-eyed

睡衣 shuìyī nightdress; pajamas; pajama jacket

睡衣裤 shuìyīkù pajamas; pajama pants

水银 shuǐyín mercury, quicksilver

水翼艇 shuǐyìtǐng hydrofoil

水域 shuǐyù waters; area of water

睡着 shuìzháo fall asleep

水准仪 shuǐzhǔn yí spirit level

水准 shuǐzhǔn standard, level

水族馆 shuǐzú guǎn aquarium

书脊 shūjí spine

书籍 shūjí books

书架 shūjià bookcase

暑假 shǔjià summer vacation

树胶 shùjiāo gum

赎金 shújīn ransom

数据 shùjù data

数据保护 shùjù bǎohù data protection

数据储存 **shùjù chǔcún** data storage

数据处理 **shùjù chǔlǐ** data processing

数据俘获 **shùjù fúhuò** data capture

数据库 **shùjù kù** database

疏浚 **shūjùn** dredge

数据载体 **shùjù zàitǐ** data carrier

熟客 **shúkè** regular visitor

漱口 **shùkǒu** gargle

漱口剂 **shùkǒujì** mouthwash

树篱 **shùlí** hedge

熟练 **shúliàn** skillful; proficient; practised ◊ proficiency

数量 **shùliàng** amount

熟练技巧 **shúliàn jìqiǎo** dexterity

树林 **shùlín** wood

数落 **shǔluò** tell off, chew out

书面 **shūmiàn** written ◊ in writing; 以书面形式 **yǐ shūmiàn xíngshì** in writing

数目 **shùmù** number, numeral; sum

吮 **shǔn** suck

顺便 **shùnbiàn** in passing

顺便过访 **shùnbiàn guòfǎng** stop by

顺便看望 **shùnbiàn kànwàng** look in on

顺便来访 **shùnbiàn láifǎng** drop in

顺便问一下 **shùnbiàn wènyīxià** by the way, incidentally

顺从 **shùncóng** obey; submit ◊ obedient; submissive; docile

顺从的人 **shùncóng de rén** conformist

顺风 **shùnfēng** tail wind

枢纽 **shūniǔ** hub; center

瞬间 **shùnjiān** moment, instant ◊ momentarily

顺口溜 **shùnkǒuliū** jingle

顺利 **shùnlì** smooth ◊ smoothly

顺势疗法 **shùnshì liáofǎ** homeopathy

顺时针 **shùn shízhēn** clockwise

吮吸 **shǔnxī** suck; 吮吸拇指 **shǔnxī mǔzhǐ** suck one's thumb

顺心 **shùnxīn** satisfactory

顺序 **shùnxù** sequence

说 **shuō** talk; speak; say; 你说呢？ **nǐ shuō ne?** what do you think?; 你说什么？ **nǐ shuō shénme?** pardon me? what did you say?; 那就是说 **nà jiùshì shuō** that is to say; 说吧 **shuō ba** go ahead; 说正经的 **shuō zhèngjing de** seriously, joking apart; 我在说正经的 **wǒ zài shuō zhèngjing de** I'm serious

说唱音乐 **shuōchàng yīnyuè** rap MUS

说定 **shuōdìng** agree on; arrange; 说定了 **shuōdìngle** and that's flat; that's settled

说法 **shuōfǎ** way of saying something; version

说服 **shuōfú** persuade, convince; 说服 X 做 Y **shuōfú X zuò Y** persuade X to do Y, talk X into doing Y

说话 **shuōhuà** speak

说话方式 **shuōhuà fāngshì** speech, way of speaking

说话能力 **shuōhuà nénglì** speech, ability to speak

说谎话 **shuō huǎnghuà** lie

说谎者 **shuōhuǎng zhě** liar

说教 **shuōjiào** preach

说明 **shuōmíng** explain ◊ explanation; caption

说明书 **shuōmíng shū** instruction manual

硕士 **shuòshì** master's (degree)

说说而已 **shuōshuo ér yǐ** all talk and no action

说笑话 **shuō xiàohuà** joke; crack a joke

说真的 **shuōzhēnde** honestly; 说真的吗？ **shuōzhènde ma?** seriously?

说正事 **shuō zhèngshì** get to the point

竖排 **shùpái** portrait *print*

书皮 **shūpí** dust cover

树皮 **shùpí** bark

薯片 **shǔpiàn** (potato) chips

鼠拼 **shǔpīn** rat race

述评 **shùpíng** comment ◊ commentary

竖起 **shùqǐ** erect, put up ◊ erection

书签 **shūqiān** bookmark

竖起耳朵 **shùqǐ ěrduo** prick up one's ears

竖琴 **shùqín** harp

熟人 **shúrén** acquaintance; friend

输入 **shūrù** input; import

输入端口 **shūrù duānkǒu** input port

疏散 **shūsàn** disperse; decentralize

书商 **shūshāng** bookseller

树梢 **shùshāo** tree top

舒适 **shūshì** cozy; comfortable

熟食 **shúshí** cooked meal

竖式 (钢琴) **shùshì (gāngqín)** upright (piano)

叔叔 **shūshu** uncle (*father's younger brother*); *also used to address non-related men*

数数 **shǔshù** count

熟睡 **shúshuì** fast asleep

输送 **shūsòng** transport; convey; inject *fuel*

书摊 **shūtān** bookstall

薯条 **shǔtiáo** (French) fries

熟透 **shútòu** well-done, cooked through

鼠尾草 **shǔwěicǎo** sage

梳洗 **shūxǐ** clean up, freshen up

熟悉 **shúxī** know; be familiar with

书写体 **shūxiětǐ** script

书写体系 **shūxiě tǐxì** writing

书信往来 **shūxìn wǎnglái** correspondence

输血 **shūxuè** (blood) transfusion

数学 **shùxué** mathematics ◊ mathematical

数学家 **shùxué jiā** mathematician

输血者 **shūxuè zhě** blood donor

输液 **shūyè** infusion

树液 **shùyè** sap

鼠疫 **shǔyì** plague

属于 **shǔyú** belong; belong to; 我不属于这里 **wǒ bù shǔyú zhèlǐ** I don't belong here

术语 **shùyǔ** terminology; term

疏远 **shūyuǎn** drift apart; alienate; distance oneself ◊ estranged

疏于练习 **shūyú liànxí** be out of practice

输者 **shūzhě** loser

树枝 **shùzhī** branch

树脂 **shùzhī** resin

树桩 **shùzhuāng** stump

梳妆台 **shūzhuāng tái** dressing table, dresser

书桌 **shūzhuō** desk

梳子 **shūzi** hairbrush; comb

数字 **shùzì** number, digit, figure ◊ digital; 四位数字 **sìwèi shùzì** four digit number

数字视频光盘 **shùzì shìpín guāngpán** DVD

嘶 **sī** neigh

撕 **sī** tear (up)

思 **sī** think; consider

私 **sī** private

丝 **sī** silk

死 **sǐ** die ◊ death ◊ dead; 死于癌症 **sǐyú áizhèng** die of cancer

寺 **sì** Buddhist temple

四 **sì** four

似 **sì** resemble, be like; seem

饲 **sì** feed, fodder

四胞胎 **sì bāotāi** quadruplets

私奔 **sībēn** elope

四边形 **sìbiān xíng** quadrangle; rectangle

四重唱 **sì chóngchàng** quartet

四重奏 **sì chóngzòu** quartet

丝绸 **sīchóu** silk

丝绸之路 **Sīchóu zhī lù** Silk Road

四川 **Sìchuān** Sichuan, Szechuan

四川盆地 **Sìchuān Péndì** Sichuan Basin

四次 **sìcì** four times

丝带 **sīdài** ribbon

斯大林 **Sīdàlín** Stalin

死定了 **sǐdìngle** doomed

司法 **sīfǎ** justice ◊ judicial

四方形 **sìfāng xíng** square

四方院 **sìfāng yuàn** quadrangle

司法权 **sīfǎquán** jurisdiction

似非而是 **sìfēi'érshì** paradoxical ◊ paradoxically

四分音符 **sì fēn yīnfú** quarternote

死不开口 **sǐ bù kāikǒu** clam up

死产 **sǐchǎn** be stillborn

撕成碎片 **sīchéng suìpiàn** shred

四分之三 **sì fēn zhī sān** three-quarters

四分之一 **sì fēn zhī yī** quarter

丝瓜 **sīguā** loofah

丝毫 **sīháo** shred, vestige

似乎 **sìhu** looks like; seems ◊ apparently; 她似乎是 … **tā sìhū shì …** she comes across as …

撕毁 **sīhuǐ** tear up

厮混 **sīhùn** play around, be unfaithful; 与 X 厮混 **yǔ X sīhùn** get mixed up with X

死胡同 **sǐ hútòng** dead end, blind alley

司机 **sījī** driver; motorist; chauffeur

四季豆 **sìjìdòu** green bean

撕开 **sīkāi** slit; rip open

思考 **sīkǎo** contemplate, think about

司库 **sīkù** treasurer

私利 **sīlì** self-interest

饲料 **sìliào** fodder

撕裂 **sīliè** rip

司炉 **sīlú** stoker, boilerman

思路 **sīlù** line of thought

思念 **sīniàn** long for, pine for

死气沉沉 **sǐqì chénchen** dead *place* ◊ dull, boring

私人 **sīrén** private, personal; intimate

死人 **sǐrén** the dead; dead person

四人帮 **Sìrénbāng** Gang of Four

私人财产 **sīrén cáichǎn** private property

私人教师 **sīrén jiàoshī** (private) tutor

私人空间 **sīrén kōngjiān** privacy

私人助理 **sīrén zhùlǐ** personal assistant

丝绒 **sīróng** velvet

私生 **sīshēng** illegitimate

私生活 **sīshēnghuó** private life

私生子 **sīshēngzǐ** illegitimate child, bastard

死尸 **sǐshī** corpse

四十 **sìshí** forty

撕碎 **sīsuì** tear to pieces

私通 **sītōng** adultery ◊ commit adultery

死亡 **sǐwáng** death; fatality

死亡率 **sǐwáng lǜ** mortality, death rate

死亡总数 **sǐwáng zǒngshù** death toll

私下 **sīxià** in private, privately

撕下 **sīxià** tear out; tear off

思想 **sīxiǎng** thought; thinking; idea; ideology

死刑 **sǐxíng** capital punishment, death penalty; execution

私刑处死 **sīxíng chùsǐ** lynch

四星级 **sìxīngjí** four-star

嘶哑 **sīyǎ** hoarse

饲养 **sìyǎng** breed ◊ breeding

饲养员 **sìyǎng yuán** breeder

司仪 **sīyí** marshal; master of ceremonies

肆意破坏 **sìyì pòhuài** vandalize

私语 **sīyǔ** whisper

寺院 **sìyuàn** temple

四月 **sìyuè** April

死者 **sǐzhě** the deceased

丝制 **sīzhì** silk

四肢 **sìzhī** limbs

丝织品 **sīzhīpǐn** silk goods

四周 **sìzhōu** all around

四足动物 **sìzú dòngwù** quadruped

松 **sōng** pine ◊ loose ◊ loosely; 松一口气 **sōng yìkǒu qì** heave a sigh of relief

送 **sòng** deliver; give; accompany, escort; 我送你到门口 **wǒ sòng nǐ dào ménkǒu** I'll see you to the door

送别 **sòngbié** see off

送别宴会 **sòngbié yànhuì** farewell party

宋朝 **Sòng Cháo** Song Dynasty

松驰 **sōngchí** slack; flabby ◊ slacken; 松弛的肌肉 **sōngchíde jīròu** flab

宋词 **Sòngcí** Song Dynasty lyric poetry

松动 **sōngdong** loose ◊ work loose; loosen up

颂歌 **sònggē** carol

送回 **sònghuí** send back

送回国 **sòng huíguó** repatriate

送货 **sònghuò** delivery

送货车 **sònghuò chē** delivery

van

送货单 sònghuò dān delivery note

送货日期 sònghuò rìqī delivery date

耸肩 sǒngjiān shrug; 他耸了耸肩就走了 tā sǒnglesǒng jiān jiù zǒule he gave a shrug and left

松紧带 sōngjǐndài elastic

松开 sōngkāi release

松垮 sōngkuǎ lax

耸立 sǒnglì tower; rise

送礼 sònglǐ offer a present; give a bribe

松木 sōngmù pine (wood)

耸人听闻 sǒngrén tīngwén lurid

松软 sōngruǎn floppy; fluffy

松手 sōngshǒu let go

松鼠 sōngshǔ squirrel

松树 sōngshù pine (tree)

送送 sòngsòng see out, see to the door

松塔 sōngtǎ (pine) cone

松香 sōngxiāng resin

松懈 sōngxiè relax

送行 sòngxíng see off

怂恿 sǒngyǒng egg on

馊 sōu sour

搜捕 sōubǔ search

搜查 sōuchá search; frisk

搜查证 sōucházhèng search warrant

搜集 sōují gather; save

搜索 sōusuǒ search; scour; scan

搜索队 sōusuǒduì search party

搜寻 sōuxún search ◊ hunt for; scour; comb; surf (the Net)

酥 sū crisp

俗 sú vulgar; common

宿 sù stay overnight

塑 sù mold; sculpt

素 sù plain; white ◊ vegetarian food

速 sù fast

酸 suān acid ◊ acidic; sour; aching; sore

算 suàn count, include

蒜 suàn garlic

酸橙 suānchéng lime

酸辣汤 suānlàtāng hot and sour soup

算命 suànmìng tell s.o.'s fortune; tell fortunes

算命者 suànmìng zhě fortune-teller

酸奶 suānnǎi yogurt

算盘 suànpan abacus

算术 suànshù arithmetic; sum

算算术 suàn suànshù add

酸味 suānwèi acidity; sourness

酸雨 suānyǔ acid rain

算帐 suànzhàng settle accounts; settle scores; 跟 X 算旧帐 gēn X suàn jiùzhàng have an old score to settle with X

酥饼 sūbǐng flaky pastry

俗不可耐 sú bù kě nài garish

素菜 sùcài vegetarian dish

速成课 sùchéng kè crash course

酥脆 sūcuì crispy; crunchy

苏打 sūdá soda

速冻 sùdòng quick-freeze ◊ quick-frozen

速度 sùdù speed, pace, rate; tempo; 速度每小时一百五十英里 sùdù měi xiǎoshí yībǎi wǔshí yīnglǐ at a speed of 150 mph

速度极限 sùdù jíxiàn speed limit

苏格兰 Sūgélán Scotland ◊ Scottish

虽 suī although

髓 suí pith

随 suí follow; 随你的便！suí nǐde biàn! suit yourself!

穗 suì ear (of corn)

碎 suì shatter ◊ shattered

岁 suì year; years old; 她五岁了 tā wǔsuì le she's five years old

随便 suíbiàn arbitrary; casual ◊ at random; at will; 随便拿 suíbiàn ná take as much as you want; help yourself; 随便你 suíbiàn nǐ if you like; suit yourself

随便看看 suíbiàn kànkan browse

随从人员 suícóng rényuán entourage

穗带 suìdài braid

隧道 suìdào tunnel

随和 suíhé easy-going

随后 suíhòu afterward,

subsequently ◊ subsequent

随机 **suíjī** random

随机抽样 **suíjī chōuyàng** random sample

碎块 **suìkuài** fragment

碎裂 **suìliè** break up; crumble

碎片 **suìpiàn** piece; flake; shred; splinter; fragment

虽然 **suīrán** although, while

碎肉 **suìròu** ground meat

随身听 **suíshēntīng** Walkman®, personal stereo

随时 **suíshí** at any time

碎石 **suìshí** gravel

随意 **suíyì** as one likes; 你要吃什么？– 随意 **nǐ yào chī shénme? – suíyì** what would you like to eat? – anything will be fine

速记 **sùjì** shorthand ◊ take shorthand

肃静！**sùjìng!** silence!

诉苦 **sùkǔ** complain

苏联 **Sūlián** Soviet Union

塑料 **sùliào** plastic

塑料袋 **sùliào dài** plastic bag

素描簿 **sùmiáo bò** sketchbook

宿命 **sùmìng** predestination

塑膜 **sùmó** shrink-wrapping

塑膜包装 **sùmó bāozhuāng** shrink-wrap ◊ shrink-wrapping

孙 **sūn** grandson

损 **sǔn** lose; damage

笋 **sǔn** bamboo shoot

损害 **sǔnhài** harm, damage; impair

损耗 **sǔnhào** wear (and tear)

损坏 **sǔnhuài** break; damage

损坏表面 **sǔnhuài biǎomiàn** deface

孙女 **sūnnǚ** granddaughter (*son's daughter*)

损伤 **sǔnshāng** damage; mutilate; 未受损伤 **wèi shòu sǔnshāng** uninjured; unscathed; undamaged

损失 **sǔnshī** damage; loss; toll

损失惨重 **sǔnshī cǎnzhòng** disastrous

孙中山 **Sūn Zhōngshān** Sun Yat-sen

孙子 **sūnzi** grandson (*son's son*)

锁 **suǒ** lock; 锁在里面 **suǒ zài lǐmiàn** lock in; 锁在外面 **suǒ zài wàimiàn** lock out

缩 **suō** shrink, contract; retract

索 **suǒ** rope

所 **suǒ** what, that which; 据我所知 **jù wǒ suǒ zhī** according to what I know ◊ *measure word for institutions*; 一所学校 **yì suǒ xuéxiào** a school

索道 **suǒdào** cable railroad

所得税 **suǒdéshuì** income tax

缩短 **suōduǎn** shorten; 缩短会议 **suōduǎn huìyì** cut a meeting short

缩格书写 **suōgé shūxiě** indent *text*

锁骨 **suǒgǔ** collarbone

缩回 **suōhuí** draw back

缩减 **suōjiǎn** decrease; cut back

锁匠 **suǒjiàng** locksmith

缩进 **suōjìn** retract

缩进排印 **suōjìn páiyìn** indent (*in text*)

锁孔 **suǒkǒng** keyhole

索赔 **suǒpéi** claim

锁起来 **suǒ qǐlái** lock away

索取 **suǒqǔ** claim

索取单 **suǒqǔ dān** coupon

琐事 **suǒshì** triviality, trifle

所述 **suǒshù** above-mentioned

缩水 **suōshuǐ** shrink

琐碎事 **suǒsuì shì** odds and ends; trivia; minor details

所谈 **suǒtán** in question

所谓 **suǒwèi** alleged; so-called

缩微胶卷 **suōwēi jiāojuǎn** microfilm

缩小 **suōxiǎo** reduce, make smaller

缩写 **suōxiě** abbreviate ◊ abbreviation

所以 **suǒyǐ** therefore; so; consequently

索引 **suǒyǐn** index

索引卡 **suǒyǐn kǎ** index card

所有 **suǒyǒu** own ◊ all; 他把所有的东西都吃了 **tā bǎ suǒyǒude dōngxi dōu chī le** he ate all of it

所有权 **suǒyǒu quán** ownership; title

所有物 **suǒyǒu wù** belongings, possessions, stuff, things

所在地 **suǒzàidì** seat; site

锁住 **suǒzhù** immobilize

俗气 **súqì** tacky

肃清 **sùqīng** mop up MIL

速溶咖啡 **sùróng kāfēi** instant coffee

宿舍 **sùshè** hostel; boarding house; dormitory

素食 **sùshí** vegetarian

素食者 **sùshí zhě** vegetarian

素食主义 **sùshí zhǔyì** vegan

素食主义者 **sùshí zhǔyì zhě** vegan

诉讼 **sùsòng** lawsuit

诉讼细节 **sùsòng xìjié** legal technicality

俗套 **sútào** corny

俗套情节 **sútào qíngjié** hokum

塑像 **sùxiàng** statue

苏醒 **sūxǐng** come around, come to ◊ revival; 使.. 苏醒 **shǐ ... sūxǐng** revive

俗艳 **súyàn** loud *color*

宿营地 **sùyíngdì** quarters

酥油 **sūyóu** butter; cream

塑造 **sùzào** form, shape

素质 **sùzhì** constitution, make-up; qualities

T

他 **tā** he; him ◊ his
她 **tā** she; her
它 **tā** it ◊ its
塔 **tǎ** tower
獭 **tǎ** otter
踏 **tà** step, tread
踏板 **tàbǎn** pedal; treadle
踏板车 **tàbǎnchē** scooter
塌鼻 **tābí** snub-nosed
她的 **tāde** her ◊ hers
他的 **tāde** his
它的 **tāde** its
塌方 **tāfāng** landslide
胎 **tāi** embryo; fetus
苔 **tái** moss
台 **tái** platform; terrace; Taiwan
太 **tài** too; very 太多饭 **tài duō fàn** too much rice; 太大 **tài dà** too big
台北 **Táiběi** Taipei
台布 **táibù** tablecloth
台词 **táicí** speech
态度 **tàidù** attitude, manner
胎儿 **tāi'ér** embryo; fetus
太妃糖 **tàifēi táng** toffee
台风 **táifēng** typhoon
泰国 **Tàiguó** Thailand ◊ Thai
太极拳 **tàijíquán** tai chi
太空 **tàikōng** (outer) space
太空舱 **tàikōng cāng** (space) capsule
胎面 **tāimiàn** tread
太平间 **tàipíngjiān** mortuary
太平洋 **Tàipíngyáng** Pacific Ocean
太平洋岸 **Tàipíngyáng àn** Pacific Rim
太平洋岸国家 **Tàipíngyáng àn guójiā** Pacific Rim countries
台球 **táiqiú** snooker; billiards
泰然自若 **tàirán zìruò** poised
泰山 **Tàishān** Mount Tai
台式机 **táishìjī** desk top computer
太太 **tàitai** Mrs ◊ wife
台湾 **Táiwān** Taiwan ◊ Taiwanese

台湾海峡 **Táiwān Hǎixiá** Taiwan Straits
台湾话 **Táiwān huà** Taiwanese
台湾人 **Táiwān rén** Taiwanese
太阳 **tàiyáng** sun
太阳电池板 **tàiyáng diànchí bǎn** solar panel
太阳镜 **tàiyáng jìng** sunglasses
太阳能 **tàiyáng néng** solar energy
太阳穴 **tàiyáng xuè** temple
踏脚石 **tàjiǎo shí** stepping stone
塔吉克 **Tǎjíkè** Tajikistan ◊ Tajiki
他妈的 **tāmāde** √ damn, fuck ◊ fucking; 去他妈的! **qù tāmāde!** fuck!; fuck him / that!
他们 **tāmen** they; them ◊ their
她们 **tāmen** they; them ◊ their (*female only*)
她们的 **tāmende** their ◊ theirs (*female only*)
他们的 **tāménde** their ◊ theirs
他们自己 **tāmen zìjǐ** themselves
摊 **tān** pool
贪 **tān** covet
瘫 **tān** paralyzed
坛 **tán** bed (*of flowers*)
谈 **tán** talk; 我会和他谈 **wǒ huì hé tā tán** I'll talk to him about it
痰 **tán** spit, spittle
弹 **tán** play *string instrument*; 弹钢琴 **tán gāngqín** play the piano; 弹吉他 **tán jítā** play the guitar
叹 **tàn** sigh
碳 **tàn** carbon
炭 **tàn** charcoal
坦白 **tǎnbái** confess ◊ frankly ◊ open; 坦白告诉我 **tǎnbái gàosù wǒ** give it to me straight
炭笔 **tànbǐ** charcoal (*for drawing*)
探测 **tàncè** probe
探测器 **tàncè qì** detector
探查 **tànchá** probe
摊贩 **tānfàn** street trader

探访者 tànfǎng zhě caller, visitor

汤 tāng soup; stock; broth

糖 táng sugar; candy

躺 tǎng lie

淌 tǎng run (of nose etc)

烫 tàng hot

唐朝 Táng Cháo Tang Dynasty

汤匙 tāngchí spoon; soup spoon

搪瓷 tángcí enamel

糖醋 tángcù sweet and sour

堂弟 tángdì cousin (younger male on father's side)

探戈舞 tāngē wǔ tango

烫发 tàngfà have a perm ◊ perm

糖粉 tángfěn confectioners' sugar

糖罐 tángguàn sugar bowl

糖果 tángguǒ candy

糖浆 tángjiāng molasses, syrup

烫焦 tàngjiāo scorch; singe

堂姐 tángjiě cousin (older female on father's side)

糖精 tángjīng saccharin

淌流 tǎngliú run (of nose)

堂妹 tángmèi cousin (younger female on father's side)

汤面 tāngmiàn noodle soup

糖尿病 tángniàobìng diabetes ◊ diabetic

唐人街 tángrénjiē Chinatown

唐三彩 tángsāncǎi Tang ceramics glazed in three colors

搪塞 tángsè stonewall, stall

烫伤 tàngshāng scald

唐诗 Tángshī Tang poetry

糖霜 tángshuāng frosting

趟水 tāngshuǐ wade; paddle

唐突草率 tángtū cǎoshuài curt

汤碗 tāngwǎn soup bowl

躺下 tǎngxia lie down

堂兄 tángxiōng cousin (older male on father's side)

躺椅 tǎngyǐ deck chair; lounger

谈话 tánhuà talk

谈话节目 tánhuà jiémù talk show

瘫痪 tānhuàn paralysis ◊ paralyze; 使 … 瘫痪 shǐ … tānhuàn immobilize

弹簧 tánhuáng spring

坍毁 tānhuǐ dilapidated

弹回来 tán huílái rebound

摊开 tānkāi open; unfold; spread

坦克 tǎnkè tank MIL

贪婪 tānlán greedy; acquisitive

谈恋爱 tán liàn'ài date

摊凉 tānliáng cool (down)

谈判 tánpàn negotiate ◊ negotiations

谈判员 tánpàn yuán negotiator

弹起 tánqǐ bounce

叹气 tànqì sigh

弹射 tánshè eject

贪食 tānshí gluttony ◊ gluttonous

贪食者 tānshí zhě glutton

坦率 tǎnshuài frank, open, candid ◊ candor

碳水化合物 tànshuǐ huàhéwù carbohydrate

探索 tànsuǒ exploration ◊ seek

探索性 tànsuǒ xìng exploratory

探索者 tànsuǒ zhě explorer

坍塌 tāntā give way

探讨 tàntǎo explore

弹跳 tántiào bounce

探听 tàntīng investigate; nose around

探望时间 tànwàng shíjiān visiting hours

贪污 tānwū embezzle ◊ embezzlement

叹息 tànxī sigh

探险 tànxiǎn expedition

贪心 tānxīn greed

弹性 tánxìng elasticity

探照灯 tànzhàodēng searchlight

摊子 tānzi stall, stand, booth

毯子 tǎnzi blanket, rug

弹奏 tánzòu play

逃 táo flee; escape

桃 táo peach

讨 tǎo discuss

套 tào set; suit; suite ◊ measure word for rooms, furniture, clothes; 一套家具 yītào jiāju a suite of furniture

逃避 táobì escape, elude; shirk ◊ evasion

逃兵 táobīng deserter

绦虫 tāochóng tapeworm

掏出 tāochū get out; cough up money

陶瓷 táocí ceramics

逃犯 **táofàn** fugitive

套服 **tàofú** suit

陶工 **táogōng** potter

讨好 **tǎohǎo** flatter ◊ flattering

讨价还价 **tǎojià huánjià** bargain, haggle

套间 **tàojiān** suite (of rooms)

掏空 **tāokōng** empty

讨论 **tǎolùn** discuss, talk over; debate ◊ discussion

讨论会 **tǎolùn huì** conference

逃跑 **táopǎo** run away, flee ◊ flight; getaway

陶器 **táoqì** ceramics, pottery, earthenware

淘气 **táoqì** naughty

掏钱 **tāoqián** cough up, pay

淘气包 **táoqìbāo** rogue; brat

陶器作坊 **táoqì zuōfang** pottery (*place*)

讨人喜欢 **tǎorén xǐhuān** endearing

淘汰 **táotài** eliminate; weed out ◊ elimination

淘汰赛 **táotàisài** knockout competition

滔滔不绝 **tāotao bùjué** torrent (*of words*)

逃脱 **táotuō** escape; 逃脱处分 **táotuō chǔfèn** get off, escape punishment

逃学 **táoxué** play hookey

讨厌 **tǎoyàn** disgusting; tiresome ◊ detest, loathe ◊ what a nuisance!; 令人讨厌 **lìngrén tǎoyàn** rotten *trick*; unsavory; bitchy

讨厌鬼 **tǎoyànguǐ** pest, so-and-so; creep

套装 **tàozhuāng** outfit

桃子 **táozi** peach

套子 **tàozi** housing; case

逃走 **táozǒu** flee, run away

逃罪 **táozuì** get away with

陶醉 **táozuì** intoxicated; high

她自己 **tā zìjǐ** herself

他自己 **tā zìjǐ** himself

它自己 **tā zìjǐ** itself

特 **tè** special

特别 **tèbié** special, specific, particular, ◊ specially, specifically, particularly

特别工作组 **tèbié gōngzuòzǔ** task force

特产 **tèchǎn** specialty

特大 **tèdà** king-size(d)

特大号 **tè dàhào** outsize

特等包厢 **tèděng bāoxiāng** dress circle

特地 **tèdì** expressly

特点 **tèdiǎn** characteristic, peculiarity

特工人员 **tègōng rényuán** secret agent

特护（部）**tèhù (bù)** intensive care (unit)

特技 **tèjì** trick; stunt

特快 **tèkuài** express

特免 **tèmiǎn** immunity, exemption

疼 **téng** pain, hurt ◊ sore; 疼不疼？**téng bùténg?** is it sore?, does it hurt?

腾出 **téngchū** vacate

藤条 **téngtiáo** wicker

疼痛 **téngtòng** hurt, pain ◊ painful

藤椅 **téngyǐ** wicker chair

特权 **tèquán** privilege

特色 **tèsè** feature, characteristic

特殊 **tèshū** special, particular; exceptional; 特殊情况 **tèshū qíngkuàng** one-off, exception; special circumstances

特务 **tèwu** secret agent

特务机关 **tèwù jīguān** secret service

特写镜头 **tèxiě jìngtóu** close-up

特性 **tèxìng** quality, trait

特有 **tèyǒu** distinctive; peculiar to

特征 **tèzhēng** attribute, characteristic

特种 **tèzhǒng** special ◊ special type

特种饮食 **tèzhǒng yǐnshí** special diet

踢 **tī** kick; 踢足球 **tī zúqiú** play soccer

梯 **tī** ladder; steps

蹄 **tí** hoof

题 **tí** subject, theme

提 **tí** carry; lift; raise; 不提 X 的事 **bù tí X de shì** keep quiet about X

体 **tǐ** body

剃 **tì** shave

替 **tì** replace; substitute ◊ in behalf of; 替我问她好 **tì wǒ wèn tā hǎo** remember me to her

天 **tiān** sky; heaven; day; 天晚了 **tiānwǎn le** it's getting late

添 **tiān** add

甜 **tián** sweet

填 **tián** fill out, fill in

田 **tián** field

舔 **tiǎn** lick; lap up

天安门广场 **Tiān'ānmén Guǎngchǎng** Tiananmen Square

填表 **tiánbiǎo** fill out a form

天才 **tiāncái** talent; genius ◊ ingenious

甜菜 **tiáncài** sugar beet

填充 **tiánchōng** stuff *turkey etc*

天窗 **tiānchuāng** skylight

田地 **tiándì** field; farmland

天鹅 **tiān'é** swan

天鹅绒 **tiān'éróng** velvet

天份 **tiānfèn** gift, talent; flair

天赋 **tiānfù** gift, talent

天沟 **tiāngōu** gutter

天黑 **tiānhēi** dark; 天黑以后 **tiānhēi yǐhòu** after dark

天花 **tiānhuā** smallpox

天花板 **tiānhuābǎn** ceiling

添加 **tiānjiā** add

添加剂 **tiānjiā jì** additive

田径 **tiánjìng** track and field; athletics

天空 **tiānkōng** sky

填料 **tiánliào** stuffing

填满 **tiánmǎn** fill up; fill in

天哪！ **tiānna!** good heavens!; oh God!

甜品 **tiánpǐn** dessert

天平 **tiānpíng** scales

天气 **tiānqì** weather; 天气很冷 **tiānqì hěnlěng** it's cold; 天气晴朗 **tiānqì qínglǎng** it's sunny

天气预报 **tiānqì yùbào** weather forecast

天然 **tiānrán** natural ◊ naturally

天然气 **tiānrán qì** natural gas

田赛 **tiánsài** field events

天生 **tiānshēng** innate ◊ naturally; 天生的 … **tiānshēngde …** be a natural …

天使 **tiānshǐ** angel

甜食 **tiánshí** confectionery

田鼠 **tiánshǔ** vole

天坛 **Tiāntán** Temple of Heaven

天堂 **tiāntáng** heaven; paradise

天体 **tiāntǐ** heavenly body

天体运行轨道 **tiāntǐ yùnxíng guǐdào** orbit

甜味剂 **tiánwèijì** sweetener

天文 **tiānwén** astronomy

天文台 **tiānwén tái** observatory

天文学 **tiānwén xué** astronomy

天文学家 **tiānwén xuéjiā** astronomer

天线 **tiānxiàn** aerial, antenna

天线塔 **tiānxiàntǎ** (radio) mast

填写 **tiánxiě** fill out, fill in, complete

天性 **tiānxìng** disposition, nature

填鸭式灌输 **tiányā shì guànshū** spoonfeed

天衣无缝 **tiān yī wú fèng** perfect

田园式 **tiányuánshì** idyllic

甜玉米 **tián yùmǐ** sweetcorn

天真 **tiānzhēn** naive; childlike

天真无邪 **tiānzhēn wúxié** childlike; innocent

天主教 **Tiānzhǔjiào** (Roman) Catholic

天主教徒 **Tiānzhǔjiào tú** (Roman) Catholic

天资 **tiānzī** aptitude

挑 **tiāo** choose, pick

条 **tiáo** strip; item ◊ *measure word for long thin things*; 一条裤子 **yìtiáo kùzi** a pair of pants; 一条香烟 **yìtiáo xiāngyān** a carton of cigarettes; 一条新闻 **yìtiáo xīnwén** a bit of news

调 **tiáo** adjust

挑 **tiǎo** push; provoke

跳 **tiào** jump, leap; hop; skip

跳板 **tiàobǎn** springboard; gangway

挑拨 **tiǎobō** provoke

挑出 **tiāochū** single out

挑刺儿 **tiāocìr** be critical ◊ critical

挑动 **tiǎodòng** stir up

跳动 **tiàodòng** beat, throb

挑逗 **tiǎodòu** provoke ◊ provocative; 挑斗 X 去做 Y **tiǎodòu X qù zuò Y** dare X to do Y

挑逗嗯哨 **tiǎodòu hūshào** wolf whistle

跳高 **tiàogāo** high jump

调羹 **tiáogēng** spoon

调合 **tiáohé** set *alarm clock etc*

挑拣 **tiāojiǎn** be selective ◊ selective

条件 **tiáojiàn** condition, term, requirement, stipulation ◊ conditional

条件反射 **tiáojiàn fǎnshè** conditioning

调节 **tiáojié** adjust

调解 **tiáojiě** mediate; reconcile ◊ mediation; reconciliation

调解人 **tiáojiě rén** mediator; troubleshooter

条款 **tiáokuǎn** clause; provision

跳栏 **tiàolán** hurdle; hurdles

跳栏运动员 **tiàolán yùndòng yuán** hurdler

调料 **tiáoliào** spice; herb; condiment; ingredient

调配饮料 **tiáopèi yǐnliào** mixer (*drink*)

调皮 **tiáopí** naughty; rude

调皮鬼 **tiáopíguǐ** little monkey, scamp

跳棋 **tiàoqí** Chinese checkers

调情 **tiáoqíng** flirt; 向 X 调情 *xiàng X tiáoqíng* make a pass at X

调情者 **tiáoqíng zhě** flirt (*person*)

跳棋盘 **tiàoqí pán** checkerboard

跳伞 **tiàosǎn** parachute; bail out

挑三拣四 **tiāosān jiǎnsì** choosey, discriminating

跳伞者 **tiàosǎn zhě** parachutist

调色剂 **tiáosè jì** toner

跳绳 **tiàoshéng** jump rope

跳水 **tiàoshuǐ** dive; diving

跳水板 **tiàoshuǐ bǎn** diving board

跳水者 **tiàoshuǐ zhě** diver

挑剔 **tiāotì** fussy, particular, choosey, picky; 挑剔食物的人 *tiāotì shíwù de rén* fussy eater

挑挑拣拣 **tiāotiāo jiǎnjiǎn** pick and choose ◊ picky, choosey

调停 **tiáotíng** arbitrate, intercede

调味 **tiáowèi** season; 给 X 调味 *gěi X tiáowèi* flavor X

调味品 **tiáowèipǐn** flavoring, seasoning

调味汁儿 **tiáowèi zhīr** dressing

条纹 **tiáowén** streak; stripe

跳舞 **tiàowǔ** dance

调谐 **tiáoxié** tune up

调谐器 **tiáoxié qì** tuner

挑衅 **tiǎoxìn** provoke ◊ provocation ◊ provocative

条形码 **tiáoxíng mǎ** bar code

挑选 **tiāoxuǎn** choose, select

调音 **tiáoyīn** tune up

跳远 **tiàoyuǎn** long jump

条约 **tiáoyuē** treaty, pact

跳跃 **tiàoyuè** jump, bound, spring

跳蚤 **tiàozao** flea

跳蚤市场 **tiàozǎo shìchǎng** flea market

挑战 **tiǎozhàn** challenge; 挑战 X 做 Y *tiǎozhàn X zuò Y* challenge X to Y

挑战者 **tiǎozhàn zhě** challenger

调整 **tiáozhěng** adjust

调制 **tiáozhì** concoct

调制解调器 **tiáozhì jiětiáoqì** modem

调制品 **tiáozhì pǐn** concoction

笤帚 **tiáozhǒu** broom

体操 **tǐcāo** gymnastics

体操家 **tǐcāojiā** gymnast

提倡 **tíchàng** advocate

提出 **tíchū** bring up, broach, raise; advance; 提出辞职通知 *tíchū cízhí tōngzhī* hand in one's notice

提词 **tící** prompt

题词 **tící** dedication ◊ dedicate

替代 **tìdài** replace; deputize for

替代演员 **tìdài yǎnyuán** double (*of actor*)

提到 **tídào** mention, touch on, refer to

剃刀 **tìdāo** shaver

踢踏舞 **tītà wǔ** tap dance

贴 **tiē** stick; 贴壁纸 *tiē bìzhǐ* wallpaper

铁 **tiě** iron

贴边 **tiēbiān** hem; seam; edge

贴标签 **tiē biāoqiān** label

铁饼 **tiěbǐng** discus

铁饭碗 **tiě fànwǎn** iron rice bowl, job for life

铁轨 **tiěguǐ** rail

铁匠 **tiějiàng** blacksmith

铁路 **tiělù** railroad

贴签 **tiēqiān** sticky label

铁锹 **tiěqiāo** shovel, spade

贴身 **tiēshēn** skin-tight ◊ cling

贴邮票 **tiē yóupiào** stamp

体罚 **tǐfá** corporal punishment

提高 **tígāo** raise, elevate; increase; improve ◊ rise

提高…等级 **tígāo … děngjí** upgrade

提高标价 **tígāo biāojià** mark up

提高价值 **tígāo jiàzhí** appreciate FIN

提高效率 **tígāo xiàolǜ** streamline

体格 **tǐgé** physique; 体格健美 **tǐgé jiànměi** athletic

体格检查 **tǐgé jiǎnchá** physical, medical check-up

提供 **tígōng** supply, provide, furnish; offer; 提供资金 **tígōng zījīn** finance

提供信息 **tígōng xìxī** inform ◊ informative

提供消息人 **tígōng xiāoxī rén** informant

剃光 **tìguāng** shaven

屉柜 **tì guì** chest of drawers

替换 **tìhuàn** substitute, replace; 替换队员 **tìhuàn duìyuán** make a substitution

替换衣服 **tìhuàn yīfu** change one's clothes

剃胡子 **tì húzi** shave

梯级 **tījí** stair; rung

提及 **tíjí** mention

体积 **tǐjī** volume

替件 **tìjiàn** replacement part

提款 **tíkuǎn** withdraw ◊ withdrawal

提炼 **tíliàn** refine

提炼厂 **tíliàn chǎng** refinery

体面 **tǐmiàn** face; dignity ◊ respectable

提名 **tímíng** nominate ◊ nomination

题目 **tímù** topic

体内 **tǐnèi** internally

厅 **tīng** hall; auditorium

听 **tīng** listen; listen to; obey; 我听你之便 **wǒ tīng nǐ zhī biàn** I am at your disposal; 听电话 **tīng diànhuà** answer the telephone

停 **tíng** stop; 停了 **tíngle** come to a stop

亭 **tíng** pavilion

挺 **tǐng** very, quite; 挺好 **tǐng hǎo** very good, terrific

停泊 **tíngbó** moor

停泊区 **tíngbó qū** moorings

听不见 **tīngbújiàn** inaudible

停车 **tíngchē** park ◊ parking

停车标志 **tíngchē biāozhì** stop sign

停车场 **tíngchē chǎng** parking lot; 室内停车场 **shìnèi tíngchē chǎng** parking garage

停车处 **tíngchē chù** parking place

听从 **tīngcóng** obey; respond

听到 **tīngdào** hear; hear about

听得见 **tīngde jiàn** audible

停电 **tíngdiàn** power cut, blackout

停顿 **tíngdùn** pause; disruption ◊ be at a standstill; 使停顿 **shǐ tíngdùn** disrupt

停放 **tíngfàng** park MOT

听话 **tīnghuà** listen; obey ◊ obedient

停火 **tínghuǒ** cease-fire

听见 **tīngjiàn** hear

听距 **tīngjù** within hearing

挺括 **tǐngkuò** crisp

听力 **tīnglì** hearing; comprehension

听起来 **tīngqǐlái** sound; 听起来很有趣 **tīngqǐlái hěn yǒuqù** that sounds interesting

听清楚 **tīng qīngchu** hear, catch

听其自然 **tīngqí zìrán** resign oneself to

听取意见 **tīngqǔ yìjiàn** canvass

挺身而出 **tǐngshēn ér chū** come forward

停尸房 **tíngshīfáng** morgue

听说… **tīngshuō …** people say …, they say that …

听天由命 **tīngtiān yóumìng** resigned

听筒 **tīngtǒng** receiver TELEC

停歇 **tíngxiē** rest

停业 **tíngyè** shut down, fold, cease trading

听诊 **tīngzhěn** sound MED

听诊器 **tīngzhěnqì** stethoscope

停职 **tíngzhí** suspension (*from duty*)

停止 **tíngzhǐ** stop, halt; let up

停滞 **tíngzhì** stagnant

挺直 **tǐngzhí** straighten up

停滞不前 **tíngzhì bù qián** come to a halt

停止生产 **tíngzhǐ shēngchǎn** discontinue

听众 **tīngzhòng** audience; listeners

停住 **tíngzhù** stop

亭子 **tíngzi** kiosk; pavilion

提起 **tíqǐ** pull up

提前 **tíqián** early, in advance

提起公诉 **tíqǐ gōngsù** prosecute

提取 **tíqǔ** withdraw; extract

体弱 **tǐruò** infirm; weak ◊ infirmity; 体弱的人 **tǐruò de rén** weakling

提神 **tíshén** freshen up; refresh oneself

提升 **tíshēng** promote

替身演员 **tìshēn yǎnyuán** stuntman

提示 **tíshì** point out; hint ◊ cue

提示符 **tíshìfú** prompt

梯田 **tītián** terraced field, terrace

体贴 **tǐtiē** nice; considerate

剃头匠 **tìtóu jiàng** barber

提问 **tíwèn** ask

体温 **tǐwēn** (body) temperature

体温过低 **tǐwēn guòdī** hypothermia

题献 **tíxiàn** dedicate

体现 **tǐxiàn** embody

提心吊胆 **tíxīn diàodǎn** be on tenterhooks

提醒 **tíxǐng** remind; 提醒X做Y **tíxǐng X zuò Y** remind X to do Y

体臭 **tǐxiù** BO, body odor

剃须刀 **tìxū dāo** razor

剃须刀刀片 **tìxū dāo dāopiàn** razor blade

剃须膏 **tìxūgāo** shaving soap

体验 **tǐyàn** experience

提议 **tíyì** suggest, propose ◊ proposal, motion

体育 **tǐyù** sport

体育版 **tǐyù bǎn** sports page

体育场 **tǐyù chǎng** stadium

体育馆 **tǐyù guǎn** gymnasium

体育记者 **tǐyù jìzhě** sports journalist

体育新闻 **tǐyù xīnwén** sports news

体育运动 **tǐyù yùndòng** sport ◊ sporting

体质 **tǐzhì** physique; constitution

体制 **tǐzhì** system

体重 **tǐzhòng** (body) weight

梯子 **tīzi** ladder

替罪羊 **tìzuìyáng** scapegoat

通 **tōng** through; 通了 **tōngle** you're through TELEC

铜 **tóng** copper

童 **tóng** child

瞳 **tóng** pupil

同 **tóng** same; similar; with; and

桶 **tǒng** barrel, drum; tub; pail

捅 **tǒng** poke, prod

统 **tǒng** unite

痛 **tòng** pain, hurt; ache ◊ sore, aching; 痛不痛? **tòng bútòng?** does it hurt?

同伴 **tóngbàn** partner

铜版画 **tóngbǎnhuà** copperplate

同胞 **tóngbāo** fellow citizen; fellow countryman

同步 **tóngbù** same speed; 使…同步 **shǐ … tóngbù** synchronize

统舱 **tǒngcāng** lower deck

通常 **tōngcháng** usual, normal ◊ usually, normally

通常开支 **tōngcháng kāizhī** overhead FIN

痛打 **tòngdǎ** thrashing, hiding ◊ lay into

同代人 **tóngdài rén** contemporary

通道 **tōngdào** passage; aisle

同等 **tóngděng** equal ◊ equally; 同等价值 **tóngděng jiàzhí** of equal value

同等人 **tóngděngrén** peer

通风 **tōngfēng** air; ventilate ◊ airy; drafty ◊ ventilation

通风报信 **tōngfēng bàoxìn** tip off

通风井 **tōngfēng jǐng** ventilation shaft

通风孔 tōngfēng kǒng vent

通风设备 tōngfēng shèbèi ventilator

同感 tónggǎn sympathy

通告 tōnggào notice

通关 tōngguān customs clearance

铜管乐队 tóngguǎn yuèduì brass band

通过 tōngguò pass, get by ◊ via, through; 通过考试 *tōngguò kǎoshì* pass an exam; 通过他安排 *tōngguò tā ānpái* arranged through him

童话 tónghuà fairy tale

通货膨胀 tōnghuò péngzhàng inflation

通货再膨胀 tōnghuò zài péngzhàng reflation

通缉 tōngjí: 被通缉 bèi tōngjí wanted

统计 tǒngjì statistics ◊ statistical

同届 tóngjiè contemporary

统计学 tǒngjì xué statistics; 从统计学角度来说 *cóng tǒngjìxué jiǎodù láishuō* statistically

统计资料 tǒngjì zīliào statistics

同居 tóngjū cohabit; 和 X 同居 *hé X tóngjū* live with X

瞳孔 tóngkǒng pupil

痛哭 tòngkū bawl, wail

恸哭 tòngkū bawl, wail

痛苦 tòngkǔ suffering; misery; distress; discomfort; 令人痛苦 *lìngrén tòngkǔ* painful; distressing

痛快一番 tòngkuài yīfān go (out) on a spree

恸哭声 tòngkūshēng wail

通力合作 tōnglì hézuò pull together

同卵双胎 tóngluǎn shuāngtāi identical twins

同盟 tóngméng alliance, confederation

同盟者 tóngméng zhě ally

同名人 tóngmíng rén namesake

童年 tóngnián childhood

同年 tóngnián same year ◊ of the same age

铜牌 tóngpái bronze medal

通气 tōngqì ventilate, air

痛切 tòngqiè poignant

通气管 tōngqìguǎn snorkel

同情 tóngqíng pity; sympathize with; empathize with; commiserate ◊ compassion

通情达理 tōngqíng dálǐ understanding

同情心 tóngqíngxīn sympathy

同时 tóngshí at the same time, simultaneously, together; in the meantime ◊ simultaneous

同事 tóngshì colleague, associate

痛惜 tòngxī deplore

通向 tōngxiàng give onto

通宵 tōngxiāo throughout the night

通晓 tōngxiǎo familiarity

通泄药 tōngxiè yào laxative

通信 tōngxìn correspond

通行费 tōngxíng fèi toll

同性恋 tóngxìngliàn homosexual ◊ homosexuality

同性恋者 tóngxìngliàn zhě homosexual; lesbian

通行权 tōngxíng quán right of way

同形异义词 tóngxíng yìyì cí homograph

通行证 tōngxíngzhèng pass

通信联络 tōngxìn liánluò correspondence

通信员 tōngxìn yuán messenger

通信者 tōngxìn zhě correspondent

同学 tóngxué classmate; fellow student

通讯录 tōngxùn lù address book

通讯社 tōngxùn shè news agency

通讯卫星 tōngxùn wèixīng communications satellite

通讯业 tōngxùn yè communications

通讯员 tōngxùn yuán correspondent

同样 tóngyàng same

童谣 tóngyáo nursery rhyme

同意 tóngyì agree, concur; consent; grant ◊ agreement; approval; 我同意这个想法 *wǒ tóngyì zhèige xiǎngfǎ* I am for the idea

统一 **tǒngyī** unite; unify ◊ unified; uniform ◊ uniformly ◊ unity; unification

同义词 **tóngyìcí** synonym

统一收费率 **tǒngyī shōufèilǜ** flat rate

同意资助 **tóngyì zīzhù** underwrite FIN

同狱犯人 **tóngyù fànrén** inmate

通知 **tōngzhī** inform, notify; report ◊ circular; notice

同志 **tóngzhì** comrade

统治 **tǒngzhì** reign; rule

统治者 **tǒngzhì zhě** ruler

童装 **tóngzhuāng** children's clothes

偷 **tōu** take, steal

头 **tóu** head

投 **tóu** hurl, fling, throw; pitch

透 **tòu** pass through

投案 **tóu'àn** give oneself up

头版 **tóubǎn** front page

头版新闻 **tóubǎn xīnwén** front page news

投标 **tóubiāo** tender

偷捕 **tōubǔ** poach

头朝下 **tóu cháoxià** head over heels

投弹手 **tóudàn shǒu** bomber (terrorist)

头等 **tóuděng** first class

头等大事 **tóuděng dàshì** a matter of paramount importance ◊ be paramount

投递 **tóudì** deliver ◊ delivery

头顶 **tóudǐng** top of the head

头顶上 **tóudǐng shàng** overhead

头顶头 **tóudǐngtóu** head-on

偷东西 **tōu dōngxi** steal

头发 **tóufa** hair; 做头发 **zuò tóufà** have one's hair done

头发花白 **tóufa huābái** gray-haired

投稿 **tóugǎo** contribute ◊ contribution

投稿人 **tóugǎo rén** contributor

头昏脑胀 **tóuhūn nǎozhàng** dizzy, giddy

投机活动 **tóujī huódòng** venture

投机买卖 **tóujī mǎimài** speculation

头巾 **tóujīn** (head)scarf

透镜 **tòujìng** lens

投机商 **tóujī shāng** speculator FIN

偷看一眼 **tōukàn yīyǎn** sneak a glance at

头靠 **tóukào** headrest

头盔 **tóukuī** helmet

偷懒 **tōulǎn** laze around; goof off

头栏 **tóulán** header

投篮 **tóulán** shoot (at the basket)

头颅 **tóulú** skull

头路 **tóulù** part (in hair)

透露 **tòulù** leak out; disclose, divulge ◊ disclosure; 未透露 **wèi tòulù** untold

头颅骨 **tóulúgǔ** skull

透露真相 **tòulù zhēnxiàng** revealing

透明 **tòumíng** see-through, transparent

头目 **tóumù** ringleader

偷拿 **tōuná** sneak, steal

头脑 **tóunǎo** mind; chief

头脑简单 **tóunǎo jiǎndān** simple(-minded)

头脑冷静 **tóunǎo lěngjìng** level-headed; 头脑敏锐的人 **tóunǎo mǐnruì de rén** clear thinker

头盘 **tóupán** starter (of meal)

头皮 **tóupí** scalp

投票 **tóupiào** vote ◊ voting; ballot

投票间 **tóupiào jiān** voting booth

投票决定 **tóupiào juédìng** ballot; vote on

投票箱 **tóupiào xiāng** ballot box

投票站 **tóupiàozhàn** polling booth

头皮屑 **tóupíxiè** dandruff

投弃 **tóuqì** jettison

偷窃 **tōuqiè** steal ◊ larceny, theft

投球 **tóuqiú** pitch

投入 **tóurù** put in, insert; plunge into; inject ◊ input; injection

透入 **tòurù** penetrate

头上空间 **tóushang kōngjiān** headroom

投手 **tóushǒu** pitcher

投手场地 **tóushǒu chǎngdì** mound

偷税 **tōushuì** evade taxes

透水汽 **tòu shuǐqì** porous

投诉 tóusù complain; make a fuss ◊ complaint

头条新闻 tóutiáo xīnwén headline news

偷听 tōutīng overhear; eavesdrop

头痛 tóutòng headache

偷偷 tōutōu furtive; 偷偷溜进房间 *tōutōu liūjìn fángjiān* sneak into the room

头衔 tóuxián title

投降 tóuxiáng yield, surrender ◊ submission

投影器 tóuyǐng qì projector

头晕 tóuyūn dizzy, giddy ◊ feel dizzy

投掷 tóuzhì throw

透支 tòuzhī advance

头重脚轻 tóuzhòng jiǎoqīng top-heavy

骰子 tóuzi dice

投资 tóuzī invest ◊ investment

投资者 tóuzī zhě investor

偷走 tōuzǒu snatch; make off with

突 tū suddenly

秃 tū bald

图 tú picture; diagram

涂 tú apply

屠 tú kill

途 tú path; road; way

徒 tú follower; disciple

土 tǔ earth; land

吐 tǔ spit

吐 tù vomit; 我要吐 *wǒ yào tù* I'm going to throw up

兔 tù rabbit; hare

图案 tú'àn pattern; design

团 tuán round ◊ gather ◊ group; society; mass; wad; expedition; regiment

团结 tuánjié unite ◊ united; 团结在 X 的周围 *tuánjié zài X de zhōuwéi* rally around X

团结一致 tuánjié yīzhì solidarity

团聚 tuánjù reunion ◊ reunite

湍流 tuānliú turbulence

团体 tuántǐ group

团圆 tuányuán reunion; get-together

团子 tuánzi dumpling

图板 túbǎn drawing board

突变 tūbiàn sudden change

图标 túbiāo icon

图表 túbiǎo chart; graph

徒步旅行 túbù lǚxíng backpack

徒步旅行者 túbù lǚxíng zhě hiker; walker; backpacker

涂层 túcéng coat

突出 tūchū stick out, project ◊ prominent; imposing; glaring; outstanding, excellent; 突出的椎间盘 *tūchūde zhuījiānpán* slipped disc

吐出 tǔchū spit (out); 吐出心里的话 *tǔchū xīnlǐ de huà* get ... off one's chest

凸窗 tūchuāng bay window

秃顶 tūdǐng bald; 他开始秃顶了 *tā kāishǐ tūdǐng le* he's going bald

图钉 túdīng thumbtack

土豆 tǔdòu potato

土豆泥 tǔdòuní mashed potatoes

土耳其 Tǔ'ěrqí Turkey ◊ Turkish

突发奇想 tūfā qíxiǎng whim

土匪 tǔfěi bandit

屠夫 túfū butcher

涂改液 túgǎiyè whiteout (*for text*)

图画 túhuà picture; drawing; painting

图画书 túhuàshū picture book

推 tuī push; jolt

腿 tuǐ leg

退 tuì move backward; retreat; retire

退步 tuìbù go backward; fall behind

推测 tuīcè suspect; assume; presume; guess

退场 tuìchǎng exit; walk out

退潮 tuìcháo ebb tide

推迟 tuīchí postpone, put off, defer; delay

推出 tuīchū bring out

退出 tuìchū withdraw, pull out, stand down, drop out; exit, quit

推辞 tuīcí decline

退掉 tuìdiào take back; 退掉 X *tuìdiào X* take X back to the store

推定 tuīdìng presumption

推动 tuīdòng push forward; promote; boost; budge

推动力 tuīdòng lì impetus

推断 **tuīduàn** conclude ◊
conclusion; 由 Y 推断出 X **yóu Y
tuīduàn chū X** conclude X from Y

腿肚子 **tuǐdùzi** calf (of leg)

推翻 **tuīfān** overthrow, topple,
overturn

颓废 **tuífèi** decadent

退格 **tuìgé** backspace (key)

推合门 **tuīhémén** swing-door

退化 **tuìhuà** degenerate into

退还 **tuìhuán** return, send back

推挤 **tuījǐ** jostle

推荐 **tuījiàn** recommend ◊
recommendation; reference; 推荐
X 任某个职位 **tuījiàn X rèn
mǒugè zhíwèi** recommend X for
a post

推荐人 **tuījiàn rén** referee

推进 **tuījìn** propel

推开 **tuīkāi** push away

退款 **tuìkuǎn** refund

推理 **tuīlǐ** deduce

推论 **tuīlùn** deduction

退落 **tuìluò** ebb

蜕皮 **tuìpí** peel; shed its skin

退去 **tuìqù** subside

退让 **tuìràng** retreat

退色 **tuìsè** faded

退烧 **tuìshāo** subside (of fever)

退缩 **tuìsuō** flinch; wince

推土机 **tuītǔ jī** bulldozer

退位 **tuìwèi** abdicate

推诿责任 **tuīwěi zérèn** pass the
buck

退伍 **tuìwǔ** discharge

退伍军人 **tuìwǔ jūnrén** veteran

推想 **tuīxiǎng** gather, understand

推销 **tuīxiāo** market, sell; plug ◊
marketing

推销员 **tuīxiāo yuán** salesman

推行 **tuīxíng** implement; pursue

退休 **tuìxiū** retire ◊ retired ◊
retirement

退休金 **tuìxiū jīn** pension

退休老人 **tuìxiū lǎorén** senior
citizen

退休年龄 **tuìxiū niánlíng**
retirement age

退休者 **tuìxiū zhě** retired person;
pensioner

退学学生 **tuìxué xuéshēng**
dropout

推移 **tuīyí** pass, go by ◊ passage (of
time)

退职金 **tuìzhí jīn** gratuity (on
retirement)

推子 **tuīzi** clippers

突击 **tūjī** rush

途经 **tújīng** by way of, via ◊ pass
through

途径 **tújìng** way, path; gateway

土块 **tǔkuài** clump

凸块儿 **tūkuàir** bump

徒劳 **túláo** thankless ◊ in vain

图利 **túlì** mercenary

涂料 **túliào** paint; 上涂料 **shàng
túliào** paint

吐露 **tùlù** confide

涂满 **túmǎn** be plastered with

涂抹 **túmǒ** smear

图谋 **túmóu** scheme

土木工程师 **tǔmù
gōngchéngshī** civil engineer

吞 **tūn** swallow

吞并 **tūnbìng** annex

臀部 **túnbù** buttocks; rump; hip

臀部牛排 **túnbù niúpái**
rumpsteak

吞饵 **tūn'ěr** bite (of fish)

囤积 **túnjī** hoard

吞没 **tūnmò** engulf

吞食 **tūnshí** devour

豚鼠 **túnshǔ** guinea pig

吞吞吐吐 **tūntun tǔtu** cagey

吞下 **tūnxià** down; keep down
food

吞咽 **tūnyàn** gulp

脱 **tuō** remove, get off; take down

拖 **tuō** drag; pull

托 **tuō** entrust

妥 **tuǒ** appropriate

拖把 **tuōbǎ** mop

驼背 **tuóbèi** hunchback; hump

拖布 **tuōbù** mop

拖长 **tuōcháng** drag out, spin out

拖车 **tuōchē** trailer; wrecker

拖船 **tuōchuán** tug

拖地 **tuōdì** mop

脱掉 **tuōdiào** slip off

拖动 **tuōdòng** drag

托儿所 **tuō'érsuǒ** day-nursery,
crèche

驼峰 **tuófēng** hump

脱光衣服 **tuōguāng yīfu** strip

脱轨 **tuōguǐ** be derailed

托架 **tuōjià** bracket (*for shelf*)

脱缰 **tuōjiāng** bolt

脱节 **tuōjié** disjointed

脱臼 **tuōjiù** dislocation

拖拉 **tuōlā** trail

拖拉机 **tuōlājī** tractor

拖缆 **tuōlǎn** towrope

脱离 **tuōlí** break away ◊ out of

脱粒 **tuōlì** thresh

脱离关系 **tuōlí guānxì** disown

脱离危险 **tuōlí wēixiǎn** out of danger

驼鹿 **tuólù** moose, elk

脱落 **tuōluò** come off; fall out; peel; shed

陀螺 **tuóluó** (spinning) top

唾沫 **tuòmo** spittle

鸵鸟 **tuóniǎo** ostrich

拖盘 **tuōpán** tray

拖欠 **tuōqiàn** be in arrears

拖欠款 **tuōqiàn kuǎn** arrears

脱去衣服 **tuōqù yīfu** strip

脱色 **tuōsè** lose its color, fade; 使脱色 **shǐ tuōsè** bleach

脱水 **tuōshuǐ** dehydrated

拖网鱼船 **tuōwǎng yúchuán** trawler

托位 **tuōwèi** dislocate

拖鞋 **tuōxié** slippers; flip-flops; mules

妥协 **tuǒxié** compromise

拖延 **tuōyán** stall

脱氧核糖核酸 **tuōyǎng hétáng hésuān** DNA, deoxyribonucleic acid

托曳 **tuōyè** haul; pull

唾液 **tuòyè** saliva

脱衣服 **tuō yīfu** undress, get undressed

脱颖而出 **tuō yǐng ér chū** come to the fore

椭圆 **tuǒyuán** oval; ellipse

托运 **tuōyùn** ship, send

托运公司 **tuōyùn gōngsī** freight company, freight forwarder

脱脂棉 **tuōzhīmián** absorbent cotton

脱脂乳 **tuōzhīrǔ** skimmed milk

拖走 **tuōzǒu** tow away

涂片 **túpiàn** smear

突破 **tūpò** breakthrough; penetration

土丘 **tǔqiū** mound

突然 **tūrán** suddenly ◊ abrupt, sudden; 突然跌落 **tūrán diēluò** plunge; 突然袭击 **tūrán xíjī** raid; pounce

土壤 **tǔrǎng** soil

土人 **tǔrén** native

屠杀 **túshā** massacre; slaughter

徒手格斗 **túshǒu gédòu** unarmed combat

图书馆 **túshūguǎn** library

图书馆员 **túshūguǎn yuán** librarian

吐痰 **tǔtán** spit

突袭 **tūxí** raid

图形 **túxíng** figure; graphic

徒刑 **túxíng** prison sentence

图形卡 **túxíngkǎ** graphics card

图形控制器 **túxíng kòngzhì qì** graphics controller

图形学 **túxíngxué** graphics

凸印 **tūyìn** emboss

涂油漆 **tú yóuqī** paint

屠宰 **túzǎi** slaughter

屠宰场 **túzǎichǎng** slaughterhouse

突增 **tūzēng** jump

图章 **túzhāng** chop, stamp, seal

途中 **túzhōng** en route

土著 **tǔzhù** native

兔子 **tùzi** rabbit; hare

T字形拐杖 **T zì xíng guǎizhàng** crutch

UW

U 形弯 **U xíngwān** U-turn

挖 **wā** dig

蛙 **wā** frog

瓦 **wǎ** roof tile

袜 **wà** socks; stockings

挖鼻孔 **wā bíkǒng** pick one's nose

挖出 **wāchū** dredge up

歪 **wāi** leaning, slanting; crooked

外 **wài** outside ◊ external; foreign; outward ◊ externally; outwardly

外币 **wàibì** foreign currency

外边 **wàibiān** outside; offside

外表 **wàibiǎo** appearance; exterior; façade; veneer ◊ outward

外部 **wàibù** outside, exterior ◊ outer; external

外出 **wàichū** go out

外出旅程 **wàichū lǚchéng** outward journey

外公 **wàigōng** grandfather (*maternal*)

外观 **wàiguān** exterior; appearance; look

外国 **wàiguó** foreign country ◊ abroad ◊ foreign

外国人 **wàiguó rén** foreigner

外行 **wàiháng** layman; layperson

外号 **wàihào** nickname

外汇 **wàihuì** foreign currency, foreign exchange

外交 **wàijiāo** diplomacy ◊ diplomatic

外交部 **Wàijiāobù** Department of State, Ministry of Foreign Affairs

外交部长 **Wàijiāobù Zhǎng** Secretary of State, Foreign Minister

外交官 **wàijiāo guān** diplomat

外交免疫力 **wàijiāo miǎnyì lì** diplomatic immunity

外交事物 **wàijiāo shìwù** foreign affairs

外交政策 **wàijiāo zhèngcè** foreign policy

外景 **wàijǐng** on location

外科 **wàikē** surgical

外壳 **wàiké** hull; husk

外科医师 **wàikē yīshī** surgeon

外来语 **wàiláiyǔ** foreign word; loan word

外贸 **wàimào** foreign trade

外面 **wàimiàn** outside ◊ external

外婆 **wàipó** grandmother (*maternal*)

歪曲 **wāiqū** distort, misrepresent; 对正义的歪曲 **duì zhèngyì de wāiqū** travesty of justice

外甥 **wàisheng** nephew (*sister's son*)

外甥女 **wàishengnǚ** niece (*sister's daughter*)

外孙女 **wàisūnnǚ** granddaughter (*daughter's daughter*)

外孙子 **wàisūnzi** grandson (*daughter's son*)

外围装置 **wàiwéi zhuāngzhì** peripheral

外星人 **wàixīng rén** alien

外衣 **wàiyī** coat

外语 **wàiyǔ** foreign language

曾外孙 **wàizēngsūn** great-grandson (*daughter's grandson*)

外祖父 **wàizǔfù** grandfather (*maternal*)

外祖父母 **wàizǔfùmǔ** grandparents (*maternal*)

外祖母 **wàizǔmǔ** grandmother (*maternal*)

瓦解 **wǎjiě** disintegrate

挖掘 **wājué** excavate ◊ excavation

挖掘机 **wājuéjī** excavator

挖空 **wākōng** excavate; dig

挖苦 **wākǔ** dry

瓦楞铁 **wǎlèngtiě** corrugated iron

瓦楞纸板 **wǎlèng zhǐbǎn** corrugated cardboard

瓦砾 **wǎlì** rubble

湾 **wān** bay

弯 **wān** bend ◊ bent

完 **wán** finish ◊ finished, over; complete; 她还没完呢 **tā hái méiwán ne** she still hasn't finished; 完了 **wánle** be through, be finished; 完了！**wánle!** that's it!; there you are!

玩 **wán** play

碗 **wǎn** bowl

晚 **wǎn** late ◊ evening; night; 天晚了 **tiānwǎn le** it's getting late

万 **wàn** ten thousand

晚安 **wǎn'ān** good night

晚报 **wǎnbào** evening paper

完毕 **wánbì** finished

晚餐 **wǎncān** dinner

完成 **wánchéng** complete; accomplish ◊ completion

完成式 **wánchéngshì** perfect tense

碗橱 **wǎnchú** cupboard

晚点 **wǎndiǎn** delayed

碗碟柜 **wǎndié guì** dresser

豌豆 **wāndòu** pea

晚饭 **wǎnfàn** supper

王 **wáng** king

网 **wǎng** net; network; web; grid; Internet; 一网鱼 **yìwǎngyú** a haul of fish

往 **wǎng** to; toward ◊ past

忘 **wàng** forget

望 **wàng** look ahead; expect

旺 **wàng** prosperous

网吧 **wǎngbā** Internet café

挽歌 **wǎngē** lament

忘恩负义 **wàng'ēn fùyì** ingratitude

往返 **wǎngfǎn** there and back

王国 **wángguó** kingdom

王后 **wánghòu** queen (*monarch's wife*)

旺火煸炒 **wànghuǒ biānchǎo** stir-fry

忘记 **wàngjì** forget

旺季 **wàngjì** high season

往来 **wǎnglái** contact; dealings; relations

网络 **wǎngluò** network; Internet

网络服务 **wǎngluò fúwù** on-line service

完工 **wángōng** complete

王牌 **wángpái** trump card

网球 **wǎngqiú** tennis; tennis ball

网球场 **wǎngqiú chǎng** tennis court

网球拍 **wǎngqiú pāi** tennis racket

网球手 **wǎngqiú shǒu** tennis player

网球网 **wǎngqiú wǎng** net (*in tennis*)

忘却 **wàngquè** forget; get over *lover etc*

网上 **wǎngshang** on-line COMPUT

往事 **wǎngshì** the past

顽固 **wángù** obstinate, stubborn; set ◊ obstinacy

汪汪叫 **wāngwang jiào** yap; bark

王位 **wángwèi** throne

往下 **wǎngxià** downward

妄想 **wàngxiǎng** delusion

妄想狂 **wàngxiǎng kuáng** paranoia

网眼 **wǎngyǎn** mesh

望远镜 **wàngyuǎn jìng** telescope; binoculars

网址 **wǎngzhǐ** web site; web page

王子 **wángzǐ** prince

妄自尊大的人 **wàngzì zūndà de rén** squirt

完好无损 **wánhǎo wúsǔn** sound, in good repair

晚会 **wǎnhuì** party; (evening) function

玩忽职守 **wánhū zhíshǒu** misconduct; negligence; malpractice

完结 **wánjié** be over

万金油 **wànjīnyóu** balm

挽救 **wǎnjiù** retrieve

玩具 **wánjù** toy

万里长城 **Wànlǐ Chángchéng** Great Wall of China

晚礼服 **wǎnlǐfú** evening dress

完美 **wánměi** perfect, flawless; beautiful ◊ perfection

完美主义者 **wánměi zhǔyì zhě** perfectionist

万能钥匙 **wànnéng yàoshi** master key, skeleton key

顽皮 **wánpí** mischievous

晚 期 **wǎnqī** terminal ◊ terminally

顽 强 **wánqiáng** stubborn; tenacious

弯 曲 **wānqū** bend ◊ crooked ◊ curve; 使 弯 曲 **shǐ wānqū** warp

完 全 **wánquán** complete; total ◊ completely, fully; 完 全 一 样 **wánquán yīyàng** exactly the same

玩 儿 **wánr** play; party; 玩 儿 开 心 点 儿 **wánr kāixīn diǎnr** have a good time

完 善 **wánshàn** perfect

晚 上 **wǎnshang** evening; 晚 上 十 一 点 **wǎnshàng shíyī diǎn** 11 o'clock at night; 晚 上 好 ! **wǎnshang hǎo!** good evening!

弯 身 **wānshēn** bend; double up

玩 世 不 恭 **wán shì bù gōng** cynically

玩 耍 **wánshuǎ** enjoy oneself

玩 童 **wántóng** urchin

弯 弯 曲 曲 **wānwan qūqu** twisty

万 无 一 失 **wàn wú yì shī** unerring

惋 惜 **wánxī** pity; 令 人 惋 惜 **lìngrén wǎnxī** lamentable

玩 笑 **wánxiào** joke

万 幸 **wànxìng** fortunate

蜿 蜒 **wānyán** wind ◊ winding; 蜿 蜒 行 进 **wānyán xíngjìn** wriggle

晚 宴 服 **wǎnyànfú** evening wear

弯 腰 **wānyāo** bend down, stoop

弯 腰 曲 背 **wānyāo qūbèi** stoop

万 一 … **wànyī … in case …**

玩 意 儿 **wányìr** trinket

玩 杂 耍 **wán záshuǎ** juggle

玩 杂 耍 的 人 **wán záshuǎ de rén** juggler

完 整 **wánzhěng** complete; thorough ◊ completely

婉 转 地 叫 **wǎnzhuǎn de jiào** warble

晚 走 **wǎnzǒu** stay behind

蛙 人 **wārén** frogman

瓦 特 **wǎtè** watt

娃 娃 **wáwa** doll

挖 心 **wāxīn** core

蛙 泳 **wāyǒng** breaststroke

袜 子 **wàzi** socks; stockings

煨 **wēi** poach

微 **wēi** small; micro-

危 **wēi** danger

违 **wéi** break; transgress; violate

围 **wéi** encircle; surround; besiege; 用 栅 栏 围 起 **yòng zhàlán wéiqǐ** fence in

唯 **wéi** only

为 **wéi** be ◊ as ◊ achievement

伪 **wěi** false

伟 **wěi** great

尾 **wěi** tail; end

喂 **wèi** hello TELEC; hey! ◊ feed *animals etc*

位 **wèi** position

为 **wèi** for; 为 … 干 杯 **wèi … gānbēi** toast, propose a toast to; 为 … 辩 护 **wèi … biànhù** stick up for

未 **wèi** not yet; not; 未 成 文 **wèi chéngwén** unwritten

味 **wèi** taste

畏 **wèi** fear

胃 **wèi** stomach

卫 **wèi** guard

尾 巴 **wěiba** tail

违 背 **wéibèi** violate; disobey; go against ◊ violation

卫 兵 **wèibīng** guard

微 波 **wēibō** microwave

微 薄 **wēibó** sparse; scanty ◊ scantily; sparsely; 微 薄 的 工 资 **wēibóde gōngzī** pittance

微 波 炉 **wēibōlú** microwave (oven)

微 不 足 道 **wēi bù zú dào** paltry, derisory

未 曾 **wèicéng** never

围 场 **wéichǎng** pound (*for strays*)

未 成 年 **wèi chéngnián** juvenile; underage

未 成 年 人 **wèichéngnián rén** minor, juvenile

维 持 **wéichí** maintain; get by; hold out

维 持 生 活 **wéichí shēnghuó** manage

微 处 理 机 **wēichǔlǐjī** microprocessor

未 出 生 **wèi chūshēng** unborn

为 此 **wèicǐ** for this reason

伟 大 **wěidà** great ◊ greatness

味 道 **wèidao** taste, flavor

尾 灯 **wěidēng** tail light

微 电 子 学 **wēidiànzǐ xué**

microelectronics

纬度 **wěidù** latitude

纬度线 **wěidùxiàn** parallel

巍峨 **wēi'é** lofty

违法 **wéifǎ** illicit, illegal ◊ illegally

违法者 **wéifǎ zhě** criminal; lawbreaker

违反 **wéifǎn** break, contravene

违犯 **wéifàn** violate, breach ◊ violation

违反合同 **wéifǎn hétóng** breach of contract

违反交通法规 **wéifǎn jiāotōng fǎguī** traffic violation

微风 **wēifēng** breeze

未付 **wèifù** nonpayment ◊ outstanding

威佛饼干 **wēifú bǐnggān** wafer

桅杆 **wéigān** mast

微光 **wēiguāng** gleam, glimmer

微观世界 **wēiguān shìjiè** microcosm

危害 **wēihài** damage

威吓 **wēihè** intimidate

维护 **wéihù** defend, stand up for; uphold; preserve ◊ maintenance

未婚 **wèihūn** unmarried

未婚夫 **wèihūnfū** fiancé

未婚妻 **wèihūnqī** fiancée

维护 **wéihù** protect, look after

危机 **wēijī** crisis

危急 **wēijí** critical; desperate ◊ critically

危及 **wēijí** endanger

未解决 **wèi jiějué** unsettled

围巾 **wéijīn** scarf

味精 **wèijīng** monosodium glutamate

未经加工 **wèijīng jiāgōng** raw, unprocessed

微晶片 **wēijīngpiàn** microchip

伪君子 **wěijūnzǐ** hypocrite

违抗 **wěikàng** defy ◊ in defiance of

胃口 **wèikǒu** appetite

围困 **wéikùn** besiege ◊ siege

未来 **wèilái** future

未来式 **wèiláishì** future tense ◊ futuristic

慰劳金 **wèiláojīn** golden handshake

为了 **wèile** for; in order to; because of; 为了我 **wèile wǒ** for my sake

微量 **wēiliàng** trace

帷幕 **wéimù** curtain

喂奶 **wèinǎi** breast-feed

为难 **wéinán** uncomfortable; distressed; 使为难 **shǐ wéinán** disconcert

味浓 **wèinóng** strong

委派 **wěipài** posting

围棋 **Wéiqí** Go

委屈 **wěiqu** injustice

围裙 **wéiqún** apron

围绕 **wéirǎo** surround; revolve around ◊ around

委任 **wěirèn** appoint

微弱 **wēiruò** feeble

伪善 **wěishàn** hypocrisy

未删节 **wèi shānjié** full-length

伪善言词 **wěishàn yáncí** cant

危慑 **wēishè** deter

卫生 **wèishēng** hygienic, sanitary ◊ hygiene

卫生带 **wèishēngdài** sanitary napkin

卫生间 **wèishēngjiān** rest room

卫生间用品 **wèishēngjiān yòngpǐn** toiletries

卫生巾 **wèishēngjīn** sanitary napkin

卫生设备 **wèishēng shèbèi** sanitation

维生素 **wéishēngsù** vitamin

卫生纸 **wèishēngzhǐ** toilet paper

为什么 **wèishénme?** why?; what for?; 为什么不？ **wèishénme bù?** why not?

危慑因素 **wēishè yīnsù** deterrent

威士忌 **wēishìjì** whiskey

卫戍部队 **wèishù bùduì** garrison

畏缩 **wèisuō** recoil; shrink from; shy away

维他命 **wéitāmìng** vitamin

维他命药片 **wéitāmìng yàopiàn** vitamin pill

胃痛 **wèitòng** stomach ache

委托 **wěituō** commission; 把Y委托给X **bǎ Y wěituōgěi X** entrust Y to X

未完待续 **wèiwán dàixù** to be continued

威望 **wēiwàng** prestige

委婉说法 **wěiwǎn shuōfǎ** euphemism

微温 **wēiwēn** lukewarm, tepid

唯物论 **wéiwùlùn** materialistic

唯物主义 **wéiwù zhǔyì** materialism

唯物主义者 **wéiwù zhǔyì zhě** materialist

危险 **wēixiǎn** danger, hazard, peril ◊ dangerous, unsafe; 处于危险境地 **chǔyú wēixiǎn jìngdì** be in jeopardy

危险人物 **wēixiǎn rénwù** security risk

危险者 **wēixiǎn zhě** menace

微小 **wēixiǎo** tiny, minute, minuscule

微笑 **wēixiào** smile; 对 ... 微笑 **duì ... wēixiào** smile at

威胁 **wēixié** threat; menace; intimidation ◊ threaten, intimidate ◊ menacing

猥亵 **wěixiè** obscene, filthy

微型 **wēixíng** pocket

卫星 **wèixīng** satellite

微型电视 **wēixíng diànshì** portable TV

卫星电视 **wèixīng diànshì** satellite TV

卫星电视盘 **wèixīng diànshì pán** satellite dish

唯心论 **wéixīn lùn** spiritualism

维修 **wéixiū** maintain; service; repair

威严 **wēiyán** majestic

喂养 **wèiyǎng** feed

偎依 **wēiyī** nestle, snuggle; cling

唯一 **wéiyī** sole, only, single ◊ solely

位于 **wèiyú** be situated; lie

委员会 **wěiyuánhuì** commission; committee

未预见到 **wèi yùjiàn dào** unforeseen

伪造 **wěizào** counterfeit, forge; falsify

伪造品 **wěizào pǐn** forgery

伪造人 **wěizào rén** forger

违章停车罚款单 **wéizhāng tíngchē fákuǎndān** parking ticket

位置 **wèizhi** location, position; locality, situation

未知 **wèizhī** unknown

未支付 **wèi zhīfù** unsettled

围住 **wéizhù** enclose

伪装 **wěizhuāng** disguise; camouflage ◊ dress up ◊ phoney; 伪装为 X **wěizhuāng wéi X** masquerade as X

位子 **wèizi** seat, place

围嘴 **wéizuǐ** bib

温 **wēn** warm

闻 **wén** smell, sniff

文 **wén** writing; language; literature; culture

蚊 **wén** mosquito

吻 **wěn** kiss

稳 **wěn** stable; steady

问 **wèn** ask; question, query

闻出 **wénchū** smell

问答比赛 **wèndá bǐsài** quiz

问答卷 **wèndá juàn** questionnaire

稳定 **wěndìng** stable ◊ stability ◊ stabilize

温度 **wēndù** temperature

温度表 **wēndùbiǎo** thermometer

温度计 **wēndùjì** thermometer

稳而有力 **wěn ér yǒulì** firm

翁 **wēng** old man

嗡鸣声 **wēngmíng shēng** drone, droning noise

稳固 **wěngù** rigid

嗡嗡作响 **wēngwēng zuòxiǎng** hum; buzz

问好 **wènhǎo** ask after; send greetings; 向她问好 **xiàng tā wènhǎo** give her my love; send her my best wishes

问号 **wènhào** question mark

温和 **wēnhé** mild; moderate; mellow ◊ mildness

温和派 **wēnhépài** moderate POL

问候 **wènhòu** send one's regards; say hello; ask after; 代我向 X 问候 **dài wǒ xiàng X wènhòu** give my regards to X

文化 **wénhuà** culture ◊ cultural

文化冲击 **wénhuà chōngjī** culture shock

文化大革命 **Wénhuà Dàgémìng** Cultural Revolution

文件 **wénjiàn** document; papers; documentation; file

文件管理程序 **wénjiàn guǎnlǐ chéngxù** file manager

文件夹 **wénjiàn jiá** folder

文具 **wénjù** stationery

文具商店 **wénjù shāngdiàn** stationery store

文科硕士 **wénkē shuòshì** Master of Arts

文科学位 **wénkē xuéwèi** arts degree

文盲 **wénmáng** illiterate

文明 **wénmíng** civilization; culture

闻名 **wénmíng** famous

温暖 **wēnnuǎn** warm

文凭 **wénpíng** qualification; diploma; certificate

文乞 **wénqǐ** hack

文人 **wénrén** egghead

温柔 **wēnróu** gentle, soft; tender

纹身 **wénshēn** tattoo

温室 **wēnshì** greenhouse, hothouse

温室气体 **wēnshì qìtǐ** greenhouse gas

温室效应 **wēnshì xiàoyìng** greenhouse effect

文书工作 **wénshū gōngzuò** paperwork

温顺 **wēnshùn** meek

问题 **wèntí** problem; question, matter; 是钱的问题 **shì qián de wèntí** it's a question of money

温习 **wēnxí** brush up; revise

蚊香 **wénxiāng** mosquito coil

问心有愧 **wèn xīn yǒu kuì** have a guilty conscience

文学 **wénxué** literature ◊ literary

问讯 **wènxùn** ask; inquire

问讯处 **wènxùn chù** information office

问讯台 **wènxùn tái** information desk

文雅 **wényǎ** refined; cultivated; elegant

瘟疫 **wēnyì** epidemic, plague

文艺 **wényì** art and literature

文章 **wénzhāng** article

蚊帐 **wénzhàng** mosquito net

稳重 **wěnzhòng** sedate; sober

稳住 **wěnzhù** steady

蚊子 **wénzi** mosquito

文字 **wénzì** writing; text

文字处理 **wénzì chǔlǐ** word processing

文字处理机 **wénzì chǔlǐjī** word processor

窝 **wō** nest; socket ◊ *measure word for broods, hives of bees etc*; 一窝蜜蜂 **yìwō mìfēng** a hive of bees

我 **wǒ** I; me ◊ my; 我是 … **wǒ shì** … TELEC it's … here

卧 **wò** lie down

握 **wò** hold; grasp

卧病在床 **wò bìng zài chuáng** be confined to one's bed

卧车 **wòchē** sleeping car

卧床不起 **wò chuáng bù qǐ** bedridden

卧倒 **wòdǎo** lie flat; drop to the ground

我的 **wǒde** my; mine

我的天啊！**wǒde tiān'a!** (oh) dear!, dear me!

握紧 **wòjǐn** clench

涡轮机 **wōlúnjī** turbine

我们 **wǒmen** we; us ◊ our; 我们别吵了 **wǒmén bié chǎole** let's not argue; 我们走吧 **wǒmén zǒu ba** let's go

我们的 **wǒménde** our ◊ ours

我们自己 **wǒmen zìjǐ** ourselves

蜗牛 **wōniú** snail

窝棚 **wōpeng** shed; hovel

卧铺 **wòpù** place to sleep, bunk (*on train*)

卧室 **wòshì** bedroom

握手 **wòshǒu** handshake ◊ shake hands

我自己 **wǒ zìjǐ** myself

污 **wū** dirt

乌 **wū** black ◊ crow

屋 **wū** house

无 **wú** nothing ◊ not; no

五 **wǔ** five

武 **wǔ** military

午 **wǔ** midday
舞 **wǔ** dance
雾 **wù** fog; mist
误 **wù** mistake
勿 **wù** do not
物 **wù** thing
五百 **wǔbǎi** five hundred
舞伴 **wǔbàn** (dance) partner
无比 **wúbǐ** incomparable
务必 **wùbì** must; 务必保证做完 X **wùbì bǎozhèng zuòwán X** see to it that X gets done
五彩 **wǔcǎi** colorful; 五彩缤纷 **wǔcǎi bīnfēn** a blaze of color
午餐 **wǔcān** lunch
午餐时间 **wǔcān shíjiān** lunchtime
无常 **wúcháng** erratic
无偿 **wúcháng** unpaid
舞场 **wǔchǎng** dance floor; dance hall
无偿债能力 **wú chángzhài nénglì** insolvent
无产阶级 **wúchǎn jiējí** proletariat
无耻 **wúchǐ** outrageous; shameless
无处 **wúchù** nowhere
无带 **wúdài** strapless
舞蹈 **wǔdǎo** dancing
误导 **wùdǎo** misguided
舞蹈编导 **wǔdǎo biāndǎo** choreographer
舞蹈家 **wǔdǎo jiā** dancer
舞蹈演员 **wǔdǎo yǎnyuán** dancer
无敌 **wúdí** invincible
污点 **wūdiǎn** mark; blot; flaw
屋顶 **wūdǐng** roof
无动于衷 **wú dòng yúzhōng** indifferent; untouched; aloof; unconcerned
无端 **wúduān** unfounded; unprovoked
无法 **wúfǎ** unable to
无法超越 **wúfǎ chāoyuè** insurmountable
无法和解 **wúfǎ héjiě** irreconcilable
无法解释 **wúfǎ jiěshì** unaccountable

irresistible
无法理解 **wúfǎ lǐjiě** be out of one's depth
无法弥补 **wúfǎ míbǔ** irreparable
午饭 **wǔfàn** lunch
无法区别 **wúfǎ qūbié** indistinguishable
无法挽回 **wúfǎ wǎnhuí** irrecoverable
无法慰藉 **wúfǎ wèijiè** inconsolable
无法想象 **wúfǎ xiǎngxiàng** inconceivable
无法形容 **wúfǎ xíngróng** indescribable
无风险 **wúfēngxiǎn** safe
无根据 **wúgénjù** groundless, baseless, unfounded
污垢 **wūgòu** dirt
无辜 **wúgū** innocent ◊ innocently
无关紧要 **wúguān jǐnyào** immaterial
乌龟 **wūguī** tortoise; turtle
无轨电车 **wúguǐ diànchē** streetcar
无故障 **wú gùzhàng** trouble-free
无害 **wúhài** harmless
无核 **wúhé** nuclear-free
无花果 **wúhuāguǒ** fig
雾化器 **wùhuà qì** atomizer
污秽 **wūhuì** grubby
污秽 **wūhuì** squalor
舞会 **wǔhuì** dance; ball; prom
误会 **wùhuì** misunderstand; misconstrue ◊ misunderstanding
屋脊 **wūjí** ridge (of roof)
污迹 **wūjì** smudge, smear; 产生污迹 **chǎnshēng wūjì** stain
无机 **wújī** inorganic
无家 **wújiā** homeless
无价 **wújià** invaluable; priceless
无家的人 **wújiāde rén** the homeless
无家具设备 **wú jiājù shèbèi** unfurnished
物件 **wùjiàn** article, item
误将 X 认作 Y **wùjiāng X rènzuò Y** mistake X for Y
五角大楼 **Wǔjiǎo Dàlóu** the Pentagon
物价上涨 **wùjià shàngzhǎng**

inflatinary

无价值 **wú jiàzhí** insignificant; worthless

误解 **wùjiě** misunderstand; misread ◊ misunderstanding, misconception; 使人误解 **shǐrén wùjiě** misleading

无戒心 **wú jièxīn** unsuspecting

无节制 **wú jiézhì** immoderate

无计划性 **wú jìhuà xìng** arbitrary

无精打采 **wújīng dǎcǎi** listless

五金商店 **wǔjīn shāngdiàn** hardware store

无脊椎动物 **wú jízhuì dòngwù** invertebrate

无拘束 **wú jūshù** unrestrained

无咖啡因 **wú kāfēiyīn** decaffeinated

无可奉告 **wúkě fènggào** no comment

无可奈何 **wúkě nàihé** helpless ◊ helplessly ◊ resignation ◊ it can't be helped

无可争辩 **wúkě zhēngbiàn** undisputed ◊ unquestionably

无可指责 **wúkě zhīzé** beyond reproach, irreproachable

无可指摘 **wúkě zhīzhāi** irreproachable

无愧 **wúkuì** worthy

无赖 **wúlài** scoundrel; scrounger

无礼 **wúlǐ** rudeness, impertinence ◊ impertinent; saucy

无力 **wúlì** feeble

武力 **wǔlì** force

物理 **wùlǐ** physics

无聊 **wúliáo** boredom; monotony ◊ boring; uninteresting

无力量 **wúlìliàng** powerless

无领长袖衫 **wúlǐng chángxiùshān** sweatshirt

无理性 **wúlǐxìng** irrational

物理学家 **wùlǐ xuéjiā** physicist

无理由 **wú lǐyóu** uncalled-for

乌龙茶 **wūlóngchá** oolong tea

无论哪个 **wúlùn nǎgè** whichever

无论哪里 **wúlùn nǎlǐ** wherever

无论如何 **wúlùn rúhé** still, in any case; no matter what

无论什么时候 **wúlùn shénme shíhòu** whenever

无论是谁 **wúlùn shì shéi** whoever

无毛 **wúmáo** hairless

雾蒙蒙 **wùméngméng** hazy

污蔑 **wūmiè** smear; slander; libel

诬蔑 **wūmiè** smear; slander; libel

无名 **wúmíng** obscure; nameless

无名指 **wúmíngzhǐ** ring finger

无内胎 **wú nèitāi** tubeless

无能 **wúnéng** incompetent; incapable; unable ◊ inability

无能为力 ... **wú néng wéilì** ... be powerless to ...

五年计划 **Wǔnián Jìhuà** Five Year Plan

误判 **wùpàn** miscarriage of justice

无偏见 **wú piānjiàn** detached

物品 **wùpǐn** object; item

武器 **wǔqì** arms, armaments; weapon

雾气 **wùqì** mist, haze

无铅 **wúqiān** unleaded

无情 **wúqíng** ruthless; callous ◊ ruthlessly; callously ◊ ruthlessness; 无情的力量 **wúqíngde lìliàng** brute force

无亲戚关系 **wú qīnqī guānxi** unrelated

无穷 **wúqióng** infinity

舞曲 **wǔqǔ** dance music

无权 **wúquán** unauthorized

污染 **wūrǎn** contaminate; pollute; infect ◊ contamination; pollution ◊ tainted

污染物质 **wūrǎn wùzhì** pollutant

无人操纵 **wúrén cāozòng** unmanned

无人承担 **wúrén chéngdān** unoccupied *post*

无人住 **wúrén zhù** unoccupied *building*

侮辱 **wǔrǔ** insult, slight

物色 **wùsè** hunt

物色人才的人 **wùsè réncái de rén** headhunter

无声 **wúshēng** silent; mute ◊ silently

无生命 **wú shēngmìng** inanimate; lifeless

无生气 **wú shēngqì** be in the doldrums

无生殖能力 **wú shēngzhí nénglì** infertility

无神论者 **wú shén lùn zhě** atheist

五十 **wǔshí** fifty

武士 **wǔshì** warrior

务实 **wùshí** pragmatic

无数 **wúshù** countless, innumerable

武术 **wǔshù** martial arts

污水 **wūshuǐ** sewage

午睡 **wǔshuì** afternoon nap

污水管 **wūshuǐ guǎn** sewer

无私 **wúsī** selfless, unselfish

五四运动 **Wǔsì yùndòng** May 4th movement

误算 **wùsuàn** miscalculate ◊ miscalculation

无所谓 **wúsuǒwèi** indifferent ◊ all the same

勿踏草坪 **wùtà cǎopíng** keep off the grass

舞台 **wǔtái** stage, platform

舞台布景 **wǔtái bùjǐng** scenery THEA

无特殊技能 **wú tèshū jìnéng** unskilled

物体 **wùtǐ** object

无条件 **wú tiáojiàn** unconditional

舞厅 **wǔtīng** ballroom; dancehall

无痛 **wútòng** painless

无头脑 **wútóunǎo** mindless

乌托邦 **wūtuōbāng** utopia

勿忘我 **wùwàngwǒ** forget-me-not

无畏 **wúwèi** fearless, intrepid

无味 **wúwèi** tasteless, insipid; dull

无危险 **wúwēixiǎn** safe

污物 **wūwù** sewage

污物处理场 **wūwù chǔlǐ chǎng** sewage plant

无武器 **wú wǔqì** unarmed

无限 **wúxiàn** infinite, unlimited, boundless; untold

无线 **wúxiàn** cordless, wireless

无线电 **wúxiàn diàn** radio, wireless

无线电话 **wúxiàn diànhuà** cordless phone; radio telephone

无线电视 **wúxiàn diànshì** terrestrial TV

无限制 **wúxiànzhì** unlimited, limitless; indefinite ◊ indefinitely

无效 **wúxiào** invalid, null and void; futile; 使无效 **shǐ wúxiào** neutralize; annul

无效率 **wúxiàolǜ** inefficient

无懈可击 **wúxiè kějī** impeccable

无心 **wúxīn** unintentionally

五星红旗 **wǔxīng hóngqí** Chinese national flag

五星级饭店 **wǔxīngjí fàndiàn** five-star hotel

污朽 **wūxiǔ** stale

无袖 **wúxiù** sleeveless

午休 **wǔxiū** lunch break, lunch hour

乌鸦 **wūyā** crow; raven

呜咽 **wūyān** sob

屋檐 **wūyán** eaves

呜咽 **wūyè** whimper

午夜 **wǔyè** midnight

呜咽声 **wūyèshēng** whimper

午夜时 **wǔyèshí** at midnight

无疑 **wúyí** no doubt, undoubtedly, doubtless; easily

无意 **wúyìde** unintentional ◊ unintentionally

五一节 **Wǔyī Jié** May Day

无意识 **wúyìshí** unconscious ◊ unconsciously

无异议 **wú yìyì** unquestioning

无意义 **wú yìyì** senseless, pointless; meaningless

无用 **wúyòng** useless

无忧虑 **wú yōulǜ** secure *feeling*

无忧无虑 **wúyōu wúlǜ** carefree, happy-go-lucky

无远见 **wú yuǎnjiàn** short-sighted

无缘无故 **wúyuán wúgù** for no reason

五月 **wǔyuè** May

无与伦比 **wú yǔ lúnbǐ** unique

乌云 **wūyún** dark clouds

无增长 **wú zēngzhǎng** zero growth

无债务 **wú zhàiwù** solvent

无障碍 **wú zhàng'ài** open

无政府状态 **wú zhèngfǔ zhuàngtài** anarchy

无知 **wúzhī** ignorance ◊ ignorant

物质 **wùzhì** matter, substance,

material

无止境 **wú zhǐjìng** endless, unending, infinite ◊ endlessly, infinitely

无中止 **wú zhōngzhǐ** without a break

无主 **wúzhǔ** unattended

无助 **wúzhù** helpless

武装 **wǔzhuāng** arms, weapons ◊ arm ◊ armed

武装力量 **wǔzhuāng lìliàng** armed forces

物主代词 **wùzhǔ dàicí** possessive pronoun

无资格 **wú zīgé** ineligible

无子女 **wú zǐnǚ** childless

无罪 **wúzuì** innocent ◊ innocence

无足轻重 **wúzú qīngzhòng** insignificant, of little importance

无组织 **wú zǔzhi** disorganized

X

X光照片 **X guāng zhàopiān** X-ray

膝 **xī** knee

吸 **xī** inhale; smoke; suck

稀 **xī** rare; sparse; thin

锡 **xī** tin

西 **xī** west ◊ western

溪 **xī** stream

熄 **xī** extinguish

席 **xí** mat; seat; place; feast

袭 **xí** attack

习 **xí** learn; study; practise

洗 **xǐ** wash, clean; shuffle *cards*; develop *photographs*

喜 **xǐ** pleasure, joy

系 **xì** system; department; faculty ◊ tie

细 **xì** fine; thin

戏 **xì** play

瞎 **xiā** blind

虾 **xiā** shrimp

峡 **xiá** strait

狭 **xiá** narrow

下 **xià** down, downward; below; under; next ◊ get off; come down (*of rain etc*); lay *eggs*; 下个星期 / 下个月 *xiàgè xīngqī* / *xiàgè yuè* next week / next month

吓 **xià** scare; 吓了 X 一跳 *xià le X yítiào* give X a scare

夏 **xià** summer

下巴 **xiàba** chin

下班 **xiàbān** finish work; go off duty

下边 **xiàbiān** beneath

下车 **xiàchē** get off; get out

下沉 **xiàchén** sink; settle

下船 **xiàchuán** disembark

下垂 **xiàchuí** droop, sag

瑕疵 **xiácī** flaw, blemish

下次 **xiàcì** next time

吓呆 **xiàdāi** petrify

下等 **xiàděng** third-rate

下等场所 **xiàděng chǎngsuǒ** dive (*bar etc*)

下跌 **xiàdiē** plunge

下定义 **xià dìngyì** define

下毒 **xiàdú** drug

下赌注 **xià dǔzhù** bet on; stake

下飞机 **xià fēijī** disembark (*from plane*)

下岗 **xiàgǎng** unemployed; laid off (*from state enterprise*) ◊ unemployment

下岗工人 **xiàgǎng gōngrén** the unemployed (*from state enterprise*)

峡谷 **xiágǔ** canyon; gorge; glen

吓唬 **xiàhu** browbeat

喜爱 **xǐ'ài** like; love ◊ beloved; fond ◊ favor; fondness

下机 **xiàjī** log off

下级 **xiàjí** subordinate

夏季 **xiàjì** summer

下降 **xiàjiàng** decrease; decline; descend; sink ◊ descent; drop; fall ◊ downward

下降趋势 **xiàjiàng qūshì** downturn

下决心 **xià juéxīn** decide; make up one's mind ◊ determined

下来 **xiàlái** come down, descend ◊ descent

夏令时 **xiàlìngshí** summer time; daylight saving time

下流 **xiàliú** indecent; profane; sleazy; smutty

下流坯 **xiàliúpī** swine (*person*)

下落不明 **xiàluò bùmíng** be missing

下毛毛雨 **xià máomao yǔ** drizzle

下面 **xiàmian** underneath; below

先 **xiān** first, beforehand

仙 **xiān** fairy; immortal

鲜 **xiān** fresh

弦 **xián** chord; string

咸 **xián** salty; savory

闲 **xián** idle ◊ leisure

嫌 **xián** dislike ◊ suspicion

显 **xiǎn** show; be obvious

线 **xiàn** line; thread; cord; 一线希望 **yíxiàn xīwàng** glimmer of hope

县 **xiàn** county

馅 **xiàn** filling

腺 **xiàn** gland

现 **xiàn** appear ◊ current, present

献 **xiàn** give; present

陷 **xiàn** trap; pitfall; snare

限 **xiàn** limit

瞎闹 **xiānào** mess around, waste time

现场 **xiànchǎng** on the spot ◊ scene of the crime

现场示范 **xiànchǎng shìfàn** reconstruct *crime*

现场直播 **xiànchǎng zhíbō** live broadcast

现成 **xiànchéng** ready-made; off the peg

县城 **xiànchéng** county town

舷窗 **xiánchuāng** porthole

现存 **xiàncún** existing; in existence; in stock, available

现代 **xiàndài** modern; contemporary ◊ modern times

现代化 **xiàndàihuà** modernize ◊ modernization

显得 **xiǎndé** appear, seem

限定 **xiàndìng** limit

限度 **xiàndù** limit

显而易见 **xiǎn ér yìjiàn** inevitable

宪法 **xiànfǎ** constitution ◊ constitutional

箱 **xiāng** box; crate; case

香 **xiāng** incense; perfume ◊ fragrant, aromatic, nice-smelling; tasty

相 **xiāng** each other

乡 **xiāng** countryside; hometown

详 **xiáng** details

响 **xiǎng** sound ◊ loud

想 **xiǎng** think; want; 好好想想！ **hǎohao xiǎngxiang!** think hard!; 我也是这么想的 **wǒ yě shì zhème xiǎng de** I think so too; 你想去看电影吗？ **nǐ xiǎng qù kàn diànyǐng ma?** would you like to go to the movies?; 想得开 **xiǎng de kāi** try to look on the

bright side of things

享 **xiǎng** enjoy

项 **xiàng** item

相 **xiàng** appearance

向 **xiàng** to; toward; 他向我走过来 **tā xiàng wǒ zǒuguòlái** he came up to me; 向 … 眨眼 **xiàng … zhǎyǎn** wink at; 向 X 挥手 **xiàng X huīshǒu** wave to X

象 **xiàng** elephant ◊ look like, resemble

像 **xiàng** look like, resemble

乡巴佬 **xiāngbālǎo** redneck

镶板 **xiāngbǎn** panel; section

向北 **xiàngběi** north ◊ northward

象鼻 **xiàngbí** (elephant's) trunk

相比 **xiāngbǐ** compare; 与 X 相比 **yǔ X xiāngbǐ** compared with X, next to X

镶边 **xiāngbiān** edge

香槟酒 **xiāngbīn jiǔ** champagne

香草 **xiāngcǎo** vanilla

相册 **xiàngcè** photo album

香肠 **xiāngcháng** sausage

镶齿冠 **xiāng chǐguàn** crown *tooth*

相处 **xiāngchǔ** mix, socialize; 他和人相处不好 **tā hé rén xiāngchù bùhǎo** he doesn't relate to people

想出 **xiǎngchū** think up

相当 **xiāngdāng** quite, considerably ◊ parallel, match; 相当大 **xiāngdāng dà** quite big; sizeable; 相当多 **xiāngdāng duō** quite a few, a lot

相当于 **xiāngdāngyú** equivalent ◊ be equivalent to; be tantamount to ◊ as much as

想到 **xiǎngdào** think of

向导 **xiàngdǎo** guide

想得开 **xiǎngdekāi** light-hearted

向东 **xiàngdōng** eastward, east

相对 **xiāngduì** relative ◊ relatively

想法 **xiǎngfa** thought, idea

相反 **xiāngfǎn** opposite, reverse; 与 … 相反 **yǔ … xiāngfǎn** contrary to …, as opposed to …

相反方向 **xiāngfǎn fāngxiàng** opposite direction

相符 **xiāngfú** correspond, match

香港 **Xiānggǎng** Hong Kong
香港回归 **Xiānggǎng huíguī** Hong Kong handover
相关 **xiāngguān** related
向后 **xiànghòu** backward
相互 **xiānghù** mutual
相互对立 **xiānghù duìlì** contradictory
相互关联 **xiānghù guānlián** interrelated
相互依赖 **xiānghù yīlài** interdependent
相互作用 **xiānghù zuòyòng** interaction
想家 **xiǎngjiā** be homesick
香蕉 **xiāngjiāo** banana
橡胶 **xiàngjiāo** rubber
相接 **xiāngjiē** interface
相近 **xiāngjìn** close
香精 **xiāngjīng** scent, perfume
镶框 **xiāngkuàng** frame
项链 **xiàngliàn** necklace
香料 **xiāngliào** spice
相貌 **xiàngmào** features (*facial*)
项目 **xiàngmù** item; project; entry (*in diary etc*)
橡木 **xiàngmù** oak (*wood*)
向南 **xiàng nán** southward
向内 **xiàngnèi** inward
想念 **xiǎngniàn** miss
相配 **xiāngpèi** match, complement
橡皮 **xiàngpí** rubber; eraser
相片 **xiàngpiàn** photo
橡皮筋 **xiàngpíjīn** elastic band
橡皮奶头 **xiàngpí nǎitóu** pacifier
香气 **xiāngqì** smell, fragrance, aroma
想起 **xiǎngqǐ** remember; think of; 使 X 想起 Y **shǐ X xiǎngqǐ Y** remind X of Y
象棋 **xiàngqí** chess
镶嵌 **xiāngqiàn** inlay; paneling ◊ set *jewel*
向前 **xiàngqián** forward, onward
想起来 **xiǎng qǐlái** think of; come up with
详情 **xiángqíng** details
项圈 **xiàngquān** collar
向日葵 **xiàngrìkuí** sunflower
相容 **xiāngróng** compatible
香山 **Xiāngshān** Fragrant Hills

向上 **xiàngshàng** up, upward
响声 **xiǎngshēng** sound
相识 **xiāngshí** know each other
享受 **xiǎngshòu** enjoy
详述 **xiángshù** discuss; expand on
橡树 **xiàngshù** oak tree
香水 **xiāngshuǐ** perfume
乡思 **xiāngsī** homesickness
相似 **xiāngsì** alike, similar ◊ be alike ◊ similarity
相似处 **xiāngsì chù** resemblance
相似之处 **xiāngsì zhī chù** parallel ◊ similarity
相同 **xiāngtóng** equal; equivalent ◊ equally
闲逛 **xiánguàng** wander, stroll
向外 **xiàngwài** outward
向往 **xiàngwǎng** yearning
香味 **xiāngwèi** perfume, scent, aroma
响尾蛇 **xiǎngwěishé** rattlesnake
详细 **xiángxì** detailed, full ◊ in detail, fully; minutely
向西 **xiàngxī** west ◊ westward
乡下 **xiāngxià** country (*as opposed to town*)
向下 **xiàngxià** down ◊ downward; underneath
乡下佬 **xiāngxiàlǎo** *pej* hick
想象 **xiǎngxiàng** imagine; envisage ◊ imagination; 我能想象出来 **wǒ néng xiǎngxiàng chūlái** I can just imagine it
想象力 **xiǎngxiànglì** imagination
乡下人 **xiāngxià rén** *pej* hillbilly
相信 **xiāngxìn** believe; believe in; trust
象牙 **xiàngyá** ivory; tusk
香烟 **xiāngyān** cigarette
象样 **xiàngyàng** respectable
想要 **xiǎngyào** wish
香油 **xiāngyóu** sesame oil
享有 **xiǎngyǒu** enjoy; 享有特权 **xiángyǒu tèquán** privileged
相遇 **xiāngyù** meet
香皂 **xiāngzào** toilet soap
象征 **xiàngzhēng** symbol, emblem, token ◊ symbolize
相撞 **xiāngzhuàng** collide; knock together
箱子 **xiāngzi** box; chest; crate;

case; trunk

陷害 xiànhài frame, stitch up

显赫 xiǎnhè influential

鲜红 xiānhóng scarlet

先后顺序 xiānhòu shùnxù order, sequence; 事情发生的先后顺序 shìqíng fāshēng de xiānhòu shùnxù the sequence of events

鲜花 xiānhuā fresh flowers

针线活 xiànhuózhēni sewing

献祭 xiànjì sacrifice

先见之明 xiānjiàn zhī míng foresight

线接头 xiàn jiētóu terminal

先进 xiānjìn advance ◊ advanced; progressive

现金 xiànjīn cash

现今 xiànjīn nowadays

现金出纳机 xiànjīn chūnà jī cash register

现金短缺 xiànjīn duǎnquē short of cash

陷阱 xiànjǐng pitfall; trap

现金折扣 xiànjīn zhékòu cash discount

现金支付 xiànjīn zhīfù cash down

先决条件 xiānjué tiáojiàn qualification

现款定金 xiànkuǎn dìngjīn cash in advance

先例 xiānlì precedent

闲聊 xiánliáo chatter; gossip

显露 xiǎnlòu be out (of secret)

显露 xiǎnlù manifest itself

线路 xiànlù circuit; line; wiring

线路板 xiànlù bǎn circuit board

线路图 xiànlù tú road map

鲜美 xiānměi delicious; succulent

鲜明 xiānmíng stark

羡慕 xiànmù envy; 令 X 羡慕 lìng X xiànmù be the envy of X

仙女 xiānnǚ fairy

险情指示灯 xiǎnqíng zhǐshìdēng hazard lights

先驱 xiānqū pioneer, forerunner

线圈 xiànquān coil

显然 xiǎnrán obvious ◊ apparently, evidently

闲人免进！ xiánrén miǎnjìn! keep out!

仙人掌 xiānrénzhǎng cactus

陷入 xiànrù become entangled in; 陷入困境 xiànrù kùnjìng be in a fix; 陷入圈套 xiànrù quāntào be trapped

先生 xiānsheng mister; sir; teacher; husband

献身于 xiànshēn yú dedicate oneself to

显示 xiǎnshì display, show

现实 xiànshí practical; realistic ◊ reality

现世 xiànshì earthly

显示器 xiǎnshìqì indicator; monitor

现实主义 xiànshí zhǔyì realism

现实主义者 xiànshí zhǔyì zhě realist

咸水 xiánshuǐ salt water

线索 xiànsuǒ clue; thread

献题 xiàntí dedication (in book)

先天性 xiāntiān xìng congenital

线条 xiàntiáo line

纤维 xiānwéi fiber

显微镜 xiǎnwēijìng microscope

纤维素 xiānwéisù cellulose

嫌恶 xiánwù distaste

纤细 xiánxì slender

闲暇 xiánxiá leisure, spare time

显现 xiǎnxiàn unfold; show up, reveal

现象 xiànxiàng phenomenon

现行 xiànxíng going, current

献血 xiànxuè donate blood

献血者 xiànxuè zhě blood donor

险崖 xiǎnyá crag

鲜艳 xiānyàn bright; vivid; colorful ◊ brightly

先验 xiānyàn transcendental

显眼 xiǎnyǎn conspicuous ◊ stand out ◊ conspicuously

嫌疑 xiányí suspicion

嫌疑犯 xiányífàn suspect

献殷勤 xiàn yīnqín make advances

现有 xiànyǒu available; in existence

先于 xiānyú precede

陷于 xiànyú get into; 陷于困境 xiànyú kùnjìng get into difficulties

弦乐器 **xiányuè qì** stringed instrument

弦乐器演奏者 **xiányuè qì yǎnzòu zhě** string player; strings

现在 **xiànzài** now, at the moment; 现在不行 ***xiànzài bùxíng*** not now

现在看来 **xiànzài kànlái** in retrospect

现在时 **xiànzàishí** present tense

闲着 **xiánzhe** twiddle one's thumbs

闲置 **xiánzhì** idle *machinery*

限制 **xiànzhì** restriction; qualify *remark*; 限制 X ***xiànzhì X*** draw the line at X

线轴 **xiànzhóu** spool

显著 **xiǎnzhù** outstanding; prominent; striking, marked

仙子 **xiānzǐ** fairy; immortal

现做的饭 **xiànzuòde fàn** cooked meal

削 **xiāo** peel, skin; cut, trim; 用刀削净 ***yòng dāo xiāojìng*** scrape

消 **xiāo** disappear

小 **xiǎo** small, little; young; 她比我小十岁 ***tā bǐ wǒ xiǎo shísuì*** she is ten years my junior; 从小 ***cóng xiǎo*** from childhood

晓 **xiǎo** dawn ◊ know

笑 **xiào** laugh

效 **xiào** effect

孝 **xiào** filial

校 **xiào** school

小报 **xiǎobào** tabloid

小便 **xiǎobiàn** urine; pee ◊ urinate; pee

笑柄 **xiàobǐng** butt, target; 变成笑柄 ***biànchéng xiàobǐng*** become a laughing stock

小病 **xiǎobìng** indisposed

小部分 **xiǎobùfen** fraction

小菜 **xiǎocài** side dish

小菜一碟 **xiǎocài yìdié** small amount

小册子 **xiǎo cèzi** booklet, brochure, pamphlet

消沉 **xiāochén** dismal

小吃 **xiǎochī** snack

小吃店 **xiǎochīdiàn** snack bar

小丑 **xiǎochǒu** clown

消除 **xiāochú** eliminate, get rid of, delete ◊ elimination, deletion

小船 **xiǎochuán** boat; launch; dinghy

哮喘 **xiāochuǎn** asthma

小袋 **xiǎodài** pouch

小刀 **xiǎodāo** pocketknife

小调 **xiǎodiào** minor MUS; D 小调 ***D xiǎodiào*** in D minor

消毒 **xiāodú** sterilize, disinfect ◊ sterile

小段儿 **xiǎoduànr** bit, length

消毒剂 **xiāodú jì** disinfectant

小儿麻痹症 **xiǎo'ér mábìzhèng** polio

效仿 **xiàofǎng** imitate; 效仿 X ***xiàofǎng X*** follow in X's footsteps

消防车 **xiāofáng chē** fire truck

消防队 **xiāofáng duì** fire department

消防队员 **xiāofáng duìyuán** fireman, firefighter

消防龙头 **xiāofáng lóngtóu** hydrant, fireplug

消费 **xiāofèi** consume ◊ expense; consumption

小费 **xiǎofèi** tip

消费品 **xiāofèi pǐn** consumer goods

消费者 **xiāofèi zhě** consumer

消费者社会 **xiāofèi zhě shèhuì** consumer society

小公共 **xiǎo gōnggòng** public minibus

小狗 **xiǎogǒu** puppy

小姑 **xiǎogū** sister-in-law (*husband's younger sister*)

效果 **xiàoguǒ** effect; 效果不佳 ***xiàoguǒ bùjiā*** ineffective

小孩 **xiǎohái** child, kid

消耗 **xiāohào** use; consume ◊ consumption

消耗量 **xiāohào liàng** consumption (*quantity used*)

小河 **xiǎohé** stream, creek

消化 **xiāohuà** digest ◊ digestion; 消化不良 ***xiāohuà bùliáng*** indigestion

笑话 **xiàohua** joke, crack

小黄瓜 **xiǎohuángguā** gherkin

消化系统 **xiāohuà xìtǒng**

digestive system

销货点 **xiāohuò diǎn** point of sale

小伙子 **xiǎo huǒzi** lad, youth

消极 **xiāojí** negative; destructive

小鸡 **xiǎojī** chick

削价 **xiāojià** cut-price

削减 **xiāojiǎn** cut, ax ◊ cutback

小轿车 **xiǎo jiàochē** sedan, saloon

小教堂 **xiǎo jiàotáng** chapel

小姐 **xiǎojie** Miss ◊ young woman; 王小姐 *Wáng xiǎojiě* Miss Wang

小径 **xiǎojìng** track, trail

宵禁令 **xiāojìn lìng** curfew

小孔 **xiǎokǒng** puncture, hole

小块儿 **xiǎokuàir** bit

效力 **xiàolì** effect

小礼服 **xiǎo lǐfú** dinner jacket

销路 **xiāolù** sales; circulation

小路 **xiǎolù** path; back road

效率 **xiàolǜ** efficiency

小旅馆 **xiǎo lǚguǎn** inn

小萝卜 **xiǎoluóbo** radish

小马 **xiǎomǎ** pony

小麦 **xiǎomài** wheat

小猫 **xiǎomāo** kitten

小米 **xiǎomǐ** millet

消灭 **xiāomiè** destroy, exterminate, eradicate; 消灭有害动物 *xiāomiè yǒuhài dòngwù* pest control

消磨时间 **xiāomó shíjiān** pass the time

酵母 **xiàomǔ** yeast

小牛 **xiǎoniú** calf

小牛肉 **xiǎo niúròu** veal

小跑 **xiǎopǎo** trot

小朋友 **xiǎo péngyǒu** children

削皮 **xiāopí** peel, pare

小气 **xiǎoqì** mean; mean-spirited

消遣 **xiāoqiǎn** amuse oneself ◊ pastime

削铅笔刀 **xiāo qiānbǐ dāo** pencil sharpener

小汽车 **xiǎo qìchē** automobile

小圈子 **xiǎo quānzi** in-group

小人书 **xiǎorén shū** picture book

笑容满面 **xiǎoróng mǎnmiàn** beam, smile

削弱 **xiāoruò** diminish

消散 **xiāosàn** lift, clear

小山坡 **xiǎoshānpō** hill

小声 **xiǎoshēng** quiet

笑声 **xiàoshēng** laugh ◊ laughter

消失 **xiāoshī** disappear; go away; pass ◊ disappearance

小时 **xiǎoshí** hour

小事 **xiǎoshì** trivial matter

消瘦 **xiāoshòu** emaciated

销售 **xiāoshòu** sell, market ◊ sales, marketing

销售点 **xiāoshòu diǎn** (sales) outlet

销售额 **xiāoshòu'é** sales figures

销售会议 **xiāoshòu huìyì** sales meeting

小数 **xiǎoshù** decimal

小书包 **xiǎoshūbāo** schoolbag, satchel

小数点 **xiǎoshù diǎn** decimal point

小睡 **xiǎoshuì** grab some sleep; snooze

孝顺 **xiàoshùn** be devoted to

小说 **xiǎoshuō** novel; fiction

小说家 **xiǎoshuō jiā** novelist

小梳妆盒 **xiǎo shūzhuāng hé** vanity case

小叔子 **xiǎoshūzi** brother-in-law (*husband's younger brother*)

小淘气 **xiǎo táoqì** bully; rascal

萧条 **xiāotiáo** depression (*economic*) ◊ depressed

小题大做 **xiǎotí dàzuò** make a fuss

小艇 **xiǎotǐng** motor launch

小提琴 **xiǎo tíqín** violin, fiddle

小提琴家 **xiǎo tíqín jiā** violinist

小桶 **xiǎotǒng** keg

小偷 **xiǎotōu** thief; burglar

小偷小摸 **xiǎotōu xiǎomō** pilfering

小团 **xiǎotuán** pellet

消退 **xiāotuì** fade

小屋 **xiǎowū** hut

消息 **xiāoxi** news

小息 **xiǎoxī** coffee break

小虾 **xiǎoxiā** shrimp

小巷 **xiǎoxiàng** lane; side street

肖像 **xiàoxiàng** portrait

消息灵通 **xiāoxī língtōng** be in the know

小心 **xiǎoxīn** be careful ◊ carefully; 要很小心 **yào hěn xiǎoxīn** it requires great care

笑星 **xiàoxīng** joker

小型公共汽车 **xiǎoxíng gōnggòng qìchē** minibus

小型客车 **xiǎoxíng kèchē** compact MOT

小型摩托车 **xiǎoxíng mótuōchē** motorscooter

小心谨慎 **xiǎoxīn jǐnshèn** guarded ◊ gingerly

小心轻放 **xiǎoxīn qīngfàng** (handle) with care

小学 **xiǎoxué** elementary school

小学老师 **xiǎoxué lǎoshī** elementary teacher

小学生 **xiǎoxuéshēng** schoolchild

小阳春 **xiǎoyángchūn** Indian summer

逍遥法外 **xiāoyáo fǎwài** get off scot-free ◊ at large

消音器 **xiāoyīn qì** silencer

校友 **xiàoyǒu** schoolmate

校园 **xiàoyuán** campus

校长 **xiàozhǎng** principal, head teacher

小折刀 **xiǎo zhédāo** pocketknife

小装置 **xiǎozhuāngzhí** gadget

小字 **xiǎozì** small print

小卒 **xiǎozú** pawn

小组 **xiǎozǔ** panel

小组委员会 **xiǎozǔ wěiyuánhuì** subcommittee

吓跑 **xiàpǎo** scare away

下坡 **xiàpō** downhill

下坡滑雪 **xiàpō huáxuě** downhill skiing

下去 **xiàqù** go down; continue; 谈下去 **tán xiàqù** talk on, continue talking

吓人 **xiàrén** frightening; 吓人一跳 **xiàrényítiào** jump, give a jump

下士 **xiàshì** corporal MIL

下属 **xiàshǔ** subordinate

下述 **xiàshù** following

下水 **xiàshuǐ** launch ◊ downstream

下水道 **xiàshuǐ dào** drains, drainage

下水系统 **xiàshuǐ xìtǒng** sanitation

下塌 **xiàtā** stay

下台 **xiàtái** step down ◊ downfall

夏天 **xiàtiān** summer ◊ in the summer

下网 **xiàwǎng** log off ◊ offline

下午 **xiàwǔ** afternoon; 下午场 **xiàwǔ chǎng** matinée, afternoon show

下午好 **xiàwǔ hǎo** good afternoon

下陷 **xiàxiàn** sink, drop; subside

狭小 **xiáxiǎo** poky

下小雨 **xià xiǎoyǔ** it's spitting (with rain)

下斜 **xiàxié** descend (of road)

下雪 **xiàxuě** snow

侠义 **xiáyì** chivalrous

狭隘 **xiáyì** narrow views etc

下一步 **xià yībù** next

下一个 **xià yīgè** next; 谁是下一个？ **shuí shì xià yīgè?** who's next?

下意识 **xiàyìshí** subconscious

下雨 **xiàyǔ** rain; 下雨了 **xiàyǔ le** it's raining

瑕瑜互见 **xiáyú hùjiàn** patchy

下载 **xiàzǎi** download

狭窄 **xiázhǎi** narrow; confined

瞎子 **xiāzi** blind person

西班牙 **Xībānyá** Spain ◊ Spanish

细胞 **xìbāo** cell

西北部 **xīběi bù** northwest

稀薄 **xībó** thin

西部 **xībù** west; western

西部片 **xībùpiān** western (movie)

西餐 **xīcān** western cuisine

细察 **xìchá** scrutinize ◊ scrutiny

细长 **xìcháng** narrow; slim

洗车处 **xǐchē chù** car wash

洗车服务 **xǐchē fúwù** valet service (for cars)

吸尘 **xīchén** vacuum

吸尘器 **xīchén qì** vacuum cleaner

洗涤 **xǐdí** clean, wash; erase tape

洗涤槽 **xǐdícáo** sink

洗涤剂 **xǐdí jì** detergent

吸毒成瘾 **xīdú chéngyǐn** be hooked on drugs

吸毒者 **xīdú zhě** drug addict

歇 **xiē** rest

斜 **xié** slanting, oblique; diagonal

鞋 **xié** shoe; footwear

携 **xié** carry; hold

邪 **xié** evil

写 **xiě** write

谢 **xiè** thank

卸 **xiè** unload

泄 **xiè** release

蟹 **xiè** crab

斜槽 **xiécáo** chute

写出 **xiěchū** write out

鞋带 **xiédài** shoelace; strap

携带 **xiédài** take (along)

懈怠 **xièdài** slack, lax

携带式电脑 **xiédài shì diànnǎo** laptop

鞋底 **xiédǐ** sole

鞋店 **xiédiàn** shoestore

鞋钉 **xiédīng** spike (*on shoe*)

协定 **xiédìng** agreement

亵渎 **xièdú** blaspheme

邪恶 **xié'è** evil, wicked; spiteful

鞋跟 **xiégēn** heel

邂逅 **xièhòu** encounter

协会 **xiéhuì** association, institute

卸货 **xièhuò** unload

鞋匠 **xiéjiang** shoemaker, cobbler

邪教 **xiéjiào** cult, sect

谢绝 **xièjué** decline, refuse

斜靠 **xiékào** prop, lean

泄漏 **xièlòu** break; leak out; give away ◊ leak, disclosure

泄露 **xièlòu** disclose, reveal ◊ disclosure, revelation

泄密 **xièmì** reveal a secret

泄密者 **xièmì zhě** telltale

斜坡 **xiépō** slope, gradient

胁迫 **xiépò** blackmail

协商 **xiéshāng** negotiate ◊ negotiation

写生 **xiěshēng** sketch

邪视 **xiéshì** leer

斜视 **xiéshì** squint; look sideways

鞋刷 **xiéshuā** shoe brush

歇斯底里 **xiēsīdǐlǐ** hysteria ◊ hysterical; 歇斯底里的发作 **xiēsīdǐlǐde fāzuò** hysterics

斜体 **xiétǐ** italic

谢天谢地！ **xiètiān xièdì!** thank goodness!

协调 **xiétiáo** harmony;

coordination ◊ coordinate ◊ matching; 和 … 不协调 **hé … bù xiétiáo** clash with

写下 **xiěxià** write down; put down; enter

卸下 **xièxià** unload

斜线 **xiéxiàn** oblique, slash

谢谢 **xièxie** thank you, thanks

写信 **xiěxìn** write a letter

斜眼 **xiéyǎn** squint

泻药 **xièyào** laxative

斜倚 **xiéyǐ** recline

协议 **xiéyì** agreement, understanding; pact

鞋油 **xiéyóu** shoe cream, shoe polish

斜着 **xiézhe** sideways

楔子 **xiēzi** wedge

写字夹板 **xiězì jiábǎn** clipboard

协奏曲 **xiézòu qǔ** concerto

写作 **xiězuò** write (*as author*) ◊ writing (*career*)

洗发剂 **xǐfà jì** shampoo

洗发精 **xǐfà jīng** shampoo

稀饭 **xīfàn** rice porridge, congee

西方 **xīfāng** western; westerly

西方国家 **Xīfāng guójiā** the West ◊ Western

西方化 **Xīfānghuà** Westernized

西方人 **Xīfāngrén** Westerner

细分 **xìfēn** subdivide

西风 **xīfēng** westerly

西服 **xīfú** suit

媳妇 **xífù** daughter-in-law

膝盖骨 **xīgàigǔ** kneecap

吸干 **xīgān** blot

细高跟鞋 **xìgāogēnxié** stilettos

西瓜 **xīguā** watermelon

吸管 **xīguǎn** (drinking) straw

习惯 **xíguàn** custom; habit ◊ be accustomed to; 不习惯 X **bù xíguàn X** be unused to X

希罕 **xīhan** rare ◊ rarity

喜好 **xǐhào** like; love

西红柿 **xīhóngshì** tomato

西湖 **Xīhú** West Lake

喜欢 **xǐhuan** like, be fond of; enjoy; take to; relish

熄火 **xīhuǒ** stall (*of engine*)

袭击 **xíjī** attack; strike

洗剂 **xǐjì** lotion

洗劫 **xǐjié** ransack

细节 **xìjié** detail

洗洁精 **xǐjié jīng** dishwashing liquid

喜剧 **xǐjù** comedy

戏剧 **xìjù** drama, play ◊ dramatic, theatrical

戏剧家 **xìjù jiā** dramatist, playwright

细菌 **xìjūn** germ, bacterium

细菌战争 **xìjūn zhànzhēng** germ warfare

戏剧性 **xìjù xìng** dramatic, exciting

喜剧演员 **xǐjù yǎnyuán** comedian

希腊 **Xīlà** Greece ◊ Greek

细浪 **xìlàng** ripple

西兰花 **xīlánhuā** broccoli

洗礼 **xǐlǐ** baptize, christen ◊ baptism

细粒 **xìlì** granule

系列 **xìliè** series; range

奚落 **xīluò** ridicule

喜马拉雅山 **Xǐmǎlāyǎshān** Himalayas

西面 **xīmiàn** west

熄灭 **xīmiè** put out; quench; go out

心 **xīn** heart; mind; center

新 **xīn** new; unused; 我是新来的 **wǒ shì xīnlái de** I'm new to the job

锌 **xīn** zinc

辛 **xīn** bitter; hard

欣 **xīn** enjoy; appreciate

信 **xìn** faith; letter ◊ believe, trust; 他信佛 **tā xìn Fó** he's a Buddhist

西南 **xīnán** southwest ◊ southwestern

西南部 **xīnán bù** southwest

洗脑 **xǐnǎo** brainwash ◊ brainwashing

新兵 **xīnbīng** recruit

心不在焉 **xīnbúzàiyān** preoccupied; absent-minded

新潮 **xīncháo** trendy

新陈代谢 **xīnchén dàixiè** metabolism

信贷限额 **xìndài xiàn'é** credit limit

心烦 **xīnfán** frustrated; annoyed

新方向 **xīn fāngxiàng** new departure, new direction

心烦意乱 **xīnfán yìluàn** get ruffled

新发展 **xīn fāzhǎn** new departure, new development

信封 **xìnfēng** envelope

信服 **xìnfú** believe; 令人信服 **lìngrén xìnfú** compelling, convincing

星 **xīng** star

兴 **xīng** rise

行 **xíng** go ◊ expedition ◊ you're on!, ok; 星期五行吗？ **xīngqī wǔ xíngma?** are you ok for Friday?; 行了！ **xíngle!** enough!, that will do!

形 **xíng** shape, form

刑 **xíng** punishment

醒 **xíng** awake ◊ rouse

擤 **xíng** blow one's nose

杏 **xìng** apricot

性 **xìng** nature, character; gender; sex ◊ -ility; 可能性 **kě'néngxìng** possibility; 灵活性 **línghuóxìng** flexibility

姓 **xìng** surname, family name

兴 **xìng** spirit

幸 **xìng** lucky, fortunate

性爱 **xìng'ài** passion

性变态 **xìngbiàntài** pervert

性别 **xìngbié** gender, sex

性病 **xìngbìng** venereal disease

擤鼻涕 **xǐng bítì** blow one's nose

形成 **xíngchéng** form; come into existence ◊ formation

行程 **xíngchéng** trip

性传播疾病 **xìng chuánbō jíbìng** sexually transmitted disease

幸存 **xìngcún** survive ◊ survival

幸存者 **xìngcún zhě** survivor

行动 **xíngdòng** act ◊ action

幸而 **xìng'ér** mercifully

刑法 **xíngfǎ** criminal law, penal law

兴奋 **xīngfèn** excited ◊ excitement ◊ get excited; 令人兴奋 **lìngrén xīngfèn** exciting

幸奋 **xìngfèn** delight; drama, excitement

兴奋剂 **xīngfèn jì** stimulant

幸福 **xìngfú** happy ◊ happiness

性感 **xìnggǎn** sexy; sultry; sensual

兴高采烈 **xìnggāo cǎiliè** elated, exuberant ◊ elation

性格 **xìnggé** character, nature

性格外向的人 **xìnggé wàixiàng de rén** extrovert

星号 **xīnghào** asterisk

型号 **xínghào** model

猩红热 **xīnghóngrè** scarlet fever

性急 **xìngjí** impatient; petulant ◊ impatiently

性交 **xìngjiāo** sexual intercourse ◊ have sex; 与 X 性交 **yǔ X xìngjiāo** have sex with X

行经 **xíngjīng** menstruate

行经期 **xíngjīngqī** menstruation

醒酒 **xǐngjiǔ** sober up

行军 **xíngjūn** march

行军床 **xíngjūn chuáng** cot

幸亏 **xìngkuī** fortunately

醒来 **xǐnglái** wake up

行李 **xíngli** luggage, baggage

行李车 **xíngli chē** baggage car; baggage cart

行李传送带 **xíngli chuánsòngdài** (baggage) carousel

行李存放处 **xínglǐ cúnfàng chù** (baggage) checkroom

行李架 **xíngli jià** luggage rack

行李领取处 **xíngli lǐngqǔ chù** baggage reclaim

行李箱 **xínglǐ xiāng** trunk (of car)

兴隆 **xīnglóng** brisk

性能 **xìngnéng** performance; efficiency

星期 **xīngqī** week

行乞 **xíngqǐ** beg, panhandle

星期二 **xīngqī'èr** Tuesday

星期六 **xīngqīliù** Saturday

性情 **xìngqíng** temperament

星期日 **xīngqīrì** Sunday

星期三 **xīngqīsān** Wednesday

星期四 **xīngqīsì** Thursday

星期天 **xīngqītiān** Sunday

星期五 **xīngqīwǔ** Friday

星期一 **xīngqīyī** Monday

兴趣 **xìngqù** interest; 引起 X 的兴趣 **yǐnqǐ X de xìngqù** interest X

行人 **xíngrén** pedestrian

杏仁 **xìngrén** almond

人行道 **xíngrén dào** sidewalk

行人区 **xíngrén qū** pedestrian precinct

形容 **xíngróng** describe; 把 X 形容成 Y **bǎ X xíngróng chéng Y** describe X as Y

形容词 **xíngróngcí** adjective

性骚扰 **xìng sāorǎo** sexual harassment

行善者 **xíngshàn zhě** benefactor

兴盛 **xīngshèng** prosperity

行驶 **xíngshǐ** drive; go; travel; journey

行使 **xíngshǐ** exercise

刑事 **xíngshì** criminal; 有刑事记录 **yǒu xíngshì jìlù** have a criminal record

形势 **xíngshì** situation

形式 **xíngshì** form GRAM; formal; 这只是一种形式 **zhè zhǐshì yìzhǒng xíngshì** it's just a formality

形式上 **xíngshì shàng** formality

形体 **xíngtǐ** figure

星条旗 **Xīngtiáo qí** Stars and Stripes

新贵 **xīnguì** upstart

兴旺 **xīngwàng** flourish ◊ flourishing, prosperous

兴旺的企业 **xīngwàng de qǐyè** going concern

行为 **xíngwéi** behavior; deed; 行为的标准 **xíngwéide biāozhǔn** morals, standards of behavior; 行为规矩 **xíngwéi guīju** well-behaved

醒悟 **xǐngwù** awaken; realize; see things as they are

星象 **xīngxiàng** horoscope

形象 **xíngxiàng** image

形象包装 **xíngxiàng bāozhuāng** packaging, marketing

行销地区 **xíngxiāo dìqū** market

猩猩 **xīngxing** ape

行星 **xíngxīng** planet

行刑人 **xíngxíng rén** executioner

形形色色 **xíngxíng sèsè** varied, diverse

行凶抢劫 **xíngxióng qiǎngjié** mug ◊ mugging

行凶抢劫者 xíngxiōng qiǎngjié zhě mugger

性欲 xìngyù sexual desire, lust

性欲高潮 xìngyù gāocháo orgasm

幸运 xìngyùn fortunate ◊ fortunately ◊ good fortune; lucky break

幸灾乐祸 xìngzāi-lèhuò malicious delight

星占 xīngzhàn horoscope

行政 xíngzhèng administration ◊ administrative

行政机关 xíngzhèng jīguān civil service

行政系统 xíngzhèng xìtǒng bureaucracy

性质 xìngzhì quality; character

形状 xíngzhuàng form, shape

行走 xíngzǒu parade

辛亥革命 Xīnhài Gémìng 1911 Revolution

信号 xìnhào signal

新婚人 xīnhūn rén newlyweds

犀牛 xīniú rhinoceros

心悸 xīnjì palpitations

信笺 xìnjiān writing paper

信件 xìnjiàn letter; correspondence

新教 Xīnjiào Protestant

信教 xìnjiào devout

新教徒 Xīnjiàotú Protestant

新加坡 Xīnjiāpō Singapore ◊ Singaporean

新界 Xīnjiè New Territories

心肌梗塞 xīnjī gěngsè heart attack

薪金 xīnjīn pay

薪金支票 xīnjīn zhīpiào paycheck

心口灼热 xīnkǒu zhuórè heartburn

辛苦 xīnkǔ arduous, strenuous

欣快感 xīnkuàigǎn euphoria

辛辣 xīnlà sharp *taste*

信赖 xìnlài trust; rely on

新郎 xīnláng bridegroom

心理 xīnlǐ psychological ◊ psychologically, mentally

心理疾病 xīnlǐ jíbìng mental illness ◊ mentally ill

心灵感应 xīnlíng gǎnyìng telepathy ◊ telepathic

心理失调 xīnlǐ shītiáo maladjusted

心力衰竭 xīnlì shuāijié heart failure

心理学 xīnlǐ xué psychology ◊ psychological ◊ psychologically

心理学家 xīnlǐ xuéjiā psychologist

心理状态 xīnlǐ zhuàngtài mentality

心满意足 xīnmǎn yìzú contented, happy

新年 Xīnnián New Year (*Western*); 新年快乐 *Xīnnián kuàilè* Happy New Year

信念 xìnniàn conviction, belief

新娘 xīnniáng bride

芯片 xīnpiàn chip COMPUT

新起点 xīn qǐdiǎn new departure

心情 xīnqíng mood, frame of mind; 心情好 *xīnqínghǎo* good-humored

心儿 xīnr core

欣然 xīnrán readily; 欣然接受 *xīnrán jiēshòu* lap up, readily accept

新任 xīnrèn incoming, newly appointed

信任 xìnrèn trust ◊ confidence ◊ trusting

欣赏 xīnshǎng appreciate ◊ appreciation

心上人 xīnshàng rén sweetheart

心神不定 xīnshén bùdìng distraught

新生 xīnshēng newborn ◊ freshman

新式 xīnshì up-to-date

信使 xìnshǐ courier

新手 xīnshǒu beginner; rookie

薪水 xīnshuǐ salary

薪水级别 xīnshuǐ jíbié salary scale

薪水名册 xīnshuǐ míngcè payroll (*staff*)

薪水总额 xīnshuǐ zǒng'é payroll (*money*)

心算 xīnsuàn mental arithmetic

心碎 xīnsuì broken-hearted; 令人

心碎 **lìngrén xīnsuì** heartbreaking

心跳 **xīntiào** heartbeat

信条 **xìntiáo** creed

信徒 **xìntú** believer

喜怒无常 **xǐnù wúcháng** moody

新闻 **xīnwén** news

新闻报导 **xīnwén bàodǎo** news; news report

新闻播音员 **xīnwén bōyīn yuán** newsreader

新闻工作者 **xīnwén gōngzuò zhě** journalist

新闻广播 **xīnwén guǎngbō** newscast

新闻广播员 **xīnwén guǎngbō yuán** newscaster; anchor man

新闻界 **xīnwénjiè** the press

新闻写作 **xīnwén xiězuò** journalism (*writing*)

新闻业 **xīnwényè** journalism (*career*)

新闻自由 **xīnwén zìyǒu** freedom of the press

欣喜 **xīnxǐ** jubilant

信息 **xìnxī** information

新鲜 **xīnxiān** fresh ◊ freshness

信箱 **xìnxiāng** mailbox

信息技术 **xìnxī jìshù** information technology, IT

新西兰 **Xīnxīlán** New Zealand

信心 **xìnxīn** confidence

心胸宽阔 **xīnxiōng kuānkuò** broad-minded

心胸狭窄 **xīnxiōng xiázǎi** narrow-minded

欣喜若狂 **xīnxǐ ruò kuáng** rapture ◊ ecstatic

信息学 **xìnxī xué** information science

新芽 **xīnyá** sprout

信仰 **xìnyǎng** belief, faith

新颖 **xīnyǐng** novelty, freshness

新颖事物 **xīnyǐng shìwù** novelty

信以为真 **xìn yǐwéi zhēn** fall for

信用 **xìnyòng** credit FIN

信用卡 **xìnyòng kǎ** credit card

信誉 **xìnyù** credibility

新月 **xīnyuè** new moon

信誉卓著 **xìnyù zhuōzhù** creditworthy

心脏 **xīnzàng** heart ◊ cardiac

心脏病 **xīnzàng bìng** heart disease

心脏停跳 **xīnzàng tíngtiào** cardiac arrest

心脏移植 **xīnzàng yízhí** heart transplant

心照不宣 **xīnzhào bù xuān** knowing; tacit ◊ knowingly

信纸 **xìnzhǐ** writing paper

胸 **xiōng** chest; bust

兄 **xiōng** elder brother

凶 **xiōng** fierce; terrible; evil

熊 **xióng** bear

雄 **xióng** male

雄辩 **xióngbiàn** eloquent ◊ eloquently

兄弟 **xiōngdì** brothers

兄弟般 **xiōngdì ban** fraternal ◊ like brothers

兄弟姐妹 **xiōngdì jiěmèi** brothers and sisters

熊蜂 **xióngfēng** bumblebee

凶狠 **xiōnghěn** vicious

雄驹 **xióngjū** colt

熊猫 **xióngmāo** panda

凶猛 **xiōngměng** fierce

胸腔 **xiōngqiāng** thorax

凶杀 **xiōngshā** murder

凶手 **xiōngshǒu** murderer, killer

雄伟 **xióngwěi** imposing; majestic ◊ majestically

雄心勃勃 **xióngxīn bóbo** ambitious

雄性 **xióngxìng** male

熊熊燃烧 **xióngxiong ránshāo** blaze

匈牙利 **Xiōngyálì** Hungary ◊ Hungarian

胸罩 **xiōngzhào** brassière

胸针 **xiōngzhēn** brooch

锡箔 **xībó** tinfoil

锡铅合金 **xīqiān héjīn** pewter

系起来 **xì qǐlái** tie up *hair*

喜鹊 **xǐque** magpie

吸入 **xīrù** breathe in, inhale

吸入器 **xīrù qì** inhaler

稀少 **xīshǎo** rare ◊ rarity

细审 **xìshěn** sift through

牺牲 **xīshēng** sacrifice

细绳 **xìshéng** string

系绳 **xìshéng** tether

牺牲品 **xīshēng pǐn** victim

稀释 **xīshì** dilute, water down

吸收 **xīshōu** absorb

洗手间 **xǐshǒu jiān** bathroom

稀疏 **xīshū** sparse

蟋蟀 **xīshuài** cricket

嬉水 **xīshuǐ** splash

习俗 **xísú** custom

细条纹 **xìtiáowén** pinstripe

系统 **xìtǒng** system; set-up ◊ systematic

系统崩溃 **xìtǒng béngkuì** system crash

系统分析者 **xìtǒng fēnxī zhě** systems analyst

羞 **xiū** shame; embarrass

修 **xiū** repair; 把车修了 **bǎ chē xiūle** get the car fixed

休 **xiū** stop; rest; 休病假 **xiū bìngjià** be on sick leave

锈 **xiù** rust

嗅 **xiù** smell, sniff

袖 **xiù** sleeve

秀 **xiù** beautiful

修补 **xiūbǔ** mend; darn; reinforce

羞耻 **xiūchǐ** disgrace, shame

羞答答 **xiū dáda** coy

修道士 **xiūdàoshì** monastic

修道院 **xiūdàoyuàn** convent; monastery

修订 **xiūdìng** update

修复 **xiūfù** restore, recondition ◊ restoration

修改 **xiūgǎi** correct, amend; modify ◊ correction, amendment; modification; 他们要修改法律 **tāmén yào xiūgǎi fǎlǜ** they are going to change the law

休会 **xiūhuì** adjourn

休假 **xiūjià** vacation; recess ◊ take a vacation; take leave; 休假一天 **xiūjià yītiān** take a day off

修剪 **xiūjiǎn** crop; prune

修剪指甲 **xiūjiǎn zhǐjiǎ** manicure

嗅觉 **xiùjué** sense of smell

休克 **xiūkè** shock; 处于休克状态 **chǔyú xiūkè zhuàngtài** be in shock

袖口 **xiùkǒu** cuff

袖口链扣 **xiùkǒu liànkòu** cuff link

羞愧 **xiūkuì** ashamed

修理 **xiūlǐ** repair, fix

秀丽 **xiùlì** beautiful; dainty

修理车间 **xiūlǐ chējiān** workshop; garage

修理工 **xiūlǐ gōng** repairman

休眠 **xiūmián** dormant

修女 **xiūnǚ** nun

羞怯 **xiūqiè** shy; sheepish

羞辱 **xiūrǔ** humiliate ◊ humiliation

修缮 **xiūshàn** renovate, do up

修饰 **xiūshì** touch up

袖手旁观 **xiùshǒu pángguān** stand by

休息 **xiūxi** rest, take a break ◊ recess; 休息吧！ **xiūxiba!** let's call it a day!

休息一下 **xiūxi yíxià** take a break

休息日 **xiūxīrì** holiday

休养 **xiūyǎng** recuperate, recover

休养疗法 **xiūyǎng liáofǎ** rest cure

休战 **xiūzhàn** truce

袖珍 **xiùzhēn** compact; midget

袖珍本 **xiùzhēn běn** pocketbook, paperback

修正 **xiūzhèng** revise, correct ◊ revision

修正主义 **xiūzhèng zhǔyì** revisionism ◊ revisionist

袖珍型 **xiùzhēn xíng** miniature

休止 **xiūzhǐ** cessation

袖子 **xiùzi** sleeve

洗碗布 **xǐwǎn bù** dishcloth

希望 **xīwàng** hope; wish; 希望如此 **xīwàng rúcǐ** I hope so

洗碗工 **xǐwǎn gōng** dishwasher (*person*)

洗碗机 **xǐwǎn jī** dishwasher (*machine*)

洗碗水 **xǐwǎn shuǐ** dishwater

席位 **xíwèi** seat POL

细微 **xìwēi** fine *distinction*

细心 **xìxīn** careful; considerate

熙熙攘攘 **xīxi rǎngrang** busy, crowded

信息学家 **xìxī xuéjiā** information scientist

吸烟 **xīyān** smoke; have a smoke ◊ smoking; 请勿吸烟 **qǐngwù**

xīyān please refrain from smoking

吸烟车厢 **xīyān chēxiāng** smoking compartment

吸烟者 **xīyān zhě** smoker

西药 **xīyào** Western medicine (*drugs etc*)

西医 **xīyī** Western medicine (*science*)

蜥蜴 **xīyì** lizard

洗衣店 **xǐyī diàn** laundry (*place*)

洗衣粉 **xǐyī fěn** soap powder, detergent

洗衣服 **xǐyīfu** get one's laundry done; do the washing

洗衣服务 **xǐyī fúwù** valet service (*for clothes*)

洗衣机 **xǐyī jī** washing machine

吸引 **xīyǐn** attract, draw; fascinate, charm; tempt

吸引力 **xīyǐn lì** attraction; appeal

习以为常 **xí yǐ wéi cháng** usual ◊ used to

洗一洗 **xǐyīxǐ** have a wash, wash up

稀有 **xīyǒu** rare

喜悦 **xǐyuè** happy

西藏 **Xīzàng** Tibet ◊ Tibetan

洗澡 **xǐzǎo** bathe; shower ◊ bathing

洗澡间 **xǐzǎo jiān** bathroom

锡纸 **xīzhǐ** tinfoil

细枝 **xìzhī** twig

西装 **xīzhuāng** suit

戏装 **xìzhuāng** costume (*actor's*)

西装上衣 **xīzhuāng shàngyī** coat (*of a suit*)

席子 **xízi** mat

须 **xū** must ◊ whiskers

需 **xū** need

虚 **xū** empty ◊ void

许 **xǔ** promise; permit

叙 **xù** narrate

序 **xù** order, sequence

续 **xù** continue

宣 **xuān** declare

旋 **xuán** rotate; spin, whirl

悬 **xuán** hang, suspend

选 **xuǎn** choose, pick; elect; highlight COMPUT; 他们选他当总统 **tāmén xuǎn tā dāng zǒngtǒng** they voted him

President

选拔 **xuǎnbá** selection

选拔赛 **xuǎnbásài** qualifier, qualifying game

宣布 **xuānbù** announce, declare, proclaim ◊ declaration

宣布无罪 **xuānbù wúzuì** exonerate

选出 **xuǎnchū** elected

宣传 **xuānchuán** promotion, publicity, propaganda ◊ promote, publicize, plug

宣传家 **xuānchuán jiā** publicist; spin doctor

悬垂 **xuánchuí** dangle

选词 **xuǎncí** word

悬而未决 **xuán ér wèi jué** be pending ◊ undecided

旋风 **xuànfēng** whirlwind

宣告 **xuāngào** announce ◊ announcement

悬挂 **xuánguà** suspend, hang

喧哗 **xuānhuá** din, racket ◊ noisy

喧哗声 **xūanhuá shēng** noise

选举 **xuǎnjǔ** election ◊ elect

选举权 **xuǎnjǔ quán** right to vote; 有选举权 *yǒu xuǎnjǔ quán* have the vote

选举日 **xuǎnjǔ rì** election day

选举投票 **xuǎnjǔ tóupiào** vote, go to the polls

选举制度 **xuǎnjǔ zhìdù** electoral system

旋律 **xuánlù** melody

选民 **xuǎnmín** elector, voter

眩目 **xuànmù** blinding

眩目电闪 **xuánmù diànshǎn** bolt of lightning

喧闹 **xuānnào** racket, tumult ◊ noisy, rowdy; tumultuous ◊ blare out

喧闹声 **xuānnào shēng** din

悬念 **xuánniàn** suspense

宣判 **xuānpàn** pass judgment; 宣判无罪 *xuānpàn wúzuì* acquit; 宣判有罪 *xuānpàn yǒuzuì* convict

选票 **xuǎnpiào** vote

轩然大波 **xuānrán dàbō** fuss, stink

选入 **xuǎnrù** vote in

悬赏 **xuánshǎng** offer a reward

宣誓 **xuānshì** swear an oath

选手 **xuǎnshǒu** competitor

悬殊 **xuánshū** disparity

旋涡 **xuánwō** whirlpool

喧嚣 **xuānxiāo** uproar, hullabaloo

悬崖 **xuányá** cliff, bluff

宣言 **xuānyán** manifest

宣扬 **xuānyáng** advertising

炫耀 **xuànyào** show off; parade, flaunt ◊ pretentious

眩晕 **xuànyùn** giddiness, vertigo

选择 **xuǎnzé** choice, option ◊ choose, select

选择过程 **xuǎnzé guòchéng** selection process

宣战 **xuānzhàn** declare war ◊ declaration of war

旋转 **xuánzhuǎn** revolve; rotate; spin; whirl ◊ revolution, rotation

旋转门 **xuánzhuǎn mén** revolving door

旋转木马 **xuánzhuǎn mùmǎ** carousel

旋转炮塔 **xuánzhuǎn pàotǎ** turret (of tank)

絮叨 **xùdao** harp on about

蓄电池 **xù diànchí** storage battery

许多 **xǔduō** many; much; a lot of

靴 **xuē** boot

学 **xué** study; learn

穴 **xué** hole; cave

雪 **xuě** snow

血 **xuè** blood

雪白 **xuěbái** snow-white

雪崩 **xuěbēng** avalanche

雪堆 **xuěduī** snowdrift

血管 **xuèguǎn** blood vessel

雪花 **xuěhuā** snowflake

学会 **xuéhuì** learn ◊ academy

血迹 **xuèjī** bloodstain

雪茄 **xuějiā** cigar

削减 **xuējiǎn** cut, trim; whittle down

血库 **xuèkù** blood bank

血块 **xuěkuài** blood clot

雪犁 **xuělí** snowplow

雪莲 **xuělián** snowdrop

雪利酒 **xuělì jiǔ** sherry

血淋淋 **xuè línlin** bloody

学年 **xuénián** academic year

学期 **xuéqī** semester, term

雪橇 **xuěqiāo** bobsleigh, bobsled; sled, sleigh

血亲 **xuèqīn** blood relative

雪球 **xuěqiú** snowball

血球 **xuèqiú** corpuscle

雪人 **xuěrén** snowman

削弱 **xuēruò** impaired ◊ weaken

学生 **xuésheng** student

学生时代 **xuésheng shídài** school days

学术 **xuéshù** academic

血栓形成 **xuěshuān xíngchéng** thrombosis

学术成就 **xuéshù chéngjiù** scholarship (work)

学说 **xuéshuō** doctrine

血统 **xuètǒng** breed; pedigree

噱头 **xuétóu** patter, spiel; publicity stunt

学徒 **xuétú** apprentice, novice

学位 **xuéwèi** (university) degree

穴位 **xuéwèi** acupuncture point

学问 **xuéwen** knowledge

雪屋 **xuěwū** igloo

学习 **xuéxí** study; learn ◊ studying; learning; 学习驾驶 **xuéxí jiàshǐ** learn to drive; 学习曲线 **xuéxí qūxiàn** learning curve

学校 **xuéxiào** school

学校假期 **xuéxiào jiàqī** school vacation

血型 **xuèxíng** blood group

血压 **xuèyā** blood pressure

血液 **xuèyè** bloodstream

血液循环 **xuèyè xúnhuán** circulation

血液样本 **xuèyè yàngběn** blood sample

学员 **xuéyuán** cadet

学院 **xuéyuàn** college; academy; school

学者 **xuézhě** scholar

血肿 **xuèzhǒng** hematoma

血中毒 **xuè zhòngdú** blood poisoning

靴子 **xuēzi** boot

虚构 **xūgòu** make up ◊ fictitious

虚构情节 **xūgòu qíngjié** embroider, embellish story

虚话 xūhuà myth, fiction

续集 xùjí sequel, continuation

虚假 xūjiǎ hollow, meaningless ◊ pretense

许久 xǔjiǔ a long time

酗酒 xùjiǔ drink, booze

酗酒者 xùjiǔ zhě alcoholic

许可 xǔkě permission, authority ◊ license, permit

许可证 xǔkě zhèng permit, warrant

畜牧 xùmù raise livestock

序幕 xùmù prolog

熏 xūn smoke

询 xún inquire

寻 xún seek

巡 xún patrol, cruise

驯 xún tame

训 xùn instruct, train

迅 xùn fast, rapid

巡边员 xúnbiān yuán linesman

训斥 xùnchì reprimand

殉道者 xùndào zhě martyr

驯服 xùnfú tame, docile

巡官 xúnguān inspector (of police)

驯化 xùnhuà domesticate

循环 xúnhuán circulate ◊ circulation; cycle

巡回 xúnhuí round (of doctor etc)

虚拟现实 xūnǐ xiànshí virtual reality

巡警 xúnjǐng patrolman

训练 xùnliàn train ◊ training

训练班 xùnliàn bān training course

训练有素 xùnliàn yǒusù skillful; polished

巡逻 xúnluó patrol

巡逻车 xúnluó chē patrol car

巡逻队 xúnluó duì patrol

荨麻 xúnmá nettle

训兽者 xùnshòu zhě trainer (of dog)

迅速 xùnsù swift, speedy; express ◊ speedily, swiftly; 他们沿路迅速前进 **tāmen yánlù xùnsù qiánjìn** they pelted along the road

迅速上升 xùnsù shàngshēng shoot up (of prices)

迅速增长 xùnsù zēngzhǎng mushroom, spread

许诺 xǔnuò promise

询问 xúnwèn inquire; interrogate ◊ inquiry; interrogation

勋章 xūnzhāng medal; decoration

寻找 xúnzhǎo search for, look for, seek

需求 xūqiú demand

序曲 xùqǔ overture

虚荣 xūróng vanity

虚弱 xūruò weak, frail, feeble ◊ frailty, weakness

叙事体 xùshì tǐ narrative

叙事者 xùshì zhě narrator

叙述 xùshù relate, narrate, tell ◊ narration, account, story

虚伪 xūwěi hypocrisy; insincerity ◊ hypocritical

虚线 xūxiàn perforated line

虚心 xūxīn open-minded

嘘嘘声 xūxu shēng boo

序言 xùyán introduction

需要 xūyào need, require; cost; take; entail ◊ requirement, need; 有需要 **yǒu xūyào** in demand

蓄意 xùyì systematically

虚张声势 xūzhāng shēngshì bravado, bluff

Y

压 **yā** press, crush ◊ pressure
鸭 **yā** duck
鸦 **yā** crow
押 **yā** mortgage; pawn
呀 **yā** (*being at loss*): 呀，这怎么办呢？ *yā, zhè zěnme bàn ne?* oh god, what am I going to do?
牙 **yá** tooth
哑 **yǎ** dumb, mute
亚 **yà** inferior; second best
牙斑 **yábān** plaque
牙齿 **yáchǐ** tooth ◊ dental
牙齿检查 **yáchǐ jiǎnchá** dental checkup
压低 **yādī** keep down *voice etc*
牙膏 **yágāo** toothpaste
雅观 **yǎguān** graceful; refined
押金 **yājīn** deposit, security
亚军 **yàjūn** runner-up
牙科 **yákē** dentistry ◊ dental
哑口无言 **yǎkǒu wúyán** speechless
压力 **yālì** pressure; stress
哑铃 **yǎlíng** dumbbell
亚麻布 **yàmá bù** linen
腌 **yān** salt; pickle; cure
烟 **yān** smoke
淹 **yān** drown
言 **yán** word; words; talking; speech
盐 **yán** salt
严 **yán** tight; rigorous
颜 **yán** face; color
研 **yán** grind; research
岩 **yán** cliff; rock
延 **yán** extend
沿 **yán** along
演 **yǎn** perform
眼 **yǎn** eye
堰 **yàn** weir
咽 **yàn** swallow
宴 **yàn** banquet, feast
燕 **yàn** swallow (*bird*)
厌 **yàn** hate; dislike
砚 **yàn** inkstone

验 **yàn** test, check
掩蔽 **yǎnbì** cover, shelter
掩蔽物 **yǎnbì wù** shelter, screen
演播室 **yǎnbō shì** (TV) studio
掩藏 **yǎncáng** hide; disguise *fear etc*
烟草 **yāncǎo** tobacco
檐槽 **yáncáo** gutter
延长 **yáncháng** extend, lengthen; prolong ◊ lengthy, protracted
延迟 **yánchí** delay
演出 **yǎnchū** perform ◊ performance
烟囱 **yāncōng** chimney; ship's funnel
烟蒂 **yāndì** cigarette butt
烟斗 **yāndǒu** pipe (*for smoking*)
厌烦 **yànfán** be fed up
羊 **yáng** sheep
洋 **yáng** ocean
阳 **yáng** yang; sun
杨 **yáng** poplar
扬 **yáng** raise
痒 **yǎng** itch
养 **yǎng** keep, rear *animals*
氧 **yǎng** oxygen
仰 **yǎng** look up
样 **yàng** style; type; sample; model
掩盖 **yǎngài** cover, cover up; mask
掩盖真相 **yǎngài zhēnxiàng** coverup
洋白菜 **yángbái cài** cabbage (*Northern China*)
样本 **yàngběn** sample, specimen
养病 **yǎngbìng** convalesce
养蚕业 **yǎngcányè** silkworm breeding
养成 **yǎngchéng** pick up *habit*; 养成习惯 **yǎngchéng ... xíguàn** take to, make a habit of
洋葱 **yángcōng** onion
阉割 **yāngē** neuter; castrate
严格 **yángé** rigorous, strict ◊ rigor, strictness

扬帆驾驶 **yángfān jiàshǐ** sailing

养父母 **yǎngfùmǔ** foster parents

羊倌 **yángguān** shepherd

阳光 **yángguāng** sunshine

阳光充足 **yángguāng chōngzú** sunny

洋鬼子 **yáng guǐzi** *pej* foreign devil, damn foreigner

氧化物 **yǎnghuà wù** oxide

养老金 **yǎnglǎo jīn** pension

养老院 **yǎnglǎo yuàn** old people's home

羊毛 **yángmáo** wool

羊毛衣物 **yángmáo yīwù** woolen clothing

阉公牛 **yān gōngniú** steer (*animal*)

羊皮 **yángpí** sheepskin

样品 **yàngpǐn** specimen, sample

氧气 **yǎngqì** oxygen

羊绒 **yángróng** cashmere

羊肉 **yángròu** mutton

阳伞 **yángsǎn** sunshade, parasol

养神 **yǎngshén** relax

扬声器 **yángshēng qì** loudspeaker

样式 **yàngshì** pattern

杨树 **yángshù** poplar tree

阳台 **yángtái** balcony; patio; terrace

验关 **yànguān** customs inspection

验光 **yànguāng** eye test

言过其实 **yán guò qí shí** exaggeration

仰望 **yǎngwàng** look up

阳萎 **yángwěi** impotence ◊ impotent

仰卧 **yǎngwò** lie on one's back

阳性 **yángxìng** positive *test result*

洋洋大作 **yángyang dàzuò** blockbuster

仰泳 **yǎngyǒng** backstroke

养育 **yǎngyù** bring up

养鱼缸 **yǎngyúgāng** aquarium

严寒 **yánhán** frosty

烟盒 **yānhé** cigarette case

咽喉 **yānhóu** gullet; larynx

掩护 **yǎnhù** camouflage

延缓 **yánhuǎn** postpone, delay

宴会 **yànhuì** dinner party; banquet

烟灰缸 **yānhuī gāng** ashtray

烟火 **yānhuǒ** fireworks

烟火表演 **yānhuǒ biǎoyǎn** firework display

眼睑 **yǎnjiǎn** eyelid

演讲 **yǎnjiǎng** lecture, talk

演讲者 **yǎnjiǎng zhě** speaker

岩礁 **yánjiāo** ledge (*on rock face*)

眼睫毛 **yǎn jiémáo** eyelash

严谨 **yánjǐn** tight

严禁 **yánjìn** forbidden

眼睛 **yǎnjīng** eye

眼镜 **yǎnjìng** glasses

眼睛疲劳 **yǎnjīng píláo** eye strain

研究 **yánjiū** study, research

研究课题 **yánjiū kètí** research project

研究生 **yánjiū shēng** postgraduate

研究员 **yánjiú yuán** researcher

厌倦 **yànjuàn** be tired of, be sick of

严峻 **yánjùn** forbidding; somber

眼科医生 **yǎnkē yīshēng** ophthalmologist

严酷 **yánkù** stark, grim

眼泪 **yǎnlèi** teardrop

眼泪汪汪 **yǎnlèi wāngwang** tearful

严厉 **yánlì** severe ◊ severely

颜料 **yánliào** paint

严厉盘问 **yánlì pánwèn** interrogate, grill

严厉批评 **yánlì pīpíng** criticize, pan

言论自由 **yánlùn zìyóu** free speech

燕麦片 **yànmài piàn** oatmeal; oats

淹没 **yānmò** flood; submerge; deluge; drown out; 淹没堤岸 **yānmò tí'àn** flood its banks

赝品 **yànpǐn** fake

延期 **yánqī** postpone; extend ◊ postponement; extension

眼球 **yǎnqiú** eyeball

烟圈儿 **yānquānr** wisp of smoke

颜色 **yánsè** color; coloring

延伸 **yánshēn** stretch, extend

岩石 **yánshí** rock

掩饰 **yǎnshì** cover up; 替X掩饰错误缺点 **tì X yǎnshì cuòwù quēdiǎn** cover up for X

验尸 **yànshī** autopsy

厌食 **yànshí** be anorexic

验尸官 **yànshī guān** coroner

厌食症 **yànshí zhèng** anorexia

演说家 **yǎnshuō jiā** orator; speaker

淹死 **yānsǐ** drown

严肃 **yánsù** serious; stern; sober; solemn ◊ severity

研讨会 **yántǎo huì** seminar

燕尾服 **yànwěifú** tail coat

烟雾 **yānwù** smog

延误 **yánwù** delay, holdup

厌恶 **yànwù** hate; have an aversion to; 令人厌恶 **lìngrén yànwù** distasteful; sickening; repulsive

演习 **yǎnxí** exercise, drill, maneuver

演戏 **yǎnxì** put on a play; perform

眼下 **yǎnxià** at present

咽峡炎 **yānxiá yán** angina

延续 **yánxù** continue, last

验血 **yànxuè** blood test

眼药水 **yǎnyàoshuǐ** eyedrops

演艺界 **yǎnyìjiè** show business

眼影膏 **yǎnyǐnggāo** eyeshadow

谚语 **yànyǔ** saying, proverb

演员 **yǎnyuán** actor; actress

演员表 **yǎnyuán biǎo** cast

言语 **yányǔ** speech

言语矫治师 **yányǔ jiǎozhì shī** speech therapist

言语缺陷 **yányǔ quēxiàn** speech defect

沿着 **yánzhe** follow, go along; stick to *path etc* ◊ down, along; 他们沿着街跑 **tāmen yánzhe jiē pǎo** they ran up the street

验证 **yànzhèng** identification ◊ test; verify

胭脂 **yānzhī** blusher

严重 **yánzhòng** severe, grave; serious; drastic ◊ gravity, seriousness

燕子 **yànzi** swallow (*bird*)

演奏 **yǎnzòu** perform, play *music* ◊ rendition, playing, performance

演奏会 **yǎnzòu huì** recital

演奏者 **yǎnzòu zhě** player, musician

烟嘴 **yānzuǐ** tip (*of cigarette*)

要 **yāo** demand

腰 **yāo** waist

妖 **yāo** monster; ghost

邀 **yāo** invite

幺 **yāo** one (*in phone numbers*)

窑 **yáo** kiln

摇 **yáo** shake

遥 **yáo** far away, distant

咬 **yǎo** bite

舀 **yǎo** scoop

药 **yào** drug, medicine; medication

要 **yào** want; need; must; will ◊ if; 你要什么都行 **nǐ yào shénme dōu xíng** you can have whatever you want; 天也许要下雨 **tiān yěxǔ yào xiàyǔ** it might rain; 我要和你谈话 **wǒ yào hé nǐ táihuà** I need to talk to you

摇摆 **yáobǎi** roll, sway; swing; toss ◊ unsteady

腰包 **yāobāo** fanny pack

腰部 **yāobù** waist

药草 **yàocǎo** herb

药草茶 **yàocǎo chá** herbal tea

舀出 **yǎochū** scoop up

腰带 **yāodài** belt; girdle

要道 **yàodào** main street

要点 **yàodiǎn** key point; core, nub

药店 **yàodiàn** pharmacy, drugstore

摇动 **yáodòng** wave; shake; flap

要饭 **yàofàn** beg

药方 **yàofāng** prescription

药房 **yàofáng** dispensary; pharmacy, drugstore

妖怪 **yāoguài** monster; ghost

摇滚乐 **yáogǔn yuè** rock music, rock and roll

摇滚乐歌星 **yáogǔn yuè gēxīng** rock star

摇晃 **yáohuang** rock; tremble; wobble ◊ shaky

咬紧 **yǎojǐn** clench

要紧 **yàojǐn** important, vital ◊ matter

药剂师 **yàojì shī** druggist, pharmacist

遥控 **yáokòng** remote control

摇篮 **yáolán** cradle

摇橹 **yáolǔ** paddle

幼苗 **yòumiáo** seedling

药片 **yàopiàn** tablet

药品 **yàopǐn** medicine

药签 **yàoqiān** swab

邀请 **yāoqǐng** invite ◊ invitation

要求 **yāoqiú** request, ask for; demand, require ◊ demand; call

要人 **yàorén** VIP

要塞 **yàosài** fort

摇上 **yáoshàng** wind up *window*

钥匙 **yàoshi** key

要是 **yàoshi** if

钥匙圈 **yàoshiquān** keyring

药水 **yàoshuǐ** tonic

腰疼 **yāoténg** lumbago

腰痛 **yāotòng** lumbago

摇头 **yáotóu** shake one's head

摇头丸儿 **yáotóuwánr** ecstasy (*drug*)

药丸 **yàowán** pill

腰围 **yāowéi** waistline

药物 **yàowù** drug

摇下 **yáoxià** wind down *window*

谣言 **yáoyán** rumor

耀眼 **yàoyǎn** dazzle ◊ dazzling

摇摇欲坠 **yáoyao yùzhuì** ramshackle

摇椅 **yáoyǐ** rocking chair

遥远 **yáoyuǎn** far away

腰子 **yāozi** kidney

鸦片 **yāpiàn** opium

鸦片战争 **Yāpiàn Zhànzhēng** Opium War

压迫 **yāpò** oppress

牙签 **yáqiān** toothpick

牙刷 **yáshuā** toothbrush

压缩 **yāsuō** compress; condense, shorten; zip up COMPUT

压缩空气 **yāsuō kōngqì** compressed air

压缩驱动器 **yāsuō qūdòngqì** zip drive

牙套 **yátào** (dental) brace

牙疼 **yáténg** toothache

牙痛 **yátòng** toothache

牙医 **yáyī** dentist

压抑 **yàyì** inhibit; repress; muffle ◊ inhibited; pent-up ◊ inhibition

压印 **yāyìn** imprint (*of credit card*)

牙龈 **yáyín** gum

压韵 **yāyùn** rhyme; 以 ... 压韵 **yǐ ... yāyùn** rhyme with ...

压制 **yāzhì** suppress, clamp down on; silence ◊ repressive

雅致 **yǎzhì** gracious, elegant

亚洲 **Yàzhōu** Asia ◊ Asian

亚洲人 **Yàzhōu rén** Asian

椰 **yē** coconut

爷 **yé** grandpa, grandfather (*paternal*)

也 **yě** too, also, as well; 她也是 **tā yě shì** so is she; 一点也不奇怪 **yìdiǎn yě bù qíguài** not in the least surprised

野 **yě** wild

液 **yè** liquid

夜 **yè** night

页 **yè** page

叶 **yè** leaf

业 **yè** business; industry

夜班 **yèbān** night shift

夜班服务员 **yèbān fúwùyuán** night porter

野餐 **yěcān** picnic

野地 **yědì** wilderness

野鸡 **yějī** unregistered, unlicensed; worthless; mickey-mouse

夜间 **yèjiān** at night; 夜间飞行 **yèjiān fēixíng** night flight; 夜间旅行 **yèjiān lǚxíng** travel by night

液晶体显示器 **yèjīngtǐ xiǎnshìqì** LCD, liquid crystal display

冶炼厂 **yěliàn chǎng** iron and steel works

叶轮机 **yèlún jī** steam turbine

页码 **yèmǎ** page number

野蛮 **yěmán** inhuman

野牛 **yěniú** buffalo

叶片 **yèpiàn** blade (*of grass*)

野人 **yěrén** savage

野生 **yěshēng** wild

野生动物保护区 **yěshēng dòngwù bǎohù qū** animal sanctuary

夜生活 **yè shēnghuó** nightlife

野生鸟兽 **yěshēng niǎoshòu** wildlife

夜市 **yèshì** night market

野兽 **yěshòu** wild beast

耶稣 **Yēsū** Jesus

液体 **yètǐ** liquid

野兔 **yětù** hare

夜晚 **yèwǎn** night

腋窝 **yèwō** armpit

夜校 **yèxiào** evening classes; night

school

野心 **yěxīn** ambition; greed

野性 **yěxìng** savage; wild

也许 **yěxǔ** may, might ◊ perhaps, possibly, maybe; 我也许迟到 **wǒ yěxǔ chídào** I might be late

液压 **yèyā** hydraulic

野丫头 **yěyātóu** tomboy

爷爷 **yéye** grandpa, grandfather (*paternal*)

夜莺 **yèyīng** nightingale

野营车 **yěyíng chē** camper (*vehicle*)

野营者 **yěyíng zhě** camper (*person*)

业余 **yèyú** amateur

业余爱好者 **yèyú àihào zhě** amateur

业余时间 **yèyú shíjiān** spare time

野猪 **yězhū** wild boar

业主 **yèzhǔ** proprietor

液状 **yèzhuàng** liquid

椰子 **yēzi** coconut

叶子 **yèzi** leaf; foliage

椰子奶 **yēzi nǎi** coconut milk

椰子树 **yēzi shù** coconut palm

夜总会 **yèzǒnghuì** nightclub; nightspot

一 **yī** one

衣 **yī** clothes; item of clothing

依 **yī** depend on ◊ according to; 依我看 **yī wǒ kàn** as far as I can see

医 **yī** medicine; doctor

姨 **yí** aunt (*mother's sister*)

遗 **yí** lose; leave behind

仪 **yí** ceremony, rite

移 **yí** move

疑 **yí** doubt, suspect

椅 **yǐ** chair

倚 **yǐ** lean on; depend on

已 **yǐ** already

以 **yǐ** by; according to; 以 X 为目标 **yǐ X wéi mùbiāo** with a view to X; 以 X 著名 **yǐ X zhùmíng** be famous for X

意 **yì** thought, idea; intention; meaning

溢 **yì** overflow

抑 **yì** suppress

易 **yì** easy ◊ change; exchange

义 **yì** justice

议 **yì** discuss

亿 **yì** hundred million

艺 **yì** art; craft

译 **yì** translate

异 **yì** different; strange; foreign

议案 **yì'àn** bill POL

一百 **yìbǎi** one hundred

一百周年 **yìbǎi zhōunián** centenary, centennial

一般 **yìbān** ordinary, usual; mediocre ◊ usually, generally

一半 **yíbàn** half

一帮 **yìbāng** gang

易饱 **yìbǎo** stodgy

贻贝 **yíbèi** mussel

一辈子 **yī bèizi** one's whole life, a lifetime

一笔 **yìbǐ** brushstroke

一边 **yìbiān** aside

易变 **yìbiàn** unsettled

一边倒 **yìbiān dǎo** one-sided

易辨认 **yìbiànrèn** legible

仪表 **yíbiǎo** dial; dashboard

疑病症患者 **yíbìngzhèng huàn zhě** hypochondriac

易剥落 **yì bōluò** flaky

一波三折 **yìbō sānzhé** stormy *relationship*

一步 **yíbù** move (*in chess*)

一部分 **yíbùfen** part; portion; fragment

一层 **yīcéng** blanket (*of snow etc*)

易察觉 **yì chájué** visible

遗产 **yíchǎn** estate; legacy

异常 **yìcháng** exceptional; unusual ◊ exceptionally; unusually

一尘不染 **yīchén bùrǎn** spotless

议程 **yìchéng** agenda

一成不变 **yì chéng búbiàn** be very set in one's ways

易冲动 **yì chōngdòng** impulsive

溢出 **yìchū** overflow, run over; slop

遗传 **yíchuán** genetic; hereditary ◊ heredity ◊ pass on

遗传工程 **yíchuán gōngchéng** genetic engineering

遗传学 **yíchuán xué** genetics

遗传学家 **yíchuán xuéjiā** geneticist

一触即发 **yíchù jífā** simmer (with

rage)

易处理 **yì chǔlǐ** manageable

一次 **yīcì** once

依次 **yīcì** in turn

以此 **yǐcǐ** for this reason; consequently; hence; thereby

一次性 **yīcìxìng** disposable ◊ one-off

依从 **yīcóng** obey

意大利 **Yìdàlì** Italy ◊ Italian

一旦 **yídàn** ever; once

一当 **yīdāng** as soon as

一道来 **yídàolái** come along, come too

胰岛素 **yídǎosù** insulin

一大早 **yídàzǎo** at daybreak

一点 **yīdiǎn** a bit, a little; 一点水 **yīdiǎn shuǐ** a little water; 一点也不奇怪 **yìdiǎn yě bù qíguài** not in the least surprised; 好一点 **hǎo yīdiǎn** a little better; 一点一点 **yīdiǎn yīdiǎn** little by little, bit by bit

疑点 **yídiǎn** question mark

一点点 **yīdiǎndian** a little bit, not a lot; vague *taste*; 我所知道的那一点点 **wǒ suǒ zhīdào de nà yīdiǎndian** the little I know

一点儿 **yìdiǎnr** a bit, a little

一定 **yídìng** definite, certain, sure ◊ definitely, certainly, surely

移动 **yídòng** move; shift; remove ◊ removal; cell phone; 缓慢移动 **huǎnmàn yídòng** edge, move slowly

一动不动 **yídòng bùdòng** stand still

移动电话 **yídòng diànhuà** cellular phone

移动性 **yídòng xìng** mobility

易读 **yìdú** readable

一段 **yíduàn** length; passage, extract; period

一段时间 **yīduàn shíjiān** session; spell ◊ for a while

一对 **yīduì** couple; duo

一方 **yìfāng** side, team

已废弃 **yǐ fèiqì** obsolete

一份 **yífèn** helping; share

衣服 **yīfu** clothes, clothing

遗腹 **yífù** posthumous

姨父 **yífù** uncle (*mother's sister's husband*)

衣服架 **yīfújià** clothes hanger

一个 **yīgè** one ◊ single; 一个面包 **yīgè miànbāo** a loaf of bread; 一个挨着一个 **yīgè āizhe yīgè** side by side

一共 **yígòng** altogether; 一共三个 **yígòng sān gè** three in all

义工 **yìgōng** volunteer

衣钩 **yīgōu** coat hook

一贯 **yíguàn** consistent

衣柜 **yīguì** closet

异国 **yìguó** foreign country

一国两制 **yìguó liǎngzhì** one country, two systems

遗憾 **yíhàn** sad ◊ regret; 遗憾... **yíhàn ...** it's a pity that ...; 令人遗憾 **lìngrén yíhàn** deplorable ◊ sadly

颐和园 **Yíhéyuán** Summer Palace

以后 **yǐhòu** later, afterward; in future; 从那以后 **cóng nà yǐhòu** ever since

易坏 **yìhuài** perishable

议会 **yìhuì** council; assembly; parliament ◊ parliamentary

一会儿 **yíhuìr** a while; 我再等一会儿 **wǒ zài děng yíhuìr** I'll wait a while longer; 一会儿见！ **yìhuìr jiàn!** see you later!

已婚 **yǐhūn** married

一伙人 **yīhuǒ rén** crowd, set

异乎寻常 **yì hū xúncháng** uncanny

遗迹 **yíjī** vestige

以及 **yǐjí** and

衣架 **yījià** coathanger

意见 **yìjiàn** opinion; suggestion; complaint; 你有什么意见？ **nǐ yǒu shénme yìjiàn?** what's your opinion?

意见分歧 **yìjiàn fēnqí** dissension

意见相左 **yìjiàn xiāngzuǒ** disagree, differ

移交 **yíjiāo** hand over

异教徒 **yìjiàotú** heathen

易激动 **yì jīdòng** temperamental

已经 **yǐjīng** already; 已经晚了 **yǐjīng wǎn le** it's getting late

易经 **Yìjīng** I-Ching, Book of

Changes

一经要求 **yījīng yāoqiú** on request

以旧换新 **yǐ jiù huàn xīn** trade in

依据 **yījù** basis; grounds

移居 **yíjū** immigrate

移居国外 **yíjū guówài** emigrate ◊ emigration

移开 **yíkāi** move away

一开始 **yīkāishǐ** from the start

一开头 **yīkāitóu** from the outset

依靠 **yīkào** rely on ◊ reliance; 依靠 X 去做 Y **yīkào X qùzuò Y** rely on X to do Y; 依靠自己 **yīkào zìjǐ** self-reliant

倚靠 **yīkào** lean against

一刻钟 **yīkèzhōng** quarter of an hour

一口 **yīkǒu** bite, mouthful

一口气地说 **yìkǒuqìde shuō** rattle off *poem, list of names*

依赖 **yīlài** depend on ◊ dependent ◊ dependence, dependency

伊拉克 **Yīlākè** Iraq ◊ Iraqi

一览表 **yìlánbiǎo** list

伊朗 **Yīlǎng** Iran ◊ Iranian

依恋 **yīliàn** be attached to, be fond of

一连串 **yìliánchuàn** stream, string, succession

医疗 **yīliáo** medical; therapeutic ◊ (medical) care

医疗保险 **yīliáo bǎoxiǎn** health insurance

一流 **yīliú** first-class, first-rate

遗留 **yíliú** leave behind; bequeath

一楼 **yīlóu** first floor, ground floor *Br*

遗漏 **yílòu** omit ◊ omission

一律 **yīlǜ** without exception

疑虑重重 **yílǜ chóngchong** tormented by doubt

一路平安 **yīlù píng'ān** have a good journey

译码 **yìmǎ** decode

衣帽间 **yīmào jiān** checkroom (*for coats*)

疫苗 **yìmiáo** vaccine

移民 **yímín** immigrate; emigrate ◊ immigrant; emigrant; immigration; emigration

移民局 **Yímínjú** Department of Immigration

一模一样 **yìmú yíyàng** identical

音 **yīn** sound; tone

因 **yīn** because ◊ reason

阴 **yīn** yin; shade; private parts ◊ overcast; 天阴了 **tiānyīnle** cloud over

银 **yín** silver

淫 **yín** lewd

瘾 **yǐn** addiction; 有 X 的瘾 **yǒu X de yǐn** be addicted to X

引 **yǐn** draw, attract

隐 **yǐn** hide

饮 **yǐn** drink

印 **yìn** print ◊ stamp

疑难 **yínàn** problematic

阴暗 **yīn'àn** gloomy; dark ◊ gloom

引爆装置 **yǐnbào zhuāngzhì** detonator, igniter

音标 **yīnbiāo** phonetics

隐藏 **yǐncáng** hide, conceal; bury ◊ hidden

阴沉 **yīnchén** threatening, overcast, dull

印出 **yìnchū** print out

印戳 **yìnchuō** stamp

因此 **yīncǐ** so; therefore; consequently; thus

阴道 **yīndào** vagina ◊ vaginal

引导 **yǐndǎo** lead, guide; educate; direct

印第安人 **Yìndì'ān rén** Indian (*Native American*)

音调 **yīndiào** note; pitch; 调准音调 **tiáo zhǔn yīndiào** tune

音调悦耳 **yīndiào yuè'ér** tuneful

引渡 **yǐndù** extradite ◊ extradition

印度 **Yìndù** India ◊ Indian

引渡公约 **yǐndù gōngyuē** extradition treaty

印度尼西亚 **Yìndùníxīyà** Indonesia ◊ Indonesian

印度人 **Yìndùrén** Indian

印度洋 **Yìndùyáng** Indian Ocean

印度支那 **Yìndùzhīnà** Indochina ◊ Indochinese

音符 **yīnfú** note

鹰 **yīng** eagle

应 **yīng** should, ought to

婴 **yīng** infant, baby

樱 **yīng** cherry

营 **yíng** camp

赢 **yíng** win; beat

迎 **yíng** welcome; meet

影 **yǐng** shadow; image

硬 **yìng** hard

应 **yìng** respond, reply; deal with; adapt to

英镑 **yīngbàng** (pound) sterling

硬邦邦 **yìng bāngbang** solid; stiff

硬币 **yìngbì** coin

迎宾员 **yíngbīn yuán** usher

应承 **yìngchéng** promise

硬扯入 **yìngchě rù** drag in; mention

英尺 **yīngchǐ** foot

英寸 **yīngcùn** inch

应得 **yīngdé** deserve; earn ◊ well-earned

赢得 **yíngdé** gain, earn; win

营地 **yíngdì** campsite

硬度 **yìngdù** hardness

婴儿 **yīng'ér** baby, infant

婴儿车 **yīng'ér chē** baby carriage, buggy

婴儿期 **yīng'ér qī** infancy, babyhood

营房 **yíngfáng** quarters, barracks

应付 **yìngfù** manage, cope; cope with

应该 **yìnggāi** should, ought to

英格兰 **Yīnggélán** England

英国 **Yīngguó** United Kingdom; Britain; England ◊ British; English; Brit

迎合 **yínghe** cater for

樱花树 **yīnghuā shù** cherry tree

营火 **yínghuǒ** bonfire

影集 **yǐngjí** photo album

硬挤 **yìngjǐ** hustle, hurry along

硬件 **yìngjiàn** hardware COMPUT

迎接 **yíngjiē** greet, welcome

应接不暇 **yìngjiē bùxiá** be swamped with

英俊 **yīngjùn** handsome, cute (*male*)

应考人 **yìngkǎo rén** (exam) candidate

盈亏平衡点 **yíngkuī pínghéng diǎn** break-even point

硬拉 **yìnglā** drag

英里 **yīnglǐ** mile

盈利 **yínglì** profit; surplus

英明 **yīngmíng** brilliant; wise

英亩 **yīngmǔ** acre

因公 **yīngōng** on business

硬盘 **yìngpán** hard disk

硬皮书 **yìngpíshū** hardback

萦绕于心 **yíngrào yú xīn** haunting

影射 **yǐngshè** allude to

应试者 **yìngshì zhě** interviewee

应受指摘 **yìngshòu zhǐzhāi** reprehensible

硬刷子 **yìngshuāzi** scrubbing brush

罂粟 **yīngsù** poppy

鹰隼 **yīngsǔn** hawk

樱桃 **yīngtáo** cherry (*fruit*)

硬通货 **yìngtōnghuò** hard currency

硬卧 **yìngwò** hard sleeper (*on train*)

鹦鹉 **yīngwǔ** parrot

影响 **yǐngxiǎng** influence; impact ◊ influence; affect

影响力 **yǐngxiǎnglì** influence; impact

硬行推销 **yìngxíng tuīxiāo** hard sell

英雄 **yīngxióng** hero

营养 **yíngyǎng** nourishment; nutrition

营养不良 **yíngyǎng bùliáng** malnutrition

营养搭配好 **yíngyǎng dāpèihǎo** well-balanced *diet*

营养品 **yíngyǎng pǐn** nutrient

硬要 **yìngyào** impose (oneself)

营业经理 **yíngyè jīnglǐ** sales manager

营业时间 **yíngyè shíjiān** business hours

影印 **yǐngyìn** photocopy

影印本 **yǐngyìn běn** photocopy

影印机 **yǐngyìn jī** photocopier

英勇 **yīngyǒng** heroic

应用 **yìngyòng** use; apply ◊ applied

英勇事迹 **yīngyǒng shìji** exploit, deed

英语 **Yīngyǔ** English (*language*)

应征 **yìngzhēng** join the army

应征入伍者 **yìngzhēng rùwǔ zhě** draftee

硬纸板 **yìng zhǐbǎn** cardboard

应支付 **yīng zhīfù** payable, due

影子 **yǐngzi** shadow

硬座 **yìngzuò** hard seat (*on train*)

银行 **yínháng** bank FIN

银行贷款 **yínháng dàikuǎn** bank loan

银行家 **yínháng jiā** banker

银行结存 **yínháng jiécún** bank balance

银行结单 **yínháng jiédān** bank statement

银行经理 **yínháng jīnglǐ** bank manager

银行利率 **yínháng lìlǜ** bank rate

银行信用卡 **yínháng xìnyòng kǎ** banker's card

银行帐户 **yínháng zhànghù** bank account

引号 **yǐnhào** quotation mark

淫秽 **yínhuì** obscene; bawdy

银婚 **yínhūn** silver wedding (anniversary)

阴间 **yīnjiān** underworld (*in mythology*)

音阶 **yīnjiē** scale MUS

音节 **yīnjié** syllable

引进 **yǐnjìn** introduce, bring in ◊ introduction

阴茎 **yīnjīng** penis

饮酒者 **yǐnjiǔ zhě** drinker

隐居处 **yǐnjū chù** retreat

阴凉 **yīnliáng** shady

音量 **yīnliàng** volume (*of radio etc*)

阴凉处 **yīnliáng chù** in the shade

音量调控 **yīnliàng tiáokòng** volume control

饮料 **yǐnliào** drink

引路 **yǐnlù** lead the way

淫乱 **yínluàn** indecent, obscene

隐瞒 **yǐnmán** conceal, cover up; disguise

阴毛 **yīnmáo** pubic hair

隐没 **yǐnmò** go in

阴谋 **yīnmóu** conspiracy, plot

阴谋者 **yīnmóu zhě** plotter

银幕 **yínmù** screen

银牌 **yínpái** silver medal

引起 **yǐnqǐ** cause; produce; inspire; arouse; 引起 X 的注意 **yǐnqǐ X de zhùyì** catch X's eye

姻亲 **yīnqīn** in-laws

引擎 **yǐnqíng** engine

引人反感 **yǐn rén fǎngǎn** obnoxious

引人入胜 **yǐn rén rù shèng** compelling

引人注目 **yǐn rén zhùmù** stand out; attract attention ◊ spectacular; striking

阴森森 **yīn sēnsen** spooky

隐士 **yǐnshì** recluse

印刷 **yìnshuā** print

印刷厂 **yìnshuā chǎng** printing works, press

印刷机 **yìnshuā jī** printing press

印刷品 **yìnshuā pǐn** printed matter

印刷商 **yìnshuā shāng** printer

印刷字体 **yìnshuā zìtǐ** print

饮水 **yǐnshuǐ** water *animals*

因素 **yīnsù** ingredient, factor

因特网 **yīntèwǎng** Internet

阴天 **yīntiān** cloudy

引退 **yǐntuì** resign, step down

易怒 **yìnù** fiery; irritable; snappy

因为 **yīnwèi** because, since ◊ on account of

淫猥 **yínwěi** lewd

引文 **yǐnwén** quotation, quote

阴险 **yīnxiǎn** devious; insidious ◊ deviously; insidiously

音箱 **yīnxiāng** speaker (*of sound system*)

音响 **yīnxiǎng** acoustics; stereo

印象 **yìnxiàng** impression

印象深刻 **yìnxiàng shēnkè** impressive

阴性 **yīnxìng** feminine GRAM; negative *test results*

隐形眼镜 **yǐnxíng yǎnjìng** contact lens

音译 **yīnyì** transliterate

引用 **yǐnyòng** quote

饮用水 **yǐnyòng shuǐ** drinking water

引诱 **yǐnyòu** seduce ◊ seduction

音域 **yīnyù** (vocal) range

音乐 **yīnyuè** music ◊ musical

音乐会 **yīnyuè huì** concert

音乐家 **yīnyuè jiā** musician

音乐片 **yīnyuè piān** musical (*movie*)

音乐学院 **yīnyuè xuéyuàn** conservatory, music school

印章 **yìnzhāng** stamp, seal (*on document*)

引证 **yǐnzhèng** cite

银制 **yínzhì** silver

银质 **yínzhì** silver

印子 **yìnzi** imprint, impression

一瞥 **yìpiē** glance, glimpse

一起 **yīqǐ** together; along; 和 … 一起 **hé … yīqǐ** with

仪器 **yíqì** apparatus; instrument

遗弃 **yíqì** jilt; walk out on

以前 **yǐqián** before; formerly, previously ◊ former, past; 以前干过吗? **yǐqián gàn guò ma?** have you done this before?; 他不再和以前一样了 **tā búzài hé yǐqián yíyàng le** he's not the same any more

一千 **yìqiān** one thousand

一千年 **yìqiānnián** millennium

一切 **yíqiè** everything; all; 一切包括在内 **yíqiè bāokuò zàinèi** inclusive

一期付款 **yīqī fùkuàn** installment

意气消沉 **yìqì xiāochén** despondent

一群 **yìqún** flock

意趣相投 **yìqù xiāngtóu** be on the same wavelength

易燃 **yìrán** combustible, inflammable

易燃烧 **yì ránshāo** flammable

一日游 **yīrìyóu** daytrip

以色列 **Yísèliè** Israel ◊ Israeli

医生 **yīshēng** doctor

一生 **yìshēng** one's whole life, a lifetime

一声不吭 **yīshēng bùkēng** stay silent

一时 **yīshí** a while, a moment

遗失 **yíshī** lose; mislay

仪式 **yíshì** ceremony; ritual

意识 **yìshí** awareness, consciousness; 意识不到 … **yìshí búdào** … be oblivious of; 意识到 **yìshí dào** be aware of, realize; 我现在才意识到 … **wǒ xiànzài cái yìshí dào** … I realize now that …

意识形态 **yìshí xíngtài** ideology ◊ ideological

艺术 **yìshù** art ◊ artistic

艺术家 **yìshù jiā** artist

艺术界 **yìshù jiè** the arts

艺术品 **yìshù pǐn** work of art

意思 **yìsi** meaning, sense; interest; 你什么意思? **nǐ shénme yìsi?** what are you driving at?

一丝不苟 **yìsī bùgǒu** scrupulous

一丝不挂 **yīsī bùguà** stark naked

伊斯兰教 **Yīsīlánjiào** Islam ◊ Islamic

遗俗 **yísú** relic

易碎 **yìsuì** fragile; brittle

遗体 **yítǐ** remains

一天 **yītiān** one day

意图 **yìtú** intention

一团 **yìtuán** jumble

一团糟 **yītuánzāo** be a mess ◊ tangle

意外 **yìwài** accidental; unexpected ◊ by chance; unexpectedly

意外发现 **yìwài fāxiàn** stumble across

遗忘 **yíwàng** oblivion ◊ leave behind

意味 **yìwèi** signify ◊ significance

意味深长 **yìwèi shēncháng** meaningful

疑问 **yíwèn** doubt; query; interrogative GRAM

译文 **yìwén** translation

一文不名 **yīwén bùmíng** penniless

衣物 **yīwù** laundry, washing ◊ wardrobe, clothes

遗物 **yíwù** relic

义务 **yìwù** obligation, duty ◊ voluntary *work*

义务教育 **yìwù jiàoyù** compulsory education

一无所有 **yīwú suǒyǒu** zilch

以下 **yǐxià** under; following; 十岁以下 **shí suì yǐxià** under ten years of age; 读以下说明 **dú yǐxià shuōmíng** read the following instructions

异想天开！ **yìxiǎng tiānkāi!** it boggles the mind!

一向 **yíxiàng** always; till now, so far; 一向准时 **yíxiàng zhǔnshì** have a good record for punctuality

一小袋 **yīxiǎodài** sachet

一小口 **yìxiǎokǒu** sip

一小片 **yīxiǎopiàn** morsel

一下子 **yīxiàzi** all at once; in one shot

一些 **yīxiē** some, a few

一系列 **yíxìliè** succession, series

疑心 **yíxīn** suspicion; 对 X 有疑心 **duì X yǒu yíxīn** be suspicious of X

异性爱 **yìxìng'ài** heterosexual

易兴奋 **yìxīngfèn** excitable

医学 **yīxué** medicine ◊ medical

以牙还牙 **yǐyá huányá** an eye for an eye; tit for tat

一眼 **yìyǎn** peek

一样 **yīyàng** just as; just the same; 和 ... 一样高 **hé ... yīyàng gāo** as high as ...; 看起来一样 **kànqǐlái yíyàng** look the same

一氧化碳 **yīyǎng huàtàn** carbon monoxide

一言为定 **yī yán wéi dìng** it's a deal

一言以蔽之 **yìyán yǐ bìzhī** in a nutshell

一一 **yīyī** one by one

意义 **yìyì** meaning, sense; point, purpose

异议 **yìyì** objection

一饮而尽 **yìyǐn ěr jìn** gulp down

易于 ... **yìyú** ... be apt to ...

医院 **yīyuàn** hospital, infirmary

议员 **yìyuán** representative; congressman

译员 **yìyuán** interpreter

意愿 **yìyuàn** wish; inclination

一月 **yīyuè** January

依仗 **yīzhàng** count on

译者 **yìzhě** translator

一针 **yīzhēn** stitch

一直 **yīzhí** all the time, all along

遗植 **yízhí** transplant; graft

遗址 **yízhǐ** ruin

一致 **yízhì** uniform, identical; unanimous ◊ uniformly;

unanimously

意指 **yìzhǐ** mean

抑制 **yìzhì** check, restrain; refrain

意志 **yìzhì** will, willpower

意志力 **yìzhìlì** willpower

一致同意 **yízhì tóngyì** unanimous

一致性 **yīzhì xìng** consistency; correspondence

一致意见 **yízhì yìjiàn** consensus

以至于 **yǐzhìyú** so that

遗嘱 **yízhǔ** legacy; will

衣着 **yīzhuó** clothes; 衣着不整 **yīzhuó bùzhěng** sloppily dressed; 衣着整洁 **yīzhuó zhěngjié** well-dressed

椅子 **yǐzi** chair

易醉 **yìzuì** heady *drink, wine etc*

异族通婚 **yìzú tōnghūn** mixed marriage

拥 **yōng** embrace; crowd

永 **yǒng** for ever

涌 **yǒng** surge

勇 **yǒng** brave

用 **yòng** use; apply ◊ with; 用早餐 **yòng zǎocān** have breakfast; 用电子邮件寄 **yòng diànzǐ yóujiàn jì** send by e-mail

拥抱 **yōngbào** cuddle; embrace, hug

用餐 **yòngcān** dine

涌出 **yǒngchū** gush, pour

用处 **yòngchù** usefulness

用错 **yòngcuò** misuse

用法 **yòngfǎ** directions; usage

用费 **yòngfèi** expenses

勇敢 **yǒnggǎn** brave, courageous, valiant ◊ bravely ◊ bravery

用光 **yòngguāng** use up, run out of

永恒 **yǒnghéng** eternal ◊ eternity

拥护 **yōnghù** welcome

用户 **yònghù** user; consumer

用坏 **yònghuài** wear out ◊ wear

用户友好 **yònghù yǒuhǎo** user-friendly

拥护者 **yōnghù zhě** supporter, sympathizer

拥挤 **yōngjǐ** crowd; jostle ◊ crowded, packed

拥挤的人群 **yōngjǐ de rénqún** crush

涌进 yǒngjìn surge forward

佣金 yòngjīn commission

用尽 yòngjìn exhaust, use up

永久 yǒngjiǔ permanent, everlasting

用具 yòngjù equipment, gear, tackle; utensil

用力 yònglì vigorous ◊ exert oneself; 用力打开 yònglì dǎkāi force *door*; 用力举起 yònglì jǔqǐ heave

用量 yòngliàng dose, dosage

勇气 yǒngqì courage, nerve; spirit

佣人 yōngrén servant

勇士 yǒngshì tough guy

用途 yòngtú use, purpose

用过 yòngguò used

用完 yòngwán run out; run out of; use up

勇往直前 yǒng wǎng zhí qián carry on undaunted

拥有 yōngyǒu own; keep

拥有者 yōngyǒu zhě owner

永远 yǒngyuǎn for ever, eternally; 他永远不会厌倦 ta yǒngyuǎn búhuì yànjuàn he never tires of it

忧 yōu worry ◊ worried

优 yōu excellent, very good

幽 yōu secluded; peaceful

油 yóu oil; fat; grease

铀 yóu uranium

疣 yóu wart

游 yóu travel; float; swim

由 yóu from; 由此发生 … yóucǐ fāshēng … it follows from this that …; 由 … 主演 yóu … zhǔyǎn feature; 由 … 组成 yóu … zǔchéng be comprised of …

邮 yóu mail; 把 X 邮给 Y bǎ X yóu gěi Y send X to Y

有 yǒu have, have got; there is; there are ◊ (*forming adjectival constructions*): 有空调 yǒu kōngtiáo air-conditioned; 有经验 yǒu jīngyàn experienced

友 yǒu friend

右 yòu right ◊ on the right

又 yòu again

幼 yòu child ◊ young

诱 yòu seduce, lure; guide, lead

呦, 呦! yōu, yōu! well, well!

又 … 又 … yòu … yòu … both … and …

幽暗 yōu'àn dark

有帮助 yǒu bāngzhù helpful

有把握 yǒu bǎwò safely ◊ self-assured

油泵 yóubèng gas pump

右边 yòubiān right-hand

有别于 yǒubiéyú differ from

幽闭恐怖症 yōubì kǒngbù zhèng claustrophobia

有病 yǒubìng ill

有必要时 yǒu bìyào shí as necessary

油布 yóubù tarpaulin

又不 yòubú nor

油菜 yóucài rape; rapeseed oil, canola

有才华 yǒu cáihuá brilliant

有才能 yǒu cáinéng accomplished

有偿雇佣 yǒucháng gùyōng paid employment

有成效 yǒu chéngxiào productive

幼虫 yòuchóng larva

忧愁 yōuchóu sad; gloomy ◊ sadness

有臭味 yǒu chòuwèi smell ◊ smelly

油船 yóuchuán (oil) tanker

邮戳 yóuchuō postmark

虚弱 yǒu chùtòng tender

由此 yóucǐ from this

有刺铁丝网 yǒucì tiěsī wǎng barbed wire

优待 yōudài favor, special treatment

邮递 yóudì mail delivery

优点 yōudiǎn merit, strength

有点 yǒudiǎn a bit, a little

有颠覆性 yǒu diānfù xìng subversive

有点儿 yǒudiǎnr a bit, a little; 有点儿难过 yǒudiǎnr nánguò a bit sad, kind of sad

邮递员 yóudì yuán mailman

有毒 yǒudú poisonous, toxic

有毒瘾者 yǒu dúyǐn zhě junkie

诱饵 yòu'ěr bait; decoy

幼儿 yòu'ér small child, infant

幼儿学校 yòu'ér xuéxiào

kindergarten

幼儿圆 yòu'éryuán kindergarten

幼儿园老师 yòu'éryuán lǎoshī kindergarten teacher

有感染力 yǒu gǎnrǎn lì catching

有根据 yǒu gēnjù valid

有关 yǒuguān concerned, relevant, pertinent ◊ concerning, re

有关系 yǒu guānxì connect

有轨电车 yǒuguǐ diànchē streetcar

有规律 yǒu guīlǜ regular, steady ◊ regularly

有害 yǒuhài harmful; mischievous

有害元素 yǒuhài yuánsù harmful substance

友好 yǒuhǎo friendly, neighborly; kind ◊ goodwill

黝黑 yǒuhēi swarthy

油画 yóuhuà oil painting

油画布 yóuhuà bù canvas

有怀疑 yǒu huáiyí dubious

油灰 yóuhuī putty

邮汇 yóuhuì money order

诱惑 yòuhuò lure, entice ◊ alluring ◊ temptation

有活力 yǒu huólì perky, cheerful

邮寄 yóujì send

有机 yǒujī organic ◊ organically

又及 yòují PS, postscript

邮件 yóujiàn mail

有价证券 yǒujià zhèngquàn bond, security

有价值 yǒu jiàzhí valuable

游击队 yóujīduì guerrilla

有结余 yǒu jiéyú in the black

有技能 yǒu jìnéng skilled

幽静 yōujìng sleepy *town*

油井 yóujǐng oil rig, oil well

有经验 yǒu jīngyàn experienced, seasoned

有竞争力 yǒu jìngzhēng lì competitive

有进取心 yǒu jìnqǔxīn enterprising, go-ahead

有技巧 yǒu jìqiǎo professional

邮寄 yóují mail, send

邮寄人 yóují rén sender

邮局 yóujú post office

游客 yóukè visitor

有可能 yǒu kěnéng possibly;

potentially ◊ be liable to

有空 yǒu kōng have time; be available; 有空吗？ yǒu kōng ma? can you spare the time?; 有空时 yǒu kōng shí at your leisure

有愧 yǒukuì guilt

有困难 yǒu kùnnán in need

由来 yóulái origin

游览 yóulǎn visit; tour; go sightseeing; 游览全中国 yóulán quán Zhōngguó travel all over China

游廊 yóuláng veranda

有了 yǒule pregnant ◊ be expecting

游乐场 yóulè chǎng amusement park

游乐园 yóulè yuán amusement park

有理 yǒulǐ reasonable; rational; in the right

有利 yǒulì advantageous; favorable

有立法权 yǒu lìfǎ quán legislative

有利可图 yǒulì kětú profitability

有礼貌 yǒu lǐmào respectful, polite, courteous, civil ◊ respectfully

幽灵 yōulíng vision

有利润 yǒu lìrùn be profitable, pay ◊ remunerative

有理由 yǒu lǐyóu justifiable

忧虑 yōulǜ worry, care ◊ worried; distracted

有逻辑 yǒu luójí logical

有毛病 yǒu máobìng faulty

优美 yōuměi lovely; graceful; dainty ◊ grace

有魅力 yǒu mèilì glamorous; attractive; magnetic

有霉味儿 yǒu méiwèir musty

有没有 … ? yǒuméiyǒu …? is there …?; are there …?

油门 yóumén accelerator

右面 yòumiàn right-hand side

游民 yóumín hobo

有名生 yǒu míngshēng reputable

幽默 yōumò humor

幽默感 yōumò gǎn sense of

humor

柚木 **yòumù** teak

有耐心 **yǒu nàixīn** patient

有那么点儿 ... **yǒu nàme diǎnr** ... sort of ...

有男性 **yǒu nánxìng** virile

有男子气 **yǒu nánzǐqì** manly

有能力 **yǒu nénglì** able ◊ be capable of

油腻 **yóunì** greasy, oily; rich, heavy

幼年童子军 **yòunián tóngzǐjūn** Brownie

有粘性 **yǒu niánxìng** adhesive

有泥浆 **yǒu níjiāng** slimy

右派 **yòupài** right; right-winger

邮票 **yóupiào** stamp

右撇子 **yòu piě zi** right-handed

有蹼的脚 **yǒu pǔ de jiǎo** webbed feet

尤其 **yóuqí** especially, in particular

有钱 **yǒuqián** rich

有前途 **yǒu qiántú** promising

有气泡 **yǒu qìpào** effervescent

有趣 **yǒuqù** fun, amusing, entertaining; interesting

有权威性 **yǒu quánwēi xìng** authoritative

有缺陷 **yǒu quēxiàn** defective

有人 **yǒurén** someone, somebody ◊ occupied; 有人敲门 **yǒurén qiāomén** there's someone at the door

诱人 **yòurén** seductive, tantalizing

友善 **yǒushàn** amicable

忧伤 **yōushāng** sorrow

有生命危险 **yǒu shēngmìng wēixiǎn** life-threatening

优势 **yōushì** superiority

有事 **yǒu shì** have on; 你今晚有事吗？ **nǐ jīnwǎn yǒushì ma?** do you have anything on for tonight?

有时 **yǒushí** sometimes, now and again

优势和劣势 **yōushì hé lièshì** the pros and cons

有施虐狂 **yǒu shīnüèkuáng** sadistic

有失体面 **yǒushī tǐmiàn** disgraceful

有失体统 **yǒu shī tǐtǒng** offensive

有诗意 **yǒu shīyì** poetic

有适应力 **yǒu shìyìng lì** adaptable

有售 **yǒushòu** be on sale

幼兽 **yòushòu** cub

游手好闲 **yóushǒu hàoxián** loaf around

又瘦又高 **yòushòu yòugāo** lanky

有说服力 **yǒu shuōfúlì** forceful, persuasive

有锁柜 **yǒu suǒguì** locker

油台 **yóutái** drilling rig

犹太 **Yóutài** Jewish

犹太人 **Yóutài rén** Jew

有弹性 **yǒu tánxìng** springy, elastic; supple

有特异功能 **yǒu tèyì gōngnéng** psychic

油田 **yóutián** oil field

有天才 **yǒu tiāncái** talented

有天赋 **yǒu tiānfù** gifted

有条不紊 **yǒutiáo bùwěn** methodical ◊ methodically

有条件 **yǒu tiáojiàn** conditional

有条理 **yǒu tiáolǐ** systematic, methodical ◊ systematically

有条纹 **yǒu tiáowén** striped

有挑战性 **yǒu tiǎozhàn xìng** challenging

游艇 **yóutǐng** yacht

游艇驾驶员 **yǒutǐng jiàshǐ yuán** yachtsman

游艇停泊港 **yóutǐng tíngbó gǎng** marina

邮筒 **yóutǒng** mailbox

有同情心 **yǒu tóngqíng xīn** compassionate

有投票权者 **yǒu tóupiào quán zhě** voter

有图案 **yǒu tú'àn** patterned

有威望 **yǒu wēiwàng** prestigious

有威胁性 **yǒu wēixié xìng** threatening

有文化 **yǒu wénhuà** be literate

游戏 **yóuxì** play; game

优先 **yōuxiān** preferential, priority ◊ take precedence, take priority

悠闲 **yōuxián** laidback

有限 **yǒuxiàn** limited

右舷 **yòuxián** starboard

有线电视 **yǒuxiàn diànshì** cable

TV
有限度 **yǒu xiàndù** qualified
邮箱 **yóuxiāng** mailbox
有香味 **yǒu xiāngwèi** fragrant
有想像力 **yǒu xiǎngxiàng lì** imaginative
有象征性 **yǒu xiàngzhēng xìng** symbolic
优先权 **yōuxiān quán** priority; 有优先权 **yǒu yōuxiān quán** have priority
优先行驶权 **yōuxiān xíngshǐ quán** right of way
有嫌疑 **yǒu xiányí** alleged
有效 **yǒuxiào** valid; effective
幼小动物 **yòuxiǎo dòngwù** pup
有效率 **yǒu xiàolǜ** efficient ◊ efficiently
游戏场 **yóuxì chǎng** playground
有些 **yǒuxiē** some; 有些人说 ... **yǒuxiē rén shuō ...** some people say that ...
忧心忡忡 **yōuxīn chóngchóng** careworn, sad
游行 **yóuxíng** march, parade
有兴趣 **yǒu xìngqù** interested
有兴致 **yǒu xìngzhì** be in the mood for
有信心 **yǒu xìnxīn** assured
有吸收能力 **yǒu xīshōu nénglì** absorbent
优秀 **yōuxiù** excellent ◊ excellence
有修养 **yǒu xiūyǎng** cultivated, cultured; cultural
有希望 **yǒu xīwàng** hopeful
有吸引力 **yǒu xīyǐn lì** attractive; charming; seductive
优雅 **yōuyǎ** graceful ◊ lightness ◊ beautifully
油烟 **yóuyān** soot
有眼力 **yǒu yǎnlì** discerning, discriminating
有烟嘴 **yǒu yānzuǐ** tipped *cigarettes*
有药性 **yǒu yàoxìng** medicinal
有益 **yǒuyì** beneficial; useful; advantageous; expedient
友谊 **yǒuyì** friendship
有意 **yǒuyì** intend ◊ intentional, conscious ◊ intentionally, deliberately; 我有意移民 **wǒ**

yǒuyì yímín I'm thinking about emigrating; 有意为 X 准备 **yǒuyì wèi X zhǔnbèi** be meant for X
右翼 **yòuyì** right wing
又一次 **yòu yīcì** once again, once more
又一个 **yòu yígè** another
有益健康 **yǒuyì jiànkāng** healthy
有影响 **yǒu yǐngxiǎng** influential
有营养 **yǒu yíngyǎng** nourishing, nutritious
友谊商店 **Yǒuyì Shāngdiàn** Friendship Store
友谊市 **yǒuyì shì** twin town
有艺术性 **yǒu yìshù xìng** artistic
有意思 **yǒu yìsi** interesting, intriguing; significant
有一天 **yǒu yītiān** one day
有意误导 X **yǒuyì wùdǎo X** string X along
有疑心 **yǒu yíxīn** suspicious
有意义 **yǒu yìyì** meaningful
游泳 **yóuyǒng** swim ◊ swimming
有用 **yǒuyòng** useful
游泳池 **yóuyǒng chí** swimming pool; 室外游泳池 **shìwài yóuyǒng chí** open-air swimming pool
游泳裤 **yóuyǒng kù** swimsuit
游泳衣 **yóuyǒng yī** swimsuit
游泳者 **yóuyǒng zhě** swimmer
忧郁 **yōuyù** gloom ◊ glum; melancholy, depressed
鱿鱼 **yóuyú** squid
由于 **yóuyú** with; through ◊ because of, due to
犹豫 **yóuyù** hesitate ◊ hesitation ◊ tentative; 犹豫不决 **yóuyù bù jué** be indecisive; 犹豫不定 **yóuyù búdìng** be indecisive; 对 X 犹豫不定 **duì X yóuyù búdìng** be undecided about X
优越 **yōuyuè** superior
有余额 **yǒu yú'é** be in credit
忧郁症 **yōuyù zhèng** depression
油炸 **yóuzhá** (deep-)fry
有战斗性 **yǒu zhàndòu xìng** militant
有朝一日 **yǒuzhāo yīrì** someday
悠着点儿! **yōu zhe diǎnr!** steady on!
有哲理 **yǒu zhélǐ** philosophical

邮政 **yóuzhèng** mail

邮政编码 **yóuzhèng biānmǎ** zip code

邮政信箱 **yóuzhèng xìnxiāng** P.O. Box

有争议 **yǒu zhēngyì** controversial

优质 **yōuzhì** high-grade

幼稚 **yòuzhì** childish, juvenile; naive ◊ childishness; child

油脂 **yóuzhī** oil; grease; fat

有志向 **yǒu zhìxiàng** ambitious

有秩序 **yǒu zhìxù** orderly

邮资 **yóuzī** postage

柚子 **yòuzi** pomelo

有资格 **yǒuzīgé** entitled

有罪 **yǒuzuì** guilt ◊ guilty

油嘴滑舌 **yóuzuǐ huáshé** glib

有尊严 **yǒu zūnyán** dignified

右座方向盘 **yòuzuò fāngxiàngpán** right-hand drive

鱼 **yú** fish

于 **yú** to; at; in; from

愚 **yú** stupid

渔 **yú** fishing

与 **yǔ** and; with; 与 ... 有关系 **yǔ ... yǒuguānxì** in connection with ...; 与 X 不同 **yǔ X bùtóng** different from X; 与 X 断绝关系 **yǔ X duànjué guānxi** finish with X

雨 **yǔ** rain; 下着雨呢 **xià zhe yǔ ne** it's raining

语 **yǔ** language ◊ *used to form language names*; 西藏语 **Xīzàng yǔ** Tibetan

羽 **yǔ** feather

玉 **yù** jade

郁 **yù** luxuriant

遇 **yù** meet, encounter

浴 **yù** bath

欲 **yù** desire

愈 **yù** over, more than; 愈快愈好 **yù kuài yù hǎo** the faster the better

预 **yù** beforehand

圆 **yuán** round ◊ circle

元 **yuán** yuan (*Chinese money*)

园 **yuán** garden

原 **yuán** original

远 **yuǎn** far; distant; 三英里远 **sān yīnglǐ yuǎn** it's three miles off

愿 **yuàn** wish

院 **yuàn** institute

渊博 **yuānbó** vast; high-powered

原材料 **yuán cáiliào** raw materials

元朝 **Yuán Cháo** Yuan Dynasty

远程 **yuǎnchéng** long-range

远处 **yuǎnchù** distant place; 在远处 **zài yuǎnchù** in the distance

元旦 **Yuándàn** New Year's Day

园丁 **yuándīng** gardener

圆顶 **yuándǐng** dome

原定 **yuándìng** default COMPUT

远东 **Yuǎndōng** Far East

缘分 **yuánfèn** destiny

原告 **yuángào** claimant, plaintiff

原告方 **yuángàofāng** prosecution

怨恨 **yuànhèn** grudge

圆滑 **yuánhuá** slick, smooth

元件 **yuánjiàn** unit

远见 **yuǎnjiàn** vision, far-sightedness 援救 **yuánjiù** rescue

援救队 **yuánjiù duì** rescue party

远距离 **yuǎn jùlí** long-distance

援军 **yuánjūn** reinforcements

原来 **yuánlái** original ◊ originally; actually; 原来你在这儿 **yuánlái nǐ zài zhèr** there you are (*finding somebody*)

原谅 **yuánliàng** forgive, excuse, pardon ◊ forgiveness; 请原谅 **qǐng yuánliàng** I beg your pardon

原料 **yuánliào** raw material; ingredient

圆领衫 **yuánlǐng shān** T-shirt

园林师 **yuánlínshī** gardener

圆明园 **Yuánmíngyuán** Old Summer Palace

圆木 **yuánmù** log

圆盘 **yuánpán** disk

圆圈 **yuánquān** circle, ring

原始 **yuánshǐ** primitive

远视 **yuǎnshì** long-sighted, far-sighted

元素 **yuánsù** element CHEM

源头 **yuántóu** source

愿望 **yuànwàng** wish, desire

鸢尾属植物 **yuānwěishǔ zhíwù** iris (*flower*)

原文 **yuánwén** original text

原先 **yuánxiān** originally

元宵节 **Yuánxiāojié** Lantern

Festival

圆形 **yuánxíng** circular, round

园艺 **yuányì** gardening; horticulture

愿意 **yuànyì** willing, ready ◊ willingness, readiness ◊ want

原因 **yuányīn** cause, reason

元音 **yuányīn** vowel

原油 **yuányóu** crude oil

远于 **yuǎnyú** beyond

远远 **yuǎnyuǎn** much, way; 远远不如 **yuǎnyuǎn bùrú** not be a patch on

源源不断 **yuányuán búduàn** inexhaustible ◊ stream

原则 **yuánzé** principle; 原则上 **yuánzé shang** in principle

院长 **yuànzhǎng** dean

圆周 **yuánzhōu** circumference

援助 **yuánzhù** aid

圆柱 **yuánzhù** column

援助 **yuánzhù** support, help

圆珠笔 **yuánzhūbǐ** ballpoint pen

圆锥体 **yuánzhuī tǐ** cone

圆柱体 **yuánzhù tǐ** cylinder

原子 **yuánzǐ** atom ◊ atomic, nuclear

院子 **yuànzi** yard; courtyard

原子弹 **yuánzǐ dàn** atom bomb

原子废物 **yuánzǐ fèiwù** atomic waste

原子核 **yuánzǐ hé** nuclear

原子核物理 **yuánzǐ hé wùlǐ** nuclear physics

原子能 **yuánzǐ néng** atomic energy

远足 **yuǎnzú** excursion; hike

原作 **yuánzuò** original

原作品 **yuán zuòpǐn** original

欲罢不能 **yùbà bùnéng** compulsive

预报 **yùbào** forecast

预备 **yùbèi** prepare

预备队员 **yùbèi duìyuán** reserve SP

预备性 **yùbèi xìng** preliminary

预测 **yùcè** forecast, projection

鱼叉 **yúchā** harpoon

鱼船 **yúchuán** fishing boat

愚蠢 **yúchǔn** stupid, foolish, idiotic ◊ stupidity, folly

鱼刺 **yúcì** fishbone

遇到 **yùdào** encounter, meet, run into

雨点儿 **yǔdiǎnr** raindrop

预定 **yùdìng** book, reserve ◊ booking, reservation; 预定房间 **yùdìng fángjiān** book a room

约 **yuē** arrange

月 **yuè** month

阅 **yuè** read

越 **yuè** surpass, exceed; 越 … 越 … **yuè … yuè …** the more … the more …; 越快越好 **yuèkuài yuèhǎo** the sooner the better

乐 **yuè** music

阅兵 **yuèbīng** parade

月饼 **yuèbǐng** mooncake

约定 **yuēdìng** agree; arrange to meet

阅读 **yuèdú** read ◊ reading; 阅读学习 **yuèdú xuéxí** read up on

阅读材料 **yuèdú cáiliào** reading matter

乐队 **yuèduì** band; orchestra

悦耳 **yuè'ěr** pleasant-sounding; musical, melodious

越发（多）**yuèfā(duō)** more and more

岳父 **yuèfù** father-in-law (*wife's father*)

月光 **yuèguāng** moonlight

月桂 **yuèguì** laurel

越过 **yuèguò** exceed, pass; get over

约会 **yuēhuì** appointment; engagement; date, rendez-vous ◊ ask out

约会对象 **yuēhuì duìxiàng** date (*person*)

月经 **yuèjīng** period; menstruation

月经带 **yuèjīng dài** sanitary napkin

月经栓 **yuèjīng shuān** tampon

月刊 **yuèkān** monthly (*publication*)

越来越 **yuè lái yuè** increasingly; 越来越多的学生 **yuè lái yuè duō de xuéshēng** more and more students; 越来越快 **yuè lái yuè kuài** faster and faster

阅览室 **yuèlǎnshì** reading room

阅历 **yuèlì** experience; 她阅历挺

深 *tā yuèlì tǐngshēn* she has been around

月亮 **yuèliàng** moon ◊ lunar

岳母 **yuèmǔ** mother-in-law (of man)

越南 **Yuènán** Vietnam ◊ Vietnamese

月票 **yuèpiào** monthly ticket

乐谱 **yuèpǔ** music, score

乐器 **yuèqì** musical instrument

月蚀 **yuèshí** lunar eclipse

约束 **yuēshù** restrain; curb; bind; restrict ◊ restriction

约束力 **yuēshù lì** binding force

越位 **yuèwèi** offside; 未越位 *wèi yuèwèi* onside

月牙形 **yuèyá xíng** crescent

越野 **yuèyě** cross-country; 越野赛 *yuèyě sài* cross-country race

乐音 **yuèyīn** tone

乐章 **yuèzhāng** movement MUS

语法 **yǔfǎ** grammar

鱼贩 **yúfàn** fishmonger

预防 **yùfáng** prevent ◊ prevention ◊ precautionary

预防措施 **yùfáng cuòshī** precaution, preventive measure

预防性 **yùfáng xìng** preventive

渔夫 **yúfū** fisherman

预付 **yùfù** advance (payment) ◊ pay in advance

鱼竿 **yúgān** fishing pole

预感 **yùgǎn** hunch; premonition

浴缸 **yùgāng** bathtub, tub

鱼肝油 **yúgān yóu** cod-liver oil

预告 **yùgào** forecast, predict

鱼钩 **yúgōu** fishhook

宇航 **yǔháng** space travel

宇航服 **yǔháng fú** spacesuit

宇航工业 **yǔháng gōngyè** aerospace industry

宇航员 **yǔháng yuán** astronaut

愈合 **yùhé** heal

迂回 **yūhuí** detour

迂回行进 **yūhuí xíngjìn** weave

与会者 **yǔhuì zhě** conventioneer

欲火中烧 **yùhuǒ zhōngshāo** smolder

淤积 **yūjī** deposit

雨季 **yǔjì** rainy season, the rains

郁积 **yùjí** smolder

预计 **yùjì** estimate; plan; 预计到达时间 *yùjì dàodá shíjiān* estimated time of arrival

预见 **yùjiàn** foresee

遇见 **yùjiàn** meet

雨夹雪 **yǔjiáxuě** sleet

余烬 **yújìn** embers

浴巾 **yùjīn** bath towel

郁金香 **yùjīnxiāng** tulip

愉快 **yúkuài** happy, joyful; 令人愉快 *lìngrén yúkuài* nice; enjoyable, pleasant

娱乐 **yúlè** entertainment, amusement; pleasure; recreation

娱乐活动 **yúlè huódòng** amusements

娱乐园 **yúlè yuán** amusement park

娱乐中心 **yúlè zhōngxīn** leisure center; arcade

预料 **yùliào** anticipate, expect; foretell ◊ anticipation

雨林 **yǔlín** rain forest

羽毛 **yǔmáo** feather; plume

浴帽 **yùmào** shower cap

羽毛球 **yǔmáo qiú** badminton; shuttlecock

玉米 **yùmǐ** corn

玉米花 **yùmǐhuā** popcorn

渔民 **yúmín** fisherman

预谋 **yùmóu** premeditated

榆木 **yúmù** elm

云 **yún** cloud

允 **yǔn** permit

熨 **yùn** iron ◊ ironing; 熨衣服 *yùn yīfu* do the ironing

韵 **yùn** rhyme

晕 **yùn** dizzy, giddy

运 **yùn** transport

孕 **yùn** pregnant

遇难 **yùnàn** be killed (in an accident); 遇难船只 *yùnàn chuánzhī* the doomed ship

匀称 **yúnchèn** regular; shapely

匀出 **yúnchū** spare

晕船 **yùnchuán** seasick ◊ get seasick

运动 **yùndòng** move; movement; campaign; sport; exercise; 作运动 *zuò yùndòng* take exercise

运动场 **yùndòng chǎng** playing field

运动会 **yùndòng huì** meet SP

运动上衣 **yùndòng shàngyī** sportscoat

运动室 **yùndòng shì** gym, gymnasium

运动鞋 **yùndòng xié** sports shoes

运动衣 **yùndòng yī** jogging suit

运动员 **yùndòng yuán** sportsman; sportswoman; athlete; player

熨斗 **yùndǒu** iron

云耳 **yún'ěr** cloud ear (*mushroom*)

运费 **yùnfèi** freight

孕妇 **yùnfù** pregnant woman

孕妇服装 **yùnfù fúzhuāng** maternity dress

运河 **yùnhé** canal

与你无关！**yǔ nǐ wúguān!** that's none of your business!, mind your own business!

晕机 **yùnjī** airsick ◊ airsickness

酝酿 **yùnniàng** brew

愚弄 **yúnòng** tease

孕期 **yùnqī** pregnancy

运气 **yùnqì** fortune; luck

云雀 **yúnquè** lark

运输 **yùnshū** transport; transportation

运输公司 **yùnshū gōngsī** shipping company; carrier

运输机 **yùnshūjī** freighter (*plane*)

运输终点站 **yùnshū zhōngdiǎnzhàn** terminal (*for containers*)

运送 **yùnsòng** ship; shipping

陨星 **yǔnxīng** meteorite

运行 **yùnxíng** move

允许 **yǔnxǔ** allow, permit

晕眩 **yūnxuàn** light-headed

熨衣板 **yùnyībǎn** ironing board

运用 **yùnyòng** use; apply

运转 **yùnzhuǎn** operate; run; function; revolve; 这东西怎么运转？**zhèi dōngxi zěnme yùnzhuǎn?** how does this thing work?

浴盆 **yùpén** bathtub

语气 **yǔqì** tone

预期寿命 **yùqī shòumìng** life expectancy

羽绒 **yǔróng** eiderdown

雨伞 **yǔsǎn** umbrella

瘀伤 **yūshāng** bruise

于是 **yúshì** then; consequently

预示 **yùshì** usher in

浴室 **yùshì** bathroom

遇事不慌 **yùshì bùhuāng** presence of mind

与世隔绝 **yǔshì géjué** seclusion

余数 **yúshù** remainder

雨水道 **yǔshuǐ dào** storm drain

预算 **yùsuàn** calculate ◊ budget

鱼网 **yúwǎng** fishing net

欲望 **yùwàng** appetite; desire; longing

余味儿 **yúwèir** aftertaste

余下 **yúxià** the rest, remainder

预先 **yùxiān** in advance; 预先计划／考虑 **yùxiān jìhuà／kǎolǜ** plan／think ahead; 四个星期的预先通知 **sìgè xīngqī de yùxiān tōngzhī** four weeks' notice

雨靴 **yǔxuē** rain boot

语言 **yǔyán** language ◊ linguistic

预言 **yùyán** prophecy; prediction ◊ predict

语言学 **yǔyán xué** linguistics

语言学家 **yǔyán xuéjiā** linguist

语言障碍 **yǔyán zhàng'ài** language barrier

渔业 **yúyè** fishing industry

雨衣 **yǔyī** raincoat

羽衣 **yǔyī** plumage

浴衣 **yùyī** bathrobe

寓意 **yùyì** moral

郁郁不乐 **yùyù búlè** mope

预约 **yùyuē** arrange; reserve ◊ advance reservation

预展 **yùzhǎn** preview

预兆 **yùzhào** omen, sign ◊ ominous

预支 **yùzhī** get money in advance

预制 **yùzhì** prefabricated

雨中 **yǔzhōng** in the rain

与众不同 **yǔzhòng bùtóng** odd one out ◊ differently ◊ distinguished, dignified

宇宙 **yǔzhòu** universe

宇宙飞船 **yǔzhòu fēichuán** spaceship, spacecraft

宇宙空间站 **yǔzhòu kōngjiān zhàn** space station

鱼子酱 **yúzǐ jiàng** caviar

Z

砸 **zá** crack *nut*

杂 **zá** mixed, assorted; miscellaneous

杂草 **zácǎo** weed

杂费 **záfèi** incidental expenses

杂货 **záhuò** groceries

杂货店 **záhuò diàn** grocery store

杂货商 **záhuò shāng** grocer

灾 **zāi** disaster

栽 **zāi** plant; fall; 他栽倒在床上 **tā zāidǎo zài chuáng shàng** he sank onto the bed

再 **zài** again; further; 再来点儿茶吗？**zài láidiǎnr chá ma?** some more tea?; 再走两英里 **zài zǒu liǎng yīnglǐ** two miles further (on)

在 **zài** at; in; on; 在盒子里 **zài hézi lǐ** in the box; 在华盛顿/中国 **zài Huáshèngdùn / Zhōngguó** in Washington / China ◊ (*continuous tense*): 在服丧 **zài fúsāng** be mourning ◊ (*with sense of be*): be at; be in; be on; 我在火车上 **wǒ zài huǒchē shang** I'm on the train

在 … 背后 **zài … bèihòu** behind

在 … 的对面 **zài … de duìmiàn** opposite

在 … 的中心 **zài … de zhōngxīn** in the center of

在 … 底下 **zài … dǐxià** underneath

在 … 附近 **zài … fùjìn** in the vicinity of

在 … 后面 **zài … hòumiàn** behind

在 … 里 **zài … lǐ** inside

在 … 里面 **zài … lǐmiàn** within

在 … 旁 **zài … páng** beside

在 … 旁边 **zài … pángbiān** beside

在 … 期间 **zài … qījiān** during

在 … 上 **zài … shàng** on, aboard

在 … 上方 **zài … shàngfāng** over

在 … 上面 **zài … shàngmian** on; above

在 … 时期 **zài … shíqī** while

在 … 条件下 **zài … tiáojiàn xià** on the understanding that

在 … 同时 **zài … tóngshí** during

在 … 下面 **zài … xiàmiàn** beneath, under

在 … 以前 **zài … yǐqián** prior to

在 … 以外 **zài … yǐwài** outside

在 … 之列 **zài … zhī liè** rank among

在 … 之间 **zài … zhījiān** between

在 … 之内 **zài … zhīnèi** within

在 … 之前 **zài … zhīqián** before

在 … 之上 **zài … zhīshàng** on top of

在 … 之中 **zài … zhīzhōng** among(st)

在 … 中 **zài … zhōng** in the middle of

在 … 最上 **zài … zuìshàng** at the top of

在岸上 **zài ànshàng** ashore

再版 **zàibǎn** reprint

在保 **zàibǎo** on bail

在场 **zàichǎng** presence ◊ be present

再次 **zàicì** again

在此日期前使用 **zàicǐ rìqī qián shǐyòng** best before date

再发 **zàifā** recurrent

灾害 **zāihài** disaster

在行 **zàiháng** knowledgeable

在乎 **zàihu** mind, care; 我不在乎咱们做什么 **wǒ bú zàihu zánmen zuò shénme** I don't mind what we do

再婚 **zàihūn** remarry

灾祸 **zāihuò** catastrophe, disaster

再见 **zàijiàn** goodbye, see you

再来 **zàilái** call back, come back again

再来一个 **zàilái yígè** encore

灾难 **zāinàn** disaster, catastrophe

栽培 **zāipéi** cultivation

再说 **zàishuō** besides

在逃 **zàitáo** be at large; 在逃罪犯 **zàitáo zuìfàn** criminal on the run

再体验 **zài tǐyàn** relive

再现 **zàixiàn** reproduce

灾星 **zāixīng** jinx

再一次 **zàiyícì** once more

再一个 **zài yígè** another

再用 **zàiyòng** reuse

载有 **zàiyǒu** carry

在于 **zàiyú** rest with

再装满 **zài zhuāngmǎn** refill

杂技 **zájì** acrobatics

杂交 **zájiāo** hybrid

杂技演员 **zájì yǎnyuán** acrobat

砸烂 **zálàn** total, write off

杂乱 **záluàn** disorder ◊ disorderly ◊ be a mess

杂乱无章 **záluàn wú zhāng** disorder; mess ◊ messy; chaotic

砸门 **zámén** hammer at the door

暂 **zàn** temporary

赞 **zàn** praise

赞成 **zànchéng** approve, agree with ◊ favorable, agreeable ◊ approval

脏 **zāng** dirty

葬 **zàng** bury

葬礼 **zànglǐ** funeral; burial

脏乱 **zāngluàn** mess

赃物 **zāngwù** loot

脏物 **zāngwù** dirt

暂缓 **zànhuǎn** wait

赞美 **zànměi** praise; compliment ◊ complimentary

赞美诗 **zànměishī** hymn

咱们 **zánmen** we; us; 咱们快走吧 **zánmen kuài zǒu ba** let's get out of here

攒钱 **zǎnqián** save money; 为 … 攒钱 **wèi … zǎnqián** save up for

赞赏 **zànshǎng** appreciate

暂时 **zànshí** temporary ◊ temporarily

暂停 **zàntíng** pause ◊ time out

赞同 **zàntóng** agree with; approve

暂行 **zànxíng** provisional, temporary ◊ temporarily

赞许 **zànxǔ** applaud ◊ consent

赞扬 **zànyáng** credit; praise; applause

赞誉 **zànyù** praise

赞助 **zànzhù** support; patronage; sponsorship

赞助人 **zànzhùrén** patron; backer

糟 **zāo** bad, terrible ◊ damn!

遭 **zāo** meet, encounter

凿 **záo** chisel

枣 **zǎo** Chinese date

早 **zǎo** morning ◊ early; beforehand; 早在一九三五年 **zǎo zài yījiǔ sānwǔ nián** back in 1935

灶 **zào** stove; hearth

噪 **zào** noise

早餐 **zǎocān** breakfast

早产 **zǎochǎn** premature birth

早晨 **zǎochén** morning ◊ in the morning; 早晨好 **zǎochén hǎo** good morning

造成 **zàochéng** form; create; 造成困难 **zàochéng kùnnán** pose a problem

造船厂 **zàochuán chǎng** shipyard

遭到 **zāodào** meet with; 遭到炮火袭击 **zāodào pàohuǒ xíjī** come under shellfire

造反 **zàofǎn** revolt

糟糕 **zāogāo** bad, terrible, awful, horrible ◊ badly, terribly ◊ damn!

早就 **zǎojiù** for a long time; a long time ago

澡盆 **zǎopén** bath

早期 **zǎoqī** early (*farther back in time*)

早日康复！ **zǎorì kāngfù!** get well soon!

早上 **zǎoshang** in the morning; 早上好 **zǎoshang hǎo** good morning

早市 **zǎo shì** early-morning market

遭受 **zāoshòu** suffer

早熟 **zǎoshú** precocious

糟蹋 **zāotà** murder

糟透 **zāotòu** abysmal, atrocious; 糟透了！ **zāotòule!** it stinks!, it's awful!

灶头 **zàotóu** burner

造物主 **Zàowù zhǔ** the Creator

噪音 **zàoyīn** noise

凿子 **záozi** chisel

枣子 **zǎozi** Chinese date

杂耍 **záshuǎ** vaudeville

杂项 **záxiàng** sundries

杂志 **zázhì** magazine, journal

杂种狗 **zázhǒng gǒu** mongrel

责 **zé** duty, responsibility

责备 **zébèi** blame; reproach; reprimand

责怪 **zéguài** blame ◊ accusation

责骂 **zémà** scold

怎 **zěn** how; why

憎 **zēng** hate

增 **zēng** add; increase

赠 **zèng** give; present

增大 **zēngdà** increase; heighten

增多 **zēngduō** increase; multiply

憎恨 **zēnghèn** hate ◊ hatred

增加 **zēngjiā** increase, boost ◊ raise; 增加体重 **zēngjiā tǐzhòng** put on weight

增进 **zēngjìn** promote

增刊 **zēngkān** supplement

赠品 **zèngpǐn** freebie

增强 **zēngqiáng** strengthen, reinforce

赠券 **zèngquàn** coupon

增湿器 **zēngshī qì** humidifier

赠送 **zèngsòng** give; present ◊ complimentary; 把 Y 赠送给 X **bǎ Y zèngsònggěi X** present Y to X

曾孙 **zēngsūn** great-grandson (son's grandson)

曾外祖父 **zēngwài zǔfù** great-grandfather (maternal)

曾外祖母 **zēngwài zǔmǔ** great-grandmother (maternal)

增长 **zēngzhǎng** grow, expand; increase ◊ growth, expansion

增值 **zēngzhí** increase in value

曾祖父 **zēngzǔfù** great-grandfather (paternal)

曾祖母 **zēngzǔmǔ** great-grandmother (paternal)

怎么 **zěnme** how; how come; 我不知该怎么办 **wǒ bùzhī gāi zěnmebàn** I don't know what to do; 怎么了？ **zěnmele?** what's wrong?, what's the matter?

怎样 **zěnyàng** how

责任 **zérèn** responsibility, duty; blame

诘问 **zéwèn** heckle

闸 **zhá** lock; sluice

眨 **zhǎ** wink; blink

炸 **zhà** blow up, explode

榨 **zhà** squeeze

榨出 **zhàchū** extract; squeeze out ◊ extraction

炸弹 **zhàdàn** bomb

炸弹攻击 **zhàdàn gōngjī** bomb attack

轧辊 **zhágǔn** roller

诈呼 **zhàhu** bluff

摘 **zhāi** pick, pluck

窄 **zhǎi** narrow

债 **zhài** debt

摘除 **zhāichú** pluck

宅第 **zháidì** mansion

债卷 **zhàijuàn** bond

摘录 **zhāilù** extract, excerpt

债券 **zhàiquàn** promissory note; bond

债权人 **zhàiquán rén** creditor

债务 **zhàiwù** debt

窄小 **zhǎixiǎo** cramped

摘要 **zhāiyào** précis

债主 **zhàizhǔ** creditor

栅栏 **zhàlán** fence; railings; bars

蚱蜢 **zhàměng** grasshopper

沾 **zhān** dip

粘 **zhān** stick, glue

毡 **zhān** felt

展 **zhǎn** develop; open up

占 **zhàn** occupy; take; constitute, make up

站 **zhàn** stand ◊ stop; station; 站直了！ **zhànzhíle!** stand up straight!

战 **zhàn** fight ◊ battle; war

站不住脚 **zhàn búzhù jiǎo** lame excuse

战场 **zhànchǎng** battlefield, battleground

展出 **zhǎnchū** exhibit, display

站点 **zhàndiǎn** web site

战斗 **zhàndòu** combat; fight

战斗机 **zhàndòu jī** warplane, fighter

战俘 **zhànfú** prisoner of war

章 **zhāng** chapter

张 **zhāng** sheet ◊ measure word for

flat things; 一张纸 **yìzhāng zhǐ** piece of paper

掌 **zhǎng** palm

涨 **zhǎng** rise

长 **zhǎng** grow ◊ head; 家长 **jiāzhǎng** head of a family

胀 **zhàng** bloated

帐 **zhàng** account

障碍 **zhàng'ài** obstacle, hurdle, stumbling block; barrier

障碍物 **zhàng'ài wù** obstacle; obstruction, barrier, cordon

涨潮 **zhǎngcháo** incoming tide ◊ come in (*of tide*)

章程 **zhāngchéng** rules; statutes

长大 **zhǎngdà** grow up; develop

账单 **zhàngdān** check, bill; invoice

丈夫 **zhàngfu** husband

长高 **zhǎnggāo** shoot up (*of children*)

掌管 **zhǎngguǎn** preside over

掌击 **zhǎngjī** smack; slap; cuff

撞击 **zhàngjī** smash

涨价 **zhǎngjià** price rise

张开 **zhāngkāi** open, unfold

张口 **zhāngkǒu** gape

蟑螂 **zhāngláng** cockroach

长满青苔 **zhǎngmǎn qīngtái** mossy

长满树木 **zhǎngmǎn shùmù** wooded

帐目 **zhàngmù** accounts; books; account

樟脑 **zhāngnǎo** camphor

长女 **zhǎngnǚ** firstborn (daughter)

长胖 **zhǎngpàng** fill out, get fatter

帐篷 **zhàngpeng** tent

掌声 **zhǎngshēng** applause

张贴 **zhāngtiē** put up, post; pin up

战国时期 **Zhànguó Shíqī** Warring States (Period)

掌握 **zhǎngwò** grasp; master; control

章鱼 **zhāngyú** octopus

长子 **zhǎngzǐ** firstborn (son)

粘合剂 **zhānhéjì** adhesive

战后 **zhànhòu** postwar

粘糊糊 **zhānhúhú** sticky

展开 **zhǎnkāi** unfold, unwind; unroll; lay out

粘扣 **Zhānkòu** Velcro®

展览 **zhǎnlǎn** display, exhibit

展览橱窗 **zhǎnlǎn chúchuāng** display cabinet

展览会 **zhǎnlǎnhuì** exhibition

站立 **zhànlì** stand

沾料 **zhānliào** dip (*food*)

站立空间 **zhànlì kōngjiān** standing room

占领 **zhànlǐng** capture; occupy ◊ occupation

战略 **zhànlüè** strategy ◊ strategic

展品 **zhǎnpǐn** exhibit

展期 **zhǎnqī** renew, extend ◊ renewal, extension

战前 **zhànqián** prewar

站起来 **zhàn qǐlái** stand up, get up; jump to one's feet; 他腾地站起来 **tā téngde zhàn qǐlái** he scrambled to his feet

占去 **zhànqù** take up *space, time*

占少数 **zhàn shǎoshù** be in the minority

战胜 **zhànshèng** conquer ◊ victorious; 战胜 X **zhànshèng X** win a victory over X

展示 **zhǎnshì** show; show off; model

战时 **zhànshí** wartime

战士 **zhànshì** soldier; warrior; fighter

战术 **zhànshù** tactics ◊ tactical

站台 **zhàntái** platform; 第十站台 **dì shí zhàntái** track 10

粘贴 **zhāntiē** paste, stick; adhere

毡头笔 **zhāntóubǐ** felt-tip (pen)

展望 **zhǎnwàng** outlook

谵妄 **zhānwàng** delirious

站位 **zhànwèi** standing room

沾污 **zhānwū** stain

占线 **zhànxiàn** busy ◊ the line is busy

战线 **zhànxiàn** front; battle line

占线声 **zhànxiàn shēng** busy signal

崭新 **zhǎnxīn** brand-new

占星术 **zhànxīng shù** astrology

占星者 **zhànxīng zhě** astrologer

暂休 **zhànxiū** adjourn

战役 **zhànyì** battle

占用 zhànyòng occupy; encroach on

占有 zhànyǒu own, have; take

占优势 zhàn yōushì dominant; predominant ◊ predominate

占有者 zhànyǒu zhě owner

沾沾自喜 zhānzhān zìxǐ gloat

粘着 zhānzhe cling to

站着 zhànzhe stand

战争 zhànzhēng war; warfare; conflict; hostilities

站住 zhànzhù stop

辗转 zhǎnzhuǎn toss and turn

辗转反侧 zhǎnzhuǎn fǎncè toss and turn

招 zhāo beckon

朝 zhāo morning

着 zháo ignite

找 zhǎo look for; ask for

罩 zhào cover

召 zhào convene; summon

照 zhào photograph; license ◊ shine; light up ◊ according to; 照 X 光 zhào X guāng take an X-ray; 照我看来 zhào wǒ kànlái in my estimation

找出 zhǎochū locate, dig out; work out *solution*

找拇 zhǎocuò find fault with

招待 zhāodài entertain; serve *customer*; 热情招待 rèqíng zhāodài hospitality

招待会 zhāodài huì reception

招待所 zhāodàisuǒ guesthouse

找到 zhǎodào find

找工作 zhǎo gōngzuò be job hunting

照顾 zhàogù look after; tend ◊ care

照管 zhàoguǎn look after

照顾不周 zhàogù bùzhōu neglect

召唤 zhāohuàn call out; beckon

召回 zhāohuí recall

找回 zhǎohuí recover, get back ◊ recovery

招魂术者 zhāohúnshù zhě spiritualist

着火 zhǎohuǒ be on fire ◊ alight, ablaze

着急 zháojí worry; be anxious

召集 zhàojí call, convene; summon

召开 zhàokāi convene; hold

照看 zhàokàn mind, watch, keep an eye on

照亮 zhàoliàng light up

照料 zhàoliào look after; coddle

着陆 zháolù touch down (*of plane*) ◊ touchdown

着迷 zháomí captivate, entrance ◊ obsession ◊ entranced; 使着迷 shǐ zháomí fascinate; 对 X 着迷 duì X zháomí be mad about X

照明 zhàomíng illuminate, light ◊ lighting

召募 zhāomù enlist

招牌 zhāopai sign

照片 zhàopiàn photograph

招聘 zhāopìn recruit ◊ recruitment

找钱 zhǎoqián change ◊ 等一下, 我给你找钱 děng yíxià, wǒ gěi nǐ zhǎoqián just a minute, I'll give you the change

朝气蓬勃 zhāoqì péngbó youthful

招认 zhāorèn confess

着色 zháosè tinted

招收 zhāoshōu intake (*of college etc*)

招手 zhāoshǒu wave; beckon

朝霞 zhāoxiá dawn

照相 zhàoxiàng take a photo

照像机 zhàoxiàng jī camera

照耀 zhàoyào shine

罩衣 zhàoyī coveralls

照一照 zhàoyīzhào shine

沼泽 zhǎozé swamp, marsh, bog

招致 zhāozhì incur; 招致麻烦 zhāozhì máfán get into trouble

兆字节 zhàozìjié megabyte

榨取 zhàqǔ bleed; drain; overburden

炸薯片 zhá shǔpiàn potato chip

炸薯条 zhá shǔtiáo fried potatoes

扎眼 zhāyǎn pierce

眨眼 zhǎyǎn blink; wink

炸药 zhàyào dynamite; gunpowder; explosive

沾沾自喜 zhāzhan zìxǐ

complacent

渣子 **zhāzi** crumb; dregs; scum (*people*)

螫 **zhē** sting

遮 **zhē** cover

折 **zhé** break; fold

褶 **zhě** fold; pleat; tuck

这 **zhè** this; these; the; 这是谁的？ **zhè shì shéide?** whose is this?

着 **zhe** (*continuing action*): 他抱着孩子 **tā bàozhe háizi** he's holding a baby ◊ (*imperative*): 听着！ **tīngzhe!** listen!

遮蔽 **zhēbì** shade; screen; blot out

螫刺 **zhēcì** sting

这次 **zhècì** this time

折叠 **zhédié** fold ◊ folding *chair etc*, collapsible

折叠椅 **zhédiéyǐ** folding chair

折断 **zhéduàn** break; break off; fracture

这个 **zhège** this ◊ this one

折合 **zhéhé** convert *unit of measurement*

这些 **zhèi** this; these

折扣 **zhékòu** discount; rebate

这里 **zhèlǐ** here

这么 **zhème** such; so; this; 这么大 **zhème dà** this big; 这么快 **zhème kuà** so quick

折磨 **zhémo** torment, torture

榛 **zhēn** hazel

针 **zhēn** needle; hand (*of clock*)

真 **zhēn** real, true

侦 **zhēn** detect

珍 **zhēn** valuable ◊ value

疹 **zhěn** rash; blotch

枕 **zhěn** pillow

镇 **zhèn** town

震 **zhèn** tremble, shake; quake; shock

阵 **zhèn** *measure word for smoke or dust*; 一阵烟／尘土 **yízhèn yān**／**chéntǔ** a cloud of smoke／dust

珍爱 **zhēn'ài** fond *memory*

珍宝 **zhēnbǎo** treasure; gem

针鼻儿 **zhēnbír** eye of a needle

侦察 **zhēnchá** reconnoiter ◊ reconnaissance

震颤 **zhènchàn** throb; tremble; twitch

真诚 **zhēnchéng** sincere ◊ sincerely ◊ sincerity

针刺 **zhēncì** acupuncture

震荡 **zhèndàng** concussion

真的 **zhēnde** really, actually; 真的吗？ **zhēnde ma?** really?

真地 **zhēnde** truly

阵地 **zhèndì** position MIL

镇定 **zhèndìng** calm, composed

镇定自若 **zhèndìng zìruò** unflappable

震动 **zhèndòng** shudder; vibrate ◊ vibration; tremor

振动 **zhèndòng** vibrate ◊ vibration

针对 **zhēnduì** be aimed at

振奋 **zhènfèn** feel inspired; 令人振奋 **lìngrén zhènfèn** rousing

阵风 **zhènfēng** gust of wind

振奋人心 **zhènfèn rénxīn** stimulating

蒸 **zhēng** steam

征 **zhēng** journey ◊ summon; levy *taxes*

争 **zhēng** struggle; contend

整 **zhěng** complete, total; all; 三点整 **sāndiǎn zhěng** at 3 o'clock sharp

挣 **zhèng** earn; struggle

正 **zhèng** positive; plus; upright; just

证 **zhèng** evidence

政 **zhèng** politics ◊ political

争辩 **zhēngbiàn** dispute; 与X争辩 **yǔ X zhēngbiàn** take issue with X

政变 **zhèngbiàn** coup

征兵 **zhēngbīng** draft MIL

政策 **zhèngcè** policy

政策准则 **zhèngcè zhǔnzé** component, aspect (*of policy*)

正常 **zhèngcháng** normal; regular ◊ normally ◊ normality; 一切正常 **yíqiè zhèngcháng** the situation is under control

正常化 **zhèngcháng huà** normalize

争吵 **zhēngchǎo** squabble, quarrel

证词 **zhèngcí** testimony

正当 **zhèngdāng** proper; legitimate; right

正当理由 **zhèngdāng lǐyóu** justification

挣得 **zhèngde** earn

正点 **zhèngdiǎn** on schedule

争斗 **zhēngdòu** fight, struggle

整顿 **zhěngdùn** regulation; arrangement

争夺 **zhēngduó** dispute; compete for / against ◊ contest

争夺者 **zhēngduó zhě** contender

蒸发 **zhēngfā** evaporate; steam

正方形 **zhèngfāng xíng** square

征服 **zhēngfu** conquer, overcome ◊ conquest

政府 **zhèngfǔ** government

政府机构 **zhèngfǔ jīgòu** public sector

征服者 **zhēngfú zhě** conqueror

整 **zhěng** complete; whole; 两点整 **liǎngdiǎn zhěng** at two o'clock prompt

整个 **zhěnggè** whole, entire

正规来说 **zhèngguī láishuō** officially, strictly (speaking)

蒸锅 **zhēngguō** steamer (for cooking)

正好 **zhènghǎo** just right

正极 **zhèngjí** positive ELEC

证件 **zhèngjiàn** papers, ID

整洁 **zhěngjié** neat, tidy

整洁漂亮 **zhěngjié piàoliàng** smart, neat, spruce

拯救 **zhěngjiù** save ◊ salvation; redemption

证据 **zhèngjù** evidence; proof

整理 **zhěnglǐ** order, arrange; sort out; clear up

整理行装 **zhěnglǐ xíngzhuāng** pack, do one's packing

争论 **zhēnglùn** argue, contend; dispute ◊ argument; controversy

正门 **zhèngmén** front entrance

正面 **zhèngmiàn** front; façade; 正面还是反面? **zhèngmiàn háishì fǎnmiàn?** heads or tails?

正面看台 **zhèngmiàn kàntái** grandstand

证明 **zhèngmíng** certify; prove,

verify ◊ certificate; confirmation; verification

征募 **zhēngmù** recruit

正派 **zhèngpài** decent; law-abiding; straight ◊ decency

整批 **zhěngpī** in bulk

正片 **zhèngpiān** feature movie

蒸汽 **zhēngqì** steam

整齐 **zhěngqí** neat, tidy; shipshape

挣钱 **zhèngqián** earn money

蒸汽电熨斗 **zhēngqì diàn yùndǒu** steam iron

蒸汽机车 **zhēngqì jīchē** steam locomotive

蒸汽浴 **zhēngqì yù** steam bath

争取 **zhēngqǔ** fight for

政权 **zhèngquán** regime

证券 **zhèngquàn** securities

证券市场 **zhèngquàn shìchǎng** stock market; securities market

正确 **zhèngquè** correct, right ◊ correctly; properly; 大致正确 **dàzhì zhèngquè** approximately right

正确性 **zhèngquè xìng** validity

证人 **zhèngrén** witness

证人席 **zhèngrén xí** witness stand

整容外科 **zhěngróng wàikē** cosmetic surgery

整容外科医生 **zhěngróng wàikē yīshēng** plastic surgeon

正如我言 **zhèngrú wǒ yán** like I said

证实 **zhèngshí** confirm; corroborate; back up ◊ confirmation

证实 **zhèngshí** confirm

正式 **zhèngshì** formal; official ◊ formally; officially

征收 **zhēngshōu** impose, levy, collect

整数 **zhěngshù** in round figures

证书 **zhèngshù** certificate; qualification

征税 **zhēngshuì** taxation

整肃 **zhěngsù** purge

整体 **zhěngtǐ** whole; 我们必须作为一个整体一起工作 **wǒmen bìxū zuòwéi yígè zhěngtǐ yìqǐ gōngzuò** we must work together as a unit

政务会委员 zhèngwùhuì wěiyuán councilor

正相反 zhèng xiāngfǎn on the contrary

整形外科 zhěngxíng wàikē plastic surgery

整形外科医生 zhěngxíng wàikē yīshēng plastic surgeon

整修 zhěngxiū renovate ◊ renovation

正要 ... zhèngyào ... be on the point of; 我正要离开，这时 ... wǒ zhèngyào líkāi, zhèishí ... I was just about to leave when ...

争议 zhēngyì conflict

正义 zhèngyì just ◊ justice

正在 zhèngzài currently in the process of

正在流行 zhèngzài liúxíng in vogue

证章 zhèngzhāng badge

征兆 zhēngzhào symptom

争执 zhēngzhí disagreement, dispute

正直 zhèngzhí be right ◊ upright, decent

政治 zhèngzhì politics ◊ political; 政治信仰 zhèngzhì xìnyǎng political beliefs

政治犯 zhèngzhì fàn political detainee

政治家 zhèngzhì jiā politician; statesman

政治局 Zhèngzhìjú Politbureau

郑重 zhèngzhòng solemn, binding

正中要害 zhèngzhòng yàohài hit the bull's eye

症状 zhèngzhuàng symptom MED; 戒毒时的症状 jièdú shí de zhèngzhuàng withdrawal symptoms

正准备 ... zhèng zhǔnbèi ... be about to ...

正字法 zhèngzìfǎ orthography

震撼 zhènhàn shake

赈济 zhènjì charity

针脚 zhēnjiǎo stitch

贞洁 zhēnjié chaste ◊ virginity

震惊 zhènjīng shock; 令人震惊 lìngrén zhènjīng shocking; appalling

镇静 zhènjìng calm, collected, composed ◊ composure

镇静剂 zhènjìng jì tranquilizer

镇静药 zhènjìng yào sedative

针灸 zhēnjiǔ acupuncture

真空 zhēnkōng vacuum

真空包装 zhēnkōng bāozhuāng vacuum-packed

真空吸尘器 zhēnkōng xīchén qì vacuum cleaner

真理 zhēnlǐ truth

珍品 zhēnpǐn gem

真品 zhēnpǐn genuine

侦破 zhēnpò solve, crack

真实 zhēnshí real; true ◊ really, actually

珍视 zhēnshì prize, value; 不够珍视 X bú gòu zhēnshì X take X for granted, not appreciate X

真是的！ zhēnshìde! really! (expressing exasperation etc)

真实性 zhēnshí xìng authenticity

诊所 zhěnsuǒ clinic

侦探 zhēntàn detective

侦探片 zhēntàn piān crime movie

侦探小说 zhēntàn xiǎoshuō detective novel

枕套 zhěntào pillowcase, pillowslip

镇痛 zhèntòng pain-killing, analgesic

针头 zhēntóu needle (for injection)

枕头 zhěntou pillow

珍惜 zhēnxí cherish, treasure

针线 zhēnxiàn needlework; needle and thread; notions

真相 zhēnxiàng fact; truth

针线活儿 zhēnxiàn huór needlework

镇压 zhènyā repress, suppress ◊ repression, suppression

针叶树 zhēnyè shù conifer

阵雨 zhènyǔ shower (of rain)

真正 zhēnzhèng authentic, real ◊ really

镇政府 zhèn zhèngfǔ town council

针织品 zhēnzhī pǐn knitwear

针织衣服 zhēnzhī yīfú knitwear

震中 **zhènzhōng** epicenter

珍珠 **zhēnzhū** pearl

珍珠母 **zhēnzhūmǔ** mother-of-pearl

榛子 **zhēnzi** hazelnut

折蓬车 **zhépéng chē** convertible

折起来 **zhé qǐlái** fold up *chair etc*

这儿 **zhèr** here

折算 **zhésuàn** conversion

折梯 **zhétī** step ladder

这些 **zhèxiē** these

哲学 **zhéxué** philosophy

哲学家 **zhéxué jiā** philosopher

遮掩 **zhēyǎn** hush up

这样 **zhèyàng** like this, this way; so; such; 我认为是这样 **wǒ rènwéi shì zhèyàng** I think so

遮阳帽 **zhēyángmào** baseball cap

折页 **zhéyè** hinge

遮阴 **zhēyīn** shade ◊ shady

之 **zhī** *fml (possessive indicator)*: 东方之珠 **dōngfāng zhī zhū** the pearl of the east

只 **zhī** *measure word for birds, animals, boats*; 两只老虎 **liǎngzhī lǎohú** two tigers

汁 **zhī** juice

支 **zhī** *measure word for pens, pencils, cigarettes and long cylindrical things*

织 **zhī** weave; knit

知 **zhī** know

脂 **zhī** fat; grease

直 **zhí** straight

职 **zhí** employment; job

植 **zhí** plant

值 **zhí** value ◊ be worth

执 **zhí** hold

只 **zhǐ** only

纸 **zhǐ** paper

指 **zhǐ** finger ◊ point to

止 **zhǐ** stop

痣 **zhì** mole *(on skin)*

掷 **zhì** toss, throw; 掷色子 **zhì shǎizi** throw dice

治 **zhì** control

志 **zhì** will, willpower

至 **zhì** to; up to ◊ reach; 十至十五人 **shí zhì shíwǔ rén** from 10 to 15 people; 星期一至五 **xīngqī yī zhì wǔ** Monday through Friday

致 **zhì** send; cause

制 **zhì** make, manufacture

智 **zhì** wisdom

质 **zhì** substance

致癌 **zhì'ái** carcinogenic

致癌物 **zhì'ái wù** carcinogen

值班 **zhíbān** be on duty

纸板 **zhǐbǎn** cardboard

纸板盒 **zhǐbǎn hé** cardboard box

纸板火柴 **zhǐbǎn huǒchái** book of matches

纸杯子 **zhǐ bēizi** paper cup

直奔 **zhíbēn** make a beeline for

纸币 **zhǐbì** (bank)bill

掷币 **zhìbì** toss a coin

支部 **zhībù** branch, chapter

只不过 **zhǐbúguò** mere ◊ merely

织布机 **zhībùjī** loom

制裁 **zhìcái** crack down on ◊ crackdown; sanction, penalty

致残 **zhìcán** maim

支撑 **zhīcheng** support, hold up; sustain

支撑起 **zhīchēngqǐ** prop up

支撑住 **zhīchěngzhù** hold out, manage

支持 **zhīchí** hold, keep in place; support; back up, endorse ◊ backing; endorsement ◊ supportive; 我支持你 **wǒ zhīchí nǐ** I'm on your side

支持者 **zhīchí zhě** follower, supporter

支出 **zhīchū** pay ◊ expenditure

指出 **zhǐchū** point out

痔疮 **zhìchuāng** piles MED

直达 **zhídá** direct, nonstop *flight etc*

纸袋 **zhǐdài** paper bag

值当 **zhídàng** be good value

知道 **zhīdao** know

直到 **zhídào** until ◊ pending; 直到七月才能完成 **zhídào qīyuè cái néng wánchéng** it won't be finished until July

指导 **zhǐdǎo** guide; instruct; coach ◊ directions, instructions; guidance; directory

指导员 **zhǐdǎo yuán** instructor

指导者 **zhǐdǎo zhě** supervisor

值得 **zhíde** deserve, merit; be

worthwhile ◊ desirable; recommended; 值得信任 **zhíde xìnrèn** trustworthy

质地 **zhìdì** texture

支点 **zhīdiǎn** pivot

指定 **zhǐdìng** specify; designate; be meant for, be aimed at; 指定教材 **zhǐdìng jiàocái** set book

制定 **zhìdìng** enact, institute

指定集合点 **zhǐdìng jíhé diǎn** rendez-vous; assembly point

制动 **zhìdòng** brake

制动信号灯 **zhìdòng xìnhào dēng** brake light

制度 **zhìdù** system

只读存储器 **zhǐdú cúnchǔ qì** ROM, read-only memory

只读档案 **zhǐdú dǎng'àn** read-only file

至多 **zhìduō** at (the) most

脂肪 **zhīfáng** fat; 含脂肪多 **hán zhīfáng duo** fatty

支付 **zhīfù** pay; 支付手段 **zhīfù shǒuduàn** means of payment

制服 **zhìfú** uniform

至高点 **zhìgāodiǎn** summit, peak (*of powers etc*)

趾高气扬 **zhǐgāo qìyáng** swagger

至高无上 **zhìgāo wúshàng** supreme

吱嘎声 **zhīgā shēng** squeak; creak

制革 **zhìgé** tan *leather*

职工 **zhígōng** workforce, staff

直观 **zhíguān** visual

直观教具 **zhíguān jiàojù** visual aid

直观显示部件 **zhíguān xiǎnshì bùjiàn** VDU, visual display unit

至关重要 **zhìguān zhòngyào** of prime importance

直航飞机 **zhíháng fēijī** through flight

治好 **zhìhǎo** cure

纸盒 **zhǐhé** carton

之后 **zhīhòu** after

指挥 **zhǐhuī** conduct ◊ bandmaster

智慧 **zhìhuì** wisdom; intelligence

指挥调度台 **zhǐhuī diàodù tái** control tower

指挥官 **zhǐhuī guān** commander

指挥家 **zhǐhuī jiā** conductor

指挥台 **zhǐhuī tái** podium

支架 **zhījià** upright; support, prop

指甲 **zhǐjia** fingernail

指甲锉 **zhǐjia cuò** nail file

指甲刀 **zhǐjia dāo** nail clippers

指甲剪 **zhǐjia jiǎn** nail scissors

指尖 **zhǐjiān** fingertip

纸浆 **zhǐjiāng** paper pulp

直角 **zhíjiǎo** right-angle; 成直角 **chéng zhíjiǎo** at right-angles to

指甲油 **zhǐjia yóu** nail polish

指甲油去除剂 **zhǐjia yóu qùchú jì** nail polish remover

枝节 **zhījié** detail

直接 **zhíjiē** direct ◊ directly, straight

直截了当 **zhíjiē liǎodàng** straightforward, direct ◊ straight out, bluntly

掷界外球 **zhì jiè wài qiú** throw-in (*in soccer*)

织锦 **zhījǐn** tapestry

纸巾 **zhǐjīn** tissue

至今 **zhìjīn** until now, up to now

直径 **zhíjìng** diameter

致敬 **zhìjìng** salute

纸卷 **zhǐjuǎn** scroll

知觉 **zhījué** consciousness; feeling MED; 失去/恢复知觉 **shīqù / huīfù zhījué** lose / regain consciousness

直觉 **zhíjué** intuition

止渴 **zhǐkě** quench one's thirst

止咳糖 **zhǐké táng** lozenge

止咳糖浆 **zhǐké tángjiāng** cough medicine, cough syrup

指控 **zhǐkòng** accuse; charge ◊ allegation

直立 **zhílì** erect, upright

治理 **zhìlǐ** administration ◊ administer, govern

致力 **zhìlì** dedication

智力 **zhìlì** intellect; intelligence ◊ intellectual

质量 **zhìliàng** quality

质量管理 **zhìliàng guǎnlǐ** quality control

质量控制 **zhìliàng kòngzhì** quality control

治疗 **zhìliáo** treatment, therapy ◊

treat

治疗学家 **zhìliáo xuéjiā** therapist

智力迟钝 **zhìlì chídùn** retarded

支离破碎 **zhīlí pòsuì** fragmentary

支流 **zhīliú** tributary

直流电 **zhíliúdiàn** direct current

智力游戏 **zhìlì yóuxì** puzzle

支路 **zhīlù** side road

指路 **zhǐlù** navigate (*in car*)

指路人 **zhǐlùrén** navigator (*in car*)

芝麻 **zhīma** sesame

芝麻油 **zhīma yóu** sesame oil

殖民地 **zhímíndì** colony ◊ colonial

知名 **zhīmíng** famous; prominent

指明 **zhǐmíng** point out

致命 **zhìmìng** lethal, fatal ◊ fatally

殖民者 **zhímín zhě** settler

指南 **zhǐnán** guidebook; manual

指南针 **zhǐnán zhēn** compass

执拗 **zhíniù** stubborn

侄女 **zhínǚ** niece (*brother's daughter*)

纸牌 **zhǐpái** playing card

制片人 **zhìpiān rén** film-maker; producer

支票 **zhīpiào** check FIN

支票本 **zhīpiào běn** checkbook

支票帐户 **zhīpiào zhànghù** checking account

质朴 **zhìpǔ** unsophisticated

志气 **zhìqì** ambition

之前 **zhīqián** before

支气管炎 **zhīqìguǎn yán** bronchitis

智穷计尽 **zhìqióng jìjìn** be at one's wits' end

支取 **zhīqǔ** withdraw

智商 **zhìshāng** IQ

至少 **zhìshǎo** at least

智胜 **zhìshèng** outwit

直升飞机 **zhíshēng fēijī** helicopter

知识 **zhīshi** knowledge; learning

指示 **zhǐshì** indicate, signal; instruct ◊ indication; directions; 指示 X 做 Y **zhǐshì X zuò Y** instruct X to do Y

只是 **zhǐshì** just, only; except that

知识分子 **zhīshí fènzǐ** intellectual

指示牌 **zhǐshì pái** road sign

直率 **zhíshuài** blunt, direct ◊ bluntly

直爽 **zhíshuǎng** direct

直说 **zhíshuō** speak one's mind

制陶术 **zhìtáoshù** pottery

直通火车 **zhítōng huǒchē** through train

止痛片 **zhǐtòng piàn** painkiller

制图 **zhìtú** draw charts; make maps

指望 **zhǐwàng** bank on ◊ expectations

职位 **zhíwèi** office, position, post

质问 **zhìwèn** question, challenge

植物 **zhíwù** plant ◊ botanical

职务 **zhíwù** duties; job

植物学 **zhíwù xué** botany

知悉 **zhīxī** knowingly

窒息 **zhìxī** suffocate ◊ suffocation; 令人窒息 **lìngrén zhìxī** stifling

支线 **zhīxiàn** branch line

直线 **zhíxiàn** straight line

纸箱 **zhǐxiāng** carton, box, pack

指向 **zhǐxiàng** direct; point at

志向 **zhìxiàng** ambition

致谢 **zhìxiè** give one's thanks

窒息而死 **zhìxī ér sǐ** suffocate

执行 **zhíxíng** carry out, execute

直系亲属 **zhíxì qīnshǔ** the immediate family

秩序 **zhìxù** order, orderliness

止血 **zhǐxuè** stop bleeding ◊ styptic

智牙 **zhìyá** wisdom tooth

直言不讳 **zhíyán búhuì** outspoken; blunt

只要 **zhǐyào** provided that; so long as

制药 **zhìyào** pharmaceutical

制药公司 **zhìyào gōngsī** pharmaceutical company

职业 **zhíyè** business; profession; occupation ◊ vocational; occupational; professional

职业介绍所 **zhíyè jièshàosuǒ** employment agency

职业人员 **zhíyè rényuán** professional

职业杀手 **zhíyè shāshǒu** hitman

质疑 **zhìyí** challenge; 对 X 有质疑 **duì X yǒu zhìyí** feel

uncomfortable about X; question the validity of X

直译 zhíyì literal translation

指引 zhǐyǐn guide, show, direct

执意做 zhíyì zuò persist in

只有 zhǐyǒu only if; nothing but; 只有几个 zhǐyǒu jǐgè just a couple; 只有最好的 zhǐyǒu zuìhǎo de nothing but the best

至于 zhìyú as for

治愈 zhìyù heal, cure

职员 zhíyuán employee; personnel

志愿 zhìyuàn voluntary ◊ volunteer

志愿者 zhìyuàn zhě volunteer

置于两侧 zhìyú liǎngcè flank

制造 zhìzào manufacture, produce ◊ manufacturing

制造厂家 zhìzào chǎngjiā producer

制造商 zhìzào shāng manufacturer

制造者 zhìzào zhě maker

指责 zhǐzé rebuke, reproach ◊ disapproval ◊ reproachful

执照 zhízhào license

执照号码 zhízhào hàomǎ license number

指针 zhǐzhēn needle (on dial); hand (on clock)

执政 zhízhèng in power

直着走 zhízhe zǒu straight ahead ◊ carry straight on

纸制 zhǐzhì paper

制止 zhìzhǐ prevent; deter; stem, block

吱吱声 zhīzhi shēng squeak (of mouse); twitter (of birds)

蜘蛛 zhīzhū spider

支柱 zhīzhù support

止住 zhǐzhù halt

蜘蛛网 zhīzhūwǎng spider's web, cobweb

侄子 zhízi nephew (brother's son)

知足 zhīzú undemanding, modest

制作 zhìzuò make, produce ◊ production

钟 zhōng clock; bell; o'clock

中 zhōng middle; medium; China ◊ be in the process of

忠 zhōng loyal; faithful

终 zhōng end

种 zhǒng species; race; sort, kind; 两种 liǎngzhǒng two kinds of

肿 zhǒng swell ◊ swollen

重 zhòng heavy

种 zhòng plant

中 zhòng hit

众 zhòng crowd

钟表匠 zhōngbiǎo jiàng watchmaker

中波 zhōngbō medium wave

中部 zhōngbù central ◊ central part

仲裁 zhòngcái arbitrate ◊ arbitration

中餐 zhōngcān Chinese food

中产阶级 zhōngchǎn jiējí middle-class ◊ the middle classes

忠诚 zhōngchéng faithful

重大 zhòngdà serious, weighty

中等 zhōngděng medium; average, middling

中等教育 zhōngděng jiàoyù secondary education

终点 zhōngdiǎn finish, end

重点 zhòngdiǎn stress; key point; emphasis; 把重点转移到 bǎ zhòngdiǎn zhuǎnyídào shift the emphasis onto

终点线 zhōngdiǎnxiàn finishing line

终点站 zhōngdiǎn zhàn terminus

中东 Zhōngdōng Middle East

仲冬 zhòngdōng midwinter

重读 zhòngdú stress, emphasize

中毒 zhòngdú poisoning

中断 zhōngduàn interrupt; break off ◊ interruption

终端产品 zhōngduān chǎnpǐn end product

终端用户 zhōngduān yònghù end-user

众多 zhòngduō mass, large amount

中耳炎 zhōng'ěr yán middle ear infection

中饭 zhōngfàn lunch

中风 zhòngfēng stroke MED

重负 zhòngfù strain, stress

忠告 **zhōnggào** advise, recommend

中共 **Zhōnggòng** Chinese Communist Party

重工业 **zhònggōngyè** heavy industry

中共中央委员会 **Zhōnggòng Zhōngyāng Wěiyuánhuì** Central Committee of the Chinese Communist Party

中国 **Zhōngguó** China ◊ Chinese

中国大陆 **Zhōngguó Dàlù** Mainland China

中国国际旅行社 **Zhōngguó Guójì Lǚxíngshè** China International Travel Service, CITS

中国话 **Zhōngguó huà** Chinese (*language*)

中国旅行社 **Zhōngguó Lǚxíngshè** China Travel Service, CTS

中国民航 **Zhóngguó Mínháng** Civil Aviation Administration of China, CAAC

中国人 **Zhōngguó rén** Chinese

中国日报 **Zhōngguó Rìbào** China Daily

中国相棋 **Zhōngguó xiàngqí** Chinese chess

中国银行 **Zhōngguó Yínháng** Bank of China

中国制造 **Zhōngguó zhìzào** made in China

中号 **zhōnghào** medium ◊ medium-sized

中和 **zhōnghé** counteract; neutralize

中华民国 **Zhōnghuá Mínguó** Republic of China, ROC

中华人民共和国 **Zhōnghuá Rénmín Gònghéguó** People's Republic of China, PRC

中级 **zhōngjí** intermediate

重击 **zhòngjī** thump, whack; hammer on

中间 **zhōngjiān** middle ◊ halfway

中间对齐 **zhōngjiān duìqí** center *text*

中兼分子 **zhōngjiān fènzi** hard core POL

中间楼层 **zhōngjiān lóucéng** mezzanine

中间名 **zhōngjiān míng** middle name

中间派 **zhōngjiān pài** center POL

中间人 **zhōngjiān rén** go-between

终究 **zhōngjiū** finally

中肯 **zhòngkěn** apt ◊ aptly

中空 **zhōngkōng** hollow

肿块 **zhǒngkuài** lump, swelling

种类 **zhǒnglèi** kind, type, variety; species

中立 **zhōnglì** disinterested; neutral

重力 **zhònglì** gravity PHYS

重量 **zhòngliàng** weight

中量级 **zhōngliàng jí** middleweight SP

重量极 **zhòngliàng jí** heavyweight SP

中立地位 **zhōnglì dìwèi** neutrality

肿瘤 **zhǒngliú** tumor

钟楼 **zhōnglóu** belfry

钟面 **zhōngmiàn** dial, face (*of clock*)

中年 **zhōngnián** middle age ◊ middle-aged

中篇小说 **zhōngpiān xiǎoshuō** novella

钟情 **zhōngqíng** loving

中秋节 **Zhōngqiūjié** Mid-Autumn Festival, Moon Festival

中人 **zhōngrén** intermediary

中日战争 **Zhōngrì Zhànzhēng** Sino-Japanese war

中山服 **zhōngshānfú** Mao jacket

终身 **zhōngshēn** lifelong; for life

终身伴侣 **zhōngshēn bànlǚ** life partner

钟声 **zhōngshēng** ring (*of bell*)

忠实 **zhōngshí** devoted

中式 **zhōngshì** Chinese-style

中士 **zhōngshì** sergeant

重视 **zhòngshì** value, attach importance to

中世纪 **Zhōngshìjì** Middle Ages ◊ medieval

重事轻说 **zhòngshì qīngshuō** understatement

忠实于 **zhōngshí yú** be devoted to

中暑 **zhòngshǔ** heatstroke; 他中暑了 **tā zhòngshǔ le** he has had too much sun

众所周知 **zhòng suǒ zhōu zhī** well-known

重听 **zhòngtīng** hard of hearing

中途 **zhōngtú** midway

中途停留 **zhōngtú tíngliú** stop over ◊ stopover

中途退出 **zhōngtú tuìchū** abort COMPUT

中途退学 **zhōngtú tuìxué** drop out (*of school*)

中尉 **zhōngwèi** lieutenant

中文 **Zhōngwén** Chinese (*language*)

中午 **zhōngwǔ** midday

仲夏 **zhòngxià** midsummer

中小学教师 **zhōngxiǎoxué jiàoshī** schoolteacher

中小学女教师 **zhōngxiǎoxué nǚ jiàoshī** schoolmistress

中小学女生 **zhōngxiǎoxué nǚ shēng** schoolgirl

中小学男教师 **zhōngxiǎoxué nán jiàoshī** schoolmaster

中小学男生 **zhōngxiǎoxué nánshēng** schoolboy

中小学学生 **zhōngxiǎoxué xuéshēng** schoolchild

中心 **zhōngxīn** center; heart

忠心 **zhōngxīn** loyal ◊ loyalty

衷心 **zhōngxīn** sincere; warm

中学 **zhōngxué** middle school; junior high school

中学生 **zhōngxuéshēng** middle school student; junior high school student

中央 **zhōngyāng** central ◊ middle

中央处理机 **zhōngyāng chùlǐ jī** CPU, central processing unit

中央电视台 **Zhōngyāng Diànshìtái** China Central Television, CCTV

中央情报局 **Zhōngyāng Qíngbào Jú** CIA, Central Intelligence Agency

中药 **zhōngyào** Chinese medicine

重要 **zhòngyào** important, significant

重要性 **zhòngyào xìng** importance, significance

中医 **zhōngyī** Chinese medicine; Chinese doctor

重音 **zhòngyīn** accent, emphasis

众议员 **zhòngyì yuán** representative

众议院 **Zhòngyì yuàn** House of Representatives

终于 **zhōngyú** finally, eventually, in the end

忠于 **zhōngyú** stand by, be loyal to

肿胀 **zhǒngzhàng** swell up ◊ swollen ◊ swelling

忠贞 **zhōngzhēn** fidelity

终止 **zhōngzhǐ** terminate ◊ termination

中止 **zhōngzhǐ** cease, discontinue

中指 **zhōngzhǐ** middle finger

终止 **zhōngzhǐ** end, finish

种植 **zhòngzhí** grow, cultivate; plant

终止日期 **zhōngzhǐ rìqī** expiry date

种植园 **zhòngzhí yuán** plantation

种子 **zhǒngzi** seed, pip

种子选手 **zhǒngzi xuǎnshǒu** seed (*in tennis*)

种族 **zhǒngzú** race, people ◊ ethnic, racial

种族隔离 **zhǒngzú gélí** racial segregation

重罪 **zhòngzuì** felony

种族平等 **zhǒngzú píngděng** racial equality

种族歧视 **zhǒngzú qíshì** racism ◊ racist

种族歧视者 **zhǒngzú qíshì zhě** racist

种族社区 **zhǒngzú shèqū** ethnic group

粥 **zhōu** rice porridge, congee

洲 **zhōu** continent

州 **zhōu** prefecture; state

周 **zhōu** week; circle

轴 **zhóu** shaft; axle

肘 **zhǒu** elbow

皱 **zhòu** crease, wrinkle

轴承 **zhóuchéng** bearing TECH

周到 **zhōudao** considerate; tactful

周恩来 **Zhōu Ēnlái** Zhou Enlai, Chou En-lai

周刊 **zhōukān** weekly magazine

咒骂 **zhòumà** curse, swear; 咒骂 X **zhòumà X** swear at X

皱眉 **zhòuméi** frown

周末 **zhōumò** weekend ◊ on the weekend

周年 **zhōunián** anniversary

周年大会 **zhōunián dàhuì** annual general meeting

周期 **zhōuqī** cycle; period

周期性 **zhōuqī xìng** periodic; cyclical

骤然下跌 **zhòurán xiàdiē** decline, slump

周围 **zhōuwéi** around ◊ surrounding ◊ surroundings

皱纹 **zhòuwén** crease, wrinkle

绉纹纸 **zhòuwén zhǐ** crepe paper

骤增 **zhòuzēng** bulge, sudden increase

州长 **zhōuzhǎng** governor

猪 **zhū** hog, pig

珠 **zhū** pearl; bead

逐 **zhú** follow

竹 **zhú** bamboo

煮 **zhǔ** boil

主 **zhǔ** main ◊ master, lord

住 **zhù** live, reside; stop ◊ (showing result): 记住 **jì zhù** remember; 抓住 **zhuā zhù** catch

柱 **zhù** pillar

祝 **zhù** wish; 祝 X 走运 **zhù X zǒuyùn** wish X well; 祝你走运！**zhù nǐ zǒuyùn!** good luck!; 祝你健康！**zhù nǐ jiànkāng!** your health!

助 **zhù** help

抓 **zhuā** grasp; scratch

爪 **zhuǎ** claw

拽 **zhuài** pull, tow

抓阄儿 **zhuājiūr** draw lots

抓牢 **zhuā láo** tighten one's grip on

专 **zhuān** special

砖 **zhuān** brick; tile

转 **zhuǎn** turn; move, transfer ◊ turning

转 **zhuàn** turn; revolve

传 **zhuàn** biography

转变 **zhuǎnbiàn** shift, change direction ◊ swing; changeover

转播 **zhuǎnbō** relay *signal*

专长 **zhuāncháng** prowess; specialty

转车 **zhuǎnchē** change (trains/buses)

转达 **zhuǎndá** communicate, pass on

转达问候 **zhuǎndá wènhòu** send one's regards

赚的钱 **zhuànde qián** earnings

转递 **zhuǎndì** forward *letter*

转动 **zhuǎndòng** turn

转动 **zhuàndòng** turn; revolve; swing

桩 **zhuāng** stake, peg

装 **zhuāng** pack; install ◊ clothing; 装胶卷 **zhuāng jiāojuǎn** load *camera*

庄 **zhuāng** village

撞 **zhuàng** hit; bang, bump, strike

壮 **zhuàng** strong

幢 **zhuàng** measure word for buildings; 一幢楼房 **yīzhuàng lóufáng** an apartment block

转告 **zhuǎngào** relay *message*

撰稿人 **zhuàngǎorén** scriptwriter

装扮 **zhuāngbàn** disguise oneself, dress up; 装扮成 **zhuāngbàn chéng** disguise oneself as, dress up as

装备 **zhuāngbèi** equipment ◊ equip; furnish

装玻璃工人 **zhuāng bōlí de gōngren** glazier

装车 **zhuāng** load *vehicle*

壮大 **zhuàngdà** healthy

装弹药 **zhuāng dànyào** load *gun*

撞倒 **zhuàngdǎo** run over, knock down; 司机把车撞到 **sījī bǎ chē zhuàngdào ...** the driver smashed into ...

装钉 **zhuāngdīng** binding

撞翻 **zhuàngfān** knock over

壮观 **zhuàngguān** grand; spectacular ◊ splendor; spectacle

装潢 **zhuānghuáng** décor; decoration

装潢工人 **zhuānghuáng**

gōngrén decorator

撞毁 zhuànghuǐ crash *car*

撞击 zhuàngjī knock, hit ◊ blow; impact

庄稼 zhuāngjia crops

装甲车 zhuāngjiǎ chē armored vehicle

撞见 zhuàngjiàn bump into; happen to see; 撞见 X 做 Y *zhuàngjiàn X zuò Y* catch X doing Y

状况 zhuàngkuàng state, condition

壮丽 zhuànglì magnificence

装满 zhuāngmǎn fill up; top up ◊ full

装配 zhuāngpèi set up

装配厂 zhuāngpèi chǎng assembly plant

装配工 zhuāngpèi gōng fitter

装配线 zhuāngpèi xiàn assembly line

装腔作势 zhuāngqiāng zuòshì pose, pretense

装软件 zhuāng ruǎnjiàn load COMPUT

装入口袋 zhuāngrù kǒudài pack, bag up

装饰 zhuāngshì decorate, adorn ◊ decoration, embellishment ◊ decorative, ornamental

装饰物 zhuāngshì wù ornament

装饰性 zhuāngshì xìng cosmetic, superficial

撞碎 zhuàngsuì smash, crash

状态 zhuàngtài condition, state; 处于交战状态 *chǔyú jiāozhàn zhuàngtài* be at war; 处于戒备状态 *chǔyú jièbèi zhuàngtài* be on the alert

装卸工 zhuāngxiè gōng stevedore

装修 zhuāngxiū decorate *room etc*

庄严 zhuāngyán dignified

装有 zhuāngyǒu be supplied with

装载 zhuāngzài load

装置 zhuāngzhì fittings

庄重 zhuāngzhòng grave, solemn

装作 zhuāngzuò pretend; pose as

转航 zhuǎnháng tack (*of yacht*)

专横 zhuānhèng high-handed

转化 zhuǎnhuà convert

转换 zhuǎnhuàn change

转机 zhuǎnjī transfer (*of passengers*)

传记 zhuànjì biography

专家 zhuānjiā expert, specialist

专家建议 zhuānjiā jiànyì expert advice

转机厅 zhuǎnjī tīng transit lounge

专科医生 zhuānkē yīshēng specialist (doctor)

专栏 zhuānlán column

专栏作家 zhuānlán zuòjiā columnist

专利 zhuānlì patent

转脸 zhuǎnliǎn turn away, look away

专门 zhuānmén special; 专门从事 *zhuānmén cóngshì* specialize; specialize in

专门知识 zhuānmén zhīshi expertise

转晴 zhuǎnqíng brighten up, clear up

转让 zhuǎnràng entrust; transfer; 把 X 转让给 Y *bǎ X zhuǎnràng gěi Y* make X over to Y

转让契据 zhuǎnràng qìjù bill of sale

专人 zhuānrén by hand

转入地下 zhuǎnrù dìxià go underground POL

转身 zhuǎnshēn turn around, spin around

砖石结构 zhuānshí jiégòu masonry

转手 zhuǎnshǒu change hands

专题 zhuāntí article, feature

砖头 zhuāntóu brick

转弯 zhuǎnwān turn the corner

转弯处 zhuǎnwān chù curve; corner, bend

转向 zhuǎnxiàng change direction; turn around; move on ◊ change of direction; U-turn

专心 zhuānxīn concentrate ◊ concentration; devotion

专心致志 zhuānxīn zhìzhì single-minded

专业 zhuānyè professional ◊

subject, field; area of expertise
专业知识 **zhuānyè zhīshi**
specialized knowledge
专业人士 **zhuānyè rénshì**
professional (*lawyer etc*)
转移 **zhuǎnyí** transfer, move;
avert
转运商 **zhuǎnyùn shāng**
forwarding agent
转折点 **zhuǎnzhé diǎn** turning
point
专政 **zhuānzhèng** dictatorship
转租 **zhuǎnzū** sublet
抓取 **zhuāqǔ** snatch
抓住 **zhuāzhù** grab, grasp; grip;
scratch
爪子 **zhuǎzi** claw; paw
主板 **zhǔbǎn** mainboard COMPUT
珠宝 **zhūbǎo** jewel; jewelry
珠宝商 **zhūbǎo shāng** jeweler
逐步 **zhúbù** progressively,
steadily; step by step; 逐步引进
zhúbù yǐnjìn phase in; 逐步中止
zhúbù zhōngzhǐ phase out
逐步发展 **zhúbù fāzhǎn**
progressive
逐步升级 **zhúbù shēngjí** escalate
贮藏 **zhùcáng** storage
注册 **zhùcè** enroll ◊ enrolment
助产士 **zhùchǎnshì** midwife
主持 **zhǔchí** present; host; front;
chair; preside; 主持会议 **zhǔchí
huìyì** chair a meeting; 主持婚礼
zhǔchí hūnlǐ conduct a wedding
主持人 **zhǔchí rén** host (*of TV
program*)
逐出 **zhúchū** eject, evict
住处 **zhùchù** place (where one
lives)
贮存 **zhùcún** store
贮存空间 **zhùcún kōngjiān**
storage space
主导 **zhǔdǎo** dominant
主祷文 **Zhǔdǎo Wén** Lord's
Prayer
驻地 **zhùdì** resident; garrison
筑堤坝 **zhùdībà** dam
注定 **zhùdìng** condemn, doom; 注
定失败 **zhùdìng shībài** doomed
to failure
主动 **zhǔdòng** initiative ◊ active

GRAM; 主动做 X **zhǔdòng zuò X**
do X on one's own initiative
主动表示 **zhǔdòng biǎoshì**
make overtures to
住房 **zhùfáng** housing
住房条件 **zhùfáng tiáojiàn**
housing conditions
祝福 **zhùfú** bless ◊ blessing
逐个 **zhúgè** one by one
主观 **zhǔguān** subjective
主管 **zhǔguǎn** supervisor, boss ◊
be in charge of, oversee
主管人员 **zhǔguǎn rényuán**
executive; management
主观愿望 **zhǔguān yuànwàng**
wishful thinking
煮过火儿 **zhǔ guòhuǒr** overcook
祝好 **zhùhǎo** best wishes,
congratulations ◊ congratulate
祝贺 **zhùhè** congratulate; 祝贺 ...
zhùhè ... congratulations on ...
追 **zhuī** chase, pursue
追赶 **zhuīgǎn** chase, pursue
追赶者 **zhuīgǎn zhě** pursuer
坠毁 **zhuìhuǐ** crash
追究 **zhuījiū** get down to
追求 **zhuīqiú** seek, pursue
追溯 **zhuīsù** date back to;
backdate ◊ retroactive
追随者 **zhuīsuí zhě** follower,
supporter
追逐 **zhuìzhú** pursue ◊ pursuit
逐渐 **zhújiàn** gradual ◊ gradually;
逐渐减少 **zhújiàn jiǎnshǎo** taper
off, decline; 逐渐习惯 **zhújiàn
xíguàn** get accustomed to; 逐渐
形成 **zhújiàn xíngchéng** evolve
珠江 **Zhūjiāng** Pearl River
珠江三角洲 **Zhūjiāng
Sānjiǎozhōu** Pearl River Delta
主教 **zhǔjiào** bishop
助教 **zhùjiào** teaching assistant
主机体 **zhǔjītǐ** mainframe
猪圈 **zhūjuàn** pigpen
主角 **zhǔjué** leading role
主考人 **zhǔkǎo rén** examiner
助理研究员 **zhùlǐ yánjiū yuán**
research assistant
注满 **zhùmǎn** fill
著名 **zhùmíng** famous,
distinguished; 以 X 著名 **yǐ X**

zhùmíng be famous for X

注明日期 **zhùmíng rìqī** date *letter etc*

珠穆朗玛峰 **Zhūmùlǎngmǎfēng** Mount Everest

准允 **zhǔn** allow ◊ accurate

准备 **zhǔnbèi** plan; prepare; fix ◊ preparation; 把 X 准备好 **bǎ X zhǔnbèi hǎo** get X ready

准备工作 **zhǔnbèi gōngzuò** preparations

准备就绪 **zhǔnbèi jiùxù** readiness

准备练习 **zhǔnbèi liànxí** warm up

准确 **zhǔnquè** accurate; precise

准确性 **zhǔnquè xìng** accuracy

准时 **zhǔnshí** punctual ◊ punctually

准许 **zhǔnxǔ** approve; 准许 X 做 Y **zhǔnxǔ X zuò Y** permit X to do Y

准予 **zhǔnyǔ** grant

准予进入 **zhǔnyǔ jìnrù** entrance, admission

准则 **zhǔnzé** principle; norm, standard

捉 **zhuō** hold; catch

桌 **zhuō** table

啄 **zhuó** peck

着 **zhuó** put on *clothes*

桌布 **zhuōbù** tablecloth

捉到 **zhuōdào** capture

拙劣 **zhuōliè** badly

着陆 **zhuólù** land (*of aircraft*) ◊ landing

桌面排版 **zhuōmiàn páibǎn** desktop publishing, DTP

捉迷藏 **zhuōmícáng** hide-and-seek

啄木鸟 **zhuómù niǎo** woodpecker

捉弄 **zhuōnòng** take in, take for a ride

酌情 **zhuóqíng** use one's discretion; 由你酌情处理 **yóu nǐ zhuóqíng chǔlǐ** deal with it at your discretion

啄食 **zhuóshí** peck at one's food

着手 **zhuóshǒu** initiate; start work

着想 **zhuóxiǎng** consider, show consideration for

卓有成效 **zhuō yǒu chéngxiào** effective; successful

卓越 **zhuōyuè** outstanding; remarkable; notable ◊ remarkably

捉住 **zhuōzhù** catch, capture

茁壮生长 **zhuózhuàng shēngzhǎng** thrive

桌子 **zhuōzi** table

猪皮 **zhūpí** pigskin

主权 **zhǔquán** sovereign, independent ◊ sovereignty, independence

主人 **zhǔrén** host; master, owner

猪肉 **zhūròu** pork

侏儒 **zhūrú** dwarf

注射 **zhùshè** inject ◊ injection, shot

注射器 **zhùshè qì** syringe

主食 **zhǔshí** staple; staple diet

注视 **zhùshì** gaze ◊ gaze at

注释 **zhùshì** note; gloss

助手 **zhùshǒu** assistant, helper

主诉 **zhǔsù** complain of MED

竹笋 **zhúsǔn** bamboo shoots

住所 **zhùsuǒ** residence; accommodations

烛台 **zhútái** candlestick

主题 **zhǔtí** subject, topic, theme ◊ topical

铸铁 **zhùtiě** cast iron

主题歌 **zhǔtí gē** theme song

助听器 **zhùtīng qì** hearing aid

主卧室 **zhǔwòshì** master bedroom

主席 **zhǔxí** chair; chairman; chairwoman; chairperson

主修 **zhǔxiū** major in, specialize in

助学金 **zhùxuéjīn** grant (*for studies*)

主演 **zhǔyǎn** star

主要 **zhǔyào** main, major; chief ◊ mainly, primarily; mostly

主页 **zhǔyè** homepage

主意 **zhǔyì** idea; 好主意 **hǎo zhúyì** good idea; inspiration

注意 **zhùyì** notice; pay attention to; 注意到 X **zhùyì dào X** take note of X; 引起 X 的注意 **yǐnqǐ X de zhùyì** catch X's eye

注意力 **zhùyìlì** attention

注意形象 **zhùyì xíngxiàng**

image-conscious
猪油 **zhūyóu** lard
主语 **zhǔyǔ** subject GRAM
住院 **zhùyuàn** go into the hospital
住院病人 **zhùyuàn bìngrén** inpatient
铸造 **zhùzào** cast
铸造厂 **zhùzào chǎng** foundry
驻扎 **zhùzhā** place, station *guard etc*; 驻扎在 **zhùzhā zài** be stationed at
住宅区 **zhùzhái qū** residential area
主张 **zhǔzhāng** cause; position ◊ advocate, stand up for; represent
注重 **zhùzhòng** attach importance to
珠子 **zhūzi** bead; pearl
竹子 **zhúzi** bamboo
柱子 **zhùzi** pillar
住嘴！**zhùzuǐ!** shut up!
资 **zī** money, funds
紫 **zǐ** purple
子 **zǐ** son; child; seed
字 **zì** word; character; handwriting
自 **zì** self ◊ from
自卑感 **zìbēi gǎn** inferiority complex
资本 **zīběn** capital
资本家 **zīběn jiā** capitalist (*businessman*)
资本支出 **zīběn zhīchū** capital expenditure
资本主义 **zīběn zhǔyì** capitalism ◊ capitalist
资本主义者 **zīběn zhǔyì zhě** capitalist
滋补 **zībǔ** nutritious
资产 **zīchǎn** asset FIN
资产阶级 **zīchǎn jiējí** bourgeoisie
自从 **zìcóng** since; 自从你走以后 **zìcóng nǐ zǒu yǐhòu** since you left
自大 **zìdà** big-headed
子弹 **zǐdàn** bullet; cartridge; pellet
子弟 **zǐdì** disciple
字典 **zìdiǎn** dictionary
自动 **zìdòng** automatic ◊ automatically; by itself
自动点唱机 **zìdòng diǎnchàngjī** jukebox

自动扶梯 **zìdòng fútī** escalator
自动化 **zìdòng huà** automation
自动驾驶仪 **zìdòng jiàshǐ yí** autopilot
自动售货机 **zìdòng shòuhuò jī** vending machine
自发 **zìfā** spontaneous
自负 **zìfù** pompous; arrogant; vain, conceited ◊ conceit
兹附上 **zīfùshàng** please find enclosed
自高自大 **zìgāo zìdà** conceited; ostentatious
资格 **zīgé** qualification; 取得资格 **qǔde zīgé** qualify; 取消资格 **qǔxiāo zīgé** disqualify; 我不够资格来决定 **wǒ bùgòu zīgé lái juédìng** I am not qualified to judge
子宫 **zǐgōng** uterus, womb
子宫切除术 **zǐgōng qiēchúshù** hysterectomy
子宫托 **zǐgōng tuō** diaphragm
自豪 **zìháo** pride ◊ proud ◊ proudly; 以 … 为自豪 **yǐ … wéi zìháo** be proud of
自己 **zìjǐ** self; oneself ◊ own ◊ by oneself; 自己做X **zìjǐ zuò X** do X by oneself; 我自己的公寓/车 **wǒ zìjǐde gōngyù / chē** a car / an apartment of my own
字迹 **zìjì** writing
字节 **zìjié** byte
资金 **zījīn** capital, money
紫禁城 **Zǐjìnchéng** Forbidden City
自己一个人 **zìjǐ yīgè rén** alone
自觉 **zìjué** conscious
自控 **zìkòng** control oneself
自来水 **zìláishuǐ** running water
自来水笔 **zìláishuǐ bǐ** fountain pen
资料保密 **zīliào bǎomì** data protection
紫罗兰 **zǐ luólán** violet (*plant*)
紫罗兰色 **zǐ luólán sè** violet (*color*)
自满 **zìmǎn** complacent, smug ◊ complacency, smugness
字面 **zìmiàn** literal ◊ literally
自鸣得意 **zìmíng déyì** self-

satisfied

字母 **zìmǔ** letter (*of alphabet*); 依字母顺序 **yī zìmǔ shùnxù** alphabetical order

字幕 **zìmù** subtitle

字母表 **zìmǔbiǎo** alphabet

自欺 **zìqī** delude oneself

子儿 **zǐr** piece (*in chess etc*)

自然 **zìrán** nature ◊ natural ◊ naturally, of course

自然保护区 **zìrán bǎohùqū** nature reserve

自然环境 **zìrán huánjìng** the environment

自然界 **zìrán jiè** natural

自然科学 **zìrán kēxué** natural science

自然科学家 **zìrán kēxué jiā** natural scientist

自然灾害 **zìrán zāihài** natural disaster

紫色 **zǐsè** purple

自杀 **zìshā** suicide ◊ commit suicide

滋生地 **zīshēng dì** breeding ground

姿势 **zīshì** position; posture; 摆姿势 **bǎi zīshì** pose

字首 **zìshǒu** monogram ◊ monogrammed

自首 **zìshǒu** turn in (*to police*)

自私 **zìsī** selfish

自私自利 **zìsī-zìlì** selfish

字体 **zìtǐ** font; typeface

紫外 **zǐwài** ultraviolet

滋味 **zīwèi** flavor, taste

自卫 **zìwèi** self-defense

自我 **zìwǒ** self; ego; 以自我为中心 **yǐ zìwǒ wéi zhōngxīn** egocentric

自我表达 **zìwǒ biǎodá** self-expression ◊ express oneself

自我控制 **zìwǒ kòngzhì** self-control

自我批评 **zìwǒ pīpíng** self-criticism

自我约束 **zìwǒ yuēshù** self-discipline

仔细 **zǐxì** careful, thorough ◊ closely; 仔细察看 **zǐxì chákàn** study, examine; investigate; 仔细

检查 **zǐxì jiǎnchá** check, go over;

仔细彻底 **zǐxì chèdǐ** scrupulous;

仔细考虑 **zǐxì kǎolǜ** deliberate; mull over

自相矛盾 **zìxiāng máodùn** paradox

自信 **zìxìn** confident; self-confident; assertive ◊ self-confidence

自行车 **zìxíngchē** bicycle

自行车架 **zìxíngchē jià** parking rack (*for bicycle*)

自信心 **zìxìnxīn** self-confidence

自选 **zìxuǎn** self-service ◊ optional

自学 **zìxué** self-study

咨询 **zīxún** advice; consultancy

咨询公司 **zīxún gōngsī** consultancy

恣意 **zìyì** wanton

自以为是 **zì yǐwéi shì** self-righteous

自由 **zìyóu** freedom, liberty ◊ free; liberal POL; 自由放荡 **zìyóu fàngdàng** run wild

自由女神像 **Zìyóu Nǚshén Xiàng** Statue of Liberty

自由市场经济 **zìyóu shìchǎng jīngjì** free market economy

自由泳 **zìyóuyǒng** crawl, freestyle

资源 **zīyuán** resource

自愿 **zìyuàn** of one's own accord; voluntary ◊ voluntarily

自治 **zìzhì** autonomy

自制 **zìzhì** homemade ◊ self-possession

自制力 **zìzhì lì** self control

自治区 **zìzhì qū** autonomous region

资助 **zīzhù** subsidize; back; stake

自传 **zìzhuàn** autobiography

自助餐 **zìzhù cān** buffet, self-service meal

自助餐馆 **zìzhù cānguǎn** self-service restaurant

自助式 **zìzhù shì** self-service

孜孜不倦 **zīzī bùjuàn** tireless

自尊 **zìzūn** self-esteem; pride, self-respect ◊ proud

自尊心 **zìzūn xīn** self-respect

鬃 **zōng** mane

踪 zōng footprint

总 zǒng total; general; main; gross FIN ◊ always

纵 zòng vertical

总部 zǒngbù head office

总裁 zǒngcái president

总的 zǒngde general, overall; 总的看来 **zǒngde kànlái** on the whole

总额 zǒng'é lump sum

总共 zǒnggòng altogether; 总共七十美元 **zǒnggòng qīshí měiyuán** that comes to $70 altogether

总公司 zǒnggōngsī parent company

综合 zōnghé comprehensive; 综合报道 **zōnghé bàodào** news round-up

纵横交错 zònghéng jiāocuò checkered

棕褐色 zōnghè sè tan (color)

综合性 zōnghé xìng full, comprehensive

纵火 zònghuǒ arson

踪迹 zōngjī track, trace

总机 zǒngjī telephone exchange

宗教 zōngjiào religion ◊ religious

总计 zǒngjì total

总结 zǒngjié summary

总经理 zǒng jīnglǐ CEO, chief executive officer, managing director

总计为 zǒngjìwéi add up to

总理 zǒnglǐ premier, prime minister

棕榈树 zōnglǘshù palm tree

棕色 zōngsè brown

纵深 zòngshēn deep

总是 zǒngshì always

棕树 zōngshù palm tree

总数 zǒngshù total; sum

总司令 zǒngsīlìng commander-in-chief

总体 zǒngtǐ overall

总统 zǒngtǒng president ◊ presidential

总统竞选 zǒngtǒng jìngxuǎn presidential campaign

总统职位 zǒngtǒng zhíwèi presidency

总帐 zǒngzhàng ledger

总之 zǒngzhī anyhow, in any case; to sum up, briefly

总指挥部 zǒng zhǐhuībù headquarters

走 zǒu walk; go; move; leave; run; navigate COMPUT; 走吧 **zǒuba** let's go; 走了 **zǒule** walk away; walk out; go ◊ gone 我得走了 **wǒ děi zǒule** I must be going

揍 zòu beat up; punch, sock

奏 zòu play musical instrument

走调 zǒudiào out of tune

走动 zǒudòng get around; move around

走狗 zǒugǒu pej running dog; yesman

走过 zǒuguò tread; walk past

走过来 zǒu guòlai approach

走后门儿 zǒu hòuménr go through the back door

走火 zǒuhuǒ go off (of gun)

走近 zǒujìn draw near

走进 zǒujìn enter

走开 zǒukāi buzz off; walk away

走廊 zǒuláng corridor; passageway; hall

走路 zǒulù walk, go on foot ◊ walking

走慢 zǒumàn lose time (of watch)

走散 zǒusàn wander off

走神 zǒushén wander (of attention)

走失 zǒushī stray

走私 zǒusī smuggle ◊ smuggling

走私者 zǒusī zhě smuggler

走投无路 zǒutóu wúlù desperate

走味儿 zǒuwèir stale

奏效 zòuxiào work, succeed

走走 zǒuzou walk, walk around

走嘴 zǒuzuǐ slip of the tongue

租 zū rent; hire; lease

卒 zú pawn (in chess)

足 zú foot ◊ enough

组 zǔ group; team, crew

祖 zǔ ancestor ◊ ancestral

阻 zǔ block; stop

阻碍 zǔ'ài hinder, impede, frustrate ◊ setback

钻 zuàn drill

钻孔 zuānkǒng bore a hole

钻石 zuànshí diamond
钻头 zuàntóu drill
组成 zǔchéng make up, comprise
组成成分 zǔchéng chéngfèn composition, make-up
租出 zūchū lease out
阻挡 zǔdǎng obstruct; keep, detain ◊ tackle SP
阻冻剂 zǔdòngjì antifreeze
组分 zǔfèn constituent, component
阻风门 zǔfēngmén choke MOT
祖父 zǔfù grandfather (*paternal*)
祖父母 zǔfùmǔ grandparents (*paternal*)
足够 zúgòu enough, sufficient, ample ◊ amply; 足够多了 zúgòu duō le that's plenty
祖国 zǔguó native country, homeland
组合 zǔhé combination ◊ group
组合成一体 zǔhéchéng yītǐ put together, assemble
组合装置 zǔhé zhuāngzhì system COMPUT
嘴 zuǐ mouth; spout
醉 zuì drunk
最 zuì most; 最漂亮 zuì piàoliàng the most beautiful; 最大 zuìdà the biggest; the eldest
罪 zuì crime
最初 zuìchū first; original; initial
嘴唇 zuǐchún lip
最底 zuìdǐ bottom ◊ minimum; lowest
最低工资 zuìdī gōngzī minimum wage
最顶 zuìdǐng top, uppermost
最多 zuìduō maximum; most ◊ at most
罪恶 zuì'è sin
罪犯 zuìfàn criminal; culprit; offender
最高 zuìgāo highest; topmost; tallest
最高档 zuì gāodǎng top gear
最高级会议 zuì gāojí huìyì summit meeting
最高权威 zuìgāo quánwēi supremacy
最高限度 zuìgāo xiàndù ceiling, limit
最高一层 zuìgāo yīcéng top floor
最高音部 zuì gāoyīn bù treble MUS
醉鬼 zuìguǐ drunk
最好 zuìhǎo best; 你最好征得同意 nǐ zuìhǎo zhēngdé tóngyì you'd best ask permission
最后 zuìhòu last, final; ultimate ◊ finally, lastly; in the end; 最后关头 zuìhòu guāntóu at the eleventh hour; 作为最后一招 zuòwéi zuìhòu yīzhāo as a last resort
最后较量 zuìhòu jiàoliàng showdown
最后结果 zuìhòu jiéguǒ upshot
最后面 zuìhòumiàn the very back; bottom (*of garden etc*)
最后期限 zuìhòu qīxiàn deadline
最后通牒 zuìhòu tōngdié ultimatum
最坏 zuìhuài worst ◊ the worst
最佳 zuìjiā best, optimum
最近 zuìjìn recent; closest ◊ recently; the other day; in the near future, soon; 最近的公共汽车站 zuìjìnde gōnggòng qìchē zhàn the nearest bus stop; 最近在忙些什么? zuìjìn zài mángxiē shénme? what are you up to these days?
最酒会 zuìjiǔhuì cocktail party
最快速度 zuìkuài sùdù top speed
最轻微 zuì qīngwēi least, slightest
罪人 zuìrén sinner; offender
最少 zuìshǎo least; minimum
最深 zuìshēn innermost; deepest
最适宜 zuì shìyí optimum, most suitable
最小 zuìxiǎo least, smallest
最喜欢 zuì xǐhuan favorite; pet
最新 zuìxīn latest; newest; 最新版本 zuìxīn bǎnběn latest edition
罪行 zuìxíng crime; offense
最优良 zuì yōuliáng state-of-the-art

最优秀 **zuì yōuxiù** top (*of class etc*)

罪有应得 **zuì yǒu yīngdé** it serves you/him right

最远 **zuìyuǎn** furthest, farthest

最糟 **zuìzāo** worst

最终 **zuìzhōng** eventual; final, ultimate ◊ eventually; in due course; ultimately, finally

最终结果 **zuìzhōng jiéguǒ** end result

最重要 **zuì zhòngyào** most important, central, paramount ◊ above all

租金 **zūjīn** rent, rental

阻力 **zǔlù** resistance

祖母 **zǔmǔ** grandmother (*paternal*)

祖母绿 **zǔmǔlǜ** emerald green

尊 **zūn** respect

遵 **zūn** follow, abide by

遵从 **zūncóng** follow, comply with ◊ compliance

尊敬 **zūnjìng** respect ◊ honored, esteemed; 尊敬的先生 **zūnjìngde xiānshēng** Dear Sir

遵守 **zūnshǒu** abide by, comply with ◊ observance; 遵守规章 **zūnshǒu guīzhāng** conform, obey the rules

遵循 **zūnxún** follow, keep to

尊严 **zūnyán** dignity

鳟鱼 **zūnyú** trout

尊重 **zūnzhòng** respect; honor

昨 **zuó** yesterday

左 **zuǒ** left

坐 **zuò** sit; sit down; catch, get *bus etc*; go by *car etc*

作 **zuò** make, do; be

做 **zuò** do; make; perform, carry out; have *operation;* 为 X 做好事 **wèi X zuò hǎoshì** do X a good turn; 做吧！**zuò ba!** go on, do it!

座 **zuò** seat ◊ stand, support ◊ *measure word for mountains and buildings*; 一座山 **yī zuò shān** a mountain

作伴 **zuòbàn** keep ... company

坐班房 **zuò bānfáng** be behind bars

作弊 **zuòbì** cheat; fix, rig

左边 **zuǒbian** left, left-hand side ◊ left-hand

左边驾驶车 **zuǒbiān jiàshǐ chē** left-hand drive

座舱 **zuòcāng** cabin, cockpit

左侧 **zuǒcè** left ◊ to the left

坐车 **zuòchē** go by car; go by train

做出 **zuòchū** arrive at *decision etc*

坐船 **zuòchuán** go by boat

做出反应 **zuòchū fǎnyìng** respond, react

作出牺牲 **zuòchū xīshēng** make sacrifices

作饭 **zuòfàn** cook

作坊 **zuōfang** workshop

作翻译 **zuò fānyì** interpret; translate

作废 **zuòfèi** expire, become invalid

坐飞机 **zuò fēijī** travel by plane, fly

做工好 **zuògōnghǎo** well-made

作广告 **zuò guǎnggào** publicize; advertize

坐骨神经痛 **zuògǔ shénjīng tòng** sciatica

坐火车 **zuò huǒchē** go by train

作家 **zuòjiā** author, writer

作料 **zuóliào** seasoning

左轮手枪 **zuǒlún shǒuqiāng** revolver

坐落 **zuòluò** be situated

做梦 **zuòmèng** dream; 做梦也想不到 **zuòmèng yě xiǎng bú dào** undreamt-of

琢磨 **zuómo** ponder

作呕 **zuò'ǒu** feel nauseous; 令人作呕 **lìngrén zuò'ǒu** nauseating, disgusting

左派 **zuǒpài** the left POL

作品 **zuòpǐn** work (*book, painting etc*); production (*play etc*); composition MUS

作评委 **zuò píngwěi** judge *competition*

坐骑 **zuòqí** mount

坐起来 **zuòqǐlái** sit up (*in bed*)

作曲家 **zuòqǔ jiā** composer

左手 **zuǒshǒu** left-hand

做手势 **zuò shǒushi** gesticulate

昨天 **zuótiān** yesterday

昨天晚上 **zuótiān wǎnshang** last night

昨晚 **zuówǎn** last night

做完 **zuòwán** finish doing

作为 **zuòwéi** as; by way of; 作为 常规 **zuòwéi chángguī** as a matter of course; 作为秘密 **zuòwéi mìmì** in confidence

座位 **zuòwèi** place, seat

作伪证 **zuò wěizhèng** perjury ◊ perjure oneself

作文 **zuòwén** composition, essay

坐卧两用床 **zuòwò liǎngyòng chuáng** couchette

坐下 **zuòxia** sit down

左舷 **zuǒxián** port(side) NAUT

作业 **zuòyè** job, task; homework, assignment

左翼 **zuǒyì** left-wing

作用 **zuòyòng** function

作用力 **zuòyòng lì** strain

座右铭 **zuòyòumíng** motto

作者 **zuòzhě** author, writer

作证 **zuòzhèng** testify, give evidence

坐直 **zuòzhí** sit up straight

做作 **zuòzuò** theatrical, exaggerated; artificial, insincere ◊ exaggerate

租契 **zūqì** lease

足球 **zúqiú** soccer

组曲 **zǔqǔ** suite MUS

阻塞 **zǔsāi** obstruct, block ◊ traffic jam

祖先 **zǔxiān** ancestor; ancestry

足音 **zúyīn** sound of footsteps

租用 **zūyòng** lease

租用车 **zūyòng chē** rental car

租约 **zūyuē** rental agreement

族长 **zúzhǎng** (tribal) chief

组织 **zǔzhī** organization ◊ organize, put together ◊ tissue ANAT

阻止 **zǔzhǐ** stop, prevent, block; 阻止 X 做 Y **zǔzhǐ X zuò Y** prevent X from doing Y

足智多谋 **zúzhì duōmóu** resourceful

组织者 **zǔzhī zhě** organizer

诅咒 **zǔzhòu** curse

组装 **zǔzhuāng** assemble, put together ◊ assembly

组装件 **zǔzhuāngjiàn** (assembly) kit

Activity & Reference Section

The following section contains two parts to help you in your learning:

Games and puzzles to help you learn to use this dictionary and practice your Chinese language skills. You'll learn about the different features of this dictionary and how to look something up effectively.

Basic words and expressions to reinforce your learning and help you master the basics.

Using Your Dictionary

Using a bilingual dictionary is important if you want to speak, read or write in a foreign language. Unfortunately, if you don't understand the symbols in your dictionary or the structure of the entries, you'll make mistakes.

What kind of mistakes? Think of some of the words you know in English that sound or look alike. For example, think about the word *ring*. How many meanings can you think of for the word *ring*? Try to list at least three:

a. _____

b. _____

c. _____

Now look up *ring* in the English side of the dictionary. There are almost ten Chinese words that correspond to the single English word *ring*. Some of these Chinese words are listed below in scrambled form.

Unscramble the jumbled Chinese words, then draw a line connecting each Chinese word or expression with the appropriate English meaning.

Chinese jumble	*English meanings*
1. 指戒	a. a circle around something
2. 圈圆	b. the sound of a bell
3. 拳场击	c. jewelry worn on the finger
4. 戏马团	d. the boxing venue
5. 钟敲	e. one of the venues at a circus
6. 声钟	f. to ring a bell

With so many Chinese words to choose from, each meaning something different, you must be careful to choose the right one to fit the context of your translation. Using the wrong word can make it hard for people to understand you. Imagine the confusing sentences you would make if you never looked beyond the first translation.

For example:

The boxer wearily entered the circle.

She always wore the circle left to her by her grandmother.

I was waiting for the phone to circle when there was a knock at the door.

If you choose the wrong meaning, you simply won't be understood. Mistakes like these are easy to avoid once you know what to look for when using your dictionary. The following pages will review the structure of your dictionary and show you how to pick the right word when you use it. Read the tips and guidelines, then complete the puzzles and exercises to practice what you have learned.

Identifying Headwords

If you are looking for a single word in the dictionary, you simply look for that word's location in alphabetical order. However, if you are looking for a phrase, or an object that is described by several words, you will have to decide which word to look up.

Two-word terms are listed by their first word. If you are looking for the Chinese equivalent of *shooting star*, you will find it under *shooting*.

So-called phrasal verbs in English are listed in separate entries following the main verb. The phrasal verbs *go ahead*, *go back*, *go off*, *go on*, *go out*, and *go up* are all found after the entry for *go*.

Idiomatic expressions are found under the key word in the expression. The phrase *in my opinion* is found in the entry for *opinion*.

On the Chinese side of the dictionary, always look for the first character no matter how long the phrase is. For example, if you want to look up the phrase 国内生产总值 (gross domestic product, GDP), simply look for the word 国, then 内, and then 生, until you locate the entire phrase.

Find the following words and phrases in your bilingual dictionary. Identify the headword that each is found under. Then, try to find all of the headwords in the word-search puzzle on the next page.

1. melting pot
2. be in shock
3. break-in
4. doggy bag
5. bring
6. pull strings
7. be in jeopardy
8. get X to do Y
9. that's a relief
10. take advantage of
11. make up for
12. speak one's mind
13. be in need of X
14. heavy smoker
15. keep an eye on something

z	s	r	u	o	v	o	l	x	q	u	e	r	p	o	u	j	k
u	h	e	d	u	a	v	c	d	x	f	n	e	e	d	e	c	i
i	o	e	z	o	v	c	d	e	z	u	i	e	j	l	j	m	u
m	c	q	t	b	s	t	r	i	n	g	u	c	e	p	i	a	y
e	k	m	e	l	t	i	n	g	p	o	t	m	o	h	r	k	s
k	n	k	b	g	t	y	z	o	i	u	n	i	p	a	s	e	f
c	f	w	i	n	g	w	s	t	z	s	d	v	a	n	t	y	g
o	s	d	f	t	b	e	s	e	r	e	a	a	r	m	y	s	e
u	p	v	a	d	v	a	n	t	a	g	e	s	d	a	o	m	t
s	e	e	e	z	g	n	k	a	w	a	b	e	y	e	e	u	y
a	a	d	h	o	i	y	b	r	i	n	g	w	o	e	l	d	s
i	k	o	e	q	m	i	d	e	l	e	k	d	l	u	r	i	q
b	d	g	a	o	e	g	l	l	y	t	a	i	o	t	u	a	l
e	z	g	v	k	a	w	a	i	s	i	m	s	e	i	e	n	f
l	w	y	y	f	u	e	o	e	b	r	e	a	k	i	n	q	g
c	e	f	g	i	i	a	m	f	o	r	c	e	d	u	i	e	a
a	n	r	y	t	n	i	u	e	p	a	r	g	n	e	n	r	w
u	z	a	d	o	g	g	y	b	a	g	l	e	s	g	r	d	e

Alphabetization

The entries in a bilingual dictionary are listed in alphabetical order. Words that begin with the same letter or letters are alphabetized from A to Z using the first unique letter in each word. Chinese words are sorted by pinyin, not character. For example, *high-class* is written in Chinese characters 高级, and in pinyin **gāojí**; *happy* in Chinese characters 高兴, and in pinyin **gāoxìng**; *to tell* in Chinese characters 告诉, and in pinyin **gàosù**. Though 高级 and 高兴 share the same first character, they are not grouped together, because according to pinyin, the alphabetical order should be **gāojí** (高级), **gàosù** (告诉), and **gāoxìng** (高兴), not 高级, 高兴, and 告诉.

Practice alphabetizing the following Chinese words. Their pinyin are listed for your reference. Rewrite the words in alphabetical order. Next to each word also write the number that is associated with it. Then follow that order to connect the dots on the next page. Not all of the dots will be used, only those whose numbers appear in the word list.

Word	Pīnyīn	No.	Word	Pīnyīn	No.
上市	shàngshì	1	润滑	rùnhuá	9
太平洋	Tàipíngyáng	11	平方	píngfāng	36
通货膨胀	tōnghuò péngzhàng	5	安静	ānjìng	28
东方	dōngfāng	12	文字	wénzì	28
安排	ānpái	23	气象	qìxiàng	2
二手	èrshǒu	27	名片	míngpiàn	20
能力	nénglì	29	疯子	fēngzi	31
东	dōng	7	平衡	pínghéng	37
人工	réngōng	15	白天	báitiān	18
女人	nǚrén	33	东北	dōngběi	21
网上	wǎngshang	35	买	mài	17
白色	báisè	14	汉语	Hànyǔ	34
动词	dòngcí	4	镜子	jìngzi	8
处理	chùlǐ	26	二	èr	22

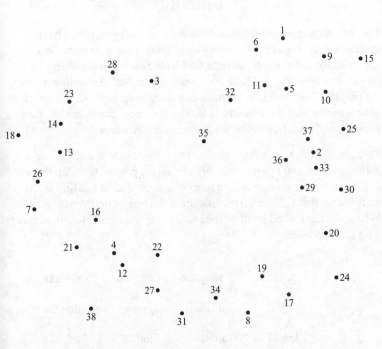

What country do you see ?

_____ _____ _____ _____ _____

Spelling

Like any dictionary, a bilingual dictionary will tell you if you have spelled a word correctly. As long as you know how to pronounce a Chinese word, it's usually easy to find its location in a dictionary by its pinyin. But how can you look up a word if you don't know how to spell the pinyin? Though it may be time-consuming, the only way to check your spelling with a dictionary is to take your best guess, or your best guesses, and look to see which appears in the dictionary.

Practice checking your spelling using the words below. Each group includes one correct pinyin and three incorrect pinyin. Look up the words and cross out the misspelled versions (the ones you do not find in the dictionary). Rewrite the correct pinyin in the blanks on the next page. When you have filled in all of the blanks, use the circled letters to reveal a mystery message.

1. 冬天	dōngtān	dōngtiān	dōntān	dōntiān
2. 今后	jīnhuò	jīnghuò	jīnhòu	jīnghòu
3. 老师	lǎoshī	loǎsī	lǒushī	loǎshī
4. 目的	mùdè	mòdè	mùdì	mòdì
5. 幸福	xìnfú	xìngfú	xìnfó	xìngfó
6. 破坏	puòhuài	puòhài	pòhuài	pòhài
7. 人民	rénmín	réngmín	rénmíng	réngmíng
8. 使用	sǐyòn	shǐyòn	sǐyòng	shǐyòng
9. 国家	gójiā	guójiā	gójāi	góujāi
10. 石头	sító	shító	sítóu	shítóu

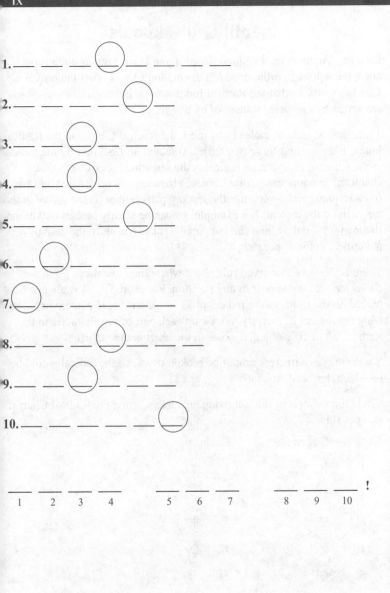

Identifying Radicals

How can you look up a Chinese word if you know how to write it but don't know how to pronounce it, i.e. you don't know what the pinyin is? This is a problem that the Radical Index solves, in which Chinese words are sorted by character instead of by pinyin.

There are two sets of tables to be used: the Radical Chart and the Radical Index. Before using these two tables, you have to first identify the radical in the Chinese character. A radical is the semantic root of a Chinese character. In many cases, one Chinese character can be divided into two or more parts, and sometimes the leading parts, either on the left or at the top, will be the radical. For example, 打 can be clearly broken down into two parts, 扌 and 丁, and the left part 扌 is its radical. In the case of 花, the radical is the upper part, 艹.

There is, however, no fixed rule about where the radical can go in a character—it may appear in any position. For example, 刂 is always placed on the right, so the radical of 到 is 刂, not 至. If you are not sure what the radical is, then try to look up each part of the character in the Radical Chart. The one that exists in the chart is the radical.

Some simple characters cannot be broken down, so the radical would be the character itself, such as 一, 大, and 目.

Circle the radicals of the following characters, using the Radical Chart if you get stuck.

	Character	**Radical**	
1.	披	(扌)	皮
2.	吓	口	下
3.	菲	艹	非
4.	怒	奴	心
5.	削	肖	刂
6.	勋	员	力
7.	坠	队	土
8.	宝	宀	玉

Using the Radical Index

Once you know the radical, you are ready to use the Radical Index to look up Chinese characters. First you have to identify the radical in the Chinese character and look for the radical number in the Radical Chart. Then refer to the Radical Index going through the list under this radical number. When you find the character in the Radical Index, you will see its pinyin pronunciation. You can then use the pinyin to look up the word in the dictionary.

Let's say you come across the word "仗" but don't know its pinyin. First, determine that the left part, "亻" is the radical and find it under the "2 strokes" section in the Radical Chart. This radical is identified as number "19," so use that number to find the radical on page 21 in the Radical Index. Going through the list, you will find the character "仗" in the middle of the left column on page 21, and its pinyin, "**zhàng,**" to its right. Now you're ready to look up the word using its pinyin in the way mentioned earlier.

Look for the radical numbers of the Chinese characters listed on the left, and find the page numbers of the words listed on the right. Then match the two words with the same number.

	Word	*Radical number*	*Word*	*Page number*
1.	玫	_____	副词	_____
2.	初	_____	可以	_____
3.	配	_____	多	_____
4.	病	_____	二	_____
5.	鳞	_____	发	_____
6.	盖	_____	甲	_____
7.	空	_____	理解	_____
8.	鑫	_____	苍	_____
9.	鼠	_____	节目	_____
10.	翻	_____	刊物	_____

Entries in Context

In this dictionary, in addition to the literal translation of each headword, entries sometimes include phrases using that word. When the headword is repeated within an English-Chinese entry, a symbol called a *swung dash* (~) takes its place. On the Chinese-English side, the headword is repeated in each phrase. For example, on page 64, the entry of 保持 (hold maintain; keep, stay) has four phrases, namely 保持沉默 (stay silent), 保持距离 (keep one's distance), 保持冷静 (keep one's cool), and 与 X 保持联络 (keep in contact with X).

Fill in the sentences below using the correct word in context. Then find the correct answers in the word search puzzle.

Hint: Each clue contains key words that will help you find the answer. Look up the bold words in each clue. You'll find the answers in expressions within each entry.

1. The sign indicating No Smoking read "**jìnzhǐ** _____".

2. The Chinese host gestured at the table and said, "Help yourself. _____ **chī**."

3. Last but not least! "**zuìhòu dàn bìngfēi zuì bù** _____ **de**."

4. Do you mind my smoking? **wǒ chōuyān nǐ bù** _____ **ma**?

5. Could you come and fix the machine please? **It's out of order.** **tā** _____ **le**.

6. What a shame! **zhēn** _____.

7. Good luck! **zhùnǐ** _____.

8. I wondered how much it cost, so I asked "**duōshǎo** _____ ?"

9. She had lost her lighter, so she asked the man next to her for a light, "**kěyǐ jiège** _____ **ma**?"

10. The police shouted to the thief, "Hands up! (**jǔqǐ** _____ **lái**)!"

11. I have brought the airline ticket and will go to China by air (**zuò** _____).

12. I wondered what time it was; I asked a friend, "**jǐ** _____ **le**?"

13. In this respect (zài zhè _____), the title of this article could be misleading.

14. Oh, don't mention it. búyòng _____ ! It was nothing!

15. You should have come here earlier; you've just missed him.
    tā _____ zǒu le.

16. Thank you so much. You shouldn't have bothered.
    tài _____ nǐle.

ì	a	e	z	ò	v	c	d	e	z	u	f	e	j	l	j	k	u
m	e	y	í	h	à	n	m	i	n	g	ē	ç	e	p	i	r	y
e	e	w	c	i	o	a	á	f	m	q	i	g	o	h	r	e	s
k	n	k	b	g	t	y	f	o	i	u	j	i	p	a	s	h	f
h	u	ǒ	i	n	g	h	á	t	z	x	ī	y	ā	n	t	y	g
ô	s	h	o	c	k	e	n	e	r	e	a	a	r	m	y	s	e
u	p	v	o	w	c	d	h	d	s	e	v	q	i	á	n	m	t
s	e	s	u	í	b	i	à	n	t	a	f	e	y	e	è	u	y
a	a	h	s	o	f	ǎ	n	d	u	ì	ā	w	o	e	l	d	k
i	z	ǒ	u	y	ù	n	d	e	l	e	n	d	l	u	r	i	è
b	d	u	c	o	s	h	ī	l	í	n	g	i	o	t	u	a	q
e	z	g	g	k	l	w	a	i	s	i	m	s	e	i	e	n	ì
l	w	y	ā	f	t	e	o	e	b	r	i	a	k	q	r	t	g
c	e	f	n	i	i	a	m	f	o	r	à	e	d	u	i	e	a
a	n	r	g	t	n	i	u	z	h	ò	n	g	y	à	o	r	w

Using Entries in Context

On both sides of the dictionary, the letters *X* and *Y* are used to indicate insertion points for other words if you are building a complete sentence using an entry in context. It's very important to pay attention to the place where these marks appear, as the insertion points may vary greatly from English to Chinese.

Look up the following phrases in your dictionary, using the words in bold. Mark the insertion points by writing *X* and/or *Y* in the correct place in each sentence.

1. How **far** is it to X?
_____到_____去_____有_____多_____远_____?

2. **cheat** X out of Y
_____从_____那_____里_____骗_____出_____

3. be **good** for X
_____对_____有_____用_____

4. X is **relative** to Y
_____与_____有_____关_____

5. **tell** X to do Y
_____叫_____做_____

6. 有 X 的倾向 (yǒu X de **qīngxiàng**)
_____be_____subject_____to_____

7. 把 X 插入 Y (bǎ X **chārù** Y)
_____insert_____into_____

8. X 比 Y 好 (X **bǐ** Y hǎo)
_____is_____better_____than_____

9. 把 X 交给 Y (bǎ X **jiāo**gěi Y)
_____send_____to_____

10. 借给 XY (**jiè**gěi X Y)
_____lend_____to_____

Word Families

Some English words have several related meanings that are represented by different words in Chinese. These related meanings belong to the same word family and are grouped together under a single English headword. Other words, while they look the same in English, do not belong to the same word family. These words are written under a separate headword.

Think back to our first example, *ring*. The translations 圆圈, 戒指, and 拳击场 all refer to related meanings of *ring* in English. They are all circular things, though in different contexts. 钟声 and 敲钟, however, refer to a totally different meaning of *ring* in English: the sound a bell makes.

The word family for *circles*, with all of its nuanced Chinese translations, is grouped together under *ring*[1]. The word family for *sounds* is grouped together under *ring*[2].

Study the lists of words below. Each group includes three Chinese translations belonging to one word family, and one Chinese translation of an identical-looking but unrelated English word. Eliminate the translation that is not in the same word family as the others.

Hint: Look up the Chinese words to find out what they mean. Then look up those translations in the English-Chinese side of your dictionary to find the word family that contains the Chinese words.

1. 好 (hǎo)	晴朗 (qínglǎng)	罚款 (fákuǎn)	细 (xì)
2. 可以 (kěyǐ)	会 (huì)	能 (néng)	罐头 (guàntóu)
3. 领导 (lǐngdǎo)	铅 (qiān)	领先 (lǐngxiān)	领头 (lǐngtóu)
4. 小姐 (xiǎojiě)	想念 (xiǎngniàn)	错过 (cuòguò)	未击中 (wèijīzhòng)
5. 休息 (xiūxi)	靠 (kào)	以…为基础 (yǐ…wéi jīchǔ)	余下 (yúxià)

Pronunciation

Though Chinese seems to sound totally different from English, many consonants and vowels sound similar if we break down the pronunciation. For example, in the Chinese pinyin system, the consonant "t" sounds just like "t" in English.

Referring to "The Pronunciation of Chinese" on pages 10-11, identify the sounds of the following letters in pinyin. If the letters sound the same as they do in English, put a check mark in the "English" column. If they don't sound the same, then write down the English letter(s) with the correct sound. At the end of this exercise, you'll discover a secret message with the checked letters.

Chinese	*English*
1. g	_____
2. r	_____
3. c	_____
4. x	_____
5. zh	_____
6. ao	_____
7. e	_____
8. ui	_____
9. a	_____
10. t	_____

_____ _____ _____ _____!

Tones

Unlike many western languages, Chinese has four pitched tones: first tone "—", a high, level tone with the volume held constant; second tone "/", rising sharply from middle register and increasing in volume; third tone "√", which starts low, then falls lower before rising again to a point slightly higher than the starting point; fourth tone "\", which starts high then drops sharply in pitch and volume.

Tone marks are placed on top of the vowel in pinyin. If a character has two or more vowels in its pinyin and the first vowel is i, u, or ü, then the mark should be placed on the second vowel. In all other cases, the tone mark appears on the first vowel.

Circle the vowel that will take tone marks.

1. an
2. gai
3. sheng
4. yuan
5. liao
6. hou
7. guang
8. chi
9. xue
10. huai

Chinese has tones because Chinese has fewer syllables and more homophonic words than other languages. Chinese has approximately 400 syllables, while English has about 12,000. So, tones help distinguish words with similar sounds, allowing them to signify different meanings.

Look up the following words in the dictionary to see how many different tone combinations can apply to the pinyin. Add the tones and write down the different English meanings.

1. guomin
2. jiaoshi
3. zhanshi
4. xiangqi
5. shixian
6. chengren
7. huangdi
8. tongzhi
9. qishi
10. muji

Parts of Speech

In English and Chinese, words are categorized into different *parts of speech*. These labels tell us what function a word performs in a sentence.

Nouns are things. *Verbs* describe actions. *Adjectives* describe nouns in sentences. For example, the adjective *pretty* tells you about the noun *girl* in the phrase a *pretty girl*. *Adverbs* also describe, but they modify verbs, adjectives, and other adverbs. The adverb *quickly* tells you more about how the action is carried out in the phrase *ran quickly*.

Prepositions specify relationships in time and space. They include words such as *in*, *on*, *before*, or *with*. *Articles* are words that accompany nouns. Words like *the* and *a* or *an* modify the noun, marking it as specific or general, and known or unknown.

Conjunctions are words like *and*, *but*, and *if* that join phrases and sentences together. *Pronouns* take the place of nouns in a sentence.

On the Chinese-English side of the dictionary, the symbol ◊ is used to separate different translations when the part of speech of each translation is different. For example, the Chinese word "花" can refer to *flower/blossom*, or can be used as a verb, meaning *spend/cost*, so you will find a ◊ between the two sets of translations.

In Chinese, the character "的" or "地" is used at the end of a word to identify adjectives and adverbs. In other words, if you want to convert an adjective into adverb, simply replace "的" with "地" at the end. However, on the Chinese-English side of the dictionary, the word "的" has been omitted in translations of adjectives.

The following activity uses words from the dictionary in a Sudoku-style puzzle. In Sudoku puzzles, the numbers 1 to 9 are used to fill in grids. All digits 1 to 9 must appear, but cannot be repeated, in each square, row, and column.

In the following puzzles, you are given a set of words for each part of the grid. Determine each word's part of speech. Then arrange the words within the square so that, in the whole puzzle, you do not repeat any part of speech within a column (vertical) or row (horizontal).

Hint: If one of the words given in the puzzle is a noun, then you know that no other nouns can be put in that row or column of the grid. Use the process of elimination to figure out where the other parts of speech can go.

Let's try a small puzzle first. Use the categories noun *n*, verb *v*, adjective *adj*, and adverb *adv* to solve this puzzle. Each section corresponds to one section of the puzzle.

Section 1

跑 (pǎo), 狗 (gǒu), 正确 (zhèngquè), 迅速地 (xùnsùdi)

Section 2

美元 (měiyuán), 秘密地 (mìmìdi), 做 (zuò), 大 (dà)

Section 3

高兴地 (gāoxìngdi), 潮湿 (cháoshī), 窗口 (chuāngkǒu), 唱歌 (chànggē)

Section 4

彩票 (cǎipiào), 可爱 (kěài), 破坏 (pòhuài), 失望地 (shīwàngdi)

	正确 (zhèngquè)		
			美元 (měiyuán)
		破坏 (pòhuài)	
高兴地 (gāoxìngdi)			

Now try a larger puzzle. For this puzzle, use the categories noun *n*, verb *v*, adjective *adj*, adverb *adv*, preposition *prep*, and pronoun *pro*.

Section 1

电梯 (diàntī), 沉着 (chénzhuó), 烧 (shāo), 他们 (tāmen), 亲切地 (qīnqièdi), 在 (zài)

Section 2

正直 (zhèngzhí), 前 (qián), 分类 (fēnlèi), 老师 (lǎoshī), 痛苦地 (tòngkǔdi), 你 (nǐ)

Section 3

里 (lǐ), 工作 (gōngzuò), 签订 (qiāndìng), 虚弱 (xūruò), 我们 (wǒmén), 成熟地 (chéngshúdi)

Section 4

洗 (xǐ), 健康 (jiànkāng), 它 (tā), 开心地 (kāixīndi), 灯 (dēng), 后 (hòu)

Section 5

外 (wài), 美丽 (měilì), 舞台 (wǔtái), 提高 (tígāo), 我 (wǒ), 渐渐 (jiànjiàn)

Section 6

家庭 (jiātíng), 他 (tā), 下 (xià), 灿烂 (cànlàn), 离开 (líkāi), 坚定地 (jiāndìngdi)

		烧 (shāo)	老师 (lǎoshī)		
电梯 (diàntī)					分类 (fēnlèi)
	签订 (qiāndìng)			灯 (dēng)	
	我们 (wǒmén)			健康 (jiànkāng)	
外 (wài)					他 (tā)
		我 (wǒ)	下 (xià)		

Running Heads

Running heads are the words printed in blue at the top of each page. The running head on the left tells you the first headword on the left-hand page. The running head on the right tells you the last headword on the right-hand page. All the words that fall in alphabetical order between the two running heads appear on those two dictionary pages.

Look up the running head on the page where each headword appears, and write it in the space provided. Then unscramble the jumbled running heads and match them with what you wrote.

Headword	Running head	Jumbled running head
1. 不安 (bù'ān)	bówù xuéjiā	sīnàoqángnhi
2. 吃 (chī)		kǒùdndguèmāi
3. 电话 (diànhuà)		ápúotāng
4. 丁香 (dīngxiāng)		āunóyujgániōgg
5. 古老 (gǔlǎo)		ǒǐnum
6. 坏人 (huàirén)		jùxwéubóiā
7. 木工 (mùgōng)		wuéhàhù
8. 牛肉 (niúròu)		guánxcénhùy
9. 批准 (pīzhǔn)		gǒnytī
10. 亲戚 (qīnqi)		hjhsùccǔúùn
11. 数目 (shùmù)		nēniàpddogà
12. 投票 (tóupiào)		híwdiǔs

Riddles

Solve the following riddles in English. Then write the Chinese pinyin of the answer on the lines. You will need the numbers below the lines for the activity "Cryptogram."

1. This cold season is followed by spring.

___ ___ ___ ___ ___ ___ ___ ___
11   26   3   17   6   13   25   3

2. You don't want to forget this type of clothing when you go to the beach.

___ ___ ___ ___ ___ ___ ___ ___ ___
5   26   14   5   26   3   17   5   13

3. This thing protects you from the rain, but it's bad luck to open it indoors!

___ ___ ___
18   25   3

4. This number comes before the number one. You need this digit to write out the numbers ten, twenty, and one million.

___ ___ ___ ___
12   13   3   17

5. The couple you call Mom and Dad.

___ ___ ___ ___ ___ ___ ___ ___
2   13   25   10   21   25   3   17

6. If you are injured or very ill, you should go to this place.

___ ___ ___ ___ ___ ___
5   13   5   14   25   3

7. This mode of transportation has only two wheels. It is also good exercise!

___ ___ ___ ___ ___ ___   ___ ___ ___
10   13   20   13   3   17   8   21   4

8. This brown drink can wake you up when you're sleepy.

$\frac{\quad}{15}$ $\frac{\quad}{25}$ $\frac{\quad}{19}$ $\frac{\quad}{4}$ $\frac{\quad}{13}$

9. This currency is used in China.

$\frac{\quad}{22}$ $\frac{\quad}{4}$ $\frac{\quad}{3}$ $\frac{\quad}{9}$ $\frac{\quad}{13}$ $\frac{\quad}{3}$ $\frac{\quad}{16}$ $\frac{\quad}{13}$

10. This part of speech modifies a verb or an adjective.

$\frac{\quad}{19}$ $\frac{\quad}{14}$ $\frac{\quad}{8}$ $\frac{\quad}{13}$

11. Wearing this in the car is a safety precaution.

$\frac{\quad}{25}$ $\frac{\quad}{3}$ $\frac{\quad}{23}$ $\frac{\quad}{14}$ $\frac{\quad}{25}$ $\frac{\quad}{3}$ $\frac{\quad}{11}$ $\frac{\quad}{25}$ $\frac{\quad}{13}$

12. Snow White bit into this red fruit and fell into a long slumber.

$\frac{\quad}{7}$ $\frac{\quad}{13}$ $\frac{\quad}{3}$ $\frac{\quad}{17}$ $\frac{\quad}{17}$ $\frac{\quad}{14}$ $\frac{\quad}{26}$

13. This professional brings letters and packages to your door.

$\frac{\quad}{5}$ $\frac{\quad}{26}$ $\frac{\quad}{14}$ $\frac{\quad}{18}$ $\frac{\quad}{13}$ $\frac{\quad}{5}$ $\frac{\quad}{14}$ $\frac{\quad}{25}$ $\frac{\quad}{3}$

14. This midday meal falls between breakfast and dinner.

$\frac{\quad}{24}$ $\frac{\quad}{14}$ $\frac{\quad}{8}$ $\frac{\quad}{25}$ $\frac{\quad}{3}$

15. A very young dog is referred to as this.

$\frac{\quad}{20}$ $\frac{\quad}{13}$ $\frac{\quad}{25}$ $\frac{\quad}{26}$ $\frac{\quad}{17}$ $\frac{\quad}{26}$ $\frac{\quad}{14}$

Cryptogram

Using your answers to the riddles, write the letter that corresponds to each number in the spaces. When you are done, you will discover an English message. What does it say?

8	21	13	3	4	18	4		21	25	18		6	21	4
	12	25	22	17	4	18	6		3	14	9	16	4	22
26	19		18	7	4	25	15	4	22	18		13	3	
	6	21	4		24	26	22	12	11					

Taiwanese Equivalents

Mandarin Chinese is the official language of both Mainland China and Taiwan. Just like American English and British English, there are some differences between the two language groups. On the English-Chinese side of the dictionary, you will find the symbol ⏎ beside an English headword when a Taiwanese equivalent is given in the Taiwanese appendix on pages 717-719.

Look up each English word in the dictionary and write down its Mandarin Chinese pinyin. Then look up the Taiwanese equivalent and write down its pinyin.

English	Mandarin Chinese pinyin	Taiwanese written in pinyin
1. Mandarin		
2. feedback		
3. bicycle		
4. chips		
5. taxi		
6. pineapple		
7. cursor		
8. college exam		
9. New Zealand		
10. North Korea		

Answer Key

Using Your Dictionary

a.-c. Answers will vary.

1. 戒指, c
2. 圆圈, a
3. 拳击场, d
4. 马戏团, e
5. 敲钟, f
6. 钟声, b

Identifying Headwords

1. melting pot
2. shock
3. break-in
4. doggy bag
5. bring
6. string
7. jeopardy
8. get
9. relief
10. advantage
11. make
12. speak
13. need
14. heavy
15. eye

```
z  s  r  u  o  v  o  l  x  q  u  e  r  p  o  u  j  k
u  h  e  d  u  a  v  c  d  x  f  n  e  e  d  e  c  i
i  o  e  z  o  v  c  d  e  z  u  i  e  j  l  j  m  u
m  c  q  t  b  s  t  r  i  n  g  u  c  e  p  i  a  y
e  k  m  e  l  t  i  n  g  p  o  t  m  o  h  r  k  s
k  n  k  b  g  t  y  z  o  i  u  n  i  p  a  s  e  f
c  f  w  i  n  g  w  s  t  z  s  d  v  a  n  t  y  g
o  s  d  f  t  b  e  s  e  r  e  a  r  m  y  s  e  t
u  p  v  a  d  v  a  n  t  a  g  e  s  d  a  o  m  t
s  e  e  z  g  n  k  a  w  a  b  e  y  e  e  u  y
a  a  d  h  o  i  y  b  r  i  n  g  w  o  e  l  d  s
i  k  o  e  q  m  i  d  e  l  e  k  d  l  u  r  i  q
b  d  g  a  o  e  g  l  l  y  t  a  i  o  t  u  a  l
e  z  g  v  k  a  w  a  i  s  i  m  s  e  i  e  n  f
l  w  y  y  f  u  e  o  e  b  r  e  a  k  i  n  q  g
c  e  f  g  i  i  a  m  f  o  r  c  e  d  u  i  e  a
a  n  r  y  t  n  i  u  e  p  a  r  g  n  e  n  r  w
u  z  a  d  o  g  g  y  b  a  g  l  e  s  g  r  d  e
```

Alphabetization

ānjìng, ānpái, báisè, báitiān, chùlǐ, dōng, dōngběi, dòngcí, dōngfāng, èr, èrshǒu, fēngzi, hànyǔ, jìngzi, mài, míngpiàn, nénglì, nǚrén, píngfāng, pínghéng, qìxiàng, réngōng, rùnhuáyóu, shàngshì, tàipíngyáng, tōnghuòpéngzhàng, wǎngzhàn, wénzì

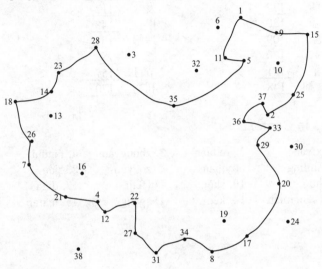

<u>C</u> <u>H</u> <u>I</u> <u>N</u> <u>A</u>

Spelling

1. dongtian
2. jinhou
3. laoshi
4. mudi
5. xingfu
6. pohuai
7. renmin
8. shiyong
9. guojia
10. shitou

<u>G</u> <u>O</u> <u>O</u> <u>D</u>   <u>F</u> <u>O</u> <u>R</u>   <u>Y</u> <u>O</u> <u>U</u>!

Radical

1. 扌
2. 口
3. 艹
4. 心
5. 刂
6. 力
7. 土
8. 宀

Radical Index

1. 玫	78	
2. 初	112	
3. 配	157	
4. 病	111	
5. 鳞	172	
6. 盖	120	
7. 空	109	
8. 鑫	170	
9. 鼠	181	
10. 翻	148	

副词	120
可以	172
多	109
二	111
发	112
甲	148
理解	181
苍	78
节目	157
刊物	170

Entries in Context

1. xīyān	**2.** suíbiàn	**3.** zhòngyào	**4.** fǎnduì
5. shīlíng	**6.** yíhàn	**7.** zǒuyùn	**8.** qián
9. huǒ	**10.** shǒu	**11.** fēijī	**12.** diǎn
13. fāngmiàn	**14.** kèqì	**15.** gāng	**16.** máfán

```
ì  a  e  z  ò  v  c  d  e  z  u  f  e  j  l  j  k  u
m  e  y  í  h  à  n  m  i  n  g  ē  ç  e  p  i  r  y
e  e  w  c  i  o  a  á  f  m  q  i  g  o  h  r  e  s
k  n  k  b  g  t  y  f  o  i  u  j  i  p  a  s  h  f
h  u  ǒ  i  n  g  h  á  t  z  x  ī  y  ā  n  t  y  g
ô  s  h  o  c  k  e  n  e  r  e  a  a  r  m  y  s  e
u  p  v  o  w  c  d  h  d  s  e  v  q  i  á  n  m  t
s  e  s  u  í  b  i  à  n  t  a  f  e  y  e  è  u  y
a  a  h  s  o  f  ǎ  n  d  u  ì  ā  w  o  e  l  d  k
i  z  ǒ  u  y  ù  n  d  e  l  e  n  d  l  u  r  i  è
b  d  u  c  o  s  h  ī  l  í  n  g  i  o  t  u  a  q
e  z  g  k  l  w  a  i  s  i  m  s  e  i  e  n  ì
l  w  y  ā  f  t  e  o  e  b  r  i  a  k  q  r  t  g
c  e  f  n  i  i  a  m  f  o  r  à  e  d  u  i  e  a
a  n  r  g  t  n  i  u  z  h  ò  n  g  y  à  o  r  w
```

Using Entries in Context

1. _____ 到 __X__ 去 _____ 有 _____ 多 _____ 远 _____?
2. _____ 从 __Y__ 那 _____ 里 _____ 骗 _____ 出 __X__
3. _____ 对 __X__ 有 _____ 用 _____
4. __X__ 与 __Y__ 有 _____ 关 _____
5. _____ 叫 __X__ 做 __Y__
6. _____ be _____ subject _____ to __X__
7. _____ insert __X__ into __Y__
8. __X__ is _____ better _____ than __Y__
9. _____ send __X__ to __Y__
10. _____ lend __X__ to __Y__

Word Families

1. 罚款 (fákuǎn)
2. 罐头 (guàntóu)
3. 铅 (qiān)
4. 小姐 (xiǎojiě)
5. 余下 (yúxià)

Pronunciation

1. ✔ go   2. ✔ rice   3. ts   4. sh   5. j
6. ow   7. ✔ yes   8. way   9. ✔ far   10. ✔ tip

<u>G</u> <u>R</u> <u>E</u> <u>A</u> <u>T</u> !

Tones

1. ⓐn
3. shⒺng
5. liⓐo
7. guⓐng
9. xⓊe

2. gⓐi
4. yuⓐn
6. hⓄu
8. chⒾ
10. huⓐi

Tones (Continued)

1. guómín　国民　(national)
   guòmǐn　过敏　(allergy)
2. jiàoshī　教师　(teacher)
   jiàoshì　教室　(classroom)
3. zhǎnshì　展示　(show; show off; model)
   zhànshí　战时　(wartime)
   zhànshì　战士　(soldier; warrior; fighter)
4. xiāngqì　香气　(smell, fragrance, aroma)
   xiǎngqǐ　想起　(remember; think of)
   xiàngqí　象棋　(chess)
5. shíxiàn　实现　(fulfill; realize; come true)
   shìxiān　事先　(beforehand)
6. chéngrén　成人　(adult)
   chéngrèn　承认　(acknowledge, recognize; admit, confess; concede)
7. huāngdì　荒地　(wasteland; heath)
   huángdì　皇帝　(emperor)
   huángdì　黄帝　(Yellow Emperor)
8. tōngzhī　通知　(inform, notify; report)
   tóngzhì　同志　(comrade)
   tǒngzhì　统治　(reign; rule)

9. qīshí　七十　(seventy)
   qíshī　骑师　(jockey)
   qíshǐ　祈使　(imperative)
   qíshì　歧视　(discriminate against)
   qǐshì　启示　(message)
10. mǔjī　母鸡　(hen)
    mùjī　目击　(witness)

Parts of Speech

狗 (gǒu) *n*	正确 (zhèngquè) *adj*	秘密地 (mìmìdi) *adv*	做 (zuò) *v*
跑 (pǎo) *v*	迅速地 (xùnsùdi) *adv*	大 (dà) *adj*	美元 (měiyuán) *n*
潮湿 (cháoshī) *adj*	窗口 (chuāngkǒu) *n*	破坏 (pòhuài) *v*	失望地 (shīwàngdi) *adv*
高兴地 (gāoxìngdi) *adv*	唱歌 (chànggē) *v*	彩票 (cǎipiào) *n*	可爱 (kěài) *adj*

他们 (tāmen) *pro*	亲切地 (qīnqièdi) *adv*	烧 (shāo) *v*	老师 (lǎoshī) *n*	前 (qián) *v*	正直 (zhèngzhí) *adj*
电梯 (diàntī) *n*	在 (zài) *prep*	沉着 (chénzhuó) *adj*	痛苦地 (tòngkǔdi) *adv*	你 (nǐ) *pro*	分类 (fēnlèi) *v*
虚弱 (xūruò) *adj*	签订 (qiāndìng) *v*	里 (lǐ) *prep*	它 (tā) *pro*	灯 (dēng) *n*	开心地 (kāixīndi) *adv*
成熟地 (chéngshúdi) *adv*	我们 (wǒmén) *pro*	工作 (gōngzuò) *n*	洗 (xǐ) *v*	健康 (jiànkāng) *adj*	后 (hòu) *prep*
外 (wài) *prep*	舞台 (wǔtái) *n*	渐渐 (jiànjiàn) *adv*	灿烂 (cànlàn) *adj*	离开 (líkāi) *v*	他 (tā) *pro*
提高 (tígāo) *v*	美丽 (měilì) *adj*	我 (wǒ) *pro*	下 (xià) *prep*	坚定地 (jiāndìngdi) *adv*	家庭 (jiātíng) *n*

Running Heads

Headword	Running head	Jumbled running head
1. 不安	bówù xuéjiā	sīnàoqángnhi
2. 吃	chéngxùyuán	kǒùdndguèmāi
3. 电话	diàndēng pào	ápúotāng
4. 丁香	dì wǔshí	āunóyujgániōgg
5. 古老	guójiā gōngyuán	òǐnum
6. 坏人	huàhé wù	jùxwéubóiā
7. 木工	mùdèngkǒudāi	wuéhàhù
8. 牛肉	nuòmǐ	guánxcénhùy
9. 批准	pútáo gān	gǒnytī
10. 亲戚	qīngshàonián	hjhsùccǔúùn
11. 数目	shùjù chǔcún	nēniàpddogà
12. 投票	tǒngyī	híwdiǔs

Riddles

1. dongtian
2. youyongyi
3. san
4. ling
5. jiazhang
6. yiyuan
7. zixingche
8. kafei
9. renminbi
10. fuci
11. anquandai
12. pingguo
13. youdiyuan
14. wucan
15. xiaogou

Cryptogram

8	21	13	3	4	18	4		21	25	18		6	21	4
C	h	i	n	e	s	e		h	a	s		t	h	e

	12	25	22	17	4	18	6		3	14	9	16	4	22
	l	a	r	g	e	s	t		n	u	m	b	e	r

26	19		18	7	4	25	15	4	22	18		13	3
o	f		s	p	e	a	k	e	r	s		i	n

6	21	4		24	26	22	12	11			
t	h	e		w	o	r	l	d			

Taiwanese Equivalents

	Mandarin Chinese pinyin	*Taiwanese written in pinyin*
1.	pǔtōnghuà	guóyǔ
2.	fǎnkuìxìnxī	huíkuì
3.	zìxíngchē	jiǎotàchē
4.	shǔpiàn	yángyúpiàn
5.	chūzūchē	jìchéngchē
6.	bōluó	fènglí
7.	guāngbiāo	yóubiāo
8.	gāokǎo	liánkǎo
9.	xīnxīlán	niǔxīlán
10.	běicháoxiǎn	běihán

BASIC CHINESE PHRASES

Essential

Hello.	你好。	nǐ hǎo
Goodbye.	再见。	zài jiàn
Yes.	是的。	shì de
No.	不是。	bú shì
OK.	好的。	hǎo de
Excuse me! *(to get attention)*	请问！	qǐng wèn
Excuse me. *(to get past)*	请让一下！	qǐng ràng yí xià
I'm sorry.	对不起。	duì bu qǐ
I'd like…	我想…	wǒ xiǎng…
How much?	多少钱?	duō shǎo qián
Where is…?	…在哪里?	…zài nǎ li
Please.	请。	qǐng
Thank you.	谢谢。	xiè xie
You're welcome.	不用谢。	bú yòng xiè
Please speak slowly.	请慢慢讲。	qǐng màn man jiǎng
Can you repeat that?	你能重复一下吗?	ní néng chóng fù yí xià ma
I don't understand.	我不明白。	wǒ bù míng bái
Do you speak English?	你说英语吗?	ní shuō yīng yǔ ma
I don't speak Chinese.	我不会说中文。	wǒ bú huì shuō zhōng wén
Where's the restroom [toilet]?	厕所在哪里?	cè suǒ zài nǎ li
Help!	救命！	jiù mìng

Getting Around

Is this the way to…?	这是去…的路吗?	zhè shì qù…de lù ma
How far is it to…?	去…有多远?	qù…yǒu duō yuǎn
Where's…?	…在哪里?	…zài nǎ li

…Street	…街	…jiē
this address	这个地址	zhè ge dì zhǐ
the highway [motorway]	高速公路	gāo sù gōng lù
Can you show me on the map?	你能在地图上指给我看吗?	nǐ néng zài dì tú shàng zhǐ gěi wǒ kàn ma
I'm lost.	我迷路了	wǒ mí lù le
straight ahead	一直向前	yì zhí xiàng qián
left	左边	zuǒ biān
right	右边	yòu biān
on/around the corner	在/转过街角	zài/zhuǎn guò jiē jiǎo
opposite	对面	duì mian
behind	后面	hòu mian
next to	旁边	páng biān
after	后	hòu
north/south	北/南	běi/nán
east/west	东/西	dōng/xī
at the traffic light	在红绿灯那儿	zài hóng lǜ dēng nà er
at the intersection	在十字路口	zài shí zì lù kǒu

Communication Difficulties

Do you speak English?	你说英语吗?	nǐ shuō yīng yǔ ma
Does anyone here speak English?	这里有谁说英语吗?	zhè li yǒu shéi shuō yīng yǔ ma
I don't speak Chinese.	我不会说中文。	wǒ bú huì shuō zhōng wén
Can you speak more slowly?	你能说慢一点吗?	nǐ néng shuō màn yì diǎn ma
Can you repeat that?	你能重复一下吗?	nǐ néng chóng fù yí xià ma
Excuse me?	请问?	qǐng wèn
What was that?	那是什么?	nà shì shén me
Can you spell it?	你能把它拼出来吗?	nǐ néng bǎ tā pīn chū lái ma

Please write it down.	请把它写下来。	qǐng bǎ tā xiě xià lái
Can you translate this into English for me?	你能把这个翻译成英语吗？	nǐ néng bǎ zhè ge fān yì chéng yīng yǔ ma
What does this/that mean?	这个 / 那个是什么意思？	zhè ge/nà ge shì shén me yì si
How do you pronounce that?	那个怎么发音？	nà ge zěn me fā yīn
Point to the phrase in the book.	在书上指出词组。	zài shū shàng zhǐ chū cí zǔ
I understand.	我明白了。	wǒ míng bái le
I don't understand.	我不明白。	wǒ bù míng bái
Do you understand?	你明白了吗？	nǐ míng bái le ma

Making Friends

Hello!	你好！	nǐ hǎo
Good morning.	早晨好。	zǎo chén hǎo
Good evening.	晚上好。	wǎn shang hǎo
My name is…	我的名字是…	wǒ de míng zi shì…
What's your name?	你叫什么名字？	nǐ jiào shén me míng zi
I'd like to introduce you to…	我想向你介绍…	wǒ xiǎng xiàng nǐ jiè shào…
Pleased to meet you.	见到你很高兴。	jiàn dào nǐ hěn gāo xìng
How are you?	你好吗？	nǐ hǎo ma
Fine, thanks. And you?	很好，谢谢。你呢？	hěn hǎo xiè xiè nǐ ne
I'm here…	我在这里…	wǒ zài zhè li…
on business	出差	chū chāi
on vacation [holiday]	度假	dù jià
studying	学习	xué xí
I'm staying for…	我要呆…	wǒ yào dāi…
I've been here…	我在这里已经…了	wǒ zài zhè li yǐ jīng…le
a day	一天	yì tiān
a week	一个星期	yí gè xīng qī

a month	一个月	yí gè yuè
Where are you from?	你从哪里来?	nǐ cóng nǎ li lái
I'm from…	我来自…	wǒ lái zì…
Have you ever been to…?	你去过…吗?	nǐ qù guò…ma
Australia	澳洲	Àozhōu
Canada	加拿大	jiā ná dà
Ireland	爱尔兰	ài ěr lán
the U.K.	英国	yīng guó
the U.S.	美国	měi guó

Relationships

Who are you with?	你和谁一起来的?	nǐ hé shuí yì qǐ lái de
I'm here alone.	我是一个人来的。	wǒ shì yí gè rén lái de
I'm with my…	我和我的…一起来的	wǒ hé wǒ de…yì qǐ lái de
husband/wife	丈夫/妻子	zhàng fu/qī zi
boyfriend/girlfriend	男/女朋友	nán/nǚ péng you
brother/sister	兄弟/姐妹	xiōng di/jiě mèi
father/mother	父亲/母亲	fù qin/mǔ qin
friend(s)/colleague(s)	朋友/同事	péng yǒu/tóng shì
When's your birthday?	你的生日是什么时候?	nǐ de shēng rì shì shén me shí hòu
How old are you?	你多大年纪了?	nǐ duō dà nián jì le
I'm…	我…	wǒ …
Are you married?	你结婚了吗?	nǐ jié hūn le ma
I'm…	我…	wǒ…
single/in a relationship	单身/有固定朋友	dān shēn/yǒu gù dìng péng you
engaged/married	订婚/结婚了	dìng hūn/jié hūn le
divorced/separated	离婚/分居了	lí hūn/fēn jū le
widowed	寡居	guǎ jū
Do you have children/grandchildren?	你有孩子/孙子吗?	nǐ yǒu hái zi/sūn zi ma

Work and School

What do you do?	你做什么工作?	nǐ zuò shén me gōng zuò
What are you studying?	你在学什么?	nǐ zài xué shén me
I'm studying Chinese.	我在学中文	wǒ zài xué zhōng wén
I…	我…	wǒ…
am a consultant	是一位顾问	shì yí wèi gù wèn
am unemployed	失业了	shī yè le
work at home	在家工作	zài jiā gōng zuò
Who do you work for?	你为谁工作?	nǐ wèi shéi gōng zuò
I work for…	我为…工作	wǒ wèi…gōng zuò
Here's my business card.	这是我的名片。	zhè shì wǒ de míng piàn

Sightseeing

Do you have information on…?	你了解…的信息吗?	nǐ liǎo jiě…de xìn xī ma
How do we get there?	我们怎么去那里?	wǒ men zěn me qù nà li
Can you recommend…?	你能推荐…吗?	nǐ néng tuī jiàn…ma
a boat trip	坐船游览	zuò chuán yóu lǎn
a bus tour	公共汽车游览	gōng gòng qì chē yóu lǎn
an excursion to…	去…的游览	qù…de yóu lǎn
a sightseeing tour	观光游览	guān guāng yóu lǎn
I'd like to go on the tour to…	我想去…游览	wǒ xiǎng qù…yóu lǎn
When's the next tour?	下次游览是什么时候?	xià cì yóu lǎn shì shén me shí hòu
Are there tours in English?	有英语导游吗?	yǒu yīng yǔ dǎo yóu ma
Is there an English guide *book/audio* guide?	有英语的旅游手册 / 录音旅游指南吗?	yǒu yīng yǔ de lǚ yóu shǒu cè/lù yīn lǚ yóu zhǐ nán ma

What time do we leave/return?	我们什么时候出发／回来？	wǒ men shén me shí hòu chū fā/huí lái
Do we have free time in…?	我们在…有自由支配时间吗？	wǒ men zài…yǒu zì yóu zhī pèi shí jiān ma
We'd like to see…	我们想看看…	wǒ men xiǎng kàn kan…
Can we stop here…?	我们可以停在这里…吗？	wǒ men kě yǐ tíng zài zhè li…ma
to take photos	照相	zhào xiàng
for souvenirs	买纪念品	mǎi jì niàn pǐn
go to the restrooms [toilets]	去洗手间	qù xǐ shǒu jiān
Can we look around?	我们可以在周围看看吗？	wǒ men kě yǐ zài zhōu wéi kàn kan ma
Is it handicapped [disabled]-accessible?	残疾人可以使用吗？	cán jí rén kě yǐ shǐ yòng ma
Wait! Someone is missing.	等一等！有人掉队了。	děng yī děng yǒu rén diào duì le

Impressions

It's…	它很…	tā hěn…
amazing	了不起	liǎo bu qǐ
beautiful	漂亮	piào liang
boring	没意思	méi yì si
interesting	有意思	yǒu yì si
magnificent	壮观	zhuàng guān
romantic	浪漫	làng màn
strange	奇怪	qí guài
stunning	让人震惊	ràng rén zhèn jīng
terrible	可怕	kě pà
ugly	难看	nán kàn
I (don't) like it.	我（不）喜欢。	wǒ (bù) xǐ huan

Sights

Where's the…?	…在哪里?	…zài nǎ li
battleground	战场	zhàn chǎng
botanical garden	植物园	zhí wù yuán
city hall	市政大厅	shì zhèng dà tīng
downtown area	市中心	shì zhōng xīn
fort	要塞	yào sài
fountain	喷泉	pēn quán
Great Hall of the People	人民大会堂	rén mín dà huì táng
library	图书馆	tú shū guǎn
market	商场	shāng chǎng
(war) memorial	（战争）纪念馆	(zhàn zhēng) jì niàn guǎn
museum	博物馆	bó wù guǎn
old town	古镇	gǔ zhèn
opera house	歌剧院	gē jù yuàn
palace	宫殿	gōng diàn
park	公园	gōng yuán
ruins	遗迹	yí jì
shopping area	购物区	gòu wù qū
theater	剧院	jù yuàn
tower	塔	tǎ
Can you show me on the map?	你能在地图上指给我看吗?	nǐ néng zài dì tú shàng zhǐ gěi wǒ kàn ma

Accommodations

Can you recommend a hotel?	你能推荐一家旅馆吗?	nǐ néng tuī jiàn yì jiā lǚ guǎn ma
I have a reservation.	我有预定。	wǒ yǒu yù dìng
My name is…	我的名字…	wǒ de míng zi…
Do you have a room…?	有…的房间吗?	yǒu… de fáng jiān ma
for one/two	一/两人	yì/liǎng rén
with a bathroom	带浴室	dài yù shì

with air conditioning	带空调	dài kōng tiáo
For…	住…	zhù
tonight	今天晚上	jīn tiān wǎn shang
two nights	两个晚上	liǎng gè wǎn shang
one week	一个星期	yí gè xīng qī
How much?	多少钱?	duō shǎo qián
Is there anything cheaper?	有没有更便宜的?	yǒu mei yǒu gèng pián yi de
When's check-out?	几点退房?	jí diǎn tuì fáng
Can I leave this in the safe?	我可以把这个留在保险柜吗?	wǒ kě yǐ bǎ zhè ge liú zài bǎo xiǎn guì ma
Can I leave my bags?	我可以把包留下吗?	wǒ kě yǐ bǎ bāo liú xià ma
Can I have my bill/ a receipt?	可以给我账单/收据吗?	kě yǐ gěi wǒ zhàng dān/shōu jù ma
I'll pay in cash/ by credit card.	我用现金/信用卡付款。	wǒ yòng xiàn jīn/xìn yòng kǎ fù kuǎn

Internet and Communications

Where's an internet café?	网吧在哪里?	wǎng bā zài nǎ li
Can I access the internet/check e-mail?	我能上网/查电子邮件吗?	wǒ néng shàng wǎng/chá diàn zǐ yóu jiàn ma
How much per (half) hour?	每(半)个小时多少钱?	měi (bàn) gè xiǎo shí duō shǎo qián
How do I connect/log on?	我怎么上网/登录?	wǒ zěn me shàng wǎng/dēng lù
A phone card, please.	请给我一张电话卡。	qǐng gěi wǒ yì zhāng diàn huà kǎ
Can I have your phone number?	可以给我你的电话号码吗?	kě yǐ gěi wǒ nǐ de diàn huà hào mǎ ma
Here's my number/ e-mail.	这是我的电话号码/电子邮件地址。	zhè shì wǒ de diàn huà hào mǎ/diàn zǐ yóu jiàn dì zhǐ
Call/E-mail me.	给我打电话/发电子邮件。	gěi wǒ dǎ diàn huà/fā diàn zǐ yóu jiàn

Hello. This is…	你好，这是…	nǐ hǎo, zhè shì…
Can I speak to…?	我可以与…讲话吗？	wǒ kě yǐ yǔ…jiǎng huà ma
Can you repeat that?	你能重复一遍吗？	nǐ néng chóng fù yí biàn ma
I'll call back later.	我等一会儿再打电话。	wǒ děng yí huì er zài dǎ diàn huà
Bye.	再见。	zài jiàn
Where's the post office?	邮局在哪里？	yóu jú zài nǎ li
I'd like to send this to…	我想把这个送到…	wǒ xiǎng bǎ zhè ge sòng dào…

Shopping

Where's the market/mall [shopping centre]?	市场／购物中心在哪里？	shì chǎng/gòu wù zhōng xīn zài nǎ li
I'm just looking.	我只是看看。	wǒ zhǐ shì kàn kan
Can you help me?	你能帮我吗？	nǐ néng bāng wǒ ma
I'm being helped.	有人帮我了。	yǒu rén bāng wǒ le
How much?	多少钱？	duō shǎo qián
That one, please.	请给我那个。	qǐng gěi wǒ nèi ge
That's all.	就这些。	jiù zhè xiē
Where can I pay?	我在哪里付款？	wǒ zài nǎ li fù kuǎn
I'll pay in cash/by credit card.	我用现金／信用卡付款。	wǒ yòng xiàn jīn/xìn yòng kǎ fù kuǎn
A receipt, please.	请给我收据。	qǐng gěi wǒ shōu jù

Stores

Where's the…?	…在哪里？	…zài nǎ li
antique store	古董店	gǔ dǒng diàn
bakery	面包店	miàn bāo diàn
bank	银行	yín háng
bookstore	书店	shū diàn
camera store	照相机商店	zhào xiàng jī shāng diàn

clothing store	服装店	fú zhuāng diàn
delicatessen	熟食店	shú shí diàn
department store	百货商店	bǎi huò shāng diàn
florist	花店	huā diàn
gift shop	礼品店	lǐ pǐn diàn
health food store	健康食品店	jiàn kāng shí pǐn diàn
jeweler	珠宝店	zhū bǎo diàn
liquor store [off-licence]	酒店	jiǔ diàn
food market	食品市场	shí pǐn shì chǎng
music store	音乐商店	yīn yuè shāng diàn
pastry shop	面包点心店	miàn bāo diǎn xīn diàn
pharmacy [chemist]	药房	yào fángfang
produce [grocery] store	食品店	shí pǐn diàn
shoe store	鞋店	xié diàn
shopping mall [shopping centre]	购物中心	gòu wù zhōng xīn
souvenir store	纪念品商店	jì niàn pǐn shāng diàn
sporting goods store	体育用品商店	tǐ yù yòng pǐn shāng diàn
supermarket	超级市场	chāo jí shì chǎng
toy store	玩具商店	wán jù shāng diàn

Services

Can you recommend…?	你能推荐…吗?	nǐ néng tuī jiàn…ma
a barber	一位理发师	yí wèi lǐ fà shī
a dry cleaner	一家干洗店	yì jiā gān xǐ diàn
a hairstylist	一位发型师	yí wèi fà xíng shī
a laundromat [launderette]	一家洗衣房	yì jiā xǐ yī fángfang
a nail salon	一家美甲沙龙	yì jiā měi jiǎ shā lóng
a spa	一家温泉	yì jiā wēn quán
a travel agency	一家旅行社	yì jiā lǚ xíng shè

Can you…this?	你能…这个吗?	nǐ néng…zhè ge ma
alter	改	gǎi
clean	洗	xǐ
fix [mend]	修	xiū
press	熨	yùn
patch	补	bǔ
When will it be ready?	什么时候做完?	shén me shí hòu zuò wán

Preferences

I'd like something…	我想要…	wǒ xiǎng yào
cheap/expensive	更便宜/更贵一点的	gèng pián yi/gèng guì yì diǎn de
larger/smaller	更大/更小一点的	gèng dà/gèng xiǎo yì diǎn de
nicer	更好一点的	gèng hǎo yì diǎn de
from this region	当地生产的	dāng dì shēng chǎn de
Around…yuan.	…元左右的。	…yuán zuǒ yòu de
Is it real?	它是真的吗?	tā shì zhēn de ma
Can you show me this/that?	你能让我看看这个/那个吗?	nǐ néng ràng wǒ kàn kan zhèi ge/nèi ge ma

Decisions

That's not quite what I want.	那个不是我要的。	nà ge bú shì wǒ yào de
No, I don't like it.	不，我不喜欢它。	bú wǒ bú xǐ huan tā
It's too expensive.	太贵了。	tài guì le
I have to think about it.	我要想想。	wǒ yào xiǎng xiǎng
I'll take it.	我要了。	wǒ yào le

Bargaining

That's too much.	太贵了。	tài guì le
I'll give you…	我给你…	wǒ gěi nǐ…
I have only…	我只有人民币。	wǒ zhǐ yǒu rén mín bì

| Is that your best price? | 是最低价吗？ | shì zuì dī jià ma |
| Can you give me a discount? | 能打折吗？ | néng dǎ zhé ma |

Paying

How much?	多少钱？	duō shǎo qián
I'll pay…	我要用…付款	wǒ yào yòng…fù kuǎn
in cash	现金	xiàn jīn
by credit card	信用卡	xìn yòng kǎ
by traveler's check [cheque]	旅行支票	lǚ xíng zhī piào
I don't have enough cash.	我的现金不够。	wǒ de xiàn jīn bú gòu
Can I use this…card?	我可以用…卡吗？	wǒ kě yǐ yòng…kǎ ma
ATM	自动取款机	zì dòng qǔ kuǎn jī
credit	信用	xìn yòng
debit	借记	jiè jì
gift	礼品	lǐ pín
How do I use this machine?	这机器怎么用？	zhè jī qì zěn me yòng
How much is left on the card?	卡上还有多少钱？	kǎ shàng hái yǒu duō shǎo qián
A receipt, please.	请给我收据。	qǐng gěi wǒ shōu jù

Clothing

I'd like…	我想要…	wǒ xiǎng yào…
Can I try this on?	我能试穿吗？	wǒ néng shì chuān ma
It doesn't fit.	不合适。	bú hé shì
It's too…	太…	tài…
big/small	大／小	dà/xiǎo
short/long	短／长	duǎn/cháng
tight/loose	紧／宽	jǐn/kuān
Do you have this in size…?	这件衣服有…号的吗？	zhè jiàn yī fu yǒu…hào de ma

I'm a size…in the U.S./U.K.	按美国 / 英国尺寸我是…。	àn měi guó/yīng guó chǐ cùn wǒ shì…
Do you have this in a bigger/smaller size?	这件衣服有大/小一点的吗?	zhè jiàn yī fu yǒu dà/ xiǎo yì diǎn de ma
Can you measure me?	你能给我量量吗?	nǐ néng gěi wǒ liáng liáng ma

Color

I'd like something…	我想要…	wǒ xiǎng yào…
light/dark	更鲜艳 / 暗一点的	gèng xiān yàn/àn yì diǎn de
beige	米黄	mǐ huáng
black	黑色	hēi sè
blue	蓝色	lán sè
brown	褐色	hè sè
green	绿色	lǜ sè
gray	灰色	huī sè
orange	橙色	chéng sè
pink	粉红色	fěn hóng sè
purple	紫色	zǐ sè
red	红色	hóng sè
white	白色	bái sè
yellow	黄色	huáng sè

Newsstand and Tobacconist

Do you sell English language newspapers?	你卖英文报纸吗?	nǐ mài yīng wén bào zhǐ ma
I'd like…	我想买…	wǒ xiǎng mǎi
a cigar	雪茄	xuě jiā
a pack/carton of cigarettes	一包 / 一条香烟	yì bāo/yì tiáo xiāng yān
a lighter	一个打火机	yí gè dǎ huǒ jī
a magazine	一本杂志	yì běn zá zhì
matches	火柴	huǒ chái
a newspaper	一份报纸	yí fèn bào zhǐ

a phone card	一张电话卡	yì zhāng diàn huà kǎ
a postcard	一张明信片	yì zhāng míng xìn piàn
a road/town map of...	...道路 / 市区地图	...dào lù/shì qū dì tú
stamps	邮票	yóu piào

Nightlife

What's there to do at night?	晚上可以做什么?	wǎn shang kě yǐ zuò shén me
Can you recommend...?	你能推荐…吗?	nǐ néng tuī jiàn… ma
a bar	一个酒吧	yí gè jiǔ bā
a cabaret	一个带歌舞表演的餐馆	yí gè dài gē wǔ biǎo yǎn de cān guǎn
a casino	一个赌场	yí gè dǔ chǎng
a dance club	舞蹈俱乐部	wǔ dǎo jù lè bù
a jazz club	爵士乐俱乐部	jué shì yuè jù lè bù
a club with Chinese music	一家有中国音乐的俱乐部	yì jiā yǒu Zhōng guó yīn yuè de jù lè bù
Is there live music?	有没有现场音乐?	yǒu mei yǒu xiàn chǎng yīn yuè
How do I get there?	我怎么去那里?	wǒ zěn me qù nà li
Is there a cover charge?	有没有附加费?	yǒu mei yǒu fù jiā fèi
Let's go dancing.	我们去跳舞吧。	wǒ men qù tiào wǔ ba

Business Travel

I'm here on business.	我在这里出差。	wǒ zài zhè li chū chāi
Here's my business card.	这是我的名片。	zhè shì wǒ de míng piàn
Can I have your card?	可以给我你的名片吗?	kě yǐ gěi wǒ nǐ de míng piàn ma
Where's the...?	…在哪里?	…zài nǎ li
business center	商业中心	shāng yè zhōng xīn
convention hall	会议厅	huì yì tīng
meeting room	会议室	huì yì shì

My name is…	我叫…	wǒ jiào…
May I introduce my colleague…	我来介绍一下同事…	wǒ lái jiè shào yí xià tóng shì…
I have a meeting/an appointment with…	我和…有一个会 / 预约	wǒ hé …yǒu yí gè huì/ yù yuē
I'm sorry I'm late.	很抱歉我迟到了。	hěn bào qiàn wǒ chí dào le
I need an interpreter.	我需要翻译。	wǒ xū yào fān yì
You can reach me at the …Hotel.	你可以在…旅馆找到我。	nǐ kě yǐ zài…lǚ guǎn zhǎo dào wǒ
I'm here until…	我要在这里呆到…	wǒ yào zài zhè lǐ dāi dào…
I need to…	我需要…	wǒ xū yào…
make a call	打电话	dǎ diàn huà
make a photocopy	复印	fù yìn
send an e-mail	发电子邮件	fā diàn zǐ yóu jiàn
send a fax	发传真	fā chuán zhēn
send a package (overnight)	寄一个（第二天送达的）包裹	jì yí gè (dì èr tiān sòng dá de) bāo guǒ
It was a pleasure to meet you.	见到你很高兴。	jiàn dào nǐ hěn gāo xìng

English - Chinese

A

a, an ◊ (*no translation*): *a bus* gōnggòng qìchē 公共汽车; *I'm a student* wǒ shì xuésheng 我是学生 ◊ (*with a measure word*) yī 一; *can I have a cup of coffee?* qǐng gěi wǒ yìbēi kāfēi? 请给我一杯咖啡?; *five men and a woman* wǔge nánde yíge nǚde 五个男的一个女的 ◊ (*per*): *$50 a time* yícì wǔshí měiyuán 一次五十美元

abandon *object*, *person* pāoqì 抛弃; *car* líqì 离弃; *plan* fàngqì 放弃

abbreviate suōxiě 缩写

abbreviation suōxiě 缩写

abdicate *v/i* tuìwèi 退位

abdomen dùzi 肚子

abdominal fùbù 腹部

abduct jiéchí 劫持

♦**abide by** zūnshǒu 遵守

ability nénglì 能力

ablaze zháohuǒ 着火

able (*skillful*) yǒu nénglì 有能力; *be ~ to* nénggòu 能够; *I wasn't ~ to see / hear* wǒ dāngshí bùnéng kàn / tīng 我当时不能看 / 听

abnormal bú zhèngcháng 不正常

aboard **1** *prep* zài ... shàng 在 ... 上 **2** *adv*: *be ~* (*on ship*) zài chuán shàng 在船上; (*on plane*) zài fēijī shàng 在飞机上; *go ~* (*on ship*) shàng chuán 上船; (*on plane*) shàng fēijī 上飞机

abolish fèichú 废除

abort *v/t mission*, *rocket launch* shǐ zhōngtú shībài 使中途失败; COMPUT *program* zhōngtú tuìchū 中途退出

abortion réngōng liúchǎn 人工流产; *have an ~* zuò rénliú 做人流

about **1** *prep* (*concerning*) guānyú ... 关于 ...; *what's it ~?* (*book*, *film*) jiǎng shénmede? 讲什么的?; (*complaint*) shénme shì? 什么事? **2** *adv* (*roughly*) dàyuē 大

约; *~ 50* dàyuē wǔshí 大约五十; *be ~ to ...* zhèng zhǔnbèi ... 正准备 ...

above **1** *prep* (*higher than*) bǐ ... gāo 比 ... 高; (*more than*) bǐ ... duō 比 ... 多; *~ all* zuì zhòngyào 最重要 **2** *adv* zài shàngtóu 在上头; *on the floor ~* lóushàng 楼上

above-mentioned suǒshù 所述

abrasion mósǔn 磨损

abrasive *personality* cūbào 粗暴

abridge jīngjiǎn 精简

abroad *live* guówài 国外; *go ~* chūguó 出国

abrupt *departure* tūrán 突然; *manner* shēngyìng 生硬

abscess nóngzhǒng 脓肿

absence (*of person*) quēxí 缺席; (*from school*) kuàngkè 旷课; (*from work*) kuànggōng 旷工; (*lack*) quēfá 缺乏

absent *adj* quēxí 缺席; (*from school*) kuàngkè 旷课; (*from work*) kuànggōng 旷工

absent-minded xīnbù zàiyān 心不在焉

absolute *power* juéduì 绝对; *idiot* shízú 十足

absolutely (*completely*) wánquán 完全; *~ not!* bù kěnéng! 不可能!; *do you agree? - ~* nǐ tóngyì ma? - tóngyì 你同意吗? - 同意

absolve shèmiǎn 赦免

absorb xīshōu 吸收; *~ed in ...* quánshén guànzhùyú ... 全神贯注于 ...

absorbent yǒu xīshōu nénglì 有吸收能力

absorbent cotton tuōzhīmián 脱脂棉

abstain (*from voting*) qìquán 弃权

abstention (*in voting*) qìquán 弃权

abstract *adj* chōuxiàng 抽象

absurd huāngtáng 荒唐

absurdity huāngtáng 荒唐
abundance fēngfù 丰富
abundant fēngfù 丰富
abuse[1] *n* (*insults*) rǔmà 辱骂; (*of child*) nüèdài 虐待; (*of thing*) lànyòng 滥用
abuse[2] *v/t* (*physically*) nüèdài 虐待; (*verbally*) rǔmà 辱骂
abusive *language* yǒu nüèdài xìng 有虐待性; **become ~** kāishǐ chòumà 开始臭骂
abysmal (*very bad*) zāotòu 糟透
abyss shēnyuān 深渊
academic 1 *n* xuézhě 学者 **2** *adj* xuéshù 学术; *person* hàoxué 好学; **~ year** xuénián 学年
academy xuéyuàn 学院
accelerate 1 *v/i* jiāsù 加速 **2** *v/t production* jiākuài 加快
acceleration (*of car*) jiāsù 加速
accelerator yóumén 油门
accent (*when speaking*) kǒuyīn 口音; (*emphasis*) zhòngyīn 重音
accentuate qiángdiào 强调
accept 1 *v/t offer, suggestion, present* jiēshòu 接受; *behavior, conditions* rěnshòu 忍受 **2** *v/i* jiēshòu 接受
acceptable kěyǐ róngrěn 可以容忍
acceptance jiēshòu 接受
access 1 *n* (*to a building*) rùkǒu 入口; (*to secrets*) jiējìn 接近; (*to one's children*) jiējìn de quánlì 接近的权利; **have ~ to** *computer* shǐyòng quán 使用权; *child* yǒu jiēchù quán 有接触权 **2** *v/t also* COMPUT shǐyòng 使用
access code COMPUT tōnglù mìmǎ 通路密码
accessible nénggòu jiējìn 能够接近
accessory (*for wearing*) yīshì fùjiàn 衣饰附件; COMPUT fùjiàn 附件; LAW bāngxiōng 帮凶
access road gōnglù zhīxiàn 公路支线
access time COMPUT shǐyòng shíjiān 使用时间
accident (*involving injury or death*) shìgù 事故; (*something not done on purpose*) bùxiǎoxīn 不小心; **by**

~ bùxiǎoxīn 不小心
accidental yìwài 意外
acclimate, acclimatize *v/t* shìyìng 适应
accommodate gěi ... tígōng zhùsuǒ 给 ... 提供住所; *special requirements* qiānjiù 迁就
accommodations zhùsuǒ 住所
accompaniment MUS bànzòu 伴奏
accompany péitóng 陪同; MUS bànzòu 伴奏
accomplice bāngxiōng 帮凶
accomplish *task* wánchéng 完成; *goal* dádào 达到
accomplished yǒu cáinéng 有才能
accord: *of one's own* **~** zìyuàn 自愿
accordance: *in* **~** *with* gēnjù 根据
according: **~** *to* gēnjù 根据
accordingly (*consequently*) yīncǐ 因此; (*appropriately*) fúhé 符合
account *n* (*financial*) zhàngmù 帐目; (*report, description*) xùshù 叙述; *give an* **~** *of* xùshù 叙述; *on no* **~** juébù 决不; *on* **~** *of* yīnwèi 因为; *take ... into* **~**, *take* **~** *of ...* kǎolǜ dào ... 考虑到 ...
♦**account for** (*explain*) jiěshì 解释; (*make up, constitute*) gòngjì dá 共计达
accountability zérèn 责任
accountable: *be held* **~** fù zérèn 负责任
accountant kuàijì 会计
accounting software cáiwù ruǎnjiàn 财务软件
accounts zhàngmù 帐目
accumulate *v/t* & *v/i* lěijī 累积
accuracy zhǔnquè xìng 准确性
accurate zhǔnquè 准确
accusation zéguài 责怪; (*public*) qiǎnzé 谴责
accuse zhǐkòng 指控; (*publicly*) qiǎnzé 谴责; *he* **~***d me of lying* tā zhǐkòng wǒ sāhuǎng 他指控我撒谎; *be* **~***d of ...* LAW bèi kònggào ... 被控告 ...
accused: *the* **~** LAW bèigào 被告
accustom: *get* **~***ed to* zhújiàn

xíguàn 逐渐习惯; **be ~ed to** xíguàn 习惯

ace (*in cards*)⇩ jiānr 尖儿; (*in tennis: shot*) fāqiú défēn 发球得分; (*pilot, designer etc*) dìyīliú 第一流

ache *n & v/i* tòng 痛

achieve huòdé chéngjiù 获得成就

achievement (*of ambition*) huòdé 获得; (*thing achieved*) chéngjiù 成就

acid *n* suān 酸

acid rain suānyǔ 酸雨

acid test *fig* guānjiàn de kǎoyàn 关键的考验

acknowledge chéngrèn 承认

acknowledg(e)ment rènkě 认可

acoustics yīnxiǎng 音响

acquaint: **be ~ed with** rènshi 认识

acquaintance (*person*) shúrén 熟人

acquire *skill, knowledge* huòdé 获得; *property* qǔdé 取得

acquisitive tānlán 贪婪

acquit LAW xuānpàn wúzuì 宣判无罪

acre yīngmǔ 英亩

acrobat zájì yǎnyuán 杂技演员

acrobatics zájì 杂技

across 1 *prep* (*on other side of: of Atlantic etc*) zài … de lìngyībiān 在 … 的另一边; (*of the street, table etc*) zài … de duìmiàn 在 … 的对面; **the post office is ~ the road from the bank** yóujú zài yínháng de duìmiàn 邮局在银行的对面 ◊ (*to other side of: of Atlantic etc*) héngguò 横过; (*of street etc*) guò 过; **he walked ~ America** tā héngguò Měiguó 他横过美国 **2** *adv* (*to other side*) guòlái 过来; **10 yards ~** shí mǎ kuān 十码宽

act 1 *v/i* THEA biǎoyǎn 表演; (*pretend*) jiǎzhuāng 假装; **~ as** línshí dānrèn 临时担任 **2** *n* (*deed*) xíngdòng 行动; (*of play*) mù 幕; (*in vaudeville*) jiémù 节目; (*pretense*) jiǎzhuāng 假装; (*law*) fǎguī 法规

acting 1 *n* (*profession*) biǎoyǎn yè

表演业; (*performance*) biǎoyǎn 表演 **2** *adj* (*temporary*) dàilǐ 代理

action xíngdòng 行动; **out of ~** (*not functioning*) shīlíng 失灵; **take ~** cǎiqǔ xíngdòng 采取行动; **bring an ~ against** LAW qǐsù 起诉

action replay TV chóngfù 重复

active huóyuè 活跃; *party member* jījí 积极; GRAM zhǔdòng 主动

activist POL jījí fènzi 积极分子

activity huódòng 活动

actor yǎnyuán 演员

actress nǚyǎnyuán 女演员

actual shíjì 实际

actually (*in fact, to tell the truth*) shíjì shàng 实际上; (*surprise*) zhēnde 真的; **~ I do know him** (*stressing converse*) shíjìshàng wǒ rènshì tā de 实际上我认识他的

acupuncture zhēnjiǔ 针灸

acute *pain* jùliè 剧烈; *sense* mǐngǎn 敏感

ad guǎnggào 广告

adapt 1 *v/t* (*for TV, movies*) gǎibiān 改编; *machine* gǎiyòng 改用 **2** *v/i* (*of person*) shìyìng 适应

adaptable *person, plant* yǒu shìyìng lì 有适应力; *vehicle etc* kě gǎiyòng 可改用

adaptation (*of play etc*) gǎibiān 改编

adapter (*electric*) jiēhé qì 接合器

add *v/t* MATH, *sugar, salt etc* jiā 加; (*say, comment*) shuō 说 **2** *v/i* (*of person*) suàn suànshù 算算术

♦ **add on** 15% *etc* jiāshàng 加上

♦ **add up 1** *v/t* jiāqǐlái 加起来 **2** *v/i fig* hélǐ 合理

addict *n* chéngyǐn zhě 成瘾者

addicted: **be ~ to X** yǒu X de yǐn 有 X 的瘾

addiction (*to drugs*) yǐn 瘾; (*to TV, chocolate etc*) chénnì 沉溺

addictive: **be ~** (*of drugs, TV, chocolate etc*) chéngyǐn 成瘾

addition MATH jiāfǎ 加法; (*to list, company etc*) bǔchōng 补充; **in ~** lìngwài 另外; **in ~ to X** chúle X zhīwài 除了 X 之外

additional fùjiā 附加

additive tiānjiā jì 添加剂

add-on fùjiàn 附件

address **1** *n* dìzhǐ 地址; **form of ~** chēnghu 称呼 **2** *v/t letter* xiě dìzhǐ 写地址; *audience* jiǎnghuà 讲话; *person* chēnghu 称呼

address book tōngxùn lù 通讯录

addressee shōuxìn rén 收信人

adequate chōngfèn 充分; (*satisfactory*) jǐn gòu mǎnyì 仅够满意

adhere jiānchí 坚持

♦adhere to *surface* niánfù 粘附; *rules* zūnshǒu 遵守

adhesive yǒu niánxìng 有粘性

adhesive plaster ⇩chuàngkětiē 创可贴

adhesive tape jiāobù 胶布

adjacent línjìn 邻近

adjective xíngróngcí 形容词

adjoining gébì 隔壁

adjourn *v/i* (*of court*) zànxiū 暂休; (*of meeting*) xiūhuì 休会

adjust *v/t* tiáozhěng 调整

adjustable kě tiáozhěng 可调整

administer *medicine* gěi 给; *company* guǎnlǐ 管理; *country* zhìlǐ 治理

administration xíngzhèng 行政; (*of company*) guǎnlǐ 管理; (*of country*) zhìlǐ 治理; (*government*) zhèngfǔ 政府

administrative xíngzhèng 行政

administrator guǎnlǐ rényuán 管理人员

admirable lìngrén qīnpèi 令人钦佩

admiral hǎijūn shàngjiàng 海军上将

admiration qīnpèi 钦佩

admire qīnpèi 钦佩

admirer chóngbài zhě 崇拜者

admissible kě yǔnxǔ 可允许

admission (*confession*) chéngrèn 承认; **~ free** miǎnfèi rùchǎng 免费入场

admit (*to a hospital, organization, school*) jiēnà 接纳; (*confess*) chéngrèn 承认; (*accept*) jiēshòu 接受

admittance: **no ~** jìnzhǐ rùnèi 禁止入内

adolescence qīngchūn qī 青春期

adolescent **1** *n* qīngshàonián 青少年 **2** *adj* qīngchūn qī 青春期

adopt *child* lǐngyǎng 领养; *plan* cǎinà 采纳

adoption (*of child*) lǐngyǎng 领养; (*of plan*) cǎinà 采纳

adorable kě'ài 可爱

adore hěn xǐhuān 很喜欢

adult **1** *n* chéngrén 成人 **2** *adj* chéngrén 成人; **~ film** chéngrén piān 成人片

adultery sītōng 私通

advance **1** *n* (*money*) tòuzhī 透支; (*in science etc*) xiānjìn 先进; MIL jìngōng 进攻; **in** ~ yùfù 预付; (*of time*) tíqián 提前; (*get money*) yùzhī 预支; **make ~s** (*progress*) jìnbù 进步; (*sexually*) xiàn yīnqín 献殷勤 **2** *v/i* MIL jìngōng 进攻; (*make progress*) jìnbù 进步 **3** *v/t theory* tíchū 提出; *sum of money* yùfù 预付; *human knowledge, a cause* cùjìn 促进

advance booking yùyuē 预约

advanced *country* xiānjìn 先进; *level* gāoděng 高等; *learner* gāojí 高级

advance payment yùfù 预付

advantage hǎochù 好处; **it's to your ~** duì nǐ yǒu hǎochù 对你有好处; **take ~ of** *opportunity* lìyòng 利用

advantageous yǒulì 有利

adventure màoxiǎn 冒险

adventurous *person* xǐhuān màoxiǎn 喜欢冒险; *investment, policy* yǒu fēngxiǎn 有风险

adverb fùcí 副词

adversary duìshǒu 对手

advertise *v/t & v/i* dēng guǎnggào 登广告

advertisement guǎnggào 广告

advertiser dēng guǎnggào zhě 登广告者

advertising xuānyáng 宣扬; (*industry*) guǎnggào yè 广告业

advertising agency guǎnggào gōngsī 广告公司

advice zīxún 咨询; **take X's ~** jiēshòu X de yìjiàn 接受X的意见

advisable kěqǔ 可取

advise *person* quàngào 劝告; *caution etc* zhōnggào 忠告; **~ X to ...** jiànyì X zuò ... 建议X做 ...

adviser gùwèn 顾问

aerial tiānxiàn 天线

aerial photography hángkōngshèyǐng 航空摄影

aerobics ⇩zēng yǎng jiànshēn fǎ 增氧健身法

aerodynamic kōngqì dònglì 空气动力

aeronautical hángkōng 航空

aerosol pēnmò 喷沫

aerospace industry yǔháng gōngyè 宇航工业

affair (*matter*) shì shì 事事; (*business*) shìwù 事务; (*love*) liàn'ài 恋爱; **foreign ~s** wàijiāo shìwù 外交事务; **have an ~ with** yǔ ... tōngjiān 与 ... 通奸

affect (*influence, concern*) yǐngxiǎng 影响; MED qīnxí 侵袭

affection àimù 爱慕

affectionate yǒu àimù xīn 有爱慕心

affinity qīnjìn 亲近

affirmative: answer in the ~ rènkě de huídá 认可的回答

affluent fùyù 富裕; **~ society** fánróng de shèhuì 繁荣的社会

afford (*financially*) fùdān de qǐ 负担得起

Afghan 1 *adj* Āfùhàn 阿富汗 **2** *n* (*person*) Āfùhàn rén 阿富汗人

Afghanistan Āfùhàn 阿富汗

afloat *boat* piāofú 漂浮

afraid: be ~ hàipà 害怕; **be ~ of** hàipà 害怕; *of upsetting s.o. etc* dānxīn 担心; **I'm ~** (*expressing regret*) kǒngpà 恐怕; **I'm ~ so** fēicháng bàoqiàn, zhèshì zhēnde 非常抱歉,这是真的; **I'm ~ not** fēicháng bàoqiàn, bùshì zhèyàng 非常抱歉,不是这样

Africa Fēizhōu 非洲

African 1 *adj* Fēizhōu 非洲 **2** *n* Fēizhōu rén 非洲人

after 1 *prep* (*in order, position, time*) zhīhòu 之后; **~ all** bìjìng 毕竟; **~ that** zài nà zhīhòu 在那之后; **it's ten ~ two** liǎngdiǎn shífēn 两点十分 **2** *adv* (*afterward*) hòulái 后来; **the day ~** dì'èrtiān 第二天

afternoon xiàwǔ 下午; **in the ~** zài xiàwǔ 在下午; **this ~** jīntiān xiàwǔ 今天下午; **good ~** ⇩xiàwǔ hǎo 下午好

after sales service shòuhòu fúwù 售后服务

aftershave nánshì hùfū yè 男士护肤液

aftertaste yúwèir 余味儿

afterward hòulái 后来

again zài 再

against *lean* kào 靠; **X ~ Y** SP X duì Y X对Y; **I'm ~ the idea** wǒ fǎnduì zhège zhǔyì 我反对这个主意; **what do you have ~ her?** nǐ duì tā yǒu shénme yìjiàn? 你对她有什么意见?; **~ the law** wéifǎ 违法

age 1 *n* (*of person, object*) niánjì 年纪; (*era*) shídài 时代; **at the ~ of** niánlíng wéi nián líng 为; **under ~** wèidào fǎdìng niánlíng 未到法定年龄; **she's five years of ~** tā wǔsuì le 她五岁了 **2** *v/i* biànlǎo 变老

agency dàilǐ chù 代理处

agenda yìchéng 议程; **on the ~** zài yìchéng shàng 在议程上

agent dàilǐ rén 代理人

aggravate (*worsen*) shǐ èhuà 使恶化

aggression qīnfàn xíngwéi 侵犯行为

aggressive hào xúnxìn 好寻衅; (*dynamic*) jījí 积极

agile línghuó 灵活

agitated jiāolù bù'ān 焦虑不安

agitation jiāolù 焦虑

agitator shàndòng zhě 煽动者

ago: 2 days ~ liǎngtiān qián 两天前; **long ~** hěnjiǔ yǐqián 很久以前; **how long ~?** duōjiǔ zhīqián? 多久之前?

agonizing nánshòu 难受

agony jídù tòngkǔ 极度痛苦

agree 1 *v/i* (*of people, figures, accounts*) tóngyì 同意; **I ~** wǒ tóngyì 我同意; *I don't ~* wǒ bù tóngyì 我不同意; *it doesn't ~ with me* (*of food*) bú shìhé wǒ bù shìhé wǒ 不适合我 **2** v/t price shāngdìng 商定; *~ that something should be done* zànchéng yīnggāi cǎiqǔ xíngdòng 赞成应该采取行动

agreeable (*pleasant*) lìngrén yúkuài 令人愉快; (*in agreement*) zànchéng 赞成

agreement (*consent*) tóngyì 同意; (*contract*) xiéyì 协议; *reach ~ on* dáchéng xiéyì 达成协议

agricultural nóngyè 农业

agriculture nóngyè 农业

ahead: *be ~ of* lǐngxiān 领先; *plan / think ~* yùxiān jìhuà / kǎolǜ 预先计划 / 考虑

aid n & v/t yuánzhù 援助

Aids àizībìng 艾滋病

ailing economy xiāotiáo 萧条

aim 1 n (*in shooting*) miáozhǔn 瞄准; (*objective*) mùbiāo 目标 **2** v/i (*in shooting*) miáozhǔn 瞄准; *~ at doing X, ~ to do X* zhìlìyú zuò X 致力于做 X **3** v/t: *be ~ed at* (*of remark etc*) zhēnduì 针对; (*of guns*) miáozhǔn 瞄准

air 1 n kōngqì 空气; *by ~ travel* zuò fēijī 坐飞机; *send mail* hángkōng 航空; *in the open ~* zài shìwài 在室外; *on the ~* RAD, TV bōsòng 播送 **2** v/t room shǐ tōngfēng 使通风; fig: views fābiǎo 发表

airbase kōngjūn jīdì 空军基地; **air-conditioned** yǒu kōngtiáo 有空调; **air-conditioning** ⇩ kōngtiáo 空调; **aircraft** fēijī 飞机; **aircraft carrier** hángkōng mǔjiàn 航空母舰; **air cylinder** shuǐfèi 水肺; **airfield** jīchǎng 机场; **air force** kōngjūn 空军; **air hostess** kōngjiě 空姐; **air letter** hángkōng xìnjiàn 航空信件; **airline** hángkōng gōngsī 航空公司; **airmail**: *by ~* jì hángkōng 寄航空; **airplane** fēijī 飞机; **air pollution** kōngqì wūrǎn 空气污染; **airport** jīchǎng 机场; **airsick**: *get ~* yǒu kōngyūnbìng 有空晕病; **airspace** kōngyù 空域; **air**

terminal jīchǎng zhōngduān 机场终端; **airtight** container mìfēng 密封; **air traffic** kōngzhōng jiāotōng 空中交通; **air-traffic control** kōngzhōng jiāotōng kòngzhì 空中交通控制; **air-traffic controller** kōngzhōng jiāotōng kòngzhì rényuán 空中交通控制人员

airy room tōngfēng 通风; attitude kōngxiǎng 空想

aisle tōngdào 通道

aisle seat kào tōngdào zuòwèi 靠通道座位

alarm 1 n jǐngzhōng 警钟; *raise the ~* bàojǐng 报警 **2** v/t shǐ kǒnghuāng 使恐慌

alarm clock nàozhōng 闹钟

Albania Ā'ěrbāníyà 阿尔巴尼亚

Albanian 1 adj Ā'ěrbāníyà 阿尔巴尼亚 **2** n (*person*) Ā'ěrbāníyà rén 阿尔巴尼亚人; (*language*) Ā'ěrbāníyà yǔ 阿尔巴尼亚语

album (*for photographs*) yǐngjí 影集; (*record*) chàngpiān 唱片

alcohol jiǔ 酒

alcoholic 1 n xùjiǔ zhě 酗酒者 **2** adj hán jiǔjīng 含酒精

alert 1 n (*signal*) jǐngbào 警报; *be on the ~* chùyú jièbèi zhuàngtài 处于戒备状态 **2** v/t shǐ jǐngjué 使警觉 **3** adj liúxīn 留心

alibi n búzài fànzuì xiànchǎng de shēnbiàn 不在犯罪现场的申辩

alien 1 n (*foreigner*) wàiguó rén 外国人; (*from space*) wàixīng rén 外星人 **2** adj mòshēng 陌生; *be ~ to X* (*not in keeping with a person's character*) yǔ X běnxìng bùfú 与 X 本性不符

alienate shūyuǎn 疏远

alight adj zháohuǒ 着火

alike 1 adj: *be ~* xiāngsì 相似 **2** adv xiāngsì 相似; *old and young ~* lǎoshào yīyàng 老少一样

alimony shànyǎng fèi 赡养费

alive: *be ~* huózhe 活着

all 1 adj dōu 都; *we ~ agree* wǒmen dōu tóngyì 我们都同意; *~ Chinese cities* Zhōngguó suǒyǒude

chéngshì 中国所有的城市
2 *pron*: **~ of us / them** wǒ / tāmen dōu 我 / 他们都; **he ate ~ of it** tā dōu chī le 他都吃了; **that's ~, thanks** jiù zhèixiē, xièxie 就这些, 谢谢; **for ~ I care** wǒ cái bùguǎn ne 我才不管呢; **for ~ I know** jù wǒ suǒzhī 据我所知; **~ at once** yíxiàzi 一下子; **~ but (nearly)** jīhū 几乎; **~ the better** gènghǎole 更好了; **~ the time** yìzhí 一直; **they're not at ~ alike** tāmen gēnběn búxiàng 他们根本不像; **not at ~!** yìdiǎnr yě bù! 一点儿也不!; **two ~ (in score)** èrpíng 二平

allegation zhǐkòng 指控
alleged *culprit* yǒu xiányí 有嫌疑; *reason* suǒwèi 所谓
allergic: **be ~ to ...** duì ... guòmǐn 对 ... 过敏
allergy guòmǐn 过敏
alleviate jiǎnqīng 减轻
alley hútòng 胡同
alliance tóngméng 同盟
alligator dùnwěnè 钝吻鳄
allocate ānpái 安排
allot fēnpèi 分配
allow (*permit*) yǔnxǔ 允许; (*calculate for*) jìsuàn 计算; **it's not ~ed** bùxíng 不行; **~ X to ...** yǔnxǔ X ... 允许 X ...
♦allow for kǎolǜ dào 考虑到
allowance (*money*) jīntiē 津贴; (*pocket money*) língyòng qián 零用钱; **make ~s** (*for thing, weather etc*) kǎolǜ dào 考虑到; (*for person*) yuánliàng 原谅
alloy héjīn 合金
all-purpose duō yòngtú 多用途; all-round quánmiàn 全面; all-time: **be at an ~ low** kōngqián wèiyǒu de dī 空前未有的低
♦allude to yǐngshè 影射
alluring yòuhuò 诱惑
all-wheel drive sìlún qūdòng 四轮驱动
ally *n* tóngméng zhě 同盟者
almond xìngrén 杏仁
almost jīhū 几乎
alone dāndú 单独

along **1** *prep*: **walk ~ this path** yánzhe zhètiáo xiǎolù zǒu 沿着这条小路走 **2** *adv* yīqǐ 一起; **~ with** hé 和; **all ~** (*all the time*) yīzhí 一直
aloud chūshēngdi 出声地
alphabet zìmǔ biǎo 字母表
alphabetical order yī zìmǔ shùnxù 依字母顺序
already yǐjīng 已经
alright: **that's ~** (*doesn't matter*) méi guānxi 没关系; (*when somebody says thank you*) búxiè 不谢; (*is quite good*) búcuò 不错; **I'm ~** (*not hurt*) wǒ méi shìr 我没事儿; (*have got enough*) gòule 够了; **~, that's enough!** déle 得了; **can I? – ~** kěyǐ ma? – kěyǐ 可以吗? – 可以
also yě 也
altar shèngtán 圣坛
alter *v/t* gǎibiàn 改变
alteration gēnggǎi 更改
alternate **1** *v/i* jiāotì 交替 **2** *adj* měigé 每隔
alternating current jiāoliúdiàn 交流电
alternative **1** *n* xuǎnzé 选择 **2** *adj* lìngyī kě xuǎnzé 另一可选择; *lifestyle, music etc* bùtóng zhǒng 不同种
alternatively huòzhě 或者
although jǐnguǎn 尽管
altitude (*of plane*) gāodù 高度; (*of mountain, city*) hǎibá 海拔
alt key COMPUT Alt jiàn Alt 键
altogether (*completely*) wánquán 完全; (*in all*) yīgòng 一共
altruistic lìrén 利人
aluminum lǚ 铝
always zǒngshì 总是; **it's ~ raining here** zhèr zǒngshì xià yǔ 这儿总是下雨
a.m. (*in the morning*) zǎochén 早晨
amalgamate *v/i* (*of companies*) hébìng 合并
amateur *n* (*unskilled*) yèyú àihào zhě 业余爱好者; sp yèyú 业余
amaze shǐ dàwéi chījīng 使大为吃惊
amazement jīngqí 惊奇

amazing (*surprising*) jīngrén 惊人; (*very good*) méizhìle 没治了

ambassador dàshǐ 大使

amber: **at ~** huáng 黄

ambiguous hánhú 含糊

ambition zhìxiàng 志向; *pej* yěxīn 野心

ambitious yǒu zhìxiàng 有志向; *plan* xióngxīn bóbo 雄心勃勃

ambulance jiùhùchē 救护车

ambush **1** *n* fújī 伏击 **2** *v/t* máifú 埋伏

amend gǎizhèng 改正

amendment xiūgǎi 修改

amends: **make ~** bǔguò 补过

amenities biànlì shèshī 便利设施

America Měiguó 美国

American **1** *adj* Měiguó 美国 **2** *n* Měiguó rén 美国人

amiable hé'ǎi kěqīn 和蔼可亲

amicable yǒushàn 友善

ammunition jūnhuǒ 军火; *fig* jìngōng shǒuduàn 进攻手段

amnesty *n* shèmiǎn 赦免

among(st) zài ... zhīzhōng 在 ... 之中

amount shùliàng 数量; (*sum of money*) jīn'é 金额

♦amount to děngyú 等于

ample chōngzú 充足

amplifier fàngdàqì 放大器

amplify *sound* fàngdà 放大

amputate jiézhī 节肢

amuse (*make laugh etc*) dòuxiào 逗笑; (*entertain*) gěi ... tígōng yúlè 给 ... 提供娱乐

amusement (*merriment*) lèqù 乐趣; (*entertainment*) yúlè 娱乐; **~s** (*games*) yúlè huódòng 娱乐活动; **to our great ~** lìng wǒmén hěn gāoxìng 令我们很高兴

amusement arcade yúlè zhōngxīn 娱乐中心

amusement park yúlè yuán 娱乐园

amusing yǒuqù 有趣

anabolic steroid héchéng dàixiè jīsù 合成代谢激素

Analects of Confucius Lúnyǔ 论语

analog COMPUT mónǐ 模拟

analogy bǐyù 比喻

analysis fēnxī 分析; (*psychoanalysis*) jīngshén fēnxī 精神分析

analyze fēnxī 分析

anarchy wúzhèngfǔ zhuàngtài 无政府状态

anatomy jiěpōu 解剖

ancestor zǔxiān 祖先

anchor NAUT **1** *n* máo 锚 **2** *v/i* pāomáo 抛锚

anchor man TV xīnwén guǎngbō yuán 新闻广播员

ancient *adj* gǔlǎo 古老

and ◊ (*joining nouns*) hé 和; **you ~ me** nǐ hé wǒ 你和我 ◊ (*joining adjectives*) yòu ... yòu ... 又 ...; **tall ~ thin** yòu gāo yòu shòu 又高又瘦 ◊ (*~ then*) ránhòu 然后; **he checked in ~ went to his room** tā dēngle jì ránhòu qùle tāde fángjiān 他登了记然后去了他的房间 ◊ (*two actions at the same time*) biān ... biān ... 边 ... 边 ...; **she was laughing ~ crying** tā yìbiān xiào yìbiān kū 她一边笑一边哭; **they were eating ~ drinking** tāmen biān chī biān hē 他们边吃边喝 ◊ (*when listing things, not translated*): **two beers ~ a coffee** liǎngge píjiǔ yíge kāfēi 两个啤酒一个咖啡 ◊: **faster ~ faster** yuèlái yuè kuài 越来越快

anemia pínxuè 贫血

anemic: **be ~** pínxuè 贫血

anesthetic *n* mázuì 麻醉

anesthetist mázuì shī 麻醉师

anger **1** *n* fènnù 愤怒 **2** *v/t* shǐ fènnù 使愤怒

angina yānxiá yán 咽峡炎

angle *n* jiǎodù 角度

angry fènnù 愤怒; **be ~ with X** duì X shēngqì 对X生气

anguish jídù tòngkǔ 极度痛苦

animal dòngwù 动物

animated huópo 活泼

animated cartoon dònghuà piān 动画片

animation (*liveliness*) huópo 活泼; (*cinematic*) dònghuà piān shèzhì 动画片摄制

animosity díyì 敌意

ankle ⇩jiǎowàn 脚腕

annex **1** n (building) kuòjiàn bùfèn 扩建部分 **2** v/t state tūnbìng 吞并

anniversary (wedding ~) zhōunián 周年

announce xuānbù 宣布

announcement xuāngào 宣告

announcer TV, RAD bōyīn yuán 播音员

annoy shǐ fánnǎo 使烦恼; **be ~ed** shēngqì 生气

annoyance (anger) fán 烦; (sth annoying) fánnǎo 烦恼

annoying nǎorén 恼人

annual adj (once a year) nián 年; (of a year) niándù 年度

annul marriage shǐ wúxiào 使无效

anonymous nìmíng 匿名

anorexia yànshí zhèng 厌食症

anorexic: **be ~** yànshí zhèng 厌食

another adj & pron (different) lìng yígè 另一个; (additional) yòu yígè 又一个; (referring to something that hasn't yet happened) zài yígè 再一个; **can I have ~ … ?** wǒ kěyǐ zài lái yíge … ma? 我可以再来一个 … 吗? ; **one ~** hùxiāng 互相

answer **1** n (to letter, person) dáfù 答复; (to problem, question) dá'àn 答案 **2** v/t letter, person dáfù 答复; question huídá 回答; **~ the door** kāimén 开门; **~ the telephone** tīng diànhuà 听电话

♦ answer back **1** v/t person huízuǐ 回嘴 **2** v/i huízuǐ 回嘴

♦ answer for fùzé 负责

answerphone ⇩lùyīn diànhuà 录音电话

ant mǎyǐ 蚂蚁

antagonism díyì 敌意

Antarctic Nánjí 南极

antenatal chǎnqián 产前

antenna (of insect) chùjiǎo 触角; (for TV) tiānxiàn 天线

antibiotic n kàngjūnsù 抗菌素

antibody kàngtǐ 抗体

anticipate yùliào 预料

anticipation yùliào 预料

antidote jiědúyào 解毒药

antifreeze zǔdòngjì 阻冻剂

Anti-Japanese War Kàng Rì Zhànzhēng 抗日战争

antipathy fǎngǎn 反感

antiquated chénjiù 陈旧

antique n gǔdǒng 古董

antique dealer gǔdǒng shāng 古董商

Anti-rightists Campaign Fǎnyòu Yùndòng 反右运动

antiseptic **1** adj kàngjūn 抗菌 **2** n kàngjūnjì 抗菌剂

antisocial bù héqún 不和群

antivirus program COMPUT kàng bìngdú chéngxù 抗病毒程序

anxiety jiāojí 焦急

anxious jiāojí 焦急; (eager) rèxīn 热心; **be ~ for …** (for news etc) jiāojí děngdài … 焦急等待 …

any **1** adj: **are there ~ diskettes / glasses?** yǒuméiyǒu cípán / bēizi? 有没有磁盘 / 杯子? ; **is there ~ bread / improvement?** yǒuméiyǒu miànbāo / jìnbù? 有没有面包 / 进步? ; **there aren't ~ diskettes / glasses** méiyǒu cípán / bēizi 没有磁盘 / 杯子; **there isn't ~ bread / improvement** méiyǒu miànbāo / jìnbù 没有面包 / 进步; **have you ~ idea at all?** nǐ dàodǐ míng bù míngbái? 你到底明不明白? ; **take ~ one you like** suí nǐ ná nǎyīgè 随你拿哪一个 **2** pron: **do you have ~?** nǐ yǒu méiyǒu? 你有没有? ; **there isn't / aren't ~ left** méi shèng de le 没剩的了; **~ of them could be guilty** tāmén zhīzhōng rèn yīgè dōu kěnéng yǒuzuì 他们之中任一个都可能有罪 **3** adv: **is that ~ better / easier?** hǎo / róngyì diǎnr le ma? 好 / 容易点儿了吗? ; **I don't like it ~ more** wǒ bù xǐhuānle 我不喜欢了

anybody (emphatic) rènhé rén 任何人; **~ can do that** rènhé rén dōu kěyǐ zuò 任何人都可以做 ◊ (with negatives): **there wasn't ~ there** méirén zài nàr 没人在那儿 ◊ (in questions, conditionals) shéi; *if ~ can help* rúguǒ shéi néng bāngmáng 如果谁能帮忙

anyhow (*summarizing*) zǒngzhī 总之; (*in any way*) wúlùn yòng hézhǒng fāngfǎ 无论用何种方法; (*at least*) zhìshǎo 至少

anyone → *anybody*

anything shénme 什么; *I didn't hear ~* wǒ méi tīngjiàn shénme 我没听见什么; *~ but* yīdiǎnr yě bù 一点儿也不; *~ else?* háiyǒu shénme? 还有什么？

anyway → *anyhow*

anywhere wúlùn nǎli 无论哪里; *I can't find it ~* wǒ nǎr dōu zhǎobùzháo 我哪儿都找不着

apart (*in distance*) jùlí 距离; *live ~* (*of people*) fēnjū 分居; *~ from* (*excepting*) chúle 除了; (*in addition to*) cǐwà 此外

apartment gōngyù 公寓

apartment block gōngyù dàshà 公寓大厦

apathetic lěngmò 冷漠

ape *n* xīngxing 猩猩

aperture PHOT guāngquān 光圈

apologize dàoqiàn 道歉

apology dàoqiàn 道歉

apostrophe GRAM piěhào 撇号

appall shǐ zhènjīng 使震惊

appalling lìngrén zhènjīng 令人震惊; *language* cūlǔ 粗鲁

apparatus qìxiè 器械

apparent míngxiǎn 明显; *become ~ that …* … kāishǐ biànde míngxiǎn … 开始变得明显

apparently hǎoxiàng 好象

appeal 1 *n* (*charm*) xīyǐn lì 吸引力; (*for funds etc*) hūyù 呼吁; LAW shàngsù 上诉 **2** *v/i* LAW shàngsù 上诉

♦ **appeal for** kěnqiè qǐngqiú 恳切请求

♦ **appeal to** (*be attractive to*) duì … yǒu xīyǐnlì 对 … 有吸引力

appear chūxiàn 出现; (*in film etc*) dēngchǎng 登场; (*of new product*) chūxiàn 出现; (*in court*) dàochǎng 到场; (*look, seem*) xiǎndé 显得; *it ~s that …* kànlái … 看来 …

appearance (*arrival*) dàolái 到来;

(*in film etc*) dēngchǎng 登场; (*in court*) chūtíng 出庭; (*look*) wàibiǎo 外表; *put in an ~* lòumiàn 露面

appendicitis lánwěiyán 阑尾炎

appendix MED lánwěi 阑尾; (*of book etc*) fùlù 附录

appetite wèikǒu 胃口; *fig* yùwàng 欲望

appetizer (*food*) kāiwèi pǐn 开胃品; (*drink*) kāiwèi jiǔ 开胃酒

appetizing kāiwèi 开胃

applaud 1 *v/i* gǔzhǎng 鼓掌 **2** *v/t* hècǎi 喝采; *fig* zànxǔ 赞许

applause gǔzhǎng 鼓掌; (*praise*) zànyáng 赞扬

apple píngguǒ 苹果

apple pie píngguǒ pài 苹果派

apple sauce píngguǒ zhīr 苹果汁儿

appliance qìxiè 器械; (*household*) jiāyòng qìxiè 家用器械

applicable *ruling* shìyòng 适用

applicant shēnqǐng zhě 申请者

application (*for job, passport, visa, university etc*) shēnqǐng 申请

-application form (*for passport, visa, university*) shēnqǐng biǎogé 申请表格

apply 1 *v/t* shǐyòng 使用; *ointment* cāyòng 搽用 **2** *v/i* (*of rule, law*) shìyòng 适用

♦ **apply for** *job, passport, university* shēnqǐng 申请

♦ **apply to** (*contact*) xiàng … shēnqǐng 向 … 申请; (*affect*) guānxì dào 关系到

appoint (*to position*) rènmìng 任命

appointment (*to position*) rènmìng 任命; (*meeting*) yuēhuì 约会

appointments diary yuēhuì rìjìběn 约会日记本

appreciate 1 *v/t* (*value*) xīnshǎng 欣赏; (*be grateful for*) gǎnjī gǎnjī 感激; (*acknowledge*) yìshí dào 意识到; *thanks, I ~ it* fēicháng gǎnxiè 非常感谢 **2** *v/i* FIN tígāo jiàzhí 提高价值

appreciation (*of kindness etc*) gǎnjī 感激; (*of music etc*) xīnshǎng 欣赏

apprehensive dānxīn 担心

apprentice xuétú 学徒

approach **1** *n* línjìn 临近; (*offer, proposal*) tíyì 提议; (*to problem*) fāngshì 方式 **2** *v/t* (*get near to*) línjìn 临近; (*contact*) liánxì 联系; *problem* chǔlǐ 处理

approachable *person* píngyì jìnrén 平易近人

appropriate *adj* qiàdàng 恰当

approval tóngyì 同意

approve **1** *v/i* zànchéng 赞成 **2** *v/t* pīzhǔn 批准

♦ approve of rèntóng 认同

approximate *adj* dàyuē 大约

approximately dàyuē 大约

APR (= *annual percentage rate*) niánlǜ 年率

apricot xìng 杏

April sìyuè 四月

apt *pupil* línglì 伶俐; *remark* qiàrú qífèn 恰如其分; *be ~ to …* yìyú … 易于 …

aptitude tiānzī 天资

aquarium (*large*) shuǐzú guǎn 水族馆; (*small, at home*) yǎngyúgāng 养鱼缸

aquatic (*water-dwelling*) shuǐqī 水栖; *sports* (*in water*) shuǐzhōng 水中; (*on water*) shuǐshàng 水上; (*under water*) shuǐxià 水下

Arab **1** *adj* Ālābó 阿拉伯 **2** *n* Ālābó rén 阿拉伯人

Arabic **1** *adj* Ālābó 阿拉伯 **2** *n* Ālābó yǔ 阿拉伯语

arable gēngzhòng 耕种

arbitrary rènyì 任意; *remark* suíbiàn 随便; *attack* wú jìhuà xìng 无计划性

arbitrate *v/i* (*in public affair*) zhòngcái 仲裁; (*in private*) tiáotíng 调停

arbitration (*in public affair*) zhòngcái 仲裁; (*in private*) tiáotíng 调停

arch *n* gǒng 拱

archeologist kǎogǔ xué jiā 考古学家

archeology kǎogǔ xué 考古学

archer gōngjiàn shǒu 弓箭手

architect jiànzhù shī 建筑师

architecture jiànzhù xué 建筑学

archives dǎng'àn 档案

archway gǒngmén 拱门

Arctic Běijí 北极

ardent qiánchéng 虔诚

area (*region*) dìqū 地区; (*of activity, job, study etc*) fànwéi 范围; (*square metres etc*) miànjī 面积

area code TELEC qūhào 区号

arena SP bǐsài chǎng 比赛场

Argentina Āgēntíng 阿根廷

Argentinian **1** *adj* Āgēntíng 阿根廷 **2** *n* Āgēntíng rén 阿根廷人

arguably kě zhēnglùn 可争论

argue **1** *v/i* (*quarrel*) chǎojià 吵架; (*reason*) zhēnglùn 争论 **2** *v/t: ~ that* jiānchí 坚持

argument (*quarrel*) chǎojià 吵架; (*reasoning*) zhēnglùn 争论

argumentative ài chǎojià 爱吵架

arid *land* pínjí 贫瘠

arise (*of situation, problem*) chéngxiàn 呈现

arithmetic suànshù 算术

arm[1] *n* (*of person*) shǒubì 手臂; (*of chair*) fúshǒu 扶手

arm[2] *v/t* wǔzhuāng 武装

armaments wǔqì 武器

armchair fúshǒu yǐ 扶手椅

armed wǔzhuāng 武装

armed forces wǔzhuāng lìliàng 武装力量

armed robbery chíxiè qiǎngjié 持械抢劫

armor hùjiǎ 护甲

armored vehicle zhuāngjiǎ chē 装甲车

armpit yèwō 腋窝

arms (*weapons*) wǔqì 武器

army jūnduì 军队

aroma xiāngwèir 香味儿

around **1** *prep* (*in circle*) wéirǎo 围绕; (*approximately*) dàyuē 大约; *it's ~ the corner* zài guǎijiǎo nàr 在拐角那儿; *we walked ~ the garden* wǒmen zài huāyuán lǐ sànbù le 我们在花园里散步了; *they all stood ~ him* tāmen dōu zhàn zài tāde zhōuwéi 他们都站在他的周围 **2** *adv* (*in the area*) zài zhèr 在这儿; (*encircling*) zhōuwéi 周围;*he lives ~ here* tā zhùzài fùjìn 他住在附近;*walk ~* zǒuzou 走走;*be ~ (somewhere near)* zài fùjìn 在附近;*there are a lot of people ~* yǒu hěnduō rén 有很多人;*she has been ~ (has traveled, is experienced)* tā yuèlì tǐngshēn 她阅历挺深

arouse *interest, suspicion* yǐnqǐ 引起;*strong feelings* huànxǐng 唤醒;*(sexually)* jīfā 激发

arrange *(put in order)* zhěnglǐ 整理;*furniture* bùzhì 布置;*flowers* chā 插;*music* gǎibiān 改编;*meeting, party, time, place etc* ānpái 安排;*I've ~d to meet her* wǒ ānpái hé tā jiànmiàn le 我安排和她见面了

♦**arrange for** ānpái 安排

arrangement *(plan)* ānpái 安排;*(agreement)* xiéyì 协议;*(layout: of furniture etc)* bùzhì 布置;*(of flowers)* chāhuā 插花;*(of music)* gǎibiān 改编

arrears tuōqiàn kuǎn 拖欠款;*be in ~ (of person)* tuōqiàn 拖欠

arrest 1 *n* dàibǔ 逮捕;*be under ~* bèibǔ 被捕 **2** *v/t* dàibǔ 逮捕

arrival dàodá 到达;*~s (at airport)* dàodá 到达

arrive dàodá 到达

♦**arrive at** *place* dǐdá 抵达;*decision etc* zuòchū 做出

arrogance àomàn 傲慢

arrogant jiāo'ào zìdà 骄傲自大

arrow jiàntóu 箭头

arson zònghuǒ 纵火

art yìshù 艺术;*the ~s* yìshù jiè 艺术界;*~s degree* wénkē xuéwèi 文科学位

art gallery huàláng 画廊

arterial road gànxiàn 干线

artery MED dòngmài 动脉

arthritis guānjié yán 关节炎

article *(item)* wùjiàn 物件;*(in newspaper)* wénzhāng 文章;*(section of law etc)* kuǎn 款;GRAM guàncí 冠词

articulate *adj person* biǎodá nénglì qiáng 表达能力强;*essay* biǎodá de qīngchǔ yǒulì 表达得清楚有力

artificial rénzào 人造;*(not sincere)* zuòzuò 做作

artificial intelligence réngōng zhìnéng 人工智能

artillery dàpào 大炮

artisan shǒuyì rén 手艺人

artist *(painter)* huàjiā 画家;*(artistic person)* yìshù jiā 艺术家

artistic *person* yǒu yìshù xìng 有艺术性;*skills* yìshù 艺术

as 1 *conj* ◊ *(while, when)* dāng … de shíhou 当…的时候;*~ I was about to leave, the phone rang again* dāng wǒ yào zǒu de shíhou, diànhuà yòu xiǎng le 当我要走的时候,电话又响了;*I saw him ~ I was cycling along* wǒ qí chēzi de shíhou kànjiàn le tā 我骑车子的时候看见了他 ◊ *(because)* yīnwéi 因为;*I didn't go ~ I wasn't feeling well* wǒ méi qù yīnwéi wǒ bú tài shūfu 我没去因为我不太舒服 ◊ *(like)* xiàng 像;*~ I said* xiàng wǒ shuōde 像我说的;*~ if* hǎoxiàng 好像;*~ usual* rútóng wǎngcháng 如同往常;*~ necessary* yǒu bìyào shí 有必要时 **2** *adv*:*~ high / pretty ~ …* hé … yíyàng gāo / piàoliang 和…一样高 / 漂亮;*~ much ~ that?* nàme duō? 那么多?**3** *prep* zuòwéi 作为;*~ a child / schoolgirl* zuòwéi háizi / nǚ xuéshēng 作为孩子 / 女学生;*work ~ a teacher / translator* dāng lǎoshī / fānyì 当老师 / 翻译;*~ for* zhìyú 至于;*~ Hamlet* bànyǎn Hāmǔláitè 扮演哈姆莱特

asap (= *as soon as possible*) jìnkuài 尽快

ash huī 灰;*~es* huī 灰;*(after cremation)* gǔhuī 骨灰

ashamed xiūkuì 羞愧;*be ~ of* wèi … diūliǎn 为…丢脸;*you should be ~ of yourself* nǐ bū hàisāo 你不害臊

ash can lājī xiāng 垃圾箱

ashore zài ànshàng 在岸上;*go ~* shàng'àn 上岸

ashtray yānhuī gāng 烟灰缸

Asia Yàzhōu 亚洲

Asian 1 *adj* Yàzhōu 亚洲 **2** *n* Yàzhōu rén 亚洲人

aside yībiān 一边; **~ from** chúle 除了

ask 1 *v/t person* wèn 问; (*invite*) jiào 叫; *question* tíwèn 提问; *favor* qǐngqiú 请求; **can I ~ you something?** kěyǐ wèn nǐ xiē shì ma? 可以问你些事吗？; **~ X for ...** gēn X yào ... 跟 X 要 ...; **~ X to ...** yào X ... 要 X ...; **~ X about Y** xiàng X dǎtīng Y 向 X 打听 Y **2** *v/i* wèn 问

♦ **ask after** *person* wènhòu 问候

♦ **ask for** yāoqiú 要求; *person* zhào zhǎo 找

♦ **ask out** (*for a drink, night out*) yuēhuì 约会

asking price yàojià 要价

asleep: be (**fast**) **~** shúshuì 熟睡; **fall ~** shuìzháo le 睡着了

asparagus lúsǔn 芦笋

aspect fāngmiàn 方面

aspirin āsīpǐlín 阿司匹林

ass¹ (*idiot*) bèndàn 笨蛋

ass² V (*buttocks*) pìgu 屁股; (*sex*) xìng 性

assassin ànshā zhě 暗杀者

assassinate ànshā 暗杀

assassination ànshā 暗杀

assault 1 *n* gōngjī 攻击; (*physical*) ōudǎ 殴打; (*verbal*) wēixié 威胁 **2** *v/t* (*physically*) ōudǎ 殴打; (*verbally*) wēixié 威胁

assemble 1 *v/t parts* zǔzhuāng 组装 **2** *v/i* (*of people*) jízhōng 集中

assembly (*of parts*) zǔzhuāng 组装; POL yìhuì 议会

assembly line zhuāngpèi xiàn 装配线

assembly plant zhuāngpèi chǎng 装配厂

assent *v/i* tóngyì 同意

assert: ~ oneself jiānchí zìjǐde lìchǎng 坚持自己的立场

assertive *person* zìxìn 自信

assess *situation* pínggū 评估; *value* gūjià 估价

asset FIN zīchǎn 资产; *fig* bǎobèi 宝贝

asshole V pìyǎnr 屁眼儿; (*idiot*) bèndàn 笨蛋

assign *person, thing* fēnpèi 分配

assignment (*task, study*) rènwù 任务

assimilate *v/t information* xīshōu 吸收; *person into group* jiēshòu 接受

assist bāngzhù 帮助

assistance bāngzhù 帮助

assistant zhùshǒu 助手

assistant director fù zhǔguǎn 副主管; (*of movie*) fù dǎoyǎn 副导演

assistant manager fù jīnglǐ 副经理

associate 1 *v/t:* **~ X with Y** X hé Y liánxiǎng zài yīqǐ X 和 Y 联想在一起 **2** *v/i:* **~ with** jiéjiāo 结交 **3** *n* tóngshì 同事

associate professor fù jiàoshòu 副教授

association xiéhuì 协会; **in ~ with** yǔ ... hézuò 与 ... 合作

assortment (*of food*) huāsè jùquán 花色俱全; (*of people*) gèshì gèyàng 各式各样

assume (*suppose*) xiǎngxiàng 想象; (*for the sake of argument*) jiǎdìng 假定

assumption shèxiǎng 设想

assurance bǎozhèng 保证; (*confidence*) xìnxīn 信心

assure (*reassure*) shǐ quèxìn 使确信

assured (*confident*) yǒu xìnxīn 有信心

asterisk xīnghào 星号

asthma xiàochuǎn 哮喘

astonish shǐ jīngyà 使惊讶; **be ~ed** jīngyà 惊讶

astonishing lìngrén jīngyà 令人惊讶

astonishment jīngyà 惊讶

astrologer zhànxīng zhě 占星者

astrology zhànxīng shù 占星术

astronaut yǔháng yuán 宇航员

astronomer tiānwén xuéjiā 天文学家

astronomical *price etc* jùdà 巨大

astronomy tiānwén xué 天文学

asylum (*mental*) jīngshén bìngyuàn 精神病院; (*political*) bìhù 庇护

at (*with places*) zài 在; **~ the cleaner's** zài gānxǐdiàn lǐ 在干洗店里; **Joe's** zài Qiáo jiālǐ 在乔家里; **~ the door** zài ménkǒu 在门口; **~ 10 dollars** biāojià shí měiyuán 标价十美元; **~ the age of 18** shíbāsuì shí 十八岁时; **~ 5 o'clock** wǔ diǎnzhōng 五点钟; **be good / bad ~ X** shàncháng / bū shàncháng yú X 擅长 / 不擅长于 X

atheist wú shén lùn zhě 无神论者

athlete yùndòng yuán 运动员

athletic tǐgé jiànměi 体格健美

athletics tiánjìng yùndòng 田径运动

Atlantic Dàxīyáng 大西洋

atlas dìtú jí 地图集

ATM (= **automated teller machine**) qǔkuǎn jī 取款机

atmosphere (*of earth*) dàqì 大气; (*ambiance*) qìfen 气氛

atmospheric pollution dàqì wūrǎn 大气污染

atom yuánzǐ 原子

atom bomb yuánzǐ dàn 原子弹

atomic yuánzǐ 原子

atomic energy yuánzǐ néng 原子能

atomic waste yuánzǐ fèiwù 原子废物

atomizer wùhuà qì 雾化器

atrocious zāotòu 糟透

atrocity bàoxíng 暴行

attach shuānláo 栓牢; **~ importance to** zhùzhòng 注重; **be ~ed to** (*fond of: thing*) yīliàn 依恋; (*person*) àimù 爱慕

attachment (*to e-mail*) fùjiàn 附件

attack **1** n (*physical*) ōudǎ 殴打; MIL xíjī 袭击; (*verbal*) pēngjī 抨击 **2** v/t (*physically*) ōudǎ 殴打; MIL xíjī 袭击; (*verbally*) pēngjī 抨击

attempt **1** n chángshì 尝试 **2** v/t shìtú 试图

attend cānjiā 参加

♦attend to chǔlǐ 处理; *customer* fúshì 服侍

attendance chūqín 出勤

attendant (*in museum*) fúwù yuán 服务员

attention zhùyìlì 注意力; **bring to the ~ of ...** shǐ ... zhùyì 使 ... 注意; **your ~ please** qǐng zhùyì 请注意; **pay ~** zhùyì 注意

attentive *listener* rèxīn 热心

attic gélóu 阁楼

attitude tàidù 态度

attn (= **for the attention of**) gěi 给

attorney lǜshī 律师; **power of ~** shòuquán 授权

attract *person, attention* xīyǐn 吸引; **be ~ed to X** (*person*) àimù X 爱慕 X

attraction xīyǐn lì 吸引力; (*romantic*) mèilì 魅力

attractive yǒu xīyǐn lì 有吸引力

attribute[1] v/t: **~ X to ...** bǎ X guīyīn yú ... 把 X 归因于 ...; **the poem has been ~d to ...** jùshuō zhèi shǒu shī wéi ... suǒzuò 据说这首诗是 ... 所作

attribute[2] tèzhēng 特征

auction n & v/t pāimài 拍卖

♦auction off pāimài diào 拍卖掉

audacious *plan* màoxiǎn 冒险

audacity fàngsì 放肆

audible tīngdejiàn 听得见

audience (*of concert etc*) tīngzhòng 听众; (*in theater, at show, TV*) guānzhòng 观众

audio *adj* lùyīn 录音

audiovisual shìtīng 视听

audit **1** n shěnjì 审计 **2** v/t shěnhé 审核; *course* pángtīng 旁听

audition n & v/i shìyǎn 试演

auditor shěnjì shī 审计师

auditorium (*of theater etc*) tīng tīng 厅

August bāyuè 八月

aunt (*own, paternal*) gū 姑; (*own, maternal*) yí 姨; (*somebody else's*) āyí 阿姨

austere jiǎnpǔ 简朴

austerity (*economic*) jīngjì jǐnsuō 经济紧缩

Australasia Àodàlāxīyà 澳大利西亚

Australia Àodàlìyà 澳大利亚

Australian **1** adj Àodàlìyà 澳大利亚 **2** n Àodàlìyà rén 澳大利亚人

Austria Àodìlì 奥地利
Austrian 1 *adj* Àodìlì 奥地利 **2** *n*
  Àodìlì rén 奥地利人
authentic *antique* zhēnzhèng 真正;
  accent dìdào 地道
authenticity zhēnshí xìng 真实性
author zuòzhě 作者
authoritative *person, manner* ài xià
  mìnglìng 爱下命令; *source of*
  information yǒu quánwēi xìng 有
  权威性
authority quánwēi 权威;
  (*permission*) xǔkě 许可;
  be an ~
  on ... shì ... de quánwēi 是 ... 的
  权威; *the authorities* dāngquán
  zhě 当权者
authorize shòuquán 授权; *be ~d*
  to ... shòuquán ... 授权 ...
autistic gūpì 孤僻
auto *n* qìchē 汽车
autobiography zìzhuàn 自传
autograph qīnbǐ qiānmíng 亲笔
  签名
automate shǐ zìdònghuà 使自动
  化
automatic 1 *adj* zìdòng 自动 **2** *n*
  (*car, gun etc*) zìdòng 自动
automatically zìdòng 自动
automation zìdòng huà 自动化
automobile xiǎo qìchē 小汽车
automobile industry qìchē yè 汽
  车业
autonomous region zìzhìqū 自治
  区
autonomy zìzhì 自治
autopilot zìdòng jiàshǐ yí 自动驾
  驶仪
autopsy yànshī 验尸
auxiliary *adj* fǔzhù 辅助
available *facility, service, book,*
  information kě dédào 可得到;
  person yǒukōng 有空
avalanche xuěbēng 雪崩
avenue dàdào 大道; *fig* lù lù 路
average 1 *adj* píngjūn 平均;
  (*ordinary*) pǔtōng 普通; (*of*
  mediocre quality) mǎmahūhū 马马
  虎虎 **2** *n* píngjūn shuǐzhǔn 平均
  水准; *above / below ~* gāoyú /

dīyú píngjūn shuǐzhǔn 高于 / 低
  于平均水准; *on ~* píngjūn
  láishuō 平均来说 **3** *v/t* píngjūn
  平均
♦ **average out** *v/t* suàn píngjūn shù
  算平均数
♦ **average out at** píngjūn shì 平均
  是
aversion: *have an ~ to* yànwù 厌
  恶
avert *one's eyes* zhuǎnyí 转移; *crisis*
  bìmiǎn 避免
aviary niǎoshè 鸟舍
aviation hángkōng 航空
avid rèxīn 热心
avoid bìmiǎn 避免
awake *adj* xǐng 醒; *it's keeping me*
  ~ ràng wǒ shuìbùzháo 让我睡不
  着
award 1 *n* (*prize*) jiǎnglì 奖励 **2** *v/t*
  jiǎnglì 奖励; *damages* pàngěi 判
  给
aware: *be ~ of X* zhīdào X 知道 X;
  become ~ of X dézhī X 得知 X
awareness yìshí 意识
away: *be ~* (*traveling, sick etc*) bùzài
  不在; *walk / run ~* zǒu / pǎo kāi
  走 / 跑开; *look ~* búkàn 不看; *it's*
  2 miles ~ liǎng yīnglǐ yuǎn 两英
  里远; *Christmas is still six weeks*
  ~ lí shèngdànjié háiyǒu liù xīngqī
  离圣诞节还有六星期; *take X*
  ~ from Y (*something from*
  somebody) cóng Y nàlǐ názǒu X 从
  Y 那里拿走 X; *put X ~* bǎ X
  fànghǎo 把 X 放好
away game SP kèfāng bǐsài 客方
  比赛
awesome F (*terrific*) ⇩ gàilemàole
  盖了帽了
awful zāogāo 糟糕
awkward (*clumsy*) bènzhuō 笨拙;
  (*difficult*) nányǐ duìfù 难以对付;
  (*embarrassing*) gāngà 尴尬; *feel ~*
  gāngà 尴尬
awning chuánpéng 船篷
ax 1 *n* fǔ 斧 **2** *v/t* *project, budget,*
  jobs etc xiāojiǎn 削减
axle lúnzhóu 轮轴

B

BA (= **Bachelor of Arts**) wén xuéshì 文学士

baby *n* yīng'ér 婴儿

baby carriage yīng'ér chē 婴儿车; **baby-sit** kānháizi 看孩子; **baby-sitter** línshí bǎomǔ 临时保姆

bachelor dānshēn hàn 单身汉

back 1 *n* (*of person*) hòubèi 后背; (*of car, bus*) hòubù 后部; (*of paper, jacket, house, book*) bèimiàn 背面; (*of drawer*) jǐn lǐmiàn 尽里面; (*of chair*) kàobèi 靠背; SP hòuwèi 后卫; **in** ~ zài hòumian 在后面; **in the ~ of the car** zài qìchē hòuzuò 在汽车后座; **at the ~ of the bus** zài gōnggòng qìchē hòuzuò 在公共汽车后座; ~ **to front** qiánhòu diāndǎo 前后颠倒; **at the ~ of beyond** zài huāngwú rényān de dìfāng 在荒无人烟的地方 2 *adj* hòu 后; ~ **road** xiǎolù 小路 3 *adv*: **please move/stand** ~ qǐng hòutuì 请后退 **2 meters ~ from the edge** lí biānyuán liǎngmǐ 离边缘两米; ~ **in 1935** zǎozài yījiǔ sānwǔ nián 早在一九三五年; **give X ~ to Y** jiāng X huángeǐ Y 将 X 还给 Y; **she'll be ~ tomorrow** tā míngtiān huílái 她明天回来; **when are you coming ~?** nǐ shénme shíhòu huílái? 你什么时候回来？; **take X ~ to the store** (*because unsatisfactory*) tuìdiào X 退掉 X; **they wrote/phoned** ~ tāmen huíxìn/dǎhuí diànhuà le 他们回信/打回电话了; **he hit me** ~ tā huíshǒu dǎwǒ 他回手打我 4 *v/t* (*support*) zhīchí 支持; *car* dǎochē 倒车; *horse* xià dǔzhù 下赌注 5 *v/i* (*of driver*) dǎochē 倒车

♦ back away hòutuì 后退

♦ back down fàngqì 放弃

♦ back off hòutuì 后退; (*from danger*) dǎ tuìtánggǔ 打退堂鼓

♦ back onto bèixiàng 背向

♦ back out (*of commitment*) sāshǒu 撒手

♦ back up 1 *v/t* (*support*) zhīchí 支持; *claim, argument* zhèngshí 证实; *file* hòubèi 后备; **be backed up** (*of traffic*) páichéng chánglóng 排成长龙 2 *v/i* (*in car*) hòutuì 后退

back burner: **put ... on the** ~ bǎ ... fàngzài yībiān 把 ... 放在一边

backdate zhuīsù 追溯

backdoor hòumén 后门

backer zànzhù rén 赞助人

backfire *v/i* fig chǎnshēng shì yǔ yuàn weí de jiéguǒ 产生事与愿违的结果; **background** bèijǐng 背景; (*of person*) jīnglì 经历; (*of situation*) bèijǐng zīliào 背景资料; **backhand** *n* (*in tennis*) fǎnshǒu jīqiú 反手击球

backing (*support*) zhīchí 支持; (*musicians*) bànzòu 伴奏; (*singers*) bànchàng 伴唱

backing group bànzòu zǔ 伴奏组; (*singers*) bànchàng zǔ 伴唱组

backlash qiánglìè fǎnyìng 强烈反应; **backlog** jīyā 积压; **backpack** 1 *n* bēibāo 背包 2 *v/i* túbù lǚxíng 徒步旅行; **backpacker** túbù lǚxíng zhě 徒步旅行者; **backpedal** fig chū'ěr fǎněr 出尔反尔; **backspace** (*key*) tuìgé 退格; **backstairs** hòu lóutī 后楼梯; **backstroke** SP yǎngyǒng 仰泳

backup also COMPUT hòubèi 后备; **take a** ~ COMPUT zuò bèiyòng cípán 做备用磁盘

backup disk COMPUT bèiyòng cípán 备用磁盘

backward 1 *adj* child chídùn 迟钝;

society luòhòu 落后; *glance* xiànghòu 向后 **2** *adv* xiànghòu 向后

backyard hòu huāyuán 后花园; *fig* hòuyuàn 后院

bacon xūn xiánròu 熏咸肉

bacteria xìjūn 细菌

bad bùhǎo 不好; *weather, conditions* èliè 恶劣; *cold, headache etc* jùliè 剧烈; *mistake, accident* yánzhòng 严重; *(rotten)* huài 坏; *it's not ~* hái kěyǐ 还可以; *that's really too ~ (shame)* tài yíhàn le 太遗憾了; *feel ~ about (guilty)* gǎndào qiànjiù 感到歉疚; *be ~ at* bù zhuāncháng yú 不专长于; *Friday's ~, how about Thursday?* xīngqīwǔ bù héshì, xīngqīsì zěnme yàng? 星期五不合适，星期四怎么样？

bad debt wúfǎ shōuhuí de huàizhàng 无法收回的坏账

bad language cūhuà 粗话

badge zhèngzhāng 证章

badger *v/t* jiūchán 纠缠

badly *behave* bùhǎo 不好; *injured, damaged* yánzhòng 严重; *perform* chà 差; *he ~ needs a haircut / rest* tā jíxū jiǎn tóufa / xiūxi 他急需剪头发／休息; *he is ~ off (poor)* tā hěn qióng 他很穷

badminton yǔmáo qiú 羽毛球

baffle shǐ kùnhuò 使困惑; *be ~d* mōbùzháo tóunǎo 摸不着头脑

baffling *mystery* nányǐ jiědá 难以解答; *software etc* shēn'ào 深奥

bag *(plastic, paper)* dàizi 带子; *(for school, traveling)* bāo 包; *(purse)* shǒutí bāo 手提包

baggage xíngli 行李

baggage car RAIL xíngli chē 行李车; **baggage cart** xíngli chē 行李车; **baggage check** cúnfàng xíngli chù 存放行李处; **baggage reclaim** xíngli língqǔ chù 行李领取处

baggy kuānsōng 宽松

bail *n* LAW bǎoshì 保释; *(money)* bǎoshì jīn 保释金; *on ~* zàibǎo 在保

◆**bail out 1** *v/t* LAW bǎoshì 保释;

fig bāngzhù dùguò nánguān 帮助渡过难关 **2** *v/i (of airplane)* tiàosǎn 跳伞

bait *n* yòu'ěr 诱饵

bake *v/t* kǎo 烤

baked potato kǎo tǔdòu 烤土豆

baker miànbāo shīfu 面包师傅

bakery miànbāo diàn 面包店

balance 1 *n* pínghéng 平衡; *(remainder)* chā'é 差额; *(of bank account)* jiécún 结存 **2** *v/t ~ the books* jiésuàn 结算 **3** *v/i* pínghéng 平衡; *(of accounts)* shōuzhī pínghéng 收支平衡

balanced *(fair)* gōngpíng 公平; *personality* pínghéng 平衡; *~ diet* jūnhéng yǐnshí 均衡饮食

balance of payments guójì shōuzhī chā'é 国际收支差额

balance of trade màoyì chā'é 贸易差额

balance sheet juésuàn biǎo 决算表

balcony *(of house)* yángtái 阳台; *(in theater)* lóutīng 楼厅

bald *man* tūdǐng 秃顶; *he's going ~* tā kāishǐ tūdǐng le 他开始秃顶了

ball qiú 球; *on the ~* jījǐng 机警; *play ~ fig* hézuò 合作; *the ~'s in his court* lúndào tā zuòchū fǎnyìng 轮到他作出反应

ball bearing gǔnzhū zhóuchéng 滚珠轴承

ballerina bāléiwǔ nǚ yǎnyuán 芭蕾舞女演员

ballet bāléiwǔ 芭蕾舞

ballet dancer bāléiwǔ yǎnyuán 芭蕾舞演员

ball game *(baseball game)* qiúsài 球赛; *that's a different ~* nà shì lìng yíjiàn shì 那是另一件事

ballistic missile dàndào dǎodàn 弹道导弹

balloon *(child's)* qìqiú 气球; *(for flight)* rè qìqiú 热气球

ballot 1 *n* tóupiào 投票 **2** *v/t members* tóupiào juédìng 投票决定

ballot box tóupiào xiāng 投票箱

ballpark (*baseball*) bàngqiú chǎng 棒球场; *be in the right ~ fig* dàzhì zhèngquè 大致正确

ballpark figure dàzhì zhèngquè de shùmù 大致正确的数目

ballpoint (*pen*) ⇩ yuánzhū bǐ 圆珠笔

balls ∨ dàn 蛋; (*courage*) yǒngqì 勇气

bamboo zhúzi 竹子

bamboo shoots zhúsǔn 竹笋

ban 1 *n* jìnlìng 禁令 **2** *v/t* jìnzhǐ 禁止

banana xiāngjiāo 香蕉

band (*musical group*) yuèduì 乐队

bandage 1 *n* bēngdài 绷带 **2** *v/t* bǎng bēngdài 绑绷带

Band-Aid® ⇩ chuàngkětiē 创可贴

bandit tǔfěi 土匪

bandwagon: *jump on the ~* gǎn làngtóu 赶浪头

bandy *legs* luóquān tuǐ 罗圈腿

bang 1 *n* (*noise*) hōngde yīshēng 轰的一声; (*blow*) měngjī 猛击 *v/t door* shuāi 摔; (*hit*) zhuàng 撞 **3** *v/i* fāchū pēngde yīxiǎng 发出砰的一响

Bangladesh Mèngjiālā 孟加拉

Bangladeshi 1 *adj* Mèngjiālā 孟加拉 **2** *n* (*person*) Mèngjiālā rén 孟加拉人

banjo bānzhuō qín 班卓琴

bank¹ (*of river*) hé'àn 河岸

bank² 1 *n* FIN yínháng 银行 **2** *v/i:* *~ with* yòng ... yínháng 用 ... 银行 **3** *v/t money* chǔcún 储存

♦ **bank on** zhǐwàng 指望; *don't ~ it* bié nàme kěndìng 别那么肯定

bank account yínháng zhànghù 银行帐户; **bank balance** yínháng jiécún 银行结存; **bank bill** chāopiào 钞票

banker yínháng jiā 银行家

banker's card yínháng xìnyòng kǎ 银行信用卡

banker's order chángqī wěituō shū 长期委托书

bank loan yínháng dàikuǎn 银行贷款; **bank manager** yínháng jīnglǐ 银行经理; **Bank of China** Zhōngguó Yínháng 中国银行;

bank rate yínháng lìlǜ 银行利率; **bankroll** *v/t* tígōng zījīn 提供资金

bankrupt 1 *adj* pòchǎn 破产; *go ~* pòchǎn 破产 **2** *v/t* pòchǎn 破产

bankruptcy pòchǎn 破产

bank statement yínháng jiédān 银行结单

banner héngfú 横幅

banns jiéhūn gōnggào 结婚公告

banquet yànhuì 宴会

banter *n* qǔxiào 取笑

baptism xǐlǐ 洗礼

baptize xǐlǐ 洗礼

bar¹ (*iron, chocolate*) tiáo 条; (*for drinks*) jiǔbā 酒吧; (*counter*) guìtái 柜台; *a ~ of soap* yīkuài féizào 一块肥皂; *be behind ~s* (*in prison*) zuò bānfáng 坐班房

bar² *v/t* jìnzhǐ 禁止

bar³ *prep* (*except*) chúle 除了

barbecue ⇩ **1** *n* shāokǎo huì 烧烤会; (*equipment*) kǎojià 烤架 **2** *v/t* kǎo 烤

barbed wire yǒucì tiěsī 有刺铁丝

barber tìtóu jiàng 剃头匠

bar code ⇩ tiáoxíng mǎ 条形码

bare *adj* (*naked*) guāng 光; (*empty:* *room*) kōng 空; *mountainside, floor* guāng tūtu 光秃秃

barefoot: *be ~* guāngjiǎo 光脚

barefoot doctor chìjiǎo yīshēng 赤脚医生

bare-headed guāngzhe tóu 光着头

barely jǐnjǐn 仅仅

bargain 1 *n* (*deal*) jiāoyì 交易; (*good buy*) piányí huò 便宜货; *it's a ~!* (*deal*) zhēn piányi! 真便宜! **2** *v/i* tǎojià huánjià 讨价还价

♦ **bargain for** (*expect*) yùliào 预料

barge *n* NAUT bóchuán 驳船

bark¹ 1 *n* (*of dog*) fèi 吠 **2** *v/i* fèi 吠

bark² (*of tree*) shùpí 树皮

barley dàmài 大麦

barn liángcāng 粮仓

barometer qìyā biǎo 气压表; *fig* qíngyǔ biǎo 晴雨表

barracks MIL yíngfáng 营房

barrel (*container*) tǒng 桶

barren *land* huāngmò 荒漠

barricade *n* lùzhàng 路障

barrier lángān 栏杆; (*cultural*) zhàng'ài 障碍; *language ~* yǔyán zhàng'ài 语言障碍

bar tender jiǔdiàn huǒjì 酒店伙计

barter 1 *n* yìhuò màoyì 易货贸易 2 *v/t* jiāohuàn 交换

base 1 *n* (*bottom end*) dǐbù 底部; (*underneath*) dǐzuò 底座; (*center*, MIL) jīdì 基地 2 *v/t* yǐ … wéi jīchǔ 以 … 为基础; *~ X on Y* yǐ Y wéi X de jīchǔ 以 Y 为 X 的基础; *be ~d in* (*in city, country*) yǐ … wéi jīdì 以 … 为基地

baseball (*ball*) bàngqiú 棒球; (*game*) bàngqiú yùndòng 棒球运动

baseball bat bàngqiú gùn 棒球棍; baseball cap bàngqiú mào 棒球帽; baseball player bàngqiú yùndòngyuán 棒球运动员

basement (*of house*) dìxiàshì 地下室; (*of store*) dǐcéng 底层

base rate FIN jīběn lìlǜ 基本利率

basic (*rudimentary*) jīběn 基本; (*fundamental*) zhǔyào 主要

basically dàzhì shuōlái 大致说来

basics: *the ~* jīběn yuánlǐ 基本原理; *get down to ~* chǎngkāi tiānchuāng shuō liànghuà 敞开天窗说亮话

basin (*for washing*) shuǐchí 水池; (*geographical*) péndì 盆地

basis jīchǔ 基础; (*of argument*) gēnjù 根据

bask shài tàiyáng 晒太阳

basket lánzi 篮子; (*in basketball*) wǎng 网

basketball lánqiú 篮球

bass 1 *n* (*part*) nán dīyīn 男低音; (*singer*) nán dīyīn gēshǒu 男低音歌手; (*instrument*) dīyīn yuèqì 低音乐器 2 *adj* nán dīyīn 男低音

bastard sīshēngzǐ 私生子; F húndàn 混蛋; *poor ~ / stupid ~* F kělián chóng / chǔndàn 可怜虫 / 蠢蛋

bat¹ 1 *n* (*for baseball*) qiúgùn 球棍;

(*for table tennis*) qiúpāi 球拍 2 *v/i* (*in baseball*) jīqiú 击球

bat²: *he didn't ~ an eyelid* tā wúdòng yúzhōng 他无动于衷

bat³ (*animal*) biānfú 蝙蝠

batch *n* pī 批

bath zǎopén 澡盆; *have a ~*, *take a ~* xǐzǎo 洗澡

bathe *v/i* (*have a bath*) xǐzǎo 洗澡

bath mat dìjīn 地巾; bathrobe yùyī 浴衣; bathroom (*for bath*) xǐzǎo jiān 洗澡间; (*for washing hands*) xǐshǒu jiān 洗手间; (*toilet*) cèsuǒ / xǐshǒu jiān 厕所 / 洗手间; bath towel yùjīn 浴巾; bathtub yùgāng 浴缸

batter *n* miànhú 面糊; (*in baseball*) jīqiú yuán 击球员

battery diànchí 电池; MOT xù diànchí 蓄电池

battle 1 *n* zhànyì 战役; *fig* dòuzhēng 斗争 2 *v/i* (*against illness etc*) bódòu 搏斗

battlefield, battleground zhànchǎng 战场

bawdy yínhuì 淫秽

bawl (*shout*) dàjiào 大叫; (*weep*) tòngkū 痛哭

♦bawl out *v/t* F chòumà yīdùn 臭骂一顿

bay (*inlet*) wān 湾

bay window tūchuāng 凸窗

be ◊ shì 是; *it's me* shì wǒ 是我; *how much is / are … ?* … duōshǎo qián? … 多少钱？; *there is*, *there are* yǒu 有; *~ careful* xiǎoxīn 小心; *don't ~ sad* bié shāngxīn 别伤心 ◊ (*not translated*): *was she there?* tā zài nàr ma? 她在那儿吗？; *I'm happy* wǒ gāoxìng 我高兴; *this book is intereresting* zhè běn shū hěn yǒuqù 这本书很有趣 ◊: *has the mailman been?* yóudìyuán láiguò le ma? 邮递员来过了吗？; *I've never been to Beijing* wǒ cóngméi qùguò Běijīng 我从没去过北京; *I've been here for hours* wǒ láile hěnjiǔ le 我来了很久了 ◊ (*tags*): *that's right, isn't it?* shìde, duìbuduì? 是的，对不

对？; *she's Chinese, isn't she?* tā shì Zhōngguó rén, shìba? 她是中国人，是吧？◊ (*auxiliary*): *I am thinking* wǒ zài xiǎng 我在想; *he was running* tā zài pǎobù 他在跑步; *you're ~ing silly* nǐ fànshǎ ne 你犯傻呢 ◊ (*obligation*): *you are to do what I tell you* nǐ yào zhào wǒ shuōde qùzuò 你要照我说的去做; *I was to tell you this* wǒ běnlái gāi gàosu nǐ 我本来该告诉你; *you were not to tell anyone* nǐ bù yīnggāi gàosu rènhé rén 你不应该告诉任何人 ◊ (*passive*): *he was killed* tā bèi shā sǐ le 他被杀死了; *they have been sold* tāmen yǐjīng bèi màidiào le 他们已经被卖掉了

♦ **be in for** *surprise, trouble etc* huì dédào 会得到

beach hǎitān 海滩

beachwear hǎibīn fúzhuāng 海滨服装

beads zhūzi 珠子

beak huì 喙

beaker wúbǐng jiǔbēi 无柄酒杯

be-all: *the ~ and end-all* liǎobuqǐ 了不起

beam 1 *n* (*in ceiling etc*) héngliáng 横梁 **2** *v/i* (*smile*) xiǎoróng mǎnmiàn 笑容满面 **3** *v/t* (*transmit*) dìngxiàng fāshè 定向发射

bean curd dòufu 豆腐

beans dòu 豆; *be full of ~* jīnglì chōngpèi 精力充沛

beansprouts dòuyá 豆芽

bear¹ (*animal*) xióng 熊

bear² 1 *v/t weight* chéngshòu 承受; *costs* chéngdān 承担; (*tolerate*) rěnshòu 忍受; *child* shēngyù 生育 **2** *v/i*: *bring pressure to ~ on* shījiā yālì 施加压力

♦ **bear out** (*confirm*) zhèngshí 证实

bearable kě róngrěn 可容忍

beard húzi 胡子

bearing (*in machine*) zhóuchéng 轴承; *that has no ~ on the case* nà hé zhègè ànjiàn méi shénme guānxi 那和这个案件没什么关系

bear market FIN dànshì 淡市

beast chùshēng 畜生

beat 1 *n* (*of heart*) tiàodòng 跳动; (*of music*) jiézòu 节奏 **2** *v/i* (*of heart*) tiàodòng 跳动; (*of rain*) qiāodǎ 敲打; *~ about the bush* guǎiwān mòjiǎo 拐弯抹角 **3** *v/t* (*in competition*) jībài 击败; (*hit*) dǎ 打; (*pound*) pāi 拍; *~ it!* F gǔnkāi 滚开！; *it ~s me* F wǒ bū míngbái 我不明白

♦ **beat up** hěnzòu 狠揍

beaten: *off the ~ track* xiǎn yǒurén shèzú 鲜有人涉足

beating (*physical*) dǎ 打

beat-up pòjiù 破旧

beautician měiróng jiā 美容家

beautiful *woman, house, day* měilì 美丽; *meal* fēngshèng kěkǒu 丰盛可口; *vacation* wánměi 完美; *story, movie* dòngrén 动人; *thanks, that's just ~!* xièxie, wǒ gòule! 谢谢，我够了！

beautifully *cooked, done* gānghǎo 刚好; *simple* yōuyǎ 优雅

beauty (*of woman, sunset*) měilì 美丽

beauty parlor měiróng yuàn 美容院

♦ **beaver away** nǔlì gōngzuò 努力工作

because yīnwèi 因为; *~ it was too expensive* yīnwèi tàiguì 因为太贵; *~ of* yóuyú 由于

beckon *v/i* zhāohuàn 召唤

become biànchéng 变成; *what's ~ of her?* tā jiūjìng zěnmeyàng? 她究竟怎么样？

bed chuáng 床; (*of flowers*) tán 坛; (*of sea, river*) chuáng 床; *go to ~* shuìjiào 睡觉; *he's still in ~* tā háiméi qǐchuáng ne 他还没起床呢; *go to ~ with* hé ... shàng-chuáng 和 ... 上床

bedclothes chuángshàng yòngpǐn 床上用品

bedding qǐnjù 寝具

bedridden wòchuáng bùqǐ 卧床不起; **bedroom** shuìfáng 睡房; **bedspread** chuángzhào 床罩; **bedtime** jiùqǐn shíjiān 就寝时间

bee mìfēng 蜜蜂

beech shānmáo jǔ 山毛榉

beef **1** *n* niúròu 牛肉; F (*complaint*) láosāo 牢骚 **2** *v/i* F (*complain*) nào 闹

♦beef up chōngshí 充实

beefburger hànbǎo bāo 汉堡包

beef noodles niúròumiàn 牛肉面

beehive fēngxiāng 蜂箱

beeline: *make a ~ for* zhíbēn 直奔

beep **1** *n* dūdū shēng 嘟嘟声 **2** *v/i* fāchū dūdū shēng 发出嘟嘟声 **3** *v/t* (*call on pager*) hū 呼

beeper kuòjī 扩机

beer píjiǔ 啤酒

beetle jiǎchóng 甲虫

before **1** *prep* (*time, space, order*) zhīqián 之前 **2** *adv* yǐqián 以前; *the week* / *day* ~ qián yīgè xīngqī / tiān 前一个星期 / 天 **3** *conj* zhīqián 之前

beforehand shìxiān 事先

beg **1** *v/i* yàofàn 要饭 **2** *v/t*: ~ *X to* ... kěnqiú X qùzuò ... 恳求 X 去做 ...

beggar qǐgài 乞丐

begin **1** *v/i* kāishǐ 开始; *to ~ with* (*at first*) běnlái 本来; (*in the first place*) shǒuxiān 首先 **2** *v/t* kāishǐ 开始

beginner chūxué zhě 初学者

beginner driver jiàshǐ xuéyuán 驾驶学员

beginning kāishǐ 开始; (*origin*) qǐyuán 起源

behalf: *on or in* ~ *of* dàibiǎo 代表; *on my* / *his* ~ dàibiǎo wǒ / tā 代表我 / 他

behave *v/i* biǎoxiàn 表现; ~ (*oneself*) shǒu guījǔ 守规矩; ~ (*yourself*)! guījǔ diǎn! 规矩点 !

behavior xíngwéi 行为

behind **1** *prep* (*in position*) zài ... hòumian 在 ... 后面; (*in progress, in order*) luòhòu 落后; *be ~ ...* (*responsible for*) zài ... bèihòu 在 ... 背后; (*support*) zhīchí 支持 **2** *adv* (*at the back*) zài hòumian 在后面; *leave, stay* liúxià 留下; *be ~ with X* zài X fāngmiàn luòhòu 在 X 方面落后

Beijing Běijīng 北京

being (*existence*) shēngcún 生存; (*creature*) shēngwù 生物

belated láichí 来迟

belch *n* & *v/i* dǎgé 打嗝

Belgian **1** *adj* Bǐlìshí 比利时 **2** *n* Bǐlìshí rén 比利时人

Belgium Bǐlìshí 比利时

belief (*trust*) xìnrèn 信任; (*religion*) xìnyǎng 信仰; (*opinion*) kànfǎ 看法

believe xiāngxìn 相信

♦believe in xiāngxìn 相信; *ghosts* xìn 信; *a person* xìnrèn 信任

believer (*also fig*) xìntú 信徒

bell (*on bike, door*) líng 铃; (*in church, school*) zhōng 钟

bellhop shìzhě 侍者

belligerent *adj* jiāozhàn zhōng 交战中

bellow **1** *n* hǒushēng 吼声; (*of bull*) hǒujiào shēng 吼叫声 **2** *v/i* nùhǒu 怒吼; (*of bull*) hǒujiào 吼叫

belly (*of person, animal*) dùzi 肚子; (*fat stomach*) pàng dùzi 胖肚子

bellyache *v/i* F bàoyuàn 抱怨

belong *v/i* shǔyú 属于; *where does this ~?* zhè yīnggāi fàngzài nǎli? 这应该放在哪里 ?; *I don't ~ here* wǒ bù shǔyú zhèlǐ 我不属于这里

♦belong to shǔyú 属于; *club, organization* shì ... chéngyuán 是 ... 成员

belongings suǒyǒu wù 所有物

beloved *adj* xǐ'ài 喜爱

below **1** *prep* zài ... de xiàmian 在 ... 的下面; (*in amount, rate, level*) dīyú 低于 **2** *adv* zài xiàmian 在下面; (*in text*) zài xiàwén zhōng 在下文中; *see* ~ rúxià 如下; *10 degrees* ~ língxià shídù 零下十度

belt yāodài 腰带; *tighten one's* ~ *fig* jiéyuē 节约

bench (*seat*) chángyǐ 长椅; (*work~*) gōngzuò tái 工作台

benchmark jīzhǔn 基准

bend **1** *n* wānqū 弯曲 **2** *v/t* wān 弯 **3** *v/i* wān 弯; (*of person*) wānshēn 弯身

♦**bend down** wānyāo 弯腰

bender F kuángyǐn 狂饮

beneath 1 *prep* zài … xiàmiàn 在 … 下面；(*in status, value*) dīyú 低于 **2** *adv* xiàbiān 下边

benefactor shīzhǔ 施主

beneficial yǒuyì 有益

benefit 1 *n* hǎochù 好处 **2** *v/t* yǒuyì yú 有益于 **3** *v/i* shòuyì 受益

benevolent císhàn 慈善

benign cíxiáng 慈祥；MED liángxìng 良性

bequeath yíliú 遗留；*fig* liúxià 留下

bereaved 1 *adj* sàngshī qīnrén 丧失亲人 **2** *n: the ~* sàngshī qīnrén de rénmen 丧失亲人的人们

berry jiāngguǒ 浆果

berserk: *go ~* fāfēng 发疯

berth (*for sleeping*) pùwèi 铺位；(*for ship*) chuántái 船台；*give X a wide ~* bìkāi X 避开 X

beside zài … pángbiān 在 … 旁边；*be ~ oneself with rage / grief* kuángnù / jí bēishāng 狂怒 / 极悲伤；*that's ~ the point* nàshì wúguān de 那是无关的

besides 1 *adv* zàishuō 再说 **2** *prep* (*apart from*) chúle 除了

best 1 *adj* zuìhǎo 最好 **2** *adv* zuìhǎo 最好；*it would be ~ if …* zuìhǎo … 最好 …；*I like her ~* wǒ zuì xǐhuān tā 我最喜欢她 **3** *n: do one's ~* jìnlì érwéi 尽力而为；*the ~* (*thing*) zuìhǎo 最好；(*person*) zuìjiā 最佳；*make the ~ of* còuhe 凑和；*all the ~!* zhù yīqiè shùnlì! 祝一切顺利！

best before date zàicǐ rìqī qián shǐyòng 在此日期前使用；*best man* (*at wedding*) nán bīnxiàng 男傧相；*best-seller* chàngxiāo shū 畅销书

bet 1 *n* dǔzhù 赌注 **2** *v/i* dǔbó 赌博；(*reckon*) dǎdǔ 打赌；*you ~!* dāngrán le! 当然了！

betray bèipàn 背叛

betrayal bèipàn 背叛

better 1 *adj* gènghǎo 更好；*get ~* gǎijìn 改进；(*in health*) hǎozhuǎn 好转；*he's ~* (*in health*) tā hǎodiǎnr le 他好点儿了 **2** *adv* gènghǎo 更好；*you'd ~ ask permission* nǐ zuìhǎo zhēngdé tóngyì 你最好征得同意；*I'd really ~ not* wǒ háishì bùyào le 我还是不要了；*all the ~ for us* duì wǒmen yǒu hǎochù 对我们有好处；*I like her ~* wǒ gèng xǐhuān tā le 我更喜欢她了

better off *adj* fùyù 富裕

between *prep* zài … zhījiān 在 … 之间；*~ you and me* nǐwǒ sīxià shuōshuo 你我私下说说

beverage *fml* yǐnliào 饮料

beware: *~ of* xiǎoxīn 小心

bewilder shǐ hútu 使糊涂

beyond 1 *prep* (*in space*) yuǎnyú 远于；(*in degree, extent*) chāochū 超出；*~ recognition* rèn bù chūlái le 认不出来了；*it's ~ me* (*don't understand*) wǒ bù míngbái 我不明白；(*can't do it*) chāochū wǒde nénglì fànwéi 超出我的能力范围 **2** *adv* gèngyuǎn 更远

Bhutan Bùdān 不丹

Bhutanese 1 *adj* Bùdān 不丹 **2** *n* (*person*) Bùdān rén 不丹人

bias *n* (*against*) piānjiàn 偏见；(*in favor of*) piāntǎn 偏袒

bias(s)ed (*against*) piānjiàn 偏见；(*in favor of*) piāntǎn 偏袒

bib (*for baby*) wéizuǐ 围嘴

Bible shèngjīng 圣经

bibliography cānkǎo shūmù 参考书目

biceps èrtóu jī 二头肌

bicker zhēngchǎo 争吵

bicycle *n* ⇩ zìxíng chē 自行车

bid 1 *n* (*at auction*) chūjià 出价；(*attempt*) qǐtú 企图 **2** *v/i* (*at auction*) chūjià 出价

biennial *adj* liǎngnián yīcì 两年一次

big 1 *adj* dà 大；(*tall*) gāo 高；*my ~ brother / sister* wǒ gēge / jiějie 我哥哥 / 姐姐；*~ name* chūmíng 出名 **2** *adv: talk ~* chuīniú 吹牛

bigamy chónghūn 重婚

big-headed zìdà 自大

bike 1 *n* zìxíng chē 自行车 **2** *v/i* qí

zìxíng chē 骑自行车

bikini bǐjīní 比基尼

bilingual shuāngyǔ 双语

bill 1 *n* zhàngdān 账单；(*money*) chāopiào 钞票；POL yì'àn 议案；(*poster*) hǎibào 海报 **2** *v/t* (*invoice*) kāi zhàngdān 开账单

billboard guǎnggào pái 广告牌

billfold qiánbāo 钱包

billiards táiqiú 台球

billion shíyì 十亿

bill of exchange huìpiào 汇票

bill of sale zhuǎnràng qìjù 转让契据

bin (*for storage*) xiāngzi 箱子

binary èrjìn zhì 二进制

bind *v/t* (*connect*) liánjiē 连接；(*tie*) bǎng 绑；(*oblige*) yuēshù 约束

binder (*for papers*) huóyè jiá 活页夹

binding 1 *adj* agreement, promise yǒu yuēshù lì 有约束力 **2** *n* (*of book*) zhuāngdīng 装钉

binoculars wàngyuǎn jìng 望远镜

biodegradable néng jìnxíng shēngwù jiàngjiě 能进行生物降解

biography zhuànjì 传记

biological shēngwù 生物；*~ parents* qīnshēng fùmǔ 亲生父母；*~ detergent* huóxìng xǐdí jì 活性洗涤剂

biology shēngwù xué 生物学

biotechnology shēngwù gōngyì xué 生物工艺学

bird niǎo 鸟

bird of prey měngqín 猛禽

bird sanctuary niǎolèi bǎohù qū 鸟类保护区

birth (*of child*) chūshēng 出生；(*labor*) fēnmiǎn 分娩；*fig* (*of country*) dànshēng 诞生；*give ~ to child* shēng háizi 生孩子；*date of ~* chūshēng rìqī 出生日期

birth certificate chūshēng zhèng 出生证；**birth control** bìyùn 避孕；**birthday** shēngri 生日；*happy ~!* shēngrì kuàile! 生日快乐！；**birthplace** chūshēng dì 出生地；**birthrate** chūshēng lǜ 出生率

biscuit bǐnggān 饼干

bisexual 1 *adj* shuāngxìng 双性 **2** *n* shuāngxìng rén 双性人

bishop zhǔjiào 主教

bit *n* (*piece*) xiǎokuàir 小块儿；(*length*) xiǎoduànr 小段儿；(*part*) bùfen 部分；COMPUT èrjìn zhì wèi 二进制位；*a ~* (*a little*) yǒudiǎnr 有点儿；(*of time*) yīhuir 一会儿；*a ~ of* (*a little*) yīdiǎn 一点；*a ~ of news / advice* yītiáo xīnwén / yīgè gàojiè 一条新闻 / 一个告诫；*~ by ~* yīdiǎn yīdiǎn 一点一点；*I'll be there in a ~* (*in a little while*) wǒ yīhuǐr huìdào 我一会儿会到

bitch 1 *n* (*dog*) mǔgǒu 母狗；F (*woman*) pōfù 泼妇 **2** *v/i* F (*complain*) fā láosāo 发牢骚

bitchy F person, remark lìngrén tǎoyàn 令人讨厌

bite 1 *n* (*of dog, snake*) yǎo 咬；(*of mosquito, flea, spider*) dīng 叮；(*of food*) yīkǒu 一口；*get a ~* (*of angler*) yú tūněr 鱼吞饵；*let's have a ~* (*to eat*) wǒmén chī diǎnr dōngxi ba 我们吃点儿东西吧 **2** *v/t* (*of dog, snake*) yǎo 咬；(*of mosquito, flea, spider*) dīng 叮 **3** *v/i* yǎo 咬；(*of mosquito, flea*) dīng 叮；(*of fish*) tūněr 吞饵

bitter taste kǔ 苦；person chōngmǎn yuànhèn 充满怨恨；weather hánlěng 寒冷；argument jīliè 激烈

bitterly: *~ cold* hánlěng 寒冷

black 1 *adj* hēi 黑；coffee etc wúnǎi 无奶；fig àndàn 暗淡 **2** *n* (*color*) hēisè 黑色；(*person*) hēirén 黑人；*in the ~* FIN yǒu jiéyú 有结余

♦**black out** *v/i* hūnmí 昏迷

black bean sauce dòubànjiàng 豆瓣酱；**blackberry** hēiméi 黑莓；**blackbird** shānniǎo 山鸟；**blackboard** hēibǎn 黑板；**black box** hēi xiázi 黑匣子；**black economy** hēishì jīngjì 黑市经济

blacken person's name fěibàng 诽谤

black eye qīngzhǒng yǎnkuàng 青肿眼眶；**black ice** hēibīng 黑冰；**blacklist 1** *n* hēi míngdān 黑名单 **2** *v/t* shàng hēi míngdān 上黑名单；**blackmail 1** *n* xiépò 胁迫；

emotional ~ gǎnqíng qiāozhà 感情敲诈 *v/t* xiépò 胁迫;
blackmailer lèsuǒ zhě 勒索者;
black market hēishì 黑市
blackness hēi'àn 黑暗
blackout ELEC tíngdiàn 停电; MED hūnmí 昏迷; **blacksmith** tiějiàng 铁匠; **black tea** hóngchá 红茶
bladder pángguāng 膀胱
blade (*of knife, sword*) rèn 刃; (*of helicopter*) jiāngyè 桨叶; (*of grass*) yèpiàn 叶片
blame 1 *n* zébèi 责备; (*responsibility*) zérèn 责任 **2** *v/t* zéguài 责怪; ~ *X for Y* yīnwèi Y zébèi X 因为 Y 责备 X
bland *smile* píngdàn 平淡; *answer* kūzào wúwèi 枯噪无味; *food* dàn 淡
blank 1 *adj page, tape* kòngbái 空白; *look* mángrán 茫然 **2** *n* (*empty space*) kòngwèi 空位; *my mind's a* ~ wǒ tóunǎo yīpiàn kòngbái 我头脑一片空白
blank check kōngtóu zhīpiào 空头支票
blanket *n* tǎnzi 毯子; *a* ~ *of* fig yīcéng 一层
♦**blare** *v/i* xuānnào 喧闹
♦**blare out 1** *v/i* xuānnào 喧闹 **2** *v/t* dàshēng fāchū 大声发出
blaspheme *v/i* xièdú 亵渎
blast 1 *n* (*explosion*) bàozhà 爆炸; (*gust*) yīgǔ 一股 **2** *v/t* yòng zhàyào zhà 用炸药炸; ~*!* gāisǐ! 该死!
♦**blast off** (*of rocket*) fāshè shàngtiān 发射上天
blast furnace gāolú 高炉
blast-off fāshè 发射
blatant míngxiǎn 明显
blaze 1 *n* (*fire*) huǒyàn 火焰; *a* ~ *of color* wǔcǎi bīnfēn 五彩缤纷 **2** *v/i* (*of fire*) xióngxiong ránshāo 熊熊燃烧
♦**blaze away** (*with gun*) měngjī 猛击
blazer nánshì biàn shàngzhuāng 男式便上装
bleach 1 *n* piǎobái jì 漂白剂 **2** *v/t hair* shǐ tuōsè 使脱色
bleak *countryside* huāngliáng 荒凉;

weather hánlěng cìgǔ 寒冷刺骨; *future* àndàn 暗淡
bleary-eyed shuìyǎn xīngsōng 睡眼惺松
bleat *v/i* (*of sheep*) miēmie jiào 咩咩叫
bleed 1 *v/i* liúxuè 流血 **2** *v/t fig* zhàqǔ 榨取
bleeding *n* liúxuè 流血
bleep 1 *n* BB shēng BB 声 **2** *v/i* fāchū BB shēng 发出 BB 声 **3** *v/t* (*call on pager*) hūhuàn 呼唤
bleeper hūjiào jī 呼叫机
blemish 1 *n* xiácī 瑕疵 **2** *v/t reputation* pòhuài 破坏
blend *n & v/i* hùnhé 混合
♦**blend in 1** *v/i* rónghé 融和 **2** *v/t* (*in cooking*) jiǎohé 搅和
blender (*machine*) jiǎohéjī 搅和机
bless zhùfú 祝福; ~ *you* (*in response to sneeze*) no equivalent; *be* ~*ed with* yǒuxìng dédào 有幸得到
blessing REL qíshén cìfú 祈神赐福; *fig* (*approval*) zànchéng 赞成
blind 1 *adj* máng 盲; *corner* kànbújiàn lìngyītóu de guǎijiǎo 看不见另一头的拐角; ~ *to* shì'ér bújiàn 视而不见 **2** *n: the* ~ mángrén 盲人 **3** *v/t* shīshīmíng 使失明; *fig* shǐ shīqù pànduàn lì 使失去判断力
blind alley sǐ hútong 死胡同
blindfold *v/t, n & adv* méngzhù yǎnjīng 蒙住眼睛
blinding xuànmù 眩目
blind spot (*in road*) mángdiǎn 盲点; *fig* wúzhī 无知
blink *v/i* (*of person*) zhǎyǎn 眨眼; (*of light*) shǎnshuò 闪烁
blip (*on radar screen*) guāngdiǎn 光点; *fig* zànshí quēxiàn 暂时缺陷
bliss kuàilè 快乐
blister 1 *n* shuǐpào 水疱 **2** *v/i* qǐ shuǐpào 起水疱; (*of paint*) qǐ qìpào 起气泡
blizzard bàofēngxuě 暴风雪
bloated zhàng 胀
blob (*of liquid*) dī 滴
bloc POL jítuán 集团
block 1 *n* kuài 块; (*in town*) jiēduàn

街段; (*of shares*) dàzōng 大宗; (*blockage*) zhàng'ài wù 障碍物 **2** *v/t* dǔsè 堵塞

♦ **block in** (*with vehicle*) dǔzhù 堵住

♦ **block out** *light* dǎngzhù 挡住

♦ **block up** *v/t sink etc* dǔsāi 堵塞

blockade *n & v/t* fēngsuǒ 封锁

blockage dǔsāi 堵塞

blockbuster yángyang dàzuò 洋洋大作

block letters dàxiě zìmǔ 大写字母

blond *adj* jīnfà 金发

blonde *n* (*woman*) jīnfà nǚláng 金发女郎

blood xuèyè 血液; **in cold ~** cánrěn 残忍

blood bank xuèkù 血库; **blood donor** ⇩ xiànxuè zhě 献血者; **blood group** xuèxíng 血型

bloodless *coup* wú liúxuè 无流血

blood poisoning xuè zhòngdú 血中毒; **blood pressure** xuèyā 血压; **blood relation, blood relative** xuèqīn 血亲; **blood sample** xuèyè yàngběn 血液样本; **bloodshed** liúxuè 流血; **bloodshot** bùmǎn xuèsī 布满血丝; **bloodstain** xuèjì 血迹; **bloodstream** xuèliú 血流; **blood test** yànxuè 验血; **blood transfusion** shūxuè 输血; **blood vessel** xuèguǎn 血管

bloody *hands etc* dàixuè 带血; *battle* xuè línlín 血淋淋

bloody mary hóng mǎlì hùnhé jiǔ 红玛丽混合酒

bloom 1 *n* huāduǒ 花朵; **in full ~** shèngkāi 盛开 **2** *v/i* kāihuā 开花; *fig* xīngwàng 兴旺

blossom 1 *n* huā 花 **2** *v/i* kāihuā 开花; *fig* fāzhǎn 发展

blot 1 *n* mòshuǐ zì 墨水渍; *fig* wūdiǎn 污点 **2** *v/t paper* xīgān 吸干; (*wipe dry*) cāgān 擦干

♦ **blot out** (*hide from view*) zhēbì 遮蔽; *memory* mǒmiè 抹灭

blotch zhěn 疹

blouse chènshān 衬衫

blow[1] *n* jī 击; (*setback*) zǔ'ài 阻碍

blow[2] **1** *v/t* (*of wind*) chuī 吹; *whistle* chuīshào 吹哨; (*spend*) làngfèi 浪费; *opportunity* shīqù 失去; **~ one's nose** xǐng bítì 擤鼻涕 **2** *v/i* (*of wind*) guāfēng 刮风; (*of whistle*) chuīshào 吹哨; (*of person*) chuīqì 吹气; (*of fuse*) shāoduàn 烧断; (*of tire*) bàozhà 爆炸

♦ **blow off** *v/t & v/i* chuīdiào 吹掉

♦ **blow out** *v/t & v/i* (*of candle*) chuīmiè 吹灭

♦ **blow over 1** *v/t* chuīdǎo 吹倒 **2** *v/i* chuīdǎo 吹倒; (*calm down*) píngxī 平息; (*of argument*) bèi dànwàng 被淡忘

♦ **blow up 1** *v/t* (*with explosives*) zhà zhà 炸; *balloon* chōngqì 充气; *photograph* fàngdà 放大 **2** *v/i* zhà 炸; (*become angry*) dàfā píqì 大发脾气

blow-dry *v/t* chuīgān 吹干; **blow job** ∨ kǒuyín 口淫; **blow-out** (*of tire*) chētāi bàozhà 车胎爆炸; F (*big meal*) měicān 美餐; **blow-up** (*of photo*) fàngdà xiàngpiān 放大相片

blue 1 *adj* lánsè 蓝色; **~ movie** huángsè diànyǐng 黄色电影 **2** *n* lánsè 蓝色

blueberry lán jiāngguǒ 蓝浆果; **blue chip** rèmén 热门; **blue-collar worker** lánlíng gōngrén 蓝领工人; **blueprint** (*also fig*) lántú 蓝图

blues MUS bólǔsī yīnyuè 勃鲁斯音乐; **have the ~** jǔsàng 沮丧

blues singer bólǔsī gēshǒu 勃鲁斯歌手

bluff 1 *n* (*deception*) xūzhāng shēngshì 虚张声势 **2** *v/i* zhàhu 诈呼

blunder 1 *n* dàcuò 大错 **2** *v/i* fàn dà cuòwù 犯大错误

blunt *adj* dùn 钝; *person* zhíshuài 直率

bluntly *speak* tǎnbái 坦白

blur *n & v/t* móhu 模糊

blurb (*on book*) jiǎnjiè 简介

♦ **blurt out** búshèn shuōchū 不慎说出

blush 1 *n* hóngsè 红色 **2** *v/i*

liǎnhóng 脸红

blusher (*cosmetic*) yānzhī 胭脂

BO (*body odor*) tǐxiù 体臭

board 1 *n* bǎn 板; (*for game*) qípán 棋盘; (*for notices*) pái 牌; **~ (of directors**) dǒngshì huì 董事会; **on ~** (*plane*) zài fēijī shàng 在飞机上; (*train*) zài huǒchē shàng 在火车上; (*boat*) zài chuán shàng 在船上; **take on ~** *comments etc* kǎolǜ 考虑; (*fully realize truth of*) yìshídào zhēnxiàng 意识到真相; **across the ~** quánmiàn 全面 **2** *v/t airplane etc* shàng 上 **3** *v/i* (*of passengers*) shànglái 上来

♦**board up** fēng 封

♦**board with** shànsù 膳宿

board and lodging chīzhù 吃住

boarder jì shànsù zhě 寄膳宿者; EDU jìsù shēng 寄宿生

board game qípán yóuxì 棋盘游戏

boarding card dēngjī kǎ 登机卡; **boarding house** sùshè 宿舍; **boarding pass** dēngjī kǎ 登机卡; **boarding school** jìsù xuéxiào 寄宿学校

board meeting dǒngshìhuì huìyì 董事会会议; **board room** huìyì shì 会议室; **boardwalk** hǎibīn rénxíngdào 海滨人行道

boast *n* & *v/i* chuīniú 吹牛

boat chuán 船; (*small, for leisure*) xiǎochuán 小船; **go by ~** zuòchuán 坐船

bob[1] (*haircut*) duǎnfà 短发

bob[2] *v/i* (*of boat etc*) piāolái piāoqù 漂来漂去

♦**bob up** tūrán chūxiàn 突然出现

bobsleigh, bobsled xuěqiāo 雪橇

bodice jǐnshēn xiōngyī 紧身胸衣

bodily 1 *adj* shēntǐ 身体 **2** *adv eject* qīnshēn 亲身

body shēntǐ 身体; (*dead*) shītǐ 尸体; **~ of water** shuǐtǐ 水体; **~ (suit**) (*undergarment*) jǐnshēn yī 紧身衣

bodyguard bǎobiāo 保镖; **body language** shēnshì yǔ 身势语; **body odor** tǐxiù 体臭; **body shop** MOT chēshēn xiūlǐ chǎng 车

身修理厂; **bodywork** MOT chēshēn 车身

boggle: **it ~s the mind!** yìxiǎng tiānkāi! 异想天开！

bogus jiǎ 假

Bohai Gulf Bóhǎi Wān 渤海湾

boil[1] (*swelling*) jiēzi 疖子

boil[2] **1** *v/t liquid, egg, vegetables* zhǔ 煮 **2** *v/i* kāi 开

♦**boil down to** guīgēn jiédǐ 归根结底

♦**boil over** (*of milk etc*) fèiyì 沸溢

boiled rice báifàn 白饭

boiled water kāishuǐ 开水

boiler guōlú 锅炉

boisterous xuānnào 喧闹

bold 1 *adj* dàdǎn 大胆 **2** *n* (*print*) cūtǐ 粗体; **in ~** yòng cūtǐ 用粗体

bolster *v/t confidence* zēngqiáng 增强

bolt 1 *n* luóshuān 螺栓; (*on door*) chāxiāo 插销; (*of lightning*) xuánmù diànshǎn 眩目电闪; **like a ~ from the blue** qíngtiān pīlì 晴天霹雳 **2** *adv*: **~ upright** bǐzhí 笔直 **3** *v/t* (*fix with bolts*) shuānzhù 栓住; (*close*) shuān 闩 **4** *v/i* (*run off*) tuōjiāng 脱缰; (*of prisoner*) táopǎo 逃跑

bomb 1 *n* zhàdàn 炸弹 **2** *v/t* hōngzhà 轰炸

bombard: **~ with questions** liánzhūpào sìdì tíchū wèntí 连珠炮似地提出问题

bomb attack zhàdàn gōngjī 炸弹攻击

bomber (*airplane*) hōngzhà jī 轰炸机; (*terrorist*) tóudàn shǒu 投弹手

bomber jacket duǎn jiákè 短夹克

bomb scare hōngzhà jǐnggào 轰炸警告

bond 1 *n* (*tie*) liánjié 联结; FIN zhàijuàn 债券 **2** *v/i* (*of glue*) niánjié 粘结

bone 1 *n* gǔtou 骨头 **2** *v/t meat, fish* qùgǔ 去骨

bonfire yínghuǒ 营火

bonsai pénjǐng 盆景

bonus (*money*) jiǎngjīn 奖金; (*something extra*) éwài pǐn 额外品

boo 1 *n* xūxu shēng 嘘嘘声 **2** *v/t actor, speaker* hè dàocǎi 喝倒彩 **3** *v/i* fāchū xūxu shēng 发出嘘嘘声

book 1 *n* shū 书; **~ of matches** zhǐbǎn huǒchái 纸板火柴 **2** *v/t (reserve)* yùdìng 预定; *(of policeman)* dēngjì 登记 **3** *v/i (reserve)* yùdìng 预定

bookcase shūjià 书架

booked up kèmǎn 客满; *person* méiyǒu shíjiān 没有时间

bookie F dǔjì rén 赌纪人

booking *(reservation)* yùdìng 预定

booking clerk shòupiào yuán 售票员

bookkeeper jìzhàng rén 记账人

bookkeeping jìzhàng 记账

booklet xiǎo cèzi 小册子

bookmaker dǔjì rén 赌纪人

Book of Changes Yìjīng 易经

books *(accounts)* zhàngmù 帐目; *do the* ~ jìzhàng 记账

bookseller shūshāng 书商; **bookstall** shūtān 书摊; **bookstore** shūdiàn 书店

boom¹ *n & v/i (in business)* fánróng 繁荣

boom² *n (noise)* lónglong shēng 隆隆声

boonies F: *out in the ~* qióngxiāng pìrǎng 穷乡僻壤

boost 1 *n (to sales, confidence)* jīlì 激励; *(to economy)* cùjìn 促进 **2** *v/t production, sales* zēngjiā 增加; *prices* tígāo 提高; *confidence, morale* zēngqiáng 增强

boot *n* xuēzi 靴子

♦**boot out** F qūchú 驱除

♦**boot up** COMPUT qǐdòng 启动

booth *(at market, fair)* huòtān 货摊; *(at exhibition)* tānzi 摊子; *(in restaurant)* cānzuò 餐座

booze *n* F jiǔ 酒

booze-up *Br* F kuánghē 狂喝

border 1 *n (between countries)* biānjiè 边界; *(edge)* biānyuán 边缘 **2** *v/t country, river* jiāojiè 交界

♦**border on** *country* jiāojiè 交界; *(be almost)* jìnsì 近似

borderline: *a ~ case of ...* liǎngkě

xìngxíng ... 两可性形 ...

bore¹ *v/t hole* zuānkǒng 钻孔

bore²1 *n (person)* mènrén 闷人; *it's such a ~* tài méijìnr le 太没劲儿了 **2** *v/t* shǐ yànfán 使厌烦

bored: *be ~* mèn 闷; *I'm ~* wǒ hěn mèn 我很闷

boredom wúliáo 无聊

boring fáwèir 乏味儿

born: *be ~* chūshēng 出生; *where were you ~?* nǐ zài nǎr chūshēng? 你在哪儿出生?; *be a ~ ...* tiānshēngde ... 天生的 ...

borrow jiè 借

boss shàngjí 上级

♦**boss around** chāilái qiǎnqù 拆来遣去

bossy ài guǎnshì 爱管事

botanical zhíwù 植物

botany zhíwù xué 植物学

botch *v/t* gǎode yītuán zāo 搞得一团糟

both 1 *adj & pron* liǎnggè 两个; *I know ~ (of the) brothers* liǎng xiōngdì wǒ dōu rènshi 两兄弟我都认识; *~ (of the) brothers were there* liǎng xiōngdì dōu zài nàr 两兄弟都在那儿; *~ of them (things)* nà liǎnggè 那两个; *(people)* nà liǎngrén 那两人 **3** *adv:* *~ ... and ...* yòu ... yòu ... 又 ... 又 ...; *is it business or pleasure? – ~* gōngzuò háishì yúlè? – liǎngyàng dōuyǒu 工作还是娱乐? – 两样都有

bother 1 *n* máfan 麻烦; *it's no ~* méi wèntí 没问题 **2** *v/t (disturb)* máfan 麻烦; *person working* dǎjiǎo 打搅; *(worry)* shǐdānxīn 使担心 **3** *v/i* guǎn 管; *don't ~ (you needn't do it)* búyòngle 不用了; *you needn't have ~ed* tài máfan nǐle 太麻烦你了

bottle 1 *n* píngzi 瓶子; *(for baby)* nǎipíng 奶瓶 **2** *v/t* zhuāngpíng 装瓶

♦**bottle up** *feelings* èzhì 遏制

bottle bank shōupíng chù 收瓶处

bottled water píngzhuāng shuǐ 瓶装水

bottleneck *n (in road, production)*

zǔsāi diǎn 阻塞点

bottle-opener kāipíng qì 开瓶器

bottom 1 *adj* zuìdī 最低 **2** *n* (*on the inside*) dǐbù 底部; (*of hill*) jiǎo脚; (*of pile*) zuìdǐ 最底; (*underside*) dǐmiàn 底面; (*of street*) zuìdǐ chù 最底处; (*of garden*) zuì hòumiàn 最后面; (*buttocks*) pìgu 屁股; *at the ~ of the screen* zài píngmù zuìdǐ chù 在屏幕最底处

♦**bottom out** dá zuìdī diǎn 达最低点

bottom line *fig* (*financial outcome*) lìrùn 利润; (*the real issue*) zhēnzhèng wèntí 真正问题

boulder dà shítóu 大石头

bounce 1 *v/t ball* tánqǐ 弹起 **2** *v/i* (*of ball*) tánqǐ 弹起; (*on sofa etc*) tǎntiào 弹跳; (*of rain etc*) sìxià fēijiàn 四下飞溅; (*of check*) bèi jù fù tuìhuí 被拒付退回

bouncer bǎmén rén 把门人

bound[1]: *be ~ to do X* (*sure to*) kěndìng zuò X 肯定做X; (*obliged to*) shòu yuēshù qǔzuò X 受约束去做X

bound[2]: *be ~ for* (*of ship*) shǐwǎng 驶往

bound[3] *n & v/i* (*jump*) tiàoyuè 跳跃

boundary biānjiè 边界

boundless wúxiàn 无限

bouquet (*flowers*) huāshù 花束; (*of wine*) fāngxiāng 芳香

bourbon bōpáng wēishìjì jiǔ 波旁威士忌酒

bout MED fāzuò 发作; (*in boxing*) jiàoliàng 较量

boutique shízhuāng shāngdiàn 时装商店

bow[1] **1** *n* (*as greeting*) jūgōng 鞠躬 **2** *v/i* jūgōng 鞠躬 **3** *v/t head* dītóu 低头

bow[2] (*knot*) húdié jié 蝴蝶结; MUS gōng 弓

bow[3] (*of ship*) chuántóu 船头

bowels jiécháng 结肠

bowl[1] (*large container*) pén 盆; (*small container for rice*) wǎn 碗

bowl[2] **1** *n* (*ball*) bǎolíng qiú 保龄球 **2** *v/i* (*in bowling*) dǎ bǎolíng qiú 打保龄球

♦**bowl over** *fig* jīngdāi 惊呆

bowling bǎolíng qiú 保龄球

bowling alley bǎolíng qiú dào 保龄球道

bow tie lǐngjié 领结

box[1] *n* (*container*) hézi 盒子; (*on form*) fānggé 方格

box[2] *v/i* quánjī 拳击

boxer quánjī shǒu 拳击手

boxing quánjī 拳击

boxing match quánjī bǐsài 拳击比赛

box office shòupiào chù 售票处

boy nánháir 男孩儿; (*son*) érzi 儿子

boycott dǐzhì 抵制

boyfriend nán péngyou 男朋友

boyish xiàng nánhái yīyàng 象男孩一样

boyscout tóngzǐ jūnduì yuán 童子军队员

brace (*on teeth*) yátào 牙套

bracelet shǒuzhuó 手镯

bracket (*for shelf*) tuōjià 托架; (*in text*) kuòhào 括号

brag *v/i* chuīniú 吹牛

braid *n* (*in hair*) biànzi 辫子; (*trimming*) suìdài 穗带

braille mángwén 盲文

brain nǎo 脑

brainless F shǎ 傻

brains (*intelligence*) nǎozi 脑子

brainstorm (*brilliant idea*) línggǎn 灵感; **brainstorming** jítǐ zìyóu tǎolùn 集体自由讨论; **brain surgeon** nǎo wàikē yīshēng 脑外科医生; **brainwash** xǐnǎo 洗脑; **brainwashing** xǐnǎo 洗脑; **brainwave** (*brilliant idea*) línggǎn 灵感

brainy F cōngmíng 聪明

braise dùn 炖

brake *n & v/i* shāchē 刹车

brake light zhìdòng xìnhào dēng 制动信号灯

brake pedal shāchē tàbǎn 刹车踏板

branch *n* (*of tree*) shùzhī 树枝; (*of bank*) fēnháng 分行; (*of company*) fēn gōngsī 分公司; (*of chain store*) fēndiàn 分店

◆**branch off** (*of road*) fēnchà 分 岔

◆**branch out** kuòchōng 扩 充

brand 1 *n* páizi 牌 子 **2** *v/t*: *be ~ed a liar* bèi qiǎnzé wéi piànzi 被 谴 责 为 骗 子

brand image shāngbiāo gàiniàn 商 标 概 念

brandish huīdòng 挥 动

brand leader míngpáir 名 牌 儿; **brand loyalty** míngpái zhōngyú gǎn 名 牌 忠 于 感; **brand name** (*famous*) míngpái shāngpǐn 名 牌 商 品; (*name of a brand*) shāngbiāo 商 标

brand-new zhǎnxīn 崭 新

brandy báilándì 白 兰 地

brass huángtóng 黄 铜

brass band tóngguǎn yuèduì 铜 管 乐 队

brassière xiōngzhào 胸 罩

brat *pej* táoqìbāo 淘 气 包

bravado xūzhāng shēngshì 虚 张 声 势

brave *adj* yǒnggǎn 勇 敢

bravery yǒnggǎn 勇 敢

brawl *n & v/i* dòu ōu 斗 殴

brawny qiángzhuàng 强 壮

Brazil Bāxī 巴 西

Brazilian 1 *adj* Bāxī 巴 西 **2** *n* Bāxī rén 巴 西 人

breach (*violation*) wéifàn 违 犯; (*in party*) fēnliè 分 裂

breach of contract LAW wéifǎn hétóng 违 反 合 同

bread *n* miànbāo 面 包

breadcrumbs miànbāo zhā 面 包 渣

breadth kuāndù 宽 度; (*of knowledge*) guǎngdù 广 度

breadwinner yǎngjiā huókǒu de rén 养 家 活 口 的 人

break 1 *n* (*in bone*) gǔzhé 骨 折; (*in wire etc*) duàntóu 断 头; (*rest*) xiūxi 休 息; (*in relationship*) fēnkāi 分 开; *give X a ~* (*opportunity*) gěi X jīhuì 给 X 机 会; *take a ~* xiūxi yīxià 休 息 一 下; *without a ~ work, travel* wú zhōngzhǐ 无 中 止 **2** *v/t machine, device, toy* sǔnhuài 损 坏; *stick, arm, leg* zhéduàn 折 断; *china, glass, egg* shǐ pòsuì 使 破

碎; *rules, law, promise* wéifǎn 违 反; *news* bàogào 报 告; *record* dǎpò 打 破 **3** *v/i* (*of machine, device, toy*) sǔnhuài 损 坏; (*of china, glass, egg*) pòsuì 破 碎; (*of stick*) zhéduàn 折 断; (*of news*) xièlòu 泄 漏; (*of storm*) tūrán dàzuò 突 然 大 作; (*of boy's voice*) biànshēng 变 声

◆**break away** *v/i* (*escape*) táopǎo 逃 跑; (*from family*) líkāi 离 开; (*from organization*) bèipàn 背 叛; (*from tradition*) tuōlí 脱 离

◆**break down 1** *v/i* (*of vehicle, machine*) chū máobìng 出 毛 病; (*of talks*) pòliè 破 裂; (*in tears*) kòngzhì bùzhù 控 制 不 住; (*mentally*) kuǎle 垮 了 **2** *v/t door* dǎlàn 打 烂; *figures* fēnlèi 分 类

◆**break even** COM shōuzhī pínghéng 收 支 平 衡

◆**break in** (*interrupt*) chāzuǐ 插 嘴; (*of burglar*) pòmén ér rù 破 门 而 入

◆**break off 1** *v/t* bāixià 掰 下; *branch* zhéduàn 折 断; *relationship* duànjué 断 绝; *they've broken it off* tāmén fēnshǒu le 他 们 分 手 了 **2** *v/i* (*stop talking*) zhōngduàn 中 断

◆**break out** (*start up, of disease*) bàofā 爆 发; (*of prisoners*) pòláo 破 牢; *he broke out in a rash* tā fā hóngzhěn 他 发 红 疹

◆**break up 1** *v/t* (*into component parts*) fēnjiě 分 解; *fight* qūsàn 驱 散 **2** *v/i* (*of ice*) suìliè 碎 裂; (*of couple*) líyì 离 异; (*of band, meeting*) fēnshǒu 分 手

breakable kě dǎpò 可 打 破

breakage pòsǔn wù 破 损 物

breakdown (*of vehicle, machine*) gùzhàng 故 障; (*of talks*) pòliè 破 裂; (*nervous ~*) bēngkuì 崩 溃; (*of figures*) fēnlèi 分 类

break-even point yíngkuī pínghéng diǎn 盈 亏 平 衡 点

breakfast *n* zǎocān 早 餐; *have ~* chī zǎocān 吃 早 餐

break-in dàoqiè 盗 窃

breakthrough tūpò 突 破

breakup (*of marriage, partnership*) fēnshǒu 分手

breast (*of woman*) rǔfáng 乳房

breastfeed *v/t* bǔrǔ 哺乳

breaststroke wāyǒng 蛙泳

breath hūxī 呼吸; ***be out of ~*** chuǎn bū guò qì lái 喘不过气来; ***take a deep ~*** shēn hūxī 深呼吸

Breathalyzer®, breath analyzer hūqì yànzuì qì 呼气验醉器

breathe 1 *v/i* hūxī 呼吸 **2** *v/t* (*inhale*) xīqì 吸气; (*exhale*) hūchū 呼出

♦**breathe in** *v/t & v/i* xīrù 吸入

♦**breathe out** *v/t & v/i* hūchū 呼出

breathing hūxī 呼吸

breathless chuǎn bū guò qì lái 喘不过气来

breathlessness chuǎn bū guò qì 喘不过气

breathtaking jīngrén 惊人

breed 1 *n* pǐnzhǒng 品种 **2** *v/t* fánzhí 繁殖; *fig* yùnniàng 酝酿 **3** *v/i* (*of animals*) fánzhí 繁殖

breeder (*of animals*) sìyǎng yuán 饲养员

breeding (*of animals*) sìyǎng 饲养

breeding ground *fig* zīshēng dì 滋生地

breeze wēifēng 微风

brew 1 *v/t beer* niàngzào 酿造; *tea* pào 泡 **2** *v/i* (*of storm, trouble*) yùnniàng 酝酿

brewer niàngzào zhě 酿造者

brewery niàngzào chǎng 酿造厂

bribe *n & v/t* huìlù 贿赂

bribery huìlù 贿赂

brick zhuāntóu 砖头

bricklayer níwǎ jiàng 泥瓦匠

bride xīnniáng 新娘

bridegroom xīnláng 新郎

bridesmaid bànniáng 伴娘

bridge[1] *n* qiáo 桥; (*of nose*) bíliáng 鼻梁; (*of ship*) jiàshǐ tái 驾驶台 **2** *v/t gap* jiànlì qiáoliáng 建立桥梁

bridge[2] (*card game*) qiáopái 桥牌

brief[1] *adj* jiǎnduǎn 简短

brief[2] **1** *n* (*mission*) rènwù 任务 **2** *v/t*: **~ X on Y** xiàng X jièshào Y 向 X 介绍 Y

briefcase gōngwén bāo 公文包

briefing jiǎnbào 简报

briefly (*for a short period of time*) yīhuìr 一会儿; (*in a few words*) jiǎndān 简单; (*to sum up*) zǒngzhī 总之

briefs (*for women*) duǎn nèikù 短内裤; (*for men*) sānjiǎo kù 三角裤

bright *color* xiānyàn 鲜艳; *light* qiángliè 强烈; *future* guāngmíng 光明; *smile* huānkuài 欢快; (*sunny*) qínglǎng 晴朗; *room* míngliàng 明亮; (*intelligent*) cōngmíng 聪明

♦**brighten up 1** *v/t* shǐ míngliàng 使明亮; (*make more lively*) shǐ huóyuè 使活跃 **2** *v/i* (*of weather*) zhuǎnqíng 转晴; (*of face, person*) gāoxìng qǐlái 高兴起来

brightly *smile* huānkuài 欢快; *shine* míngliàng 明亮; *colored* xiānyàn 鲜艳

brightness (*of weather*) míngliàng 明亮; (*of smile*) huānkuài 欢快; (*intelligence*) cōngmíng 聪明

brilliance (*of person*) cáihuá 才华; (*of color*) guāngcǎi 光彩

brilliant *sunshine etc* míngliàng 明亮; (*very good*) jiéchū 杰出; (*very intelligent*) yǒu cáihuá 有才华; *idea* yīngmíng 英明

brim (*of container*) biānyuán 边缘; (*of hat*) màoyán 帽檐

brimful mǎn 满

bring *object* (*not immediate*) dàilái 带来; *object* (*more immediate*) nálái 拿来; *person* dài 带; *peace, happiness, misery* dàilái 带来; **~ it here, will you?** nádào zhèrlái, xíngma? 拿到这儿来, 行吗?; **can I ~ a friend?** wǒ néng dàige péngyǒu láima? 我能带个朋友来吗?

♦**bring about** dàilái 带来

♦**bring around** (*from a faint*) huīfù zhījué 恢复知觉; (*persuade*) shuōfú 说服

♦**bring back** (*return*) huán 还; (*re-introduce*) huīfù 恢复; *memories* shǐ huíyì qǐ 使回忆起; (*cause to* *come back*) lìng … huílái 令 … 回来

♦**bring down** *fence, tree* shǐ dǎoxià 使倒下; *government* shǐ kuǎtái 使垮台; *bird, airplane* shèluò 射落; *rates, inflation, price* shǐ jiàngdī 使降低

♦**bring in** *interest, income* zhèng 挣; *legislation* yǐnjìn 引进; *verdict* xuānbù 宣布; (*involve*) shǐ jièrù 使介入

♦**bring out** (*produce: book*) chūbǎn 出版; *video, CD, new product* tuīchū 推出

♦**bring to** (*from a faint*) huīfù zhījué 恢复知觉

♦**bring up** *child* yǎngyù 养育; *subject* tíchū 提出; (*vomit*) ǒutù 呕吐

brink qiàobì biānyuán 峭壁边缘; **on the ~** *fig* jíjiāng 即将

brisk *person* huópo 活泼; *voice* shēngyìng 生硬; *walk* qīngkuài 轻快; *trade* xīnglóng 兴隆

bristles (*on chin*) húzi chá 胡子楂; (*of brush*) máo 毛

bristling: be ~ with (*of person*) húnshēn dùshì 浑身都是; (*of street*) bùmǎn 布满

Britain Yīngguó 英国; (*formal use*) Dà Bùlièdiān 大不列颠

British 1 *adj* Yīngguó 英国; (*formal use*) Dà Bùlièdiān 大不列颠 **2** *n*: **the ~** Yīngguó rén 英国人; (*formal use*) Dà Bùlièdiān rén 大不列颠人

Briton Yīngguó rén 英国人; (*formal use*) Dà Bùlièdiān rén 大不列颠人

brittle yìsuì 易碎

broach *subject* tíchū 提出

broad 1 *adj street, shoulders, hips* kuān 宽; *smile* kuānróng 宽容; (*general*) gàikuò xìng 概括性; **in ~ daylight** guāngtiān huàrì 光天化日 **2** *n* F (*woman*) niángrmen 娘儿们

broadcast *n & v/t* guǎngbō 广播

broadcaster bōyīn yuán 播音员

broadcasting bōyīn 播音

broaden 1 *v/i* biànkuān 变宽 **2** *v/t*

shǐ kuòdà 使扩大; **~ the mind** shǐ shìyě kāikuò 使视野开阔

broadjump tiàoyuǎn 跳远

broadly: **~ speaking** dàtǐ láishuō 大体来说

broadminded xīnxiōng kuānkuò 心胸宽阔

broccoli xīlánhuā 西兰花

brochure xiǎo cèzi 小册子

broil *v/t* kǎo 烤

broiler *n* (*on stove*) kǎopán 烤盘; (*chicken*) nènjī 嫩鸡

broke F (*temporarily*) méiyǒu yīgè zǐr 没有一个子儿; (*long term*) bùmíng yīwén 不明一文; **go ~** (*go bankrupt*) pòchǎn 破产

broken *adj* chū máobìng 出毛病; *glass, window* pòsuì 破碎; *neck, arm* gǔzhé 骨折; *home, marriage* pòliè 破裂; *English* jiéjie bāba 结结巴巴

broken-hearted xīnsuì 心碎

broker jīngjì rén 经纪人

bronchitis qìguǎn yán 气管炎

bronze *n* (*metal*) qīngtóng 青铜; (*~ medal*) tóngpái 铜牌

brooch xiōngzhēn 胸针

brood *v/i* (*of person*) shēng mènqì 生闷气

broom tiáozhǒu 笤帚

broth (*soup*) tāng 汤; (*stock*) liàotāng 料汤

brothel jìyuàn 妓院

brother (*own, elder*) gēge 哥哥; (*own, younger*) dìdi 弟弟; (*somebody else's, elder or younger*) xiōngdì 兄弟; **they're ~s** tāmén shì xiōngdì 他们是兄弟; **~s and sisters** xiōngdì jiěmèi 兄弟姐妹

brother-in-law (*elder sister's husband*) jiěfu 姐夫; (*younger sister's husband*) mèifu 妹夫; (*husband's younger brother*) xiǎoshūzi 小叔子; (*husband's older brother*) dàbózi 大伯子; (*wife's older brother*) nèixiōng 内兄; (*wife's younger brother*) nèidì 内弟; **they're brothers-in-law** tāmén shì liánjīnr 他们是连襟

brotherly xiōngdì bān 兄弟般

brow (*forehead*) nǎoménr 脑门儿;

(*of hill*) pōdǐng 坡顶

browbeat xiàhu 吓唬

brown 1 *n* zōngsè 棕色 **2** *adj* zōngsè 棕色; (*tanned*) shàihēile 晒黑了 **3** *v/t & v/i* (*in cooking*) shàngshǎi 上色

brownbag: ~ *it* zìdài wǔfàn shàngbān 自带午饭上班

Brownie yòunián tóngzǐjūn 幼年童子军

brownie (*cake*) xiǎo qiǎokèlì dàngāo 小巧克力蛋糕

brown-nose *v/t* F pāi mǎpì 拍马屁

browse (*in store*) suíbiàn kànkan 随便看看; ~ *through a book* suíbiàn fānyuè běnshū 随便翻阅本书

browser COMPUT liúlǎn qì 浏览器

bruise 1 *n* cuòshāng 挫伤 **2** *v/t person* dǎqīng 打青; *fruit* pèngshāng 碰伤; (*emotionally*) shānghài 伤害 **3** *v/i* (*of person*) yúshāng 瘀伤; (*of fruit*) pèngshāng 碰伤

bruising *adj fig* yǒu shānghài xìng 有伤害性

brunch zǎowǔcān 早午餐

brunette zōngfà nǚzǐ 棕发女子

brunt: *bear the ~ of ... ...* shǒudāng qíchōng ... 首当其冲

brush 1 *n* shuā 刷; (*conflict*) xiǎo chōngtū 小冲突 **2** *v/t* shuā 刷; (*touch lightly*) qīngchù 轻触; (*move away*) chúqù 除去

♦**brush against** cājí 擦及

♦**brush aside** bùlǐ 不理

♦**brush off** shuāidiào 刷掉; *criticism* bùtīng 不听

♦**brush up** chóngwēn 重温

brushoff F dīngzi 钉子; *get the ~* pèng dīngzi 碰钉子

brusque shēngyìng 生硬

Brussels sprouts qiúyá gānlán 球芽甘蓝

brutal cánrěn 残忍

brutality bàoxíng 暴行

brutally cánrěn 残忍; *be ~ frank* chèdǐdi tǎnbái 彻底地坦白

brute chùshēng 畜生

brute force wúqíngde lìliàng 无情的力量

bubble *n* qìpào 气泡

bubble gum pàopao táng 泡泡糖

buck[1] F (*dollar*) kuài kuài 块

buck[2] *v/i* (*of horse*) měngrán gōngbèi yuèqǐ 猛然弓背跃起

buck[3]: *pass the ~* tuīwěi zérèn 推诿责任

bucket shuǐtǒng 水桶

buckle[1] **1** *n* dāgōu 搭钩 **2** *v/t belt* jìxì 系

buckle[2] *v/i* (*of wood, metal*) biànxíng 变形

bud *n* BOT huālěi 花蕾

Buddha Fó 佛

Buddhism Fójiào 佛教

Buddhist 1 *n* Fójiào tú 佛教徒; *he's a ~* tā xìn Fó 他信佛 **2** *adj* Fójiào 佛教

Buddhist temple sì 寺

buddy F huǒbàn 伙伴; (*form of address*) gērmen 哥儿们

budge 1 *v/t* tuīdòng 推动; (*make reconsider*) shǐ gǎibiàn zhǔyì 使改变主意 **2** *v/i* yídòng 移动; (*change one's mind*) gǎibiàn zhǔyì 改变主意

budgerigar hǔpí yīngwǔ 虎皮鹦鹉

budget 1 *n* yùsuàn 预算; (*of a family*) kāizhī 开支; *be on a ~* jīngdǎ xìsuàn jìngdǎ xìsuàn 精打细算 **2** *v/i* zuò yùsuàn 作预算

♦**budget for** jìsuàn 计算

buff[1] *adj color* tǔhuángsè 土黄色

buff[2]: *a movie / jazz ~* yīgè diànyǐng / juéshì yuè mí 一个电影 / 爵士乐迷

buffalo yěniú 野牛; *water ~* shuǐniú 水牛

buffer RAIL fángzhuàng shān 防撞栅; COMPUT huǎnchōng qì 缓冲器; *fig* huǎnhé zuòyòng 缓和作用

buffet[1] (*meal*) zìzhù cān 自助餐

buffet[2] *v/t* (*of wind*) pāidǎ 拍打

bug 1 *n* (*insect*) kūnchóng 昆虫; (*virus*) bìngdú 病毒; (*spying device*) qiètīng qì 窃听器; COMPUT gùzhàng 故障 **2** *v/t telephones, room* zhuāng qiètīng qì 装窃听

器;F (*annoy*) shǐ nǎonù 使恼怒

buggy (*for baby*) yīng'ér chē 婴儿车

build 1 *n* (*of person*) shēncái 身材 **2** *v/t* jiànzào 建造

♦**build up 1** *v/t strength* zēngqiáng 增强; *relationship* fāzhǎn 发展; *collection* zhújiàn zàochéng 逐渐造成 **2** *v/i* zhújiàn jījù 逐渐积聚

builder (*person*) jiànzhù gōngrén 建筑工人; (*company*) jiànzhù gōngsī 建筑公司

building jiànzhù 建筑; (*activity*) jiànzào 建造

building site jiànzhù gōngdì 建筑工地

building trade jiànzhù yè 建筑业

build-up (*accumulation*) jījù 积聚; (*publicity*) yúlùn zhǔnbèi 舆论准备

built-in nèizhuāng 内装; *flash* nèihán 内含

built-up area jiànzhù qū 建筑区

bulb BOT qiújīng 球茎; (*light ~*) diàndēng pào 电灯泡

bulge 1 *n* (*sudden increase*) zhòuzēng 骤增 **2** *v/i* (*of pocket*) gǔgu nāngnang 鼓鼓囊囊; (*of wall, eyes*) péngzhàng 膨胀

bulk dà duōshù 大多数; **in ~** zhěngpī 整批

bulky *parcel* tǐjī dà 体积大; *sweater* féidà 肥大

bull (*animal*) gōngniú 公牛

bulldoze (*demolish*) chǎnpíng 铲平; **~ X into Y** *fig* xiépò X zuò Y 胁迫 X 作 Y

bulldozer tuītǔ jī 推土机

bullet zǐdàn 子弹

bulletin bùgào 布告

bulletin board (*on wall*) bǔgào bǎn 布告板; COMPUT gōnggào pái 公告牌

bullet point (*in printing*) biāotídiǎn 标题点

bullet-proof fángdàn 防弹

bull market FIN shàngzhǎng hángqíng 上涨行情

bull's-eye bǎxīn 靶心; **hit the ~** zhèngzhòng yàohài 正中要害

bullshit *n & v/i* V húshuō bādào 胡说八道

bully 1 *n* èbà 恶霸; (*child*) xiǎo táoqì 小淘气 **2** *v/t* qīfu 欺负

bum F **1** *n* (*tramp*) lǎnhàn 懒汉; (*worthless person*) méiyòng de dōngxi 没用的东西 **2** *adj* (*useless*) sōu 馊 **3** *v/t cigarette etc* qǐqiú 乞求

♦**bum around** F (*travel*) piāobó liúlàng 漂泊流浪; (*be lazy*) fānfan lǎn 犯犯懒

bumblebee xióngfēng 熊蜂

bump 1 *n* (*swelling*) zhǒngkuàir 肿块儿; (*in road*) tūkuàir 凸块儿; **get a ~ on the head** tóushàng zhǒngle yīkuàir 头上肿了一块儿 **2** *v/t* zhuàng 撞

♦**bump into** *table* zhuàng 撞; (*meet*) pèngjiàn 碰见

♦**bump off** F (*murder*) gǎodiào 搞掉

♦**bump up** F *prices* měngtái wùjià 猛抬物价

bumper 1 *n* MOT bǎoxiǎn gàng 保险杠 **2** *adj harvest* fēngshèng 丰盛; (*extremely good*) jíhǎo 极好

bumpy diānbō 颠簸

bun (*hairstyle*) jìzi 髻子; (*for eating*) xiǎoyuán miànbāo 小圆面包

bunch (*of people*) huǒ huǒ 伙; (*of keys*) chuàn 串; **a ~ of flowers** yīshù huā 一束花; **a ~ of grapes** yīchuàn pútáo 一串葡萄; **thanks a ~** (*ironic*) duō xièle! 多谢了!

bundle (*of clothes*) bāo bāo 包; (*of wood*) kǔn 捆

♦**bundle up** *v/t* bǎ ... bāo qǐlái 把 ... 包起来; (*dress warmly*) chuānde nuǎnhuó 穿得暖和

bungle *v/t* gǎozāo 搞糟

bunk *n* chuángpù 床铺

bunk beds shuāngcéng chuáng 双层床

buoy *n* hángbiāo 航标

buoyant *fig* yúkuài 愉快; *economy* fánróng 繁荣

burden 1 *n* fùzhòng 负重; *fig* fùdān 负担 **2** *v/t*: **~ X with Y** yòng Y lái fánnǎo X 用 Y 来烦恼 X

bureau (*chest of drawers*) dǒuchú 斗橱; (*office*) bànshì chù 办事处

bureaucracy (*red tape*) guānliáo zhǔyì 官僚主义; (*system*) xíngzhèng xìtǒng 行政系统

bureaucrat guānliáo 官僚

bureaucratic guānliáo 官僚

burger hànbǎobāo 汉堡包

burglar xiǎotōu 小偷

burglar alarm ⇩ fángqiè jǐngbào qì 防窃警报器

burglarize dàoqiè 盗窃

burglary dàoqiè 盗窃

burial zànglǐ 葬礼

burly kuíwú 魁梧

Burma Miǎndiàn 缅甸

Burmese 1 *adj* Miǎndiàn 缅甸 **2** *n* (*person*) Miǎndiàn rén 缅甸人; (*language*) Miǎndiàn yǔ 缅甸语

burn 1 *n* shāoshāng 烧伤 **2** *v/t* shāo 烧; *toast, meat* shāojiāo 烧焦; (*of sun*) shàishāng 晒伤; (*consume*) shāo 烧 **3** *v/i* shāozháo 烧着; (*of house*) shāohuǐ 烧毁; (*of toast*) shāojiāo 烧焦; (*get sunburnt*) shàishāng 晒伤

♦**burn down** *v/t & v/i* shāohuǐ 烧毁

♦**burn out: burn oneself out** shǐ zìjǐ jīngpí lìjìn 使自己筋疲力尽; *a burned-out car* shāohuǐ de chē 烧毁的车

burner (*on cooker*) zàotóu 灶头

burp *n, v/i & v/t* dǎgé 打嗝

burst 1 *n* (*in water pipe*) lièkǒu 裂口; (*of gunfire*) sǎoshè 扫射; *a ~ of energy* néngliàng bàofā 能量爆发 **2** *adj tire* bàoliè 爆裂 **3** *v/t balloon* bàoliè 爆裂 **4** *v/i* (*of balloon, tire*) bàoliè 爆裂; *~ into a room* chuǎngrù 闯入; *~ into tears* tūrán dàkū 突然大哭; *~ out laughing* tūrán dàxiào 突然大笑

bury máizàng 埋葬; (*conceal*) yǐncáng 隐藏; *be buried under ...* (*covered by*) máizài ... zhīxià 埋在 ... 之下; *~ oneself in work* máitóu yú gōngzuò 埋头于工作

bus 1 *n* gōnggòng qìchē 公共汽车; (*long distance*) chángtú qìchē 长途汽车 **2** *v/t* yòng gōnggòng qìchē zǎisòng 用公共汽车载送

busboy shìyìng shēng 侍应生

bush (*plant*) guànmù 灌木; (*land*) huāngyě 荒野

bushed F (*tired*) píláo bùkān 疲劳不堪

bushy *beard* nóngmì 浓密

business (*trade*) shēngyi 生意; (*company*) gōngsī 公司; (*work*) gōngzuò 工作; (*sector*) zhíyè 职业; (*affair, matter*) shìjiàn 事件; (*as subject of study*) shāngyè 商业; *on ~* yīngōng 因公; *that's none of your ~!, mind your own ~!* yǔ nǐ wúguān! 与你无关!

business card míngpiàn 名片;

business class shāngwù cāng 商务舱; **business hours** yíngyè shíjiān 营业时间; **businesslike** gāo xiàoyì 高效益; **business lunch** shāngyè wǔcān 商业午餐; **businessman** shāngrén 商人; **business meeting** shāngyè huìyì 商业会议; **business school** shāngyè xuéxiào 商业学校; **business studies** shāngyè xué 商业学; **business trip** chūchāi 出差; **businesswoman** nǚshāngrén 女商人

bus station gōnggòng qìchē zōngzhàn 公共汽车总站

bus stop chēzhàn 车站

bust[1] *n* (*of woman*) xiōng 胸

bust[2] F **1** *adj* (*broken*) dǎsuì 打碎; *go ~* pòchǎn 破产 **2** *v/t* dǎsuì 打碎

♦**bustle around** mánglù 忙碌

bust-up F pòliè 破裂

busty fēngmǎn 丰满

busy 1 *adj* máng 忙; *street* yǒu shēngqì 有生气; *store, restaurant*: (*making money*) shēngyì xīnglóng 生意兴隆; (*full of people*) xīxi rǎngrang 熙熙攘攘; TELEC zhànxiàn 占线; *be ~ doing X* mángzhe zuò X 忙着作X **2** *v/t*: *~ oneself with* zìjǐ mángyú 自己忙于

busybody ài guǎn xiánshì de rén 爱管闲事的人

busy signal zhànxiàn shēng 占线声

but 1 *conj* dànshì 但是; *~ that's*

not fair! shízài tàibù gōngpíng le! 实在太不公平了！; *it's not me ~ my father you want* nǐ yào zhǎode shì wǒ bàba ér búshì wǒ 你要找的是我爸爸而不是我; *~ then* (*again*) dàn lìngyī fāngmiàn 但另一方面 **2** *prep*: *all ~ him* chúle tā zhīwài suǒyǒu rén 除了他之外所有人; *the last ~ one* dàoshǔ dìèr gè 倒数第二个; *the next ~ one* jiēzhe dìèr 接着第二; *~ for you* méiyǒu nǐ 没有你; *nothing ~ the best* zhǐyǒu zuìhǎo de 只有最好的

butcher màiròu de 卖肉的; (*murderer*) túfū 屠夫

butt 1 *n* (*of cigarette*) yāndì 烟蒂; (*of joke*) xiàobǐng 笑柄; F (*buttocks*) pìgu 屁股 **2** *v/t* yòng tóu zhuàng 用头撞; (*of goat, bull*) yòng tóu dǐng 用头顶

♦ **butt in** chāzuǐ 插嘴

butter ⇩ **1** *n* huángyóu 黄油 **2** *v/t* mǒ huángyóu 抹黄油

♦ **butter up** F fèngcheng 奉承

butterfly (*insect*) húdié 蝴蝶

buttocks túnbù 臀部

button 1 *n* kòuzi 扣子; (*on machine*) ànniǔ 按钮; (*badge*) huīzhāng 徽章 **2** *v/t* kòu kòuzi 扣扣子

buttonhole 1 *n* (*in suit*) kòuyǎnr 扣眼儿 **2** *v/t* qiángliú jiāotán 强留交谈

buxom fēngmǎn 丰满

buy 1 *n* piányí huò 便宜货 **2** *v/t* mǎi 买; *can I ~ you a drink?* wǒ néng gěinǐ mǎi bēi yǐnliào ma? 我能给你买杯饮料吗？; *$50 doesn't ~ much* wǔshí měiyuán mǎibùliǎo shénme 五十美元买不了什么

♦ **buy off** (*bribe*) shōumǎi 收买

♦ **buy out** COM mǎixià quánbù gǔfèn 买下全部股份

♦ **buy up** dàliàng mǎijìn 大量买进

buyer mǎijiā 买家; (*for department store etc*) cǎigòu yuán 采购员

buzz 1 *n* zàoyīn 噪音; F (*thrill*) xīngfèn gǎn 兴奋感 **2** *v/i* (*of insect*) fāchū wēngweng shēng 发出嗡嗡声; (*with buzzer*) àn fēngmíng qì 按蜂鸣器 **3** *v/t* (*with buzzer*) àn fēngmíng qì jiào 按蜂鸣器叫

♦ **buzz off** F zǒukāi 走开

buzzer fēngmíng qì 蜂鸣器

by 1 *prep* (*agency*) bèi 被; (*near, next to*) kàojìn 靠近; (*no later than*) bù chíyú 不迟于; (*past*) jīngguò 经过; (*mode of transport*) chéng 乘; *side ~ side* yīgè āizhe yīgè 一个挨着一个; *~ day / night* zài báitiān / wǎnshàng 在白天 / 晚上; *~ bus / train* chéng gōnggòng qìchē / huǒchē 乘公共汽车 / 火车; *~ the hour / ton* yǐ xiǎoshí / dūn jìsuàn 以小时 / 吨计算; *~ my watch* ànzhào 按照; *a play ~ ...* yóu ... xiěde jùzuò 由 ... 写的剧作; *~ oneself* zìjǐ 自己; *~ a couple of minutes* yǐ jǐ fēnzhōng zhīchā 以几分钟之差; **2** *~ 4* (*measurement*) èr chéng sì 二乘四; *~ this time tomorrow* míngtiān zhègè shíhòu 明天这个时候 **2** *adv*: *~ and ~* (*soon*) guò yīhuìr 过一会儿

bye(-bye) zàijiàn 再见

bygone: *let ~s be ~s* guòqùde shì ràngtā guòqù ba 过去的事让它过去吧

bypass 1 *n* (*road*) pánglù 旁路; MED fēnliú shù 分流术 **2** *v/t* ràoguò 绕过

by-product fù chǎnpǐn 副产品

bystander pángguān zhě 旁观者

byte zìjié 字节

byword: *be a ~ for ...* chéngwéi ... de dàihào 成为 ... 的代号

C

CAAC (= *Civil Aviation Admini-stration of China*) Zhōngguó Mínháng 中国民航

cab (*taxi*) chūzū qìchē 出租汽车; (*van-type ~*) miàndī miàn de 面的; (*in Taiwan*) jìchéngchē 计程车; (*of truck*) jiàshǐ shì 驾驶室

cab driver chūzū qìchē sījī 出租汽车司机; (*of van-type cab*) miàndī sījī 面的司机; (*in Taiwan*) jìchéngchē sījī 计程车司机

cabaret gēwǔ biǎoyǎn 歌舞表演

cabbage (*in northern China*) yángbái cài 洋白菜; (*in southern China*) juǎnxīn cài 卷心菜

cabin (*of plane*) zuòcāng 座舱; (*of ship*) chuáncāng 船舱

cabin crew jīzǔ rényuán 机组人员

cabinet (*cupboard*) guìzi 柜子; (*display ~*) chénlièguì 陈列柜; POL nèigé 内阁

cable (*of electrical appliance, telephone*) diànxiàn 电线; (*for securing*) gāngsī shéng 钢丝绳; **~** (**TV**) yǒuxiàn diànshì 有线电视

cable car lǎnchē 缆车

cab stand chūzūchē zhàn 出租车站

cache COMPUT gāosù huǎncún 高速缓存

cactus xiānrénzhǎng 仙人掌

cadaver shītǐ 尸体

CAD-CAM jìsuànjī fǔzhù shèjì hé zhìzào 计算机辅助设计和制造

caddie 1 *n* (*in golf*) qiútóng 球童 **2** *v/i:* **~ for ...** dāng ... de qiútóng 当 ... 的球童

cadet xuéyuán 学员

cadge: **~ X from Y** gēn Y qǐqiú X 跟 Y 乞求 X

cadre gànbu 干部

café xiǎo fànguǎnr 小饭馆

cafeteria shítáng 食堂

caffeine kāfēiyīn 咖啡因

cage lóng 笼

cagey tūntun tǔtu 吞吞吐吐

cahoots: **be in ~ with ...** gēn ... tónghuǒ 跟 ... 同伙

cake 1 *n* dàngāo 蛋糕; ***be a piece of ~*** *fig* hěn róngyì 很容易 **2** *v/i* (*of mud, blood*) jiékuàir 结块儿

calcium gaì 钙

calculate (*work out*) gūjì 估计; (*in arithmetic*) jìsuàn 计算

calculating jīngmíng 精明

calculation jìsuàn jiēguǒ 计算结果

calculator jìsuàn qì 计算器

calendar rìlì 日历

calf[1] (*young cow*) xiǎoniú 小牛

calf[2] (*of leg*) tuǐdùzi 腿肚子

caliber (*of gun*) kǒujìng 口径; ***a man of his ~*** xiàng tā nàyàng yǒu nénglì de rén 像他那样有能力的人

call 1 *n* (*phone ~*) diànhuà 电话; (*shout*) hǎnjiào 喊叫; (*demand*) yāoqiú yāoqiú 要求; ***there's a ~ for you*** yǒu nǐde diànhuà 有你的电话; ***give X a call*** gěi X dǎ diànhuà 给 X 打电话 **2** *v/t* (*on phone*) dǎ diànhuà gěi 打电话给; (*summon*) jiào 叫; *meeting* zhàojí 召集; (*by court*) chuán 传; (*describe as*) shuōchéng shì 说成是; (*shout*) dàhǎn 大喊; ***what have they ~ed the baby?*** tāmen gěi háizi qǐ shénme míngzi? 他们给孩子起什么名字?; **~ *the manager*** zhǎo jīnglǐ lái 找经理来; ***but we ~ him Old Li*** dàn wǒmen jiào tā Lǎo Lǐ 但我们叫他老李; **~ *X names*** mà X 骂 X **3** *v/i* (*on phone*) dǎ diànhuà 打电话; (*shout*) hūhǎn 呼喊; (*visit*) lái lai 来

♦ **call at** (*stop at*) qù 去; (*of train*) zài ... tíngchē 在 ... 停车

◆ **call back 1** *v/t (on phone)* huí diànhuà 回电话; **call X back** *(summon)* jiào X huíqù 叫 X 回去 **2** *v/i (on phone)* zài dǎ diànhuà 再打电话; *(make another visit)* zàilái 再来

◆ **call for** *person* jiē jiē 接; *goods* qùná qù 去拿; *(demand)* yāoqiú 要求; *(require)* bìxū yào 必须要

◆ **call in 1** *v/t expert* qǐng qǐng 请; **call X in** *(summon by person in authority)* jiào X jìnqù 叫 X 进去 **2** *v/i (phone)* dǎ diànhuà lái 打电话来; **~ sick** dǎ diànhuà qǐng bìngjià 打电话请病假

◆ **call off** *(cancel)* qǔxiāo 取消

◆ **call on** *(urge)* dūncù 敦促; *(visit)* bàifǎng 拜访

◆ **call out** *(shout)* dàhǎn 大喊; *(summon)* zhāohuàn 召唤

◆ **call up** *v/t (on phone)* dǎ diànhuà gěi 打电话给; COMPUT dǎkāi 打开

caller *(on phone)* dǎ diànhuà zhě 打电话者; *(visitor)* tànfǎng zhě 探访者

call girl jìnǚ 妓女

calligraphy shūfǎ 书法

callous wúqíng 无情

calm 1 *adj sea, weather* píngjìng 平静; *person* lěngjìng 冷静 **2** *n (of countryside)* ānjìng 安静; *(of person)* lěngjìng 冷静

◆ **calm down 1** *v/t:* **calm X down** shǐ X lěngjìng xiàlái 使 X 冷静下来 **2** *v/i (of sea, weather, person)* píngjìng xiàlái 平静下来

calorie kǎlùlǐ 卡路里

Cambodia Jiǎnpǔzhài 柬埔寨

Cambodian 1 *adj* Jiǎnpǔzhài 柬埔寨 **2** *n (person)* Jiǎnpǔzhài rén 柬埔寨人

camcorder shèxiàn jī 摄像机

camera zhàoxiàng jī 照像机

cameraman shèyǐng shī 摄影师

camouflage 1 *n* wěizhuāng 伪装 **2** *v/t* yǎnhù 掩护

camp 1 *n* yíng yíng 营 **2** *v/i* lùyíng 露营

campaign 1 *n* yùndòng 运动; **presidential ~** zǒngtǒng jìngxuǎn 总统竞选 **2** *v/i* gǎo yùndòng 搞运动

campaigner huódòngjiā 活动家

camper *(person)* yěyíng zhě 野营者; *(vehicle)* yěyíng chē 野营车

camping lùyíng 露营

campsite yíngdì 营地

campus xiàoyuán 校园

can¹ ◊ *(ability)* néng 能; **I ~'t** wǒ bùnéng 我不能; **~'t you see?** nǐ nándào méi kànjiàn? 你难道没看见？; **I ~'t see** wǒ kànbújiàn 我看不见; **~ you hear me?** nǐ tīngde jiàn wǒ ma? 你听得见我吗？; **~ he call me back?** tā néng gěi wǒ huí diànhuà ma? 他能给我回电话吗？; **as fast as you ~** yuèkuài yuèhǎo 越快越好; **as well as you ~** jìnliàng ba 尽量吧; **you ~'t be serious!** bié kāi wánxiào le! 别开玩笑了！; **~ I help you?** wǒ néng bāng nǐ máng ma? 我能帮你忙吗?; **~ you help me?** nǐ néng bāng wǒ ma? 你能帮我吗？; **~ I have a beer / coffee?** qǐng lái bēi píjiǔ / kāfēi? 请来杯啤酒 / 咖啡？; **that ~'t be right** bù kěnéng 不可能 ◊ *(with skills)* huì 会; **~ you speak French?** nǐ huì shuō Fǎyǔ ma? 你会说法语吗？ ◊ *(permission)* kěyǐ 可以; **~ I take this one?** wǒ kěyǐ ná zhèige ma? 我可以拿这个吗？

can² **1** *n (for drinks etc)* guàntóu 罐头 **2** *v/t (put in ~)* guànzhuāng 罐装

Canada Jiānádà 加拿大

Canadian 1 *adj* Jiānádà 加拿大 **2** *n* Jiānádà rén 加拿大人

canal *(waterway)* yùnhé 运河

canary *(bird)* jīnsīquè 金丝雀

cancel qǔxiāo 取消

cancellation qǔxiāo 取消

cancer áizhèng 癌症

c & f (= **cost and freight**) chéngběn jiā yùnfèi 成本加运费

c & i (= **cost and insurance**) chéngběn jiā bǎoxiǎn fèi 成本加保险费

candid tǎnshuài 坦率

candidacy hòuxuǎn 候选

candidate (*for position*) hòuxuǎn rén 候选人; (*in exam*) yìngkǎo rén 应考人

candle làzhú 蜡烛

candlestick zhútái 烛台

candor tǎnshuài 坦率

candy táng 糖

cannabis dàmá 大麻

canned *fruit, tomatoes* guànzhuāng 罐装; **~ laughter** (*recorded*) yùlù xiàoshēng 预录笑声

cannibalize *old car etc* chāijiàn 拆件

cannot → **can**[1]

canoe dúmù zhōu 独木舟

can opener kāiguàn qì 开罐器

cant wěishàn yáncí 伪善言词

can't → **can**[1]

canteen (*in factory*) shítáng 食堂

Canton Guǎngdōng 广东

Cantonese 1 *adj* Guǎngdōng 广东 **2** *n* Guǎngdōng rén 广东人; (*language*) Guǎngdōnghuà 广东话

canvas (*for painting*) yóuhuà bù 油画布; (*material*) fānbù 帆布

canvass 1 *v/t* (*seek opinion of*) tīngqǔ yìjiàn 听取意见 **2** *v/i* POL lāpiào 拉票

canyon xiágǔ 峡谷

cap (*hat*) màozi 帽子; (*of bottle, lens*) gàizi 盖子; (*of pen*) bǐmào 笔帽

capability (*of person*) nénglì 能力; (*of military*) lìliàng 力量

capable nénggàn 能干; **be ~ of** yǒu nénglì 有能力

capacity (*of container, building*) róngliàng 容量; (*of elevator*) fùhè liàng 负荷量; (*of car engine*) róngliàng 容量; (*of factory*) chǎnliàng 产量; (*ability*) nénglì 能力; **in my ~ as ...** yǐwǒ ... de shēnfèn 以我 ... 的身份

capital *n* (*of country*) shǒudū 首都; (*capital letter*) dàxiě zìmǔ 大写字母; (*money*) zījīn 资金

capital expenditure zīběn zhīchū 资本支出; **capital gains tax** zīběn shōuyì shuì 资本收益税; **capital growth** zīběn

chéngzhǎng 资本成长

capitalism zīběn zhǔyì 资本主义

capitalist 1 *adj* zīběn zhǔyì 资本主义 **2** *n* (*believer*) zīběn zhǔyì zhě 资本主义者; (*businessman*) zīběn jiā 资本家

capital letter dàxiě zìmǔ 大写字母

capital punishment sǐxíng 死刑

capitulate ràngbù 让步

capsize 1 *v/i* fānchuán 翻船 **2** *v/t* shǐ fānchuán 使翻船

capsule (*of medicine*) jiāonáng 胶囊; (*space ~*) tàikōng cāng 太空舱

captain *n* (*of ship*) chuánzhǎng 船长; (*of aircraft*) jīzhǎng 机长; (*of team*) duìzhǎng 队长

caption *n* (*to photo*) shuōmíng 说明

captivate zháomí 着迷

captive fúlǔ 俘虏

captivity bèi guān qǐlái 被关起来

capture 1 *n* (*of city*) zhànlǐng 占领; (*of criminal*) zhuōdào 捉到; (*of animal*) bǔhuò 捕获 **2** *v/t person,* zhuōdào 捉到; *animal* bǔhuò 捕获; *city, building* gōngxià 攻下; (*win: market share*) huòdé 获得; (*portray: mood*) miáohuì 描绘; **~ the moment** zhuāzhù nàyī chànà 抓住那一刹那

car chē 车; (*of train*) chēxiāng 车厢; **by ~** zuòchē 坐车

carafe píng 瓶

carat kèlā 克拉

carbohydrate tànshuǐ huàhéwù 碳水化合物

carbonated *drink* qìpào 起泡

carbon monoxide yīyǎng huàtàn 一氧化碳

carburetter, carburetor qìhuàqì 汽化器

carcinogen zhì'ái wù 致癌物

carcinogenic zhì'ái 致癌

card (*to mark special occasion*) kǎpiàn 卡片; (*post~*) míngxìnpiànr 明信片儿; (*business ~*) míngpiànr 名片儿; (*playing ~*) zhǐpái 纸牌

cardboard yìng zhǐbǎn 硬纸板

cardiac xīnzàng 心脏

cardiac arrest xīnzàng tíngtiào 心脏停跳

cardigan kāijīn máoyī 开襟毛衣

card index kǎpiàn mùlù 卡片目录

card key kǎpiàn yàoshí 卡片钥匙

care 1 *n* (*of baby, pet, elderly, sick*) zhàogù 照顾; (*medical ~*) yīliáo 医疗; (*worry*) yōulǜ 忧虑; **~ of** (*on envelope*) fánjiāo 烦交; **take ~** (*be cautious*) xiǎoxīn 小心; **take ~** (*of yourself*)! (*goodbye*) bǎozhòng! 保重！; **take ~ of** baby, dog zhàogù 照顾; tool, house, garden àihù 爱护; (*deal with*) chǔlǐ 处理; project fùzé 负责; **take ~ of the check** fùzhàng 付账; (*handle*) **with ~** (*on label*) xiǎoxīn qīngfàng 小心轻放 **2** *v/i* guānxīn 关心; **if you really ~d** (*were concerned*) yàoshì nǐ zhēnde guānxīn dehuà 要是你真的关心的话; **I don't ~!** wǒbú zàihu! 我不在乎！; **I couldn't ~ less** wǒ yìdiǎn yě bú zàihū 我一点也不在乎

♦ **care about** guānxīn 关心

♦ **care for** (*look after*) zhàogù 照顾; (*like, be fond of*) xǐhuān 喜欢; **would you ~ ... ?** nǐ yào ... ma? 你要...吗?

career (*profession*) shìyè 事业; (*path through life*) jīnglì 经历

carefree wúyōu wúlǜ 无忧无虑

careful (*cautious*) jǐnshèn 谨慎; (*thorough*) zǐxì 仔细; person xìxīn 细心; (*be*) **~!** xiǎoxīn! 小心！

carefully (*with caution*) xiǎoxīn 小心; worded etc jīngxīn 精心

careless person cūxīn 粗心; work cǎoshuài 草率; **you are so ~!** nǐ tài dàyì le! 你太大意了！

caress *n & v/t* àifǔ 爱抚

caretaker kānguǎn rén 看管人

careworn yōuxīn chōngchong 忧心忡忡

cargo huòwù 货物

caricature *n* (*picture*) fěngcì huà 讽刺画; (*in writing*) fěngcì wénzhāng 讽刺文章

caring *adj* yǒu àixīn 有爱心

carnage dà túshā 大屠杀

carnation kāngnǎixīn 康乃馨

carnival miàohuì 庙会

carol *n* sònggē 颂歌

carousel (*at airport*) xínglǐ chuánsòngdài 行李传送带; (*at fairground*) xuánzhuǎn mùmǎ 旋转木马

carp (*fish*) lǐyú 鲤鱼

carpenter mùjiàng 木匠

carpet dìtǎn 地毯

carpool *n* héhuǒ yòngchē 合伙用车; **car port** qìchēpéng 汽车棚; **car rental** chūzū qìchē gōngsī 出租汽车公司

carrier (*company*) yùnshū gōngsī 运输公司; (*of disease*) dàijùn zhě 带菌者

carrot húluóbo 胡萝卜

carry 1 *v/t* (*in hand*) ná 拿; (*on back*) bēi 背; (*hold in front*) bàozhe 抱; (*move: goods*) bānyùn 搬运; (*have on one's person*) dàizhe 带着; (*of pregnant woman*) huáizhe 怀着; disease dài ... dejùn 带...的菌; (*of ship, plane, bus etc*) zàiyǒu 载有; proposal tōngguò 通过; **get carried away** chōnghūn le tóu 冲昏了头 **2** *v/i* (*of sound*) chuánsòng 传送

♦ **carry on 1** *v/i* (*continue*) jiēzhe zuò 接着做; (*talking*) diédiebùxiū 喋喋不休; (*make a fuss*) chǎonào 吵闹 **2** *v/t* (*conduct*) jìxù 继续

♦ **carry on with** (*have an affair with*) hé ... yǒu àimèi guānxī 和...有暧昧关系

♦ **carry out** survey etc jìnxíng 进行; orders etc zhíxíng 执行

car seat (*for child*) háitóng qìchē zuòyǐ 孩童汽车座椅

cart (*horsedrawn*) mǎchē 马车; (*for baggage*) xínglǐ chē 行李车

cartel liánhé qǐyè 联合企业

carton (*for storage, transport*) zhǐxiāng 纸箱; (*for milk, eggs etc*) zhǐhé 纸盒; **a ~ of cigarettes** yītiáo xiāngyān 一条香烟

cartoon (*in newspaper, magazine*) fěngcì huà 讽刺画; (*on TV, film*) kǎtōng piàn 卡通片

cartridge (*for gun*) zǐdàn 子弹

carve *meat* qiē 切; *wood* kè 刻

carving (*figure*) diāokè pǐn 雕刻品

car wash xǐchēchù 洗车处

case[1] (*container*) hé 盒; (*of Scotch, wine*) xiāng 箱; (*suitcase*) píxiāng 皮箱

case[2] *n* (*instance*) lìzi 例子; (*argument*) gēnjù 根据; (*for police, attorney*) ànjiàn 案件; MED bìnglì 病例; **in ~ ...** wànyī ... 万一 ...; **in any ~** zǒngzhī 总之; **in that ~** jìrán zhèyàng 既然这样

case history MED bìngshǐ 病史

cash 1 *n* xiànjīn 现金; **short of ~** xiànjīn duǎnquē 现金短缺; **~ down** xiànjīn zhīfù 现金支付; **pay (in) ~** fù xiànjīn 付现金; **~ in advance** xiànkuǎn dìngjīn 现款定金; **~ on delivery** jiāohuò fùkuǎn 交货付款 **2** *v/t check* duìxiàn 兑现

♦**cash in on** cóngzhōng huòlì 从中获利

cash cow jīnkù 金库; **cash desk** fùkuǎn tái 付款台; **cash discount** xiànjīn zhékòu 现金折扣; **cash flow** liúdòng jījīn 流动基金

cashier *n* (*in store etc*) chūnà yuán 出纳员

cash machine qǔkuǎn jī 取款机

cashmere *adj* yángróng 羊绒

cash register xiànjīn chūnà jī 现金出纳机

casino dǔchǎng 赌场

casket (*coffin*) guāncai 棺材

cassette cídài 磁带

cassette player lùyīnjī 录音机

cassette recorder lùyīnjī 录音机

cast 1 *n* (*of play*) yǎnyuán biǎo 演员表; (*mold*) móxíng 模型 **2** *v/t metal* jiāozhù 浇铸; *play* fēnpèi juésè 分配角色; **~ X as ...** *actor* fēnpèi X bànyǎn ... 分配X扮演 ...; **~ doubt on** lìngrén huáiyí 令人怀疑

♦**cast off** *v/i* (*of ship*) jiělǎn 解缆

caste zhǒngxìng 种姓

caster (*on chair etc*) jiǎolún 脚轮

cast iron *n* shēngtiě 生铁

cast-iron *adj* shēngtiě 生铁

castle chéngbǎo 城堡

castrate yāngē 阉割

casual (*chance, offhand, not formal*) suíbiàn 随便; (*not permanent*) línshí 临时

casualty shāngwáng rénshì 伤亡人士

casual wear biànfú 便服

cat māo 猫

catalog *n* mùlù 目录

catalyst *fig* dǎohuǒ xiàn 导火线

catalytic converter cuīhuà zhuǎnhuà qì 催化转化器

catastrophe zāinàn 灾难

catch 1 *n* jiē 接; (*of fish*) bǔhuò wù 捕获物; (*locking device*) shuān 闩; (*problem*) wèntí 问题 **2** *v/t ball* jiēzhù 接住; *escaped prisoner* zhuōzhù 捉住; (*get on: bus, train*) zuò 坐; (*not miss: bus, train*) gǎnshàng 赶上; *fish with rod* diàodào 钓到; *fish with net* bǔdào 捕到; (*in order to speak to*) zhǎodào 找到; (*hear*) tīng qīngchǔ 听清楚; *illness* rǎnshàng 染上; **~ (a) cold** dé gǎnmào 得感冒; **~ X's eye** (*of person, object*) yǐnqǐ X de zhùyì 引起X的注意; **~ sight of, ~ a glimpse of** kànjiàn 看见; **~ X doing Y** zhuàngjiàn X zuò Y 撞见X做Y

♦**catch on** (*become popular*) shòu huānyíng 受欢迎; (*understand*) lǐjiě 理解

♦**catch up** *v/i* gǎnshàng 赶上

♦**catch up on** míbǔ 弥补

catch-22: **it's a ~ situation** jìntuì liǎngnán 进退两难

catcher (*in baseball*) jiēshǒu 接手

catching *disease* chuánrǎn xìng 传染性; *fear, panic* yǒu gǎnrǎn lì 有感染力

catchy *tune* róngyì shàngkǒu 容易上口

category fànchóu 范畴

♦**cater for** (*meet the needs of*) yínghé 迎合; (*provide food for*) bāobàn 包办

caterer jiǔxí chéngbàn rén 酒席承办人

caterpillar máochóng 毛虫

cathedral dà jiàotáng 大教堂

Catholic 1 *adj* Tiānzhǔjiào 天主教 2 *n* Tiānzhǔ jiàotú 天主教徒

catsup fānqié jiàng 蕃茄酱

cattle niú 牛

catty èdú 恶毒

cauliflower càihuā 菜花

cause 1 *n* yuányīn 原因; (*grounds*) lǐyóu 理由; (*aim of movement, charity etc*) zhǔzhāng 主张 2 *v/t* yǐnqǐ 引起

caution 1 *n* (*carefulness*) jǐnshèn 谨慎; ~ *is advised* jǐnshèn yīxiē 谨慎一些 2 *v/t* (*warn*) jǐnggào 警告

cautious jǐnshèn 谨慎

cave dòng 洞

♦cave in (*of roof*) dǎotā 倒塌

caviar yúzǐ jiàng 鱼子酱

cavity (*in tooth*) qǔchǐ 龋齿

cc (= *carbon copy*) 1 *n* fùběn 副本 2 *v/t* fùběn gěi 副本给

CCTV (= *China Central Television*) Zhōngyāng Diànshìtái 中央电视台

CD (*compact disc*) guāngpán 光盘

CD-ROM guāngpán 光盘

CD-ROM drive guāngqū 光驱

cease *v/t* & *v/i* zhōngzhǐ 中止

cease-fire tínghuǒ 停火

ceiling (*of room*) tiānhuābǎn 天花板; (*limit*) zuìgāo xiàngdù 最高限度

celebrate 1 *v/i* qìngzhù 庆祝 2 *v/t* qìngzhù 庆祝; (*observe*) guò 过

celebrated zhùmíng 著名

celebration qìngzhù huì 庆祝会

celebrity míngrén 名人

celery qíncài 芹菜

cell (*for prisoner*) láofáng 牢房; BIO xìbāo 细胞; COMPUT dānyuán 单元

cellar dìjiào 地窖

cello dà tíqín 大提琴

cellophane bōli zhǐ 玻璃纸

cell(ular) phone ⇩ shǒutí diànhuà 手提电话

Celsius shèshì 摄氏

cement 1 *n* shuǐní 水泥 2 *v/t* yòng shuǐní hú 用水泥糊; *friendship* jiāqiáng 加强

cemetery mùdì 墓地

censor *v/t* shān'gǎi 删改

censorship shěnchá zhìdù 审查制度

cent fēn 分

centenary, centennial yìbǎi zhōunián 一百周年

center 1 *n* zhōngxīn 中心; POL zhōngjiān pài 中间派; *in the ~ of ...* zài ... de zhōngxīn 在 ... 的中心 2 *v/t* fàngzài zhōngyāng 放在中央; *text* zhōngjiān duìqí 中间对齐

♦center on jízhōng yú 集中于

centigrade shèshì 摄氏; *10 degrees ~* shèshì shídù 摄氏十度

centimeter límǐ 厘米

central zhōngbù 中部; *location, apartment* zhōngyāng 中央; (*main*) zhǔyào 主要; *be ~ to X* shì X de zhōngxīn yàodiǎn 是 X 的中心要点

Central Committee of the Chinese Communist Party Zhōnggòng Zhōngyāng Wěiyuánhuì 中共中央委员会

central heating nuǎnqì 暖气

centralize *decision making* jízhōng 集中

central processing unit zhōngyāng chǔlǐ jī 中央处理机

central locking MOT zhōngyāng suǒchē 中央锁车

century shìjì 世纪

CEO (= *Chief Executive Officer*) zǒng jīnglǐ 总经理

ceramic cí 磁

ceramics (*objects*) táocí 陶瓷

cereal (*grain*) gǔlèi 谷类

ceremonial 1 *adj* diǎnlǐ 典礼 2 *n* diǎnlǐ 典礼

ceremony (*event*) diǎnlǐ 典礼; (*ritual*) yíshì 仪式

certain (*sure*) kěndìng 肯定; (*particular*) mǒuzhǒng 某种; *it's ~ that ...* kěndìng ... 肯定 ...; *a ~ Mr S.* yígè jiào S xiānshēng de rén 一个叫 S 先生的人; *make ~* quèdìng 确定; *know / say for ~* kěyǐ kěndìng 可以肯定

certainly (*definitely*) yídìng 一定;

(*of course*) méi wèntí 没问题；~ **not!** juéduì bùxíng! 绝对不行！

certainty (*confidence*) quèxìn 确信；(*inevitability*) bìrán xìng 必然性；**it's a ~** kěndìng 肯定

certificate (*qualification*) zhèngshù 证书；(*official paper*) zhèngmíng 证明

certified public accountant hégé kuàijì shī 合格会计师

certify zhèngmíng 证明

Cesarean n pōufù 剖腹

cessation xiūzhǐ 休止

c/f (= **cost and freight**) chéngběn jiā yùnfèi 成本加运费

CFC (= **chlorofluorocarbon**) hánlǜ fútīng 含氯氟烃

chain 1 n liàntiáo 链条；(*of stores, hotels*) liánsuǒ diàn 连锁店 **2** v/t：~ **X to Y** bǎ X shuānzài Y shàng 把 X 拴在 Y 上

chain reaction liánsuǒ fǎnyìng 连锁反应；**chain smoke** yìzhī jiē yìzhī de chōuyān 一支接一支地抽烟；**chain smoker** yānbù líkǒu de rén 烟不离口的人；**chain store** liánsuǒdiàn 连锁店

chair 1 n yǐzi 椅子；(*arm ~*) fúshǒu yǐ 扶手椅；(*at university*) jiàoshòu zhíwèi 教授职位；**the ~** (*electric ~*) diànyǐ 电椅；(*at meeting*) zhǔxí 主席；**go to the ~** zuò diànyǐ 坐电椅；**take the ~** zhǔchí huìyì 主持会议 **2** v/t meeting zhǔchí 主持

chair lift shēngjiàng yǐ 升降椅

chairman zhǔxí 主席

Chairman Mao Máo Zhǔxí 毛主席

chairperson, chairwoman zhǔxí 主席

chalk (*for writing*) fěnbǐ 粉笔；(*in soil*) báihuī 白灰

challenge 1 n (*difficulty, in race, competition*) tiǎozhàn 挑战 **2** v/t (*defy*) fǎnduì 反对；(*call into question*) zhìyí 质疑；~ **X to Y** tiǎozhàn X zuò Y 挑战 X 做 Y

challenger tiǎozhàn zhě 挑战者

challenging job, undertaking yǒu tiǎozhàn xìng 有挑战性

chambermaid nǚ fúwùyuán 女服务员

Chamber of Commerce shānghuì 商会

chamois (*leather*) jǐpí 麂皮

champagne xiāngbīn jiǔ 香槟酒

champion 1 n SP guànjūn 冠军；(*of cause*) hànwèi zhě 捍卫者 **2** v/t (*cause*) zhīchí 支持

championship (*event*) jǐnbiāosài 锦标赛；(*title*) guànjūn 冠军

chance (*possibility*) kěnéng 可能；(*opportunity*) jīhuì 机会；(*risk*) fēngxiǎn 风险；(*luck*) jīyù 机遇；**by ~** yìwài 意外；**take a ~** màoxiǎn 冒险；**I'm not taking any ~s** wǒ bùcún jiàoxìng zhīxīn 我不存侥幸之心

Chancellor (*in Germany*) Zǒnglǐ 总理；~ (**of the Exchequer**) (*in Britain*) Cáizhèngdàchén 财政大臣

chandelier diàodēng 吊灯

Changbai Mountain Chángbáishān 长白山

change 1 n (*alteration: to plan, idea, script*) gǎibiàn 改变；(*in society, climate, condition*) biànhuà 变化；(*small coins*) língqián 零钱；(*from purchase*) zhǎoqián 找钱；(*different situation etc*) gēnghuàn 更换；**for a ~** huàn kǒuwèi 换口味；**a ~ of clothes** tìhuàn yīfu 替换衣服 **2** v/t (*alter*) gǎibiàn 改变；bankbill, trains, planes, one's clothes, (*replace*) huàn 换 **3** v/i biàn 变；(*put on different clothes*) huàn yīfu 换衣服；(*take different train/bus*) huàn 换

channel (*on TV, radio*) píndào 频道；(*waterway*) hǎixiá 海峡

chant 1 n hǎnjiào 喊叫 **2** v/i gāohū 高呼

chaos hùnluàn 混乱

chaotic hùnluàn 混乱

chapel xiǎo jiàotáng 小教堂

chapped gānliè 干裂

chapter (*of book*) zhāng 章；(*of organization*) zhībù 支部

character (*nature*) běnxìng 本性；(*person*) rén 人；(*in book, play*) rénwù 人物；(*personality*) xìnggé

性格; (*for writing Chinese etc*) zì 字; **he's a real ~** tā hěn yǒu gèxìng 他很有个性

characteristic 1 *n* tèdiǎn 特点 **2** *adj* diǎnxíng 典型

characterize (*be typical of*) diǎnfàn 典范; (*describe*) miáoshù 描述

charbroiled kǎo kǎo 烤烤

charcoal (*for barbecue*) mùtàn 木炭; (*for drawing*) tànbǐ 炭笔

charge 1 *n* (*fee*) fèiyòng 费用; LAW kònggào 控告; **free of ~** miǎnfèi 免费; **will that be cash or ~?** xiànjīn háishì jìzhàng? 现金还是记账？; **be in ~** fùzé 负责; **take ~** jiēguǎn 接管 **2** *v/t sum of money* shōufèi 收费; (*put on account*) jìzhàng 记账; LAW zhǐkòng 指控; *battery* chōngdiàn 充电 **3** *v/i* (*of troops*) chōngfēng 冲锋; (*of animal*) jìngōng 进攻

charge account shēzhàng hùkǒu 赊账户口

charge card jìzhàng kǎ 记账卡

charisma mèilì 魅力

charitable *institution, donation, person* císhàn 慈善

charity (*assistance*) zhènjì 赈济; (*organization*) císhàng jīgòu 慈善机构

charm 1 *n* (*appealing quality*) mèilì 魅力; (*on bracelet etc*) xiǎo zhuāngshì pǐn 小装饰品 **2** *v/t* (*delight*) xīyǐn 吸引

charming mírén 迷人; *idea* yǒu xīyǐn lì 有吸引力

charred shāojiāo 烧焦

chart (*diagram*) túbiǎo 图表; (*map: for sea*) hánghǎi tú 航海图; (*for airplane*) hángkōng tú 航空图; **the ~s** MUS liúxíng chàngpiān xuǎnmù 流行唱片选目

charter *v/t* bāozū 包租

charter flight bāojī 包机

chase 1 *n* zhuīzhú 追逐 **2** *v/t* zhuī 追

♦**chase away** gǎnzǒu 赶走

chaser (*drink*) suí lièjiǔ yǐhòu hēde dīdùjiǔ 随烈酒以后喝的低度酒

chassis (*of car*) dǐpán 底盘

chat 1 *n* liáotiān 聊天 **2** *v/i* liáo 聊

chatter 1 *n* diédie bùxiū 喋喋不休 **2** *v/i* (*talk*) xiánliáo 闲聊; (*of teeth*) dǎzhàn 打颤

chatterbox ráoshé zhě 饶舌者

chatty *person* jiàntán 健谈; *letter* jiācháng xiánhuà 家常闲话

chauffeur *n* sījī 司机

chauvinist (*male ~*) dà nánrén zhǔyì zhě 大男人主义者

cheap *adj* (*inexpensive*) piányi 便宜; (*nasty*) dījí 低级; (*mean*) xiǎoqì 小气

cheat 1 *n* (*person*) piànzi 骗子 **2** *v/t* piàn 骗; **~ X out of Y** cóng Y nàli piànchū X 从 Y 那里骗出 X **3** *v/i* (*in exam*) zuòbì 作弊; (*in cards etc*) gǎoguǐ 搞鬼; **~ on one's husband** gěi zhàngfu dài lǜ màozi 给丈夫戴绿帽子

check[1] *n & adj* (*in pattern*) fānggé 方格

check[2] FIN zhīpiào 支票; (*in restaurant etc*) zhàngdān 账单; **the ~ please** zhàngdān 账单

check[3] **1** *n* (*to verify sth*) jiǎnchá 检查; **keep in ~, hold in ~** kòngzhì 控制; **keep a ~ on** héduì 核对 **2** *v/t* (*verify*) cháchá 查查; (*machinery*) jiǎnchá 检查; (*restrain*) yìzhì 抑制; (*stop*) kòngzhì zhù 控制住; (*with a ~mark*) dǎgōu 打勾; (*coat, package etc*) cúnfàng 存放 **3** *v/i* cháchá 查查; **~ for** jiǎnchá 检查

♦**check in** (*at airport*) lǐng dēngjī kǎ 领登机卡; (*at hotel*) dēngjì 登记

♦**check off** héduì 核对

♦**check on** chákàn 察看

♦**check out 1** *v/i* (*of hotel*) ⇓ jiézhàng 结账 **2** *v/t* (*look into*) diàochá 调查; *club, restaurant etc* shìshi 试试

♦**check up on** diàochá 调查

♦**check with** (*of person*) wèn 问; (*tally: of information, facts*) fúhé 符合

checkbook zhīpiào běn 支票本

checked *material* gézi 格子

checkerboard tiàoqí pán 跳棋盘

checkered *pattern* zònghéng-jiāocuò 纵横交错; *career* bǎojīng cāngsāng 饱经沧桑

checkers tiàoqí 跳棋

check-in (*counter*) lǐng dēngjī kǎ guìtái 领登机卡柜台

checking account zhīpiào zhànghù 支票帐户

check-in time lìng dēngjī kǎ shíjiān 领登机卡时间

checklist qīngdān 清单; **check mark** gōuhào 勾号; **checkmate** *n* jiāngsǐ 将死; **checkout** (*in supermarket*) guìtái chū 柜台出; **check-out time** (*from hotel*) ⇩ jiézhàng shíjiān 结账时间; **checkpoint** (*military, police*) guānqiǎ 关卡; **checkroom** (*for coats*) yīmào jiān 衣帽间; (*for baggage*) xínglǐ cúnfàng chù 行李存放处; **checkup** *medical* jiànkāng jiǎnchá 健康检查; *dental* yáchǐ jiǎnchá 牙齿检查

cheek miànjiá 面颊

cheekbone quángǔ 颧骨

cheer 1 *n* huānhū 欢呼; **~s!** (*toast*) gānbēi! 干杯！**2** *v/t* shòu huānyíng 受欢迎 **3** *v/i* hècǎi 喝采

♦**cheer on** hècǎi 喝采

♦**cheer up 1** *v/i* gāoxìng qǐlái 高兴起来; **~!** gǔ qǐ jìnr lái! 鼓起劲儿来！**2** *v/t*: **cheer X up** ràng X gāoxìng 让 X 高兴

cheerful kuàihuó 快活

cheering huānhū 欢呼

cheerleader lālāduì yuán 啦啦队员

cheese ⇩ nǎilào 奶酪

cheeseburger nǎilào hànbǎobāo 奶酪汉堡包

cheesecake ⇩ nǎilào dàngāo 奶酪蛋糕

chef chúshī 厨师

chemical 1 *adj* huàxué 化学 **2** *n* huàxué zhìpǐn 化学制品

chemical warfare huàxué zhàn 化学战

chemist huàxué jiā 化学家

chemistry huàxué 化学; *fig* mòqì 默契

chemotherapy huàxué liáofǎ 化学疗法

cherish *memory, hope* zhēnxī 珍惜

cherry (*fruit*) yīngtáo 樱桃; (*tree*) yīnghuā shù 樱花树

chess xiàngqí 象棋

chessboard qípán 棋盘

chest (*of person*) xiōng 胸; (*box*) xiāngzi 箱子

chestnut lìzi 栗子; (*tree*) lìzi shù 栗子树

chest of drawers tì guì 屉柜

chew *v/t* jiáo 嚼; (*of dog, rats*) kěn 啃

♦**chew out** F shǔluò 数落

chewing gum kǒuxiāng táng 口香糖

Chiang Kai-shek Jiǎng Jièshí 蒋介石

chick xiǎojī 小鸡; F (*girl*) niū 妞

chicken 1 *n* jī 鸡; (*food*) jīròu 鸡肉; F dǎnxiǎo guǐ 胆小鬼 **2** *adj* F (*cowardly*) dǎnxiǎo 胆小

♦**chicken out** dǎ tuìtánggǔ 打退堂鼓

chickenfeed F méi yóushui 没油水

chicken pox shuǐdòu 水痘

chief 1 *n* (*head*) tóunǎo 头脑; (*of tribe*) zúzhǎng 族长 **2** *adj* zhǔyào 主要

chiefly zhǔyào 主要

chilblain dòngchuāng 冻疮

child háizi 孩子; *pej* yòuzhì 幼稚

childbirth shēngchǎn 生产

childhood tóngnián 童年

childish *pej* yòuzhì 幼稚

childless wú zǐnǚ 无子女

childlike tiānzhēn wúxié 天真无邪

Children's Day Értóngjié 儿童节

chill 1 *n* (*in air*) lěngqì 冷气; (*illness*) gǎnmào 感冒 **2** *v/t* (*wine*) lěngcáng 冷藏

chilli (*pepper*) làjiāo 辣椒

chilly *weather* hánlěng 寒冷; *welcome* lěngdàn 冷淡; **I'm ~** wǒ yǒudiǎn lěng 我有点冷

chime *v/i* míng 鸣

chimney yāncōng 烟囱

chimpanzee hēi xīngxing 黑猩猩

chin xiàba 下巴

china cíqì 磁器; (*material*) cí 磁

China Zhōngguó 中国

China Central Television Zhōngyāng Diànshìtái 中央电视台; **China Daily** Zhōngguó Rìbào 中国日报; **China International Travel Service** Zhōngguó Guójì Lǚxíngshè 中国国际旅行社; **China Travel Service** Zhōngguó Lǚxíngshè 中国旅行社; **Chinatown** (*in other countries*) Tángrénjiē 唐人街

Chinese 1 *adj* Zhōngguó 中国; (*in Chinese*) Zhōngwén 中文 2 *n* (*written language*) Zhōngwén 中文; (*spoken language*) Zhōngguóhuà 中国话; (*person*) Zhōngguórén 中国人

Chinese character hànzì 汉字; **Chinese checkers** tiàoqí 跳棋; **Chinese chess** xiàngqí 象棋; **Chinese doctor** zhōngyī 中医; **Chinese dumpling** jiǎozi 饺子; **Chinese foot** (*measurement*) chǐ 尺; **Chinese inch** (*measurement*) cùn 寸; **Chinese leaf** / **cabbage** báicài 白菜; **Chinese leek** jiǔcài 韭菜; **Chinese medicine** zhōngyī 中医; (*herbs, drugs*) zhōngyào 中药; **Chinese New Year** Chūnjié 春节; **Chinese New Year's Day** Chūyī 初一; **Chinese New Year's Eve** Chúxī 除夕; **Chinese onion** cōng 葱; **Chinese-style** Zhōngshì 中式

chink (*gap*) fèng 缝; (*sound*) dīngdāng shēng 叮当声

chip 1 *n* (*fragment*) suìxiè 碎屑; (*damage*) liè kǒu 裂口; (*in gambling*) chóumǎ 筹码; COMPUT xīnpiàn 芯片; *potato* ~*s* ⇩ shǔpiàn 薯片 2 *v/t* (*damage*) nòng pò yīdiǎn 弄破一点

♦ **chip in** (*interrupt*) chāzuǐ 插嘴; (*with money*) chūqián 出钱

chiropractor ànmójìshī 按摩技师

chirp *v/i* jījī jiào 唧唧叫

chisel *n* záozi 凿子

chivalrous xiáyì 侠义

chives jiǔcài 韭菜

chlorine lǜ 氯

chockfull yōngjǐ 拥挤

chocolate qiǎokèlì 巧克力; *hot* ~ rè qiǎokèlì 热巧克力

chocolate cake qiǎokèlì dàngāo 巧克力蛋糕

choice 1 *n* xuǎnzé 选择; (*selection*) gèsè gèyàng 各色各样; (*preference*) xuǎnzé 选择; *I had no* ~ wǒ méiyǒu xuǎnzé yúdì 我没有选择余地 2 *adj* (*top quality*) jīngxuǎn 精选

choir héchàngtuán 合唱团

choke 1 *n* MOT zǔfēngmén 阻风门 2 *v/i* qiǎ 卡; *he* ~*d on a bone* tā qiǎle gǔtóu 他卡了骨头 3 *v/t* qiā bózi 掐脖子

cholesterol dǎngùchún 胆固醇

choose 1 *v/t* xuǎnzé 选择 2 *v/i* tiāoxuǎn 挑选

choosey F tiāotì 挑剔

chop 1 *n* kǎn 砍; (*meat*) páigǔ 排骨; (*seal*) túzhāng 图章 2 *v/t wood* kǎn 砍; *meat, vegetables* duò 跺

♦ **chop down** (*tree*) kǎndǎo 砍倒

chopper (*tool*) kǎndǎo 砍刀; F (*helicopter*) zhíshēng fēijī 直升飞机

chopsticks kuàizi 筷子

chord MUS xián 弦

chore (*household task*) jiāwù 家务

choreographer wǔdǎo biāndǎo 舞蹈编导

choreography biān wǔ shù 编舞术

chorus (*singers*) héchàng tuán 合唱团; (*of song*) héchàng 合唱

Chou En-lai Zhōu Ēnlái 周恩来

Christ Jīdū 基督; ~*!* wǒde tiān ya! 我的天呀!

christen xǐlǐ 洗礼

Christian 1 *n* Jīdū tú 基督徒 2 *adj* Jīdū jiào 基督教; *attitude* Jīdū jī 基督

Christianity Jīdūjiào 基督教

Christian name míng 名

Christmas Shèngdànjié 圣诞节; *at* ~ Shèngdànjié qījiān 圣诞节期间; *Merry* ~*!* Shèngdàn kuàilè! 圣诞快乐!

Christmas card Shèngdàn kǎ 圣

诞卡; **Christmas Day** Shèngdànjié 圣诞节; **Christmas Eve** Shèngdàn yè 圣诞夜; **Christmas present** Shèngdàn lǐwù 圣诞礼物; **Christmas tree** Shèngdàn shù 圣诞树

chrome, chromium gè 铬

chronic mànxìng 慢性

chronological shíjiān shùnxù 时间顺序; *in ~ order* àn shíjiān shùnxù 按时间顺序

chrysanthemum júhuā 菊花

chubby féipàng 肥胖

chuck *v/t* F rēng 扔

♦**chuck out** *object* rēngdiào 扔掉; *person* hōng 轰

chuckle 1 *n* qīngxiào 轻笑 **2** *v/i* gēgē de xiào 咯咯地笑

chunk dàkuài 大块

church jiàotáng 教堂

chute xiécáo 斜槽; (*for garbage*) lājī dào 垃圾道

CIA (= *Central Intelligence Agency*) Zhōngyāng Qíngbào Jú 中央情报局

cider píngguǒ jiǔ 苹果酒

CIF (= *cost insurance freight*) chéngběn jiā bǎoxiǎn fèi 成本加保险费

cigar xuějiā 雪茄

cigarette xiāngyān 香烟

cinema (*Br: building*) diànyǐng yuàn 电影院; (*as institution*) diànyǐng 电影

cinnamon ròuguì 肉桂

circle 1 *n* yuánquān 圆圈; (*group*) quānzi 圈子 **2** *v/t* (*draw circle around*) dǎquān 打圈 **3** *v/i* (*of plane, bird*) pánxuán 盘旋

circuit *Elec* xiànlù 线路; (*lap*) quān 圈

circuit board xiànlù bǎn 线路板

circuit breaker duànlù kāiguān 断路开关

circular 1 *n* (*giving information*) tōngzhī 通知 **2** *adj* yuánxíng 圆形

circulate 1 *v/i* xúnhuán 循环 **2** *v/t* (*memo*) chuányuè 传阅

circulation BIO xúnhuán 循环; (*of newspaper, magazine*) xiāolù 销路

circumference yuánzhōu 圆周

circumstances qíngkuàng 情况; (*financial*) jīngjì qíngkuàng 经济情况; *under no ~* juébùnéng 决不能; *under the ~* zài zhèzhǒng qíng kuàng xià 在这种情况下

circus mǎxìtuán 马戏团

cistern shuǐxiāng 水箱

citizen gōngmín 公民

citizenship guójí 国籍

CITS (= *China International Travel Service*) Zhōngguó Guójì Lǚxíngshè 中国国际旅行社

city chéngshì 城市; *~ center* shì zhōngxīn 市中心; *~ hall* shìzhèng tīng 市政厅

civic *adj* chéngshì 城市; *pride, responsibilities* gōngmín 公民

civil (*as opposed to military*) mínjiān 民间; *disobedience etc* gōngmín 公民; (*polite*) yǒu lǐmào 有礼貌

civil engineer tǔmù gōngchéngshī 土木工程师

civilian 1 *n* píngmín 平民 **2** *adj clothes* biànzhuāng 便装

civilization wénmíng 文明

civilize *person* jiàodǎo 教导

civil rights gōngmín quán 公民权; **civil servant** gōngwùyuán 公务员; **civil service** xíngzhèng jīguān 行政机关; **civil war** nèizhàn 内战

claim 1 *n* (*request*) suǒpéi 索赔; (*right*) quánlì 权利; (*assertion*) zhǔzhāng 主张 **2** *v/t* (*ask for as a right*) suǒqǔ 索取; (*assert*) shēngchēng 声称; *lost property* lǐng 领; *they have ~ed responsibility for the attack* tāmén duì zhècì gōngjī biǎoshì fùzérèn 他们对这次攻击表示负责任

claimant shēnqǐng rén 申请人; LAW yuángào 原告

clam gélí 蛤蜊

♦**clam up** F sǐbù kāikǒu 死不开口

clammy *hands* niánhūhu 黏糊糊; *weather* mēnrè 闷热

clamor (*noise*) xuānhuáshēng 喧哗声; (*outcry*) hūshēng 呼声

♦**clamor for** chǎozheyào 吵着要

clamp 1 *n* (*fastener*) jiāzi 夹子 **2** *v/t*

(*fasten*) jiājǐn 夹紧

♦**clamp down** yāzhì 压制

♦**clamp down on** duì … jiāyǐ kòngzhì 对 … 加以控制

clan jiāzú 家族

clandestine mìmì 秘密

clang 1 *n* kēngqiāngshēng 铿锵声 **2** *v/i* kēngde yīshēng 铿地一声

clap 1 *v/i* (*applaud*) pāishǒu 拍手 **2** *v/t* pāi 拍

clarify chéngqīng 澄清

clarinet dānhuángguǎn 单簧管

clarity qīngxīdù 清晰度

clash 1 *n* chōngtú 冲突; (*of personalities*) bù xiétiáo 不协调 **2** *v/i* fāshēng chōngtū 发生冲突; (*of opinions*) bùyīzhì 不一致; ~ **with** … (*of events*) hé … fāshēng chōngtú 和 … 发生冲突; (*of colors*) hé … bù xiétiáo 和 … 不协调

clasp 1 *n* jiāzi 夹子 **2** *v/t* (*in hand*) jǐnwò 紧握

class 1 *n* (*lesson*) kè 课; (*group of people*) bān 班; (*category*) děngjí 等级; (*social* ~) jiēcéng 阶层 **2** *v/t* guīlèi 归类

classic 1 *adj* (*typical*) diǎnxíng 典型; (*definitive*) quánwēi xìng 权威性 **2** *n* jīngdiǎn zuòpǐn 经典作品

classical *music* gǔdiǎn 古典

classification (*act*) děngjí 等级; (*category*) fēnlèi 分类

classified *information* jīmì 机密

classified ad(**vertisement**) fēnlèi guǎnggào 分类广告

classify (*categorize*) fēnlèi 分类

classmate tóngxué 同学; **classroom** jiàoshì 教室; **class warfare** jiējí dòuzhēng 阶级斗争

classy F gāojí 高级

clatter 1 *n* huālā 哗啦 **2** *v/i* kuāngdāng kuāngdāng xiǎng 哐当哐当响

clause (*in agreement*) tiáokuǎn 条款; GRAM cóngjù 从句

claustrophobia yōubì kǒngbù zhèng 幽闭恐怖症

claw 1 *n* (*of lobster, crab*) qiánzi 钳子; (*of cat, woman*) zhuǎzi 爪子 **2** *v/t* (*scratch*) zhuā 抓

clay niántǔ 粘土

clean 1 *adj* gānjìng 干净 **2** *adv* F (*completely*) wánquán 完全 **3** *v/t* *teeth, shoes* shuā 刷; *house, room* dǎsǎo 打扫; *car, hands, face, clothes* xǐ 洗; **have … ~ed** bǎ … náqù xǐ 把 … 拿去洗

♦**clean out** *room, cupboard* dǎsǎo gānjìng 打扫干净; **clean X out** *fig* bǎ X shū guāng le 把 X 输光了

♦**clean up 1** *v/t* shōushí gānjìng 收拾干净 **2** *v/i* dǎsǎo 打扫; (*wash*) shūxǐ 梳洗; (*on stock market etc*) fācái 发财

cleaner (*person*) qīngjié gōng 清洁工; **dry ~** gānxǐ diàn 干洗店

cleaning woman qīngjié nǚgōng 清洁女工

cleanse (*skin*) qīngjié 清洁

cleanser (*for skin*) qīngjié jì 清洁剂

clear 1 *adj* *explanation, photograph, voice* qīngchu 清楚; (*obvious*) míngxiǎn 明显; *weather, sky* qínglǎng 晴朗; *water, eyes* qīngchè 清澈; *skin* guāngjié 光洁; *conscience* qīngbái 清白; **a ~ thinker** tóunǎo mǐnruì de rén 头脑敏锐的人; **I'm not ~ about it** wǒ bù dà míngbái 我不大明白; **I didn't make myself ~** wǒ méi jiǎng qīngchu 我没讲清楚 **2** *adv*: **stand ~ of** bùyào kàojìn 不要靠近; **steer ~ of** bǎochí jùlí 保持距离 **3** *v/t* *roads etc* qīngchú 清除; (*acquit*) chéngqīng 澄清; (*authorize*) yǔnxǔ 允许; (*earn*) zhèng 挣; **~ one's throat** qīng sǎngzi 清嗓子 **4** *v/i* (*of sky, mist*) qíngle 晴了; (*of face*) kāilǎng 开朗

♦**clear away** *v/t* shōushi 收拾

♦**clear off** *v/i* táopǎo 逃跑; ~**!** gǔnkāi! 滚开！

♦**clear out 1** *v/t* (*cupboard*) qīnglǐ 清理 **2** *v/i* táopǎo 逃跑

♦**clear up 1** *v/i* (*tidy up*) shōushi 收拾; (*of weather*) zhuǎnqíng 转晴; (*of illness, rash*) xiāoshī 消失 **2** *v/t* (*tidy*) shōushi 收拾; *mystery, problem* jiějué 解决

clearance (*space*) kōngjiān 空间; (*authorization*) xǔkě 许可

clearance sale qīngcāng dà pāimài 清仓大拍卖

clearly (*with clarity*) qīngchu 清楚; (*evidently*) míngxiǎn 明显

clemency réncí 仁慈

clench *teeth* yǎojǐn 咬紧; *fist* wòjǐn 握紧

clergy shénzhí rényuán 神职人员

clergyman mùshī 牧师

clerk (*administrative*) zhíyuán 职员; (*in store*) fúwùyuán 服务员

clever *person, animal, idea* cōngmíng 聪明; *gadget, device* qiǎomiào 巧妙

click 1 *n* COMPUT diǎnjī 点击 **2** *v/i* kādāshēngxiǎng 咔嗒声响

♦**click on** COMPUT àn 按

client gùkè 顾客

cliff xuányá 悬崖

climate qìhòu 气候; *economic ~* jīngjì qìhòu 经济气候

climax *n* gāocháo 高潮

climb 1 *n* (*up mountain*) pāndēng 攀登 **2** *v/t* pá 爬 **3** *v/i* (*in mountains etc*) pá 爬; *fig* (*inflation etc*) shàngshēng 上升

♦**climb down** pá xiàlái 爬下来; *fig* ràngbù 让步

climber (*person*) dēngshān zhě 登山者

clinch: *~ a deal* dáchéng jiāoyì 达成交易

cling (*of clothes*) tiēshēn 贴身

♦**cling to** (*of child*) zhānzhe 粘着; *ideas, tradition* gùshǒu 固守

clingfilm bǎoxiān zhǐ 保鲜纸

clingy *child, boyfriend* chánrén 缠人

clinic zhěnsuǒ 诊所

clinical línchuáng 临床

clink 1 *n* (*noise*) dīngdāngshēng 叮当声 **2** *v/i* dīngdāng zuòxiǎng 叮当作响

clip¹ 1 *n* (*fastener*) jiāzi 夹子 **2** *v/t* jiā 夹; *~ X to Y* bǎ X jiādào Y shàng 把 X 夹到 Y 上

clip² 1 *n* (*extract*) jiǎnjí 剪辑 **2** *v/t* *hair, hedge, grass* jiǎn 剪

clipboard xiězì jiábǎn 写字夹板;

COMPUT jiǎntiē bǎn 剪贴板

clippers (*for hair*) tuīzi 推子; (*for nails*) zhǐjiǎdāo 指甲刀; (*for gardening*) jiǎncǎo qián 剪草钳

clipping (*from newspaper*) jiǎnbào 剪报

cloak *n* dǒupeng 斗篷

clock zhōng 钟; (*speedometer*) jìchéng qì 记程器

clock radio shōuyīnjī nàozhōng 收音机闹钟

clockwise shùn shízhēn 顺时针

clockwork fātiáo 发条; *it went like ~* yíqiè shùnlì 一切顺利

♦**clog up 1** *v/i* dǔzhù 堵住 **2** *v/t* sāizhù 塞住

close¹ 1 *adj family, friend* qīnmì 亲密; *resemblance* xiāngjìn 相近 **2** *adv* jìn 近; *~ at hand* zài shēnbiān 在身边; *~ by* fùjìn 附近; *it's ~ to the stores* lí shāngdiàn jìn, hěn fāngbiàn 离商店近，很方便; *be ~ to X* (*as a friend etc*) hé X qīnjìn 和 X 亲近

close² 1 *v/t* guān 关; (*permanently: business*) guānbì 关闭 **2** *v/i* (*of door, store*) guānmén 关门; (*of window*) guān 关; (*of eyes*) bìshàng 闭上; (*of store: permanently*) guānbì 关闭

♦**close down** *v/t & v/i* guānbì 关闭

♦**close in** *v/i* pòjìn 迫近

♦**close up 1** *v/t building* fēngbì 封闭 **2** *v/i* (*move closer*) kàolǒng 靠拢

closed *store* guānmén 关门; *eyes* bìshàng 闭上

closed-circuit television bìlù diànshì 闭路电视

closely *listen, watch* zǐxì 仔细; *cooperate* mìqiè 密切

closet yīguì 衣柜

close-up tèxiě jìngtóu 特写镜头

closing time guānmén shíjiān 关门时间

closure guānbì 关闭

clot 1 *n* (*of blood*) xuèkuài 血块 **2** *v/i* (*of blood*) jiékuài 结块

cloth (*fabric*) bùliào 布料; (*for kitchen, cleaning*) mābù 抹布

clothes yīfu 衣服

clothes brush shuāzi 刷子
clothes hanger yījià 衣架
clothing yīfu 衣服
cloud n yún 云; **a ~ of smoke / dust** yízhèn yān / chéntǔ 一阵烟 / 尘土
♦cloud over (of sky) tiānyīnle 天阴了
cloudburst qīngpéndàyǔ 倾盆大雨
cloudy yīntiān 阴天
clout fig (influence) yǐngxiǎng 影响
clown (in circus) xiǎochǒu 小丑; (joker) chǒujiǎo 丑角; pej chǔncái 蠢材
club n (weapon) mùgùn 木棍; (golf iron) qiúgān 球杆; (organization) jùlèbù 俱乐部
clue xiànsuǒ 线索; **I haven't a ~** wǒ wánquán bù zhidào 我完全不知道
clued-up zàiháng 在行
clump n (of earth) tǔkuài 土块; (group) cuō 撮
clumsiness bènzhuō 笨拙
clumsy person bènshǒu bènjiǎo 笨手笨脚
cluster 1 n (of people) qún qún 群; (of houses) pái pái 排 2 v/i (of people) jùjí 聚集; (of houses) jízhōng 集中
clutch 1 n MOT líhéqì 离合器 2 v/t jǐnwò 紧握
♦clutch at shìtú zhuāzhù 试图抓住
Co. (= **Company**) gōngsī 公司
c / o (= **care of**) fánjiāo 烦交
coach 1 n (trainer) jiàoliàn 教练 2 v/t zhǐdǎo 指导
coagulate (of blood) níngjié 凝结
coal méi 煤
coalition liánméng 联盟
coal-mine méikuàng 煤矿
coarse fabric cūcāo 粗糙; hair cūyìng 粗硬; (vulgar) cūsú 粗俗
coast n hǎibiān 海边; **at the ~** zài hǎibiān 在海边
coastal línhǎi 临海
coastguard hǎi'àn jǐngwèi duì 海岸警卫队; (person) hǎi'àn jǐngwèi 海岸警卫
coastline hǎi'àn xiàn 海岸线

coat 1 n wàiyī 外衣; (over~) dàyī 大衣; (of animal) máopí 毛皮; (of paint etc) céng 层 2 v/t (cover) jiāshàng yīcéng 加上一层
coathanger yījià 衣架
coating céng 层
coax hǒng 哄
cobweb zhīzhūwǎng 蜘蛛网
cocaine kěkǎyīn 可卡因
cock n (chicken) gōngjī 公鸡; (any male bird) gōngniǎo 公鸟
cockeyed idea etc huāngmiù 荒谬
cockpit (of plane) zuòcāng 座舱
cockroach zhāngláng 蟑螂
cocktail jīwěijiǔ 鸡尾酒
cocoa (plant) kěkě shù 可可树; (drink) kěkě 可可
coconut (to eat) yēzi 椰子
coconut milk yēzi nǎi 椰子奶
coconut palm yēzi shù 椰子树
COD (= **collect on delivery**) huòdào fùkuǎn 货到付款
coddle sick person zhàoliào 照料; child jiāoshēng guànyǎng 娇生惯养
code n mìmǎ 密码
co-educational nánnǚ héxiào 男女合校
coerce qiǎngpò 强迫
coexist gòngcún 共存
coexistence gòngchǔ 共处
coffee kāfēi 咖啡
coffee break xiǎoxī 小息; coffee maker kāfēi jī 咖啡机; coffee pot kāfēi hú 咖啡壶; coffee shop kāfēi diàn 咖啡店; coffee table chájī 茶几
coffin guāncai 棺材
cog lúnchǐ 轮齿
cognac báilándì 白兰地
cogwheel qiàn chǐlún 嵌齿轮
cohabit tóngjū 同居
coherent liánguàn 连贯
coil 1 n (of rope) juǎn 卷 2 v/t juǎn 卷; **~ (up)** juǎn qǐlái 卷起来
coin n yìngbì 硬币
coincide qiǎohé 巧合
coincidence qiǎohé 巧合
coke F (cocaine) kěkǎyīn 可卡因
Coke® kěkǒu kělè 可口可乐
cold 1 adj lěng 冷; **I'm (feeling) ~**

wǒ juéde hěnlěng 我觉得很冷;
***it's ~** tiānqì hěnlěng 天气很冷;
in ~ blood lěngkù 冷酷; **get ~
feet** dǎ tuìtánggǔ 打退堂鼓 **2** *n*
hánlěng 寒冷; *I have a ~* wǒ
gǎnmàole 我感冒了
cold boiled water liáng kāishuǐ
凉开水; **cold-blooded** lěngxuè 冷
血; *fig* lěngkù 冷酷; **cold cuts**
lěngpán 冷盘; **cold noodles**
lěngmiàn 冷面; **cold sore**
zuǐbiān pàozhěn 嘴边疱疹
coleslaw (*northern China*) liángbàn
yángbáicài 凉拌洋白菜;
(*southern China*) liángbàn
juǎnxīncài 凉拌卷心菜
colic jiǎotòng 绞痛
collaborate (*in research, etc*) hézuò
合作; (*with enemy*) gōujié 勾结
collaboration hézuò 合作; (*with
enemy*) gōujié 勾结
collaborator hézuò zhě 合作者;
(*with enemy*) gōujié zhě 勾结者
collapse dǎotā 倒塌; (*of person*)
bēngkuì 崩溃
collapsible zhédié 折迭
collar lǐngzi 领子; (*for dog, cat*)
xiàngquān 项圈
collarbone suǒgǔ 锁骨
colleague tóngshì 同事
collect 1 *v/t person* jiē 接; *tickets,
cleaning etc* ná 拿; (*gather, as
hobby*) shōují 收集 **2** *v/i* (*gather
together*) jízhōng 集中 **3** *adv*: *call
~* shòuhuàrén fùfèi 受话人付费
collect call shòuhuàrén fùfèi 受话
人付费
collected *works, poems etc* quánjí
全集; *person* zhènjìng 镇静
collection (*of art*) shōucángpǐn 收
藏品; (*fashions*) shízhuāng
zhǎnlǎn 时装展览; (*in church*)
mùjuān 募捐
collective 1 *adj* gòngtóng 共同;
POL jítǐ 集体 **2** *n* POL jítǐ 集体
collective bargaining jítǐ xiédìng
集体协定
collector shōucáng jiā 收藏家
college xuéyuàn 学院
college exam ⇩ gāokǎo 高考
collide pèngzhuàng 碰撞

collision xiāngzhuàng 相撞
colloquial kǒuyǔ 口语
colon (*punctuation*) màohào 冒号;
ANAT jiécháng 结肠
colonel shàngxiào 上校
colonial *adj* zhímíndì 殖民地
colonize *country* kāituò zhímíndì
开拓殖民地
colony zhímíndì 殖民地
color 1 *n* yánsè 颜色; (*in cheeks*)
liǎnsè 脸色; *in ~* (*movie etc*) cǎisè
彩色; *~s* MIL jūnqí 军旗 **2** *v/t
one's hair* rǎnsè 染色 **3** *v/i* (*blush*)
liǎnhóng 脸红
color-blind sèmáng 色盲
colored *adj person* hēi 黑
color fast bú tuìsè 不褪色
colorful xiānyàn 鲜艳; *account*
jīngcǎi 精彩
coloring yánsè 颜色; (*of the skin*)
fūsè 肤色
color photograph cǎicè zhàopiàn
彩色照片; **color scheme** sècǎi
shèjì 色彩设计; **color TV** cǎisè
diànshì 彩色电视
colt xióngjū 雄驹
column liè 列; (*architectural*)
yuánzhù 圆柱; (*of text*) lán 栏;
(*newspaper feature*) zhuānlán 专栏
columnist zhuānlán zuòjiā 专栏
作家
coma hūnmí 昏迷
comb 1 *n* shūzi 梳子 **2** *v/t* shū 梳;
area sōuxún 搜寻
combat 1 *n* zhàndòu 战斗 **2** *v/t* yǔ
... zuò dòuzhēng 与 ... 做斗争
combination zǔhé 组合; (*of safe*)
mìmǎ 密码
combine 1 *v/t ingredients* hùnhé 混
合; *~ X with Y* jiāngù X hé Y 兼
顾 X 和 Y **2** *v/i* (*of chemical
elements*) huàhé 化合
combine harvester liánhé
shōugējī 联合收割机
combustible yìrán 易燃
combustion ránshāo 燃烧
come (*toward speaker*) lái 来;
(*toward listener*) qù 去; (*of train,
bus*) láile 来了; *don't ~ too close*
bié tài kàojìn 别太靠近; *in the
years to ~* zài jīnhòu jǐnián 在今

后几年; **how ~?** F zěnme? 怎
么？

♦ **come about** (*happen*) fāshēng 发
生

♦ **come across 1** *v/t items* wúyì
zhōng fāxiàn 无意中发现；
person wúyì zhōng yùdào 无意中
遇到 **2** *v/i*: **it didn't ~** (*of idea,
humor*) méi rén míngbái 没人明
白; **she comes across as …** tā
sìhū shì … 她似乎是 …

♦ **come along** (*come too*) yīdàolái
一道来; (*turn up*) láidào 来到;
(*progress*) jìnzhǎn 进展

♦ **come apart** kě chāizhuāng 可拆
装; (*break*) suìle 碎了

♦ **come around** (*to s.o.'s home*) lái
来; (*regain consciousness*) sūxǐng
苏醒

♦ **come away** (*leave*) líkāi 离开;
(*of button etc*) diàole 掉了

♦ **come back** huílái 回来; **it came
back to me** wǒ xiǎng qǐláile 我想
起来了

♦ **come by 1** *v/i* bàifǎng 拜访 **2** *v/t*
(*acquire*) dédào 得到

♦ **come down** xià lái 下来; (*in
price, amount etc*) xiàjiàng 下降;
(*of rain, snow*) xià 下; **he came
down the stairs** tā zǒuxià lóutī 他
走下楼梯

♦ **come for** (*attack*) gōngjí 攻击;
(*collect: thing*) láiqǔ 来取; (*collect:
person*) láijiē 来接

♦ **come forward** (*present oneself*)
tǐngshēn érchū 挺身而出

♦ **come from** láizì 来自

♦ **come in** zǒu jìnlái 走进来; (*of
train*) dàodá 到达; (*of tide*) zhǎngcháo 涨潮; **~!** qǐngjìn! 请进！;
the horse came in fourth nà mǎ
pǎole dìsì 那马跑了第四

♦ **come in for**: **~ criticism** shòudào
pīpíng 受到批评

♦ **come in on**: **~ a deal** jiārù jiāoyì
加入交易

♦ **come off** (*of handle etc*) tuōluò 脱
落

♦ **come on** (*progress*) jìnzhǎn 进
展; **~!** kuàidiǎnr! 快点儿！; (*in
disbelief*) bùkěnéng 不可能

♦ **come out** (*of person*) chū 出; (*of
sun, results, product*) chūlái 出来;
(*of stain*) xiāoshī 消失; (*of book,
record*) fāxíng 发行

♦ **come to 1** *v/t place* dàodá 到达;
(*of hair, dress, water*) dádào 达到;
that comes to $70 zǒnggòng qīshí
měiyuán 总共七十美元 **2** *v/i*
(*regain consciousness*) sūxǐng 苏醒

♦ **come up** shàngqù 上去; (*of sun*)
shēng qǐlái 升起来; **something
has ~** yǒushì fāshēng 有事发生

♦ **come up with** *new idea etc* xiǎng
qǐlái 想起来

comeback: **make a ~** dōngshān
zàiqǐ 东山再起

comedian xǐjù yǎnyuán 喜剧演
员; *pej* chǒujiǎo 丑角

comedown luòpò 落泊

comedy xǐjù 喜剧

comet huìxīng 彗星

comeuppance: **he'll get his ~** tā
huì dédào bàoyìng 他会得到报
应

comfort 1 *n* xiǎngshòu 享受;
(*consolation*) ānwèi 安慰 **2** *v/t*
ānwèi 安慰

comfortable *chair, house, room*
shūfu 舒服; **be ~** (*of person*) shūfu
舒服; (*financially*) fùyù 富裕

comic 1 *n* (*to read*) mànhuà 漫画
2 *adj* yǒuqù 有趣

comical huájī 滑稽

comic book mànhuà shū 漫画书

comics liánhuán mànhuà 连环漫
画

comma dòuhào 逗号

command 1 *n* mìnglìng 命令 **2** *v/t*
mìnglìng 命令

commander zhǐhuīguān 指挥官

commander-in-chief zǒngsīlìng
总司令

commemorate jìniàn 纪念

commemoration: **in ~ of …** jìniàn
… 纪念 …

commence *v/t & v/i* kāishǐ 开始

comment 1 *n* yìjiàn 意见; **no ~**
wúkě fènggào 无可奉告 **2** *v/i*
fābiǎo yìjiàn 发表意见

commentary pínglùn 评论

commentator pínglùn jiā 评论家

commerce shāngyè 商业

commercial 1 *adj* shāngyè 商业 **2** *n* (*ad*) guǎnggào 广告

commercial break guǎnggào 广告

commercialize *v/t* shāngyè huà 商业化

commercial traveler lǚxíng tuīxiāo yuán 旅行推销员

commiserate tóngqíng 同情

commission 1 *n* (*payment*) yòngjīn 佣金; (*job*) chēngbāo 承包; (*committee*) wěiyuánhuì 委员会 **2** *v/t* (*for a job*) wěituō 委托

commit *money* chéngnuò 承诺; **~ a crime** fànzuì 犯罪; **~ oneself** tóurù 投入

commitment zérèn 责任

committee wěiyuánhuì 委员会

commodity shāngpǐn 商品

common (*not rare*) píngcháng 平常; (*shared*) gòngtóng 共同; **in ~** gòngtóng zhīchù 共同之处; **have something in ~ with X** hé X yǒu gòngtóng zhīchù 和 X 有共同之处

common law wife tóngjū qīzi 同居妻子; **commonplace** *adj* píngyōng 平庸; **common sense** chángshì 常识

commotion sāodòng 搔动

communal gōngyòng 公用

commune gōngshè 公社

communicate 1 *v/i* (*have contact, make self understood*) gōutōng 沟通 **2** *v/t* zhuǎndá 转达

communication gōutōng 沟通

communications tōngxùn yè 通讯业

communications satellite tōngxùn wèixīng 通讯卫星

communicative *person* ài shuōhuà 爱说话

Communism Gòngchǎnzhǔyì 共产主义

Communist 1 *adj* Gòngchǎnzhǔyì 共产主义 **2** *n* Gòngchǎndǎngyuán 共产党员

Communist China Zhōnggòng 中共

Communist Party Gòngchǎndǎng 共产党

community shèqū 社区

commute 1 *v/i* (*to work*) chéngchē shàngbān 乘车上班; **he ~s to work in Tianjin** tā chéngchē qù Tiānjīn shàngbān 他乘车去天津上班 **2** *v/t* LAW jiǎnxíng 减刑

commuter chéngchē shàngbān zhě 乘车上班者; **the trains are packed with ~s** huǒchē jǐmǎnle chéngchē shàngbān zhě 火车挤满了乘车上班者

commuter traffic shàngxiàbān jiāotōng 上下班交通

commuter train shàngxià bān huǒchē 上下班火车

compact 1 *adj* xiùzhēn 袖珍 **2** *n* MOT xiǎoxíng kèchē 小型客车

compact disc MUS jīguāng chàngpiān 激光唱片; COMPUT guāngpán 光盘

companion bànlǚ 伴侣

companionship péibàn 陪伴

company COM gōngsī 公司; (*companionship*) péibàn 陪伴; (*guests*) kèrén 客人

company car gōngsī chē 公司车

company law gōngsī fǎ 公司法

comparable (*which can be compared*) kě bǐjiào 可比较; (*similar*) lèisì 类似

comparative 1 *adj* (*relative*) xiāngduì 相对; *study* bǐjiào 比较; **~ form** GRAM bǐjiào jí 比较级 **2** *n* GRAM bǐjiào jí 比较级

comparatively xiāngduì éryán 相对而言

compare 1 *v/t* bǐjiào 比较; **~ X with Y** jiāng X yǔ Y xiāng bǐjiào 将X与Y相比较; **~d with X** yǔ X xiāngbǐ 与X相比 **2** *v/i* bǐjiào 比较

comparison bǐjiào 比较; **there's no ~** méidebǐ 没的比

compartment (*cupboard*) chúguì 橱柜; (*for credit cards etc*) jiácéng 夹层

compass luópán yí 罗盘仪; (*pair of*) **~es** yuánguī 园规

compassion tóngqíng 同情

compassionate yǒu tóngqíng xīn

有同情心

compatibility fúhé xìng 符合性

compatible *people* hédelái 合得来; *blood types, life styles* fúhé 符合; COMPUT xiāngróng 相容; **we're not ~** wǒmén hébùlái 我们合不来

compel (*force*) qiǎngpò 强迫; *I felt ~led to …* wǒ bùdebù … 我不得不 …

compelling *argument* lìngrén xìnfú 令人信服; *movie, book* yǐnrén rùshèng 引人入胜

compensate 1 *v/t* (*with money*) péicháng 赔偿 **2** *v/i*: **~ for** bǔcháng 补偿

compensation (*money*) péicháng 赔偿; (*reward*) hǎochù 好处; (*comfort*) ānwèi 安慰

compete jìngzhēng 竞争; (*take part*) cānjiā 参加; **~ for** zhēngduó 争夺

competence, competency nénglì 能力

competent *person* chèngzhí 称职; *work* hégé 合格; **I'm not ~ to judge** wǒ bùgòu zīgé qù pànduàn 我不够资格去判断

competition (*contest, competing*) jìngzhēng 竞争; SP bǐsài 比赛; (*competitors*) duìshǒu 对手; **the government wants to encourage ~** zhèngfǔ yào gǔlì jìngzhēng 政府要鼓励竞争

competitive (*able to compete: price, offer*) yǒu jìngzhēng lì 有竞争力; (*liking to compete*) hào jìngzhēng 好竞争; *profession, sport* jìngzhēnglì hěnqiáng 竞争力很强

competitor (*in contest*) bǐsài zhě 比赛者; COM jìngzhēng duìshǒu 竞争对手

compile biānzhì 编制

complacency zìmǎn 自满

complacent zhānzhan zìxǐ 沾沾自喜

complain *v/i* bàoyuàn 抱怨; (*to store, manager*) tóusù 投诉; **~ of** MED zhǔsù 主诉; **~ about X** bàoyuàn X 抱怨 X

complaint tóusù 投诉; MED jíbìng 疾病

complement *v/t* xiāngpèi 相配; **they ~ each other** tāmen hěn xiāngchèn 他们很相衬

complementary hùwéi bǔchōng 互为补充

complete 1 *adj* (*total*) shízú 十足; (*full*) wánzhěng 完整; (*finished*) wángōng 完工 **2** *v/t building, course, task etc* wánchéng 完成; *form* tiánxiě 填写

completely wánquán 完全

completion wánchéng 完成

complex 1 *adj* fùzá 复杂 **2** *n* PSYCH bìngtài kǒngjù 病态恐惧; (*of buildings*) zhōngxīn 中心

complexion (*facial*) miànsè 面色

compliance zūncóng 遵从

complicate shǐ fùzá huà 使复杂化

complicated fùzá 复杂

complication kùnnan 困难; **~s** MED bìngfā zhèng 并发症

compliment 1 *n* zànměi 赞美 **2** *v/t* zànměi 赞美

complimentary *speech* zànměi 赞美; (*free*) miǎnfèi 免费; (*in restaurant, hotel*) zèngsòng 赠送; **be very ~ about** jíkǒu chēngzàn 极口称赞

compliments slip biàntiáo 便条

comply fúcóng 服从; **~ with …** zūnshǒu … 遵守 …

component bùfèn 部分

compose *v/t* zǔchéng 组成; MUS chuàngzuò 创作; **be ~d of X** yóu X zǔchéng 由 X 组成; **~ oneself** shǐ zìjǐ píngjìng xiàlái 使自己平静下来

composed (*calm*) píngjìng 平静

composer MUS zuòqǔ jiā 作曲家

composition (*make-up*) zǔchéng chéngfèn 组成成分; MUS zuòpǐn 作品; (*essay*) zuòwén 作文

composure zhènjìng 镇静

compound *n* CHEM huàhé wù 化合物

compound interest fùlì 复利

comprehend (*understand*) lǐjiě 理解

comprehension lǐjiě 理解

comprehensive zōnghé xìng 综合性

comprehensive insurance zǒngkuò bǎoxiǎn 总括保险

compress 1 *n* MED fūbù 敷布 **2** *v/t air, gas, information* yāsuō 压缩

comprise (*consist of*) bāohán 包含; (*make up*) gòuchéng 构成; **be ~d of ...** yóu ... zǔchéng 由 ... 组成

compromise 1 *n* tuǒxié 妥协 **2** *v/i* tuǒxié 妥协 **3** *v/t principles* fàngqì 放弃; *reputation etc* sǔnhài 损害; **~ oneself** liánlèi zìjǐ 连累自己

compulsion PSYCH qiángpò xìng shénjīng zhì 强迫性神经质

compulsive *behavior* bùyóu zìzhǔ 不由自主; *reading* yùbà bùnéng 欲罢不能

compulsory yìwù 义务; *class* bìxiū 必修; **~ education** yìwù jiàoyù 义务教育

computer diànnǎo 电脑; **it's on ~** zài diànnǎo shang 在电脑上

computer-controlled diànnǎo kòngzhì 电脑控制

computer game diànzǐ yóuxì 电子游戏

computerize diànnǎo huà 电脑化

computer literate huìyòng diànnǎo 会用电脑; **computer science** jìsuànjī kēxué 计算机科学; **computer scientist** jìsuànjī kēxué jiā 计算机科学家

computing diànnǎo shǐyòng 电脑使用

comrade (*friend*) péngyou 朋友; POL tóngzhì 同志

comradeship yǒuyì 友谊

con F **1** *n* piànjú 骗局 **2** *v/t* piàn 骗

conceal *fact, truth etc* yǐnmán 隐瞒; *object* yǐncáng 隐藏

concede *v/t* (*admit*) chéngrèn 承认

conceit zìfù 自负

conceited zìgāo zìdà 自高自大

conceivable kě xiǎngxiàng 可想象

conceive *v/i* (*of woman*) huáiyùn 怀孕; **~ of** (*imagine*) shèxiǎng 设想

concentrate 1 *v/i* (*on task*) jízhōng jīnglì 集中精力 **2** *v/t one's attention, energies* jízhōng 集中

concentrated *juice etc* nóngsuō 浓缩

concentration zhuānxīn 专心

concept gàiniàn 概念

conception (*of child*) huáiyùn 怀孕

concern 1 *n* (*anxiety*) dānyōu 担忧; (*care*) guānxīn 关心; (*business*) shìwù 事务; (*company*) gōngsī 公司 **2** *v/t* (*involve*) shèjí 涉及; (*worry*) dānyōu 担忧; **~ oneself with** guǎn 管

concerned (*anxious*) gǎndào bù ān 感到不安; (*caring*) guānxīn 关心; (*involved*) yǒuguān 有关; **as far as I'm ~** jiù wǒ ér yán 就我而言

concerning *prep* yǒuguān 有关

concert yīnyuè huì 音乐会

concerted (*joint*) liánhé 联合

concertmaster shǒuxí xiǎo tíqín yǎnzòu zhě 首席小提琴演奏者

concerto xiézòu qǔ 协奏曲

concession (*giving in*) ràngbù 让步

conciliatory ānfǔ 安抚

concise jiǎnmíng 简明

conclude 1 *v/t* (*deduce*) tuīduàn chū 推断出; (*end*) jiéshù 结束; **~ X from Y** yóu Y tuīduàn chū X 由 Y 推断出 X **2** *v/i* jiéshù 结束

conclusion (*deduction*) jiélùn 结论; (*end*) jiéwěi 结尾; **in ~** zuìhòu 最后

conclusive juédìng xìng 决定性

concoct *meal, drink* tiáozhì 调制; *excuse, story* biānzào 编造

concoction (*food, drink*) tiáozhì pǐn 调制品

concrete[1] *adj* (*not abstract*) jùtǐ 具体

concrete[2] *n* hùnníngtǔ 混凝土

concubine qiè 妾

concur *v/i* tóngyì 同意

concussion zhèndàng 震荡

condemn *action* qiǎnzé 谴责; *building* xuāngào ... bù shìyú jūzhù 宣告 … 不 适 于 居 住; (*doom*) zhùdìng 注定; **~ to death** pàn sǐxíng 判死刑

condemnation (*of action*) qiǎnzé 谴责

condensation (*on walls, windows*) lěngníng wù 冷凝物

condense 1 v/t (*make shorter*) yāsuō 压缩 **2** v/i (*of steam*) shǐ lěngníng 使冷凝

condensed milk liànrǔ 炼乳

condescend: he ~ed to speak to me tā fàngxià jiàzi hé wǒ jiǎnghuà 他放下架子和我讲话

condescending (*patronizing*) bào cì'ēn tàidù 抱赐恩态度

condition 1 n (*state, of health*) zhuàngtài 状态; MED bìng 病; (*requirement, term*) tiáojiàn 条件; **~s** (*circumstances*) tiáojiàn 条件; **on ~ that …** zhǐyào … 只要 … **2** v/t PSYCH shǐ xíngchéng tiáojiàn fǎnshè 使形成条件反射

conditional 1 adj acceptance yǒu tiáojiàn 有条件; **~ on …** shì … érdìng 视 … 而定 **2** n GRAM tiáojiàn 条件

conditioner (*for hair*) hùfà jì 护发剂; (*for fabric*) qiānwēi bǎohù jì 纤维保护剂

conditioning PSYCH tiáojiàn fǎnshè 条件反射

condo → **condominium**

condolences diàoyàn 吊唁

condom ⇩ bìyùn tào 避孕套

condominium = gòngxiáng gōnggòng shèshī de gōngyù 共享公共设施的公寓

condone actions kuānróng 宽容

conducive: ~ to yǒu zhùyú 有助于

conduct 1 n (*behavior*) jǔzhǐ 举止 **2** v/t (*carry out*) shíshī 实施; ELEC chuándǎo 传导; MUS zhǐhuī 指挥; **~ oneself** biǎoxiàn 表现

conducted tour dǎoyóu lǚyóu 导游旅游

conductor MUS zhǐhuī jiā 指挥家; (*on train*) lièchē zhǎng 列车长

cone (*in geometry*) yuánzhuī tǐ 圆锥体; (*of pine tree*) sōngtǎ 松塔;

(*on highway*) zhuīxíng lùbiāo 锥性路标; **an ice-cream ~** dànjuǎn bīngqílín 蛋卷冰淇淋

confectioner tiánpǐn shāng 甜品商

confectioners' sugar tángfěn 糖粉

confectionery (*candy*) tiánshí 甜食

confederation tóngméng 同盟

confer 1 v/t (*bestow*) shòuyǔ 授予 **2** v/i (*discuss*) jiāohuàn yìjiàn 交换意见

conference tǎolùn huì 讨论会

conference room huìyì tīng 会议厅

confess 1 v/t sin, guilt chéngrèn 承认; crime tǎnbái 坦白; REL chàn-huǐ 忏悔; **I – I don't know** wǒ chéngrèn wǒ bù zhīdào 我承认我不知道 **2** v/i chéngrèn 承认; (*to priest*) chànhuǐ 忏悔; (*to police*) tǎnbái 坦白; **~ to a weakness for X** chéngrèn xǐ'ài X 承认喜爱 X

confession gòngrèn 供认; (*to police*) rènzuì shū 认罪书; REL chànhuǐ 忏悔

confessional REL gàojiě shì 告解室

confessor REL gàojiě shénfù 告解神父

confide 1 v/t tùlù 吐露 **2** v/i: **~ in …** (*trust*) xìnrèn … 信任 …

confidence (*assurance*) xìnxīn 信心; (*trust, secret*) xìnrèn 信任; **in ~** zuòwéi mìmì 作为秘密

confident (*self-assured*) zìxìn 自信; (*convinced*) kěndìng 肯定

confidential jīmì 机密

confine (*imprison*) jiānjìn 监禁; (*restrict*) júxiàn yú 局限于; **be ~d to one's bed** wòbìng zàichuáng 卧病在床

confined space xiázhǎi 狭窄

confinement (*imprisonment*) jiānjìn 监禁; MED fēnmiǎn 分娩

confirm v/t quèdìng 确定; theory, statement, fears zhèngshí 证实

confirmation zhèngmíng 证明; (*of theory statement, fears*) zhèngshí 证实

confirmed (*inveterate*) jiāndìng 坚定

confiscate mòshōu 没收

conflict 1 n (*disagreement*) zhēngyì 争议; (*clash*) chōngtū 冲突; (*war*) zhànzhēng 战争 2 v/i (*clash*) chōngtū 冲突

conform zūnshǒu guīzhāng 遵守规章; (*of product*) fúhé 符合; ~ *to government standards* fúhé zhèngfǔ biāozhǔn 符合政府标准

conformist n shùncóng de rén 顺从的人

confront (*face*) miànduì 面对; (*tackle*) shǐ duìzhì 使对质

confrontation chōngtū 冲突

Confucianism Rújiā 儒家

Confucius Kǒngzǐ 孔子

confuse hùnxiáo 混淆; ~ *X with Y* bǎ X dāngchéng Y 把 X 当成 Y

confused kùnhuò 困惑

confusing lìngrén hútú 令人糊涂

confusion (*muddle, chaos*) hùnxiáo 混淆

congeal (*of blood, fat*) nínggù 凝固

congenial (*pleasant*) lìngrén yúkuài 令人愉快; *a ~ host* hàokè de zhǔrén 好客的主人

congenital MED xiāntiān xìng 先天性

congested *roads* dǔsè 堵塞

congestion (*on roads*) dǔsè 堵塞; (*in chest*) chōngxuè 充血; *traffic ~* jiāotōng dǔsè 交通堵塞

congratulate zhùhè 祝贺

congratulations zhùhè 祝贺; ~ *on ...* zhùhè ... 祝贺 ...

congregate (*gather*) jùjí 聚集

congregation REL jiàotáng jíhuì 教堂集会

congress (*conference*) dàibiǎo dàhuì 代表大会; *Congress* (*of US*) Guóhuì 国会

Congressional Guóhuì 国会

Congressman Guóhuì yìyuán 国会议员

conifer zhēnyè shù 针叶树

conjecture n (*speculation*) cāicè 猜测

conjugate v/t GRAM lièjǔ cíxíng biànhuà 列举词形变化

conjunction GRAM liánjiē cí 连接词; *in ~ with* liántóng 连同

conjunctivitis jiémó yán 结膜炎

♦ conjure up (*produce*) biàn móshù bān biànchū 变魔术般变出; (*evoke*) lìngrén xiǎngqǐ 令人想起

conjurer, conjuror (*magician*) móshù shī 魔术师

conjuring tricks móshù 魔术

con man piànzi 骗子

connect (*join*) liánjiē 连接; TELEC jiētōng 接通; (*link*) yǒu guānxi 有关系; (*to power supply*) jiētōng diànlù 接通电路

connected: *be well-~* duō guànxi hù 多关系户; *be ~ with ...* yǔ ... yǒu guānxi 与 ... 有关系

connecting flight ⇩ liányùn fēijī 联运飞机

connection (*in wiring*) liánjiē 连接; (*link, personal contact*) guānxi 关系; (*when traveling*) liányùn 联运; *in ~ with ...* yǔ ... yǒuguānxi 与 ... 有关系

connector COMPUT liánjiē qì 连接器

connoisseur hángjia 行家

conquer zhēngfú 征服; *fig* (*fear etc*) zhànshèng 战胜

conqueror zhēngfú zhě 征服者

conquest (*of territory*) zhēngfú 征服

conscience liángxīn 良心; *a guilty ~* nèijiù 内疚; *it has been on my ~* wǒ yīzhí gǎndào nèijiù 我一直感到内疚

conscientious rènzhēn 认真

conscientious objector jù fú bīngyì zhě 拒服兵役者

conscious *adj* (*aware*) zìjué 自觉; (*deliberate*) yǒuyì 有意; MED qīngxǐng 清醒; *be ~ of ...* yìshí dào ... 意识到 ...

consciousness (*awareness*) yìshí 意识; MED zhījué 知觉; *lose / regain ~* shīqù / huīfù zhījué 失去 / 恢复知觉

consecutive liánxù 连续

consensus yīzhì yìjiàn 一致意见

consent 1 n zànxǔ 赞许 2 v/i tóngyì 同意

consequence (result) hòuguǒ 后果

consequently (therefore) suǒyǐ 所以

conservation (preservation) bǎohù 保护

conservationist n tíchàng fánghù zhě 提倡防护者

conservative adj (conventional), estimate bǎoshǒu 保守; clothes lǎoqì 老气

conservatory (for plants) nuǎnfáng 暖房; MUS yīnyuè xuéyuàn 音乐学院

conserve 1 n (jelly) guǒjiàng 果酱 2 v/t energy, strength bǎocún 保存

consider (regard) rènwéi 认为; (show regard for, think about) kǎolǜ 考虑; it is ~ed to be ... zhòngsuǒ zhōuzhī ... 众所周知 ...

considerable xiāngdāng dà 相当大

considerably zài hěndà chéngdù shàng 在很大程度上

considerate tǐtiē 体贴

consideration (thought) kǎolǜ 考虑; (thoughtfulness, concern) guānxīn 关心; (factor) yào kǎolǜ de shì 要考虑的事; take X into ~ kǎolǜ X 考虑 X

consignment COM huòwù 货物

♦consist of bāokuò 包括

consistency (texture) niánchóu dù 黏稠度; (unchangingness) yīzhì xìng 一致性

consistent (unchanging) yīguàn 一贯

consolation ānwèi 安慰

console v/t ānwèi 安慰

consonant n GRAM fǔyīn 辅音

consortium hézǔ 合组

conspicuous xiǎnyǎn 显眼

conspiracy yīnmóu 阴谋

conspire mìmóu 密谋

constant (continuous) bùduàn 不断

consternation jīngkǒng 惊恐

constipated biànmì 便秘

constipation biànmì 便秘

constituent n (component) zǔfèn 组分

constitute (account for) zhàn 占; (represent) gòuchéng 构成

constitution POL xiànfǎ 宪法; (of person) tǐzhì 体质

constitutional adj POL xiànfǎ 宪法

constraint (restriction) xiànzhì 限制

construct v/t building etc jiànzào 建造

construction (of building etc) jiànzào 建造; (building, trade etc) jiànzhù 建筑; under ~ zài jiànzào zhōng 在建造中

construction industry jiànzhù yè 建筑业; construction site shīgōng gōngdì 施工工地; construction worker jiànzhù gōngrén 建筑工人

constructive yǒu jiànshè xìng 有建设性

consul lǐngshì 领事

consulate lǐngshì guǎn 领事馆

consult (seek the advice of) hé ... shāngliàng 和 ... 商量

consultancy (company) zīxún gōngsī 咨询公司; (advice) zīxún 咨询

consultant (adviser) gùwèn 顾问

consultation cuōshāng 磋商

consume (eat, drink) shíyòng 食用; (use) hàoyòng 耗用

consumer (purchaser) gùke 顾客

consumer confidence gùke xìnxīn 顾客信心; consumer goods xiāofèi pǐn 消费品; consumer society xiāofèi zhě shèhuì 消费者社会

consumption (of energy) xiāohào 消耗; (quantity used) xiāohào liàng 消耗量

contact 1 n (person) shóurén 熟人; (communication, physical) jiēchù 接触; keep in ~ with X yǔ X bǎochí liánluò 与 X 保持联络 2 v/t liánluò 联络

contact lens yǐnxíng yǎnjìng 隐形眼镜

contact number liánxì diànhuà 联

系电话

contagious chuánrǎn 传染; *fig* mànyán 蔓延

contain *tears, laughter* kòngzhì 控制; *it ~ed my camera* wǒde zhàoxiàngjī zài lǐmiàn 我的照像机在里面; *~ oneself* kòngzhì zìjǐ 控制自己

container (*recipient*) róngqì 容器; COM ⇩ jízhuāng xiāng 集装箱

container ship ⇩ jízhuāng xiāng chuán 集装箱船

contaminate wūrǎn 污染

contamination wūrǎn 污染

contemplate *v/t* (*look at*) zhùshì 注视; (*think about*) sīkǎo 思考

contemporary 1 *adj* dāngdài 当代 **2** *n* tóngdài rén 同代人; (*at school*) tóngjiè 同届

contempt qīngmiè 轻蔑; *be beneath ~* bùzhí yīgù 不值一顾

contemptible bēiliè 卑劣

contemptuous biǎoshì qīngmiè 表示轻蔑

contend: *~ for ...* jìngzhēng ... 竞争 ...; *~ with ...* yìngfu ... 应付 ...

contender (*in sport, competition*) jìngzhēng zhě 竞争者; (*against champion*) zhēngduó zhě 争夺者; POL jìngxuǎn rén 竞选人

content[1] *n* nèiróng 内容

content[2] **1** *adj* mǎnzú 满足 **2** *v/t*: *~ oneself with ...* mǎnzú yú ... 满足于 ...

contented mǎnzú 满足

contention (*assertion*) lùndiǎn 论点; *be in ~ for ...* zhēngduó ... 争夺 ...

contentment mǎnzú 满足

contents (*of house, letter, bag etc*) nèiróng 内容

contest[1] (*competition*) bǐsài 比赛; (*struggle, for power*) zhēngduó 争夺

contest[2] *v/t leadership etc* jìngzhēng 竞争; (*oppose*) duì ... tíchū zhìyí 对 ... 提出质疑

contestant cānsài zhě 参赛者

context shàngxià wén 上下文; *look at X in* ~ gēnjù jùtǐ huánjìng lái kǎolǜ X 根据具体环境来考

虑 X; *look at X out of* ~ tuōlí jùtǐ huánjìng lái kǎolǜ X 脱离具体环境来考虑 X

continent *n* dàlù 大陆

contingency bùcè shìjiàn 不测事件

continual bùduàn 不断

continuation xùjí 续集

continue 1 *v/t* jìxù 继续; *to be ~d* wèiwán dàixù 未完待续 **2** *v/i* jìxù 继续

continuity liánguàn xìng 连贯性

continuous bùtíng 不停

contort *face, body* niǔqū 扭曲

contour lúnkuò 轮廓

contraception bìyùn 避孕

contraceptive *n* (*device*) bìyùn qì 避孕器; (*pill*) bìyùn yào 避孕药

contract[1] *n* hétóng 合同

contract[2] **1** *v/i* (*shrink*) shōusuō 收缩 **2** *v/t illness* gǎnrǎn 感染

contractor chéngbāo rén 承包人

contractual hétóng 合同

contradict *statement* yǔ ... yǒu máodùn 与 ... 有矛盾; *person* fǎnbó 反驳

contradiction máodùn 矛盾

contradictory *account* xiānghù duìlì 相互对立

contraption F qíyì jīqì 奇异机器

contrary[1] **1** *adj* duìlì 对立; *~ to ...* yǔ ... xiāngfǎn 与 ... 相反 **2** *n*: *on the* ~ zhèng xiāngfǎn 正相反

contrary[2] (*perverse*) hào yǔ rén zuòduì 好与人作对

contrast 1 *n* duìzhào 对照 **2** *v/t* duìzhào 对照 **3** *v/i* xíngchéng duìbǐ 形成对比

contrasting jiérán xiāngfǎn 截然相反

contravene wéifǎn 违反

contribute 1 *v/i* (*with money, material*) juānxiàn 捐献; (*with time*) gòngxiàn 贡献; (*to magazine, paper*) tóugǎo 投稿; (*to discussion*) fābiǎo yìjiàn 发表意见; *~ to* (*help to cause*) cùchéng 促成 **2** *v/t money* juānxiàn 捐献; *time, suggestion* gòngxiàn 贡献

contribution (*money*) juānxiàn 捐献; (*to political party, debate, of* time, effort) gòngxiàn 贡献; (to magazine) tóugǎo 投稿

contributor (of money) juānkuǎn rén 捐款人; (to magazine) tóugǎo rén 投稿人

contrive cémóu 策谋

control 1 n (of country, emotion etc) kòngzhì 控制; **be in ~ of ...** kòngzhì zhe ... 控制着 ...; **bring X under ~** déyǐ kòngzhì X 得以控制 X; **get out of ~** shīqù kòngzhì 失去控制; **lose ~ of X** shīqù kòngzhì X de nénglì 失去控制 X 的能力; **lose ~ of oneself** shīqù zìkòng 失去自控; **the situation is under ~** yīqiè zhèngcháng 一切正常; **circumstances beyond our ~** wǒmén wúfǎ kòngzhì de yīnsù 我们无法控制的因素; **~s** (of aircraft, vehicle) cāozòng zhuāngzhì 操纵装置; (restrictions) guǎnzhì cuòshī 管制措施 **2** v/t (govern) kòngzhì 控制; (restrict) xiànzhì 限制; (regulate) guǎnlǐ 管理; **~ oneself** (not get angry, emotional) zìkòng 自控; (not overeat etc) kèzhì zìjǐ 克制自己

control center kòngzhì zhōngxīn 控制中心; **control freak** F kòngzhì kuáng 控制狂; **control key** COMPUT kòngzhìjiàn 控制键

controlled substance shòu guǎnzhì yàowù 受管制药物

controlling interest FIN kònggǔ quányì 控股权益

control panel kòngzhì pán 控制盘

control tower zhǐhuī diàodù tái 指挥调度台

controversial yǒu zhēngyì 有争议

controversy zhēnglùn 争论

convalesce yǎngbìng 养病

convalescence liáoyǎng qī 疗养期

convene v/t zhàojí 召集

convenience (of having sth, location) fāngbiàn 方便; (of arrangement, time) shìyí 适宜; **at your/my ~** zài nǐ/wǒ fāngbiàn de

shíhòu 在你/我方便的时候; **all (modern) ~s** suǒyǒu xiàndàihuà shèbèi 所有现代化设备

convenience food fāngbiàn shípǐn 方便食品

convenience store fāngbiàn xiǎo shāngdiàn 方便小商店

convenient location, device fāngbiàn 方便; time, arrangement héshì 合适

convent nǚ xiūdào yuàn 女修道院

convention (tradition) shèhuì xísú 社会习俗; (conference) dàhuì 大会

conventional person, ideas, method píngcháng 平常

convention center huìyì zhōngxīn 会议中心

conventioneer yǔhuì zhě 与会者

conversant: be ~ with ... shúxī ... 熟悉 ...

conversation jiāotán 交谈

conversational kǒuyǔ 口语

converse n (opposite) xiāngfǎn 相反

conversely lìngyī fāngmiàn 另一方面

conversion (of figures, money) zhésuàn 折算

conversion table huànsuàn biǎo 换算表

convert 1 n guīfù zhě 归附者 **2** v/t house, room etc gǎijiàn 改建; unit of measurement zhéhé 折合; energy zhuǎnhuà 转化; person gǎibiàn xìnyǎng 改变信仰

convertible n (car) zhépéng chē 折蓬车

convey (transmit) chuándì 传递; (give) biǎoshì 表示; (express) biǎodá 表达; (carry) shūsòng 输送

conveyor belt chuánsòng dài 传送带

convict 1 n qiúfàn 囚犯 **2** v/t LAW xuānpàn yǒuzuì 宣判有罪; **~ X of Y** yǐ Y zuìxíng xuānpàn X 以 Y 罪行宣判 X

conviction LAW dìngzuì 定罪;

(*belief*) quèxìn 确信

convince (*persuade*) shuōfú 说服; **I'm ~d that ...** wǒ kěndìng ... 我肯定 ...

convincing lìngrén xìnfú 令人信服

convivial (*friendly*) huānlè 欢乐

convoy (*of ships*) chuánduì 船队; (*of vehicles*) chēduì 车队

convulsion MED chōuchù 抽搐

cook 1 *n* chúshī 厨师 **2** *v/t* zuò 做; (*roast, bake*) kǎo 烤; (*steam*) zhēng 蒸; (*stir fry*) chǎo 炒 **a ~ed meal** xiànzuòde fàn 现做的饭 **3** *v/i* (*of person*) zuòfàn 做饭; (*roast, bake*) kǎo 烤; (*steam*) zhēng 蒸; (*stir fry*) chǎo 炒

cookbook pēngrèn shū 烹饪书

cookery pēngtiáo 烹调

cookie qǔqí 曲奇

cooking (*food*) fàncài 饭菜

cool 1 *n*: **keep one's ~** bǎochí lěngjìng 保持冷静; **lose one's ~** F shīqù kòngzhì 失去控制 **2** *adj* **weather, breeze** liángshuǎng 凉爽; **drink** liáng 凉; (*calm*) lěngjìng 冷静; (*unfriendly*) lěngmò 冷漠; F (*great*) kù 酷 **3** *v/i* (*of food*) tānliáng 摊凉; (*of tempers*) píngxī 平息; (*of interest*) shīqù rèqíng 失去热情 **4** *v/t*: **~ it** F lěngjìng xiàlái 冷静下来

♦ **cool down 1** *v/i* (*of food, stove*) tānliáng 摊凉; (*of weather*) liángkuài qǐlái 凉快起来; (*of person*) liángkuài 凉快; *fig* (*of tempers*) píngxī 平息 **2** *v/t* **food** shǐ biànliáng 使变凉; *fig* shǐ píngxī 使平息

cooperate hézuò 合作

cooperation hézuò 合作

cooperative 1 *n* COM hézuò shè 合作社 **2** *adj* COM hézuò 合作; (*helpful*) lèyì pèihé 乐意配合

coordinate **activities** xiétiáo 协调

coordination (*of activities, body*) xiétiáo 协调

cop F tiáozi 条子

cope yìngfu 应付; **~ with ...** yìngfu ... 应付 ...

copier (*machine*) fùyìn jī 复印机

copilot fù jiàshǐ yuán 副驾驶员

copious **notes** hěnduō 很多; **amount of food** fēngshèng 丰盛

copper *n* (*metal*) tóng 铜

copy 1 *n* (*imitation*) fùzhì pǐn 复制品; (*duplicate*) fùběn 副本; (*photocopy*) fùyìn jiàn 复印件; (*of book*) běn 本; (*of record, CD*) pán 盘; (*written material*) gǎozi 稿子; **make a ~ of a file** COMPUT fùzhì yīfèn dǎng'àn 复制一份档案 **2** *v/t* (*imitate*) fǎngzào 仿造; (*duplicate*) fùxiě 复写; (*photocopy*) fùyìn 复印; COMPUT: **file** fùzhì 复制; (*in writing*) chāoxiě 抄写; (*in order to cheat*) chāoxí 抄袭; **~ a key** pèi yàoshi 配钥匙

copy cat F fǎngxiào zhě 仿效者; **copycat crime** fǎngzhì fànzuì 仿制犯罪; **copyright** *n* bǎnquán 版权; **copy-writer** (*in advertising*) guǎnggào wénzì zhuàngǎo rén 广告文字撰稿人

coral shānhú 珊瑚

cord (*string*) shéng 绳; (*cable*) xiàn 线

cordial *adj* rèqíng 热情

cordless phone wúxiàn diànhuà 无线电话

cordon jǐngjiè xiàn 警戒线

♦ **cordon off** fēngsuǒ 封锁

cords (*pants*) dēngxīnróng kù 灯芯绒裤

corduroy dēngxīnróng 灯芯绒

core 1 *n* (*of fruit*) xīnr 心儿; (*of problem*) yàodiǎn 要点; (*of organization, party*) héxīn 核心 **2** *v/t* **fruit** wāxīn 挖心 **3** *adj* **issue, meaning** zuì zhòngyào 最重要

cork (*in bottle*) píngsāi 瓶塞; (*material*) ruǎnmù 软木

corkscrew ⇩ luósī qǐzi 螺丝起子

corn yùmǐ 玉米

corner 1 *n* (*of page*) jiǎo 角; (*of room*) jiǎoluò 角落; (*of table*) zhuōjiǎo 桌角; (*of street*) jiējiǎo 街角; (*bend: on road*) zhuǎnwān 转弯; (*in soccer*) jiǎoqiú 角球; **in the ~** zài jiǎoluò lǐ 在角落里; **on**

the ~ (*of street*) zài jiējiǎo 在街角
2 *v/t person* shǐ zǒutóu wúlù 使走
投无路；**~ the market** lǒngduàn
shìchǎng 垄断市场 **3** *v/i* (*of
driver, car*) guǎiwānr 拐弯儿
corner kick (*in soccer*) jiǎoqiú 角
球
cornstarch diànfěn 淀粉
corny F *joke* sútào 俗套；F *gesture*
duōchóu shàngǎn 多愁善感
coronary 1 *adj* guànzhuàng
dòngmài 冠状动脉 **2** *n* (*coronary
thrombosis*) guànzhuàng dòngmài
xuèshuān 冠状动脉血栓；(*heart
attack*) guànxīnbìng 冠心病
coroner yànshī guān 验尸官
corporal *n* xiàshì 下士
corporal punishment tǐfá 体罚
corporate COM jítuán 集团；**~
image** gōngsī xíngxiàng 公司形
象；**sense of ~ loyalty** gōngsī
guāngróng gǎn 公司光荣感
corporation (*business*) gǔfèn
yǒuxiàn gōngsī 股份有限公司
corps bùduì 部队
corpse sǐshī 死尸
corpulent féipàng 肥胖
corpuscle xuèqiú 血球
corral *n* chùlán 畜栏
correct 1 *adj* zhèngquè 正确 **2** *v/t*
jiūzhèng 纠正；*proofs, homework*
xiūgǎi 修改
correction xiūgǎi 修改
correspond (*match*) xiāngfú 相符；
(*write letters*) tōngxìn 通信；**~ to ...**
děngyú ... 等于 ...；**~ with ...**
(*match*) fúhé ... 符合 ...
correspondence (*matching*) yī
zhìxìng 一致性；(*letters*) xìnjiàn
信件；(*exchange of letters*) tōngxìn
liánluò 通信联络
correspondent (*letter writer*)
tōngxìn zhě 通信者；(*reporter*)
tōngxùn yuán 通讯员
corresponding (*equivalent*)
duìděng 对等
corridor (*in building*) zǒuláng 走廊
corroborate zhèngshí 证实
corrode *v/t & v/i* fǔshí 腐蚀
corrosion fǔshí 腐蚀
corrugated cardboard wǎlèng

zhǐbǎn 瓦楞纸板
corrugated iron wǎlèng tiě 瓦楞
铁
corrupt 1 *adj* fǔbài 腐败；COMPUT
pòhuài 破坏 **2** *v/t* shǐ duòluò 使
堕落；(*bribe*) huìlù 贿赂
corruption shòuhuì 受贿
cosmetic *adj* měiróng 美容；*fig*
zhuāngshì xìng 装饰性
cosmetics huàzhuāng pǐn 化妆品
cosmetic surgeon zhěngróng
wàikē yīshēng 整容外科医生
cosmetic surgery zhěngróng
wàikē 整容外科
cosmonaut yǔháng yuán 宇航员
cosmopolitan *city* shìjiè xìng 世界
性
cost 1 *n* (*price*) jiàgé 价格；(*in
finance*) chéngběn 成本；*fig* dàijià
代价；**~s** COM fèiyòng 费用 **2** *v/t*
$50 etc xūyào 需要；*time* shǐ
sàngshī 使丧失；FIN: *project* gūjià
估价；**how much does it ~?**
duōshao qián? 多少钱？；**it ~
them $500** tāmen huāle wǔbǎi
měijīn 他们花了五百美金；**it ~
me my health** wǒde jiànkāng
yīncǐ ér shòusǔn 我的健康因此
而受损
cost and freight COM huòjià jiā
yùnjià 货价加运价；**cost-
conscious** jiéyuē 节约；**cost-
effective** huásuàn 划算；**cost,
insurance and freight** COM
huòjià, bǎoxiǎn jiā yùnjià 货
价, 保险加运价
costly *mistake* dàijià cǎnzhòng 代
价惨重
cost of living shēnghuó fèiyòng 生
活费用
cost price chéngběn jiàgé 成本价
格
costume (*for actor*) xìzhuāng 戏装
costume jewelry jiǎ zhūbǎo 假珠
宝
cot (*camp-bed*) xíngjūn chuáng 行
军床
cottage cūnshè 村舍
cottage cheese nóngjiā xiān
gānlào 农家鲜干酪
cotton 1 *n* miánhua 棉花 **2** *adj*

miánbù 棉布

♦**cotton on** F míngbái 明白

♦**cotton on to** F duì ... chǎnshēng hǎogǎn 对 ... 产生好感

♦**cotton to** F xǐhuān 喜欢

cotton candy miánhuā táng 棉花糖

couch n cháng shāfā 长沙发

couch potato pào diànshì de rén 泡电视的人

couchette zuòwò liǎngyòng chuáng 坐卧两用床

cough n & v/i késou 咳嗽

♦**cough up 1** v/t blood etc ké 咳；F money tāochū 掏出 **2** v/i F (pay) tāoqián 掏钱

cough medicine, cough syrup zhǐké tángjiāng 止咳糖浆

could: ~ I have my key? kěyǐ gěiwǒ yàoshi ma? 可以给我钥匙吗？；~ you help me? láojià bāngbang máng 劳驾帮帮忙；this ~ be the our bus yěxǔ shì wǒménde gōnggòng qìchē 也许是我们的公共汽车；you ~ be right méizhǔnr nǐshì duìde 没准儿你是对的；I ~n't say for sure wǒ bùnéng kěndìng 我不能肯定；he ~ have got lost tā kěnéng mílù le 他可能迷路了；you ~ have warned me! zǎo bù shuō! 早不说！

council (assembly) yìhuì 议会；(authority) zhèngfǔ 政府

councilman zhèngwùhuì wěiyuán 政务会委员

councilor zhèngwùhuì wěiyuán 政务会委员

counsel 1 n (advice) quàngào 劝告；(lawyer) lùshī 律师 **2** v/t course of action tíyì 提议；person fǔdǎo 辅导

counseling fǔdǎo 辅导

counselor (adviser) fǔdǎo yuán 辅导员；LAW lùshī 律师

count 1 n (number arrived at) zǒngshù 总数；(action of ~ing) shùshù 数数；(in baseball, boxing) huīji cìshù 挥击次数；keep ~ of ... shǔ ... de quèqiè shùmù 数 ... 的确切数目；lose ~ of ...

shǔbùqīng ... 数不清 ...；at the last ~ zuìhòu yīcì shǔde shíhòu 最后一次数的时候 **2** v/i (to ten etc) shǔ 数；(calculate) jìsuàn 计算；(be important) yǒu zhòngyào yìyì 有重要意义；(qualify) suàn 算 **3** v/t (~ up) shǔ 数；(calculate) jìsuàn 计算；(include) bāokuò 包括

♦**count on** yīkào 依靠

countdown dào shǔshù 倒数数

countenance v/t zànchéng 赞成

counter[1] (in store, café) guìtái 柜台；(in game) chóumǎ 筹码

counter[2] **1** v/t fǎnjī 反击 **2** v/i (retaliate) fǎnbó 反驳

counter[3]: run ~ to ... yǔ ... bùxiāng fúhé 与 ... 不相符合

counteract zhōnghé 中和

counter-attack 1 n fǎnjī 反击 **2** v/i jìnxíng fǎnjī 进行反击

counterbalance pínghéng lì 平衡力；**counterclockwise** nì shízhēn 逆时针；**counterespionage** fǎn jiàndié huódòng 反间谍活动

counterfeit v/t & adj wěizào 伪造

counterpart (person) duìfāng 对方

counterproductive qǐ fǎn zuòyòng 起反作用

countersign v/t huìqiān 会签

countless shǔbu jìn 数不尽

country (nation) guójiā 国家；(as opposed to town) xiāngxià 乡下；in the ~ zài xiāngxià 在乡下

country and western MUS xiāngcūn yǔ xībù yīnyuè 乡村与西部音乐；**countryman** (fellow ~) tóngbāo 同胞；**countryside** nóngcūn 农村

county (in US & China) xiàn 县

coup POL zhèngbiàn 政变；fig piàoliàng de yīju piàoliang de yìjǔ 漂亮的一举

couple (married) fūqī 夫妻；(man & woman) qínglǚ 情侣；(two people) yīduì 一对；just a ~ zhǐyǒu jǐgè 只有几个；a ~ of (people) jǐgè 几个；a ~ of days jǐtiān 几天；a ~ of matters jǐjiàn shì 几件事；a ~ of tickets jǐzhāng piào 几张票

coupon (form) suǒqǔ dān 索取

单; (*voucher*) zèngquàn 赠券
courage yǒngqì 勇气
courageous yǒnggǎn 勇敢
courier (*messenger*) xìnshǐ 信使;
  (*with tourist party*) dǎoyóu 导游
course *n* (*series of lessons*) kèchéng
  课程; (*part of meal*) dàocài 道菜;
  (*of ship, plane*) hángxiàng 航向;
  (*for horse race, golf*) chǎng 场; (*for
  cross-country running, skiing*) dào
  道; **of ~** (*certainly*) dāngrán 当然;
  (*naturally*) zìrán 自然; **of ~ not**
  dāngrán bù 当然不; **~ of action**
  cǎiqǔ de xíngdòng 采取的行动;
  ~ of treatment liáochéng 疗程; **in
  the ~ of …** zài … qījiān 在 … 期
  间
court *n* LAW fǎtíng 法庭;
  (*courthouse*) fǎyuàn 法院; SP
  chǎng 场; **take X to ~** hé X dǎ
  guānsī 和 X 打官司
court case fǎtíng ànjiàn 法庭案
  件
courteous yǒu lǐmào 有礼貌
courtesy lǐmào 礼貌
courthouse fǎyuàn 法院; **court
  martial 1** *n* jūnshì fǎtíng 军事法
  庭 **2** *v/t* yǐ jūnfǎ shěnpàn 以军法
  审判; **court order** fǎlìng 法令;
  courtroom shěnpàn shì 审判室;
  courtyard yuànzi 院子
cousin (*older male on father's side*)
  tángxiōng 堂兄; (*younger male on
  father's side*) tángdì 堂弟; (*older
  female on father's side*) tángjiě 堂
  姐; (*younger female on father's side*)
  tángmèi 堂妹; (*older male on
  mother's side*) biǎoxiōng 表兄;
  (*younger male on mother's side*)
  biǎodì 表弟; (*older female on
  mother's side*) biǎojiě 表姐;
  (*younger female on mother's side*)
  biǎomèi 表妹
cove (*small bay*) xiǎo hǎnwān 小海
  湾
cover 1 *n* (*protective*) zhào 罩; (*of
  book, magazine*) fēngmiàn 封面;
  (*for bed*) bèizi 被子; (*shelter*)
  yǎnbì 掩蔽; (*insurance*) bǎoxiǎn
  保险; **take ~ from the rain** bìyǔ
  蔽雨 **2** *v/t* fùgài 覆盖; (*hide*)

yǎngài 掩盖; (*of insurance policy*)
bǎoxiǎn 保险; *distance* xíngshì 行
驶; (*of journalist*) bàodào 报道;
with his hands ~ed in …
mǎnshǒu dōushì … 满手都是 …
♦**cover up 1** *v/t* gàizhù 盖住; *fig*
yǎngài 掩盖 **2** *v/i fig* yǐnmán 隐
瞒; **~ for X** tì X yǎnshì cuòwù
quēdiǎn 替 X 掩饰错误缺点
coverage (*by media*) bàodào 报道
covering letter fùxìn 附信
covert mìmì 秘密
coverup (*concealment*) yǎnshì 掩饰
cow *n* mǔniú 母牛
coward dǎnxiǎo guǐ 胆小鬼
cowardice dǎnxiǎo 胆小
cowardly dǎnxiǎo 胆小
cowboy niúzǎi 牛仔
cower quánsuō 蜷缩
coy (*evasive*) hánhu qící 含糊其
辞; (*flirtatiously*) xiū dáda 羞答答
cozy shūshì 舒适
CPU (= ***central processing unit***)
zhōngyāng chùlǐ jī 中央处理机
crab *n* pángxiè 螃蟹
crack 1 *n* lièfèng 裂缝; (*joke*)
xiàohua 笑话 **2** *v/t cup, glass* shǐ
chǎnshēng lièfèng 使产生裂缝;
nut zá 砸; *code* pòyì 破译; F
(*solve*) zhēnpò 侦破; **~ a joke**
shuō xiàohuà 说笑话 **3** *v/i* liè 裂;
get ~ing kāishǐ gàn 开始干
♦**crack down on** zhìcái 制裁
♦**crack up** (*have breakdown*)
kuǎdiào 垮掉; F (*laugh*) pěngfù
dàxiào 捧腹大笑
crackbrained yúchǔn 愚蠢
crackdown zhìcái 制裁
cracked *cup, glass* pòliè 破裂; F
(*crazy*) fēngkuáng 疯狂
cracker (*to eat*) bócuì bǐnggān 薄
脆饼干
crackle *v/i* (*of fire*) huālā 哗啦
cradle *n* (*for baby*) yáolán 摇篮
craft[1] NAUT chuán 船
craft[2] (*skill*) gōngyì 工艺; (*trade*)
zhíyè 职业
craftsman shǒuyì rén 手艺人
crafty jiǎohuá 狡猾
crag (*rocky*) xiǎnyá 险崖
cram *v/t* sāi 塞

cramped *room, apartment* zhǎixiǎo 窄小

cramps chōujīn 抽筋

cranberry yuèjú 越橘

crane 1 *n* (*machine*) qǐzhòng jī 起重机 **2** *v/t*: **~ one's neck** shēncháng bózi 伸长脖子

crank *n* (*strange person*) guàirén 怪人

crankshaft qǔzhóu 曲轴

cranky (*bad-tempered*) bàozào 暴躁

crap F shǐ 屎; (*bad quality goods*) pòlàn 破烂; (*nonsense*) húshuō 胡说

crash 1 *n* (*noise*) huālā shēng 哗啦声; (*of thunder*) pīlì 劈雳; (*accident*), COMPUT shìgù 事故; (*plane ~*) fēijī shīshì 飞机失事; COM dǎobì 倒闭 **2** *v/i* (*of wave*) huālā yīshèng jī 哗啦一声击; (*of vase*) pādi yīshēng diào 啪地一声掉; (*of thunder*) tūrán fāchū jùxiǎng 突然发出巨响; (*of car*) zhuàng 撞; (*of airplane*) zhuìhuǐ 坠毁; (COM: *of market*) bàodiē 暴跌; COMPUT chū shìgù 出事故; F (*sleep*) guòyè 过夜 **3** *v/t car* zhuànghuǐ 撞毁

♦ **crash out** F (*fall asleep*) shuìzháo 睡着

crash course sùchéng kè 速成课;

crash diet kuàisù jiǎnféi 快速减肥; **crash helmet** fángzhuàng tóukuī 防撞头盔; **crash landing** shuāijī zháolù 摔机着陆

crate (*packing case*) xiāngzi 箱子

crater (*of volcano*) huǒshān kǒu 火山口

crave kěwàng 渴望

craving kěwàng 渴望; **a ~ for ...** fēicháng xiǎngyào ... 非常想要 ...

crawl 1 *n* (*in swimming*) zìyóuyǒng 自由泳; **at a ~** (*very slowly*) fēicháng huǎnmàn 非常缓慢 **2** *v/i* (*on floor*) pá 爬; (*move slowly*) huǎnmàn xíngjìn 缓慢行进

♦ **crawl with** jǐmǎn 挤满

crayon làbǐ 蜡笔

craze kuángrè 狂热; **the latest ~** zuì shímáo de kuángrè 最时髦的狂热

crazy *adj* fāfēng 发疯; **be ~ about ...** duì ... zháomí 对 ... 着迷

creak 1 *n* zhīgā zhīgā shēng 吱嘎吱嘎声 **2** *v/i* zhīgā zhīgā zuòxiǎng 吱嘎吱嘎作响

cream 1 *n* (*for skin, coffee, cake*) rǔshuāng 乳霜; (*color*) mǐsè 米色 **2** *adj* (*color*) mǐsè 米色

cream cheese nǎiyóu gānlào 奶油干酪

creamer (*jug*) nǎizhōng 奶盅; (*for coffee*) nǎifěn 奶粉

creamy (*with lots of cream*) duō nǎiyóu 多奶油

crease 1 *n* (*accidental*) zhòuwén 皱纹; (*deliberate*) kùxiàn 裤线 **2** *v/t* (*accidentally*) nòngzhòu 弄皱

create 1 *v/t* (*make*) chuàngzào 创造; (*lead to*) yǐnqǐ 引起 **2** *v/i* (*be creative*) chuàngxīn 创新

creation chuàngzào 创造; REL chuàngzào tiāndì 创造天地; (*something created*) chuàngzàode zuòpǐn 创造的作品

creative yǒu chuàngzào nénglì 有创造能力

creator chuàngzào zhě 创造者; (*author*) zuòzhě 作者; (*founder*) fāqǐ rén 发起人; **the Creator** REL Zàowù zhǔ 造物主

creature (*animal*) dòngwù 动物; (*person*) rén 人

credibility (*of person*) xìnyù 信誉; (*of story*) kěxìn xìng 可信性

credible (*believable*) kě xiāngxìn 可相信; *candidate etc* kě xìnrèn 可信任

credit 1 *n* FIN shēqiàn 赊欠; (*use of ~ cards*) xìnyòng 信用; (*honor*) zànyáng 赞扬; (*payment received*) dàifāng 贷方; **be in ~** yǒu yú'é 有余额; **get the ~ for X** yǒuyú X dédào zànyáng 由于 X 得到赞扬 **2** *v/t* (*believe*) xiāngxìn 相信; **~ an amount to an account** cúnrù zhànghù 存入帐户

creditable zhíde zànyáng 值得赞扬

credit card xìnyòng kǎ 信用卡

credit limit (*of credit card*) xìndài xiàn'é 信贷限额

creditor zhàizhǔ 债主

creditworthy xìnyù zhuózhù 信誉卓著

credulous qīngxìn 轻信

creed (*beliefs*) xìntiáo 信条

creek (*stream*) xiǎohé 小河

creep 1 *n pej* tǎoyàn guǐ 讨厌鬼 **2** *v/i* nièshǒu nièjiǎo de zǒu 蹑手蹑脚地走

creeper BOT púfú zhíwù 匍匐植物

creeps: *the house / he gives me the* ~ zhè fángzi / tā shǐwǒ húnshēn qǐ jīpí gēda 这房子 / 他使我浑身起鸡皮疙瘩

creepy lìngrén máogǔ sǒngrán 令人毛骨悚然

cremate huǒhuà 火化

cremation huǒhuà 火化

crematorium huǒhuà chǎng 火化场

crescent *n* (*shape*) yuèyá xíng 月牙形

crest (*of hill*) dǐng 顶; (*of bird*) ròuguàn 肉冠

crestfallen jǔsàng 沮丧

crevice lièfèng 裂缝

crew *n* (*of ship, airplane*) quántǐ gōngzuò rényuán 全体工作人员; (*of repairmen etc*) zǔ 组; (*crowd, group*) yīhuǒ rén 一伙人

crew cut píngtóu 平头

crew neck shuǐshǒu lǐng 水手领

crib *n* (*for baby*) xiǎohái chuáng 小孩床

crick: ~ *in the neck* jǐngbù tòngxìng jìngluán 颈部痛性痉挛

cricket (*insect*) xīshuài 蟋蟀

crime (*offence*) zuìxíng 罪行; (*shameful act*) lìngrén yíhàn de shì 令人遗憾的事; *the* ~ *rate* fànzuì lǜ 犯罪率

criminal 1 *n* zuìfàn 罪犯 **2** *adj* xíngshì 刑事; (*shameful*) lìngrén yíhàn 令人遗憾

crimson *adj* shēnhóng sè 深红色

cringe xiàde wànghòu suō 吓得往后缩

cripple 1 *n* (*disabled person*) cánjí rénshì 残疾人士 **2** *v/t person* shòushāng zhì cán 受伤至残; *fig* shǐ xiànyú tānhuàn 使陷于瘫痪

crisis wēijī 危机

crisp *adj weather, air* liángshuǎng 凉爽; *lettuce, apple* xīnxiān ér cuìshēng 新鲜而脆生; *bacon, toast* cuì 脆; *new shirt, bills* tǐngkuò 挺括

criterion (*standard*) biāozhǔn 标准

critic pínglùn jiā 评论家

critical (*making criticisms*) tiāocìr 挑刺儿; (*serious*) wēijí 危急; *moment etc* jǐnyào 紧要; MED yánzhòng 严重

critically *speak etc* yǒu pīpíng xìng 有批评性; ~ *ill* bìngde hěn yánzhòng 病得很严重

criticism pīpíng 批评

criticize *v/t* pīpíng 批评

croak 1 *n* (*of frog*) guāgua jiāoshēng 呱呱叫声; (*of person*) dīyǎ de shuōhuà shēng 低哑的说话声 **2** *v/i* (*of frog*) guāgua jiào 呱呱叫; (*of person*) dīyǎ di shuōhuà 低哑地说话

crockery táoqì 陶器

crocodile èyú 鳄鱼

crony F mìyǒu 密友

crook *n* (*dishonest*) piànzi 骗子

crooked (*not straight*) wānqū 弯曲; (*dishonest*) bù lǎoshí 不老实

crop 1 *n* shōucheng 收成; *fig* pī 批; ~*s* zhuāngjia 庄稼 **2** *v/t hair, photo* xiūjiǎn 修剪

♦**crop up** (*be mentioned*) tídào 提到; (*happen unexpectedly*) yìwài de fāshēng 意外地发生

cross 1 *adj* (*angry*) shēngqì 生气 **2** *n* (*X*) chāzi 叉子; (*Christian symbol*) shízìjià 十字架 **3** *v/t* (*go across*) chuānguò 穿过; ~ *oneself* REL yòng shǒu huà shízì 用手画十字; ~ *one's legs* jiāochā shuāngtuǐ 交叉双腿; *keep one's fingers ~ed* qíqiú zǒuyùn 祈求走运; *it never ~ed my mind* wǒ gēnběn jiù méiyǒu xiǎng 我根本就没有想 **4** *v/i* (*go across the road*) guò mǎlù 过马路; (*of lines*) jiāochā 交叉

♦**cross off**, **cross out** qǔxiāo 取消

crossbar (*of goal*) héngmù 横木; (*of bicycle*) chējià héngliáng 车架横梁; (*in high jump*) hénggān 横杆

cross-country (**skiing**) yuèyě (huáxuě) 越野 (滑雪)

crossed check huàxiàn zhīpiào 划线支票

cross-examine LAW fǎn jiéwèn 反诘问

cross-eyed nèi xiéshì 内斜视

crossing NAUT héngdù 横渡

crossroads shízì lùkǒu 十字路口; **cross-section** (*of people*) jùyǒu dàibiǎo xìng de gèsè rénwù 具有代表性的各色人物; **crosswalk** ⇩ rénxíng héngdào 人行横道; **crossword** (**puzzle**) zònghéng tiánzì mí 纵横填字迷

crouch *v/i* dūn 蹲

crow *n* (*bird*) wūyā 乌鸦; **as the ~ flies** yán zhíxiàn 沿直线

crowd *n* rénqún 人群; (*at sports event*) guānzhòng 观众

crowded yōngjǐ 拥挤

crown 1 *n* (*on tooth*) chǐguàn 齿冠 2 *v/t* tooth xiāng chǐguàn 镶齿冠

crucial guānjiàn 关键

crude 1 *adj* (*vulgar*) cūlǔ 粗鲁; (*unsophisticated*) jiǎnlòu 简陋 2 *n*: **~** (**oil**) yuányóu 原油

cruel cánrěn 残忍

cruelty cánrěn 残忍

cruise 1 *n* hángxíng 航行 2 *v/i* (*in ship*) hángxíng 航行; (*of car*) huǎnmàn xúnxíng 缓慢巡行; (*of plane*) yǐ jīngjì xúnxíng sùdù fēixíng 以经济巡行速度飞行

cruise liner dàxíng yóutǐng 大型游艇

cruising speed jūnsù 均速

crumb zhāzi 渣子

crumble 1 *v/t* nòngsuì 弄碎 2 *v/i* (*of bread, stonework*) suìliè 碎裂; *fig* (*of opposition etc*) bēngkuì 崩溃

crumple 1 *v/t* (*crease*) nòngzhòu 弄皱 2 *v/i* (*collapse*) dǎoxià 倒下

crunch 1 *n*: **when it comes to the ~** F dāng guānjiàn shíkè dàolái shí 当关键时刻到来时 2 *v/i* (*of snow, gravel*) gāzhī zuòshēng 嘎吱作声

crusade *n fig* yùndòng 运动

crush 1 *n* (*crowd*) yōngjǐ de rénqún 拥挤的人群; **have a ~ on** rèliàn 热恋 2 *v/t* yā 压; (*crease*) nòngzhòu 弄皱; **they were ~ed to death** tāmén bèi yā sǐle 他们被压死了 3 *v/i* (*crease*) zhòu 皱

crust (*on bread*) miànbāo pí 面包皮

crutch (*for injured person*) T zì xíng guǎizhàng T字形拐杖

cry 1 *n* (*call*) hǎnjiào 喊叫; **have a ~** kū yīchǎng 哭一场 2 *v/t* (*call*) hǎnjiào 喊叫 3 *v/i* (*weep*) kū 哭

♦**cry out** 1 *v/t* dàshēng shuōchū 大声说出 2 *v/i* hǎnjiào 喊叫

♦**cry out for** (*need*) pòqiè xūyào 迫切需要

crystal (*mineral*) shuǐjīng 水晶; (*glass*) jīngzhì bōli 晶质玻璃

crystallize 1 *v/t* jiéjīng 结晶 2 *v/i* (*of thoughts etc*) jiéjīng 结晶

CTS (= **China Travel Service**) Zhōngguó Lǚxíngshè 中国旅行社

cub yòushòu 幼兽

Cuba Gǔbā 古巴

Cuban 1 *adj* Gǔbā 古巴 2 *n* Gǔbā rén 古巴人

cube (*shape*) lìfāng xíng 立方形

cubic lìfāng 立方

cubic capacity TECH róngjī liàng 容积量

cubicle (*changing room*) gēngyī shì 更衣室

cucumber huángguā 黄瓜

cuddle *n & v/t* yōngbào 拥抱

cuddly kitten etc dòurén lián'ài 逗人怜爱; (*liking cuddles*) xǐhuān lǒulou bàobao 喜欢搂搂抱抱

cue *n* (*for actor etc*) tíshì 提示; (*for pool*) qiúgān 球杆

cuff 1 *n* (*of shirt*) xiùkǒu 袖口; (*of pants*) kùjiǎo fānbiān 裤角翻边; (*blow*) zhǎngjī 掌击; **off the ~** wèijīng zhǔnbèi 未经准备 2 *v/t* (*hit*) zhǎngjī 掌击

cuff link xiùkǒu liànkòu 袖口链扣

culinary pēngtiáo 烹调

culminate: ~ *in* ... yǐ ... gàozhōng 以 ... 告终

culmination dǐngdiǎn 顶点

culprit zuìfàn 罪犯

cult (*sect*) zōngpài 宗派

cultivate *land* gēngzuò 耕作; *person* péiyǎng 培养

cultivated *person* yǒu xiūyǎng 有修养

cultivation (*of land*) gēngzuò 耕作

cultural (*relating to the arts*) yǒu xiūyǎng 有修养; (*relating a country's identity*) wénhuà 文化

Cultural Revolution Wénhuà Dàgémìng 文化大革命

culture *n* (*artistic*) wénmíng 文明; (*of a country*) wénhuà 文化

cultured (*cultivated*) yǒu xiūyǎng 有修养

culture shock wénhuà chōngjī 文化冲击

cumbersome léizhuì 累赘

cunning *n* & *adj* jiǎohuá 狡猾

cup *n* bēi 杯; (*trophy*) bēi 杯; *a ~ of tea* yībēi chá 一杯茶

cupboard guìzi 柜子

curable kěyī 可医

curator guǎnzhǎng 馆长

curb 1 *n* (*of street*) lùyuán 路缘; (*on powers etc*) yuēshù 约束 2 *v/t* kòngzhì 控制

curdle *v/i* (*of milk*) níngjié 凝结

cure 1 *n* MED liáofǎ 疗法 2 *v/t* MED zhìhǎo 治好; *meat, fish* yān 腌

curfew xiāojìn lìng 宵禁令

curiosity (*inquisitiveness*) hàoqí xīn 好奇心

curious (*inquisitive*) hàoqí 好奇; (*strange*) qítè 奇特

curiously (*inquisitively*) hàoqí 好奇; (*strangely*) qíguài 奇怪; *~ enough* qíguàide shì 奇怪的是

curl 1 *n* (*in hair*) quánfà 鬈发; *~ of smoke* yānquānr 烟圈儿 2 *v/t hair* juǎn 卷; (*wind*) chánrào 缠绕 3 *v/i* (*of hair*) juǎn 卷; (*of leaf, paper etc*) quánqū 蜷曲

♦**curl up** quánqū 蜷曲

curly *tail* quánqū 鬈曲; *~ hair* quánfà 鬈发

currant (*dried fruit*) xiǎo pútáo gān 小葡萄干

currency (*money*) huòbì 货币; *foreign ~* wàihuì 外汇

current 1 *n* (*in sea*) jīliú 激流; ELEC diànliú 电流; (*of opinions etc*) qīngxiàng 倾向 2 *adj* (*present*) mùqián 目前

current affairs, current events shíshì 时事

current affairs program shíshì tǎolùn jiémù 时事讨论节目

currently mùqián 目前

curriculum kèchéng 课程

curse 1 *n* (*spell*) zǔzhòu 诅咒; (*swearword*) zhòumà 咒骂 2 *v/t* zǔzhòu 诅咒; (*swear at*) zhòumà 咒骂 3 *v/i* (*swear*) màrén 骂人

cursor COMPUT ⇩ guāngbiāo 光标

cursory cūlüè 粗略

curt tángtū cǎoshuài 唐突草率

curtail jiéduǎn 截短

curtain chuānglián 窗帘; THEA wéimù 帷幕

curve 1 *n* qūxiàn 曲线 2 *v/i* (*bend*) wānqū 弯曲

cushion 1 *n* (*for couch etc*) kàodiàn 靠垫 2 *v/t blow, fall* huǎnhé ... de chōngjī 缓和 ... 的 冲击

custard dànnǎi hù 蛋奶糊

custody (*of children*) fúyǎng quán 扶养权; *in ~* LAW bèi jūliú 被拘留

custom (*tradition*) xíguàn 习惯; COM huìgù 惠顾; *as was his ~* àn tā píngcháng xíguàn 按他平常习惯

customary chángguī 常规; *it is ~ to ...* chángguī shàng ... 常规上 ...

customer gùkè 顾客

customer relations gùkè guānxi 顾客关系

customs hǎiguān 海关

customs clearance tōngguān 通关; **customs inspection** yànguān 验关; **customs officer** hǎiguān guānyuán 海关官员

cut 1 *n* (*with knife, scissors*) qiēkǒu 切口; (*injury*) shāngkǒu 伤口; (*of garment, hair*) kuǎnshì 款式; (*reduction*) xiāojiǎn 削减; *my hair needs a ~* wǒ gāi jiǎn tóufà le 我该剪头发了 **2** *v/t* qiē 切; (*reduce*) xiāojiǎn 削减; COMPUT: *text* jiǎnqiē 剪切; *get one's hair ~* jiǎn tóufà 剪头发

♦ **cut back 1** *v/i* (*in costs*) suōjiǎn 缩减 **2** *v/t employees* cáiyuán 裁员

♦ **cut down 1** *v/t tree* kǎndǎo 砍倒 **2** *v/i* (*in smoking etc*) jiǎnshǎo 减少

♦ **cut down on:** *~ smoking / drinking* shǎo chōuyān / hējiǔ 少抽烟 / 喝酒

♦ **cut off** (*with knife, scissors etc*) jiǎndiào 剪掉; (*isolate*) géjué 隔绝; TELEC duànxiàn 断线; *we were cut off* diànhuà duànxiàn le 电话断线了

♦ **cut out** (*with scissors*) jiǎnchū 剪出; *alcohol, smoking* jiè jiè 戒戒; (*eliminate*) páichú 排除; *cut that out!* F gòule! 够了！; *be ~ for X* shìhé yú X 适合于 X

♦ **cut up** *v/t meat etc* qiēsuì 切碎

cutback xiāojiǎn 削减

cute (*pretty*) kě'ài 可爱; (*sexually attractive, male*) yīngjùn 英俊; (*sexually attractive, female*) piàoliàng 漂亮; (*smart, clever*) shuǎ xiǎo cōngmíng 耍小聪明

cuticle biǎopí 表皮

cut-price xiāojià 削价

cut-throat *competition* cánkù 残酷

cutting 1 *n* (*from newspaper etc*) jiǎnjí 剪辑 **2** *adj remark* shāngrén gǎnqíng 伤人感情

cyberspace diànnǎo kōngjiān 电脑空间

cycle 1 *n* (*bicycle*) zìxíngchē 自行车; (*series of events*) xúnhuán 循环 **2** *v/i* qí zìxíngchē 骑自行车

cycling qí zìxíngchē 骑自行车

cyclist qí zìxíngchē de rén 骑自行车的人

cylinder (*container*) yuántǒng róngqì 园筒容器; (*in engine*) qìgāng 汽缸

cylindrical yuánzhù xíng 圆柱形

cynic fènshì jísú zhě 愤世嫉俗者

cynical fènshì jísú 愤世嫉俗

cynicism fènshì jísú 愤世嫉俗

cyst nángzhǒng 囊肿

Czech 1 *adj* Jiékè 捷克; *the ~ Republic* Jiékè Gònghéguó 捷克共和国 **2** *n* (*person*) Jiékè rén 捷克人; (*language*) Jiékè yǔ 捷克语

D

DA (= *district attorney*) dìfāng jiǎnchá guān 地方检查官
dab 1 *n* (*small amount*) shǎoliàng 少量 **2** *v/t* (*remove*) qīngcā 轻搽; (*apply*) cā 搽
♦ **dabble in** suíbiàn gǎogao 随便搞搞
dad bà ba 爸爸
dagger bǐshǒu 匕首
daily 1 *n* (*paper*) rìbào 日报 **2** *adj* měirì 每日
dainty yōuměi 优美
dairy products rǔzhì pǐn 乳制品
dais tái tái 台台
dam 1 *n* (*for water*) shuǐbà 水坝 **2** *v/t river* zhùdībà 筑堤坝
damage 1 *n* sǔnshī 损失; *fig* (*to reputation etc*) sǔnhài 损害 **2** *v/t* sǔnhuài 损坏; *fig* (*reputation etc*) sǔnshāng 损伤
damages LAW péicháng 赔偿
damaging yǒu pòhuài xìng 有破坏性
dame F (*woman*) nǚrén 女人
damn 1 *interj* gāisǐ 该死 **2** *n: I don't give a ~!* wǒ cái bùguǎn ne! 我才不管呢! **3** *adj* gāisǐ 该死 **4** *adv* zhēn 真 **5** *v/t* (*condemn*) qiǎnzé 谴责; *~ it!* zhēn qìsǐ rén! 真气死人! ; *I'm ~ed if ...* wǒ cái bù ... 我才不...
damned → **damn**
damp *building, cloth* shī 湿
dampen nòng shī 弄湿
dance 1 *n* tiàowǔ 跳舞; (*social event*) wǔhuì 舞会 **2** *v/i* tiàowǔ 跳舞; *would you like to ~?* kěyǐ qǐngnǐ tiàowǔ ma? 可以请你跳舞吗?
dancer wǔdǎo jiā 舞蹈家; (*performer*) wǔdǎo yǎnyuán 舞蹈演员
dancing wǔdǎo 舞蹈
dandruff tóupíxiè 头皮屑

Dane Dānmài rén 丹麦人
danger wēixiǎn 危险; *out of ~* (*of patient*) tuōlí wēixiǎn 脱离危险
dangerous wēixiǎn 危险; *assumption* màoxiǎn 冒险
dangle 1 *v/t* yáohuang yáohuǎng 摇晃 **2** *v/i* xuánchuí 悬垂
Danish 1 *adj* Dānmài 丹麦 **2** *n* (*language*) Dānmài yǔ 丹麦语
Danish (pastry) Dānmài dàngāo 丹麦蛋糕
dare 1 *v/i* gǎn 敢; *how ~ you!* nǐgǎn! 你敢! **2** *v/t: ~ X to do Y* tiǎodòu X qù zuò Y 挑斗 X 去做 Y
daring *adj* dàdǎn 大胆
dark 1 *n* hēi'àn 黑暗; *after ~* tiānhēi yǐhòu 天黑以后; *keep X in the ~ fig* bú gàosù X 不告诉 X **2** *adj room, night* hēi 黑; *hair, eyes* shēn yánsè 深颜色; *~ green / blue* shēn lǜ / lán 深绿 / 蓝
darken (*of sky*) biàn hēi 变黑
dark glasses hēi yǎnjìng 黑眼镜
darkness hēi'àn 黑暗
darling 1 *n* qīn'ài de 亲爱的 **2** *adj* qī'ài 亲爱
darn[1] *n* (*mend*) bǔdīng 补丁 **2** *v/t* (*mend*) bǔ 补
darn[2], **darned** → **damn**
dart 1 *n* (*for throwing*) fēibiāo 飞标 **2** *v/i* měngchōng 猛冲
dash 1 *n* (*punctuation*) pòzhé hào 破折号; (*small amount*) shǎoliàng 少量; (MOT: *dashboard*) yíbiǎo bǎn 仪表板; *a ~ of brandy* shǎoliàng báilándì 少量白兰地; *make a ~ for* jíchōng 急冲 **2** *v/i* jíchōng 急冲 **3** *v/t hopes* pòmiè 破灭
♦ **dash off 1** *v/i* gǎnkuài líkāi 赶快离开 **2** *v/t* (*write quickly*) cōngmáng xiě 匆忙写
dashboard yíbiǎo bǎn 仪表板

data shùjù 数据

database shùjù kù 数据库; **data capture** shùjù fúhuò 数据俘获; **data processing** shùjù chǔlǐ 数据处理; **data protection** zīliào bǎomì 资料保密; **data storage** shùjù chǔcún 数据储存

date¹ (*fruit*) zǎo 枣

date² 1 *n* rìqī 日期; (*meeting*) yuēhuì 约会; (*person*) yuēhuì duìxiàng 约会对象; **what's the ~ today?** jīntiān jǐhào? 今天几号？; **out of ~** *clothes* guòshí 过时; *passport* guòqī 过期; **up to ~** zuìxīn 最新 2 *v/t letter, cheque* zhùmíng rìqī 注明日期; (*go out with*) tán liàn'ài 谈恋爱; **that ~s you** (*shows your age*) xiǎnshì nǐde niánlíng 显示你的年龄

dated guòshí 过时

daub *v/t* luàntú 乱涂

daughter nǚ'ér 女儿

daughter-in-law érxífu 儿媳妇

daunt *v/t* shǐ qìněi 使气馁

dawdle màntūntun de zuò 慢吞吞地做

dawn 1 *n* pòxiǎo 破晓; *fig* (*of new age*) kāiduān 开端 2 *v/i*: **it ~ed on me that ...** wǒ yìshí dào ... 我意识到 ...

day tiān 天; **what ~ is it today?** jīntiān xīngqī jǐ? 今天星期几？; **~ off** fàngjià 放假; **by ~** báitiān 白天; **~ by ~** yī tiāntian di 一天天地; **the ~ after** dì'èr tiān 第二天; **the ~ after tomorrow** hòutiān 后天; **the ~ before** qián yī tiān 前一天; **the ~ before yesterday** qiántiān 前天; **~ in ~ out** měitiān 每天; **in those ~s** nà shíhòu 那时候; **one ~** yǒu yìtiān 有一天; **the other ~** (*recently*) zuìjìn 最近; **let's call it a ~!** xiūxība! 休息吧！

daybreak pòxiǎo 破晓; **daydream** 1 *n* báirì mèng 白日梦 2 *v/i* báirì zuòmèng 白日做梦; **daylight** rìguāng 日光; **daytime: in the ~** báitiān 白天; **daytrip** yīrìyóu 一日游

daze: **in a ~** bùzhī suǒcuò 不知所措

dazed (*by good / bad news*) bùzhī suǒcuò 不知所措; (*by a blow*) fāhūn 发昏

dazzle *v/t* (*of light*) huǎng 晃; *fig* mízhù 迷住

dead 1 *adj person, plant* sǐ 死; *battery, phone, bulb* shīlíng 失灵; F (*place*) sǐqì chénchen 死气沉沉 2 *adv* F (*very*) hěn 很; **~ beat**, **~ tired** jīnpí lìjìn 筋疲力尽; **that's ~ right** hěn zhèngquè 很正确 3 *n*: **the ~** (*dead people*) sǐrén 死人; **in the ~ of night** shēnyè 深夜

deaden *pain, sound* shǐ jiǎnshǎo 使减少

dead end (*street*) sǐ hútong 死胡同; **dead-end job** méi qiántú de gōngzuò 没前途的工作; **dead heat** tóngshí dàodá zhōngdiǎn 同时到达终点; **deadline** qīxiàn 期限; (*for newspaper, magazine*) zuìhòu qīxiàn 最后期限; **deadlock** *n* (*in talks*) jiāngjú 僵局

deadly *adj* (*fatal*) zhìmìng 致命; F (*boring*) sǐqì chénchen 死气沉沉

deaf lóng 聋

deaf-and-dumb lóngyǎ 聋哑

deafen shǐ tīng bū jiàn 使听不见

deafening jí dàshēng 极大声

deafness lóng 聋

deal 1 *n* jiāoyì 交易; **it's a ~** (*we have reached an agreement*) chéngjiāo 成交; (*it's a promise*) méi wèntí 没问题; **a good ~** (*bargain*) hǎo jiàqián 好价钱; **a great ~** (*a lot*) hěnduō 很多; **a great ~ of** (*lots*) hěnduō 很多 2 *v/t cards* fāpái 发牌; **~ a blow to** dǎjī 打击

♦ **deal in**: **~ X** (*trade in*) zuò X mǎimài 做 X 买卖

♦ **deal out** *cards* fāpái 发牌

♦ **deal with** (*handle*) chǔlǐ 处理; (*do business with*) dǎ jiāodào 打交道

dealer (*merchant*) shāngrén 商人; (*drug ~*) fàndú zhě 贩毒者; (*in card game*) fāpái zhě 发牌者

dealing (*drug ~*) fàndú 贩毒

dealings (*business*) jiāowǎng 交往

dean (*of college*) yuànzhǎng 院长

dear *adj* qīn'ài 亲爱; (*expensive*) guì 贵; *Dear Sir* zūnjìngde xiānshēng 尊敬的先生; *Dear Wang Li* qīn'àide Wáng Lì 亲爱的王丽; (*oh*) ~!, ~ *me!* wǒde tiān'a! 我的天啊！

dearly *love* shēn 深

death sǐwáng 死亡

death penalty sǐxíng 死刑

death toll sǐwáng zǒngshù 死亡总数

debatable kě zhēnglùn 可争论

debate 1 *n* (*between opposing sides*) biànlùn 辩论; (*discussion*) tǎolùn 讨论 2 *v/i* (*discuss*) tǎolùn 讨论; (*between opposing sides*) biànlùn 辩论 3 *v/t* biànlùn 辩论

debauchery fàngdàng 放荡

debit 1 *n* jièfāng 借方 2 *v/t account* jièfāng 借方; ~ *his account with $30* zài tāde jièfāng zhàngshang jì sānshí měiyuán 在他的借方帐上记三十美元

debris cánjī 残迹

debt zhài 债; *be in* ~ (*financially*) qiànzhài 欠债

debtor jièfāng 借方

debug *room* chāichú qiètīngqì 拆除窃听器; COMPUT chúcuò 除错

début *n* shǒuyǎn 首演

decade shínián 十年

decadent tuífèi 颓废

decaffeinated wú kāfēiyīn 无咖啡因

decanter xì jǐng píng 细颈瓶

decapitate shìshǒu fēnlí 尸首分离

decay 1 *n* (*process, matter*) fǔlàn 腐烂; (*of civilization*) shuāituì 衰退; (*in teeth*) làn làn 烂烂 2 *v/i* fǔlàn 腐烂; (*of civilization*) shuāituì 衰退; (*of teeth*) làn làn 烂烂

deceased: *the* ~ sǐzhě 死者

deceit qīpiàn 欺骗

deceitful bù lǎoshi 不老实

deceive qīpiàn 欺骗

December shí'èryuè 十二月

decency zhèngpài 正派; *he had the* ~ *to ...* tā qǐmǎ zhīdào qù ... 他起码知道去 ...

decent *person* zhèngpài 正派; *salary, price* kě jìshòu 可接受; *size* gòudà 够大; *meal, sleep* zúgòu 足够; *I'm not* ~ *yet!* (*adequately dressed*) wǒ hái méi chuānhǎo yīfu ne! 我还没穿好衣服呢！

decentralize *administration* shūsàn 疏散

deception qīpiàn 欺骗

deceptive kàobuzhù 靠不住

deceptively: *it looks* ~ *simple* kànqǐlái jiǎndān 看起来简单

decibel fēnbèi 分贝

decide 1 *v/t* (*make up one's mind*) juédìng 决定; (*conclude*) xià juéxīn 下决心; (*settle*) pànjué 判决 2 *v/i* juédìng 决定; *you* ~ nǐ lái juédìng 你来决定

decided (*definite*) jiānjué 坚决; (*obvious*) míngxiǎn 明显

decider (*match etc*) juédìng sài 决定赛

decimal *n* xiǎoshù 小数

decimal point xiǎoshù diǎn 小数点

decimate èshā dà bùfen 扼杀大部分

decipher jiě mìmǎ 解密码

decision juédìng 决定; *come to a* ~ xià juéxīn 下决心

decision-maker dāngquán zhě 当权者

decisive guǒduàn 果断; (*crucial*) juédìng xìng 决定性

deck (*of ship*) jiǎbǎn 甲板; (*of cards*) yīfù zhǐpái 一副纸牌

deckchair jiǎbǎn yòng yǐ 甲板用椅

declaration (*statement*) shēngmíng 声明; (*of independence*) xuānbù 宣布; ~ *of war* xuānzhàn 宣战

declare *state* shēngmíng 声明; *independence* xuānbù 宣布; (*at customs*) chéngbào 呈报; ~ *war* xuānzhàn 宣战

decline 1 *n* (*fall*) xiàjiàng 下降; (*in standards*) jiàngdī 降低; (*in health*) shuāituì 衰退 2 *v/t invitation* xièjué 谢绝; ~ *to comment* / *accept* xièjué fābiǎo yìjiàn / jìshòu 谢绝发表意见 / 接

受 **3** v/i (*refuse*) xièjué 谢绝; (*decrease*) jiǎnshǎo 减少; (*of health*) shuāituì 衰退

declutch qǔxià líhéqì 取下离合器

decode yìmǎ 译码

decompose fǔlàn 腐烂

décor zhuānghuáng 装潢

decorate (*with paint, paper*) zhuāngxiū 装修; (*adorn*) zhuāngshì 装饰; *soldier* shòuxūn 授勋

decoration (*paint, paper*) zhuānghuáng 装潢; (*ornament*) zhuāngshì 装饰

decorative zhuāngshì 装饰

decorator (*interior ~*) zhuānghuáng gōngrén 装潢工人

decoy n yòu'ěr 诱饵

decrease 1 n xiàjiàng 下降 **2** v/t suōjiǎn 缩减 **3** v/i xiàjiàng 下降

dedicate *book etc* tíxiàn 题献; ~ **oneself to …** xiànshēn yú … 献身于 …

dedication (*in book*) xiàntí 献题; (*to cause, work*) zhìlì 致力

deduce tuīlǐ 推理

deduct: ~ **X from Y** cóng Y zhōng jiǎnqù X 从 Y 中减去 X

deduction (*from salary*) kòuchú 扣除; (*conclusion*) tuīlùn 推论

deed n (*act*) xíngwéi 行为; LAW qìyuē 契约

deep *hole, water, color* shēn 深; *shelf* zòngshēn 纵深; *voice* shēnchén 深沉; *thinker* shēnrù 深入; ~ **trouble** shēnxiàn kùnjìng 身陷困境

deepen 1 v/t bǎ … jiāshēn 把 … 加深 **2** v/i biànshēn 变深; (*of crisis, mystery*) jiāzhòng 加重

deep freeze n bīngxiāng 冰箱; **deep-frozen food** lěngdòng shípǐn 冷冻食品; **deep-fry** yóuzhá 油炸

deer lù 鹿

deface sǔnhuài biǎomiàn 损坏表面

defamation fěibàng 诽谤

defamatory fěibàng 诽谤

default adj COMPUT yuándìng 原定

defeat 1 n (*conquering*) jībài 击败;

(*losing*) shībài 失败 **2** v/t jībài 击败; (*of task, problem*) cuòbài 锉败

defeatist adj *attitude* shībài zhǔyì 失败主义

defect n quēxiàn 缺陷

defective yǒu quēxiàn 有缺陷

defend bǎowèi 保卫; *cause* hànwèi 捍卫; (*stand by*) wéihù 维护; (*justify*) biànhù 辩护; ~ **X** LAW wèi X biànhù 为 X 辩护

defendant bèigào 被告

defense n bǎowèi 保卫; SP fángshǒu 防守; LAW bèigào 被告; (*justification*) biànhù 辩护; (*of cause*) hànwèi 捍卫; **come to X's** ~ bāngzhù X 帮助 X

defense budget POL guófáng kāizhī 国防开支

defense lawyer biànhù lǜshī 辩护律师

defenseless gūlì wúyuán 孤立无援

defense player SP shǒuwèi duìyuán 守卫队员; **Defense Secretary** POL guófáng bùzhǎng 国防部长; **defense witness** LAW biànhù zhèngrén 辩护证人

defensive 1 n: **on the** ~ cǎiqǔ shǒushì 采取守势; **go on the** ~ cǎiqǔ shǒushì 采取守势 **2** adj *weaponry* fángyù 防御; *person* zìwǒ biànhù 自我辩护

defer v/t tuīchí 推迟

deference jìngyì 敬意

deferential biǎoshì jìngyì 表示敬意

defiance duìkàng 对抗; **in** ~ **of** wéikàng 违抗

defiant tiǎozhàn 挑战

deficiency (*lack*) quēfá 缺乏

deficient: **be** ~ **in** quēfá 缺乏

deficit kuīsǔn 亏损

define *word* xià dìngyì 下定义; *objective* míngquè 明确

definite *date, answer, improvement* míngquè 明确; (*certain*) kěndìng 肯定; **are you** ~ **about that?** nǐ néngbùnéng kěndìng? 你能不能肯定?; **nothing** ~ **has been arranged** zuìhòu ānpái hái méiyǒu quèdìng 最后安排还没有

确定

definite article dìngguàncí 定冠词

definitely kěndìng 肯定

definition (of word) dìngyì 定义; (of objective) chǎnshù 阐述

definitive quánwēi xìng 权威性

deflect ball, blow shǐ zhuǎnxiàng 使转向; criticism niǔzhuǎn 扭转; (from course of action) niǔzhuǎn fāngxiàng 扭转方向; **be ~ed from** shǐ cóng … zhuǎnbiàn fāngxiàng 使从 … 转变方向

deform shǐ chéng jīxíng 使成畸形

deformity jīxíng 畸形

defraud piànqǔ 骗取

defrost v/t food jiědòng 解冻; fridge huàbīng 化冰

deft língqiǎo 灵巧

defuse bomb chāichú yǐnxìn 拆除引信; situation tiáojiě 调解

defy wéikàng 违抗

degenerate v/i duòluò 堕落; **~ into** tuìhuà 退化

degrade shǐ diūliǎn 使丢脸

degrading position, work dījí 低级

degree (from university) xuéwèi 学位; (of temperature, angle, latitude) dù 度; (amount) chéngdù 程度; **by ~s** zhújiàn 逐渐; **get one's ~** huòdé xuéwèi 获得学位

dehydrated tuōshuǐ 脱水

de-ice chúbīng 除冰

de-icer (spray) chúbīng qì 除冰器

deign: **~ to …** qūzūn … 屈尊 …

deity shén 神

dejected jǔsàng 沮丧

delay 1 n yánchí 延迟 2 v/t tuīchí 推迟; **be ~ed** bèi dāngē 被耽搁 3 v/i tuīchí 推迟

delegate 1 n dàibiǎo 代表 2 v/t task, person shòuquán 授权

delegation (of task, people) shòuquán 授权

delete shānqù 删去; COMPUT shānchú 删除; (cross out) huàdiào 划掉

deletion (act) xiāochú 消除; (that deleted) shānchú 删除

deli shóushí diàn 熟食店

deliberate 1 adj gùyì 故意 2 v/i

zǐxì kǎolǜ 仔细考虑

deliberately gùyì 故意

delicacy (of fabric) jīngzhì 精致; (of problem) mǐngǎn 敏感; (of health) xūruò 虚弱; (tact) jǐnshèn 谨慎; (food) měishí 美食

delicate fabric jīngzhì 精致; problem mǐngǎn 敏感; health xūruò 虚弱

delicatessen shóushí diàn 熟食店

delicious hǎochī 好吃; **that was ~** zhēn hǎochī 真好吃

delight n xìngfèn 兴奋

delighted gāoxìng 高兴

delightful evening yúkuài 愉快; person kě'ài 可爱

delimit huàqīng jièxiàn 划清界线

delirious MED zhānwàng 谵妄; (ecstatic) jídù xīngfèn 极度兴奋

deliver sòng 送; message dìjiāo 递交; baby shēng 生; **~ a speech** jiǎnghuà 讲话

delivery (of goods, mail) sònghuò 送货; (of baby) fēnmiǎn 分娩

delivery date sònghuò rìqī 送货日期; **delivery note** sònghuò dān 送货单; **delivery van** sònghuò chē 送货车

delude qīpiàn 欺骗; **~ oneself** zìqī 自欺

deluge 1 n dàyǔ 大雨; fig fēngyōng érzhì 蜂拥而至 2 v/t fig yānmò 淹没

delusion wàngxiǎng 妄想

de luxe adj háohuá 豪华

demand 1 n yāoqiú 要求; COM xūqiú 需求; **in ~** yǒu xūyào 有需要 2 v/t yāoqiú 要求

demanding job gāo yāoqiú 高要求; person kēkè 苛刻

demented jīngshén cuòluàn 精神错乱

demise qùshì 去世; fig mièwáng 灭亡

demitasse xiǎobēi 小杯

demo (protest) shìwēi 示威; (of video etc) shìfàn 示范

democracy mínzhǔ 民主

democrat mínzhǔ zhǔyì zhě 民主主义者; **Democrat** POL Mínzhǔ dǎngrén 民主党人

democratic mínzhǔ 民主

demo disk shìfàn dié 示范碟

demolish *building* chāihuǐ 拆毁;
argument cuīhuǐ 摧毁

demolition (*of building*) chāihuǐ 拆
毁; (*of argument*) cuīhuǐ 摧毁

demon móguǐ 魔鬼

demonstrate 1 *v/t* (*prove*)
zhèngmíng 证明; *machine* shìfàn
示范 2 *v/i* (*politically*) shìwēi 示威

demonstration (*show*) xiǎnshì 显
示; (*protest*) shìwēi 示威; (*of
machine*) shìfàn 示范

demonstrative: *be ~* gǎnqíng
wàilù 感情外露

demonstrator (*protester*) shìwēi
zhě 示威者

demoralized qìněi 气馁

demoralizing lìngrén xièqì 令人
泄气

den (*study*) shūfáng 书房

Deng Xiaoping Dèng Xiǎopíng 邓
小平

Deng Xiaoping theory Dèng
Xiǎopíng lǐlùn 邓小平理论

denial (*of rumour, accusation*)
fǒurèn 否认; (*of request*) jùjué 拒
绝

denim niúzǎi bù 牛仔布

denims (*jeans*) niúzǎikù 牛仔裤

Denmark Dānmài 丹麦

denomination (*of money*) miàn'é
面额; (*religious*) jiàopài 教派

dense (*thick*) nónghòu 浓厚;
foliage chóumì 稠密; *crowd* mìjí
密集; (*stupid*) chídùn 迟钝

densely: *~ populated* rénkǒu mìjí
人口密集

density (*of population*) chóumì dù
稠密度

dent 1 *n* āochù 凹处 2 *v/t* shǐ āoxià
使凹下

dental *treatment* yáchǐ 牙齿;
hospital yákē 牙科

dentist yáyī 牙医

dentures jiǎyá 假牙

deny *charge, rumour* fǒurèn 否认;
right, request jùjué 拒绝

deodorant ⇩ chúxiù jì 除臭剂

depart líkāi 离开; *~ from* (*deviate
from*) wéibèi 违背

department (*of company, store*)
bùmén 部门; (*of university*) xì 系;
(*of government*) bù 部; *Department of Defense* Guófáng bù 国
防部; *Department of the Interior*
Nèizhèng bù 内政部; *Depart-
ment of State* Guówùyuàn 国务
院

department store bǎihuò
shāngchǎng 百货商场

departure (*leaving*) dòngshēn 动
身; (*of train, bus*) chūfā 出发; (*of
person from job*) líkāi 离开;
(*deviation*) piānlí 偏离; *a new ~*
(*for government, organization*) xīn
qǐdiǎn 新起点; (*for company*) xīn
fāzhǎn 新发展; (*for actor, artist,
writer*) xīn fāngxiàng 新方向

departure lounge hòujī shì 候机
室

departure time qǐchéng shíjiān 启
程时间

depend: *that ~s* shì qíngxíng ér
dìng 视情形而定; *it ~s on the
weather* kàn tiānqì ba 看天气
吧; *I ~ on you* wǒ kàozhe nǐle 我
靠着你了

dependable kěkào 可靠

dependence, dependency yīlài
依赖

dependent 1 *n* yīkào zhě 依靠者
2 *adj* yīkào 依靠

depict (*in painting, writing*)
miáoshù 描述

deplorable lìngrén yíhàn 令人遗
憾

deplore tòngxī 痛惜

deport qūchú chūjìng 驱除出境

deportation qūchú chūjìng 驱除
出境

deportation order qūchú lìng 驱
除令

deposit 1 *n* (*in bank*) cúnchǔ 存储;
(*of mineral*) chénjī 沉积; (*on
purchase*) dìngjīn 定金 2 *v/t money*
cúnchǔ 存储; (*put down*) gē 搁;
silt, mud yūjī 淤积

deposition LAW xuānshì zhèng 宣
誓证

depot (*train station*) huǒchē zhàn

火车站; (*bus station*) qìchē zhàn 汽车站; (*for storage*) cāngkù 仓库

depreciate *v/i* FIN biǎnzhí 贬值

depreciation FIN biǎnzhí 贬值

depress *person* shǐ yōuyù 使忧郁

depressed *person* yōuyù 忧郁

depressing lìngrén shāngxīn 令人伤心

depression MED yōuyù zhèng 忧郁症; (*economic*) xiāotiáo 萧条; (*meteorological*) dīyā qū 低压区

deprive: ~ *X of Y* cóng X nàlǐ názǒu Y 从 X 那里拿走 Y

deprived pínkùn 贫困

depth (*of water, shelf, thought*) shēndù 深度; (*of voice*) dīchén dù 低沉度; (*of color*) nóngdù 浓度; **in ~** (*thoroughly*) shēnrù 深入; **in the ~s of winter** lóngdōng jìjié 隆冬季节; **be out of one's ~** (*in water*) zài shuǐ shēnde mòdǐng chù 在水深得没顶处; *fig* (*in discussion etc*) wúfǎ lǐjiě 无法理解

deputation shòuquán 授权

♦**deputize for** tìdài 替代

deputy dàilǐ 代理

deputy leader fù zǒngguǎn 副总管

derail: **be ~ed** (*of train*) tuōguǐ 脱轨

deranged fākuáng 发狂

derelict *adj* shīxiū 失修

deride qǔxiào 取笑

derision qǔxiào 取笑

derisive *remarks, laughter* cháonòng 嘲弄

derisory *amount, salary* wēibù zúdào 微不足道

derivative (*not original*) pàishēng 派生

derive *v/t* dédào 得到; **be ~d from** (*of word*) qǐyuán yú 起源于

derogatory biǎnyì 贬义

descend 1 *v/t* xiàlái 下来; **be ~ed from** shì ... de hòuyì 是 ... 的后裔

descend 2 *v/i* (*of airplane*) xiàjiàng 下降; (*of road*) xiàxié 下斜; (*of mood, darkness*) lǒngzhào 笼罩

descendant hòuyì 后裔

descent (*from mountain*) xiàlái 下来; (*of airplane*) xiàjiàng 下降; (*ancestry*) zǔxiān 祖先; **of Chinese** ~ huáyì 华裔

describe miáoshù 描述; **~ X as Y** bǎ X xíngróng chéng Y 把 X 形容成 Y

description miáoxiě 描写; (*of criminal*) miáoshù 描述

desegregate qǔxiāo zhǒngzú gélí 取消种族隔离

desert[1] *n also fig* shāmò 沙漠

desert[2] **1** *v/t* (*abandon*) pāoqì 抛弃 **2** *v/i* (*of soldier*) kāi xiǎochāi 开小差

deserted huāngliáng 荒凉

deserter MIL táobīng 逃兵

desertion (*abandoning*) pāoqì 抛弃; MIL kāi xiǎochāi 开小差

deserve yīngdé 应得

design 1 *n* (*subject, of an object*) shèjì 设计; (*drawing*) shèjì tú 设计图; (*pattern*) tú'àn 图案 **2** *v/t* *building, car, machine* shèjì 设计; **not ~ed for heavy use** zhǐ xiàn qīngyòng 只限轻用

designate *v/t person* rènmìng 任命; *area* zhǐdìng 指定

designer (*of building, car, ship, audio*) shèjì shī 设计师

designer clothes míngpái fúzhuāng 名牌服装

design fault shèjì shīwù 设计失误

design school shèjì xuéyuàn 设计学院

desirable *residence* chèngxīn rúyì 称心如意; (*to be recommended*) zhíde 值得

desire *n* (*wish*) yuànwàng 愿望; (*sexual*) xìngyù 性欲

desk shūzhuō 书桌; (*in hotel*) wènxùn tái 问讯台

desk clerk jiēdàiyuán 接待员; **desktop computer** COMPUT ⇩ táishìjī 台式机; **desktop publishing** zhuōmiàn páibǎn 桌面排版

desolate *adj place* huāngliáng 荒凉

despair 1 *n* juéwàng 绝望; **in** ~

juéwàng 绝望 2 v/i juéwàng 绝望; **~ of** duì ... búbào xīwàng 对 ... 不抱希望

desperate person zǒutóu wúlù 走投无路; action gūzhù yīzhì 孤注一掷; situation wēijí 危急; **be ~ for a drink / cigarette** pòqiè xūyào yǐnliào / xiāngyān 迫切需要饮料 / 香烟

desperation gūzhù yīzhì 孤注一掷; **an act of ~** gūzhù yīzhì zhījǔ 孤注一掷之举

despise kànbùqǐ 看不起

despite jǐnguǎn 尽管

despondent yìqì xiāochén 意气消沉

despot bàojūn 暴君

dessert tiánpǐn 甜品

destination mùdìdì 目的地

destiny yuánfèn 缘分

destitute pínkùn 贫困

destroy cuīhuǐ 摧毁

destroyer (boat) qūchú jiàn 驱除舰

destruction pòhuài 破坏

destructive power pòhuài xìng 破坏性; criticism xiāojí 消极; child táoqì 淘气

detach fēnkāi 分开

detachable kě fēnkāi 可分开

detached (objective) wú piānjiàn 无偏见

detachment (objectivity) bùpiān bùyǐ 不偏不倚

detail n (small point) zhījié 枝节; (piece of information) xìjié 细节; (irrelevancy) suǒsuì xiǎoshì 琐碎小事; **in ~** xiángxì 详细

detailed xiángxì 详细

detain (hold back) dāngé dānge 耽搁; (as prisoner) jūliú 拘留

detainee: political ~ zhèngzhì fàn 政治犯

detect chájué 察觉; (of device) jiǎncè 检测

detection (of criminal, crime) zhēnchá 侦察; (of smoke etc) jiǎncè 检测

detective (policeman) zhēntàn 侦探

detective novel zhēntàn xiǎoshuō 侦探小说

detector tàncè qì 探测器

détente POL huǎnhé 缓和

detention (imprisonment) jūliú 拘留

deter (frighten) wēishè 危慑; (stop) zhìzhǐ 制止; **~ X from doing Y** zǔzhǐ X zuò Y 阻止 X 做 Y

detergent xǐdí jì 洗涤剂

deteriorate èhuà 恶化

determination (resolution) juéxīn 决心

determine (establish) chámíng 查明

determined xià juéxīn 下决心; effort jiānjué 坚决

deterrent n wēishè yīnsù 危慑因素

detest tǎoyàn 讨厌

detonate 1 v/t shǐ bàozhà 使爆炸 **2** v/i bàozhà 爆炸

detour n yūhuí 迂回; (diversion) ràodào xíngshǐ 绕道行驶

♦**detract from** achievement, enjoyment yǒusǔn yú 有损于; appearance of sth shǐ jiǎnsè 使减色

detriment: to the ~ of duì ... búlì 对 ... 不利

detrimental búlì 不利

deuce (in tennis) píngjú 平局

devaluation (of currency) biǎnzhí 贬值

devalue currency biǎnzhí 贬值

devastate also fig cuīhuǐ 摧毁

devastating cuīhuǐ xìng 摧毁性

develop 1 v/t film chōngxǐ 冲洗; land, site jiànshè 建设; activity, business kuòdà 扩大; (originate) fāmíng 发明; (improve on) gǎijìn 改进; illness, cold kāishǐ 开始 **2** v/i (grow) fāzhǎn 发展; (of person) zhǎngdà 长大

developer (of property) búdòngchǎn shāng 不动产商

developing country fāzhǎn zhōng guójiā 发展中国家

development (of film) chōngxǐ 冲洗; (of land, site) jiànshè 建设; (of business, country) fāzhǎn 发展; (event) shìjiàn 事件; (origination)

device (*tool*) qìjù 器具

devil móguǐ 魔鬼

devious (*sly*) jiǎohuá 狡猾

devise fāmíng 发明

devoid: ~ *of* wánquán méiyǒu 完全没有

devote *time, effort* gòngxiàn 贡献

devoted *son etc* zhōngshí 忠实; *be ~ to X* (*to parents, grandparents*) xiàoshùn X 孝顺 X; (*to any other person*) zhōngshí yú X 忠实于 X

devotion zhuānxīn 专心

devour *food* lángtūn hǔyàn 狼吞虎咽; *book* zháomí 着迷

devout qiánchéng 虔诚

dew lùshuǐ 露水

dexterity shúliàn jìqiǎo 熟练技巧

diabetes tángniàobìng 糖尿病

diabetic 1 *n* tángniàobìng huànzhě 糖尿病患者 **2** *adj* tángniàobìng 糖尿病

diagonal *adj* xié xié 斜斜

diagram tú tú 图图

dial 1 *n* (*of clock*) zhōngmiàn 钟面; (*of meter*) yíbiǎo 仪表; TELEC bōhào pán 拨号盘 **2** *v/i* TELEC bōhào 拨号 **3** *v/t* TELEC: *number* bō bō 拨拨

dialect fāngyán 方言

dialog duìhuà 对话

dial tone bōhàoyīn 拨号音

diameter zhíjìng 直径

diametrically: ~ *opposed* jiérán xiāngfǎn 截然相反

diamond (*jewel*) zuànshí 钻石; (*in cards*) fāngkuàir 方块儿; (*shape*) língxíng 菱形

diaper niàobù 尿布

diaphragm ANAT gémó 隔膜; (*contraceptive*) zǐgōng tuō 子宫托

diarrhea fùxiè 腹泻, lādùzi 拉肚子 F

diary rìjì 日记

dice 1 *n* tóuzi 骰子 **2** *v/t* (*cut*) qiē chéng dīng 切成丁

dichotomy liǎng duìlì 两对立

dictate *v/t letter, novel* kǒushòu 口授

dictation kǒushòu 口授

dictator POL dúcái zhě 独裁者

dictatorial *tone of voice* mìnglìng shì 命令式; *person, power* dúcái 独裁

dictatorship zhuānzhèng 专政

dictionary zìdiǎn 字典

die sǐ 死; ~ *of cancer* / *AIDS* sǐyú áizhèng / àizībìng 死于癌症 / 艾滋病; *I'm dying to know* / *leave* wǒ jí xiǎng zhīdào / líkāi 我极想知道 / 离开

♦ **die away** (*of noise*) zhújiàn xiāoshī 逐渐消失

♦ **die down** (*of noise*) jiàngdī 降低; (*of storm*) jiǎnruò 减弱; (*of fire*) biànruò 变弱; (*of excitement*) píngxī 平息

♦ **die out** (*of custom, species*) mièjué 灭绝

diesel (*fuel*) cháiyóu 柴油

diet 1 *n* (*regular food*) shíwù 食物; (*for losing weight*) jiǎnféi shípǐn 减肥食品; (*for health reasons*) tèzhǒng yǐnshí 特种饮食 **2** *v/i* (*to lose weight*) jiǎnféi 减肥

differ (*be different*) bùtóng 不同; (*disagree*) yìjiàn xiāngzuǒ 意见相左

difference chābié 差别; (*disagreement*) fēnqí 分歧; *it doesn't make any* ~ (*doesn't change anything*) méi shénme chābié 没什么差别; (*doesn't matter*) méi shénme guānxi 没什么关系

different bùtóng 不同

differentiate: ~ *between* qūfēn 区分

differently yǔzhòng bùtóng 与众不同

difficult bù róngyì 不容易

difficulty kùnnan 困难; *with* ~ chīlì 吃力

dig 1 *v/t* wā 挖 **2** *v/i*: *it was ~ging into me* juérù wǒ 掘入我

♦ **dig out** (*find*) zhǎochū 找出

♦ **dig up** juéqǐ 掘起; *information* cháchū 查出

digest *v/t* xiāohuà 消化; *information* línghuì 领会

digestible *food* kě xiāohuà 可消化

digestion xiāohuà 消化
digit (*number*) shùzì 数字; *a four ~ number* sìwèi shùzì 四位数字
digital shùzì 数字
dignified yǒu zūnyán 有尊严
dignitary dáguān guìrén 达官贵人
dignity zūnyán 尊严
digress zànshí lítí 暂时离题
digression zànshí lítí 暂时离题
dike (*wall*) dī 堤
dilapidated tānhuǐ 坍毁
dilate (*of pupils*) kuòzhāng 扩张
dilemma jìntuì liǎngnán 进退两难; *be in a ~* chùyú jìntuì liǎngnán de jìngdì 处于进退两难的境地
diligent qínfèn 勤奋
dilute *v/t* xīshì 稀释
dim 1 *adj room, light* hūn'àn 昏暗; *outline* bù xiǎnzhù 不显著; (*stupid*) shǎ 傻; *prospects* bēiguān 悲观 **2** *v/t*: *~ the headlights* shǐ chē qiándēng àndàn 使车前灯暗淡 **3** *v/i* (*of lights*) biàn àndàn 变暗淡
dimension (*measurement*) chǐcun 尺寸
diminish 1 *v/t value* shǐ jiǎnshǎo 使减少; *authority* xiāoruò 削弱 **2** *v/i* biànshǎo 变少
diminutive 1 *n* àichēng 爱称 **2** *adj* xiǎo 小
dimple jiǔwō 酒窝
dim sum diǎnxin 点心
din *n* xuānnào shēng 喧闹声
dine yòngcān 用餐
diner (*person*) yòngcān zhě 用餐者; (*restaurant*) xiǎo cānguǎn 小餐馆
dinghy xiǎochuán 小船
dingy *atmosphere* hūn'àn 昏暗; (*dirty*) zāng 脏
dining car cānchē 餐车; **dining room** cānshì 餐室; **dining table** cānzhuō 餐桌
dinner (*in the evening*) wǎncān 晚餐; (*at midday*) wǔcān 午餐; (*gathering*) yànhuì 宴会
dinner guest yànhuì kèrén 宴会客人; **dinner jacket** xiǎo lǐfú 小礼服; **dinner party** yànhuì 宴会
dinosaur kǒnglóng 恐龙
dip 1 *n* (*swim*) yóuyǒng 游泳; (*for food*) zhānliào 沾料; (*in road*) āoxiàn 凹陷 **2** *v/t zhān* 沾; *~ the headlights* diǎn chē qiándēng àndàn 使车前灯暗淡 **3** *v/i* (*of road*) qīngxié 倾斜
diploma wénpíng 文凭
diplomacy wàijiāo 外交; (*tact*) lǎoliàn 老练
diplomat wàijiāo guān 外交官
diplomatic wàijiāo 外交; (*tactful*) lǎoliàn 老练
dire (*urgent*) pòbù jídài 迫不及待
direct 1 *adj* zhíjiē 直接; *flight, train* zhídá 直达; *person* zhíshuǎng 直爽 **2** *v/t* (*to a place*) zhǐyǐn 指引; *play, movie* dǎoyǎn 导演; *attention* zhǐxiàng 指向
direct current ELEC zhíliú 直流
direction fāngxiàng 方向; (*of movie, play*) dǎoyǎn 导演; *~s* (*instructions*) zhǐshì 指示; (*to a place*) fāngwèi 方位; (*for use*) zhǐdǎo 指导; (*for medicine*) yòngfǎ 用法
direction indicator MOT fāngwèi zhǐshì 方位指示
directly 1 *adv* (*straight*) zhíjiē 直接; (*soon*) hěnkuài 很快; (*immediately*) lìjí 立即 **2** *conj* yīdāng 一当
director (*of company*) zhǔguǎn 主管; (*of play, movie*) dǎoyǎn 导演
directory zhǐdǎo 指导; TELEC diànhuà bù 电话簿
dirt (*grime*) zāng dōngxi 脏东西
dirt cheap hěn piányi 很便宜
dirty 1 *adj* zāng 脏; (*pornographic*) huángsè 黄色 **2** *v/t* nòngzāng 弄脏
dirty trick bēibǐ xíngwéi 卑鄙行为
disability cánjí 残疾
disabled 1 *n* cánjí rénshì 残疾人士 **2** *adj* cánjí 残疾
disadvantage (*drawback*) bùlì zhīchù 不利之处; *be at a ~* chīkuī 吃亏
disadvantaged shèhuì dìwèi dīxià

社会地位低下

disadvantageous búlì 不利

disagree (*of person*) bù tóngyì 不同意

♦**disagree with**: *~X* (*of person*) yǔ X yìjiàn bù yīzhì 与X意见不一致; (*of food*) yǔ X bù xiāngyí 与X不相宜

disagreeable lìngrén bù yúkuài 令人不愉快

disagreement bùtóng yìjiàn 不同意见; (*argument*) zhēngzhí 争执

disappear xiāoshī 消失; (*run away*) pǎodiào 跑掉

disappearance (*of item*) xiāoshī 消失; (*of person*) shīzōng 失踪

disappoint shǐ shīwàng 使失望

disappointed shīwàng 失望

disappointing lìngrén shīwàng 令人失望

disappointment shīwàng 失望

disapproval zhǐzé 指责

disapprove bù zànchéng 不赞成; *~ of* bù zànchéng 不赞成

disarm 1 *v/t robber* jiěchú wǔqì 解除武器; *militia* shǐ sàngshī shānghài nénglì 使丧失伤害能力 **2** *v/i* cáijūn 裁军

disarmament (*of militia*) jiěchú wǔzhuāng 解除武装; (*of country*) cáijūn 裁军

disarming shǐrén xiāochú huáiyí 使人消除怀疑

disaster zāinàn 灾难

disaster area shòuzāi dìqū 受灾地区; *fig* (*person*) mǎdàhā 马大哈

disastrous sǔnshī cǎnzhòng 损失惨重

disbelief: *in ~* bùkě xiāngxìn 不可相信

disc (*CD*) guāngdié 光碟

discard *old clothes etc* rēngdiào 扔掉; *boyfriend, theory* pāoqì 抛弃

discern *improvement* chájué 察觉; (*make out*) biànchū 辨出

discernible kě biànrèn chū 可辨认出

discerning yǒu yǎnlì 有眼力

discharge 1 *n* (*from hospital*) chūyuàn 出院; (*from army*) tuìwǔ 退伍; (*of waste*) páichū 排出 **2** *v/t* (*from hospital*) yǔnxǔ chūyuàn 允许出院; (*from army*) qiǎnsàn 遣散; (*from job*) kāichú 开除; *waste* páichū 排出

disciple (*religious*) zǐdì 子弟

disciplinary chéngjiè xìng 惩戒性

discipline 1 *n* jìlǜ 纪律 **2** *v/t child, dog, employee* chéngfá 惩罚

disc jockey DJ DJ

disclaim fǒurèn 否认

disclose tòulù 透露

disclosure (*of information, name*) tòulù 透露; (*about scandal etc*) xièlòu 泄露

disco dísīkē 迪斯科; (*place*) ⇩ dítīng 迪厅

discolor shǐ biànsè 使变色

discomfort *n* (*pain*) tòngkǔ 痛苦; (*embarrassment*) bú zìzài 不自在

disconcert shǐ wéinán 使为难

disconcerted jiǒngpò 窘迫

disconnect (*detach: hose, electrical / gas appliance*) shǐ bù jiētōng 使不接通; *supply, telephones* qiēduàn 切断; *I was ~ed* TELEC wǒ bèi qiēduàn le 我被切断了

disconsolate jǔsàng 沮丧

discontent bùmǎn 不满

discontented bù mǎnyì 不满意

discontinue *product* tíngzhǐ shēngchǎn 停止生产; *bus, train service, magazine* zhōngzhǐ 中止

discord MUS bù xiétiáo 不协调; (*in relations*) bù héxié 不和谐

discotheque dísīkē 迪斯科; (*place*) ⇩ dítīng 迪厅

discount 1 *n* zhékòu 折扣 **2** *v/t goods* dǎ zhékòu 打折扣; *theory* bù kǎolǜ 不考虑

discourage (*dissuade*) quànzǔ 劝阻; (*dishearten*) shǐ jǔsàng 使沮丧

discover fāxiàn 发现

discoverer fāxiàn zhě 发现明者

discovery fāxiàn 发现

discredit *v/t person* shǐ sàngshī míngyù 使丧失名誉; *theory* shǐrén bù xiāngxìn 使人不相信

discreet *person* jǐnshèn 谨慎; *restaurant* kǎolǜ zhōudào 考虑周到

discrepancy chācuò 差错

discretion pànduàn nénglì 判断能力; **at your ~** yóu nǐ zhuóqíng chǔlǐ 由你酌情处理

discriminate: **~ against** qíshì 歧视; **~ between** (*distinguish*) qūbié 区别

discriminating yǒu yǎnlì 有眼力

discrimination (*sexual, racial etc*) qíshì 歧视

discus SP tiěbǐng 铁饼

discuss tǎolùn 讨论; (*of article*) xiángshù 详述

discussion tǎolùn 讨论

disease jíbìng 疾病

disembark *v/i* (*from plane*) xià fēijī 下飞机; (*from ship*) xià chuán 下船

disenchanted: **~ with** duì ... shīqù xìngqù 对 ... 失去兴趣

disengage fàngkāi 放开

disentangle jiětuō kāi 解脱开

disfigure shǐ huǐróng 使毁容

disgrace **1** *n* xiūchǐ 羞耻; **a ~** (*person*) bù guāngcǎi de rén 不光彩的人; **it's a ~** bùzhí hàisào 不知害臊; **in ~** diūliǎn 丢脸 **2** *v/t* shǐ diūliǎn 使丢脸

disgraceful *behaviour, situation* yǒushī tǐmiàn 有失体面

disgruntled bùmǎn 不满

disguise **1** *n* wěizhuāng 伪装; (*costume, make-up*) jiǎ miànjù 假面具 **2** *v/t* yǐnmán 隐瞒; *fear, anxiety* yǎncáng 掩藏; **~ oneself as** zhuāngbàn chéng 装扮成; **he was ~d as** tā jiǎzhuāng shì 他假装是

disgust **1** *n* jíwéi fǎngǎn 极为反感 **2** *v/t* shǐ fǎngǎn 使反感

disgusting *habit, smell, food* lìngrén zuò'ǒu 令人作呕

dish (*part of meal*) cài cài 菜; (*container*) diézi 碟子

dishcloth xǐwǎn bù 洗碗布

disheartened jǔsàng 沮丧

disheartening lìngrén shāngxīn 令人伤心

disheveled bù zhěngqí 不整齐

dishonest bù chéngshí 不诚实

dishonesty bù chéngshí 不诚实

dishonor *n* chǐrǔ 耻辱; **bring ~ on** dàilái chǐrǔ 带来耻辱

dishonorable kěchǐ 可耻

dishwasher (*machine*) xǐwǎn jī 洗碗机; (*person*) xǐwǎn gōng 洗碗工

dishwashing liquid xǐjiéjīng 洗洁精

dishwater xǐwǎn shuǐ 洗碗水

disillusion *v/t* shǐ huànxiǎng pòmiè 使幻想破灭

disillusionment huànmiè 幻灭

disinclined bú yuànyì 不愿意

disinfect xiāodú 消毒

disinfectant xiāodú jì 消毒剂

disinherit bōduó jìchéng quán 剥夺继承权

disintegrate lièkāi 裂开; (*of marriage, building*) wǎjiě 瓦解

disinterested (*unbiassed*) zhōnglì 中立

disjointed tuōjié 脱节

disk (*shape*) yuánpán 圆盘; COMPUT ⇩ cípán 磁盘; **on ~** chǔcún zài cípán shàng 储存在磁盘上

disk drive COMPUT ⇩ cípán dàijī 磁盘带机

diskette ⇩ ruǎn cípán 软磁盘

dislike **1** *n* fǎngǎn 反感 **2** *v/t* bù xǐhuān 不喜欢

dislocate *shoulder* tuōwèi 脱位

dislodge shǐ yídòng 使移动

disloyal bù zhōngchéng 不忠诚

disloyalty bùzhōng 不忠

dismal *weather* zāogāo 糟糕; *news, prospect* lìngrén jǔsàng 令人沮丧; *person* (*sad*) yōuxīn chōngchong 忧心忡忡; *person* (*negative*) xiāochén 消沉; *failure* bēicǎn 悲惨

dismantle *object* chāi 拆; *organization* shǐ jiětǐ 使解体

dismay **1** *n* (*alarm*) jīng'è 惊愕; (*disappointment*) shīwàng 失望 **2** *v/t* shǐ huīxīn 使灰心

dismiss *employee* jiěgù 解雇; *suggestion, idea* bù kǎolù 不考虑; *possibility* bú fàngzài xīnshàng 不放在心上

dismissal (*of employee*) jiěgù 解雇

disobedience bù fúcóng 不服从
disobedient juéjiàng 倔强
disobey wéibèi 违背
disorder (*untidiness*) záluàn 杂乱; (*unrest*) bàoluàn 暴乱; MED shītiáo 失调
disorderly *room, desk* záluàn 杂乱; *mob* bù shǒu zhìxù 不守秩序
disorganized wú zǔzhi 无组织
disoriented míhuo 迷惑
disown tuōlí guānxì 脱离关系
disparaging biǎnyì 贬抑
disparity xuánshū 悬殊
dispassionate (*objective*) bù piānxīn 不偏心
dispatch *v/t* (*send*) fāchū 发出
dispensary (*in pharmacy*) yàofáng 药房
dispense: ~ *with* shěngquè 省却
disperse 1 *v/t* qūsàn 驱散 2 *v/i* (*of crowd*) shūsàn 疏散; (*of mist*) qūsàn 驱散
displace (*supplant*) páijǐ 排挤
display 1 *n* zhǎnlǎn 展览; (*of emotion*) biǎoshì 表示; (*in store window*) chénliè 陈列; COMPUT xiǎnshì 显示; *be on ~* (*at exhibition*) zhǎnlǎn 展览; (*be for sale*) chénliè 陈列 2 *v/t emotion* xiǎnshì 显示; (*at exhibition*) zhǎnlǎn 展览; (*for sale*) chénliè 陈列; COMPUT xiǎnshì 显示
display cabinet (*in museum, store*) zhǎnlǎn chúchuāng 展览橱窗
displease shǐ bù gāoxìng 使不高兴
displeasure bùmǎn 不满
disposable *diapers, contact lenses* yīcìxìng 一次性; ~ *income* shèngyú shōurù 剩余收入
disposal rēngdiào 扔掉; (*of pollutants, nuclear waste*) chǔlǐ 处理; *I am at your* ~ wǒ tīng nǐ zhī biàn 我听你之便; *put X at Y's* ~ ràng Y zìyóu zhīpèi X 让 Y 自由支配 X
dispose: ~ *of* rēngdiào 扔掉
disposed: *be* ~ *to do X* (*willing*) yuànyì zuò X 愿意做 X; *be well* ~ *toward X* duì X yǒu hǎogǎn 对 X 有好感

disposition (*nature*) qīngxiàng 倾向
disproportionate bùchéng bǐlì 不成比例
disprove fǎnzhèng 反证
dispute 1 *n* zhēnglùn 争论; (*between the two countries*) zhēngbiàn 争辩; (*industrial*) zhēngzhí 争执 2 *v/t* zhēnglùn 争论; (*fight over*) zhēngduó 争夺
disqualify qǔxiāo zīgé 取消资格
disregard *n* & *v/t* hūshì 忽视
disrepair: *in a state of* ~ shīxiū 失修
disreputable shēngmíng bàihuài 声名败坏; *area* shēngyù bùhǎo 声誉不好
disrespect bù zūnzhòng 不尊重
disrespectful bù lǐmào 不礼貌
disrupt *train service* shǐ tíngdùn 使停顿; *meeting, class* pòhuài 破坏; (*intentionally*) rǎoluàn 扰乱
disruption (*of train service*) tíngdùn 停顿; (*of meeting, class*) pòhuài 破坏; (*intentional*) rǎoluàn 扰乱
disruptive pòhuài xìng 破坏性
dissatisfaction bùmǎn 不满
dissatisfied bù mǎnyì 不满意
dissension yìjiàn fēnqí 意见分歧
dissent 1 *n* chí yìyì 持异议 2 *v/i*: ~ *from* chàng fǎndiào 唱反调
dissident *n* chí bùtóng zhèngjiàn zhě 持不同政见者
dissimilar bùtóng 不同
dissociate: ~ *oneself from X* fǒurèn zìjǐ hé X yǒu guānxi 否认自己和 X 有关系
dissolute fàngdàng 放荡
dissolve *v/t* & *v/i* róngjiě 溶解
dissuade quànzhǐ 劝止; ~ *X from Y* quànzǔ X bùyào qù zuò Y 劝阻 X 不要去做 Y
distance 1 *n* jùlí 距离; *in the* ~ zài yuǎnchù 在远处 2 *v/t*: ~ *oneself from X* shǐ zìjǐ yǔ X bǎochí jùlí 使自己和 X 保持距离
distant *place, time, relative* yuǎn 远; *fig* (*aloof*) bǎochí yīdìngde jùlí 保持一定的距离
distaste xiánwù 嫌恶
distasteful lìngrén yànwù 令人厌恶

distinct (*clear*) míngxiǎn 明显；
(*different*) bùtóng 不同；*as ~ from*
X yǔ X bùtóng 与X不同

distinction (*differentiation*) qūbié
区别；*hotel / product of* ~ gāo
zhìliàng lǚguǎn / chǎnpǐn 高质量
旅馆 / 产品

distinctive tèyǒu 特有

distinctly qīngchǔ 清楚；
(*decidedly*) míngxiǎn 明显

distinguish (*see*) biànbié 辨别；~
between X and Y qūfēn X hé Y
区分X和Y

distinguished (*famous*) zhùmíng
著名；(*dignified*) yǔzhòng bùtóng
与众不同

distort wāiqū 歪曲

distract *person* shǐ fēnxīn 使分心；
attention fēnsàn zhùyì lì 分散注
意力

distracted (*worried*) yōulǜ 忧虑

distraction (*of attention*) fēnshén
wù 分神物；(*amusement*) yúlè 娱
乐；*drive X to* ~ shǐ X fēnxīn 使X
分心

distraught xīnshén bùdìng 心神
不定

distress 1 *n* (*mental suffering*)
kǔnǎo 苦恼；(*physical pain*)
tòngkǔ 痛苦；*in* ~ (*ship, aircraft*)
wēinàn zhōng 危难中 **2** *v/t*
(*upset*) shāngxīn 伤心

distress signal qiújiù xìnhào 求救
信号

distribute fēngěi 分给；*leaflets*
sànfā 散发；*wealth* fēnpèi 分配；
COM jīngxiāo 经销

distribution (*handing out*) fēnfā 分
发；(*of wealth*) fēnpèi 分配；COM
jīngxiāo 经销

distribution arrangement COM
jīngxiāo hétóng 经销合同

distributor COM jīngxiāo shāng 经
销商

district qū 区

district attorney dìfāng jiǎnchá
guān 地方检查官

distrust *n & v/t* huáiyí 怀疑

disturb (*interrupt*) dǎjiǎo 打搅；
(*upset*) dānyōu 担忧；*do not* ~
qǐngwù dǎjiǎo 请勿打搅

disturbance (*interruption*) gānrǎo
干扰；~*s* sāoluàn 骚乱

disturbed (*concerned, worried*)
dānxīn 担心；*mentally* ~ jīngshén
shīcháng 精神失常

disturbing lìngrén shāngxīn 令人
伤心

disused fèiqì 废弃

ditch 1 *n* kēng 坑 **2** *v/t* F (*get rid of*)
pāoqì 抛弃

dive 1 *n* tiàoshuǐ 跳水；
(*underwater*) qiánshuǐ 潜水；(*of
plane*) fǔchōng 俯冲；F (*bar etc*)
xiàděng chǎngsuǒ 下等场所；
take a ~ (*of dollar etc*) tūrán
xiàjiàng 突然下降 **2** *v/i* tiàoshuǐ
跳水；(*underwater*) qiánshuǐ 潜
水；(*of plane*) fǔchōng 俯冲

diver (*off board*) tiàoshuǐ zhě 跳水
者；(*underwater*) qiánshuǐ zhě 潜
水者

diverge chàkāi 岔开

diverse duōyàng huà 多样化

diversification COM duōzhǒng
jīngyíng 多种经营

diversify *v/i* COM duōzhǒng
jīngyíng 多种经营

diversion (*for traffic*) gǎixiàn 改
线；(*to distract attention*) qiānzhì 牵
制

diversity duōyàng huà 多样化

divert *traffic* gǎixiàn 改线；~ *attention* fēnsàn zhùyì lì 分散注
意力

divest ~ *X of Y* gěi X bōduó Y 给X
剥夺Y

divide fēn 分；*fig: country, family*
fēnliè 分裂

dividend FIN gǔxī 股息；*pay ~s fig*
lìng shòuyì 令受益

divine REL shén 神；F gài le mào le
盖了帽了

diving (*from board*) tiàoshuì 跳水；
(*scuba* ~) qiánshuǐ 潜水

diving board tiàoshuǐ bǎn 跳水板

divisible kě chú jìn 可除尽

division MATH chúfǎ 除法；(*split: in
party etc*) fēnliè 分裂；(*splitting
into parts*) fēngē 分割；(*of
company*) bùmén 部门

divorce 1 *n* líhūn 离婚；*get a* ~

líhūn 离婚 **2** *v/t & v/i* líhūn 离婚

divorced líhūn 离婚; **get ~d** líhūn 离婚

divorcee líhūn zhě 离婚者

divulge tòulù 透露

DIY (= **do-it-yourself**) zìjǐ dòngshǒu 自己动手

DIY store zìjǐ dòngshǒu shāngdiàn 自己动手商店

dizzy: feel ~ tóuyūn 头晕

DNA (= **deoxyribonucleic acid**) tuōyǎng hétáng hésuān 脱氧核糖核酸

do 1 *v/t* zuò 做; *one's hair* shū 梳; *the beds* pū 铺; *French, chemistry etc* xuéxí 学习; *100mph etc* xíngshǐ 行驶; **what are you ~ing tonight?** nǐ jīnwǎn gànshénme? 你今晚干什么？; **I don't know what to ~** wǒ bùzhī gāi zěnme bàn 我不知该怎么办; **no, I'll ~ it** bùyòng, wǒ lái ba 不用，我来吧; **~ it right now!** mǎshàng jiù gàn! 马上就干！; **have you done this before?** yǐqián gàn guò ma? 以前干过吗？; **have one's hair done** zuò tóufà 做头发 **2** *v/i* (*be suitable, enough*) yě kěyǐ 也可以; **that will ~!** xíng! 行了！; **~ well** (*of person*) chénggōng 成功; (*of business*) chāngshèng 昌盛; **well done!** (*congratulations!*) gōngxǐ! 恭喜！; **how ~ you ~?** nǐ hǎoma? 你好吗? **3** *auxiliary:* **~ you know him?** nǐ rènshi tā ma? 你认识他吗？; **I don't know** wǒ bù zhīdào 我不知道; **~ you like … ? – yes I ~** nǐ xǐhuān … ma? – wǒ xǐhuān 你喜欢…吗？– 我喜欢; **he works hard, doesn't he?** tā gōngzuò hái nǔlì, shìba? 他工作还努力，是吧？; **don't you believe me?** nǐ nándào bù xiāngxìn wǒ? 你难道不相信我？; **you ~ believe me, don't you?** nǐ quèshí xiāngxìn wǒ, shìba? 你确实相信我，是吧？; **you don't know the answer, ~ you? – no I don't** nǐ bù zhīdào dá'àn, shìba? – wǒ bù zhīdào 你不知道答案，是吧？– 我不知道

♦ **do away with** fèichú 废除

♦ **do in: I'm done in** F wǒ lèisǐ le 我累死了

♦ **do out of: do X out of Y** piànXY 骗XY

♦ **do up** (*renovate*) gǎizhuāng 改装; (*fasten*) jìláo 系牢; *buttons* kòuhǎo 扣好; *laces* bǎng xiédài 绑鞋带

♦ **do with: I could ~ …** wǒ xiǎngyào … 我想要…; **he won't have anything to ~ it** (*won't get involved*) tā bùxiǎng jièrù 他不想介入

♦ **do without 1** *v/i* méiyǒu yěxíng 没有也行 **2** *v/t* bù xūyào 不需要

docile *person* shùncóng 顺从; *animal* xùnfú 驯服

dock[1] **1** *n* NAUT chuánwù 船坞 **2** *v/i* (*of ship*) kào mǎtóu 靠码头; (*of spaceship*) duì jiē chù 对接处

dock[2] LAW bèigào xí 被告席

dockyard chuánchǎng 船厂

doctor *n* MED yīshēng 医生; (*form of address*) yīshēng 医生

doctorate bóshì 博士

doctrine jiàotiáo 教条

docudrama jìshí diànshì jù 记实电视剧

document *n* wénjiàn 文件

documentary (*program*) jìlù piān 纪录片

documentation wénjiàn 文件

dodge *v/t blow* shǎnkāi 闪开; *person, issue* duǒbì 躲避; *question* bìkāi 避开

doe (*deer*) mǔlù 母鹿

dog 1 *n* gǒu 狗 **2** *v/t* (*of bad luck*) bànsuí 伴随

dog catcher zhuā gǒu rén 抓狗人

dog-eared *book* juǎnjiǎo 卷角

dogged gùzhí 固执

doggie (*in children's language*) gǒugǒu 狗狗

doggy bag gǒu shí dài 狗食袋

doghouse: be in the ~ shòu lěngyù 受冷遇

dogma jiàotiáo 教条

dogmatic jiàotiáo zhǔyì 教条主义

do-gooder Léi Fēng shūshu 雷锋
叔叔

dog tag MIL shēnfèn shíbié pái 身
份识别牌

dog-tired lèi sǐ le 累死了

do-it-yourself zìjǐ dòngshǒu 自己
动手

doldrums: *be in the ~* (*of economy*)
wú shēngqì 无生气

♦**dole out** shǎoliàng pèijǐ 少量配
给

doll (*toy*) wáwa 娃娃; F (*woman*)
měimào shàonǚ 美貌少女

♦**doll up:** *get dolled up* dǎbàn 打
扮

dollar měiyuán 美元

dollop *n* yīdìng liàng 一定量

dolphin hǎitún 海豚

dome (*of building*) yuándǐng 圆顶

domestic *adj chores* jiātíng 家庭;
news, policy guónèi 国内; (*for
agriculture*) jiāchù 家畜

domesticate *animal* xùnhuà 驯化;
be ~d (*of person*) zuò jiāwù 做家
务

domestic flight guónèi hángbān
国内航班

dominant zhǔyào 主要; *member*
zhǔdǎo 主导; BIO zhàn yōushì 占
优势

dominate kòngzhì 控制; *landscape*
gāosǒng yú 高耸于

domination kòngzhì 控制

domineering bàdào 霸道

donate *money* juān 捐; *toys, books,*
MED juānxiàn 捐献; *time, energy*
fùchū 付出

donation (*of money, toys, books*),
MED juānxiàn 捐献; (*of time,
energy*) fùchū 付出

donkey lǘ 驴

donor (*of money*), MED juānxiàn
zhě 捐献者

donut ⇩ zhá miànbǐngquān 炸面
饼圈

doom *n* (*fate*) mìngyùn 命运;
(*ruin*) zāinàn 灾难

doomed *project* zhùdìng shībài 注
定失败; *we are ~* (*bound to fail*)
wǒmen sǐdìng le 我们死定了;
the ~ ship / *plane* yùnàn
chuánzhī / fēijī 遇难船只 / 飞机

door mén 门; (*entrance*) dàmén 大
门; *there's someone at the ~*
yǒurén qiāomén 有人敲门

doorbell ménlíng 门铃; **doorknob** mén bǎshǒu 门把手;
doorman shǒumén rén 守门人;
doormat méndiàn 门垫; **doorstep** ménjiē 门阶; **doorway**
rùkǒu 入口

dope 1 *n* (*drugs*) dúpǐn 毒品;
(*idiot*) shǎzi 傻子; (*information*)
qíngbào 情报 **2** *v/t* shǐ mázuì 使
麻醉

dormant *plant* xiūmián 休眠; *~
volcano* jìng huǒshān 静火山

dormitory sùshè 宿舍

dosage yòngliàng 用量

dose *n* yòngliàng 用量

dot *n* (*also in e-mail*) diǎn 点; *on
the ~* (*exactly*) zhǔnshí 准时

♦**dote on** chǒng'ài 宠爱

dotted line diǎnxiàn 点线

double 1 *n* (*amount*) shuāngbèi 双
倍; (*person*) chóngyǐng 重影; (*of
movie star*) tìdài yǎnyuán 替代演
员; (*room*) shuāngrén fáng 双人
房 **2** *adj* (*twice as much*) liǎngbèi
两倍; *whisky* jiābèi 加倍; *sink,
oven* shuāng 双; *doors* liǎngchóng
两重; *layer* liǎngcéng 两层; *in ~
figures* liǎngwèi shù 两位数
3 *adv* liǎngbèi 两倍; **4** *v/t* jiābèi
加倍; (*fold*) duìzhé 对折 **5** *v/i*
fānyīfān 翻一番

♦**double back** *v/i* (*go back*) fǎnhuí
返回

♦**double up** (*in pain*) wānshēn 弯
身; (*share*) héyòng 合用

double-bass dīyīn tíqín 低音提
琴; **double bed** shuāngrén
chuáng 双人床; **double-
breasted** shuāngpái kòushì 双排
扣式; **doublecheck** *v/t & v/i*
fùchá 复查; **double chin**
shuāngxiàba 双下巴; **double
click** COMPUT shuāngjī 双击;
doublecross *v/t* qīpiàn 欺骗;
double glazing shuāngcéng bōli
双层玻璃; **double-quick:** *in ~
time* jíkuài 极快; **double room**

shuāngrén fáng 双人房
doubles (*in tennis*) shuāngdǎ 双打
doubt 1 *n* yíwèn 疑问; (*uncertainty*) yóuyù 犹豫; *be in ~* nányǐ quèdìng 难以确定; *no ~* (*probably*) wúyí 无疑 **2** *v/t* huáiyí 怀疑
doubtful *remark, look* zhíde huáiyí 值得怀疑; *be ~* (*of person*) ná bùzhǔn 拿不准; *it is ~ whether* nányǐ yùliào 难以预料
doubtfully huáiyí 怀疑
doubtless wúyí 无疑
dough shēngmiàn tuán 生面团; F (*money*) qián 钱
dove gēzi 鸽子; *fig* zhǔhé pài rénwù 主和派人物
dowdy bù xiāosǎ 不潇洒
Dow Jones Average Dào Qióng píngjūn zhí 道琼平均值
down[1] *n* (*feathers*) róng róng 绒绒
down[2] **1** *adv* (*downward, onto the ground*) xià 下; *~ there* zài xiàbiān 在下边; *fall ~* shuāidǎo 摔倒; *$200 ~* (*as deposit*) xiànfù èrbǎi měiyuán 现付二百美元; *~ south* zài nánfāng 在南方; *be ~* (*of price, rate*) xiàjiàng 下降; (*of numbers, amount*) jiǎnshǎo 减少; (*not working*) shīlíng 失灵; F (*depressed*) qíngxù dīluò 情绪低落 **2** *prep* xiàngxià 向下; (*along*) yánzhe 沿着; *it fell ~ the hole* diào kūlonglǐ le 掉窟窿里了; *go ~ this street* yánzhe zhèitiáo jì zǒu 沿着这条街走; *there are stores all ~ the street* mǎnjì dōushì shāngdiàn 满街都是商店; *he walked ~ the hill* tā xià shān le 他下山了 **3** *v/t* (*swallow*) tūnxià 吞下; (*destroy*) jībài 击败
down-and-out *n* qióngkùn liáodǎo 穷困潦倒; **downcast** (*dejected*) jǔsàng 沮丧; **downfall** *n* kuǎtái 垮台; (*reason for ~*) kuǎtái de yuányīn 垮台的原因; (*of politician*) xiàtái 下台; **downgrade** *v/t* jiàngdī děngjí 降低等级; *employee* jiàngzhí 降职; **downhearted** jǔsàng 沮丧; **downhill** *adv* xiàpō 下坡; *go ~ fig*

zǒu xiàpō lù 走下坡路; *~ skiing* xiàpō huáxuě 下坡滑雪; **download** COMPUT xiàzǎi 下载; **downmarket** *adj* dījí 低级; **down payment** dìngjīn 定金; **downplay** *v/t* qīngmiáo dànxiě 轻描淡写; **downpour** qīngpén dàyǔ 倾盆大雨; **downright 1** *adj* lie, idiot shízú 十足 **2** *adv* dangerous, stupid etc shízài shì 实在是; **downside** (*disadvantage*) quēxiàn 缺陷; **downsize** *v/t* car shēngchǎn xiǎoxíng 生产小型; *company* cáiyuán cáiyuán 裁员 **2** *v/i* (*of company*) cáiyuán 裁员; **downstairs** *adj & adv* lóuxià 楼下; **down-to-earth** *approach* jiǎotà shídì 脚踏实地; *person* shíshì qiúshì 实事求是; **down-town** *adj & adv* shì zhōngxīn 市中心; **downturn** (*in economy*) xiàjiàng qūshì 下降趋势
downward 1 *adj glance* xiàngxià 向下; *trend* xiàjiàng 下降 **2** *adv* wǎngxià 往下
doze *n & v/i* dǎdùnr 打盹儿
♦**doze off** dǎ kēshuì 打瞌睡
dozen shí'èr 十二, dá dǎ 打; *~s of X* F jǐshíge X 几十个 X
drab dāndiào 单调
draft 1 *n* (*of air*) guòtáng fēng 过堂风; (*of document*) cǎogǎo 草稿; MIL zhēngbīng 征兵; *~* (*beer*), *beer on ~* shēng píjiǔ 生啤酒 **2** *v/t document* qǐ cǎogǎo 起草稿; MIL zhēngbīng 征兵
draft dodger táobì bīngyì zhě 逃避兵役者
draftee yìngzhēng rùwǔ zhě 应征入伍者
draftsman huìtú yuán 绘图员; (*of plan*) qǐcǎo rén 起草人
drafty tōngfēng 通风
drag 1 *n*: *it's a ~ having to ...* yào zuò ... shízài shì tài méijìnr le 要做 ... 实在是太没劲儿了; *he's a ~* tā méi shénme jìn 他没什么劲; *the main ~* jiēdào 街道; *in ~* nánbàn nǚzhuāng 男扮女装 **2** *v/t* (*pull*) lā 拉; *person, oneself* yìnglā 硬拉; (*search*) sǎo 扫;

COMPUT tuōdòng 拖动 **3** *v/i* (*of time*) tuō 拖 ; (*of show, movie*) méijìnr 没劲儿; **~ X into Y** (*involve*) yìng bǎ X lāchě jìn Y 硬把 X 拉扯进 Y; **~ X out of Y** (*get information from*) cóng Y nàlǐ nádào X 从 Y 那里拿到 X

♦ **drag away: *drag oneself away from the TV*** qiángpò zìjǐ bùkàn diànshì 强迫自己不看电视

♦ **drag in** (*into conversation*) yìngchě rù 硬扯入

♦ **drag on** (*last long time*) tuō 拖

♦ **drag out** (*prolong*) tuōcháng 拖长

♦ **drag up** (*mention*) lǎotí 老提

dragon lóng 龙; *fig* pōfù 泼妇

Dragon Boat Festival Duānwǔjié 端午节

dragonfly qīngtíng 蜻蜓

drain 1 *n* (*pipe*) xiàshuǐ guǎndào 下水管道; (*under street*) xiàshuǐ dào 下水道; **a ~ on resources** hàofèi cáifù zhīwù 耗费财富之物 **2** *v/t water* lǜ 滤; *oil* páigān 排干; *vegetables* páigān shuǐfèn 排干水分; *land* shǐ gānhé 使干涸; *glass, tank* dàoguāng 倒光; (*exhaust: person*) jīnpí lìjìn 筋疲力尽 **3** *v/i* (*of dishes*) dīshuǐ 滴水

♦ **drain away** (*of liquid*) páiqù 排去

♦ **drain off** *water* páiqù 排去

drainage (*drains*) xiàshuǐ dào 下水道; (*of water from soil*) páishuǐ 排水

drainpipe páishuǐ guǎn 排水管

drama (*art form, play in theater*) xìjù 戏剧; (*play on TV*) jiémù 节目; (*dramatic event*) xìjùxìng shìjiàn 戏剧性事件; (*excitement*) xīngfèn 兴奋

dramatic xìjù 戏剧; (*exciting*) xìjù xìng 戏剧性; *gesture* zuòzuò 做作

dramatist jùzuò jiā 剧作家

dramatization (*play*) gǎibiān chéng xìjù 改编成戏剧

dramatize *story* gǎibiān chéng xìjù 改编成戏剧; *fig* zuòzuò 做作

drape *v/t cloth, coat* guà 挂; **~d in** (*covered with*) fùgài 覆盖

drapery bùshì 布饰

drapes chuānglián 窗帘

drastic (*extreme*) yánzhòng 严重; *measures* jíduān 极端; *change* jídà 极大

draw 1 *n* (*in match, competition*) píngjú 平局; (*in lottery*) kāijiǎng 开奖; (*attraction*) xīyǐn 吸引 **2** *v/t picture, map* huà 画; *cart, curtain* lā 拉; *lottery ticket* chōu 抽; *gun, knife* chōuchū 抽出; (*attract*) xīyǐn 吸引; (*lead*) jiào 叫; (*from bank account*) tíkuǎn 提款 **3** *v/i* huàhuà 画画; (*in match, competition*) dǎ píngjú 打平局; **~ near** (*of person*) zǒujìn 走近; (*of date*) línjìn 临近

♦ **draw back 1** *v/i* (*recoil*) suōhuí 缩回 **2** *v/t* (*pull back*) lākāi 拉开

♦ **draw on 1** *v/i* (*advance*) línjìn 临近 **2** *v/t* (*make use of*) lìyòng 利用

♦ **draw out** *billfold, money* qǔchū 取出

♦ **draw up 1** *v/t document* qǐcǎo 起草; *chair* lā guòlái 拉过来 **2** *v/i* (*of vehicle*) tíng 停

drawback bìduān 弊端

drawer[1] (*of desk etc*) chōuti 抽屉

drawer[2]: **she is a good ~** tā hěnhuì huàhuàr 她很会画画儿

drawing (*picture*) huà 画; (*skill*) huìtú 绘图

drawing board túbǎn 图板; ***go back to the ~*** chóngxīn kāishǐ 重新开始

drawl *n* màn tūntun de jiǎnghuà 慢吞吞地讲话

dread *v/t* hàipà 害怕

dreadful zāogāo 糟糕

dreadfully (*extremely*) jíduān 极端; *behave* zāogāo 糟糕

dream 1 *n* mèng 梦 **2** *adj house etc* mèngzhōng 梦中 **3** *v/t & v/i* zuòmèng 做梦; (*day~*) mèngxiǎng 梦想

♦ **dream up** píngkōng xiǎngchū 凭空想出

dreamer (*day~*) mèngxiǎng jiā 梦想家

dreamy *voice, look* jīngshen huǎnghū 精神恍惚

dreary chénmèn 沉闷

dredge *harbour, canal* shūjùn 疏浚
♦**dredge up** *fig* wāchū 挖出
dregs *(of coffee)* zhāzi 渣子; *the ~ of society* shèhuì zhāzǐ 社会渣滓
drench *v/t* shǐ shītòu 使湿透; *get ~ed* bèi yǔlín 被雨淋
dress 1 *n (for woman)* ↓ liányīqún 连衣裙; *(clothing)* fúzhuāng 服装 **2** *v/t wound* fūguǒ 敷裹; *~ X person* gěi X chuān yīfu 给 X 穿衣服; *get ~ed* chuān yīfu 穿衣服 **3** *v/i (get ~ed)* chuān yīfu 穿衣服; *(well, in black etc)* chuānzhe 穿著
♦**dress up** *v/i* dǎbàn 打扮; *(wear a disguise)* wěizhuāng 伪装; *~ as* zhuāngbàn chéng 装扮成
dress circle tèděng bāoxiāng 特等包厢
dresser *(dressing table)* shūzhuāng tái 梳妆台; *(in kitchen)* wǎndié guì 碗碟柜
dressing *(for salad)* tiáowèi zhīr 调味汁儿; *(for wound)* fūliào 敷料
dressing room *(in theater)* huàzhuāng shì 化装室
dressing table shūzhuāng tái 梳妆台
dressmaker cáifeng 裁缝
dress rehearsal cǎipái 彩排
dressy jiǎngjiu 讲究
dribble *v/i (of person, baby)* liú kǒushuǐ 流口水; *(of water)* dī dī 滴; SP dàiqiú 带球
dried *fruit etc* gān 干; *~ bean curd* gāndòufu 干豆腐
drier *(machine)* shuǎigān jī 甩干机
drift 1 *n (of snow)* xuěduī 雪堆 **2** *v/i (of snow)* xuě chéngduī 雪成堆; *(of ship)* piāofú 漂浮; *(go off course)* piāobó 漂泊; *(of person)* liúdàng 流荡
♦**drift apart** *(of couple)* shūyuǎn 疏远
drifter liúlàng zhě 流浪者
drill 1 *n (tool)* zuàn 钻; *(exercise)* yǎnxí 演习; MIL cāoliàn 操练 **2** *v/t hole* zuàn 钻 **3** *v/i (for oil)* zuàn 钻; MIL cāoliàn 操练
drilling rig *(platform)* yóutái 油台
drily *remark* lěng bīngbīng 冷冰冰
drink 1 *n* yǐnliào 饮料; *a ~ of*

water yīdiǎn shuǐ 一点水; *go for a ~* qù hē diǎn dōngxi 去喝点东西 **2** *v/t* hē 喝 **3** *v/i* hē 喝; *(consume alcohol)* hējiǔ 喝酒; *I don't ~* wǒ bù hējiǔ 我不喝酒
♦**drink up** *v/t & v/i* hēguāng 喝光
drinkable kěyǐ hē 可以喝
drinker yǐnjiǔ zhě 饮酒者
drinking *(of alcohol)* hējiǔ 喝酒
drinking water yǐnyòng shuǐ 饮用水
drip 1 *n (liquid)* dī 滴; MED diǎndī 点滴 **2** *v/i* dī 滴
dripdry dīgān 滴干
dripping: *~ (wet)* quánbù shītòu 全部湿透
drive 1 *n (journey)* lǚtú 旅途; *(outing)* dōufēng 兜风; *(energy)* jīnglì 精力; COMPUT cípán dàijī 磁盘带机; *(campaign)* yùndòng 运动; *left-/right-hand ~* MOT zuǒ/yǒu zuǒ jiàshǐ 左/右座驾驶 **2** *v/t vehicle* jiàshǐ 驾驶; *(own)* yōngyǒu 拥有; *(take in car)* yòng chē sòng 用车送; TECH qūdòng 驱动; *that noise/he is driving me mad* nàge zàoyīn/tā lìngwǒ fāfēng 那个噪音/他令我发疯 **3** *v/i* jiàshǐ 驾驶
♦**drive at:** *what are you driving at?* nǐ shénme yìsi? 你什么意思?
♦**drive away 1** *v/t* qūchē líkāi 驱车离开; *(chase off)* hōng 哄 **2** *v/i* qūchē líkāi 驱车离开
♦**drive in** *v/t nail* qiāojìn 敲进
♦**drive off** *v/i* qūchē líkāi 驱车离开
driver sījī 司机
driver's license jiàshǐ zhízhào 驾驶执照
driveway qìchē dào 汽车道
driving 1 *n* jiàshǐ 驾驶 **2** *adj rain* měngliè 猛烈
driving force dònglì 动力; **driving instructor** jiàshǐ jiàoliàn 驾驶教练; **driving lesson** xuéchē kèchéng 学车课程; **driving school** ↓ jiàshǐ xuéxiào 驾驶学校; **driving test** jiàzhí kǎoshì 驾驶考试

drizzle 1 *n* máomao yǔ 毛毛雨
2 *v/i* xià máomao yǔ 下毛毛雨

drone *n* (*noise*) wēngmíng shēng 嗡鸣声

droop *v/i* xiàchuí 下垂; (*of plant*) kūwěi 枯萎

drop 1 *n* (*of rain*) dī 滴; (*small amount*) yīdiǎn 一点; (*in price, temperature*) diē tiē 跌; (*in number*) xiàjiàng 下降 **2** *v/t* rēng 扔; (*and lose*) diūshī 丢失; *person from car* ràng ... xiàchē 让 ... 下车; *person from team* chúqù 除去; (*stop seeing*) duànjué guānxi 断绝关系; *charges, demand etc* qǔxiāo 取消; (*give up*) fàngqì 放弃; **~ a line to** jì fēng duǎn xìn 寄封短信 **3** *v/i* diēluò 跌落; (*decline*) xiàjiàng 下降; (*of wind*) jiǎnhuǎn 减缓

♦ **drop in** (*visit*) shùnbiàn láifǎng 顺便来访

♦ **drop off 1** *v/t person* ràng ... xiàchē 让 ... 下车; (*deliver*) shùnbiàn sòng 顺便送 **2** *v/i* (*fall asleep*) shuìzháo 睡着; (*decline*) zhújiàn xiàjiàng 逐渐下降

♦ **drop out** (*withdraw*) tuìchū 退出; (*of school*) zhōngtú tuìxué 中途退学

dropout (*from school*) tuìxué xuéshēng 退学学生; (*from society*) tuìchū shìsú zhě 退出世俗者

drops (*for eyes*) yǎn yàoshuǐ 眼药水

drought gānhàn 干旱

drown 1 *v/i* yānsǐ 淹死 **2** *v/t person* yānsǐ 淹死; *sound* yānmò 淹没; **be ~ed** yānsǐ 淹死

drowsy fākùn 发困

drudgery dāndiào 单调

drug 1 *n* MED yào 药; (*illegal*) dúpǐn 毒品; **be on ~s** yǒu xīdú shìhào 有吸毒嗜好 **2** *v/t* xiàdú 下毒

drug addict xīdú chéngyǐn zhě 吸毒成瘾者; **drug dealer** fàndú zhě 贩毒者; **drug trafficking** fàndú 贩毒

druggist yàojì shī 药剂师

drugstore yàofáng 药房

drum 1 *n* MUS gǔ 鼓; (*container*) tǒng 桶

♦ **drum into: drum X into Y** xiàng Y qiángdiào X 向 Y 强调 X

♦ **drum up: ~ support** zhāolǎn zhīchí 招揽支持

drummer gǔshǒu 鼓手

drumstick MUS gǔchuí 鼓槌; (*of poultry*) jītuǐ 鸡腿

drunk 1 *n* zuìguǐ 醉鬼 **2** *adj* hēzuìle 喝醉了; **get ~** hēzuì 喝醉

drunken *voices, laughter* hēzuì 喝醉; **~ party** zuìjiǔ huì 醉酒会

drunk driving jiǔhòu kāichē 酒后开车

dry 1 *adj skin, clothes, weather, wine* gān 干; (*ironic*) wākǔ 挖苦; (*alcohol banned*) jìnjiǔ 禁酒 **2** *v/t dishes* cāgān 擦干 **3** *v/i* liànggān 晾干

♦ **dry out** (*of alcoholic*) jièjiǔ 戒酒

♦ **dry up** (*of river*) gānkū 干枯; (*be quiet*) bìzuǐ 闭嘴

dry-clean *v/t* gānxǐ 干洗

dry cleaner gānxǐ diàn 干洗店

dry cleaning (*clothes*) gānxǐ yīwù 干洗衣物

dryer (*machine*) shuǎigān jī 甩干机

DTP (= **desktop publishing**) zhuōmiàn páibǎn 桌面排版

dual shuāng 双

dub *movie* pèiyīn 配音

dubious kào būzhù 靠不住; (*having doubts*) yǒu huáiyí 有怀疑

duck 1 *n* yā 鸭 **2** *v/i* duǒcáng 躲藏 **3** *v/t one's head* dītóu 低头; *question* huíbì 回避

dud *n* (*false bill*) jiǎ chāopiào 假钞票

due (*owed*) qiàn 欠; (*proper*) shìdàng 适当; **is there a train ~?** huǒchē shìbùshì gāiláile? 火车是不是该来了?; **when is the baby ~?** háizi shénme shíhòu chūshēng? 孩子什么时候出生?; **~ to** (*because of*) yóuyú 由于; **be ~ to X** (*be caused by*) yīn X ér chǎnshēng 因 X 而产生; **in ~ course** zuìzhōng 最终

dull *weather* yīn chénchén 阴沉沉; *sound* bù qīngcuì 不清脆; *pain* dùn 钝; (*boring*) dāndiào 单调

duly (*as expected*) zhǔnshí 准时; (*properly*) shìdàng 适当

dumb (*mute*) yǎ 哑; (*stupid*) shǎ 傻

dump 1 n (*for garbage*) lājī zhàn 垃圾站; (*unpleasant place*) guǐdìfāng 鬼地方 **2** v/t (*deposit*) qīngdào 倾倒; (*dispose of*) rēng 扔; *toxic waste, nuclear waste* diūqì 丢弃

dumpling tuánzi 团子

dune shāqiū 沙丘

dung fènbiàn 粪便

dungarees lián yīkù 连衣裤

dunk *biscuit* diǎn 点

duo MUS yīduì 一对

duplex (*apartment*) ⇩ èrliánshì gōngyù 二连式公寓

duplicate 1 n fùjiàn 复件; *in ~* liǎngfèn 两份 **2** v/t (*copy*) fùzhì 复制; (*repeat*) chóngfù 重复

duplicate key fùzhì yàoshi 复制钥匙

durable *material* láo 牢; *relationship* chíjiǔ 持久

duration qījiān 期间

duress: *under ~* zài xiépò xià 在胁迫下

during: *~ X* zài X qījiān 在 X 期间

dusk huánghūn 黄昏

dust 1 n chéntǔ 尘土 **2** v/t: *~ X with Y* (*sprinkle*) bǎ Y sǎzài X shàng 把 Y 洒在 X 上

dust cover (*for furniture*) jiājù zhào 家具罩; (*for book*) shūpí 书皮

duster (*cloth*) mābù 抹布

dust jacket (*of book*) shūjí hùfēng 书籍护封

dustpan bòji 簸箕

dusty duō chéntǔ 多尘土

Dutch 1 adj Hélán 荷兰; *go ~* gèzì fùkuǎn 各自付款 **2** n (*language*) Hélán yǔ 荷兰语; *the ~* Hélán rénmín 荷兰人民

duty zérèn 责任; (*task*) rènwù 任务; (*on goods*) shuì 税; *be on ~* zhíbān 值班; *be off ~* xiàbān 下班

duty-free 1 adj miǎnshuì 免税 **2** n miǎnshuì wùpǐn 免税物品

duty-free store miǎnshuì shāngdiàn 免税商店

DVD COMPUT ⇩ shùzì shìpín guāngpán 数字视频光盘

dwarf 1 n zhūrú 侏儒 **2** v/t shǐ xiǎnde ǎixiǎo 使显得矮小

♦**dwell on** lǎoshì xiǎngzhe 老是想着

dwindle jiǎnshǎo 减少

dye 1 n rǎnliào 染料 **2** v/t rǎnsè 染色

dying *person* chuísǐ 垂死; *industry, tradition etc* jíjiāng mièjué 即将灭绝

dynamic *person* jīnglì chōngpèi 精力充沛

dynamism (*energy*) dònglì 动力

dynamite n zhàyào 炸药

dynamo TECH diàndòng jī 电动机

dynasty cháodài 朝代; *Ming Dynasty* Míngcháo 明朝

dyslexia sòngdú kùnnán 诵读困难

dyslexic 1 adj sòngdú kùnnán 诵读困难 **2** n sòngdú kùnnán bìnghuànzhě 诵读困难病患者

E

each 1 *adj* měigè 每个 2 *adv* fēnbié 分别; **they're $1.50 ~** měigè yī měiyuán wǔshí měifēn 每个一美元五十美分 3 *pron* měigè 每个; **~ other** bǐcǐ 彼此

eager kěwàng 渴望; **be ~ to do X** rèzhōngyú zuò X 热衷于做 X

eager beaver rèxīnchángde rén 热心肠的人

eagerly rèqiè 热切

eagerness rèxīn 热心

eagle yīng 鹰

ear (*of person, animal*) ěrduǒ 耳朵; (*of corn*) suì 穗

earache ěrtòng 耳痛

eardrum gǔmó 鼓膜

early 1 *adj* (*not late*) zǎo 早; (*ahead of time*) tíqián 提前; (*farther back in time*) zǎoqī 早期; (*in the near future*) xùnsù 迅速 2 *adv* (*not late*) zǎo 早; (*ahead of time*) tíqián 提前

early bird (*in morning*) zǎochén 早晨; (*who arrives early*) xiānxíng zhě 先行者

earmark *money* bōchū 拨出; **~ X for Y** wèi Y ānpái X 为 Y 安排 X

earn zhèng 挣; *holiday, drink etc* yīngdé 应得; *respect* yíngdé 赢得

earnest rènzhēn 认真; **in ~** rènzhēn 认真

earnings zhuànde qián 赚的钱

earphones ěrjī 耳机; **ear-piercing** *adj* cì'ěr 刺耳; **earring** ěrhuán 耳环; **earshot: within ~** zài tīnglì fànwéi zhīnèi 在听力范围之内; **out of ~** bú zài tīnglì fànwéi zhīnèi 不在听力范围之内

earth (*soil*) tǔ 土; (*world, planet*) dìqiú 地球; **where on ~ ... ?** dàodǐ zài nǎr ... ? 到底在哪儿 ... ?

earthenware *n* táoqì 陶器

earthly xiànshì 现世; **it's no ~ use ... ...** wánquán wúyòng ... 完全无用

earthquake dìzhèn 地震

earth-shattering lìngrénzhènjīng 令人震惊

ease 1 *n* róngyì 容易; **be at (one's) ~, feel at ~** gǎndào shūfu 感到舒服; **be or feel ill at ~** gǎndào bù shūfu 感到不舒服 2 *v/t* (*relieve*) fàngsōng 放松 3 *v/i* (*of pain*) jiǎnqīng 减轻

♦ease off 1 *v/t* (*remove*) xiǎoxīn yídiào 小心移掉 2 *v/i* (*of pain, rain*) jiǎnhuǎn 减缓

easel (*for blackboard*) hēibǎnjià 黑板架; (*for artist*) huàjià 画架

easily (*with ease*) róngyì 容易; (*by far*) wúyí 无疑

east 1 *n* dōngfāng 东方 2 *adj* dōng 东 3 *adv travel* xiàng dōngfāng 向东方

East China Sea Dōnghǎi 东海

Easter Fùhuójié 复活节

Easter egg Fùhuójié cǎidàn 复活节彩蛋

easterly cóng dōng láide 从东来的

eastern dōngbù 东部; (*Oriental*) Dōngfāng 东方

easterner (*from the east coast*) dōnghǎi'àn de rén 东海岸的人

eastward(s) xiàngdōng 向东

easy (*not difficult*) róngyì 容易; (*relaxed*) fàngsōng 放松; **take things ~** (*slow down*) bùjǐnzhǎng 不紧张; **take it ~!** (*calm down*) biéjǐnzhāng! 别紧张

easy chair ānlèyǐ 安乐椅

easy-going suíhé 随和

eat *v/t & v/i* chī 吃

♦eat out chūqù chī 出去吃

♦eat up *food* chīguāng 吃光; *fig* hàojìn 耗尽

eatable kěchī 可吃

eaves wūyán 屋檐

eavesdrop tōutīng 偷听

ebb *v/i* (*of tide*) tuìluò 退落

♦**ebb away** *fig* (*of courage, strength*) jiǎnshǎo 减少

ebb tide tuìcháo 退潮

eccentric 1 *adj* gǔguài 古怪 **2** *n* gǔguài de rén 古怪的人

echo 1 *n* huíshēng 回声 **2** *v/i* huídàng 回荡 **3** *v/t words* chóngfù 重复; *views* chóngshēn 重申

eclipse 1 *n* (*of sun*) rìshí 日蚀; (*of moon*) yuèshí 月蚀 **2** *v/t fig* shèngguò 胜过

ecological shēngtài 生态

ecological balance shēngtài pínghéng 生态平衡

ecologically friendly lǜsè 绿色

ecologist shēngtàixuéjiā 生态学家

ecology shēngtàixué 生态学

economic jīngjì 经济

economical (*cheap*) jīngjì 经济; (*thrifty*) jiéshěng 节省

economically (*in terms of economics*) jīngjì shang 经济上; (*thriftily*) jiéjiǎn 节俭

economics (*science*) jīngjìxué 经济学; (*financial aspects*) jīngjì qíngkuàng 经济情况

economist jīngjìxuéjiā 经济学家

economize jǐnsuō kāizhī 紧缩开支

♦**economize on** jiéshěng 节省

economy (*of a country*) jīngjì 经济; (*saving*) jiéshěng 节省

economy class jīngjìcāng 经济舱; **economy drive** jiéyuē xíngdòng 节约行动; **economy size** jīngjìzhuāng 经济装

ecosystem shēngtài xìtǒng 生态系统

ecstasy kuángxǐ 狂喜; (*drug*) yáotóuwánr 摇头丸儿

ecstatic xīnxǐ ruò kuáng 欣喜若狂

eczema shīzhěn 湿疹

edge 1 *n* (*of knife*) fēng fēng 锋锋; (*of table, road etc*) biānyuán 边缘; (*in voice*) cì'ěr 刺耳; **on** ~ jízào 急躁 **2** *v/t* xiāngbiān 镶边 **3** *v/i* (*move slowly*) huǎnmàn yídòng 缓慢移动

edgewise: *I couldn't get a word in* ~ wǒ chābúshàng huà 我插不上话

edgy jízào 急躁

edible kě shíyòng 可食用

edit *text, file, book, newspaper* biānjí 编辑; *TV program* jiǎnjí 剪辑; *movie* jiǎnjiē 剪接

edition bǎnběn 版本

editor *of text, book, newspaper, TV program, movie* biānjí 编辑; *sports / political* ~ tǐyù / zhèngzhì lán biānjí 体育 / 政治栏编辑

editorial 1 *adj* biānjí 编辑 **2** *n* shèlùn 社论

EDP (= *electronic data processing*) diànzǐ shùjù chǔlǐ 电子数据处理

educate *child* jiàoyù 教育; *consumers* yǐndǎo 引导

educated *person* shòuguò jiàoyù 受过教育

education jiàoyù 教育

educational jiàoyù 教育; *informative* yǒu jiàoyù yìyì 有教育意义

eel mán 鳗

eerie guàiyì 怪异

effect *n* xiàoguǒ 效果; *negative* hòuguǒ 后果; **take** ~ (*of medicine, drug*) shēngxiào 生效; **come into** ~ (*of law*) shíshī 实施

effective (*efficient*) yǒuxiào 有效; (*striking*) chǎnshēng shēnkè yìnxiàng 产生深刻印象; ~ **May 1** cóng wǔyuè yīrì qǐ shēngxiào 从五月一日起生效

effeminate nǚrénqì 女人气

effervescent yǒu qìpào 有气泡; *personality* huóyuè 活跃

efficiency xiàolǜ 效率

efficient yǒu xiàolǜ 有效率

efficiently yǒu xiàolǜ 有效率

effort (*struggle*) fèilì 费力; (*attempt*) nǔlì 努力; *make an ~ to do X* nǔlì zuò X 努力做 X

effortless róngyì 容易

effrontery wúchǐ 无耻

effusive guòyú jīdòng 过于激动

e.g. lìrú 例如

egalitarian *adj* píngděngzhǔyì 平等主义

egg (*of hen*) jīdàn 鸡蛋; (*of bird*) dàn 蛋

♦**egg on** sǒngyǒng 怂恿

eggcup jīdānbēi 鸡蛋杯; **egg fried rice** dànchǎofàn 蛋炒饭; **egghead** wénrén 文人; **eggplant** qiézi 茄子; **eggshell** dànké 蛋壳

ego PSYCH zìwǒ 自我; (*self-esteem*) zìzūn 自尊

egocentric yǐ zìwǒ wéi zhōngxīn 以自我为中心

Egypt Āijí 埃及

Egyptian 1 *adj* Āijí 埃及 **2** *n* Āijí rén 埃及人

eiderdown (*quilt*) yǔróng 羽绒

eight bā 八

eighteen shíbā 十八

eighteenth dì shíbā 第十八

eighth dì bā 第八

eightieth dì bāshí 第八十

eighty bāshí 八十

either 1 *adj* rèn yīgè 任一个; (*both*) liǎng 两 **2** *pron* nǎge dōuxíng 哪个都行 **3** *adv*: **I won't go ~** wǒ yě bú qù 我也不去 **4** *conj*: **~ ... or** huòzhě ... huòzhě 或者 ... 或者

eject 1 *v/t* zhúchū 逐出 **2** *v/i* (*from plane*) tánshè 弹射

eke out yányòng 延用

el (*elevated railroad*) gāojià tiělù 高架铁路

elaborate 1 *adj* jīngxīn zhìzuò 精心制作 **2** *v/i* xiángjìn jiěshì 详尽解释

elapse liúshì 流逝

elastic 1 *adj* yǒu tánxìng 有弹性 **2** *n* sōngjǐndài 松紧带

elastic band xiàngpíjīn 橡皮筋

elasticity tánxìng 弹性

elasticized dài sōngjǐn 带松紧

elated xìnggāocǎiliè 兴高采烈

elation xìnggāocǎiliè 兴高采烈

elbow 1 *n* zhǒu 肘 **2** *v/t*: **~ out of the way** yòng zhǒu jǐchū yìtiáo lù 用肘挤出一条路

elder 1 *adj* niánzhǎng 年长 **2** *n* niánzhǎngzhě 年长者

elderly shàng niánjì 上年纪

eldest 1 *adj*: **the ~ brother** dàgē 大哥; **the ~ sister** dàjiě 大姐 **2** *n*: **the ~** zuìdà 最大

elect *v/t* xuǎn 选; **~ to do X** xuǎnzé zuò X 选择做 X

elected xuǎnchū 选出

election xuǎnjǔ 选举

election campaign jìngxuǎn huódòng 竞选活动

election day xuǎnjǔrì 选举日

elective kěxuǎn 可选

elector xuǎnmín 选民

electoral system xuǎnjǔ zhìdù 选举制度

electorate quántǐ xuǎnmín 全体选民

electric diàn 电; *fig* shǐrén tūrán xīngfèn 使人突然兴奋

electrical diàn 电

electric blanket diànrètǎn 电热毯

electric chair diànyǐ 电椅

electrician diàngōng 电工

electricity diàn 电

electrify shǐ diànqìhuà 使电气化; *fig* cìjī 刺激

electrocute diànsǐ 电死

electrode diànjí 电极

electron diànzǐ 电子

electronic diànzǐ 电子

electronic data processing diànzǐ shùjù chǔlǐ 电子数据处理

electronic mail diànzǐ yóujiàn 电子邮件

electronics diànzǐxué 电子学

elegance gāoyǎ 高雅

elegant gāoyǎ 高雅

element CHEM yuánsù 元素

elementary (*rudimentary*) chūjí 初级

elementary school xiǎoxué 小学

elementary teacher xiǎoxué lǎoshī 小学老师

elephant dàxiàng 大象

elevate tígāo 提高

elevated railroad gāojià tiělù 高架铁路

elevation (*altitude*) hǎibá 海拔

elevator diàntī 电梯

eleven shíyī 十一

eleventh dì shíyī 第十一; *at the ~ hour* zuìhòu guāntóu 最后关头

eligible hégé 合格

eligible bachelor héyì nánshì 合意男士

eliminate (*get rid of*) chúdiào 除掉; (*rule out*) páichú 排除; (*kill*) gàndiào 干掉; *be ~d* (*from competition*) bèi táotài 被淘汰

elimination (*from competition*) táotài 淘汰; (*of poverty*) xiāochú 消除; (*murder*) gàndiào 干掉

elite 1 *n* jīngyīng 精英 2 *adj* gāoděng 高等

elk tuólù 驼鹿

ellipse tuǒyuán 椭圆

elm yúmù 榆木

elope sībēn 私奔

eloquence kǒucái 口才

eloquent xióngbiàn 雄辩

eloquently xióngbiàn 雄辩

else: *anything ~?* hái yào biéde ma? 还要别的吗？; *if you've got nothing ~ to do* rúguǒ nǐ méiyǒu biéde shì yào zuò 如果你没有别的事要做; *no one ~* méiyǒu biérén 没有别人; *everyone ~ is going* biérén dōu qù 别人都去; *who ~ was there?* hái yǒu shéi zài nàr? 还有谁在那儿？; *someone ~* biérén 别人; *something ~* biéde dōngxi 别的东西; *let's go somewhere ~* zánmen qù biéde dìfāng ba 咱们去别的地方吧; *or ~* (*otherwise*) fǒuzé 否则

elsewhere biéchù 别处

elude *escape from* táobì 逃避; *avoid* duǒbì 躲避

elusive nányǐ pǔzhuō 难以扑捉

emaciated xiāoshòu 消瘦

e-mail 1 *n* diànzǐ yóujiàn 电子邮件 2 *v/t person* dǎ diànzǐ yóujiàn 打电子邮件; *text* yòng diànzǐ yóujiàn jì 用电子邮件寄

e-mail address diànzǐ xìnxiāng 电子信箱

emancipated *woman* jiěfàng 解放

emancipation jiěfàng 解放

embalm bǎocún 保存

embankment *of river* dī'àn 堤岸; RAIL lùdī 路堤

embargo *n* jìnyùn 禁运

embark *v/i* shàngchuán 上船
♦embark on kāishǐ 开始

embarrass shǐ gāngà 使 ... 尴尬

embarrassed gāngà 尴尬

embarrassing lìngrén gāngà 令人尴尬

embarrassment gāngà 尴尬

embassy dàshǐguǎn 大使馆

embellish zhuāngshì 装饰; *story* jiāgōng 加工

embers yújìn 余烬

embezzle dàoyòng 盗用

embezzlement dàoyòng 盗用

embitter shǐkǔnǎo 使苦恼

emblem xiàngzhēng 象征

embodiment huàshēn 化身

embody tǐxiàn 体现

embolism shuānsè 栓塞

emboss *metal* fútū 浮凸; *paper, fabric* tūyìn 凸印

embrace 1 *n* yōngbào 拥抱 2 *v/t* (*hug*) yōngbào 拥抱; (*take in*) bāokuò 包括 3 *v/i* (*of two people*) yōngbào 拥抱

embroider cìxiù 刺绣; *fig* xūgòu qíngjié 虚构情节

embroidery cìxiù 刺绣

embryo pēitāi 胚胎

emerald (*precious stone*) lǜbǎoshí 绿宝石; (*color*) zǔmǔlǜ 祖母绿

emerge (*appear*) chūxiàn 出现; *it has ~d that ...* jùxī ... 据悉 ...

emergency jǐnjí qíngkuàng 紧急情况; *in an ~* yùdào jǐnjí qíngkuàng 遇到紧急情况

emergency exit jǐnjí chūkǒu 紧急出口

emergency landing jǐnjí zháoluò 紧急着落

emigrant *n* yímín 移民

emigrate yíjū guówài 移居国外

emigration yíjū guówài 移居国外

eminent jiéchū 杰出

eminently fēicháng 非常

emission (*of gases*) páifàng 排放

emotion qínggǎn 情感

emotional *problems, development*

qínggǎn 情感; (*full of emotion*) fùyú qínggǎn 富于情感

empathize: ~ with tóngqíng 同情

emperor huángdì 皇帝

emphasis zhòngdiào 重调

emphasize qiángdiào 强调

emphatic kěndìng 肯定

empire dìguó 帝国

employ gùyōng 雇佣; (*use*) shǐyòng 使用; **he's ~ed as a ...** tā bèi gù zuò ... 他被雇作 ...

employee gùyuán 雇员

employer gùzhǔ 雇主

employment zhíyè 职业; (*work*) gōngzuò 工作; **be seeking ~** zài qiúzhí 在求职

employment agency zhíyè jièshàosuǒ 职业介绍所

empress huánghòu 皇后

emptiness kōngxū 空虚

empty 1 *adj* kōng 空; *promises* kōngdòng 空洞 **2** *v/t pockets* tāokōng 掏空; *drawer* dàokōng 倒空; *glass, bottle* dào 倒 **3** *v/i (of room, street)* biànkōng 变空

emulate gǎnchāo 赶超

enable shǐde néngzuò 使得能做

enact *law* zhìdìng 制定; THEA yǎnchū 演出

enamel *n* tángcí 搪瓷; (*on tooth*) fàlángzhì 珐琅质; (*paint*) cíqī 瓷漆

enchanting *smile, village, person* mírén 迷人

encircle bāowéi 包围

enclose (*in letter*) fùjiàn 附件; *area* wéizhù 围住; **please find ~d ...** zīfùshàng ... 兹附上 ...

enclosure (*with letter*) fùjiàn 附件

encore *n* zàilái yīgè 再来一个

encounter 1 *n* xièhòu 邂逅 **2** *v/t person* jiēchù 接触; *problem, resistance* yùdào 遇到

encourage gǔlì 鼓励

encouragement gǔlì 鼓励

encouraging lìngrén gǔwǔ 令人鼓舞

♦**encroach on** *land* qīnzhàn 侵占; *rights* qīnfàn 侵犯; *time* zhànyòng 占用

encyclopedia bǎikēquánshū 百科全书

end 1 *n* (*extremity*) jìntóu 尽头; (*conclusion*) jiéwěi 结尾; (*purpose*) mùdì 目的; **in the ~** zuìhòu 最后; **for hours on ~** chíxùbúduàn 持续不断; **stand X on ~** zhílì X 直立 X; **at the ~ of July** qīyuèmò 七月末; **put an ~ to** jiéshù 结束 **2** *v/t & v/i* jiéshù 结束

♦**end up** jiéguǒ 结果

endanger wēijí 危及

endangered species bīnlín mièjuéde wùzhǒng 濒临灭绝的物种

endearing tǎorén xǐhuān 讨人喜欢

endeavor 1 *n* nǔlì 努力 **2** *v/t* jìnlì 尽力

ending jiéjú 结局; GRAM cíwěi 词尾

endless wúzhǐjìng 无止境

endorse *check* bèishū 背书; *candidacy* zhīchí 支持; *product* cùxiāo 促销

endorsement (*of check*) bèiqiān 背签; (*of candidacy*) zhīchí 支持; (*of product*) cùxiāo 促销

end product zhōngduān chǎnpǐn 终端产品

end result zuìzhōng jiéguǒ 最终结果

endurance rěnnàilì 忍耐力

endure 1 *v/t* rěnnài 忍耐 **2** *v/i* (*last*) chíxù 持续

enduring chíjiǔ 持久

end-user zhōngduān yònghù 终端用户

enemy dírén 敌人

energetic jùliè 剧烈; *person* yǒu jīngshen 有精神; *fig: measures* jījí 积极

energy (*gas, electricity etc*) néngyuán 能源; (*of person*) jīnglì 精力

energy-saving *device* jiénéng 节能

enforce shíshī 实施

engage 1 *v/t* (*hire*) pìnyòng 聘用 **2** *v/i* TECH niēhé 啮合

♦**engage in** cóngshì 从事

engaged (*to be married*) dìnghūn 订婚; **get ~** dìnghūn 订婚

engagement (*appointment*) yuēhuì 约会; (*to be married*) dìnghūn 订婚; MIL jiāozhàn 交战

engagement ring dìnghūn jièzhǐ 订婚戒指

engaging *smile, person* xīyǐnrén 吸引人

engine yǐnqíng 引擎

engineer 1 *n* gōngchéngshī 工程师; NAUT lúnjīzhǎng 轮机长; RAIL gōngchéngshī 工程师 **2** *v/t fig* (*meeting etc*) qiǎomiàode ānpái 巧妙地安排

engineering gōngchéng 工程

England Yīnggélán 英格兰

English 1 *adj* Yīngguó 英国 **2** *n* (*language*) Yīngyǔ 英语; **the ~** Yīnggélán rén 英格兰人

Englishman Yīnggélán nánzǐ 英格兰男子

Englishwoman Yīnggélán nǚzǐ 英格兰女子

engrave diāokè 雕刻

engraving (*drawing*) bǎnhuà 版画; (*design*) diāokè 雕刻

engrossed: **~ in** quánshén guànzhùyú 全神贯注于

engulf tūnmò 吞没

enhance zēngqiáng 增强

enigma mí mí 谜

enigmatic shénmì 神秘

enjoy xǐhuan 喜欢; **~ oneself** guòde kuàilè 过得快乐; **~!** (*said to somebody eating*) chīhǎo! 吃好!

enjoyable lìngrén yúkuài 令人愉快

enjoyment lèqù 乐趣

enlarge kuòdà 扩大

enlargement kuòdà 扩大

enlighten qǐdí 启迪

enlist 1 *v/i* MIL bàomíng cānjūn 报名参军 **2** *v/t* zhāomù 召募; **~ the help of X** jiào X bāngmáng 叫 X 帮忙

enliven shǐhuóyuè 使活跃

enormity (*size*) pángdà 庞大; (*wickedness*) qióngxiōngjí'è 穷凶极恶

enormous jùdà 巨大; *satisfaction, patience* jídà 极大

enormously fēicháng 非常

enough 1 *adj* zúgòu 足够 **2** *pron* zúgòu 足够; **will $50 be ~?** wǔshí měiyuán gòu le ma? 五十美元够了吗?; **I've had ~!** wǒ shòugòu le 我受够了!; **that's ~, calm down!** xíngle lěngjìngdiǎnr 行了, 冷静点儿! **3** *adv* zúgòu 足够; **strangely ~** qíguài 奇怪的是

enquire, enquiry → **inquire, inquiry**

enraged jīnù 激怒

enrich *vocabulary* kuòdà 扩大; *somebody's life* fēngfù 丰富

enroll *v/i* zhùcè 注册

enrolment zhùcè 注册

ensure bǎozhèng 保证

entail qiānshè 牵涉

entangle: **become ~d in** (*in rope*) chánràozài 缠绕在; (*in love affair*) xiànrù 陷入

enter 1 *v/t room, house* jìnrù 进入; *competition* cānjiā 参加; *person, horse in race* bàomíng 报名; *write down* xiěxià 写下; COMPUT jiànrù 键入 **2** *v/i* jìnrù 进入; THEA shàngchǎng 上场; (*in competition*) bàomíng 报名 **3** *n* COMPUT huíchējiàn 回车健

enterprise (*initiative*) jìnqǔxīn 进取心; (*venture*) qǐyè 企业

enterprising yǒu jìnqǔxīn 有进取心

entertain 1 *v/t* (*amuse*) shǐrén kuàilè 使人快乐; (*consider: idea*) yuànyì kǎolù 愿意考虑 **2** *v/i* (*have guests*) zhāodài 招待

entertainer biǎoyǎnzhě 表演者

entertaining *adj* yǒuqù 有趣

entertainment yúlè 娱乐

enthrall mízhù 迷住

enthusiasm rèqíng 热情

enthusiast rèzhōngzhě 热中者

enthusiastic rèxīn 热心

entice yòuhuò 诱惑

entire zhěnggè 整个

entirely wánquán 完全

entitle fùyù quánlì 赋予权利

entitled *book* dìngmíng 定名

entrance *n* (*doorway*) rùkǒu 入口;

(*fact of entering*) jìnrù 进入; THEA chūchǎng 出场; (*admission*) zhǔnyǔ jìnrù 准予进入

entranced zháomí 着迷

entrance fee rùchǎngfèi 入场费

entrant cānjiā zhě 参加者

entrenched *attitudes* gēnshēndìgù 根深蒂固

entrepreneur qǐyèjiā 企业家

entrepreneurial yǒu chuàngyè cáinéng 有创业才能

entrust: *~ X with Y, ~ Y to X* bǎ Y wěituōgěi X 把 Y 委托给 X

entry (*way in*) rùkǒu 入口; (*admission*) jìnrù 进入; (*for competition*) cānjiāzhě 参加者; (*in diary, accounts*) xiàngmù 项目

entry form cānsàibiǎo 参赛表

entry visa rùjìng qiānzhèng 入境签证

envelop bāozhù 包住

envelope xìnfēng 信封

enviable zhídé xiànmù 值得羡慕

envious mǎnhuái jídù 满怀嫉妒; *be ~ of X* xiànmù X 羡慕 X

environment (*nature*) zìrán huánjìng 自然环境; (*surroundings*) huánjìng 环境

environmental yǒuguān huánjìng 有关环境

environmentalist huánjìng bǎohùlùn zhě 环境保护论者

environmentally friendly lùsè 绿色

environmental pollution huánjìng wūrǎn 环境污染

environmental protection huánjìng bǎohù 环境保护

environs jìnjiāo 近郊

envisage xiǎngxiàng 想象

envoy shǐzhě 使者

envy 1 *n* jídù 嫉妒; *be the ~ of X* lìng X xiànmù 令 X 羡慕 **2** *v/t*: dùxiàn 妒羡; *~ X Y* xiànmù X de Y 羡慕 X 的 Y

epic 1 *n* shǐshī 史诗 **2** *adj journey* shǐshībān 史诗般; *a task of ~ proportions* zhòngdà rènwù 重大任务

epicenter ⇩ zhènzhōng 震中

epidemic liúxíngxìng 流行性

epilepsy diānxiánzhèng 癫痫症

epileptic *n* diānxián 癫痫

epileptic fit diānxián fāzuò 癫痫发作

epilog jiéwěi bùfen 结尾部分

episode (*of story, soap opera*) yījí 一集; (*happening*) shìjiàn 事件

epitaph mùzhìmíng 墓志铭

epoch jìyuán 纪元

epoch-making huàshídài 划时代

equal 1 *adj* xiāngtóng 相同; *be ~ to* (*a task*) néngshèngrèn 能胜任 **2** *n* děngtóng 等同 **3** *v/t* (*with numbers*) děngyú 等于; (*be as good as*) búxùnsè 不逊色

equality píngděng 平等

equalize 1 *v/t* jūnhéng 均衡 **2** *v/i* SP bānpíng bǐfēn 扳平比分

equalizer SP píngfēnqiú 平分球

equally tóngděng 同等; *~, ...* cǐwài, ... 此外 ...

equate: *~ X with Y* děngtóng X hé Y 等同 X 和 Y

equation MATH děngshì 等式

equator chìdào 赤道

equilibrium pínghéng 平衡

equinox: *Spring ~* Chūnfēn 春分; *Autumn ~* Qiūfēn 秋分

equip: *~X* zhuāngbèi X 装备 X; *he's not ~ped to handle it* fig tā wúlì chǔlǐ cǐshì 他无力处理此事

equipment zhuāngbèi 装备

equity COM pǔtōnggǔ 普通股

equivalent 1 *adj* xiāngtóng 相同; *be ~ to* xiāngdāngyú 相当于 **2** *n*: *X is the ~ of Y* X xiāngdāngyú Y X 相当于 Y

era jìyuán 纪元

eradicate gēnchú 根除

erase (*with eraser*) cādiào 擦掉; *tape* xǐdiào 洗掉; COMPUT shānchú 删除

eraser (*for blackboard*) hēibǎncā 黑板擦; (*for pencil*) xiàngpí 橡皮

erect 1 *adj* zhílì 直立 **2** *v/t* shùqǐ 竖起

erection (*of building etc*) shùqǐ 竖起; (*of penis*) bóqǐ 勃起

erode qīnshí 侵蚀; *fig: rights, power* qīnfàn 侵犯

erosion qīnshí 侵蚀; *fig* qīnfàn 侵犯

erotic sèqíng 色情

eroticism xìngyù 性欲

errand chāishǐ 差使; *run ~s* pǎotuǐ 跑腿

erratic wúcháng 无常

error cuòwù 错误

error message COMPUT cuòwù xìnxī 错误信息

erupt (*of volcano*) bàofā 爆发; (*of violence*) tūrán fāshēng 突然发生; (*of person*) fāhuǒ 发火

eruption (*of volcano*) bàofā 爆发; (*of violence*) tūrán fāshēng 突然发生

escalate zhúbù shēngjí 逐步升级

escalation shēngjí 升级

escalator zìdòngfútī 自动扶梯

escape 1 *n* (*of prisoner, animal*) táotuō 逃脱; (*of gas*) lòuchū 漏出; *have a narrow ~* jiǔsǐyìshēng 九死一生 **2** *v/i* (*of prisoner, animal*) táotuō 逃脱; (*of gas*) lòuchū 漏出 **3** *v/t: the word ~s me* wǒ xiǎngbùqǐlái zhèigè cí le 我想不起来这个词了

escape chute tuōxiǎn huátī 脱险滑梯

escort 1 *n* péitóng 陪同; (*guard*) hùwèi 护卫 **2** *v/t* (*socially*) péi péi 陪陪; (*act as guard to*) hùwèi 护卫

especially yóuqí 尤其

espionage jiàndié huódòng 间谍活动

essay *n* duǎnwén 短文

essential *adj* bìyào 必要

essentially jīběnshàng 基本上

establish *company* chénglì 成立; (*create*) chuàngzào 创造; (*determine*) quèdìng 确定; *~ oneself as* wèi zìjǐ yíngdé 为自己赢得

establishment (*firm, store etc*) jīgòu 机构; *the Establishment* dāngquánpài 当权派

estate (*area of land*) dìchǎn 地产; (*possessions of dead person*) yíchǎn 遗产

esthetic měiguān 美观

estimate *n & v/t* gūjì 估计

estimation: *he has gone up / down in my ~* zēngjiā / jiàngdī duì tā de zūnjìng 增加 / 降低对他的尊敬; *in my ~* (*opinion*) zhào wǒ kànlái 照我看来

estranged *wife, husband* shūyuǎn 疏远

estuary hékǒuwān 河口湾

ETA (= *estimated time of arrival*) yùjì dàodá shíjiān 预计到达时间

etching shíkèshù 蚀刻术

eternal yǒnghéng 永恒

eternity yǒnghéng 永恒

ethical dàodé 道德

ethics lúnlǐxué 伦理学

ethnic zhǒngzú 种族

ethnic group zhǒngzú shèqū 种族社区

ethnic minority shǎoshù mínzú 少数民族

euphemism wěiwǎn shuōfǎ 委婉说法

euphoria xīnkuàigǎn 欣快感

Europe Ōuzhōu 欧洲

European 1 *adj* Ōuzhōu 欧洲 **2** *n* Ōuzhōu rén 欧洲人

euthanasia ānlèsǐ 安乐死

evacuate (*clear people from*) chèkōng 撤空; (*leave*) chèlí 撤离

evade bìkāi 避开

evaluate pínggū 评估

evaluation pínggū 评估

evangelist fúyīn chuándào zhě 福音传道者

evaporate (*of water*) zhēngfā 蒸发; (*of confidence*) xiāoshī 消失

evasion táobì 逃避

evasive bùtǎnshuài 不坦率

eve qiánxī 前夕

even 1 *adj* (*regular*) jūnyún 均匀; (*level*) píng 平; (*number*) ǒushù 偶数; *get ~ with X* bàofù X 报复 X **2** *adv* shènzhì 甚至; *~ bigger / better* gèngdà / hǎo 更大 / 好; *not ~* lián ... yěbù 连 ... 也不; *~ so* jǐnguǎn rúcǐ 尽管如此; *~ if* jíshǐ 即使 **3** *v/t: ~ the score* lāpíng bǐfēn 拉平比分

evening wǎnshang 晚上; *in the ~* wǎnshang 晚上; *this ~* jīntiān wǎnshang 今天晚上; *good ~* wǎnshang hǎo 晚上好

evening class yèxiào 夜校; **evening dress** (*for man, woman*) wǎnlǐfú 晚礼服; **evening paper** wǎnbào 晚报

evenly (*regularly*) jūnyún 均匀

event shìjiàn 事件; SP bǐsài xiàngmù 比赛项目; *at all ~s* wúlùn rúhé 无论如何

eventful yǒu xǔduō dàshì 有许多大事

eventual zuìzhōng 最终

eventually zhōngyú 终于

ever *adv* (*with past or perfect tense questions*) céngjīng 曾经; (*with past or perfect tense negative*) cónglái 从来; (*with conditionals*) yídàn 一旦; (*for emphasis*) dàodǐ 到底; *did you ~ go abroad before you were 15?* shíwǔ suì yǐqián nǐ céngjīng chūguò guó ma? 十五岁以前你曾经出过国吗?; *have you ~ been to ... ?* nǐ céng dàoguò ... ma? 你曾到过 ... 吗?; *he hasn't ~ been there* tā cónglái méi qùguò nàr 他从来没去过那儿; *if you ~ come to China, give me a call* nǐ yàoshì yídàn lái Zhōngguó, gěi wǒ dǎge diànhuà 你要是一旦来中国, 给我打个电话; *for ~* yǒngyuǎn 永远; *~ since* cóng nà yǐhòu 从那以后; *~ since he came to China ...* cóng tā lái Zhōngguó yǐhòu ... 从他来中国以后 ...

Everest: *Mount ~* ⇩ Zhūmùlǎngmǎfēng 珠穆朗玛峰

evergreen *n* chángqīng 常青

everlasting yǒngjiǔ 永久

every měiyī 每一; *~ other day* měigéyìtiān 每隔一天; *~ now and then* ǒu'ěr 偶尔

everybody měigèrén 每个人

everyday měitiān 每天

everyone měigèrén 每个人

everything yíqiè 一切

everywhere gèchù 各处; (*wherever*) dàochù 到处

evict zhúchū 逐出

evidence hénjì 痕迹; LAW zhèngjù 证据; *give ~* chūzhèng 出证

evident míngxiǎn 明显

evidently (*clearly*) míngxiǎn 明显; (*apparently*) xiǎnrán 显然

evil 1 *adj* xié'è 邪恶 **2** *n* è 恶

evoke *image* huànqǐ 唤起

evolution jìnhuà 进化

evolve *v/i* (*of animals*) jìnhuà 进化; (*develop*) zhújiàn xíngchéng 逐渐形成

ewe mǔyáng 母羊

ex- qián 前

ex *n* F (*former wife*) qiánqī 前妻; (*former husband*) qiánfū 前夫

exact *adj* quèqiè 确切

exactly qiàqià 恰恰; *~!* jiùshì! 就是!; *not ~* bù quánshì 不全是

exaggerate 1 *v/t* kuādà 夸大 **2** *v/i* kuāzhāng 夸张

exaggeration yán guò qí shí 言过其实

exam kǎoshì 考试; *take an ~* cānjiā kǎoshì 参加考试; *pass/ fail an ~* tōngguò/bùtōngguò kǎoshì 通过/不通过考试

examination (*of facts etc*) diàochá 调查; (*of patient*) jiǎnchá 检查; EDU kǎoshì 考试

examine *study* diàochá 调查; *patient* jiǎnchá 检查; EDU kǎo 考

examiner EDU zhǔkǎorén 主考人

example lìzi 例子; *for ~* bǐrú 比如; *set a good/bad ~* shùlì hǎo/bùhǎo bǎngyàng 树立好/不好榜样

exasperate rěnǎo 惹恼

excavate *v/t* (*dig*) wājué 挖掘; (*of archeologist*) fājué 发掘

excavation wājué 挖掘

excavator wājuéjī 挖掘机

exceed (*be more than*) chāoguò 超过; (*go beyond*) chāochū 超出

exceedingly jíduān 极端

excel 1 *v/i* shàncháng 擅长; *~ at X* shàncháng X 擅长 X **2** *v/t*: *~ one- self* shèngguò guòqù 胜过过去

excellence yōuxiù 优秀

excellent hěn hǎo 很好

except chúle 除了; *~ for* chúle X yǐwài 除了 X 以外; *~ that ...*

zhǐshì … 只是 …

exception lìwài 例外; **with the ~ of** chúle 除了; **take ~ to** fǎnduì 反对

exceptional (*very good*) jiéchū 杰出; (*special*) tèshū 特殊

exceptionally (*extremely*) yìcháng 异常

excerpt jiélù 节录

excess 1 *n* guòdù 过度; **eat / drink to ~** chī / hē wúdù 吃 / 喝无度; **in ~ of** duōyú 多于 **2** *adj* duōyú 多余

excess baggage chāozhòngde xíngli 超重的行李

excess fare bǔpiàofèi 补票费

excessive guòfèn 过分

exchange 1 *n* (*of views, information*) jiāohuàn 交换; (*between schools*) jiāoliú 交流; **in ~** zuòwéi jiāohuàn 作为交换; **in ~ for** yònglái huànqǔ 用来换取 **2** *v/t* (*in store*) gēnghuàn 更换; *addresses* hùhuàn 互换; *currency* duìhuàn 兑换; **~ X for Y** yòng X huàn Y 用 X 换 Y

exchange rate FIN duìhuànlǜ 兑换率

excitable yìxīngfèn 易兴奋

excite (*make enthusiastic*) jīdòng 激动

excited xīngfèn 兴奋; **get ~** xīngfèn 兴奋; **get ~ about X** wèi X gǎndào xīngfèn 为 X 感到兴奋

excitement xīngfèn 兴奋

exciting lìngrén xīngfèn 令人兴奋

exclaim jīngjiào 惊叫

exclamation gǎntàn 感叹

exclamation point gǎntànhào 感叹号

exclude (*not include*) páichú zàiwài 排除在外; *possibility* páichú 排除; (*bar. from club etc*) páichì 排斥

excluding chúle 除了

exclusive *hotel, restaurant* dútè 独特; *rights* dúyǒu 独有; *interview* dújiā 独家

excruciating *pain* jùliè 剧烈

excursion yuǎnzú 远足

excuse 1 *n* jièkǒu 借口 **2** *v/t* (*forgive*) yuánliàng 原谅; **please ~ me** (*allow to leave*) shīpéi 失陪; **~ X from Y** miǎnchú X zuò Y 免除 X 做 Y; **~ me** (*to get attention*) qǐngwèn 请问; (*to get past*) láojià 劳驾; (*interrupting somebody*) hěn bàoqiàn 很抱歉

execute *criminal* chǔjué 处决; *plan* shíshī 实施

execution (*of criminal*) sǐxíng 死刑; (*of plan*) shíshī 实施

executioner xíngxíngrén 行刑人

executive *n* zhǔguǎn rényuán 主管人员

executive briefcase zhǔguǎn rényuán gōngshìbāo 主管人员公事包

executive washroom zhǔguǎn guànxǐshì 主管盥洗室

exemplary mófàn 模范

exempt: be ~ from miǎnchú 免除

exercise 1 *n* (*physical*) duànliàn 锻炼; EDU liànxí 练习; MIL yǎnxí 演习; **take ~** zuò yùndòng 作运动 **2** *v/t muscle* duànliàn 锻炼; *dog* liù 遛; *caution, restraint* yìngyòng 应用 **3** *v/i* duànliàn 锻炼

exercise book EDU liànxíběn 练习本

exert *authority* xíngshǐ 行使; **~ oneself** yònglì 用力

exertion fèilì 费力

exhale hūchū 呼出

exhaust 1 *n* (*fumes*) fèiqì 废气; (*pipe*) páiqìguǎn 排气管 **2** *v/t* (*tire*) shǐpíjuàn 使疲倦; (*use up*) yòngjìn 用尽

exhaust fumes páichūde fèiqì 排出的废气

exhausted (*tired*) jīnpílìjìn 筋疲力尽

exhausting lìngrénpíjuàn 令人疲倦

exhaustion láolèi guòdù 劳累过度

exhaustive chèdǐ 彻底

exhaust pipe páiqìguǎn 排气管

exhibit 1 *n* (*in exhibition*) zhǎnpǐn 展品 **2** *v/t* (*of gallery*) zhǎnlǎn 展览; (*of artist*) zhǎnchū 展出; (*give evidence of*) xiǎnchū 显出

exhibition zhǎnlǎnhuì 展览会; (*of bad behavior*) chūchǒu 出丑; (*of skill*) biǎoyǎn 表演

exhibitionist fēngtóu zhǔyì zhě 风头主义者

exhilarating lìngrén yúkuài 令人愉快

exile 1 *n* liúwáng 流亡; (*person*) qùguó zhě 去国者 **2** *v/t* liúfàng 流放

exist cúnzài 存在; **~ on X** kào X shēngcún 靠X生存

existence cúnzài 存在; (*life*) shēngcún 生存; **in ~** xiàncún 现存; **come into ~** xíngchéng 形成

existing xiàncún 现存

exit 1 *n* (*way out*) chūkǒu 出口; (*from highway*) chūlù 出路; THEA tuìchǎng 退场 **2** *v/i* COMPUT tuìchū 退出

exonerate xuānbù wúzuì 宣布无罪

exorbitant guògāo 过高

exotic fùyǒu yìguó qíngdiào 富有异国情调

expand 1 *v/t* kuòdà 扩大 **2** *v/i* zēngzhǎng 增长; (*of metal*) péngzhàng 膨胀

♦**expand on** xiángshù 详述

expanse guǎngkuò 广阔

expansion zēngzhǎng 增长; (*of metal*) péngzhàng 膨胀

expect 1 *v/t* qīdài 期待; *baby* huáiyùn 怀孕; (*suppose*) rènwéi 认为; (*demand*) yāoqiú 要求 **2** *v/i*: **be ~ing** yǒule 有了; **I - so** wǒ xiǎng huì de 我想会的

expectant huáiyǒu xīwàng 怀有希望

expectant mother zhǔn mǔqīn 准母亲

expectation qīwàng 期望; **~s** (*demands*) zhǐwàng 指望

expedient *n* yǒuyì 有益

expedition tànxiǎn 探险; (*group*) tuán 团; (*to do shopping, sightseeing*) xíng 行

expel *person* kāichú 开除

expend *energy* huāfèi 花费

expendable *person* kě xiāofèi 可消耗

expenditure huāfèi 花费

expense xiāofèi 消费; **at the company's ~** yóu gōngsī fùfèi 由公司付费; **a joke at my ~** kāi wǒde wánxiào 开我的玩笑; **at the ~ of his health** zài sǔnhài tā shēntǐ de qíngkuàng xià 在损害他身体的情况下

expense account bàoxiāo zhànghù 报销帐户

expenses yòngfèi 用费

expensive ángguì 昂贵

experience 1 *n* (*event*) jīnglì 经历; (*in life*) tǐyàn 体验; (*in particular field*) jīngyàn 经验 **2** *v/t pain, pleasure* gǎnjué 感觉; *problem, difficulty* yùdào 遇到

experienced yǒujīngyàn 有经验

experiment 1 *n* shìyàn 试验 **2** *v/i* shíyàn 实验; **~ on X** (*on animals etc*) yòng X zuò shíyàn 用X做实验; **~ with** (*try out*) shìyàn 试验

experimental yòngyú shíyàn 用于实验

expert 1 *adj* shúliàn 熟练 **2** *n* zhuānjiā 专家

expert advice zhuānjiā jiànyì 专家建议

expertise zhuānmén zhīshi 专门知识

expire dàoqī 到期

expiry qīmǎn 期满

expiry date zhōngzhǐ rìqī 终止日期

explain 1 *v/t* shuōmíng 说明 **2** *v/i* jiěshì 解释

explanation jiěshì 解释

explicit *instructions* míngquè 明确

explicitly *state, forbid* míngquè 明确

explode *v/i & v/t bomb* bàozhà 爆炸

exploit[1] *n* yīngyǒng shìji 英勇事迹

exploit[2] *v/t person* bōxuē 剥削; *resources* lìyòng 利用

exploitation (*of person*) bōxuē 剥削

exploration tànsuǒ 探索

exploratory *surgery* tànsuǒxìng 探索性

explore *country etc* kǎochá 考察

possibility tàntǎo 探讨

explorer tànsuǒ zhě 探索者

explosion bàozhà 爆炸; (*in population*) jīzēng 激增

explosive *n* zhàyào 炸药

export 1 *n* (*action*) chūkǒu 出口; (*item*) chūkǒuwù 出口物 **2** *v/t goods* chūkǒu 出口; COMPUT dǎochū 导出

export campaign chūkǒu xuānchán 出口宣传

exporter chūkǒushāng 出口商

expose (*uncover*) lùchū 露出; *scandal* jiēlù 揭露; *person* jiēchuān 揭穿; ~ *X to Y* ràng X shòudào Y 让 X 受到 Y

exposure bàolù 暴露; MED tǐwēn guòdī 体温过低; (*of dishonest behavior*) jiēchuān 揭穿; (*part of film*) bàoguāng 曝光

express 1 *adj* (*fast*) xùnsù 迅速; (*explicit*) míngquè 明确 **2** *n* (*train*) tèkuài 特快; (*bus*) kuàisù 快速 **3** *v/t* (*speak of, voice*) biǎoshì 表示; *feelings* biǎodá 表达; ~ *oneself well* qīngchǔ biǎodá zìjǐde yìsi 清楚表达自己的意思; ~ *oneself* (*emotionally*) zìwǒ biǎodá 自我表达

express elevator tèkuài diàntī 特快电梯

expression (*voiced*) biǎoshì 表示; (*on face*) biǎoqíng 表情; (*phrase*) biǎodáfǎ 表达法; (*expressiveness*) gǎnqíng 感情

expressive fùyǒu biǎoqíng 富有表情

expressly (*explicitly*) qīngchǔ biǎomíng 清楚表明; (*deliberately*) tèdì 特地

expressway gāosù gōnglù 高速公路

expulsion (*from school*) kāichú 开除; (*of diplomat*) qūzhú 驱逐

exquisite (*beautiful*) jīngměi 精美

extend 1 *v/t* kuòdà 扩大; *runway, path* yáncháng 延长; *contract, visa* yánqī 延期; *thanks, congratulations* biǎoshì 表示 **2** *v/i* (*of garden etc*) shēnzhǎn 伸展

extension (*to house*) kuòjiàn 扩建; (*of contract, visa*) yánqī 延期; TELEC fēnjī 分机

extension cable dǎoxiàn 导线

extensive guǎngfàn 广泛

extent chéngdù 程度; *to such an ~ that* dàodá rúcǐ chéngdù yǐzhìyú 到达如此程度以致于; *to a certain ~* zài yídìng chéngdù shang 在一定程度上

exterior 1 *adj* wàibù 外部 **2** *n* (*of building*) wàiguān 外观; (*of person*) wàibiǎo 外表

exterminate *vermin* xiāomiè 消灭; *race* mièjué 灭绝

external (*outside*) wàimiàn 外面

extinct *species* juézhǒng 绝种

extinction juézhǒng 绝种

extinguish *fire* pūmiè 扑灭; *cigarette* xīmiè 熄灭

extinguisher mièhuǒqì 灭火器

extort ~ *money from X* lèsuǒ X de jīnqián 勒索 X 的金钱

extortion lèsuǒ 勒索

extortionate guògāo 过高

extra 1 *n* (*sth ~*) éwàide shìwù 额外的事物 **2** *adj* éwài 额外; *be ~* (*cost more*) lìngwài shōufèi 另外收费 **3** *adv* géwài 格外

extra charge fùjiāfèi 附加费

extract 1 *n* xuǎnlù 选录 **2** *v/t* qǔchū 取出; *oil, juice* zhàchū 榨出; *coal* wā 挖; *tooth* báchū 拔出; *information* huòqǔ 获取

extraction (*process*) zhàchū 榨出; (*of tooth*) báchū 拔出

extradite yǐndù 引渡

extradition yǐndù 引渡

extradition treaty yǐndù gōngyuē 引渡公约

extramarital hūnwài 婚外

extraordinarily yìcháng 异常

extraordinary bùpíngcháng 不平常

extravagance shēchǐ 奢侈

extravagant (*with money*) huīhuò 挥霍

extreme 1 *n* jíduān 极端 **2** *adj* jídù 极度; *views* piānjī 偏激

extremely jíqí 极其

extremist *n* jíduānzhǔyì zhě 极端主义者

extricate jiějiù 解救

extrovert *n* xìnggé wàixiàng de rén 性格外向的人

exuberant xìnggāocǎiliè 兴高采烈

exult kuángxǐ 狂喜

eye **1** *n* yǎnjīng 眼睛; (*of needle*) zhēnbír 针鼻儿; ***keep an ~ on*** (*look after*) zhàokàn 照看; (*monitor*) guānchá 观察 **2** *v/t* qiáo 瞧

eyeball yǎnqiú 眼球; eyebrow méimao 眉毛; eyeglasses yǎnjìng 眼镜; eyelash jiémáo 睫毛; eyelid yǎnjiǎn 眼睑; eyeliner yǎnxiànyè 眼线液; eyeshadow yǎnyǐnggāo 眼影膏; eyesight shìlì 视力; eyesore bú shùnyǎn 不顺眼; eye strain yǎnjīng píláo 眼睛疲劳; eyewitness mùjīzhě 目击者

F

F (= *Fahrenheit*) Huáshì 华氏

fabric bùliào 布料

fabulous jí hǎo 极好

façade (*of building*) zhèngmiàn 正面; (*of person*) wàibiǎo 外表

face 1 n liǎn 脸; ~ *to* ~ miàn duì miàn 面对面; *lose* ~ diūliǎn 丢脸 2 v/t person, the sea miànduì 面对

facelift miànbù lāpí shǒushù 面部拉皮手术

face value piàomiàn jiàzhí 票面价值; *take X at* ~ cóng biǎomiàn shang kàn X 从表面上看X

facilitate shǐ ... biànlì 使 ... 便利

facilities shèshī 设施

fact shìshí 事实; *in* ~, *as a matter of* ~ shíjì shang 实际上

factor yīnsù 因素

factory gōngchǎng 工厂

faculty (*hearing etc*) nénglì 能力; (*at university*) xì 系

fade v/i (*of colors*) xiāotuì 消退

faded color, jeans tuìsè 退色

fag F (*homosexual*) tóngxìngliàn 同性恋

Fahrenheit Huáshì 华氏

fail 1 v/i shībài 失败 2 v/i: ~ *an exam* kǎoshì bù jígé 考试不及格

failure shībài 失败

faint 1 adj bù míngxiǎn 不明显 2 v/i hūndǎo 昏倒

fair[1] n COM jiāoyìhuì 交易会

fair[2] adj hair qiǎnsè 浅色; complexion báixī 白皙; (*just*) gōngzhèng 公正; *it's not* ~ zhè bù gōngpíng 这不公平

fairly treat gōngzhèng 公正; (*quite*) xiāngdāng 相当

fairness (*of treatment*) gōngzhèng 公正

fairy xiānzǐ 仙子

fairy tale shénhuà gùshì 神话故事

faith xìnxīn 信心; REL xìnyǎng 信仰

faithful zhōngchéng 忠诚; *be* ~ *to one's partner* duì pèi'ǒu zhōngchéng 对配偶忠诚

fake 1 n yànpǐn 赝品 2 adj fǎngzhì 仿制

fall[1] (*autumn*) qiūtiān 秋天

fall[2] 1 v/i (*of person*) shuāidǎo 摔倒; (*of government*) kuǎtái 垮台; (*of prices, temperature, exchange rate*) xiàjiàng 下降; (*of night*) láilín 来临; *it* ~*s on a Tuesday* nà tiān shì xīngqī'èr 那天是星期二; ~ *ill* shēngbìng 生病 2 n (*of person*) shuāijiāo 摔跤; (*of government, minister*) dǎotái 倒台; (*in price, temperature*) xiàjiàng 下降

♦fall back on yīkào 依靠

♦fall down dǎoxià 倒下

♦fall for person àishang 爱上; (*be deceived by*) xìnyǐwéizhēn 信以为真

♦fall out (*of hair*) diàoluò 掉落; (*argue*) nào bièniu 闹别扭

♦fall over dǎoxià 倒下

♦fall through (*of plans*) luòkōng 落空

fallout fàngshèchén 放射尘

false cuòwù 错误

false teeth jiǎyá 假牙

falsify wěizào 伪造

fame míngyù 名誉

familiar (*intimate*) qīnjìn 亲近; form of address qīnqiè 亲切; *be* ~ *with X* shúxī X 熟悉X

familiarity (*with subject etc*) tóngxiǎo 通晓

familiarize shǐ shúxī 使熟悉; ~ *oneself with X* shǐ zìjǐ shúxī yíxià X 使自己熟悉一下X

family jiātíng 家庭

family doctor jiātíng yīshēng 家庭医生; family name xìng 姓;

family planning jìhuà shēngyù 计划生育

famine jīhuang 饥荒

famous zhùmíng 著名; **be ~ for X** yǐ X zhùmíng 以 X 著名

fan[1] n (supporter) mí 迷

fan[2] **1** n (for cooling, electric) diànshàn 电扇; (handheld) shànzi 扇子 **2** v/t: **~ oneself** gěi zìjǐ shānfēng 给自己扇风

fanatic kuángrè zhě 狂热者

fanatical kuángrè 狂热

fan belt MOT fēngshàn pídài 风扇皮带

fancy adj design jīngzhì 精致

fancy dress qítè fúzhuāng 奇特服装

fancy-dress party huàzhuāng wǎnhuì 化妆晚会

fang jiānyá 尖牙

fanny pack yāobāo 腰包

fantastic (very good) bàngjíle 棒极了; (very big) jùdà 巨大

fantasy huànxiǎng 幻想

far adv yuǎn 远; (much) fēicháng 非常; **~ away** yáoyuǎn 遥远; **how ~ is it to X?** dào X qù yǒu duōyuǎn? 到 X 去有多远？; **as ~ as the corner / hotel** dào jiǎoluò / bīnguǎn nàme yuǎn 到角落 / 宾馆那么远; **as ~ as I can see** yī wǒ kàn yīwǒ 依我看; **as ~ as I know** jùwǒsuǒzhī 据我所知; **you've gone too ~** (in behavior) nǐzuòde guòfèn 你做得过分; **so ~ so good** dào mùqián wéizhǐ, yíqiè dōu hěn shùnlì 到目前为止，一切都很顺利

farce (ridiculous goings-on) nàojù 闹剧

fare n (for travel) piàojià 票价

Far East Yuǎndōng 远东

farewell n cíbié 辞别

farewell party sòngbié yànhuì 送别宴会

farfetched qiānqiáng 牵强

farm n nóngchǎng 农场

farmer nóngfū 农夫

farmhouse nóngshè 农舍

farmworker nóngchǎng gōngrén 农场工人

farsighted yǒu yuǎnjiàn 有远见; (optically) yuǎnshì 远视

fart F **1** n pì 屁 **2** v/i fàngpì 放屁

farther adv gèngyuǎn 更远

farthest travel etc zuìyuǎn 最远

fascinate v/t shǐ zháomí 使着迷; **be ~d by X** bèi X xīyǐnzhù 被 X 吸引住

fascinating mírén 迷人

fascination (with subject) chīmí 痴迷

fascism fǎxīsī zhǔyì 法西斯主义

fascist 1 n fǎxīsī zhǔyì zhě 法西斯主义者 **2** adj fǎxīsī 法西斯

fashion n shíshàng 时尚; (manner) fāngshì 方式; **in ~** liúxíng 流行; **out of ~** guòshí 过时

fashionable clothes, person, idea shímáo 时髦

fashion-conscious yǒu shíshàng yìshí 有时尚意识

fashion designer shízhuāng shèjìshī 时装设计师

fast[1] **1** adj kuài 快; **be ~** (of clock) kuài 快 **2** adv kuài 快; **stuck ~** dǔzhùle 堵住了; **~ asleep** shúshuì 熟睡

fast[2] n (not eating) jìnshí 禁食

fasten 1 v/t shǐ gùdìng 使固定; **~ X onto Y** bǎ X gùdìng zài Y shang 把 X 固定在 Y 上 **2** v/i (of dress etc) jì 系

fastener (for dress) lāliàn 拉链; (for lid) jǐngàiqì 紧盖器

fast food kuàicān 快餐; **fast-food restaurant** kuàicāndiàn 快餐店; **fast forward 1** n (on video etc) kuàijìnjiàn 快进健 **2** v/i kuàijìn 快进; **fastlane** kuàisù chēdào 快速车道; **fast train** kuàichē 快车

fat 1 adj pàng 胖 **2** n (on meat) zhīfáng 脂肪

fatal zhìmìng 致命; error wúkě wǎnjiù 无可挽救

fatality sǐwáng 死亡

fatally: be ~ injured shòu zhìmìng shāng 受致著伤

fate mìngyùn 命运

father n fùqin 父亲

fatherhood shēnwéirénfù 身为人父

father-in-law (*woman's*) gōnggōng 公公; (*man's*) yuèfù 岳父

fatherly sì fùqīn 似父亲

fathom *n* NAUT yīngxún 英寻

fatigue *n* píjuàn 疲倦

fatso F pàngzi 胖子

fatty 1 *adj* hán zhīfáng duo 含脂肪多 **2** *n* F (*person*) pàngzi 胖子

faucet lóngtóu 龙头

fault *n* (*defect*) máobìng 毛病; *it's your/my ~* shì nǐde/wǒde cuò 是你的/我的错; *find ~ with X* zhǎo X de cuò 找X的错

faultless wánměi 完美

faulty *products* yǒu máobìng 有毛病

favor *n* xǐ'ài 喜爱; *in ~ of X* (*resign, withdraw*) duì X yǒulì 对X有利; *be in ~ of ...* zhīchí ... 支持 ...; *do X a ~* bāng X ge máng 帮X个忙; *do me a ~!* (*don't be stupid*) bàituō! 拜托!

favorable *reply etc* zànchéng 赞成

favorite 1 *n* zuì xǐhuān 最喜欢; (*food*) piān'ài 偏爱 **2** *adj* zuì xǐhuān 最喜欢

fax 1 *n* chuánzhēn 传真; *send X by ~* bǎ X yòng chuánzhēn chuánsòng 把X用传真传送 **2** *v/t* yòng chuánzhēn chuán 用传真传; *~ X to Y* bǎ X chuánzhēn gěi Y 把X传真给Y

FBI (= *Federal Bureau of Investigation*) Liánbāng Diàochájú 联邦调查局

fear 1 *n* kǒngjù 恐惧 **2** *v/t* hàipà 害怕

fearless wúwèi 无畏

feasibility study kěxíngxìng yánjiū 可行性研究

feasible qièshí kěxíng 切实可行

feast *n* shèngyàn 盛宴

feat jìyì 技艺

feather yǔmáo 羽毛

feature 1 *n* (*on face*) róngmào 容貌; (*of city, building, plan, style*) tèsè 特色; (*article in paper*) zhuāntí 专题; (*movie*) zhèngpiān 正片; *make a ~ of X* qiángdiào X 强调X **2** *v/t* (*of movie*) yóu ... zhǔyǎn 由 ... 主演

February èryuè 二月

federal liánbāngzhì 联邦制

federation liánbāng 联邦

fed up *adj* F yànfán 厌烦; *be ~ with X* yīn X ér yànfán 因X而厌烦

fee fèiyòng 费用; (*of lawyer, doctor, consultant*) chóujīn 酬金; (*for entrance*) fèi 费; (*for membership*) huìfèi 会费

feeble *person* xūruò 虚弱; *attempt* wúlì 无力; *laugh* wēiruò 微弱

feed *v/t* gōngyǎng 供养; *animal* wèi 喂

feedback ⇩ fǎnkuì xìnxī 反馈信息

feel 1 *v/t* (*touch*) chùmō 触摸; (*sense*) gǎndào 感到; *pain, pleasure, sensation* gǎnzhī 感知; (*think*) rènwéi 认为 **2** *v/i* (*of cloth etc*) gěirén gǎnjué 给人感觉; *it ~s like silk/cotton* mōqǐlái xiàng sī/miánhuā 摸起来像丝/棉花; *your hand ~s hot/cold* nǐde shǒu mōqǐlái rè/liáng 你的手摸起来热/凉; *I ~ hungry/tired* wǒ gǎnjué è/lèi le 我感觉饿/累了; *how are you ~ing today?* nǐ jīntiān gǎnjué zěnmeyàng? 你今天感觉怎么样?; *how does it ~ to be rich?* fùyǒu shì shénme gǎnjué? 富有是什么感觉?; *do you ~ like a drink/meal?* xiǎng bù xiǎng hē/chīdiǎnr shénme? 想不想喝/吃点儿什么?; *I ~ like going/staying* wǒ xiǎng zǒu/dāi zài zhèr 我想走/呆在这儿; *I don't ~ like it* wǒ bù xiǎngyào 我不想要

♦ **feel up to** rènwéi yǒu nénglì zuò 认为有能力做

feeler (*of insect*) chùjiǎo 触角

feelgood factor lèguān xīnlǐ 乐观心理

feeling (*of happiness*) gǎnjué 感觉; (*emotion*) gǎnqíng 感情; (*sensation*) zhījué 知觉; *what are your ~s about X?* nǐ shì zěnme xiǎng de? 你是怎么想的?; *I have mixed ~s about him* wǒ duì tā yǒu hěn máodùnde gǎnqíng 我

对他有很矛盾的感情
fellow (*man*) jiāhuo 家伙
fellow citizen tóngbāo 同胞;
　fellow countryman tóngbāo 同
　胞;**fellow man** quánrénlèi 全人
　类
felony zhòngzuì 重罪
felt *n* máozhān 毛毡
felt tip, **felt-tip(ped) pen**
　zhāntóubǐ 毡头笔
female 1 *adj animal, plant* cíxìng 雌
　性; (*referring to people*) nǚxìng 女
　性 **2** *n* (*of animals, plants*) cíxìng
　dòngzhíwù 雌性动植物;
　(*person*) nǚxìng 女性; *pej* (*woman*)
　nǚrén 女人
feminine 1 *adj qualities* yǒu nǚxìng
　qìzhì 有女性气质; GRAM yīnxìng
　阴性; **she's very ~** tā hěn yǒu
　nǚrén wèidào 她很有女人味道
　2 *n* GRAM yīnxìng 阴性
feminism ⇩ nǚquán zhǔyì 女权
　主义
feminist ⇩ **1** *n* nǚquán zhǔyì zhě
　女权主义者 **2** *adj* nǚquán zhǔyì 女权
fen (*Chinese money*) fēn 分
fence *n* zhàlán 栅栏
♦ **fence in** *land* yòng zhàlán wéiqǐ
　用栅栏围起
fencing SP jíjiàn 击剑
fend: **~ for oneself** dúlì shēnghuó
　独立生活
fender MOT yìzǐbǎn 翼子板
ferment[1] *v/i* (*of liquid*) fājiào 发酵
ferment[2] *n* (*unrest*) dòngdàng bù'ān
　动荡不安
fermentation fājiào 发酵
fern jué 蕨
ferocious cánrěn 残忍
ferry *n* dùchuán 渡船
fertile *soil* féiwò 肥沃; *woman,*
　animal néng shēngyù 能生育
fertility (*of soil*) féiwò 肥沃; (*of*
　woman, animal) fányù 繁育
fertility drug cùyùnyào 促孕药
fertilize *v/t ovum* shǐ shòujīng 使受
　精
fertilizer (*for soil*) féiliào 肥料
fervent *admirer* rèchéng 热诚
fester *v/i* (*of wound*) huànnóng 化脓
festival jiérì 节日

festive jiérì 节日
festivities huānqìng 欢庆
fetch *person* jiē 接; *thing* ná 拿;
　price màidé 卖得
fetus tāi'ér 胎儿
feud *n* shìchóu 世仇
fever fāshāo 发烧
feverish fāshāo 发烧; *fig:*
　excitement jīdòng 激动
few 1 *adj* (*not many*) hěnshǎo 很少;
　a ~ (*things*) jǐgè 几个; *quite a ~*, *a*
　good ~ (*a lot*) xiāngdāngduō 相当
　多 **2** *pron* (*not many*) shǎoshù jǐgè
　少数几个; *a ~* (*some*) yìxiē 一些;
　quite a ~, *a good ~* (*a lot*) xǔduō
　许多
fewer *adj* gèngshǎo 更少; *~ than*
　... shǎoyú ... 少于 ...
fiancé wèihūnfū 未婚夫
fiancée wèihūnqī 未婚妻
fiasco chèdǐde shībài 彻底的失
　败
fib *n* xiǎohuǎng 小谎
fiber *n* xiānwéi 纤维
fiberglass bōlí xiānwéi 玻璃纤维;
fiber optic guāng xiān 光纤;**fi-**
ber optics guāngdǎo xiānwéi 光
　导纤维
fickle biànhuà wúcháng 变化无常
fiction (*novels*) xiǎoshuō 小说;
　(*made-up story*) biānzàode shì 编
　造的事
fictitious xūgòu 虚构
fiddle 1 *n* F (*violin*) xiǎotíqín 小提
　琴 **2** *v/i:* *~ with* bǎinòng 摆弄;
　around with húluàn bǎinòng 胡
　乱摆弄 **3** *v/t accounts, results*
　cuàngǎi 篡改
fidelity zhōngzhēn 忠贞
fidget *v/i* fánzào bù'ān 烦躁不安
field *n* tiándì 田地; (*for sport*)
　chǎng 场; (*competitors in race*)
　cānsài zhě 参赛者; (*of research,*
　knowledge etc) lǐngyù 领域; *that's*
　not my ~ nà búzài wǒde fànwéi
　zhīnèi 那不在我的范围之内
field events tiánsài 田赛
fierce *animal* xiōngměng 凶猛;
　wind, storm qiángliè 强烈
fiery *personality* yìnù 易怒; *temper*
　bàozào 暴躁

fifteen shíwǔ 十五
fifteenth dìshíwǔ 第十五
fifth dìwǔ 第五
fiftieth dì wǔshí 第五十
fifty wǔshí 五十
fifty-fifty *adv* duìbàn 对半
fig wúhuāguǒ 无花果
fight 1 *n* zhàndòu 战斗; *fig (for survival, championship)* zhēngdòu 争斗; *(in boxing)* quánjī 拳击 **2** *v/t enemy, person* yǔ … dǎzhàng 与 … 打仗; *(in boxing)* jiāofēng 交锋; *a disease, injustice* zuò dòuzhēng 作斗争 **3** *v/i* dǎjià 打架
♦**fight for** *one's rights, cause* zhēngqǔ 争取
fighter zhànshì 战士; *(airplane)* zhàndòujī 战斗机; *(boxer)* quánjīshǒu 拳击手; *she's a ~* tāshìge fèndòu zhě 她是个奋斗者
figurative *use of word* bǐyù 比喻; *art* yòng túxíng biǎoxiàn 用图形表现
figure 1 *n (digit)* shùzì 数字; *(of person)* xíngtǐ 形体; *(form, shape)* túxíng 图形 **2** *v/t* F *(think)* rènwéi 认为
♦**figure on** F *(plan)* jìhuà 计划
♦**figure out** *(understand)* lǐjiě 理解; *calculation* jìsuànchū 计算出
figure skating huāyàng huábīng 花样滑冰
file¹ 1 *n (of documents)* dàng'àn 档案; COMPUT wénjiàn 文件 **2** *v/t documents* zhěnglǐ 整理
♦**file away** *documents* jiāng … guīdàng 将 … 归档
file² *n (for wood, fingernails)* cuòdāo 锉刀
file cabinet dàng'ànxiāng 档案箱
file manager COMPUT wénjiàn guǎnlǐ chéngxù 文件管理程序
Filipino 1 *adj* Fēilǜbīn 菲律宾 **2** *n (person)* Fēilǜbīn rén 菲律宾人
fill 1 *v/t* zhùmǎn 注满 **2** *n: eat one's ~* chīgebǎo 吃个饱
♦**fill in** *form* tiánxiě 填写; *hole* tiánmǎn 填满
♦**fill in for** línshí tìdài 临时替代
♦**fill out 1** *v/t form* tiánxiě 填写

2 *v/i (get fatter)* zhǎngpàng 长胖
♦**fill up 1** *v/t* zhuāngmǎn 装满 **2** *v/i (of stadium, theater)* chōngmǎn 充满
fillet *n* lǐjǐ 里脊
fillet steak lǐjǐ niúpái 里脊牛排
filling 1 *n (in sandwich)* xiàn 馅; *(in tooth)* bǔyá 补牙 **2** *adj food* róngyi bǎorén 容易饱人
filling station jiāyóuzhàn 加油站
film 1 *n (for camera)* jiāojuǎn 胶卷; *(movie)* diànyǐng 电影 **2** *v/t person, event* pāishè 拍摄
film-maker zhìpiàn rén 制片人
film star diànyǐng míngxīng 电影明星
filter 1 *n* guòlǜqì 过滤器 **2** *v/t coffee, liquid* guòlǜ 过滤
♦**filter through** *(of news reports)* mànmàn chuánkāi 慢慢传开
filter tip *(cigarette)* guòlǜzuǐ 过滤嘴
filth huìwù 污物
filthy āngzāng 肮脏; *language etc* wěixiè 猥亵
fin *(of fish)* qí 鳍
final 1 *adj (last)* zuìhòu 最后; *decision* quèdìng 确定 **2** *n* SP juésài 决赛
finalist cānjiā juésài zhě 参加决赛者
finalize *plans, design* quèdìng 确定
finally zuìhòu 最后; *(at last)* zhōngyú 终于
finance 1 *n* jīnróng 金融 **2** *v/t* tígōng zījīn 提供资金
financial jīnróng 金融
financier jīnróngjiā 金融家
find *v/t* zhǎodào 找到; *if you ~ it too hot / cold* rúguǒ nǐ juédé tài rè / lěng 如果你觉得太热 / 冷; *~ X innocent / guilty* LAW cáidìng X wúzuì / yǒuzuì 裁定 X 无罪 / 有罪
♦**find out 1** *v/t* huòzhī 获知 **2** *v/i (inquire)* cháxún 查询; *(discover)* liǎojiědào 了解到
fine¹ *adj day, weather* qínglǎng 晴朗; *wine, performance, city* hǎo 好; *distinction* xìwēi 细微; *line* xì 细; *how's that? – that's ~* nǐ kàn zěnmeyàng? – hǎo 你看怎么样 ? –

好; *that's ~ by me* wǒ juédé kěyǐ 我觉得可以; *how are you? – ~* nǐ hǎo ma? – hěn hǎo 你好吗？ – 很好

fine² **1** *n* (*penalty*) fájīn 罚金 **2** *v/t* fákuǎn 罚款

finger *n* shǒuzhǐ 手指

fingernail shǒuzhǐjiǎ 手指甲; **fingerprint** shǒuyìn 手印; **fingertip** zhǐjiān 指尖; *have X at one's ~s* duì X liǎo rú zhǐzhǎng 对 X 了如指掌

finicky *person* guòfèn tiāotì 过分挑剔; *design, pattern* guòfèn jiǎngjiu xìjié 过分讲究细节

finish 1 *v/t* jiéshù 结束; *~ doing X* zuòwán X 做完 X **2** *v/i* jiéshù 结束 **3** *n* (*of product*) zuìhòu bùfen 最后部分; (*of race*) zhōngdiǎn 终点

♦**finish off** *v/t*: *~ a drink / meal / one's work* bǎ shèngxiàde he / chī / zuòwán 把剩下的喝 / 吃 / 做完

♦**finish up** *v/t food* chīwán 吃完; *he finished up liking it / living there* tā hòulái xǐhuān tā le / zhù zài nàr le 他后来喜欢它了 / 住在那儿了

♦**finish with**: *~ X with boyfriend etc* yǔ X duànjué guānxi 与 X 断绝关系

finishing line zhōngdiǎnxiàn 终点线

Finland Fēnlán 芬兰

Finn Fēnlán rén 芬兰人

Finnish 1 *adj* Fēnlán 芬兰 **2** *n* (*language*) Fēnlán yǔ 芬兰语

fir lěngshān 冷杉

fire 1 *n* huǒ 火; (*electric, gas*) nuǎnlú 暖炉; (*blaze*) shīhuǒ 失火; (*bonfire, campfire etc*) gōuhuǒ 篝火; *be on ~* zháohuǒ 着火; *catch ~* shāozháo 烧着; *set X on ~*, *set ~ to X* gěi X fànghuǒ 给 X 放火 **2** *v/i* (*shoot*) shèjī 射击 **3** *v/t* F (*dismiss*) jiěgù 解雇; *be ~d* bèi chǎo yóuyú le 被炒鱿鱼了

fire alarm huǒjǐng jǐngbào 火警警报; **firearm** qiāngzhī 枪支; **firecracker** biānpào 鞭炮; **fire**

department xiāofángduì 消防队; **fire escape** ānquán chūkǒu 安全出口; **fire extinguisher** mièhuǒqì 灭火器; **firefighter** xiāofángduìyuán 消防队员; **fireplace** bìlú 壁炉; **fire truck** xiāofángchē 消防车; **firewood** mùchái 木柴; **fireworks** yānhuǒ 烟火; (*display*) yānhuǒ biǎoyǎn 烟火表演

firm¹ *adj grip, handshake* wěn ér yǒulì 稳而有力; *flesh, muscles* jiēshí 结实; *voice, decision* jiāndìng 坚定; *a ~ deal* yíxiàng kěndìng de xiéyì 一项肯定的协议

firm² *n* COM gōngsī 公司

first 1 *adj* dìyī 第一; *who's ~ please?* shéi shì dìyīgè? 谁是第一个？ **2** *n* dìyīgè 第一个 **3** *adv arrive, finish* dìyī 第一; (*beforehand*) xiān 先; *~ of all* (*for one reason*) shǒuxiān 首先; *at ~* qǐchū 起初

first aid jíjiù 急救; **first-aid box**, **first-aid kit** jíjiùxiāng 急救箱; **first-born** *adj* zhǎngzǐ(nǚ) 长子(女); **first class 1** *adj ticket, compartment* tóuděng 头等; (*very good*) yīliú 一流 **2** *adv travel* tóuděng 头等; **first floor** yīlóu 一楼; **first-hand** *adj* qīnshēn 亲身

firstly shǒuxiān 首先

first name míngzi 名字

first-rate yīliú 一流

fiscal cáizhèng 财政

fiscal year cáizhèng niándù 财政年度

fish 1 *n* yú 鱼 **2** *v/i* diàoyú 钓鱼

fishbone yúcì 鱼刺

fisherman yúfū 渔夫

fishing bǔyú 捕鱼

fishing boat yúchuán 鱼船; **fishing line** diàosī 钓丝; **fishing rod** diàoyúgān 钓鱼杆

fish stick yútiáo 鱼条

fishy F (*suspicious*) kěyí 可疑

fist quán 拳

fit¹ *n* MED hūnjué 昏厥; *a ~ of rage / jealousy* yìgǔ nùhuǒ / jídù qíngxù 一股怒火 / 嫉妒情绪

fit² *adj* (*physically*) jiànkāng 健康;

(*morally*) qiàdàng 恰当; **keep ~** jiànshēn 健身

fit³ 1 *v/t* (*of clothes*) héshì 合适; (*attach*) ānzhuāng 安装 **2** *v/i* (*of clothes*) héshì 合适; (*of piece of furniture etc*) róngdexià 容得下 **3** *n*: **it is a good ~** hěn héshì 很合适; **it's a tight ~** yǒudiǎnr jǐn 有点儿紧

♦**fit in** (*of person in group*) héqún 合群; **it fits in with our plans** zhè yǔ wǒmende jìhuà yízhì 这与我们的计划一致

fitful *sleep* bù wěndìng 不稳定
fitness (*physical*) jiànkāng 健康
fitness center jiànshēn zhōngxīn 健身中心
fitted carpet gùdìnghǎode dìtǎn 固定好的地毯
fitted kitchen yǒu gùdìng shèbèi de chúfáng 有固定设备的厨房
fitter *n* zhuāngpèigōng 装配工
fitting *adj* qiàdàng 恰当
fittings zhuāngzhì 装置
five wǔ 五
Five Year Plan Wǔnián Jìhuà 五年计划
fix 1 *n* (*solution*) jiějué 解决; **be in a ~** F xiànrù kùnjìng 陷入困境 **2** *v/t* (*attach*) dìngláo 钉牢; (*repair*) xiūlǐ 修理; (*arrange: meeting etc*) ānpái 安排; *lunch* zhǔnbèi 准备; (*dishonestly: match etc*) zuòbì 作弊; **~ X onto Y** bǎ X gùdìng zài Y shang 把 X 固定在 Y 上; **I'll ~ you a drink** wǒ gěi nǐ nòng diǎn yǐnliào 我给你弄点饮料

♦**fix up** *meeting* ānpái 安排; **it's all fixed up** dōu shì ānpái hǎode 都是安排好的

fixed (*in one position*) gùdìng 固定; *timescale, exchange rate* quèdìng búbiàn 确定不变
fixture (*in room*) gùdìng zhuāngzhì 固定装置
flab (*on body*) sōngchíde jīròu 松弛的肌肉
flabbergast: **be ~ed** F dàchīyìjīng 大吃一惊
flabby *muscles, stomach* sōngchí 松弛

flag¹ *n* qí 旗
flag² *v/i* (*tire*) píjuàn 疲倦
flair (*talent*) tiānfèn 天份; **have a natural ~ for X** duì X yǒu tiānfèn 对 X 有天份
flake *n* suìpiàn 碎片
♦**flake off** *v/i* bōluò 剥落
flaky yì bōluò 易剥落
flaky pastry sūbǐng 酥饼
flamboyant *personality* ài xuànyào 爱炫耀
flame *n* huǒyàn 火焰
flammable yì ránshāo 易燃烧
flan guǒxiànbǐng 果馅饼
flank 1 *n* (*of horse etc*) lèibù 肋部; MIL cèyì 侧翼 **2** *v/t* zhìyú liǎngcè 置于两侧; **be ~ed by X** liǎngcè yǒu X 两侧有 X
flap 1 *n* (*of envelope, pocket*) kǒugài 口盖; (*of table*) huódòngbiān 活动边; **be in a ~** F jǐnzhāng huāngluàn 紧张慌乱 **2** *v/t wings* jīnyì 襟翼 **3** *v/i* (*of flag etc*) yáodòng 摇动
flare 1 *n* (*distress signal*) shǎnguāng zhuāngzhì 闪光装置; (*in dress*) lābazhuàng 喇叭状 **2** *v/t nostrils* gǔqǐ 鼓起
♦**flare up** (*of violence*) tūqǐ 突起; (*of illness, rash*) fùfā 复发; (*of fire*) biànwàng 变旺; (*get very angry*) fānù 发怒
flash 1 *n* (*of light*) shǎnshuò 闪烁; PHOT shǎnguāngdēng 闪光灯; **in a ~** F shǎndiànbān 闪电般; **have a ~ of inspiration** língjīyídòng 灵机一动; **~ of lightning** shǎndiàn 闪电 **2** *v/i* (*of light*) shǎnliàng 闪亮 **3** *v/t headlights* yòng guāng liánluò 用光联络
flashback (*in movie*) shǎnhuí 闪回
flashbulb shǎnguāng dēngpào 闪光灯泡
flasher MOT shǎnguāng zhǐshìdēng 闪光指示灯
flashlight shǒudiàntǒng 手电筒; PHOT shǎnguāngdēng 闪光灯
flashy *pej* huāshao 花哨
flask nuǎnpíng 暖瓶
flat 1 *adj surface, land* píngtǎn 平坦; *beer* pǎoqì 跑气; *battery* yòngwán

diàn 用完电; *tire* qì bùzú 气不足; *shoes* píngdǐ 平底; *sound, tone* píngdàn 平淡; **and that's ~** F shuōdìngle 说定了 **2** *adv* MUS yǐ dīdiào 以低调; **~ out** *work, run, drive* jiéjìnquánlì 竭尽全力

flat-chested píngxiōng 平胸

flat rate tǒngyī shōufèilǜ 统一收费率

flatten *v/t land, road* biànpíng 变平; (*by bombing, demolition*) jīdǎo 击倒

flatter *v/t* fèngcheng 奉承

flattering *comments* tǎohǎo 讨好; *color, clothes* shǐrén gèng piàoliàng 使人更漂亮

flattery fèngcheng 奉承

flavor 1 *n* wèidao 味道 **2** *v/t*: **~ X** *food* gěi X tiáowèi 给 X 调味

flavoring tiáowèipǐn 调味品

flaw *n* xiácī 瑕疵

flawless wánměi 完美

flea tiàozao 跳蚤

flee *v/i* táopǎo 逃跑

fleet *n* NAUT jiànduì 舰队; (*of taxis, trucks*) chēduì 车队

fleeting *visit etc* duǎnzàn 短暂; **catch a ~ glimpse of** piējiàn 瞥见

flesh ròutǐ 肉体; (*of fruit*) guǒròu 果肉; **meet / see X in the ~** jiàndào X běnrén 见到 X 本人

flex *v/t muscles* huódòng 活动

flexible línghuó 灵活; **I'm quite ~** (*about arrangements, timing*) wǒ kěyǐ jīdòng 我可以机动

flick *v/t tail* qīngtán 轻弹; **he ~ed a fly off his hand** tā gǎndiàole shǒushangde cángying 他赶掉了手上的苍蝇; **she ~ed her hair out of her eyes** tā bōkāi le yǎnqiánde tóufa 她拨开了眼前的头发

♦**flick through** *book, magazine* liúlǎn 浏览

flicker *v/i* (*of light, candle, computer screen*) shǎndòng 闪动

flies (*on pants: zipper*) lāliànr 拉链儿; (*buttons*) kāikòu 开扣

flight (*in airplane*) hángbān 航班; (*flying*) fēixíng 飞行; (*fleeing*) táopǎo 逃跑; **~ (of stairs)** lóutīde

yíduàn 楼梯的一段

flight crew jīzǔ rényuán 机组人员; **flight deck** fēixíng jiǎbǎn 飞行甲板; **flight number** hángbānhào 航班号; **flight path** fēixíng lùxiàn 飞行路线; **flight recorder** fēixíng jìlùyí 飞行记录仪; **flight time** (*departure*) qǐfēi shíjiān 起飞时间; (*duration*) fēixíng shíjiān 飞行时间

flighty qīngfú 轻浮

flimsy *structure, furniture* bù jiēshi 不结实; *dress, material* qīng'érbó 轻而薄; *excuse* bù zúxìn 不足信

flinch tuìsuō 退缩

fling *v/t* rēng 扔; **~ oneself into a chair** zāidào yǐzi shang 栽到椅子上

♦**flip through** *book, magazine* liúlǎn 浏览

flipper (*for swimming*) jiǎopǔ 脚蹼

flirt 1 *v/i* tiáoqíng 调情 **2** *n* tiáoqíng zhě 调情者

flirtatious ài tiáoqíng 爱挑情

float *v/i* piāofú 漂浮; FIN fúdòng 浮动

flock *n* (*of sheep*) yìqún 一群

flog *v/t* (*whip*) biāndǎ 鞭打

flood 1 *n* hóngshuǐ 洪水 **2** *v/t* (*of river*) yānmò 淹没; **~ its banks** (*of river*) yānmò tī'àn 淹没堤岸

flooding hóngshuǐ fànlàn 洪水泛滥

floodlight *n* fànguāngdēng 泛光灯

floor *n* dìbǎn 地板; (*story*) lóucéng 楼层

floorboard yíkuài dìbǎn 一块地板; **floor cloth** pū dìbǎn de hòubù 铺地板的厚布; **floor lamp** luòdìdēng 落地灯

flop 1 *v/i* měngrán tǎngxià 猛然躺下; F (*fail*) chèdǐ shībài 彻底失败 **2** *n* F (*failure*) chèdǐ shībài 彻底失败

floppy *adj* (*not stiff*) sōngruǎn 松软; (*weak*) xūruò 虚弱

floppy (disk) ⇩ ruǎnpán 软盘

floppy drive COMPUT ruǎnqū 软驱

florist huāshāng 花商

flour miànfěn 面粉

flourish *v/i* fánróng 繁荣

flourishing *trade* xīngwàng 兴旺

flow 1 *v/i (of river, electric current, traffic)* liúdòng 流动; *(of work)* jìnxíng 进行 **2** *n (of river)* liúdòng 流动; *(of information, ideas)* jiāoliú 交流

flowchart liúchéngtú 流程图

flower 1 *n* huā 花 **2** *v/i* kāihuā 开花

flowerbed huātán 花坛

flowerpot huāpén 花盆

flowery *pattern* duōhuā 多花; *style of writing* cízǎo huálì 词藻华丽

flu liúgǎn 流感

fluctuate *v/i* bōdòng 波动

fluctuation bōdòng 波动

fluency *(in a language)* liúlì 流利

fluent *adj* liúlì 流利; *he speaks ~ Chinese* tā jiǎng yìkǒu liúlìde Hànyǔ 他讲一口流利的汉语

fluently *speak, write* liúlì 流利

fluff: *a bit of ~ (material)* yìdiǎn róngmáo 一点绒毛

fluffy *adj material, hair* péngsōng 蓬松; *clouds* sōngruǎn 松软; *~ toy* sōngruǎnde wánjù 松软的玩具

fluid *n* liútǐ 流体

flunk *v/t* F *subject* bù jígé 不及格

fluorescent *light* fā yíngguāng 发荧光

flush 1 *v/t toilet* chōngxǐ 冲洗; *~ X down the toilet* bǎ X chōngjìn cèsuǒ 把 X 冲进厕所 **2** *v/i (of toilet)* chōngxǐ 冲洗; *(go red in the face)* biànhóng 变红 **3** *adj (level)* qípíng 齐平; *be ~ with X* yǔ X wángquán qípíng 与 X 完全齐平

♦ **flush away** *(down toilet)* chōngdiào 冲掉

♦ **flush out** *rebels etc* gǎnchū 赶出

fluster *v/t* shǐ jǐnzhāng 使紧张; *get ~ed* jǐnzhāng 紧张

flute chángdí 长笛

flutter *v/i (of bird, wings)* bǎichì 摆翅; *(of flag)* piāodòng 飘动; *(of heart)* pūdòng 扑动

fly[1] *n (insect)* cāngying 苍蝇

fly[2] *n (on pants: zipper)* lāliànr 拉链儿; *(buttons)* kāikòu 开扣

fly[3] **1** *v/i (of bird, airplane)* fēixíng 飞行; *(in airplane)* chéngjī 乘机; *(of flag)* piāoyáng 飘扬; *(rush)* fēipǎo 飞跑; *~ into a rage* bórán dànù 勃然大怒 **2** *v/t airplane* jiàshǐ 驾驶; *airline* dāchéng 搭乘; *(transport by air)* kōngyùn 空运

♦ **fly away** *(of bird, airplane)* fēizǒu 飞走

♦ **fly back** *v/i (travel back)* fēihuí 飞回

♦ **fly in 1** *v/i (of airplane, passengers)* fēidào 飞到 **2** *v/t supplies etc* kōngyùn 空运

♦ **fly off** *(of hat etc)* fēituō 飞脱

♦ **fly out** *v/i* chéng jī qù chéngjī 乘机去

♦ **fly past** *(in formation)* biānduì fēixíng 编队飞行; *(of time)* fēishì 飞逝

flying *n* fēixíng 飞行

foam *n (on liquid)* pàomò 泡沫

foam rubber pàomò xiàngjiāo 泡沫橡胶

FOB (= *free on board*) lí'àn jiàgé 离岸价格

focus *n (of attention)* jízhōng 集中; PHOT jiāojù 焦距; *be in ~ / out of ~* PHOT zài / búzài jiāodiǎn shang 在 / 不在焦点上

♦ **focus on** *problem, issue* jízhōng yú 集中于; PHOT jùjiāo yú 聚焦于

fodder sìliào 饲料

fog wù 雾

foggy duōwù 多雾

foil[1] *n (silver ~ etc)* xīzhǐ 锡纸

foil[2] *v/t (thwart)* cuòbài 挫败

fold[1] **1** *v/t paper etc* zhédié 折叠; *~ one's arms* hébào shuāngbì 合抱双臂 **2** *v/i (of business)* tíngyè 停业 **3** *n (in cloth etc)* zhě 褶

♦ **fold up 1** *v/t* zhé qǐlái 折起来 **2** *v/i (of chair, table)* néng zhédié 能折叠

fold[2] *n (for sheep etc)* yánglán 羊栏

folder *also* COMPUT wénjiànjiá 文件夹

folding zhédié 折叠; *~ chair* zhédiéyǐ 折叠椅

foliage yèzi 叶子

folk *(people)* rénmen 人们; *my ~ (family)* wǒde jiārén 我的家人; *come in, ~s* F dàjiā qǐngjìn 大家

请进

folk dance ⇩ mínjiānwǔ 民间舞; **folk music** mínyuè 民乐; **folk singer** míngēshǒu 民歌手; **folk song** míngē 民歌

follow 1 v/t person gēnsuí 跟随; road yánzhe ... qiánjìn 沿着 ... 前进; guidelines, instructions zūnxún 遵循; TV series, news liánxù kàn 连续看; (understand) míngbái 明白; **~ me** gēn wǒ lái 跟我来 **2** v/i gēnzhe 跟着; (logically) bìrán fāshēng 必然发生; **it ~s from this that ...** yóucǐ fāshēng ... 由此发生 ...; **as ~s** rúxià 如下

♦**follow up** v/t letter, inquiry hòuxù 后续

follower (of politician etc) zhuīsuí zhě 追随者; (of football team) zhīchí zhě 支持者; (of TV program) zhōngshí guānzhòng 忠实观众

following 1 adj day, night jiēzhe 接着; points xiàshù 下述; pages yǐxià 以下 **2** n (people) yìpī zhīchí zhě 一批支持者; **the ~** rúxià 如下

follow-up meeting gēnzōng huìyì 跟踪会议

follow-up visit (to doctor etc) liánxùde bàifǎng 连续的拜访

folly (madness) yúchǔn 愚蠢

fond (loving) xǐ'ài 喜爱; memory zhēn'ài 珍爱; **be ~ of** xǐhuan 喜欢

fondle àifǔ 爱抚

fondness xǐ'ài 喜爱

font (for printing) zìtǐ 字体

food (formal word) shíwù 食物; (informal word) chīde 吃的

food freak F dàchī 大吃; **food mixer** shíwù jiǎobànqì 食物搅拌器; **food poisoning** shíwù zhòngdú 食物中毒

fool n chǔnrén 蠢人; **make a ~ of oneself** shǐ zìjǐ chūchǒu 使自己出丑

♦**fool around** húnào 胡闹; (sexually) yǒu wàiyù 有外遇

♦**fool around with** knife, drill etc bǎinòng 摆弄

foolish yúchǔn 愚蠢

foolproof búhuì chūcuò 不会出错

foot jiǎo 脚; (measurement) yīngchǐ 英尺; **on ~** bùxíng 步行; **at the ~ of the page / hill** zài yè / shān jiǎo xià 在页 / 山角下; **put one's ~ in it** F (by saying sth) lìngrénnánkān shuō cuòhuà 说错话; (by doing sth) zuò cuòshì 做错事

football měishì zúqiú 美式足球; (soccer) zúqiú 足球; (ball) zúqiú 足球; **football player** měishì zúqiú duìyuán 美式足球队员; (soccer) qiúyuán 球员; **footbridge** bùxíngqiáo 步行桥

footer COMPUT jiǎozhù 脚注

foothills shānlù xiǎoqiū 山麓小丘

footing (basis) jīchǔ 基础; **lose one's ~** shīzú diēdǎo 失足跌倒; **be on the same / a different ~** píngděng / bù píngděng de dìwèi 平等 / 不平等的地位; **be on a friendly ~ with X** yǔ X guānxi róngqià 与 X 关系融洽

footlights jiǎodēng 脚灯; **footnote** jiǎozhù 脚注; **footpath** xiǎolù 小路; **footprint** jiǎoyìn 脚印; **footstep** jiǎobù 脚步; **follow in X's ~s** xiàofǎng X 效仿 X; **footwear** xié 鞋

for ◊ (purpose, destination etc) wèile 为了; **save up ~ a vacation** wèile dùjià zǎnqián 为了度假攒钱; **study ~ an exam** wèile kǎoshì xuéxí 为了考试学习; **a train ~ X** qù X de huǒchē 去 X 的火车; **clothes ~ children** tóngzhuāng 童装; **it's too big / small ~ you** nǐ chuān tài dà / xiǎo 你穿太大 / 小; **here's a letter ~ you** zhè shì nǐde xìn 这是你的信; **this is ~ you** zhè shì gěi nǐde 这是给你的; **what is there ~ lunch?** wǔcān chī shénme? 午餐吃什么?; **the steak is ~ me** niúpái shì wǒde 牛排是我的; **what is this ~?** zhè shì gàn shénme yòngde? 这是干什么用的?; **what ~?** wèishénme? 为什么? ◊ (time) **~ three days / two hours** sān tiān / liǎnggè xiǎoshí 三天 / 两个

小时; **please get it done ~ Monday** qǐng zài xīngqīyī yǐqián zuòwán 请在星期一以前做完 ◊ (*distance*): **I walked ~ a mile** wǒ zǒule yìyīnglǐ 我走了一英里; **it stretches ~ 100 miles** liánmián yìbǎi yīnglǐ 连绵一百英里 ◊ (*in favor of*): **I am ~ the idea** wǒ tóngyì zhèige xiǎngfǎ 我同意这个想法 ◊ (*instead of, in behalf of*): **let me do that ~ you** wǒ gěi nǐ zuò ba 我给你做吧; **we are agents ~ X** wǒmen shì X de dàilǐrén 我们是X的代理人 ◊ (*in exchange for*): **I bought it ~ $25** wǒ huāle èrshíwǔ měiyuán mǎide 我花了二十五美元买的; **how much did you sell it ~?** nǐ duōshao qián màide? 你多少钱卖的？

forbid jìnzhǐ 禁止; **~ X to do Y** jìnzhǐ X zuò Y 禁止X做Y

forbidden yánjìn 严禁; **smoking / parking ~** jìnzhǐ xīyān / tíngchē 禁止吸烟 / 停车

Forbidden City Zǐjìnchéng 紫禁城

forbidding yánjùn 严峻

force 1 *n* (*violence*) wǔlì 武力; (*of explosion, wind, punch*) lìliàng 力量; **come into ~** (*of law etc*) shēngxiào 生效; **the ~s** MIL bùduì 部队 **2** *v/t* door, lock yònglì dǎkāi 用力打开; **~ X to do Y** qiángpò X zuò Y 强迫X做Y; **~ X open** qiángxíng dǎkāi X 强行打开X

forced laugh, smile miǎnqiǎng 勉强; confession bèipò 被迫

forced landing pòjiàng 迫降

forceful argument qiángyǒulì 强有力; speaker yǒu shuōfúlì 有说服力; character jiānqiáng 坚强

forceps qiánzi 钳子

forcible entry yòng qiánglì 用强力; argument yǒu shuōfúlì 有说服力

ford *n* héliú qiǎnchù 河流浅处

fore: come to the ~ tuō yǐng ér chū 脱颖而出

foreboding bùxiángde yùgǎn 不祥的预感; **forecast 1** *n* yùcè 预测;

(*of weather*) yùbào 预报 **2** *v/t* yùbào 预报; **forecourt** (*of garage*) jiāyóuchù 加油处; **forefathers** zǔxiān 祖先; **forefinger** shízhǐ 食指; **foregone: that's a ~ conclusion** nà shì bìránde 那是必然的; **foreground** qiánbù 前部; **forehand** (*in tennis*) zhèngshǒu dǎo 正手打; **forehead** é 额

foreign wàiguó 外国

foreign affairs wàijiāo shìwù 外交事物

foreign currency wàibì 外币

foreigner wàiguórén 外国人

foreign exchange wàihuì 外汇; **foreign language** wàiyǔ 外语; **Foreign Office** *Br* Wàijiāobù 外交部; **foreign policy** wàijiāo zhèngcè 外交政策; **Foreign Secretary** *Br* Wàijiāobùzhǎng 外交部长

foreman lǐngbān 领班; **foremost** zuì zhòngyào 最重要; **forerunner** xiānqū 先驱; **foresee** yùjiàn 预见; **foreseeable** kě yùjiàn 可预见; **in the ~ future** zài kě yùjiànde wèilái 在可预见的未来; **foresight** xiānjiàn zhī míng 先见之明

forest sēnlín 森林

forestry sēnlínxué 森林学

foretaste qiǎncháng 浅尝

foretell yùliào 预料

forever *adv* yǒngyuǎn 永远

foreword qiányán 前言

forfeit *v/t* right, privilege etc sàngshī 丧失

forge *v/t* (*counterfeit*) wěizào 伪造; signature mófǎng 模仿

forger wěizàorén 伪造人

forgery (*bank bill*) jiǎ chāopiào 假钞票; (*document*) wěizàopǐn 伪造品

forget wàngjì 忘记

forgetful jiànwàng 健忘

forget-me-not (*flower*) wùwàngwǒ 勿忘我

forgive 1 *v/t* yuánliàng 原谅 **2** *v/i* liàngjiě 谅解

forgiveness yuánliàng 原谅

fork *n* chāzi 叉子; (*in road*) fēnchàchù 分岔处

♦**fork out** *v/i* F (*pay*) chūqián 出钱

forklift (**truck**) chāchē 叉车

form 1 *n* (*shape*) xíngzhuàng 形状; (*document*) biǎogé 表格 **2** *v/t* (*in clay etc*) sùzào 塑造; *friendship* jiànlì 建立; *opinion* xíngchéng 形成; *past tense etc* xíngshì 形式 **3** *v/i* (*take shape, develop*) xíngchéng 形成

formal zhèngshì 正式; *recognition etc* guānfāng 官方

formality guīfàn 规范; *it's just a ~* zhè zhǐshì yìzhǒng xíngshì 这只是一种形式

formally *adv speak, behave* zhèngshì 正式; *recognized* guānfāng 官方

format 1 *v/t diskette* shǐ géshìhuà 使格式化; *document* ānpái ... bǎnshì 安排 ... 版式 **2** *n* (*size: of magazine, paper etc*) kāibĕn 开本; (*make-up: of program*) fēnggé 风格

formation (*act of forming*) xíngchéng 形成; (*of airplanes*) biānduì 编队

formative lìyú chéngzhǎng 利于成长; *in his ~ years* zài tā xìnggé xíngchéng de shíqí 在他性格形成的时期

former yǐqián 以前; *the ~* qiánzhě 前者

formerly yǐqián 以前

formidable kĕpà 可怕

formula MATH gōngshì 公式; CHEM fēnzǐshì 分子式; (*for success etc*) mìjué 秘诀

formulate (*express*) biǎodá 表达

fort MIL yàosài 要塞

forth: *back and ~* láihuí 来回; *and so ~* dĕngdĕng 等等

forthcoming (*future*) jíjiāng fāshēng 即将发生; *personality* rèxīn 热心

fortieth dìsìshí 第四十

fortnight *Br* bàngeyuè 半个月

fortress MIL chéngbǎo 城堡

fortunate xìngyùn 幸运

fortunately xìngkuī 幸亏

fortune yùnqì 运气; (*lot of money*) dàbǐde qián 大笔的钱

fortune-teller suànmìng zhě 算命者

forty sìshí 四十

forward 1 *adv* xiàngqián 向前 **2** *adj pej* zhíjiéliǎodàng 直截了当 **3** *n* SP qiánfēng 前锋 **4** *v/t letter* zhuǎndì 转递

forwarding agent COM zhuǎnyùnshāng 转运商

fossil huàshí 化石

foster child lǐngyǎngde háizi 领养的孩子

foster parents yǎngfùmǔ 养父母

foul 1 *n* SP fànguī xíngwéi 犯规行为 **2** *adj smell, taste* nánwén 难闻; *weather* èliè 恶劣 **3** *v/t* SP fànguī 犯规

found *v/t school etc* chuàngbàn 创办

foundation (*of theory etc*) jīchǔ 基础; (*of organization*) chénglì 成立; (*organization*) jījīnhuì 基金会

foundations (*of building*) dìjī 地基

founder *n* chuàngjiànrén 创建人

foundry zhùzàochǎng 铸造厂

fountain pēnquán 喷泉

four sì 四

four-star *hotel etc* sìxīngjí 四星级

fourteen shísì 十四

fourteenth dìshísì 第十四

fourth dìsì 第四

fowl qín 禽

fox *n* húli 狐狸

fraction xiǎobùfen 小部分; (*decimal*) fēnshù 分数

fracture 1 *n* gǔzhé 骨折 **2** *v/t* zhéduàn 折断

fragile yìsuì 易碎

fragment *n* yíbùfen 一部分

fragmentary zhīlípòsuì 支离破碎

fragrance fāngxiāng 芳香

fragrant yǒu xiāngwèi 有香味

Fragrant Hills Xiāngshān 香山

frail xūruò 虚弱

frame 1 *n* kuàng 框; *~ of mind* xīnqíng 心情 **2** *v/t picture* gěi ... xiāngkuàng 给 ... 镶框; F *person* xiànhài 陷害

framework kuàngjià 框架

France Fǎguó 法国

frank tǎnshuài 坦率

frankly tǎnbái 坦白; *~, it's not worth it* tǎnbáide shuō, bù zhídé 坦白地说, 不值得

frantic fāfēng 发疯

fraternal xiōngdìban 兄弟般; *~ love* shǒuzú zhī qíng 手足之情

fraud qīpiàn 欺骗; (*person*) piànzi 骗子

fraudulent qīpiànxìng 欺骗性

frayed *cuffs* mósǔn 磨损

freak 1 *n* (*unusual event*) fǎncháng xiànxiàng 反常现象; (*two-headed person, animal etc*) jīxíng 畸形; F (*strange person*) guàirén 怪人; *movie/jazz ~* F diànyǐng/ juéshìyuè mí 电影/爵士乐迷 **2** *adj wind, storm etc* yìcháng qiángl, 异常强烈

freckle quèbān 雀斑

free 1 *adj* (*at liberty*) zìyóu 自由; (*no cost*) miǎnfèi 免费; *room, table* kòngyú 空余; *are you ~ this afternoon?* nǐ jīntiān xiàwǔ yǒukòng ma? 你今天下午有空吗？; *~ and easy* bùjū xíngshì 不拘形式; *for ~* (*travel, get something*) miǎnfèi 免费 **2** *v/t prisoners* shìfàng 释放

freebie F zèngpǐn 赠品

freedom zìyóu 自由

freedom of the press xīnwén zìyóu 新闻自由

free kick (*in soccer*) rènyì qiú 任意球; **freelance 1** *adj* gètǐ 个体 **2** *adv: I work ~* wǒ shì gètǐhù 我是个体户; **freelancer** gètǐhù 个体户; **free market economy** zìyóu shìchǎng jīngjì 自由市场经济; **free sample** miǎnfèi yàngpǐn 免费样品; **free speech** yánlùn zìyóu 言论自由; **freeway** gāosù gōnglù 高速公路; **freewheel** *v/i* (*on bicycle*) guànxìng huáxíng 惯性滑行

freeze 1 *v/t food, river* lěngdòng 冷冻; *wages, bank account* dòngjié 冻结; *video* zàntíng 暂停 **2** *v/i* (*of water*) nínggù 凝固

♦**freeze over** (*of river*) quánmiàn jiébīng 全面结冰

freezer lěngdòngshì 冷冻室

freezing 1 *adj* jílěng 极冷; *it's ~ out here* dòngsǐ rén le 冻死人了; *it's ~* (*cold*) (*of weather, water*) lěngjíle 冷极了; *I'm ~* (*cold*) wǒ dòngsǐle 我冻死了 **2** *n* língdù 零度; *10 below ~* língxià shídù 零下十度

freezing compartment lěngdòngxiāng 冷冻箱

freezing point bīngdiǎn 冰点

freight *n* huòwù 货物; (*costs*) yùnfèi 运费

freight car (*on train*) huòchēxiāng 货车厢

freighter (*ship*) huòchuán 货船; (*airplane*) yùnshūjī 运输机

freight train huòyùn lièchē 货运列车

French 1 *adj* Fǎguó 法国 **2** *n* (*language*) Fǎyǔ 法语; *the ~* Fǎguó rén 法国人

French doors luòdìchuāng 落地窗; **French fries** shǔtiáo 薯条; **Frenchman** Fǎguó nánrén 法国男人; **Frenchwoman** Fǎguó nǚrén 法国女人

frequency pínlù 频率; (*of radiowave*) bōduàn 波段

frequent[1] *adj* jīngcháng 经常

frequent[2] *v/t bar* chángqù 常去

frequently shícháng 时常

fresh *fruit, meat etc* xīnxiān 新鲜; (*cold*) liángshuǎng 凉爽; (*new*) xīn 新; (*impertinent*) cūlǔ 粗鲁 *~ start* chóngxīn kāishǐ 重新开始

♦**freshen up 1** *v/i* shūxǐ 梳洗 **2** *v/t room, paintwork* shǐ … huànrán yì xīn 使 … 焕然一新

freshman xīnshēng 新生

freshness (*of fruit, meat*) xīnxiān 新鲜; (*of style, approach*) xīnyǐng 新颖; (*of weather*) liángshuǎng 凉爽

fresh orange (*juice*) xīnxiānde júzizhī 新鲜的橘子汁

freshwater *adj* dànshuǐ 淡水

fret *v/i* fánzào 烦躁

friction PHYS mócā 摩擦; (*between people*) chōngtū 冲突

friction tape juéyuán jiāobù 绝缘

胶布

Friday xīngqīwǔ 星期五

fridge bīngxiāng 冰箱

fried egg jiāndàn 煎蛋; **fried noodles** chǎomiàn 炒面; **fried potatoes** shǔtiáo 薯条; **fried rice** chǎofàn 炒饭

friend péngyou 朋友; *make ~s (of one person)* jiāo péngyǒu 交朋友; *(of two people)* chéngwéi péngyǒu 成为朋友; *make ~s with X* yǔ X jiāo péngyǒu 与 X 交朋友

friendly *adj atmosphere* yǒuhǎo 友好; *person* héshàn 和善; *(easy to use)* qīnhéxìng 亲和性; *be ~ with X (be friends)* yǔ X guānxi róngqià 与 X 关系融洽

friendship yǒuyì 友谊

Friendship Store Yǒuyì Shāngdiàn 友谊商店

fries shǔtiáo 薯条

fright jīngxià 惊吓; *give X a ~* xià le X yítiào 吓了 X 一跳

frighten *v/t* jīngxià 惊吓; *be ~ed* hàipà 害怕; *don't be ~ed* bié hàipà 别害怕; *be ~ed of X* hàipà X 害怕 X

frightening xiàrén 吓人

frigid *(sexually)* lěngdàn 冷淡

frill *(on dress etc)* shìbiān 饰边; *(fancy extra)* fùjiāwù 附加物

fringe *(on dress, curtains etc)* shìbiān 饰边; *(in hair)* liúhǎi 刘海儿; *(edge)* biānyuán 边缘

frisk *v/t* sōuchá 搜查

frisky *puppy etc* huópo yǒulì 活泼有力

♦**fritter away** *time, fortune* xiāohào 消耗

frivolous *person, pleasures* fūqiǎn 肤浅

frizzy *hair* juǎn 卷

frog wā 蛙

frogman wārén 蛙人

from ◊ *(in time)*: *~ 9 to 5 (o'clock)* cóng jiǔdiǎn dào wǔdiǎn 从九点到五点; *~ the 18th century* cóng shíbā shìjì qǐ 从十八世纪起; *~ today on* cóng jīntiān qǐ 从今天起; *~ next Tuesday* cóng xiàge xīngqī èr qǐ 从下个星期二起

◊ *(in space)*: *~ here to there* cóng zhèr dào nàr 从这儿到那儿; *we drove here ~ Shanghai* wǒmen cóng Shànghǎi kāichē láide 我们从上海开车来的 ◊ *(origin)*: *a letter ~ Jo* Qiáo de láixìn 乔的来信; *a gift ~ the management* guǎnlǐ bùmén sòngde lǐwù 管理部门送的礼物; *it doesn't say who it's ~* méiyǒu shǔmíng 没有署名; *I am ~ New Jersey* wǒ láizì Xīn Zéxī zhōu 我来自新泽西州; *made ~ bananas* yòng xiāngjiāo zuòde 用香蕉做的 ◊ *(because of)*: *tired ~ the journey* yīn lǚxíng ér píláo 因旅行而疲劳; *it's ~ overeating* shì yóu dàliàng jìnshí yǐnqǐde 是由大量进食引起的

front 1 *n (of building, book)* zhèngmiàn 正面; *(cover organization)* huǎngzi 幌子; MIL qiánxiàn 前线; *(of weather)* fēngfēng 锋; *in ~* zài qiánmian 在前面; *(in a race)* lǐngxiān 领先; *in ~ of X* zài X de qiánmian 在 X 的前面; *at the ~ of X* zài X de qiánbù 在 X 的前部 **2** *adj wheel, seat* qiánmian 前面 **3** *v/t TV program* zhǔchí 主持

front cover fēngmiàn 封面; **front door** qiánmén 前门; **front entrance** zhèngmén 正门

frontier biānjiāng 边疆; *fig (of knowledge, science)* jíxiàn 极限

front page *(of newspaper)* tóubǎn 头版; **front page news** tóubǎn xīnwén 头版新闻; **front row** qiánpái 前排; **front seat passenger** *(in car)* qiánpáizuò chéngkè 前排座乘客; **front-wheel drive** qiánlún qūdòng 前轮驱动

frost *n* shuāng 霜

frostbite dòngshāng 冻伤

frostbitten dòngshāng 冻伤

frosted glass móshā bōlí 磨砂玻璃

frosting *(on cake)* tángshuāng 糖霜

frosty *weather* yánhán 严寒; *fig: welcome* lěngdàn 冷淡

froth *n* pàomò 泡沫

frothy *cream etc* qǐ pàomò 起泡沫

frown *n & v/i* zhòuméi 皱眉

frozen *feet etc* bīngliáng 冰凉; *landscape* bīngfēng 冰封; *food* lěngdòng 冷冻; *I'm* ~ F wǒ dònghuài le 我冻坏了

frozen food lěngdòng shípǐn 冷冻食品

fruit shuǐguǒ 水果

fruitful *talks etc* chénggōng 成功

fruit juice guǒzhī 果汁

fruit salad shuǐguǒ sèlā 水果色拉

frustrate *v/t person* shǐ ... jǔsàng 使 ... 沮丧; *plans* zǔ'ài 阻碍

frustrated *look, sigh* jǔsàng 沮丧

frustrating shǐrén xīnfán 使人心烦

frustratingly *slow, hard* lìngrén huīxīn 令人灰心

frustration huīxīn 灰心; *sexual* ~ xìng shēnghuó shīyì 性生活失意; *the ~s of modern life* xiàndài shēnghuó de bújìnrényì 现代生活的不尽人意

fry *v/t* (*stir-*~) chǎo 炒; (*deep-*~) yóuzhá 油炸

fuck *v/t* V (*screw*) cào 操; ~! māde! 妈的！; ~ *him/that!* qù tāmāde! 去他妈的！

♦**fuck off** V: ~! gǔnkāi! 滚开！

fucking V tāmāde 他妈的

fuel *n* ránliào 燃料

fugitive táofàn 逃犯

fulfill *v/t* shíxiàn 实现; *feel* ~*ed* gǎndào mǎnzú 感到满足

fulfilling *job* lìngrén mǎnyì 令人满意

fulfillment (*of contract etc*) lǚxíng 履行; (*moral, spiritual*) mǎnzú 满足

full *bottle* zhuāngmǎn 装满; *hotel, bus* mǎnyuán 满员; *diskette* mǎn 满; *account, report* xiángxì 详细; *life* chōngshí 充实; *schedule, day* fánmáng 繁忙; ~ *of X* (*of water etc*) chōngmǎn X 充满X; (*of tourists etc*) dàochù shì 到处是; (*of errors*) quánshì 全是; ~ *up* *hotel etc* kèmǎn 客满; (*with food*) chī bǎo le 吃饱了; *pay in* ~

quánbù fùqīng 全部付清

full coverage (*insurance*) zǒngkuò bǎoxiǎn 总括保险; **full-grown** chéngshú 成熟; **full-length** *dress* quáncháng 全长; *movie* wèi shānjié 未删节; **full moon** mǎnyuè 满月; **full stop** jùhào 句号; **full-time 1** *adj worker, job* quánrìzhì 全日制 **2** *adv work* quánrì 全日

fully *booked* quánbù 全部; *recovered* wánquán 完全; *understand, explain* quánmiàn 全面; *describe* xiángxì 详细

fumble *v/t catch, job* bènzhuóde chǔlǐ 笨拙地处理

♦**fumble around** mōsuǒde zhǎo 摸索地找

fume: *be fuming* F (*be very angry*) dànù 大怒

fumes fèiqì 废气

fun lèqù 乐趣; *it was great* ~ hěn kāixīn 很开心; *bye, have* ~! zàijiàn, jìnqíng wánr ba! 再见，尽情玩儿吧！; *for* ~ wèile wán 为了玩; *make* ~ *of X* qǔxiào X 取笑X

function 1 *n* zuòyòng 作用; (*reception etc*) jíhuì 集会 **2** *v/i* yùnzhuǎn 运转; ~ *as X* qǐ X de zuòyòng 起X的作用

fund 1 *n* jījīn 基金 **2** *v/t project etc* bōkuǎn 拨款

fundamental (*basic*) jīběn 基本; (*substantial*) běnzhì 本质; (*crucial*) shífēn zhòngyào 十分重要

fundamentally *different, altered* cóng gēnběn shang 从根本上

funeral zànglǐ 葬礼

funeral home bìnyíguǎn 殡仪馆

funicular (*railway*) lǎnsuǒ tiědào 缆索铁道

funnel *n* (*of ship*) yāncōng 烟囱

funnily (*oddly*) qíguài 奇怪; (*comically*) huájī 滑稽; ~ *enough* qíguàide shì qíguài de 奇怪的是

funny (*comical*) kěxiào 可笑; (*odd*) gǔguài 古怪

fur máopí 毛皮

furious (*angry*) fènnù 愤怒; *at a* ~ *pace* fēikuàide 飞快地

furnace lúzi 炉子

furnish *room* zhuāngbèi 装备; (*supply*) tígōng 提供

furniture jiāju 家具; *a piece of ~* yíjiàn jiāju 一件家具

furry *animal* máopí fùgài 毛皮覆盖

further 1 *adj* (*additional*) jìnyíbù 进一步; (*more distant*) gèngyuǎn 更远; *until ~ notice* lìngxíng tōngzhī 另行通知; *have you anything ~ to say?* nǐ hái yǒu shénme yào shuō de ma? 你还有什么要说的吗？ **2** *adv walk, drive* gèngyuǎn 更远; *~, I want to say …* cǐwài, wǒ yào shuō … 此外，我要说…; *2 miles ~* (**on**) zài zǒu liǎng yīnglǐ 再走两英里 **3** *v/t cause etc* cùjìn 促进

furthest *adj & adv* zuìyuǎn 最远

furtive *glance* tōutōu 偷偷

fury (*anger*) bàonù 暴怒

fuse ELEC **1** *n* bǎoxiǎnsī 保险丝 **2** *v/i* bǎoxiǎnsī shǎoduàn 保险丝烧断 **3** *v/t* shǎoduàn bǎoxiǎnsī 烧断保险丝

fusebox bǎoxiǎnsī hé 保险丝盒

fuselage jīshēn 机身

fuse wire bǎoxiǎnsī xiàn 保险丝线

fusion rónghé 熔合

fuss *n* dàjīng xiǎoguài 大惊小怪; *make a ~* (*complain*) tóusù 投诉; (*behave in exaggerated way*) xiǎotí dàzuò 小题大做; *make a ~ of* (*be very attentive to*) guòyú guānzhù 过于关注

fussy *person* tiāotì 挑剔; *design etc* tài duō zhuāngshì 太多装饰; *a ~ eater* tiāotì shíwù de rén 挑剔食物的人

futile wúxiào 无效

future *n* (*of person, company*) qiántú 前途; (*of humanity, earth*) wèilái 未来; GRAM jiānglàishí 将来时; *in ~* yǐhòu 以后

futures FIN qīhuò 期货

futures market FIN qīhuò shìchǎng 期货市场

futuristic *design* wèiláishì 未来式

fuzzy *hair* juǎn 卷; (*out of focus*) móhu 模糊

G

gadget xiǎozhuāngzhì 小装置

gag 1 n dǔ zuǐ bù 堵嘴布; (joke)
xiàohua 笑话 2 v/t person sāizhù
… de zuǐ 塞住 … 的 嘴; the press
yāzhì 压制

gain v/t (acquire) yíngdé 赢得; ~
speed jiāsù 加速; ~ 10 pounds
tǐzhòng zēngjiāle shí bàng 体重
增加了十磅

gale dàfēng 大风

gallant yǒu shēnshì fēngdù 有绅
士风度

gall bladder dǎnnáng 胆囊

gallery (for art) huàláng 画廊; (in
theater) dǐngcéng lóuzuò 顶层楼
座

galley (on ship) chuán shàng
chúfáng 船上厨房

gallon jiālún 加仑; ~s of tea
dàliàng de chá 大量的茶

gallop v/i fēipǎo 飞跑

gallows jiǎoxíngjià 绞刑架

gallstone dǎnjiéshí 胆结石

gamble dǔbó 赌博

gambler dǔtú 赌徒

gambling dǔbó 赌博

game n (match) bǐsài 比赛; (sport)
yùndòng 运动; (children's) yóuxì
游戏; (in tennis) yìjú 一局

gang yìbāng 一帮

♦ gang up on héhuǒ gōngjī 合伙
攻击

Gang of Four Sìrénbāng 四人帮

gangster dǎitú 歹徒

gangway tiàobǎn 跳板

gap (in wall) lièfèng 裂缝; (for
parking) kòngr 空儿; (in figures)
chājù 差距; (in time, conversation)
jiànxì 间隙; (between two people's
characters) chāyì 差异

gape v/i (person) zhāngkǒu 张口;
(hole) lièkāi 裂开

♦ gape at mùdèng kǒudāi de
níngshì 目瞪口呆地凝视

gaping adj hole lièkāi 裂开

garage for parking chēkù 车库; for
gas jiāyóuzhàn 加油站; for repairs
qìchē xiūlǐzhàn 汽车修理站

garbage ⇩ lājī 垃圾; fig (nonsense)
fèihuà 废话

garbage can lājīxiāng 垃圾箱;
garbage collection shōu lājī 收
垃圾; garbage dump lājī zhàn
垃圾站

garden huāyuán 花园

gardener yuándīng 园丁;
(professional) yuánlínshī 园林师

gardening yuányì 园艺

gargle v/i shùkǒu 漱口

garish súbùkěnài 俗不可耐

garland n huāhuán 花环

garlic dàsuàn 大蒜

garment fúzhuāng 服装

garnish v/t diǎnzhuì 点缀

garrison n (place) zhùdì 驻地;
(troops) wèishù bùduì 卫戍部队

garter diàowàdài 吊袜带

gas n qìtǐ 气体; (gasoline) qìyóu 汽
油

gash n qièkǒu 切口

gasket diànpiàn 垫片

gasoline qìyóu 汽油

gasp 1 n chuǎnxī 喘息 2 v/i
qìchuǎn 气喘; ~ for breath
chuǎnqì 喘气

gas pedal yóuménr 油门儿; gas
pump yóubèng 油泵; gas sta-
tion jiāyóuzhàn 加油站; gas
works méiqìchǎng 煤气厂

gate (of house, castle) dàmén 大门;
(at airport) dēngjīkǒu 登机口

gatecrash bùqǐngzìdào 不请自到

gateway ménkǒu 门口; fig tújìng
途径

gather 1 v/t facts, information sōují
搜集; am I to ~ that ... ? wǒ
yīnggāi lǐjiě wéi ... ? 我应该理
解为 ... ?; ~ speed jiāsù 加速

2 *v/i* (*understand*) tuīxiǎng 推想

♦**gather up** *possessions* jīlěi 积累

gathering (*group of people*) jùhuì 聚会

gaudy huāshao 花哨

gauge 1 *n* jìliángqì 计量器 **2** *v/t* cèdìng 测定

gaunt qiáocuì 憔悴

gauze bóshā 薄纱

gay *n & adj* (*homosexual*) tóngxìngliàn 同性恋

gaze 1 *n* zhùshì 注视 **2** *v/i* níngshì 凝视

♦**gaze at** níngshì 凝视

GB (= *Great Britain*) Dà Bùlièdiān 大不列颠

GDP (= *gross domestic product*) guónèi shēngchǎn zǒngzhí 国内生产总值

gear *n equipment* yòngjù 用具; *in vehicles* chǐlún 齿轮; *~ lever*, *~shift* biànsùgǎnr 变速杆

gel (*for hair*) rǔ 乳; (*for shower*) yè 液

gem zhēnbǎo 珍宝; *fig* (*book etc*) zhēnpǐn 珍品; *you're a ~* (*person*) nǐ zhēn hǎo 你真好

gender xìngbié 性别

gene jīyīn 基因; *it's in his ~s* tā shēnglái rúcǐ 他生来如此

general 1 *n* (*in army*) jiāngjūn 将军; *in ~* dàtǐshang 大体上 **2** *adj* (*overall, miscellaneous*) zǒngde 总的; (*widespread*) pǔbiàn 普遍

general election pǔxuǎn 普选

generalization gàikuò 概括; *that's a ~* nà shì gè gàikuò 那是个概括

generalize gàikuò 概括

generally yìbānde 一般地

generate (*create*) chǎnshēng 产生; (*in linguistics*) shēngchéng 生成; *~ electricity* fādiàn 发电

generation dài 代; *~ gap* dàigōu 代沟

generator fādiànjī 发电机

generosity dàfang 大方

generous (*with money*) dàfang 大方; (*not too critical*) kuānhóng dàliàng 宽宏大量; *portion etc* dàliàng 大量

genetic yíchuán 遗传

genetically yíchuán yīnzi shang 遗传因子上

genetic engineering yíchuán gōngchéng 遗传工程

genetic fingerprint gètǐ yíchuán xìngzhēng 个体遗传性征

geneticist yíchuánxuéjiā 遗传学家

genetics yíchuánxué 遗传学

Genghis Khan Chéngjísīhàn 成吉思汗

genial *person, company* qīnqiè 亲切

genitals shēngzhíqì 生殖器

genius tiāncái 天才

gentle wēnróu 温柔

gentleman shēnshì 绅士

gents (*toilet*) nányòngwèishēngjiān 男用卫生间

genuine zhēnpǐn 真品; (*sincere*) zhēnchéng 真诚

geographical *features* dìlǐ 地理

geography (*of area*) dìxíng 地形; (*subject*) dìlǐxué 地理学

geological dìzhì 地质

geologist dìzhìxué zhě 地质学者

geology (*of area*) dìzhì 地质; (*subject*) dìzhìxué 地质学

geometric(al) jǐhéxué 几何学

geometry jǐhé 几何

geriatric 1 *adj* lǎonián 老年 **2** *n* lǎoniánbìngxué 老年病学

germ bìngjūn 病菌; *of idea etc* méngyá 萌芽

germ warfare xìjūn zhànzhēng 细菌战争

German 1 *adj* Déguó 德国 **2** *n* (*person*) Déguó rén 德国人; (*language*) Déyǔ 德语

Germany Déguó 德国

gesticulate zuò shǒushì 做手势

gesture *n* (*with hand*) shǒushì 手势; *fig* (*of friendship*) biǎoshì 表示

get (*obtain*) dédào 得到; (*fetch*) gěi ... ná gěi ... 拿; (*receive: letter*) shōudào 收到; (*receive: knowledge, respect etc*) huòdé 获得; (*catch: bus, train etc*) zuò 坐; (*arrive*) dào 到; (*understand*) míngbái 明白; *can I ~ you a*

drink? nǐ xiǎng hē shénme? 你想喝什么?; ~ **going** (*leave*) zǒu 走 ◊ (*become, grow*): ~ **tired** / ~ **old** lèi le / lǎo le 累了 / 老了 ◊ (*causative*) bǎ … 把…; ~ **one's hair cut** bǎ tóufa jiǎn le 把头发剪了; ~ **the car fixed** bǎ chē xiūle 把车修了; ~ **X ready** bǎ X zhǔnbèi hǎo 把 X 准备好; ~ **X to do Y** jiào X zuò Y 叫 X 做 Y ◊ (*have opportunity*): **I got to meet him** tā wǒ yǒu jīhuì jiàndào 我有机会见到他; **did you ~ to go there?** nǐ yǒu jīhuì qù nàr le ma? 你有机会去那儿了吗 ? ◊: ~ **to know** rènshi 认识 ◊: **have got** yǒu 有: **have you got any children?** nǐ yǒu háizi ma? 你有孩子吗?; **I've got three tickets** wǒ yǒu sānzhāng piào 我有三张票; **I've got a headache** wǒ tóutòng 我头痛; **have you got time?** nǐ yǒu shíjiān ma? 你有时间吗 ? ◊: **have got to** (*must*) bìxū 必须; **I have got to study** / **see him** wǒ bìxū xuéxí / kàn tā 我必须学习 / 看他; **I don't want to, but I've got to** wǒ bùdébù 我不得不

◆**get around** (*travel*) lǚxíng 旅行; (*be mobile*) zǒudòng 走动

◆**get along** (*progress*) jìnzhǎn 进展; (*come to party etc*) dào 到; (*with somebody*) yú … chùdelái 与 … 处得来

◆**get at** (*criticize*) pīpíng 批评; (*imply, mean*) yìzhǐ 意指

◆**get away 1** *v/i* (*leave*) líkāi 离开 **2** *v/t*: **get X away from Y** bǎ X cóng Y názǒu 把 X 从 Y 拿走

◆**get away with** táozuì 逃罪

◆**get back 1** *v/i* (*return*) huídào 回到; **I'll ~ to you on that** wǒ yíhuìr zài huídá nǐde wèití 我一会儿再回答你的问题 **2** *v/t* (*obtain again*) chóngxīn dédào 重新得到

◆**get by** (*pass*) tōngguò 通过; (*financially*) wéichí 维持

◆**get down 1** *v/i* (*from ladder etc*) xiàlái 下来; (*duck*) wān yāo 弯腰 **2** *v/t* (*depress*) jiào rén jǔsàng 叫人沮丧

◆**get down to** (*start: work*) kāishǐ rènzhēn duìdài 开始认真对待; (*reach: real facts*) zhuījiū 追究

◆**get in 1** *v/i* (*arrive: of train, plane*) dàodá 到达; (*come home*) dàojiā 到家; (*to car*) jìnrù 进入; **how did they ~?** (*of thieves, snakes etc*) tāmen zěnme jìnlaide? 他们怎麼进来的 ? **2** *v/t* (*to suitcase etc*) fàngjìnqù 放进去

◆**get off 1** *v/i* (*from bus etc*) cóng … xiàlái 从 … 下来; (*finish work*) xià bān 下班; (*not be punished*) táotuō chǔfèn 逃脱处分 **2** *v/t* (*remove*) nádiào 拿掉; **top, boots, clothes** tuō 脱; ~ **the grass!** wùtà cǎopíng! 勿踏草坪 !

◆**get off with** (*Br: sexually*) yǔ … jiéshí 与 … 结识; ~ **a small fine** jiāo diǎnr fájīn jiù liǎoshì le 交点儿罚金就了事了

◆**get on 1** *v/i* (*be friendly*) chùdelái 处得来; (*advance: of time*) bù zǎo le 不早了; (*become old*) lǎo le 老了; (*make progress*) jìnzhǎn 进展; ~ **to the train** / **bus** / **one's bike** shàng chē 上车; ~ **to the airplane** shàng fēijī 上飞机; **it's getting on** tiānwǎn le 天晚了; **he's getting on** tā shàngle niánjì 他上了年纪; **he's getting on for 50** tā kuài wǔshí le 他快五十了 **2** *v/t*: ~ **the bus** / **one's bike** shàng chē 上车; **get one's hat on** dài shàng màozi 戴上帽子; **I can't get these pants on** wǒ chuān bú shàng kùzi 我穿不上裤子

◆**get out 1** *v/i* (*of car etc*) chūlái 出来; ~ **of prison** chūyù 出狱; ~! gǔnchūqù! 滚出去 ! ; **let's ~ of here** zánmen kuài zǒu ba 咱们快走吧; **I don't ~ much these days** jìnlái wǒ bú tài chūqù 近来我不太出去 **2** *v/t* nail, something jammed nòngchū 弄出; stain chúqù 除去; gun, pen tāochū 掏出

◆**get over** fence yuèguò 越过; lover etc wàngquè 忘却; disappointment kèfú 克服

◆**get over with**: **let's get it over**

with zánmen kuàidiǎnr bǎ tā nòngwán ba 咱们快点儿把它弄完吧

♦ **get through** (*on telephone*) dǎtōng 打通; (*make self understood*) ràng rén tīng dǒng 让人听懂

♦ **get up 1** *v/i* (*in morning*) qǐchuáng 起床; (*from chair etc*) zhànqǐlái 站起来; (*of wind*) dà qǐlái 大起来 **2** *v/t* (*climb: hill*) pá 爬

♦ **get up to: what have you been getting up to?** nǐ zuìjìn gànshénme? 你最近干什么？

getaway (*from robbery*) táopǎo 逃跑; **~ car** qiántáochē 潜逃车

get-together jùhuì 聚会

ghastly (*horrible*) kěpà 可怕

gherkin xiǎohuángguā 小黄瓜

ghetto shǎoshùmínzú jūzhùqū 少数民族居住区

ghost guǐ 鬼

ghostly guǐyíyàng 鬼一样

giant 1 *n* jùrén 巨人 **2** *adj* pángdà 庞大

gibberish fèihuà 废话

giblets nèizàng 内脏

giddiness xuànyùn 眩晕

giddy tóuyūn 头晕

gift lǐwù 礼物

gifted yǒu tiānfù 有天赋

giftwrap bāozhuāng shāngpǐn 包装商品

gigabyte COMPUT qiānzhào zìjié 千兆字节

gigantic jùdà 巨大

giggle 1 *v/i* gēgē de xiào 咯咯地笑 **2** *n* shǎxiào 傻笑

gill (*of fish*) sāi 鳃

gilt *n* dùjīn cáiliào 镀金材料; **~s** FIN jīnbiānr gǔpiào 金边儿股票

gimmick guǐbǎxì 鬼把戏

gin dùsōngzǐjiǔ 杜松子酒; **~ and tonic** ⇩ kuíníng dùsōngzǐjiǔ 奎宁杜松子酒

ginger *n* (*spice*) jiāng 姜

gingerbread jiāngbǐng 姜饼

ginseng rénshēn 人参

gipsy jípǔsàirén 吉普赛人

giraffe chángjǐnglù 长颈鹿

girder *n* dàliáng 大梁

girl nǚhái 女孩

girlfriend (*of boy*) nǚ péngyou 女朋友; (*of girl*) nǚxìng péngyou 女性朋友

girlie magazine huángsè zázhì 黄色杂志

girl scout nǚ tóngzǐjūn 女童子军

gist yàozhǐ 要旨

give gěi 给; (*supply: electricity etc*) gōngjǐ 供给; **~ a talk** zuò jiǎngzuò 作讲座; **~ a lecture** jiǎngkè 讲课; **~ a cry** dàshēng hūhǎn 大声呼喊; **~ her my love** xiàng tā wènhǎo 向她问好

♦ **give away** (*as present*) sòng 送; (*betray*) xièlòu 泄漏; **give oneself away** bàolù zìjǐ 暴露自己

♦ **give back** huán 还

♦ **give in 1** *v/i surrender* qūfú 屈服 **2** *v/t* (*hand in*) jiāochū 交出

♦ **give off** *smell, fumes* fāchū 发出

♦ **give onto** (*open onto*) tōngxiàng 通向

♦ **give out 1** *v/t leaflets etc* fēnfā 分发; **~ a groan** shēnyín 呻吟 **2** *v/i* (*of supplies, strength*) yòngwán 用完

♦ **give up 1** *v/t smoking etc* jiè 戒; **give oneself up** (*to police etc*) tóu'àn 投案 **2** *v/i* (*cease habit*) jiè 戒; (*stop making effort*) fàngqì 放弃

♦ **give way** (*of bridge etc*) bēngkuì 崩溃

given name míngzi 名字

glacier bīngchuān 冰川

glad gāoxìng 高兴

gladly yúkuài 愉快

glamor mèilì 魅力

glamorous yǒu mèilì 有魅力

glance 1 *n* yìpiē 一瞥 **2** *v/i* sǎoshì 扫视

♦ **glance at** sǎoshì 扫视

gland xiàn 腺

glandular fever línbāxiàn rè 淋巴腺炎

glare 1 *n* (*of sun, headlights*) qiángliède guāng 强烈的光 **2** *v/i* (*of sun, headlights*) shǎnyào 闪耀

♦ **glare at** nùmù ér shì 怒目而视

glaring *adj mistake* tūchū 突出

glass (*material*) bōli 玻璃; (*for drink*) bōlibēi 玻璃杯

glasses (*eye~*) yǎnjìng 眼镜

glasshouse nuǎnfáng 暖房

glaze n guānghuámiàn 光滑面

♦**glaze over** (*of eyes*) biànde móhu 变得模糊

glazed *expression* dāizhì 呆滞

glazier zhuāng bōlí gōngrén 装玻璃工人

glazing chuāngyòngbōlí 窗用玻璃

gleam 1 n wēiguāng 微光 2 v/i shǎnshuò 闪烁

glee kuàilè 快乐

gleeful lìngrén xīngfèn 令人兴奋

glib yóuzuǐhuáshé 油嘴滑舌

glide huáxiáng 滑行

glider huáxiáng jī 滑翔机

gliding n (*sport*) huáxiáng yùndòng 滑翔运动

glimmer 1 n (*of light*) wēiguāng 微光; **a ~ of hope** yíxiàn xīwàng 一线希望 2 v/i fāwēiguāng 发微光

glimpse 1 n yìpiē 一瞥; **catch a ~ of** piējiàn 瞥见 2 v/t piējiàn 瞥见

glint 1 n shǎnshuò 闪烁 2 v/i (*of light*) fāwēiguāng 发微光; (*of eyes*) shǎnxiàn mǒuzhǒng shénsè 闪现某种神色

glisten v/i shǎnguāng 闪光

glitter v/i shǎnshǎn fāguāng 闪闪发光

glitterati yǒu míngqì de ren 有名气的人

gloat v/i zhānzhānzìxǐ 沾沾自喜; **~ over** xīngzāilèhuò de kǎolǜ ... 幸灾乐祸地考虑

global (*worldwide*) quánqiú 全球; (*without exceptions*) pǔbiàn 普遍

global economy quánqiú jīngjì 全球经济; **global market** quánqiú shìchǎng 全球市场; **global warming** quánqiú qìwēn shēnggāo 全球气温升高

globe (*the earth*) dìqiú 地球; (*model of earth*) dìqiúyí 地球仪

gloom (*darkness*) yīn'àn 阴暗; (*mood*) yōuyù 忧郁

gloomy *room* yīn'àn 阴暗; *mood, person* yōuchóu 忧愁

glorious *weather, day* qínglǎng 晴朗; *victory* guāngróng 光荣

glory n róngyù 荣誉

gloss n (*shine*) guāngzé 光泽; (*general explanation*) zhùshì 注释

glossary cíhuìbiǎo 词汇表

gloss paint yǒuguāng túliào 有光涂料

glossy 1 adj *paper* guānghuá 光滑 2 n (*magazine*) guāngmiàn 光面

glove shǒutào 手套

glow 1 n (*of light, fire*) guānghuī 光辉; (*in cheeks*) hóngrùn 红润 2 v/i (*of light, fire*) fāguāng 发光; (*of cheeks*) xiànchū hóngrùn 现出红润

glowing *description* rèqíng 热情

glue 1 n jiāo 胶 2 v/t zhān 粘; **~ X to Y** bǎ X zhānzài Y shàng 把 X 粘在 Y 上

glum yōuyù 忧郁

glutinous rice nuòmǐ 糯米

glutton tānshí zhě 贪食者

gluttony tānshí 贪食

GMT (= *Greenwich Mean Time*) Gélínwēizhì biāozhǔn shíjiān 格林威治标准时间

gnarled *branch* niǔqū 扭曲; *hands* gǔjié línxún 骨节嶙峋

gnat ruì 蚋

gnaw v/t *bone* kěn 啃

GNP (= *gross national product*) guómín shēngchǎn zǒngzhí 国民生产总值

Go (*game*) wéiqí 围棋

go 1 n: **on the ~** mánglù 忙碌 2 v/i qù 去; (*leave: of train, plane, of people*) líkāi 离开; (*work, function*) yùnzhuǎn 运转; (*become*) biànde 变得; (*come out: of stain etc*) diào 掉; (*cease: of pain etc*) méile 没了; (*match: of colors etc*) pèi 配; **~ shopping / jogging** qù mǎi dōngxi / mànpǎo 去买东西 / 慢跑; **I must be ~ing** wǒ děi zǒule 我得走了; **let's ~** zǒuba 走吧; **~ for a walk** qù sànbù 去散步; **~ to bed** shàngchuáng 上床; **~ to school** shàngxué 上学; **how's the work ~ing?** gōngzuò jìnzhǎn rúhé? 工作进展如何？;

they're ~ing for $50 (*being sold at*) yǐ wǔshí měiyuán chūshòu 以 五 十 美元 出售; **hamburger to ~** hànbǎobāo, dàizǒu 汉 堡包, 带 走; **be all gone** (*finished*) yòng-wánle 用 完 了; **be ~ing to do X** yàozuò X 要做 X

♦ **go ahead** (*and do something*) gàn(shuō)ba 干 (说) 吧; (*on you go*) qùba 去 吧

♦ **go ahead with** *plans etc* àn … jìnxíng 按 … 进行

♦ **go along with** *suggestion* zàntóng 赞同

♦ **go at** (*attack*) gōngjī 攻击

♦ **go away** (*of person*) líkāi 离 开; (*of rain*) tíng 停; (*of pain, clouds*) xiāoshī 消失

♦ **go back** (*return*) huíqù 回 去; (*date back*) zhuīsù 追溯; **~ to sleep** zài shuì 再睡; **we ~ a long way** wǒmen xiāngshí duōnián le 我们 相识多年了

♦ **go by** (*of car, people*) guòqu 过 去; (*of time*) tuīyí 推移

♦ **go down** xiàqù 下 去; (*of sun, ship*) luòxià 落 下; (*of swelling*) xiāoqù 消去; **~ well / badly** (*of suggestion etc*) shòu / búshòu huānyíng 受 / 不受欢迎

♦ **go for** (*attack*) xíjī 袭击; (*like*) xǐhuān 喜欢

♦ **go in** (*to room, house*) jìnqù 进去; (*of sun*) yǐnmò 隐 没; (*fit: of part etc*) ān 安

♦ **go in for** *competition, race* cánjiā 参加; (*like, take part in*) kù'ài 酷 爱

♦ **go off 1** *v/i* (*leave*) líkāi 离开; (*of bomb*) bàozhà 爆炸; (*of gun*) zǒuhuǒ 走 火; (*of alarm*) xiǎngqǐ 响 起; (*of milk etc*) huàile 坏 了 **2** *v/t* (*stop liking*) bú zài xǐhuān 不 再喜欢

♦ **go on** (*continue*) jìxù 继续; (*happen*) fāshēng 发 生; **what's going on?** fāshēng shénme shì le? 发生 什么事了?; **~, do it!** (*encouraging*) zuò ba! 做吧！

♦ **go on at** (*nag*) láodao 唠叨

♦ **go out** (*of person*) chūqù 出 去;

(*of light, fire*) xīmiè 熄灭

♦ **go over** *v/t* (*check*) zǐxì jiǎnchá 仔 细检查; (*do again*) zài guò yíbiàn 再过一遍

♦ **go through** *v/t illness, hard times* jīnglì 经历; (*check*) jiǎnchá 检查; (*read through*) liúlǎn 浏览

♦ **go under** (*sink*) chénmò 沉 没; (*of company*) pòchǎn 破产

♦ **go up** (*climb*) shàngqù 上 去; *mountain* pāndēng 攀登; (*of prices*) shàngzhǎng 上 涨

♦ **go without 1** *food etc* méiyǒu yě xíng 没 有也行 **2** *v/i* rěnshòu méiyǒu 忍受没有

goad *v/t* cìjī 刺激

go-ahead 1 *n* xǔkě 许可; **get the ~** dédào xǔkě 得到许可 **2** *adj* (*enterprising, dynamic*) yǒujìnqǔxīn 有进取心

goal (*sport: target*) mùbiāo 目标; (*sport: point*) bǐfēn 比分; (*objective*) mùbiāo 目 标

goalkeeper shǒuményuán 守门员

goalpost ménzhù 门柱

goat shānyáng 山羊

♦ **gobble up** lángtūnhǔyàn 狼 吞 虎咽

go-between zhōngjiānrén 中间人

Gobi Desert ⇩ Gēbìtān 戈壁滩

god shén 神; **thank God!** xiètiānxièdì! 谢天谢地！; **oh God!** tiānna! 天哪！

goddess nǔshén 女神

godfather (*in mafia*) bāngtóu 帮 头

godforsaken *place, town* dǎoméi 倒霉

goggles hùmùjìng 护目镜

going *adj price etc* xiànxíng 现 行; **~ concern** xīngwàng de qǐyè 兴 旺 的企业

goings-on fāshēng de shìqíng 发 生的事情

gold 1 *n* huángjīn 黄 金; (*~ medal*) jīnpái 金 牌 **2** *adj* jīn 金

golden *sky, hair* jīnsè 金 色; **~ handshake** wèiláojīn 慰 劳 金; **~ wedding anniversary** jīnhūn jìniàn 金婚纪念

goldfish jīnyú 金鱼

goldsmith jīnshǒushìshāng 金首

饰商

golf gāo'ěrfū 高尔夫

golf club (*organization*) gāo'ěrfū jùlèbù 高尔夫俱乐部; (*stick*) gāo'ěrfū qiúgùn 高尔夫球棍

golf course gāo'ěrfū qiúchǎng 高尔夫球场

golfer dǎ gāo'ěrfūqiúde ren 打高尔夫球的人

gong luó 锣; (*in wrestling*) míngluó lìng 鸣锣令

good *person, weather, movie, news, child* hǎo 好; *food* hǎochī 好吃; *a ~ many* xǔduō 许多; *be ~ at ...* shànyú ... 善于 ...; *be ~ for X* duì X yǒuyòng 对 X 有用

goodbye zàijiàn 再见; *say ~ to X, wish X ~* gàobié X 告别 X

good-for-nothing *n* méiyòng de rén 没用的人; **Good Friday** Fùhuójié Xīngqīwǔ 复活节星期五; **good-humored** xīnqínghǎo 心情好; **good-looking** *woman, man* hǎokàn 好看; **good-natured** píqi hǎo 脾气好

goodness (*moral*) shànxíng 善行; (*of fruit etc*) jīnghuá 精华; *thank ~!* xiètiānxièdì! 谢天谢地！

goods COM shāngpǐn 商品

goodwill yǒuhǎo 友好

goody-goody *n* chǎnmèi zhě 谄媚者

gooey nián 粘

goof *v/i* F nòngzāole 弄糟了

goose é 鹅

gooseberry cùlì 醋栗

gooseflesh jīpí gēda 鸡皮疙瘩

gorge **1** *n* xiágǔ 峡谷 **2** *v/t*: *~ oneself on ...* dàchī ... 大吃 ...

gorgeous *weather* fēnghé rìlì 风和日丽; *dress, woman, hair* piàoliang 漂亮; *smell* hěn xiāng 很香

gorilla dàxīngxing 大猩猩

go-slow dàigōng 怠工

Gospel (*in Bible*) Fúyīn 福音

gossip **1** *n* liúyán fēiyǔ 流言蜚语; (*person*) chángshé 长舌 **2** *v/i* xiánliáo 闲聊

govern zhìlǐ 治理

government zhèngfǔ 政府

governor zhōuzhǎng 州长

gown (*long dress*) chángfú 长服; (*wedding dress*) jiéhūn lǐfú 结婚礼服; (*of academic, judge, priest*) lǐfúshì chángpáo 礼服式长袍; (*of surgeon*) dàguà 大褂

grab *v/t* zhuāzhù 抓住; *~ some food* suíbiàn chīxiē kuàicān 随便吃些快餐; *~ some sleep* xiǎoshuì 小睡

grace yōuměi 优美

graceful yōuyǎ 优雅

gracious *person* réncí 仁慈; *style, living* yǎzhì 雅致

grade **1** *n* (*quality*) děngjí 等级; EDU niánjí 年级 **2** *v/t* gěi ... fēnlèi 给 ... 分类

grade crossing píngmiàn jiāochā 平面交叉

gradient xiépō 斜坡

gradual zhújiàn 逐渐

gradually zhújiàn 逐渐

graduate *n* bìyèshēng 毕业生

graduation bìyè 毕业

graffiti húluàn túmǒ 胡乱涂抹

graft *n* BOT jiàjiē 嫁接; MED yízhí 移植; F (*hard work*) xīnkǔ de huór 辛苦的活儿

grain lì 粒; (*in wood*) mùwén 木纹; *go against the ~* gégé bú rù 格格不入

gram kè 克

grammar yǔfǎ 语法

grammatical héhū yǔfǎ 合乎语法

grand **1** *adj* zhuàngguān 壮观; F (*very good*) hǎojíle 好极了 **2** *n* F ($1000) yìqiān 一千

grandad (*paternal*) yéye 爷爷; (*maternal*) wàigōng 外公

grandchild (*son's son*) sūnzi 孙子; (*son's daughter*) sūnnǚ 孙女; (*daughter's son*) wàisūnzi 外孙子; (*daughter's daughter*) wàisūnnǚ 外孙女

Grand Canal Dàyùnhé 大运河

granddaughter (*son's daughter*) sūnnǚ 孙女; (*daughter's daughter*) wàisūnnǚ 外孙女

grandeur hóngwěi 宏伟

grandfather (*paternal*) zǔfù 祖父; (*maternal*) wàizǔfù 外祖父;

grandma (*paternal*) nǎinai 奶奶；
(*maternal*) lǎolao 姥姥；**grandmother** (*paternal*) zǔmǔ 祖母；
(*maternal*) wàizǔmǔ 外祖母；
grandpa (*paternal*) yéye 爷爷；
(*maternal*) wàigōng 外公；**grandparents** (*paternal*) zǔfùmǔ 祖父
母；(*maternal*) wàizǔfùmǔ 外祖父
母；**grand piano** dàgāngqín 大钢
琴；**grandson** (*son's son*) sūnzi 孙
子；(*daughter's son*) wàisūnzi 外孙
子；**grandstand** zhèngmiàn
kàntái 正面看台

granite huāgāngshí 花岗石

granny (*paternal*) nǎinai 奶奶；
(*maternal*) wàipó 外婆

grant 1 *n money* bōkuǎn 拨款；
(*money: for university, school*)
zhùxuéjīn 助学金 2 *v/t wish,
peace* shòuyǔ 授予；*visa* zhǔnyǔ
准予；*request* tóngyì 同意；***take X
for ~ed*** (*assume to be true*) rènwéi
X lǐ suǒ dāngrán 认为 X 理所当
然；(*not appreciate fully*) bú gòu
zhēnshì X 不够珍视 X

granulated sugar shātáng 砂糖

granule xìlì 细粒

grape pútao 葡萄

grapefruit pútaoyòu 葡萄柚；
grapefruit juice pútaoyòuzhī 葡
萄柚汁；**grapevine**: ***hear X
through the ~*** xiǎodào tīngláide
X 小道听来的 X

graph túbiǎo 图表

graphic 1 *adj description etc*
shēngdòng 生动 2 *n* COMPUT
túxíng 图形

graphics COMPUT túxíngxué 图形
学

graphics card COMPUT túxíngkǎ
图形卡

graphics controller COMPUT
túxíng kòngzhìqì 图形控制器

♦grapple with *attacker* yǔ ...
gédòu 与 ... 格斗；*problem etc*
jìnlì jiějué 尽力解决

grasp 1 *n* (*physical*) zhuā 抓；
(*mental*) zhǎngwò 掌握 2 *v/t*
(*physically*) zhuāzhù 抓住；
(*understand*) lǐjiě 理解

grass cǎo 草

grasshopper zhàměng 蚱蜢；
grasslands cǎoyuán 草原；
grass widow yǔ zhàngfu chángqī
fēnjū de nǚzi 与丈夫长期分居
的女子

grassy duōcǎo 多草

grate[1] *n* (*metal*) lúgé 炉格

grate[2] 1 *v/t* (*in cooking*) mósuì 磨碎
2 *v/i* (*of sounds*) cāxiǎng 擦响

grateful gǎnjī 感激；***be ~ to X*** duì
X xīncún gǎnjī 对 X 心存感激

grater cāzi 擦子

gratification mǎnzú 满足

gratify shǐmǎnzú 使满足

grating 1 *n* (*on drain etc*) gé gé 格格
2 *adj sound, voice* cì'ěr 刺耳

gratitude gǎn'ēn 感恩

gratuity xiǎofèi 小费

grave[1] *n* fénmù 坟墓

grave[2] *adj error* yánzhòng 严重；
face, voice zhuāngzhòng 庄重

gravel *n* lìshí 砾石

gravestone mùbēi 墓碑

graveyard mùdì 墓地

gravity PHYS zhònglì 重力

gravy ròuzhī 肉汁

gray *adj* huīsè 灰色；***he / his hair is
going ~*** tóufa báile 头发白了

gray-haired tóufa huābái 头发花
白

graze[1] *v/i* (*of cow, horse*) chīcǎo 吃
草

graze[2] 1 *v/t arm etc* cāshāng 擦伤
2 *n* mùcǎo 牧草

grease yóu 油

greasy *food* yóuzhī guòduō 油脂
过多；*hair, skin, hands, plate* yóunì
油腻

great *mistake, misunderstanding,
disappointment* hěndà 很大；*open
space* guǎngkuò 广阔；*sum of
money* dàliàng 大量；(*major:
composer, writer*) wěidà 伟大；
(*very good*) hěnbàng 很棒；***~ to
see you!*** jiàndào nǐ zhēn gāoxìng!
见到你真高兴！

great-grandfather (*paternal*)
zēngzǔfù 曾祖父；(*maternal*)
zēngwàizǔfù 曾外祖父；**great-
grandmother** (*paternal*)
zēngzǔmǔ 曾祖母；(*maternal*)

zēngwàizǔmǔ 曾外祖母; **Great Hall of the People** Rénmín Dàhuìtáng 人民大会堂; **Great Leap Forward** Dàyuèjìn 大跃进

greatly fēicháng 非常

greatness wěidà 伟大

Great Wall (**of China**) (Wànlǐ) Chángchéng (万里) 长城

greed tānxīn 贪心

greedy tānlán 贪婪

green lǜsè 绿色; (*environmentally*) lǜsè 绿色

greengrocer shūcài shuǐguǒ shāng 蔬菜水果商; **greenhorn** shēngshǒu 生手; **greenhouse** wēnshì 温室; **greenhouse effect** wēnshì xiàoyìng 温室效应; **greenhouse gas** wēnshì qìtǐ 温室气体; **green tea** lǜchá 绿茶

greet yíngjiē 迎接

greeting wènhòu 问候

grenade shǒuliúdàn 手榴弹

grid wǎng 网

gridiron SP měishì zúqiúchǎng 美式足球场

gridlock (*in traffic*) jiāotōng dǔsè 交通堵塞

grief bēishāng 悲伤

grievance láosāo 牢骚

grieve bēitòng 悲痛; **~ for X** āidào X 哀悼 X

grill 1 *n* (*for cooking*) kǎojià 烤架; (*window*) gézi 格子 **2** *v/t food* kǎo 烤; (*interrogate*) yánlì pánwèn 严厉盘问

grille gézi 格子

grim kěbù 可怖

grimace *n* guàixiàng 怪相

grime chéngòu 尘垢

grimy āngzāng 肮脏

grin 1 *n* liězuǐ 咧嘴 **2** *v/i* lòuchǐ'ěrxiào 露齿而笑

grind *v/t coffee, meat* niǎnsuì 碾碎

grip 1 *n* (*on rope etc*) jǐnwò 紧握; **be losing one's ~** (*losing one's skills*) sàngshī nénglì 丧失能力 **2** *v/t* zhuāzhù 抓住

gristle ruǎngǔ 软骨

grit *n* (*dirt*) cūshā 粗砂; (*for roads*) shālì 砂砾

groan 1 *n* shēnyínshēng 呻吟声 **2** *v/i* shēnyín 呻吟

grocer záhuòshāng 杂货商

groceries záhuò 杂货

grocery store záhuòdiàn 杂货店

groin fùgǔgōu 腹股沟

groom 1 *n* (*for bride*) xīnláng 新郎; (*for horse*) mǎfū 马夫 **2** *v/t horse* shuā 刷; (*train, prepare*) péixùn 培训; **well ~ed** (*in appearance*) xiūshì de hǎo 修饰得好

groove cáo 槽

grope 1 *v/i* (*in the dark*) ànzhōng mōsuǒ 暗中摸索 **2** *v/t* (*sexually*) mōsuǒ 摸索

♦ **grope for** *door handle, the right word* xúnzhǎo 寻找

gross *adj* (*coarse, vulgar*) cūsú 粗俗; *exaggeration* shízú 十足; FIN zǒng 总; **~ domestic product** guónèi shēngchǎn zǒngzhí 国内生产总值; **~ national product** guómín shēngchǎn zǒngzhí 国民生产总值

ground 1 *n* dìmiàn 地面; (*reason*) lǐyóu 理由; ELEC dìxiàn 地线; **on the ~** zài dìshang 在地上 **2** *v/t* ELEC shǐjiēdì 使接地

ground control dìmiàn kòngzhì 地面控制

ground crew dìqín rényuán 地勤人员

groundless wúgēnjù 无根据

ground meat suìròu 碎肉; **groundnut** luòhuāshēng 落花生; **ground plan** píngmiàntú 平面图; **ground staff** SP qiúchǎng guǎnlǐyuán 球场管理员; (*at airport*) dìqín rényuán 地勤人员; **groundwork** jīchǔ gōngzuò 基础工作

group 1 *n* zǔ 组; **divide ... into ~s** bǎ ... fēnzǔ 把 ... 分组 **2** *v/t* (*put together*) zǔhé 组合; (*classify*) fēnlèi 分类

grow 1 *v/i* (*of child, animal*) chéngzhǎng 成长; (*of plants*) shēngzhǎng 生长; (*of hair, beard*) liú 留; (*of number, amount*) zēngzhǎng 增长; (*of business*)

fāzhǎn 发展；*~ old / ~ tired*
(*become*) lǎo le / lèi le 老了 / 累了
2 *v/t flowers* zhòngzhí 种植

♦**grow up** (*of person*) zhǎngdà 长
大；(*of city etc*) kuòdà 扩大；*~!* bié
xiàng háizi sìde! 别象孩子似
的！

growl 1 *n* páoxiàoshēng 咆哮声
2 *v/i* páoxiào 咆哮

grown-up 1 *n* chéngrén 成人 **2** *adj*
chéngshú 成熟

growth (*of person*) chéngzhǎng 成
长；(*of company*) fāzhǎn 发展；
(*increase*) zēngzhǎng 增长；MED
liú 瘤

grub (*of insect*) qícáo 蛴螬

grubby wūhuì 污秽

grudge 1 *n* yuànhèn 怨恨；*bear
a ~* jìhèn 记恨 **2** *v/t: ~ a person
...* duì mǒurén de ... 妒忌某人
的 ...

grudging miǎnqiǎng 勉强

grueling *climb, task* shǐ rén
jīnpílìjìn 使人筋疲力尽

gruff cūbào 粗暴

grumble bàoyuàn 抱怨

grumbler ài fā láosāo de rén 爱发
牢骚的人

grunt 1 *n* hūlushēng 呼噜声 **2** *v/i*
zuò hūlushēng 作呼噜声

guarantee 1 *n* bǎozhèng 保证；*~
period* bǎozhèngqī 保证期 **2** *v/t*
dānbǎo 担保

guarantor dānbǎorén 担保人

guard 1 *n* (*security ~*) jǐngwèi 警卫；
MIL wèibīng 卫兵；(*in prison*)
kānshǒu 看守；*be on one's ~
against* dīfang 提防 **2** *v/t* shǒuwèi
守卫

♦**guard against** fángzhǐ 防止

guarded *reply* xiǎoxīn jǐnshèn 小
心谨慎

guardian LAW jiānhùrén 监护人

guerrilla yóujīduì 游击队

guess 1 *n* cāicè 猜测 **2** *v/t answer*
cāixiǎng 猜想；*I ~ so / not* kěnéng
可能 **3** *v/i* cāi 猜

guesswork tuīcè 推测

guest kèrén 客人

guesthouse zhāodàisuǒ 招待所

guestroom kèfáng 客房

guffaw *n & v/i* kuángxiào 狂笑

guidance zhǐdǎo 指导

guide 1 *n* (*person*) dǎoyóu 导游；
(*book*) zhǐnán 指南 **2** *v/t* xiàngdǎo
向导

guidebook zhǐnán 指南

guided missile dǎodàn 导弹

guided tour (*in museum, art gallery*)
yǒu dǎoyóu de cānguān 有导游
的参观

guidelines fāngzhēn 方针

guilt (*legal, moral*) yǒukuì 有愧；
(*guilty feeling*) nèijiù 内疚

guilty LAW yǒuzuì 有罪；
(*responsible*) chéngdān zérèn 承担
责任；*smile* nèijiù 内疚；*have a ~
conscience* wèn xīn yǒu kuì 问心
有愧

guinea pig túnshǔ 豚鼠；*fig* gòng
shìyàn yòng de rén 供试验用的
人

guitar jítā 吉他

guitarist tán jítā de rén 弹吉他的
人

gulf hǎiwān 海湾；*fig* fēnqí 分歧

gull ōu 鸥

gullet yānhóu 咽喉

gullible yì shòupiàn 易受骗

gulp 1 *n* (*of water etc*) tūnyàn 吞咽
2 *v/i* (*in surprise*) chījīng 吃惊

♦**gulp down** *drink* yìyǐn ér jìn 一
饮而尽；*breakfast, food*
lángtūnhǔyàn 狼吞虎咽

gum[1] (*in mouth*) chǐyín 齿龈

gum[2] *n* (*glue*) shùjiāo 树胶；
(*chewing ~*) kǒuxiāngtáng 口香糖

gun qiāng 枪

♦**gun down** qiāngdǎ 枪打

gun fire pàohuǒ 炮火；**gunman**
(*robber*) chíqiāng dǎitú 持枪歹
徒；**gunshot** shèjī 射击；**gunshot
wound** qiāngshāng 枪伤

gurgle *v/i* (*of baby*) gēgē de xiào 咯
咯地笑；(*of drain*) gǔgǔ de liú 汩
汩地流

gush *v/i* (*of liquid*) yǒngchū 涌出

gushy F (*very enthusiastic*) guòfèn
duōqíng 过分多情

gust zhènfēng 阵风

gusty *weather* fēngdà 风大；*~ wind*
dàfēng 大风

gut 1 *n* nèizàng 内脏; F (*stomach*) dùzi 肚子; **~s** F (*courage*) dǎnliàng 胆量 **2** *v/t* (*of fire*) huǐhuài … de nèibù huǐhuài … 的内部

gutter (*on sidewalk*) yáncáo 檐槽; (*on roof*) tiāngōu 天沟

guy F jiāhuo 家伙; *hey, you ~s* hèi, nǐmen 嘿，你们

gym (*sports club*) tǐyùguǎn 体育馆; (*in school*) yùndòngshì 运动室

gym shoes yùndòngxié 运动鞋

gymnasium tǐyùguǎn 体育馆; (*in school*) yùndòngshì 运动室

gymnast tǐcāojiā 体操家

gymnastics tǐcāo 体操

gynecologist fùkē yīshēng 妇科医生

gypsy jípǔsàiren 吉普赛人

H

habit xíguàn 习惯
habitable shìyú jūzhù 适于居住
habitat qīxīdì 栖息地
habitual guàncháng 惯常; *smoker, drinker* jīngcháng 经常
hack *n poor writer* wénqí 文乞
hacker COMPUT hēikè 黑客
hackneyed chénfǔ 陈腐
haddock hēixiànxuě 黑线鳕
haggard qiáocuì 憔悴
haggle tǎojià huánjià 讨价还价
hail *n* bīngbáo 冰雹
hailstorm báobào 雹暴
Hainan Island Hǎinán Dǎo 海南岛
hair tóufa 头发; (*on body, animal*) máo 毛
hairbrush shūzi 梳子; haircut lǐfà 理发; hairdo fàshì 发式; hairdresser lǐfàshī 理发师; *at the ~* zài lǐfàdiàn 在理发店; hairdrier, hairdryer chuīfēngqì 吹风器
hairless wúmáo 无毛
hairpin fàjiá 发夹; hairpin curve jízhuǎnwān 急转弯; hair-raising máogǔ sǒngrán 毛骨悚然; hair remover chúmáojì 除毛剂; hair-splitting *n* wúyì ěr suǒsuì de fēnxī 无益而琐碎的分析; hairstyle fàxíng 发型
hairy *arm, animal* duōmáo 多毛; F (*frightening*) jí rén 急人
half 1 *n* yíbàn 一半; *~ past ten*, *after ten* shídiǎnbàn 十点半; *~ an hour* bànge xiǎoshí 半个小时; *~ a pound* bànbàng 半磅 2 *adj* bàn 半 3 *adv* yíbàn 一半
half-hearted sānxīn'èryì 三心二意; half term xuéqī zhōngxiū 学期中休; half time 1 *n* SP bànchǎng 半场 2 *adj*: *~ job* bànrì gōngzuò 半日工作; halfway 1 *adj stage, point* bàntú 半途 2 *adv* zhōngjiān 中间; *the bookstore is ~ down Zhongshan Avenue* shūdiàn zài Zhōngshān dàjiē de zhōngjiān 书店在中山大街的中间;
hall (*large room*) dàtīng 大厅; (*hallway in house*) zǒuláng 走廊
halo guānghuán 光环
halt 1 *v/i* tíngzhǐ 停止 2 *v/t* zhìzhù 止住 3 *n*: *come to a ~* tíngzhì bù qián 停滞不前
halve *v/t* fēnchéng liǎngbàn 分成两半
ham huǒtuǐ 火腿
hamburger ⇩ hànbǎobāo 汉堡包
hammer 1 *n* chuízi 锤子 2 *v/i* chuídǎ 锤打; *~ at the door* zámén 砸门
hammock diàochuáng 吊床
hamper[1] *n* (*for food*) fànkuāng 饭筐
hamper[2] *v/t* (*obstruct*) zǔ'ài 阻碍
hamster cāngshǔ 仓鼠
Han Hàn 汉; (*nationality*) Hànzú 汉族
Han Dynasty Hàncháo 汉朝
hand 1 *n* shǒu 手; (*of clock*) zhēn 针; (*worker*) gōngrén 工人; *at ~, to ~* zài shēnbiān 在身边; *at first ~* dìyīshǒu 第一手; *by ~ write* yòngshǒu 用手; *deliver* zhuānrén 专人; *on the one ~ ... , on the other ~ ...* yìfāngmiàn ... lìngyìfāngmiàn ... 一方面 ... 另一方面 ...; *in ~* (*being done*) zài chǔlǐ zhōng 在处理中; *on your right ~* yòumiàn 右面; *~s off!* bié pèng! 别碰！; *~s up!* jǔqǐshǒulái! 举起手来！; *change ~s* zhuǎnshǒu 转手
♦hand down chuánxiàlái 传下来
♦hand in jiāochū 交出
♦hand on chuánxiàqù 传下去
♦hand out fēnfā 分发
♦hand over yíjiāo 移交; *to*

authorities shàngjiāo 上交

handbag *Br* shǒutíbāo 手提包; **handbook** shǒucè 手册; **handbrake** *Br* shǒuzhá 手轧; **handcuffs** shǒukào 手铐

handicap *n* zhàng'ài 障碍

handicapped (*physically*) cánjí 残疾; **~ by lack of funds** yóuyú zījīn ér shòuzǔ 由于资金而受阻

handicraft shǒugōngyì 手工艺

handiwork shǒugōng 手工

handkerchief shǒujuàn 手绢

handle 1 *n* bǎshou 把手 **2** *v/t goods* bānyùn 搬运; *case, deal* chǔlǐ 处理; *difficult person* duìfu 对付; **let me ~ this** wǒ lái chǔlǐ ba 我来处理吧

handlebars chēbǎ 车把

hand luggage shǒutí xíngli 手提行李; **handmade** shǒugōng zhìzuò 手工制作; **handrail** fúshǒu 扶手; **handshake** wòshǒu 握手

hands-off bùgānshè 不干涉

handsome shuài 帅

hands-on qīnzì dòngshǒu 亲自动手

handwriting zì 字

handwritten shǒuxiě 手写

handy *tool, device* fāngbiàn 方便; *it might come in ~* yěxǔ huì yǒuyòng 也许会有用

hang 1 *v/t picture* guà 挂; *person* diàosǐ 吊死 **2** *v/i* (*of dress, hair*) chuíxià 垂下 **3** *n*: **get the ~ of X** zhǎodào X de qiàomén 找到 X 的窍门

♦**hang around** xiánguàng 闲逛

♦**hang on** (*wait*) děngdeng 等等

♦**hang on to** (*keep*) bǎoliú 保留

♦**hang up** TELEC guàduàn 挂断

hangar fēijīkù 飞机库

hanger *for clothes* yīfújiā 衣服架

hang glider (*person*) xuánguà shì huáxiáng zhě 悬挂式滑翔者; (*device*) xuánguà shì huáxiángjī 悬挂式滑翔机

hang gliding xuánguà shì huáxiáng yùndòng 悬挂式滑翔运动

hangover (jiǔhòu) tóutòng (酒后) 头痛

♦**hanker after** kěwàngyǒu 渴望有

hankie, hanky *F* shǒujuàn 手绢

haphazard ǒuránxìng 偶然性

happen fāshēng 发生; *if you ~ to see him* rúguǒ nǐ pèngqiǎo jiàndào tā 如果你碰巧见到他; *what has ~ed to you?* nǐ zěnme le? 你怎么了?

♦**happen across** ǒurán fāxiàn 偶然发现

happening shìjiàn 事件

happily gāoxìng 高兴; (*luckily*) xìngyùn 幸运

happiness xìngfú 幸福

happy kuàilè 快乐

happy-go-lucky wúyōuwúlǜ 无忧无虑

happy hour kuàilè shíjiān 快乐时间

harass sāorǎo 骚扰

harassed jiāozào 焦躁

harassment sāorǎo 骚扰; *sexual ~* xìngsāorǎo 性骚扰

harbor 1 *n* gǎngwān 港湾 **2** *v/t criminal* bāobì 包庇; *grudge* huáiyǒu 怀有

hard yìng 硬; (*difficult*) nán 难; *facts, evidence* bùrónghuáiyí 不容怀疑; **~ of hearing** zhòngtīng 重听

hardback yìngpíshū 硬皮书; **hard-boiled** *egg* zhǔ de lǎo 煮得老; **hard copy** dǎyìn wénběn 打印文本; **hard core** POL zhōngjiān fènzi 中兼分子; **hard currency** ⇩ yìngtōnghuò 硬通货; **hard disk** ⇩ yìngpán 硬盘

harden 1 *v/t* shǐbiànyìng 使变硬 **2** *v/i* (*glue*) biànyìng 变硬; (*attitude*) mánhèng 蛮横

hardheaded jiǎng shíjì 讲实际

hardliner qiángyìng lùxiàn zhě 强硬路线者

hardly jīhūbù 几乎不

hardness yìngdù 硬度; (*difficulty*) nándù 难度

hard seat (*on train*) yìngzuò 硬座

hardsell yìngxíng tuīxiāo 硬行推销

hardship jiānnán 艰难

hard sleeper (*on train*) yìngwò 硬卧; **hard up** quēqián 缺钱; **hardware** jīnshǔ qìjù 金属器具; COMPUT yìngjiàn 硬件; **hardware store** wǔjīn shāngdiàn 五金商店; **hard-working** qínmiǎn 勤勉

hardy qiángzhuàng 强壮

hare yětù 野兔

harm 1 *n* sǔnhài 损害; *it wouldn't do any ~ to ...* ... méi shénme huàichù ... 没什么坏处 2 *v/t* sǔnhài 损害

harmful yǒuhài 有害

harmless wúhài 无害

harmonious héxié 和谐

harmonize shǐ héxié 使和谐

harmony MUS héshēng 和声; (*in relationship etc*) xiétiáo 协调

harp shùqín 竖琴

♦ **harp on about** F xùdao 絮叨

harpoon *n* yúchā 鱼叉

harsh jiānkè 尖刻

harvest *n* shōuhuò 收获

hash: *make a ~ of X* F bǎ X nòngzāo 把 X 弄糟

hash browns shǔtiáo 薯条

hashish dàmá 大麻

haste cāngcù 仓促

hasty cǎoshuài 草率

hat màozi 帽子

hatch *n* (*for serving food*) chuāngkǒu 窗口; (*on ship*) cāngkǒu 舱口

♦ **hatch out** (*of eggs*) fūchū 孵出

hatchet duǎnbǐng xiǎofǔ 短柄小斧

hate *n* & *v/t* zēnghèn 憎恨

hatred zēnghèn 憎恨

haughty àomàn 傲慢

haul 1 *n*: *a ~ of fish* yìwǎngyú 一网鱼 2 *v/t* (*pull*) tuōyè 托曳

haulage tuōyùn 托运

haulage company tuōyùn gōngsī 托运公司

haulier tuōyùn gōngsī 托运公司

haunch tuǐtúnbù 腿臀部

haunt 1 *v/t* chángdào 常到; *this place is ~ed* zhè dìfang nàoguǐ 这地方闹鬼 2 *n* cháng qù de dìfang 常去的地方

haunting *tune* yíngrào yú xīn 萦绕于心

have ◊ (*own*) yǒu 有; *I ~ three tickets* wǒ yǒu sānzhāng piào 我有三张票 ◊ *breakfast, lunch* chī 吃 ◊: *can I ~ a cup of coffee?* qǐng gěiwǒ yìbēi kāfēi? 请给我一杯咖啡?; *can I ~ more time?* qǐng zài gěiwǒ yìxiē shíjiān? 请再给我一些时间?; *do you ~ ...?* nǐ yǒu ... ma? 你有 ...吗? ◊ (*must*): *~ (got) to* bìxū 必须 *I have to study* / *see him* wǒ bìxū xuéxí/kàn tā 我必须学习/看他; ◊ (*causative*): *I had my hair cut* wǒ bǎ tóufa jiǎnle 我把头发剪了; *I'll ~ the car repaired* wǒ yào bǎ chē xiūle 我要把车修了 ◊ (*past tense*): *I ~ eaten* wǒ chīguò le 我吃过了; *~ you seen her?* nǐ jiàndào tā le ma? 你见到她了吗?

♦ **have back**: *when can I have it back?* shénme shíhou huángěi wǒ? 什么时候还给我?; *it's good to have you back* nǐ huíláile zhēnhǎo 你回来了真好

♦ **have on** (*wear*) chuān 穿; (*have planned*) yǒu shì 有事; *do you have anything on for tonight?* nǐ jīnwǎn yǒushì ma? 你今晚有事吗?

haven *fig* bìnànsuǒ 避难所

havoc hàojié 浩劫; *play ~ with X* jiāng X gǎode yītuán zāo 将 X 搞得一团糟

haw (*berry*) shānzhā 山楂

hawk yīngsǔn 鹰隼; *fig* qiángyìng pài rénwù 强硬派人物

hay gāncǎo 干草

hay fever huāfěnrè 花粉热

hazard *n* wēixiǎn 危险

hazard lights MOT xiǎnqíng zhǐshìdēng 险情指示灯

hazardous màoxiǎn 冒险

haze bówù 薄雾

hazel (*tree*) zhēn 榛

hazelnut zhēnzi 榛子

hazy *view, image* wùméngméng 雾蒙蒙; *memories* móhu 模糊; *I'm a bit ~ about it* wǒ duìcǐ bú tài qīngchǔ 我对此不太清楚

he tā 他

head 1 *n* tóu 头; (*boss, leader*) lǐngdǎo 领导; (*of school*) xiàozhǎng 校长; (*of beer*) pàomò 泡沫; (*of nail*) dīngmào 钉帽; (*of queue, line*) qiánmiàn 前面; *$15 a ~* měikè shíwǔ měiyuán 每客十五美元; *~s or tails?* zhèngmiàn háishì fǎnmiàn? 正面还是反面?; *at the ~ of the list* míngdān shang dìyīwèi 名单上第一位; *~ over heels fall* tóu cháoxià 头朝下; *fall in love* shēnshēn 深深; *lose one's ~* (*go crazy*) fāfēng 发疯 **2** *v/t* (*lead*) lǐngdǎo 领导; *ball* yòng tóu dǐng 用头顶

headache tóutòng 头痛

header (*in soccer*) dǐngqiú 顶球; (*in document*) tóulán 头栏

headhunter COM wùsè réncái de rén 物色人才的人

heading (*in list*) biāotí 标题

headlamp qiándēng 前灯; **headlight** qiándēng 前灯; **headline** (*in newspaper*) dàzì biāotí 大字标题; *make the ~s* chéngwéi tóutiáo xīnwén 成为头条新闻; **headlong** *adv fall* tóu xiàng qián 头向前; **headmaster** xiàozhǎng 校长; **headmistress** xiàozhǎng 校长; **head office** (*of company*) zǒngbù 总部; **head-on** *adv & adj crash* tóudǐngtóu 头顶头; **headphones** ěrjī 耳机; **headquarters** zǒng zhǐhuībù 总指挥部; **headrest** tóukào 头靠; **headroom** *for vehicle under bridge* jìngkōng gāodù 净空高度; *in car* tóushang kōngjiān 头上空间; **headscarf** tóujīn 头巾; **headstrong** rènxìng 任性; **head teacher** xiàozhǎng 校长; **head waiter** fúwùyuán zhǎng 服务员长; **headwind** nìfēng 逆风

heady *drink, wine etc* yìzuì 易醉

heal *v/t & v/i* yùhé 愈合

health jiànkāng 健康; *your ~!* zhù nǐ jiànkāng! 祝你健康!

health club jiànshēn jùlèbù 健身俱乐部; **health food** jiànkāng shípǐn 健康食品; **~ store**

jiànkāng shípǐndiàn 健康食品店; **health insurance** jiànkāng bǎoxiǎn 健康保险; **health resort** liáoyǎngdì 疗养地

healthy *person* jiànkāng 健康; *food, lifestyle* yǒuyì jiànkāng 有益健康; *economy* zhuàngdà 壮大

heap *n* duī 堆

♦**heap up** *v/t* duījī 堆积

hear tīngjiàn 听见

♦**hear about** tīngdào 听到

♦**hear from** (*have news from*) dédào xiāoxī 得到消息

hearing tīnglì 听力; LAW shěnxùn 审讯; *within ~* tīngjù 听距; *out of ~* tīngbúdào 听不到

hearing aid zhùtīngqì 助听器

hearsay: *by ~* chuánwén 传闻

hearse língchē 灵车

heart xīn 心; (*of problem*) shízhì 实质; (*of city, organization*) zhōngxīn 中心; *know X by ~* shóujì X 熟记 X

heart attack xīnzàngbìng 心脏病; **heartbeat** xīntiào 心跳; **heartbreaking** lìngrén xīnsuì 令人心碎; **heartburn** xīnkǒu zhuórè 心口灼热; **heart failure** xīnlì shuāijié 心力衰竭; **heartfelt** *sympathy* fāzì nèixīn 发自内心

hearth bìlú 壁炉

heartless wúqíng 无情

heartrending *plea, sight* shāngxīn 伤心

hearts (*in cards*) hóngtáo 红桃

heart throb F ǒuxiàng 偶像

heart transplant xīnzàng yízhí 心脏移植

hearty *meal* fēngshèng 丰盛; *person* rèchén 热忱; *~ appetite* hǎo wèikǒu 好胃口

heat rè 热

♦**heat up** jiārè 加热

heated *swimming pool* jiā le rè 加了热; *discussion* rèliè 热烈

heater fārèqì 发热器

heath huāngdì 荒地

heathen *n* yìjiàotú 异教徒

heating nuǎnqì 暖气

heat-resistant kàngrè 抗热; **heatstroke** zhòngshǔ 中暑;

heatwave rèlàng 热浪

heave v/t (lift) yònglì jùqǐ 用力举起

heaven tiāntáng 天堂; *good ~s!* tiānna! 天哪！

heavy zhòng 重; *rain* dà 大; *traffic* yōngjǐ 拥挤; *accent* zhòng 重; *food* yóunì 油腻; *financial loss* chénzhòng 沉重; *loss of life, bleeding* dàliàng 大量; *~ smoker* yān chōu de duō de rén 烟抽得多的人; *~ drinker* jiǔ hē de duō de rén 酒喝得多的人

heavy-duty jìnyòng 禁用

heavyweight SP zhòngliàngjí 重量极

heckle v/t jiéwèn 诘问

hectic mánglù 忙碌

hedge n shùlí 树篱

hedgehog cìwei 刺猬

heed: *pay ~ to* zhùyì 注意

heel (of foot) jiǎohòugēn 脚后跟; (of shoe) xiégēn 鞋跟

heel bar xiūxiébù 修鞋部

hefty zhòng 重

height gāodù 高度; (of season) shèng 盛

heighten *effect, tension* zēngdà 增大

heir jìchéngrén 继承人

heiress nǚ jìchéngrén 女继承人

helicopter zhíshēngfēijī 直升飞机

hell dìyù 地狱; *what the ~ are you doing / do you want?* F nǐ jiūjìng zài gàn shénme / yào shénme? 你究竟在干什么 / 要什么？; *go to ~!* F qùnǐde! 去你的！; *a ~ of a lot* F duōde bùdéliǎo 多得不得了; *he's one ~ of a nice guy* F zhèi jiāhuo zhēn búcuò 这家伙真不错

hello nǐ hǎo 你好; TELEC wéi 喂

helm NAUT duò 舵

helmet tóukuī 头盔

help n & v/t bāngzhù 帮助; *~!* jiùmìng! 救命！; *can you ~ me?* jiègè shǒu, xíngma? 借个手，行吗？; *~ oneself* (to food) suíbiàn chī 随便吃; *I can't ~ it* wǒ rěnbúzhù 我忍不住; *I couldn't ~*

laughing wǒ jīnbúzhù xiàole 我禁不住笑了

helper zhùshǒu 助手

helpful yǒu bāngzhù 有帮助

helping (of food) yífèn 一份

helpless (unable to cope) bùnéng zìzhù 不能自助; (powerless) wúzhù 无助

help screen COMPUT jiěyí píngmù 解疑屏幕

hem n (of dress etc) zhébiān 折边

hemisphere bànqiú 半球

hemorrhage n & v/i chūxiě 出血

hemp dàmá 大麻

hen mǔjī 母鸡

henchman pej púcóng 仆从

henpecked qīguǎnyán 妻管严; *~ husband* yǒu qīguǎnyán de zhàngfu 有妻管严的丈夫

hepatitis gānyán 肝炎

her 1 adj tāde 她的; *~ ticket* tāde piào 她的票 2 pron tā 她; *I know ~* wǒ rènshi tā 我认识她; *this is for ~* zhè shì gěi tā de 这是给她的

herb yàocǎo 药草

herb(al) tea yàocǎochá 药草茶

herbal medicine cǎoyào 草药

herd n shòuqún 兽群

here zhèr 这儿; *~'s to you!* (toast) wèi nǐ gānbēi! 为你干杯！; *~ you are* (giving sth) gěi nǐ 给你; *~ we are!* (finding sth) zài zhèr! 在这儿！

hereditary disease yíchuán 遗传

heritage shìxí yíchǎn 世袭遗产

hermit jūshì 居士

hernia MED shàn 疝

hero yīngxióng 英雄

heroic yīngyǒng 英勇

heroin hǎiluòyīn 海洛因

heroine nǚyīngxióng 女英雄

heron cānglù 苍鹭

herpes MED pàozhěn 疱疹

herring fēiyú 鲱鱼

hers tāde 她的; *a friend of ~* tāde péngyǒu 她的朋友

herself tā zìjǐ 她自己; *she hurt ~* tā nòngshāngle zìjǐ 她弄伤了自己; *by ~* tā dúzì 她独自

hesitate yóuyù 犹豫

hesitation yóuyù 犹豫

heterosexual *adj* yìxìng'ài 异性爱

heyday quánshèngqī 全盛期

hi nǐ hǎo 你好

hibernate dōngmián 冬眠

hiccup *n* dǎgér 嗝儿; (*minor problem*) xiǎowèntí 小问题; *have the ~s* dǎgér 打嗝儿

hick *pej* F xiāngxiàlǎo 乡下佬

hick town *pej* F qióngxiāng pìrǎng 穷乡僻壤

hidden *meaning* nèihán 内涵; *treasure* yǐncáng 隐藏

hide[1] *v/t & v/i* cáng 藏

hide[2] *n* (*of animal*) duǒcángchù 躲藏处

hide-and-seek zhuōmícáng 捉迷藏

hideaway pìjìngchù 僻静处

hideous kěpà 可怕; *crime* hài rén tīngwén 骇人听闻; *face* chǒulòu 丑陋

hiding[1] (*beating*) tòngdǎ 痛打

hiding[2]: *be in ~* duǒcángzhe 躲藏着; *go into ~* duǒcáng qǐlái 躲藏起来

hiding place duǒcángchù 躲藏处

hierarchy děngjí zhìdù 等级制度

hi-fi gāo bǎozhēn diànqì 高保真电器

high 1 *adj building, mountain, temperature, price, note, salary, speed* gāo 高; *quality* gāojí 高级; *society* shàngliú 上流; (*on drugs*) táozuì 陶醉; *~ wind* jìnfēng 劲风; *have a very ~ opinion of* duì ... yǒu hěn gāo píngjià 对 ... 有很高评价; *it is ~ time ...* gāi shì ... de shíhou le 该是 ... 的时候了 2 *n* MOT gāo 高; (*in statistics*) gāofēng 高峰; EDU zhōngxué 中学 3 *adv* gāo 高; *~ in the sky* gāogāo zài kōng 高高在空; *that's as ~ as we can go* (*in offer*) zhè shì wǒmen chū de zuìgāo jià 这是我们出的最高价

highbrow *adj* gāodiào 高调;

highchair gāojiǎoyǐ 高脚椅;

highclass gāojí 高级; **high diving** gāokōng tiàoshuǐ 高空跳水;

high-frequency gāopín 高频;

high-grade yōuzhì 优质; **high-handed** zhuānhèng 专横; **high-heeled** gāogēn 高跟; **high jump** tiàogāo 跳高; **high-level** gāo jiēcéng 高阶层; **high life** háohuáde shēnghuó fāngshì 豪华的生活方式

highlight 1 *n* (*main event*) zuìjīngcǎi chǎngmiàn 最精采场面; (*in hair*) rǎnsè 染色 2 *v/t* (*with pen*) yòng sèbǐ huà 用色笔划; COMPUT xuǎn 选

highlighter (*pen*) ⇩ cǎibǐ 彩笔

highly *desirable, likely* fēicháng 非常; *be ~ paid* xīnshuǐ gāo 薪水高; *think ~ of X* duì X píngjià hěn gāo 对 X 评价很高

high performance *drill* dàgōnglǜ 高效率; *battery* gāonéng 高能; **high-pitched** gāoyīndiào 高音调; **high point** (*of life, career*) dǐngfēng 顶峰; **high-powered** *engine* dàgōnglǜ 大功率; *intellectual* yuānbó 渊博; *salesman* chíyǒu yàozhí 持有要职; **high pressure** 1 *n* (*weather*) gāoyā 高压 2 *adj* TECH gāoyā 高压; *salesman* qiángxíng tuīxiāo 强行推销; *job, lifestyle* yǒu hěn dà yālì 有很大压力; **high priest** dà jìsī 大祭司; **high school** zhōngxué 中学; **high society** shàngliú shèhuì 上流社会; **high-speed train** gāosù huǒchē 高速火车; **high-strung** shífēn mǐngǎn 十分敏感; **high tech** *n & adj* gāoxīn jìshù 高新技术; **high technology** gāoxīn jìshù 高新技术; **high-tension** *cable* gāoyā 高压; **high tide** gāocháo 高潮; **high water** gāocháo 高潮; **highway** gōnglù 公路; **high wire** (*in circus*) gāngsīshéng 钢丝绳

hijack *v/t* jiéchí 劫持; *~ a plane* jiéjī 劫机; *~ a bus* jiéchē 劫车

hijacker (*of plane*) jiéjī zhě 劫机者; (*of bus*) jiéchē zhě 劫车者

hike[1] 1 *n* yuǎnzú 远足 2 *v/i* bùxíng 步行

hike[2] *n* (*in prices*) jíjù táigāo 急遽抬高

hiker túbù lǚxíng zhě 徒步旅行者

hilarious fēicháng huájī 非常滑稽

hill xiǎoshānpō 小山坡; (*slope*) shānpō 山坡

hillbilly *pej* F xiāngxiàrén 乡下人

hillside shānpō 山坡

hilltop xiǎoshān shāndǐng 小山山顶

hilly yǒu pō 有坡

hilt jiànbǐng 剑柄

him tā 他

Himalayas Xǐmǎlāyǎshān 喜马拉雅山

himself tā zìjǐ 他自己; *he hurt ~* tā nòngshāngle zìjǐ 他弄伤了自己; *by ~* tā dúzì 他独自

hinder zǔzhǐ 阻止

hindrance zhàng'ài 障碍

hindsight: *with ~* shìhòude rènshi 事后的认识

hinge zhéyè 折页

hint (*clue*) tíshì 提示; (*piece of advice*) tíyì 提议; (*implied suggestion*) ànshì 暗示; (*of red, sadness etc*) lüèwēi 略微

hip túnbù 臀部

hip pocket pìdōur 屁兜儿

hippopotamus hémǎ 河马

hire *v/t* zū 租

his 1 *adj* tāde 他的 **2** *pron* tāde 他的; *a friend of ~* tāde péngyǒu 他的朋友

Hispanic 1 *adj* Lādīng Měizhōu 拉丁美洲 **2** *n* Lādīng Měizhōu rén 拉丁美洲人

hiss *v/i* (*of snake*) fā sīsī shēng 发嘶嘶声; (*of audience*) fā xūshēng 发嘘声

historian lìshǐxuéjiā 历史学家

historic yǒu lìshǐ yìyì 有历史意义

historical yǒuguān lìshǐ 有关历史

history lìshǐ 历史

hit 1 *v/t person, ball* dǎ 打; (*collide with*) zhuàng 撞; *he was ~ by a bullet* tā bèi zǐdàn dǎzhòng le 他被子弹打中了; *it suddenly ~ me* (*I realized*) wǒ tūrán yìshí dào 我突然意识到 **2** *n* (*blow*) dǎjī 打击; MUS liúxíng chàngpiàn 流行唱片; (*success*) jùdà chénggōng 巨大成功

♦ **hit back** fǎnjī 反击

♦ **hit on** *idea* pèngqiǎo zhǎodào 碰巧找到

♦ **hit out at** (*criticize*) pēngjī 抨击

hit-and-run: *~ accident* zhàoshì zhě táopǎo shìgù 肇事者逃跑事故; *~ driver* zhàoshì zhě táopǎo sījī 肇事者逃跑司机

hitch 1 *n* (*problem*) wèntí 问题; *without a ~* méiyǒu wèntí 没有问题 **2** *v/t* shuānzhù 拴住; *~ X to Y* bǎ X shuān zài Y shang 把 X 拴在 Y 上; *~ a ride* dā biànchē 搭便车 **3** *v/i* (*hitchhike*) miǎnfèi dāchē 免费搭车

♦ **hitch up** *wagon, trailer* lā 拉

hitchhike miǎnfèi dāchē 免费搭车; **hitchhiker** miǎnfèi dāchē de rén 免费搭车的人; **hitchhiking** miǎnfèi dāchē 免费搭车

hi-tech *n* & *adj* gāoxīn jìshù 高新技术

hitlist hēimíngdān 黑名单; **hitman** zhíyè shāshǒu 职业杀手; **hit-or-miss** pèng yùnqì 碰运气; **hit squad** tèshū rènwù zǔzhī 特殊任务组织

HIV rénlèi sàngshī miǎnyìlì bìngdú 人类丧失免疫力病毒

hive (*for bees*) fēngfáng 蜂房

♦ **hive off** *v/t* (COM: *separate off*) chéngwéi dāndúde tuántǐ 成为单独的团体

HIV-positive dàiyǒu rénlèi sàngshī miǎnyìlì bìngdú 带有人类丧失免疫力病毒

hoard 1 *n* mìcángde qiáncái 密藏的钱财 **2** *v/t* jiàocáng 窖藏

hoarse sīyǎ 嘶哑

hoax *n* qīpiàn 欺骗

hobble *v/i* pánshān 蹒跚

hobby shìhào 嗜好

hobo liúlànghàn 流浪汉

hockey (*ice ~*) bīngqiú 冰球

hog *n* (*pig*) zhū 猪

hoist 1 *n* qǐzhòngjī 起重机 **2** *v/t* (*lift*) shēngqǐ 举起; *flag* shēng 升

hokum (*nonsense*) fèihuà 废话; (*sentimental stuff*) sútào qíngjié 俗

套情节

hold 1 *v/t (in hands)* ná 拿; *(support, keep in place)* zhīchí 支持; *passport, license* chíyǒu 持有; *prisoner, suspect* guānyā 关押; *(contain)* chéngyǒu 盛有; *job, post* rèn 任; *course* bǎochí 保持; **~ one's breath** bǐngzhù hūxī 屏住呼吸; **he can ~ his drink** tā hěn néng hē 他很能喝; **~ X responsible** shǐ X fùzé 使 X 负责; **~ that ...** *(believe, maintain)* rènwéi ... 认为...; **~ the line** TELEC qǐng bié guàduàn 请别挂断 **2** *n (in ship, plane)* huòcāng 货舱; **catch or take ~ of X** zhuāzhù X 抓住X; **lose one's ~ on X** *(on rope)* zhuābúzhù X 抓不住X

♦**hold against: hold X against Y** yīn X jìhèn Y 因 X 记恨 Y

♦**hold back 1** *v/t crowds* lánzhù 拦住; *facts, information* yǐnmán 隐瞒 **2** *v/i (not tell all)* yǐnmán 隐瞒

♦**hold on** *(wait, TELEC)* děngyíxià 等一下; **now ~ a minute!** biézháojí! 别着急！

♦**hold on to** *(keep)* bǎoliú 保留; *belief* jiānchí 坚持

♦**hold out 1** *v/t hand* shēnchū 伸出; *prospect* jùyǒu 具有 **2** *v/i (of supplies)* wéichí 维持; *(trapped miners etc)* zhīchéngzhù 支撑住

♦**hold up** *v/t hand* shēnchū 伸出; *bank etc* qiǎngjié 抢劫; *(make late)* dāngē 耽搁; **hold X up as an example** bǎ X zuò lìzi 把 X 做例子

♦**hold with** *(approve of)* zànchéng 赞成

holder *(container)* hé bǎo 盒; *(of passport, ticket, record etc)* chíyǒu zhě 持有者

holding company gǔdōng gōngsī 股东公司

holdup *(robbery)* qiǎngjié 抢劫; *(delay)* yánwù 延误

hole dòng dòng 洞

holiday *(single day)* xiūxīrì 休息日; *(period)* jiàqī 假期; **take a ~** xiūjià 休假

holidaymaker dùjiàde rén 度假的人

Holland Hélán 荷兰

hollow *object* zhōngkōng 中空; *cheeks* āoxiàn 凹陷; *promise* xūjiǎ 虚假

holly dōngqīng 冬青

holocaust dà pòhuài 大破坏

hologram quánxítú 全息图

holster yāodài tào 腰带套

holy shénshèng 神圣

Holy Spirit Shènglíng 圣灵

Holy Week Fùhuójié qián yìzhōu 复活节前一周

home 1 *n* jiā 家; *(native country)* zǔguó 祖国; *(town, part of country)* jiāxiāng 家乡; *(for old people)* lǎorényuàn 老人院; **at ~** *(in my house)* zài jiā 在家; *(in my country)* zài guónèi 在国内; SP běnyíng 本营; **make yourself at ~** bié jūshù 别拘束; **at ~ and abroad** guónèiwài 国内外; **work from ~** zài jiā gōngzuò 在家工作 **2** *adv* jiā 家; **go ~** huíjiā 回家; *(to own country)* huíguó 回国

home address jiātíng zhùzhǐ 家庭住址; **homecoming** guījiā 归家; **home computer** jiāyòng diànnǎo 家用电脑

homeless *adj* wújiā 无家; **the ~** wújiāde rén 无家的人

homeloving liànjiā 恋家

homepage COMPUT zhǔyè 主页

homely *(homeloving)* yǒu jiā de qìfēn 有家的气氛; *(not good-looking)* bù piàoliàng 不漂亮

homemade zìzhì 自制; **home match** zài běndì dǎ de bǐsài 在本地打的比赛; **home movie** jiātíng lùxiàng 家庭录像

homeopathy shùnshì liáofǎ 顺势疗法

homesick: be ~ xiǎngjiā 想家

home town jiāxiāng 家乡

homeward *adv (to own house)* xiàng jiā zǒu 向家走; *(to own country)* xiàng běnguó zǒu 向本国走

homework EDU zuòyè 作业

homeworking COM zài jiā gōngzuò 在家工作

homicide *(crime)* móushā 谋杀;

(*police department*) mìng'ānbù 命案部

homograph tóngxíngyìyìcí 同形异义词

homophobia tóngxìngliàn zèngwù gǎn 同性恋憎恶感

homosexual *n & adj* tóngxìngliàn 同性恋

honest chéngshí 诚实

honestly shuōzhēnde 说真的; **~!** zhēnshìde! 真是的！

honesty chéngshí 诚实

honey fēngmì 蜂蜜; F (*darling*) qīn'àide 亲爱的

honeycomb cháopí 巢脾

honeymoon *n* mìyuè 蜜月

Hong Kong Xiānggǎng 香港; **~ handover** Xiānggǎng huíguī 香港回归

honk *v/t horn* àn lǎba 按喇叭

honor 1 *n* róngyù 荣誉 **2** *v/t* gěiyǐ róngyù 给以荣誉

honorable guāngróng 光荣

hood (*over head*) dōumào 兜帽; (*over cooker*) chōu yóuyān jī 抽油烟机; MOT qìchē yǐnqíng gàizi 汽车引擎盖子; F (*gangster*) huàidàn 坏蛋

hoodlum ègùn 恶棍

hoof tí 蹄

hook (*to hang clothes on*) guàgōu 挂钩; (*for fishing*) yúgōu 鱼钩; **off the ~** TELEC bú guà diànhuà 不挂电话

hooked: be ~ on X bèi X mízhù 被X迷住; **be ~ on drugs** xīdú chéngyǐn 吸毒成瘾

hooker F jìnǚ 妓女

hookey: play ~ táoxué 逃学

hooligan liúmáng 流氓

hooliganism liúmáng xíngwéi 流氓行为

hoop gū 箍

hoot *v/t & v/i* (*of car horn*) àn lǎba 按喇叭; (*of owl*) māotóuyīngjiào 猫头鹰叫

hop[1] *n* (*plant*) shémácǎo 蛇麻草

hop[2] *v/i* (*of people*) dānjiǎotiào 单脚跳; (*of animals*) shuāngjiǎotiào 双脚跳

hope 1 *n* xīwàng 希望; **there's no ~ of that** nà shì bùkěnéng de 那是不可能的 **2** *v/t* xīwàng 希望; **I ~ you like it** wǒ xīwàng nǐ xǐhuān tā 我希望你喜欢它; **~ for X** qīwàng X 期望X; **I ~ so** xīwàng rúcǐ 希望如此; **I ~ not** wǒ bù xīwàng zhèyàng 我不希望这样

hopeful (*optimistic*) lèguān 乐观; (*promising*) yǒu xīwàng 有希望

hopefully *say* bàoyǒu xīwàng 抱有希望; (*I/ we hope*) dànyuàn 但愿

hopeless *position, propect* méiyǒu xīwàng 没有希望; (*useless: person*) méi qiántú 没前途

horizon dìpíngxiàn 地平线

horizontal shuǐpíng 水平

hormone hé'ěrméng 荷尔蒙

horn (*of animal*) jiǎo 角; MOT qìchē lǎba 汽车喇叭

hornet dàhuángfēng 大黄蜂

horn-rimmed spectacles yǒu jiǎozhìjià de yǎnjìng 有角质架的眼镜

horny F yǒu xìng chōngdòng 有性冲动

horoscope xīngzhàn 星占

horrible zāogāo 糟糕

horrify: I was horrified wǒ bèi xiàhuàile 我被吓坏了

horrifying *experience* kěpà 可怕; *idea, prices* lìngrén zhènjīng 令人震惊

horror kǒngbù 恐怖; **the ~s of war** zhànzhēngde kǒngbù 战争的恐怖

horror movie kǒngbù diànyǐng 恐怖电影

hors d'œuvre cānqiánde xiǎochī 餐前的小吃

horse mǎ 马

horseback: on ~ qímǎ 骑马; **horse chestnut** qīyèshùshǔ zhíwù 七叶树属植物; **horse-power** mǎlì 马力; **horse race** sàimǎ 赛马; **horseshoe** mǎtítiě 马蹄铁

horticulture yuányì 园艺

hose ruǎnguǎn 软管

hospice jiùjìyuàn 救济院

hospitable hàokè 好客

hospital yīyuàn 医院; **go into the**

~ zhùyuàn 住院

hospitality rèqíng zhāodài 热情招待

host n (*at party, reception*) zhǔrén 主人; (*of TV program*) zhǔchírén 主持人

hostage rénzhì 人质; *be taken ~* bèi kòuzuò rénzhì 被扣作人质

hostage taker kòuyā rénzhì de rén 扣押人质的人

hostel (*for students*) xiàowài jìsùshè 校外寄宿舍; (*youth ~*) lǚdiàn 旅店

hostess (*at party, reception*) nǚzhǔrén 女主人; (*on airplane*) kōngjiě 空姐; (*in bar*) nǚzhāodài 女招待

hostile díduì 敌对

hostility (*of attitude*) díyì 敌意; *hostilities* zhànzhēng 战争

hot *weather, water, object, food* rè 热; (*spicy*) là 辣; *I'm ~* wǒ hěn rè 我很热; F (*good*) jíhǎo 极好

hot dog hóngcháng miànbāo 红肠面包

hotel bīnguǎn 宾馆

hot key COMPUT kuàijiéjiàn 快捷键; **hotplate** diànlú 电炉; **hot spot** (*military, political*) rèdiǎn 热点

hour xiǎoshí 小时

hourly *adj* měixiǎoshí 每小时

house n fángzi 房子; *at your ~* zài nǐjiā 在你家

houseboat chuánwū 船屋; **housebreaking** rùshì qiǎngjié 入室抢劫; **household** jiāshǔ 家属; **household name** jiāyùhùxiǎo 家喻户晓; **house husband** jiātíng zhǔnán 家庭主男; **housekeeper** guǎnjiā 管家; **housekeeping** (*activity*) jiāwù guǎnlǐ 家务管理; (*money*) jiāwù kāixiāo 家务开消; **House of Representatives** Zhòngyìyuàn 众议院; **housewarming** (**party**) qìngzhù qiānjū de jùhuì 庆祝迁居的聚会; **housewife** jiātíng zhǔfù 家庭主妇; **housework** jiāwù 家务

housing zhùfáng 住房; TECH xiāng 箱

housing conditions zhùfáng tiáojiàn 住房条件

hovel máoshè 茅舍

hover áoxiáng 翱翔

hovercraft qìdiànchuán 气垫船

how zěnme 怎么; *~ are you?* nǐ hǎo ma? 你好吗？; *~ about ... ?* ... zěnmeyàng? ... 怎么样？; *~ much?* duōshao? 多少？; *~ much is it?* (*cost*) duōshao qián? 多少钱？; *~ many?* jǐgè? 几个？; *~ often?* duō jīngcháng? 多经常？; *~ funny / sad!* duō huájì / bēiāi! 多滑稽 / 悲哀！

however bùguò 不过; *~ big / rich / small they are* bùguǎn tāmen duō dà / fù / xiǎo 不管他们多大 / 富 / 小

howl v/i (*of dog*) háojiào 嚎叫; (*of person in pain*) āiháo 哀号; (*with laughter*) kuángxiào 狂笑

hub (*of wheel*) lúngǔ 轮毂; COMPUT jíxiànqì 集线器

hubcap gǔgài 毂盖

♦ **huddle together** quánsuō zài yìqǐ 蜷缩在一起

hue yánsè 颜色

huff: *be in a ~* fā píqì 发脾气

hug v/t yōngbào 拥抱

huge jùdà 巨大

hull wàiké 外壳

hullabaloo xuānxiāo 喧器

hum 1 v/t *song, tune* hēngchàng 哼唱 **2** v/i (*of person*) fā hēnghēngshēng 发哼哼声; (*of machine*) fā wēngwēngshēng 发嗡嗡声

human 1 n rén 人 **2** *adj* rénlèi 人类; *strengths, weaknesses etc* rénxìng 人性; *~ error* rénwéide cuòwù 人为的错误

human being rén 人

humane réndào 人道

humanitarian réndàozhǔyì zhě 人道主义者

humanity (*human beings*) rénxìng 人性; (*of attitude etc*) réncí 仁慈

human race rénlèi 人类

human resources (*department*) rénlèi zīyuán 人类资源

humble *attitude, person* qiānbēi 谦

卑; *origins* dīwēi 低微; *meal* jiǎndān 简单; *house* jiǎnlòu 简陋

humdrum dāndiào 单调

humid shīrè 湿热

humidifier zēngshīqì 增湿器

humidity shīdù 湿度

humiliate xiūrǔ 羞辱

humiliating diūliǎn 丢脸

humiliation xiūrǔ 羞辱

humility qiāngōng 谦恭

humor (*comical*) yōumò 幽默; (*mood*) qíngxù 情绪; *sense of ~* yōumògǎn 幽默感

humorous huīxié 诙谐

hump 1 *n* (*of camel*) tuófēng 驼峰; (*of person*) tuóbèi 驼背; (*on road*) xiépō 斜坡 **2** *v/t* (*carry*) bēizhe 背着

hunch (*idea*) yùgǎn 预感

hundred bǎi 百

hundredth dì yìbǎi 第一百

hundredweight yīngdàn 英担

Hungarian 1 *adj* Xiōngyálì 匈牙利 **2** *n* (*person*) Xiōngyálì rén 匈牙利人; (*language*) Xiōngyálì yǔ 匈牙利语

Hungary Xiōngyálì 匈牙利

hunger jī'è 饥饿

hung-over jiǔhòu tóutòng 酒后头痛

hungry jī'è 饥饿; *I'm ~* wǒ è le 我饿了

hunk: *great ~* F (*man*) kuíwú 魁梧

hunky-dory F rúyì 如意

hunt 1 *n* (*for animals*) shòuliè 狩猎; (*for a new leader, actor*) wùsè 物色; (*for criminal, missing child*) xúnzhǎo 寻找 **2** *v/t animal* lièqǔ 猎取

♦**hunt for** sōuxú 搜寻

hunter (*as sport*) lièshǒu 猎手; (*for living*) lièrén 猎人

hunting dǎliè 打猎

hurdle SP tiàolán 跳栏; *fig* (*obstacle*) zhàng'ài 障碍

hurdler SP tiàolán yùndòngyuán 跳栏运动员

hurdles SP tiàolán 跳栏

hurl měngzhì 猛掷

hurray! hǎowa! 好哇！

hurricane jùfēng 飓风

hurried cōngcōng 匆匆

hurry 1 *n* cōngmáng 匆忙; *be in a ~* jímáng 急忙 **2** *v/i* kuàidiǎnr 快点儿

♦**hurry up 1** *v/i* kuàidiǎnr 快点儿；*~!* gǎnjǐn! 赶紧! **2** *v/t* cuīcù 催促

hurt 1 *v/i* tòng 痛; *does it ~?* tòng bútòng? 痛不痛？ **2** *v/t* shāng 伤; (*emotionally*) shānggǎnqíng 伤感情

husband zhàngfu 丈夫

hush *n* chénmò 沉默; *~!* biéchūshēng! 别出声!

♦**hush up** *scandal etc* zhēyǎn 遮掩

husk (*of peanuts etc*) wàiké 外壳

husky *adj* shāyǎ 沙哑

hustle 1 *n* jǐ 挤; *~ and bustle* rènào 热闹 **2** *v/t person* yìngjǐ 硬挤

hut péngwū 棚屋

hyacinth fēngxìnzǐ 风信子

hybrid *n* (*plant, animal*) zájiāo 杂交

hydrant xiāofáng lóngtóu 消防龙头

hydraulic yèyā 液压

hydro ... shuǐ 水

hydroelectric shuǐlì fādiàn 水力发电

hydrofoil (*boat*) shuǐyìtǐng 水翼艇

hydrogen qīng 氢; *~ bomb* qīngdàn 氢弹

hygiene wèishēng 卫生

hygienic wèishēng 卫生

hymn zànměishī 赞美诗

hype *n* dàchuī dàléi 大吹大擂

hyperactive huódòng guòdù 活动过度; **hypermarket** dà xíng chāojí shìchǎng 大型超级市场; **hypersensitive** guòmǐn 过敏; **hypertension** guòdù jǐnzhāng 过度紧张; MED gāoxuèyā 高血压; **hypertext** COMPUT chāowénběn 超文本

hyphen liánzìhào 连字号

hypnosis cuīmiánshù 催眠术

hypnotherapy cuīmián liáofǎ 催眠疗法

hypnotize: *~ X* shǐ X jìnrù cuīmián zhuàngtài 使 X 进入催眠状态

hypochondriac *n* yíbìngzhèng huàn zhě 疑病症患者

hypocrisy xūwěi 虚伪

hypocrite wěijūnzǐ 伪君子
hypocritical xūwěi 虚伪
hypothermia tǐwēn guòdī 体温过低
hypothesis jiǎshè 假设
hypothetical jiǎshè 假设
hysterectomy zǐgōng qiēchúshù 子宫切除术

hysteria xiēsīdǐlǐ 歇斯底里
hysterical *person, laugh* xiēsīdǐlǐ 歇斯底里; (*very funny*) huájī kěxiào 滑稽可笑; **become** ~ biànde xiēsīdǐlǐ 变得歇斯底里
hysterics xiēsīdǐlǐde fāzuò 歇斯底里的发作; (*laughter*) kuángxiào 狂笑

I

I wǒ 我

ice bīng 冰; **break the ~** *fig* dǎpò chénmò 打破沉默

♦ice up (*of engine, wings*) jiébīng 结冰

iceberg bīngshān 冰山

icebox bīngxiāng 冰箱; **ice-breaker** (*ship*) pòbīngchuán 破冰船; **ice cream** bīngqílín 冰淇淋; **ice-cream parlor** bīngqílín diàn 冰淇淋店; **ice cube** bīngkuài 冰块

iced *drink* jiābīng 加冰

iced coffee bīngkāfēi 冰咖啡

ice hockey bīngqiú 冰球

ice rink bīngchǎng 冰场

I-Ching Yìjīng 易经

icicle bīngzhù 冰柱

icon (*cultural*) shèngxiàng 圣像; COMPUT túbiāo 图标

icy *road, surface* huá 滑; *welcome* lěngdàn 冷淡

idea zhǔyì 主意; **good ~!** hǎo zhǔyì! 好主意！; **I have no ~** wǒ bù zhīdào 我不知道; **it's not a good ~ to do X** zuò X bú tài shìhé 做 X 不太适合

ideal (*perfect*) lǐxiǎng 理想

idealistic lǐxiǎnghuà 理想化

identical yìmúyíyàng 一模一样; **~ twins** tóngluǎn shuāngtāi 同卵双胎

identification yànzhèng 验证; (*papers etc*) shēnfen zhèngmíng 身分证明

identify jiànbié 鉴别

identity shēnfen 身分; **~ card** shēnfenzhèng 身分证

ideology sīxiǎng 思想

ideological yìshíxíngtài 意识形态

idiom (*saying*) xíyǔ 习语

idiomatic (*natural*) dìdào 地道; **she speaks quite ~ English** tā néng jiǎng yìkǒu dìdào de yīngwén 她能讲一口地道的英文

idiosyncrasy pǐxìng 癖性

idiot báichī 白痴

idiotic yúchǔn 愚蠢

idle 1 *adj person* lǎnguǐ 懒鬼; *threat* shuōshuō ér yǐ 说说而已; *machinery* xiánzhì 闲置; **in an ~ moment** xiánxiáshí 闲暇时 2 *v/i* (*engine*) kōngzhuàn 空转

♦idle away *the time etc* dǎfa 打发

idol ǒuxiàng 偶像

idolize chóngbài 崇拜

idyllic tiányuánshì 田园式

if rúguǒ 如果

igloo xuěwū 雪屋

ignite 1 *v/t* diǎnrán 点燃 2 *v/i* zháo 着

ignition (*in car*) fādòng zhuāngzhì 发动装置; **~ key** dǎhuǒ yàoshi 打火钥匙

ignorance wúzhī 无知

ignorant wúzhī 无知; (*rude*) cūlǔ 粗鲁

ignore hūluè 忽略

ill yǒubìng 有病; **fall ~, be taken ~** shēngbìng 生病; **feel ~ at ease** júcùbù'ān 局促不安

illegal fēifǎ 非法

illegible biànrèn bùqīng 辨认不清

illegitimate *child* sīshēng 私生

ill-fated búxìng 不幸

illicit wéifǎ 违法

illiterate wénmáng 文盲

ill-mannered jǔzhǐ cūlǔ 举止粗鲁

ill-natured píqi huài 脾气坏

illness jíbìng 疾病

illogical bù hé luójí 不合逻辑

ill-tempered píqi huài 脾气坏

ill-treat nüèdài 虐待

illuminate *building etc* zhàomíng 照明

illuminating *remarks etc* qǐfāxìng 启

发性

illusion huànxiǎng 幻象

illustrate *book* chātú 插图; (*with examples*) shuōmíng 说明

illustration (*picture*) chātú 插图; (*with examples*) lìzhèng 例证

illustrator huìtúrén 绘图人

ill will èyì 恶意

image (*picture*) huàmiàn 画面; (*exact likeness*) xiāngxiàng 相象; (*of politician, company*) xíngxiàng 形象

image-conscious zhùyì xíngxiàng 注意形象

imaginable kěyǐ xiǎngxiàng 可以想象; *the biggest / smallest size ~* kěyǐ xiǎngxiàngchū de zuìdà / zuìxiǎo chǐcùn 可以想象出的最大 / 最小尺寸

imaginary jiǎxiǎng 假想

imagination xiǎngxiàng 想象; *it's all in your ~* dōu shì nǐ xiǎngxiàng de 都是你想象的

imaginative jùyǒu xiǎngxiànglì 具有想象力

imagine xiǎngxiàng 想象; *I can just ~ it* wǒ néng xiǎngxiàng chūlái 我能想象出来; *you're imagining things* nǐ shì zài húsīluànxiǎng 你是在胡思乱想

imbecile dīnéng'ér 低能儿

IMF (= *International Monetary Fund*) Guójì Huòbì Jījīn 国际货币基金

imitate mófǎng 模仿

imitation (*copying*) mófǎng 模仿; (*something copied*) fǎngzào 仿造

immaculate chúnjié 纯洁

immaterial (*not relevant*) wúguān jǐnyào 无关紧要

immature bù chéngshú 不成熟

immediate jíkè 即刻; *the ~ family* zhíxì qīnshǔ 直系亲属; *in the ~ neighborhood* jìnlín 紧邻

immediately lìjí 立即; *~ after the bank / church* yí guò yínháng / jiàotáng 一过银行 / 教堂

immense jùdà 巨大

immerse jìnpào 浸泡; *~ oneself in studies etc* chénjìn 沉浸

immersion heater diàn rèshuǐqì 电热水器

immigrant *n* yímín 移民

immigrate yíjū 移居

immigration (*act*) yímín 移民; *Immigration* (*government office*) yímínjú 移民局

imminent pòjìn 迫近

immobilize *factory, person* shǐ ... tānhuàn 使 ... 瘫痪; *car* suǒzhù 锁住

immoderate wú jiézhì 无节制

immoral bú dàodé 不道德

immorality bú dàodé 不道德

immortal bùxiǔ 不朽

immortality bùxiǔ 不朽

immune (*to illness, infection*) miǎnyì 免疫; (*from ruling, requirement*) miǎnchú 免除

immune system MED miǎnyì xìtǒng 免疫系统

immunity (*to infection*) miǎnyì 免疫; (*from ruling*) tèmiǎn 特免; *diplomatic ~* wàijiāo miǎnyì lì 外交免疫力

impact *n* (*of meteorite, vehicle*) zhuàngjī 撞击; (*of new manager etc*) yǐngxiǎnglì 影响力; (*effect*) yǐngxiǎng 影响

impair sǔnhài 损害

impaired xuēruò 削弱

impartial gōngzhèng 公正

impassable *road* bùtōng 不通

impasse (*in negotiations etc*) jiāngjú 僵局

impassioned *speech, plea* jīdòng 激动

impassive lěngdàn 冷淡

impatience bú nàixīn 不耐心

impatient bú nàixīn 不耐心

impatiently bú nàixīn 不耐心

impeccable *turnout* wúxièkějī 无懈可击; *English, Chinese* jīngtōng 精通

impeccably *dressed* wánměi 完美; *pronounce, speak* wánměi 完美

impede zǔ'ài 阻碍

impediment (*in speech*) kǒuchī 口吃

impending pò zài méijié 迫在眉睫

impenetrable cì bù chuān 刺不穿

imperative 1 *adj* jǐnjí 紧急 **2** *n* GRAM qíshǐ 祈使

imperceptible nányǐ chájué 难以察觉

imperfect 1 *adj* bù wánměi 不完美 **2** *n* GRAM bù wánzhěng 不完整

imperial huángdì 皇帝

imperialism dìguó zhǔyì 帝国主义

impersonal bú jù réngéxìng 不具人格性

impersonate (*as a joke*) jiǎbàn 假扮; (*illegally*) màochōng 冒充

impertinence wúlǐ 无礼

impertinent wúlǐ 无礼

imperturbable chéngzhuó lěngjìng 沉着冷静

impervious; ~ **to X** duì X wúdòngyúzhōng 对 X 无动于衷

impetuous qīngshuài 轻率

impetus (*of campaign etc*) tuīdònglì 推动力

implement 1 *n* gōngjù 工具 **2** *v/t measures etc* shíshī 实施

implicate: ~ **X in Y** xiǎnshì X shèjí Y 显示 X 涉及 Y

implication ànshì 暗示

implicit hánxù 含蓄; *trust* juéduì 绝对

implore kěnqiú 恳求

imply ànzhǐ 暗指

impolite bù lǐmào 不礼貌

import *n* & *v/i* jìnkǒu 进口

importance zhòngyàoxìng 重要性

important zhòngyào 重要

importer jìnkǒushāng 进口商

impose *tax* zhēngshōu 征收; ~ **oneself on X** yìng chánzhe X 硬缠着 X

imposing tūchū 突出

impossibility bù kěnéngxìng 不可能性

impossible bù kěnéng 不可能

impostor màomíng dǐngtì de rén 冒名顶替的人

impotence yángwěi 阳萎

impotent yángwěi 阳萎

impoverished pínkùn 贫困

impractical *person* bú xiànshí 不现实; *suggestion* bù shíjì 不实际

impress: ~ **X** (*impress another person*) gěi X liúxià shēnkè yìnxiàng 给 X 留下深刻印象; *be* **~ed by X** X gěi rén liúxià shēnkè yìnxiàng X 给人留下深刻印象; *I'm not ~ed* wǒ bù mǎnyì 我不满意

impression yìnxiàng 印象; (*impersonation*) huájī de mófǎng 滑稽的模仿; *make a good* / *bad* **~ on X** gěi X liúxià hǎo / huài yìnxiàng 给 X 留下好 / 坏印象; *I get the* **~ that …** wǒ juéde … 我觉得 …

impressionable yì shòu yǐngxiǎng 易受影响

impressive gěi rén yǐ shēnkè yìnxiàng 给人以深刻印象

imprint *n* (*of credit card*) yāyìn 压印

imprison jiānjìn 监禁

imprisonment jiānjìn 监禁

improbable bú dà kěnéng 不大可能

improper *behavior* bú qiàdàng 不恰当

improve 1 *v/t* gǎijìn 改进; *skills, Chinese* tígāo 提高; *relations* gǎishàn 改善 **2** *v/i* (*of health*) hǎozhuǎn 好转; (*of Chinese skills, life*) tígāo 提高

improvement gǎijìn 改进

improvize *v/i* jíxìng 即兴

impudent cūlǔ 粗鲁

impulse chōngdòng 冲动; *do X on an* **~** yìshí chōngdòng zuò X 一时冲动做 X; ~ **buy** chōngdòng gòuwù 冲动购物

impulsive yì chōngdòng 易冲动

impunity: *with* **~** bú shòu chěngfá 不受惩罚

impure *thoughts* āngzāng 肮脏; *substance* bùchún 不纯

in 1 *prep* ◊ zài lǐmiàn 在里面; ~ *Washington* / *China* zài Huáshèngdùn / Zhōngguó 在华盛顿 / 中国; ~ *the street* zài jiēshang 在街上; ~ *the box* zài hézi lǐ 在盒子里; *put it* **~** *your pocket* bǎ tā fàng zài nǐde dōulǐ

把它放在你的兜里; **wounded**
~ **the leg** / **arm** tuǐ / gēbo shòu
shāng 腿 / 胳膊受伤◊: ~ **1999**
yījiǔjiǔjiǔ nián 19 99 年; ~ **two**
hours (from now) liǎng ge xiǎoshí
yǐhòu 两个小时以后; (over
period of) liǎng ge xiǎoshí 两个小
时; **I haven't seen him ~ three**
years wǒ sānnián méi kànjiàn tāle
我三年没看见他了; ~ **the**
morning zǎoshang 早上; ~ **the**
summer xiàtiān 夏天; ~ **August**
bāyuè 八月◊: ~ **English** / **Chinese**
yòng Yīngyǔ / Hànyǔ 用英语 / 汉
语; ~ **a loud voice** dàshēng 大声;
~ **his style** yǐ tāde fāngshì 以他的
方式; **dressed** ~ **yellow** chuān
huángsè yīfu 穿黄色衣服◊: ~
crossing the road (while) guò
mǎlù shí 过马路时; ~ **agreeing**
to this (by virtue of) yídàn tóngyì
zhège 一旦同意这个◊: ~ **his**
novel zài tāde xiǎoshuō lǐ 在他的
小说里; ~ **Confucius** zài
Kǒngzǐde zhùzuò lǐ 在孔子的著
作里◊: **three** ~ **all** yígòng sān gè
一共三个; **one** ~ **ten** shífēnzhīyī
十分之一 **2** adv (at home, in the
building etc) zài lǐmian 在里面;
(arrived: train) dàodá 到达; (in its
position) zài lǐtou 在里头; ~ **here**
zài zhèr 在这儿 **3** adj
(fashionable, popular) liúxíng 流行
inability wúnéng 无能
inaccessible nán jiējìn 难接近
inaccurate bù jīngquè 不精确
inactive bù huóyuè 不活跃
inadequate bùshì dàng 不适当
inadvisable bù míngzhì 不明智
inanimate wú shēngmìng 无生命
inapplicable bú shìyòng 不适用
inappropriate bú shìdàng 不适当
inarticulate kǒuchǐ bùqīng 口齿
不清
inattentive bù jīngxīn 不经心
inaudible tīngbújiàn 听不见
inaugural speech jiùzhí 就职
inaugurate kāimù 开幕
inborn shēnglái 生来
inbreeding jìnqīn fánzhí 近亲繁
殖

inc. (= **incorporated**) gōngsī 公司
incalculable damage shǔbuqīng 数
不清
incapable wú nénglì 无能力; **be ~**
of doing X bùnéng zuò X 不能做
X
incendiary device ránshāodàn 燃
烧弹
incense[1] n xiāng 香
incense[2] v/t jīnù 激怒
incentive dònglì 动力
incessant liánxù 连续
incessantly bùtíng 不停
incest luànlún 乱伦
inch n yīngcùn 英寸
incident shìjiàn 事件
incidental bǔchōng 补充; ~ **ex-**
penses záfèi 杂费
incidentally shùnbiàn shuō yíxià
顺便说一下
incinerator fénhuàlú 焚化炉
incision qiēkāi 切开
incisive mind, analysis jiānruì 尖锐
incite shāndòng 煽动; ~ **X to do Y**
shāndòng X zuò Y 煽动 X 做 Y
inclement weather èliè 恶劣
inclination tendency, liking yìyuàn
意愿
incline: **be ~d to do X** yǒu zuò X
de qīngxiàng 有做 X 的倾向
inclose → **enclose**
include bāokuò 包括
including prep bāokuò 包括
inclusive adj & prep price bāokuò
zàinèi 包括在内; ~ **of X** bāokuò
X zàinèi 包括 X 在内 **3** adv yíqiè
bāokuò zàinèi 一切包括在内;
from Monday to Thursday ~ cóng
zhōuyī dào zhōusì 从周一到周
四
incoherent bù liánguàn 不连贯
income shōurù 收入
income tax suǒdéshuì 所得税
incoming flight jídá 即达;
phonecall, mail shōudào 收到;
president xīnrèn 新任; ~ **tide**
zhǎngcháo 涨潮
incomparable bùkě bǐnǐ 不可比
拟
incompatibility bù xiāngfú 不相
符

incompatible bù xiāngfú 不相符

incompetence bú chènzhí 不称职

incompetent bú chènzhí 不称职

incomplete bù wánzhěng 不完整

incomprehensible bùkě lǐjiě 不可理解

inconceivable wúfǎ xiǎngxiàng 无法想象

inconclusive fēi jiélùnxìng 非结论性

incongruous bù xiétiáo 不协调

inconsiderate kǎolǜ bùzhōu 考虑不周

inconsistent bù yízhì 不一致

inconsolable wúfǎ wèijiè 无法慰藉

inconspicuous bù xiǎnyǎn 不显眼

inconvenience n bù fāngbiàn 不方便

inconvenient bù fāngbiàn 不方便

incorporate bāohán 包含

incorporated COM gōngsī 公司

incorrect bú zhèngquè 不正确

incorrectly bú zhèngquè 不正确

incorrigible bùkě jiùyào 不可救药

increase 1 v/t zēngjiā 增加 2 v/i tígāo 提高 3 n zēngjiā 增加

increasing zēngjiā 增加

increasingly yuèláiyuè 越来越

incredible (amazing, very good) lìngrén nányǐ zhìxìn 令人难以置信

incriminate xiǎnde yǒuzuì 显得有罪; ~ oneself shòuliánlèi 受连累

incubator (for chicks) fūhuàqì 孵化器; (for babies) héngwēn yùyīng xiāng 恒温育婴箱

incur zhāozhì 招致

incurable bùkě zhìyù 不可治愈

indebted: be ~ to X qiàn X zhài 欠 X 债

indecent xiàliú 下流

indecisive yóuyù bù jué 犹豫不决

indecisiveness yóuyùbùjué 犹豫不决

indeed (in fact) shìshí shàng 事实上; (yes, agreeing) díquèshì 的确是; very much ~ fēicháng 非常

indefinable nányǐ miáoshù 难以描述

indefinite bú quèdìng 不确定; ~ article GRAM búdìngguàncí 不定冠词

indefinitely wú xiànqī 无限期

indelicate bù jīngxì 不精细

indent 1 n (in text) suōjìn páiyìn 缩进排印 2 v/t line suōgé shūxiě 缩格书写

independence dúlì 独立

Independence Day Dúlìrì 独立日

independent dúlì 独立

independently deal with dúlì 独立; ~ of dāndú 单独

indescribable nányǐ xíngróng 难以形容; (very bad) zāo de wúfǎ xíngróng 糟得无法形容

indescribably wúfǎ xíngróng 无法形容; ~ bad zāo de wúfǎ xíngróng 糟得无法形容; ~ beautiful měi de wúfǎ xíngróng 美得无法形容

indestructible bùnéng sǔnhuài 不能损坏

indeterminate bú quèdìng 不确定

index (for book) suǒyǐn 索引

index card suǒyǐnkǎ 索引卡; index finger shízhǐ 食指; index-linked àn shēnghuó zhǐshù tiáozhěng 按生活指数调整

India Yìndù 印度

Indian 1 adj Yìndù 印度 2 n Yìndù rén 印度人; (American) Yìndì'ān rén 印第安人

Indian summer xiǎoyángchūn 小阳春

indicate 1 v/t biǎomíng 表明 2 v/i (when driving) zhǐshì 指示

indication zhǐshì 指示

indicator (on car) fāngxiàng zhǐshìqì 方向指示器

indict kònggào 控告

indifference mò bù guānxīn 漠不关心

indifferent mò bù guānxīn 漠不关心; (mediocre) yìbān 一般

indigestible bùnéng xiāohuà 不能

消化

indigestion xiāohuà bùliáng 消化不良

indignant fènkǎi 愤慨

indignation fènkǎi 愤慨

indirect jiànjiē 间接

indirectly jiànjiē 间接

indiscreet qīngshuài 轻率

indiscretion (act) qīngshuài 轻率

indiscriminate rènyì ér wéi 任意而为

indispensable bùkě quēshǎo 不可缺少

indisposed (not well) xiǎobìng 小病

indisputable bùróng zhìyí 不容置疑

indisputably bùróng zhìyí 不容置疑

indistinct móhu 模糊

indistinguishable wúfǎ qūbié 无法区别

individual 1 n gèrén 个人 **2** adj (separate) dāndú 单独; (personal) gèrén 个人

individualist gèrénzhǔyǐ zhě 个人主义者

individually gèzì 各自

indivisible bùkě fēngē 不可分割

indoctrinate guànshū 灌输

indolence lǎnduò 懒惰

indolent lǎnduò 懒惰

Indochina Yìndùzhīnà 印度支那

Indochinese adj Yìndùzhīnà 印度支那

Indonesia Yìndùníxīyà 印度尼西亚

Indonesian 1 adj Yìndùníxīyà 印度尼西亚 **2** n (person) Yìndùníxīyà rén 印度尼西亚人

indoor shìnèi 室内

indoors zài shìnèi 在室内

indorse → endorse

induction ceremony jiùzhí yíshì 就职仪式

indulge 1 v/t (oneself, one's tastes) fàngzòng zìjǐ 放纵自己 **2** v/i: ~ **in X** jìnqíng xiǎngshòu X 尽情享受 X

indulgence (of tastes, appetite etc) fàngzòng 放纵; (lax attitude)

shūhū 疏忽

indulgent (not strict enough) bù yángé 不严格

industrial gōngyè 工业

industrial action gōngyè xíngdòng 工业行动

industrial dispute láozī jiūfēn 劳资纠纷

industrialist shíyèjiā 实业家

industrialize 1 v/t shǐ gōngyèhuà 使工业化 **2** v/i gōngyèhuà 工业化

industrial waste gōngyè fèiliào 工业废料

industrious qínmiǎn 勤勉

industry gōngyè 工业

ineffective xiàoguǒ bùjiā 效果不佳

ineffectual person dīnéng 低能

inefficient wúxiàolǜ 无效率

ineligible wúzīgé 无资格

inept bùshúliàn 不熟练

inequality bùpíngděng 不平等

inescapable nánmiǎn 难免

inestimable nányǐ gūliàng 难以估量

inevitable xiǎn ér yìjiàn 显而易见

inevitably bùkě bìmiǎn 不可避免

inexcusable bùkě yuánliàng 不可原谅

inexhaustible person jīnglì chōngpèi 精力充沛; supply yuányuán búduàn 源源不断

inexpensive piányi 便宜

inexperienced méi jīngyàn 没经验

inexplicable fèijiě 费解

inexpressible joy nán yǐ biǎoshù 难以表述

infallible juéduì kěkào 绝对可靠

infamous chòumíng yuǎnyáng 臭名远扬

infancy (of person) yīng'érqī 婴儿期; (of state, institution) chūjí jiēduàn 初级阶段

infant yīng'ér 婴儿

infantile pej háiziqì 孩子气

infantry bùbīng 步兵

infantry soldier bùbīng 步兵

infatuated: be ~ **with X** míliàn X 迷恋 X

infect (*of person*) yǐngxiǎng 影响; *food, water* wūrǎn 污染; *become ~ed* gǎnrǎn 感染

infected *wound* gǎnrǎn 感染

infection chuánrǎn 传染

infectious *disease* chuánrǎn 传染; *fig: laughter* gǎnrǎn 感染

infer: *~ X from Y* cóng Y tuīduànchū X 从 Y 推断出 X

inferior *quality* lièzhì 劣质; (*in rank, military*) dìwèidī 地位低; (*in company, workmanship*) zhíwèidī 职位低

inferiority (*in quality*) lièzhì 劣质

inferiority complex zìbēigǎn 自卑感

infertile bùnéng fányù 不能繁育

infertility wú shēngzhí nénglì 无生殖能力

infidelity bùzhōng 不忠

infiltrate *v/t* dǎrù 打入

infinite wúxiàn 无限

infinitive búdìngshì 不定式

infinity wúqióng 无穷

infirm tǐruò 体弱

infirmary yīyuàn 医院

infirmity tǐruò 体弱

inflame jīdòng 激动

inflammable yìrán 易燃

inflammation MED fāyán 发炎

inflatable *dinghy* kě chōngqì 可充气

inflate *v/t tire, dinghy* chōngqì 充气; *economy* péngzhàng 膨胀

inflation tōnghuò péngzhàng 通货膨胀

inflationary (*of inflation*) wùjià shàngzhǎng 物价上涨; (*causing inflation*) dǎozhì tōnghuò péngzhàng 导致通货膨胀

inflection (*of voice*) biànyīn 变音

inflexible *attitude, person* gùzhí 固执

inflict: *~ X on Y* shǐ Y zāoshòu X 使 Y 遭受 X

in-flight fēixíngzhōng 飞行中; *~ entertainment* fēixíngzhōng tígōng de yúlè huódòng 飞行中提供的娱乐活动

influence 1 *n* yǐngxiǎng 影响; (*power to influence*) yǐngxiǎnglì 影响力; *be a good/bad ~ on X* duì X yǒu hǎo/huài yǐngxiǎng 对 X 有好/坏影响 **2** *v/t* yǐngxiǎng 影响

influential yǒu yǐngxiǎng 有影响

influenza liúxíngxìng gǎnmào 流行性感冒

inform 1 *v/t* tōngzhī 通知; *~ X of Y* bǎ Y tōngzhī gěi X 把 Y 通知给 X; *please keep me ~ed* qǐng chuándá gěi wǒ 请传达给我 **2** *v/i* gàofā 告发; *~ on X* gàofā X 告发 X

informal fēi zhèngshì 非正式

informality fēi zhèngshì 非正式

informant tígōng xiāoxirén 提供消息人

information xìnxī 信息

information science xìnxīxué 信息学; **information scientist** xìnxīxuéjiā 信息学家; **information technology** xìnxī jìshù 信息技术

informative tígōng xìnxī 提供信息

informer gàofārén 告发人

infra-red *adj* hóngwàixiàn 红外线

infrastructure jīchǔ jiégòu 基础结构

infrequent shǎoyǒu 少有

infuriate jīnù 激怒

infuriating lìngrén shēngqì 令人生气

infuse *v/i* (*of tea*) pào 泡

infusion (*herb tea*) jìnpào 浸泡

ingenious jīngmíng 精明

ingenuity jīngmíng 精明

ingot dìng 锭

ingratiate: *~ oneself with X* qǔyuè X 取悦 X

ingratitude wàng'ēnfùyì 忘恩负义

ingredient (*for cooking*) yuánliào 原料; *fig* (*for success*) yīnsù 因素

in-group xiǎoquānzi 小圈子

inhabit jūzhù 居住

inhabitable shìyú jūzhù 适于居住

inhabitant jūmín 居民

inhale 1 *v/t* xīrù 吸入 **2** *v/i* (*when smoking*) xīqì 吸气

inhaler xīrùqì 吸入器

inherit jìchéng 继承

inheritance jìchéng 继承

inhibit *growth, conversation etc* zǔzhǐ 阻止

inhibited yàyì 压抑

inhibition yāyì 压抑

inhospitable (*of people*) lěngdàn 冷淡; (*of place*) huāngliáng 荒凉

in-house *adj & adv* zài gōngsī nèi 在公司内

inhuman yěmán 野蛮

initial 1 *adj* zuìchū 最初 **2** *n* xìngmíng shǒu zìmǔ 姓名首字母 **3** *v/t* (*write initials on*) qiān xìngmíng shǒu zìmǔ 签姓名首字母

initially kāishǐ 开始

initiate *v/t* zhuóshǒu 着手

initiation kāichuàng 开创

initiative zhǔdòngxìng 主动性; *do X on one's own* ~ zhǔdòng zuò X 主动做X

inject *medicine, drug* zhùshè 注射; *fuel* shūsòng 输送; *capital* tóurù 投入

injection MED zhùshè 注射; (*of fuel*) shūsòng 输送; (*of capital*) tóurù 投入

injure shānghài 伤害

injured 1 *adj leg* shòushāng 受伤; *feelings* shòushānghài 受伤害 **2** *n*: *the* ~ shòushāng zhě 受伤者

injury shānghài 伤害

injustice fēizhèngyì 非正义

ink mòshuǐ 墨水

inkjet (*printer*) pēnmò (dǎyìnjī) 喷墨 (打印机)

inland nèilù 内陆

in-laws yīnqīn 姻亲

inlay *n* xiāngqiàn 镶嵌

inlet (*of sea*) hǎiwān 海湾; (*in machine*) rùkǒu 入口

inmate (*of prison*) fànrén 犯人; (*of mental hospital*) bìngyǒu 病友

inn xiǎolǚguǎn 小旅馆

innate tiānshēng 天生

inner nèibù 内部

inner city jiùchéngqū 旧城区

Inner Mongolia Nèi Měnggǔ 内蒙古

Inner Mongolian Grasslands Nèi Měnggǔ Dà Cǎo Yuán 内蒙古大草原

innermost zuìshēn 最深

inner tube nèitāi 内胎

innocence (*of child*) tiānzhēn 天真; LAW wúzuì 无罪

innocent *child* tiānzhēn 天真; LAW wúzuì 无罪

innovation géxīn 革新

innovative géxīn 革新

innovator géxīn zhě 革新者

innumerable shǔbuqīng 数不清

inoculate jiēzhǒng 接种

inoculation jiēzhǒng 接种

inoffensive bù chùfàn rén 不触犯人

inorganic wújī 无机

input *n & v/t* (*into project etc*) tóurù 投入; COMPUT shūrù 输入

input port COMPUT shūrù duānkǒu 输入端口

inquest shěnxùn 审讯

inquire xúnwèn 询问; ~ *into X* diàochá X 调查X

inquiry xúnwèn 询问

inquisitive hàoqí 好奇

insane fēngkuáng 疯狂

insanitary bù wèishēng 不卫生

insanity fēngkuáng 疯狂

insatiable bùnéng mǎnzú 不能满足

inscription míngwén 铭文

inscrutable shénmì 神秘

insect kūnchóng 昆虫

insecticide shāchóngjì 杀虫剂

insect repellent fángchóngyào 防虫药

insecure bù ānquán 不安全

insecurity bù ānquángǎn 不安全感

insensitive bù mǐngǎn 不敏感

insensitivity bù língmǐnxìng 不灵敏性

inseparable *two issues* bùkě fēngē 不可分割; *two people* fēnbùkāi 分不开

insert 1 *n* (*in magazine etc*) fùjiāwù 附加物 **2** *v/t* chārù 插入; ~ *X into Y* bǎ X chārù Y 把X插入Y

insertion (*act*) chārù 插入

inside 1 *n* (*of house, box*) nèibù 内部; (*of road*) lǐcè 里侧; *somebody*

***on the* ~** nèibùrén 内部人; *~ out* lǐmiàn fāndào wàimiàn 里面翻到外面; *turn X* ~ *out* bǎ X lǐ fān wài 把 X 里翻外; *know X* ~ *out* chèdǐ liǎojiě X 彻底了解 X **2** *prep* zài … lǐ 在 … 里; *~ the house* zài wūlǐ 在屋里; *~ of 2 hours* bú dào liǎng xiǎoshí 不到两小时 **3** *adv stay, remain* zài lǐmiàn 在里面; *go, carry* lǐmiàn 里面; *we went* ~ wǒmen jìn lǐmiàn le 我们进里面了 **4** *adj* nèibù 内部; *~ information* nèibù xiāoxi 内部消息; *~ lane* SP lǐquān pǎodào 里圈跑道; (*on road*) lǐdào 里道; *~ pocket* lǐbiāndōu 里边兜

insider nèibùrén 内部人

insider trading FIN nèimù jiāoyì 内幕交易

insides lǐmiàn 里面

insidious yǐnfú 隐伏

insight dòngchá 洞察

insignificant wú jiàzhí 无价值

insincere bù zhēnchéng 不真诚

insincerity xūwěi 虚伪

insinuate (*imply*) ànshì 暗示

insist jiānchí 坚持; *please keep it, I* ~ nǐ yídìng yào liúzhe 你一定要留着

♦ **insist on** jiānjué yāoqiú 坚决要求

insistent jiānchí 坚持

insolent mánhèng 蛮横

insoluble *problem* bùnéng jiějué 不能解决; *substance* bù róngjiě 不溶解

insolvent wú chángzhài nénglì 无偿债能力

insomnia shīmián 失眠

inspect *work, tickets, baggage* jiǎnchá 检查; *building, factory, school* shìchá 视察

inspection (*of work, tickets, baggage*) jiǎnchá 检查; (*of building, factory, school*) shìchá 视察

inspector (*in factory*) jiǎncháyuán 检查员; (*on buses*) chápiàoyuán 查票员; (*of police*) xúnguān 巡官

inspiration línggǎn 灵感; (*very good idea*) hǎo zhǔyi 好主意

inspire (*cause: respect etc*) yǐnqǐ 引起; *be ~d by X* cóng X dédào línggǎn 从 X 得到灵感

instability (*of character, economy*) bù wěndìng 不稳定

install *computer, telephone, software* ānzhuāng 安装

installation (*of new equipment, software etc*) ānzhuāng 安装; *military* ~ jūnshì zhuāngbèi 军事装备

installment (*of story, TV drama etc*) jí集; (*payment*) yīqī fùkuàn 一期付款

installment plan fēnqī fùkuǎn 分期付款

instance (*example*) lìzi 例子; *for* ~ lìrú 例如

instant 1 *adj* lìjí 立即 **2** *n* shànà 刹那; *in an* ~ yíhuìr 一会儿

instantaneous jíkè 即刻

instant coffee sùróng kāfēi 速溶咖啡

instantly jíkè 即刻

instant noodles ⇩ fāngbiànmiàn 方便面

instead dàitì 代替; *I'll take that one* ~ nà wǒ ná nèige ba 那我拿那个吧; *I haven't got tea, would you like coffee* ~? wǒ méiyǒu chá, nǐ hē kāfēi xíng ma? 我没有茶, 你喝咖啡行吗?; *he didn't go home, he went to the bar* ~ tā méi huíjiā, tā qù jiǔbā le 他没回家, 他去酒吧了; *~ of* ér búshì 而不是

instep jiǎobèi 脚背

instinct běnnéng 本能

instinctive běnnéng 本能

institute 1 *n* xiéhuì 协会; (*special home*) yuàn 院 **2** *v/t new law, inquiry* zhìdìng 制定

institution (*governmental*) jīgòu 机构; (*something traditional*) fēngsú xíguàn 风俗习惯; (*setting up*) jiànlì 建立

instruct (*order*) zhǐshì 指示; (*teach*) zhǐdǎo 指导; *~ X to do Y* (*order*) zhǐshì X zuò Y 指示 X 做 Y

instruction shuōmíng 说明; *~s for use* shǐyòng shuōmíngshū 使用

说明书

instruction manual shuōmíngshū 说明书

instructive yǒu zhǐdǎo yìyì 有指导意义

instructor zhǐdǎoyuán 指导员

instrument MUS yuèqì 乐器; (gadget, tool) qìjù 器具

insubordinate bùfúcóng 不服从

insufficient búgòu 不够

insulate ELEC shǐ juéyuán 使绝缘; (against cold) shǐ gérè 使隔热

insulation ELEC juéyuán cáiliào 绝缘材料; (against cold) gérè 隔热

insulin yídǎosù 胰岛素

insult n & v/t wǔrǔ 侮辱

insurance bǎoxiǎn 保险

insurance company bǎoxiǎn gōngsī 保险公司

insurance policy bǎoxiǎndān 保险单

insure v/t gěi ... bǎoxiǎn 给 ... 保险

insured: be ~ed cānjiā bǎoxiǎn 参加保险

insurmountable wúfǎ chāoyuè 无法超越

intact (not damaged) wèishòusǔn 未受损

intake (of college etc) zhāoshōu 招收

integrate v/t róngwéiyìtǐ 融为一体

integrated circuit jíchéng diànlù 集成电路

integrity (honesty) chéngshí 诚实

intellect zhìlì 智力

intellectual 1 adj zhìlì 智力 2 n zhīshífènzǐ 知识分子

intelligence zhìlì 智力; (news) qíngbào 情报

intelligence service qíngbàojú 情报局

intelligent cōngmíng 聪明

intelligible kě lǐjiě 可理解

intend dǎsuàn 打算; ~ to do X (do on purpose) zhǐzài zuò X 旨在做 X; (plan to do) dǎsuàn zuò X 打算做 X; that's not what I ~ed nà bù shì wǒde yìtú 那不是我的意图

intense sensation, pleasure, heat, pressure jùliè 剧烈; personality rèqíng 热情; concentration gāodù 高度

intensify 1 v/t effect, pressure jiāqiáng 加强 2 v/i (pain) jiājù 加剧; (fighting) biànqiángliè 变强烈

intensity (of sensation, heat, pain) qiángliè 强烈; (of fighting) jīliè 激烈

intensive study, training, treatment qiánghuà 强化

intensive care (unit) tèhù (bù) 特护(部)

intensive course (of language study) jīngdúkè 精读课

intent: be ~ on doing X (determined to do) jiānjué zuò X 坚决做 X; (concentrating on) jízhōng jīnglì zuò X 集中精力做 X

intention yìtú 意图; I have no ~ of ... (refuse to) wǒ gēnběn bù xiǎng ... 我根本不想 ...

intentional yǒuyì 有意

intentionally yǒuyì 有意

interaction xiānghù zuòyòng 相互作用

interactive jiāohùshì 交互式

intercede tiáotíng 调停

intercept ball lánjié 拦截; message jiéchá 截查; missile jiéjī 截击

interchange n (of highways) jiāochādào 交叉道

interchangeable kěhùhuàn 可互换

intercom duìjiǎngjī 对讲机

intercourse (sexual) xìngjiāo 性交

interdependent xiānghù yīlài 相互依赖

interest 1 n xìngqù 兴趣; FIN lìxī 利息; take an ~ in X duì X yǒu xìngqù 对 X 有兴趣 2 v/t: ~ X yǐnqǐ X de xìngqù 引起 X 的兴趣; does that offer ~ you? nǐ duì zhèigè tiáojiàn gǎn xìngqù ma? 你对这个条件感兴趣吗?

interested yǒu xìngqù 有兴趣; be ~ in X duì X yǒu xìngqù 对 X 有兴趣; thanks, but I'm not ~ xièxiè, dàn wǒ bù gǎn xìngqù 谢谢, 但我不感兴趣

interesting yǒuqù 有趣

interest rate lìxīlǜ 利息率
interface 1 n jièmiàn 界面 **2** v/i
xiāngjiē 相接
interfere gānshè 干涉
♦**interfere with** controls nònghuài
弄坏; plans gānrǎo 干扰
interference gānshè 干涉; (on
radio) gānrǎo 干扰
interior 1 adj nèibù 内部 **2** n (of
house) nèibù 内部; (of country)
nèilù 内陆; **Department of the
Interior** Nèizhèngbù 内政部
interior decoration nèibù
zhuāngxiū 内部装修; **interior
design** shìnèi shèjì 室内设计;
interior designer shìnèi shèjì zhě
室内设计者
interlude (at theater, concert)
mùjiān 幕间; (period) shíjiān 时
间
intermediary n zhōngrén 中人
intermediate adj zhōngjí 中级
intermission (in theater, movie
theater) mùjiān xiūxī 幕间休息
intern v/t jūliú 拘留
internal nèibù 内部; trade guónèi
国内
internal combustion engine
nèiránjī 内燃机
internally (in body) tǐnèi 体内;
(within organization) nèibù 内部
Internal Revenue (**Service**)
Guónèi Shuìshōu (bù) 国内税收
(部)
international 1 adj guójì 国际 **2** n
(match) guójì bǐsài 国际比赛;
(player) guójì bǐsài xuǎnshǒu 国
际比赛选手
International Court of Justice
Guójì Fǎtíng 国际法庭
International Labor Day Guójì
Láodòngjié 国际劳动节
internationally guójì 国际
International Monetary Fund
Guójì Huòbì Jījín Zǔzhī 国际货
币基金组织
Internet yīntèwǎng 因特网,
wǎngluò 网络; **on the ~** zài
wǎngluò shàng 在网络上
Internet café wǎngbā 网吧
internist nèikē yīshēng 内科医生

interpret 1 v/t (linguistically) kǒuyì
口译; piece of music, comment etc
jiěshì 解释 **2** v/i zuò fānyì 作翻
译
interpretation (linguistic) kǒuyì 口
译; (of piece of music, of meaning)
lǐjiě 理解
interpreter kǒuyì zhě 口译者
interrelated facts xiānghù guānlián
相互关联
interrogate xúnwèn 询问
interrogation xúnwèn 询问
interrogative n GRAM yíwèn 疑问
interrogator shěnwèn zhě 审问者
interrupt 1 v/t speaker dǎduàn 打断
2 v/i chāhuà 插话
interruption zhōngduàn 中断
intersect v/t & v/i jiāochā 交叉
intersection (crossroads) shízì
lùkǒu 十字路口
interstate n zhōujìjiān 州际间
interval jiàngé 间隔; (in theater, at
concert) jiànxiē 间歇
intervene (of person, police etc)
jièrù 介入
intervention jièrù 介入
interview 1 n (on TV, in paper)
cǎifǎng 采访; (for job) miànshì 面
试 **2** v/t (on TV, for paper) cǎifǎng
采访; (for job) miànshì 面试
interviewee (on TV) bèi cǎifǎng
zhě 被采访者; (for job) yìngshì
zhě 应试者
interviewer (on TV, for paper)
cǎifǎng zhě 采访者; (for job)
miànshì zhě 面试者
intestine chángzi 肠子
intimacy (of friendship) qīnmì 亲
密; (sexual) qīnnì 亲昵
intimate friend qīnmì 亲密;
(sexually) qīnnì 亲昵; thoughts
sīrén 私人
intimidate wēixié 威胁
intimidation wēixié 威胁
into dào ... lǐ 到 ... 里; **he walked
~ the store** tā zǒu dào diànlǐ 他走
到店里; **he put it ~ his suitcase**
tā bǎ tā fàngzài tāde yīxiāng lǐ 他
把它放在他的衣箱里; **trans-
late ~ English** fānyì chéng Yīngyǔ
翻译成英语; **turn ~** biànchéng

变成; **be ~ X** F (*like*) xǐhuān X 喜欢 X; (*be involved with*) chīmí X 痴迷 X; **when you're ~ the job** dāng nǐ shúxi zhè gōngzuò de shíhòu 当你熟悉这工作的时候

intolerable bùnéng rěnshòu 不能忍受

intolerant bù róngrěn 不容忍

intoxicated táozuì 陶醉

intransitive bù jíwù 不及物

intravenous jìngmàinèi 静脉内

intrepid wúwèi 无畏

intricate fùzá 复杂

intrigue 1 *n* cèhuà 策划 **2** *v/t* yǐnqǐ hàoqíxīn 引起好奇心; **I would be ~d to know …** wǒ huì yǒu xìngqù dézhī … 我会有兴趣得知 …

intriguing yǒu yìsi 有意思

introduce jièshào 介绍; *new technique etc* yǐnjìn 引进; **may I ~ …?** wǒ lái jièshào yíxià … … 我来介绍一下 …

introduction (*to person, new food, sport etc*) jièshào 介绍; (*in book*) xùyán 序言; (*of new techniques etc*) yǐnjìn 引进

introvert *n* nèixiàng xìnggé de rén 内向性格的人

intrude *v/i* qīnfàn 侵犯

intruder qīnfàn zhě 侵犯者

intrusion qīnfàn 侵犯

intuition zhíjué 直觉

invade qīnlüè 侵略

invalid[1] *adj* wúxiào 无效

invalid[2] *n* MED bìngruò 病弱

invalidate *claim, theory* shǐ wúxiào 使无效

invaluable *help, contributor* wújià 无价

invariably (*always*) búbiàn 不变

invasion qīnlüè 侵略

invent fāmíng 发明

invention fāmíng 发明

inventive yǒu fāmíng cáinéng 有发明才能

inventor fāmíng zhě 发明者

inventory mùlù 目录

inverse *adj order* xiāngfǎn 相反

invert dàozhì 倒置

inverted commas yǐnhào 引号

invertebrate *n* wú jízhuī dòngwù 无脊椎动物

invest *v/t & v/i* tóuzī 投资

investigate diàochá 调查

investigation diàochá 调查

investigative journalism diàochá bàodào 调查报道

investment tóuzī 投资

investor tóuzī zhě 投资者

invigorating *climate* shǐrén shuǎngkuài 使人爽快

invincible wúdí 无敌

invisible bùkějiàn 不可见

invitation yāoqǐng 邀请

invite yāoqǐng 邀请; **can I ~ you for a meal?** wǒ kěyǐ qǐng nǐ chī dùn fàn ma? 我可以请你吃顿饭吗？

invoice 1 *n* zhàngdān 帐单 **2** *v/t customer* kāi zhàngdān 开帐单

involuntary fēiběnyì 非本意

involve *hard work, expense* xūyào 需要; (*concern*) shèjí 涉及; **what does it ~?** nà xūyào shénme? 那需要什么？; **get ~d with X** juǎnrù X 卷入 X; (*emotionally, romantically*) yǔ X yǒu gǎnqíng 与 X 有感情

involved (*complex*) fùzá 复杂

involvement (*in a project etc*) chāshǒu 插手; (*in a crime, accident*) juǎnrù 卷入

invulnerable búyì shòushāng 不易受伤

inward 1 *adj* nèibù 内部 **2** *adv* xiàngnèi 向内

inwardly nèixīn 内心

iodine diǎn 碘

IOU (= *I owe you*) jièjù 借据

IQ (= *intelligence quotient*) zhìshāng 智商

Iran Yīlǎng 伊朗

Iranian 1 *adj* Yīlǎng 伊朗 **2** *n* (*person*) Yīlǎng rén 伊朗人; (*language*) Yīlǎng yǔ 伊朗语

Iraq Yīlākè 伊拉克

Iraqi 1 *adj* Yīlākè 伊拉克 **2** *n* (*person*) Yīlākè rén 伊拉克人

Ireland Ài'ěrlán 爱尔兰

iris (*of eye*) hóngmó 虹膜; (*flower*) yuānwěishǔ zhíwù 鸢尾属植物

Irish Ài'ěrlán 爱尔兰

Irishman Ài'ěrlán nánzǐ 爱尔兰男子

Irishwoman Ài'ěrlán nǚzǐ 爱尔兰女子

iron 1 *n* (*substance*) tiě 铁; (*for clothes*) yùndǒu 熨斗 **2** *v/t shirts etc* yùn 熨

ironic(**al**) fěngcì 讽刺

ironing yùn 熨; ***do the ~*** yùn yīfu 熨衣服

ironing board yùnyībǎn 熨衣板

ironworks gāngtiěchǎng 钢铁厂

iron rice bowl (*job for life*) tiě fànwǎn 铁饭碗

irony fěngcì 讽刺

irrational wúlǐxìng 无理性

irreconcilable wúfǎ héjiě 无法和解

irrecoverable wúfǎ wǎnhuí 无法挽回

irregular *intervals* bùguīlǜ 不规律; *sizes* bùguīzé 不规则; *behavior* bùguīfàn 不规范

irrelevant bùxiānggān 不相干

irreparable wúfǎ míbǔ 无法弥补

irreplaceable *object, person* bùkě tìdài 不可替代

irrepressible *sense of humor* bùnéng yìzhì 不能抑制; *person* bùjūshù 不拘束

irreproachable wúkě zhǐzé 无可指责

irresistible wúfǎ kàngjù 无法抗拒

irrespective: ***~ of X*** búgù X 不顾 X

irresponsible búfùzérèn 不负责任

irretrievable bùkě wǎnhuí 不可挽回

irreverent bùqiánchéng 不虔诚

irrevocable bùkě qǔxiāo 不可取消

irrigate guàngài 灌溉

irrigation guàngài 灌溉

irrigation canal guàngàiqú 灌溉渠

irritable fánzào 烦躁

irritate rěnù 惹怒

irritating fánrén 烦人

irritation fánzào 烦燥

Islam Yīsīlánjiào 伊斯兰教

Islamic Yīsīlánjiào 伊斯兰教

island dǎo 岛; (*traffic*) ~ ānquándǎo 安全岛

islander dǎoyǔrén 岛屿人

isolate (*separate*) gélí 隔离; (*cut off*) gūlì 孤立; (*identify*) fēngé 分隔

isolated *house* gūlì 孤立; *occurrence* dānyī 单一

isolation (*of a region*) gélí 隔离; ***in ~*** dāndú 单独

isolation ward gélíjiān 隔离间

Israel Yǐsèliè 以色列

Israeli 1 *adj* Yǐsèliè 以色列 **2** *n* (*person*) Yǐsèliè rén 以色列人

issue 1 *n* (*matter*) shìqing 事情; (*result*) jiéguǒ 结果; (*of magazine*) qī 期; ***the point at ~*** zhēnglùnde wèntí 争论的问题; ***take ~ with X*** yǔ X zhēngbiàn 与 X 争辩 **2** *v/t supplies, coins, passports, visa* fāxíng 发行; *warning* fābiǎo 发表

IT (= *information technology*) xìnxī jìshù 信息技术

it tā 它 ◊ (*not translated*): ***~'s on the table*** zài zhuōzi shang 在桌子上; ***~'s raining*** xiàyǔ le 下雨了; ***~'s me / him*** shì wǒ / tā 是我 / 他; ***~'s yellow*** shì huángde 是黄的; ***~'s Charlie here*** TELEC wǒ shì Chálǐ 我是查理; ***~'s your turn*** gāi nǐ de le 该你的了; ***that's ~!*** (*that's right*) duìle! 对了！; (*finished*) wánle! 完了！

Italian 1 *adj* Yìdàlì 意大利 **2** *n* (*person*) Yìdàlì rén 意大利人; (*language*) Yìdàlì yǔ 意大利语

italic xiétǐ 斜体

Italy Yìdàlì 意大利

itch 1 *n* yǎng 痒 **2** *v/i* fāyǎng 发痒

item tiáo 条

itemize *invoice* fēnxiàng lièjǔ 分项列举

itinerary lǚxíng jìhuà 旅行计划

its tāde 它的

itself tā zìjǐ 它自己; ***by ~*** (*alone*) dúzì 独自; (*automatically*) zìdòng 自动

ivory (*substance*) xiàngyá 象牙

ivy chángchūnténg 常春藤

J

jab *v/t* chuō 戳

jack MOT qiānjīndǐng 千斤顶; *(in cards)* gōu 钩

♦ **jack up** MOT yòng qiānjīndǐng dǐng 用千斤顶顶

jacket *(coat)* jiákè 茄克; *(of book)* hùfēng 护封

jacket potato kǎo tǔdòu 烤土豆

jack-knife *v/i* wānchéng V zì xíng 弯成V字形

jackpot lěijī de dǔzhù 累积的赌注; ***hit the ~*** fā dàcái 发大财

jade *n* yù 玉

jagged cēncī bùqí 参差不齐

jail *n* jiānyù 监狱

jam¹ guǒjiàng 果酱

jam² **1** *n* MOT shīlíng 失灵; F *(difficulty)* kùnjìng 困境; ***be in a ~*** xiànrù kùnjìng 陷入困境 **2** *v/t* *(ram)* bǎ ... sāijìn 把 ... 塞进; *(cause to stick)* qiǎzhù 卡住; *broadcast* gānrǎo 干扰; ***be ~med*** *(of roads)* dǔsè 堵塞; *(of door, window)* qiǎzhù 卡住 **3** *v/i* *(stick)* qiǎzhù 卡住; *(squeeze)* jǐjìn 挤进

jam-packed yōngjǐ 拥挤

janitor kānménrén 看门人

January yīyuè 一月

Japan Rìběn 日本

Japanese **1** *adj* Rìběn 日本 **2** *n* *(person)* Rìběn rén 日本人; *(language)* Rìyǔ 日语

jar¹ *n* *(container)* guàn 罐

jar² *v/i* *(of noise)* cì'ěr 刺耳; ***~ on*** cìjī 刺激

jargon hánghuà 行话

jasmine tea mòlìhuāchá 茉莉花茶

jaundice huángdǎn 黄疸

jaw *n* hé 颌

jaywalker luànchuǎng mǎlù de rén 乱闯马路的人

jaywalking luànchuǎng mǎlù 乱闯马路

jazz juéshìyuè 爵士乐

♦ **jazz up** F diǎnzhuì 点缀

jealous dùjì 妒忌; ***be ~ of ...*** dùjì ... 妒忌 ...

jealousy dùjì 妒忌

jeans niúzǎikù 牛仔裤

jeep jípǔchē 吉普车

jeer **1** *n* cháonòng 嘲弄 **2** *v/i* qǐhòng 起哄; ***~ at*** cháoxiào 嘲笑

jelly guǒdòng 果冻

jelly bean ruǎntáng 软糖

jellyfish hǎizhé 海蜇

jeopardize shǐ xiànyú kùnjìng 使陷于困境

jeopardy: ***be in ~*** chǔyú wēixiǎn jìngdì 处于危险境地

jerk¹ **1** *n* měngrán yídòng 猛然一动 **2** *v/t* měnglā 猛拉

jerk² F chǔnrén 蠢人

jerky *movement* hūdònghūtíng 忽动忽停

jersey *(sweater)* jǐnshēn tàoshān 紧身套衫; *(fabric)* yōují xìmáoshā 优级细毛纱

jest **1** *n* xiàohuà 笑话; ***in ~*** kāi wánxiào 开玩笑 **2** *v/i* kāi wánxiào 开玩笑

Jesus Yēsū 耶稣

jet **1** *n* *(of water)* pēnshèliú 喷射流; *(nozzle)* guǎnzuǐ 管嘴; *(airplane)* pēnqìshì 喷气式 **2** *v/i* *(travel)* fēi 飞

jet-black hēi yòu liàng 黑又亮; jet engine pēnqì fādòngjī 喷气发动机; jetlag shíchā fǎnyìng 时差反应

jettison tóuqì 投弃; *fig* fàngqì 放弃

jetty fángbōdī 防波堤

Jew Yóutàirén 犹太人

jewel zhūbǎo 珠宝; *fig (person)* shòu zhēnshì de rén 受珍视的人

jeweler zhūbǎoshāng 珠宝商

jewelry zhūbǎo 珠宝

Jewish Yóutài 犹太

jiao (*Chinese money*) jiǎo 角

jiffy: *in a ~* F yíhuìr 一会儿

jigsaw (*puzzle*) pīntú yóuxì 拼图游戏

jilt yíqì 遗弃

jingle 1 *n* (*song*) shùnkǒuliū 顺口溜 **2** *v/i* (*of keys, coins*) fā dīngdāngshēng 发叮当声

jinx (*person*) zāixīng 灾星; (*bad luck*) èyùn 厄运; *there's a ~ on this project* zhèige xiàngmù yǒu fángrén de dōngxi 这个项目有妨人的东西

jitters: *get the ~* F gǎndào jǐnzhāng 感到紧张

jittery F jǐnzhāng 紧张

job (*employment*) gōngzuò 工作; (*task*) rènwù 任务; *out of a ~* shīyè 失业; *it's a good ~ you ...* xìngkuī nǐ ... 幸亏你 ...; *you'll have a ~* (*it'll be difficult*) nǐ yǒu huór gànle 你有活儿干了

job description gōngzuò zhízé shuōmíng 工作职责说明; **job satisfaction** gōngzuò de mǎnzúgǎn 工作的满足感; **job hunt:** *be ~ing* zhǎo gōngzuò 找工作

jobless méi gōngzuò 没工作

jockey *n* qíshǒu 骑师

jog 1 *n* mànpǎo 慢跑; *go for a ~* qù mànpǎo 去慢跑 **2** *v/i* (*as exercise*) mànpǎo 慢跑 **3** *v/t elbow etc* qīngtuī 轻推; *~ X's memory* yǐnqǐ X de huíyì 引起 X 的回忆

jogger (*person*) mànpǎo de rén 慢跑的人; (*shoe*) yùndòngxié 运动鞋

jogging mànpǎo 慢跑; *go ~* qù mànpǎo 去慢跑

jogging suit yùndòngyī 运动衣

john F (*toilet*) cèsuǒ 厕所

join 1 *n* liánjiēchù 联结处 **2** *v/i* (*of roads, rivers*) huìhé 汇合; (*become a member*) cānjiā 参加 **3** *v/t* (*connect*) liánjiē 连接; *person* yǔ ... huìmiàn 与 ... 会面; *club* cānjiā 参加; (*go to work for*) jiārù 加入; (*of road*) huìhé 汇合

♦ **join in** cānjiā 参加

♦ **join up** MIL cānjūn 参军

joiner mùgōng 木工

joint 1 *n* ANAT guānjié 关节; (*in woodwork*) liánjiēchù 连接处; (*of meat*) dàkuài ròu 大块肉; F (*place*) dìfang 地方; (*of cannabis*) dàmáyān 大麻烟 **2** *adj* (*shared*) gòngtóng 共同

joint account liánhé zhànghù 联合帐户; **joint-stock company** gǔfèn gōngsī 股份公司; **joint venture** hézī qǐyè 合资企业

joke 1 *n* (*story*) gùshì 故事; (*practical ~*) xiàohua 笑话; *play a ~ on X* kāi X de wánxiào 开 X 的玩笑; *it's no ~* búshì nàozhe wánr de 不是闹着玩儿的 **2** *v/i* (*pretend*) shuō xiàohuà 说笑话; (*having a ~*) yìqǐ shuōxiào 一起说笑

joker (*person*) xiàoxīng 笑星; *pej* shǎguā 傻瓜; (*in cards*) bǎidá 百搭

joking: *~ apart* shuō zhèngjing de 说正经的

jokingly kāi wánxiào 开玩笑

jolly yúkuài 愉快

jolt 1 *n* (*jerk*) diānbǒ 颠簸 **2** *v/t* (*push*) tuī 推

♦ **jot down** cōngcōng jìxià 匆匆记下

journal (*magazine*) zázhì 杂志; (*diary*) rìjì 日记

journalism (*writing*) xīnwén xiězuò 新闻写作; (*trade*) xīnwényè 新闻业

journalist xīnwén gōngzuò zhě 新闻工作者

journey *n* lǚxíng 旅行

joy kuàilè 快乐

jubilant xīnxǐ 欣喜

jubilation huānxīn 欢欣

judge 1 *n* LAW fǎguān 法官; (*in competition*) píngwěi 评委 **2** *v/t* pànduàn 判断; *competition* zuò píngwěi 作评委

judgment LAW cáijué 裁决; (*opinion*) kànfǎ 看法; (*good sense*) juéduànlì 决断力

judicial sīfǎ 司法

judicious míngzhì 明智

judo róudào 柔道

jug hú 壶

juggle wán záshuǎ 玩杂耍; *fig* bēnbō 奔波

juggler wán záshuǎ de rén 玩杂耍 的人

juice zhī 汁

juicy duōzhī 多汁; *news, gossip* yǒuqù 有趣

jukebox zìdòng diǎnchàngjī 自动 点唱机

July qīyuè 七月

jumble *n* yìtuán 一团

jumble up húluànde hùnzài yìqǐ 胡 乱地混在一起

jump 1 *n* tiào 跳; (*increase*) tūzēng 突增; *give a ~* (*of surprise*) xiàrényítiào 吓人一跳 2 *v/i* tiào 跳; (*in surprise*) jīngtiào 惊跳; (*increase*) měngzēng 猛增; *~ to one's feet* zhàn qǐlái 站起来; *~ to conclusions* juédìng cōngcōng zuò juédìng 匆匆做决定 3 *v/t fence etc* tiàoyuè 跳跃; F (*attack*) tūrán gōngjī 突然攻击

◆ jump at *opportunity* pòbùjídài de zhuāzhù 迫不及待地抓住

jumper (SP: *person*) tiàoyuè de rén 跳跃的人

jumpy jǐnzhāng 紧张

junction (*of roads*) jiāochā lùkǒu 交叉路口

June liùyuè 六月

jungle cónglín 丛林

junior 1 *adj* (*subordinate*) dìwèi dī 地位低; (*younger*) dī 低 2 *n* (*in rank*) dìwèi jiào dī zhě 地位较低 者; *she is ten years my ~* tā bǐ wǒ xiǎo shísuì 她比我小十岁

junk fèipǐn 废品; (*boat*) fānchuán 帆船

junk food ⇩ kuàicān 快餐

junkie yǒu dúyǐn zhě 有毒瘾者

junk mail lājī yóujiàn 垃圾邮件

junkyard fèipǐnzhàn 废品站

jurisdiction LAW sīfǎquán 司法权

juror péishěnyuán 陪审员

jury péishěntuán 陪审团

just 1 *adj law* gōngzhèng 公正; *war, cause* zhèngyì 正义 2 *adv* (*barely*) gānggāng 刚刚; (*exactly*) qiàhǎo 恰好; (*only*) zhǐshì 只是; *I've ~ seen her* wǒ gānggāng kàndào tā 我刚刚看到她; *~ about* (*almost*) jīhū 几乎; *I was ~ about to leave when ...* wǒ zhèngyào líkāi, zhèishí ... 我正要 离开, 这时...; *~ like that* (*abruptly*) mòmíng qí miào 莫名 其妙; (*exactly like that*) jiù nèiyàng 就那样; *~ now* (*a few moments ago*) gāngcái gāngcái 刚才; (*at the moment*) xiànzài xiànzài 现在; *~ you wait!* nǐ děngzhe ba! 你等着吧！; *~ be quiet!* bié chūshēng! 别出声！

justice gōngpíng 公平; (*of cause*) zhèngyì 正义

justifiable kě zhèngmíng wéi zhèngdāng 可证明为正当

justifiably yǒu lǐyóu 有理由

justification zhèngdāng lǐyóu 正 当理由

justify zhèngmíng ... shì zhèngdāng 证明 ... 是正当; *text* shēnmíng yuányóu 申明缘由

justly (*fairly*) gōngzhèng 公正; (*rightly*) zhèngquè 正确

◆ jut out *v/i* shēnchū 伸出

juvenile 1 *adj* wèi chéngnián 未成 年; *pej* yòuzhì 幼稚 2 *n fml* wèi chéngnián zhě 未成年者

juvenile delinquency shàonián fànzuì 少年犯罪

juvenile delinquent shàoniánfàn 少年犯

K

k (= *kilobyte*) qiānzìjié 千字节; (= *thousand*) qiān 千

karaoke kǎlā O K 卡拉 OK

karate kōngshǒudào 空手道

karate chop kōngshǒudàode zhǎngcèpī 空手道的掌侧劈

Kazakh 1 *adj* Hāsàkèsītǎn 哈萨克斯坦 2 *n* (*person*) Hāsàkèsītǎn rén 哈萨克斯坦人

Kazakhstan Hāsàkèsītǎn 哈萨克斯坦

keel *n* NAUT lónggǔ 龙骨

keen rèqiè 热切; (*intense*) qiángliè 强烈

keep 1 *n* (*maintenance*) shēngjì 生计; for ~s F yǒngyuǎn 永远 2 *v/t* bǎoliú 保留; (*not give back*) yōngyǒu 拥有; (*not lose*) bǎozhù 保住; (*detain*) zǔdǎng 阻挡; (*in specific place*) cúnfàng 存放; *family* gōngyǎng 供养; *animals* yǎng 养; ~ a promise bǎoshǒu chéngnuò 保守承诺; ~ ... company péibàn ... 陪伴 ...; ~ X waiting ràng X děng 让 X 等; ~ ... to oneself (*not tell*) bǎ ... bǎozhù mìmì 把 ... 保住秘密; ~ X from Y bùràng Y zhīdào X 不让 Y 知道 X; ~ on trying jìxù chángshì 继续尝试; ~ on interrupting zǒngshì gānrǎo 总是干扰 3 *v/i* (*remain*) bǎochí 保持; (*of food, milk*) bǎozhì 保质

♦ keep away 1 *v/i* bú kàojìn 不靠近; ~ from X bié kàojìn X 别靠近 X 2 *v/t* shǐ rén bú kàojìn 使人不靠近

♦ keep back *v/t* (*hold in check*) zǔzhǐ 阻止; *information* yǐnmán 隐瞒

♦ keep down *v/t* *voice, noise* yādī 压低; *costs, inflation etc* bǎochí dīshuǐpíng 保持低水平; *food* tūnxià 吞下

♦ keep in (*in hospital*) liúzài 留在; (*in school*) fá xuéshēng liúxiào 罚学生留校

♦ keep off 1 *v/t* (*avoid*) bìmiǎn 避免; ~ the grass! wùtà cǎopíng! 勿踏草坪! 2 *v/i* (*of rain*) wèixià 未下

♦ keep out *v/i* bìkāi 避开; ~! (*as sign*) xiánrén miǎnjìn! 闲人免进!

♦ keep to *path, rules* zūnxún 遵循

♦ keep up 1 *v/i* (*when walking, running etc*) gēnshàng 跟上 2 *v/t* *pace, payments* gēnshang 跟上; *bridge* zhīchēng 支撑; *pants* tí 提

♦ keep up with *tóngsù shàngshēng* 同速上升; (*stay in touch with*) yǔ X bǎochí liánxì 与 X 保持联系

keeping: in ~ with yízhì 一致

keg xiǎotǒng 小桶

kennel gǒuwō 狗窝

kennels yǎnggǒuchǎng 养狗场

kernel héxīn 核心

kerosene méiyóu 煤油

ketchup fānqiéjiàng 番茄酱

kettle hú 壶

key 1 *n* (*to door, drawer*) yàoshi 钥匙; COMPUT, MUS jiàn 键 2 *adj* (*vital*) guānjiàn 关键 3 *v/t* COMPUT jiànrù 键入

♦ key in *data* yòng jiànpán shūrù 用键盘输入

keyboard COMPUT, MUS jiànpán 键盘; keyboarder COMPUT cāozuò jiànpán de rén 操作键盘的人; keycard yàoshi kǎ 钥匙卡

keyed-up jǐnzhāng 紧张

keyhole suǒkǒng 锁孔; keynote speech dìng jīdiào de yǎnshuō 定基调的演说; keyring yàoshiquān 钥匙圈

kick 1 *n* tī 踢; F (*thrill*) kuàigǎn 快感; (*just*) for ~s F wèile qǔlè 为了取乐 2 *v/t* tī 踢; F *habit* jièchú 戒

除 **3** *v/i* tī 踢

♦**kick around** *v/t ball* tīzhewánr 踢着玩儿; (*treat harshly*) shuǎnòng 耍弄; F (*discuss*) shāngtán 商谈

♦**kick in 1** *v/t F money* gòngxiàn 贡献 **2** *v/i* (*of boiler etc*) kāishǐ qǐdòng 开始启动

♦**kick off** *v/i* kāiqiú 开球; F (*start*) kāishǐ 开始

♦**kick out** qūzhú 驱逐; *be kicked out of the company* / *army* bèi qūzhúchū gōngsī / bùduì 被驱逐出公司 / 部队

♦**kick up**: *~ a fuss* nàoshì 闹事

kickback F (*bribe*) huíkòu 回扣

kickoff kāiqiú 开球

kid F **1** *n* (*child*) xiǎoháir 小孩儿; *~ brother* / *sister* dìdi / mèimei 弟弟 / 妹妹 **2** *v/t* kāi wánxiào 开玩笑 **3** *v/i* kāi wánxiào 开玩笑; *I was only ~ding* wǒ zhǐshì zài kāi wánxiào 我只是在开玩笑

kidder F huì kāi wánxiào de rén 会开玩笑的人

kidnap bǎngjià 绑架

kidnap(p)er bǎngjià zhě 绑架者

kidnap(p)ing bǎngjià 绑架

kidney ANAT shèn 肾; (*food*) yāozi 腰子

kill *v/t* shāsǐ 杀死; *plant* nòngsǐ 弄死; *time* xiāomó 消磨; *be ~ed in an accident* zài shìgù zhōng sàngshēng 在事故中丧生; *~ oneself* zìshā 自杀

killer (*murderer*) xiōngshǒu 凶手; (*cause of death*) zhìmìngde dōngxi 致命的东西

killing móushā 谋杀; *make a ~* (*lots of money*) dàzǒucáiyùn 大走财运

killingly: *~ funny* F jíwéiyǒuqù 极为有趣

kiln yáo 窑

kilo gōngjīn 公斤

kilobyte qiānzìjié 千字节; **kilogram** gōngjīn 公斤; **kilometer** gōnglǐ 公里

kimono héfú 和服

kind[1] *adj* yǒuhǎo 友好

kind[2] *n* zhǒnglèi 种类; (*make*) pǐnpái 品牌; *what ~ of ... ?* shén-

meyàngde ... ? 什么样的 ... ?; *all ~s of people* gèzhǒnggèyàngde rén 各种各样的人; *nothing of the ~* háowú xiāngsì zhīchù 毫无相似之处; *~ of sad* / *strange* F yǒudiǎnr nánguò / qíguài 有点儿难过 / 奇怪

kindergarten yòu'éryuán 幼儿园

kind-hearted hǎoxīn 好心

kindly 1 *adj* yǒuhǎo 友好 **2** *adv* réncí 仁慈; (*please*) qǐng 请

kindness hǎoyì 好意

king guówáng 国王

kingdom wángguó 王国

king-size(d) F tèdà 特大

kink (*in hose etc*) niǔjié 扭结

kinky F biàntài 变态

kiosk shòuhuòtíng 售货亭

Kirg(h)iz 1 *adj* Jíěrjísī 吉尔吉斯 **2** *n* (*person*) Jíěrjísī rén 吉尔吉斯人; (*language*) Jíěrjísī yǔ 吉尔吉斯语

kiss 1 *n* wěn 吻 **2** *v/t* wěn 吻 **3** *v/i* qīnwěn 亲吻

kit (*equipment*) chéngtào yòngpǐn 成套用品; (*for assembly*) zǔzhuāngjiàn 组装件

kitchen chúfáng 厨房

kitchenette xiǎochúfáng 小厨房

kitchen sink: *everything but the ~* F chúle guōtái 除了锅台

kite fēngzheng 风筝; *fly a ~* fàng fēngzheng 放风筝

kitten xiǎomāo 小猫

kitty (*fund*) gòngtóngde zījīn 共同的资金

klutz F (*clumsy person*) bènzhuóde rén 笨拙的人

KMT Guómíndǎng 国民党

knack juéqiào 诀窍

knead *dough* róu 揉

knee *n* xī 膝

kneecap *n* xīgàigǔ 膝盖骨

kneel guìxià 跪下

knick-knacks xiǎoshìwù 小饰物

knife 1 *n* dāo 刀 **2** *v/t* yòngdāocì 用刀刺

knit 1 *v/t* zhī 织 **2** *v/i* biānzhī 编织

♦**knit together** (*of broken bone*) láogùde zhǎngzài yìqǐ 牢固地长在一起

knitting (*something being knitted*) biānzhīwù 编织物; (*activity*) biānzhī 编织

knitwear zhēnzhī yīfú 针织衣服

knob (*on door*) lāshǒu 拉手

knock 1 *n* (*on door*) qiāo 敲; (*blow*) zhuàngjī 撞击 **2** *v/t* (*hit*) jī 击; (*criticize*) pīpíng 批评 **3** *v/i* (*on the door*) qiāo 敲

♦ **knock around 1** *v/t* (*beat*) cūbàode dǎ 粗暴地打 **2** *v/i* F (*travel*) mànyóu 漫游

♦ **knock down** (*of car*) zhuàngdǎo zài dìshang 撞倒在地上; *object, building etc* chāichú 拆除; F (*reduce the price of*) jiàngjià 降价

♦ **knock out** (*make unconscious*) shǐ hūnmí 使昏迷; (*of medicine*) mázuì 麻醉; *power lines etc* jīdǎo 击倒

♦ **knock over** bàndǎo 绊倒; (*of car*) zhuàngdǎo 撞倒

knockdown: *a* ~ *price* dīlián 低廉

knockout *n* (*in boxing*) jīdǎo 击倒; (*competition*) táotàisài 淘汰赛

knot 1 *n* jié 结 **2** *v/t* dǎjié 打结

knotty *problem* jíshǒu 棘手

know zhīdao 知道; *person* rènshi 认识; *place* shúxī 熟悉; *language* dǒng 懂; (*recognize*) rènchū 认出 **2** *v/i*: *I don't* ~ wǒ bù zhīdào 我不知道; *yes, I* ~ shì, wǒ zhīdào 是，我知道 **3** *n*: *be in the* ~ xiāoxi língtōng 消息灵通

knowhow jìnéng 技能

knowing xīnzhào bù xuān 心照不宣

knowingly (*wittingly*) zhīxī 知悉; *smile etc* xīnzhào bù xuān 心照不宣

know-it-all F zì yǐwéi wúsuǒbùzhī de rén 自以为无所不知的人

knowledge zhīshí 知识; *to the best of my* ~ jùwǒsuǒzhī 据我所知; *have a good* ~ *of X* jīngtōng X 精通 X

knowledgeable zàiháng 在行

knuckle zhǐguānjié 指关节

♦ **knuckle down** káishǐ rènzhēn gōngzuò 开始认真工作

♦ **knuckle under** qūfú 屈服

KO jīdǎo 击倒

Korea (*South*) Nán Hán 南韩; (*North*) Běi Cháoxiǎn 北朝鲜

Korean 1 *adj* (*South*) Nán Hán 南韩; (*North*) Běi Cháoxiǎn 北朝鲜 **2** *n* (*South*) Nán Hán rén 南韩人; (*North*) Běi Cháoxiǎn rén 北朝鲜人; (*language*) Cháoxiǎn yǔ 朝鲜语

kosher REL hélí 合礼; F zhèngdāng 正当

Kowloon Jiǔlóng 九龙

kudos róngyù 荣誉

kung-fu gōngfu 功夫

Kyrgyzstan Jíěrjísī 吉尔吉斯

L

lab shíyàn shì 实验室
label 1 n biāoqiān 标签 **2** v/t baggage tiē biāoqiān 贴标签
labor n (work) láodòng 劳动; (workers) gōngrén 工人; (in pregnancy) fēnmiǎn 分娩; **be in ~** zài fēnmiǎn zhōng 在分娩中
laboratory shíyàn shì 实验室
laboratory technician shíyàn shì jìshī 实验室技师
Labor Day Láodòngjié 劳动节
labored style, speech bú zìrán 不自然
laborer láodòng zhě 劳动者
laborious (difficult) fèilì 费力
labor union gōnghuì 工会
labor ward chǎnfáng 产房
lace 1 n (material) huābiān 花边; (for shoe) xiédài 鞋带
♦ **lace up** shoes bǎngdài 绑带
lack 1 n quēshǎo 缺少 **2** v/t quēfá 缺乏 **3** v/i quēfá 缺乏; **be ~ing** quēfá 缺乏
lacquer n (for hair) dìng fàjiāo 定发胶
lacquerware qīqì 漆器
lad xiǎo huǒzi 小伙子
ladder tīzi 梯子
laden zhuāngmǎnle 装满了
ladies room nǚcè 女厕
ladle n cháng bǐngsháo 长柄勺
lady nǚshì 女士
ladybug piáochóng 瓢虫
lag v/t pipes zhuāng wàitào 装外套
♦ **lag behind** luòhòu 落后
lager chénzhǔ píjiǔ 陈贮啤酒
lagoon huánjiāo hú 环礁湖
laidback yōuxián 悠闲
lake hú 湖
lamb (animal) gāoyáng 羔羊; (meat) gāoyáng ròu 羔羊肉
lame person qué 瘸; excuse zhàn búzhù jiǎo 站不住脚
lament 1 n (speech) dàocí 悼词; (song) wǎngē 挽歌; (music) āiyuè 哀乐 **2** v/t wèi … ér bēitòng 为 … 而悲痛
lamentable lìngrén wǎnxī 令人惋惜
laminated yóu bópiàn diéchéng 由薄片迭成; **~ glass** céngyā bōli 层压玻璃
lamp dēng 灯
lamppost lùdēng zhù 路灯柱
lampshade dēngzhào 灯罩
land 1 n tǔdì 土地; (shore) lùdì 陆地; (country) guójiā 国家; **by ~** yóu lùlù 由陆路; **on ~** zài lùdì 在陆地; **work on the ~** (as farmer) gàn nónghuó 干农活 **2** v/t airplane zhuólù 着陆; job dédào 得到 **3** v/i (airplane) zhuólù 着陆; (ball, something thrown) luò luò 落落
landing (of airplane) zhuólù 着陆; (top of staircase) (lóutī) píngtái (楼梯) 平台
landing field fēijī qǐjiàng chǎng 飞机起降场; **landing gear** qǐluò zhuāngzhì 起落装置; **landing strip** jiǎnbiàn jīchǎng 简便机场
landlady (of bar) lǎobǎnniáng 老板娘; (of apartment etc) fángdōng 房东; **landlord** (of bar) lǎobǎn 老板; (of apartment etc) fángdōng 房东; **landmark** lùbiāo 路标; fig lǐchéng bēi 里程碑; **land owner** dìzhǔ tǔdì 地主; **landscape 1** n fēngjǐng 风景; (painting) fēngjǐng huà 风景画 **2** adv print héngpái 横排; **landslide** níshí liú 泥石流; **landslide victory** yādǎo duōshù de xuǎnpiào 压倒多数的选票
lane (in country) xiǎoxiàng 小巷; (alley) hútong 胡同; (on freeway) hángdào 行道
language yǔyán 语言
lank hair píngzhí 平直

lanky *person* yòushòu yòugāo 又瘦
又高
lantern dēnglóng 灯笼
Lantern Festival Yuánxiāojié 元
宵节
Lao Lǎowō yǔ 老挝语
Laos ⇩ Lǎowō 老挝
Laotian 1 *adj* Lǎowō 老挝 **2** *n*
(*person*) Lǎowō rén 老挝人
lap¹ *n* (*of track*) quān 圈
lap² *n* (*of water*) pōlàng pāidǎ shēng
波浪拍打声
♦**lap up** *drink, milk* tiǎn 舔; *flattery*
xīnrán jiēshòu 欣然接受
lap³ *n* (*of person*) dàtuǐ 大腿
lapel fānlǐng 翻领
laptop COMPUT ⇩ xiédài shì
diànnǎo 携带式电脑
larceny tōuqiè 偷窃
lard zhūyóu 猪油
larder shípǐn chǔcáng shì 食品储
藏室
large *building, country, hands, head*
dà 大; *sum of money* duō 多; **at ~**
(*of criminal*) xiāoyáo fǎwài 逍遥
法外; (*of wild animal*) wèi bèibǔ
未被捕
largely (*mainly*) zhǔyào 主要
lark (*bird*) yúnquè 云雀
larva yòuchóng 幼虫
laryngitis hóuyán 喉炎
larynx yānhóu 咽喉
laser jīguāng 激光
laser beam jīguāng guāngshù 激
光光束
laser printer jīguāng dǎyìn jī 激光
打印机
lash¹ *v/t* (*with whip*) biāndǎ 鞭打
♦**lash down** (*with rope*) bǎngzhù
绑住
lash² *n* (*eyelash*) yǎn jiémáo 眼睫
毛
last¹ *adj* (*in series*) zuìhòu 最后;
(*preceding*) shàng yīcì 上一次; **~
but one** dàoshǔ dì'èrgè 倒数第
二个; **~ night** zuówǎn 昨晚; **~
but not least** zuìhòu dàn bìngfēi
zuì bú zhòngyàode 最后但并非
最不重要的; **at ~** zhōngyú 终
于; *Last Emperor* Mòdài Huángdì
末代皇帝

last² *v/i* chíxù 持续
lastly zuìhòu 最后
latch *n* ménshuān 门闩
late (*behind time*) chídào 迟到; (*in
day*) wǎn 晚; *it's getting ~* yǐjīng
wǎn le 已经晚了; *of ~* zuìjìn 最
近; *the ~ 19th/20th century*
shíjiǔ/èrshí shìjì mòqī 十九/二
十世纪末期
lately zuìjìn 最近
later *adv* hòulái 后来; *see you ~!*
yìhuǐr jiàn! 一会儿见！; *~ on*
yǐhòu 以后, hòulái 后来
latest *news, girlfriend* zuìxīn 最新
lathe chēchuáng 车床
lather (*from soap*) pàomòr 泡沫
儿; (*sweat*) hànmòr 汗沫儿
Latin America Lādīng Měizhōu 拉
丁美洲
Latin American 1 *adj* Lādīng
Měizhōu 拉丁美洲 **2** *n* Lādīng
Měizhōu rén 拉丁美洲人
latitude (*geographical*) wěidù 纬
度; (*freedom to maneuver*)
kuānróng dù 宽容度
latter hòuzhě 后者
laugh 1 *n* xiàoshēng 笑声; *it was a
~* kāiwánxiào 开玩笑 **2** *v/i* xiào
笑
♦**laugh at** cháoxiào 嘲笑
laughing stock: *make oneself a ~*
shǐ zìjǐ chéngwéi xiàobǐng 使自己
成为笑柄; *become a ~*
biànchéng xiàobǐng 变成笑柄
laughter xiàoshēng 笑声
launch 1 *n* (*boat, without engine*)
xiǎochuán 小船; (*with engine*)
xiǎotǐng 小艇; (*of rocket*) fāshè 发
射; (*of ship*) xiàshuǐ 下水; (*of
product*) fāxíng 发行 **2** *v/t rocket*
fāshè 发射; *ship* shǐchuán xiàshuǐ
使船下水; *new product* fāxíng 发
行
launch(ing) ceremony (*for new
product*) fāxíng qìngzhù 发行庆
祝
launch(ing) pad fāshè tái 发射台
launder xǐ 洗
laundromat zìzhù xǐyī diàn 自助
洗衣店
laundry (*place*) xǐyī diàn 洗衣店;

(*clothes*) yīwù 衣物; ***get one's ~ done*** xǐ yīfu 洗衣服

laurel yuèguì 月桂

lavatory (*place*) cèsuǒ 厕所; (*equipment*) mǎtǒng 马桶

lavender xūnyīcǎo 熏衣草

lavish *adj* huīhuò 挥霍

law fǎlìng 法令; (*as subject*) fǎlǜ 法律; ***against the ~*** fànfǎ 犯法; ***forbidden by ~*** fǎlǜ bùzhǔn 法律不准

law court fǎtíng 法庭

lawful héfǎ 合法

lawless méiyǒu fǎjì 没有法纪

lawn cǎopíng 草坪

lawn mower gécǎo jī 割草机

lawsuit sùsòng 诉讼

lawyer lǜshī 律师

lax sōngkuǎ 松垮

laxative *n* tōngxiè yào 通泄药

lay *v/t* (*put down*) fàngxià 放下; *eggs* xià 下; ∨ (*sexually*) shuì 睡

♦**lay into** (*attack*) tòngdǎ 痛打

♦**lay off** *workers* jiěgù 解雇

♦**lay on** (*provide*) zhǔnbèi 准备

♦**lay out** *objects* ānpái 安排; *page* zhǎnkāi 展开

lay-by (*on road*) lùpáng tíngchē chù 路旁停车处

layer *n* céng 层

layman fēi zhuānyè rényuán 非专业人员

layout *n* bùjú 布局; COMPUT géshì 格式

♦**laze around** lǎnsǎn 懒散

lazy *person* lǎn 懒; *day* lìngrén lǎnsǎn 令人懒散

lb (= ***pound(s)***) bàng 磅

LCD (= ***liquid crystal display***) yèjīngtǐ xiǎnshìqì 液晶体显示器

lead[1] **1** *v/t procession, race* lǐngtóu 领头; *company, team* lǐngdǎo 领导; (*guide, take*) dàilǐng 带领 **2** *v/i* (*in race, competition*) lǐngxiān 领先; (*provide leadership*) lǐngdǎo 领导; ***a street ~ing off the square*** cóng guǎngchǎng fāchū de yìtiáo jiē 从广场发出的一条街; ***where is this ~ing?*** zhè yǐndào nǎr? 这引到哪儿? **3** *n* (*in race*)

lǐngxiān 领先; ***be in the ~*** lǐngxiān 领先; ***take the ~*** jū shǒuwèi 居首位; ***lose the ~*** luòhòu 落后

♦**lead on** (*go in front*) zǒuzài qiánmiàn 走在前面

♦**lead up to** yǐndào 引到

lead[2] *n* (*for dog*) jiāngsheng 缰绳

lead[3] *n* (*substance*) qiān 铅

leader lǐngxiù 领袖

leadership (*of party etc*) lǐngdǎo dìwèi 领导地位; ***under his ~*** zài tāde lǐngdǎo xià 在他的领导下; ***skills of ~*** lǐngdǎo jìqiǎo 领导技巧

leadership contest lǐngdǎo dìwèi jìngzhēng 领导地位竞争

lead-free *gas* bù hán qiān 不含铅

leading *adj runner* dìyī 第一; *company, product* lǐngxiān 领先

leading-edge *adj technology* lǐngxiān 领先

leaf yèzi 叶子

♦**leaf through** fānyuè 翻阅

leaflet dānzhāng 单张

league (*group*) liánméng 联盟; (*in sport*) liánsài 联赛

leak 1 *n* lòu 漏; (*of information*) xièlòu 泄漏 **2** *v/i* lòu 漏

♦**leak out** (*of air, gas*) lòuqì 漏气; (*of news*) xièlòu 泄漏

leaky *pipe, boat* lòu 漏

lean[1] **1** *v/i* (*be at an angle*) wāi 歪; ***~ against X*** kàozhe X 靠着 X **2** *v/t* kàozhe 靠着; ***~ X against Y*** bǎ X kàozài Y shàng 把 X 靠在 Y 上

lean[2] *adj meat* shòu 瘦; *style, prose* jiǎnjié 简洁

leap 1 *n* tiào 跳; ***a great ~ forward*** jìnle yī dàbù 进了一大步 **2** *v/i* tiào 跳

leap year rùnnián 闰年

learn xuéxí 学习; ***~ how to do X*** xuéxí zuò X 学习做 X

learner xuésheng 学生

learning *n* (*knowledge*) zhīshì 知识; (*act*) xuéxí 学习

learning curve xuéxí qǔxiàn 学习曲线; ***be on the ~*** zài xuéxí qǔxiàn shàng 在学习曲线上

lease 1 *n* zūqì 租契 **2** *v/t apartment, equipment* zū 租

♦**lease out** zūchū 租出

lease purchase zūjiè gòumǎi 租借购买

leash n (for dog) jiāngsheng 缰绳

least 1 adj movement zuì qīngwēi 最轻微; reason zuìxiǎo 最小; amount zuìshǎu 最少 **2** adv zuìbù 最不 **3** n zuìshǎo 最少; **not in the ~ surprised / disappointed** yìdiǎn yěbù qíguài / shīwàng 一点也不奇怪 / 失望; **at ~** zhìshǎo 至少

leather n & adj pí pí 皮皮

leave 1 n (vacation) jiàqī 假期; **on ~** fàngjià 放假 **2** v/t city, place líkāi 离开; person yǔ … fēnshǒu 与 … 分手; husband, wife pāoqì 抛弃; food on plate shèngxia 剩下; scar, memory liúxià 留下; (forget, leave behind) wàngjì 忘记; **let's ~ things as they are** xiànzài jiù zhèyàng ba 现在就这样吧; **how did you ~ things with him?** nǐ zěnme hé tā jiāodài de 你怎么和他交待的？; **~ X alone** (not touch) biépèng X 别碰 X; (not interfere with) bù dǎjiǎo 不打搅; (not damage) bié nònghuài le 别弄坏了; **be left** shèngxia 剩下; **there is nothing left** méishèng shénme 没剩什么 **2** v/i (of person) líkāi 离开; (of airplane) qǐfēi 起飞; (of train, bus) chūfā 出发; (of ship) qǐháng 启航

♦**leave behind** (intentionally) yíliú 遗留; (forget) yíwàng 遗忘

♦**leave on** hat dàizhe 带着; coat chuānzhe 穿着; TV, computer biéguān 别关

♦**leave out** word, figure shěnglüè 省略; (not put away) liúzhe 留着; **leave me out of this** bié suànwǒ 别算我

leaving party gàobié huì 告别会

lecture 1 n jiǎngzuò 讲座 **2** v/i (at university) jiāo 教

lecture hall jiǎngyǎn tīng 讲演厅

lecturer jiǎngshī 讲师

LED (= **light-emitting diode**) fāguāng èrjí guǎn 发光二极管

ledge (on rock face) yánjiāo 岩礁; (of window) chuāngtái 窗台

ledger COM zǒngzhàng 总帐

leek jiǔcōng 韭葱

leer n (sexual) xiéshì 邪视; (evil) hán èyìde yìpiē 含恶意的一瞥

left 1 adj zuǒ 左 **2** n zuǒbiān 左边; POL zuǒpài 左派; **on the ~** zài zuǒbiān 在左边; **on the ~ of …** zài … de zuǒbiān 在 … 的左边; **to the ~** turn, look zài zuǒcè 在左侧 **3** adv turn, look zài zuǒcè 在左侧

left-hand zài zuǒbiān 在左边; bend zuǒbiān 左边; **left-hand drive** zuǒbiān jiàshǐ chē 左边驾驶车; **left-handed** guànyòng zuǒshǒu 惯用左手; **left-overs** (food) shèngcài 剩菜; **left-wing** POL zuǒyì 左翼

leg tuǐ 腿; **pull X's ~** gēn X kāi wánxiào 跟 X 开玩笑

legacy yíchǎn 遗产

legal (allowed) héfǎ 合法; (relating to the law) fǎlǜ 法律

legal adviser fǎlǜ zīxún yuán 法律咨询员

legalism (philosophy) fǎjiā 法家

legalist philosophy fǎjiā 法家

legality héfǎ xìng 合法性

legalize shǐhéfǎ 使合法

legend chuánshuō 传说

legendary chūmíng 出名

legible yìbiànrèn 易辨认

legislate lìfǎ 立法

legislation (laws) fǎguī 法规; (passing of laws) lìfǎ guòchéng 立法过程

legislative powers lìfǎ 立法; assembly yǒu lìfǎ quán 有立法权

legislature POL lìfǎ jīgòu 立法机构

legitimate héfǎ 合法

leg room shēnjiǎo kōngjiān 伸脚空间

leisure kòngxián 空闲; **at your ~** yǒu kòng shí 有空时

leisure center yúlè zhōngxīn 娱乐中心

leisurely pace cóngróng 从容

leisure time kòngyú shíjiān 空余时间

lemon níngméng 柠檬

lemonade níngméng shuǐ 柠檬水

lemon juice níngméng zhīr 柠檬汁儿

lemon tea níngméng chá 柠檬茶

lend: ~ *X to Y* jiègěi Y X 借给 Y X

length chángdù 长度; (*piece: of material etc*) yíduàn 一段; *at ~ describe, explain* xiángxì de 详细地; (*eventually*) zuìzhōng 最终

lengthen shǐ biàncháng 使变长

lengthy *speech* rǒngcháng 冗长; *stay* mànchángi 漫长

lenient kuāndà 宽大

Lenin Liéníng 列宁

lens (*of camera*) jìngtóu 镜头; (*contact lens, of eyeglasses, of eye*) yǎnjìng 眼镜

lens cover (*of camera*) jìngtóu gài 镜头盖

Lent Dàzhāijié 大斋节

lentil bīngdòu 兵豆

lentil soup bīngdòutāng 兵豆汤

leopard bào 豹

leotard jǐnshēnyī 紧身衣

lesbian *n* nǚtóng xìngliàn zhě 女同性恋者

less: *eat* / *talk* ~ shǎo chī / shuō 少吃 / 说; ~ *interesting* / *serious* méi nàme yǒuqù / rènzhēn 没那么有趣 / 认真; *it cost* ~ bǐjiào piányi 比较便宜; ~ *than $200* shǎoyú liǎngbǎi měiyuán 少于两百美元

lesson kè 课

let *v/t* (*allow*) ràng 让; ~ *X do Y* ràng X zuò Y 让 X 做 Y; ~ *me go!* ràng wǒ zǒu! 让我走！; ~ *him come in* ràng tā jìnlái 让他进来; ~*'s go* / *stay* wǒmen zǒu ba / bùzǒu ba 我们走吧 / 不走吧; ~*'s not argue* wǒmen bié chǎole 我们别吵了; ~ *alone* gèng bù yòng shuō 更不用说; ~ *go of* (*of rope, handle*) fàngkāi 放开

◆ **let down** *hair* fàngsōng 放松; *blinds* fàngxià 放下; *skirt, pants* fàngcháng 放长; *let X down* (*disappoint*) ràng X shīwàng 让 X 失望

◆ **let in**: *let X in* (*to house*) ràng X jìnlái 让 X 进来

◆ **let off** (*not punish*) fàngguò 放过;

(*from car*) xiàchē 下车

◆ **let out** (*of room, building*) chūzū 出租; *jacket etc* fàngdà 放大; ~ *a cry* shīshēng 失声

◆ **let up** *v/i* (*stop*) tíngzhǐ 停止

lethal zhìmìng 致命

lethargic lǎnsǎn 懒散

letter (*of alphabet*) zìmǔ 字母; (*in mail*) xìnjiàn 信件

letterhead (*heading*) xìnzhǐ táitóu 信纸台头; (*headed paper*) táitóu xìnzhǐ 台头信纸

letter of credit COM shāngyè xìnyòng shū 商业信用书

lettuce shēngcài yè 生菜叶

letup: *without a* ~ méiyǒu zhōngzhǐ 没有中止

leukemia báixuè bìng 白血病

level 1 *adj field, surface* píngtǎn 平坦; (*in competition, scores*) bìngjìn 并进; *draw* ~ *with ...* hé ... lāpíng 和 ... 拉平 **2** *n* (*on scale*) shuǐpíng 水平; (*in hierarchy*) jíbié 级别; (*amount, quantity*) lǜ 率; (*of alcohol in blood etc*) nóngdù 浓度; *on the* ~ (*on level ground*) zài píngmiàn shàng 在平面上; (*honest*) tǎnshuài 坦率

level-headed tóunǎo lěngjìng 头脑冷静

lever 1 *n* gànggǎn 杠杆 **2** *v/t* yòng gànggǎn yídòng 用杠杆儿移动; ~ *X open* bǎ X qiàokāi 把 X 撬开

leverage gànggǎnr lìliàng 杠杆儿力量; (*influence*) yíngxiǎng 影响

levy *v/t taxes* zhēngshōu 征收

lewd yínwěi 淫猥

Lhasa Lāsà 拉萨

liability (*responsibility*) zérèn 责任; (*likeliness*) kěnéng xìng 可能性

liability insurance dìsān fāng bǎoxiǎn 第三方保险

liable (*answerable*) fùzé 负责; *be* ~ *to* (*likely*) yǒu kěnéng 有可能

◆ **liaise with** yǔ ... jiànlì liánxì 与 ... 建立联系

liaison (*contacts*) liánluò 联络

liar shuōhuǎng zhě 说谎者

libel *n* & *v/t* fěibàng 诽谤

liberal *adj* (*broad-minded*) dàfāng

大方; (*generous: portion etc*)
kāngkǎi 慷慨; POL zìyóu 自由
liberate jiěfàng 解放
liberated *woman* bèi jiěfàng 被解
放
liberty zìyóu 自由; *at ~* (*prisoner etc*) huòdé zìyóu 获得自由; *be at ~ to do X* yǒu quánlìzuò X 有权利做 X
librarian túshū guǎnyuán 图书馆员
library túshūguǎn 图书馆
Libya Lìbǐyà 利比亚
Libyan 1 *adj* Lìbǐyà 利比亚 **2** *n* Lìbǐyà rén 利比亚人
license 1 *n* zhízhào 执照 **2** *v/t bar* xǔkě 许可; ~ *a company to produce ...* xǔkě gōngsī shēngchǎn ... 许可公司生产...
license number zhízhào hàomǎ 执照号码
license plate (*of car*) chēpái 车牌
lick 1 *n* shétiǎn 舌舔 **2** *v/t* tiǎn 舔; ~ *one's lips* chuíxián 垂涎
licking: *get a ~* F (*defeat*) bèi dǎbài 被打败
lid gàizi 盖子
lie[1] **1** *n* (*untruth*) huǎnghuà 谎话 **2** *v/i* shuō huǎnghuà 说谎话
lie[2] *v/i* (*of person: on back*) tǎng 躺; (*on stomach*) pā 趴; (*of object*) píng fàngzhe 平放着; (*be situated*) wèiyú 位于
♦ **lie down** tǎngxià 躺下
lie-in: *have a ~* Br shuì lǎnjiào 睡懒觉
lieutenant zhōngwèi 中尉
life shēngmìng 生命; (*of machine*) shòumìng 寿命; *all her ~* tā yí bèizi 她一辈子; *that's ~!* jiùshì rénshēng! 这就是人生！
life belt jiùshēng quān 救生圈
lifeboat jiùshēng tǐng 救生艇;
life expectancy yùqī shòumìng 预期寿命; **lifeguard** jiùshēng yuán 救生员; **life history** shēnghuó shǐ 生活史; **life insurance** rénshòu bǎoxiǎn 人寿保险; **life jacket** jiùshēng yī 救生衣
lifeless wú shēngmìng 无生命

lifelike shēngdòng 生动; **lifelong** zhōngshēn 终身; **life preserver** (*for swimmer*) shuǐshàng jiùshēng gōngjù 水上救生工具; **life-saving** *adj medical equipment, drug* jiùshēng 救生; **lifesized** yǔ yuánwù yìbān dàxiǎo 与原物一般大小; **life-threatening** yǒu shēngmìng wēixiǎn 有生命危险;
lifetime shòumìng 寿命; *in my ~* zài wǒ yìshēng zhōng 在我一生中
lift 1 *v/t* jǔqǐ 举起 **2** *v/i* (*fog*) xiāosàn 消散 **3** *n* (*Br: elevator*) diàntī 电梯; (*in car*) dā biànchē 搭便车; *give X a ~* ràng X dāchē 让 X 搭车
♦ **lift off** *v/i* (*of rocket*) fāshè 发射
ligament rèndài 韧带
light[1] **1** *n* guāngxiàn 光线; (*lamp*) dēng 灯; *in the ~ of* jiànyú 鉴于; *have you got a ~?* kěyǐ jiège huǒ ma? 可以借个火吗？ **2** *v/t fire, cigarette* diǎnhuǒ 点火; (*illuminate*) zhàomíng 照明 **3** *adj* (*not dark*) míngliàng 明亮
♦ **light up 1** *v/t* (*illuminate*) zhàoliàng 照亮 **2** *v/i* (*start to smoke*) diǎnyān 点烟
light[2] **1** *adj* (*not heavy*) qīng 轻 **2** *adv*: *travel ~* méi shénme xíngli 没什么行李
light bulb diàndēng pào 电灯泡
lighten[1] *v/t color* huǎnhé 缓和
lighten[2] *v/t load* shǐ biànqīng 使变轻
♦ **lighten up** (*of person*) fàngsōng 放松
lighter (*for cigarettes*) dǎhuǒ jī 打火机
light-headed (*dizzy*) yūnxuàn 晕眩; **light-hearted** xiǎngdekāi 想得开; **lighthouse** dēngtǎ 灯塔
lighting zhàomíng 照明
lightly *touch* qīngqīng 轻轻; *get off ~* qīngyì táotuō chéngfá 轻易逃脱惩罚
lightness[1] (*of room, color*) yōuyǎ 优雅
lightness[2] (*in weight*) qīng 轻
lightning shǎndiàn 闪电

lightning conductor bìléi dǎoxiàn 避雷导线

light pen guāngbǐ 光笔

lightweight (*in boxing*) qīngliàng jí 轻量级

light year guāngnián 光年

likable kě'ài 可爱

like[1] **1** *prep* xiàng 象; **be ~ X** (*in looks, character*) xiàng X 象 X; **what is she ~?** (*in looks, character*) tā zhǎngde shénmeyàng? 她长得什么样? ; **it's not ~ him** (*not his character*) bú xiàng tā 不象他 **2** *conj* F (*as*) rú 如; **~ I said** zhèngrú wǒyán 正如我言

like[2] *v/t* xǐhuan 喜欢; **I ~ it** wǒ xǐhuan wǒ 喜欢; **I ~ her** wǒ xǐhuan tā 我喜欢她; **I would ~ ...** wǒ xiǎngyào ... 我想要...; **I would ~ to ...** wǒ xīwàng ... 我希望...; **would you ~ ...?** nǐyào ... ma? 你要...吗? ; **would you ~ to ...?** nǐyào ... ma? 你要...吗? ; **to do X** xǐhào X 喜好 X; **if you ~** suíbiàn nǐ 随便你

likeable kě'ài 可爱

likelihood kěnéng xìng 可能性; **in all ~** duōbànr 多半儿

likely (*probable*) kěnéng 可能; **not ~!** méiménr! 没门儿!

likeness (*resemblance*) lèisì 类似

liking: to your ~ hé nǐ kǒuwèir 合你口味儿; **take a ~ to X** kāishǐ xǐhuān X 开始喜欢 X

lilac (*flower*) dīngxiāng huā 丁香花; (*color*) dàn zǐsè 淡紫色

lily bǎihé huā 百和花

lily of the valley línglán 铃兰

limbs sìzhī 四肢

lime[1] (*fruit, tree*) suānchéng 酸橙

lime[2] (*substance*) shíhuī 石灰

limegreen lùhuáng sè 绿黄色

limelight: be in the ~ yǐnrén zhùmù 引人注目

limit 1 *n* xiàndù 限度; **within ~s** zài yídìng fànwéi nèi 在一定范围内; **off ~s** jìnzhǐ rùnèi 禁止入内; **that's the ~!** shízài tài guòfèn le! 实在太过分了! **2** *v/t* xiànzhì 限制

limitation júxiàn 局限

limited company yǒuxiàn gōngsī 有限公司

limo, limousine gāojí jiàochē 高级轿车

limp[1] *adj* material róuruǎn 柔软; *body* ruò 弱

limp[2] *n* bǒxíng 跛行; **he has a ~** tā bǒxíng 他跛行

line[1] *n* (*on paper, road*) xiàntiáo 线条; TELEC diànhuà xiàn 电话线; (*of people, trees*) pái 排; (*of text*) háng 行; (*of business*) zhíyè 职业; **the ~ is busy** zhànxiàn 占线; **hold the ~** qǐng shāoděng yìhuǐr 请稍等一会儿; **draw the ~ at X** xiànzhì X 限制 X; **~ of inquiry** diàochá fāngfa 调查方法; **~ of reasoning** sīlù 思路; **stand in ~** páiduì 排队; **in ~ with ...** (*conforming with*) fúhé ... 符合...; **he's out of ~** (*not doing the proper thing*) tā tài guòfènle 他太过分了

line[2] *v/t* (*with material*) ānchènlǐ 安衬里

♦ **line up** *v/i* páiduì 排队

linen (*material*) yàmá bù 亚麻布; (*sheets etc*) chuángshàng yòngpǐn 床上用品

liner (*ship*) bānchuán 班船

linesman SP xúnbiān yuán 巡边员

linger (*of person*) dòuliú 逗留; (*of pain*) áizhe 挨着

lingerie nǚ nèiyī 女内衣

linguist yǔyán xuéjiā 语言学家

linguistic yǔyán 语言

lining (*of clothes*) chènlǐ 衬里; (*of pipe*) chènliào 衬料; (*of brakes*) chèndiàn 衬垫

link 1 *n* (*connection*) liánjiē 连接; (*in chain*) yìjié 一节 **2** *v/t* liánjiē 连接

♦ **link up** *v/i* huìhé 会合; TV liánjiē 联接

lion shīzi 狮子

lip zuǐchún 嘴唇

lipread *v/i* chúndú 唇读

lipstick kǒuhóng 口红

liqueur lìkǒu jiǔ 利口酒

liquid 1 *n* yètǐ 液体 **2** *adj* yèzhuàng 液状

liquidation qīngsuàn 清算; **go into**

~ pòchǎn 破产

liquidity liúdòng chǎn 流动产

liquor jiǔjīng yǐnliào 酒精饮料

liquorice gāncǎo 甘草

liquor store mài jiǔdiàn 卖酒店

lisp 1 *n* kǒuchǐ bùqīng 口齿不清 **2** *v/i* kǒuchǐ bùqīng de shuōhuà 口齿不清地说话

list 1 *n* yīlán biǎo 一览表 **2** *v/t* biānliè 编列

listen tīng 听

♦ **listen in** pángtīng 旁听

♦ **listen to** *radio, person* tīng 听

listener (*to radio*) tīngzhòng 听众; *he's a good ~* tā hěn liúxīn tīng 他 很留心听

listings magazine jiémù biǎo 节 目表

listless wújīng dǎcǎi 无精打采

liter gōngshēng 公升

literal wánquán yīzhào yuánwén 完全依照原文; ~ *translation* zhíyì 直译

literary wénxué 文学

literate: *be* ~ yǒu wénhuà 有文化

literature wénxué 文学

litter lājī 垃圾; (*of animal*) yīwō 一窝

little 1 *adj* xiǎo 小; *the ~ ones* xiǎo péngyǒu 小朋友 **2** *n* shǎoxǔ 少许; *the – I know* wǒ suǒ zhīdào de nà yī diǎndian 我所知道的那一点点; *a ~* yīdiǎn 一点; *a ~ bread / wine* yīdiǎn miànbāo / jiǔ 一点面包 / 酒; *a ~ is better than nothing* zǒng bǐ méiyǒu yào qiáng 总比没有要强 **3** *adv* shǎoxǔ 稍许; ~ *by* zhújiàn de 逐渐地; *a ~ better / bigger* hǎo / dà yīdiǎn 好 / 大一点; *a ~ before 6* bǐ liùdiǎn zǎo yīdiǎn 比六点早一点

Little Red Book Máo Zhǔxí Yǔlù 毛主席语录

live[1] *v/i* (*reside*) zhùzài 住在; (*be alive*) shēnghuó 生活

♦ **live on 1** *v/t rice, bread* kào … shēnghuó 靠 … 生活 **2** *v/i* (*continue living*) huó xiàqù 活下去

♦ **live up**: *live it up* kuánghuān 狂欢

♦ **live up to** bú kuìyú 不愧于

♦ **live with**: ~ *X* (*with a person*) hé X tóngjū 和 X 同居

live[2] *adj broadcast* shíkuàng 实况; ~ *ammunition* shídàn 实弹

livelihood shēngjì 生计

lively huópo 活泼

liver MED gānzàng 肝藏; (*food*) gān 肝

livestock shēngchù 牲畜

livid (*angry*) fēicháng shēngqì 非常生气

living 1 *adj* huóde 活的 **2** *n* móushēng 谋生; *earn one's* ~ móushēng 谋生; *standard of* ~ shēnghuó shuǐpíng 生活水平

living room kètīng 客厅

lizard xīyì 蜥蜴

load 1 *n* fùdān 负担; ELEC fùzài 负载; ~*s of* dàliàng 大量 **2** *v/t car, truck* zhuāng 装; *camera* zhuāng jiāojuǎn 装胶卷; *gun* zhuāng dànyào 装弹药; COMPUT: *software* zhuāng ruǎnjiàn 装软件; ~ *X onto Y* bǎ X zhuāngdào Y shàng 把 X 装到 Y 上

loaded F (*very rich*) hěn yǒuqián 很有钱; (*drunk*) hēzuì le 喝醉了

loaf cháng miànbāo 长面包; *a ~ of bread* yīgè miànbāo 一个面包

♦ **loaf around** yóushǒu hàoxián 游手好闲

loafer (*shoe*) píngdǐ píbiànxié 平底皮便鞋

loan 1 *n* dàikuǎn 贷款; *on* ~ jièyòng 借用 **2** *v/t* jiè 借; ~ *X Y* jiègěi X Y 借给 X Y

loathe tǎoyàn 讨厌

lobby (*in hotel, theater*) méntīng 门厅; POL yuànwài huódòng jítuán 院外活动集团

lobster lóngxiā 龙虾

local 1 *adj* dìfang 地方; *I'm not* ~ wǒ búshì běndìde 我不是本地的 **2** *n* (*person*) běndì rén 本地人

local anesthetic júmá 局麻; **local call** TELEC qūnèi diànhuà 区内电话; **local government** dìfang zhèngfǔ 地方政府

locality suǒzàiqū 所在区

locally *live, work* zài dāngdì 在当

地

local produce dāngdì tèchǎn 当地特产

local time dāngdì shíjiān 当地时间

locate *new factory etc* shèzhì 设置; (*identify position of*) zhǎochū 找出; *be -d* zài mǒuchù 在某处

location (*siting*) dìngwèi 定位; (*identifying position of*) wèizhi 位置; *on ~ movie* wàijǐng 外景

lock[1] (*of hair*) lǚ 缕

lock[2] **1** *n* (*on door*) suǒ 锁 **2** *v/t door* suǒ 锁; *~ X in position* bǎ X gùdìng 把 X 固定

♦ **lock away** suǒ qǐlái 锁起来

♦ **lock in** *person* suǒ zài lǐmiàn 锁在里面

♦ **lock out** (*of house*) suǒzài wàimiàn 锁在外面; *I've locked myself out* wǒ bǎ zìjǐ suǒ zài ménwài le 我把自己锁在门外了

♦ **lock up** (*in prison*) jūjìn 拘禁

locker yǒu suǒguì 有锁柜

locket xiǎo hé 小盒

locksmith suǒjiàng 锁匠

locust huángchóng 蝗虫

lodge 1 *v/t complaint* shēnsù 申诉 **2** *v/i* (*of bullet, ball*) qiǎzhù 卡住

lodger fángkè 房客

loft gélóu 阁楼

lofty *heights* wēi'é 巍峨; *ideals* gāo'ào 高傲

log (*wood*) yuánmù 圆木; (*written record*) jìlù 记录

♦ **log off** (*from computer system*) xiàjī 下机; (*from network, database*) xiàwǎng 下网

♦ **log on** (*to computer system*) shàngjī 上机; (*to network, database*) shàngwǎng 上网

♦ **log on to** *computer system* shàngjī 上机; *network, database* shàngwǎng 上网

logbook rìzhì 日志

log cabin mùwū 木屋

logic luójí 逻辑

logical yǒu luójí 有逻辑

logistics hòuqín xué 后勤学

logo biāozhì 标志

loiter xiánguàng 闲逛

London Lúndūn 伦敦

loneliness (*of person*) gūdú gǎn 孤独感; (*of place*) jìmò gǎn 寂寞感

lonely *person* gūdú 孤独; *place* jìmò 寂寞

loner bù héqún de rén 不合群的人

long[1] **1** *adj road, leg time, wait* cháng 长; *journey* yuǎn 远; *it's a ~ way* hěnyuǎn a 很远啊 **2** *adv* chángjiǔ 长久; *don't be ~* kuàidiǎnr huílái 快点儿回来; *5 weeks is too ~* wǔge xīngqī tàicháng le 五个星期太长了; *will it take ~?* shìbúshì yào hěn cháng shíjiān? 是不是要很长时间？; *that was ~ ago* nàshì hěnjiǔ yǐqián le 那是很久以前了; *~ before then* lǎozǎo 老早; *before ~* bùjiǔ 不久; *we can't wait any ~er* wǒmén bùnéng zài děng le 我们不能再等了; *he no ~er works here* tā búzài zhèlǐ gōngzuò le 他不在这里工作了; *so ~ as* (*provided*) zhǐyào 只要; *so ~!* mànzǒu! 慢走！

long[2] *v/i: ~ for X* pànwàng X 盼望 X; *be ~ing to do X* kěwàng zuò X 渴望做 X

long-distance *adj phonecall* chángtú 长途; *race, flight* yuǎn jùlí 远距离

longing *n* kěwàng 渴望

longitude jīngdù 经度

long jump tiàoyuǎn 跳远; **Long March** Chángzhēng 长征; **long-range** *missile* yuǎnchéng 远程; *forecast* chángyuǎn 长远; **long-sighted** yuǎnshì 远视; **long-sleeved** chángxiù 长袖; **long-standing** chángjiǔ chíxù 长久持续; **long-term** *adj* chángqī 长期; **long wave** chángpō 长波

loo *Br* cèsuǒ 厕所

look 1 *n* (*appearance*) wàiguān 外观; (*glance*) kàn 看; *give X a ~* kàn X yìyǎn 看 X 一眼; *have a ~ at X* (*examine*) kànyíkàn X 看一看 X; *can I have a ~?* wǒ néng kàn yíxià ma? 我能看一下吗？; *can I* *have a ~ around?* wǒ néng kànkan ma? 我能看看吗？；*~s (beauty)* měimào 美貌 **2** *v/i* kàn 看；*(search)* xúnzhǎo 寻找；*(seem)* sìhū 似乎；*you ~ tired/different* nǐ kànqǐlái hěn lèi/bù yíyàng 你看起来很累/不一样

◆**look after** zhàogù 照顾

◆**look around** *museum, city* guānguāng 观光

◆**look at** kàn 看；*(examine)* jiǎnchá 检查；*(consider)* kàn 看

◆**look back** huígù 回顾

◆**look down on** kànbùqǐ 看不起

◆**look for** zhǎo 找

◆**look forward to** qīdài 期待

◆**look in on** *(visit)* shùnbiàn kànwàng 顺便看望

◆**look into** *(investigate)* diàochá 调查

◆**look on 1** *v/i (watch)* pángguān 旁观 **2** *v/t:* **~ X as** *(consider)* bǎ X kànzuò 把 X 看作

◆**look onto** *garden, street* cháoxiàng 朝向

◆**look out** *v/i (of window etc)* cháo wàikàn 朝外看；*(pay attention)* liúshén 留神；**~!** xiǎoxīn! 小心！

◆**look out for** xúnzhǎo 寻找；*(be on guard against)* dāngxīn 当心

◆**look out of** *window* cháo wàikàn 朝外看

◆**look over** *house, translation* zǐxì jiǎnchá 仔细检查

◆**look through** *magazine, notes* liúlǎn 浏览

◆**look to** *(rely on)* yīkào 依靠

◆**look up 1** *v/i (from paper etc)* xiàng shàngkàn 向上看；*(improve)* hǎozhuǎn 好转；*things are looking up* yǒu hǎozhuǎn 有好转 **2** *v/t word, phone number* chákàn 查看；*(visit)* bàifǎng 拜访

◆**look up to** *(respect)* zūnjìng 尊敬

lookout *(person)* kānshǒu 看守；*be on the ~ for* xúnzhǎo 寻找

◆**loom up** yǐnyuē di chūxiàn 隐约地出现

loony F **1** *n* fēngzi 疯子 **2** *adj* fēngkuáng 疯狂

loop *n* quān 圈

loophole *(in law etc)* lòudòng 漏洞

loose *connection, wire, button* sōng 松；*clothes* kuānsōng 宽松；*morals* fàngdàng 放荡；*wording* bù yángé 不严格；*~ change* língqián 零钱；*~ ends* *(of problem, discussion)* shìqíng shàngwèi wánchéng de xìjié 事情尚未完成的细节

loosely *tied* sōng 松；*worded* bù yángé 不严格

loosen *collar, knot* jiěkāi 解开

loot 1 *n* zāngwù 赃物 **2** *v/i* luèduó 掠夺

looter luèduó zhě 掠夺者

◆**lop off** kǎndiào 砍掉

lop-sided bù pínghéng 不平衡

Lord *(God)* Shàngdì 上帝；*~'s Prayer* Zhǔdǎo Wén 主祷文

lorry *Br* huòchē 货车

lose 1 *v/t object* diūshī 丢失；*match* shū 输；*I'm lost* wǒ mílù le 我迷路了；*get lost!* gǔndàn! 滚蛋！**2** *v/i* SP shūdiào 输掉；*(of clock)* zǒumàn 走慢

◆**lose out** shīlì 失利

loser SP shūzhě 输者；*(in life)* shībài zhě 失败者

loss *(of object)* sǔnshī 损失；*(of loved one)* sàngshī 丧失；*(in business)* kuīsǔn 亏损；*make a ~* kuīsǔn 亏损；*be at a ~* bù zhī suǒcuò 不知所措

lost shīqù 失去

lost-and-found *(office)* shīwù zhāolǐng chù 失物招领处

lot: *a ~, ~s* hěnduō 很多；*a ~ of, ~s of* hěnduō 很多；*a ~ better/a ~ easier* hǎo de duō/róngyì de duō 好得多/容易得多

lotion xǐjì 洗剂

loud *music, voice, noise* xiǎng 响；*color* súyàn 俗艳

loudspeaker yángshēng qì 扬声器

lounge qǐjū shì 起居室

◆**lounge around** xiánguàng 闲逛

lounge suit xīzhuāng 西装

louse shīzi 虱子

lousy *meal, weather, vacation* bù zěnme yàng 不怎么样；*thing to do* tǎoyàn 讨厌；*I feel ~* wǒ bù shūfú 我不舒服

lout liúmáng 流氓
lovable kě'ài 可爱
love 1 *n* ài 爱; (*in tennis*) língfēn 零分; **be in ~** zài liàn'ài zhīzhōng 在恋爱之中; **fall in ~ with** àishàng 爱上; **make ~** zuò'ài 作爱; **yes, my ~** hǎode, wǒ qīn àide 好的，我亲爱的 **2** *v/t person, country, wine* ài 爱; **~ to do X** xǐ ài zuò X 喜爱作 X
love affair fēngliú yùnshì 风流韵事; **lovelife** àiqíng shēnghuó 爱情生活; **love letter** qíngshū 情书
lovely *face, hair* měilì 美丽; *color* piàoliang 漂亮; *tune* yōuměi 优美; *person, meal* hěn hǎo 很好; *vacation, weather* lìngrén yúkuài 令人愉快; **we had a ~ time** wǒmén kě kāixīn le 我们可开心了
lover qíngrén 情人
loving *adj* zhōngqíng 钟情
low 1 *adj bridge, wall* ǎi 矮; *salary, price, voice* dī 低; *quality* chà 差; **be feeling ~** gǎndào qíngxù bùhǎo 感到情绪不好; **be ~ on gas / tea** méi duōshǎo méiqì / cháyè 没多少煤气／茶叶 **2** *n* (*in weather*) dī qìyā qū 低气压区; (*in sales, statistics*) zuì dīdiǎn 最低点
lowbrow *adj* quēfá wénhuà sùyǎng 缺乏文化素养; **low-calorie** dī kǎlùlì 低卡路里; **low-cut** *dress* dī lǐngkǒu 低领口
lower *boat, something to the ground* fàngxià 放下; *flag* jiàng 降; *hemline* fàng 放; *pressure, price* jiàngdī 降低
low-fat dīzhīfáng 低脂肪; **lowkey** dīdiào 低调; **lowlands** dīdì 低地; **low-pressure area** dīyā dìqū 低压地区; **low season** dànjì 淡季; **low tide** dīcháo 低潮
loyal zhōngxīn 忠心
lozenge (*shape*) língxíng 菱形; (*tablet*) zhǐké táng 止咳糖
Ltd (= *limited*) yǒuxiàn gōngsī 有限公司
lubricant rùnhuá jì 润滑剂
lubricate rùnhuá 润滑

lubrication rùnhuá 润滑
lucid (*clear*) míngliǎo 明了; (*sane*) shénzhì qīngxǐng 神志清醒
luck yùnqì 运气; *bad* ~ èyùn 恶运; *hard* ~! dǎoméi! 倒霉！; *good* ~ xìngyùn 幸运; *good* ~! zhùnǐ zǒuyùn! 祝你走运！
♦**luck out** F jiǎoxìng chénggōng 侥幸成功
luckily xìngyùnde 幸运地
lucky *person* xìngyùn 幸运; *day, number* jíxiáng 吉祥; *coincidence* jiǎoxìng 侥幸; *you were* ~ nǐ zhēn zǒuyùn 你真走运; *he's* ~ *to be alive* tā jiǎoxìng déyǐ táoshēng 他侥幸得以逃生; *that's* ~! zhēn zǒuyùn! 真走运！
ludicrous huāngtáng 荒唐
luggage xíngli 行李
lukewarm *water* wēiwēn 微温; *reception* bú rèqíng 不热情
lull 1 *n* (*in storm, fighting*) zànshí píngxī 暂时平息; (*in conversation*) jiānxiē 间歇; **~ X into a false sense of security** shǐ X chǎnshēng bù zhēnshíde ānquán gǎn 使 X 产生不真实的安全感
lullaby cuīmián qǔ 催眠曲
lumbago yāoténg 腰疼
lumber *n* (*timber*) mùcái 木材
luminous guāngmíng 光明
lump (*of sugar*) kuài 块; (*swelling*) zhǒngkuài 肿块
♦**lump together** bǎ ... guībìng zài yìqǐ 把 ... 归并在一起
lump sum zǒng'é 总额
lumpy āotū bùpíng 凹凸不平
lunacy jíduān yúchǔn 极端愚蠢
lunar yuèliang 月亮
lunatic *n* fēngzi 疯子
lunch wǔcān 午餐; *have* ~ chī wǔcān 吃午餐
lunch box ⇩ wǔcān hé 午餐盒; **lunch break** wǔxiū 午休; **lunch hour** wǔxiū 午休; **lunchtime** wǔcān shíjiān 午餐时间
lung fèi 肺
lung cancer fèi'ái 肺癌
♦**lunge at** chōngjī 冲击
lurch *v/i* (*of person*) pánshān 蹒跚; (*of ship*) qīngxié 倾斜

lure *n & v/t* yòuhuò 诱惑
lurid *color* huǒhóng 火红; *details* sǒngrén tīngwén 耸人听闻
lurk (*of person*) qiáncáng 潜藏; (*of doubt*) qiánzài 潜在
luscious *fruit, dessert* gānměi 甘美; *woman, man* xìnggǎn 性感
lust *n* xìngyù 性欲

luxurious háohuá 豪华
luxury *n & adj* háohuá 豪华
lychee lìzhī 荔枝
lymph gland línbājié 淋巴结
lynch sīxíng chùsǐ 私刑处死
lynx shānmāo 山猫
lyricist cí zuòzhě 词作者
lyrics gēcí 歌词

M

MA (= *Master of Arts*) wénkē shuòshì 文科硕士

ma'am nǔshì 女士

Macanese 1 *adj* Àomén 澳门 **2** *n* (*person*) Àomén rén 澳门人

Macao Àomén 澳门

machine 1 *n* jīqì 机器 **2** *v/t* (*on sewing machine*) féngrènjī 缝纫机; TECH jīzhì 机制

machine gun *n* jīqiāng 机枪

machine-readable kě jīdú 可机读

machinery (*machines*) jīqì 机器

machismo nánzǐ qìgài 男子气概

macho dànánzǐqì 大男子气

mackintosh yǔyī 雨衣

macro COMPUT hóng huìbiān 宏汇编

mad (*insane*) fēng 疯; (*angry*) nǎohuǒ 恼火; **be ~ about X** (*keen on*) duì X zháomí 对X着迷; **drive X ~** shǐ X fāfēng 使X发疯; **go ~** (*become insane*) fāfēng 发疯; (*with enthusiasm*) kuángrèqǐlái 狂热起来; **like ~ run, work** pīnmìng 拼命

madden (*infuriate*) shǐrén nǎohuǒ 使人恼火

maddening shǐrén nǎohuǒ 使人恼火

made-to-measure dìngzuò 定做

madhouse *fig* yí piàn hùnluàn 一片混乱

madly fēngkuáng 疯狂; **~ in love** rèliàn 热恋

madman fēngrén 疯人

madness jīngshén shīcháng 精神失常

Mafia: **the ~** hēishǒudǎng 黑手党

magazine (*printed*) zázhì 杂志

maggot qū 蛆

magic 1 *n* mófǎ 魔法; (*tricks*) móshù 魔术; **like ~** móshùbān 魔术般 **2** *adj* juémiào 绝妙

magical *powers* mófǎ 魔法;

moment miàobùkěyán 妙不可言

magician (*performer*) móshùshī 魔术师

magic spell fúzhòu 符咒

magic trick móshù 魔术

magnanimous kāngkǎi 慷慨

magnet císhí 磁石

magnetic yǒucíxìng 有磁性; *fig*: *personality* yǒumèilì 有魅力

magnetism (*of person*) mèilì 魅力

magnificence zhuànglì 壮丽

magnificent zhuàngguān 壮观

magnify fàngdà 放大; *difficulties* kuādà 夸大

magnifying glass fàngdàjìng 放大镜

magnitude dàxiǎo 大小

magpie xǐque 喜鹊

mah-jong májiàng 麻将

maid nǔpú 女仆; (*in hotel*) fúwùyuán 服务员

maiden name niángjiāxìng 娘家姓

maiden voyage shǒuháng 首航

mail 1 *n* yóuzhèng 邮政; **put X in the ~** yóujì X 邮寄X **2** *v/t letter* yóujì 邮寄; *person* yóudìyuán 邮递员

mailbox (*in street*) yóutǒng 邮筒; (*for house, e-mail*) xìnxiāng 信箱

mailman yóudìyuán 邮递员;

mail-order catalog yóugòu mùlù 邮购目录; **mail-order firm** yóugòu shāngpǐn gōngsī 邮购商品公司

maim zhìcán 致残

main *adj* zhǔyào 主要

mainboard COMPUT zhǔbǎn 主板; **mainframe** COMPUT zhǔjītǐ 主机体; **mainland** dàlù 大陆; **on the ~** zài dàlù shang 在大陆上; **mainland China** Zhōngguó dàlù 中国大陆

mainly zhǔyào 主要

main road dàlù 大路
main street zhǔjiē 主街
maintain peace, law and order wéichí 维持; pace, speed, ship bǎochí 保持; machine, house bǎoyǎng 保养; family gōngyǎng 供养; innocence, guilt jiānchí 坚持; ~ that duànyán 断言
maintenance (of machine, house) bǎoyǎng 保养; (money) fǔyǎngfèi 抚养费; (of law and order) wéihù 维护
majestic wēiyán 威严
major 1 adj (significant) zhǔyào 主要; in C ~ MUS C dàdiào C 大调 **2** n MIL shàoxiào 少校
♦ **major in** zhǔxiū 主修
majority dàduōshù 大多数; POL duōdéde piàoshù 多得的票数; be in the ~ zhàn duōshù 占多数
make 1 n (brand) páizi 牌子 **2** v/t zuò 做; (earn) zhèng 挣; MATH děngyú 等于; ~ X do Y (force to) pòshǐ X zuò Y 迫使 X 做 Y; (cause to) cùshǐ X zuò Y 促使 X 做 Y; you can't ~ me do it nǐ bùnéng pòshǐ wǒ zuò zhèijiànshì 你不能迫使我做这件事; ~ X happy / angry shǐ X gāoxìng / shēngqì 使 X 高兴 / 生气; ~ a decision zuò juédìng 做决定; ~ a telephone call dǎ ge diànhuà 打个电话; made in China Zhōngguó zhìzào 中国制造; ~ it (catch bus, train) gǎnshàng 赶上; (succeed) huòdé chénggōng 获得成功; (survive) cúnhuó 存活; sorry, I can't ~ it tomorrow (come) duìbùqǐ, wǒ míngr qùbùliǎo 对不起, 我明儿去不了; what time do you ~ it? nǐ biǎo jǐdiǎnle? 你表几点了 ?; ~ believe jiǎzhuāng 假装; ~ do with X yòng X jiāngjiù 用 X 将就; what do you ~ of it? nǐ juédé zěnmeyàng? 你觉得怎么样 ?
♦ **make for**: ~ X (go toward) cháo X yídòng 朝 X 移动
♦ **make off** táozǒu 逃走
♦ **make off with** (steal) tōuzǒu 偷走
♦ **make out** list xiěchū 写出; check

kāichū 开出; (see) biànrèn 辨认; (imply) ànshì 暗示
♦ **make over**: make X over to Y bǎ X zhuǎnràng gěi Y 把 X 转让给 Y
♦ **make up 1** v/i (of woman, actor) huàzhuāng 化妆; (after quarrel) héjiě 和解 **2** v/t story, excuse biānzào 编造; face huàzhuāng 化妆; (constitute) zhàn 占; be made up of X yóu X zǔchéng 由 X 组成; ~ one's mind xià juéxīn 下决心; make it up (after quarrel) héhǎo 和好
♦ **make up for** míbǔ 弥补
make-believe n jiǎxiǎng 假想
maker zhìzào zhě 制造者
makeshift dàiyòngpǐn 代用品
make-up (cosmetics) huàzhuāngpǐn 化妆品
maladjusted xīnlǐ shītiáo 心理失调
malaria nüèji 疟疾
Malay (person) Mǎláixīyà rén 马来西亚人; (language) Mǎlái yǔ 马来语
Malaysia Mǎláixīyà 马来西亚
Malaysian Mǎláixīyà 马来西亚
male 1 adj (masculine) nánxìng 男性; animal, bird, fish xióng, gōng 雄, 公 **2** n (man) nánrén 男人; (animal, bird, fish) xióngxìng 雄性
male chauvinist (pig) dànánzǐ zhǔyì zhě 大男子主义者
male nurse nán hùshì 男护士
malevolent èdú 恶毒
malfunction 1 n shīlíng 失灵 **2** v/i fāshēng gùzhàng 发生故障
malice èyì 恶意
malicious èyì 恶意
malignant tumor èxìng 恶性
mall (shopping ~) gòuwù zhōngxīn 购物中心
malnutrition yíngyǎng bùliáng 营养不良
malpractice wánhūzhíshǒu 玩忽职守
maltreat nüèdài 虐待
maltreatment nüèdài 虐待
mammal bǔrǔ dòngwù 哺乳动物
mammoth adj (enormous) jùdà 巨大

man *n* nánrén 男人; (*human being*) rén 人; (*humanity*) rénlèi 人类; (*in checkers*) qízǐ 棋子

manage 1 *v/t business* jīngyíng 经营; *money* guǎn 管; *suitcase* nádòng 拿动; **~ to ...** zuòchéng ... 做成 ... **2** *v/i* (*cope*) yìngfù 应付; (*financially*) wéichí shēnghuó 维持生活; **can you ~?** nǐ néngxíng ma? 你能行吗?

manageable yì chǔlǐ 易处理

management (*managing*) guǎnlǐ 管理; (*managers*) zhǔguǎn rényuán 主管人员; **under his ~** zài tāde guǎnlǐ xià 在他的管理下

management buyout guǎnlǐ rényuán shōumǎi 管理人员收买; **management consultant** jīngyíng gùwèn 经营顾问; **management studies** guǎnlǐxué 管理学; **management team** guǎnlǐ rényuán 管理人员

manager jīnglǐ 经理

managerial jīngyíng 经营

managing director zǒngjīnglǐ 总经理

Manchu (*nationality*) Mǎnzú 满族

Manchuria Mǎnzhōu 满洲

Mandarin (*language*) ⇩ Pǔtōnghuà 普通话

mandarin (*in China*) guānlì 官吏

mandarin orange júzi 橘子

mandate (*authority*) shòuquán 授权; (*task*) shǐmìng 使命

mandatory qiángzhì 强制

mane (*of horse*) zōng 鬃

maneuver 1 *n* xíngdòng 行动 **2** *v/t* shèfǎ yídòng 设法移动

mangle *v/t* (*crush*) huǐhuài 毁坏

manhandle *person* cūbàode duìdài 粗暴地对待; *object* yònglì yídòng 用力移动

manhood (*maturity*) chéngnián 成年; (*virility*) nánzǐhànqì 男子汉气

man-hour gōngzuò shí 工作时

manhunt jīná 缉拿

mania (*craze*) pǐhào 癖好

maniac kuángrén 狂人

manicure *n* xiūjiǎn zhǐjiǎ 修剪指甲

manifest 1 *adj* míngxiǎn 明显

2 *v/t* xuānyán 宣言; **~ itself** xiǎnlù 显露

manipulate *person* bǎibù 摆布; *bones* jiǎozhèng 矫正; *equipment* cāozòng 操纵

manipulation (*of person*) bǎibù 摆布; (*of bones*) jiǎozhèng 矫正

manipulative ài cāozòng rén 爱操纵人

mankind rénlèi 人类

manly yǒu nánzǐqì 有男子气

man-made rénzào 人造

mannequin (*for clothes*) réntǐ móxíng 人体模型

manner (*of doing sth*) fāngshì 方式; (*attitude*) tàidù 态度

manners: *good / bad ~* yǒu / méiyǒu lǐmào 有 / 没有礼貌; *have no ~* méilǐmào 没礼貌

manpower láodònglì 劳动力

mansion zháidì 宅第

mantelpiece, mantelshelf bìlútái 壁炉台

manual 1 *adj* shǒugōng 手工 **2** *n* zhǐnán 指南

manufacture 1 *n* zhìzào 制造 **2** *v/t equipment* zhìzào 制造

manufacturer zhìzàoshāng 制造商

manufacturing (*industry*) zhìzào 制造

manure féiliào 肥料

manuscript shǒugǎo 手稿

many 1 *adj* xǔduō 许多; *~ times* xǔduō cì 许多次; *not ~ people / taxis* méiyǒu duōshao rén / chūzūchē 没有多少人 / 出租车; *too ~ problems / beers* tàiduō wèntí / píjiǔ 太多问题 / 啤酒 **2** *pron* xǔduō rén 许多人; *a great ~, a good ~* xiāngdāng duō 相当多; *how ~ do you need?* nǐ xūyào duōshao? 你需要多少?

mao (*Chinese money*) máo 毛

Mao badge Máo Zhǔxí xiàngzhāng 毛主席像章; **Mao jacket** Zhōngshānfú 中山服; **Mao Tse-tung, Mao Zedong** Máo Zédōng 毛泽东; **Mao Zedong thought** Máo Zédōng sīxiǎng 毛泽东思想

map 504

map *n* dìtú 地图

♦map out chóuhuà 筹划

maple fēng 枫

mar pòhuài 破坏

marathon (*race*) mǎlāsōng 马拉松

marble (*material*) dàlǐshí 大理石

March sānyuè 三月

march 1 *n* xíngjūn 行军; (*demonstration*) yóuxíng 游行 2 *v/i* (*in protest*) yóuxíng 游行

mare mǔmǎ 母马

margarine rénzào huángyóu 人造黄油

margin (*of page*) kòngbái 空白; (COM: *profit margin*) yínglì 盈利; *by a narrow* ~ hěnxiǎode chāshù 很小的差数

marginal (*slight*) hěnxiǎo 很小

marginally (*slightly*) shāowēi 稍微

marihuana, marijuana dàmá 大麻

marina yóutǐng tíngbó gǎng 游艇停泊港

marinade *n* yānpàozhī 腌泡汁

marinate yānpào 腌泡

marine 1 *adj* hǎiyáng 海洋 2 *n* MIL hǎilùbīng 海陆兵

marital hūnyīn 婚姻

maritime hǎishàng 海上

mark 1 *n* (*stain*) wūdiǎn 污点; (*sign, token*) biāozhì 标志; (*trace*) jìxiàng 迹象; EDU fēnshù 分数; *leave one's* ~ liúxià chíjiǔ yìnxiàng 留下持久印象 2 *v/t* (*stain*) liú hénjì yú 留痕迹于; EDU pīgǎi 批改; (*indicate*) biāomíng 标明; (*commemorate*) jìniàn 纪念 3 *v/i* (*of fabric*) liúyǒu wūjì 留有污迹

♦mark down *goods* jiàngdī biāojià 降低标价

♦mark out (*with a line etc*) huàxiàn biāochū 划线标出; *mark X out fig* (*set apart*) shǐ X yǔ zhòng bùtóng 使X与众不同

♦mark up *price* tígāo biāojià 提高标价; *goods* zài chéngběn shang jiājià 在成本上加价

marked (*definite*) míngquè 明确

marker (*highlighter*) biāojìbǐ 标记笔

market 1 *n* jíshì 集市; (*for particular commodity*) shìchǎng 市场; (*outlet*) xíngxiāo dìqū 行销地区; (*stock* ~) zhèngquàn shìchǎng 证券市场; *on the* ~ shàngshì 上市 2 *v/t* xiāoshòu 销售

market economy shìchǎng jīngjì 市场经济

market forces shìchǎng lìliàng 市场力量

marketing tuīxiāo 推销

market leader shìchǎng zhǔdǎo 市场主导; market-place shìchǎng 市场; market research shìchǎng diàochá 市场调查; market share shìchǎng zhànyǒulǜ 市场占有率

mark-up jiàgé tígāo 价格提高

marmalade chéngzijiàng 橙子酱

marquee dàzhàngpéng 大帐篷

marriage (*institution*) hūnyīnzhì 婚姻制; (*state of being married*) hūnyīn 婚姻; (*event*) hūnlǐ 婚礼

marriage certificate jiéhūn zhèngshū 结婚证书

marriage counselor hūnyīn gùwèn 婚姻顾问

married yǐhūn 已婚; *be ~ to X* yǔ X jiéhūn 与X结婚

marry jiéhūn 结婚; (*of priest*) zhǔchí hūnlǐ 主持婚礼; *get married* jiéhūn 结婚

marsh zhǎozé 沼泽

marshal *n* (*police officer*) jǐngchá 警察; (*official*) sīyí 司仪

marshmallow miánhuātáng 棉花糖

marshy yǒu zhǎozé 有沼泽

martial arts wǔshù 武术

martial law jièyánlìng 戒严令

martyr *n* xùndào zhě 殉道者

martyred miǎnqiǎng 勉强

marvel *n* qíyìde shìwù 奇异的事物

♦marvel at dàwéijīngyà 大为惊讶

marvelous jíhǎo 极好

Marx Mǎkèsī 马克思

Marxism Mǎkèsīzhǔyì 马克思主义

Marxist 1 *adj* Mǎkèsīzhǔyì 马克思主义 2 *n* Mǎkèsīzhǔyì zhě 马

克思主义者

Marxism-Leninism Mǎlièzhǔyì 马列主义

Marxist-Leninist Mǎlièzhǔyì zhě 马列主义者

mascara jiémáogāo 睫毛膏

mascot jíxiángde rénwù 吉祥的人物

masculine *also* GRAM nánzǐqì 男子气

masculinity (*virility*) yángxìng 阳性

mash *v/t* dǎochénghúzhuàng 捣成糊状

mashed potatoes tǔdòuní 土豆泥

mask 1 *n* miànjù 面具 **2** *v/t feelings* yǎngài 掩盖

masochism shòunüèkuáng 受虐狂

masochist shòunüèkuáng zhě 受虐狂者

mason níwǎjiàng 泥瓦匠

masonry (*stonework*) zhuānshí jiégòu 砖石结构; (*skill*) shígōng jìqiǎo 石工技巧

masquerade 1 *n fig* jiǎzhuāng 假装 **2** *v/i*: ~ **as X** wěizhuāng wéi X 伪装为X

mass[1] **1** *n* (*great amount*) zhòngduō 众多; (*body*) tuán 团; **the ~es** qúnzhòng 群众; **~es of** hěnduō 很多 **2** *v/i* jíjié 集结

mass[2] REL zuò mísa 作弥撒

massacre 1 *n* dàtúshā 大屠杀; F (*in sport*) cǎnbài 惨败 **2** *v/t* túshā 屠杀; F (*in sport*) yǐ xuánshū bǐfēn zhànshèng 以悬殊比分战胜

massage 1 *n* ànmó 按摩 **2** *v/t* zuò ànmó 作按摩; *figures* tiáozhěng 调整

massage parlor ànmóyuàn 按摩院

masseur nán ànmóshī 男按摩师

masseuse ànmó xiǎojiě 按摩小姐

massive jùdà 巨大

mass media dàzhòng chuánméi 大众传媒; **mass-produce** dàliàng shēngchǎn 大量生产; **mass production** dàliàng shèngchǎn 大量生产

mast (*of ship*) chuánwéi chuán qiáng 船桅; (*for radio signal*) tiānxiàntǎ 天线塔

master 1 *n* (*of dog*) zhǔrén 主人; (*of ship*) chuánzhǎng 船长; **be a ~ of X** zhǎngwò X 掌握X **2** *v/t skill, language* jīngtōng 精通; *situation* kòngzhì 控制

master bedroom zhǔwòshì 主卧室

master key wànnéng yàoshi 万能钥匙

masterly gāomíng 高明

mastermind 1 *n* juécè zhě 决策者 **2** *v/t* mùhòu cèhuà 幕后策划; **Master of Arts** wénkē shuòshì 文科硕士; **master of ceremonies** sīyí 司仪; **masterpiece** jiézuò 杰作; **master's (degree)** shuòshì 硕士

mastery jīngtōng 精通

masturbate shǒuyín 手淫

mat *n* (*for floor*) diàn 垫; (*for table*) gérèdiàn 隔热垫

match[1] (*for cigarette*) huǒchái 火柴

match[2] **1** *n* (*competition*) bǐsài 比赛; **be no ~ for X** bùnéng yǔ X pǐdí 不能与X匹敌; **meet one's ~** qígǔ xiāngdāng 旗鼓相当 **2** *v/t* (*be the same as*) yǔ ... yīyàng 与 ... 一样; ~ **X** (*equal*) yǔ X pǐdí 与X匹敌 **3** *v/i* (*of colors, patterns*) xiāngpèi 相配

matchbox huǒcháihé 火柴盒

matching *adj* xiétiáo 协调

mate 1 *n* (*of animal*) ǒu 偶; NAUT fùshǒu 副手 **2** *v/i* jiāopèi 交配

material 1 *n* (*fabric*) bùliào 布料; (*substance*) cáiliào 材料 **2** *adj* wùzhì 物质

materialism wéiwù zhǔyì 唯物主义

materialist wéiwù zhǔyì zhě 唯物主义者

materialistic wéiwùlùn 唯物论

materialize chéngxiàn 呈现

materials yuánliào 原料

maternal mǔqīn fāngmiàn 母亲方面

maternity mǔxìng 母性

maternity dress yùnfù fúzhuāng

孕妇服装；**maternity leave**
chǎnjià 产假；**maternity ward**
chǎnkē bìngfáng 产科病房

math shùxué 数学

mathematical *calculations, formula*
shùxué 数学；*mind, person* luójí
逻辑

mathematician shùxuéjiā 数学家

mathematics shùxué 数学

matinée xiàwǔchǎng 下午场

matriarch nǚzúzhǎng 女族长

matrimony hūnyīn 婚姻

matt cūmiàn 粗面

matter (*affair*) shìqing 事情；PHYS
wùzhì 物质；*as a ~ of course*
lǐsuǒdāngrán 理所当然；*as a ~
of fact* shìshí shang 事实上；
what's the ~? zěnmele? 怎么
了？；*no ~ what she says* bùguǎn
tā shuō shénme 不管她说什么
2 *v/i* yàojǐn 要紧；*it doesn't ~*
méiguānxì 没关系

matter-of-fact búdònggǎnqíng 不
动感情

mattress chuángdiàn 床垫

mature 1 *adj* chéngshú 成熟 **2** *v/i*
(*of person*) chéngshú 成熟；(*of
insurance policy etc*) dàoqī 到期

maturity chéngshú 成熟

maximize zēngzhì zuìdà xiàndù 增
至最大限度

maximum 1 *adj* zuìgāo/dà 最高/
大 **2** *n* zuìduō 最多

May wǔyuè 五月

may ◊ (*possibility*) yěxǔ 也许；*it ~
rain* kěnéng huì xiàyǔ 可能会下
雨；*you ~ be right* nǐ yěxǔ duì 你
也许对；*it ~ not happen* zhèshìr
kěnéng búhuì fāshēng 这事儿可
能不会发生 ◊ (*permission*) kěyǐ
可以；*I help / smoke?* wǒ kěyǐ
bāngmáng/xīyān ma? 我可以帮
忙/吸烟吗？；*you ~ if you like*
nǐ yuànyì de huà, kěyǐ 你愿意的
话，可以

maybe kěnéng 可能

May Day Wǔyī Jié 五一节

mayo, mayonnaise ◊
dànhuángjiàng 蛋黄酱

mayor shìzhǎng 市长

maze mígōng 迷宫；*fig* qūjìng 曲

径

MB (= *megabyte*) zhàozìjié 兆字
节

MBA (= *Master of Business Administration*) ◊ gōngshāng
guǎnlǐxué shuòshì 工商管理学
硕士

MBO (= *management buyout*)
guǎnlǐ rényuán shōumǎi 管理人
员收买

MD (= *Doctor of Medicine*) dàifū
大夫

me wǒ 我；*it's ~* shì wǒ 是我

meadow cǎopíng 草坪

meager shǎoliàng 少量

meal cān 餐

mealtime jìncān shíjiān 进餐时间

mean¹ (*with money*) lìnsè 吝啬；
(*nasty*) bēibǐ 卑鄙

mean² **1** *v/t* (*intend*) yìzhǐ 意指；
(*signify*) biǎoshì 表示；*~ to do X*
dǎsuàn zuò X 打算做 X；*be ~t for*
(*of remark*) zhǐdìng 指定；*be ~t
for X* yǒuyì wèi X zhǔnbèi 有意
为 X 准备；*doesn't it ~ anything
to you?* (*doesn't it matter?*) zhè
nándào yǔ nǐ wúguān ma? 这难
道与你无关吗？ **2** *v/i*：*~ well*
huái hǎoyì 怀好意

meaning (*of word*) hányì 含义

meaningful (*comprehensible*) yǒu
yìyì 有意义；(*constructive*) jījí 积
极；*glance* yìwèi shēncháng 意味
深长

meaningless *sentence etc* wúyìyì 无
意义；*gesture* kōngdòng 空洞

means (*financial*) cáiyuán 财源；
(*way*) fāngfǎ 方法；*~ of transport*
jiāotōng gōngjù 交通工具；*by all
~* (*certainly*) dāngrán kěyǐ 当然可
以；*by no ~ rich / poor* gēnběn bù
fù/qióng 根本不富/穷；*by ~ of*
yòng 用

meantime: *in the ~* tóngshí 同时

measles mázhěn 麻疹

measure 1 *n* (*step*) cuòshī 措施；
(*certain amount*) chéngdù 程度
2 *v/t* cèliáng 测量 **3** *v/i* yǒu ...
cháng/kuān 有 ... 长/宽；*it ~s 15
yards by 5 yards* cháng shíwǔ mǎ,
kuān wǔ mǎ 长十五码，宽五码

♦measure out liángchū 量出
♦measure up to: ~ **X** dádào X de biāozhǔn 达到 X 的标准
measurement (*action*) cèliáng 测量; (*dimension*) chǐcun 尺寸; ***system of*** ~ dùliánghéng 度量衡
meat ròu 肉
meatball ròuwánzi 肉丸子
meatloaf ròugāo 肉糕
mechanic jìgōng 技工
mechanical *device* jīxiè 机械; *gesture* dāibǎn 呆板
mechanically jīxiè 机械; *do sth* dāibǎn 呆板
mechanism jīxiè zhuāngzhì 机械装置
mechanize shǐ jīxièhuà 使机械化
medal jiǎngzhāng 奖章
medalist jiǎngzhāng huòdé zhě 奖章获得者
meddle gānshè 干涉
media: *the* ~ dàzhòng chuánméi 大众传媒
media hype méitǐ xuànrǎn 媒体渲染
median strip zhōngyāng fēnchēdài 中央分车带
mediate tiáojiě 调解
mediation tiáojiě 调解
mediator tiáojiěrén 调解人
medical 1 *adj* yīliáo 医疗 2 *n* tǐgé jiǎnchá 体格检查
medical certificate jiànkāng zhèngshū 健康证书
Medicare yīliáo bǎozhàng fāng'àn 医疗保障方案
medicated hán yàowù 含药物
medication yào 药
medicinal yǒu yàoxìng 有药性
medicine (*science*) yīxué 医学; (*medication*) yào 药
medieval zhōngshìjì 中世纪
mediocre píngyōng 平庸
mediocrity (*of work etc*) píngyōng 平庸; (*person*) píngyōngde rén 平庸的人
meditate dǎzuò 打坐
meditation dǎzuò 打坐
medium 1 *adj* (*average*) zhōngděng 中等; *steak* bāfēnshóu 八分熟 2 *n* (*in size*) zhōnghào 中号;

(*vehicle*) méijiè 媒介; (*spiritualist*) língméi 灵媒
medium-sized zhōnghào 中号
medium wave RAD zhōngbō 中波
medley (*assortment*) hùnhé 混合
meek wēnshùn 温顺
meet 1 *v/t* jiàn 见; (*collect*) jiē 接; (*of eyes*) xiāngyù 相遇; (*satisfy*) dádào 达到; ~ **X** (*in competition*) yǔ X bǐsài 与 X 比赛 2 *v/i* jiànmiàn 见面; (*in competition*) bǐsài 比赛; (*of eyes*) xiāngyù 相遇; (*of committee etc*) jùhé 聚合 3 *n* SP yùndònghuì 运动会
♦meet with *person* huìwù 会晤; *opposition, approval etc* zāodào 遭到
meeting huìyì 会议; *he's in a* ~ tā zài kāihuì 他在开会
meeting place huìchǎng 会场
megabyte COMPUT zhào 兆
Mekong River Méigōnghé 湄公河
melancholy *adj* yōuyù 忧郁
mellow 1 *adj* róuhé 柔和 2 *v/i* (*of person*) wēnhé 温和
melodious yuè'ěr 悦耳
melodramatic gǎnqíng kuāzhāng 感情夸张
melody xuánlǜ 旋律
melon guā 瓜
melt *v/t & v/i* rónghuà 融化
♦melt away *fig* xiāoshī 消失
♦melt down *v/t metal* rónghuǐ 熔毁
melting pot *fig* rónglú 熔炉
member chéngyuán 成员; ~ *of Congress* guóhuì yìyuán 国会议员
membership chéngyuán zīgé 成员资格; (*number of members*) chéngyuán rénshù 成员人数
membership card chéngyuánzhèng 成员证
membrane mó 膜
memento jìniànpǐn 纪念品
memo bèiwànglù 备忘录
memoirs huíyìlù 回忆录
memorable zhídé jìniàn 值得纪念
memorial 1 *adj* jìniàn 纪念 2 *n*

jìniànbēi 纪念碑

Memorial Day Zhènwáng Jiàngshì jìniànrì 阵亡将士纪念日

memorize jìzhù 记住

memory (*recollection*) jìyì 记忆; (*power of recollection*) jìyìlì 记忆力; (COMPUT: *device*) cúnchǔqì 存储器; (COMPUT: *capacity*) cúnchǔlì 存储力; *have a good / bad ~* jìyìlì hǎo / huài 记忆力好 / 坏; *in ~ of X* zuòwéi duì X de jìniàn 作为对X的纪念

menace 1 n (*threat*) wēixié 威胁; (*person*) wēixiǎn zhě 危险者 **2** v/t wēixié 威胁

menacing wēixié 威胁

mend 1 v/t xiūlǐ 修理 **2** n xiūlǐ 修理; *be on the ~* (*after illness*) zài hǎozhuǎn zhōng 在好转中

menial adj dīxià 低下

meningitis nǎomóyán 脑膜炎

menopause juéjīngqī 绝经期

men's room náncè 男厕

menstruate xíngjīng 行经

menstruation xíngjīngqī 行经期

mental jīngshén 精神; F (*crazy*) fēng 疯

mental arithmetic xīnsuàn 心算; **mental cruelty** jīngshén nüèdài 精神虐待; **mental hospital** jīngshénbìngyuàn 精神病院; **mental illness** jīngshénbìng 精神病

mentality xīnlǐ zhuàngtài 心理状态

mentally (*inwardly*) zài nè ixīn 在内心; *calculate etc* xīnlǐ 心里; *~ handicapped* dīnéng 低能; *~ ill* xīnlǐ jíbìng 心理疾病

mention 1 n tíjí 提及 **2** v/t tídào 提到; *don't ~ it* búyòng kèqì 不用客气

mentor liángshīyìyǒu 良师益友

menu (*for food*, COMPUT) càidān 菜单

mercenary 1 adj túlì 图利 **2** n MIL gùyōngbīng 雇佣兵

merchandise huòpǐn 货品

merchant shāngrén 商人

merciful réncí 仁慈

mercifully (*thankfully*) xìng'ér 幸而

merciless wúqíng 无情

mercury shuǐyín 水银

mercy réncí 仁慈; *be at X's ~* rènyóu X bǎibù 任由X摆布

mere adj zhǐbúguò 只不过

merely jǐnjǐn 仅仅

merge v/i (*of two lines etc*) héwéiyìtǐ 合为一体; (*of companies*) hébìng 合并

merger COM hébìng 合并

merit 1 n (*worth*) jiàzhí 价值; (*advantage*) yōudiǎn 优点 **2** v/t zhíde 值得

merry yúkuài 愉快; *Merry Christmas!* Shèngdàn kuàilè! 圣诞快乐!

merry-go-round xuánzhuǎn mùmǎ 旋转木马

mesh n wǎngyǎn 网眼

mess n (*untidiness*) zāngluàn 脏乱; (*trouble*) kùnjìng 困境; *be a ~* (*of room, desk, hair*) záluàn 杂乱; (*of situation, life*) yītuánzāo 一团糟

♦**mess around 1** v/i xiānào 瞎闹 **2** v/t person hùnong 糊弄

♦**mess around with** bǎinòng 摆弄; *s.o.'s wife* sītōng 私通

♦**mess up** room, papers nòngluàn 弄乱; task gǎozāo 搞糟; plans, marriage gǎohuài 搞坏

message (*of movie, book*) qǐshì 启示; *can I leave a ~?* wǒ kěyǐ liúyán ma? 我可以留言吗?

messenger (*courier*) tōngxìnyuán 通信员

messy room língluàn 凌乱; person lāta 邋遢; job zāng 脏; divorce, situation fùzá 复杂

metabolism xīnchéndàixiè 新陈代谢

metal n & adj jīnshǔ 金属

metallic (sì) jīnshǔ (似) 金属

meteor liúxīng 流星

meteoric fig fēisù 飞速

meteorite yǔnxīng 陨星

meteorological qìxiàng 气象

meteorologist qìxiàngxuéjiā 气象学家

meteorology qìxiàngxué 气象学

meter¹ (*for measuring*) biǎo 表；
(*parking* ~) qì 器
meter² (*unit of length*) mǐ 米
method fāngfǎ 方法
methodical yǒutiáolǐ 有条理
methodically yǒutiáobùwěn 有条
不紊
meticulous jíjīngxì 极精细
metric gōngzhì 公制
metropolis dà dūshì 大都市
metropolitan *adj* dà dūshì 大都市
mew → *miaow*
Mexican 1 *adj* Mòxīgē 墨西哥
2 *n* Mòxīgē rén 墨西哥人
Mexico Mòxīgē 墨西哥
mezzanine (**floor**) zhōngjiān
lóucéng 中间楼层
miaow 1 *n* miāo 喵 2 *v/i* zuò
miāomiāo shēng 作喵喵声
mickey mouse *adj* F *course,
qualification* yějī 野鸡
microchip wēijīngpiàn 微晶片；
microcosm wēiguān shìjiè 微观
世界；microelectronics
wēidiànzǐxué 微电子学；micro-
film suōwēi jiāojuǎn 缩微胶卷；
microphone màikèfēng 麦克风；
microprocessor wēichǔlǐjī 微处
理机；microscope xiǎnwēijìng
显微镜；microscopic jíwēixiǎo
极微小；microwave (*oven*)
wēibōlú 微波炉
midair: *in* ~ zài bànkōngzhōng 在
半空中
midday zhōngwǔ 中午
middle 1 *adj* zhōngjiān 中间 2 *n*
zhōngyāng 中央；*in the* ~ *of X*
(*floor, room*) zài X zhōngyāng 在 X
中央；*in the* ~ *of* (*period of time*)
zài … zhōng 在 … 中；*be in the* ~
of doing X zhèngzài zuò X
dāngzhōng 正在做 X 当中
middle-aged zhōngnián 中年；
Middle Ages Zhōngshìjì 中世
纪；middle-class *adj* zhōngchǎn
jiējí 中产阶级；middle classes
zhōngchǎn jiējí 中产阶级；Mid-
dle East Zhōngdōng 中东；Mid-
dle Kingdom Zhōngguó 中国；
middleman jīngjìrén 经纪人；
middle name zhōngjiānmíng 中

间名；middleweight *n* (*boxer*)
zhōngliàngjí 中量级
middling zhōngděng 中等
midget *adj* xiùzhēn 袖珍
midnight wǔyè 午夜；*at* ~ wǔyèshí
午夜时；midsummer zhòngxià
仲夏；midway zhōngtú 中途；
midweek *adv* lǐbài zhōng 礼拜
中；Midwest Zhōngxībù 中西
部；midwife zhùchǎnshì 助产士；
midwinter zhòngdōng 仲冬
might¹ yěxǔ 也许；*I* ~ *be late* wǒ
yěxǔ chídào 我也许迟到；*it* ~
rain tiān yěxǔ yào xiàyǔ 天也许
要下雨；*it* ~ *never happen* zhè
yěxǔ yǒngyuǎn búhuì fāshēng 这
也许永远不会发生；*I* ~ *have
lost it* wǒ yěxǔ bǎ tā gěi diūle 我
也许把它给丢了；*he* ~ *have
left* tā yěxǔ yǐjīng zǒule 他也许
已经走了；*you* ~ *as well spend
the night here* nǐ háibùrú jiù zài
zhèr guòyè 你还不如就在这儿
过夜；*you* ~ *have told me!* nǐ zá
méi gàosu wǒ! 你咋没告诉我！
might² *n* (*power*) lìliàng 力量
mighty 1 *adj* qiángyǒulì 强有力
2 *adv* F (*extremely*) jíqí 极其
migraine piāntóutòng 偏头痛
migrant worker liúdòng gōngrén
流动工人
migrate qiānyí 迁移
migration qiānjū 迁居
mike màikèfēng 麦克风
mild wēnhé 温和
mildew méi 霉
mildly shìdù 适度
mildness wēnhé 温和
mile yīnglǐ 英里；~*s better* / *easier*
hǎo / róngyì déduō 好 / 容易得多
mileage lǐchéng 里程
milestone *fig* lǐchéngbēi 里程碑
militant 1 *adj* yǒu zhàndòuxìng 有
战斗性 2 *n* jījí fènzi 积极分子
military 1 *adj* jūnshì 军事 2 *n*: *the*
~ jūnduì 军队
military academy jūnshì xuéyuàn
军事学院
militia mínbīng 民兵
milk 1 *n* nǎi 奶 2 *v/t* jǐnǎi 挤奶
milk chocolate niúnǎi qiǎokèlì 牛

奶巧克力

milk shake nǎixī 奶昔

mill n (*for grain*) mòfáng 磨坊; (*for textiles*) máofǎngchǎng 毛纺厂

♦ **mill around** luànzhuàn 乱转

millennium yīqiānnián 一千年

milligram(me) háokè 毫克

millimeter háomǐ 毫米

million bǎiwàn 百万; **hundred** ~ yì 亿

millionaire bǎiwànfùwēng 百万富翁

mime v/t dǎ yǎyǔ 打哑语

mimic 1 n hào xuéyàng zhě 好学样者 **2** v/t mófǎng 模仿

mince v/t qiēsuì 切碎

mincemeat ròuxiàn 肉馅

mind 1 n tóunǎo 头脑; **it's all in your** ~ dōu zài nǐde nǎohǎilǐ 都在你的脑海里; **be out of one's** ~ fāfēng 发疯; **bear** or **keep X in** ~ jìzhù X 记住X; **I've a good** ~ **to** ... wǒ zhēn xiǎng ... 我真想 ...; **change one's** ~ gǎibiàn zhǔyì 改变主意; **it didn't enter my** ~ gēnběn méi xiǎngdào 根本没想到; **give X a piece of one's** ~ zébèi X 责备X; **make up one's** ~ juédìng 决定; **have X on one's** ~ guàlù X 挂虑X; **keep one's** ~ **on X** zhuānxīnyú X 专心于X **2** v/t (*look after*) zhàokàn 照看; (*object to*) jièyì 介意; (*heed*) liúxīn 留心; **I don't** ~ **what we do** wǒ bú zàihu zánmen zuò shénme 我不在乎咱们做什么; **do you** ~ **if I smoke?, do you** ~ **my smoking?** wǒ chōuyān nǐ bù fǎnduì ma? 我抽烟你不反对吗？; **would you** ~ **opening the window?** qǐng bǎ chuāngzi dǎkāi hǎoma? 请把窗子打开好吗？; ~ **the step!** zhùyì jiǎoxià! 注意脚下！; ~ **your own business!** bùguǎn nǐde shì! 不关你的事！ **3** v/i: ~**!** (*be careful*) dāngxīn 当心; **never** ~**!** méiguānxi! 没关系！; **I don't** ~ wǒ wúsuǒwèi 我无所谓

mind-boggling jīngrén 惊人

mindless *violence* wútóunǎo 无头脑

mine[1] *pron* wǒde 我的; **a friend of** ~ wǒde péngyǒu 我的朋友

mine[2] **1** n (*for coal etc*) kuàng 矿 **2** v/i (*for coal etc*) kāicǎi 开采; ~ **for** kāicǎi 开采

mine[3] **1** n (*explosive*) dìléi 地雷 **2** v/t pūléi 铺雷

minefield MIL bùléiqū 布雷区; *fig* qiánzài kùnnánqū 潜在困难区

miner kuànggōng 矿工

mineral n kuàngwù 矿物

mineral water kuàngquánshuǐ 矿泉水

minesweeper NAUT sǎoléi tǐng 扫雷艇

Ming Dynasty Míngcháo 明朝

mingle v/i (*of sounds, smells*) hùnhé 混合; (*at party*) jiāowǎng 交往

mini (*skirt*) chāoduǎnqún 超短裙

minibus xiǎoxíng gōnggòngqìchē 小型公共汽车

miniature adj xiùzhēnxíng 袖珍型

minimal zuìxiǎo 最小

minimize jiānzhì zuìxiǎo 减至最小; (*downplay*) jìnkěnéng jiǎnshǎo 尽可能减少

minimum 1 adj zuìshǎo 最少 **2** n zuìdī xiàndù 最低限度

minimum wage zuìdī gōngzī 最低工资

mining kuàngyè 矿业

miniskirt chāoduǎnqún 超短裙

minister POL bùzhǎng 部长; REL mùshī 牧师

ministerial bùzhǎng 部长

ministry POL bù 部

mink (*fur*) diāopí 貂皮; (*coat*) diāopí dàyī 貂皮大衣

minor 1 adj cìyào 次要; **in D** ~ MUS D xiǎodiào D小调 **2** n LAW wèichéngniánrén 未成年人

minority shǎoshù 少数; **be in the** ~ zhànshǎoshù 占少数

mint n (*herb*) bòhe 薄荷; (*chocolate*) bòhe diǎnxīn 薄荷点心; (*hard candy*) bòhe táng 薄荷糖

minus 1 n (~ *sign*) jiǎnhào 减号 **2** prep jiǎnqù 减去

minuscule wēixiǎo 微小

minute[1] n (*of time*) fēnzhōng 分钟

in a ~ (soon) yíhuìr 一会儿; *just a ~* děngyíxià 等一下

minute² *adj (tiny)* wēixiǎo 微小; *(detailed)* xiángxì 详细; *in ~ detail* jùtǐ xìzhì 具体细致

minutely *(in detail)* xiángxì 详细

minutes *(of meeting)* jìlù 记录

miracle qíjì 奇迹

miraculous qíjìbān 奇迹般

miraculously qíjì 奇迹

mirage hǎishì shènlóu 海市蜃楼

mirror 1 *n* jìngzi 镜子; MOT *(rear-view)* hòushìjìng 后视镜; *(wing)* dàoguāngjìng 到光镜 **2** *v/t* fǎnshè 反射

misanthropist yànwù rénlèi zhě 厌恶人类者

misapprehension: *be under a ~* zài wùjiě de qíngkuàng xià 在误解的情况下

misbehave jǔzhǐbúdàng 举止不当

misbehavior búdàngde jǔzhǐ 不当的举止

miscalculate *v/t & v/i* wùsuàn 误算

miscalculation wùsuàn 误算

miscarriage MED liúchǎn 流产; *~ of justice* wùpàn 误判

miscarry *(of plan)* shībài 失败

miscellaneous gèzhǒng gèyàng 各种各样

mischief *(naughtiness)* èzuòjù 恶作剧

mischievous *(naughty)* wánpí 顽皮; *(malicious)* yǒuhài 有害

misconception wùjiě 误解

misconduct wánhū zhíshǒu 玩忽职守

misconstrue wùhuì 误会

misdemeanor qīngzuì 轻罪

miser shǒucáinú 守财奴

miserable *(unhappy)* nánguò 难过; *weather, performance* lìngrén búkuài 令人不快

miserly *amount* shǎodékělián 少得可怜

misery *(unhappiness)* tòngkǔ 痛苦; *(wretchedness)* bēicǎn 悲惨

misfire *(of joke, scheme)* wèidé yùqīxiàoguǒ 未得预期效果

misfit *(in society)* yǔ shèhuì gégébúrù de rén 与社会格格不入的人

misfortune búxìng 不幸

misgivings gùlù 顾虑

misguided wùdǎo 误导

mishandle chǔlǐbúdàng 处理不当

mishap búxìng shìgù 不幸事故

misinterpret qūjiě 曲解

misinterpretation qūjiě 曲解

misjudge *person, situation* cuòwù gūjì 错误估计

mislay yíshī 遗失

mislead yǐndǎocuò 引导错

misleading shǐrén wùjiě 使人误解

mismanage guǎnlǐ búshàn 管理不善

mismanagement búdàngde guǎnlǐ 不当的管理

mismatch pèihé búdàng 配合不当

misplaced *loyalty, enthusiasm* cuòwùde fùchū 错误地付出

misprint *n* cuòyìn 错印

mispronounce fācuò 发错

mispronunciation fāyīn cuòwù 发音错误

misread *word, figures* dúcuò 读错; *situation* wùjiě 误解

misrepresent wāiqū 歪曲

miss¹: *Miss Wang* Wáng xiǎojiě 王小姐

miss² **1** *n* SP wèijīzhòng 未击中; *give X a ~ meeting, party etc* búqù X 不去 X **2** *v/t (not hit)* wèijīzhòng 未击中; *(emotionally)* xiǎngniàn 想念; *bus, train, plane* méigǎnshàng 没赶上; *(not notice, fail to take)* cuòguò 错过; *(not be present at)* bùchūxí 不出席; *you've just ~ed him (not met)* tā gāng zǒule 他刚走了 **3** *v/i* wèijīzhòng 未击中

misshapen jīxíng 畸形

missile *(guided)* dǎodàn 导弹

missing diūshī 丢失; *be ~* xiàluòbùmíng 下落不明

mission *(task)* rènwù 任务; *(people)* shǐmìngtuán 使命团

missionary REL chuánjiàoshì 传教士

misspell pīnxiěcuò 拼写错

mist bówù 薄雾

♦ **mist over** (*of eyes*) móhu 模糊

♦ **mist up** (*of window etc*) méngshàng shuǐqì 蒙上水汽

mistake 1 *n* cuòwù 错误; *make a ~* fàn cuòwù 犯错误; *by ~* cuòwùde 错误地 **2** *v/t* xuǎncuò 选错; *~ X for Y* wùjiāng X rènzuò Y 误将 X 认作 Y

mistaken: *be ~* nòngcuò 弄错

mister xiānsheng 先生

mistress (*lover*) qíngfù 情妇; (*of servant, dog*) nǚzhǔrén 女主人

mistrust 1 *n* búxìnrèn 不信任 **2** *v/t* huáiyí 怀疑

misty *weather* bówù lǒngzhào 薄雾笼罩; *eyes* móhu 模糊; *color* méngménglónglóng 朦朦胧胧

misunderstand wùjiě 误解

misunderstanding (*mistake*) wùjiě 误解; (*argument*) zhēngzhí 争执

misuse 1 *n* wùyòng 误用 **2** *v/t* yòngcuò 用错

mitigating circumstances jiǎnqīngde qíngjié 减轻的情节

mitt (*in baseball*) bàngqiú shǒutào 棒球手套

mitten liánzhǐ shǒutào 连指手套

mix 1 *n* (*mixture*) hùnhé 混合; (*in cooking*) hùnhéwù 混合物; (*cooking: ready to use*) hùnhé pèiliào 混合配料 **2** *v/t* hùnhé 混合; *cement* jiǎohuo 搅和 **3** *v/i* (*socially*) xiāngchǔ 相处

♦ **mix up** gǎoluàn 搞乱; *mix X up with Y* hùnxiáo X hé Y 混淆 X 和 Y; *be mixed up* (*emotionally*) míwǎng 迷惘; (*of figures, papers*) nòngluàn 弄乱; *be mixed up in X* yǔ X yǒu qiānlián 与 X 有牵连; *get mixed up with X* yǔ X sīhùn 与 X 厮混

♦ **mix with** (*associate with*) jiāowǎng 交往

mixed *feelings* fùzá 复杂; *reactions, reviews* gèzhǒng gèyàng 各种各样

mixed marriage yìzú tōnghūn 异族通婚

mixer (*for food*) jiǎobànqì 搅拌器; (*drink*) tiáopèi yǐnliào 调配饮料; *she's a good ~* tā hěn héqún 她很合群

mixture hùnhé(wù) 混合 (物); (*medicine*) fùfāngyào 复方药

mix-up hùnluàn 混乱

moan 1 *n* (*of pain*) shēnyín 呻吟; (*complaint*) láosao 牢骚 **2** *v/i* (*in pain*) shēnyín 呻吟; (*complain*) bàoyuàn 抱怨

mob 1 *n* bàomín 暴民 **2** *v/t* bāowéi 包围

mobile 1 *adj person* kě línghuó zǒudòng 可灵活走动; (*that can be moved*) kěyídòng 可移动 **2** *n* (*for decoration*) fēngdòng shìwù 风动饰物; *Br* (*phone*) yídòng 移动, dàgēdà 大哥大

mobile home huódòng zhùfáng 活动住房

mobile phone *Br* yídòng 移动; (*formal use*) shǒutí diànhuà 手提电话

mobility yídòngxìng 移动性

mobster dǎitú 歹徒

mock 1 *adj* mónǐ 摹拟 **2** *v/t* qǔxiào 取笑

mockery (*derision*) cháonòng 嘲弄; (*travesty*) duì zhèngyì de wāiqū 对正义的歪曲

mock-up (*model*) dàmóxíng 大模型

mode (*form*) fāngshì 方式; COMPUT cāozuò fāngfǎ 操作方法

model 1 *adj employee, husband* mófàn 模范; *boat, plane* móxíng 模型 **2** *n* (*miniature*) chúxíng 雏型; (*pattern*) móshì 模式; (*fashion ~*) mótèr 模特儿; *male ~* nán mótèr 男模特儿 **3** *v/t* zhǎnshì 展示 **4** *v/i* (*for designer, artist*) zuò mótèr 作模特儿

modem tiáozhì jiětiáoqì 调制解调器

moderate 1 *adj* shìdù 适度; POL wēnhé 温和 **2** *n* POL wēnhépài 温和派 **3** *v/t* biànhéhuǎn 变和缓 **4** *v/i* jiǎnruò 减弱

moderately shìdù 适度

moderation (*restraint*) jiézhì 节制; *in* ~ shìdù 适度

modern xiàndài 现代

modernization xiàndàihuà 现代化

modernize 1 *v/t* shǐxiàndàihuà 使现代化 **2** *v/i* (*of business, country*) xiàndàihuà 现代化

modest *house, apartment* pǔsù 朴素; (*small*) búdà 不大; (*not conceited*) qiānxùn 谦逊

modesty (*of house, apartment*) pǔsù 朴素; (*of wage, improvement*) shìdù 适度; (*lack of conceit*) qiānxùn 谦逊

modification xiūgǎi 修改

modify xiūgǎi 修改

modular *furniture* dāntǐ shèjì 单体设计

module dāntǐ 单体; (*space* ~) cāng 舱

moist cháoshī 潮湿

moisten nòngshī 弄湿

moisture shīrùn 湿润

moisturizer (*for skin*) rùnfūshuāng 润肤霜

molar móyá 磨牙

molasses tángjiāng 糖浆

mold[1] *n* (*on food*) méi 霉

mold[2] **1** *n* múzi 模子 **2** *v/t clay etc* jiāozhù 浇铸; *character, person* lèixíng 类型

moldy *food* fāméi 发霉

mole (*on skin*) zhì 痣

molecular fēnzǐ 分子

molecule fēnzǐ 分子

molest *child, woman* sāorǎo 骚扰

mollycoddle nì'ài 溺爱

molten rónghuà 熔化

mom F mā 妈

moment piànkè 片刻; *at the* ~ xiànzài 现在; *for the* ~ zànshí 暂时

momentarily (*for a moment*) shùnjiān 瞬间; (*in a moment*) jíkè 即刻

momentary duǎnzàn 短暂

momentous jízhòngyào 极重要

momentum dònglì 动力

monarch jūnzhǔ 君主

monastery xiūdàoyuàn 修道院

monastic xiūdào 修道

Monday xīngqīyī 星期一

monetary huòbì 货币

money qián 钱

money-lender fàngzhài zhě 放债者; **money market** jīnróng shìchǎng 金融市场; **money order** huìkuǎndān 汇款单

Mongolia Měnggǔ 蒙古

Mongolian 1 *adj* Měnggǔ 蒙古 **2** *n* (*person*) Měnggǔ rén 蒙古人

mongrel zázhǒnggǒu 杂种狗

monitor 1 *n* COMPUT jiānshìqì 监视器 **2** *v/t* chíxù guānchá 持续观察

monk héshàng 和尚; *become a* ~ chūjiā 出家

monkey hóu 猴; F (*child*) tiáopíguǐ 调皮鬼

♦**monkey around with** F bǎinòng 摆弄

monkey wrench huódòng bānshǒu 活动扳手

monogram *n* zìshǒu 字首

monogrammed zìshǒu 字首

monolog dúbái 独白

monopolize lǒngduàn 垄断

monopoly dúzhàn 独占

monosodium glutamate wèijīng 味精

monotonous dāndiào fáwèi 单调乏味

monotony wúliáo 无聊

monsoon jìfēng 季风

monsoon season jìfēng yǔjì 季风雨季

monster *n* yāoguài 妖怪

monstrosity jīxíng 畸形

monstrous jīxíng 畸形

month yuè 月

monthly 1 *adj* měiyuè 每月 **2** *adv* měiyuè yícì 每月一次 **3** *n* (*magazine*) yuèkān 月刊

monument jìniànbēi 纪念碑

mood (*frame of mind*) xīnqíng 心情; (*bad* ~) huàiqíngxù 坏情绪; (*of meeting, country*) qìfēn 气氛; *be in a good / bad* ~ qíngxù hǎo / huài 情绪好 / 坏; *be in the* ~ *for* yǒu xìngzhì 有兴致

moody xǐnùwúcháng 喜怒无常

moon *n* yuèliang 月亮

moonlight 1 *n* yuèguāng 月光

2 *v/i* F jiānzhí 兼职
moonlit yǒu yuèguāng 有月光
moor *v/t boat* tíngbó 停泊
moorings tíngbó qū 停泊区
moose tuólù 驼鹿
mop 1 *n* tuōbù 拖布 **2** *v/t floor* tuōdì 拖地; *eyes, face* cā 擦
♦**mop up** cājìng 擦净; MIL sùqīng 肃清
mope yùyùbúlè 郁郁不乐
moral 1 *adj* dàodé 道德; *person, behavior* jiǎngdàodé 讲道德 **2** *n* (*of story*) yùyì 寓意; **~s** xíngwéide biāozhǔn 行为的标准
morale shìqì 士气
morality měidé 美德
morbid bìngtài 病态
more 1 *adj* gèngduō 更多; *we need ~ time* wǒmen xūyao géngduo de shíjiān 我门需要更多的时间; *some ~ tea?* zài láidiǎnr chá ma? 再来点儿茶吗？; *~ and ~ students / time* yuèláiyuè-duōde xuésheng / shíjiān 越来越多的学生 / 时间 **2** *adv* gèng(duō) 更（多）; *~ important* gèng zhòngyào 更重要; *~ often* gèng pínfán 更频繁; *~ and ~* yuèfā(duō) 越发（多）; *~ or less* dàzhì 大致; *once ~* zàiyícì 再一次; *~ than* duōyú 多于; *I don't live there any ~* wǒ búzài zhù nàrle 我不再住那儿了 **3** *pron* gèngduōde shùliàng 更多的数量; *do you want some ~?* nǐ hái yàodiǎnr ma? 你还要点儿吗？; *a little ~* zài lái yìdiǎndiǎn 再来一点点
moreover érqiě 而且
morgue tíngshīfáng 停尸房
morning (*before 10am*) zǎochén 早晨; (*between 10am and 12pm*) shàngwǔ 上午; *in the ~* (*before 10am*) zǎochén 早晨; (*between 10am and 12pm*) shàngwǔ 上午; (*tomorrow: before 10am*) míngtiān zǎochén 明天早晨; (*tomorrow: between 10am and 12pm*) míngtiān shàngwǔ 明天上午; *this ~* (*before 10am*) jīntiān zǎochén 今天早晨; (*usually between 10am and 12pm*) jīntiān shàngwǔ 今天上午; *tomorrow ~* (*before 10am*) míngtiān zǎochén 明天早晨; (*between 10am and 12pm*) míngtiān shàngwǔ 明天上午; *good ~* (*before 10am*) zǎochén hǎo 早晨好; (*between 10am and 12pm*) shàngwǔ hǎo 上午好
moron shǎguā 傻瓜
morose guāipǐ 乖僻
morphine mǎfēi 吗啡
morsel: *a ~ of* yīxiǎopiàn 一小片
mortal 1 *adj* bìsǐ 必死; *blow* zhìmìng 致命; *enemy* bùgòngdài-tiān 不共戴天 **2** *n* rén 人
mortality bùmiǎnyīsǐ 不免一死, sǐwáng lǜ 死亡率
mortar[1] MIL pǎijīpào 迫击炮
mortar[2] (*cement*) shājiāng 砂浆
mortgage 1 *n* dǐyā 抵押 **2** *v/t* dǐyā jièkuǎn 抵押借款
mortician bìnyíyè zhě 殡仪业者
mortuary tàipíngjiān 太平间
mosaic mǎsàikè 马赛克
Moscow Mòsīkē 莫斯科
mosquito wénzi 蚊子
mosquito coil wénxiāng 蚊香
mosquito net wénzhàng 蚊帐
moss tái 苔
mossy zhǎngmǎn qīngtái 长满青苔
most 1 *adj* duōshù 多数 **2** *adv* (*very*) hěn 很; *the ~ beauti-ful / interesting* zuì piàoliàng / yǒuqù 最漂亮 / 有趣; *that's the one I like ~* nàge shì wǒ zuì xǐhuān de 那个是我最喜欢的; *~ of all* zuì zhòngyào 最重要 **3** *pron* dàduōshù 大多数; *at (the) ~* zhìduō 至多; *make the ~ of* jìnliàng lìyòng 尽量利用
mostly zhǔyào 主要
motel qìchē lǚguǎn 汽车旅馆
moth é 蛾
mother 1 *n* mǔqīn 母亲 **2** *v/t* xiàng mǔqīnbān zhàogù 像母亲般照顾
motherboard COMPUT mǔbǎn 母板; **motherhood** mǔqīn shēnfèn 母亲身份; **mother-in-law** (*of man*) yuèmǔ 岳母; (*of woman*)

pópó 婆婆

motherly mǔxìng 母性

mother-of-pearl zhēnzhūmǔ 珍珠母; **Mother's Day** Mǔqīnjié 母亲节; **mother tongue** mǔyǔ 母语

motif zhuāngshì shìyàng 装饰式样

motion 1 n (movement) yùndòng 运动; (proposal) tíyì 提议; **put or set things in ~** zuò bìyào de ānpái 作必要的安排 **2** v/t: **he ~ed me forward** tā shìyì wǒ qiánxíng 他示意我前行

motionless búdòng 不动

motivate person cùdòng 促动

motivation dònglì 动力

motive dòngjī 动机

motor fādòngjī 发动机

motorbike mótuōchē 摩托车; **motorboat** qìchuán 汽船; **motorcade** qìchē chángliè 汽车长列; **motorcycle** mótuōchē 摩托车; **motorcyclist** qí mótuōchē de rén 骑摩托车的人; **motor home** zhùfáng qìchē 住房汽车

motorist sījī 司机

motor rickshaw bèngbèngchē 蹦蹦车; **motorscooter** xiǎoxíng mótuōchē 小型摩托车; **motor vehicle** jīdòngchē 机动车

motto zuòyòumíng 座右铭

mound (hillock) tǔqiū 土丘; (in baseball) tóushǒu chǎngdì 投手场地; (pile) duī 堆

mount 1 n (mountain) shān 山; (horse) zuòqí 坐骑 **2** v/t steps pá 爬; horse, bicycle qíshàng 骑上; campaign fāqǐ 发起; photo, painting biǎotiē 裱贴 **3** v/i zēngzhǎng 增长

♦**mount up** jíjù 积聚

mountain shān 山

mountain bike shāndìchē 山地车

mountaineer dēngshānjiā 登山家

mountaineering dēngshān yùndòng 登山运动

mountainous duōshān 多山

mourn 1 v/t dàoniàn 悼念 **2** v/i āidào 哀悼; **~ for X** dàoniàn X 悼念 X

mourner āidào zhě 哀悼者

mournful bēi'āi 悲哀

mourning fúsāng 服丧; **be in ~** zài fúsāng 在服丧; **wear ~** chuān sāngfú 穿丧服

mouse shǔ 鼠; COMPUT ⇩ shǔbiāo 鼠标

mouse mat COMPUT shǔbiāodiàn 鼠标垫

mouth n (of person) zuǐ 嘴; (of river) hékǒu 河口

mouthful (of food, drink) yīkǒu 一口

mouthorgan kǒuqín 口琴; **mouthpiece** (of instrument) chuīkǒu 吹口; (spokesperson) hóushé 喉舌; **mouthwash** shùkǒujì 漱口剂; **mouthwatering** lìngrén chuíxián 令人垂涎

move 1 n (in chess, checkers) yíbù 一步; (step, action) jǔcuò 举措; (change of house) bānjiā 搬家; **get a ~ on!** gǎnkuài! 赶快！ **don't make a ~!** bùxǔdòng! 不许动！ **2** v/t object yídòng 移动; (transfer) zhuǎnyí 转移; (emotionally) gǎndòng 感动 **3** v/i dòng 动; (transfer) zhuǎn 转; **~ house** bānjiā 搬家

♦**move around** (in room) zǒudòng 走动; (from place to place) qiānyí 迁移

♦**move away** yíkāi 移开; (move house) bānzǒu 搬走

♦**move in** bānjìn 搬进

♦**move on** (to another town) jìxù xíngjìn 继续行进; (to another job) diào tiáo 调; (to another subject) zhuǎnxiàng 转向

♦**move out** (of house) bānchū 搬出; (of area) chèlí 撤离

♦**move up** (in league) tíshēng 提升; (make room) nuódòng 挪动

movement dòngzuò 动作; (organization) yùndòng 运动; MUS yuèzhāng 乐章

movers bānyùn gōngrén 搬运工人

movie diànyǐng 电影; **go to a ~/ the ~s** qù kàn diànyǐng 去看电影

moviegoer guānzhòng 观众

movie theater diànyǐngyuàn 电影院

moving (*which can move*) huódòng 活动; (*emotionally*) gǎnrén 感人

mow *grass* gē 割

♦**mow down** sǎomiè 扫灭

mower yìcǎojī 刈草机

moxibustion jiǔshù 灸术

MP (= *Military Policeman*) jūnjǐng 军警

mph (= *miles per hour*) yīnglǐ shísù 英里时速

Mr xiānsheng 先生; ~ *Wang* Wáng xiānsheng 王先生

Mrs tàitai 太太; ~ *Wang* Wáng tàitai 王太太

Ms nǚshì 女士; ~ *Wang* Wáng nǚshì 王女士

much 1 *adj* xǔduō 许多; ~ *money* xǔduō qián 许多钱; *there's not* ~ *difference* méiyǒu duōshao chābié 没有多少差别; *as* ~ *X as Y* (*same amount as*) hé Y yíyàng duō de X 和 Y 一样多的X **2** *adv* hěn 很; *he is* ~ *admired* tā hěn lìngrén xiànmù 他很令人羡慕; *I don't like him* ~ wǒ bútài xǐhuan tā 我不太喜欢他; ~ *better* hǎo de duō 好得多; ~ *cheaper* piányi de duō 便宜得多; *very* ~ fēicháng 非常; *thank you very* ~ fēicháng gǎnxiè 非常感谢; *too* ~ guòduō 过多; *you talk too* ~ nǐ shuōde guòduō 你说得过多 **3** *pron* duōshǎo 多少; *nothing* ~ méi shénme 没什么; *as* ~ *as ...* gēn ... yíyàng (duō) 跟 ... 一样 (多); *I lost as* ~ *as you did* wǒ gēn nǐ shūde yíyàng duō 我跟你输的一样多; *do as* ~ *as you can* jìnliàng zuò ba 尽量做吧; *take as* ~ *as you want* suíbiàn ná 随便拿; *as* ~ *as ten thousand dollars* duōdá yíwàn měiyuán 多达一万美元; *I thought as* ~ wǒ jiùshì zhènme xiǎngde 我就是这么想的

muck (*dirt*) zāngwù 脏物

mucus niányè 粘液

mud ní 泥

muddle 1 *n* hùnluàn 混乱 **2** *v/t*

nòng hútu 弄糊涂

♦**muddle up** gǎoluàn 搞乱

muddy *adj* nínìng 泥泞

muffin sōngbǐng 松饼

muffle yāyì 压抑

♦**muffle up** *v/i* chuān hòu yīdiǎn 穿厚一点

muffler MOT páiqì xiāoshēngqì 排汽消声器

mug¹ *n* (*for tea, coffee*) dàbēi 大杯; F (*face*) liǎndànr 脸蛋儿

mug² *v/t* (*attack*) xíngxiōng qiǎngjié 行凶抢劫

mugger xíngxiōng qiǎngjié zhě 行凶抢劫者

mugging xíngxiōng qiǎngjié 行凶抢劫

muggy mēnrè 闷热

mule (*animal*) luó luo 骡骡; (*slipper*) tuōxié 拖鞋

♦**mull over** zǐxì kǎolǜ 仔细考虑

multilingual shǐyòng duōzhǒng yǔyán 使用多种语言

multimedia *n* duōméitǐ 多媒体

multinational 1 *adj* guójì 国际 **2** *n* COM duōguó 多国

multiple *adj* duōgè 多个

multiplication zēngduō 增多

multiply 1 *v/t* chéng 乘 **2** *v/i* zēngjiā 增加

mumble 1 *n* gūnong 咕哝 **2** *v/t* gūnong 咕哝 **3** *v/i* hánhude shuō 含糊地说

mumps sāixiànyán 腮腺炎

munch 1 *v/t* yònglì jǔjué 用力咀嚼 **2** *v/i* dàjǔdàjué 大咀大嚼

municipal shìzhèng 市政

mural *n* bìhuà 壁画

murder 1 *n* móushā 谋杀 **2** *v/t person* móushā 谋杀; *song* zāotà 糟蹋

murderer xiōngshǒu 凶手

murderous *rage, look* shāqì téngténg 杀气腾腾

murmur 1 *n* dīyǔshēng 低语声 **2** *v/t* dīyǔ 低语

muscle jīròu 肌肉

muscular *pain, strain* jīròu 肌肉; *person* jīròu fādá 肌肉发达

muse *v/i* chénsī 沉思

museum bówùguǎn 博物馆

mushroom 1 *n* mógū 蘑菇 **2** *v/i* xùnsù zēngzhǎng 迅速增长

music yīnyuè 音乐; (*in written form*) yuèpǔ 乐谱

musical 1 *adj* yīnyuè 音乐; *person* yǒu yuègǎn 有乐感; *voice* yuè'ěr 悦耳 **2** *n* (*movie*) yīnyuèpiān 音乐片; (*on stage*) gēwǔjù 歌舞剧

musical instrument yuèqì 乐器

musician yīnyuèjiā 音乐家

mussel yíbèi 贻贝

must ◊ (*necessity*): *I ~ be on time* wǒ bìxū zhǔnshí 我必须准时; *I ~* wǒ bìxūděi ... 我必须得 ...; *I ~n't be late* wǒ bùnéng chídào 我不能迟到 ◊ (*probability*): *it ~ be about 6 o'clock* dàgài liùdiǎnzhōng le 大概六点钟了; *they ~ have arrived by now* tāmen xiànzài kěndìng dàole 他们现在肯定到了

mustache bāzì hú 八字胡

mustard jièmò 芥末

musty yǒu méiwèir 有霉味儿

mute *adj animal* wúshēng 无声

muted jiǎnruò 减弱

mutilate sǔnshāng 损伤

mutiny 1 *n* pànluàn 叛乱 **2** *v/i* fǎnpàn 反叛

mutter 1 *v/i* gūnong 咕哝 **2** *v/t* dīshēng shuō 低声说

mutton yángròu 羊肉

mutual xiānghù 相互

muzzle 1 *n* (*of animal*) bíkǒu bùfēn 鼻口部分; (*for dog*) kǒutào 口套 **2** *v/t*: *~ the press* qiánzhì xīnwén 钳制新闻

my wǒde 我的

myopic jìnshì 近视

myself wǒzìjǐ 我自己; *by ~* dúzì 独自

mysterious shénmì 神秘

mysteriously bùkě sīyì 不可思议

mystery mí 谜

mystify míhuo 迷惑

myth shénhuà 神话; *fig* xūhuà 虚话

mythical cúnzài yú shénhuà zhōng 存在于神话中

mythology shénhuàxué 神话学

N

nab (*take for oneself*) qiǎng 抢
nag 1 *v/i* (*of person*) láodao bùtíng
唠叨不停 **2** *v/t* fán fáng; **~X to do
Y** méiwán méiliǎo de yào X qùzuò
Y 没完没了地要X去做Y
nagging *person* hào láodao 好唠
叨; *doubt* kùnrǎo 困扰; *pain*
lìngrén fánnǎo 令人烦恼
nail (*for wood*) dīng 钉; (*on finger,
toe*) zhǐjia 指甲
nail clippers zhǐjia dāo 指甲刀;
nail file zhǐjia cuò 指甲锉; **nail
polish** zhǐjia yóu 指甲油; **nail
polish remover** zhǐjia yóu qùchú
jì 指甲油去除剂; **nail scissors**
zhǐjia jiǎn 指甲剪; **nail varnish**
zhǐjia yóu 指甲油
naive tiānzhēn 天真
naked luǒtǐ 裸体; *to the ~ eye*
yòng ròuyǎn láikàn 用肉眼来看
name 1 *n* míngzi 名字; *what's
your ~?* nǐ jiào shénme míngzi? 你
叫什么名字？; (*formal use*)
qǐngwèn guìxìng? 请问贵姓？;
call X ~s jiào X wàihào 叫X外号;
make a ~ for oneself chéngmíng
成名 **2** *v/t* qǐmíng 起名
♦**name for: *name X for Y*** yǐ Y de
míngzi wèi X qǐmíng 以Y的名字
为X起名
namely jí 即
namesake tóngmíng rén 同名人
nametag (*on clothing etc*) biāoqiān
标签
nanny *n* bǎomǔ 保姆
nap *n* xiǎoshuì 小睡; *have a ~*
dǎdǔnr 打盹儿
nape: ~ of the neck hòu bójǐng 后
脖颈
napkin (*table ~*) cānjīn 餐巾;
(*sanitary*) wèishēngjīn 卫生巾
narcotic *n* mázuì pǐn 麻醉品
narcotics agent fǎndú jǐng 反毒警
narrate xùshù 叙述

narration (*telling*) xùshù 叙述
narrative 1 *n* (*story*) gùshì 故事
2 *adj poem, style* xùshì tǐ 叙事体
narrator xùshì zhě 叙事者
narrow *street, bed etc* xiázhǎi 狭窄;
views, mind xiáyì 狭隘; *victory*
miǎnqiáng 勉强
narrowly *win* miǎnqiángde 勉强
地; *~ escape X* miǎnqiáng de
táotuō X 勉强地逃脱X
narrow-minded xīnxiōng xiázǎi 心
胸狭窄
nasal *voice* bíyīn zhòng 鼻音重
nasty *person, thing to say* bēibǐ 卑
鄙; *smell, weather* èliè 恶劣; *cut,
wound, disease* yánzhòng 严重
nation guójiā 国家
national 1 *adj currency, identity,
issues* guólì 国立; *newspaper, security* guójiā 国家; *economic
indicators* guómín 国民; *pride*
àiguó 爱国 **2** *n* guómín 国民
national anthem guógē 国歌
National Day Guóqìngjié 国庆节
national debt guózhài 国债
nationalism mínzú zhǔyì 民族主
义
Nationalist Party (*KMT*) Guómíndǎng 国民党
nationality guójí 国籍
nationalize *industry etc* shǐ guóyǒu
huà 使国有化
national park guójiā gōngyuán 国
家公园
National People's Congress
Quánguó Rénmín Dàibiǎo Dàhuì
全国人民代表大会
native 1 *adj* (*of a country*) běnguó
本国; (*of a place*) běndì 本地; *~
language* (*of a nation*) běnguó yǔ
本国语; (*mother tongue*) mǔyǔ 母
语 **2** *n* dāngdì rén 当地人;
(*tribesman*) tǔrén 土人
native country zǔguó 祖国

native speaker jiǎng běnguóyǔ de rén 讲本国语的人

NATO (= *North Atlantic Treaty Organization*) Běiyuē 北约

natural zìrán 自然; *resources, forces* zìrán jiè 自然界; *death* zìrán 自然; *flavor* fēi rénzào 非人造; *a ~ blonde* tiānshēng jīn tóufà rén 天生金头发人

natural gas tiānrán qì 天然气

naturalist bówù xuéjiā 博物学家

naturalize: *become ~d* jiārù guójí 加入国籍

naturally (*of course*) dāngrán 当然; *behave, speak* zìrán de 自然地; (*by nature*) tiānshēng 天生

natural science zìrán kēxué 自然科学

natural scientist zìrán kēxué jiā 自然科学家

nature zìrán 自然; (*of person*) xìnggé 性格; (*of problem*) běnzhì 本质

nature reserve zìrán bǎohùqū 自然保护区

naughty táoqì 淘气; *photograph, word etc* bùdétí 不得体

nausea ěxin 恶心

nauseate *fig* (*disgust*) shǐ ěxin 使恶心

nauseating *smell, taste* lìngrén zuò'ǒu 令人作呕; *person* ròumá 肉麻

nauseous: *feel ~* juéde ěxīn 觉得恶心

nautical hánghǎi 航海

nautical mile hǎilǐ 海里

naval hǎijūn 海军

naval base hǎijūn jīdì 海军基地

navel dùqí 肚脐

navigable *river* kě tōngháng 可通航

navigate *v/i* (*in ship, airplane*) cèháng 测航; (*in car*) zhǐlù 指路; COMPUT zǒu 走

navigation (*nautical, in airplane*) hángxíngxué 航行学; (*in car*) lǐnglù 领路; (*skills*) yǐndǎo 引导

navigator (*on ship*) hánghǎi jiā 航海家; (*in airplane*) jiàshǐ yuán 驾驶员; (*in car*) zhǐlùrén 指路人

navy hǎijūn 海军

navy blue *n & adj* hǎijūn lán 海军兰

near 1 *adv* jìn 近 **2** *prep* jiējìn 接近; *~ the bank* jìn yínháng 近银行; *do you go ~ the bank?* nǐ huìbúhuì zǒu yínháng nàbiān? 你会不会走银行那边？ **3** *adj* jìn 近; *the ~est bus stop* zuìjìnde gōnggòng qìchē zhàn 最近的公共汽车站; *in the ~ future* bùyuǎnde jiānglái 不远的将来

nearby *adv live* zài fùjìn 在附近

nearly jīhū 几乎

near-sighted jìnshì 近视

neat *room, desk* zhěngjié 整洁; *person* zhěngqí 整齐; *whiskey* chún 纯; *solution* qiǎomiào 巧妙; F (*terrific*) tǐnghǎo 挺好

necessarily yídìng 一定

necessary bìbù kěshǎo 必不可少; *it is ~ to X* yǒu bìyào zuò X 有必要做X

necessitate xūyào 需要

necessity (*being necessary*) bìyào xìng 必要性; (*sth necessary*) bìxū pǐn 必需品

neck bózi 脖子

necklace xiàngliàn 项链; **neckline** (*of dress*) lǐngkǒu 领口; **necktie** lǐngdài 领带

née mǔjiā xìng 母家姓

need 1 *n* xūyào 需要; *if ~ be* rúguǒ yǒu xūyào dehuà 如果有需要的话; *in ~* yǒu kùnnán 有困难; *be in ~ of X* xūyào X 需要X; *there's no ~ to be rude / upset* méi bìyào zhème cūlǔ / shāngxīn 没必要这么粗鲁 / 伤心 **2** *v/t* xūyào 需要; *you'll ~ to buy one* nǐ yǒu bìyào mǎi yígè 你有必要买一个; *you don't ~ to wait* nǐ bùbì děngzhe 你不必等着; *I ~ to talk to you* wǒ yào hé nǐ tánihuà 我要和你谈话; *~ I say more?* wǒ háiyǒu shénme kěshuōde? 我还有什么可说的？

needle (*for sewing*) zhēn 针; (*for injection*) zhēntóu 针头; (*on dial*) zhǐzhēn 指针

needlework zhēnxiàn huór 针线

活儿

needy qióng 穷

negative 1 *adj verb, sentence* fǒudìng 否定; *attitude, person* xiāojí 消极; ELEC fùdiàn 负电 **2** *n:* **answer in the ~** jǐyǔ fǒudìngde huídá 给予否定的回答

neglect 1 *n* hūlüè 忽略 **2** *v/t garden, one's health* zhàogù bùzhōu 照顾不周; *~ to do X* méiyǒu zuò X 没有做X

neglected *gardens, author* búshòu zhòngshì 不受重视; *feel ~* gǎndào búshòu zhòngshì 感到不受重视

negligence wánhū zhíshǒu 玩忽职守

negligent cūxīn dàyì 粗心大意

negligible *quantity, amount* kěyǐ hūlüè 可以忽略

negotiable *salary, contract* kě xiéshāng 可协商

negotiate 1 *v/i* xiéshāng 协商 **2** *v/t deal, settlement* xiéshāng 协商; *obstacles* jiějué 解决; *bend in road* tōngguò 通过

negotiation xiéshāng 协商

negotiator tánpàn yuán 谈判员

Negro (*person*) Hēi rén 黑人

neigh *v/i* sī 嘶

neighbor línjū 邻居

neighborhood (*in town*) dìqū 地区; *in the ~ of ...* fig dàyuē ... 大约 ...

neighboring *house, state* fùjìn 附近

neighborly yǒuhǎo 友好

neither 1 *adj* liǎngzhě dōubù 两者都不; *~ answer was correct* liǎng ge dá'àn dōu búduì 两个答案都不对 **2** *pron* něige dōu bù 哪个都不; *in the end I bought ~* zuìhòu wǒ něige dōu méi mǎi 最后我哪个都没买; *~ of them recognized me* tāmenliǎ shéi dōu méi rènchū wǒ lai 他们俩谁都没认出我来 **3** *adv:* ~ *... nor ...* jìbù ... yěbù ... 既不 ... 也不 ... **4** *conj* yěbù 也不; *~ do I* wǒ yě bù 我也不

neon light níhóng dēng 霓虹灯

Nepal Níbó'ěr 尼泊尔

Nepalese 1 *adj* Níbó'ěr 尼泊尔 **2** *n* (*person*) Níbó'ěr rén 尼泊尔人; (*language*) Níbó'ěr yǔ 尼泊尔语

nephew (*brother's son*) zhízi 侄子; (*sister's son*) wàisheng 外甥

nerd F guàirén 怪人

nerve shénjīng 神经; (*courage*) yǒngqì 勇气; (*impudence*) dǎliàng 胆量; *it's bad for my ~s* duì wǒde shénjīng bùhǎo 对我的神经不好; *get on X's ~s* shǐ X xīnfán yìluàn 使X心烦意乱

nerve-racking shǐrén xīnfán 使人心烦

nervous *person* jǐnzhāng 紧张; *twitch* shénjīng xìng 神经性; *be ~ about doing X* hàipà zuò X 害怕做X

nervous breakdown jīngshén bēngkuì 精神崩溃

nervous energy jīnglì chōngpèi 精力充沛

nervousness jǐnzhāng 紧张

nervous wreck hěn jǐnzhāng derén 很紧张的人

nervy (*fresh*) dàdǎn 大胆

nest *n* cháo 巢

nestle shūshìde āndùn xiàlái 舒适地安顿下来

net¹ (*for fishing*) yúwǎng 鱼网; (*for tennis*) wǎngqiú wǎng 网球网

net² *adj price, amount* chún 纯; *weight* jìng 净

net curtain shā chuānglián 纱窗帘

net profit jìnglì 净利

nettle xúnmá 荨麻

network (*of contacts, cells*) liánluò wǎng 联络网; COMPUT wǎngluò 网络

neurologist shénjīngbìng xuéjiā 神经病学家

neurosis shénjīng jīnéng bìng 神经机能病

neurotic *adj* shénjīng zhì 神经质

neuter *v/t animal* yāngē 阉割

neutral 1 *adj country* zhōnglì 中立; *color* fēi cǎisè 非彩色 **2** *n* (*gear*) kōngdǎng 空档; *in ~* zài kōngdǎng 在空档

neutrality zhōnglì dìwèi 中立地位

neutralize *effect of drug etc* shǐ zhōnghé 使中和; *argument* shǐ wúxiào 使无效

never ◊ (*in past*) cónglái méi 从来没; *I've ~ eaten this* wǒ cónglái méi chīguo zhèige 我从来没吃过这个 ◊ (*in present*) cónglái bù 从来不; *she ~ goes to the movies* tā cónglái búqù kàn diànyǐng 她从来不去看电影 ◊ (*in future tenses*) juébúhuì 绝不会; *she will ~ marry him* tā juébúhuì gēn tā jiéhūn 她绝不会跟他结婚 ◊ (*in disbelief*) bùkěnéng 不可能; *you're ~ going to believe this* nǐ búhuì xiāngxìn zhè jiàn shì 你不会相信这件事; *you ~ promised, did you?* nǐ cónglái méiyǒu xǔnuòguò, shìba? 你从来没有许诺过, 是吧?

never-ending méiwán 没完

nevertheless dànshì 但是

new xīn 新; *this system is still ~ to me* wǒ duì zhège xìtǒng háishì bù shúxì 我对这个系统还是不熟悉; *I'm ~ to the job* wǒ shì xīnlái de 我是新来的; *that's nothing ~* méiyǒu shénme kě qíguàide 没有什么可奇怪的

newborn *adj* xīnshēng 新生

newcomer xīnlái derén 新来的人

newly (*recently*) zuìjìn 最近

newly-weds xīnhūn rén 新婚人

new moon xīnyuè 新月

news xīnwén 新闻; (*on TV, radio*) xīnwén bàodǎo 新闻报导; *that's ~ to me* wǒ méi tīngshuō guò zhèjiànshì 我没听说过这件事

news agency tōngxùnshè 通讯社; **newscast** TV xīnwén guǎngbō 新闻广播; **newscaster** TV xīnwén guǎngbōyuán 新闻广播员; **newsdealer** bàokān jīngshòu rén 报刊经售人; **news flash** jǐnjí xīnwén bàodào 紧急新闻报道

newspaper bàozhǐ 报纸

newsreader TV *etc* xīnwén bōyīn yuán 新闻播音员; **news report** xīnwén bàodào 新闻报道; **newsstand** bàotānr 报摊儿; **newsvendor** bàofàn 报贩

New Territories (*in Hong Kong*) Xīnjiè 新界

New Year Xīnnián 新年; (*Chinese*) Chūnjié 春节; *Happy ~!* Xīnnián kuàilè! 新年快乐!

New Year's Day (*Jan 1*) Yuándàn 元旦; (*Chinese*) Chūyī 初一

New Year's Eve (*Dec 31*) Yuándàn Qiányè 元旦前夜; (*Chinese*) Chúxī 除夕

New York Niǔyuē 纽约

New Zealand ⇩ Xīnxīlán 新西兰

New Zealander ⇩ Xīnxīlán rén 新西兰人

next 1 *adj* (*in time, space*) xià yīgè 下一个; *the ~ week / month he came back again* xiàgè xīngqī / xiàgè yuè tā zàilái 下个星期/下个月他再来; *who's ~?* shuí shì xià yīgè? 谁是下一个?

2 *adv* xià yībù 下一步; *~ to X* (*beside*) zài X de pángbiān 在X的旁边; (*in comparison with*) yǔ X xiāngbǐ 与X相比

next door *adj & adv* gébì 隔壁

next of kin zuìjìnde qīnshǔ 最近的亲属

nibble *v/t* kěn 啃

nice *person* tǐtiē 体贴; *day, weather, meal, food, party, trip, vacation* lìngrén yúkuài 令人愉快; *house, hair* piàoliang 漂亮; *be ~ to your sisters* duì nǐ jiěmèi hǎodiǎnr 对你姐妹好点儿; *that's very ~ of you* nǐ tàihǎole 你太好了

nicely *presented etc* jīngxīn de 精心地; (*pleasantly*) héyí di 合宜地

niceties: *social ~* shèjiāo lǐjié 社交礼节

niche (*in market*) quēkǒu 缺口; (*special position*) héshìde wèizhì 合适的位置

nick *n* (*cut*) kèhén 刻痕; *in the ~ of time* qiàhǎo 恰好

nickel niè 镍

nickname *n* wàihào 外号

niece (*brother's daughter*) zhínǚ 侄女; (*sister's daughter*) wài shengnǚ

外甥女

niggardly *adj amount, person* xiǎoqì 小气

night yè 夜; *tomorrow* ~ míngyè 明夜; *(evening)* míngwǎn 明晚; *11 o'clock at* ~ wǎnshàng shíyī diǎn 晚上十一点; *travel by* ~ yèjiān lǚxíng 夜间旅行; *during the* ~ yèjiān 夜间; *stay the* ~ guòyè 过夜; *a room for 2/3 ~s* yīgè fángjiān, liǎngsān yè 一个房间，两三夜; *work* ~*s* shàng yèbān 上夜班; *good* ~ wǎn'ān 晚安; *in the middle of the* ~ bànyè sāngēng 半夜三更

nightcap *(drink)* shuìqián jiǔ 睡前酒; **nightclub** yèzǒnghuì 夜总会; **nightdress** shuìyī 睡衣; **nightfall**: *at* ~ huánghūn 黄昏; **night flight** yèjiān fēixíng 夜间飞行; **nightgown** shuìyī 睡衣

nightingale yèyīng 夜莺

nightlife yè shēnghuó 夜生活

nightly 1 *adj* yèjiān 夜间 **2** *adv* zài yèjiān 在夜间

nightmare èmèng 恶梦; *fig* kěpàde jīngyàn 可怕的经验; **night-market** yèshì 夜市; **night porter** yèbān fúwùyuán 夜班服务员; **night school** yèxiào 夜校; **night shift** yèbān 夜班; **nightshirt** shuìyī 睡衣; **nightspot** yèzǒnghuì 夜总会; **nighttime**: *at* ~, *in the* ~ zài yèjiān 在夜间

nil líng 零

nimble jīlíng 机灵

nine jiǔ 九

nineteen shíjiǔ 十九

nineteenth dìshíjiǔ 第十九

ninetieth dìjiǔshí 第九十

ninety jiǔshí 九十

ninth dìjiǔ 第九

nip *n (pinch)* qiā 掐; *(bite)* yǎo 咬

nipple rǔtóu 乳头

nitrogen dàn 氮

no 1 *adv* bù 不; *do you understand? – – * ~ nǐ dǒng ma? – bùdǒng 你懂吗？–不懂; *does he agree? – – * ~ tā tóngyì ma? – bù tóngyì 他同意吗？–不同意 **2** *adj* méiyǒu 没有; *there's* ~

coffee/tea left méiyǒu kāfēi/chá le 没有咖啡/茶了; *I have* ~ *family/money* wǒ méiyǒu jiātíng/qián 我没有家庭/钱; *I'm* ~ *linguist/expert* wǒ bùshì yúyán xuéjiā/zhuānjiā 我不是语言学家/专家; ~ *smoking/parking* jìnzhǐ xīyān/tíngchē 禁止吸烟/停车

nobility guìzú 贵族

noble *adj* gāoguì 高贵

nobody méirén 没人; ~ *knows* méirén zhīdào 没人知道; *there was* ~ *at home* méirén zàijiā 没人在家

nod *n & v/i* diǎntóu 点头
♦ **nod off** *(fall asleep)* dǎ kēshuì 打瞌睡

no-hoper bù zhōngyòng derén 不中用的人

noise shēngyīn 声音; *(loud, unpleasant)* zàoyīn 噪音

noisy xuānhuá 喧哗

nominal *amount* míngyì shàng 名义上

nominate *(appoint)* tímíng 提名; ~ *X for a post (propose)* tuījiàn X rèn mǒugè zhíwèi 推荐X任某个职位

nomination *(appointment)* rènmìng 任命; *(proposal)* tímíng 提名; *(person proposed)* bèi tímíng rén 被提名人

nominee bèi tímíng rén 被提名人

non ... bù ... 不 ...

nonalcoholic bù hán jiǔjīng 不含酒精

nonaligned bù jiéméng 不结盟

nonchalant mòbù guānxīn 漠不关心

noncommissioned officer fēi shòumìng guānyuán 非受命官员

noncommittal *person, response* bù mínglǎng 不明朗

nondescript méiyǒu tèzhēng 没有特征

none méi yīgè 没一个; ~ *of the students* méi yīgè xuéshēng 没一个学生; ~ *of the chocolate* méi yìzhǒng qiǎokèlì 没一种巧克

力; *there is / are ~ left*
méishèngde 没剩的
nonentity wúzú qīngzhòng 无足
轻重
nonetheless rán'ér 然而
　nonexistent bù cúnzài 不存在;
　nonfiction fēi xiǎoshuō 非小说;
　non(in)flammable bùrán 不燃;
　noninterference, noninterven-
　tion bù gānyù 不干预; non-iron
　shirt miǎnyùntàng 免熨烫
no-no: *that's a ~* bùxíngde 不行
的
no-nonsense *approach* rènzhēn 认
真
nonpayment wèifù 未付; non-
　polluting fēi wūrǎn 非污染;
　nonresident *n* kèrén 客人; non-
　returnable bù kětuì 不可退
nonsense húshuō 胡说; *don't talk
~* bié húshuō 别胡说; *~, it's
easy!* húshuō, zhèhěn róngyì! 胡
说, 这很容易!
nonskid *tires* fánghuá 防滑; non-
　slip *surface* bùhuá 不滑; non-
　smoker (*person*) bù xīyān zhě 不
　吸烟者; nonstandard fēi
　chángguī 非常规; nonstick *pan*
　bùzhān 不粘; nonstop 1 *adj*
　flight, train zhídá 直达; *chatter*
　bùtíng 不停 2 *adv fly, travel* zhídá
　直达; *chatter, argue* bùtíng 不停;
　nonswimmer búhuì yóuyǒng zhě
　不会游泳者; nonunion *adj*
　bùshǔ gōnghuì 不属工会; non-
　violence fēi bàolì 非暴力; non-
　violent fēi bàolì 非暴力
noodles miàntiáo 面条
noodle soup tāngmiàn 汤面
nook jiǎoluò 角落
noon zhōngwǔ 中午; *at ~* zài
zhōngwǔ 在中午
noose quāntào 圈套
nor yòubú 又不; *~ do I* wǒ yěbù 我
也不
norm zhǔnzé 准则
normal zhèngcháng 正常
normality zhèngcháng 正常
normalize *relationships* zhèngcháng
huà 正常化
normally (*usually*) yībān de 一般

地; (*in a normal way*) zhèngcháng
de 正常地
north 1 *n* běibù 北部; *to the ~ of
X* X yǐběi X 以北 2 *adj* běibù 北
部 3 *adv travel* xiàngběi 向北; *~
of X* X běibù X 北部
North America Běiměi 北美
North American 1 *adj*
　Běiměizhōu 北美洲 2 *n*
　Běiměizhōu rén 北美洲人
northeast *n* dōngběi bù 东北部
northerly *adj* běi 北
northern běifāng 北方
northerner běifāng rén 北方人
North Korea ⇩ Běicháoxiān 北朝
鲜
North Korean ⇩ 1 *adj* Běicháo-
　xiān 北朝鲜 2 *n* Běicháoxiān rén
　北朝鲜人
North Pole Běijí 北极
northward *travel* xiàngběi 向北
northwest *n* xīběi bù 西北部
Norway Nuówēi 挪威
Norwegian 1 *adj* Nuówēi 挪威
　2 *n* (*person*) Nuówēi rén 挪威人;
　(*language*) Nuówēi yǔ 挪威语
nose bízi 鼻子; *it was right under
my ~* jiù zài wǒ yǎnqián 就在我
眼前
♦nose around tàntīng 探听
nosebleed liú bíxuè 流鼻血
nostalgia huáijiù 怀旧
nostalgic huáijiù 怀旧
nostril bíkǒng 鼻孔
nosy hàoguǎn xiánshì 好管闲事
not ◊ (*present and future*) bù 不; *~
this one, that one* búshì zhèige,
shì nèige 不是这个, 是那个; *~
now* xiànzài bùxíng 现在不行; *~
there* nàr bùxíng 那儿不行; *~
like that* bùnéng nàyàng 不能那
样; *~ before Tuesday / next week*
xīngqī èr / xià xīngqī qián bùxíng
星期二 / 下星期前不行; *~ for
me, thanks* wǒ bùyào, xièxiè 我
不要, 谢谢; *~ a lot* yīdiǎndian
一点点; *it's ~ allowed* bù yúnxǔ
没成呢 / 不允许; *I don't know*
wǒ bù zhīdào 我不知道; *I am ~
American* wǒ búshì Měiguó rén
我不是美国人; *I'm ~ going* wǒ

búqù 我不去; *it won't be cold tomorrow* míngtiān bùnéng lěng 明天不能冷◊ (*past tense, and with yǒu*) méi 没; *he didn't help* tā méi bāngmáng 他没帮忙; *he wasn't there* tā méi zài 他没在; *I haven't told him yet* wǒ hái méi gàosu ta 我还没告诉他; *I don't have that book* wǒ méiyǒu nèi běn shū 我没有那本书; *we don't have a car* wǒmen méiyǒu chē 我们没有车

notable zhuóyuè 卓越

notary gōngzhèng rén 公证人

notch āokǒu 凹口

note *n* (*short letter*) biàntiáo 便条; MUS yīndiào 音调; (*memo to self*) jìlù 记录; (*comment on text*) zhùshì 注释; *take ~s* jì bǐjì 记笔记; *take ~ of X* zhùyì dào X 注意到 X

♦**note down** jìlù xiàlái 记录下来

notebook *also* COMPUT bǐjì běn 笔记本

noted zhùmíng 著名

notepad biàntiáo běn 便条本

notepaper biàntiáo zhǐ 便条纸

nothing méiyǒu shénme 没有什么; *~ for me thanks* wǒ shénme yě búyào xièxie 我什么也不要谢谢; *there was ~ to eat* méiyǒu shénme chīde 没有什么吃的; *there's ~ left* méiyǒu shénme le 没有什么了; *~ works in this office* bāngōngshì lǐ shénme dōu huài le 办公室里什么都坏了; *~ but* zhǐ 只; *there's ~ but work in his life* tā shēnghuó zhōng zhǐyǒu gōngzuò 他生活中只有工作; *he wants ~ but the best* tā zhǐ yào zuìhǎo de 他只要最好的; *~ much* méi duōshǎo 没多少; *for ~* (*for free*) miǎnfèi 免费; (*for no reason*) wúyuán wúgù 无缘无故; *I'd like ~ better* zuì hǎole 最好了

notice 1 *n* (*on bulletin board, in street, in newspaper*) tōnggào 通告; (*advance warning*) yùxiān tōngzhī 预先通知; (*to leave job*) cízhí tōngzhī 辞职通知; (*to leave house*) zūpíng tōngzhī 租凭通知;

at short ~ tūrán 突然; *until further ~* zài lìngxíng tōngzhī zhīqián 在另行通知之前; *give X his / her ~* (*to quit job*) xiàng X tíchū cízhí tōngzhī 向 X 提出辞职通知; (*to leave house*) xiàng X tíchū tuìfáng tōngzhī 向 X 提出退房通知; *hand in one's ~* (*to employer*) tíchū cízhí tōngzhī 提出辞职通知; *four weeks' ~* sìge xīngqī de yùxiān tōngzhī 四个星期的预先通知; *take ~ of X* zhùyì X 注意 X; *take no ~ of X* búyào guǎn X 不要管 X **2** *v/t* zhùyì 注意

noticeable míngxiǎn 明显

notify tōngzhī 通知

notion kànfǎ 看法

notions zhēnxiàn 针线

notorious shēngmíng lángjí 声名狼籍

nougat jiá jiānguǒ táng 夹坚果糖

nought *Br* líng 零

noun míngcí 名词

nourishing yǒu yíngyǎng 有营养

nourishment yíngyǎng 营养

novel *n* xiǎoshuō 小说

novelist xiǎoshuō jiā 小说家

novelty (*being novel*) xīnyǐng 新颖; (*sth novel*) xīnyǐng shìwù 新颖事物

November shíyī yuè 十一月

novice xuétú 学徒

now xiànzài 现在; *~ and again, ~ and then* yǒushí yǒu时; *by ~* zhèshí 这时; *from ~ on* cóng xiànzài kāishǐ 从现在开始; *right ~* cǐkè 此刻; *just ~* (*at this moment*) xiànzài 现在; (*a little while ago*) gāngcái 刚才; *~, ~!* déla, déla! 得啦, 得啦！; *~, where did I put it?* nàme, wǒ bǎ tā fàng zài nǎrle? 那么, 我把它放在哪儿了？

nowadays xiànjīn 现今

nowhere wúchù 无处; *it's ~ near finished* lí wánchéng hái zǎozhe ne 离完成还早着呢

nozzle pēnzuǐ 喷嘴

nuclear yuánzǐhé 原子核

nuclear energy hénéng 核能;

nuclear fission hé lièbiàn 核裂变; **nuclear-free** wúhé 无核; **nuclear physics** yuánzǐhé wùlǐ 原子核物理; **nuclear power** hénéng 核能; **nuclear power station** hénéng zhàn 核能站; **nuclear reactor** hé fǎnyìng duī 核反应堆; **nuclear waste** hé fèiwù 核废物; **nuclear weapons** hé wǔqì 核武器

nude 1 *adj* luǒtǐ 裸体 **2** *n* (*painting*) luǒtǐ huà 裸体画; *in the ~* chì luǒluo 赤裸裸

nudge *v/t* qīngtuī 轻推

nudist *n* luǒtǐ zhǔyì zhě 裸体主义者

nuisance fánrén 烦人; *make a ~ of oneself* lìngrén tǎoyàn 令人讨厌; *what a ~!* tǎoyàn! 讨厌！

nuke *v/t* yòng hé wǔqì gōngjī 用核武器攻击

null and void wúxiào 无效

numb mámù 麻木; (*emotionally*) chídùn 迟钝

number 1 *n* (*figure*) shùmù 数目; (*quantity*) ruògān 若干; (*of hotel room, house, phone number etc*) shùzì 数字 **2** *v/t* (*put a number on*) biānhào 编号

numeral shùmù 数目

numerate jìshù nénglì qiáng 计数能力强

numerous xǔduō 许多

nun nígū 尼姑; *become a ~* chūjiā 出家

nurse hùshì 护士

nursery tuō'érsuǒ 托儿所; (*for plants*) miáopǔ 苗圃

nursery rhyme tóngyáo 童谣; **nursery school** yòu'éryuán 幼儿园; **nursery school teacher** yòu'éryuán lǎoshī 幼儿园老师

nursing hùlǐ 护理

nursing home (*for old people*) lǎorén yuàn 老人院

nut jiānguǒ 坚果; (*for bolt*) luómǔ 螺母; *~s* F (*testicles*) dàn 蛋

nutcrackers jiānguǒ qián 坚果钳

nutrient *n* yíngyǎng pǐn 营养品

nutrition yíngyǎng 营养

nutritious yǒu yíngyǎng 有营养

nuts *adj* F (*crazy*) fēng 疯; *be ~ about X* míliàn X 迷恋 X

nutshell: *in a ~* yìyán yǐ bìzhī 一言以蔽之

nutty *taste* jiānguǒ wèir 坚果味儿; F (*crazy*) fēngkuáng 疯狂

nylon nílóng 尼龙

O

oak (*tree*) xiàngshù 橡树; (*wood*) xiàngmù 橡木

oar jiǎng 桨

oasis lǜzhōu 绿洲; *fig* shìwài táoyuán 世外桃源

oath LAW shìyán 誓言; (*swearword*) zǔzhòu 诅咒; **on ~** zài shìyán de yuēshù xià 在誓言的约束下

oatmeal yànmàipiàn 燕麦片

oats yànmàipiàn 燕麦片

obedience fúcóng 服从

obedient fúcóng 服从

obey fúcóng 服从

obituary *n* fùgào 讣告

object[1] *n* (*thing*) wùtǐ 物体; (*aim*) mùdì 目的; GRAM bīnyǔ 宾语

object[2] *v/i* fǎnduì 反对

♦object to fǎnduì 反对

objection fǎnduì 反对

objectionable (*unpleasant*) tǎoyàn 讨厌

objective 1 *adj* kèguān 客观 2 *n* mùbiāo 目标

obligation yìwù 义务; **be under an ~ to X** duì X yǒu yìwù 对 X 有义务

obligatory bìxū 必须

oblige: **much ~d!** duōxièle! 多谢了!

obliging lèyú zhùrén 乐于助人

oblique 1 *adj reference* hánhu qící 含糊其辞 2 *n* (*in punctuation*) xiéxiàn 斜线

obliterate *city* huǐmiè 毁灭; *memory* chúqù 除去

oblivion (*being forgotten*) yíwàng 遗忘; **fall into ~** jiànbèi wàngquè 渐被忘却

oblivious: **be ~ of ...** yìshí búdào ... 意识不到 ...

oblong *adj* chángfāngxíng 长方形

obnoxious yǐnrén fǎngǎn 引人反感

obscene yínhuì 淫秽; *salary, poverty* guòfèn 过分

obscure (*hard to see*) hūn'àn 昏暗; (*hard to understand*) nánjiě 难解; (*little known*) wúmíng 无名

observance (*of festival*) zūnshǒu 遵守

observant liúxīn 留心

observation (*of nature, stars*) guānchá 观察; (*comment*) yìjiàn 意见

observatory tiānwén tái 天文台

observe *behavior* zhùyì 注意; *people* kàndào 看到; *nature* guāncè 观测

observer (*of human nature etc*) guānchá zhě 观察者; (*at conference, elections*) guāncháyuán 观察员

obsess: **be ~ed with X** duì X zháomí 对 X 着迷

obsession pǐ癖; (*with a person, hobby*) zháomí 著迷

obsessive *behavior* guòfèn 过分

obsolete yǐ fèiqì 已废弃

obstacle (*physical*) zhàng'ài wù 障碍物; (*to progress etc*) zhàng'ài 障碍

obstetrician chǎnkē yīshī 产科医师

obstinacy wángù 顽固

obstinate wángù 顽固

obstruct *road, passage* zǔsè 阻塞; *investigation, police* zǔdǎng 阻挡

obstruction (*on road etc*) zhàng'ài wù 障碍物

obstructive *behavior* fáng'ài 妨碍

obtain dédào 得到

obtainable *products* kě huòdé 可获得

obvious (*evident, not subtle*) míngxiǎn 明显

obviously míngxiǎnde 明显地; **~!** dāngránle! 当然了!

occasion jīhuì 机会

occasional ǒu'ěr 偶尔

occasionally ǒurán 偶然

occult 1 *adj* shénmì 神秘 **2** *n:* **the ~** mìshù 秘术

occupant (*of vehicle*) chéngkè 乘客; (*of house*) jūzhù zhě 居住者

occupation (*job*) zhíyè 职业; (*of country*) zhànlǐng 占领

occupy *one's time, mind* zhànyòng 占用; *position in company* chōngrèn 充任; *country* zhànlǐng 占领

occur fāshēng 发生; *it ~red to me that ...* wǒ xiǎngdào ... 我想到 ...

occurrence chūxiàn 出现

ocean hǎiyáng 海洋

o'clock: *at five/six ~* wǔ/liù diǎnzhōng 五/六点钟

October shíyuè 十月

octopus zhāngyú 章鱼

odd (*strange*) qíguài 奇怪; (*not even*) jīshù 奇数; *the ~ one out* yǔzhòng bùtóng 与众不同; *50 ~* dàgài wǔshí 大概五十

odds: *be at ~ with X* yǔ X duìlì 与 X 对立

odds and ends (*objects*) língxīng cánwù 零星残物; (*things to do*) suǒsuì shì 琐碎事

odometer lǐchéng biǎo 里程表

odor qìwèi 气味

of: *the name ~ the street/hotel* jiē/lǚguǎn de míngzi 街/旅馆的名字; *the color ~ the car* qìchē yánsè 汽车颜色; *the works ~ Dickens* Dígèngsī zhùzuò 狄更斯著作; *five/ten minutes ~ twelve* shí'èr diǎn chà wǔ/shí fēn 十二点差五/十分; *die ~ cancer/a stroke* sǐyú áizhèng/zhòngfèng 死于癌症/中风; *love ~ money/adventure* duì qián/màoxiǎn de xǐ'ài 对钱/冒险的喜爱; *~ the three this is ...* sāngè zhīzhōng zhèshì ... 三个之中这是 ...

off 1 *prep:* *~ the main road* (*away from*) líkāi dà mǎlù 离开大马路; (*leading off*) cóng dà mǎlù fēnchà chūlái 从大马路分岔出来; *$20 ~ the price* jiǎnjià èrshí měiyuán 减价二十美元; *he's ~ his food* tā bùchī dōngxi 他不吃东西

2 *adv:* *be ~* (*of light*) méi kāidēng 没开灯; (*of TV, machine*) méikāi 没开; (*of brake*) méi shàng zhá 没上闸; (*of lid, top*) méi gàizhe gàir 没盖着盖儿; (*not at work*) méi shàngbān 没上班; (*canceled*) qǔxiāo 取消; *we're ~ tomorrow* (*leaving*) wǒmén míngtiān líkāi 我们明天离开; *I'm ~ to New York* wǒ qù Niǔyuē 我去纽约; *with his pants ~* tā bù chuān kùzi 他不穿裤子; *with his hat ~* tā bù dài màozi 他不戴帽子; *take a day ~* xiūjià yītiān 休假一天; *it's 3 miles ~* sān yīnglǐ yuǎn 三英里远; *it's a long way ~* (*in the distance*) hái yuǎn zhene 还远着呢; (*in future*) hái qiě zhene 还且着呢; *drive/walk ~* kāizǒu/zǒukāi 开走/走开 **3** *adj:* *the ~ switch* guānbì jiàn 关闭键

offend *v/t* (*insult*) màofàn 冒犯

offender LAW zuìfàn 罪犯

offense LAW zuìxíng 罪行

offensive 1 *adj behavior, remark, smell* tǎoyàn 讨厌 **2** *n* MIL (*attack*) gōngjī 攻击; *go onto the ~* cǎiqǔ gōngjī 采取攻击

offer 1 *n* tígōng 提供 **2** *v/t* tígōng 提供; *~ X Y* gěi X Y 给 X Y

offhand *adj attitude* bùjū lǐjié 不拘礼节

office (*building*) bàngōnglóu 办公楼; (*room*) bàngōngshì 办公室; (*position*) zhíwèi 职位

office block bàngōng dàlóu 办公大楼

office hours bàngōng shíjiān 办公时间

officer MIL jūnguān 军官; (*in police*) jǐngguān 警官

official 1 *adj organization, statement view, theory* guānfāng 官方; (*confirmed*) zhèngshì 正式 **2** *n* guānyuán 官员

officially (*strictly speaking*) zhèngguī láishuō 正规来说

off-line *adj working, input* xiàwǎng 下网; *go ~* líxiàn 离线; **off-peak** *rates, season* dīfēng shíjiān 低峰时间; *~ electricity* dīfēng shíjiān gōngdiàn 低峰时间供电; **off-season 1** *adj rates, vacation* dànjì 淡季 **2** *n* dànjì 淡季; **offset** *v/t losses, disadvantage* dǐxiāo 抵消; **offside 1** *adj wheel etc* wàibiān 外边 **2** *adv* SP yuèwèi 越位; **offspring** hòudài 后代; **off-white** *adj* huībái sè 灰白色

often jīngcháng 经常

oil 1 *n* (*for machine, food, skin*) yóu 油; (*as resource*) shíyóu 石油 **2** *v/t hinges, bearings* jiāyóu 加油

oil company shíyóu gōngsī 石油公司; **oil painting** yóuhuà 油画; **oil rig** yóujǐng 油井; **oil tanker** yóuchuán 油船; **oil well** yóujǐng 油井

oily yǒuyóu 有油; *food* yóunì 油腻

ointment ruǎngāo 软膏

ok kěyǐ 可以; *can I?* – ~ kěyǐ ma? – kěyǐ 可以吗？- 可以; *is it ~ with you if …?* … nǐ bù jièyì ba? … 你不介意吧？; *that's ~ by me* wǒ tóngyì 我同意; *are you ~?* (*well, not hurt*) nǐ méishìr ba? 你没事儿吧？; *are you ~ for Friday?* xīngqī wǔ xíngma? 星期五行吗？; *he's ~* (*is a good guy*) tā tǐnghǎo 他挺好; *is this bus ~ for …?* zhè gōnggòng qìchē qù … ma? 这公共汽车去 … 吗？

old lǎo 老; (*previous*) jiù 旧; *how are you/is he?* nǐ/tā duōdà niánji le? 你/他多大年纪了？; *he's getting ~* tā shàng niánji le 他上年纪了

old age lǎonián 老年

old-fashioned guòshí 过时

Old Summer Palace Yuánmíngyuán 圆明园

olive gǎnlǎn 橄榄

olive oil gǎnlǎn yóu 橄榄油

Olympic Games Àoyùnhuì 奥运会

omelet jiān dànjuǎn 煎蛋卷

ominous yùzhào 预兆

omission yílòu 遗漏

omit yílòu 遗漏; ~ *to do X* wàngjì zuò X 忘记做 X

on 1 *prep*: ~ *the table/wall* zài zhuō/qiáng shàng 在桌/墙上; ~ *the bus/train* gōnggòng qìchē/huǒchē lǐ 公共汽车/火车里; ~ *TV/the radio* diànshì shàng/guǎngbō lǐ 电视上/广播里; ~ *Sunday* xīngqī tiān 星期天; ~ *the 1st of …* … dìyī tiān … 第一天; *this is ~ me* (*I'm paying*) wǒ lái fùqián 我来付钱; ~ *his arrival/departure* tā dàodá/líkāi shí 他到达/离开时 **2** *adv*: *be ~* (*of light*) kāidēng 开灯; (*of TV, computer etc*) kāi 开; (*of brake*) shàngzhá 上闸; (*of lid, top*) gàizhe gàir 盖着盖儿; (*of program: being broadcast*) kāiyǎn 开演; (*of meeting etc: be scheduled to happen*) jìnxíng 进行; *what's ~ tonight?* (*on TV etc*) jīnwǎn yǒu shénme jiémù? 今晚有什么节目？; (*what's planned?*) jīnwǎn gàn shénme? 今晚干什么？; *with his jacket ~* tā chuānzhe wàiyī 他穿着外衣; *with his hat ~* tā dàizhe màozi 他戴着帽子; *you're ~* (*I accept your offer etc*) xíng 行; ~ *you go* (*go ahead*) nǐ gànba 你干吧; *walk/talk ~* zǒu/tán xiàqù 走/谈下去; *and so ~* děngdeng 等等; ~ *and ~ talk etc* méiwán méiliǎo 没完没了 **3** *adj*: *the ~ switch* kāiqǐ jiàn 开启键

once 1 *adv* (*one time*) yīcì 一次; (*formerly*) céngjīng 曾经; ~ *again*, ~ *more* yòu yīcì 又一次; *at ~* (*immediately*) lìjí 立即; *all at ~* (*suddenly*) tūrán 突然; (*all*) *at ~* (*together*) yīqǐ 一起; ~ *upon a time there was …* cóngqián yǒu … 从前有 … **2** *conj*: ~ *you have finished* nǐ yī wánle yǐhòu 你一完了以后

one 1 *n* (*number*) yī 一; (*in phone numbers*) yāo 幺 **2** *adj* yīgè 一个; ~ *day* yītiān 一天; ~ *country, two systems* yīguó liǎngzhì 一国两制 **3** *pron* yīgè 一个; *which ~?* nǎ yīgè? 哪一个？; ~ *by ~ enter, deal with* yīyī 一一; ~ *another* hùxiāng 互相; *the little ~s* xiǎo péngyǒu mén 小朋友们 **4** *personal pron*: *what can ~ say?*

háiyǒu shénme kě shuō de? 还有什么可说的？

one child policy jìhuà shēngyù 计划生育; **one-off** n (unique event, person) yīcì xìng 一次性; (exception) tèshū qíngkuàng 特殊情况; **one-parent family** dānshēn fùmǔ jiātíng 单身父母家庭

oneself zìjǐ 自己; **do X by ~** zìjǐ zuò X 自己做 X

one-sided discussion, fight yībiān dǎo 一边倒; **one-way street** dānxíng dào 单行道; **one-way ticket** dānchéng piào 单程票

onion yángcōng 洋葱

on-line adj shàngwǎng 上网; **be ~** zài wǎngshang 在网上; **go ~ (to)** shàngwǎng 上网

on-line service COMPUT wǎngluò fúwù 网络服务

onlooker pángguān zhě 旁观者

only 1 adv zhǐ 只; **not ~ X but also Y** bù jǐnjin X, Y yěshì 不仅仅 X, Y 也是; **~ just** gānggang 刚刚 **2** adj wéiyī 唯一; **~ son / daughter** dúzǐ / nǚ 独子 / 女

onset jiànglín 降临

onside adv SP wèi yuèwèi 未越位

onto: put X ~ Y bǎ X fàngdào Y shàng 把 X 放到 Y 上

onward xiàngqián 向前; **from ... ~** ... zhīhòu ... 之后

oolong tea wūlóngchá 乌龙茶

ooze 1 v/i (of liquid, mud) shènchū 渗出 **2** v/t: **he ~s charm** tā xiǎnde hěnyǒu mèilì 他显得很有魅力

opaque glass bù tòumíng 不透明

OPEC (= **Organization of Petroleum Exporting Countries**) Shíyóu Shūchūguó Zǔzhī 石油输出国组织

open 1 adj door, store, file kāizhe 开着; (honest, frank) tǎnbái 坦白; relationship wú zhàng'ài 无障碍; countryside kōngkuàng 空旷; **in the ~ air** lùtiān 露天 **2** v/t door, store, window, bottle kāi 开; book, paper tānkāi 摊开; COMPUT: file dǎkāi 打开; meeting kāishǐ 开始; **~ a bank account** kāi hù 开户 **3** v/i (of door, store, flower) kāi 开

♦ **open up** v/i (of person) fàngkāi 放开

open-air adj meeting, concert lùtiān 露天; **~ pool** shìwài yóuyǒng chí 室外游泳池; **open-door policy** kāifàng zhèngcè 开放政策; **open-ended** contract etc bú gùdìng 不固定

opening (in wall etc) kòngxì 空隙; (beginning: of movie, novel etc) kāishǐ 开始; (job going) kòngquē 空缺

openly (honestly, frankly) tǎnshuài 坦率

open-minded xūxīn 虚心; **open plan office** tǒngyī bàngōngshì 统一办公室; **open ticket** fēi gùdìng piào 非固定票

opera gējù 歌剧; **Peking Opera** Jīngjù 京剧

opera glasses xiǎo wàngyuǎnjìng 小望远镜; **opera house** gējù yuàn 歌剧院; **Peking Opera House** Jīngjù Yuàn 京剧院; **opera singer** gējù jiā 歌剧家

operate 1 v/i (of company) jīngyíng 经营; (of airline, bus service) guǎnlǐ 管理; (of machine) yùnzhuǎn 运转; MED dòng shǒushù 动手术 **2** v/t machine cāozuò 操作

♦ **operate on** MED gěi ... kāidāo 给 ... 开刀

operating instructions cāozuò shǒuzé 操作手则; **operating room** MED shǒushù shì 手术室; **operating system** COMPUT cāozuò xìtǒng 操作系统

operation MED shǒushù 手术; (of machine) cāozuò 操作; **~s** (of company) jīngyíng 经营; **have an ~** MED zuò shǒushù 做手术

operator TELEC jiēxiàn shēng 接线生; (of machine) cāozuò zhě 操作者; (tour ~) lǚxíng dàiyíng zhě 旅行代营者

ophthalmologist yǎnkē yīshēng 眼科医生

opinion (view) kànfǎ 看法; **what's your ~?** nǐ yǒu shénme yìjiàn? 你有什么意见？; **in my ~** zài wǒ

kànlái 在我看来
opium yāpiàn 鸦片
Opium War Yāpiàn Zhànzhēng 鸦片战争
opponent duìshǒu 对手
opportunity jīhuì 机会
oppose fǎnduì 反对; **be ~d to ...** fǎnduì ... 反对 ...; **as ~d to X** yǔ X xiāngfǎn 与 X 相反
opposite 1 *adj side of road, end of town* duìmiàn 对面; *direction, meaning* xiāngfǎn 相反; *views, characters* duìkàng 对抗; **the ~ sex** yìxìng 异性 **2** *n* fǎnmiàn 反面
opposition (*to plan*) fǎnduì 反对; *Br* POL zàiyědǎng 在野党
oppress *the people* yāpò 压迫
oppressive *rule, dictator* bàonüè 暴虐; *weather* chénzhòng 沉重
optical illusion cuòshì 错视
optician yǎnjìng diàn 眼镜店
optimism lèguān 乐观
optimist lèguān zhě 乐观者
optimistic lèguān 乐观
optimum 1 *adj* zuì shìyí 最适宜 **2** *n* zuìjiā tiáojiàn 最佳条件
option xuǎnzé 选择, xuǎnxiàng 选项
optional kě xuǎnzé 可选择
optional extras kě xuǎnzé de fùjiājiàn 可选择的附加件
or huò 或; **~ else!** bùrán dehuà děngzhe qiáo! 不然的话等着瞧!
oral exam kǒushì 口试; **oral hygiene** kǒuqiāng wèishēng 口腔卫生; **oral sex** kǒuyín 口淫
orange 1 *adj* (*color*) chéng 橙 **2** *n* (*fruit*) chéng 橙; (*color*) chéngsè 橙色
orangeade chéngzhīr 橙汁儿
orange juice ⇩ chéngzhīr 橙汁儿
orator yǎnshuōjiā 演说家
orbit 1 *n* (*of earth*) tiāntǐ yùnxíng guǐdào 天体运行轨道; **send X into ~** jiāng X sòngrù guǐdào 将 X 送入轨道 **2** *v/t the earth* rào guǐdào yùnxíng 绕轨道运行
orchard guǒyuán 果园

orchestra guǎnxián yuèduì 管弦乐队
orchid lánhuā 兰花
ordeal kǔnànde jīnglì 苦难的经历
order 1 *n* (*command*) mìnglìng 命令; (*sequence*) cìxù 次序; (*being well arranged*) zhìxù 秩序; (*for goods*) dìnggòu 定购; (*in restaurant*) dìng càidān 定菜单; **in ~ to** wèile ... 为了 ...; **out of ~** (*not functioning*) shīlíng 失灵; (*not in sequence*) cìxù diāndǎo 次序颠倒 **2** *v/t* (*put in sequence etc*) ānpái 安排; *goods* dìnghuò 定货; *meal* jiàocài 叫菜; **~ X to do Y** mìnglìng X qù zuò Y 命令 X 去做 Y **3** *v/i* (*in restaurant*) diǎncài 点菜
orderly 1 *adj* yǒu zhìxù 有秩序 **2** *n* (*in hospital*) qínzá gōng 勤杂工
ordinary pǔtōng 普通
ore kuàngshí 矿石
organ ANAT qìguān 器官; MUS fēngqín 风琴
organic *food, fertilizer* zìrán 自然
organism shēngwù 生物
organization jīgòu 机构; (*organizing*) zǔzhī 组织
organize zǔzhī 组织
organizer (*person*) zǔzhī zhě 组织者
orgasm xìngyù gāocháo 性欲高潮
Orient Dōngfāng 东方
orient *v/t* (*direct*) cháo X de fāngxiàng 朝 X 的方向; **~ oneself** (*get bearings*) rènqīng xíngshì 认清形势
Oriental 1 *adj* Dōngfāng 东方 **2** *n* Dōngfāng rén 东方人
origin qǐyuán 起源; **person of Chinese ~** Huáyì 华裔; **idea of Chinese ~** qǐyuán yú Zhōngguóde sīxiǎng 起源于中国的思想
original 1 *adj* (*not copied*) yuánzuò 原作; (*first*) zuìchū 最初 **2** *n* (*painting etc*) yuán zuòpǐn 原作品
originality dúchuànglì 独创力
originally yuánxiān 原先
originate 1 *v/t scheme, idea* fāmíng

发明 **2** v/i (of idea, belief) fāqǐ 发起; (of family) láizì yú 来自于

originator (of scheme etc) fāqǐrén 发起人; **he's not an ~** tā bùshì gè fāmíngjiā 他不是个发明家

ornament zhuāngshì wù 装饰物

ornamental zhuāngshì 装饰

ornate style huá ér bùshí 华而不实

orphan gū'ér 孤儿

orphanage gū'ér yuàn 孤儿院

orthopedic adj jiǎoxíng wàikē 矫形外科

ostentatious style, behavior zìgāo zìdà 自高自大; clothes kuāzhāng 夸张

other 1 adj (referring to people) qítā 其他; (referring to things, animals) qítā 其它; **the ~ day** (recently) nàtiān 那天; **every ~ day** / **person** měi liángtiān / gèrén zhōng de yīgè 每两天 / 个人中的一个 **2** n lìng yīgè 另一个; **the ~s** (people) qítāde 其他的; (things, animals) qítāde 其它的

otherwise bùrán dehuà 不然的话; (differently) bùtóng 不同

otter shuǐtǎ 水獭

ought: **I** / **you ~ to know** wǒ / nǐ yīnggāi zhīdào 我 / 你应该知道; **you ~ to have done it** nǐ zǎo yīnggāi zuòle 你早应该做了

ounce àngsī 盎司

our wǒmen 我们

ours wǒménde 我们的; **a friend of ~** wǒménde péngyǒu 我们的朋友

ourselves wǒmen zìjǐ 我们自己; **by ~** wǒmen zìjǐ 我们自己

oust (from office) miǎnzhí 免职

out: **be ~** (of light) guāndiào 关掉; (of fire) xīmiè 熄灭; (of flower) shèngkāi 盛开; (of sun) chūlái 出来; (not at home, not in building) búzài 不在; (of calculations) cuò 错; (be published) chūbǎn 出版; (of secret) xiǎnlòu 显露; (no longer in competition) táotài 淘汰; (no longer in fashion) guòshí 过时; **~ here in Dallas** zài zhèlǐ Dálāsī 在这里达拉斯; **he's ~ in the gar-**

den tā zài huāyuán lǐ 他在花园里; (get) **~!** chūqù! 出去 ！; (get) **~ of my room!** gǔnchū wǒ fángjiān! 滚出我房间 ！; **that's ~** (out of the question) bùxíng 不行; **he's ~ to win** (fully intending to) tā fēi yíng bùkě 他非赢不可

outboard motor chuánwěi diàndòngjī 船尾电动机

outbreak (of violence, war) bàofā 爆发

outburst (emotional) bèngfā 迸发

outcast n bèi yíqì zhě 被遗弃者

outcome jiéguǒ 结果

outcry qiángliè kàngyì 强烈抗议

outdated guòshí 过时

outdo shèngguò 胜过

outdoor toilet, activities, life shìwài 室外

outdoors adv shìwài 室外

outer wall etc wàibù 外部

outer space tàikōng 太空

outfit (clothes) tàozhuāng 套装; (company, organization) zǔzhī 组织

outgoing flight chūháng 出航; personality kāilǎng 开朗

outgrow old ideas chāoguò 超过

outing (trip) chūyóu 出游

outlet (of pipe) chūkǒu 出口; (for sales) xiāoshòu diǎn 销售点; ELEC chāzuò 插座

outline 1 n (of person, building etc) lúnkuò 轮廓; (of plan, novel) cǎotú 草图 **2** v/t plans etc dǎ cǎotú 打草图

outlive huóde bǐ … gèngjiǔ 活得比 … 更长

outlook (prospects) zhǎnwàng 展望

outlying areas biānyuǎn 边远

outnumber: **X ~s Y by … times** X bǐ Y dà … bèi X 比 Y 大 … 倍

out of ◊ (motion): **run ~ the house** pǎochū wūwài 跑出屋外 ◊ (position): **20 miles ~ Nanjing** Nánjīng yǐwài èrshí yīnglǐ 南京以外二十英里 ◊ (cause): **~ jealousy** / **curiosity** yóuyú jídù / hàoqí 由于嫉妒 / 好奇 ◊ (without): **we're ~ gas** wǒmén chē méi yóu le 我们车没油了◊ (*from a group*): **5 ~ 10** shífēn zhīwǔ 十分之五

out-of-date guòshí 过时
out-of-the-way huāngpì 荒僻
outperform bǐ ... hǎo 比 ... 好
output 1 *n* (*of factory*) chǎnliàng 产量; COMPUT shūchū 输出 **2** *v/t* (*produce*) shēngchǎn 生产; COMPUT: *signal* fāchū 发出
outrage 1 *n* (*feeling*) gōngfèn 公愤; (*act*) bàoxíng 暴行 **2** *v/t* yǐnqǐ fènkǎi 引起愤慨; *I was ~d to hear X* dāng wǒ tīngdào X shí gǎndào shífēn fènnù 当我听到 X 时感到十分愤怒
outrageous *acts* wúchǐ 无耻; *prices* guòfèn 过分
outright 1 *adj winner* chèdǐ 彻底 **2** *adv win* chèdǐ 彻底; *kill* jísǐ 即死
outrun (*run faster than*) pǎode gèngkuài 跑得更快; (*run for longer than*) pǎode gèngjiǔ 跑得更久
outset kāishǐ 开始; *from the ~* yī kāitóu 一开头
outside 1 *adj surface, wall, lane* wàibù 外部 **2** *adv sit, go* wàimiàn 外面 **3** *prep* zài ... yǐwài 在 ... 以外; (*apart from*) chúle 除了 **4** *n* (*of building, case etc*) wàimiàn 外面; *at the ~* zuìduō 最多
outside broadcast lùyīn shìwài bōyīn 录音室外播音
outsider lěngmén 冷门
outsize *adj clothing* tè dàhào 特大号
outskirts jiāoqū 郊区
outspoken zhíyán búhuì 直言不讳
outstanding *success, quality* xiǎnzhù 显著; *writer, athlete* jiéchū 杰出; FIN: *invoice, sums* wèifù 未付
outward *adj appearance* wàibiǎo 外表; *~ journey* wàichū lǚchéng 外出旅程
outward-going kāilǎng 开朗
outwardly xiàngwàide 向外地
outweigh bǐ ... zhòngyào 比 ... 重要

outwit zhìshèng 智胜
oval *adj* tuǒyuán 椭圆
ovary luǎncháo 卵巢
oven kǎoxiāng 烤箱
over 1 *prep* (*across*) guò 过; (*more than*) chāoguò 超过; (*above*) zài ... shàngfāng 在 ... 上方; (*during*) zài ... qījiān 在 ... 期间; *travel all ~ China* yóulán quán Zhōngguó 游览全中国; *you find them all ~ China* tāmén biànbù Zhōngguó 它们遍布中国; *let's talk ~ a drink / meal* wǒmén biān hē / chī biān tán 我们边喝 / 吃边谈; *we're ~ the worst* wǒmén yǐjīng dùguòle zuì kùnnán de shíkè 我们已经渡过了最困难的时刻 **2** *adv*: *be ~* (*finished*) wánjié 完结; (*left*) shèngyú 剩余; *~ to you* (*your turn*) gāi nǐ le 该你了; *~ in Europe* zài Ōuzhōu 在欧洲; *~ here* zài zhèlǐ 在这里; *~ there* zài nàlǐ 在那里; *it hurts all ~* wǒ húnshēn dōu téng 我浑身都疼; *painted white all ~* quánbù shuā báisè 全部刷白色; *it's all ~* quánwánle 全完了; *~ and ~ again* lǚcì 屡次; *do X ~* (*again*) zàicì zuò X 再次做 X
overall 1 *adj length* zǒngtǐ 总体 **2** *adv* cóng tóu zhì wěi 从头至尾
overawe: *be ~d by X* bèi X xiàzhù 被 X 吓住
overboard: *man ~!* yǒurén luòshuǐ! 有人落水！; *go ~ for X* duì X kuángrè zhuīqiú 对 X 狂热追求
overcast *day, sky* duōyún 多云
overcharge *v/t customer* guògāo yàojià 过高要价
overcoat dàyī 大衣
overcome *difficulties, shyness* zhēngfú 征服; *be ~ by emotion* búnéng zìzhì 不能自制
overcrowded yōngjǐ 拥挤
overdo (*exaggerate*) kuāzhāng 夸张; (*in cooking*) zhǔ guòhuǒr 煮过火儿; *you're ~ing things* guòyú láolèi 过于劳累
overdone *meat* guòhuǒ 过火
overdose *n* guòliàng 过量

overdraft chāozhī 超支; *have an ~* yǒu chāozhī 有超支

overdraw *account* chāozhī 超支; *be \$800 ~n* chāozhī bābǎi měiyuán 超支八百美元

overdrive MOT chāosù 超速

overdue *apology, alteration* qīdài yǐjiǔ 期待以久

overestimate *abilities, value* guògāo gūjì 过高估计

overexpose *photograph* guòdù gǎnguāng 过度感光

overflow 1 *n* (*pipe*) fànlàn 泛滥 **2** *v/i* (*of water*) shǐ yìchù 使溢出

overgrown *garden* cùyè cóngshēng 簇叶丛生; *he's an ~ baby* tā shuǎ xiǎohái píqì 他耍小孩脾气

overhaul *v/t engine* dàxiū 大修; *plans* chèdǐ jiǎnchá 彻底检查

overhead 1 *adj lights* tóudǐng shàng 头顶上; *railroad* jiàkōng 架空 **2** *n* FIN tōngcháng kāizhī 通常开支

overhear tōutīng 偷听

overjoyed kuángxǐ 狂喜

overland *adj & adv* jīngguò lùdì 经过陆地

overlap *v/i* (*of tiles, periods of time etc*) chóngdié 重迭; (*of theories*) fùhé 复合; ELEC fùhé guòzhòng 负荷过重

overlook (*of tall building etc*) fǔshì 俯视; (*not see*) hūlüè 忽略

overly guòdùde 过度地; *not ~ ...* méi guòdùde ... 没过度地 ...

overnight *adv* yèjiān 夜间

overnight bag guòyè dài 过夜袋

overpaid fùqián guòduō 付钱过多

overpass lìtǐ jiāochā 立体交叉

overpower *v/t* (*physically*) jībài jíbài 击败

overpowering *smell* nóngliè 浓裂; *sense of guilt* qiángliè 强烈

overpriced yàojià guògāo 要价过高

overrated guògāo gūjì 过高估计

overrule *decision* fǒujué 否决

overrun *country* qīnzhàn 侵占; *time* chāoshí 超时; *be ~ with* mànyán 蔓延

overseas *adj & adv* hǎiwài 海外

overseas Chinese Huáqiáo 华侨

oversee jiānshì 监视

oversight shūhū 疏忽

oversleep shuì guòtóu 睡过头

overtake (*in work, development*) chāoguò 超过; *Br* MOT chāochē 超车

overthrow tuīfān 推翻

overtime *work* jiābān 加班

overture MUS xùqǔ 序曲; *make ~s to* tíchū jiànyì 提出建议

overturn 1 *v/t vehicle, object* fānzhuàn 翻转; *government* tuīfān 推翻 **2** *v/i* (*of vehicle*) fān 翻

overweight chāozhòng 超重

overwhelm (*with work*) bèi gōngzuò yāde chuǎnbù guòqì 被工作压得喘不过气; (*with emotion*) bùzhī suǒcuò 不知所措; *be ~ed by* (*by response*) jīngxǐ jiāojí 惊喜交集

overwork 1 *n* guòdù gōngzuò 过度工作 **2** *v/i* gōngzuò guòdù 工作过度 **3** *v/t: ~ X* shǐ X píláo guòdù 使X疲劳过度

owe *v/t* qiàn 欠; *~ X \$500* qiàn X wǔbǎi měiyuán 欠X五百美元; *~ X an apology* yīng xiàng dàoqiàn 应向X道歉; *how much do I ~ you?* wǒ qiàn nǐ duōshǎo? 我欠你多少?

owing to yóuyú 由于

owl māotóuyīng 猫头鹰

own[1] *v/t* yōngyǒu 拥有

own[2] **1** *adj* zìjǐ 自己 **2** *pron: an apartment of my ~* wǒ zìjǐde gōngyù 我自己的公寓; *on my / his ~* wǒ / tā zìjǐ 我 / 他自己

♦ **own up** tǎnbái de chéngrèn 坦白地承认

owner yōngyǒu zhě 拥有者

ownership suǒyǒu quán 所有权

ox niú 牛

oxide yǎnghuà wù 氧化物

oxygen yǎngqì 氧气

oyster háo 蚝

oyster sauce háoyóu 蚝油

ozone chòuyǎng 臭氧

ozone layer chòuyǎng céng 臭氧层

P

pace 1 *n* (*step*) bù 步; (*speed*) sùdù 速度 2 *v/i*: **~ up and down** duóbù 踱步

pacemaker MED qǐbóqì 起博器; SP dìng sùdù zhě 定速度者

Pacific: **the ~** (**Ocean**) Tàipíngyáng 太平洋

Pacific Rim: **the ~** Tàipíngyáng àn 太平洋岸; **~ countries** Tàipíngyáng guójiā 太平洋岸国家

pacifier (*for baby*) xiàngpí nǎitóu 橡皮奶头

pacifism hépíng zhǔyì 和平主义

pacifist *n* hépíng zhǔyì zhě 和平主义者

pacify ānfǔ 安抚

pack 1 *n* (*back~*) bēibāo 背包; (*of cereal, food*) dài 袋; (*of cigarettes*) bāo 包; (*of cards*) fù 副 2 *v/t* bag jiāng dōngxi zhuāngrù 将东西装入; *item of clothing etc* fàngrù xínglǐ 放入行李; *goods* bāozhuāng 包装; *groceries* zhuāngrù kǒudài 装入口袋 3 *v/i* zhěnglǐ xíngzhuāng 整理行装

package 1 *n* (*parcel*) bāoguǒ 包裹; (*of offers etc*) zhěngdài cáiliào 整袋材料 2 *v/t* (*in packs*) dǎbāo 打包; (*for promotion*) bāozhuāng 包装

package deal (*for vacation*) bāobàn lǚxíng 包办旅行

package tour bāobàn lǚxíng 包办旅行

packaging (*of product*) bāozhuāng 包装; (*of rock star etc*) xíngxiàng bāozhuāng 形象包装

packed (*crowded*) mǎnyuán 满员

packet bāo 包

pact xiéyì 协议

pad¹ 1 *n* (*piece of cloth etc*) diànliào 垫料; (*for writing*) biànjiānběn 便笺本 2 *v/t* (*with material*) diànchèn 垫衬; *speech, report* pīncòu 拼凑

pad² *v/i* (*move quietly*) qīngqīng zǒu 轻轻走

padded *jacket, shoulders* dài chèndiàn 带衬垫

padding (*material*) chènliào 衬料; (*in speech etc*) fèihuà 废话

paddle¹ 1 *n* (*for canoe*) lǔ 橹 2 *v/i* (*in canoe*) yáolǔ 摇橹

paddle² *v/i* (*in water*) tāngshuǐ 趟水

paddock xiǎowéichǎng 小围场

paddy dàozi 稻子

paddy field dàotián 稻田

padlock 1 *n* guàsuǒ 挂锁 2 *v/t* gate yòng guàsuǒ suǒ 用挂锁锁; **~ X to Y** yòng guàsuǒ bǎ X suǒ zài Y shàng 用挂锁把 X 锁在 Y 上

page¹ *n* (*of book etc*) yè 页; **~ number** yèmǎ 页码

page² *v/t* (*call*) ⇩ chuánhū 传呼

pager ⇩ chuánhūjī 传呼机

pagoda bǎotǎ 宝塔

paid employment yǒucháng gùyōng 有偿雇佣

pail tǒng 桶

pain téngtòng 疼痛; **be in ~** tòng 痛; **take ~s to ...** fèi kǔxīn ... 费苦心 ...; **X is a ~ in the neck** F X zhēn fánrén X 真烦人

painful *arm, leg etc* téngtòng 疼痛; (*distressing*) lìngrén tòngkǔ 令人痛苦; (*laborious*) fèishì 费事

painfully (*extremely, acutely*) tèbié 特别

painkiller zhǐtòngpiàn 止痛片

painless wútòng 无痛

painstaking zǐxì 仔细

paint 1 *n* (*for wall, car*) túliào 涂料; (*for artist*) yánliào 颜料 2 *v/t* wall etc shàng túliào 上涂料; *picture* yòng yánliào huà 用颜料画 3 *v/i* (*as art form*) huìhuà 绘画

paintbrush (*for wall, ceiling*) qīshuā 漆刷; (*of artist*) huàbǐ 画笔

painter (*decorator*) fěnshuāgōng 粉
刷工; (*artist*) huàjiā 画家

painting (*activity*) huìhuà 绘画;
(*picture*) túhuà 图画

paintwork (*in room*) fěnshuā 粉
刷; (*of car*) qī 漆

pair duì 对; *a ~ of shoes / sandals*
yìshuāng xié / liángxié 一双鞋 / 凉
鞋

pajama jacket shuìyī 睡衣

pajama pants shuìkù 睡裤

pajamas shuìyīkù 睡衣裤

Pakistan Bājīsītǎn 巴基斯坦

Pakistani 1 *adj* Bājīsītǎn 巴基斯
坦 2 *n* Bājīsītǎn rén 巴基斯坦人

pal F (*friend*) gēmenr 哥们儿; *hey
~, got a light?* lǎoxiōng, jiège
huǒr? 老兄，借个火儿？

palace gōngdiàn 宫殿

palate è 腭

palatial fùlì 富丽

pale *person* cāngbái 苍白; *~ pink /
blue* dànfěn / lánsè 淡粉 / 蓝色

pallet huòbǎn 货板

pallor liǎnsè cāngbái 脸色苍白

palm[1] (*of hand*) shǒuzhǎng 手掌

palm[2] (*tree*) zōnglǘshù 棕榈树

palpitations MED xīnjì 心悸

paltry wēibùzúdào 微不足道

pamper fàngzòng 放纵

pamphlet xiǎocèzi 小册子

pan 1 *n* (*for cooking*) guō 锅 2 *v/t* F
(*criticize severely*) yánlì pīpíng 严
厉批评

♦ pan out (*develop*) fāzhǎn 发展

pancake bóbǐng 薄饼

panda xióngmāo 熊猫

pandemonium dà hùnluàn 大混
乱

pane (*of glass*) kuài 块

panel (*section*) xiāngbǎn 镶板;
(*people*) xiǎozǔ 小组

paneling xiāngqiàn 镶嵌

panhandle *v/i* F xíngqǐ 行乞

panic 1 *n* kǒnghuāng 恐慌 2 *v/i*
shòujīng 受惊; *don't ~* biéhuāng
别慌

panic buying FIN kǒnghuāng
gòumǎi 恐慌购买; panic selling
FIN kǒnghuāng pāoshòu 恐慌抛
售; panic-stricken jīnghuāng

shīcuò 惊惶失措

panorama quánjǐng 全景

panoramic *view* quánjǐng 全景

pansy (*flower*) sānsèjǐn 三色堇; F
jiǎxiǎozi 假小子

pant *v/i* chuǎnxī 喘息

panties nèikù 内裤

pants kùzi 裤子

pantyhose liánkùwà 连裤袜

paper 1 *n* (*material*) zhǐ 纸;
(*news~*) bàozhǐ 报纸; (*wall~*) bìzhǐ
壁纸; (*academic*) lùnwén 论文;
(*examination ~*) kǎoshìjuàn 考试
卷; ~s (*documents*) wénjiàn 文件;
(*identity ~s*) zhèngjiàn 证件; *a
piece of ~* yìzhāng zhǐ 一张纸
2 *adj* zhǐzhì 纸制 3 *v/t room, walls*
biǎohú 裱糊

paperback píngzhuāngshū 平装
书; paper bag zhǐdài 纸袋; paper clip huíxíngzhēn 回形针;
paper cup zhǐ bēizi 纸杯子;
paperwork wénshū gōngzuò 文
书工作

par (*in golf*) biāozhǔn gānshù 标准
杆数; *be on a ~ with X* yǔ X
tóngděng zhòngyào 与X同等重
要; *feel below ~* gǎnjué bú tài hǎo
感觉不太好

parachute 1 *n* jiàngluòsǎn 降落
伞 2 *v/i* tiàosǎn 跳伞 3 *v/t troops,
supplies* (yòng jiàngluòsǎn) kōngtóu (用降落伞) 空投

parachutist tiàosǎn zhě 跳伞者

parade 1 *n* (*procession*) yuèbīng 阅
兵 2 *v/i* xíngzǒu 行走 3 *v/t knowledge, new car* xuànyào 炫耀

paradise *Biblical* lèyuán 乐园; *fig*
tiāntáng 天堂

paradox zìxiāng máodùn 自相矛
盾

paradoxical sì fēi ér shì 似非而
是

paradoxically sì fēi ér shì 似非而
是

paragraph duànluò 段落

parallel 1 *n* (*line*) píngxíngxiàn 平
行线; (*of latitude*) wěidùxiàn 纬
度线; *fig* xiāngsì zhī chù 相似之
处; *do two things in ~* tóngshí zuò
liǎngjiàn shì 同时做两件事

2 *adj line* píngxíng 平行; *fig* tóngshí fāshēng 同时发生 **3** *v/t* (*match*) xiāngdāng 相当

paralysis tānhuàn 瘫痪

paralyze tānhuàn 瘫痪; *fig* bù zhī suǒ cuò 不知所措

paramedic hùlǐ rényuán 护理人员

parameter jièxiàn 界限

paramilitary 1 *adj* zhǔn jūnshì 准军事 **2** *n* zhǔn jūnshì bùduì chéngyuán 准军事部队成员

paramount zuì zhòngyào 最重要; *be* ~ tóuděng dàshì 头等大事

paranoia wàngxiǎngkuáng 妄想狂

paranoid *adj* duōyí 多疑

paraphernalia záqīzábāde dōngxi 杂七杂八的东西

paraphrase shìyì 释义

paraplegic *n* xiàshēn tānhuàn de rén 下身瘫痪的人

parasite jìshēngchóng 寄生虫; *fig* kào jiùjì wéishēng 靠救济为生

parasol yángsǎn 阳伞

paratrooper sǎnbīng 伞兵

parcel *n* bāoguǒ 包裹

♦**parcel up** bāoqǐ 包起

parch *v/t* shǐ jiāogān 使焦干; *be ~ed* (*of person*) kě jíle 渴极了

pardon 1 *n* LAW shèmiǎn 赦免; *I beg your* ~? (*what did you say*) nǐ shuō shénme? 你说什么？; *I beg your* ~ (*I'm sorry*) qǐng yuánliàng 请原谅 **2** *v/t* yuánliàng 原谅; LAW shèmiǎn 赦免; ~ *me?* nǐ shuō shénme? 你说什么？

pare (*peel*) xiāopí 削皮

parent jiāzhǎng 家长

parental fùmǔ 父母

parent company zǒnggōngsī 总公司

parent-teacher association jiāzhǎng jiàoshī liányìhuì 家长教师联谊会

park¹ (*area*) gōngyuán 公园

park² MOT **1** *v/t* tíngfàng 停放 **2** *v/i* tíngchē 停车

parka fēngxuě dàyī 风雪大衣

parking MOT tíngchē 停车; *no* ~ jìnzhǐ tíngchē 禁止停车

parking brake shǒuzhá 手轧;

parking garage shìnèi tíngchēchǎng 室内停车场; **parking lot** tíngchēchǎng 停车场; **parking meter** tíngchē jìshí shōufèiqì 停车计时收费器; **parking place** tíngchēchù 停车处; **parking ticket** wéizhāng tíngchē fákuǎndān 违章停车罚款单

parliament yìhuì 议会

parliamentary yìhuì 议会

parole 1 *n* jiǎshì 假释; *be on* ~ huòdé jiǎshì 获得假释 **2** *v/t* zhǔnxǔ jiǎshì 准许假释

parrot yīngwǔ 鹦鹉

parsley ōuqín 欧芹

part 1 *n* yíbùfen 一部分; (*section, area*) bùfen 部分; (*of machine*) língjiàn 零件; (*in play, movie*) juésè 角色; MUS shēngbù 声部; (*in hair*) fèng 缝; *take* ~ *in* cānjiā 参加 **2** *adv* (*partly*) bùfēn 部分 **3** *v/i* fēnkāi 分开 **4** *v/t*: ~ *one's hair* jiāng tóufà fēnkāi 将头发分开

♦**part with** *things* chūràng 出让

part exchange bùfen dǐjià jiāoyìfǎ 部分抵价交易法; *take X in* ~ yǐ bùfēn dǐjià jiāoyìfǎ gòumǎi X 以部分抵价交易法购买X

partial (*incomplete*) bù wánquán 不完全; *be* ~ *to* piān'ài 偏爱

partially bùfen 部分

participant cānjiā zhě 参加者

participate cānjiā 参加; ~ *in X* cānjiā X 参加X

participation cānjiā 参加

particle PHYS lìzǐ 粒子; (*small amount*) yìdiǎnr 一点儿

particular (*specific*) tèbié 特别; (*special*) tèshū 特殊; (*fussy*) tiāotì 挑剔; *in* ~ yóuqí 尤其

particularly tèbié 特别

parting (*of people*) líbié 离别

partition 1 *n* (*screen*) píngfēng 屏风; (*of country*) fēnliè 分裂 **2** *v/t* *country* fēnliè 分裂

♦**partition off** gékāi 隔开

partly bùfen 部分

partner COM héhuǒrén 合伙人; (*in relationship*) tóngbàn 同伴; (*in particular activity*) dādàng 搭档

partnership COM héhuǒ jīngyíng 合伙经营; (*in particular activity*) dādàng guānxi 搭档关系

part of speech cíxìng 词性; **part owner** gòngyǒu zhě 共有者; **part-time 1** *adj* jiānzhí 兼职 **2** *adv* work jiānzhí 兼职

party 1 *n* (*celebration*) qìngzhùhuì 庆祝会; POL dǎng 党; (*group of people*) zǔ 组; **be a ~ to** cānyù 参与 **2** *v/i* F wánr 玩儿

party member dǎngyuán 党员

pass 1 *n* (*for getting into a place*) tōngxíngzhèng 通行证; SP chuánqiú 传球; (*in mountains*) guān'ài 关隘; **make a ~ at X** xiàng X tiáoqíng 向X调情 **2** *v/t* (*hand*) dì 递; (*go past*) jīngguò 经过; (*overtake*) yuèguò 越过; (*go beyond*) chāoguò 超过; (*approve*) biǎojué tōngguò 表决通过; SP chuánqiú 传球; **~ an exam** tōngguò kǎoshì 通过考试; **~ sentence** LAW pànxíng 判刑; **~ the time** xiāomó shíjiān 消磨时间 **3** *v/i* (*of time*) tuīyí 推移; (*in exam*) jígé 及格; SP chuándì 传递; (*go away*) xiāoshī 消失

♦**pass around** hùxiāng chuán 互相传

♦**pass away** (*die*) qùshì 去世

♦**pass by** *v/t & v/i* (*go past*) jīngguò 经过

♦**pass on 1** *v/t* information, book chuándì 传递 **2** *v/i* (*die*) qùshì 去世

♦**pass out** (*faint*) hūnjué 昏厥

♦**pass through** town tújīng 途经

♦**pass up** opportunity fàngguò 放过

passable road kě tōngguò 可通过; (*acceptable*) guòdequ 过得去

passage (*corridor*) tōngdào 通道; (*from poem, book*) yīduàn 一段; (*of time*) tuīyí 推移

passageway zǒuláng 走廊

passenger chéngkè 乘客

passenger seat chéngkè zuòwèi 乘客座位

passer-by guòlùrén 过路人

passion (*emotion*) qínggǎn 情感; (*sexual desire*) xìng'ài 性爱; (*fervor*) rèqíng 热情

passionate lover rèliàn 热恋; (*fervent*) rèqíng 热情

passive 1 *adj* bèidòng 被动 **2** *n* GRAM bèidòng yǔtài 被动语态; **in the ~** bèidòng xíngshì 被动形式

pass mark jígéfēn 及格分

passport hùzhào 护照

passport control hùzhào jiǎncháchù 护照检查处

password kǒulìng 口令

past 1 *adj* (*former*) yǐqián 以前; **the ~ few days** jìnjǐtiān 近几天; **that's all ~ now** nà dōu yǐjīng guòqù le 那都已经过去了 **2** *n* guòqù 过去; **in the ~** zài guòqù 在过去 **3** *prep* (*in time*) chíyú 迟于; (*in position*) jīngguò 经过; **it's half – two** xiànzài liǎngdiǎnbàn 现在两点半 **4** *adv*: **run / walk ~** pǎo / zǒuguò 跑 / 走过

paste 1 *n* (*adhesive*) jiànghu 糨糊 **2** *v/t* (*stick*), COMPUT zhāntiē 粘贴

pastel 1 *n* (*color*) qīngdànsè 清淡色 **2** *adj* qīngdàn 清淡

pastime xiāoqiǎn 消遣

pastor jiàoqū mùshī 教区牧师

past participle guòqù fēncí 过去分词

pastrami wǔxiāng xūnniúròu 五香熏牛肉

pastry (*for pie*) yóusū miàntuán 油酥面团; (*small cake*) sūpí gāodiǎn 酥皮糕点

past tense guòqùshí 过去时

pasty *adj* complexion cāngbái 苍白

pat 1 *n* qīngpāi 轻拍; **give X a ~ on the back** *fig* xiàng X biǎoshì zhùhè 向X表示祝贺 **2** *v/t* pāipāi 拍拍

patch 1 *n* (*on clothing*) bǔdīng 补丁; (*period of time*) yīduàn shíqī 一段时期; (*area*) bùfen 部分; **be not a ~ on** F yuǎnyuǎn bùrú 远远不如 **2** *v/t* clothing dǎ bǔdīng 打补丁

♦**patch up** (*repair temporarily*) línshí xiūlǐ 临时修理; quarrel jiějué 解决

patchwork 1 n (needlework) zápīn huābù 杂拼花布 **2** adj quilt zápīn huābù miánbèi 杂拼花布棉被

patchy quality bùyízhì 不一致; work, performance xiáyúhùjiàn 瑕瑜互见

patent 1 adj míngxiǎn 明显 **2** n (for invention) zhuānlì 专利 **3** v/t invention qǔdé zhuānlìquán 取得专利权

patent leather qīpí 漆皮

patently (clearly) míngxiǎn 明显

paternal relative fùxì 父系; pride, love fùqīnbān 父亲般

paternalism jiāzhǎng zhǔyì 家长主义

paternalistic jiāzhǎng zuòfēng 家长作风

paternity fùqīn shēnfèn 父亲身分

path xiǎolù 小路; fig tújìng 途径, lùjìng 路径

pathetic (invoking pity) zhāorén liánmǐn 招人怜悯; F (very bad) kěbēi 可悲

pathological bìngtài 病态

pathologist bìnglǐxuéjiā 病理学家

pathology bìnglǐxué 病理学

patience nàixīn 耐心

patient 1 n bìngrén 病人 **2** adj yǒu nàixīn 有耐心; **just be ~!** nàixīn diǎnr! 耐心点儿!

patiently nàixīn 耐心

patio píngtái 平台

patriot àiguó zhě 爱国者

patriotic àiguó 爱国

patriotism àiguó zhǔyì 爱国主义

patrol 1 n xúnluóduì 巡逻队; **be on ~** zài xúnluó zhōng 在巡逻中 **2** v/t streets, border xúnluó 巡逻

patrol car xúnluóchē 巡逻车; **patrolman** xúnjǐng 巡警; **patrol wagon** qiúchē 囚车

patron (of store, movie house) gùkè 顾客; (of artist, charity etc) zànzhùrén 赞助人

patronage (of artist, charity etc) zànzhù 赞助

patronize person gāorén yīděngde duìdài 高人一等地对待

patronizing gāorén yīděng 高人一等

patter 1 n (of rain etc) pādāshēng 啪嗒声; F (of salesman) xuétóu 噱头 **2** v/i pāidǎ 拍打

pattern n (on wallpaper, fabric) tú'àn 图案; (for knitting, sewing) yàngshì 样式; (model) móxíng 模型; (in behavior, events) fāngshì 方式

patterned yǒu tú'àn 有图案

paunch dà dùzi 大肚子

pause 1 n tíngdùn 停顿 **2** v/i tíngdùn 停顿 **3** v/t tape zàntíng 暂停

pave pū 铺; **~ the way for X** fig wèi X chuàngzào tiáojiàn 为X创造条件

pavement (roadway) lùmiàn 路面

paving stone pūlù shíbǎn 铺路石板

paw 1 n (of animal) zhuǎzi 爪子; F (hand) shǒuzhuǎzi 手爪子 **2** v/t F yòng shǒu luànmō 用手乱摸

pawn¹ n (in chess) zú 卒; fig xiǎozú 小卒

pawn² v/t diǎndàng 典当

pawnbroker dàngpù lǎobǎn 当铺老板

pawnshop dàngpù 当铺

pay 1 n xīnjīn 薪金; **in the ~ of X** shòugù yú X 受雇于X **2** v/t employee fùqián gěi 付钱给; sum, bill fù 付; **~ attention** zhùyì 注意; **~ X a compliment** biǎoyáng X 表扬X **3** v/i fùzhàng 付帐; (be profitable) yǒu lìrùn 有利润; **it doesn't ~ to do X** zuò X débùchángshī 做X得不偿失; **~ for X** (purchase) fù X fèi 付X费; **you'll ~ for this!** fig nǐ děngzhe qiáoba! 你等着瞧吧!

♦**pay back** person huánqián 还钱; loan chánghuán 偿还; (get revenge on) bàofù 报复

♦**pay in** (to bank) cúnrù 存入

♦**pay off 1** v/t debt chángqīng 偿清; corrupt official huìlù 贿赂 **2** v/i (be profitable) yǒu bàocháng 有报偿

♦**pay up** quánbù fùqīng 全部付清

payable yīng zhīfù 应支付

pay check xīnjīn zhīpiào 薪金支票

payday fāxīnrì 发薪日

payee shōukuǎnrén 收款人

pay envelope gōngzīdài 工资袋

payer fùkuǎnrén 付款人

payment (*of bill*) fùkuǎn 付款; (*money*) fùchūde kuǎnxiàng 付出的款项

pay phone gōngyòng diànhuà 公用电话

payroll (*money*) xīnshuǐ zǒng'é 薪水总额; (*employees*) xīnshuǐ míngcè 薪水名册; **be on the ~** shì gùyuán 是雇员

PC (= **personal computer**) gèrén diànnǎo 个人电脑; (= **politically correct**) wú zhèngzhì cuòwù 无政治错误

pea wāndòu 豌豆

peace (*as opposed to war*) hépíng 和平; (*quietness*) níngjìng 宁静

peaceable person héqi 和气

Peace Corps Hépíngduì 和平队

peaceful píngjìng 平静

peacefully ānjìng 安静

peach táozi 桃子

peacock kǒngquè 孔雀

peak 1 n (*of mountain*) shāndǐng 山顶; (*mountain*) shānfēng 山峰; *fig* dǐngfēng 顶峰 **2** v/i dádào dǐngfēng 达到顶峰

peak consumption gāofēng xiāohào 高峰消耗

peak hours gāofēng shíjiān 高峰时间

peanut huāshēng 花生; *get paid ~s* F zhèng bù liǎo jǐfēn qián 挣不了几分钱; *that's ~s to him* F nà duì tā láishuō búsuàn shénme 那对他来说不算什么

peanut butter huāshēngjiàng 花生酱

pear lí 梨

pearl zhēnzhū 珍珠

Pearl River Zhūjiāng 珠江

Pearl River Delta Zhūjiāng sānjiǎozhōu 珠江三角洲

peasant nóngmín 农民

pebble luǎnshí 卵石

pecan měizhōu shānhétáo 美洲山核桃

peck 1 n (*bite*) zhuó 啄; (*kiss*) cōngcōngyīwěn 匆匆一吻 **2** v/t (*bite*) zhuó 啄; (*kiss*) cōngcōngde wěn 匆匆地吻

peculiar (*strange*) qíguài 奇怪; **~ to** (*special*) tèyǒu 特有

peculiarity (*strangeness*) guàiyì 怪异; (*special feature*) dútèxìng 独特性

pedal 1 n (*of bike*) tàbǎn 踏板 **2** v/i (*turn ~s*) cǎi tàbǎn 踩踏板; (*cycle*) qí 骑

pedal rickshaw dàoqílǘ 倒骑驴

pedantic shūdāiziqì 书呆子气

pedestal (*for statue*) jīzuò 基座

pedestrian n xíngrén 行人

pedestrian crosswalk rénxíng héngdào 人行横道

pedestrian precinct xíngrénqū 行人区

pediatrician érkēxuéjiā 儿科学家

pediatrics érkēxué 儿科学

pedicab sānlúnchē 三轮车

pedigree 1 n (*of dog, racehorse*) chúnzhǒng 纯种; (*of person*) xuètǒng 血统 **2** adj chúnzhǒng 纯种

pee v/i F sāniào 撒尿

peek 1 n yìyǎn 一眼 **2** v/i piējiàn 瞥见

peel 1 n guǒpí 果皮 **2** v/t fruit, vegetables xiāopí 削皮 **3** v/i (*of nose, shoulders*) tuōluò 脱落; (*of paint*) bōluò 剥落

peep → **peek**

peephole kuīkǒng 窥孔

peer[1] n (*equal*) tóngděngrén 同等人

peer[2] v/i níngshì 凝视; **~ through the mist** xiàng wùzhōng zhāngwàng 向雾中张望; **~ at** zǐxìkàn 仔细看

peeved F nǎonù 恼怒

peg n (*for hat, coat*) guàgōu 挂钩; (*for tent*) zhuāng 桩; **off the ~** xiànchéng 现成

pejorative biǎnyì 贬抑

Peking Běijīng 北京

Peking duck Běijīng kǎoyā 北京烤鸭

Peking Opera Jīngjù 京剧

pellet xiǎotuán 小团; (*bullet*) zǐdàn 子弹

pelt 1 *v/t*: ~ *X with Y* jiāng Y tóuxiàng X 将 Y 投向 X **2** *v/i*: *they ~ed along the road* tāmen yánlù xùnsù qiánjìn 他们沿路迅速前进; *it's ~ing down* dàyǔ piáopō 大雨瓢泼

pelvis gǔpén 骨盆

pen[1] *n* (*ballpoint*) yuánzhūbǐ 圆珠笔; (*fountain ~*) zìláishuǐbǐ 自来水笔

pen[2] (*enclosure*) juàn 圈

pen[3] F (*penitentiary*) láo 牢

penalize búlìyú 不利于

penalty chéngfá 惩罚; SP fáqiú 罚球

penalty area SP fáqiúqū 罚球区

penalty clause wéiyuē fákuǎn de guīdìng 违约罚款的规定

pencil qiānbǐ 铅笔

pencil sharpener xiāoqiānbǐ dāo 削铅笔刀

pendant (*necklace*) chuíshì 垂饰

pending 1 *prep* zhídào 直到 **2** *adj*: *be* ~ (*awaiting a decision*) xuán ér wèi jué 悬而未决; (*about to happen*) pòjìn 迫近

penetrate chuāntòu 穿透; *market* dǎrù 打入

penetrating *stare* shēnmíng zhēnxiàng 深明真相; *scream* jiānruì 尖锐; *analysis* yǒu dòngchálì 有洞察力

penetration tūpò 突破

pen friend bǐyǒu 笔友

penicillin qīngméisù 青霉素

peninsula bàndǎo 半岛

penis yīnjīng 阴茎

penitence chànhuǐ 忏悔

penitent *adj* hòuhuǐ 后悔

penitentiary jiānyù 监狱

pen name bǐmíng 笔名

pennant jǐnbiāoqí 锦标旗

penniless yīwénbùmíng 一文不名

penpal bǐyǒu 笔友

pension yǎnglǎojīn 养老金

♦**pension off** bèipò tuìxiū 被迫退休

pension fund yǎnglǎo jījīn 养老基金

pension scheme yǎnglǎojīn fāng'àn 养老金方案

pensive chénsī 沉思

Pentagon: *the* ~ Wǔjiǎo Dàlóu 五角大楼

penthouse dǐngcéng gōngyù 顶层公寓

pent-up yāyì 压抑

penultimate dàoshǔ dì'èr 倒数第二

peony mǔdān 牡丹

people rén 人; (*race*, *tribe*) mínzú 民族; *the* ~ rénmín 人民; *the American* ~ Měiguó rénmín 美国人民; ~ *say that* ... tīngshuō ... 听说 ...

People's Commune Rénmín Gōngshè 人民公社; **People's Congress** Rénmín Dàibiǎo Dàhuì 人民代表大会; **People's Daily** Rénmín Rìbào 人民日报; **People's Liberation Army** Jiěfàngjūn 解放军; **People's Republic of China** Zhōnghuá Rénmín Gònghéguó 中华人民共和国

pepper (*spice*) hújiāofěn 胡椒粉; (*vegetable*) làjiāo 辣椒

peppermint (*candy*) bòhetáng 薄荷糖; (*flavoring*) hújiāo bòhe 胡椒薄荷

pep talk gǔlìde huà 鼓励的话

per měi 每

per annum měinián 每年

perceive (*with senses*) juéchá 觉察; (*view*, *interpret*) lǐjiě 理解

percent bǎifēnzhī 百分之; *one hundred* ~ bǎifēnzhī bǎi 百分之百

percentage bǎifēnbǐ 百分比

perceptible kě juéchá 可觉察

perceptibly kàndechū 看得出

perception (*through senses*) gǎnzhī nénglì 感知能力; (*of situation*) kànfǎ 看法; (*insight*) dòngchálì 洞察力

perceptive *person*, *remark* yǒu dòngchálì 有洞察力

perch 1 *n* (*for bird*) qīxīchù 栖息处 **2** *v/i* (*of bird*) qīxī 栖息; (*of* *person*) dāzuò 搭坐

percolate *v/i (of coffee)* guòlǜ 过滤

percolator guòlǜshì kāfēihú 过滤式咖啡壶

percussion dǎjīyuè 打击乐

percussion instrument dǎjī yuèqì 打击乐器

perfect 1 *n* GRAM wánchéngshì 完成式 **2** *adj* wánměi 完美 **3** *v/t* wánshàn 完善

perfection wánměi 完美; **to ~** qiàdào hǎochù 恰到好处

perfectionist wánměi zhǔyì zhě 完美主义者

perfectly jíjiā 极佳; (*totally*) wánquán 完全

perforated dǎkǒng 打孔

perforated line xūxiàn 虚线

perforations chǐkǒng 齿孔

perform 1 *v/t (carry out)* zuò 做; (*of actor, musician etc*) biǎoyǎn 表演 **2** *v/i (of actor, musician, dancer)* biǎoyǎn 表演; (*of machine*) yùnzhuǎn 运转

performance (*by actor, musician etc*) biǎoyǎn 表演; (*of employee, company etc*) biǎoxiàn 表现; (*by machine*) xìngnéng 性能

performance car gāonéng qìchē 高能汽车

performer biǎoyǎn zhě 表演者

perfume (*for woman*) xiāngshuǐ 香水; (*of flower*) xiāngwèi 香味

perfunctory fūyǎn 敷衍

perhaps yěxǔ 也许

peril wēixiǎn 危险

perilous duōxiǎn 多险

perimeter zhōubiān 周边

perimeter fence zhōubiān zhàlan 周边栅栏

period (*time*) yíduàn 一段; (*menstruation*) yuèjīng 月经; (*punctuation mark*) jùhào 句号; **I don't want to, ~!** wǒ bùxiǎng zuò, jiù zhèiyàng! 我不想做，就这样！

periodic zhōuqīxìng 周期性

periodical *n* qīkān 期刊

periodically dìngqī 定期

peripheral 1 *adj (not crucial)* cìyào 次要 **2** *n* COMPUT wàiwéi zhuāngzhì 外围装置

periphery biānyuán 边缘

perish (*of rubber*) fǔlàn 腐烂; (*of person*) mò 殁

perishable *adj food* yìhuài 易坏

perjure: **~ oneself** zuò wěizhèng 作伪证

perjury zuò wěizhèng 作伪证

perk *n (of job)* dàiyù 待遇

♦**perk up 1** *v/t* shǐ ... kuàihuó 使 ... 快活 **2** *v/i* huóyuè qǐlái 活跃起来

perky (*cheerful*) yǒu huólì 有活力

perm *n & v/t* tàngfà 烫发

permanent *adj* yǒngjiǔ 永久

permanently chángqī 长期

permissible róngxǔ 容许

permission xǔkě 许可

permissive fàngrèn 放任

permit 1 *n* xǔkězhèng 许可证 **2** *v/t* róngxǔ 容许; **~ X to do Y** zhǔnxǔ X zuò Y 准许 X 做 Y

perpendicular *adj* chuízhí 垂直

perpetual chíxù 持续

perpetually búduàn 不断

perpetuate shǐ yǒngcún 使永存

perplex shǐ kùnhuò 使困惑

perplexed kùnhuò 困惑

perplexity kùnhuò 困惑

persecute *oppress* pòhài 迫害

persecution pòhài 迫害

perseverance jiānchíbúxiè 坚持不懈

persevere jiānchí zuò 坚持做

persist chíxù 持续; **~ in** zhíyì zuò 执意做

persistence (*perseverance*) jiānchíbúxiè 坚持不懈; (*continuation*) jìxù cúnzài 继续存在

persistent *person* gùzhí 固执; *questions, rain, unemployment etc* chíxù búduàn 持续不断

persistently (*continually*) liánxù búduàn 连续不断

person rén 人; **in ~** qīnzì 亲自

personal (*private*) sīrén 私人; (*relating to a particular individual*) gèrén 个人; **don't make ~ remarks** bié tánlùn biérén 别谈论别人

personal assistant sīrén zhùlǐ 私人助理; **personal computer**

gèrén diànnǎo 个人电脑; **personal hygiene** gèrén wèishēng 个人卫生

personality gèxìng 个性; (*celebrity*) míngrén 名人

personally (*for my part*) jiù wǒ láishuō 就我来说; (*in person*) qīnzì 亲自; ***don't take it*** ~ bié wèicǐ fánnǎo 别为此烦恼

personal pronoun rénchēng dàicí 人称代词

personal stereo suíshēntīng 随身听

personnel (*employees*) zhíyuán 职员; (*department*) rénshì bùmén 人事部门

personnel manager rénshìbù zhǔrèn 人事部主任

perspiration hànshuǐ 汗水

perspire chūhàn 出汗

persuade *person* shuōfú 说服; ~ ***X to do Y*** shuōfú X zuò Y 说服X做Y

persuasion quànshuō 劝说

persuasive yǒu shuōfúlì 有说服力

pertinent yǒuguān 有关

perturb shǐ bù'ān 使不安

perturbing lìngrén bù'ān 令人不安

pervasive *influence, ideas* pǔbiàn cúnzài 普遍存在

perverse (*awkward*) bèilǐ 背理

perversion (*sexual*) biàntài xīnlǐ 变态心理

pervert *n* (*sexual*) xìngbiàntài 性变态

pessimism bēiguān 悲观

pessimist bēiguān zhě 悲观者

pessimistic bēiguān 悲观

pest (*bird*) hàiniǎo 害鸟; (*insect*) hàichóng 害虫; (*animal*) hàishòu 害兽; F tǎoyànguǐ 讨厌鬼

pest control xiāomiè yǒuhài dòngwù 消灭有害动物

pester jiūchán 纠缠; ~ ***X to do Y*** chánzhe X zuò Y 缠着X做Y

pesticide shāchóngjì 杀虫剂

pet 1 *n* (*animal*) chǒngwù 宠物; (*favorite*) chǒng'ér 宠儿 **2** *adj* (*favorite*) zuì xǐhuān 最喜欢 **3** *v/t*

animal fǔmō 抚摸 **4** *v/i* (*of couple*) àifǔ 爱抚

petal huābàn 花瓣

♦**peter out** jiànjiàn xiāoshī 渐渐消失

petite jiāoxiǎo 娇小

petition *n* qǐngyuànshū 请愿书

petrified shòujīngxià 受惊吓

petrify xiàdāi 吓呆

petrochemical shíyóu huàxué chǎnpǐn 石油化学产品

petroleum shíyóu 石油

petty *person, behavior* xiǎoqì 小气; *details, problem* suǒsuì 琐碎

petty cash língyòng xiànjīn 零用现金

petulant xìngjí 性急

pew jiàotáng chángyǐ 教堂长椅

pewter xīqiān héjīn 锡铅合金

pharmaceutical zhìyào 制药

pharmaceuticals zhìyào gōngsī 制药公司

pharmacist (*in store*) yàoshāng 药商

pharmacy (*store*) yàofáng 药房

phase jiēduàn 阶段

♦**phase in** zhúbù yǐnjìn 逐步引进

♦**phase out** zhúbù zhōngzhǐ 逐步中止

PhD (= ***Doctor of Philosophy***) bóshì 博士

phenomenal fēifán 非凡

phenomenally jīngrén 惊人

phenomenon xiànxiàng 现象

philanthropic réncí 仁慈

philanthropist císhànjiā 慈善家

philanthropy réncí 仁慈

Philippines: *the* ~ Fēilǜbīn 菲律宾

philistine *n* yìmáng 艺盲

philosopher zhéxuéjiā 哲学家

philosophical yǒu zhélǐ 有哲理

philosophy zhéxué 哲学

phobia kǒngbùzhèng 恐怖症

phoenix fènghuáng 凤凰

phone 1 *n* diànhuàjī 电话机 **2** *v/t* & *v/i* dǎ diànhuà 打电话

phone book diànhuàbù 电话簿

phone booth diànhuàtíng 电话亭; **phonecall** diànhuà 电话;

phone number diànhuà hàomǎ 电话号码

phon(e)y *adj* wěizhuāng 伪装

photo *n* xiàngpiàn 相片

photo album xiàngcè 相册;
  photocopier yǐngyìnjī 影印机;
  photocopy 1 *n* yǐngyìnběn 影印
  本 2 *v/t* yǐngyìn 影印

photogenic shàngxiàng 上相

photograph 1 *n* zhàopiàn 照片
  2 *v/t* pāishè 拍摄

photographer shèyǐngshī 摄影师

photography shèyǐng 摄影

phrase 1 *n* piànyǔ 片语 2 *v/t*
  cuòcí 措词

phrasebook duǎnyǔ shǒucè 短语
  手册

physical 1 *adj* (*relating to the body*)
  shēntǐ 身体 2 *n* MED tǐgé jiǎnchá
  体格检查

physical handicap cánjí 残疾

physically shēntǐ shang 身体上

physician yīshēng 医生

physicist wùlǐxuéjiā 物理学家

physics wùlǐ 物理

physiotherapist lǐliáo yīshēng 理
  疗医生

physiotherapy lǐliáo 理疗

physique tǐgé 体格

pianist gāngqínjiā 钢琴家

piano gāngqín 钢琴

pick 1 *n*: **take your** ~ xuǎnba 选吧
  2 *v/t* (*choose*) xuǎn 选; *flowers,*
  fruit cǎi 采; ~ **one's nose** wā bíkǒng 挖鼻孔 3 *v/i*: ~ **and choose**
  tiāotiāojiǎnjiǎn 挑挑拣拣

♦pick at: ~ **one's food** xiǎokǒu chī
  dōngxi 小口吃东西

♦pick on (*treat unfairly*) qīfu 欺负;
  (*select*) xuǎn 选

♦pick out (*identify*) rènchū 认出

♦pick up 1 *v/t* náqǐ 拿起; (*from*
  ground) jiǎnqǐ 拣起; (*collect*)
  qǔhuí 取回; (*from airport etc*) jiē
  接; (*in car*) ràngrén dā biànchē 让
  人搭便车; (*in sexual sense*)
  gōuyǐn 勾引; *language, skill*
  xuéhuì 学会; *habit* yǎngchéng 养
  成; *illness* gǎnrǎn 感染; (*buy*) mǎi
  买; *criminal* dàibǔ 逮捕; ~ **the tab**
  mǎidān 买单 2 *v/i* (*improve*)
  hǎozhuǎn 好转

picket 1 *n* (*of strikers*) jiūcháduì 纠

察队 2 *v/t* shèzhì jiūchá 设置纠
察

picket fence jiānbǎntiáo zhàlan 尖
  板条栅栏

picket line jiūcháxiàn 纠察线

pickle *v/t* yānzì 腌渍

pickles pàocài 泡菜

pickpocket páshǒu 扒手

pick-up (truck) qīngxíng xiǎohuòchē 轻型小货车

picky F tiāotì 挑剔

picnic *n* & *v/i* yěcān 野餐

picture 1 *n* (*photo*) zhàopiàn 照
  片; (*painting*) huìhuà 绘画;
  (*illustration*) chātú 插图; (*movie*)
  diànyǐng 电影; **keep X in the** ~
  shǐ X liǎojiě shíqíng 使 X 了解实
  情 2 *v/t* xiǎngxiàng 想象

picture book túhuàshū 图画书

picture postcard míngxìnpiàn 明
  信片

picturesque rúhuà 如画

pie pài 派

piece (*fragment*) suìpiàn 碎片;
  (*component*) bùfen 部分; (*in board*
  game) zǐr 子儿; **a ~ of pie** / **bread**
  yíkuài pài / miànbāo 一块派 / 面
  包; **a ~ of advice** yíxiàng jiànyì 一
  项建议; **go to ~s** jīngshén bēngkuì 精神崩溃; **take to ~s** chāikāi
  拆开

♦piece together *broken plate*
  zǔzhuāng 组装; *facts, evidence*
  pīncòu 拼凑

piecemeal *adv* yíbùfen yíbùfen 一
  部分一部分

piecework *n* jìjiàn gōngzuò 计件
  工作

pierce (*penetrate*) cìtòu 刺透; *ears*
  zhāyǎn 扎眼

piercing *noise* jiānlì 尖利; *eyes* ruìlì
  锐利; *wind* cìgǔ 刺骨

pig zhū 猪; (*unpleasant person*) húndàn 混蛋

pigeon gēzi 鸽子

pigheaded wángù 顽固

pigpen (*also fig*) zhūjuàn 猪圈

pigskin zhūpí 猪皮

pigtail mǎwěibiàn 马尾辫

pile duī 堆; **a ~ of work** xǔduō 许
  多

♦**pile up 1** *v/i* (*of work, bills*) jījù 积聚 **2** *v/t* duīchéngduī 堆成堆

piles MED zhìchuāng 痔疮

pile-up MOT liánhuán pèngzhuàng 连环碰撞

pilfering xiǎotōu xiǎomō 小偷小摸

pilgrim cháoshèng zhě 朝圣者

pilgrimage cháoshèng zhī xíng 朝圣之行

pill yào 药; ***the ~*** kǒufú bìyùnyào 口服避孕药; ***be on the ~*** chī bìyùnyào 吃避孕药

pillar zhùzi 柱子

pillion (*of motor bike*) mótuōchē hòuzuò 摩托车后座

pillow *n* zhěntou 枕头

pillowcase, pillowslip zhěntào 枕套

pilot 1 *n* (*of airplane*) fēixíngyuán 飞行员 **2** *v/t airplane* jiàshǐ 驾驶

pilot plant shìyàn qū 试验区

pilot scheme shìyàn fāng'àn 试验方案

pimp *n* lāpítiáode nánrén 拉皮条的男人

pimple fěncì 粉刺

PIN (= ***personal identification number***) mìmǎ 密码

pin 1 *n* (*for sewing*) dàtóuzhēn 大头针; (*in bowling*) mùzhù 木柱; (*badge*) huīzhāng 徽章; ELEC chātóu 插头 **2** *v/t* (*hold down*) ànzhù 按住; (*attach*) yòng zhēn gùdìng 用针固定

♦**pin down: pin X down to a date** jiào X dìngge shíjiān 叫X定个时间

♦**pin up** *notice* zhāngtiē 张贴

pincers áo áo 螯螯; ***a pair of ~*** yìbǎ qiánzi 一把钳子

pinch 1 *n* niē 捏; (*of salt, sugar etc*) yìniē 一捏; ***at a ~*** bìyàoshí 必要时 **2** *v/t* niē 捏 **3** *v/i* (*of shoes*) jiājiǎo 夹脚

pine *n* (*tree*) sōngshù 松树; (*wood*) sōngmù 松木

♦**pine for** sīniàn 思念

pineapple ⇓ bōluó 菠萝

ping 1 *n* pēngde yìshēng 砰的一声 **2** *v/i* fāchū pēngde yìshēng 发

出砰的一声

ping-pong pīngpāngqiú 乒乓球

pink (*color*) fěnhóngsè 粉红色

pinnacle *fig* dǐngfēng 顶峰

pinpoint míngquè zhǐchū 明确指出

pins and needles fāmá 发麻

pinstripe *adj* xìtiáowén 细条纹

pint pǐntuō 品脱

pin-up (***girl***) měinǚ 美女

pinyin pīnyīn 拼音

pioneer 1 *n fig* chuàngshǐrén 创始人 **2** *v/t* shǒuchàng 首倡

pioneering *adj work* kāituò 开拓

pious qiánchéng qiánchéng 虔诚

pip *n* (*of fruit*) zhǒngzi 种子

pipe 1 *n* (*for smoking*) yāndǒu 烟斗; (*for water, gas, sewage*) guǎnzi 管子 **2** *v/t* yòng guǎndào shūsòng 用管道输送

♦**pipe down** ānjìng 安静

piped music bèijǐng yīnyuè 背景音乐

pipeline guǎndào 管道; ***in the ~*** jíjiāng fāshēng 即将发生

piping hot gùntàng 滚烫

pirate *v/t software etc* dàobǎn 盗版

piss 1 *v/i* F (*urinate*) sāniào 撒尿 **2** *n* F niào 尿

pissed F (*annoyed*) nǎonù 恼怒; *Br* (*drunk*) hēzuìle 喝醉了

pistol shǒuqiāng 手枪

piston huósāi 活塞

pit *n* (*hole*) kēng 坑; (*coal mine*) kuàngkēng 矿坑

pitch[1] *n* MUS yīndiào 音调

pitch[2] **1** *v/i* (*in baseball*) tóuqiú 投球 **2** *v/t tent* dā 搭; *ball* tóu 投

pitch black qīhēi 漆黑

pitcher[1] (*baseball player*) tóushǒu 投手

pitcher[2] (*container*) guàn 罐

piteous kělián 可怜

pitfall xiànjǐng 陷阱

pith (*of citrus fruit*) suí suǐ 髓

pitiful *sight* lìngrén liánmǐn 令人怜悯; *excuse, attempt* kěbǐ 可鄙

pitiless wúqíng 无情

pittance wēibóde gōngzī 微薄的工资

pity 1 *n* tóngqíng 同情; ***it's a ~***

that ... yíhàn ... 遗憾 ...; what a ~! zhēn yíhàn！真遗憾！; *take ~ on* chūyú tóngqíng ér bāngzhù 出于同情而帮助 **2** *v/t person* tóngqíng 同情

pivot 1 *v/i* zài zhīdiǎn shang zhuàndòng 在支点上转动 **2** *n* zhīdiǎn 支点

pizza bǐsà 比萨

PLA (= *People's Liberation Army*) Jiěfàngjūn 解放军

PLA soldier Jiěfàngjūn 解放军

placard biāoyǔpái 标语牌

place 1 *n* dìfang 地方; (*bar, restaurant*) cānyǐnchù 餐饮处; (*apartment, house*) jiā 家; (*in book*) yè 页; (*in race, competition*) míngcì 名次; (*seat*) zuòwèi 座位; *at my / his ~* zài wǒ / tā nàr 在我／他那儿; *in ~ of* dàitì 代替; *feel out of ~* gǎndào bù xiāngchèn 感到不相称; *take ~* fāshēng 发生; *in the first ~* (*firstly*) shǒuxiān 首先; (*in the beginning*) kāishǐ 开始 **2** *v/t* (*put*) fàng 放; (*identify*) wánquán rèndìng 完全认定; *~ an order* dìnghuò 订货

place mat cānjù diàn 餐具垫

placid ānjìng 安静

plague 1 *n* wēnyì 瘟疫 **2** *v/t* (*bother*) fánrǎo 烦扰

plain¹ *n* píngyuán 平原

plain² **1** *adj* (*clear, obvious*) qīngchǔ 清楚; (*not fancy*) qīngdàn 清淡; (*not pretty*) pǔtōng 普通; (*not patterned*) méiyǒu tú'àn 没有图案; (*blunt*) shuàizhí 率直; *~ chocolate* chún qiǎokèlì 纯巧克力 **2** *adv* xiǎnrán 显然; *it's ~ crazy* zhēnshì fēngkuáng 真是疯狂

plain clothes: *in ~* chuān biànyī 穿便衣

plainly (*clearly*) qīngchǔ 清楚; (*bluntly*) zhíshuài 直率; (*simply*) pǔsù 朴素

plain-spoken zhíyánbúhuì 直言不讳

plaintiff yuángào 原告

plaintive āishāng 哀伤

plait 1 *n* (*in hair*) biànzi 辫子 **2** *v/t hair* biān biànzi 编辫子

plan 1 *n* (*project, intention*) jìhuà 计划; (*drawing*) shèjìtú 设计图 **2** *v/t* (*prepare*) zhǔnbèi 准备; (*design*) shèjì 设计; *~ to do X*, *~ on doing X* dǎsuàn zuò X 打算做 X **3** *v/i* dìng jìhuà 订计划

plane¹ (*airplane*) fēijī 飞机

plane² (*tool*) bàozi 刨子

planet xíngxīng 行星

plank (*of wood*) mùbǎn 木板; *fig* (*of policy*) zhèngcè zhǔnzé 政策准则

planning jìhuà 计划; *at the ~ stage* zài chóuhuà zhōng 在筹划中

plant¹ **1** *n* zhíwù 植物 **2** *v/t* zhòng 种

plant² *n* (*factory*) chǎng 厂; (*equipment*) shèbèi 设备

plantation dà zhòngzhíyuán 大种植园

plaque (*on wall*) shìbǎn 饰板; (*on teeth*) yábān 牙斑

plaster 1 *n* (*on wall, ceiling*) huīní 灰泥 **2** *v/t wall, ceiling* yòng huīní túmǒ 用灰泥涂抹; *be ~ed with* túmǎn 涂满

plaster cast shígāo bēngdài 石膏绷带

plastic 1 *n* sùliào 塑料 **2** *adj* (*made of ~*) sùliào 塑料

plastic bag sùliàodài 塑料袋; **plastic money** xìnyòngkǎ 信用卡; **plastic surgeon** zhěngxíng wàikē yīshēng 整形外科医生; **plastic surgery** zhěngxíng wàikē 整形外科

plate *n* (*for food*) pánzi 盘子; (*sheet of metal*) bóbǎncái 薄板材

plateau gāoyuán 高原

platform (*stage*) wǔtái 舞台; (*of railway station*) ⇩ zhàntái 站台; *fig* (*political*) zhènggāng 政纲

platinum *n* & *adj* bó 铂

platitude chéncí làndiào 陈词滥调

platonic *relationship* chún yǒuyì 纯友谊

platoon (*of soldiers*) pái 排

platter (*for meat, fish*) dà qiǎnpán 大浅盘

plausible sìhū yǒu dàolǐ 似乎有道理

play 1 n (in theater, on TV) jù 剧; (of children) yóuxì 游戏; TECH huódòng 活动; SP bǐsàide biǎoxiàn 比赛的表现 **2** v/i (of children) wánr 玩儿; (of musician) tánzòu 弹奏; (SP: perform) dǎ 打; (SP: take part) cānsài 参赛 **3** v/t musical instrument tán 弹; piece of music yǎnzòu 演奏; game wánr 玩儿; opponent yǔ … bǐsài yǔ … 比赛; (perform: Macbeth etc) biǎoyǎn 表演; particular role bànyǎn 扮演; ~ a joke on X kāi X de wánxiào 开 X 的玩笑

play around (be unfaithful) sīhùn 厮混

♦**play down** dànhuà 淡化

♦**play up** (of machine) chū gùzhàng 出故障; (of child) rě máfan 惹麻烦; (of tooth, bad back etc) gěi rén tòngkǔ 给人痛苦

playact (pretend) jiǎzhuāng 假装

playback huífàng 回放

playboy huāhuāgōngzǐ 花花公子

player SP yùndòng yuán 运动员; (musician) yǎnzòu zhě 演奏者; (actor) yǎnyuán 演员

playful punch etc nàozhe wánr 闹着玩儿

playground yóuxìchǎng 游戏场

playing card zhǐpái 纸牌

playing field yùndòngchǎng 运动场

playmate yóuxìde huǒbàn 游戏的伙伴

playwright jùzuòjiā 剧作家

plaza (for shopping) gòuwù zhōngxīn 购物中心

plea n kěnqiú 恳求

plead v/i qǐngqiú 请求; ~ for kěnqiú 恳求; ~ guilty / not guilty fú / bùfú zuì 服 / 不服罪; ~ with X qǐngqiú X 请求 X

pleasant lìngrén yúkuài 令人愉快

please 1 adv qǐng 请; more tea? – yes, ~ hái yào chá ma? – hǎode, xièxiè 还要茶吗 ? – 好的, 谢谢; ~ do méiwèntí 没问题 **2** v/t shǐ gāoxìng 使高兴; ~ yourself

qǐngbiàn 请便

pleased gāoxìng 高兴; ~ to meet you hěn gāoxìng rènshí nǐ 很高兴认识你

pleasing shǐrén yúkuài 使人愉快

pleasure (happiness, satisfaction) kuàilè 快乐; (as opposed to work) yúlè 娱乐; (delight) lèqù 乐趣; it's a ~ (you're welcome) méiguānxi 没关系; with ~ dāngrán 当然

pleat n (in skirt) zhě 褶

pledge 1 n (promise) bǎozhèng 保证; Pledge of Allegiance Zhōngchéng Xuānshì 忠诚宣誓 **2** v/t (promise) chéngnuò 承诺

plentiful dàliàng 大量

plenty (abundance) fùzú 富足; ~ of xǔduō 许多; that's ~ zúgòu duō le 足够多了; there's ~ for everyone yǒudeshì gěi dàjiā 有的是给大家

pliable kěsù 可塑

pliers qiánzi 钳子; a pair of ~ yìbǎ qiánzi 一把钳子

plight kùnjìng 困境

plod v/i (walk) jiānnán xíngzǒu 艰难行走

♦**plod along** (with a job) huǎnmàn jìnxíng 缓慢进行

plodder (at work, school) chénmèn kǔgàn de rén 沉闷苦干的人

plot[1] n (land) xiǎokuài tǔdì 小块土地

plot[2] **1** n (conspiracy) yīnmóu 阴谋; (of novel) qíngjié 情节 **2** v/t mìmóu 密谋 **3** v/i mìmóu 密谋

plotter yīnmóu zhě 阴谋者; COMPUT huìtúyí 绘图仪

plow 1 n lí 犁 **2** v/t & v/i gēngdì 耕地

♦**plow back** profits fǎn tóuzī 反投资

pluck v/t eyebrows zhāichú 摘除; chicken bámáo 拔毛

♦**pluck up**: ~ courage gǔqǐ yǒngqì 鼓起勇气

plug 1 n (for sink, bath) sāizi 塞子; (electrical) chātóu 插头; (spark ~) huǒhuāsāi 火花塞; (for new book etc) xuānchuán 宣传 **2** v/t hole yòng sāizi dǔ 用 塞子 堵; *new book etc* tuīxiāo 推销

♦**plug away** F nǔlì búxiè 努力不懈

♦**plug in** *v/t* jiētōng diànyuán 接通电源

plum 1 *n* lǐzi 李子 **2** *adj job* yōuyuè 优越

plumage yǔyī 羽衣

plumb *adj* chuízhí 垂直

plumber shuǐnuǎngōng 水暖工

plumbing (*pipes*) guǎndào zhuāngzhì 管道装置

plume *n* yǔmáo 羽毛

plummet (*of airplane*) kuàisù luòxià 快速落下; (*of share prices*) dàdiē 大跌

plump *adj* féipàng 肥胖

♦**plump for** xuǎnzé 选择

plunge 1 *n* měngrán diēluò 猛然跌落; (*in prices*) xiàdiē 下跌; *take the* ~ cǎiqǔ dàdǎn cuòshī 采取大胆措施 **2** *v/i* tūrán diēluò 突然跌落; (*of prices*) xiàdiē 下跌 **3** *v/t* tóurù 投入; *the city was ~d into darkness* zhèi chéngshì xiànrù yípiàn hēi'àn zhōng 这城市陷入一片黑暗中; *the news ~d him into despair* tā tīngdào nà xiāoxi jiù xiànrùle juéwàng 他听到那消息就陷入了绝望

plunging: ~ *neckline* shēn V zì lǐng 深 V 字领

plural 1 *adj* fùshù xíngshì 复数形式 **2** *n* fùshù 复数

plus 1 *prep* jiāshàng 加上 **2** *adj* duō 多; *$500* ~ wǔbǎiduō měiyuán 五百多美元 **3** *n* (*symbol*) jiāhào 加号; (*advantage*) hǎochù 好处 **4** *conj* (*moreover, in addition*) érqiě 而且

plush háohuá 豪华

plywood jiāohébǎn 胶合板

p.m. xiàwǔ 下午

pneumatic chōngqì 充气

pneumatic drill fēngzuàn 风钻

pneumonia fèiyán 肺炎

poach[1] *v/t* (*cook*) wēi 煨

poach[2] **1** *v/i* tōubǔ 偷捕 **2** *v/t salmon etc* tōubǔ 偷捕

poached egg wò jīdàn 卧鸡蛋

P.O. Box yóuzhèng xìnxiāng 邮政信箱

pocket 1 *n* kǒudài 口袋; *line one's own* ~*s* fā wāicái 发歪财; *be out of* ~ péiqián 赔钱 **2** *adj* (*miniature*) wēixíng 微型 **3** *v/t* jùwéijǐyǒu 据为己有

pocketbook (*woman's*) xiǎo shǒutíbāo 小手提包; (*wallet*) qiánbāo 钱包; (*book*) píngzhuāngshū 平装书; **pocket calculator** xiǎo jìsuànqì 小计算器; **pocketknife** xiǎo zhédāo 小折刀

podium zhǐhuītái 指挥台

poem shī 诗

poet shīrén 诗人

poetic *person, description* yǒu shīyì 有诗意

poetic justice yīngdéde jiǎngchéng 应得的奖惩

poetry shīgē 诗歌

poignant tòngqiè 痛切

point 1 *n* (*of pencil, knife*) jiānduān 尖端; (*in competition, exam*) fēn 分; (*purpose*) yìyì 意义; (*moment*) shíkè 时刻; (*in argument, discussion*) guāndiǎn 观点; (*in decimals*) diǎn 点; *beside the* ~ lítí 离题; *be on the* ~ *of* zhèngyào ... 正要 ...; *get to the* ~ shuō zhèngshì 说正事; *the* ~ *is ...* wèntí shì ... 问题是 ...; *there's no* ~ *in waiting / trying* děng / shì gēnběn méiyòng 等 / 试根本没用 **2** *v/i* zhǐ 指 **3** *v/t gun* duìzhǔn 对准

♦**point at** (*with finger*) zhǐxiàng 指向

♦**point out** *sights* shǐ zhùyì 使注意; *advantages etc* zhǐchū 指出

♦**point to** (*with finger*) yòngshǒu zhǐ 用手指; *fig* (*indicate*) ànshì 暗示

point-blank 1 *adj refusal, denial* zhíjiéliǎodàng 直截了当; *at* ~ *range* zài jìnjùlí nèi 在近距离内 **2** *adv refuse, deny* duànrán 断然

pointed jiānruì 尖锐

pointer (*for teacher*) jiàobiān 教鞭; (*hint*) diǎnzi 点子; (*sign, indication*) jìxiàng 迹象

pointless wúyìyì 无意义; *it's* ~

trying to do X chángshì zuò X gēnběn méiyòng 尝试做 X 根本没用

point of sale (*place*) xiāohòudiǎn 销货点; (*promotional material*) cùxiāo zīliào 促销资料

point of view guāndiǎn 观点

poise zìzhì 自制

poised *person* tàiránzìruò 泰然自若

poison 1 *n* dúyào 毒药 **2** *v/t* dúhài 毒害

poisonous yǒudú 有毒

poke 1 *n* tǒng 捅 **2** *v/t* (*prod*) tǒng 捅; (*stick*) shēnchū 伸出; **~** ***fun at*** cháoxiào 嘲笑; **~** ***one's nose into*** gānyù 干预

♦**poke around** xúnzhǎo 寻找

poker (*card game*) pūkèpái 扑克牌

poky (*cramped*) xiáxiǎo 狭小

Poland Bōlán 波兰

polar dìjí 地极

polar bear běijíxióng 北极熊

polarize *v/t* liǎngjí fēnhuà 两极分化

Pole Bōlán rén 波兰人

pole[1] (*of wood, metal*) gān gǎn 杆杆

pole[2] (*of earth*) dìjí 地极

polevault chēnggān tiàogāo 撑竿跳高

police *n* jǐngfāng 警方

policeman jǐngchá 警察; **police state** jǐngchá guójiā 警察国家; **police station** jǐngchájú 警察局; **policewoman** nǚjǐngchá 女警察

policy[1] zhèngcè 政策

policy[2]: ***insurance ~*** bǎoxiǎndān 保险单

polio xiǎo'ér mábìzhèng 小儿麻痹症

Polish 1 *adj* Bōlán 波兰 **2** *n* (*language*) Bōlán yǔ 波兰语

polish 1 *n* (*product*) cāguāngjì 擦光剂 **2** *v/t* cāliàng 擦亮; *speech* rùnsè 润色

♦**polish off** *food* chīguāng 吃光

♦**polish up** *skill* tígāo 提高

polished *performance* xùnliàn-yǒusù 训练有素

Politbureau Zhèngzhìjú 政治局

polite yǒu lǐmào 有礼貌

politely lǐmào 礼貌

politeness lǐmào 礼貌

political zhèngzhì 政治

politically correct wú zhèngzhì cuòwù 无政治错误

politician zhèngzhìjiā 政治家

politics zhèngzhì 政治; ***what are his ~?*** tā yǒu shénme zhèngzhì xìnyǎng? 他有什么政治信仰？

poll 1 *n* (*survey*) mínyì cèyàn 民意测验; ***the ~s*** (*election*) xuǎnjǔ 选举; ***go to the ~s*** (*vote*) xuǎnjǔ tóupiào 选举投票 **2** *v/t people* diàochá 调查; *votes* huòdé 获得

pollen huāfěn 花粉

pollen count huāfěn jìshù 花粉计数

polling booth tóupiàozhàn 投票站

pollster mínyì cèyàn zhě 民意测验者

pollutant wūrǎn wùzhì 污染物质

pollute wūrǎn 污染

pollution wūrǎn 污染

polo neck (*sweater*) yuán gāo fānlǐng 圆高翻领

polo shirt gāolǐngshān 高领衫

polyethylene jùyǐxī 聚乙烯

polyester jùzhǐxiánwéi 聚酯纤维

polystyrene jùběnyǐxī 聚苯乙烯

polyunsaturated hányǒu duōchóng bùbǎohé huàhéwù 含有多重不饱和化合物

pompous zìfù 自负

pond chítáng 池塘

ponder *v/i* shēnsī 深思

pony xiǎomǎ 小马

ponytail mǎwěifà 马尾发

poodle juǎnmáo xiǎogǒu 卷毛小狗

pool[1] (*swimming ~*) chí 池; (*of water, blood*) tān 摊

pool[2] (*game*) ⇩ pǔ'ěrdànzǐxì 普尔弹子戏

pool[3] **1** *n* (*common fund*) gòngtóng chǔjīn 共同储金 **2** *v/t resources* jíhé 集合

pool hall pǔ'ěrdànzǐxì tīng 普尔弹子戏厅

pool table pǔ'ěrdànzǐxì zhuō 普尔弹子戏桌

pooped F jīnpílìjìn 筋疲力尽

poor 1 *adj* (*not wealthy*) pínqióng 贫穷; (*not good*) bùhǎo 不好; (*unfortunate*) búxìng 不幸; *be in ~ health* shēntǐ bùhǎo 身体不好; *~ old Tony!* kěliánde Tuōní! 可怜的托尼! **2** *n*: *the ~* qióngrén 穷人

poorly 1 *adv* hěnzāo 很糟 **2** *adj* (*unwell*) bùshūfu 不舒服

pop¹ 1 *n* (*noise*) pēngde yīshēng 砰的一声 **2** *v/i* (*of balloon etc*) fāchū pēngde yīshēng 发出砰的一声 **3** *v/t cork* báchū 拔出; *balloon* bàopò 爆破

pop² 1 *n* MUS liúxíng yīnyuè 流行音乐 **2** *adj* liúxíng 流行

pop³ (*father*) bà ba 爸爸

pop⁴ *v/t* (*put*) fàng 放

♦**pop up** *v/i* (*appear suddenly*) tūrán chūxiàn 突然出现

popcorn yùmǐhuā 玉米花

pope jiàohuáng 教皇

poplar yángshù 杨树

poppy yīngsù 罂粟

Popsicle® bàngbàngbīng 棒棒冰

pop song liúxíng gēqǔ 流行歌曲

popular shòu huānyíng 受欢迎; *belief, support* pǔbiàn 普遍

popularity (*of person*) shēngwàng 声望

populate jūzhù 居住

population rénkǒu 人口

porcelain *n & adj* cí 瓷

porch ménláng 门廊

porcupine háozhū 豪猪

pore (*of skin*) máokǒng 毛孔

♦**pore over** xìkàn 细看

pork zhūròu 猪肉

porn *n* huángsè zuòpǐn 黄色作品

porn(o) *adj* huángsè 黄色

pornographic huángsè 黄色

pornography sèqíng zuòpǐn 色情作品

porous tòu shuǐqì 透水汽

port¹ *n* (*town*) gǎngshì 港市; (*area*) gǎngkǒu 港口; COMPUT duānkǒu 端口

port² *adj* (*left-hand*) zuǒxián 左舷

portable 1 *adj* shǒutíshì 手提式 **2** *n* COMPUT bǐjìběn 笔记本; *~ TV*

wēixíng diànshì 微型电视

porter (*at railroad station*) bānyùngōng 搬运工; (*doorman in hotel*) ménwèi 门卫

porthole NAUT xiánchuāng 舷窗

portion *n* yíbùfen 一部分; (*of food*) fèn 份

portrait 1 *n* (*painting, photograph*) xiàoxiàng 肖像; (*depiction*) miáoxiě 描写 **2** *adv print* shùpái 竖排

portray (*of artist*) huà 画; (*of photographer*) pāi 拍; (*of actor*) bànyǎn 扮演; (*of author*) miáoshù 描述

portrayal (*by actor*) bànyǎn 扮演; (*by author*) miáoshù 描述

Portugal Pútáoyá 葡萄牙

Portuguese 1 *adj* Pútáoyá 葡萄牙 **2** *n* (*person*) Pútáoyá rén 葡萄牙人; (*language*) Pútáoyá yǔ 葡萄牙语

pose 1 *n* (*pretense*) zhuāngqiāng zuòshì 装腔作势 **2** *v/i* (*for artist, photographer*) bǎi zīshì 摆姿势; *~ as* zhuāngzuò 装作 **3** *v/t*: *~ a problem / a threat* zàochéng kùnnán / wēixié 造成困难/威胁

position 1 *n* (*location*) wèizhi 位置; (*stance*) zīshì 姿势; (*in race, competition*) wèi 位; (*occupied by soldiers*) zhèndì 阵地; (*point of view*) lìchǎng 立场; (*situation*) chǔjìng 处境; (*job*) zhíwèi 职位; (*status*) dìwèi 地位 **2** *v/t* ānfàng 安放

positive *attitude* lèguān 乐观; *response* biǎoshì tóngyì 表示同意; *medical test* yángxìng 阳性; GRAM kěndìng 肯定; ELEC zhèngjí 正极; *be ~* (*sure*) quèdìng 确定

positively (*decidedly*) shífēn kěndìng 十分肯定; (*definitely*) juéduì 绝对

possess chíyǒu 持有

possession (*ownership*) chíyǒu 持有; (*thing owned*) cáichǎn 财产; *~s* suǒyǒuwù 所有物

possessive *person* xiǎnshì zhànyǒuyù 显示占有欲

possessive pronoun GRAM wùzhǔ dàicí 物主代词

possibility kěnéng xìng 可能性

possible kěnéng 可能; *the shortest / quickest ~ ...* jìn kěnéng zuìduǎn / zuìkuài ... 尽可能最短 / 最快 ...; *the best ~ ...* jìn kěnéng zuìhǎo ... 尽可能最好 ...

possibly kěnéng 可能; (*perhaps*) yěxǔ 也许; *that can't ~ be right* nà bù kěnéng duì 那不可能对; *could you ~ tell me ... ?* nǐ néngbùnéng gàosù wǒ ... ? 你能不能告诉我 ... ?

post[1] **1** *n* (*of wood, metal*) gānzi 杆子 **2** *v/t notice* zhāngtiē 张贴; *profits* gōngbù 公布; *keep X ~ed* ràng X zhīdào 让 X 知道

post[2] **1** *n* (*place of duty*) zhíwèi 职位 **2** *v/t soldier, employee* pàiwǎng 派往; *guards* bùzhì 布置

postage yóuzī 邮资

postal yóudì 邮递

postcard míngxìnpiàn 明信片

postdate tiánwǎn rìqī 填晚日期

poster hǎibào 海报

posterior *n hum* (*buttocks*) pìgu 屁股

posterity hòudài 后代

postgraduate 1 *n* yánjiūshēng 研究生 **2** *adj* dàxué bìyèhòu 大学毕业后

posthumous *novel* zuòzhě sǐhòu chūbǎn 作者死后出版; *award* sǐhòu huòdé 死后获得; *baby* yífù 遗腹

posthumously sǐhòu fāshēng 死后发生

posting (*assignment*) wěipài 委派

postmark yóuchuō 邮戳

postmortem yànshī 验尸

post office yóujú 邮局

postpone tuīchí 推迟

postponement yánqī 延期

posture zīshì 姿势

postwar zhànhòu 战后

pot[1] (*for cooking in*) guō 锅; (*for coffee, tea*) hú 壶; (*for plant*) pén 盆

pot[2] F (*marijuana*) dàmá 大麻

potato tǔdòu 土豆

potato chips ⇩ zháshǔpiàn 炸薯片

potent *drug, medicine* xiàolì dà 效力大; *ruler* qiángyǒulì 强有力

potential 1 *adj* kěnéng chūxiàn 可能出现 **2** *n* qiánlì 潜力

potentially yǒu kěnéng 有可能

pothole (*in road*) kēngwā 坑洼

potter *n* táogōng 陶工

pottery (*activity*) zhìtáoshù 制陶术; (*items*) táoqì 陶器; (*place*) táoqì zuōfang 陶器作坊

potty *n* (*for baby*) biànpén 便盆

pouch (*bag*) xiǎodài 小袋

poultry (*birds*) jiāqín 家禽; (*meat*) jiāqínròu 家禽肉

pounce *v/i* (*of animal*) měngpū 猛扑; *fig* tūrán xíjī 突然袭击

pound[1] *n* (*weight*) bàng 磅

pound[2] (*for strays*) wéichǎng 围场; (*for cars*) mòshōu chēliàng chù 没收车辆处

pound[3] *v/i* (*of heart*) jùliè tiàodòng 剧烈跳动; *~ on* (*hammer on*) zhòngjī 重击

pound sterling yīngbàng 英镑

pour 1 *v/t liquid* dào 倒 **2** *v/i* yǒngchū 涌出; *it's ~ing* (*with rain*) dàyǔqīngpén 大雨倾盆

♦ **pour out** *liquid* dàochū 倒出; *troubles* qīngsù 倾诉

pout *v/i* juēzuǐ 撅嘴

poverty pínkùn 贫困

poverty-stricken pínkùn bùkān 贫困不堪

powder 1 *n* fěnmò 粉末; (*for face*) fěn 粉 **2** *v/t face* chāfěn 搽粉

powder room nǚcèsuǒ 女厕所

power 1 *n* (*strength*) lì 力; (*authority*) quánlì 权力; (*energy*) néngliàng 能量; (*electricity*) diàn 电; *in ~* POL zhízhèng 执政; *fall from ~* POL shīshì 失势 **2** *v/t*: *be ~ed by X* yóu X zuò dònglì 由 X 作动力

power-assisted yǒu dònglì yuánzhù 有动力援助; **power cable** diànyuán diànlǎn 电源电缆; **power cut** tíngdiàn 停电

powerful qiángyǒulì 强有力

powerless wúlìliàng 无力量; *be ~ to ...* wúnéngwéilì ... 无能为力 ...

power line diànxiàn 电线; **power outage** tíngdiàn 停电; **power**

station fādiànzhàn 发电站;
power steering gāonéng zhuǎnxiàng 高能转向; **power unit**
néngliàng dānwèi 能量单位
PR (= *public relations*) gōngguān
公关
practical *experience* shíjì 实际;
person xiànshí 现实; (*functional*)
shíyòng 实用
practical joke èzuòjù 恶作剧
practically *behave, think* shíshìqiú-
shì 实事求是; (*almost*) jīhū 几乎
practice 1 *n* shíjiàn 实践, liànxí
练习; (*rehearsal*) páiliàn 排练;
(*custom*) chángguī 常规; *in ~* (*in
reality*) shíjì shang 实际上; *be out
of ~* shūyúliànxí 疏于练习 **2** *v/i*
xùnliàn 训练 **3** *v/t* liànxí 练习;
law, medicine zhíyè 执业
pragmatic wùshí 务实
pragmatism shíyòngzhǔyì 实用主
义
prairie dàcǎoyuán 大草原
praise 1 *n* zànyù 赞誉 **2** *v/t*
chēngzàn 称赞
praiseworthy zhídé chēngzàn 值
得称赞
prank *n* èzuòjù 恶作剧
prattle *v/i* xiánliáo 闲聊
pray qídǎo 祈祷
prayer dǎogào 祷告
PRC (= *People's Republic of
China*) Zhōnghuá Rénmín Gònghéguó 中华人民共和国
preach 1 *v/i* (*in church*) bùdào 布
道; (*moralize*) shuōjiào 说教 **2** *v/t*:
~ a sermon bùdào 布道
preacher chuándàorén 传道人
precarious bù wěndìng 不稳定
precariously bù wěngù 不稳固
precaution yùfáng cuòshī 预防措
施
precautionary *measure* yùfáng 预
防
precede *v/t* (*in time*) xiānyú 先于;
(*walk in front of*) lǐngxiān zǒu 领
先走
precedence: *take ~* yōuxiān 优
先; *take ~ over ...* lǐngxiānyú ...
领先于 ...
precedent *n* xiānlì 先例

preceding *week* qiányī 前一;
chapter shàngyī 上一
precinct (*district*) qūyù 区域
precious bǎoguì 宝贵
precipitate *v/t crisis* jiāsù 加速
précis *n* zhāiyào 摘要
precise zhǔnquè 准确
precisely jīngquè 精确
precision jīngquè 精确
precocious *child* zǎoshú 早熟
preconceived *idea* shìxiān xíngchéng 事先形成
precondition bìbèi 必备
predator (*animal*) shíròu dòngwù
食肉动物
predecessor (*in job*) qiánrènzhě
前任者; (*machine*) qiányī xínghào
前一型号
predestination sùmìng 宿命
predicament jiǒngkuàng 窘况
predict yùyán 预言
predictable kě yùyán 可预言
prediction yùyán 预言
predominant zhàn yōushì 占优势
predominantly zhǔyào 主要
predominate zhàn yōushì 占优势
prefabricated yùzhì 预制
preface *n* qiányán 前言
prefecture (*in ancient China*) zhōu
州
prefer gèng xǐhuān 更喜欢; *~ X to
Y* yǔ Y xiāngbǐ gèng xǐhuān X 与
Y 相比更喜欢 X; *~ to do*
nìngyuàn zuò 宁愿做
preferable gèng chènxīn 更称心;
be ~ to gèng shìyí 更适宜
preferably gèng kěqǔ 更可取
preference piān'ài 偏爱
preferential yōuxiān 优先
prefix qiánzhuì 前缀
pregnancy yùnqī 孕期
pregnant huáiyùn 怀孕
prehistoric shǐqián 史前
prejudice 1 *n* piānjiàn 偏见 **2** *v/t*
person yǐngxiǎng 影响; *chances*
xuēruò 削弱
prejudiced piānxīn 偏心
preliminary *adj* yùbèixìng 预备性
premarital hūnqián 婚前
premature: *~ birth* zǎochǎn 早产
premeditated yùmóu 预谋

premier n (*prime minister*) zǒnglǐ 总理

première n shǒucì gōngyǎn 首次公演

premises dìfang 地方

premium n (*in insurance*) bǎoxiǎnfèi 保险费

premonition yùgǎn 预感

prenatal chǎnqián 产前

preoccupied xīnbúzàiyān 心不在焉

preparation (*act*) zhǔnbèi 准备; *in ~ for X* wèi X zuòhǎo zhǔnbèi 为 X 作好准备; *~s* zhǔnbèi gōngzuò 准备工作

prepare 1 v/t zhǔnbèi 准备; *be ~d to do X* (*willing*) yuànyì zuò X 愿意做 X **2** v/i zhǔnbèi 准备

preposition jiècí 介词

preposterous huāngmiù 荒谬

prerequisite bìbèi 必备

prescribe (*of doctor*) kāi yàofāng 开药方

prescription MED yàofāng 药方

presence zàichǎng 在场; *in the ~ of X* zài X miànqián 在 X 面前

presence of mind yùshì bùhuāng 遇事不慌

present[1] **1** adj (*current*) mùqián 目前; *be ~* zàichǎng 在场 **2** n dāngqián 当前; *the ~* xiànzài 现在; GRAM xiànzàishí 现在时; *at ~* cǐkè 此刻

present[2] **1** n (*gift*) lǐwù 礼物 **2** v/t award, bouquet shòuyǔ 授予; program zhǔchí 主持; *~ X with Y*, *~ Y to X* bǎ Y zèngsònggěi X 把 Y 赠送给 X

presentation (*to audience*) bàogào 报告

present-day dāngjīn 当今

presently (*at the moment*) xiànzài 现在; (*soon*) bùjiǔ 不久

preservation bǎochí 保持

preservative n fángfǔjì 防腐剂

preserve 1 n (*domain*) lǐngyù 领域 **2** v/t standards, peace etc wéihù 维护; wood etc bǎohù 保护; food bǎocún 保存

preside v/i (*at meeting*) zhǔchí 主持

presidency zǒngtǒng zhíwèi 总统职位

president POL zǒngtǒng 总统; (*of company*) dǒngshìzhǎng 董事长

presidential zǒngtǒng 总统

press 1 n: *the ~* xīnwénjiè 新闻界 **2** v/t button àn 按; (*urge*) dūncù 敦促; (*squeeze*) jǐyā 挤压; clothes yùn 熨 **3** v/i: *~ for* cuīcù 催促

press conference jìzhě zhāodàihuì 记者招待会

pressing adj pòqiè 迫切

pressure 1 n yālì 压力; *be under ~* chéngshòu yālì 承受压力; *be under ~ to do X* pòyú yālì zuò X 迫于压力做 X **2** v/t qiǎngpò 强迫

prestige wēiwàng 威望

prestigious yǒu wēiwàng 有威望

presumably dàgài 大概

presume tuīcè 推测; *~ to do* màomèi zuò 冒昧做

presumption (*of innocence, guilt*) tuīdìng 推定

presumptuous màoshī 冒失

pre-tax nàshuì qián 纳税前

pretend 1 v/t zhuāngzuò 装作 **2** v/i jiǎzhuāng 假装

pretense xūjiǎ 虚假

pretentious xuànyào 炫耀

pretext jièkǒu 借口

pretty 1 adj piàoliang 漂亮 **2** adv (*quite*) xiāngdāng 相当

prevail (*triumph*) zhànshèng 战胜

prevailing shèngxíng 盛行

prevent fángzhǐ 防止; *~ X (from) doing Y* zǔzhǐ X zuò Y 阻止 X 做 Y

prevention yùfáng 预防

preventive yùfángxìng 预防性

preview n (*of movie, exhibition*) yùzhǎn 预展

previous qiányī 前一

previously yǐqián 以前

prewar zhànqián 战前

prey n lièwù 猎物

♦ **prey on** bǔshí 捕食; fig (*of conman etc*) lièqǔ 猎取

price 1 n jiàgé 价格 **2** v/t COM dìngjià 定价

priceless wújià 无价

price war jiàgézhàn 价格战

pricey ángguì 昂贵

prick[1] **1** *n* (*pain*) cì 刺 **2** *v/t* (*jab*) chuō 戳

prick[2] *n* ∨ (*penis*) jība 鸡巴; (*person*) chǔnrén 蠢人

♦**prick up**: ~ **one's ears** (*of dog*) shùqǐ ěrduo 竖起耳朵; (*of person*) tūrán kāishǐ zhùyì tīng 突然开始注意听

prickle (*on plant*) cì 刺

prickly *beard*, *plant* duōcì 多刺; (*irritable*) yìnù 易怒

prickly heat fèizi 痱子

pride 1 *n* (*in person*, *achievement*) zìháo 自豪; (*self-respect*) zìzūn 自尊 **2** *v/t*: ~ **oneself on X** yǐ X wéi zìháo 以 X 为自豪

priest mùshī 牧师

primarily zhǔyào 主要

primary 1 *adj* zhǔyào 主要 **2** *n* POL chūxuǎn 初选

prime 1 *n*: **be in one's** ~ zhèngzhí shèngnián 正值盛年 **2** *adj* *example*, *reason* zhǔyào 主要; **of** ~ **importance** zhìguān zhòngyào 至关重要

prime minister shǒuxiàng 首相

prime time TV huángjīn shíjiān 黄金时间

primitive yuánshǐ 原始; *conditions* jiǎnlòu 简陋

prince wángzǐ 王子

princess gōngzhǔ 公主

principal 1 *adj* zhǔyào 主要 **2** *n* (*of school*) xiàozhǎng 校长

principally zhǔyào 主要

principle (*in moral sense*) zhǔnzé 准则; (*rule*) yuánzé 原则; **on** ~ yījù zìjǐ de yuánzé 依据自己的原则; **in** ~ yuánzé shang 原则上

print 1 *n* (*in book etc*) yìnshuā zìtǐ 印刷字体; PHOT zhàopiàn 照片; **out of** ~ juébǎn 绝版 **2** *v/t* yìnshuā 印刷; COMPUT dǎyìn 打印; (*in block capitals*) dàxiě 大写

♦**print out** yìnchū 印出

printed matter yìnshuāpǐn 印刷品

printer (*person*) yìnshuāshāng 印刷商; (*machine*) ⇩ dǎyìnjī 打印机

printing press yìnshuājī 印刷机

printout dǎyìnchū de zīliào 打印出的资料

prior 1 *adj* shìxiān 事先 **2** *prep*: ~ **to** zài ...yǐqián 在 ... 以前

prioritize (*put in order of priority*) huàfēn qīngzhònghuǎnjí 划分轻重缓急; (*give priority to*) jǐyǔ yōuxiān 给予优先

priority yàowèi 要位; **have** ~ yǒu yōuxiānquán 有优先权

prison jiānyù 监狱

prisoner qiúfàn 囚犯; **take X** ~ fúlǔ X 俘虏 X

prisoner of war zhànfú 战俘

privacy sīrén kōngjiān 私人空间

private 1 *adj* sīrén 私人 **2** *n* MIL shìbīng 士兵; **in** ~ sīxià 私下

privately (*in private*) sīxià 私下; *funded*, *owned* gèrén 个人; (*inwardly*) nèixīn 内心

private sector mínyíng qǐyè 民营企业

privilege (*special treatment*) tèquán 特权; (*honor*) róngxìng 荣幸

privileged xiángyǒu tèquán 享有特权; (*honored*) róngxìng 荣幸

prize 1 *n* jiǎngshǎng 奖赏 **2** *v/t* zhēnshì 珍视

prizewinner huòjiǎng zhě 获奖者

prizewinning huòjiǎng 获奖

pro[1] *n*: **the** ~**s and cons** yōushì hé lièshì 优势和劣势

pro[2] → **professional**

pro[3]: **be** ... (*in favor of*) zànchéng ... 赞成 ...

probability kěnéng xìng 可能性

probable hěn kěnéng 很可能

probably yěxǔ 也许

probation (*in job*) shìyòng 试用; LAW huǎnxíng 缓刑

probation officer huǎnxíng jiāndūguān 缓刑监督官

probation period (*in job*) shìyòngqī 试用期

probe 1 *n* (*investigation*) diàochá 调查; (*scientific*) tàncè 探测 **2** *v/t* tànchá 探查; (*investigate*) diàochá 调查

problem wèntí 问题; **no** ~ méi

wèntí 没问题

procedure bùzhòu 步骤

proceed 1 v/i (go: of people) qiánxíng 前行; (of work etc) jìnzhǎn 进展 **2** v/t: **~ to do X** jìxù zuò X 继续做 X

proceedings (events) jìnchéng 进程

proceeds shōurù 收入

process 1 n guòchéng 过程; **in the ~** (while doing it) zài … de guòchéng zhōng 在 … 的过程中 **2** v/t food, raw materials jiāgōng 加工; data chǔlǐ 处理; application etc shěnchá 审查

procession hángliè 行列

processor COMPUT chǔlǐqì 处理器

proclaim xuānbù 宣布

prod n & v/t tǒng 捅

prodigy: (infant) ~ shéntóng 神童

produce 1 n chǎnpǐn 产品 **2** v/t commodity shēngchǎn 生产; (bring about) yǐnqǐ 引起; (bring out) náchū 拿出; play, movie, TV program zhìzuò 制作

producer (of commodity) zhìzào chǎngjiā 制造厂家; (of play, movie, TV program) zhìpiānrén 制片人

product chǎnpǐn 产品; (result) jiéguǒ 结果

production chǎnliàng 产量; (of play, movie, TV program) zhìzuò 制作; (play, movie, TV program) zuòpǐn 作品

production capacity shēngchǎn nénglì 生产能力

production costs shēngchǎn chéngběn 生产成本

productive duōchǎn 多产; meeting yǒu chéngxiào 有成效

productivity shēngchǎnlì 生产力

profane language xiàliú 下流

profess shēngchēng 声称

profession zhíyè 职业

professional 1 adj (not amateur), advice, help zhuānyè 专业; piece of work yǒu jìqiǎo 有技巧; **turn ~** biànchéng zhuānyè 变成专业 **2** n (doctor, lawyer etc, expert) zhuānyè rénshì 专业人士; (not an amateur) zhíyè rényuán 职业人员

professionally play sport zuòwéi zhuānyè 作为专业; (well, skillfully) zhuānyè 专业

professor jiàoshòu 教授

proficiency jīngtōng 精通

proficient jīngtōng 精通

profile (of face) cèmiàn 侧面; (description) jièshào 介绍

profit 1 n lìrùn 利润 **2** v/i: **~ by**, **~ from** cóngzhōng xīqǔ yìchù 从中吸取益处

profitability yǒulìkětú 有利可图

profitable kěhuò lìrùn 可获利润

profit margin lìrùnlǜ 利润率

profound shēnqiè 深切

profoundly shēnshēn 深深

prognosis yùhòu 预后

program 1 n jìhuà 计划; (on radio, TV) jiémù 节目; COMPUT chéngxù 程序; (in theater) jiémùdān 节目单 **2** v/t COMPUT biān chéngxù 编程序

programmer COMPUT chéngxùyuán 程序员

progress 1 n jìnbù 进步; **make ~** yǒu jìnbù 有进步; **in ~** jìnxíngzhōng 进行中 **2** v/i (advance in time) jìnzhǎn 进展; (move on) jìnxíng 进行; (make progress) qǔdé jìnbù 取得进步; **how is the work ~ing?** gōngzuò jìnzhǎnde zěnmeyàng? 工作进展得怎么样？

progressive adj (enlightened) kāimíng 开明; (which progresses) zhúbù fāzhǎn 逐步发展

progressively zhúbù 逐步

prohibit jìnzhǐ 禁止

prohibition jìnzhǐ 禁止; **Prohibition** jìnjiǔ shíqī 禁酒时期

prohibitive prices gāode mǎibùqǐ 高得买不起

project¹ n (plan) jìhuà 计划; (undertaking) xiàngmù 项目; EDU kètí 课题; (housing area) ⇩ tǒngjiàn zhùzháiqū 统建住宅区

project² 1 v/t figures, sales jìhuà 计划; movie fàngyìng 放映 **2** v/i (stick out) tūchū 突出

projection (forecast) yùcè 预测

projector (*for slides*) fàngyìngjī 放映机

proletariat wúchǎn jiējí 无产阶级

prolific *writer*, *artist* duōchǎn 多产

prolong yáncháng 延长

prom (*school dance*) wǔhuì 舞会

prominent *nose*, *chin* tūchū 突出; (*significant*) xiǎnzhù 显著

promiscuity xìng luànjiāo 性乱交

promiscuous xìngluàn 性乱

promise 1 *n* chéngnuò 承诺 2 *v/t* xǔnuò 许诺; ~ *to* ... xǔnuò zuò ... 许诺做 ...; ~ *X to Y* xǔnuò gěi Y X 许诺给 Y X 3 *v/i* bǎozhèng 保证

promising yǒu qiántú 有前途

promote *employee* jìnshēng 晋升; (*encourage*, *foster*) zēngjìn 增进; COM xuānchuán 宣传

promoter (*of sports event*) chuàngbànrén 创办人

promotion (*of employee*) jìnjí 晋级; (*of scheme*, *idea*) xuānchuán 宣传; COM cùxiāo 促销

prompt 1 *adj* (*on time*) zhǔnshí 准时; (*speedy*) jíshí 及时 2 *adv*: *at two o'clock* ~ liǎngdiǎnzhěng 两点正 3 *v/t* (*cause*) jīqǐ 激起; *actor* tící 提词 4 *n* COMPUT tíshìfú 提示符

promptly (*on time*) jíshí 及时; (*immediately*) lìjí 立即

prone: *be* ~ *to* yìyú zuò 易于做

pronoun dàicí 代词

pronounce *word* fāyīn 发音; (*declare*) xuānbù 宣布

pronounced *accent* míngxiǎn 明显; *views* míngquè 明确

pronunciation fāyīn 发音

proof *n* zhèngjù 证据; (*of book*) jiàoyàng 校样

prop 1 *v/t* xiékào 斜靠 2 *n* (*in theater*) dàojù 道具

♦ prop up zhīchēngqǐ 支撑起; *regime* zhīchí 支持

propaganda xuānchuán 宣传

propel tuījìn 推进

propellant (*in aerosol*) qǐ tuījìn zuòyòng 起推进作用

propeller (*of boat*) luóxuánjiǎng 螺旋桨

proper (*real*) zhēnzhèng 真正; (*correct*) qiàdàng 恰当; (*fitting*) shìdàng 适当

properly (*correctly*) zhèngquè 正确; (*fittingly*) shìdàng 适当

property cáichǎn 财产; (*land*) fángdìchǎn 房地产

property developer fángdìchǎn kāifārén 房地产开发人

prophecy yùyán 预言

prophesy zuò yùyán 作预言

proportion bǐlì 比例，bùfen 部分; ~s (*dimensions*) miànjī 面积

proportional chéng bǐlì 成比例

proposal (*suggestion*) tíyì 提议; (*of marriage*) qiúhūn 求婚

propose 1 *v/t* (*suggest*) jiànyì 建议; (*plan*) jìhuà 计划 2 *v/i* (*make offer of marriage*) qiúhūn 求婚

proposition 1 *n* jiànyì 建议 2 *v/t* *woman* tíchū xìngyàoqiú 提出性要求

proprietor yèzhǔ 业主

proprietress nǚ yèzhǔ 女业主

prose sǎnwén 散文

prosecute *v/t* LAW tíqǐ gōngsù 提起公诉

prosecution LAW qǐsù 起诉; (*lawyers*) yuángàofāng 原告方

prosecutor gōngsùrén 公诉人

prospect 1 *n* (*chance*, *likelihood*) kěnéng 可能; (*thought of sth in the future*) qīwàng 期望; ~s qiánjǐng 前景 2 *v/i*: ~ *for gold* kāntàn 勘探

prospective kěnéng 可能

prosper chénggōng 成功

prosperity xīngshèng 兴盛

prosperous xīngwàng 兴旺

prostitute *n* jìnǚ 妓女; *male* ~ nánjì 男妓

prostitution màiyín 卖淫

prostrate: *be* ~ *with grief* bēitòngyùjué 悲痛欲绝

protect *v/t* bǎohù 保护

protection bǎohù 保护

protection money bǎohùfèi 保护费

protective yǒu bǎohùxìng 有保护性

protector bǎohù zhě 保护者

protein dànbáizhì 蛋白质

protest 1 *n* kàngyì 抗议; (*demonstration*) shìwēi 示威 **2** *v/t* shēnmíng 申明; (*object to*) fǎnduì 反对 **3** *v/i* shēngbiàn 声辩; (*demonstrate*) shìwēi 示威

Protestant 1 *n* Xīnjiàotú 新教徒 **2** *adj* Xīnjiào 新教

protester shìwēi zhě 示威者

protocol lǐyí 礼仪

prototype móxíng 模型

protracted yáncháng 延长

protrude *v/i* tūchū 凸出

proud jiāo'ào 骄傲; (*independent*) zìzūn 自尊; **be ~ of** yǐ … wéi zìháo 以 … 为自豪

proudly zìháo 自豪

prove zhèngmíng 证明

proverb yànyǔ 谚语

provide tígōng 提供; **~ Y to X, ~ X with Y** wèi X tígōng Y 为X提供Y; **~d (that)** (*on condition that*) zhǐyào 只要

♦**provide for** *family* gōngyǎng 供养; **~ X** (*of law etc*) guīdìng X 规定 X

province shěng 省

provincial *city* shěng 省; *pej* (*attitude*) shǒujiù 守旧

provision (*supply*) gōngyìng 供应; (*of law, contract*) tiáokuǎn 条款

provisional línshí 临时

proviso fùdài tiáojiàn 附带条件

provocation tiǎoxìn 挑衅

provocative tiǎoxìn 挑衅; (*sexually*) tiǎodòu 挑逗

provoke (*cause*) yǐnqǐ 引起; (*annoy*) jīnù 激怒

prow NAUT chuánshǒu 船首

prowess zhuāncháng 专长

prowl *v/i* (*of tiger etc*) qīngqīng yídòng 轻轻移动; (*of burglar*) qiánxíng 潜行

prowler guǐguǐsuìsuìde rén 鬼鬼祟祟的人

proximity línjìn 邻近

proxy (*authority*) dàilǐ quán 代理权; (*person*) dàilǐ rén 代理人

prude jiǎzhèngjing 假正经

prudence shěnshèn 审慎

prudent shěnshèn 审慎

prudish jiǎzhèngjing 假正经

prune[1] *n* xīméifǔ 西梅脯

prune[2] *v/t plant* xiūjiǎn 修剪; *fig* xuējiǎn 削减

pry dǎtīng 打听

♦**pry into** cìtàn 刺探

PS (= *postscript*) òují 又及

PSB (= *Public Security Bureau*) Gōng'ān Jú 公安局

pseudonym huàmíng 化名

psychiatric jīngshénbìng 精神病

psychiatrist jīngshénkē yīshēng 精神科医生

psychiatry jīngshénbìngxué 精神病学

psychic *adj* yǒu tèyì gōngnéng 有特异功能

psychoanalysis jīngshén fēnxī 精神分析

psychoanalyst jīngshén fēnxīxué-jiā 精神分析学家

psychoanalyze zuò jīngshén fēnxī 作精神分析

psychological xīnlǐ 心理

psychologically xīnlǐ 心理

psychologist xīnlǐxuéjiā 心理学家

psychology xīnlǐxué 心理学

psychopath jīngshén biàntài zhě 精神变态者

puberty qīngchūnqī 青春期

pubic hair yīnmáo 阴毛

public 1 *adj* gōngzhòng 公众 **2** *n*: **the ~** mínzhòng 民众; **in ~** dāngzhòng 当众

publication (*of book, report*) chūbǎn 出版; (*by newspaper*) kānchū 刊出; (*book, newspaper*) chūbǎnwù 出版物

publicity xuānchuán 宣传

publicize (*make known*) xuānchuán 宣传; COM zuò guǎnggào 作广告

publicly dāngzhòng 当众

public minibus xiǎo gōnggòng 小公共; **public prosecutor** gōngsùrén 公诉人; **public relations** gōngguān 公关; **public school** gōngxué 公学; **public sector** zhèngfǔ jīgòu 政府机构; **Public Security Bureau** Gōng'ān Jú 公安局

publish chūbǎn 出版

publisher chūbǎnshè 出版社

publishing chūbǎnyè 出版业

publishing company chūbǎn gōngsī 出版公司

puddle n shuǐkēng 水坑

puff 1 n (of wind, smoke) yīgǔ 一股 **2** v/i (pant) chuǎnxī 喘息; **~ on a cigarette** yīkǒuyīkǒude chōuyān 一口一口地抽烟

puffy eyes, face péngzhàng 膨胀

pull 1 n (on rope) lā 拉; F (appeal) xīyǐnlì 吸引力; F (influence) yǐngxiǎnglì 影响力 **2** v/t (drag) lā 拉; (tug) chě 扯; tooth bá 拔; muscle lāshāng 拉伤 **3** v/i zhuài 拽

♦ **pull apart** (separate) lākāi 拉开

♦ **pull away** v/t chōukāi 抽开

♦ **pull down** (lower) lāxià 拉下; (demolish) chāihuǐ 拆毁

♦ **pull in** v/i (of bus, train) jìn zhàn 进站

♦ **pull off** leaves etc lādiào 拉掉; F deal zuòchéng shì 做成事

♦ **pull out 1** v/t chōuchū 抽出; troops chèlí 撤离 **2** v/i (of an agreement, a competition) tuìchū 退出; (of troops) chèlí 撤离; (of ship) shǐchū 驶出

♦ **pull through** (from an illness) kāngfù 康复

♦ **pull together 1** v/i (cooperate) tōnglìhézuò 通力合作 **2** v/t: **pull oneself together** kòngzhì zìjǐ 控制自己

♦ **pull up 1** v/t (raise) tíqǐ 提起; plant, weeds báqǐ 拔起 **2** v/i (of car etc) tíng 停

pulley huálún 滑轮

pullover jǐnshēn tàoshān 紧身套衫

pulp guǒròu 果肉; (for paper-making) zhǐjiāng 纸浆

pulpit bùdàotán 布道坛

pulsate (of heart, blood) bódòng 搏动; (of rhythm) chàndòng 颤动

pulse màibó 脉搏

pump 1 n (machine) ⇩ bèng 泵; (gas ~) qìyóubèng 汽油泵 **2** v/t yòng bèng chōuyā 用泵抽压

♦ **pump up** gěi ... chōngqì 给 ... 充气

pumpkin nánguā 南瓜

pun shuāngguānyǔ 双关语

punch 1 n (blow) jīdǎ 击打; (implement) dǎkǒngjī 打孔机 **2** v/t (with fist) yòng quán jī 用拳击; hole, ticket dǎ kǒng 打孔

punch line miàoyǔ 妙语

punctual zhǔnshí 准时

punctuality shǒushí 守时

punctually zhǔnshí 准时

punctuate jiā biāodiǎn 加标点

punctuation biāodiǎn fúhào yòngfǎ 标点符号用法

punctuation mark biāodiǎn fúhào 标点符号

puncture 1 n xiǎokǒng 小孔 **2** v/t chuān kǒng 穿孔

pungent cìbí 刺鼻

punish person chéngfá 惩罚

punishing pace, schedule chīlì 吃力

punishment chéngfá 惩罚

puny person ruòxiǎo 弱小

pup yòuxiǎo dòngwù 幼小动物

pupil[1] (of eye) tóngkǒng 瞳孔

pupil[2] (student) xuésheng 学生

puppet mù'ǒu 木偶

puppet government kuǐlěi zhèngfǔ 傀儡政府

puppet show mù'ǒuxì 木偶戏

puppy xiǎogǒu 小狗

purchase[1] n & v/t gòumǎi 购买

purchase[2] (grip) jǐnwò 紧握

purchaser mǎizhǔ 买主

pure silk, wool chún 纯; air, water jiéjìng 洁净; white etc chúncuì 纯粹; sound chúnzhèng 纯正; (morally) chúnjié 纯洁

purely wánquán 完全

purge 1 n (of political party) zhěngsù 整肃 **2** v/t qīngchú 清除

purify water jìnghuà 净化

puritan qīngjiàotú 清教徒

puritanical qīngjiàotúshì 清教徒式

purity chúndù 纯度; (moral) chúnjié 纯洁

purple adj zǐsè 紫色

Purple Heart MIL Zǐxīn Xúnzhāng 紫心勋章

purpose (aim, object) mùdì 目的;

on ~ gùyì 故意
purposeful jiāndìng 坚定
purposely yǒuyì 有意
purr *v/i* (*of cat*) hūlushēng 呼噜声
purse *n* (*pocketbook*) shǒudài 手袋
pursue *v/t person* zhuīzhú 追逐;
  career zhuīqiú 追求; *course of
  action* jìxù jìnxíng 继续进行
pursuer zhuīgǎn zhě 追赶者
pursuit (*chase*) zhuīgǎn 追赶; (*of
  happiness etc*) zhuīqiú 追求;
  (*activity*) huódòng 活动; *those in
  ~* nàxiē zhuībǔ de rén 那些追捕
  的人
pus nóng 脓
push 1 *n* (*shove*) tuī 推; (*of button*)
  àn 按 **2** *v/t* (*shove*) tuī 推; *button*
  àn 按; (*pressurize*) bīpò 逼迫;
  drugs fàndú 贩毒; *be ~ed for X*
  (*be short of*) X jǐn X 紧; *be ~ing 40*
  kuài sìshí le 快四十了 **3** *v/i* tuī
  推
♦**push along** *cart etc* xiàng qián tuī
  向前推
♦**push away** tuīkāi 推开
♦**push off 1** *v/t lid* tuīdiào 推掉
  2 *v/i* (*leave*) líkāi 离开; *~!* zǒukāi!
  走开！
♦**push on** *v/i* (*continue*) jìxù qiánjìn
  继续前进
♦**push up** *prices* shàngtiáo 上调
push-button yòng ànniǔ cāozòng
  用按钮操纵
pusher (*of drugs*) dúpǐn fànzi 毒品
  贩子
push-up fǔ wòchēng 俯卧撑
pushy kèqiú 苛求
puss, pussy (**cat**) māomī 猫咪
put fàng 放; *question* wèn 问; *~ the
  cost at ...* gūjià ... 估价 ...
♦**put aside** *money* chǔcún 储存;
  work fàngzài yībiān 放在一边
♦**put away** (*in closet etc*) shōuqǐlái
  收起来; (*in institution*) guānjìn 关
  进; (*consume*) hē 喝; *money* chǔcún 储存; *animal* jiéguǒ 结果
♦**put back** (*replace*) fànghuí yuánchù 放回原处
♦**put by** *money* chǔcún 储存
♦**put down** fàngxià 放下; *deposit*
  fù dìngjīn 付定金; *rebellion*

zhènyā 镇压; (*belittle: person*)
qīngshì 轻视; (*in writing*) xiěxià 写
下; *put one's foot down* (*in car*)
cǎi yóuménr 踩油门儿; (*be firm*)
jiāndìng 坚定; *put X down to Y*
(*attribute*) bǎ X guīyīn yú Y 把X
归因于Y
♦**put forward** *idea etc* jiànyì 建议
♦**put in** fàngjìnqù 放进去; *time*
  fùchū 付出; *request, claim*
  chéngjiāo 呈交
♦**put in for** shēnqǐng 申请
♦**put off** *light, radio, TV* guāndiào
  关掉; (*postpone*) tuīchí 推迟;
  (*deter*) shǐ rén búzuò 使人不做;
  (*repel*) gǎndào fǎngǎn 感到反感;
  put X off Y shǐ X bù xǐhuān Y 使X
  不喜欢Y
♦**put on** *light, radio, TV* dǎkāi 打
  开; *tape, music* fàng 放; *jacket,
  shoes* chuān 穿; *make-up* cháyòng
  搽用; *brake* shā 刹; (*perform*)
  yǎnchū 演出; (*assume*) jiǎzhuāng
  假装; *~ weight* zēngjiā tǐzhòng 增
  加体重; *she's just putting it on*
  tā zhǐshì zhuāng de 她只是装底
♦**put out** *hand* shēnchū 伸出; *fire*
  xīmiè 熄灭; *light* guāndiào 关掉
♦**put through** (*on phone*) jiētōng
  接通
♦**put together** (*assemble*) zǔhéchéng yītǐ 组合成一体;
  (*organize*) zǔzhī 组织
♦**put up** *v/t hand* jǔqǐ 举起; (*give a
  bed to*) gōngyìng shísù 供应食宿;
  (*erect*) shùqǐ 竖起; *prices* tígāo 提
  高; *poster, notice* zhāngtiē 张贴;
  money tígōng 提供; *~ for sale*
  chūshòu 出售
♦**put up with** (*tolerate*) rěnshòu 忍
  受
putty yóuhuī 油灰
puzzle 1 *n* (*mystery*) mí 谜; (*game*)
  zhìlì yóuxì 智力游戏; (*jigsaw ~*)
  pīntú wánjù 拼图玩具;
  (*crossword ~*) zònghéng zìmí 纵横
  字谜 **2** *v/t* shǐkùnhuò 使困惑
puzzling lìngrén fèijiě 令人费解
PVC jùlǜyǐxī 聚氯乙烯
pylon diànlǎntǎ 电缆塔
pyramid selling chuánxiāo 传销

Q

Qin Dynasty Qín Cháo 秦朝

Qing Dynasty Qīng Chao 清朝

quack¹ 1 n (of duck) guāgua yīshēng 呱呱一声 2 v/i guāgua jiào 呱呱叫

quack² F (bad doctor) jiānghú yīshēng 江湖医生

quadrangle (figure) sìbiān xíng 四边形; (courtyard) sìfāng yuàn 四方院

quadruped sìzú dòngwù 四足动物

quadruple v/i chéng sìbèi 成四倍

quadruplets sì bāotāi 四胞胎

quaint little cottage gǔyǎ xiǎoqiǎo 古雅小巧; (slightly eccentric: ideas etc) gǔguài 古怪

quake 1 n (earthquake) dìzhèn 地震 2 v/i (of earth) dìzhèn 地震; (with fear) duōsuo 哆嗦

qualification (from university etc) wénpíng 文凭; (of remark etc) xiānjué tiáojiàn 先决条件; **have the right ~s for a job** yǒu zuò yīfèn gōngzuò de zīgé 有做一份工作的资格

qualified doctor, engineer etc hégé 合格; (restricted) yǒu xiàndù 有限度; **I am not ~ to judge** wǒ bùgòu zīgé lái juédìng 我不够资格来决定

qualify 1 v/t (of degree, course etc) shǐ jùyǒu zīgé 使具有资格; remark etc xiànzhì 限制 2 v/i (get degree etc) qǔde zīgé 取得资格; (in competition) qǔde bǐsài zīgé 取得比赛资格; **our team has qualified for the semi-final** wǒmén duì huòdé cānjiā bànjuésài de zīgé 我们队获得参加半决赛的资格; **that doesn't ~ as ...** nà bùsuàn ... 那不算 ...

quality zhìliàng 质量; (characteristic) tèxìng 特性

quality control (activity) zhìliàng kòngzhì 质量控制; (department) zhìliàng guǎnlǐ 质量管理

qualm dānyōu 担忧; **have no ~s about ...** bù dānyōu ... 不担忧 ...

quantify yòng shùliàng biǎoshì 用数量表示

quantity liàng 量

quarantine gélí 隔离

quarrel n & v/i chǎozuǐ 吵嘴

quarrelsome ài chǎojià 爱吵架

quarry (for mining) cǎishíchǎng 采石场

quart kuātuō 夸脱

quarter 1 n sìfēn zhīyī 四分之一; (part of town) dìqū 地区; **a ~ of an hour** yīkèzhōng 一刻钟; **a ~ to 5** chà yīkè wǔdiǎn 差一刻五点; **~ past 5** wǔdiǎn yīkè 五点一刻 2 v/t fēnchéng sìfèn 分成四份

quarterback SP sìfēnwèi 四分卫; quarterfinal sìfēn zhīyī juésài 四分之一决赛; quarterfinalist jìnrù sìfēn zhīyī juésài zhě 进入四分之一决赛者

quarterly adj & adv jìdù 季度

quarternote MUS sìfēn yīnfú 四分音符

quarters MIL yíngfáng 营房

quartet (instrumentalists) sì chóngzòu 四重奏; (singers) sì chóngchàng 四重唱

quartz shíyīng 石英

quaver 1 n (in voice) chàndǒu 颤抖 2 v/i (of voice) chàndǒu 颤抖

queen nǚwáng 女王; (monarch's wife) wánghòu 王后

queen bee fēngwáng 蜂王

queer (peculiar) gǔguài 古怪

quench flames xīmiè 熄灭; **~ one's thirst** zhǐkě 止渴

query 1 n yíwèn 疑问 2 v/t (express doubt about) duì ... biǎoshì yíwèn 对 ... 表示疑问;

(*check*) wèn 问; ~ **X with Y** wèn Y yǒuguān X 问 Y 有关 X

question 1 *n* wèntí 问题; **in ~** (*being talked about*) suǒtán 所谈; (*in doubt*) bèi huáiyí 被怀疑; **it's a ~ of money** / **time** shì qián / shíjiān de wèntí 是钱 / 时间的问题; **that's out of the ~** bù kěnéng 不可能 **2** *v/t person* wèn 问; LAW shěnwèn 审问; (*doubt*) huáiyí 怀疑

questionable *honesty* kě huáiyí 可怀疑; *figures*, *statement* bù kěxìn 不可信

questioning *look*, *tone* cháwèn 查问

question mark yídiǎn 疑点

questionnaire wèndá juàn 问答卷

quick kuài 快; **be ~!** kuàidiǎnr! 快点儿 !; **let's have a ~ drink** wǒmén kuàizhe hē diǎnr ba 我们快着喝点儿吧; **can I have a ~ look?** wǒ néngbūnéng kàn yīyǎn? 我能不能看一眼 ?; **that was ~!** zhème kuài! 这么快 !

quicksand liúshā 流沙; **quicksilver** shuǐyín 水银; **quickwitted** jīmǐn 机敏

quiet *voice*, *music* xiǎoshēng 小声; *engine* dī zàoyīn 低噪音; *street* ānjìng 安静; *life*, *town* píngjìng 平静; **keep ~ about X** bù tí X de shì 不提 X 的事; **~!** bìzuǐ! 闭嘴 !

♦ **quieten down 1** *v/t children*, *class* shǐ ānjìng 使安静 **2** *v/i* (*of children*) ānjìng xiàlái 安静下来; (*of political situation*) píngjìng xiàlái 平静下来

quilt (*on bed*) bèizi 被子

quinine kuíníng 奎宁

quip 1 *n* qiàopí huà 俏皮话 **2** *v/i* shuō qiàopí huà 说俏皮话

quirky gǔguài 古怪; *machine* bù wěndìng 不稳定

quit 1 *v/t job* cízhí 辞职; **~ doing X** fàngqì zuò X 放弃做 X **2** *v/i* (*leave job*) cízhí 辞职; COMPUT tuìchū 退出

quite (*fairly*) xiāngdāng 相当; (*completely*) wánquán 完全; **not ~ ready** méi wánquán zhǔnbèi hǎo 没完全准备好; **I didn't ~ understand** wǒ bū tài míngbái 我不太明白; **is that right? – not ~** duìma? – bù wánquán 对吗 ? – 不完全; **~!** zhèngshì zhèyàng! 正是这样 ! ; **~ a lot** hěn duō 很多; **it was ~ a surprise** / **change** zhēn jīngrén / biànhuà xiāngdāng dà 真惊人 / 变化相当大

quits: **be ~ with X** (*person*) yǔ X liǎngqīng 与 X 两清

quiver *v/i* chàndǒu 颤抖

quiz 1 *n* wèndá bǐsài 问答比赛 **2** *v/t* pánwèn 盘问

quiz program wèndá bǐsài jiémù 问答比赛节目

quota dìngliàng 定量

quotation (*from author*) yǐnwén 引文; (*price*) bàojià 报价; **give X a ~ for Y** gěi X tígōng yīgè Y de bàojià 给 X 提供一个 Y 的报价

quotation marks yǐnhào 引号

quote 1 *n* (*from author*) yǐnwén 引文; (*price*) bàojià 报价; (*quotation mark*) yǐnhào 引号 **2** *v/t text* yǐnyòng 引用; *price* bàojià 报价 **3** *v/i*: **~ from an author** yǐnyòng yīgè zuòjiā de zuòpǐn 引用一个作家的作品

R

rabbit tùzi 兔子
rabies kuángquǎn bìng 狂犬病
raccoon huànxióng 浣熊
race[1] n (of people) zhǒngzú 种族
race[2] 1 n SP jìngsài 竞赛; **the ~s**
(horse ~s) pǎomǎ 跑马 2 v/i (run
fast) jíxíng jíxíng 疾行; SP cānjiā jìngsài
参加竞赛; **he ~d through his
meal / work** tā xùnsù chīwánle
fàn / zuòwánle gōngzuò 他迅速
吃完了饭 / 做完了工作 3 v/t:
I'll ~ you wǒ hé nǐ bǐsài 我和你
比赛
racecourse pǎomǎ dào 跑马道;
racehorse bǐsài yòng mǎ 比赛用
马; **racetrack** pǎodào 跑道
racial zhǒngzú zhǒng 种族; **~ equality**
zhǒngzú píngděng 种族平等
racing jìngsài 竞赛
racing car sàichē 赛车
racing driver sàichē yùndòngyuán
赛车运动员
racism zhǒngzú qíshì 种族歧视
racist 1 n zhǒngzú qíshì zhě 种族
歧视者 2 adj zhǒngzú qíshì 种族
歧视
rack 1 n (for parking bikes) zìxíngchē jià 自行车架; (for bags on
train) xíngli jià 行李架; (for CDs)
chàngpiān jià 唱片架 2 v/t: ~
one's brains jiǎojìn nǎozhī 绞尽
脑汁
racket[1] SP qiúpāi 球拍
racket[2] (noise) xuānnào 喧闹;
(criminal activity) piànjú 骗局
radar léidá 雷达
radiant smile, appearance hóngguāng mǎnmiàn 红光满面
radiate v/i (of heat, light) guāngmáng sìshè 光芒四射
radiation PHYS fàngshè 放射
radiator (in room) nuǎnqì 暖气;
(in car) qǔnuǎn qì 取暖器
radical 1 adj chèdǐ 彻底; POL views

jījìn 激进 2 n POL jījìn zhǔyì zhě
激进主义者
radicalism POL jījìn zhǔyì 激进主
义
radically chèdǐ 彻底
radio shōuyīnjī 收音机; **on the ~**
shōuyīnjī lǐ 收音机里; **by ~** yòng
wúxiàndiàn 用无线电
radioactive fàngshè xìng 放射性;
radioactivity fàngshè xìng 放射
性; **radio alarm** shōuyīnjī nàozhōng 收音机闹钟; **radio sta-
tion** guǎngbō diàntái 广播电台;
radio taxi wúxiàn chūzūchē 无线
出租车; **radio telephone** wúxiàn diànhuà 无线电话; **radiotherapy** fàngshè liáofǎ 放射疗
法
radish xiǎoluóbo 小萝卜
radius bànjìng 半径
raffle n chōujiǎng 抽奖
raft mùpái 木排
rafter chuánzi 椽子
rag (for cleaning etc) mābù 抹布
rage 1 n kuángnù 狂怒; **be in a ~**
fānù 发怒; **all the ~** fēngxíng
yīshí 风行一时 2 v/i (of person)
fānù 发怒; (of storm) kuángbào
狂暴
ragged edge pòlàn 破烂; appearance luàn péngpeng 乱蓬蓬;
clothes lánlǚ 褴褛
raid 1 n (by troops, police) tūxí 突
袭; (by robbers) qiǎngjié 抢劫; FIN
jítǐ pāoshòu 集体抛售 2 v/t (of
troops, police) tūrán sōuchá 突然
搜查; (of robbers) tūrán xíjī 突然
袭击
raider (on bank etc) qiǎngjié fàn 抢
劫犯
rail (on track) tiěguǐ 铁轨; (hand~)
fúshǒu 扶手; (for towel) máojīn
jià 毛巾架; **by ~** (of people) zuò
huǒchē 坐火车; (of goods) yòng

tiělù 用铁路

railings (*around park etc*) lángān 栏杆

railroad tiělù 铁路

railroad station huǒchē zhàn 火车站

rain 1 *n* yǔ 雨; *in the* ~ yǔzhōng 雨中; *the* ~*s* yǔjì 雨季 **2** *v/i* xiàyǔ 下雨; *it's* ~*ing* xià zhe yǔ ne 下着雨呢

rainbow cǎihóng 彩虹; **rain-check**: *can I take a* ~ *on that?* (*take up offer later*) shìfǒu kěyǐ tuīchí? 是否可以推迟？; **raincoat** yǔyī 雨衣; **raindrop** yǔdiǎnr 雨点儿; **rainfall** jiàngyǔ liàng 降雨量; **rain forest** yǔlín 雨林; **rainstorm** bàofēngyǔ 暴风雨

rainy duōyǔ 多雨; *it's* ~ lǎo xiàyǔ 老下雨

rainy season yǔjì 雨季

raise 1 *n* (*in salary*) zēngjiā 增加 **2** *v/t shelf etc* shēnggāo 升高; *offer* tígāo 提高; *children* fǔyǎng 抚养; *question* tíchū 提出; *money* chóují 筹集

raisin pútáo gān 葡萄干

rake *n* (*for garden*) pázi 耙子

rally *n* (*meeting, reunion*) jíhuì 集会; MOT gōnglù sàichē 公路赛车; (*in tennis*) liánxù duìdǎ 连续对打

♦**rally round 1** *v/i* jíhé qǐlái 集合起来 **2** *v/t*: ~ *X* tuánjié zài X de zhōuwéi 团结在 X 的周围

RAM (= *random access memory*) nèicún 内存

ram 1 *n* gōngyáng 公羊 **2** *v/t ship, car* zhuàng 撞

ramble 1 *n* (*walk*) mànbù 漫步 **2** *v/i* (*walk*) mànbù 漫步; (*when speaking*) dōnglā xīchě 东拉西扯; (*talk incoherently*) màntán 漫谈

rambler (*walker*) mànbù zhě 漫步者

rambling 1 *n* (*walking*) mànbù 漫步; (*in speech*) dōnglā xīchě 东拉西扯 **2** *adj speech* màntán 漫谈

ramp pōdào 坡道; (*for raising vehicle*) xiépō 斜坡; (*unevenness in road*) qīngxié lùmiàn 倾斜路面

rampage 1 *v/i* héngchōng zhízhuàng 横冲直撞 **2** *n*: *go on the* ~ bàotiào rúléi 暴跳如雷

rampart bìlěi 壁垒

ramshackle yáoyao yùzhuì 摇摇欲坠

ranch dà mùchǎng 大牧场

rancher mùchǎng zhǔ 牧场主

rancid hāla 哈喇

rancor jīyuàn 积怨

R & D (= *research and development*) yánfā 研发

random 1 *adj* suíjī 随机; ~ *sample* suíjī chōuyàng 随机抽样 **2** *n*: *at* ~ suíbiàn 随便

range 1 *n* (*of products*) xìliè 系列; (*of gun*) shèchéng 射程; (*of airplane*) zuìdà xíngchéng 最大行程; (*of voice*) yīnyù 音域; (*of mountains*) shānmài 山脉 **2** *v/i*: ~ *from X to Y* zài X yǔ Y zhījiān 在 X 与 Y 之间

ranger (*for park and forest*) hùlínyuán 护林员; (*police in thinly populated area*) qíjǐng 骑警

rank 1 *n* MIL jūnxián 军衔; (*in society*) děngjí 等级; *the* ~*s* MIL shìbīng 士兵 **2** *v/t* pái 排

♦**rank among** zài ... zhī liè 在 ...之列

ransack xǐjié 洗劫

ransom shújīn 赎金; *hold X to* ~ bǎngpiào 绑票

rant *v/i*: ~ *and rave* kǒutù kuángyán 口吐狂言

rap 1 *n* (*at door etc*) kòují shēng 叩击声; MUS shuōchàng yīnyuè 说唱音乐 **2** *v/t table etc* kòují 叩击

♦**rap at** *window etc* qiāo 敲

rape *n* & *v/t* qiángjiān 强奸

rape victim qiángjiān shòuhài zhě 强奸受害者

rapid kuài 快

rapidity kuàisù 快速

rapids jíliú 急流

rapist qiángjiān fàn 强奸犯

rapture xīnxǐ ruòkuáng 欣喜若狂

rapturous huānxǐ 欢喜

rare hǎnjiàn 罕见; *steak* chūshú 初熟

rarely hěnshǎo 很少

rarity xīshǎo 稀少

rascal xiǎo táoqì 小淘气

rash[1] MED pízhěn 皮疹

rash[2] *action, behavior* lǔmǎng 鲁莽

raspberry xuángōuzi 悬钩子

rat lǎoshǔ 老鼠

rate 1 *n (of exchange)* bǐlǜ 比率; *(of pay)* lǜ 率; *(price)* jiàgé 价格; *(speed)* sùdù 速度; *~ of interest* FIN lìxī lǜ 利息率; *at this ~ (at this speed)* zhào zhèyàng de sùdù 照这样的速度; *(carrying on like this)* zhào zhèyàng 照这样 **2** *v/t (consider, rank)* rènwéi 认为

rather xiāngdāng 相当; *I would ~ stay here* wǒ qíngyuàn zài zhèr zhù 我情愿在这儿住; *or would you ~ … ?* nǐ shìfǒu gèng xǐhuān …? 你是否更喜欢 … ?

ration 1 *n* pèijǐ liàng 配给量 **2** *v/t supplies* dìngliàng gōngyìng 定量供应

rational hélǐ 合理

rationality hélǐ xìng 合理性

rationalization *(of production etc)* hélǐ huà 合理化

rationalize 1 *v/t production etc* shǐ hélǐ huà 使合理化; *emotions, one's actions etc* jiěshì 解释 **2** *v/i* zhǎo jièkǒu 找借口

rat race shǔpīn 鼠拼

rattle 1 *n (noise)* gāga shēng 嘎嘎声; *(toy)* bōlànggǔ 拨浪鼓 **2** *v/t chains etc* shǐ fāchū gāga shēng 使发出嘎嘎声 **3** *v/i (of chains etc)* fāchū gāga shēng 发出嘎嘎声; *(of crates)* fāchū gāla galā shēng 发出嘎拉嘎拉声

♦**rattle off** *poem, list of names* yìkǒuqìde shuō 一口气地说

rattlesnake xiǎngwěishé 响尾蛇

ravage: *~d by war* shòudào zhàn-zhēng de chuàngshāng 受到战争的创伤

rave *v/i (talk deliriously)* jiǎng húhuà 讲胡话; *(talk wildly)* húchě hú zhā 胡扯; *~ about X (be very enthusiastic)* kuángrè de tánlùn X 狂热地谈论 X

raven dà wūyā 大乌鸦

ravenous *appetite* èhuàile 饿坏了

rave review jiāokǒu chēngzàn 交口称赞

ravine shēngǔ 深谷

raving: *~ mad* fēngle 疯了

ravishing mírén 迷人

raw *meat, vegetable* shēng 生; *sugar, iron* wèijīng jiāgōng 未经加工

raw materials yuán cáiliào 原材料

ray guāngxiàn 光线; *a ~ of hope* yīxiàn xīwàng 一线希望

razor tìxū dāo 剃须刀

razor blade tìxū dāo dāopiàn 剃须刀刀片

re COM yǒuguān 有关

reach 1 *n: within ~* zài fùjìn 在附近; *out of ~* ná būdào 拿不到 **2** *v/t city etc* dàodá 到达; *(go as far as)* dào 到; *decision, agreement, conclusion* dédào 得到

♦**reach out** shēnchū shǒu 伸出手

react fǎnyìng 反应

reaction fǎnyìng 反应

reactionary *n & adj* POL fǎndòng pài 反动派

reactor *(nuclear)* fǎnyìng duī 反应堆

read 1 *v/t book. disk* dú 读; *Chinese* rènshi 认识 **2** *v/i* yuèdú 阅读; *~ to X* dúgěi X tīng 读给 X 听

♦**read out** *(aloud)* lǎngsòng 朗诵

♦**read up on** yuèdú xuéxí 阅读学习

readable *handwriting* yìdú 易读

reader *(person)* dúzhě 读者

readily *admit, agree* xīnrán 欣然

readiness *(for action)* zhǔnbèi jiùxù 准备就绪; *(to agree)* yuànyì 愿意

reading *(activity)* yuèdú 阅读; *(from meter etc)* dúshù 读数

reading matter yuèdú cáiliào 阅读材料

readjust 1 *v/t equipment, controls* tiáozhěng 调整 **2** *v/i (to conditions)* shìyìng 适应

read-only file COMPUT zhǐdú dǎng·àn 只读档案

read-only memory COMPUT zhǐdú cúnchǔ qì 只读存储器

ready (*prepared*) zhǔnbèi hǎo 准备好; (*willing*) yuànyì 愿意; **get** (*oneself*) ~ zhǔnbèi hǎo 准备好; **get X ~** bǎ X zhǔnbèi hǎo 把 X 准备好

ready-made *stew, solution etc* xiànchéng 现成

ready-to-wear xiànchéng yīfu 现成衣服

real *adj* zhēn 真

real estate fángdì chǎn 房地产

realism xiànshí zhǔyì 现实主义

realist xiànshí zhǔyì zhě 现实主义者

realistic xiànshí 现实

reality xiànshí 现实

realization (*of ideal, hope*) shíxiàn 实现

realize *v/t truth, importance* yìshí dào 意识到; *ideal, hope* shíxiàn 实现; FIN zhuànde 赚得; **I ~ now that ...** wǒ xiànzài cái yìshí dào ... 我现在才意识到 ...

really zhēnzhèng 真正; (*very*) hěn 很; **~?** zhēnde ma? 真的吗？; **not ~** (*not much*) bù zěnme yàng 不怎么样

real time COMPUT shíshí 实时

realtor búdòng chǎn zhōngjiān shāng 不动产中间商

reap shōugē 收割

reappear chóngxiàn 重现

rear 1 *n* hòumian 后面 **2** *adj legs* hòu 后; *seats, wheels, lights* hòumian 后面

rearm *v/t & v/i* chóngxīn wǔzhuāng 重新武装

rearmost zuìhòu 最后

rearrange *flowers, furniture* chóngxīn bǎifàng 重新摆放; *schedule, meetings* chóngxīn ānpái 重新安排

rear-view mirror hòushì jìng 后视镜

reason 1 *n* (*faculty*) lǐzhì 理智; (*cause*) yuányīn 原因 **2** *v/i*: **~ with** hé ... jiǎnglǐ 和 ... 讲理

reasonable *person, behavior* hélǐ 合理; *price* gōngpíng 公平; **a ~ number of people** bùshǎo rén 不少人

reasonably *act, behave* hélǐ de 合理地; (*quite*) jīhū 几乎

reassure dǎxiāo yílǜ 打消疑虑

reassuring lìngrén yǒu xìnxīn 令人有信心

rebate (*money back*) zhékòu 折扣

rebel *n* fǎnpàn zhě 反叛者; **~ troops** fǎnpàn jūnduì 反叛军队

rebellion fǎnpàn 反叛

rebellious bù fúguǎn 不服管

rebound *v/i* (*of ball etc*) tán huìlái 弹回来

rebuff *n* cuòzhé 挫折

rebuild chóngjiàn 重建

rebuke *v/t* zhǐzé 指责

recall *v/t ambassador* zhàohuí 召回; (*remember*) jìqǐ 记起

recapture MIL duóhuí 夺回; *criminal* zàicì zhuāhuò 再次抓获

receding: **~ hair** kāishǐ tūtóu 开始秃头

receipt shōujù 收据; **acknowledge ~ of X** quèrèn shōudào X 确认收到 X; **~s** FIN shōurù 收入

receive shōudào 收到

receiver (*of letter*) shōuxìn rén 收信人; TELEC tīngtǒng 听筒; (*for radio*) shōuyīnjī 收音机

receivership: **be in ~** pòchǎn 破产

recent zuìjìn 最近

recently zuìjìn 最近

reception (*in hotel, company*) jiēdài chù 接待处; (*formal party*) zhāodài huì 招待会; (*welcome*) huānyíng 欢迎; (*for radio, mobile phone*) jiēshōu lì 接收力

reception desk jiēdài chù 接待处

receptionist jiēdài yuán 接待员

receptive: **be ~ to X** yì jiēshòu X 易接受 X

recess (*in wall etc*) āochù 凹处; EDU xiūxi 休息; (*of parliament*) xiūjià 休假

recession (*economic*) bù jǐngqì 不景气

recharge *battery* chōngdiàn 充电

recipe càipǔ 菜谱

recipient (*of parcel etc*) jiēshōu rén 接收人; (*of payment*) shōukuǎn rén 收款人

reciprocal hùhuì 互惠

recital MUS yǎnzòu huì 演奏会

recite *poem* bèisòng 背诵; *details, facts* xùshù 叙述

reckless búgù hòuguǒ 不顾后果

reckon (*think, consider*) rènwéi 认为

♦**reckon with**: *have X to* ~ duìfu X 对付 X

reclaim *land from sea* shōuhuí 收回

recline *v/i* xiéyǐ 斜倚

recluse yǐnshì 隐士

recognition (*of state, achievements*) chéngrèn 承认; *changed beyond* ~ biànde rènbùchū 变得认不出

recognizable rèndechū 认得出

recognize *person, voice, tune* rènde 认得; *symptoms* biànrèn chū 辨认出; POL: *state* chéngrèn 承认; *it can be* ~d *by* ... píng ... biànrèn chū 凭 ... 辨认出

recollect huíyì 回忆

recollection huíyì 回忆

recommend tuījiàn 推荐

recommendation tuījiàn 推荐

recompense *n* bǔcháng 补偿; LAW péicháng 赔偿

reconcile *people, differences* tiáojiě 调解; *facts* shǐ yīzhì 使一致; ~ *oneself to* ... gānxīn yú ... 甘心于 ...; *be* ~d (*of two people*) héhǎo 和好

reconciliation (*of people, differences*) tiáojiě 调解; (*of facts*) yīzhì 一致

recondition xiūfù 修复

reconnaissance MIL zhēnchá 侦察

reconsider 1 *v/t offer, one's position* chóngxīn kǎolù 重新考虑 **2** *v/i* chóngxīn kǎolù 重新考虑

reconstruct *city, one's life* chóngjiàn 重建; *crime* xiànchǎng shìfàn 现场示范

record 1 *n* MUS chàngpiān 唱片; SP jìlù 纪录; (*written document, in database*) jìlù 记录; ~s dǎngàn 档案; *say sth off the* ~ fēi guānfāng de shuō 非官方地说; *have a criminal* ~ yǒu xíngshì jìlù 有刑事记录; *have a good* ~ *for punctuality* yíxiàng zhǔnshì 一向

准时 **2** *v/t* (*on tape etc*) lù 录

record-breaking dǎpò jìlù 打破纪录

recorder MUS shùdí 竖笛

record holder jìlù bǎochí zhě 纪录保持者

recording lùyīn 录音

recording studio lùyīn shì 录音室

record player diànchàngjī 电唱机

recoup *financial losses* míbǔ 弥补

recover 1 *v/t sth lost, stolen goods* zhǎohuí 找回; *composure* huīfù 恢复 **2** *v/i* (*from illness*) huīfù 恢复

recovery (*of sth lost, stolen goods*) zhǎohuí 找回; (*from illness*) huīfù 恢复; *he has made a good* ~ tā huīfù de hěnhǎo 他恢复得很好

recreation yúlè 娱乐

recruit 1 *n* MIL xīnbīng 新兵; (*to company*) xīnlái de 新来的 **2** *v/t new staff* zhāopìn 招聘; MIL zhēngmù 征募

recruitment zhāopìn 招聘

recruitment drive dà guīmó zhāopìn 大规模招聘

rectangle chángfāng xíng 长方形

rectangular chángfāng xíng 长方形

recuperate huīfù yuánqì 恢复元气

recur zàicì chūxiàn 再次出现

recurrent zàifā 再发

recycle huíshōu 回收

recycling huíshōu 回收

red hóng 红; *in the* ~ yǒu chìzì 有赤字

Red Army Hóngjūn 红军; **Red China** Hóngsè Zhōngguó 红色中国; **Red Cross** Hóngshízì 红十字

redden *v/i* (*blush*) biànhóng 变红

redecorate *v/t* chóngxīn zhuāngxiū 重新装修

redeem *debt* fùqīng 付清; *sinners* miǎnzuì 免罪

redeeming *adj*: ~ *feature* wéiyī kěqǔ zhīchù 唯一可取之处

redevelop *part of town* chóngxīn fāzhǎn 重新发展

Red Guard Hóngwèibīng 红卫兵;

red-handed: *catch X ~* dāngchǎng bǔhuò X 当场捕获 X；
redhead yǒu hóng tóufà de rén
有红头发的人；**red-hot** rè
téngteng 热腾腾；**red light** (*at
traffic light*) hóngdēng 红灯；**red
light district** hóngdēng qū 红灯
区；**red meat** niú yáng ròu 牛羊
肉；**redneck** xiāngbālǎo 乡巴佬；
red pepper làjiāo 辣椒；**red
tape** guānliáo chéngxù 官僚程
序

reduce jiàngdī 降低

reduction jiǎnshǎo 减少

redundant (*unnecessary*) duōyú 多
余

reed BOT lúwěi 芦苇

reef (*in sea*) jiāo 礁

reef knot suōfān jié 缩帆结

reek *v/i* fā chòuqì 发臭气；*~ of ...*
yǒu ... wèir 有 ... 味儿

reel *n* (*of film, thread*) juǎn 卷

refer 1 *v/t*: *~ a decision / problem
to s.o.* bǎ juédìng / wèntí jiāogěi
mǒurén 把决定 / 问题交给某
人 2 *v/i*: *~ to ...* (*allude to*) tídào ...
提到 ...；(*to dictionary etc*) cānkǎo
... 参考 ...

referee SP cáipàn 裁判；(*for job*)
tuījiàn rén 推荐人

reference (*allusion*) shèjí 涉及；
(*for job*) tuījiàn 推荐；(*~ number*)
cānkǎo hàomǎ 参考号码；*with ~
to* guānyú 关于

reference book cānkǎo shū 参考
书

referendum gōngmín tóupiào 公
民投票

refill *v/t* tank, glass zài zhuāngmǎn
再装满

refine oil, sugar tíliàn 提炼；
technique shǐ jīngměi 使精美

refined manners, language wényǎ 文
雅

refinery tíliàn chǎng 提炼厂

reflation tōnghuò zài péngzhàng
通货再膨胀

reflect 1 *v/t* light fǎnshè 反射；*be
~ed in ...* fǎnshè zài ... zhīzhōng
反射在 ... 之中 2 *v/i* (*think*)
fǎnxǐng 反省

reflection (*in water, glass etc*) fǎnshè 反射；(*consideration*) fǎnxǐng
反省

reflex (*in body*) fǎnyìng nénglì 反
应能力

reflex reaction zìdòng fǎnyìng 自
动反应

reform *n & v/t* gǎigé 改革

refrain[1] *v/i* yìzhì 抑制；*please ~
from smoking* qǐngwù xīyān 请勿
吸烟

refrain[2] *n* (*in song*) fùgē 副歌；(*in
poem*) diéjù 迭句

refresh person shǐ jīngshén
zhènzuò 使精神振作；*feel ~ed*
gǎndào jīngshén zhènzuò 感到精
神振作

refresher course fùxí kèchéng 复
习课程

refreshing drink qīngshuǎng 清爽；
experience qīngxīn yuèmù 清新悦
目

refreshments chádiǎn 茶点

refrigerate lěngcáng 冷藏

refrigerator bīngxiāng 冰箱

refuel *v/t & v/i* jiā ránliào 加燃料

refuge bìhù 庇护；*take ~* (*from
storm etc*) duǒbì 躲避

refugee nànmín 难民

refund *n & v/t* tuìkuǎn 退款

refusal jùjué 拒绝

refuse: *~ to do X* jùjué zuò X 拒绝
做 X

regain control, lost territory, the lead
chónghuò 重获

regard 1 *n*: *have great ~ for*
zūnzhòng 尊重；*in this ~* zài zhèi
fāngmiàn 在这方面；*with ~ to*
guānyú 关于；(*kind*) *~s* wènhòu
问候；*give my ~s to X* dài wǒ
wènhòu X 代我问候 X；*with no
~ for ...* bù kǎolù ... 不考虑 ...
2 *v/t*: *~ X as Y* bǎ X kànzuò Y 把 X
看作 Y；*as ~s X* guānyú X 关于 X

regarding guānyú 关于

regardless háowú gùjì 毫无顾忌；
~ of búgù 不顾

regime (*government*) zhèngquán 政
权

regiment *n* tuán 团

region dìqū 地区；*in the ~ of* dàyuē

大约
regional dìqū 地区
register 1 n dēngjì bú 登记簿
2 v/t birth, death dēngjì 登记;
vehicle shàngpái 上牌; letter
guàhào 挂号; emotion xiǎnshì 显
示; **send a ~ed letter** jì guàhào
xìn 寄挂号信 **3** v/i (for a course,
with police) dēngjì 登记
registered letter guàhào xìn 挂号
信
registrar (of births etc) dēngjì rén
登记人
registration (for a course) zhùcè 注
册; (with police) dēngjì 登记
regret 1 v/t hòuhuǐ 后悔 **2** n yíhàn
遗憾
regrettable búxìng 不幸
regrettably búxìng 不幸
regular 1 adj flights dìngqī 定期;
intervals, habits yǒu guīlǜ 有规律;
pattern, shape yúnchèn 匀称;
(normal, ordinary) pǔtōng 普通
2 n (at bar etc) chángkè 常客
regulate kòngzhì 控制
regulation (rule) guīzhāng 规章
rehabilitate ex-criminal gǎixiéguīzhèng 改邪归正
rehearsal páiyǎn 排演
rehearse v/t & v/i páiyǎn 排演
reign n & v/i tǒngzhì 统治
reimburse bǔcháng 补偿
rein jiāngsheng 缰绳
reincarnation línghún zhuǎnshì 灵
魂转世
reinforce structure xiūbǔ 修补;
beliefs jiāqiáng 加强
reinforced concrete gāngjīn hùnníng tǔ 钢筋混凝土
reinforcements MIL yuánjūn 援军
reinstate person in office shǐ fùzhí
使复职; paragraph in text chóng-
xīn bǔshàng 重新补上
reject v/t jùjué 拒绝
rejection jùjué 拒绝
relapse MED jiùbìng fùfā 旧病复
发; **have a ~** jiùbìng fùfā 旧病复
发
relate 1 v/t story xùshù 叙述; **~ X
to Y** jiǎng X yǔ Y liánxì qǐlái 将X
与Y联系起来 **2** v/i: **~ to ...** (be

connected with) yǔ ... yǒu guānlián
与 ... 有关联; **he doesn't ~ to
people** tā hé rén xiāngchǔ bùhǎo
他和人相处不好
related (by family) yǒu qīnshǔ
guānxì 有亲属关系; events, ideas
etc xiāngguān 相关
relation (in family) qīnshǔ 亲属;
(connection) guānxi 关系; **business / diplomatic ~s** shāngyè /
wàijiāo guānxi 商业 / 外交关系
relationship guānxi 关系; **have a
~** (sexual) fāshēng guānxi 发生关
系
relative 1 n qīnqi 亲戚 **2** adj
xiāngduì 相对; **X is ~ to Y** X yǔ Y
yǒuguān X与Y有关
relatively xiāngduì 相对
relax 1 v/i fàngsōng 放松; **~!,
don't get angry** xiǎng kāi diǎnr,
bié shēngqì! 想开点儿，别生
气！**2** v/t muscle fàngsōng 放松;
pace of work sōngxiè 松懈
relaxation fàngsōng 放松
relay 1 v/t message zhuǎngào 转告;
radio, TV signals zhuǎnbō 转播
2 n: **~ (race)** jiēlì sài 接力赛
release 1 n (from prison) shìfàng
释放; (of CD etc) fāxíng 发行
2 v/t prisoner shìfàng 释放;
parking brake sōngkāi 松开;
information gōngbù 公布
relent ràngbù 让步
relentless (determined) búxiè 不
懈; rain etc wúqíng 无情
relevance guānlián 关联
relevant yǒuguān 有关
reliability kěkào xìng 可靠性
reliable kěkào 可靠
reliably kěndìng 肯定; **I am
informed that ...** wǒ dédào kěkào
xiāoxi shuō ... 我得到可靠消息
说 ...
reliance yīkào 依靠; **~ on ...** yīkào
... 依靠 ...
relic (object) yíwù 遗物; (of tradition) yísú 遗俗
relief kuānwèi 宽慰; **that's a ~**
tàihǎole 太好了; **in ~** (in art)
fúdiāo 浮雕
relieve pressure, pain jiǎnqīng 减

轻; (*take over from*) jiētì 接替; **be ~d** (*at news etc*) kuānwèi 宽慰

religion zōngjiào 宗教

religious zōngjiào 宗教

religiously (*conscientiously*) rènzhēn 认真

relish 1 *n* (*sauce*) bàncài zhīr 伴菜汁儿 **2** *v/t* idea, prospect xǐhuan 喜欢

relive the past, an event zài tǐyàn 再体验

relocate *v/i* (*of business, employee*) bānqiān 搬迁

reluctance miǎnqiǎng 勉强

reluctant miǎnqiǎng 勉强; **be ~ to do X** bù qíngyuàn zuò X 不情愿做 X

reluctantly miǎnqiǎng 勉强

♦**rely on** yīkào 依靠; **~ X to do Y** yīkào X qùzuò Y 依靠 X 去做 Y

remain (*be left*) shèngxia 剩下; (*stay*) dāizài 呆在; (*continue*) réngrán 仍然; **~ silent / loyal** bǎochí chénmò / zhōngchéng 保持沉默 / 忠诚

remainder (*rest*) yúxià 余下; MATH yúshù 余数

remains (*of body*) yítǐ 遗体

remand 1 *v/t*: **~ X in custody** jūliú X 拘留 X **2** *n*: **be on ~** huányā 还押

remark 1 *n* huà 话 **2** *v/t* pínglùn 评论

remarkable fēifán 非凡

remarkably fēifán 非凡

remarry *v/i* zàihūn 再婚

remedy *n* MED liáofǎ 疗法; *fig* bǔjiù 补救

remember 1 *v/t* s.o., sth jìde 记得; **~ to lock the door** jìzhù suǒmén 记住锁门; **~ me to her** tì wǒ wèn tā hǎo 替我问她好 **2** *v/i* jìde 记得; **I don't ~** wǒ bú jìde 我不记得

remind *v/t*: **~ X to do Y** tíxǐng X zuò Y 提醒 X 做 Y; **~ X of Y** (*call to mind*) shǐ X xiǎngqǐ Y 使 X 想起 Y

reminder tíxǐng wù 提醒物; (COM: *for payment*) cuīzhàng dān 催账单

reminisce huáijiù 怀旧

reminiscent: **be ~ of X** huíyì qǐ X 回忆起 X

remnant cánjī 残迹

remorse àohuǐ 懊悔

remorseless person, pace, demands wúqíng 无情

remote village piānpì 偏僻; possibility, connection jíxiǎo 极小; (*aloof*) lěngmò 冷漠; ancestor jiǔyuǎn 久远

remote access COMPUT yuǎnchéng tōnglù 远程通路

remote control yáokòng 遥控

remotely related, connected shūyuǎn 疏远; **just ~ possible** yǒu jíxiǎo kěnéng xìng 有极小可能性

removal (*of garbage, demonstrators*) yídòng 移动; (*of doubt*) páichú 排除; (*from home*) qiānjū 迁居

remove yídòng 移动; top, lid nákāi 拿开; growth, tumor qùchú 去除; coat etc tuō 脱; doubt, suspicion jiěchú 解除

remuneration bàochóu 报酬

remunerative yǒu lìrùn 有利润

rename chóngxīn mìngmíng 重新命名

render service jǐyǔ 给予; **~ X helpless / unconscious** shǐ X gūlì wúyuán / hūnmí 使 X 孤立无援 / 昏迷

rendering (*of piece of music*) yǎnzòu 演奏

rendez-vous (*romantic*) yuēhuì 约会; MIL zhǐdìng jíhé diǎn 指定集合点

renew contract, license zhǎnqī 展期; discussions chóngxīn kāishǐ 重新开始; **feel ~ed** gǎndào jīnglì chōngpèi 感到精力充沛

renewal (*of contract etc*) zhǎnqī 展期; (*of discussions*) chóngxīn kāishǐ 重新开始

renminbi FIN rénmínbì 人民币

renounce *v/t* title, rights xuānbù fàngqì 宣布放弃

renovate zhěngxiū 整修

renovation zhěngxiū 整修

renown shēngyù 声誉

renowned zhùmíng 著名

rent 1 *n* zūjīn 租金; *for ~* chūzū 出租 **2** *v/t apartment, car, equipment* zū 租; (*~ out*) chūzū 出租

rental (*for apartment, for TV etc*) zūjīn 租金

rental agreement zūyuē 租约

rental car zūyòng chē 租用车

rent-free *adv* miǎnzū 免租

reopen 1 *v/t business, store* chóngxīn kāizhāng 重新开张; *negotiations* zài jìnxíng 再进行; LAW: *case* chóngshěn 重审 **2** *v/i* (*of theater etc*) chóngxīn kāizhāng 重新开张

reorganization (*of business*) gǎizǔ 改组; (*of room, schedule*) chóngxīn ānpái 重新安排

reorganize *business* gǎizǔ 改组; *room, schedule* chóngxīn ānpái 重新安排; *chapter* gǎibiān 改编

rep COM dàilǐ shāng 代理商

repaint chóngxīn shuā yóuqī 重新刷油漆

repair 1 *v/t* xiūlǐ 修理 **2** *n* xiūlǐ 修理; *in a good / bad state of ~* wánhǎo wúsǔn / pòsǔn 完好无损 / 破损

repairman xiūlǐ gōng 修理工

repatriate sòng huíguó 送回国

repay *money* chánghuán 偿还; *person* bàodá 报答

repayment fùhuíkuǎn 付回款

repeal *v/t law* fèichú 废除

repeat 1 *v/t sth said, performance, experience* chóngfù 重复; *am I ~ing myself?* wǒ shìbúshì chóngfù le? 我是不是重复了? **2** *v/i* chóngfù 重复; *I ~, do not touch it* wǒ zàishuō yícì, biépèng wǒ zài shuō yícì, biépèng wǒ zàishuō yícì, biépèng wǒ zàishuō 一次,别碰我再说一次 **3** *n* (*TV program etc*) chóngbō 重播

repeat business COM huítóu shēngyì 回头生意

repeated fǎnfù 反复

repeat order COM chóngfù dìnghuò 重复定货

repel *v/t invaders, attack* jītuì 击退; *insects* qūgǎn 驱赶; (*disgust*) shǐ yànwù 使厌恶

repellent 1 *n* (*insect ~*) qūchóng jì 驱虫剂 **2** *adj* lìngrén yànwù 令人厌恶

repent *v/i* hòuhuǐ 后悔

repercussions yǐngxiǎng 影响

repetition chóngfù 重复

repetitive chóngfù 重复

replace (*put back*) fànghuí 放回; (*take the place of*) tìdài 替代

replacement (*person*) dàitì rén 代替人; (*thing*) dàitì wù 代替物

replacement part tìjiàn 替件

replay 1 *n* (*recording*) chóngfàng 重放; (*match*) chóngsài 重赛 **2** *v/t match* chóngsài 重赛

replica fùzhì pǐn 复制品

reply *n, v/t & v/i* huídá 回答

report 1 *n* (*account*) bàogào 报告; (*by journalist*) bàodào 报道 **2** *v/t facts* bàodào 报道; (*to authorities*) tōngzhī 通知; *~ one's findings to X* jiāng diàochá jiéguǒ huìbào gěi X 将调查结果汇报给 X; *~ X to the police* xiàng jǐngfāng gàofā X 向警方告发 X; *he is ~ed to be in Hong Kong* jù shuō tā zài Xiānggǎng 据说他在香港 **3** *v/i* (*of journalist*) bàodào 报道; (*present oneself*) bàodào 报到; *who do you ~ to?* (*in business*) shuí shì nǐde shàngjí? 谁是你的上级?

report card huìbào 汇报

reporter jìzhě 记者

repossess COM shōuhuí 收回

reprehensible yīngshòu zhǐzhāi 应受指摘

represent (*act for*) dàibiǎo 代表; (*stand for*) zhǔzhāng 主张; (*of images in painting etc*) miáohuì 描绘

representative 1 *n* dàibiǎo rén 代表人; COM dàilǐ shāng 代理商; POL zhòngyìyuán 众议员 **2** *adj* (*typical*) diǎnxíng 典型

repress *revolt* zhènyā 镇压; *feelings, natural urges* yāyì 压抑; *laugh* rěnzhe 忍着

repression POL zhènyā 镇压

repressive POL yāzhì 压制

reprieve *n & v/t also fig* huǎnxíng 缓刑

reprimand v/t shēnchì 申斥

reprint 1 n zàibǎn 再版 **2** v/t chóngyìn 重印

reprisal bàofù xíngwéi 报复行为; **take ~s** jìnxíng bàofù xíngwéi 进行报复行为

reproach 1 n zébèi 责备; **be beyond ~** wúkě zhǐzé 无可指责 **2** v/t zhǐzé 指责

reproachful zhǐzé 指责

reproduce 1 v/t atmosphere, mood zàixiàn 再现 **2** v/i BIO fánzhí 繁殖

reproduction BIO fánzhí 繁殖; (of sound, images) fùzhì 复制; (piece of furniture) fùzhì pǐn 复制品

reproductive BIO fánzhí 繁殖

reptile páxíng dòngwù 爬行动物

republic gònghé guó 共和国

republican 1 n gònghé zhǔyì zhě 共和主义者; POL **Republican** Gònghé dàngrén 共和党人 **2** adj gònghé zhǔyì 共和主义

Republic of China Zhōnghuá Mínguó 中华民国

repudiate (deny) fǒudìng 否定

repulsive lìngrén yànwù 令人厌恶

reputable yǒu míngshēng 有名声

reputation míngyù 名誉; **have a good / bad ~** yǒuhǎo / huài míngshēng 有好 / 坏名声

request 1 n yāoqiú 要求; **on ~** yǐjīng yāoqiú 一经要求 **2** v/t yāoqiú 要求

require (need) xūyào 需要; **it ~s great care** yào hěn xiǎoxīn 要很小心; **as ~d by law** àn fǎlǜ guīdìng 按法律规定; **guests are ~d to ...** kèrénmen bìxū ... 客人们必须 ...

required (necessary) bìyào 必要

requirement (need) xūyào 需要; (condition) tiáojiàn 条件

reroute airplane etc gēnggǎi xiànlù 更改线路

rerun tape fùyìng 复映

rescue 1 n yuánjiù 援救; **come to X's ~** yuánjiù X 援救 X **2** v/t yuánjiù 援救

rescue party yuánjiù duì 援救队

research n yánjiū 研究

♦**research into** yánjiū 研究

research and development yánjiū yǔ fāzhǎn 研究与发展

research assistant zhùlǐ yánjiū yuán 助理研究员

researcher yánjiú yuán 研究员

research project yánjiū kètí 研究课题

resemblance xiāngsì chù 相似处

resemble xiàng 像

resent bùmǎn 不满

resentful bùmǎn 不满

resentment bùmǎn 不满

reservation (of room, table) yùdìng 预定; (mental) bǎoliú 保留; (special area) bǎohù dìqū 保护地区; **I have a ~** wǒ yǒuge yùdìng 我有个预定

reserve 1 n (store) chǔbèi 储备; (aloofness) hánxù 含蓄; SP yùbèi duìyuán 预备队员; **~s** FIN chǔbèi jīn 储备金; **keep X in ~** chǔbèi X dàiyòng 储备 X 待用 **2** v/t seat, table yùdìng 预定; judgment bǎoliú 保留

reserved person, manner nèixiàng 内向; table, seat bèi yùdìng 被预定

reservoir (for water) shuǐkù 水库

reside zhù 住

residence (house etc) zhùsuǒ 住所; (stay) jūzhù 居住

residence permit jūliúzhèng 居留证

resident 1 n jūmín 居民 **2** adj (living in a building) zhùdì 驻地

residential district zhùzhái qū 住宅区

residue cánzhā 残渣

resign 1 v/t position cízhí 辞职; **~ oneself to** tīngqí zìrán 听其自然 **2** v/i (from job) cízhí 辞职

resignation (from job) cízhí 辞职; (mental) wúkě nàihé 无可奈何

resigned tīngtiān yóumìng 听天由命; **we have become ~ to the fact that ...** wǒmen yǐjīng jiēshòu ... 我们已经接受 ...

resilient personality dáguān 达观; material nàiyòng 耐用

resin sōngxiāng 松香

resist 1 v/t enemy, s.o.'s advances
dǐkàng 抵抗; new measures dǐzhì
抵制; **~ temptation** bùshòu
yòuhuò 不受诱惑 **2** v/i dǐkàng
抵抗

resistance (to enemy, advances)
dǐkàng 抵抗; (to new measures)
zǔlù 阻力; (to disease, heat etc)
dǐkàng lì 抵抗力

resistant material jiāngù 坚固; **~
to heat / rust** fángrè / xiù 防热 / 锈

resolute jiānjué 坚决

resolution (decision) juéyì 决议;
(made at New Year etc) juédìng 决
定; (determination) juéxīn 决心;
(of problem) jiějué fāngfǎ 解决方
法; (of image) qīngxī dù 清晰度

resolve problem, mystery jiějué 解
决; **~ to do X** juédìng zuò X 决定
做 X

resort 1 n (place) dùjià shèngdì 度
假胜地; **as a last ~** zuòwéi
zuìhòu yīzhāo 作为最后一招

resounding success, victory chèdǐ
彻底

resource zīyuán 资源; **we don't
have the ~s for such a big contract** wǒmen méiyǒu zuò zhème
dà hétóng de zīyuán 我们没有
做这么大合同的资源

resourceful zúzhì duōmóu 足智
多谋

respect 1 n zūnjìng 尊敬; (consideration) zūnzhòng 尊重; **show ~
to** duì ... biǎoshì zūnzhòng 对 ...
表示尊重; **with ~ to** guānyú 关
于; **in this / that ~** zài zhè / nà
fāngmiàn 在这 / 那方面; **in
many ~s** zài xǔduō fāngmiàn 在
许多方面; **pay one's last ~s to
s.o.** xiàng sǐzhě gàobié 向死者告
别 **2** v/t person, s.o.'s opinion,
privacy zūnzhòng 尊重; law
zūnshǒu 遵守

respectable person tǐmiàn 体面;
bar xiàngyàng 象样

respectful yǒu lǐmào 有礼貌

respectfully yǒu lǐmào 有礼貌

respective gèzì 各自

respectively fēnbié 分别

respiration hūxī 呼吸

respirator MED réngōng hūxī qì 人
工呼吸器

respite huǎnhé 缓和; **without ~**
bùtíng 不停

respond (answer) dáfù 答复;
(react) zuòchū fǎnyìng 做出反应;
(to treatment) fǎnyìng 反应

response (answer) dáfù 答复;
(reaction) fǎnyìng 反应

responsibility zérèn 责任; **accept
~ for** fù zé 负责; (duty) zérèn 责
任; **a job with more ~** yǒu
gèngduō zérèn de gōngzuò 有更
多责任的工作

responsible (to blame) fùzé 负责;
(liable, for children, production etc)
fùzé 负责; (trustworthy, showing
seriousness) kěkào 可靠;
(involving responsibility: job) xūyào
fùzé 需要负责

responsive audience yì shòu gǎndòng 易受感动; brakes mǐngǎn
敏感

rest¹ 1 n xiūxi 休息 **2** v/i xiūxi 休
息; **~ on ...** (be based on) yǐ ... wéi
jīchǔ 以 ... 为基础; (lean against)
gē zài ... shàng 搁在 ... 上; **it all
~s with him** dōu zàiyú tāle 都在
于他了 **3** v/t (lean, balance etc)
kào 靠

rest² n: **the ~** yúxià 余下

restaurant cānguǎn 餐馆

restaurant car cānchē 餐车

rest cure xiūyǎng liáofǎ 休养疗
法

rest home yǎnglǎo yuàn 养老院

restless bù ānfèn 不安分; **have a
~ night** méi shuì hǎo 没睡好

restoration xiūfù 修复

restore building etc xiūfù 修复

restrain dog, troops yuēshù 约束;
emotions yìzhì 抑制; **~ oneself**
kòngzhì zìjǐ 控制自己

restraint (moderation) jiézhì 节制

restrict xiànzhì 限制; **I'll ~ myself
to ...** (in speech, book) wǒ jǐn tán
... 我仅谈 ...

restricted view shòu xiànzhì 受限
制

restricted area MIL jìndì 禁地

restriction xiànzhì 限制

rest room wèishēngjiān 卫生间

result n jiéguǒ 结果; *as a ~ of this* yīncǐ 因此

♦**result from** qǐyú 起于

♦**result in** dǎozhì 导致

resume v/t huīfù 恢复

résumé lǚlì 履历

resurface 1 v/t *roads* lìng pū lùmiàn 另铺路面 **2** v/i (*reappear*) chóngxīn chūxiàn 重新出现

resurrection REL fùhuó 复活

resuscitate shǐ sūxǐng 使苏醒

retail 1 adv yǐ língshòu fāngshì 以零售方式 **2** v/i: *~ at* ... língshòu jià wéi ... 零售价为 ...

retail price língshòu jià 零售价

retailer língshòu shāng 零售商

retain bǎoliú 保留

retainer FIN pìnjīn 聘金

retaliate bàofù 报复

retaliation bàofù 报复

retarded (*mentally*) zhìlì chídùn 智力迟钝

retire v/i (*from work*) tuìxiū 退休

retired tuìxiū 退休

retirement tuìxiū 退休

retirement age tuìxiū niánlíng 退休年龄

retiring miǎntiǎn 缅腆

retort n & v/i fǎnbó 反驳

retrace *footsteps* shùn yuánlù fǎnhuí 顺原路返回

retract v/t *claws* suōjìn 缩进; *undercarriage* shōusuō 收缩; *statement* shōuhuí 收回

retreat 1 v/i MIL chètuì 撤退; (*in discussion etc*) tuìràng 退让 **2** n MIL chètuì 撤退; (*place*) yǐnjū chù 隐居处

retrieve wǎnjiù 挽救

retriever (*dog*) lièquǎn 猎犬

retroactive *law etc* zhuīsù 追溯

retrograde *move, decision* hòutuì 后退

retrospect n: *in ~* xiànzài kànlái 现在看来

retrospective huígù 回顾

return 1 n (*coming back, going back*) fǎnhuí 返回; (*giving back*) tuìhuán 退还; COMPUT fǎnhuí 返回; (*in tennis*) huíqiú 回球; *by ~*

(*of post*) lìjí huífù 立即回复; *~s* (*profit*) lìrùn 利润; *many happy ~s (of the day)* zhù nǐ chángshòu 祝你长寿 **2** v/t (*give back*) tuìhuán 退还; (*put back*) fànghuí 放回; *favor, invitation* huíbào 回报 **3** v/i (*go back, come back*) fǎnhuí 返回; (*of good times, doubts etc*) huífù 回复

return flight huíchéng fēijī 回程飞机

return journey huíchéng 回程

reunification tǒngyī 统一

reunion tuánjù 团聚

reunite v/t tǒngyī 统一

reusable kě zài yòng 可再用

reuse zàiyòng 再用

rev n huízhuǎn 回转; *~s per minute* měi fēnzhōng huízhuǎn cìshù 每分钟回转次数

♦**rev up** v/t *engine* cǎi yóuménr 踩油门儿

revaluation chóngxīn píngjià 重新评价

reveal (*make visible*) xiǎnshì 显示; *secret, truth* jiēlù 揭露; *feelings* lùchū 露出

revealing *remark* tòulù zhēnxiàng 透露真相; *dress* lùtǐ 露体

revelation n xièlù 泄露

revenge n bàofù 报复; *take one's ~* wèi zìjǐ bàochóu 为自己报仇

revenue shōurù 收入

reverberate (*of sound*) huíxiǎng 回响

revere chóngjìng 崇敬

Reverend mùshī 牧师

reverent qiánchéng 虔诚

reverse 1 adj *sequence* diāndǎo 颠倒 **2** n (*opposite*) xiāngfǎn 相反; (*back*) bèimiàn 背面; MOT dàodǎng 倒档 **3** v/t *sequence* diāndǎo 颠倒; *vehicle* dàochē 倒车 **4** v/i MOT dàochē 倒车

review 1 n (*of book, movie*) pínglùn 评论; (*of troops*) jiǎnyuè 检阅; (*of situation etc*) shěnchá 审查 **2** v/t *book, movie* pínglùn 评论; *troops* jiǎnyuè 检阅; *situation etc* shěnchá 审查; EDU fùxí 复习

reviewer (*of book, movie*) pínglùn

jiā 评论家

revise v/t opinion xiūzhèng 修正; text jiàozhèng 校正

revision (of opinion) xiūzhèng 修正; (of text) jiàozhèng 校正

revisionism POL xiūzhèng zhǔyì 修正主义

revival (of custom, old style etc) fùxīng 复兴; (of patient) sūxǐng 苏醒

revive 1 v/t custom, old style etc fùxīng 复兴; patient shǐ sūxǐng 使苏醒 2 v/i (of business, exchange rate etc) shǐ shàngshēng 使上升

revoke law fèichú 废除; license qǔxiāo 取消

revolt 1 n fǎnkàng 反抗 2 v/i zàofǎn 造反

revolting (disgusting) ěxin 恶心

revolution POL etc gémìng 革命; (turn) xuánzhuǎn 旋转; **1911 Revolution** Xīnhài Gémìng 辛亥革命; **1949 Revolution** Jiěfàng 解放

revolutionary 1 n POL gémìng jiā 革命家 2 adj spirit, forces gémìng 革命; new ideas chuàngxīn 创新

revolutionize chèdǐ biàngé 彻底变革

revolve v/i xuánzhuǎn 旋转

revolver zuǒlún shǒuqiāng 左轮手枪

revolving door xuánzhuǎn mén 旋转门

revue THEA shíshì fěngcì jù 时事讽刺剧

revulsion fǎngǎn 反感

reward 1 n (financial) shǎngjīn 赏金; (benefit derived) bàochóu 报酬 2 v/t (financially) jiǎnglì 奖励

rewarding experience zhíde zuò 值得做

rewind v/t film, tape dǎo 倒

rewrite v/t chóngxiě 重写

rhetoric huálìde cízǎo 华丽的词藻

rhetorical question fǎnwèn 反问

rheumatism fēngshī bìng 风湿病

rhinoceros xīniú 犀牛

rhubarb cài yòng dàhuáng 菜用大黄

rhyme 1 n yùn 韵 2 v/i yāyùn 压韵; ~ with ... yǐ ... yāyùn 以 ... 压韵

rhythm jiézòu 节奏

rib lèigǔ 肋骨

ribbon sīdài 丝带

rice mǐ 米

rice bowl fànwǎn 饭碗; rice cooker diànfànguō 电饭锅; ricefield dàotián 稻田; rice noodles mǐfěn 米粉; rice porridge zhōu 粥; rice wine mǐjiǔ 米酒

rich 1 adj (wealthy) yǒuqián 有钱; food yóunì 油腻 2 n: the ~ fùrén 富人

rickshaw rénlìchē 人力车

rid: get ~ of garbage, unwanted furniture rēngdiào 扔掉; foreign accent, excess weight, illusions bǎituō 摆脱

riddle míyǔ 谜语

ride 1 n (on horse) qímǎ 骑马; (in vehicle) chèngchē jīhuì 乘车机会; (journey) lǚtú 旅途; **do you want a ~ into town?** xiǎng dāchē jìnchéng ma? 想搭车进城吗？; **thanks for the ~** xièxie nǐ jiào wǒ dāchē 谢谢你叫我搭车 2 v/t horse, bike qí 骑 3 v/i (on horse) qímǎ 骑马; (on bike) qí zìxíngchē 骑自行车; (in vehicle) chèngchē 乘车

rider (on horse) qímǎ rén 骑马人; (on bike) qí zìxíngchē rén 骑自行车人

ridge (raised strip) jǐ 脊; (of mountain) shānjǐ 山脊; (of roof) wūjí 屋脊

ridicule 1 n xīluò 奚落 2 v/t fěngcì 讽刺

ridiculous huāngmiù 荒谬

ridiculously huāngmiù 荒谬

riding (on horseback) qímǎ 骑马

rifle n láifù qiāng 来复枪

rift (in earth) lièxì 裂隙; (in party etc) fēnliè 分裂

rig 1 n (oil ~) yóujǐng 油井; (truck) qiānyǐn tuōchē 牵引拖车 2 v/t elections cāozòng 操纵

right 1 adj (correct) zhèngquè 正

确; (*proper, just*) zhēngdāng 正当; (*suitable*) héshì 合适; (*not left*) yòu 右; **be ~** (*of answer*) zhèngquè 正确; (*of person*) zhèngzhí 正直; (*of clock*) zhǔnquè 准确; **that's ~!** duì a! 对啊！; **put things ~** jiūzhèng cuòwù 纠正错误; **that's not ~** (*not allowed, not fair*) nà bùxíng 那不行; → **alright**
2 *adv* (*directly*) jiù 就; (*correctly*) zhèngquè 正确; (*completely*) chèdǐ 彻底; (*not left*) yǒu yòu 有右; **~ now** (*immediately*) mǎshàng 马上; (*at the moment*) xiànzài 现在 **3** *n* (*civil, legal etc*) quánlì 权利; (*not left*) yòu yòu 右; POL yòupài 右派; **on the ~** zài yòubiān 在右边; POL zài yòuyì nàbiān 在右翼那边; **turn to the ~, take a ~** xiàng yòu guǎi 向右拐; **be in the ~** yǒulǐ 有理; **know ~ from wrong** qūbié hǎohuài 区别好坏

right-angle zhíjiǎo 直角; **at ~s to ...** chéng zhíjiǎo ... 成直角

rightful *heir, owner etc* héfǎ 合法

right-hand *adj* yòubiān 右边; **on the ~ side** zài yòubiān 在右边; **right-hand drive** MOT yòuzuò fāngxiàngpán 右座方向盘; **right-handed** yòu piě zi 右撇子; **right-hand man** délì zhùshǒu 得力助手; **right of way** (*in traffic*) yōuxiān xíngshǐ quán 优先行驶权; (*across land*) tōngxíng quán 通行权; **right wing** *n* POL, SP yòuyì 右翼; **right-wing** *adj* POL yòuyì 右翼; **~ extremism** POL jíyòu zhǔyì 极右主义; **right-winger** POL yòupài 右派

rigid *material* jiānyìng 坚硬; *principles* wěngù 稳固; *attitude* kèbǎn 刻板

rigor (*of discipline*) yángé 严格; **the ~s of the winter** dōngrì de jiānxīn 冬日的艰辛

rigorous *discipline* yángé 严格; *tests, analysis* jīngquè 精确

rim (*of wheel*) lúnyuán 轮缘; (*of cup*) biān 边; (*of eyeglasses*) jìngkuàng 镜框

ring¹ (*circle*) yuánquān 圆圈; (*on

finger*) jièzhi 戒指; (*in boxing*) quánjī chǎng 拳击场; (*at circus*) mǎxì quān 马戏圈

ring² **1** *n* (*of bell*) zhōngshēng 钟声; (*of voice*) shēngdiào 声调 **2** *v/t bell* qiāozhōng 敲钟 **3** *v/i* (*of bell*) míng 鸣; **please ~ for attention** ànlíng zhāohuàn fúwù 按铃召唤服务

ringleader tóumù 头目
ring-pull lāhuán 拉环
rink liūbīng chǎng 溜冰场
rinse **1** *n* (*for hair color*) rǎnsè 染色 **2** *v/t clothes, dishes, hair* piǎoxǐ 漂洗

riot **1** *n* bàoluàn 暴乱 **2** *v/i* nàoshì 闹事
rioter nàoshì zhě 闹事者
riot police pínglúan jǐngchá 平乱警察

rip **1** *n* (*in cloth etc*) sīliè 撕裂 **2** *v/t cloth etc* sīliè 撕裂; **~ X open** sīkāi X 撕开 X

♦ **rip off** F *customers* shōufèi guògāo 收费过高; (*cheat*) qiāo zhúgàng 敲竹杠

ripe *fruit* shóu 熟
ripen *v/i* (*of fruit*) chéngshóu 成熟
ripeness (*of fruit*) shóu 熟
rip-off *n* F bōxuē 剥削
ripple (*on water*) xìlàng 细浪

rise **1** *v/i* (*from chair etc*) qǐlái 起来; (*of sun*) shēngqǐ 升起; (*of rocket*) fāshè 发射; (*of price, temperature*) shàngzhǎng 上涨; (*of water level*) shàngshēng 上升 **2** *n* (*in price, temperature*) shàngzhǎng 上涨; (*in water level*) shàngshēng 上升; (*in salary*) tígāo 提高

risk **1** *n* fēngxiǎn 风险; **take a ~** màoxiǎn 冒险 **2** *v/t* mào ... fēngxiǎn 冒 ... 风险; **let's ~ it** wǒmen shìshiba 我们试试吧

risky màoxiǎn 冒险
ritual *n & adj* yíshì 仪式
rival **1** *n* duìshǒu 对手 **2** *v/t* yǔ ... jìngzhēng 与 ... 竞争; **I can't ~ that** wǒ bǐ bú guò 我比不过

rivalry jìngzhēng 竞争
river héliú 河流
riverbed héchuáng 河床

riverside hébiān 河边

rivet 1 *n* mǎodīng 铆钉 **2** *v/t* mǎojiē 铆接; **~ X to Y** bǎ X dīngláo dào Y shàng 把 X 钉牢到 Y 上

RMB (= **renminbi**) rénmínbì 人民币

road lù 路; *it's just down the ~* jiù zài nàbiān 就在那边

roadblock lùzhàng 路障; **road hog** kāichē zài lù zhōngjiān 开车在路中间; **road holding** (*of vehicle*) gāosù jiàshǐ nénglì 高速驾驶能力; **road map** xiànlù tú 线路图; **roadside**: *at the ~* zài lùbiān 在路边; **roadsign** lùbiāo 路标; **roadway** gōnglù 公路; **roadworthy** shìyú gōnglù xíngshǐ 适于公路行驶

roam mànyóu 漫游

roar 1 *n* (*of traffic, engine*) hōngmíng shēng 轰鸣声; (*of lion*) páoxiào 咆哮; (*of person*) dàshēng chǎo 大声吵 **2** *v/i* (*of engine*) hōngmíng 轰鸣; (*of lion*) páoxiào 咆哮; (*of person*) dàshēng chǎo 大声吵; **~ with laughter** dàshēng xiào 大声笑

roast 1 *n* (*of beef etc*) kǎoròu 烤肉 **2** *v/t* kǎo 烤 **3** *v/i* (*of food*) kǎo 烤; **we're ~ing** F wǒmen rèsǐle 我们热死了

roast beef kǎo niúròu 烤牛肉

roast pork kǎo zhūròu 烤猪肉

rob *person, bank* qiǎngjié 抢劫; *I've been ~bed* wǒ bèi qiǎngjié le 我被抢劫了

robber qiǎngjié zhě 抢劫者

robbery qiǎngjié 抢劫

robe (*of judge*) guānfú 官服; (*of priest*) fǎyī 法衣; (*bath~*) yùyī 浴衣

robin dōng'é 冬鹅

robot jīqìrén 机器人

robust *person, health* jiànzhuàng 健壮; *material, structure* jiāngù 坚固

ROC (= **Republic of China**) Zhōnghuá Mínguó 中华民国

rock 1 *n* yánshí 岩石; MUS yáogǔn yuè 摇滚乐; *on the ~s drink* chānbīng 掺冰; *marriage* jíjiāng pòliè 即将破裂 **2** *v/t baby, cradle*

qīngyáo 轻摇; (*surprise*) shǐ zhènjīng 使震惊 **3** *v/i* (*on chair*) yáodòng 摇动; (*of boat*) yáohuang 摇晃

rock bottom: *reach ~* zǒurù zuìdīdiǎn 走入最低点

rock-bottom *adj prices* zuìdī 最低

rocket 1 *n* huǒjiàn 火箭 **2** *v/i* (*of prices etc*) jùzēng 剧增

rocking chair yáoyǐ 摇椅

rock'n'roll yáogǔn yuè 摇滚乐

rock star yáogǔn yuè gēxīng 摇滚乐歌星

rocky *beach, path* duō yánshí 多岩石

rod gùn 棍; (*for fishing*) gān 竿

rodent nièchǐmù dòngwù 啮齿目动物

rogue táoqìbāo 淘气包

role juésè 角色

role model bǎngyàng 榜样

roll 1 *n* (*bread*) xiǎo yuán miànbāo 小圆面包; (*of film*) juǎn 卷; (*of thunder*) lónglong shēng 隆隆声; (*list, register*) míngcè 名册 **2** *v/i* (*of ball etc*) gǔn 滚; (*of boat*) yáobǎi 摇摆 **3** *v/t*: **~ X into a ball** bǎ X juǎn chéngqiú 把 X 卷成球

♦ **roll over 1** *v/i* fānshēn 翻身 **2** *v/t person, object* fān 翻; (*renew, extend*) yánxù 延续

♦ **roll up 1** *v/t sleeves* juǎnqǐ 卷起 **2** *v/i* (*arrive*) chūxiàn 出现

roll call diǎnmíng 点名

roller (*for hair*) juǎnfà juǎn 卷发卷

roller blade *n* sìlún hànbīng xié 四轮旱冰鞋; **roller blind** juǎnlián 卷帘; **roller coaster** guò shān chē 过山车; **roller skate** *n* hànbīng xié 旱冰鞋

rolling pin gǎnmiànzhàng 擀面杖

ROM (= **read only memory**) zhǐ dú cúnchǔ qì 只读存储器

Roman Catholic 1 *n* Tiānzhǔjiào tú 天主教徒 **2** *adj* Tiānzhǔjiào 天主教

romance (*affair*) fēngliú yùnshì 风流韵事; (*novel, movie*) chuánqí 传奇

romantic làngmàn 浪漫

roof wūdǐng 屋顶

roof rack MOT chēdǐng jià 车顶架

room fángjiān 房间; (*space*) kōngjiān 空间; ***there's no ~ for X*** méi yǒu X de dìfang 没有 X 的地方

room clerk jiēdài yuán 接待员; **roommate** shìyǒu 室友; **room service** fángjiān fúwù 房间服务

roomy *house etc* dàchǎng 宽敞; *clothes* dà 大

root gēn 根; (*of word*) cígēn 词根; ***~s*** (*of person*) gēnjī 根基

♦**root out** (*get rid of*) sǎochú 扫除; (*find*) zhǎodào 找到

rope shéng 绳

♦**rope off** yòng shéngzi gékāi 用绳子隔开

rose BOT méigui 玫瑰

rostrum jiǎngtái 讲台

rosy *cheeks* hóngrùn 红润; *future* guāngmíng 光明

rot 1 *n* (*in wood, teeth*) fǔlàn 腐烂 **2** *v/i* (*of food, wood, teeth*) fǔlàn 腐烂

rota lúnzhí biǎo 轮值表

rotate *v/i* (*of blades, earth*) xuánzhuǎn 旋转

rotation (*around the sun etc*) xuánzhuǎn 旋转; ***do in ~*** lúnliú zuò 轮流做

rotten *food, wood etc* fǔlàn 腐烂; *trick, thing to do* lìngrén tǎoyàn 令人讨厌; *weather, luck* jíhuài 极坏

rough 1 *adj surface* bùpíng 不平; *hands, skin* cūcāo 粗糙; *voice* shāyǎ 沙哑; (*violent*) cūbào 粗暴; *crossing, seas* jiānnán 艰难; (*approximate*) dàgài 大概; ***~ draft*** cǎogǎo 草稿 **2** *adv*: ***sleep ~*** lùsù jiētóu 露宿街头 **3** *n* (*in golf*) zhàng'ài qūyù 障碍区域 **4** *v/t*: ***~ it*** còuhe 凑合

roughage (*in food*) cū sìliào 粗饲料

roughly (*approximately*) dàyù 大约

roulette lúnpán dǔ 轮盘赌

round 1 *adj* yuán 圆; ***in ~ figures*** zhěngshù 整数 **2** *n* (*of postman, doctor*) xúnhuí 巡回; (*of toast*) piàn 片; (*of drinks*) lún 轮; (*of competition*) chǎng 场; (*in boxing match*) huíhé 回合 **3** *v/t the corner* ràoxíng 绕行 **4** *adv & prep* → **around**

♦**round off** *edges* bǎ ... xiūyuán 把 ... 修圆; *meeting, night out* jiéshù 结束

♦**round up** *figure* bǎ ... tiáogāo chéng zhěngshù 把 ... 调高成整数; *suspects, criminals* dōubǔ 兜捕

roundabout *adj route, way of saying sth* jiànjiē 间接

round trip láihuí lǚxíng 来回旅行

round trip ticket láihuí piào 来回票

round-up (*of cattle*) gǎnlǒng 赶拢; (*of suspects, criminals*) dōubǔ 兜捕; (*of news*) zōnghé bàodào 综合报道

rouse (*from sleep*) xǐng 醒; *interest, emotions* shāndòng 煽动

rousing *speech, finale* lìngrén zhènfèn 令人振奋

route lùxiàn 路线

routine 1 *adj* chángguī 常规 **2** *n* chángguī 常规; ***as a matter of ~*** zuòwéi chángguī 作为常规

row¹ (*line*) pái 排; (*in spreadsheet etc*) háng 行; ***5 days in a ~*** jiēlián wǔ tiān 接连五天

row² 1 *v/t boat* huá 划 **2** *v/i* huáchuán 划船

rowboat huátǐng 划艇

rowdy hào chǎonào 好吵闹

row house páifáng 排房

royal *adj* huángjiā 皇家

royalty (*royal persons*) huángzú 皇族; (*on book, recording*) chōubǎn fèi 筹办费

rub *v/t* cuō 搓

♦**rub down** (*to clean*) cāshuā 擦刷

♦**rub off 1** *v/t dirt* cādiào 擦掉; *paint etc* módiào 磨掉 **2** *v/i*: ***it rubs off on you*** duì nǐ yǒu yǐngxiǎng 对你有影响

♦**rub out** (*with eraser*) móqù 磨去

rubber 1 *n* (*material*) xiàngpí 橡皮 **2** *adj* xiàngjiāo 橡胶

rubbish *Br* lājī 垃圾; (*poor quality item*) pòlàn 破烂; (*nonsense*) húshuō 胡说

rubble cūshí 粗石
ruby (*jewel*) hóng bǎoshí 红宝石
rucksack bèibāo 背包
rudder duò 舵
ruddy *complexion* hóngrùn 红润
rude cūlǔ 粗鲁; *it is ~ to …* … shì cūlǔ de … 是粗鲁的; *I didn't mean to be ~* wǒ bìngbúshì gùyì wúlǐ 我并不是故意无礼
rudeness wúlǐ 无礼
rudimentary jīběn 基本
rudiments jīběn yuánlǐ 基本原理
ruffian ègùn 恶棍
ruffle 1 *n* (*on dress*) zhě zhě 褶 **2** *v/t hair* nòngluàn 弄乱; *clothes* nòngzhòu 弄皱; *person* shǐ xīnfán yìluàn 使心烦意乱; *get ~d* xīnfán yìluàn 心烦意乱
rug xiǎo dìtǎn 小地毯; (*blanket*) tǎnzi 毯子
rugged *scenery, cliffs* qíqū 崎岖; *face* cūguǎng 粗犷; *resistance* jiānqiáng 坚强
ruin 1 *n*: *~s* fèixū 废墟; *in ~s* (*of city, building*) chéng fèixū 成废墟; (*of marriage*) pòliè 破裂; (*of plans*) pòchǎn 破产 **2** *v/t party, birthday, vacation, plans* pòhuài 破坏; *reputation* huǐhuài 毁坏; *be ~ed* (*financially*) pòchǎn 破产
rule 1 *n* (*of club, game*) guīzé 规则; (*of monarch*) tǒngzhì 统治; (*for measuring*) chǐdù 尺度; *as a ~* tōngcháng 通常 **2** *v/t country* tǒngzhì 统治; *the judge ~d that …* fǎguān pàndìng … 法官判定 … **3** *v/i* (*of monarch*) tǒngzhì 统治
♦**rule out** páichú 排除
ruler (*for measuring*) chǐzi 尺子; (*of state*) tǒngzhì zhě 统治者
ruling 1 *n* cáijué 裁决 **2** *adj party* dāngquán 当权
rum (*drink*) lǎngmǔ jiǔ 朗姆酒
rumble *v/i* (*of stomach*) lónglong zuòxiǎng 隆隆作响; (*of train in tunnel*) lùlu shǐguò 辘辘驶过
♦**rummage around** fānxún 翻寻
rummage sale jiùwù chūshòu 旧物出售
rumor 1 *n* yáoyán 谣言 **2** *v/t*: *it is ~ed that …* yǒu yáoyán shuō … 有谣言说 …

rump (*of animal*) túnbù 臀部
rumple *clothes, paper* nòngzhòu 弄皱
rumpsteak túnbù niúpái 臀部牛排
run 1 *n* (*on foot*) pǎobù 跑步; (*in car*) xíngchéng 行程; (*in tights*) chōusī 抽丝; (THEA: *of play*) liánxù yǎnchū 连续演出; *go for a ~* pǎobù 跑步; *go for a ~ in the car* zuòchē qù dōu gè quān 坐车去兜个圈; *make a ~ for it* táopǎo 逃跑; *a criminal on the ~* zàitáo zuìfàn 在逃罪犯; *in the short / long ~* cóng duǎnqī / chángyuǎn láikàn 从短期/长远来看; *a ~ on the dollar* měiyuán jǐduì 美元挤兑 **2** *v/i* (*of person, animal*) pǎo 跑; (*of river*) liú 流; (*of trains etc*) xíngshǐ 行驶; (*of paint, makeup*) tǎngliú 淌流; (*of nose, eyes*) tǎng 淌; (*of tap*) kāi 开; (*of play*) liánxù yǎnchū 连续演出; (*of engine, machine, software*) yùnzhuǎn 运转; (*in election*) jìngxuǎn 竞选; *~ for President* jìngxuǎn zǒngtǒng 竞选总统 **3** *v/t race* jìngsài 竞赛; *3 miles etc* pǎo 跑; *business, hotel, project etc* guǎnlǐ 管理; *software* yùnzhuǎn 运转; *car* yōngyǒu 拥有; *can I ~ you to the station?* wǒ kěyǐ kāichē sòng nǐ qù chēzhàn ma? 我可以开车送你去车站吗？; *he ran his eye down the page* tā liúlǎn le zhè yīyè 他浏览了这一页
♦**run across** (*meet*) pèngjiàn 碰见; (*find*) zhǎodào 找到
♦**run away** táopǎo 逃跑
♦**run down 1** *v/t* (*knock down*) zhuàngdǎo 撞倒; (*criticize*) biǎndī 贬低; *stocks* jiǎnshǎo 减少 **2** *v/i* (*of battery*) hàojìn 耗尽
♦**run into** (*meet*) pèngjiàn 碰见; *difficulties* yùdào 遇到
♦**run off 1** *v/i* táopǎo 逃跑 **2** *v/t* (*print off*) dǎyìn 打印
♦**run out** (*of contract*) qīmǎn 期满; (*of time*) yòngwán 用完; (*of*

supplies) hàojìn 耗尽

♦**run out of** *time* yòngwán 用完; *patience* shīqù 失去; *supplies* yòngguāng 用光; *I ran out of gas* wǒ chē méi yóu le 我车没油了

♦**run over 1** *v/t* (*knock down*) zhuàngdǎo 撞倒; *can we ~ the details again?* wǒmén zàikàn yībiàn xiángqíng hǎoma? 我们再看一遍详情好吗？ **2** *v/i* (*of water etc*) yìchū 溢出

♦**run through** (*rehearse*) páiliàn 排练; (*go over*) liúlàn 浏览

♦**run up** *v/t debts, large bill* lěijī 累积; *clothes* gǎnzhì 赶制

run-down *person* píjuàn 疲倦; *part of town* pòjiù 破旧; *building* shīxiū 失修

rung (*of ladder*) tījí 梯级

runner (*athlete*) sàipǎo zhě 赛跑者

runner-up yàjūn 亚军

running 1 *n* SP sàipǎo 赛跑; (*of business*) jīngyíng 经营 **2** *adj*: *for two days ~* liánxù liǎngtiān 连续两天

running dog *pej* zǒugǒu 走狗

running water (*from tap*) zìláishuǐ 自来水; (*flowing*) liúshuǐ 流水

runny *liquid* liúdòng 流动; *~ nose* liú bítì 流鼻涕

run-up SP yùbèi jiēduàn 预备阶段; *in the ~ to* zài yùbèi jiēduàn qījiān 在预备阶段期间

runway pǎodào 跑道

rupture 1 *n* pòliè 破裂 **2** *v/i* (*of pipe etc*) pòliè 破裂

rural nóngcūn 农村

rush 1 *n* tūjī 突击; *do ... in a ~* cōngmáng zuò ... 匆忙做...; *be in a ~* máng 忙; *what's the big ~?* máng shénme? 忙什么？ **2** *v/t person* cuī 催; *meal* kuàichī 快吃; *~ X to the hospital* bǎ X huǒsù sòngjìn yīyuàn 把 X 火速送进医院 **3** *v/i* gǎn gǎn 赶

rush hour gāofēng shíjiān 高峰时间

Russia Éluósī 俄罗斯

Russian 1 *adj* Éluósī 俄罗斯 **2** *n* (*person*) Éluósī rén 俄罗斯人; (*language*) Éyǔ 俄语

rust 1 *n* xiù 锈 **2** *v/i* shēngxiù 生锈

rustle 1 *n* (*of silk, leaves*) shāshā-shēng 沙沙声 **2** *v/i* (*of silk, leaves*) shāshā zuòxiǎng 沙沙作响

♦**rustle up** F *meal* cōngcōng zuò 匆匆做

rust-proof *adj* fángxiù 防锈

rust remover chúxiùjì 除锈剂

rusty shēngxiù 生锈; *French, math etc* shēngshū 生疏; *I'm a little ~* wǒ yǒudiǎnr shēng le 我有点儿生了

rut (*in road*) chēzhé 车辙; *fig* chángguī 常规; *be in a ~* guò kèbǎnde shēnghuó 过刻板的生活

ruthless wúqíng 无情

ruthlessness wúqíng 无情

rye hēimài 黑麦

rye bread hēimài miànbāo 黑麦面包

S

sabbatical *n* (*of academic*) xiūjiànián 休假年

sabotage *n & v/t* pòhuài 破坏

saccharin *n* tángjīng 糖精

sachet (*of shampoo, cream etc*) yīxiǎodài 一小袋

sack 1 *n* dà kǒudài 大口袋 2 *v/t* jiěgù 解雇

sacred shénshèng 神圣

sacrifice 1 *n* (*act*) xīshēng 牺牲; (*person, animal sacrificed*) jìpǐn 祭品; *make ~s fig* zuòchū xīshēng 作出牺牲 2 *v/t* xiànjì 献祭; *one's freedom etc* xīshēng 牺牲

sad *person, face, song* bēishāng 悲伤; *state of affairs* yíhàn 遗憾

saddle *n* ānzi 鞍子

sadism shīnüèdàikuáng 施虐狂

sadist nüèdàikuáng zhě 虐待狂者

sadistic yǒu shīnüèkuáng 有施虐狂

sadly *look, sing etc* yōuchóu 忧愁; (*regrettably*) lìngrén yíhàn 令人遗憾

sadness yōuchóu 忧愁

safe 1 *adj* (*not dangerous*) ānquán 安全; (*not in danger*) wúwēixiǎn 无危险; *investment, prediction* wúfēngxiǎn 无风险 2 *n* bǎoxiǎnguì 保险柜

safeguard 1 *n* ānquán zhuāngzhì 安全装置; *as a ~ against X* zuòwéi fángzhǐ X de bǎohù cuòshī 作为防止X的保护措施 2 *v/t* bǎohù 保护

safekeeping: *give X to Y for ~* bǎ X gěi Y tuǒshàn bǎoguǎn 把X给Y妥善保管

safely *arrive* píng'ān 平安; *complete tests etc* yǒu bǎwò 有把握; *drive* ānquán 安全; *assume* kěndìng 肯定

safety ānquán 安全; (*of investment, prediction*) bǎoxiǎn 保险; *be in ~* chùyú ānquán zhuàngtài 处于安全状态

safety belt ānquándài 安全带; safety-conscious yǒu ānquán yìshí 有安全意识; safety first ānquán dìyī 安全第一; safety pin biézhēn 别针

sag 1 *n* (*in ceiling etc*) xiàchuí 下垂 2 *v/i* (*of ceiling, rope*) xiàchuí 下垂; (*of output, tempo*) xiàjiàng 下降

sage (*herb*) shǔwěicǎo 鼠尾草

sail 1 *n* fān 帆; (*trip*) hángchéng 航程; *go for a ~* chéngchuán yóulǎn 乘船游览 2 *v/t* yacht jiàshǐ 驾驶 3 *v/i* jiàshǐchuán 驾驶船; (*depart*) qǐháng 启航

sailboard 1 *n* fānbǎn 帆板 2 *v/i* zuò fānbǎn yùndòng 作帆板运动

sailboarding fānbǎn yùndòng 帆板运动

sailboat fānchuán 帆船

sailing SP fānchuán yùndòng 帆船运动

sailing ship fānchuán 帆船

sailor (*in the navy*) hǎiyuán 海员; SP shuǐshǒu 水手; *be a good / bad ~* bùcháng / chángcháng yùnchuán de rén 不常/常常晕船的人

saint shèngtú 圣徒

sake: *for my / your ~* wèile wǒ / nǐ 为了我/你; *for the ~ of X* wèile X 为了X

salad ⇩ sèlā 色拉

salad dressing ⇩ sèlā tiáowèizhī 色拉调味汁

salary xīnshuǐ 薪水

salary scale xīnshuǐ jíbié 薪水级别

sale xiāoshòu 销售; (*reduced prices*) liánshòu 廉售; *for ~* (*sign*) dàishòu 待售; *be on ~* yǒushòu 有售; (*at reduced prices*) liánjià chūshòu 廉价出售

sales (*department*) xiāoshòu 销售

sales clerk (*in store*) shòuhuòyuán 售货员; sales figures xiāoshòu'é 销售额; salesman tuīxiāoyuán 推销员; sales manager yíngyè jīnglǐ 营业经理; sales meeting xiāoshòu huìyì 销售会议

saliva tuòyè 唾液

salmon dàmǎhāyú 大马哈鱼

saloon MOT xiǎojiàochē 小轿车; (*bar*) jiǔbā 酒吧

salt yán 盐

saltcellar yánpíng 盐瓶

salty xián 咸

salutary *experience* yǒuyì 有益

salute 1 *n* MIL jìnglǐ 敬礼 2 *v/t & v/i* zhìjìng 致敬

salvage *v/t* (*from wreck*) qiǎngjiù 抢救

salvation zhěngjiù 拯救

Salvation Army Jiùshìjūn 救世军

same 1 *adj* tóngyàng 同样 2 *pron*: *I'll have the ~ as you* hé nǐ yīyàng 和你一样; *Happy New Year – the ~ to you* Xīnnián kuàilè – Xīnnián kuàilè 新年快乐－新年快乐; *he's not the ~ any more* tā búzài hé yǐqián yíyàng le 他不再和以前一样了; *all the ~* jǐnguǎn rúcǐ 尽管如此; *men are all the ~* nánrén dōu yíyàng 男人都一样; *it's all the ~ to me* duì wǒ láishuō dōu yíyàng 对我来说都一样 3 *adv*: *look / sound the ~* kànqǐlái / tīngqǐlái yíyàng 看起来/听起来一样

sample *n* yàngběn 样本

sanatorium liáoyǎngyuàn 疗养院

sanction 1 *n* (*approval*) pīzhǔn 批准; (*penalty*) zhìcái 制裁 2 *v/t* (*approve*) tóngyì 同意

sanctity shénshèng 神圣

sanctuary REL shèngdì 圣地; (*for wild animals*) yěshēng dòngwù bǎohù qū 野生动物保护区

sand 1 *n* shā 沙 2 *v/t* (*with sandpaper*) yòng shāzhǐ móguāng 用砂纸磨光

sandal liángxié 凉鞋

sandbag shādài 沙袋; sandblast pēnshā qīngxǐ 喷沙清洗; sand dune shāqiū 沙丘

sander (*tool*) dǎmójī 打磨机

sandpaper 1 *n* shāzhǐ 砂纸 2 *v/t* yòng shāzhǐ móguāng 用砂纸磨光; sandpit shākēng 沙坑; sandstone shāyán 沙岩

sandwich 1 *n* sānmíngzhì 三明治 2 *v/t*: *be ~ed between two ...* shòujiáyú liǎng ... zhījiān 受夹于两 ... 之间

sandy *beach, soil* duōshā 多沙; *hair* shāsè 沙色

sane shénzhì zhèngcháng 神志正常

sanitarium liáoyǎngyuàn 疗养院

sanitary *conditions* wèishēng 卫生; *installations* qīngjié 清洁

sanitary napkin wèishēngjīn 卫生巾

sanitation (*sanitary installations*) wèishēng shèbèi 卫生设备; (*removal of waste*) xiàshuǐ xìtǒng 下水系统

sanitation department huánjìng wèishēng bùmén 环境卫生部门

sanity shénzhì zhèngcháng 神志正常

Santa Claus Shèngdàn Lǎorén 圣诞老人

sap 1 *n* (*in tree*) shùyè 树液 2 *v/t s.o.'s energy* xuēruò 削弱

sapphire *n* (*jewel*) lánbǎoshí 蓝宝石

sarcasm jīfěng 讥讽

sarcastic jīfěng 讥讽

sardine shādīngyú 沙丁鱼

sash (*on dress, uniform*) jiāndài 肩带; (*in window*) chuānkuàng 窗框

Satan Sādàn 撒旦

satellite wèixīng 卫星

satellite dish wèixīng diànshì pán 卫星电视盘

satellite TV wèixīng diànshì 卫星电视

satin duànzi 缎子

satire fěngcì 讽刺

satirical hán fěngcì yìwèi 含讽刺意味

satirist fěngcì zhě 讽刺者

satisfaction mǎnzú 满足; **get ~ out of X** cóng X zhōng dédào mǎnzú 从 X 中得到满足; **a feeling of ~** mǎnyìde gǎnjué 满意的感觉; **is that to your ~?** nǐ duì cǐ mǎnyì ma? 你对此满意吗？

satisfactory lìngrén mǎnyì 令人满意; (just good enough) fúhé yāoqiú 符合要求; **this is not ~** zhè hái búgòu hǎo 这还不够好

satisfy customers shǐ mǎnyì 使满意; needs, hunger, sexual desires mǎnzú 满足; conditions fúhé 符合; **I am satisfied that he ...** (convinced) wǒ xiāngxìn tā ... 我相信他...; **I hope you're satisfied!** wǒ xiǎng nǐ gāi mǎnyì le ba! 我想你该满意了吧！

Saturday xīngqīliù 星期六

sauce jiàng 酱

saucepan píngdǐguō 平底锅

saucer chábēidié 茶杯碟

saucy person wúlǐ 无礼; dress tòuguāng 透光

Saudi (Arabia) Shātè Ālābó 沙特阿拉伯

Saudi (Arabian) 1 adj Shātè Ālābó 沙特阿拉伯 **2** n (person) Shātè Ālābó rén 沙特阿拉伯人

sauna ⇩ zhēngqìyù 蒸汽浴

saunter mànbù 漫步

sausage xiāngcháng 香肠

savage 1 adj animal yěxìng 野性; attack cánkù 残酷; criticism èdú 恶毒 **2** n yěrén 野人

save 1 v/t (rescue) jiù 救; money chǔcún 储存; time jiéshěng 节省; (collect) sōují 搜集; COMPUT cúnpán 存盘; goal jiùqiú 救球; **~ as** COMPUT cúnwéi 存为; **you could ~ yourself a lot of effort** nǐ kěyǐ jiéshěng hěnduō jīnglì 你可以节省很多精力 **2** v/i (put money aside) zǎnqián 攒钱; SP jiùqiú 救球 **3** n SP jiùqiú 救球

♦**save up for** wèi ... zǎnqián 为 ... 攒钱

saving (amount saved) jiéshěng 节省; (activity) cúnqián 存钱

savings cúnkuǎn 存款

savings account chǔxù zhànghù 储蓄帐户

savings bank chǔxū yínháng 储蓄银行

savior REL jiùshìzhǔ 救世主

savor 1 n fēngwèi 风味 **2** v/t pǐncháng 品尝

savory adj (not sweet) xián 咸

saw 1 n (tool) jù 锯 **2** v/t jùkāi 锯开

♦**saw off** jùdiào 锯掉

sawdust jùmò 锯末

saxophone sàkèsīguǎn 萨克斯管

say 1 v/t shuō 说; **can I ~ something?** wǒ kěyǐ fābiǎo yīxià wǒde yìjiàn ma? 我可以发表一下我的意见吗？; **that is to ~** nà jiùshì shuō 那就是说; **what do you ~ to that?** nǐ juédé nàyàng rúhé? 你觉得那样如何？ **2** n: **have one's ~** biǎodá yìjiàn 表达意见

saying yànyǔ 谚语

scab jiā 痂

scaffold(ing) jiǎoshǒujià 脚手架

scald v/t tàngshāng 烫伤

scale[1] (on fish) línpiàn 鳞片

scale[2] **1** n (size) guīmó 规模; (on thermometer etc) kèdù 刻度; (of map) bǐlì 比例; MUS yīnjiē 音阶; **on a larger / smaller ~** gèngdà / gèngxiǎo guīmó 更大/更小规模 **2** v/t cliffs etc pāndēng 攀登

scale drawing bǐlì huìtú 比例绘图

scales (for weighing) tiānpíng 天平

scalp n tóupí 头皮

scalpel shǒushùdāo 手术刀

scalper ⇩ piàofànzi 票贩子

scan 1 v/t horizon, page sǎoshì 扫视; MED sǎomiáo 扫描; COMPUT sōusuǒ 搜索 **2** n MED sǎomiáo 扫描

♦**scan in** COMPUT sōusuǒ jìnrù 搜索进入

scandal liúyán fēiyǔ 流言蜚语

scandalous affair diūliǎn 丢脸; prices lìngrén zhènjīng 令人震惊

scanner MED sǎomiáoqì 扫描器; COMPUT sǎomiáoyí 扫描仪

scantily adv: **~ clad** chuānzhuó dānbó 穿着单薄

scanty *clothes* dānbó 单薄

scapegoat tìzuìyáng 替罪羊

scar 1 *n* shāngbā 伤疤 **2** *v/t* liúxià shānghén 留下伤痕

scarce (*in short supply*) duǎnquē 短缺; **make oneself ~** bìkāi 避开

scarcely jīhūbù 几乎不

scarcity quēfá 缺乏

scare 1 *v/t* jīngxià 惊吓; **be ~d of X** hàipà X 害怕 X **2** *n* (*panic, alarm*) jīngkǒng 惊恐; **give X a ~** gěi X xiàle yī tiào 给 X 吓了一跳

♦**scare away** xiàpǎo 吓跑

scarecrow dàocǎorén 稻草人

scarf (*around neck*) wéijīn 围巾; (*over head*) tóujīn 头巾

scarlet xiānhóng 鲜红

scarlet fever xīnghóngrè 猩红热

scary *music, movie* hěn kǒngbù 很恐怖

scathing kèbó 刻薄

scatter 1 *v/t leaflets, seeds* sǎ 撒; **be ~ed all over the room** fángjiānlǐ dàochù dōushì 房间里到处都是 **2** *v/i* (*of crowd etc*) sànkāi 散开

scatterbrained jiànwàng 健忘

scattered *showers* língxīng 零星; *family, villages* fēnsàn 分散

scenario qíngkuàng 情况

scene THEA chǎng 场; (*view, sight*) qíngjǐng 情景; (*of accident, crime etc*) shìfā dìdiǎn 事发地点; (*of novel, movie*) chǎngjǐng 场景; (*argument*) chǎonào 吵闹; **make a ~** dàchǎo dànào 大吵大闹; **~s** THEA bùjǐng 布景; **jazz / rock ~** juéshìyuè / yáogǔnyuè lǐngyù 爵士乐 / 摇滚乐领域; **behind the ~s** zài mùhòu 在幕后

scenery jǐngsè 景色; THEA wǔtái bùjǐng 舞台布景

scent *n* (*smell*) xiāngwèi 香味; (*perfume*) xiāngjīng 香精; (*of animal*) xiùjì 臭迹

schedule 1 *n* (*of events*) chéngxùbiǎo 程序表; (*of work*) jìhuàbiǎo 计划表; (*for trains*) shíkèbiǎo 时刻表; (*of lessons*) kèchéngbiǎo 课程表; **be on ~** (*of work, of workers, of train etc*) àn yùdìng shíjiān 按预定时间; **be behind ~** (*of work, of workers, of train etc*) luòhòuyú yùdìng jìhuà 落后于预定计划 **2** *v/t* (*put on schedule*) lièrù jìhuà 列入计划; **it's ~d for completion next month** dìngyú xiàgèyuè wánchéng 定于下个月完成

scheduled flight dìngqī hángbān 定期航班

scheme 1 *n* (*plan*) jìhuà 计划; (*plot*) yīnmóu 阴谋 **2** *v/i* (*plot*) túmóu 图谋

scheming *adj* guǐjì duōduān 诡计多端

schizophrenia jīngshén fēnlièzhèng 精神分裂症

schizophrenic 1 *n* jīngshén fēnlièzhèng huànzhě 精神分裂症患者 **2** *adj* jīngshén fēnliè 精神分裂

scholar xuézhě 学者

scholarship (*work*) xuéshù chéngjiù 学术成就; (*financial award*) jiǎngxuéjīn 奖学金

school xuéxiào 学校; (*university*) xuéyuàn 学院

schoolbag xiǎoshūbāo 小书包

schoolboy zhōngxiǎoxué nánshēng 中小学男生; **schoolchildren** zhōngxiǎoxué xuésheng 中小学学生; **school days** xuésheng shídài 学生时代; **schoolgirl** zhōngxiǎoxué nǚ xuésheng 中小学女生; **schoolmate** xiàoyǒu 校友; **schoolteacher** zhōngxiǎoxué jiàoshī 中小学教师

sciatica zuògǔ shénjīngtòng 坐骨神经痛

science kēxué 科学

science fiction kēhuàn 科幻

scientific kēxué 科学

scientist kēxuéjiā 科学家

scissors jiǎnzi 剪子

scoff[1] *v/t* (*eat fast*) tānlánde chī 贪婪地吃; (*eat whole lot*) chīguāng 吃光

scoff[2] *v/i* jīxiào 讥笑

♦**scoff at** cháoxiào 嘲笑

scold *v/t child, husband* zémà 责骂

scoop 1 *n* (*implement*) chǎnzi 铲子; (*story*) qiǎngxiān bàodào 抢先

报道 **2** v/t (*pick up*) yǎochū 舀出

♦**scoop up** pěngqǐ 捧起

scooter (*with motor*) xiǎoxíng mótuōchē 小型摩托车; (*child's*) tàbǎnchē 踏板车

scope fànwéi 范围; (*freedom, opportunity*) jīhuì 机会

scorch v/t tàngjiāo 烫焦

scorching hot rèsǐle 热死了

score 1 n SP bǐfēn 比分; (*written music*) yuèpǔ 乐谱; (*of movie etc*) pèiyuè 配乐; ***what's the ~?*** bǐfēn shì duōshǎo? 比分是多少？; ***have a ~ to settle with X*** gēn X suàn jiùzhàng 跟 X 算旧帐 **2** v/t *goal, point* défēn 得分; (*cut: line*) huàhén 划痕 **3** v/i défēn 得分; (*keep the score*) jìfēn 记分; ***that's where he ~s*** nà shì tāde qiángxiàng 那是他的强项

scorer (*of goal, point*) défēn yùndòngyuán 得分运动员; (*scorekeeper*) jìfēnyuán 记分员

scorn 1 n bǐshì 鄙视; ***pour ~ on X*** yòng qīngmiède kǒuwěn tán X 用轻蔑的口吻谈 X **2** v/t *idea, suggestion* àomànde jùjué 傲慢地拒绝

scornful qīngmiè 轻蔑

Scot Sūgélán rén 苏格兰人

Scotch (*whiskey*) wēishìjì 威士忌

Scotland Sūgélán 苏格兰

Scottish Sūgélán 苏格兰

scot-free: ***get off ~*** xiāoyáo fǎwài 逍遥法外

scoundrel wúlài 无赖

scour[1] (*search*) sōuxún 搜寻

scour[2] *pans* shuājìng 刷净

scout n (*boy ~*) tóngzǐjūn 童子军

scowl 1 n nùróng 怒容 **2** v/i nùshì 怒视

scram F pǎo 跑

scramble 1 n (*rush*) mángluàn 忙乱 **2** v/t *message* rǎopín 扰频 **3** v/i (*climb*) pāndēng 攀登; ***he ~d to his feet*** tā téngde zhàn qǐlái 他腾地站起来

scrap 1 n (*metal*) fèijīnshǔ 废金属; (*fight*) dǎjià 打架; (*little bit*) shǎoliàng 少量 **2** v/t *plan, project, paragraph etc* fèidiào 废掉

scrapbook jiǎntiēbù 剪贴簿

scrape 1 n (*on paintwork etc*) guācā 刮擦 **2** v/t *paintwork* guādiào 刮掉; *one's arm* cāshāng 擦伤; *vegetables* yòng dāo xiāojìng 用刀削净; ***~ a living*** miǎnqiǎng wéichí shēnghuó 勉强维持生活

♦**scrape through** (*in exam etc*) miǎnqiǎng jígé 勉强及格

scrap heap fèiliàoduī 废料堆; ***good for the ~*** háowúyòngchù 毫无用处

scrap metal fèijīnshǔ 废金属

scrappy *work* záluànwúzhāng 杂乱无章

scratch 1 n (*mark*) huàhén 划痕; ***have a ~*** (*to stop itching*) sāoyǎng 搔痒; ***start from ~*** cónglíng kāishǐ 从零开始; ***not up to ~*** búgòuhǎo 不够好

scratch 2 v/t (*mark: skin, paint*) zhuāshāng 抓伤; (*because of itch*) sāoyǎng 搔痒 **3** v/i (*of cat, nails*) zhuā 抓

scrawl 1 n liáocǎode zìjì 潦草的字迹 **2** v/t luànxiě 乱写

scream 1 n jiānjiàoshēng 尖叫声 **2** v/i jiānjiào 尖叫

screech 1 n (*of tires*) jiānlìshēng 尖利声; (*scream*) jiānjiàoshēng 尖叫声 **2** v/i (*of tires*) fāchū jiānlìshēng 发出尖利声; (*scream*) fāchū jiānjiàoshēng 发出尖叫声

screen 1 n (*in room, hospital*) gélián 隔帘; (*protective*) yǎnbiwù 掩避物; (*in movie theater*) yínmù 银幕; COMPUT píngmù 屏幕; ***on the ~*** (*in movie theater*) zài yínmùshang 在银幕上; ***on (the) ~*** COMPUT zài píngmùshang 在屏幕上 **2** v/t (*protect, hide*) zhēbì 遮蔽; *movie* fàngyìng 放映; (*for security reasons*) shěnchá 审查

screenplay diànyǐng jùběn 电影剧本; **screen saver** COMPUT píngmù bǎohùqì 屏幕保护器; **screen test** shìjìng 试镜

screw 1 n luósīdīng 螺丝钉; ∨ (*sex*) xìngjiāo 性交 **2** v/t ∨ gèn … shuìjiào 跟 … 睡觉; F (*cheat*) qīpiàn 欺骗；~ **X** to **Y** yòng luósīdīng bǎ X nǐngzài Y shàng 用 螺丝钉把X拧在Y上

♦ **screw up 1** *v/t eyes* niǔqū 扭曲；*piece of paper* róuchéntuán 揉成团；F (*make a mess of*) dǎluàn 打乱 **2** *v/i* F (*make a bad mistake*) nòngzāo 弄糟

screwdriver luósīdāo 螺丝刀

screwed up F (*psychologically*) shénjīng 神经

screw top (*on bottle*) xuángài 旋盖

scribble 1 *n* liáocǎode zìjì 潦草的字迹 **2** *v/t* (*write quickly*) cǎocǎo shūxiě 草草书写 **3** *v/i* luànxiě 乱写

script (*for play etc*) jiǎoběn 脚本；(*form of writing*) shūxiětǐ 书写体

scripture: the (**Holy**) **Scriptures** Shèngjīng 圣经

scriptwriter zhuàngǎorén 撰稿人

scroll *n* (*manuscript*) zhǐjuǎn 纸卷

♦ **scroll down** *v/i* COMPUT chuízhí xiàyí 垂直下移

♦ **scroll up** *v/i* COMPUT chuízhí shàngyí 垂直上移

scrounger wúlài 无赖

scrub *v/t floors, hands* cāxǐ 擦洗

scrubbing brush (*for floor*) yìngshuāzi 硬刷子；(*for hands*) xǐshǒushuā 洗手刷

scruffy lātā 邋遢

♦ **scrunch up** *plastic cup etc* niǎnsuì 捻碎

scruples gùlù 顾虑；**have no ~ about doing X** duì zuò X wúsuǒ gùjì 对做X无所顾忌

scrupulous (*with moral principles*) shěnshèn 审慎；(*thorough*) zǐxì chèdǐ 仔细彻底；*attention to detail* yìsībùgǒu 一丝不苟

scrutinize (*examine closely*) xìchá 细察

scrutiny xìchá 细察；**come under ~** bèishěnchá 被审查

scuba diving dài shuǐfèi qiánshuǐ 戴水肺潜水

scuffle *n* niǔdǎ 扭打

sculptor diāokè (sù) jiā 雕刻（塑）家

sculpture *n* (*art*) diāokè (sù) 雕刻（塑）；(*sth sculpted*) diāosù 雕塑

scum (*on liquid*) fúgòu 浮垢；*pej* (*people*) zhāzi 渣子

scythe *n* chángbǐng dàliándāo 长柄大廉刀

sea dàhǎi 大海；**by the ~** zài hǎibiān 在海边

seafaring *nation* hǎishàng 海上；

seafood hǎiwèi 海味；**seafront** bīnhǎiqū 滨海区；**seagoing** *vessel* shìyú yuǎnháng 适于远航；**seagull** hǎi'ōu 海鸥

seal[1] *n* (*animal*) hǎibào 海豹

seal[2] *n* (*on document*) yìnzhāng 印章；TECH mìfēng 密封 **2** *v/t container* mìfēng 密封

♦ **seal off** *area* fēngsuǒ 封锁

sea level: above / **below ~** hǎibá / dīyú hǎipíngmiàn 海拔 / 低于海平面

seam *n* (*on garment*) fèng 缝；(*of ore*) kuàngcéng 矿层

seaman shuǐshǒu 水手

seamstress nǚcáifeng 女裁缝

seaport hǎigǎng 海港

sea power (*nation*) hǎijūn qiáng-guó 海军强国

search 1 *n* sōuxún 搜寻 **2** *v/t city, files* sōuchá 搜查

♦ **search for** xúnzhǎo 寻找

searching *adj look, question* jiānruì ér shēnkè 尖锐而深刻

searchlight tànzhàodēng 探照灯；**search party** sōusuǒduì 搜索队；**search warrant** sōucházhèng 搜查证

seasick yùnchuán 晕船；**get ~** yùnchuán 晕船；**seaside** hǎibīn 海滨；**at the ~** zài hǎibīn 在海滨；**go to the ~** qù hǎibīn 去海滨

seaside resort hǎibīn shèngdì 海滨胜地

season *n* (*winter etc*) jìjié 季节；(*for tourism etc*) wàngjì 旺季

seasoned *wood* fēnggān 风干；*traveler etc* yǒu jīngyàn 有经验

seasoning zuóliào 作料

season ticket chángqīpiào 长期票

seat 1 *n* zuòwèi 座位；(*of pants*) túnbù 臀部；POL xíwèi 席位；

please take a ~ qǐng luòzuò 请落坐 **2** *v/t (have seating for)* zuòdexià 坐得下; *please remain* ~*ed* jiùzuò wùdòng 就座勿动

seat belt ānquándài 安全带

sea urchin hǎidǎn 海胆

seaweed hǎidài 海带

secluded rénjīhǎnzhì 人际罕至

seclusion yǔshìgéjué 与世隔绝

second 1 *n (of time)* yī miǎozhōng 一秒钟; *just a* ~ děngyíxià 等一下 **2** *adj* dì'èr 第二 **3** *adv come in* yǐ dì'èrwèi 以第二位 **4** *v/t motion* fùyì 附议

secondary cìyào 次要; *of* ~ *importance* cìyào 次要

secondary education zhōngděng jiàoyù 中等教育

second best *adj* dì'èr hǎo 第二好; **second biggest** dì'èr dà 第二大; **second class** *adj ticket* èrděng 二等; **second gear** MOT èrdǎng 二档; **second hand** *(on clock)* miǎozhēn 秒针 **second-hand** èrshǒu 二手

secondly qícì 其次

second-rate èrliú 二流

second thoughts: *I've had* ~ wǒ gǎibiàn zhǔyì le 我改变主意了

secrecy bǎomì 保密

secret 1 *n* mìmì 秘密; *do X in* ~ mìmì zuò X 秘密做 X **2** *adj garden, passage* mìmì 秘密; *work, department* bǎomì 保密

secret agent tègōng rényuán 特工人员

secretarial *tasks, job* mìshū 秘书

secretary mìshū 秘书; POL bùzhǎng 部长

Secretary of State Guówùqīng 国务卿

secrete *(give off)* fēnmì 分泌; *(hide away)* yǐncáng 隐藏

secretion *(of liquid)* fēnmì 分泌; *(liquid secreted)* fēnmìwù 分泌物; *(hiding)* cángnì 藏匿

secretive ài bǎomì 爱保密

secretly mìmì 秘密

secret police mìmì jǐngchá 秘密警察

secret service tèwù jīguān 特务机关

sect pàibié 派别

section bùfen 部份

sector bùmén 部门

secular shìsú 世俗

secure 1 *adj shelf etc* láogù 牢固; *feeling* wú yōulǜ 无忧虑; *job, contract* yǒu bǎozhèng 有保证 **2** *v/t shelf etc* gùdìngzhù 固定住; *s.o.'s help, finances* dédào 得到

security *(in job)* bǎozhàng 保障; *(for investment)* bǎozhèng 保证; *(at airport etc)* ānquán 安全; *(department responsible for* ~*)* bǎo'ānbù 保安部; *(of beliefs etc)* wěngù 稳固; *securities* FIN zhèngquàn 证券; *securities market* FIN zhèngquàn shìchǎng 证券市场

security alert ānquán jǐngtì 安全警惕; **security check** ānquán jiǎnchá 安全检查; **security-conscious** yǒu ānquán yìshí 有安全意识; **security forces** bǎo'ān bùduì 保安部队; **security guard** bǎo'ān rényuán 保安人员; **security risk** *(person)* wēixiǎn rénwù 危险人物

sedan xiǎo jiàochē 小轿车

sedative *n* zhènjìngyào 镇静药

sediment chéndiànwù 沉淀物

seduce *(sexually)* gōuyǐn 勾引

seduction *(sexual)* yǐnyòu 引诱

seductive *dress* yòurén 诱人; *offer* yǒu xīyǐnlì 有吸引力

see kànjiàn 看见; *(understand)* míngbái 明白; *I* ~ wǒ míngbái le 我明白了; *can I* ~ *the manager?* wǒ kěyǐ jiàn jīnglǐ ma? 我可以见经理吗？; *you should* ~ *a doctor* nǐ yīnggāi qù kàn yīshēng 你应该去看医生; ~ *X home* sòng X huíjiā 送 X 回家; *I'll* ~ *you to the door* wǒ sòng nǐ dào ménkǒu 我送你到门口; ~ *you!* zàijiàn! 再见！

♦ **see about** *(look into)* chǔlǐ 处理

♦ **see off** *(at airport etc)* sòngxíng 送行; *(chase away)* gǎnpǎo 赶跑

♦ **see out** *see X out (to the door)* sòngsòng X 送送 X

♦ **see to** (*deal with*) chǔlǐ 处理; *~ it that X gets done* wùbì bǎozhèng zuòwán X 务必保证做完 X

seed zhǒngzi 种子; (*in tennis*) zhǒngzi xuǎnshǒu 种子选手; **go to ~** (*of person, district*) shuāibài 衰败

seedling yòumiáo 幼苗

seedy *bar, district* pòjiù 破旧

seeing (*that*) jìrán 既然

seek 1 *v/t employment* xúnzhǎo 寻找; *truth* zhuīqiú 追求 **2** *v/i* tànsuǒ 探索

seem kànqǐlái 看起来; *it ~s that ...* kànqǐlái sìhū ... 看起来似乎 ...

seemingly kànshàngqu 看上去

seep (*of liquid*) lòuchū 漏出

♦ **seep out** (*of liquid*) shènlòu 渗漏

seesaw qiāoqiāobǎn 跷跷板

see-through *dress, material* tòumíng 透明

segment bàn 瓣

segmented língsuì 零碎

segregate gélí 隔离

segregation gélí 隔离

seismology dìzhènxué 地震学

seize *person, arm* zhuāzhù 抓住; *opportunity* bǎwò 把握; (*of customs, police etc*) kòuyā 扣押

♦ **seize up** (*of engine*) qiǎzhù 卡住

seizure MED fāzuò 发作; (*of drugs etc*) kòuyā 扣押

seldom hǎnjiàn 罕见

select 1 *v/t* xuǎnzé 选择 **2** *adj* (*exclusive*) gāojí 高级

selection (*choosing*) xuǎnzé 选择; (*that / those chosen*) xuǎnchūde 选出的; (*assortment*) kě gōng tiāoxuǎn 可供挑选

selection process xuǎnzé guòchéng 选择过程

selective tiāojiǎn 挑拣

self zìjǐ 自己

self-addressed envelope xiě yǒu zìjǐ dìzhǐ de xìnfēng 写有自己地址的信封; **self-assured** yǒu bǎwò 有把握; **self-catering apartment** zìchuī gōngyù 自炊公寓; **self-centered** yǐ zìwǒ wéi zhōngxīn 以自我为中心; **self-**confessed** zìjǐ tǎnbái 自己坦白; **self-confidence** zìxìn 自信; **self-confident** zìxìn 自信; **self-conscious** búzìrán 不自然; **self-contained** *apartment* shèbèi qíquán 设备齐全; **self control** zìzhìlì 自制力; **self-criticism** zìwǒ pīpíng 自我批评; **self-defense** zìwèi 自卫; **self-discipline** zìwǒ yuēshù 自我约束; **self-doubt** zìwǒ kùnhuò 自我困惑; **self-employed** gètǐ 个体; **self-evident** bùyán'éryù 不言而喻; **self-interest** sīlì 私利

selfish zìsī 自私

selfless wúsī 无私

self-made man báishǒuqǐjiāde rén 白手起家的人; **self-possessed** chénzhuó 沉着; **self-reliant** yīkào zìjǐ 依靠自己; **self-respect** zìzūn 自尊; **self-righteous** *pej* zìyǐwéishì 自以为是; **self-satisfied** *pej* zìmíngdéyì 自鸣得意; **self-service** *adj* zìzhùshì 自助式; **self-service restaurant** zìzhù cānguǎn 自助餐馆; **self-study** zìxué 自学

sell 1 *v/t* mài 卖; *you have to ~ yourself* nǐ děi tuīxiāo zìjǐ 你得推销自己 **2** *v/i* (*of products*) xiāoshòu 销售

seller màifāng 卖方

selling *n* COM xiāoshòu 销售

selling point COM shāngpǐn tèsè 商品特色

semen jīngyè 精液

semester xuéqī 学期

semi (*truck*) jiǎojiēchē 铰接车

semicircle bànyuánxíng 半圆形; **semicircular** bànyuánxíng 半圆形; **semiconductor** ELEC bàndǎotǐ 半导体; **semifinal** bànjuésài 半决赛

seminar yántǎohuì 研讨会

semiskilled bànshúliàn 半熟练

senate cānyìyuàn 参议院

senator cānyìyuán 参议员

send *v/t* (*by mail*) yóujì 邮寄; (*by mail, e-mail, fax etc*) fā 发; *~ X to Y* bǎ X yóu fāgěi Y 把 X 邮发给 Y; *~ X to see Y* jiào X qù jiàn Y 叫 X

去见 Y; **~ her my best wishes** xiàng tā wènhǎo 向她问好

♦ **send back** sònghuí 送回; *food in restaurant* tuìhuán 退还

♦ **send for** *doctor*, *help* pàirén qùzhǎo 派人去找

♦ **send in** *troops* pàiqiǎn 派遣; *next interviewee* jiào … jìnqù 叫 … 进去; *application form* jìqù 寄去

♦ **send off** *letter*, *fax etc* fāchū 发出

♦ **send up** (*mock*) qǔxiào 取笑

sender (*of letter*) yóujìrén 邮寄人

senile shuāilǎo 衰老

senility shuāilǎo zhuàngtài 衰老状态

senior (*older*) niánzhǎng 年长; (*in rank*) gāojí 高级; **be ~ to X** (*in rank*) bǐ X zīgé lǎo 比 X 资格老

senior citizen lǎorén 老人

sensation (*feeling*) gǎnjué 感觉; (*surprise event*) hōngdòng 轰动; **be a ~** (*very good*) hěn bàng 很棒

sensational *news*, *discovery* hōngdòng 轰动; (*very good*) juémiào 绝妙

sense 1 *n* (*meaning*) yìyì 意义; (*purpose*, *point*) yìsi 意思; (*common ~*) jiànshi 见识; (*of sight*, *smell etc*) guānnéng 官能; (*feeling*) gǎnjué 感觉; **in a ~** zài mǒuzhǒng yìyì shang 在某种意义上; **talk ~, man!** hēi, shuōdiǎnr yǒu dàoli de huà! 嘿，说点儿有道理的话！; **it doesn't make ~** zhè méi dàolǐ 这没道理; **there's no ~ in trying / waiting** chángshì / děngdài méiyǒu yòng 尝试 / 等待没有用 **2** *v/t s.o.'s presence* yìshídào 意识到

senseless (*pointless*) wú yìyì 无意义

sensible *person*, *decision* míngzhì 明智; *advice* hélǐ 合理

sensitive ~ skin jiāonèn 娇嫩; *person* mǐngǎn 敏感

sensitivity (*of skin*, *person*) mǐngǎnxìng 敏感性

sensual xìnggǎn 性感

sensuality ròuyù 肉欲

sensuous cìjī gǎnguān 刺激感官

sentence 1 *n* GRAM jùzi 句子;

LAW túxíng 徒刑 **2** *v/t* LAW pànxíng 判刑

sentiment (*sentimentality*) róunuò qínggǎn 柔懦情感; (*opinion*) yìjiàn 意见

sentimental shānggǎn 伤感

sentimentality róunuò qíngdiào 柔懦情调

sentry shàobīng 哨兵

separate 1 *adj* dúlì 独立; **keep X ~ from Y** fēnkāi X hé Y 分开 X 和 Y **2** *v/t* fēnkāi 分开; **~ X from Y** bǎ X yǔ Y fēnkāi 把 X 与 Y 分开 **3** *v/i* (*of couple*) fēnjū 分居

separated *couple* fēnshǒu 分手

separately *pay* fēnzhe 分着; *treat*, *deal with* fēnbié 分别

separation fēnlí 分离; (*of couple*) fēnshǒu 分手

September jiǔyuè 九月

septic gǎnrǎn 感染; **go ~** (*of wound*) shòu gǎnrǎn 受感染

sequel xùjí 续集

sequence *n* shùnxù 顺序; **in ~** àn shùnxù 按顺序; **out of ~** bú àn shùnxù 不按顺序; **the ~ of events** shìqíng fāshēng de xiānhòu shùnxù 事情发生的先后顺序

serene níngjìng 宁静

sergeant zhōngshì 中士

serial *n* liánxù gùshi 连续故事

serialize *novel on TV* liánbō 连播

serial killer liánxù shārénfàn 连续杀人犯; **serial number** (*of product*) biānhào 编号; **serial port** COMPUT chuànxíng duānkǒu 串行端口

series (*of numbers*, *events*, *errors*) xìliè 系列

serious *illness*, *situation*, *damage* yánzhòng 严重; (*person: earnest*) rènzhēn 认真; *company* zhèngshì 正式; **I'm ~** wǒ zài shuō zhèngjīngde 我在说正经的; **listen, this is ~** tīngzhe, zhè shì zhèngshìr 听着，这是正事儿; **we'd better take a ~ look at it** wǒmen zuì hǎo hǎohǎo kànyíxià 我们最好好好看一下

seriously *injured*, *understaffed*

yánzhòng 严重; ~ *intend to ...* zhēnde xiǎng 真的想...; ~*?* shuōzhènde ma? 说真的吗？; *take X ~* rènzhēn duìdài X 认真对待 X

sermon jiǎngdào 讲道

servant púrén 仆人

serve 1 *n* (*in tennis*) fāqiú 发球 **2** *v/t food, meal* duānshang 端上; *customer in store* zhāodài 招待; *one's country, the people* fúwù 服务; *it ~s you* / *him right* nǐ / tā zuì yǒu yīngdé 你 / 他罪有应得 **3** *v/i* (*give out food*) shàng cài 上菜; (*as politician etc*) gòngzhí 供职; (*in tennis*) fāqiú 发球

♦**serve up** *meal* tígōng 提供

server (*in tennis*) fāqiúrén 发球人; COMPUT fúwùqì 服务器

service 1 *n* (*to customers, community*) fúwù 服务; (*for vehicle, machine*) wéixiū 维修; (*in tennis*) fāqiú 发球; *the ~s* jūnduì 军队 **2** *v/t vehicle, machine* wéixiū 维修

service area fúwùqū 服务区

service charge (*in restaurant, club*) fúwùfèi 服务费; **service industry** fúwù hángyè 服务行业; **serviceman** MIL jūnrén 军人; **service provider** COMPUT fúwù tígōng zhě 服务提供者; **service sector** fúwù hángyè 服务行业; **service station** jiāyóuzhàn 加油站

sesame oil xiāngyóu 香油

session (*of Congress etc*) huìyì 会议; (*with psychiatrist, consultant etc*) yíduàn shíjiān 一段时间

set 1 *n* (*of tools, books etc*) tào 套; (*group of people*) yìhuǒrén 一伙人; MATH jíhé 集合; THEA: *scenery* bùjǐng 布景; (*where a movie is made*) pāishè chǎngdì 拍摄场地; (*in tennis*) pán 盘; *television ~* diànshì jī 电视机 **2** *v/t* (*place*) fàng 放; *movie, novel etc* yǐ ... wéi bèijǐng 以 ... 为背景; *date, time, limit* dìng 定; *mechanism* tiáozhěng 调整; *alarm clock* tiáohé 调合; *broken limb* jiēhǎo 接好; *jewel* xiāngqiàn 镶嵌; (*type~*) páibǎn 排

版; ~ *the table* bǎifàng cānjù 摆放餐具; ~ *a task for X* gěi X yígè rènwù 给 X 一个任务 **3** *v/i* (*of sun*) luò 落; (*of glue*) níngjié 凝结 **4** *adj views, ideas* wángù 顽固; *be dead ~ on X* jiānjué zuò X 坚决做 X; *be very ~ in one's ways* yìchéng búbiàn 一成不变; ~ *book* / *reading* (*in course*) zhǐdìng jiàocái / yuèdú cáiliào 指定教材 / 阅读材料; ~ *meal* dìngcān 定餐

♦**set apart** *set X apart from Y* shǐ X yǔ Y bùtóng 使 X 与 Y 不同

♦**set aside** (*for future use*) bōchū 拨出

♦**set back** (*in plans etc*) zǔài jìnchéng 阻碍进程; *it set me back $400* huāle wǒ sìbǎi měiyuán 花了我四百美元

♦**set off 1** *v/i* (*on journey*) chūfā 出发 **2** *v/t explosion, chain reaction* dǎozhì 导致

♦**set out 1** *v/i* (*on journey*) chūfā 出发; ~ *to do X* (*intend*) yǒu mùdì de zuò X 有目的地做 X **2** *v/t ideas, proposal* chénshù 陈述; *goods* bǎifàng 摆放

♦**set to** (*start on a task*) kāishǐ gàn 开始干

♦**set up 1** *v/t new company* chénglì 成立; *system* jiànlì 建立; *equipment, machine* zhuāngpèi 装配; *market stall* shèlì 设立; F (*frame*) shè quāntào 设圈套 **2** *v/i* (*in business*) chénglì 成立

setback zǔài 阻碍

setting (*of novel etc*) bèijǐng 背景; (*of house*) huánjìng 环境

settle 1 *v/i* (*of liquid*) chéngqīng 澄清; (*of dust*) xiàchén 下沉; (*to live*) dìngjū 定居; (*of bird*) tíngxiē 停歇 **2** *v/t dispute, issue* jiějué 解决; *s.o.'s debts* chánghuán 偿还; *check* jiésuàn 结算; *that ~s it!* nà jiù dìng le! 那就定了！

♦**settle down** *v/i* (*stop being noisy*) ānjìng 安静; (*stop wild living*) āndìng xiàlái 安定下来; (*in an area*) dìngjū 定居

♦**settle for** (*take, accept*) miǎnqiǎng rènkě 勉强认可

settlement (*of claim, debt*) qīngcháng 清偿;(*of dispute*) jiějué 解决;(*payment*) chángfù 偿付

settler (*in new country*) zhímín zhě 殖民者

set-up (*structure*) xìtǒng 系统;(*relationship*) guānxi 关系;F (*frameup*) kēnghài 坑害

seven qī 七

seventeen shíqī 十七

seventeenth dìshíqī 第十七

seventh dìqī 第七

seventieth dìqīshí 第七十

seventy qīshí 七十

sever *v/t arm, cable etc* qiēduàn 切断; *relations* zhōngduàn 中断

several *adj & pron* jǐgè 几个

severe *illness, penalty* yánzhòng 严重; *teacher, face* yánlì 严厉; *winter, weather* èliè 恶劣

severely *punish* yánlì 严厉; *speak, stare* kèkè 刻刻; *injured, disrupted* yánzhòng 严重

severity (*of illness, penalty*) yánzhòng 严重;(*of look etc*) yánsù 严肃

sew 1 *v/t* féng 缝 **2** *v/i* féngrèn 缝纫

♦**sew on** *button* féngshang 缝上

sewage wūwù 污物

sewage plant wūwù chǔlǐchǎng 污物处理场

sewer wūshuǐguǎn 污水管

sewing (*skill*) féngrèn 缝纫;(*that being sewn*) xiànhuózhēni 针线活

sewing machine féngrènjī 缝纫机

sex (*act*) xìngjiāo 性交;(*gender*) xìngbié 性别; *have ~ with X* yǔ X xìngjiāo 与 X 性交

sexual xìng fāngmiàn 性方面

sexual intercourse xìngjiāo 性交

sexually transmitted disease xìng chuánbō jíbìng 性传播疾病

sexy xìnggǎn 性感

SEZ (= *special economic zone*) jīngjì tèqū 经济特区

shabby *coat etc* hánsuān 寒酸; *treatment* bù gōngpíng 不公平

shack péngzi 棚子

shade 1 *n* (*for lamp*) dēngzhào 灯罩;(*of color*) sèdù 色度;(*on window*) liánzi 帘子; *in the ~* yīnliángchù 阴凉处 **2** *v/t* (*from sun, light*) zhēbì 遮蔽

shadow *n* yǐngzi 影子

shady *spot* yīnliáng 阴凉; *character, dealings* kàobúzhù 靠不住

shaft (*of axle*) zhóu 轴;(*of mine*) kuàngjǐng 矿井

shaggy *hair, dog* cūnóng péngsōng 粗浓蓬松

shake 1 *n: give X a good ~* bǎ X hǎohǎo yáohuàng yíxià 把 X 好好摇晃一下 **2** *v/t* yáo 摇; *~ hands* wòshǒu 握手; *~ hands with X* yǔ X wòshǒu 与 X 握手; *~ one's head* yáotóu 摇头 **3** *v/i* (*of hands, voice*) chàndǒu 颤抖;(*of building*) huàngdòng 晃动

shaken (*emotionally*) fādǒu 发抖

shake-up chóngzǔ 重组

shaky *table etc* yáohuàng 摇晃;(*after illness, shock*) ruò弱; *grasp of sth, grammar etc* bù zhāshí 不扎实

shall: *I ~ do my best* wǒ jiāng jìnwǒsuǒnéng 我将尽我所能; *~ we go now?* wǒmen xiànzài zǒuba? 我们现在走吧？

shallow *water* qiǎn 浅; *person* qiǎnbó 浅薄

shallow fry jiān 煎

shame 1 *n* xiūchǐ 羞耻; *bring ~ on X* gěi X dàilái chǐrǔ 给 X 带来耻辱; *what a ~!* zhēn yíhàn! 真遗憾！; *~ on you!* zhēn kěchǐ! 真可耻！ **2** *v/t* shǐ diūliǎn 使丢脸; *~ X into doing Y* shǐ X gǎndào xiūkuì ér zuò Y 使 X 感到羞愧而做 Y

shameful bù tǐmiàn 不体面

shameless bú yào liǎn 不要脸

shampoo 1 *n* xǐfàjīng 洗发精; *a ~ and set* xǐ tóufa bìng zuò tóufa 洗头发并做头发 **2** *v/t* gěirén xǐtóufa 给人洗头发

Shandong Peninsula Shāndōng Bàndǎo 山东半岛

Shanghai Shànghǎi 上海

shape 1 *n* xíngzhuàng 形状 **2** *v/t clay, s.o.'s life* sùzào 塑造; *the* *future* cùchéng 促成

shapeless *dress etc* wú dìngxíng 无定形

shapely *figure* yúnchèn 匀称

share 1 *n* yífèn 一份; FIN gǔfèn 股份; **do one's ~ of the work** zuò yīngzuòde gōngzuò 做应做的工作 **2** *v/t* fēnxiǎng 分享; *s.o.'s feelings, opinions* gòngtóng jùyǒu 共同具有 **3** *v/i* fēnxiǎng 分享; **do you mind sharing with Patrick?** (*bed, room, table*) nǐ yǔ Pàtèlǐkè gòngyòng hǎoma? 你与帕特里克共用好吗?

♦ **share out** píngfēn 平分

shareholder gǔdōng 股东

shark shā 鲨

sharp 1 *adj knife* fēnglì 锋利; *mind* língmǐn 灵敏; *pain* jùliè 剧烈; *taste* xīnlà 辛辣 **2** *adv* MUS piāngāo 偏高; **at 3 o'clock ~** sāndiǎn zhěng 三点整

sharpen *knife* shǐ fēnglì 使锋利; *skills* tígāo 提高

sharp practise bēibǐ jiāoyì 卑鄙交易

shatter 1 *v/t glass* fěnsuì 粉碎; *illusions* pòmiè 破灭 **2** *v/i* (*of glass*) dǎsuì 打碎

shattered F (*exhausted*) jīnpílìjìn 筋疲力尽; (*very upset*) fēicháng nánguò 非常难过

shattering *news, experience* lìngrén zhènjīng 令人震惊; *effect* lìngrén jīngtàn 令人惊叹

shave 1 *v/t* guā 刮 **2** *v/i* guāliǎn 刮脸 **3** *n:* **have a ~** guāliǎn 刮脸; **that was a close ~** nà zhēnshì jiāoxìng tuōxiǎn 那真是侥幸脱险

♦ **shave off** *beard* guādiào 刮掉; (*from piece of wood*) bàoqù yìcéng 刨去一层

shaven *head* tìguāng 剃光

shaver (*electric*) tìdāo 剃刀

shaving brush húshuā 胡刷

shaving soap tìxūgāo 剃须膏

shawl pījiān 披肩

she tā 她

shears dàjiǎndāo 大剪刀

sheath *n* (*for knife*) qiào 鞘;

shed[1] *v/t blood, tears* liú 流; *leaves* tuōluò 脱落; **~ light on X** *fig* shǐ X gèng qīngchǔ xiē 使X更清楚些

shed[2] *n* péng 棚

sheep miányáng 绵羊

sheepdog mùyángquǎn 牧羊犬

sheepish xiūqiè 羞怯

sheepskin *adj lining* yángpí 羊皮

sheer *adj madness, luxury* shízú 十足; *drop, cliffs* jìnhū chuízhí 近乎垂直

sheet (*for bed*) chuángdān 床单; (*of paper*) zhāng 张; (*of metal, glass*) bǎn 板

shelf jià 架; **shelves** jià 架

shell 1 *n* (*of mussel, egg, tortoise etc*) ké 壳; MIL pàodàn 炮弹; **come out of one's ~** *fig* búzài xiūqiè 不再羞怯 **2** *v/t peas* bāoké 剥壳; MIL pàojī 炮击

shellfire pàohuǒ 炮火; **come under ~** zāodào pàohuǒ xíjī 遭到炮火袭击

shellfish bèilèi 贝类

shelter 1 *n* (*refuge*) bìhù 庇护; (*construction*) yǎnbìwù 掩蔽物 **2** *v/i* (*from rain, bombing etc*) duǒbì 躲避 **3** *v/t* (*protect*) bǎohù 保护

sheltered *place* kě bì fēngyǔ 可避风雨; **lead a ~ life** guòzhe wúyōuwúlǜde shēnghuó 过着无忧无虑的生活

shepherd *n* mùyángrén 牧羊人

sherry xuělìjiǔ 雪利酒

shield 1 *n* dùn 盾; (*sports trophy*) dùnxíng jǐnbiāo 盾形锦标; TECH hùbǎn 护板 **2** *v/t* (*protect*) bǎohù 保护

shift 1 *n* (*in attitude, thinking*) gǎibiàn 改变; (*switchover*) zhuǎnbiàn 转变; (*in direction of wind etc*) zhuǎnxiàng 转向; (*period of work*) bān 班 **2** *v/t* (*move*) yídòng 移动; *stains etc* nòngdiào 弄掉; **~ the emphasis onto** bǎ zhòngdiǎn zhuǎnyídào 把重点转移到 **3** *v/i* (*move*) nuódòng 挪动; (*in attitude, opinion*) gǎibiàn 改变; (*of wind*) zhuǎnbiàn 转变; **that's ~ing!** F tàikuàile! 太快了!

shift key COMPUT huàndǎngjiàn 换档键

shift work lúnbānde gōngzuò 轮班的工作

shifty pej bū duì jìnr 不对劲儿

shifty-looking pej guǐgui suìsui 鬼鬼祟祟

shimmer v/i fā shǎnshuò de wēiguāng 发闪烁的微光

shin n jìngbù 胫部

shine 1 v/i (of sun, moon) zhàoyào 照耀; (of shoes, polish) fāguāng 发光; fig (of student etc) chūzhòng 出众 2 v/t flashlight etc zhàoyīzhào 照一照 3 n (on shoes etc) guāngzé 光泽

shingle (on beach) hǎibīn shāshí 海滨砂石

shingles MED dàizhuàng pàozhěn 带状疱疹

shiny surface fāliàng 发亮

ship 1 n chuán 船 2 v/t (send) yùnsòng 运送; (send by sea) hǎiyùn 海运

shipment (consignment) huòwù 货物

shipowner chuánzhǔ 船主

shipping (sea traffic) chuánbó 船舶; (sending) yùnsòng 运送; (sending by sea) hǎiyùn 海运

shipping company yùnshū gōngsī 运输公司

shipshape adj zhěngqí 整齐;
shipwreck 1 n hǎinàn 海难 2 v/t shǐ rén zāoyù hǎinàn 使人遭遇海难; **be ~ed** yù hǎinàn 遇海难;
shipyard zàochuánchǎng 造船厂

shirk táobì 逃避

shirt chènshān 衬衫; **in his ~ sleeves** tā chuānzhe chènshān, méi chuān wàiyī 他穿着衬衫，没穿外衣

shit F n shǐ 屎; (bad quality goods, work) gǒushǐ bùrú 狗屎不如; **I need a ~** wǒ děi qù lāshǐ 我得去拉屎 2 v/i lāshǐ 拉屎 3 interj māde 妈的

shitty F zāogāo 糟糕

shiver v/i chàndǒu 颤抖

shock 1 n zhènjīng 震惊; ELEC chùdiàn 触电; **be in ~** MED chǔyú

xiūkè zhuàngtài 处于休克状态 2 v/t shǐrén zhènjīng 使人震惊; **be ~ed by X** bèi X xià le yítiào 被 X 吓了一跳

shock absorber MOT jiǎnzhènqì 减震器

shocking behavior, poverty lìngrén zhènjīng 令人震惊; F (very bad) hěn zāo 很糟

shoddy goods lièzhì 劣质; behavior bēiliè 卑劣

shoe xié 鞋

shoelace xiédài 鞋带; **shoestore** xiédiàn 鞋店; **shoestring: do X on a ~** yòng jíshǎo de qián zuò X 用极少的钱做 X

♦**shoo away** children, chicken fā xūshēng gǎnzǒu 发嘘声赶走

shoot 1 n BOT nènyá 嫩芽 2 v/t shèzhòng 射中; (and kill) qiāngbì 枪毙; movie pāishè 拍摄; **~ X in the leg** X tuǐshang zhòngle yídàn X 腿上中了一弹

♦**shoot down** airplane jīluò 击落; suggestion bódǎo 驳倒

♦**shoot off** (rush off) pǎodiào 跑掉

♦**shoot up** (of prices) xùnsù shàngshēng 迅速上升; (of children) zhǎnggāo 长高; (of new suburbs, buildings etc) xùnsù jiànqǐ 迅速建起

shooting star liúxīng 流星

shop 1 n shāngdiàn 商店; **talk ~** shuō hánghuà 说行话 2 v/i mǎi dōngxi 买东西; **go ~ping** qù mǎi dōngxi 去买东西

shopkeeper diànzhǔ 店主

shoplifter rùdiàn xíngqiè 入店行窃

shopper gòuwùrén 购物人

shopping (activity) gòuwù 购物; (items) mǎidào de dōngxi 买到的东西; **do one's ~** gòuwù 购物

shopping mall gòuwù zhōngxīn 购物中心

shop steward gōnghuì fāyánrén 工会发言人

shore àn 岸; **on ~** (not at sea) ànshang 岸上

short 1 adj (in height) ǎi 矮; road,

distance, time duǎn 短; **be ~ of** quēfá 缺乏 **2** *adv*: **cut a vacation / meeting ~** suōduǎn jiàqī / huìyì 缩短假期 / 会议; **stop a person ~** shǐrén de tánhuà gārán ér zhǐ 使人的谈话嘎然而止; **go ~ of** qiànquē 欠缺; **in ~** jiǎn ér yánzhī 简而言之

shortage quēfá 缺乏

short circuit *n* duǎnlù 短路; **shortcoming** quēdiǎn 缺点; **short cut** jiéjìng 捷径

shorten *v/t* *dress, hair etc* nòngduǎn 弄短; *chapter, article* biànduǎn 变短; *vacation, work day* suōduǎn 缩短

shortfall chìzì 赤字; **shorthand** *n* sùjì 速记; **shortlist** *n* (*of candidates*) juéxuǎn 决选; **short-lived** duǎnzàn 短暂

shortly (*soon*) bùjiǔ 不久; **~ before that** jiù zài nà yǐqián 就在那以前

shorts duǎnkù 短裤; (*underwear for men*) sānjiǎo kù 三角裤

shortsighted jìnshi 近视; *fig* wú yuǎnjiàn 无远见; **short-sleeved** duǎnxiù 短袖; **short-staffed** rényuán bùzú 人员不足; **short story** duǎnpiān xiǎoshuō 短篇小说; **short-tempered** ài fā píqì 爱发脾气; **short-term** duǎnqī 短期; **short time**: **be on ~** (*of workers*) chǔyú duāngōng shíqī 处于短工时期; **short wave** duǎnbō 短波

shot (*from gun*) shèjīshēng 射击声; (*photograph*) jìngtóu 镜头; (*injection*) zhùshè 注射; **be a good / poor ~** hǎo / chàjìn de shèshǒu 好 / 差劲的射手; **like a ~** *accept, run off* háobùyóuyù 毫不犹豫; **in one ~** *drink, write etc* yíxiàzi 一下子

shotgun lièqiāng 猎枪

should yīnggāi 应该; **what ~ I do?** wǒ gāi zuò shénme? 我该做什么?; **you ~n't do that** nǐ bù yīnggāi nàme zuò 你不应该那么做; **that ~ be long enough** nà yīnggāi gòucháng le 那应该够长

了; **you ~ have heard him!** nǐ zhēn yīnggāi tīngtīng tā shuōde! 你真应该听听他说的!

shoulder *n* jiānbǎng 肩膀

shoulder blade jiānjiǎgǔ 肩胛骨

shout 1 *n* hǎnshēng 喊声 **2** *v/i* jiàohǎn 叫喊 **3** *v/t* *order* mìnglìng 命令

♦**shout at** duì ... hǎn 对 ... 喊

shouting *n* hǎnjiào 喊叫

shove 1 *n* zhuàng 撞 **2** *v/t* bān 搬 **3** *v/i* jǐ 挤

♦**shove in** *v/i* (*in line-up*) jiāxiēr 加楔儿

♦**shove off** *v/i* F (*go away*) zǒukāi 走开

shovel *n* tiěqiāo 铁锹

show 1 *n* THEA, TV jiémù 节目; (*display*) biǎolù 表露; **on ~** (*at exhibition*) zài zhǎnlǎn 在展览; **it's all done for ~** *pej* dōu shì wèi gěi biérén kàn de 都是为给别人看的 **2** *v/t* *passport, ticket* chūshì 出示; *interest, emotion* biǎodá 表达; (*at exhibition*) zhǎnshì 展示; *movie* diànyǐng 电影; **~ X to Y** bǎ X gěi Y kàn 把 X 给 Y 看 **3** *v/i* (*be visible*) kàndejiàn 看得见; (*of movie*) shàngyìng 上映; **does it ~?** néng kànchūlái ma? 能看出来吗?

♦**show off 1** *v/t skills* zhǎnshì 展示 **2** *v/i pej* xuànyào 炫耀

♦**show up 1** *v/t s.o.'s shortcomings etc* xiǎnxiànchū 显现出; **don't show me up in public** (*embarrass*) bié dāngzhòng ràng wǒ chūchǒu 别当众让我出丑 **2** *v/i* (*arrive, turn up*) dàolái 到来; (*be visible*) kàndejiàn 看得见

show business yǎnyìjiè 演艺界

showdown zuìhòu jiàoliàng 最后较量

shower 1 *n* (*of rain*) zhènyǔ 阵雨; (*to wash*) línyù 淋; **take a ~** línyù 淋浴 **2** *v/i* línyù 淋浴 **3** *v/t*: **~ X with compliments / praise** jiélì zànshǎng / biǎoyáng X 竭力赞赏 / 表扬 X

shower bath línyù 淋浴; **shower cap** yùmào 浴帽; **shower**

curtain línyùlián 淋浴帘；
  showerproof *adj* fángyǔ 防雨
show jumping mǎpí zhàng'ài
  yùndòng 马匹障碍运动
show-off ài xuányào de rén 爱炫
  耀的人
showroom shāngpǐn chénlièshì 商
  品陈列室
showy *jacket, behavior* kuāyào 夸
  耀
shred 1 *n* (*of paper etc*) suìpiàn 碎
  片；(*of evidence etc*) sīháo 丝毫
  2 *v/t paper* sīchéng suìpiàn 撕成
  碎片；(*in cooking*) qiēchéng
  xiǎotiáo 切成小条
shredder (*for documents*) qiēsuìjī
  切碎机
shrewd jīngmíng 精明
shriek 1 *n* jiānjiào 尖叫 **2** *v/i*
  jiānshēng shuōchū 尖声说出
shrimp xiǎoxiā 小虾
shrine shénkān 神龛
shrink *v/i* (*of material*) suōshuǐ 缩
  水；(*of level of support etc*) jiǎnruò
  减弱
shrink-wrap sùmó bāozhuāng 塑
  膜包装
shrink-wrapping (*process*) sùmó
  bāozhuāng 塑膜包装；(*material*)
  sùmó 塑膜
shrivel wěisuō 萎缩
shrub guànmù 灌木
shrubbery guànmùcóng 灌木丛
shrug 1 *n* sǒngjiān 耸肩；*he gave
  a ~ and left* tā sǒnglesǒng jiān jiù
  zǒule 他耸了耸肩就走了 **2** *v/i*
  sǒngjiān 耸肩 **3** *v/t:* **~ one's
  shoulders** sǒngjiān 耸肩
shudder 1 *n* (*of fear, disgust*) fādǒu
  发抖；(*of earth etc*) zhèndòng 震
  动 **2** *v/i* (*with fear, disgust*) fādǒu
  发抖；(*of earth, building*)
  zhèndòng 震动
shuffle 1 *v/t cards* xǐ 洗 **2** *v/i* (*in
  walking*) jiǎo cèng dì 脚蹭地
shun duǒbì 躲避
shut 1 *v/t* guān 关 **2** *v/i* guān 关；
  they were ~ tāmen yǐjīng guānle
  他们已经关了
♦**shut down 1** *v/t business* tíngyè
  停业；*computer* guānjī 关机 **2** *v/i*

(*of business*) guānbì 关闭；(*of
  computer*) guānjī 关机
♦**shut up** *v/i* (*be quiet*) ānjìng 安
  静；*~!* zhùzuǐ! 住嘴！
shutter (*on window*) chuāngbǎn 窗
  板；PHOT kuàiménr 快门儿
shuttle *v/i* chuānsuō 穿梭
shuttlebus (*at airport*) chuānsuō
  yíngyùn 穿梭营运；**shuttlecock**
  SP yǔmáo qiú 羽毛球；**shuttle
  service** chuānsuō yèwù 穿梭业
  务
shy hàixiū 害羞
shyness miǎntiǎn 腼腆
Siamese twins liántǐ shuāngbāotāi 连体双胞胎
Sichuan Basin Sìchuān Péndì 四
  川盆地
sick shēngbìng 生病；*sense of
  humor* cánkù 残酷；*society* bìngtài
  病态；*I feel ~* (*about to vomit*) wǒ
  gǎndào ěxīn 我感到恶心；*I'm
  going to be ~* (*vomit*) wǒ yào tù 我
  要吐；*be ~ of* (*fed up with*)
  gǎndào yànwù 感到厌恶
sicken 1 *v/t* (*disgust*) shǐrén gǎndào
  yànwù 使人感到厌恶 **2** *v/i:* **be
  ~ing for** déle … bìng 得了 … 病
sickening *adj* lìngrén yànwù 令人
  厌恶
sickle liándāo 镰刀
sick leave bìngjià 病假；*be on ~*
  xiū bìngjià 休病假
sickly *person* duōbìng 多病；*color*
  bú jiànkāng 不健康
sickness jíbìng 疾病；(*vomiting*)
  ǒutù 呕吐
side *n* (*of box, house*) cèmiàn 侧面；
  (*of room, field*) biān 边；(*of
  mountain*) miàn 面；(*of person*) lèi
  肋；SP yìfāng 一方；*take ~s* (*favor
  one side*) piānxiàng 偏向；*take ~s
  with* zhīchí 支持；*I'm on your ~*
  wǒ zhīchí nǐ 我支持你；*~ by ~*
  bìngpái 并排；*at the ~ of the
  road* zài lùbiān 在路边；*on the
  big / small ~* piān dà / xiǎo 偏大 /
  小
♦**side with** zhīchí 支持
sideboard (*furniture*) cānjùguì 餐
  具柜；**sideburns** liánbìn húzi 连

鬓胡子；**side dish** xiǎocài 小菜；

side effect fùzuòyòng 副作用；

sidelight MOT cèdēng 侧灯；

sideline 1 *n* fùyè 副业 **2** *v/t*: **feel ~d** gǎndào bèi hūshì 感到被忽视；**side street** xiǎoxiàng 小巷；

sidetrack *v/t* chàkāi 岔开；**get ~ed** bèi chàkāi 被岔开；**sidewalk** xíngréndào 人行道；**sidewalk café** lùbiān kāfēiguǎn 路边咖啡馆；**sideways** *adv* xiézhe 斜着

siege wéikùn 围困；**lay ~ to** bāowéi 包围

sieve *n* shāizi 筛子

sift *v/t corn, ore* shāi 筛

♦ **sift through** *details, data* xìshěn 细审

sigh 1 *n* tànxī 叹息；**heave a ~ of relief** sōng yìkǒu qì 松一口气 **2** *v/i* tànqì 叹气

sight *n* qíngjǐng 情景；(*power of seeing*) shìlì 视力；**~s** (*of city*) míngshèng 名胜；**catch ~ of** kànjiàn 看见；**know by ~** miànshú 面熟；**within ~ of X** zài X shìyě zhī nèi 在 X 视野之内；**out of ~** zài shìchéng zhī wài 在视程之外；*fig* F gàilemàole 盖了帽了；**what a ~ you are!** kàn nǐ shì shénme xíngxiàng! 看你是什么形象！；**lose ~ of** *objective etc* hūlüè 忽略

sightseeing guānguāng 观光；**go ~** qù guānguāng 去观光

sightseeing tour guānguāng lǚyóu 观光旅游

sightseer guānguāngkè 观光客

sign 1 *n* (*indication*) jìxiàng 迹象；(*road ~*) zhǐshìpái 指示牌；(*outside store, on building*) zhāopai 招牌；**it's a ~ of the times** shídàide biāozhì 时代的标志 **2** *v/t & v/i* qiānzì 签字

♦ **sign up** *v/i* (*join the army*) yìngzhēng 应征

signal 1 *n* xìnhào 信号；**be sending out all the right / wrong ~s** fāchū zhèngquè / cuòwù de ànshì 发出正确／错误的暗示 **2** *v/i* (*of driver*) zhǐshì 指示

signatory qiānyuēfāng 签约方

signature qiānmíng 签名

signature tune kāishǐqǔ 开始曲

significance (*importance*) zhòngyàoxìng 重要性；(*meaning*) yìyì 意义

significant *event etc* zhòngyào 重要；(*quite large*) dàliàng 大量

signify yìwèi 意味

sign language shǒushì yǔyán 手势语言

signpost lùbiāo 路标

silence 1 *n* chénmò 沉默；**in ~ work, march** ānjìng 安静；**~!** sùjìng! 肃静！ **2** *v/t* yāzhì 压制

silencer (*on gun*) xiāoyīnqì 消音器

silent ānjìng 安静；*movie* wúshēng 无声；**stay ~** (*not comment*) yīshēng bùkēng 一声不吭

silent partner bùrù shíyè de gǔdōng 不入实业的股东

silhouette *n* lúnkuò 轮廓

silicon ⇩ guī 硅

silicon chip ⇩ guīpiàn 硅片

silk 1 *n* sīchóu 丝绸 **2** *adj shirt etc* sīzhì 丝制

Silk Road Sīchóu zhī lù 丝绸之路

silly shǎ 傻

silver 1 *n* yín 银；(**~ medal**) yínpái 银牌 **2** *adj ring* yínzhì 银制；*hair* huībái 灰白

silver-plated dùyín 镀银

similar xiāngsì 相似

similarity xiāngsì 相似

simmer *v/i* (*in cooking*) dùn 炖；(*with rage*) yíchùjífā 一触即发

♦ **simmer down** ānjìngxiàlái 安静下来

simple (*easy*) jiǎndān 简单；*person* tóunǎo jiǎndān 头脑简单

simplicity jiǎndān 简单

simplified characters jiǎntǐzì 简体字

simplify shǐ jiǎndān 使简单

simplistic guòyú jiǎndānhuà 过于简单化

simply (*absolutely*) juéduì 绝对；(*in a simple way*) jiǎndān 简单；**it is ~ the best** jiǎnzhí shì zuìhǎode 简直是最好的

simulate mónǐ 摹拟

simultaneous tóngshí 同时

simultaneously tóngshí 同时

sin **1** *n* zuì'è 罪恶 **2** *v/i* fànyǒu zuì'è 犯有罪恶

since **1** *prep* zìcóng 自从; **~ last week** zìcóng shàngzhōu yǐlái 自从上周以来 **2** *adv* zìnà yǐhòu 自那以后; *I haven't seen him ~* zìnà yǐhòu, wǒ zài méi jiànguò tā 自那以后，我再没见过他 **3** *conj* (*expressions of time*) cóng … yǐlái 从 … 以来; (*seeing that*) jìrán 既然; **~ you left** zìcóng nǐ zǒu yǐhòu 自从你走以后; *~ you don't like it* jìrán nǐ bù xǐhuan 既然你不喜欢

sincere chéngzhì 诚挚

sincerely chéngzhì 诚挚; *hope* zhēnchéng 真诚; *Yours ~* jǐnqǐ 谨启

sincerity zhēnchéng 真诚

sinful xié'è 邪恶

sing chàng 唱

Singapore Xīnjiāpō 新加坡

Singaporean **1** *adj* Xīnjiāpō 新加坡 **2** *n* (*person*) Xīnjiāpō rén 新加坡人

singe *v/t* shāojiāo 烧焦

singer gēshǒu 歌手

single **1** *n* (*sole*) wéiyī 唯一; (*not double*) yígè 一个; (*not married*) dúshēn 独身; *there wasn't a ~ …* yígè … dōu méiyǒu 一个 … 都没有; *in ~ file* chéngdānháng 成单行 **2** *n* MUS dānqǔ chàngpiàn 单曲唱片; *~s* (*in tennis*) dāndǎ 单打

♦single out (*choose*) tiāochū 挑出; (*distinguish*) shǐrén chūzhòng 使人出众

single-breasted dānpáikòu 单排扣; single-handed **1** *adj* dānqiāng pīmǎ 单枪匹马 **2** *adv* dúzì 独自; single-minded zhuānxīnzhìzhì 专心致志; single mother dānshēn mǔqīn 单身母亲; single parent dānqīn 单亲; single parent family dānqīn jiātíng 单亲家庭

singular GRAM **1** *adj* dānshù 单数 **2** *n* dānshù xíngshì 单数形式; *in*

the ~ dānshù xíngshì 单数形式

sinister xié'è 邪恶

sink **1** *n* xǐdícáo 洗涤槽 **2** *v/i* (*of ship, object*) chénmò 沉没; (*of sun*) luòxià 落下; (*of interest rates, pressure etc*) xiàjiàng 下降; *he sank onto the bed* tā zāidǎo zài chuáng shàng 他栽倒在床上 **3** *v/t ship* chénmò 沉没; *funds* xiàjiàng 下降

♦sink in *v/i* (*of liquid*) shènrù 渗入; *it still hasn't really sunk in* (*of realization*) háishì méiyǒu zhēnzhèng yìshí dào 还是没有真正意识到

sinner zuìrén 罪人

Sino- Zhōng- 中

Sino-Japanese war Zhōng Rì Zhànzhēng 中日战争

sinologist Hànxuéjiā 汉学家

sinology Hànxué 汉学

Sino-Tibetan Hàn Zàng 汉藏

sinusitis MED dòuyán 窦炎

sip **1** *n* yìxiǎokǒu 一小口 **2** *v/t* xiǎokǒu hē 小口喝

sir xiānsheng 先生

siren bàojǐngqì 报警器

sirloin niúyāoròu 牛腰肉

sister (*older*) jiějie 姐姐; (*younger*) mèimei 妹妹

sister-in-law (*wife's elder sister*) qīzǐ 妻姊; (*wife's younger sister*) qīmèi 妻妹; (*husband's elder sister*) dàgūjiě 大姑姐; (*husband's younger sister*) xiǎogū 小姑; (*younger brother's wife*) dìmèi 弟妹; (*older brother's wife*) sǎozi 嫂子

sit *v/i* zuò 坐

♦sit down zuòxia 坐下

♦sit up (*in bed*) zuòqǐlái 坐起来; (*straighten back*) zuòzhí 坐直; (*wait up at night*) áoyè 熬夜

sitcom TV qíngjǐng xǐjù 情景喜剧

site **1** *n* chǎngdì 场地 **2** *v/t new offices etc* zédìng wèizhi 择定位置

sitting (*of committee, court*) kāitíng 开庭; (*for artist*) gōngrén huàxiàng huò pāizhào de shíjiān 供人

画像或拍照的时间; (for meals) shíjiānduàn 时间段

sitting room kètīng 客厅

situated: be ~ zuòluòzài 坐落在

situation xíngshì 形势; (of building etc) wèizhi 位置

six liù 六

sixteen shíliù 十六

sixteenth dìshíliù 第十六

sixth dìliù 第六

sixtieth dìliùshí 第六十

sixty liùshí 六十

size dàxiǎo 大小; (of jacket, shoes) hàomǎ 号码

♦**size up** gūliáng 估量

sizeable xiāngdāng dà 相当大

sizzle fā sīsī shēng 发咝咝声

skate 1 n (for ice) huábīng 滑冰; (roller skate) huá hànbīng 滑旱冰 **2** v/i (on ice) huábīng 滑冰; (roller skating) huá hànbīng 滑旱冰

skateboard n huábǎn 滑板

skater huábīngrén 滑冰人

skating huábīng 滑冰

skeleton kūlóu 骷髅

skeleton key wànnéng yàoshi 万能钥匙

skeptic huáiyílùn zhě 怀疑论者

skeptical huáiyí 怀疑

skepticism huáiyí tàidù 怀疑态度

sketch 1 n cǎotú 草图; THEA huájī duǎnjù 滑稽短剧 **2** v/t xiěshēng 写生

sketchbook sùmiáobù 素描簿

sketchy knowledge etc fúqiǎn 肤浅

ski n & v/i huáxuě 滑雪

skid 1 n shāchē 刹车 **2** v/i dǎhuá 打滑

skier huáxuě zhě 滑雪者

skiing huáxuě 滑雪

ski lift diàosuǒ yùnshūchē 吊索运输车

skill jìqiǎo 技巧

skilled yǒujìnéng 有技能

skilled worker jìgōng 技工

skillful shúliàn 熟练

skim surface lüèguò 掠过; milk piēqù 撇去

♦**skim off** the best tíqǔ 提取

♦**skim through** text liúlǎn 浏览

skimmed milk tuōzhīrǔ 脱脂乳

skimpy account etc qùfá 缺乏; little dress bàolù 暴露

skin 1 n pífū 皮肤 **2** v/t qùpí 去皮

skin diving qiányóu yùndòng 潜游运动

skinny píbāogǔ 皮包骨

skin-tight jǐnshēn 紧身

skip 1 n (little jump) bèng 蹦 **2** v/t (omit) lüèguò 略过

ski pole huáxuězhàng 滑雪杖

skipper NAUT chuánzhǎng 船长; (of team) duìzhǎng 队长

skirt n qúnzi 裙子

ski run huáxuědào 滑雪道

ski tow diàosuǒ yùnshūchē 吊索运输车

skull tóulúgǔ 头颅骨

sky tiānkōng 天空

skylight tiānchuāng 天窗; **skyline** kōngzhōng lúnkuò xiàn 空中轮廓线; **skyscraper** mótiāndàlóu 摩天大楼

slab (of stone) hòubǎn 厚板; (of cake etc) yídàkuài 一大块

slack rope sōngchí 松驰; discipline xièdài 懈怠; person bùrènzhēn 不认真; work cūxīn 粗心; period qīngdàn 清谈

slacken v/t rope sōngchí 松驰; pace fàngmàn 放慢

♦**slacken off** v/i (of trading) jiǎnhuǎn 减缓; (of pace) fàngmàn 放慢

slacks kuānsōng kù 宽松裤

slam 1 v/t door pēngde guānshang 砰地关上 **2** v/i (of door etc) fāchū pēngshēng 发出砰声

♦**slam down** shuāi 摔

slander n & v/t fěibàng 诽谤

slang lǐyǔ 俚语; (of a specific group) hánghuà 行话

slant 1 v/i qīngxié 倾斜 **2** n xiépō 斜坡; (given to a story) guāndiǎn 观点

slanting qīngxié 倾斜

slap n & v/t zhǎngjī 掌击

slash 1 n (cut) kǎnhén 砍痕; (in punctuation) xiéxiàn 斜线 **2** v/t skin etc luànkǎn 乱砍; prices, costs dà xùjiǎn 大削减; ~ **one's wrists**

gēwàn 割腕

slate n (type of rock) bǎnyán 板岩; (for writing on) shíbǎn 石板

slaughter 1 n (of animals) túshā 屠杀; (of people, troops) shālù 杀戮 **2** v/t animals túshā 屠杀; people, troops shālù 杀戮

slave n núlì 奴隶

slay shā 杀

slaying (murder) móushā 谋杀

sleazy bar, characters xiàliú 下流

sled(ge) n xuěqiāo 雪橇

sledge hammer dàchuí 大锤

sleep 1 n shuìjiào 睡觉; *go to ~* qù shuìjiào 去睡觉; *I need a good ~* wǒ xūyào hǎohǎo shuìyíjiào 我需要好好睡一觉; *I couldn't get to ~* wǒ shuìbùzháo 我睡不着 **2** v/i shuì 睡

♦ **sleep in** (sleep late) shuìgè lǎnjiào 睡个懒觉

♦ **sleep on** v/t proposal, decision dài cìrì juédìng 待次日决定

♦ **sleep with** (have sex with) yǔ ... shuìjiào 与 ... 睡觉

sleeping bag shuìdài 睡袋; **sleeping car** wòchē 卧车; **sleeping pill** ānmiányào 安眠药

sleepless night bùmián 不眠

sleep walker mèngyóu zhě 梦游者

sleepy yawn kùnjuàn 困倦; town yōujìng 幽静; *I'm ~* wǒ kùn le 我困了

sleet n yǔjiáxuě 雨夹雪

sleeve (of jacket etc) xiùzi 袖子

sleeveless wúxiù 无袖

sleigh n xuěqiāo 雪橇

sleight of hand qiǎomiàode shǒufǎ 巧妙的手法

slender figure, arms xiānxì 纤细; chance wēixiǎo 微小; income, margin wēibó 微薄

slice 1 n (of bread, tart) piàn 片; fig (of profits etc) fènr 份儿 **2** v/t loaf etc qiēchéng báopiàn 切成薄片

sliced bread qiēpiàn miànbāo 切片面包

slick 1 adj performance bùfèilì 不费力; pej (cunning) yuánhuá 圆滑 **2** n (of oil) fúyóu 浮油

slide 1 n (for kids) huátī 滑梯; PHOT huàndēngpiàn 幻灯片 **2** v/i huá 滑; (drop: of exchange rate etc) xiàjiàng 下降 **3** v/t nuó nuó 挪

sliding door lāmén 拉门

slight 1 adj person, figure miáotiáo 苗条; (small) xiǎo 小; *no, not in the ~est* bù, yìdiǎnr yě bù 不, 一点儿也不 **2** n (insult) wǔrǔ 侮辱

slightly shāowēi 稍微

slim 1 adj miáotiáo 苗条; chance wēixiǎo 微小 **2** v/i jiǎnféi 减肥

slime níjiāng 泥浆

slimy liquid yǒu níjiāng 有泥浆

sling 1 n (for arm) xuándài 悬带 **2** v/t (throw) rēng 扔

slip 1 n (on ice etc) shuāijiāo 摔跤; (mistake) cuòwù 错误; *a ~ of paper* yīxiǎokuài zhǐ 一小块纸; *a ~ of the tongue* zǒuzuǐ 走嘴; *give X the ~* bǎituō X 摆脱 X **2** v/i (on ice etc) huá 滑; (decline: of quality etc) xiàjiàng 下降; *he ~ped out of the room* tā liūchūle fángjiān 他溜出了房间 **3** v/t (put) qīngfàng 轻放; *he ~ped it into his brief-case* tā qīngqīngde bǎ tā fàng jìng wénjìanbāo lǐ 他轻轻地把它放进文件包里

♦ **slip away** (of time) liúshì 流逝; (of opportunity) shìqù 逝去; (die quietly) qiāorán qùshì 悄然去世

♦ **slip off** v/t jacket etc tuōdiào 脱掉

♦ **slip out** v/i (go out) liūchūqù 溜出去

♦ **slip up** (make mistake) chū chācuò 出差错

slipped disc tūchūde zhuījiānpán 突出的椎间盘

slipper tuōxié 拖鞋

slippery huá 滑

slipshod cūxīn 粗心

slit 1 n (tear) kǒuzi 口子; (hole) lièfèng 裂缝; (in skirt) kāichà 开叉 **2** v/t sīkāi 撕开

slither v/i huálái huáqù 滑来滑去

slobber v/i liú kǒushuǐ 流口水

slogan kǒuhào 口号

slop v/t yìchū 溢出

slope 1 n pō 坡; (of mountain) xiépō 斜坡; *built on a ~* zài pōshang jiàn de 在坡上建的 **2** v/i qīngxié 倾斜; ***the road ~s down to the sea*** dàolù xiàng hǎimiàn qīngxié 道路向海面倾斜

sloppy *work* cǎoshuài 草率; (*in dress*) yīzhuó bùzhěng 衣着不整; (*too sentimental*) yōngsú shānggǎn 庸俗伤感

slot *n* fèngxì 缝隙; (*in schedule*) ānpáide shíjiān 安排的时间

♦**slot in 1** v/t shǐ chārù 使插入 **2** v/i chārù 插入

slot machine (*for vending*) ⇩ tóubìshòuhuòjī 投币售货机

slouch v/i lǎnsǎn 懒散

slovenly lātā 邋遢

slow màn 慢; ***be ~*** (*of clock*) mànle 慢了

♦**slow down 1** v/t jiǎnmàn 减慢 **2** v/i mànxiàlái 慢下来

slowdown (*in production*) xiàjiàng 下降

slow motion: in ~ màndòngzuò 慢动作

slug *n* (*animal*) kuòyú 蛞蝓

sluggish xíngdòng chíhuǎn 行动迟缓

slum *n* pínmínkū 贫民窟

slump 1 *n* (*in trade*) xiāotiáoqī 萧条期 **2** v/i (*economically*) zhòurán xiàdiē 骤然下跌; (*collapse: of person*) chénzhòngde dǎoxià 沉重地倒下

slur 1 *n* (*on s.o.'s character*) dǐhuǐ 诋毁 **2** v/t *words* hánhubùqīngde shuōhuà 含糊不清地说话

slurred *speech* hánhubùqīng 含糊不清

slush bànróngxuě 半融雪; *pej* (*sentimental stuff*) gǎnshāngde dōngxi 感伤的东西

slush fund hēiqián 黑钱

slut fàngdàng nǚzǐ 放荡女子

sly jiǎohuá 狡猾; ***on the ~*** mìmì 秘密

smack 1 *n* zhǎngjī 掌击 **2** v/t *child* zhǎngjī 掌击; *bottom* pāidǎ 拍打

small 1 *adj* xiǎo 小 **2** *n:* ***the ~ of the back*** hòuyāo 后腰

small change língqián 零钱;

small hours língchén shífēn 凌晨时分; **smallpox** tiānhuā 天花

small print xiǎozì 小字; **small talk** liáotiān 聊天

smart 1 *adj* (*elegant*) piàoliang 漂亮; (*intelligent*) cōngmǐn 聪敏; *pace* mǐnjié 敏捷; ***get ~ with X*** gēn X shuǎ huátóu 跟 X 耍滑头 **2** v/i (*hurt*) cìtòng 刺痛

smart card ⇩ shuākǎ 刷卡

♦**smarten up** v/t shǐ gèng yǒu tiáolǐ 使更有条理

smash 1 *n* (*noise*) huālā yīshēng 哗啦一声; (*car crash*) zhuàngsuì 撞碎; (*in tennis*) kòuqiú 扣球 **2** v/t (*break*) dǎsuì 打碎; (*hit hard*) zhàngjī 撞击; ***~ X to pieces*** bǎ X zhuàngsuì 把 X 撞碎 **3** v/i (*break*) pòsuì 破碎; ***the driver ~ed into ...*** sījī bǎ chē zhuàngdào ... 司机把车撞到 ...

smash hit F jíwéi hōngdòng 极为轰动

smattering (*of a language*) yīzhībànjiě 一知半解

smear 1 *n* (*of ink etc*) wūjì 污迹; MED túpiàn 涂片; (*on character*) wūmiè 污蔑 **2** v/t *paint etc* túmǒ 涂抹; *character* fěibàng 诽谤

smear campaign fěibàng huódòng 诽谤活动

smell 1 *n* qìwèi 气味; ***it has no ~*** tā méiyǒu qìwèi 它没有气味; ***sense of ~*** xiùjué 嗅觉 **2** v/t wénchū 闻出 **3** v/i (*unpleasantly*) yǒu chòuwèi 有臭味; (*sniff*) wén 闻; ***what does it ~ of?*** tā yǒu shénme wèir? 它有什么味儿？; ***you ~ of beer*** nǐ yǒu píjiǔwèi 你有啤酒味

smelly yǒu chòuwèi 有臭味

smile *n & v/i* wēixiào 微笑

♦**smile at** duì ... wēixiào 对 ... 微笑

smirk *n &v/i* jiānxiào 尖笑

smog yānwù 烟雾

smoke 1 *n* yān 烟; ***have a ~*** xīyān 吸烟 **2** v/t *cigarettes* xī 吸; *bacon* yòng yānxūn 用烟熏 **3** v/i xīyān 吸烟; ***I don't ~*** wǒ bù xīyān 我不吸烟

smoker (*person*) xīyānde rén 吸烟的人

smoking xīyān 吸烟; *no ~* jìnzhǐ xīyān 禁止吸烟

smoking compartment RAIL xīyān chēxiāng 吸烟车厢

smoky *room*, *air* duōyān 多烟

smolder (*of fire*) huǎnmàn ránshāo 缓慢燃烧; *fig* (*with anger*) yùjí 郁积; (*with desire*) yùhuǒzhōngshāo 欲火中烧

smooth 1 *adj surface*, *skin*, *sea* guānghuá 光滑; *ride* píngwěn 平稳; *transition* shùnlì 顺利; *pej* (*person*) yuánhuá 圆滑 **2** *v/t hair* shǐ guānghuá 使光滑

♦ **smooth down** (*with sandpaper etc*) móguāng 磨光

♦ **smooth out** *paper*, *cloth* lāpíng 拉平

♦ **smooth over**: *smooth things over* shǐ shìqíng huǎnjiě 使事情缓解

smother *flames* mēnzhù 闷住; *person* shǐ zhìxī 使窒息; *~ X with kisses* bùtíngde qīnwěn X 不停地亲吻 X; *~ bread with jam* bǎ guǒjiàng hòuhòude fàngzài miànbāo shang 把果酱厚厚地放在面包上

smudge 1 *n* wūjì 污迹 **2** *v/t* nòngzāng 弄脏

smug zìmǎn 自满

smuggle *v/t* zǒusī 走私

smuggler zǒusī zhě 走私者

smuggling zǒusī 走私

smutty *joke*, *sense of humor* xiàliú 下流

snack *n* xiǎochī 小吃

snack bar xiǎochīdiàn 小吃店

snag (*problem*) xiǎo wèntí 小问题

snail wōniú 蜗牛

snake *n* shé 蛇

snap 1 *n* kāchāshēng 喀嚓声; PHOT zhàopiàn 照片 **2** *v/t* (*break*) duànliè 断裂; (*say sharply*) lìshēng shuō 厉声说 **3** *v/i* (*break*) pāde zhéduàn 啪地折断 **4** *adj decision*, *judgment* kuàisù 快速

♦ **snap up** *bargains* qiǎnggòu 抢购

snappy *person*, *mood* yìnù 易怒

decision, *response* lìluò 利落; (*elegant*) shímáo 时髦

snapshot zhàopiàn 照片

snarl 1 *n* (*of dog*) nùhǒu 怒吼 **2** *v/i* chánjié 缠结

snatch 1 *v/t* duódé 夺得; (*steal*) tōuzǒu 偷走; (*kidnap*) bǎngjià 绑架 **2** *v/i* zhuāqǔ 抓取

snazzy shuài 帅

sneak 1 *v/t* (*remove*, *steal*) tōuná 偷拿; *~ a glance at* tōukàn yīyǎn 偷看一眼 **2** *v/i*: *~ into the room* / *out of the room* tōutōu liūjìn / liūchū fángjiān 偷偷溜进 / 溜出房间

sneakers fānbùxié 帆布鞋

sneaking *adj*: *have a ~ suspicion that ...* xīnzhōng yǒu nányǐ xiāochú de cāiyí ... 心中有难以消除的猜疑 ...

sneaky F (*crafty*) guǐguǐsuìsuì 鬼鬼祟祟

sneer *n & v/i* lěngxiào 冷笑

sneeze 1 *n* pēntì 喷嚏 **2** *v/i* dǎ pēntì 打喷嚏

sniff 1 *v/i* (*to clear nose*) yòng bí xīqì 用鼻吸气; (*of dog*) xiù 嗅 **2** *v/t* (*smell*) wén 闻

sniper jūjīshǒu 狙击手

snitch 1 *n* (*telltale*) bānnòngshìfēi de rén 搬弄是非的人 **2** *v/i* (*tell tales*) gàomì 告密

snob shìlìyǎn 势利眼

snobbish shìlì 势利

snooker ⇩ táiqiú 台球

♦ **snoop around** kuīchá 窥察

snooty mùzhōngwúrén 目中无人

snooze 1 *n* kēshuì 瞌睡; *have a ~* xiǎoshuì 小睡 **2** *v/i* dǎ kēshuì 打瞌睡

snore *v/i* dǎ hān 打鼾

snoring *n* hānshēng 鼾声

snorkel *n* tōngqìguǎn 通气管

snort *v/i* (*of bull*, *horse*) pēnbíxī 喷鼻息; (*of person*: *disdainfully*) fāhēngshēng 发哼声

snout (*of pig*, *dog*) kǒubíbù 口鼻部

snow 1 *n* xuě 雪 **2** *v/i* xià xuě 下雪

♦ **snow under**: *be snowed under with work* gōngzuò mángbúguòlái

工作忙不过来

snowball *n* xuěqiú 雪球; snow-bound bèi xuě kùnzhù 被雪困住; snow chains MOT fáng huá liàn 防滑链; snowdrift xuěduī 雪堆; snowdrop xuělián 雪莲; snowflake xuěhuā 雪花; snowman xuěrén 雪人; snowplow xuělí 雪犁; snowstorm bàofēngxuě 暴风雪

snowy *weather* duōxuě 多雪; *roads, hills* jīxuě 积雪

snub *n & v/t* dàimàn 怠慢

snub-nosed tābí 塌鼻

snug nuǎnhuo 暖和; (*tight-fitting*) jǐnshēn 紧身

♦snuggle down quánfú 蜷伏

♦snuggle up to wēiyīzhe 偎依着

so 1 *adv*: ~ *hot / cold* tàirè / lěng 太热 / 冷; *not ~ much* búnàme 不那么; ~ *much better / easier* hǎo / róngyi duōle 好 / 容易多了; *eat / drink ~ much* chī / hē hěnduō 吃 / 喝很多; *I miss you ~* wǒ hěn xiǎng nǐ 我很想你; ~ *am I / do I* wǒ yě shì 我也是; ~ *is she / does she* tā yě shì 她也是; *and ~ on* děngděng 等等 2 *pron*: *I hope / think ~* wǒ xīwàng rúcǐ / wǒ rènwéi shì zhèiyàng 我希望如此 / 我认为是这样; *you didn't tell me – I did ~* nǐ méi gàosu wǒ – wǒ gàosù nǐ le 你没告诉我 – 我告诉你了; *50 or ~* dàyù wǔshí 大约五十 3 *conj* (*for that reason*) yīncǐ 因此; (*in order that*) shǐde 使得; *and ~ I missed the train* jiùzhèiyàng wǒ méi gǎnshang huǒchē 就这样我没赶上火车; ~ (*that*) *I could come too* nà jiùshì shuō wǒ yě néng qù 那就是说我也能去; ~ *what?* nà yòu zěnmeyàng? 那又怎么样?

soak *v/t* (*steep*) pào 泡; (*of water, rain*) jìnshī 浸湿

♦soak up *liquid* xīshōu 吸收

soaked shītòu 湿透

so-and-so F (*unknown person*) mǒumǒu rén 某某人; (*annoying person*) tǎoyànguǐ 讨厌鬼

soap *n* (*for washing*) féizào 肥皂

soap (*opera*) féizào jù 肥皂剧

soapy *water* hán féizào 含肥皂

soar (*of rocket*) shēngrù 升入; (*of bird, plane*) áoxiáng 翱翔; (*of prices*) měngzēng 猛增

sob 1 *n* wūyàn 呜咽 2 *v/i* chōuqì 抽泣

sober (*not drunk*) qīngxǐng 清醒; (*serious*) yánsù 严肃

♦sober up xǐngjiǔ 醒酒

so-called suǒwèi 所谓

soccer zúqiú 足球

sociable héqún 合群

social *adj* shèhuì 社会; (*recreational*) shèjiāo 社交

socialism shèhuì zhǔyì 社会主义

socialist 1 *adj* shèhuì zhǔyì 社会主义 2 *n* shèhuì zhǔyì zhě 社会主义者

socialize shèjiāo 社交

social work shèhuì gōngzuò 社会工作

social worker shègōng 社工

society shèhuì 社会; (*organization*) shètuán 社团

sociology shèhuì xué 社会学

sock¹ (*for wearing*) wàzi 袜子

sock² 1 *n* (*punch*) quán 拳 2 *v/t* (*punch*) zòu 揍

socket (*electrical*) chāzuò 插座; (*of arm, eye*) wō 窝

soda (~ *water*) sūdá 苏打; (*ice-cream* ~) bīngqílíng sūdá shuǐ 冰淇淋苏打水; (*soft drink*) ruǎnxìng yǐnliào 软性饮料

sofa shāfā 沙发

sofa bed shāfā chuáng 沙发床

soft *pillow, chair* ruǎn 软; *voice* wēnróu 温柔; *music* yuè'ěr 悦耳; *light, color* róuhé 柔和; *skin* róuhuá 柔滑; (*lenient*) kuānhòu 宽厚; *have a ~ spot for X* piān'ài X 偏爱 X

soft drink ruǎnxìng yǐnliào 软性饮料

soften 1 *v/t position* huǎnhé 缓和; *impact, blow* jiǎnqīng 减轻 2 *v/i* (*of butter, ice cream*) biànruǎn 变软

softly (*quietly*) dīshēng 低声

soft seat (*on train*) ruǎnzuò 软座

soft sleeper (*on train*) ruǎnwò 软卧

software ruǎnjiàn 软件

soggy shīrùn 湿润

soil 1 *n* (*earth*) tǔrǎng 土壤 **2** *v/t* nòngzāng 弄脏

solar energy tàiyáng néng 太阳能

solar panel tàiyáng diànchí bǎn 太阳电池板

soldier shìbīng 士兵

sole[1] *n* (*of foot*) jiǎodǐ bǎn 脚底板); (*of shoe*) xiédǐ 鞋底

sole[2] *adj* wéiyī 唯一; ~ *responsibility* dāndú fùzé 单独负责

solely jǐnjǐn 仅仅

solemn (*serious*) yánsù 严肃; *promise* zhèngzhòng 郑重

solid *adj* (*hard*) yìng bāngbang 硬梆梆; (*without holes*) wú kòngxì 无空隙; *gold, silver* chún 纯; (*sturdy*) láogù 牢固; *evidence* chōngfèn 充分; *support* chèdǐ 彻底

solidarity tuánjié yīzhì 团结一致

solidify *v/i* gùhuā 固化

solitaire (*card game*) ⇩ dānrén zhǐpái xì 单人纸牌戏

solitary *life, activity* gūdú 孤独; (*single*) gū línglíng 孤零零

solitude dúzì yīrén 独自一人

solo 1 *n* (*of instrumentalist*) dúzòu qǔ 独奏曲; (*of singer*) dúchàng qǔ 独唱曲 **2** *adj* dānrén 单人

soloist (*instrumentalist*) dúzòu yǎnyuán 独奏演员; (*singer*) dúchàng yǎnyuán 独唱演员

soluble *substance* kěróng 可溶; *problem* kě jiějué 可解决

solution jiědá 解答; (*mixture*) róngyè 溶液

solve jiějué 解决

solvent *adj* (*financially*) wú zhàiwù 无债务

somber *dark* huī'àn 灰暗; (*serious*) yánjùn 严峻

some 1 *adj* yīxiē 一些; ~ *people say that ...* yǒuxiē rén shuō ... 有些人说...; *would you like ~ water / cookies?* nǐ yào diǎn shuǐ /

qǔqíbǐng ma? 你要点水 / 曲奇饼吗? **2** *pron* yīxiē 一些; ~ *of the group* zǔlǐ de yīxiē rén 组里的一些人; *would you like ~?* nǐ yào diǎnrma? 你要点儿吗?; *give me ~* gěiwǒ diǎnr 给我点儿 **3** *adv* (*a bit*) shāowēi 稍微; *we'll have to wait ~* wǒmen yào děnghuìr 我们要等会儿

somebody yǒurén 有人

someday yǒuzhāo yīrì 有朝一日

somehow (*by some means*) xiǎng bànfa 想办法; (*for some unknown reason*) bùzhī zěnde 不知怎的

someone yǒurén 有人

someplace → **somewhere**

somersault 1 *n* jīndǒu 筋斗 **2** *v/i* fān jīndǒu 翻筋斗

something dōngxi 东西; *would you like ~ to drink / eat?* nǐ yàobùyào hē / chī diǎnr dōngxi? 你要不要喝 / 吃点儿东西?; *is ~ wrong?* zěnme le? 怎么了?

sometime gǎirì 改日; ~ *last year* qùnián mǒugè shíhòu 去年某个时候

sometimes yǒushí 有时

somewhere 1 *adv* mǒugè dìfang 某个地方 **2** *pron* mǒuchù 某处

son érzi 儿子

song gēqǔ 歌曲

Song Dynasty Sòng Cháo 宋朝

Song Dynasty lyrics Sòngcí 宋词

songwriter cíqǔ zuòjiā 词曲作者

son-in-law nǚxù 女婿

son of a bitch *n* F húndàn 混蛋

soon (*in no time*) hěnkuài 很快; (*early*) zǎo 早; *soon after* bùjiǔ zhīhòu 不久之后; *as ~ as ...* yī ... jiù ... 就...; *as ~ as possible* jǐnkuài 尽快; ~*er or later* chízǎo 迟早; *the ~er the better* yuèkuài yuèhǎo 越快越好

soot yóuyān 油烟

soothe *pain* jiǎnqīng 减轻; *person* ānwèi 安慰

sophisticated *person* jīngtōng shìgù 精通世故; *tastes, lifestyle* bùluò sútào 不落俗套; *machine* jīngmì 精密

sophomore èrniánjí 二年级

soprano *n* gāoyīn 高音

sordid *affair, business* bēibì 卑鄙

sore **1** *adj* (*painful*) téng 疼；F (*angry*) nǎohuǒ 恼火；*is it ~?* téng bùténg? 疼不疼？ **2** *n* chuāng 疮

sorghum gāoliáng 高粱

sorrow *n* (*sad things*) shāngxīn shì 伤心事；(*sadness*) yōushāng 忧伤

sorry (*regretful*) hòuhuǐ 后悔；(*sad*) nánguò 难过；*I'm ~ that ...* (*apology*) duìbuqǐ ... 对不起 ...；(*expressing sympathy*) hěn yíhàn ... 很遗憾 ...；(*I'm*) ~! duìbuqǐ! 对不起！；*I feel ~ for her* wǒ wèi tā gǎndào nánguò 我为她感到难过

sort **1** *n* zhǒng 种；*~ of ...* F yǒu nàme diǎnr ... 有那么点儿 ...；*is it finished? – ~ of* F wánlema? – chàbùdò 完了吗？–差不多 **2** *v/t* fēnlèi 分类；COMPUT páiliè 排列

♦**sort out** *papers* zhěnglǐ 整理；*problem* jiějué 解决

so-so *adv* còuhe 凑和

soul REL línghún 灵魂；*fig* (*of a nation etc*) jīngshén 精神；(*character*) shēngqì 生气；(*person*) rén 人

sound[1] *adj* (*sensible*) hélǐ 合理；(*healthy*) jiànkāng 健康；*business* qiángzhuàng 强壮；(*strong, not damaged*) wánhǎo wúsǔn 完好无损；*a ~ sleep* hānshuì 酣睡

sound[2] **1** *n* shēngyīn 声音；(*noise*) shēng 声 **2** *v/t* (*pronounce*) fāyīn 发音；MED tīngzhěn 听诊；*~ one's horn* àn lǎba 按喇叭 **3** *v/i*: *that ~s interesting* tīngqǐlái hěn yǒuqù 听起来很有趣；*that ~s like a good idea* tīngqǐlái xiàng hǎo zhǔyì 听起来象好主意；*she ~ed unhappy* tā hǎoxiàng bù gāoxìng 她好像不高兴

sound card COMPUT shēngkǎ 声卡

soundly *sleep* shóu 熟；*beaten* chèdǐ 彻底

soundproof *adj* géyīn 隔音

soundtrack pèiyuè 配乐

soup tāng 汤

soup bowl tāngwǎn 汤碗

sour *adj apple, orange* suān 酸；*milk* sōu 馊；*expression, comment* jiān-suān kèbó 尖酸刻薄

source *n* láiyuán 来源；(*of river*) yuántóu 源头；(*person*) xiāoxirén 消息人

south **1** *adj* nán 南 **2** *n* nánbù 南部；*to the ~ of X* zài X de nánbiān 在 X 的南边 **3** *adv* wǎngnán 往南

South Africa Nánfēi 南非；**South African 1** *adj* Nánfēi 南非 **2** *n* Nánfēi rén 南非人；**South America** Nánměi 南美；**South American 1** *adj* Nánměi 南美 **2** *n* Nánměi rén 南美人；**South China Sea** Nánhǎi 南海；**South Korea** Nánhán 南韩；**South Korean 1** *adj* Nánhán 南韩 **2** *n* Nánhán rén 南韩人；**southeast 1** *n* dōngnán bù 东南部 **2** *adj* dōngnán 东南 **3** *adv* wǎng dōngnán 往东南；*it's ~ of X* zài X de dōngnán fāng 在 X 的东南方；**Southeast Asia** Dōngnán yà 东南亚；**Southeast Asian** *adj* Dōngnán yà 东南亚；**south-eastern** dōngnán 东南

southerly *adj* nán 南

southern nán 南

southward *adv* xiàng nán 向南

southwest 1 *n* xīnán bù 西南部 **2** *adj* xīnán 西南 **3** *adv* wǎng xīnán 往西南；*it's ~ of X* zài X de xīnán fāng 在 X 的西南方

southwestern xīnán 西南

souvenir jìniàn pǐn 纪念品

sovereign *adj state* zhǔquán 主权

sovereignty (*of state*) zhǔquán 主权

Soviet Union Sūlián 苏联

sow[1] *n* (*female pig*) mǔzhū 母猪

sow[2] *v/t seeds* bōzhǒng 播种

soy bean huángdòu 黄豆；**soy bean oil** dòu yóu 豆油；**soy milk** dòujiāng 豆浆；**soy sauce** jiàng-yóu 酱油

space *n* (*beyond earth*) tàikōng 太空；(*area*) kòngbái 空白；(*room*) kōngjiān 空间

♦**space out** bǎ ... jiàngé kāi 把 ... 间隔开

space bar COMPUT kònggé jiàn 空隔键; spacecraft yǔzhòu fēichuán 宇宙飞船; spaceship yǔzhòu fēichuán 宇宙飞船; space shuttle ⇩ hángtiān fēijī 航天飞机; space station yǔzhòu kōngjiān zhàn 宇宙空间站; spacesuit yǔháng fú 宇航服

spacious kuānchang 宽敞

spade (for digging) qiāo 锹; ~s (in card game) hēitáo 黑桃

Spain Xībānyá 西班牙

span v/t kuà 跨; (of bridge) héngkuà 横跨

Spaniard Xībānyá rén 西班牙人

Spanish 1 adj Xībānyá 西班牙 2 n (language) Xībānyá yǔ 西班牙语

spank dǎ pìgǔ 打屁股

spare 1 v/t time, money yúnchū 匀出; (do without) shěngdiào 省掉; can you ~ the time? yǒukōngma? 有空吗？; there were five to ~ (left over, in excess) yǒu wǔge shèngxià 有五个剩下 2 adj money duōyú 多余; (extra) bèiyòng 备用 3 n (part) língjiàn 零件

spare ribs páigǔ 排骨; spare room kèfáng 客房; spare time yèyú shíjiān 业余时间; spare tire MOT bèiyòng lúntāi 备用轮胎; spare wheel bèiyòng chēlún 备用车轮

spark n huǒxīng 火星

sparkle v/i shǎnyào 闪耀

sparkling wine qìjiǔ 汽酒

spark plug huǒhuāsāi 火花塞

sparrow máquè 麻雀

sparse vegetation xīshū 稀疏

sparsely: ~ populated rényān xīshǎo 人烟稀少

spatter v/t mud, paint jiàn jiàn 溅

speak 1 v/i shuōhuà 说话; we're not ~ing (to each other) (we've quarreled) wǒmen nào bièniu 我们闹别扭; ~ing TELEC wǒshì 我是 2 v/t foreign language huìjiǎng 会讲; ~ one's mind zhíshuō 直说

♦ speak to yǔ ... tánhuà 与 ... 谈话; (make a speech) fāyán 发言

♦ speak for dàibiǎo ... jiǎnghuà 代表 ... 讲话; speaking for myself jù wǒ lái kàn 据我来看

♦ speak out dàdǎn di shuō 大胆地说

♦ speak up (speak louder) dàshēng diǎn 大声点

♦ speak with yǔ ... tánhuà 与 ... 谈话

speaker (at conference) yǎnjiǎng zhě 演讲者; (orator) yǎnshuō jiā 演说家; (of sound system) yīnxiāng 音箱

spearmint bòhe 薄荷

special tèshū 特殊; (particular) tèbié 特别

special economic zone jīngjì tèqū 经济特区

specialist zhuānjiā 专家

specialize zhuānmén cóngshì 专门从事; ~ in ... zhuānmén cóngshì ... 专门从事 ...

specially tèbié 特别

specialty (of company etc) zhuāncháng 专长; (of restaurant) náshǒu hǎocài 拿手好菜

species zhǒnglèi 种类

specific tèbié 特别

specifically tèbié 特别

specifications (of machine etc) guīgé 规格

specify zhǐdìng 指定

specimen yàngpǐn 样品

speck (of dust, soot) lì 粒

spectacle (impressive sight) zhuàngguān 壮观; (a pair of) ~s (yífù) yǎnjìng（一副）眼镜

spectacular adj (stunning) zhuàngguān 壮观; (impressive) yǐnrén zhùmù 引人注目

spectator guānzhòng 观众

spectrum fig fànwéi 范围

speculate v/i cāicè 猜测; FIN zuò tóujī mǎimài 做投机买卖

speculation cāicè 猜测; FIN tóujī mǎimài 投机买卖

speculator FIN tóujī shāng 投机商

speech (address) jiǎnghuà 讲话; (in play) táicí 台词; (ability to speak) shuōhuà nénglì 说话能力; (way of speaking) shuōhuà fāngshì

说话方式

speechless (*with shock, surprise*)
yīshí jiǎng bùchū huà lái 一时讲
不出话来

speech defect yányǔ qùxiàn 言语
缺陷; **speech therapist** yányǔ
jiǎozhì shī 言语矫治师; **speech
writer** yǎnjiǎnggǎo zhuànxiě rén
演讲稿撰写人

speed 1 *n* sùdù 速度; *at a ~ of
150 mph* sùdù měi xiǎoshí yībǎi
wǔshí yīnglǐ 速度每小时一百
五十英里 **2** *v/i* (*drive quickly*)
jíshǐ 疾驶; (*walk quickly*) kuàizǒu
快走; (*drive too quickly*) chāosù 超
速

♦**speed by** fēiguò 飞过

♦**speed up** *v/t & v/i* jiākuài sùdù 加
快速度

speedboat kuàitǐng 快艇

speedily xùnsù 迅速

speeding *n* (*when driving*) chāosù
超速

speeding fine chāosù xíngshǐ
fákuǎn 超速行驶罚款

speed limit ⇩ sùdù jíxiàn 速度极
限

speedometer lǐchéng jì 里程计

speedy xùnsù 迅速

spell¹ *v/t & v/i* pīn 拼

spell² *n* (*period of time*) yīduàn
shíjiān 一段时间

spellbound rùmí 入迷; **spellcheck** COMPUT pīnxiě cháncuò 拼
写查错; *do a ~ on ...* jiǎnchá ...
de pīnxiě 检查 ... 的拼写;
spellchecker COMPUT pīnxiě
cháncuò chéngxù 拼写查错程序

spelling pīnxiě 拼写

spend *money* huāqián 花钱; *time*
dùguò 度过

spendthrift *n pej* dàshǒu dàjiǎo de
rén 大手大脚的人

sperm jīngzǐ 精子; (*semen*) jīngyè
精液

sperm bank jīngzǐ kù 精子库

sphere qiútǐ 球体; *fig* lǐngyù 领
域; *~ of influence* shìlì fànwéi 势
力范围

spice *n* (*seasoning*) xiāngliào 香料

spicy *food* duō xiāngliào 多香料

spider zhīzhū 蜘蛛

spiderweb zhīzhū wǎng 蜘蛛网

spike *n* jiāntóu 尖头; (*on shoes*)
xiédīng 鞋钉

spill *v/t & v/i* sǎ 洒

spin¹ 1 *n* (*turn*) xuánzhuǎn 旋转
2 *v/t* xuánzhuǎn 旋转 **3** *v/i* (*of
wheel*) xuánzhuǎn 旋转; *my head
is ~ning* wǒ tóuhūn nǎozhàng 我
头昏脑胀

spin² *v/t wool, cotton* fǎng 纺; *web*
jiéwǎng 结网

♦**spin around** (*of person*) zhuǎnshēn 转身

♦**spin out** tuōcháng 拖长

spinach bōcài 菠菜

spinal jízhù 脊柱

spinal column jízhù 脊柱

spin doctor xuānchuán jiā 宣传
家; **spin-dry** *v/t* shuǎigān 甩干;
spin-dryer shuǎigān jī 甩干机

spine (*of person, animal*) jízhù 脊
柱; (*of book*) shūjí 书脊; (*on plant,
hedgehog*) cì 刺

spineless (*cowardly*) méi gǔqì 没
骨气

spin-off pàishēng chǎnpǐn 派生产
品

spiral 1 *n* luóxuán 螺旋 **2** *v/i* (*rise
quickly*) jíjù shàngshēng 急剧上
升

spiral staircase luóxuán shì lóutī
螺旋式楼梯

spire jiāntǎ 尖塔

spirit *n* (*as opposed to body*)
jīngshén 精神; (*of dead person*)
línghún 灵魂; (*energy*) huólì 活
力; (*courage*) yǒngqì 勇气;
(*attitude*) tàidù 态度; *we did it in
a ~ of cooperation / friendliness*
wǒmen yǐ hézuò / yǒuhǎo de
jīngshén chūfā 我们以合作 / 友
好的精神出发

spirited (*energetic*) shēngqì bóbo 生
气勃勃

spirit level shuǐzhǔn yí 水准仪

spirits¹ (*alcohol*) lièjiǔ 烈酒

spirits² (*morale*) qíngxù 情绪; *be
in good / poor ~* jīngshén hǎo /
huài 精神好 / 坏

spiritual *adj* shén 神

spiritualism wéilíng lùn 唯灵论

spiritualist n zhāohúnshù zhě 招魂术者

spit v/i (of person) tǔtán 吐痰; **it's ~ting with rain** xià xiǎoyǔ 下小雨

♦ **spit out** food, liquid tùchū 吐出

spite n èyì 恶意; **in ~ of** jǐnguǎn 尽管

spiteful huáiyǒu èyì 怀有恶意

spitting image: **be the ~ of X** hé X jiǎnzhí yīmó yīyàng 和 X 简直一模一样

splash 1 n (noise) pūtōng 扑通; (small amount of liquid) yīdiǎnr 一点儿; (of color) bāndiǎn 斑点 **2** v/t person jiàn jiàn 溅; water, mud pō 泼 **3** v/i xǐshuǐ 嬉水; (of water) fēijiàn 飞溅

♦ **splash down** (of spacecraft) jiànluò 溅落

♦ **splash out** (in spending) dàshǒu dàjiǎo de huāqián 大手大脚地花钱; **I splashed out on a round the world trip** wǒ dàshǒu dàjiǎo de huāqián zài yīgé huánqiú lǚxíng shàng 我大手大脚地花钱在一个环球旅行上

splendid jíhǎo 极好

splendor (of achievement) guānghuī cànlàn 光辉灿烂; (of building, ceremony) zhuàngguān 壮观

splint n MED jiábǎn jiá 夹板夹

splinter 1 n cì 刺 **2** v/i fēnliè 分裂

splinter group xiǎo pàibié 小派别

split 1 n (damage) lièkǒu 裂口; (disagreement) fēnliè 分裂; (division, share) fēngē 分割 **2** v/t (damage) lièkāi 裂开; logs pī 劈; (cause disagreement in) fēnliè 分裂; (divide) fēn 分 **3** v/i (tear) lièkāi 裂开; (disagree) fēnliè 分裂

♦ **split up** v/i (of couple) fēnshǒu 分手

split personality PSYCH fēnliè réngé 分裂人格

splitting headache jùliè de tóutòng 剧烈的头痛

spoil v/t child chǒnghuài 宠坏; party, fun pòhuài ... de xìngzhì pò huài ...的兴致; cooking, essay etc nòngzāo 弄糟

spoilsport F bàixìng zhě 败兴者

spoilt adj child chǒnghuài 宠坏; **be ~ for choice** tàiduō xuǎnzé le 太多选择了

spoke (of wheel) chētiáo 车条

spokesman fāyánrén 发言人

spokesperson fāyánrén 发言人

spokeswoman fāyánrén 发言人

sponge n hǎimián 海绵

♦ **sponge off, sponge on** F kào ... báichī shí 靠...白吃食

sponger F jìshēng chóng 寄生虫

sponsor 1 n dānbǎo rén 担保人 **2** v/t dānbǎo 担保

sponsorship dānbǎo 担保

spontaneous zìfā 自发; person zìrán 自然

spooky F yīn sēnsen 阴森森

spool n (for film) juǎnpán 卷盘; (for thread) xiànzhóu 线轴

spoon n sháo 勺

spoonfeed fig tiányā shì guànshū 填鸭式灌输

spoonful: **two ~s of sugar** liǎng sháo táng 两勺糖

sporadic língsǎn 零散

sport n tǐyù yùndòng 体育运动

sporting event tǐyù yùndòng 体育运动; (fair, generous) dàfang 大方; **a ~ gesture** dàfang de jǔdòng 大方的举动

sportscar pǎochē 跑车; **sportscoat** yùndòng shàngyī 运动上衣; **sports journalist** tǐyù jìzhě 体育记者; **sportsman** yùndòng yuán 运动员; **sports news** tǐyù xīnwén 体育新闻; **sports page** tǐyù bǎn 体育版; **sportswoman** yùndòng yuán 运动员

sporty person àihào yùndòng 爱好运动; clothes huāshao 花哨

spot[1] (pimple) fěncì 粉刺; (caused by measles etc) qiūzhěn 丘疹; (part of pattern) bāndiǎnr 斑点儿

spot[2] (place) dìdiǎn 地点; **on the ~** (in the place in question) zài xiànchǎng 在现场; (immediately) dāngchǎng 当场; **put X on the ~** shǐ X nánkān 使 X 难堪

spot[3] v/t (notice) zhǎodào 找到; (identify) biànrèn 辨认

spot check chōuyàng jiǎnchá 抽样检查; *carry out spot checks* jìnxíng chōuyàng jiǎnchá 进行抽样检查

spotless yīchén bùrǎn 一尘不染

spotlight n jùguāng dēng 聚光灯

spotted *fabric* huādiǎn 花点

spotty (*with pimples*) duō fěncì 多粉刺

spouse *fml* pèi'ǒu 配偶

spout 1 n zuǐ 嘴 **2** v/i (*of liquid*) pēnchū 喷出

sprain n & v/t niǔshāng 扭伤

Spratley Islands Nánshā Qúndǎo 南沙群岛

sprawl v/i shēnkāi sìzhī 伸开四肢; (*of city*) mànyán 蔓延; *send X ~ing* (*of punch*) bǎ X shuāi pā zài dìshàng 把 X 摔趴在地上

sprawling *city, suburbs* mànyán 蔓延

spray 1 n (*of sea water*) lànghuā 浪花; (*from fountain*) shuǐhuā 水花; (*paint*) pēnqī 喷漆; (*for hair*) pēnfà jiāo 喷发胶; (*container*) pēnwù qì 喷雾器 **2** v/t pēn 喷; *~ X with Y* gěi X pēn Y 给 X 喷 Y

spraygun pēnqiāng 喷枪

spread 1 n (*of disease, religion etc*) mànyán 蔓延; F (*big meal*) shèngyàn 盛宴 **2** v/t (*lay*) tānkāi 摊开; *butter, news, rumor, disease* chuánbō 传播; *arms, legs* shēnzhǎn 伸展 **3** v/i (*of fire*) mànyán 蔓延; (*of rumor, news, disease*) chuánbō 传播; (*of butter*) mǒ mǒ 抹抹

spreadsheet COMPUT biǎogé 表格

spree: *go* (*out*) *on a ~* F tòngkuài yīfān 痛快一番; *go on a shopping ~* dàmǎi tèmǎi yīfān 大买特买一番

sprightly huópo 活泼

spring[1] n (*season*) chūntiān 春天

spring[2] n (*device*) tánhuáng 弹簧

spring[3] n (*stream*) quán 泉

spring[4] n & v/i (*jump*) tiàoyuè 跳跃

♦ **spring from** láizì 来自

springboard tiàobǎn 跳板;

spring chicken: *she's no ~* hum tā shàngle niánjì 她上了年纪;

spring-cleaning dà sǎochú 大扫除; **Spring Festival** Chūnjié 春节; **springtime** chūntiān 春天

springy *mattress, ground* yǒu tánxìng 有弹性; *walk* qīngkuài 轻快

sprinkle v/t sǎ 撒; *~ X with Y* jiāng X sǎzài Y shàng 将 X 撒在 Y 上

sprinkler (*for garden*) pēnsǎ qì 喷撒器; (*in ceiling*) pēnshuǐ zhuāngzhì 喷水装置

sprint n & v/i bēnpǎo 奔跑

sprinter SP duǎnpǎo yùndòng yuán 短跑运动员

sprout 1 v/i (*of seed*) fāyá 发芽 **2** n xīnyá 新芽; (*Brussels*) *~s* qiúzhuàng gānlán 球状甘蓝

spruce *adj* zhěngjié piàoliàng 整洁漂亮

spur n fig jīlì 激励; *on the ~ of the moment* píng yìshíde chōngdòng 凭一时的冲动

♦ **spur on** (*encourage*) jīlì ... qiánjìn 激励 ... 前进

spurt 1 n (*in race*) chōngcì 冲刺; *put on a ~* jiāsù fēibēn 加速飞奔 **2** v/i (*of liquid*) pēnshè 喷射

spy 1 n jiàndié 间谍 **2** v/i cóngshì jiàndié huódòng 从事间谍活动 **3** v/t F fāxiàn 发现

♦ **spy on** ànzhōng jiānshì 暗中监视

squabble n & v/i zhēngchǎo 争吵

squalid āngzāng 肮脏

squalor wūhuì 污秽

squander *money* huīhuò 挥霍

square 1 *adj* (*in shape*) fāng 方; *~ mile / yard* píngfāng yīnglǐ / mǎ 平方英里 / 码 **2** n (*shape*) sìfāng xíng 四方形; (*in town*) guǎngchǎng 广场; (*in board game*) gé 格; MATH píngfāng 平方; *we're back to ~ one* wǒmen yòu huídào qǐdiǎn le 我们又回到起点了

square root píngfāng gēn 平方根

squash[1] n (*vegetable*) nánguā 南瓜

squash[2] n (*game*) bìqiú 壁球

squash[3] v/t (*crush*) yālàn 压烂

squat 1 *adj* (*in shape*) ǎi 矮 **2** v/i (*sit*) dūn 蹲; (*illegally*) shànzì zhànyòng 擅自占用

squatter shànzì zhàndì zhě 擅自占地者

squeak 1 n (of mouse) zhīzhi shēng 吱吱声; (of hinge) zhīgā shēng 吱嘎声 **2** v/i (of mouse) zhīzhi jiào 吱吱叫; (of hinge, shoes) zhīgā zuòxiǎng 吱嘎作响

squeal 1 n cháng ér jiān de jiàoshēng 长而尖的叫声 **2** v/i fāchū cháng ér jiān de jiàoshēng 发出长而尖的叫声

squeamish jiāoqì 娇气

squeeze 1 n (of hand, shoulder) jǐnwò 紧握 **2** v/t (press) jǐ jǐ; package etc yònglì niē 用力捏; shoulder, hand jǐnwò 紧握; (remove juice from) zhà 榨

♦ **squeeze in 1** v/i (to a car etc) jǐ jǐ **2** v/t sāi 塞

♦ **squeeze up** v/i (to make space) jǐjǐn 挤紧

squid yóuyú 鱿鱼

squint n xiéyǎn 斜眼

squirm (wriggle) niǔdòng 扭动; (in embarrassment) júcù bù'ān 局促不安

squirrel n sōngshǔ 松鼠

squirt 1 v/t pēnshè 喷射 **2** n pej F wàngzì zūndà de rén 妄自尊大的人

stab 1 n F chángshì 尝试 **2** v/t person cì 刺

stability wěndìng 稳定

stabilize 1 v/t prices, currency wěndìng 稳定; boat pínghéng 平衡 **2** v/i (of prices etc) wěndìng 稳定

stable[1] n (for horses) mǎjiù 马厩

stable[2] adj wěndìng 稳定

stack 1 n (pile) dié 叠; (smokestack) dà yāncōng 大烟囱 **2** v/t bǎ ... diéchéng duī 把 ... 叠成堆

stadium tǐyùchǎng 体育场

staff n (employees) gùyuán 雇员; (teachers) jiàoyuán 教员

staffroom (in school) jiàoyuán shì 教员室

stage[1] (in life, project etc) jiēduàn 阶段; (of journey) duàn lù 段路

stage[2] **1** n THEA wǔtái 舞台; **go on the ~** dāng yǎnyuán 当演员 **2** v/t play biǎoyǎn 表演; demonstration, strike jǔxíng 举行

stage door jùchǎng hòumén 剧场后门

stagger 1 v/i diēdie zhuàngzhuang 跌跌撞撞 **2** v/t (amaze) shǐ chījīng 使吃惊; coffee breaks etc cuòkāi 错开

staggering lìngrén chījīng 令人吃惊

stagnant water bù liúdòng 不流动; economy tíngzhì 停滞

stagnate fig (of person, mind) bù fāzhǎn 不发展

stag party hūnqián nánzi jùhuì 婚前男子聚会

stain 1 n (dirty mark) wūjì 污迹; (for wood) rǎnsè jì 染色剂 **2** v/t (dirty) zhānwū 沾污; wood rǎnsè 染色 **3** v/i (of wine etc) chǎnshēng wūjì 产生污迹; (of fabric) yìcún wūjì 易存污迹

stained-glass window cǎisè bōli chuāng 彩色玻璃窗

stainless steel n búxiùgāng 不锈钢

stain remover qùwū jì 去污剂

stair tījí 梯级; **the ~s** lóutī 楼梯

staircase lóutī 楼梯

stake 1 n (of wood) zhuāng 桩; (when gambling) dǔzhù 赌注; (investment) gǔfèn 股份; **be at ~** zài wēixiǎn zhōng 在危险中 **2** v/t tree yòng zhuāng zhīchēng 用桩支撑; money xià dǔzhù 下赌注; person zīzhù 资助

stale bread zǒuwèir 走味儿; air mēn 闷; fig: news guòshí 过时

stalemate (in chess) jiāngjú 僵局; fig jiāngjú 僵局

Stalin Sīdàlín 斯大林

stalk[1] n (of fruit, plant) gěng 梗

stalk[2] v/t (follow) gēnzōng 跟踪

stalker (of person) gēnzōng zhě 跟踪者

stall[1] n (at market) tānzi 摊子; (for cow, horse) péng 棚

stall[2] **1** v/i (of engine) xīhuǒ 熄火; (of vehicle, plane) pāomáo 抛锚; (play for time) tuōyán 拖延 **2** v/t engine xīhuǒ 熄火; people fūyǎn 敷衍

stallion mǔmǎ 牡马

stalwart *adj support, supporter* jiāndìng 坚定

stamina nàilì 耐力

stammer *n & v/i* jiēba 结巴

stamp¹ **1** *n* (*for letter*) yóupiào 邮票; (*device*) yìnchuō 印戳; (*mark made with device*) yìn 印 **2** *v/t letter* tiē yóupiào 贴邮票; *document, passport* gàizhāng 盖章

stamp² *v/t*: **~ one's feet** duòjiǎo 跺脚

♦**stamp out** (*eradicate*) xiāomiè 消灭

stampede *n* (*of cattle etc*) jīngpǎo 惊跑; (*of people*) fēngyōng 蜂拥

stance (*position*) tàidù 态度

stand 1 *n* (*at exhibition*) tānzi 摊子; (*witness ~*) zhèngrén xí 证人席; (*support, base*) zuò 座; **take the ~** LAW zuòzhèng 作证 **2** *v/i* (*be situated: of person*) zhànlì 站立; (*of object*) bèi fàngzhì 被放置; (*of building*) sǒnglì 耸立; (*as opposed to sit*) zhànzhe 站着; (*rise*) qǐlì 起立; **~ still** yídòng bùdòng 一动不动; **where do I ~ with you?** wǒmen jiūjìng shì shénme guānxi? 我们究竟是什么关系? **3** *v/t* (*tolerate*) rěnshòu 忍受; (*put*) shùfàng 竖放; **you don't ~ a chance** nǐ gēnběn méi jīhuì 你根本没机会; **~ one's ground** jiānchí zìjǐ de lìchǎng 坚持自己的立场

♦**stand back** hòutuì 后退

♦**stand by 1** *v/i* (*not take action*) xiùshǒu pángguān 袖手旁观; (*be ready*) zuò hǎo zhǔnbèi 作好准备 **2** *v/t person* zhīchí 支持; *decision* jiānchí 坚持

♦**stand down** (*withdraw*) tuìchū 退出

♦**stand for** (*tolerate*) róngrěn 容忍; (*represent*) dàibiǎo 代表

♦**stand in for** dàitì 代替

♦**stand out** yǐnrén zhùmù 引人注目

♦**stand up 1** *v/i* zhàn qǐlái 站起来 **2** *v/t*: **stand X up** F (*on date*) ràng X báiděng 让X白等

♦**stand up for** wéihù 维护

♦**stand up to** miànduì 面对

standard 1 *adj* (*usual*) chángguī 常规 **2** *n* (*level of excellence*) shuǐzhǔn 水准; (*expectation*), TECH biāozhǔn 标准; **be up to ~** fúhé biāozhǔn 符合标准; **not be up to ~** bù fúhé biāozhǔn 不符合标准

standard of living shēnghuó shuǐzhǔn 生活水准

standardize *v/t* shǐ biāozhǔn huà 使标准化

standby: on ~ (*for flight*) hòubǔ 候补

standby passenger hòubǔ lǚkè 候补旅客

standing *n* (*in society etc*) dìwèi 地位; (*repute*) shēngyù 声誉; **a musician / politician of some ~** zhuōyuè de yīnyuèjiā / zhèngzhìjiā 卓越的音乐家 / 政治家

standing room zhànlì kōngjiān 站立空间

standoffish lěngmò 冷漠; **standpoint** guāndiǎn 观点; **standstill** **be at a ~** tíngdùn 停顿; **bring ... to a ~** shǐ ... tíngdùn 使 ... 停顿

staple¹ *n* (*foodstuff*) zhǔshí 主食

staple² **1** *n* (*fastener*) dìngshūdīng 订书钉 **2** *v/t* dīng 钉

staple diet zhǔshí 主食

staple gun tiěsī dìngshūjī 铁丝订书机

stapler dìngshūjī 订书机

star 1 *n* (*in sky*) xīng 星; *fig* míngxīng 明星 **2** *v/t* (*of movie*) zhǔyǎn 主演 **3** *v/i* (*in movie*) zhǔyǎn 主演

starboard *adj* yòuxián 右舷

stare 1 *n* níngshì 凝视 **2** *v/i* mùbù zhuǎnjīng de kàn 目不转睛地看; **~ at** dīngzhe 盯着

starfish hǎixīng 海星

stark 1 *adj landscape* huāngliáng 荒凉; *room, surroundings* kōng luòluo 空落落; *reminder, etc* yánkù 严酷; *contrast* xiānmíng 鲜明 **2** *adv*: **~ naked** yīsī bùguà 一丝不挂

starling liángniǎo 椋鸟

Stars and Stripes Xīngtiáo qí 星

条旗

start 1 *n* (*beginning*) kāitóu 开头;
get off to a good / bad ~ (*in race,
marriage, career*) yīkāishǐ hěnhǎo /
zāo 一开始很好 / 糟; ***from the ~***
yīkāishǐ 一开始; ***well, it's a ~!***
qǐmǎ kāigètóu! 起码开个头!
2 *v/i* kāishǐ 开始; (*of engine, car*)
fādòng 发动; ***~ing from tomor-
row*** cóng míngtiān kāishǐ 从明天
开始 **3** *v/t* kāishǐ 开始; *engine, car*
fādòng 发动; *business* chuàngbàn
创办; ***~ to do X***, ***~ doing X*** kāishǐ
zuò X 开始做 X

starter (*part of meal*) tóupán 头盘;
(*of car*) qǐdòng zhuāngzhì 起动装
置

starting point (*for walk, discussion,
thesis*) chūfā diǎn 出发点

starting salary qǐshǐ gōngzī 起始
工资

startle: ***~ X*** shǐ X xià yītiào 使 X 吓
一跳

startling jīngrén 惊人

starvation jī'è 饥饿

starve *v/i* ái'è 挨饿; ***~ to death*** èsǐ
饿死; ***I'm starving*** F wǒ èsǐ le 我
饿死了

state¹ 1 *n* (*of car, house etc*)
zhuàngkuàng 状况; (*part of
country*) zhōu 州; (*country*) guójiā
国家; ***the States*** Měiguó 美国
2 *adj capital etc* zhōu 州;
(*ceremonial*) zhèngshì 正式; ***~
banquet*** guóyàn 国宴

state² *v/t* shēngmíng 声明

State Department Guówù Yuàn
国务院

statement (*to police*) kǒugōng 口
供; (*announcement*) shēngmíng 声
明; (*bank ~*) jiésuàn dān 结算单

state of emergency jǐnjí
zhuàngtài 紧急状态

state-of-the-art *adj* zuì yōuliáng
最优良

statesman zhèngzhì jiā 政治家

state trooper zhōu jǐngchá 州警
察

state visit guówù fǎngwèn 国务访
问

static (electricity) jìngdiàn 静电

station 1 *n* RAIL huǒchē zhàn 火车
站; RAD, TV diàntái 电台 **2** *v/t
guard etc* zhùzhā 驻扎; ***be ~ed at***
(*of soldier*) zhùzhā zài 驻扎在

stationary jìngzhǐ 静止

stationery wénjù 文具

station wagon kèhuò liǎngyòng
jiàochē 客货两用轿车

statistical tǒngjì 统计

statistically cóng tǒngjìxué jiǎodù
láishuō 从统计学角度来说

statistics (*science*) tǒngjì xué 统计
学; (*figures*) tǒngjì zīliào 统计资
料

statue sùxiàng 塑像

Statue of Liberty Zìyóu Nǚshén
Xiàng 自由女神像

status dìwèi 地位

status symbol shēnfènde xiàngzhēng 身份的象征

statute fǎlìng 法令

staunch *adj* jiāndìng 坚定

stay 1 *n* dòuliú 逗留 **2** *v/i* (*in a
place*) dòuliú 逗留; (*in a condition*)
bǎochí 保持; ***~ at home*** dāi zài
jiā lǐ 呆在家里; ***~ in a hotel*** dāi
zài lǚguǎn 呆在旅馆; ***~ right
there!*** biédòng! 别动!; ***~ put***
(*don't move*) bié zǒukāi 别走开; ***~
put in*** (*in job, city*) yǒngyuǎn
dāizài 永远呆在

♦ **stay away** líkāi 离开

♦ **stay away from** bù jiējìn 不接
近

♦ **stay behind** wǎnzǒu 晚走

♦ **stay up** (*not go to bed*) bù qùshuì
不去睡

steadily *improve etc* zhújiàn 逐渐

steady 1 *adj* (*not shaking*) píngwěn
平稳; (*regular*) yǒu guīlǜ 有规律;
(*continuous*) chíxù 持续 **2** *adv*: ***be
going ~*** zuò qínglǚ 做情侣; ***~ on!***
yōu zhe diǎnr! 悠着点儿! **3** *v/t*
wěnzhù 稳住

steak niúpái 牛排

steal 1 *v/t money etc* tōu 偷 **2** *v/i*
(*be a thief*) tōu dōngxi 偷东西;
(*move quietly*) qiāoqiaode xíngzǒu
悄悄地行走

stealthy qiāoqiao 悄悄

steam 1 *n* zhēngqì 蒸汽 **2** *v/t food*

zhēng 蒸

♦ **steam up 1** *v/i* (*of window etc*) méngshàng shuǐqì 蒙上水汽 **2** *v/t*: **be steamed up** F nǎohuǒ 恼火

steamed bread mántou 馒头

steamer (*for cooking*) zhēngguō 蒸锅

steam iron zhēngqì diàn yùndǒu 蒸汽电熨斗

steel *n* & *adj* gāng 钢

steep¹ *adj* hill etc dǒu 陡; F *prices* guì 贵

steep² *v/t* (*soak*) pào 泡

steeple jiāntǎ 尖塔

steeplechase (*in athletics*) yuèyě sài 越野赛

steer¹ *n* (*animal*) yān gōngniú 阉公牛

steer² *v/t car, boat* jiàshǐ 驾驶; *person* yǐndǎo 引导; *conversation* diàozhuǎn 掉转

steering (*of motor vehicle*) jiàshǐ jīgòu 驾驶机构

steering wheel fāngxiàng pán 方向盘

stem¹ *n* (*of plant*) gàn 干; (*of glass*) jīng 茎; (*of pipe*) bǐng 柄; (*of word*) cígàn 词干

♦ **stem from** qǐyuán yú 起源于

stem² *v/t* (*block*) zhìzhǐ 制止

stemware bōli qìmǐn 玻璃器皿

stench èchòu 恶臭

step 1 *n* (*pace*) bù 步; (*stair*) jiētī 阶梯; (*measure*) cuòshī 措施; (*decision*) juédìng 决定; **~ by ~** zhúbùde 逐步地 **2** *v/i* (*put feet in/on sth*) cǎi 踩; (*walk forward*) zǒu 走

♦ **step down** (*from post etc*) ràngwèi 让位

♦ **step out** (*go out for a short time*) chūqù yīhuìr 出去一会儿

♦ **step up** *v/t* (*increase*) jiākuài 加快

stepbrother jìxiōngdì 继兄弟; **stepdaughter** jìnǚ 继女; **stepfather** jìfù 继父; **stepladder** zhétī 折梯; **stepmother** jìmǔ 继母

stepping stone tàijiǎo shí 踏脚石; *fig* jìnshēn zhījiē 进身之阶

stepsister (*same father different mother*) tóngfù yìmǔ jiěmèi 同父异母姐妹; (*same mother different father*) tóngmǔ yìfù jiěmèi 同母异父姐妹

stepson jìzǐ 继子

stereo *n* (*sound system*) yīnxiǎng 音响

stereotype *n* chéngjiàn 成见

sterile *woman, man* bùyù 不育; MED xiāodú 消毒

sterilize *woman* jiézhá 结扎; *equipment* xiāodú 消毒

sterling *n* FIN yīngbàng 英镑

stern *adj* yánsù 严肃

steroids jīsù 激素

stethoscope tīngzhěnqì 听诊器

Stetson® Sītàisēn Zhānmào 斯泰森毡帽

stevedore zhuāngxiè gōng 装卸工

stew *n* dùn shípǐn 炖食品

steward (*on plane, ship*) chéngwùyuán 乘务员

stewardess (*on plane, ship*) chéngwùyuán 乘务员

stick¹ *n* (*wood*) mùgùn 木棍; (*of policeman*) jǐnggùn 警棍; (*walking ~*) guǎizhàng 拐杖; **the ~s** F xiāngxià 乡下

stick² **1** *v/t* (*with adhesive*) niánzhù 粘住; F (*put*) fàng 放 **2** *v/i* (*jam*) qiǎ zhù le 卡住了; (*adhere*) niánzhù 粘住

♦ **stick around** F dāi yīhuìr 呆一会儿

♦ **stick by**: **~ X** F zhōngyú X 忠于 X

♦ **stick out** *v/i* (*protrude*) tūchū 突出; (*be noticeable*) xiǎnyǎn 显眼

♦ **stick to** (*adhere to*) niánzài ... shàngmiàn 粘在 ... 上面; F (*keep to*) jiānchí 坚持; *path, road* yánzhe 沿着; F (*follow*) jǐnsuí 紧随

♦ **stick together** F dāi zài yīqǐ 呆在一起

♦ **stick up** *poster, leaflet* shùqǐ 竖起

♦ **stick up for** F wèi ... biànhù 为 ... 辩护

♦ **stick with** F jiānchí 坚持

sticker biāoqiān 标签

sticking plaster hùchuànggāo 护

创膏

stick-in-the-mud mòshǒu chéng-guī zhě 墨守成规者

sticky hands, surface nián hūhu 黏糊糊; *a ~ label* tiēqiān 贴签

stiff 1 adj brush, cardboard, leather yìng bāngbāng 硬邦邦; muscle, body jiāngyìng 僵硬; mixture, paste chóu 稠; (in manner) jūjǐn 拘谨; drink nóngliè 浓裂; fine, penalty yánlì 严厉; competition jīliè 激烈 **2** adv: *be scared ~* F hěn hàipà 很害怕; *be bored ~* F mènsǐle 闷死了

stiffen v/i biànde jǐnzhāng 变得紧张
♦ **stiffen up** (of muscle) biàn jiāngyìng 变僵硬

stifle v/t yawn, laugh rěnzhe 忍着; criticism, debate èshā 扼杀

stifling lìngrén zhìxī 令人窒息

stigma chǐrǔ 耻辱

stilettos (shoes) xì gāo gēnxié 细高跟鞋

still¹ 1 adj píngjìng 平静 **2** adv: *keep ~!* bié dònglái dòngqù! 别动来动去！; *stand ~!* biédòng! 别动！

**still² ** adv (yet) hái 还; (nevertheless) wúlùn rúhé 无论如何; *do you ~ want it?* ní háiyào ma? 你还要吗？; *she ~ hasn't finished* tā hái méiwán ne 她还没完呢; *she might ~ come* tā kěnéng réngrán huìlái 她可能仍然会来; *they are ~ my parents* tāmén zǒng háishì wǒde fùmǔ a 他们总还是我的父母啊; *~ more* (even more) gèngduō 更多

stillborn: *be ~* sǐchǎn 死产

stilted bú zìrán 不自然

stilts (under house) chēngzhù 撑柱

stimulant xīngfèn jì 兴奋剂

stimulate person cìjī 刺激; growth, demand cùjìn 促进

stimulating zhènfèn rénxīn 振奋人心

stimulation jīlì 激励

stimulus (incentive) dònglì 动力

sting 1 n (from bee, jellyfish) zhēcì 螫刺 **2** v/t (of bee, jellyfish) zhē 螫

3 v/i (of eyes) fātòng 发痛; (of scratch) gǎndào cìtòng 感到刺痛

stinging remark, criticism kèbó 刻薄

stingy F kōuménr 抠门儿

stink 1 n (bad smell) chòuwèir 臭味儿; F (fuss) xuānrán dàbō 轩然大波; *make a ~* dànào yīchǎng 大闹一场 **2** v/i (smell bad) dài chòuwèir 带臭味儿; F (be very bad) zāoitòule 糟透了

stint n guīdìng de rènqī 规定的任期; *do a ~ in the army* fú bīngyì 服兵役
♦ **stint on** jiéshěng 节省

stipulate guīdìng 规定

stipulation tiáojiàn 条件

stir 1 n: *give the soup a ~* jiǎo yī jiǎo tāng 搅一搅汤; *cause a ~* fig yǐnqǐ yīchǎng fēngbō 引起一场风波 **2** v/t jiǎobàn 搅拌 **3** v/i (of sleeping person) nuódòng 挪动
♦ **stir up** crowd shāndòng 煽动; bad memories huíyì qǐ 回忆起

stir-crazy: *be ~* F juānhuàile 圈坏了

stir-fry v/t wànghuǒ biānchǎo 旺火煸炒

stirring music, speech jīdòng rénxīn 激动人心

stitch 1 n (in sewing) zhēnjiǎo 针脚; (in knitting) yīzhēn 一针; *~es* MED féngzhēn 缝针; *have a ~* tūrán jùtòng 突然剧痛 **2** v/t sew féng 缝
♦ **stitch up** wound féng qǐlái 缝起来

stitching (stitches) xiàn 线

stock 1 n (reserves) chǔcún 储存; (COM: of store) huò 货; (animals) shēngchù 牲畜; FIN gǔpiào 股票; (food) tāng 汤; *in - / out of ~* yǒu / wúhuò 有 / 无货; *take ~* pínggū 评估 **2** v/t COM bèiyǒu 备有
♦ **stock up on** chǔbèi 储备

stockbroker gǔpiào jīngjìrén 股票经纪人; **stock exchange** gǔpiào jiāoyìsuǒ 股票交易所; **stockholder** gǔdōng 股东

stocking chángtǒngwà 长统袜

stock market gǔpiào shìchǎng 股票市场; **stockmarket crash** gǔpiào shìchǎng bàodiē 股票市场暴跌; **stockpile 1** n (of food, weapons) chǔbèi wùzī 储备物资 **2** v/t chǔbèi 储备; **stockroom** cāngkù 仓库; **stocktaking** pándiǎn 盘点

stocky ǎizhuàng 矮壮

stock-still: stand ~ yīdòng búdòng 一动不动

stodgy food yìbǎo 易饱

stomach 1 n (insides) dùzi 肚子; (abdomen) fùbù 腹部 **2** v/t (tolerate) rěnshòu 忍受

stomach-ache dùzi téng 肚子疼

stone n (material, pebble) shítou 石头; (precious ~) bǎoshí 宝石

stoned F (on drugs) mázuì 麻醉

stone-deaf wánquán lóng 完全聋

stonewall v/i F tángsè 搪塞

stony ground, path duōshí 多石

stool (seat) dèngzi 凳子

stoop¹ **1** n wānyāo qūbèi 弯腰曲背 **2** v/i (bend down) wānyāo 弯腰; (have bent back) hāyāo 哈腰

stoop² n (porch) ménláng 门廊

stop 1 n (for train, bus) zhàn 站; **come to a** ~ tíngle 停了; **put a** ~ **to** tíngzhǐ 停止 **2** v/t (put an end to, cease) tíngzhǐ 停止; (prevent) zǔzhǐ 阻止; person in street lánzhù 拦住; car, bus, train, etc: of driver tíng 停; of pedestrian lánzhù 拦住; ~ **talking immediately!** mǎshàng zhùzuǐ! 马上住嘴！; **I** ~**ped her from leaving** wǒ búràng tā ǒzu 我不让她走; **it has** ~**ped raining** yǔtíngle 雨停了; ~ **a check** tíngzhǐ duìfù zhīpiào 停止兑付支票 **3** v/i tíng 停

♦**stop by** (visit) shùnbiàn guòfǎng 顺便过访

♦**stop off** zhōngtú tíngliú 中途停留

♦**stop over** zhōngtú tíngliú 中途停留

♦**stop up** sink dǔsāi 堵塞

stopgap línshí tìdài 临时替代; **stoplight** (traffic light) hónglǜdēng 红绿灯; (brake light) shāchē

dēng 刹车灯; **stopover** dòuliú 逗留; (in air travel) zhōngtú tíngliú 中途停留

stopper (for bath, basin) sāizi 塞子; (for bottle) píngsāi 瓶塞

stopping: no ~ (sign) bùzhǔn tíngchē 不准停车

stop sign tíngchē biāozhì 停车标志

stopwatch miǎobiǎo 秒表

storage zhùcáng 贮藏; **put X in** ~ bǎ X zhùcáng qǐlái 把 X 贮藏起来; **be in** ~ zài zhùcáng kù 在贮藏库

storage capacity COMPUT cúnchǔ róngliàng 存储容量

storage space zhùcún kōngjiān 贮存空间

store 1 n shāngdiàn 商店; (stock) chǔbèi 储备; (storehouse) cāngkù 仓库 **2** v/t cúnfàng 存放; COMPUT chǔcún 储存

storefront línjiē diànpù 临街店铺; **storehouse** cāngkù 仓库; **storekeeper** diànzhǔ 店主; **storeroom** cāngkù 仓库; **store window** shāngdiàn chúchuāng 商店橱窗

storm n bàofēngyǔ 暴风雨

storm drain yǔshuǐ dào 雨水道; **storm window** wàichóng chuāng 外重窗; **storm warning** fēngbào jǐngbào 风暴警报

stormy weather yǒu bàofēngyǔ 有暴风雨; relationship yìbō sānzhé 一波三折

story¹ (tale) gùshì 故事; (account) xùshù 叙述; (newspaper article) bàodào 报道; F (lie) huǎnghuà 谎话

story² (of building) céng 层

stout adj person féipàng 肥胖; boots nàichuān 耐穿

stove (for cooking) lúzi 炉子; (for heating) jiārè qì 加热器

stow chǔcáng 储藏

♦**stow away** v/i (on ship) wúpiào tōuchéng 无票偷乘

stowaway wúpiào tōuchéng zhě 无票偷乘者

straight 1 adj line, hair zhí 直; back

bǐzhí 笔直; (*honest, direct*) tǎnshuài 坦率; (*not criminal*) zhèngpài 正派; *whiskey etc* chún 纯; (*tidy*) zhěngqí 整齐; (*conservative*) bǎoshǒu 保守; (*not homosexual*) fēi tóngxìngliàn 非同性恋; *be a ~ A student* chéngjì yōuxiùde xuésheng 成绩优秀的学生
2 *adv* (*in a straight line*) jìngzhí 径直; (*directly, immediately*) zhíjiē 直接; (*clearly*) zhèngquè 正确; *stand up ~!* zhànzhíle! 站直了！; *look X ~ in the eye* dīngzhe X de yǎnjīng 盯着 X 的眼睛; *go* ~ F (*of criminal*) gǎixié guīzhèng 改邪归正; *give it to me ~* F tǎnbái gàosù wǒ 坦白告诉我; *~ ahead be situated* jiùzài qiánmiàn 就在前面; *walk, drive* zhízhe zǒu 直着走; *look* xiàngqián kàn 向前看; *carry ~ on* (*of driver etc*) zhízhe zǒu 直着走; *~away, ~ off* mǎshàng 马上; *~ out* zhíjiēliǎodàng 直截了当; *~ up* (*without ice*) bù jiābīng 不加冰

straighten *v/t* nòngzhí 弄直
♦ **straighten out 1** *v/t situation* jiěshì qīng 解释清 **2** *v/i* (*of road*) biànzhí 变直
♦ **straighten up** tǐngzhí 挺直

straightforward (*honest, direct*) zhíjiéliǎodàng 直截了当; (*simple*) jiǎndān 简单

strain[1] *n* (*on rope, engine, heart*) zuòyòng lì 作用力; (*on person*) zhòngfù 重负 **2** *v/t* (*injure*) shāng shāng 伤; *fig: finances, budget* shījiā yālì 施加压力

strain[2] *v/t vegetables* lùgān 滤干; *oil, fat etc* guòlù 过滤

strainer (*for vegetables etc*) guòlù qì 过滤器

strait hǎixiá 海峡

straitlaced gǔbǎn 古板

strand[1] *n* (*of hair, wool, thread*) lǚ 缕

strand[2] *v/t* shǐ chǔyú kùnjìng 使处于困境; *be ~ed* chǔyú kùnjìng 处于困境

strange (*odd, curious*) qíguài 奇怪; (*unknown, foreign*) mòshēng 陌生

strangely (*oddly*) qíguài 奇怪; *~ enough* chūhū yìliào 出乎意料

stranger (*person you don't know*) mòshēng rén 陌生人; *I'm a ~ here myself* wǒ duì zhèlǐ yě hěn mòshēng 我对这里也很陌生

strangle *person* èsǐ 扼死

strap *n* (*of schoolbag*) shūbāo dài 书包带; (*of bra, dress*) jiāndài 肩带; (*of watch*) biǎodài 表带; (*of shoe*) xiédài 鞋带
♦ **strap in** jìhǎo ānquándài 系好安全带

strapless wúdài 无带

strategic zhànlüè 战略

strategy zhànlüè 战略

straw[1] cǎo 草; *that's the last ~!* zuìzhōng shǐrén wúfǎ rěnshòu! 最终使人无法忍受！

straw[2] (*for drink*) xīguǎn 吸管

strawberry cǎoméi 草莓

stray 1 *adj animal* shīsàn 失散; *bullet* liúdàn 流弹 **2** *n* (*dog*) zǒushī de gǒu 走失的狗; (*cat*) zǒushī de māo 走失的猫 **3** *v/i* (*of animal, child*) zǒushī 走失; *fig* (*of eyes, thoughts*) bùyóu zìzhǔ 不由自主

streak (*of dirt, paint*) tiáowén 条纹; *fig* (*of nastiness etc*) gèxingde yímiàn 个性的一面; *he's got a cruel ~* tā yǒudiǎnr cánrěn 他有点儿残忍 **2** *v/i* (*move quickly*) fēibēn 飞奔 **3** *v/t: be ~ed with ...* yǒu ... de hénjì 有 ... 的痕迹

stream 1 *n fig* (*of people, complaints*) yìliánchuàn 一连串; *come on ~* kāishǐ shēngchǎn 开始生产 **2** *v/i* yuányuán búduàn 源源不断; *sunlight ~ed into the room* yángguāng zhàoshè rù fángjiān 阳光照射入房间

streamer héngfú 横幅

streamline *v/t fig* tígāo xiàolù 提高效率

streamlined *car, plane* liúxiànxíng 流线型; *fig: organization* gāo xiàolù 高效率

street jiēdào 街道

streetcar yǒuguǐ diànchē 有轨电车; **streetlight** jiēdēng 街灯;

streetpeople piāobó jiētóu rénshì 漂泊街头人士；**streetwalker** jìnǚ 妓女；**streetwise** adj yǒu chéngshì shēnghuó nénglì 有城市生活能力

strength (of person: physical) lìqì 力气；fig (strong point) yōudiǎn 优点；(of wind, current) qiángdù 强度；(of emotion, friendship etc) lìliàng 力量；(of organization, country, currency) shílì 实力

strengthen 1 v/t jiāqiáng 加强 **2** v/i biànqiáng 变强

strenuous jiānkǔ 艰苦

stress 1 n (emphasis) zhòngdiǎn 重点；(tension) yālì 压力；**be under ~** shòudào yālì 受到压力 **2** v/t syllable zhòngdú 重读；importance etc qiángdiào 强调；**I must ~ that ...** wǒ bìxū qiángdiào ... 我必须强调 ...

stressed out F jiāotóulàn'é 焦头烂额

stressful jǐnzhāng 紧张

stretch 1 n (of land, water) piàn 片；**at a ~** (non-stop) liánxù 连续 **2** adj fabric kě shēnsuō 可伸缩 **3** v/t material shēnzhǎn 伸展；small income jiéyù 节约；F rules hūlüè 忽略；**he ~ed out his hand** tā shēnchū shǒu lái 他伸出手来；**a job that ~es me** yīfèn yǒu tiǎozhàn xìng de gōngzuò 一份有挑战性的工作 **4** v/i (to relax muscles) shēn lǎnyāo 伸懒腰；(to reach sth) shēnshǒu 伸手；(spread) yánshēn 延伸；(of fabric: give) shēnsuō 伸缩；(of fabric: sag) chēngcháng 撑长；**~ from X to Y** (extend) cóng X yánshēn zhì Y 从 X 延伸至 Y

stretcher dānjià 担架

strict person instructions, rules yángé 严格

strictly yángé 严格；**it is ~ forbidden** juéduì bù yúnxǔ 绝对不允许

stride 1 n dàbù 大步；**take ... in one's ~** cóngróngzìrúde chǔlǐ ... 从容自如地处理 ... **2** v/i dàbù zǒu 大步走

strident jiānruì cì'ěr 尖锐刺耳；fig: demands shēngsīlìjié 声嘶力竭

strike 1 n (of workers) bàgōng 罢工；(in baseball) hǎoqiú 好球；(of oil) fāxiàn 发现；**be on ~** zài bàgōng 在罢工；**go on ~** jǔxíng bàgōng 举行罢工 **2** v/i (of workers) bàgōng 罢工；(attack) xíjī 袭击；(of disaster) jiànglín 降临；(of clock) qiāoxiǎng 敲响 **3** v/t (hit) zhuàng 撞；fig (of disaster, illness) qīnxí 侵袭；match huá 划；(of idea, thought) chūxiànyú nǎozhōng 出现于脑中；oil fāxiàn 发现；**she struck me as being ...** tā gěi wǒde yìnxiàng shì ... 她给我的印象是 ...

♦**strike out** v/t huàdiào 划掉

strikebreaker pòhuài bàgōng zhě 破坏罢工者

striker (person on strike) bàgōng zhě 罢工者

striking (marked) xiǎnzhù 显著；(eye-catching) yǐnrén zhùmù 引人注目

string n (cord) xìshéng 细绳；(of violin, cello etc) xián 弦；(of tennis racket) bēngshéng 绷绳；**~s** (musicians) xiányuèqì yǎnzòu zhě 弦乐器演奏者；**pull ~s** lā guānxi 拉关系；**a ~ of** (series) yìliánchuàn 一连串

♦**string along 1** v/i gēnsuí 跟随 **2** v/t: **string X along** yǒuyì wùdǎo X 有意误导 X

♦**string up** F diàosǐ 吊死

stringed instrument xiányuèqì 弦乐器

stringent yángé 严格

string player xiányuèqì yǎnzòu zhě 弦乐器演奏者

strip 1 n chángtiáo 长条；(comic ~) liánhuánhuà 连环画 **2** v/t (remove) chúqù 除去；(undress) bōguāng yīfu 剥光衣服；**~ X of Y** bōduó X de Y 剥夺 X 的 Y **3** v/i (undress) tuōqù yīfu 脱去衣服；(of stripper) tuōguāng yīfu 脱光衣服

strip club tuōyīwǔ yèzǒnghuì 脱

衣舞夜总会

stripe tiáowén 条纹; (*indicating rank*) jíbié tiáowén 级别条纹

striped yǒu tiáowén 有条纹

stripper tuōyīwǔ biǎoyǎn zhě 脱衣舞表演者

strip show tuōyīwǔ biǎoyǎn 脱衣舞表演

striptease tuōyīwǔ 脱衣舞

strive 1 *v/t*: **~ to do X** nǔlì zuò X 努力做 X **2** *v/i* fèndòu 奋斗; **~ for** lìzhēng 力争

stroke 1 *n* MED zhòngfēng 中风; (*when writing*) bǐhuà 笔画; (*when painting*) yìbǐ 一笔; (*style of swimming*) yóufǎ 游法; **~ of luck** zǒuyùn 走运; **she never does a ~** (*of work*) tā cónglái bù gōngzuò 她从来不工作 **2** *v/t* fǔmō 抚摸

stroll 1 *n* sànbù 散步 **2** *v/i* xiánzǒu 闲走

stroller (*for baby*) yīng'érchē 婴儿车

strong *person* qiángzhuàng 强壮; *structure* jiāngù 坚固; *candidate* qiáng qiáng 强强; *support, supporter* jiāndìng 坚定; *wind* qiángjìn 强劲; *drink* lièxìng 烈性; *tea, coffee* nóng 浓; *taste, smell* wèinóng 味浓; *views, objections* jiānjué 坚决; *currency* jiāntǐng 坚挺

stronghold *fig* gēnjùdì 根据地

strongly qiángliè 强烈

strong-minded yìzhì jiānqiáng 意志坚强

strong-willed yìzhì jiānjué 意志坚决

structural gòujià 构架

structure 1 *n* (*sth built*) jiànzhùwù 建筑物; (*way in which sth has been put together*) jiégòu 结构 **2** *v/t* jìhuà 计划

struggle 1 *n* (*fight*) zhēngdòu 争斗; (*hard time*) jiānnán 艰难 **2** *v/i* (*with a person*) gédòu 格斗; (*have a hard time*) nǔlì 努力 **3** *v/t*: **~ to do X** zhēngzhá zuò X 挣扎做 X

strum luàntán 乱弹

strut *v/i* dàyáodàbǎide zǒu 大摇大摆地走

stub 1 *n* (*of cigarette*) yāndì 烟蒂;

(*of check, ticket*) cúngēn 存根 **2** *v/t*: **I ~bed my toe** wǒ cǎidào wǒde jiǎozhǐ 我踩到我的脚趾

♦**stub out** niǎnmiè 碾灭

stubble (*on man's face*) húcházi 胡茬子

stubborn gùzhí 固执; *defense* wánqiáng 顽强

stubby cū'ér duǎn 粗而短

stuck: **be ~ on X** F duì X yǒu xìngqu 对 X 有兴趣

stuck-up F bǎi jiàzi 摆架子

student xuésheng 学生; (*at college, university*) dàxuéshēng 大学生

student nurse shíxí hùshì 实习护士

student teacher shíxí jiàoshī 实习教师

studio (*of artist, sculptor*) gōngzuòshì 工作室; (*recording ~*) lùyīnpéng 录音棚; (*film ~*) shèyǐngpéng 摄影棚; (*TV ~*) yǎnbōshì 演播室

studious hàoxué 好学

study 1 *n* (*room*) shūfáng 书房; (*learning*) xuéxí 学习; (*investigation*) yánjiū 研究 **2** *v/t* (*at school, university*) gōngdú 攻读; (*examine*) zǐxì chákàn 仔细察看 **3** *v/i* xuéxí 学习

stuff 1 *n* (*objects, things*) dōngxi 东西; (*belongings*) suǒyǒuwù 所有物 **2** *v/t turkey* tiánchōng 填充; **~ X into Y** bǎ X sāijìn Y 把 X 塞进 Y

stuffed toy tiánliào wánjù 填料玩具

stuffing (*for turkey, in chair etc*) tiánliào 填料

stuffy *room* mèn 闷; *person* gǔbǎn 古板

stumble *v/i* bànjiǎo 绊脚

stumble across *v/t* yìwài fāxiàn 意外发现

stumble over *v/t* bàndǎo 绊到; *words* chūcuò 出错

stumbling block zhàng'ài 障碍

stump 1 *n* (*of tree*) shùzhuāng 树桩 **2** *v/t* (*of question, questioner*) nánzhù 难住

♦**stump up** F fùchū 付出

stun (*of blow*) dǎhūn 打昏; (*of*

news) dàchīyìjīng 大吃一惊

stunning (*amazing*) lìngrén jīngyì 令人惊异; (*very beautiful*) jí piàoliàng 极漂亮

stunt *n* (*for publicity*) xuétóu 噱头; (*in movie*) tèjì 特技

stuntman (*in movie*) tìshēn yǎnyuán 替身演员

stupefy mùdèngkǒudāi 目瞪口呆

stupendous jíhǎo 极好

stupid yúchǔn 愚蠢

stupidity yúchǔn 愚蠢

stupor shénzhì bùqīng 神志不清

sturdy jiēshi 结实

stutter *v/i* jiēba 结巴

sty (*for pig*) zhūjuàn 猪圈

style *n* (*method, manner*) fēnggé 风格; (*fashion*) liúxíng kuǎnshì 流行款式; (*fashionable elegance*) gédiào 格调; **go out of** ~ búzài liúxíng 不再流行

stylish yǒu gédiào 有格调

subcommittee xiǎozǔ wěiyuánhuì 小组委员会

subcompact (**car**) chāoxiǎoxíng qìchē 超小型汽车

subconscious: the ~ (**mind**) qiányìshí 潜意识

subcontract *v/t* fēnbāo hétóng 分包合同

subcontractor fēnbāorén 分包人

subdivide *v/t* xìfēn 细分

subdued *lighting* róuhé 柔和; *voice* dīluò 低落

subheading fùbiāotí 副标题

subject 1 *n* (*of country*) gōngmín 公民; (*topic*) zhǔtí 主题; (*branch of learning*) kēmù 科目; GRAM zhǔyǔ 主语; **change the ~** gǎibiàn huàtí 改变话题 **2** *adj*: **be ~ to X** yǒu X de qīngxiàng 有X的倾向; **~ to availability** shòuwán wéizhǐ 售完为止 **3** *v/t* shǐ ... zāoshòu 使 ... 遭受

subjective zhǔguān 主观

sublet *v/t* zhuǎnzū 转租

submachine gun chōngfēngqiāng 冲锋枪

submarine qiántǐng 潜艇

submerge 1 *v/t* yānmò 淹没 **2** *v/i* (*of submarine*) qiánrù 潜入

submission (*surrender*) tóuxiáng 投降; (*to committee etc*) chéngwén 呈文

submissive shùncóng 顺从

submit *v/t plan, proposal* chéngjiāo 呈交

subordinate 1 *adj employee, role etc* xiàjí 下级 **2** *n* xiàshǔ 下属

subpoena 1 *n* chuánpiào 传票 **2** *v/t person* chuánhuàn 传唤

♦**subscribe to** *magazine etc* dìngyuè 订阅; *theory* zànchéng 赞成

subscriber (*to magazine*) dìngyuè zhě 订阅者

subscription dìng dìng 订订

subsequent suíhòu 随后

subsequently hòulái 后来

subside (*of flood waters*) tuìqù 退去; (*of high winds*) píngxī 平息; (*of building*) xiàxiàn 下陷; (*of fears, panic*) jiǎnruò 减弱

subsidiary *n* fùshǔ gōngsī 附属公司

subsidize zīzhù 资助

subsidy bǔzhù 补助

♦**subsist on** kào ... shēnghuó 靠 ... 生活

subsistence farmer zìjǐ nóngchǎngzhǔ 自给农场主

subsistence level pínkùn shuǐzhǔn 贫困水准

substance (*matter*) wùzhì 物质

substandard dīyú biāozhǔn 低于标准

substantial xiāngdāng dà 相当大

substantially (*considerably*) kěguān 可观; (*in essence*) shízhì shang 实质上

substantiate *adj* zhèngmíng 证明

substantive *adj* shíjì 实际

substitute 1 *n dài tìpǐn* 代替品; SP tìhuàn zhě 替换者 **2** *v/t*: **X for Y** yòng X qǔdài Y 用X取代Y **3** *v/i*: **~ for X** dàitì X 代替X

substitution (*act*) qǔdài 取代; **make a** ~ SP tìhuàn duìyuán 替换队员

subtitle 1 *n* zìmù 字幕 **2** *v/t movie* gěi ... jiā zìmù 给 ... 加字幕

subtle qiǎomiào 巧妙

subtract *v/t number* jiǎnqù 减去; ~

X from Y cóng Y zhōng jiǎnqù X 从 Y 中减去 X

suburb jiāoqū 郊区; **the ~s** shìjiāo 市郊

suburban jiāoqū 郊区

subversive 1 adj yǒu diānfùxìng 有颠覆性 **2** n diānfù fènzǐ 颠覆分子

subway dìtiě 地铁

subzero adj xiàlíngí 零下

succeed 1 v/i (be successful) chénggōng 成功; (to throne) jíwèi 即位; **~ in doing X** chénggōngde zuò X 成功地做 X **2** v/t (come after, monarch) jiērèn 继任

succeeding jiēxiàlái 接下来

success chénggōng 成功; **be a ~** chénggōng 成功

successful chénggōng 成功

successfully chénggōng 成功

succession (sequence) yíxìliè 一系列; (to the throne) jíwèi 即位; **in ~** yígè jiē yígè 一个接一个

successive jiēlián búduàn 接连不断

successor jìrènrén 继任人

succinct jiǎnyào 简要

succulent meat, fruit xiānměi 鲜美

succumb (give in) qūfú 屈服; **~ to temptation** qūcóngyú yòuhuò 屈从于诱惑

such 1 adj (of that kind) zhèyàng 这样; **~ a** (so much of a) nàme 那么; **~ as** xiàng ... yíyàng 像 ... 一样; **there is no ~ word as ...** méiyǒu rú ... zhèmege cí 没有如 ... 这么个词 **2** adv zhème 这么; **as ~** àn qí běnshēn yìyì 按其本身意义

suck lollipop, hard candy shǔnxī 吮吸; **~ one's thumb** shǔnxī mǔzhǐ 吮吸拇指; **~ X from Y** cóng Y xīchū X 从 Y 吸出 X

♦**suck up** moisture xīshōu 吸收

♦**suck up to** F fèngcheng 奉承

sucker F (person) qīngxìn zhě 轻信者; F (lollipop) bàngbàngtáng 棒棒糖

sucking pig rǔzhū 乳猪

suction chōuxī 抽吸

sudden yìwài 意外; **all of a ~** tūrán 突然

suddenly tūrán 突然

suds (soap ~) pàomò 泡沫

sue v/t kònggào 控告

suede n róngmiàngé 绒面革

suffer 1 v/i (be in great pain) shòukǔ 受苦; (deteriorate) biànchà 变差; **be ~ing from** huànyǒu 患有 **2** v/t loss zāoshòu 遭受; setback jīngshòu 经受

suffering n tòngkǔ 痛苦

sufficient zúgòu 足够

sufficiently chōngzú 充足

suffocate 1 v/i zhìxī ér sǐ 窒息而死 **2** v/t shǐ ... zhìxī 使 ... 窒息

suffocation zhìxī 窒息

sugar 1 n shítáng 食糖 **2** v/t jiātáng 加糖

sugar bowl tángguàn 糖罐

sugar cane gānzhe 甘蔗

suggest v/t jiànyì 建议; **I ~ that we stop now** wǒ jiànyì wǒmen xiànzài tíngxià 我建议我们现在停下

suggestion jiànyì 建议

suicide zìshā 自杀; **commit ~** zìshā 自杀

suit 1 n xīzhuāng 西装; (in cards) huāsè pái 花色牌 **2** v/t (of clothes, color) shìhé 适合; **~ yourself!** suí nǐde biàn! 随你的便！; **be ~ed for X** shìhé X 适合 X

suitable shìyí 适宜

suitcase shǒutí yīxiāng 手提衣箱

suite (of rooms) tàojiān 套间; (furniture) yītào jiājù 一套家具; MUS zǔqǔ 组曲

sulfur liúhuáng 硫磺

sulk v/i shēng mènqì 生闷气

sulky shēng mènqì 生闷气

sullen mènmènbúlè 闷闷不乐

sultry climate mēnrè 闷热; (sexually) xìnggǎn 性感

sum (total) zǒngshù 总数; (amount) shùmù 数目; (in arithmetic) suànshù 算术; **a large ~ of money** amount yí dà bǐ qián 一大笔钱; **~ insured** amount bǎoxiǎn jīn'é 保险金额; **the ~ total of his efforts** tā yíqiè nǔlìde jiéguǒ 他一切努力的结果

♦**sum up 1** v/t (summarize) gàikuò

概括; (assess) píngjià 评价 **2** v/i LAW gàishù 概述

summarize v/t gàikuò 概括

summary n zǒngjié 总结

summer xiàtiān 夏天

Summer Palace Yíhéyuán 颐和园

summit (of mountain) shāndǐng 山顶; fig zhìgāodiǎn 至高点; POL zuì gāojí huìyì 最高级会议

summon staff, ministers zhàojí 召集; meeting zhàokāi 召开

♦ **summon up** strength fāhuī 发挥

summons LAW chuánpiào 传票

sump (for oil) rùnhuáyóuxiāng 润滑油箱

sun tàiyáng 太阳; in the ~ zài yángguāng xià 在阳光下; out of the ~ zài bèiyīnchù 在背阴处; he has had too much ~ tā zhòngshǔ le 他中暑了

sunbathe shài tàiyáng 晒太阳; **sunblock** fángshàigāo 防晒膏; **sunburn** shàibān 晒斑; **sunburnt** shàishāng 晒伤

Sunday xīngqīrì 星期日

sundial rìguī 日晷

sundries záxiàng 杂项

sunglasses mòjìng 墨镜

sunken cheeks āoxiàn 凹陷

sunny day yángguāng chōngzú 阳光充足; disposition kāilǎng 开朗; it is ~ tiānqì qínglǎng 天气晴朗

sunrise rìchū 日出; **sunset** rìluò 日落; **sunshade** yángsǎn 阳伞; **sunshine** yángguāng 阳光; **sunstroke** zhòngshǔ 中暑; **suntan** shàihēi 晒黑; get a ~ shàichéng gǔtóngsè 晒成古铜色

Sun Yat-sen Sūn Zhōngshān 孙中山

super 1 adj F jíhǎo 极好 **2** n (janitor) guǎnlǐyuán 管理员

superb bàngjíle 棒极了

superficial comments, analysis fúqiǎn 肤浅; person qiǎnbó 浅薄; wounds biǎopí 表皮

superfluous duōyú 多余

superhuman efforts chāohūchángrén 超乎常人

superintendent (of apartment block) guǎnlǐyuán 管理员

superior 1 adj (better) gènghǎo 更好; pej (attitude) yǒu yōuyuègǎn 有优越感 **2** n (in organization, society) shàngjí 上级

supermarket chāojí shìchǎng 超级市场

supernatural 1 adj powers chāozìrán 超自然 **2** n: the ~ chāozìrán de shìwù 超自然的事物

superpower POL chāojí dàguó 超级大国

supersonic flight, aircraft chāoyīnsù 超音速

superstition míxìn sīxiǎng 迷信思想

superstitious person míxìn 迷信

supervise jiāndū 监督

supervisor (at work) zhǐdǎo zhě 指导者

supper wǎnfàn 晚饭

supple róuruǎn 柔软

supplement (extra payment) fùjiāfèi 附加费

supplier COM gōngyìngshāng 供应商

supply 1 n gōngyìng 供应; ~ and demand gōngyìng yǔ xūqiú 供应与需求; supplies gōngyìngpǐn 供应品 **2** v/t goods tígōng 提供; ~ X with Y xiàng X tígōng Y 向 X 提供 Y; be supplied with ... zhuāngyǒu ... 装有 ...

support 1 n (for structure) zhīzhù 支柱; (backing) zhīchí 支持 **2** v/t building, structure zhīcheng 支撑; (financially) yuánzhù 援助; (back) zhīchí 支持

supporter yōnghù zhě 拥护者; (of football team etc) zhīchí zhě 支持者

supportive zhīchí 支持

suppose (imagine) liàoxiǎng 料想; I ~ so wǒ kàn shì zhèyàng 我看是这样; be ~d to ... (be meant to) yīnggāi ... 应该 ...; (be said to be) jùshuō ... 据说 ...; you are not ~d to ... (not allowed to) nǐ bùgāi ... 你不该 ...

suppository MED shuānjì 栓剂

suppress *rebellion etc* zhènyā 镇压

suppression zhènyā 镇压

supremacy zuìgāo quánwēi 最高权威

supreme *being, commander* zhìgāowúshàng 至高无上; *effort, courage, delight* jídà 极大

Supreme Court Gāojí Fǎtíng 高级法庭

surcharge fùjiāfèi 附加费

sure 1 *adj*: **I'm ~** wǒ néng quèdìng 我能确定; **I'm not ~** wǒ bú quèdìng 我不确定; **be ~ about X** duì X néng quèdìng 对 X 能确定; **make ~ that …** chámíng … 查明 … **2** *adv*: **~ enough** guǒrán rúcǐ 果然如此; **it ~ is hot today** jīntiān quèshí rè 今天确实热; **~!** dāngrán! 当然!

surely yídìng 一定; (*gladly*) dāngrán 当然

surf 1 *n* (*on sea*) jīlàng 激浪 **2** *v/t* *the Net* sōuxún 搜寻

surface 1 *n* (*of table, object*) biǎomiàn 表面; (*of water*) shuǐmiàn 水面; **on the ~** *fig* biǎomiàn shang 表面上 **2** *v/i* (*of swimmer, submarine*) fúdào shuǐmiàn 浮到水面; (*appear*) chóngxīn chūxiàn 重新出现

surface mail pǔtōng yóujiàn 普通邮件

surfboard chōnglàngbǎn 冲浪板

surfer (*on sea*) chōnglàng zhě 冲浪者

surfing chōnglàng yùndòng 冲浪运动; **go ~** zuò chōnglàng yùndòng 作冲浪运动

surge *n* (*in electric current*) diànliú jíchōng 电流急冲; (*in demand, interest, growth etc*) jīzēng 激增

♦ **surge forward** (*of crowd*) yǒngjìn 涌进

surgeon wàikē yīshī 外科医师

surgery shǒushù 手术; **undergo ~** jiēshòu shǒushù zhìliáo 接受手术治疗

surgical wàikē 外科

surly guāilì 乖戾

surmount *difficulties* kèfú 克服

surname xìng 姓

surpass chāoguò 超过

surplus 1 *n* guòshèng 过剩 **2** *adj* shèngyú 剩余

surprise 1 *n* jīngqí 惊奇; **it'll come as no ~ to hear that …** tīngdào … bùzú wéiqí 听到 … 不足为奇 **2** *v/t* shǐ … chījīng 使 … 吃惊; **be / look ~d** chīle yìjīng / kànqǐlái chīle yìjīng 吃了一惊 / 看起来吃了一惊

surprising lìngrén jīngyà 令人惊讶

surprisingly chūrényìwài 出人意外

surrender 1 *v/i* (*of army*) tóuxiáng 投降 **2** *v/t* (*hand in: weapons etc*) jiāochū 交出 **3** *n* tóuxiáng 投降; (*handing in*) jiāochū 交出

surrogate mother dàimǔ 代母

surround 1 *v/t* bāowéi 包围; **be ~ed by X** bèi X bāowéi 被 X 包围 **2** *n* (*of picture etc*) biānyuán 边缘

surrounding *adj* zhōuwéi 周围

surroundings huánjìng 环境

survey 1 *n* (*of modern literature etc*) gàikuàng 概况; (*of consumer habits*) diàochá 调查; (*of building*) jiàndìng 鉴定 **2** *v/t* (*look at*) shěnshì 审视; *building* jiàndìng 鉴定

surveyor jiàndìngrén 鉴定人

survival xìngcún 幸存

survive 1 *v/i* (*of species*) cúnhuó 存活; (*of patient*) yǒuxìng cúnhuó 有幸存活; **how are you? – I'm surviving** nǐ hǎo ma?- wǒ miǎnqiǎng huózhe 你好吗?-我勉强活着; **his two surviving daughters** tāde liǎnggè huózhede nǚ'ér 他的两个活着的女儿 **2** *v/t accident, operation* xìngcún 幸存; (*outlive*) bǐ … chángmíng 比 … 长命

survivor xìngcún zhě 幸存者; **he's a ~** *fig* tā shì yígè jīngdeqǐ fēngshuāng de rén 他是一个经得起风霜的人

susceptible (*emotionally*) yìshòu gǎndòng 易受感动; **be ~ to the cold / heat** duì lěng / rè mǐngǎn 对冷 / 热敏感

suspect 1 *n* xiányífàn 嫌疑犯

2 v/t person huáiyí 怀疑; (suppose) juéde 觉得

suspected murderer xiányí 嫌疑; **the ~ cause** bèi huáiyí de yuányīn 被怀疑的原因

suspend (hang) xuánguà 悬挂; (from office, duties) lèlìng tíngzhí 勒令停职

suspenders (for pants) diàokùdài 吊裤带

suspense jǐnzhānggǎn 紧张感

suspension (in vehicle) jiǎnzhèn zhuāngzhì 减震装置; (from duty) tíngzhí 停职

suspension bridge diàoqiáo 吊桥

suspicion huáiyí 怀疑

suspicious (causing suspicion) kěyí 可疑; (feeling suspicion) yǒu yíxīn 有疑心; **be ~ of X** duì X yǒu yíxīn 对 X 有疑心

sustain zhīcheng 支撑

swab 1 n yàoqiān 药签 **2** v/t yòng yàoqiān cā 用药签擦

swagger n zhǐgāoqìyáng 趾高气扬

swallow¹ 1 v/t liquid, food yàn 咽 **2** v/i yànshí 咽食

swallow² (bird) yànzi 燕子

swamp 1 n zhǎozé 沼泽 **2** v/t yānmò 淹没; **be ~ed with X** X yìngjiēbùxiá X 应接不暇

swampy ground shīruǎn 湿软

swan tiān'é 天鹅

swap 1 v/t jiāohuàn 交换; **~ X for Y** yòng X huàn Y 用 X 换 Y **2** v/i huàn 换

swarm 1 n (of bees) dàqún 大群 **2** v/i (of ants, tourists etc) mìjí 密集; **the town was ~ing with X** chéngshìlǐ dàochù dōu shì X 城市里到处都是 X

swarthy face, complexion yǒuhēi 黝黑

swat v/t insect, fly zhòngpāi 重拍

sway 1 n (influence, power) yǐngxiǎng 影响 **2** v/i yáobǎi 摇摆

swear v/i (use swearword) zhòumà 咒骂; (promise) fāshì 发誓; LAW xuānshì 宣誓; **~ at X** zhòumà X 咒骂 X

♦**swear in** witness shǐ ... xuānshì 使 ... 宣誓

swearword màrénhuà 骂人话

sweat 1 n hànshuǐ 汗水; **covered in ~** dàhànlínlí 大汗淋漓 **2** v/i chūhàn 出汗

sweater máoyī 毛衣

sweatshirt wúlǐng chángxiùshān 无领长袖衫

sweaty hands, smell hànlínlín 汗淋淋

Swede Ruìdiǎn rén 瑞典人

Sweden Ruìdiǎn 瑞典

Swedish 1 adj Ruìdiǎn 瑞典 **2** n (language) Ruìdiǎn yǔ 瑞典语

sweep 1 v/t floor, leaves sǎo 扫 **2** n (long curve) wānyán 蜿蜒

♦**sweep up** v/t mess, crumbs sǎolǒng 扫拢

sweeping adj generalization, statement lǒngtǒng 笼统; changes yǒu guǎngfàn yǐngxiǎng 有广泛影响

sweet adj taste, tea tián 甜; F (kind) hǎoxīn 好心; F (cute) rěrén xǐ'ài 惹人喜爱

sweet and sour adj tángcù 糖醋

sweetcorn tián yùmǐ 甜玉米

sweeten v/t drink, food shǐ ... biàntián 使 ... 变甜

sweetener (for drink) tiánwèijì 甜味剂

sweetheart xīnshàng rén 心上人

swell 1 v/i (of limb etc) zhǒngzhàng 肿胀 **2** adj F (good) jíhǎo 极好 **3** n (of the sea) qǐfú 起伏

swelling n MED zhǒngkuài 肿块

sweltering heat, day kùrè 酷热

swerve v/i (of driver, car) tūrán zhuǎnxiàng 突然转向

swift adj xùnsù 迅速

swim 1 v/i yóuyǒng 游泳; **go ~ming** qù yóuyǒng 去游泳; **my head is ~ming** wǒ tóuyūnmùxuàn 我头晕目眩 **2** n yóuyǒng 游泳; **go for a ~** qù yóuyǒng 去游泳

swimmer yóuyǒng zhě 游泳者

swimming yóuyǒng 游泳

swimming pool yóuyǒngchí 游泳池

swimsuit yóuyǒngyī 游泳衣

swindle 1 n piànjú 骗局 **2** v/t: **~ X**

out of Y cóng Y piàndé X 从 Y 骗得 X

swine F (*person*) xiàliúpī 下流坯

swing 1 *n* zhuǎnbiàn 转变; (*for child*) qiūqiān 秋千; **~ to the Democrats** zhuǎn ér zhīchí Mínzhǔdǎng 转而支持民主党 **2** *v/t* huīdòng 挥动; *hips* yáobǎi 摇摆 **3** *v/i* bǎidòng 摆动; (*turn*) zhuàndòng 转动; (*of public opinion etc*) biàndòng 变动

swing-door tuīhémén 推合门

Swiss 1 *adj* Ruìshì 瑞士 **2** *n* (*person*) Ruìshì rén 瑞士人

switch 1 *n* (*for light*) kāiguān 开关; (*change*) biànhuà 变化 **2** *v/t* (*change*) huàn 换 **3** *v/i* (*change*) gǎihuàn 改换

♦**switch off** *v/t & v/i lights, engine, PC, TV* guāndiào 关掉

♦**switch on 1** *v/t lights, engine, PC, TV* kāi 开 **2** *v/i* kāijī 开机

switchboard diànhuà jiāohuàntái 电话交换台

switchover (*to new system*) zhuǎnbiàn 转变

Switzerland Ruìshì 瑞士

swivel *v/i* (*of chair, monitor etc*) xuánzhuàn 旋转

swollen zhǒngzhàng 肿胀

swoop *v/i* (*of bird*) měngpū 猛扑

♦**swoop down on** *prey* měngpū xiàng 猛扑向

♦**swoop on** (*of police etc*) tūrán sōuchá 突然搜查

sword jiàn 剑

sycamore xīkèmò shù 西克莫树

syllable yīnjié 音节

syllabus dàgāng 大纲

symbol (*character*) fúhào 符号; (*in poetry etc*) xiàngzhēng 象征

symbolic yǒu xiàngzhēngxìng 有象征性

symbolism (*in poetry, art*) xiàngzhēng shǒufǎ 象征手法

symbolize xiàngzhēng 象征

symmetric(**al**) duìchèn 对称

symmetry duìchèn 对称

sympathetic (*showing pity*) biǎoshì tóngqíng 表示同情; (*understanding*) lǐjiě rén 理解人; **be ~ toward a person / an idea** duì rén / xiǎngfǎ biǎoshì tóngqíng, zhīchí 对人 / 想法表示同情、支持

♦**sympathize with** *person, views* tóngqíng 同情

sympathizer POL yōnghù zhě 拥护者

sympathy (*pity*) tóngqíngxīn 同情心; (*understanding*) lǐjiě 理解; ***don't expect any ~ from me!*** bié zhǐwàng wǒ kělián nǐ! 别指望我可怜你!

symphony jiāoxiǎngyuè 交响乐

symptom MED zhèngzhuàng 症状; *fig* zhēngzhào 征兆

symptomatic: be ~ of X MED shì Xde zhèngzhuàng 是 X 的症状; *fig* shì Xde zhēngzhào 是 X 的征兆

synchronize *watches* shǐ ... tóngshí 使 ... 同时; *operations* shǐ ... tóngbù 使 ... 同步

synonym tóngyìcí 同义词

syntax jùfǎ 句法

synthetic rénzào 人造

syphilis méidú 梅毒

syringe zhùshèqì 注射器

syrup tángjiāng 糖浆

system (*method*) xìtǒng 系统; (*orderliness*) chéngxù 程序; (*computer*) zǔhé zhuāngzhì 组合装置; ***the braking / fuel injection / digestive ~*** shāchē / ránliào shūrù / xiāohuà xìtǒng 刹车 / 燃料输入 / 消化系统

systematic *approach, person* yǒu tiáolǐ 有条理

systematically *analyze, study* yǒu tiáolǐ 有条理; *destroy* xùyì 蓄意

system crash xìtǒng bēngkuì 系统崩溃

systems analyst COMPUT xìtǒng fēnxī zhě 系统分析者

Szechuan Sìchuān 四川

T

tab *n* lāshé 拉舌; (*in text*) fáng-mŏshé 防抹舌

table *n* zhuōzi 桌子; (*of figures*) biǎo 表

tablecloth zhuōbù 桌布

tablespoon cānsháor 餐勺儿

tablet yàopiànr 药片儿

table tennis pīngpāngqiú 乒乓球

tabloid *n* (*newspaper*) xiǎobào 小报

taboo *adj* bìhuì 避讳

tacit xīnzhào bù xuān 心照不宣

tack 1 *n* (*nail*) píngtóudīng 平头钉 2 *v/t* (*sew*) bēng 绷 3 *v/i* (*of yacht*) zhuǎnháng 转航

tackle 1 *n* (*equipment*) yòngjù 用具; SP zǔdǎng 阻挡 2 *v/t* SP jiéqiú 截球; *problem* chǔlǐ 处理; *intruder* zhuāzhù 抓住

tacky *paint, glue* nián 粘; (*cheap, poor quality*) súqì 俗气; *behavior* bù yǎguān 不雅观

tact jīzhì 机智

tactful détǐ 得体

tactical zhànshù 战术

tactics cèlüè 策略

tactless bù détǐ 不得体

tadpole kēdǒu 蝌蚪

tag (*label*) biāoqiān 标签

Tai: *Mount* ~ Tàishān 泰山

tai chi tàijíquán 太极拳

tail *n* wěiba 尾巴

tail coat yànwěifú 燕尾服

tail light wěidēng 尾灯

tailor cáifeng 裁缝

tailor-made *suit* dìngzuò 定做; *solution* shìdàng 适当

tail wind shùnfēng 顺风

tainted *food* wūrǎn 污染

Taipei Táiběi 台北

Taiwan Táiwān 台湾

Taiwanese 1 *adj* Táiwān 台湾 2 *n* (*person*) Táiwān rén 台湾人; (*dialect*) Táiwān huà 台湾话

Taiwan Straits Táiwān Hǎixiá 台湾海峡

Tajik Tǎjíkè rén 塔吉克人

Tajiki 1 *adj* Tǎjíkè 塔吉克 2 *n* (*language*) Tǎjíkè yǔ 塔吉克语

Tajikistan Tǎjíkè 塔吉克

take *v/t* (*remove*) ná 拿; (*steal*) tōu 偷; (*transport*) sòng 送; (*accompany*) péi 陪; (*accept: money, gift, credit cards*) jiēshòu 接受; (*study: math, French*) xué 学; *photograph* zhàoxiàng 照相; *exam, degree* kǎo 考; *shower* línyù 淋浴; *stroll* sànbù 散步; *s.o.'s temperature* liáng 量; (*endure*) rěnshòu 忍受; (*require*) xūyào 需要; *how long does it ~?* yào duōcháng shíjiān? 要多长时间？; *I'll ~ it* (*when shopping*) wǒ mǎi le 我买了
- ♦ **take after** xiàng 像
- ♦ **take away** *pain* jiěchú 解除; *object* názǒu 拿走; MATH jiǎn 减; *take X away from Y* cóng Y nàlǐ názǒu X 从Y那里拿走X
- ♦ **take back** (*return: object*) tuìdiào 退掉; *person* sòng 送; (*accept back: husband etc*) jiēshòu 接受; *that takes me back* (*of music, thought etc*) shǐ wǒ huíyìqǐ 使我回忆起
- ♦ **take down** (*from shelf*) qǔxià 取下; *scaffolding* chāidiào 拆掉; *pants* tuō 脱; (*write down*) xiěxià 写下
- ♦ **take in** (*take indoors*) ná jìnlái 拿进来; (*give accommodation*) shōuliú 收留; (*make narrower*) gǎixiǎo 改小; (*deceive*) qīpiàn 欺骗; (*include*) bāokuò 包括
- ♦ **take off** 1 *v/t clothes, hat* qǔxià 取下; *10% etc* jiàngjià 降价; (*mimic*) mófǎng 模仿; *can you take a bit off here?* (*to barber*) néngbùnéng zài zhèlǐ jiǎn yìdiǎnr? 能不能在

这里剪一点儿？; *take a day / week off* fàngjià yītiān / yīxīngqī 放假一天 / 一星期 **2** *v/i (of airplane)* qǐfēi 起飞; *(become popular)* fēiyuè 飞跃

♦ **take on** *job* dānrèn 担任; *staff* pìnyòng 聘用

♦ **take out** *(from bag, pocket)* náchū 拿出; *stain* qùdiào 去掉; *tooth* qǔchū 取出; *appendix, word from text* shānchú 删除; *money from bank* qǔ 取; *(to dinner etc)* dài ... chūqù 带 ... 出去; *insurance policy* bànlǐ 办理; *take it out on X (s.o.)* zài X de shēnshàng bàofù 在 X 的身上报复

♦ **take over 1** *v/t company etc* jiānbìng 兼并; *tourists ~ the town* mǎn zhèn dōushì lǚkè 满镇都是旅客 **2** *v/i (of new management etc)* jiēguǎn 接管; *(do sth in s.o.'s place)* jiēshǒu 接手

♦ **take to** *(like)* xǐhuan 喜欢; *(form habit of)* yǎngchéng ... xíguàn 养成 ... 习惯

♦ **take up** *carpet etc* jiēqǐ 揭起; *(carry up)* ná shàngqù 拿上去; *(shorten: dress etc)* shōuduǎn 收短; *hobby* kāishǐ 开始; *judo, new language* kāishǐ xuéxí 开始学习; *offer* jiēshòu 接受; *new job* kāishǐ cóngshì 开始从事; *space, time* zhànqù 占去; *I'll take you up on your offer* wǒ jiēshòu nǐde tíyì 我接受你的提议

take-home pay shídé gōngzī 实得工资

takeoff *(of airplane)* qǐfēi 起飞; *(impersonation)* mófǎng 模仿;

takeover COM jiānbìng 兼并;

takeover bid jiānbìng tóubiāo 兼并投标

takings shōurù 收入

talcum powder shuǎngshēnfěn 爽身粉

tale gùshì 故事

talent tiāncái 天才

talented yǒu tiāncái 有天才

talk 1 *v/i* tánhuà 谈话; *can I ~ with ...?* qǐngzhǎo ...? 请找 ... ?; *I'll ~ to him about it* wǒ huì hé tā

tán wǒ huì hé tā tán **2** *v/t English etc* shuō 说; *business, politics* tán 谈; *~ X into doing Y* shuōfú X zuò Y 说服 X 做 Y **3** *n (conversation)* jiāotán 交谈; *(lecture)* yǎnjiǎng 演讲; *he's all ~ pej* tā zhǐshì kōngtán 他只是空谈

♦ **talk over** tǎolùn 讨论

talkative jiàntán 健谈

talk show tánhuà jiémù 谈话节目

tall gāo 高

tall order gāo yāoqiú 高要求

tall story kuādàde gùshì 夸大的故事

tame *animal* xùnfú 驯服; *joke etc* píngdàn 平淡

♦ **tamper with** sǔnhuài 损坏

tampon ⇩ yuèjīng shuān 月经栓

tan 1 *n (from sun)* rì shài fūsè 日晒肤色; *(color)* zōnghè sè 棕褐色 **2** *v/i (in sun)* shài hēi 晒黑 **3** *v/t leather* róu 鞣

tandem *(bike)* qiánhòu shuāngzuò zìxíngchē 前后双座自行车

Tang Dynasty Táng Cháo 唐朝

tangerine gānjú 柑桔

tangle *n* yītuánzāo 一团糟

♦ **tangle up** : *get tangled up (of string etc)* chán zài yìqǐ 缠在一起

tango *n* tāngē wǔ 探戈舞

Tang poetry Tángshī 唐诗

tank chúshuǐ chí 储水池; MOT xiāng 箱; MIL tǎnkè 坦克; *(for skin diver)* shuǐfèi 水肺

tanker *(ship)* yóuchuán 油船; *(truck)* guànchē 罐车

tanned shài hēi 晒黑

tantalizing yòurén 诱人

tantamount : *be ~ to* xiāngdāngyú 相当于

tantrum fā píqì 发脾气

Tao Dào 道

Taoism *(philosophy)* Dàojiā 道家; *(religion)* Dàojiào 道教

Taoist priest Dàoshì 道士

tap 1 *n* lóngtóu 龙头 **2** *v/t (knock)* qīngqiāo 轻敲; *phone* qiètīng 窃听

♦ **tap into** *resources* lìyòng 利用

tap dance *n* tīda wǔ 踢踏舞

tape 1 *n* (*for recording*) cídài 磁带; (*sticky*) jiāodài 胶带 **2** *v/t conversation etc* lùyīn 录音; (*with sticky tape*) zhān 粘

tape deck lùyīnzuò 录音座; **tape drive** COMPUT cídài qūdòngqì 磁带驱动器; **tape measure** juǎnchǐ 卷尺

taper *v/i* jiǎnxiǎo 减小

♦ **taper off** (*of production*) zhújiàn tíngzhǐ 逐渐停止; (*of figures*) zhújiàn jiǎnshǎo 逐渐减少

tape recorder lùyīnjī 录音机

tape recording lùyīn 录音

tapestry zhījǐn 织锦

tapeworm tāochóng 绦虫

tar *n* bǎiyóu 柏油

tardy huǎnmàn 缓慢

target 1 *n* (*in shooting, for sales, production*) mùbiāo 目标 **2** *v/t market* bǎ ... zuòwéi mùbiāo 把 ... 作为目标

target date mùbiāo rìqī 目标日期; **target group** COM duìxiàng zǔ 对象组; **target market** duìxiàng shìchǎng 对象市场

tariff (*price*) jiàmùbiǎo 价目表; (*tax*) shuì 税

tarmac (*at airport*) pǎodào 跑道

tarnish *v/t metal* shǐ ... shīqù guāngzé 使 ... 失去光泽; *reputation* sǔnhuài 损坏

tarpaulin yóubù 油布

tart *n* guǒxiànr bǐng 果馅儿饼

task rènwù 任务

task button rènwùniǔ 任务钮

task force tèbié gōngzuòzǔ 特别工作组

tassel liúsū 流苏

taste 1 *n* (*sense, of food etc*) wèidao 味道; (*in clothes, art etc*) pǐnwèi 品味; *he has no ~* tā méiyǒu shěnměi yǎnguāng 他没有审美眼光 **2** *v/t food* cháng 尝; (*experience: freedom etc*) chángshì 尝试

tasteful yǒu shěnměi yǎnguāng 有审美眼光

tasteless *food* méiwèir 没味儿; *remark, person* cūsú 粗俗

tasty xiāng 香

tattered *clothes, book* pòlàn 破烂

tatters: in ~ (*of clothes*) pòpo lànlan 破破烂烂; (*of reputation, career*) chèdǐ cuīhuǐ 彻底摧毁

tattoo *n* wénshēn 纹身

taunt *n & v/t* cháoxiào 嘲笑

taut jǐn 紧

tax 1 *n* shuì 税; *before / after ~* shuì qián / hòu 税前 / 后 **2** *v/t people, product* chōushuì 抽税

taxation (*act of taxing*) zhēngshuì 征税; (*taxes*) shuìshōu 税收

tax code shuìwù hàomǎ 税务号码; **tax-deductible** kě jiǎnshuì 可减税; **tax-free** miǎnshuì 免税

taxi ⇩ chūzūchē 出租车

taxidriver chūzūchē sījī 出租车司机

taxi rank, taxi stand chūzūchē tíngchēchù 出租车停车处

tax inspector shuìwù diàocháyuán 税务调查员; **tax payer** nàshuì rén 纳税人; **tax return** (*form*) nàshuì dān 纳税单

tea (*drink*) chá 茶; (*meal*) chádiǎn 茶点; *black ~* hóngchá 红茶; *green ~* lǜchá 绿茶

teabag chábāo 茶包

teach 1 *v/t person, subject* jiāo 教; *~ X to do Y* jiāo X zuò Y 教 X 做 Y **2** *v/i* jiāoshū 教书

teacher lǎoshī 老师

teacher training jiàoshī péixùn 教师培训

teaching (*profession*) jiāoxué 教学

teaching aid jiàojù 教具

teaching assistant zhùjiào 助教

tea cloth chájīn 茶巾; **teacup** chábēi 茶杯; **tea drinker** hēchárén 喝茶人; **tea house** cháguǎnr 茶馆儿

teak yòumù 柚木

tea leaf cháyè 茶叶

team zǔ 组

team spirit jítǐ jīngshén 集体精神

teamster kǎchē sījī 卡车司机

teamwork ⇩ pèihé 配合

teapot cháhú 茶壶

tear¹ 1 *n* (*in cloth etc*) lièkǒu 裂口 **2** *v/t paper, cloth* sī 撕; *be torn between two alternatives* yóuyù bùjué 犹豫不决 **3** *v/i* (*run fast,* *drive fast*) jí bēn 急奔

♦**tear up** *paper* sī 撕; *agreement* sīhuǐ 撕毁

tear² (*in eye*) lèi 泪; **burst into ~s** fàngshēng dàkū 放声大哭; **be in ~s** kū 哭

teardrop yǎnlèi 眼泪

tearful yǎnlèi wāngwang 眼泪汪汪

tear gas cuīlèi qì 催泪气

tearoom cháshì 茶室

tease *v/t* dòunòng 逗弄

tea service, tea set chájù 茶具

teaspoon cháchí 茶匙

teat rǔtóu 乳头

tea towel cā wǎn bù 擦碗布

technical jìshù xìng 技术性

technicality (*technical nature*) zhuānmén xìng 专门性; LAW sùsòng xìjié 诉讼细节; *that's just a ~* nà zhǐshì xìjié éryǐ 那只是细节而已

technically (*strictly speaking*) yángé láishuō 严格来说

technician jìshùyuán 技术员

technique fāngfǎ 方法

technological jìshù 技术

technology jìshù 技术

technophobia kǒng jìshù bìng 恐技术病

tedious shǐrén yànfán 使人厌烦

tee *n* (*in golf*) qiúzuò 球座

teem: *be ~ing with rain* qīngpén dàyǔ 倾盆大雨; *be ~ing with tourists / ants* chōngmǎn yóukè / mǎyǐ 充满游客 / 蚂蚁

teenage *fashions* qīngshàonián 青少年; *~ boy / girl* shàonán / nǚ 少男 / 女

teenager qīngshàonián 青少年

teens: *be in one's ~* shíjǐsuì 十几岁; *reach one's ~* jìnrù qīngshàonián shíqī 进入青少年时期

telecommunications diànxìn 电信

telegram diànbào 电报

telegraph pole diànxiàn gān 电线杆

telepathic xīnlíng gǎnyìng 心灵感应; *you must be ~!* nǐ kěndìng shì xīnlíng gǎnyìng! 你肯定是心灵感应！

telepathy xīnlíng gǎnyìng 心灵感应

telephone 1 *n* diànhuà 电话; *be on the ~* (*be speaking*) jiǎng diànhuà 讲电话; (*possess a phone*) yǒu diànhuà 有电话 **2** *v/t & v/i* dǎ diànhuà 打电话

telephone booth diànhuà tíng 电话亭; **telephone call** diànhuà 电话; **telephone directory** diànhuà běn 电话本; **telephone exchange** zǒngjī 总机; **telephone number** diànhuà hàomǎ 电话号码

telephoto lens shèyuǎn jìngtóu 摄远镜头

telesales diànhuà tuīxiāo 电话推销

telescope wàngyuǎnjìng 望远镜

televise diànshì bōfàng 电视播放

television diànshì 电视; (*set*) diànshì jī 电视机; *on ~* diànshì shang 电视上; *watch ~* kàn diànshì 看电视

television program diànshì jiémù 电视节目; **television set** diànshì jī 电视机; **television studio** diànshì shèyǐng shì 电视摄影室

tell 1 *v/t story, lie* jiǎng 讲; *the difference* qūfēn 区分; *~ X Y* gàosù X Y 告诉 X Y; *don't ~ Mom* bié gàosù māma 别告诉妈妈; *could you ~ me the way to ...?* qǐng gàosù wǒ zěnme qù ...? 请告诉我怎么去 ... ？; *~ X to do Y* jiào X zuò Y 叫 X 做 Y; *you're ~ing me!* háiyòng nǐ shuō! 还用你说！ **2** *v/i* (*have effect*) chǎnshēng xiàoguǒ 产生效果; *the heat is ~ing on him* qìwēn duì tā chǎnshēng yǐngxiǎng 气温对他产生影响; *time will ~* shíjiān zì huì dìnglùn 时间自会定论

♦**tell off** (*reprimand*) shǔluò 数落

teller (*in bank*) chūnàyuán 出纳员

telltale 1 *adj signs* xièlòu 泄露 **2** *n* xièmìzhě 泄密者

temp 1 *n* (*employee*) línshígōng 临

时工 **2** v/i dǎ línshígōng 打临时工

temper (bad ~) píqi 脾气;**be in a ~** fā píqi 发脾气;**keep one's ~** nàzhe xìngzi 捺着性子;**lose one's ~** fā píqi 发脾气

temperament xìnggé 性格

temperamental (moody) yì jīdòng 易激动

temperature wēndù 温度;(fever) fāshāo 发烧;**have a ~** fāshāo 发烧

temple[1] REL miàoyǔ 庙宇

temple[2] ANAT tàiyángxué 太阳穴

Temple of Heaven Tiāntán 天坛

tempo sùdù 速度

temporarily zànshí 暂时

temporary zànshí 暂时

tempt xīyǐn 吸引

temptation yòuhuò 诱惑

tempting yǒu xīyǐnlì 有吸引力

ten shí 十

tenacious jiānrèn 坚韧

tenant (of building) fángkè 房客;(of farm, land) diànhù 佃户

tend[1] v/t (look after) zhàogù 照顾

tend[2]: **~ to do ...** qīngxiàng yú zuò ... 倾向于做...;**~ toward ...** qīngxiàng yú ... 倾向于...

tendency qīngxiàng 倾向

tender[1] adj (sore) xūruò 虚弱;(affectionate) wēnróu 温柔;steak ruǎn 软

tender[2] n COM tóubiāo 投标

tenderness (soreness) xūruò 虚弱;(of kiss etc) wēnróu gǎn 温柔感;(of steak) ruǎn 软

tendon jiànjiàn 腱

tennis wǎngqiú 网球

tennis ball wǎngqiú 网球;**tennis court** wǎngqiú chǎng 网球场;**tennis player** wǎngqiú shǒu 网球手;**tennis racket** wǎngqiú pāi 网球拍

tenor n MUS nángāoyīn 男高音

tense[1] n GRAM shítài 时态

tense[2] adj muscle jǐn 紧;voice, person, moment jǐnzhāng 紧张

♦**tense up** v/i (of muscles) bēngjǐn 绷紧;(of person) jǐnzhāng 紧张

tension (of rope) lālì 拉力;(in atmosphere, voice) jǐnzhāng 紧张;(in movie, novel) jǐnyào guāntóu 紧要关头

tent zhàngpeng 帐篷

tentacle chùshǒu 触手

tentative yóuyù 犹豫

tenterhooks: **be on ~** tíxīn diàodǎn 提心吊胆

tenth dìshí 第十

tepid water, reaction wēiwēn 微温

term (period of time) shíqī 时期;EDU xuéqī 学期;(condition) tiáojiàn 条件;(word) cí 词;**be on good/bad ~s with X** yǔ X guānxi hǎo/huài 与 X 关系好/坏;**in the long/short ~** cháng/duǎnqī 长/短期;**come to ~s with X** duì X cǎiqǔ jiāngjiù tàidù 对 X 采取将就态度

terminal 1 n (at airport) chūrùjìng kǒu 出入境口;(for buses) zhōngdiǎnzhàn 终点站;(for containers) yùnshū zhōngdiǎnzhàn 运输终点站;ELEC xiàn jiētóu 线接头;COMPUT diànnǎo zhàn 电脑站 **2** adj illness wǎnqī 晚期

terminally adv wǎnqī 晚期;**~ ill** bìngzhèng wǎnqī 病症晚期

terminate 1 v/t contract zhōngzhǐ 终止;pregnancy liúchǎn 流产 **2** v/i zhōngzhǐ 终止

termination (of contract) zhōngzhǐ 终止;(of pregnancy) réngōng liúchǎn 人工流产

terminology shùyǔ 术语

terminus (for buses, trains) zhōngdiǎn zhàn 终点站

terrace (of houses) páifáng 排房;(on hillside) tītián 梯田;(patio) yángtái 阳台

terracotta chìtáo 赤陶

terracotta warriors bīngmǎyǒng 兵马俑

terrain dìshì 地势

terrestrial 1 n dìqiú jūmín 地球居民 **2** adj television wúxiàn diànshì 无线电视;(of the earth) lùdì 陆地

terrible kěpà 可怕

terribly (very) hěn 很

terrific liǎobuqǐ 了不起

terrifically (*very*) hěn 很

terrify kǒnghè 恐吓; **be terrified** hàipà 害怕

terrifying kěpà 可怕

territorial lǐngtǔ 领土

territorial waters lǐnghǎi 领海

territory lǐngtǔ 领土; *fig* lǐngyù 领域

terror kǒngjù 恐惧

terrorism kǒngbù zhǔyì 恐怖主义

terrorist kǒngbù fènzi 恐怖分子

terrorist organization kǒngbù jīgòu 恐怖机构

terrorize kǒnghè 恐吓

test 1 *n* (*of equipment, scientific*) cèyàn 测验; (*exam*) kǎoyàn 考验 2 *v/t machine, theory* cèyàn 测验; *student* kǎo 考

testament (*to s.o.*) shízhèng 实证; *Old / New Testament* REL Jiù / Xīnyù Quánshū 旧 / 新约全书

testicle gāowán 睾丸

testify *v/i* LAW zuòzhèng 作证

testimonial jièshào xìn 介绍信

test tube shìguǎn 试管

test-tube baby shìguǎn yīng'ér 试管婴儿

testy bàozào 暴躁

tetanus pòshāngfēng 破伤风

tether 1 *v/t horse* shuān 拴 2 *n* xìshéng 系绳; *be at the end of one's ~* shānqióng shuǐjìn 山穷水尽

text yuánwén 原文

textbook kèběn 课本

textile fǎngzhī 纺织

texture zhìdì 质地

Thai 1 *adj* Tàiguó 泰国 2 *n* (*person*) Tàiguó rén 泰国人; (*language*) Tàiguó yǔ 泰国语

Thailand Tàiguó 泰国

than bǐ 比; *bigger / faster ~ me* bǐ wǒ dà / kuài 比我大 / 快

thank *v/t* xiè 谢; *~ you* xièxie 谢谢; *no ~ you* búyòng, xièxie 不用, 谢谢

thanks gǎnxiè 感谢; *~!* xièxie 谢谢; *~ to* guīgōng yú 归功于

thankful gǎnjī 感激

thankfully gǎnjī 感激; (*luckily*) xìngkuī 幸亏

thankless *task* túláo 徒劳

Thanksgiving (**Day**) Gǎn'ēn jié 感恩节

that 1 *adj* nàge 那个; *~ one* nàge 那个 2 *pron* nà 那; *what's ~?* nàshì shénme? 那是什么？; *who's ~?* nàshì shuí? 那是谁？; *~'s mine* nàshì wǒde 那是我的; *~'s tea* nàshì chá 那是茶; *~'s very kind* nǐ tài hǎo le 你太好了; *I think ~ ...* wǒ xiǎng ... 我想 ...; *the person / car ~ you see* nǐ kànjiànde nàgè rén / nà liàng chē 你看见的那个人 / 那辆车 4 *adv* (*so*) nàme 那么; *~ big / expensive* nàme dà / guì 那么大 / 贵

thaw *v/i* huà 化

the ◊ (*no translation*): *~ border* biānjiè 边界; *~ embassy* dàshǐguǎn 大使馆; *is that ~ ring he gave you?* nà shì tā gěi nǐ de jièzhi ma? 那是他给你的戒指吗？; *~ capital of France* Fǎguó de shǒudū 法国的首都 ◊ (*when previous reference has been made*) zhè 这, nèi 那; *~ old man* nèige lǎotóu 那个老头; *~ blue bag is mine* zhè lánsè de bāo shì wǒde 这蓝色的包是我的 ◊: *~ sooner ~ better* yuèkuài yuèhǎo 越快越好

theater jùchǎng 剧场

theatrical xìjù 戏剧; (*overdone*) zuòzuò 做作

theft tōuqiè 偷窃

their tāmende 他们的; (*his or her*) tā / tāde 他 / 她的

theirs tāmende 他们的; *a friend of ~* tāmende péngyǒu 他们的朋友

them tāmen 他们; (*him or her*) tā / tā 他 / 她

theme zhǔtí 主题

theme park yóulè yuán 游乐园

theme song zhǔtí gē 主题歌

themselves: *by ~* (*alone*) tāmen zìjǐ 他们自己

then (*at that time*) nàshí 那时; (*after that*) érhòu 而后; (*deducing*) nàme

那么；*by* ~ dào nàshí 到那时

theology shénxué 神学

theoretical lǐlùn 理论

theory lǐlùn 理论；*in* ~ lǐlùn shàng láishuō 理论上来说

therapeutic yīliáo 医疗

therapist zhìliáo xuéjiā 治疗学家

therapy liáofǎ 疗法

there nàr 那儿；*over* ~/*down* ~ zài nàr/xiàmiàn nàr 在那儿/下面那儿；~ *is*/*are* ... yǒu ... 有 ...；*is*/*are* ~ ...? yǒu ... ma? 有 ... 吗？；~ *is*/*are not* ... méiyǒu ... 没有 ...；~ *you are* (*giving sth*) gěinǐ 给你；(*finding sth*) yuánlái nǐ zài zhèr 原来你在这儿；(*completing sth*) wánle 完了；~ *and back* láihuí 来回；~ *he is!* tā zài nàr! 他在那儿！；~, ~! hǎole, hǎole! 好了，好了！

thereabouts dàyù 大约

therefore yīncǐ 因此

thermometer wēndùjì 温度计

thermos flask bǎowēnpíng 保温瓶

thermostat héngwēnqì 恒温器

these *adj & pron* zhèxie 这些

thesis lùnwén 论文

they tāmen 他们；(*he or she*) tā 他/她；~ *say that* ... tīngshuō ... 听说 ...；~ *are going to change the law* tāmen yào xiūgǎi fǎlù 他们要修改法律

thick *hair* mì 密；*soup* chóu 稠；*crowd* chóumì 稠密；*fog* duō 多；*wall, book* hòu 厚；F (*stupid*) bèn 笨

thicken *sauce* shǐ biànchóu 使变稠

thickset ǎizhuàng 矮壮

thickskinned *fig* liǎnpí hòu 脸皮厚

thief xiǎotōu 小偷

thigh dàtuǐ 大腿

thimble dǐngzhēn 顶针

thin *hair, soup* xī 稀；*coat* báo 薄；*line* xì 细；*person* shòu 瘦

thing dōngxi 东西；~*s* (*belongings*) suǒyǒuwù 所有物；*how are* ~*s?* zuìjìn zěnyàng? 最近怎样？；*good* ~ *you told me* xìngkuī nǐ gàosù wǒle 幸亏你告诉我了；

what a ~ *to do*/*say!* zěnme néng nàme zuò/shuō ne! 怎么能那么做/说呢！

thingumajig F (*item*) dōngxi 东西；(*person*) nèirén 那人

think xiǎng 想；*I* ~ *so* wǒ rènwéi rúcǐ 我认为如此；*I don't* ~ *so* wǒ bú rènwéi rúcǐ 我不认为如此；*I* ~ *so too* wǒ yě shì zhème xiǎng de 我也是这么想的；*what do you* ~? nǐ shuō ne? 你说呢？；*what do you* ~ *of it?* nǐ duì cǐ yǒu hé xiǎngfǎ? 你对此有何想法？；*I can't* ~ *of anything more* wǒ xiǎngbùchū qítādele 我想不出其它的了；~ *hard!* hǎohao xiǎngxiang! 好好想想！；*I'm* ~*ing about emigrating* wǒ yǒuyì yímín 我有意移民

♦**think over** kǎolù 考虑

♦**think through** kǎolù 考虑

♦**think up** *plan* xiǎngchū 想出

third 1 *adj* dìsān 第三 **2** *n* dìsān gè 第三个；(*fraction*) sānfēnzhīyī 三分之一

thirdly dìsān 第三

third-party insurance dìsān fāng bǎoxiǎn 第三方保险；**third-rate** xiàděng 下等；**Third World** Dìsān Shìjiè 第三世界

thirst kě 渴

thirsty: *be* ~ kě 渴

thirteen shísān 十三

thirteenth dìshísān 第十三

thirtieth dìsānshí 第三十

thirty sānshí 三十

this 1 *adj* zhège 这个；~ *one* zhège 这个 **2** *pron* zhège 这个；~ *is good* zhè hǎo 这好；~ *is* ... (*introducing s.o.*) zhèshì ... 这是 ...；TELEC wǒshì ... 我是 ... **3** *adv* zhème 这么；~ *big*/*high* zhème dà/gāo 这么大/高

thorn cì 刺

thorough *search* chèdǐ 彻底；*knowledge* wánzhěng 完整；*person* búyànqífán 不厌其烦

thoroughbred (*horse*) chúnzhǒng 纯种

those *adj & pron* nàxiē 那些

though 1 *conj* (*although*) jǐnguǎn

尽管; **~ it might fail** jǐnguǎn kěnéng shībài 尽管可能失败; **as ~** hǎoxiàng 好象 2 *adv* rán'ér 然而; **it's not finished ~** hái méi wánne 还没完呢

thought (*single*) xiǎngfa 想法; (*collective*) sīxiǎng 思想

thoughtful *look, face, person* chénsī 沉思; *book* jīng rènzhēn tuīqiāo 经认真推敲; (*considerate*) xìxīn 细心

thoughtless cūxīn 粗心

thousand qiān 千; **~s of** wúshù 无数; **ten ~** wàn 万

thousandth 1 *n* dì yī qiān gè 第一千个; (*fraction*) qiānfēnzhīyī 千分之一 2 *adj* dì yī qiān gè 第一千个

thrash *v/t* chōu 抽; SP dǎbài 打败
♦**thrash around** (*with arms etc*) fánzào bù'ān de dònglái dòngqù 烦躁不安地动来动去
♦**thrash out** *solution* jiějué wèntí 解决问题

thrashing tòngdǎ 痛打; SP cǎnbài 惨败

thread 1 *n* xiàn 线; (*of screw*) luówén 螺纹 2 *v/t needle* chuānxiàn 穿线; *beads* chuān 穿

threadbare lánlǚ 褴褛

threat wēixié 威胁

threaten wēixié 威胁

threatening *gesture, tone* yǒu wēixié xìng 有威胁性; *sky* yīnchén 阴沉

three sān 三

Three Gorges Sānxiá 三峡; **Three Kingdoms** Sānguó 三国; **three-quarters** *n* sì fēn zhī sān 四分之三

thresh *v/t corn* tuōlì 脱粒

threshold (*of house*) ménkǎn 门槛; (*of new age*) kāiduān 开端; **on the ~ of** zài ... de kāiduān 在 ... 的开端

thrift jiéyù 节约

thrifty jiéyù 节约

thrill 1 *n* xìngfèn 兴奋 2 *v/t* shǐ ... xìngfèn 使 ... 兴奋; **be ~ed** gāoxìng 高兴

thriller (*movie*) jīngxiǎn diànyǐng 惊

险电影; (*novel*) jīngxiǎn xiǎoshuō 惊险小说

thrilling lìngrén máogǔ sǒngrán 令人毛骨悚然

thrive (*of plant*) zhuózhuàng shēngzhǎng 茁壮生长; (*of business, economy*) fánróng 繁荣

throat hóulóng 喉咙

throat lozenges rùnhóu táng 润喉糖

throb 1 *n* (*of heart*) tiàodòng 跳动; (*of music*) zhènchàn 震颤 2 *v/i* (*of heart*) tiàodòng 跳动; (*of music*) zhènchàn 震颤

thrombosis xuěshuān xíngchéng 血栓形成

throne wángwèi 王位

throng *n* rénqún 人群

throttle 1 *n* (*on motorbike, boat*) jiéliú fá 节流阀 2 *v/t* (*strangle*) qiā zhù bózi 掐住脖子
♦**throttle back** *v/i* guānxiǎo yóumén jiǎnsù 关小油门减速

through 1 *prep* (*across*) chuānguò 穿过; (*during*) zài ... qījiān 在 ... 期间; (*thanks to*) yóuyú 由于; **go ~ the city** chuānguò shìqū 穿过市区; **~ the winter / summer** dōng / xiàjì qījiān 冬 / 夏季期间; **Monday ~ Friday** xīngqī yī zhì wǔ 星期一至五; **arranged ~ him** tōngguò tā ānpái 通过他安排 2 *adv*: **wet ~** shī tòule 湿透了; **watch a movie ~** cóngtóu dàowěi kànwán yìchǎng diànyǐng 从头到尾看完一场电影; **read a book ~** cóngtóu dàowěi dúwán yìběn shū 从头到尾读完一本书 3 *adj*: **be ~** (*of couple*) wánle 完了; (*have arrived: of news etc*) dàodá 到达; **you're ~** TELEC tōngle 通了; **I'm ~ with X** (*finished with a person*) wǒ yǔ X juéjiāo 我与X绝交; (*finished with a task*) wǒ wánchéng le X 我完成了X

through flight zhíháng fēijī 直航飞机

throughout 1 *prep* guànchuān 贯穿 2 *adv* (*in all parts*) dàochù 到处

through train zhítōng huǒchē 直通火车

throw 1 *v/t* rēng 扔; (*of horse*) shuāidǎo 摔倒; (*disconcert*) shǐ ... cānghuáng shīcuò 使 ... 仓皇失措; *party* jǔxíng 举行 **2** *n* tóuzhì 投掷

♦ **throw away** rēngdiào 扔掉

♦ **throw out** *old things* rēngdiào 扔掉; *husband, drunk etc* niǎnzǒu 撵走; *plan* fǒujué 否决

♦ **throw up 1** *v/t ball* pāoqǐ 抛起 **2** *v/i* (*vomit*) ǒutù 呕吐

throw-away *remark* suíyì 随意; (*disposable*) yīcì xìng 一次性

throw-in SP zhì jiè wài qiú 掷界外球

thru → **through**

thrush (*bird*) dōngniǎo 鸫鸟

thrust *v/t* (*push hard*) měngtuī 猛推; ~ *X into Y's hands* bǎ X sāirù Y shǒu zhōng 把 X 塞入 Y 手中; ~ *one's way through the crowd* chuǎngguò rénqún 闯过人群

thud *n* pēng de yìshēng 砰的一声

thug ègùn 恶棍

thumb 1 *n* mǔzhǐ 拇指 **2** *v/t:* ~ *a ride* dāchē 搭车

thumbtack túdīng 图钉

thump 1 *n* (*blow*) zhòngjī 重击; (*noise*) pēng 砰 **2** *v/t person* zhòngjī 重击; ~ *one's fist on the table* yòng quántóu chuí zhuōzi 用拳头捶桌子 **3** *v/i* (*of heart*) měngtiào 猛跳; ~ *on the door* pāimén 拍门

thunder *n* dǎléi 打雷

thunderstorm léiyǔ 雷雨

thundery *weather* yào dǎléi 要打雷

Thursday xīngqī sì 星期四

thus yīncǐ 因此

thwart *person, plans* héngxiàng 横向

thyroid (**gland**) jiǎzhuàngxiàn 甲状腺

Tiananmen (*incident*) liùsì 六四; (*square*) Tiān'ānmén 天安门

Tiananmen Square Tiān'ānmén Guǎngchǎng 天安门广场

Tibet Xīzàng 西藏

Tibetan 1 *adj* Xīzàng 西藏 **2** *n* (*person*) Xīzàng rén 西藏人; (*language*) Xīzàng yǔ 西藏语

Tibetan Plateau Qīng Zàng Gāoyuán 青藏高原

tick 1 *n* (*of clock*) dīdā 滴答; (*checkmark*) dǎgōu 打勾 **2** *v/i* (*of clock*) dīdā dīdā xiǎng 滴答滴答响

♦ **tick off** (*reprimand*) xùnchì 训斥

ticket piào 票

ticket collector shòupiào yuán 售票员; **ticket inspector** chápiào yuán 查票员; **ticket machine** shòupiàojī 售票机; **ticket office** (*at station, theater*) shòupiàochù 售票处

tickle 1 *v/t person* gēzhi 胳肢 **2** *v/i* (*of material*) fāyǎng 发痒; (*of person*) shǐ fāyǎng 使发痒

ticklish *person* pàyǎng 怕痒

tidal wave làngcháo 浪潮

tide cháo 潮; **high** ~ gāocháo 高潮; **low** ~ dīcháo 低潮; **the** ~ **is in / out** zhǎngcháo / luòcháo 涨潮 / 落潮

tidy *person, habits* zhěngjié 整洁; *room, house* zhěngqí 整齐

♦ **tidy up 1** *v/t room, shelves* shōushi 收拾; **tidy oneself up** bǎ zìjǐ shōushi yīxià 把自己收拾一下 **2** *v/i* shōushi 收拾

tie 1 *n* (*necktie*) lǐngdài 领带; (SP: *even result*) píngjú 平局; **he doesn't have any** ~**s** tā méiyǒu rènhé liánxi 他没有任何联系 **2** *v/t knot* dǎjié 打结; *hands* jì 系; ~ *two ropes together* bǎ liǎngtiáo shéngzi jì zài yìqǐ 把两条绳子系在一起 **3** *v/i* SP chéng píngjú 成平局

♦ **tie down** (*with rope*) kǔnzhù 捆住; (*restrict*) yùshù 约束

♦ **tie up** *person* bǎngzhù 绑住; *laces* jìzhù 系住; *boat* bó 泊; *hair* xì qǐlái 系起来; **I'm tied up tomorrow** (*busy*) míngtiān wǒ yǒushì 明天我有事

tier (*of hierarchy*) céng 层; (*in stadium*) pái 排

tiger lǎohǔ 老虎

tight 1 *adj clothes*, (*hard to move*) jǐn 紧; *security* yán; (*properly shut*)

yán 严; (*not leaving much time*)
jǐncòu 紧凑; F (*drunk*) zuì 醉
2 *adv hold* jǐn 紧; *shut* yán 严
tighten *screw* shǐ ... biànjǐn 使 ...
变紧; *control* shǐ ... yángé 使 ...
严格; *security* shǐ ... yánjǐn 使 ...
严谨; **~ one's grip on** ... zhuā láo
... 抓牢 ...
♦**tighten up** *v/i* (*in discipline*,
security) yánjǐn qǐlái 严谨起来
tight-fisted kōuménr 抠门儿
tightrope bēngsuǒ 绷索
tile cízhuān 瓷砖
till[1] → **until**
till[2] (*cash register*) shōukuǎn tái 收
款台
till[3] *v/t soil* gēngzhòng 耕种
tilt 1 *v/t* shǐ qīngxié 使倾斜 **2** *v/i*
qīngxié 倾斜
timber mùcái 木材
time shíjiān 时间; (*occasion*) cì cì 次;
~ is up dào shíjiān le 到时间了;
for the ~ being zànshí 暂时; **have
a good ~** kāixīn 开心; **have a
good ~!** wánr kāixīn diǎnr! 玩儿
开心点儿！; **what's the ~?**,
what ~ is it? jǐdiǎnle? 几点了？;
the first ~ dìyīcì 第一次; **four ~s**
sìcì 四次; **~ and again** duōcì 多
次; **all the ~** yīzhí 一直; **two /
three at a ~** yīcì liǎng / sāngè 一次
两 / 三个; **at the same ~** *speak*,
reply etc tóngshí 同时; (*however*)
dànshì 但是; **in ~** jíshí 及时; **on ~**
ànshí 按时; **in no ~** lìkè 立刻
time bomb dìngshí zhàdàn 定时
炸弹; **time clock** (*in factory*)
jìshízhōng 计时钟; **time-
consuming** huā shíjiān 花时间;
time-lag shíjiān jiāngé 时间间
隔; **time limit** qīxiàn 期限
timely jíshí 及时
time out SP zàntíng 暂停
timer dìngshíqì 定时器
timesaving *n* jiéshěng shíjiān 节省
时间; **timescale** (*of project*)
shíjiān fànwéi 时间范围; **time
switch** dìngshíqì 定时器; **timetable** shíjiān biǎo 时间表;
timewarp (kēhuàn zhōng)
zhuǎnshí（科幻中）转时; **time**

zone shíqū 时区
timid miǎntiǎn 腼腆
timing (*choosing a time*) shíjiān
xuǎnzé 时间选择; (*of actor,
dancer*) shíjiān fēncùn 时间分寸
tin (*metal*) xī 锡
tinfoil xīpó 锡箔
tinge *n* (*of color*) wēirǎn 微染; (*of
sadness*) dài ... qìxī 带 ... 气息
tingle *v/i* yǒu cìtòng gǎn 有刺痛
感
♦**tinker with** bǎinòng 摆弄
tinkle *n* (*of bell*) dīngdāng shēng 丁
当声
tinsel jīnyín sī 金银丝
tint 1 *n* (*of color*) dànsè 淡色; (*in
hair*) rǎnsè 染色 **2** *v/t hair* rǎnsè
染色
tinted *eyeglasses* fǎnguāng 反光;
paper zháosè 着色
tiny jíxiǎo 极小
tip[1] *n* (*of stick, finger*) jiān 尖; (*of
mountain*) shāntóu 山头; (*of
cigarette*) yānzuǐ 烟嘴
tip[2] **1** *n* (*piece of advice*) quàngào 劝
告; (*money*) xiǎofèi 小费 **2** *v/t
waiter etc* gěi xiǎofèi 给小费
♦**tip off** tōngfēng bàoxìn 通风报
信
♦**tip over** *jug, liquid* dào 倒; *he
tipped water all over me* tā dào
de wǒ mǎn shēn dōu shì shuǐ 他
倒得我满身都是水
tipped *cigarettes* yǒu yānzuǐ 有烟
嘴
tippy-toe: *on ~* yòng jiǎojiān 用脚
尖
tipsy shāozuì 稍醉
tire[1] (*on wheel*) chētāi 车胎
tire[2] **1** *v/t* láolèi 劳累 **2** *v/i* láolèi 劳
累; *he never ~s of it* tā yǒngyuǎn
būhuì yànjuàn 他永远不会厌
倦
tired lèi 累; *be ~ of X* duì X
yànjuàn 对 X 厌倦
tireless *efforts* zīzī būjuàn 孜孜不
倦
tiresome (*annoying*) tǎoyàn 讨厌
tiring pífá 疲乏
tissue ANAT zǔzhī 组织; (*handkerchief*) zhǐjīn 纸巾

tissue paper ⇩ báozhǐ 薄纸

tit¹ (bird) shānquè 山雀

tit²: ~ for tat yǐyá huányá 以牙还牙

tit³ ∨ (breast) nǎizi 奶子

title (of novel etc) piānmíng 篇名; (of person) tóuxiánr 头衔儿; LAW suǒyǒu quán 所有权

titter v/i shǎxiào 傻笑

to 1 prep dào 到; ~ China dào Zhōngguó 到中国; ~ Hangzhou dào Hángzhōu 到杭州; let's go ~ my place zánmen dào wǒ nàr qù ba 咱们到我那儿去吧; walk ~ the station zǒu dào chēzhàn 走到车站; ~ the north / south of X dào X de běi / nánbiān 到 X 的北 / 南边; give X ~ Y jiāng X gěi Y 将 X 给 Y; from Monday ~ Wednesday cóng xīngqīyī dào xīngqīsān 从星期一到星期三; from 10 ~ 15 people shí zhì shíwǔ rén 十至十五人 2 with verbs: ~ speak, ~ shout jiǎnghuà, hǎnjiào 讲话，喊叫; learn ~ drive xuéxí jiàshǐ 学习驾驶; nice ~ eat hǎochī 好吃; too heavy ~ carry tàizhòng 太重; ~ be honest with you hé nǐ shíshuō le ba 和你实说了吧 3 adv: ~ and fro láihuí 来回

toad làiháma 癞蛤蟆

toadstool sǎnjūn 伞菌

toast 1 n kǎo miànbāo 烤面包; (drinking) gānbēi 干杯; propose a ~ to wèi ... gānbēi 为 ... 干杯 2 v/t (when drinking) wèi ... gānbēi 为 ... 干杯

tobacco yāncǎo 烟草

toboggan n píngdǐ xuěqiāo 平底雪橇

today jīntiān 今天

toddle (of child) xiǎoháir xíngzǒu 小孩儿行走

toddler xiǎoháir 小孩儿

toe 1 n jiǎozhǐ 脚指 2 v/t: ~ the line fúcóng mìnglìng 服从命令

toffee tàifēi táng 太妃糖

tofu dòufu 豆腐

together yīqǐ 一起; (at the same time) tóngshí 同时

toil n kǔgàn 苦干

toilet cèsuǒ 厕所; go to the ~ qù cèsuǒ 去厕所

toilet paper cèzhǐ 厕纸

toiletries wèishēngjiān yòngpǐn 卫生间用品

token (sign) xiàngzhēng 象征; (for gambling) fǔbì 辅币; (gift ~) shāngpǐn quàn 商品券

tolerable pain etc kěyǐ rěnshòu 可以忍受; (quite good) guòdeqù 过得去

tolerance kuānróng 宽容

tolerant kuānróng 宽容

tolerate noise róngxǔ 容许; person róngrěn 容忍; I won't ~ it! wǒ bùnéng róngrěn! 我不能容忍！

toll¹ v/i (of bell) míng 鸣

toll² (deaths) sǐwáng rénshù 死亡人数

toll³ (for bridge, road) tōngxíng fèi 通行费; TELEC diànhuà fèi 电话费

toll booth shōufèichù 收费处; toll-free TELEC miǎnfèi diànhuà 免费电话; toll road shōufèi gōnglù 收费公路

tomato (in northern China) xīhóngshì 西红柿; (in southern China) fānqié 蕃茄

tomato ketchup fānqiéjiàng 蕃茄酱

tomb fénmù 坟墓

tomboy yěyātóu 野丫头

tombstone mùbēi 墓碑

tomcat gōngmāo 公猫

tomorrow míngtiān 明天; the day after ~ hòutiān 后天; ~ morning míngchén 明晨

ton dūn 吨

tone (of color) fēnggé 风格; (of musical instrument) yuèyīn 乐音; (of conversation etc) yǔqì 语气; (of neighborhood) qìfēn 气氛; ~ of voice shēngdiào 声调

♦tone down demands, criticism huǎnhé 缓和

toner tiáosè jì 调色剂

tongs qiánzi 钳子; (for hair) juǎnfà qián 卷发钳

tongue n shétou 舌头

tonic MED yàoshuǐ 药水

tonic (water) ⇩ tānglìshuǐ 汤力水

tonight jīnwǎn 今晚

tonsil biǎntáotǐ 扁桃体

tonsillitis biǎntáoxiàn yán 扁桃腺炎

too (*also*) yě 也; (*excessively*) tài 太; *me* ~ wǒ yě 我也; ~ *big* / *hot* tài dà / rè 太大 / 热; ~ *much rice* tàiduō fàn 太多饭; *eat* ~ *much* chī tàiduō 吃太多

tool gōngjù 工具

toolbar COMPUT gōngjùgé 工具格

tooth yáchǐ 牙齿

toothache yáténg 牙疼

toothbrush yáshuā 牙刷

toothless méiyá 没牙

toothpaste yágāo 牙膏

toothpick yáqiān 牙签

top 1 *n* (*of mountain, tree*) dǐng 顶; (*upper part*) shàngbù 上部; (*lid: of bottle etc, pen*) gài g 盖; (*of the class, league*) zuì yōuxiù 最优秀; (*clothing*) shàngyī 上衣; (MOT: *gear*) zuì gāodǎng 最高档; *on ~ of* zài … zhī shàng 在 … 之上; *at the ~ of* zài … zuìshàng 在 … 最上; *at the ~ of the mountain* zài shāndǐng 在山顶; *get to the ~* (*of company etc*) shēng zhì zuìgāo zhíwèi 升至最高职位; *be over the ~* (*exaggerated*) guòhuǒ 过火 **2** *adj branches* zuìdǐng 最顶; *floor* zuìgāo yīcéng 最高一层; *management, official* gāojí 高级; *player* jiānzi 尖子; *speed, note* zuìgāo 最高 **3** *v/t*: *~ped with cream* shàng jiā nǎiyóu 上加奶油

top hat gāodǐngmào 高顶帽

topheavy tóuzhòng jiǎoqīng 头重脚轻

♦ **top up** *glass, tank* zhuāng mǎn 装满

topic tímù 题目

topical zhǔtí 主题

topless *adj* luǒxiōng 裸胸

topmost *branches, floor* zuìgāo 最高

topping (*on pizza*) dǐngcéng fùjiā wù 顶层附加物

topple 1 *v/i* dǎo 倒 **2** *v/t government* tuīfān 推翻

top secret *adj* juémì 绝密

topsy-turvy *adj* (*in disorder*) luànqī bāzāo 乱七八糟; *world* diāndǎo hēibái 颠倒黑白

torch (*with flame*) huǒbǎ 火把

torment 1 *n* zhémo 折磨 **2** *v/t person, animal* zhémo 折磨; *~ed by doubt* yílǜ chóngchong 疑虑重重

tornado lóngjuǎn fēng 龙卷风

torrent jīliú 激流; (*of lava*) róngliú 熔流; (*of abuse, words*) tāotao bùjué 滔滔不绝

torrential: ~ *rain* bàoyǔ 暴雨

tortoise wūguī 乌龟

torture *n* & *v/t* zhémo 折磨

toss 1 *v/t ball* zhì 掷; *rider* shuāidǎo 摔倒; *salad* bànyún 拌匀; ~ *a coin* zhìbì 掷币 **2** *v/i*: ~ *and turn* zhǎnzhuǎn fǎncè 辗转反侧

total 1 *n* zǒngshù 总数 **2** *adj sum, amount* zǒng 总; *disaster, idiot* juéduì 绝对; *stranger* wánquán 完全 **3** *v/t* F *car* zálàn 砸烂

totalitarian jíquán zhǔyì 极权主义

totally wánquán 完全

tote bag dà shǒutí bāo 大手提包

totter (*of person*) pánshān 蹒跚

touch 1 *n* (*act of touching*) chùmō 触摸; (*sense*) chùjué 触觉; (*little bit*) shǎoxǔ 少许; SP biānxiàn wài 边线外; *lose* ~ *with X* (*s.o.*) yǔ X shīqù liánxì 与X失去联系; *keep in* ~ *with X* (*s.o.*) yǔ X bǎochí liánxì 与X保持联系; *we kept in* ~ wǒmén bǎochí liánxì 我们保持联系; *be out of* ~ tuōjié 脱节 **2** *v/t* chùmō 触摸; (*emotionally*) shǐ gǎndòng 使感动 **3** *v/i* mō 摸; (*of two lines etc*) jiēchù 接触

♦ **touch down** *v/i* (*of airplane*) zháolù 着陆; SP chùdì 触地

♦ **touch on** (*mention*) tídào 提到

♦ **touch up** *photo* xiūshì 修饰; (*sexually*) dòngshǒu dòngjiǎo 动手动脚

touchdown (*of airplane*) zháolù 着陆; SP chùdì 触地

touching *adj* gǎnrén 感人

touch judge SP biānxiàn cáipànyuán 边线裁判员

touchline SP biānxiàn 边线

touchy *person* mǐngǎn 敏感

tough *person* jiānqiáng 坚强; *meat* bú yì jǔjiáo 不易咀嚼; *question, exam* nán 难; *material* jiānrèn 坚韧; *punishment* wúqíng 无情

tough guy yǒngshì 勇士

tour 1 *n* lǚyóu 旅游 2 *v/t area* cānguān 参观

tourism lǚyóu yè 旅游业

tourist lǚyóu zhě 旅游者

tourist (information) office lǚyóu zīliào chù 旅游资料处

tournament jǐnbiāo sài 锦标赛

tour operator lǚyóu gōngsī 旅游公司

tousled *hair* péngluàn 蓬乱

tow 1 *v/t car, boat* zhuài 拽 2 *n* zhuài 拽; *give X a ~* bāng X zhuài 帮 X 拽

♦**tow away** *car* tuōzǒu 拖走

toward *prep* xiàng 向

towel máojīn 毛巾

tower *n* tǎ 塔

town zhèn 镇

town council zhèn zhèngfǔ 镇政府

town hall zhèn zhèngfǔ dàlóu 镇政府大楼

towrope tuōlǎn 拖缆

toxic yǒudú 有毒

toy wánjù 玩具

♦**toy with** *object* bǎinòng 摆弄; *idea* bú dà rènzhēnde kǎolǜ 不大认真地考虑

trace 1 *n* (*of substance*) wēiliàng 微量 2 *v/t* (*find*) xúnzhǎo 寻找; (*follow: footsteps*) gēnzōng 跟踪; (*draw*) miáohuì 描绘

track *n* (*path*) xiǎojìng 小径; (*for racing*) pǎodào 跑道; RAIL guǐdào 轨道; *~ 10* RAIL dì shí zhàntái 第十站台; *keep ~ of X* jìlù X 记录 X

♦**track down** *criminal* gēnzōng zhuībǔ 跟踪追捕; *copy of a book* cházhǎo dào 查找到

tracksuit chángxiù yùndòngfú 长袖运动服

tractor ⇩ tuōlājī 拖拉机

trade 1 *n* (*commerce*) màoyì 贸易; (*profession, craft*) hángyè 行业 2 *v/i* (*do business*) jīngyíng 经营; *~ in X* zuò X de mǎimài 做 X 的买卖 3 *v/t* (*exchange*) jiāohuàn 交换; *~ X for Y* yòng X huàn Y 用 X 换 Y

♦**trade in** *v/t* (*when buying*) yǐ jiù huàn xīn 以旧换新

trade fair màoyìhuì 贸易会; **trademark** shāngbiāo 商标; **trade mission** màoyì dàibiǎotuán 贸易代表团

trader shāngrén 商人

trade secret shāngyè mìmi 商业秘密

tradesman (*plumber etc*) shǒugōngyì zhě 手工艺者

trade(s) union gōnghuì 工会

tradition chuántǒng 传统

traditional chuántǒng 传统

traditional characters fántǐzì 繁体字

traditionally chuántǒng 传统

traffic *n* (*on roads*) jiāotōng 交通; (*at airport*) jiāoliú liàng 交流量; (*in drugs*) fànmài 贩卖

♦**traffic in** *drugs* fànmài 贩卖

traffic circle huánxíng jiāochā 环形交叉; **traffic cop** F jiāotōng jǐng 交通警; **traffic island** jiāotōng dǎo 交通岛; **traffic jam** jiāotōng dǔsè 交通堵塞; **traffic light** hónglǜdēng 红绿灯; **traffic police** jiāotōng jǐng 交通警; **traffic sign** jiāotōng biāozhì 交通标志

tragedy bēijù 悲剧

tragic búxìng 不幸

trail 1 *n* (*path*) xiǎojìng 小径; (*of blood*) hénjì 痕迹 2 *v/t* (*follow*) gēnzōng 跟踪; (*tow*) tuōlā 拖拉 3 *v/i* (*lag behind*) luòhòu 落后

trailer (*pulled by vehicle*) tuōchē 拖车; (*mobile home*) péngchē 篷车; (*of movie*) diànyǐng yùgào piān 电影预告片

train¹ *n* huǒchē 火车; *go by ~* zuò huǒchē 坐火车

train² 1 *v/t team, athlete, dog* xùnliàn 训练

训练; *employee* péixùn 培训 **2** *v/i*
(*of team, athlete*) xùnliàn 训练; (*of
teacher etc*) péixùn 培训

trainee shíxí shēng 实习生

trainer SP jiàolián yuán 教练员;
(*of dog*) xùnshòu zhě 训兽者

trainers Br (*shoes*) yùndòng xié 运
动鞋

training (*of new staff*) péixùn 培训;
SP xùnliàn 训练; **be in ~** SP
xùnliàn zhōng 训练中; **be out of
~** SP jìngjì zhuàngtài bùjiā 竞技状
态不佳

training course péixùn kèchéng
培训课程

training scheme péixùn jìhuà 培
训计划

train station huǒchē zhàn 火车站

trait tèxìng 特性

traitor pàntú 叛徒

tramp 1 *n* (*Br. hobo*) yóumín 游民
2 *v/i* chénzhòng de zǒu 沉重地走

trample *v/t*: **be ~d to death** zhòng
cǎi zhì sǐ 重踩至死; **be ~d un-
derfoot** zhòngcǎi 重踩

♦ **trample on** *person, object* cǎi 踩

trampoline bēngchuáng 绷床

trance huǎnghū 恍惚; **go into a ~**
chūshénr 出神儿

tranquil níngjìng 宁静

tranquility níngjìng 宁静

tranquilizer zhènjìngjì 镇静剂

transact *deal, business* jiāoyì 交易

transaction jiāoyì 交易

transatlantic héngkuà Dàxīyáng
横跨大西洋

transcendental xiānyàn 先验

transcript jìlù 纪录

transfer 1 *v/t* diàodòng 调动;
passengers zhuǎnjī 转机; *one's
custom to another company etc*
zhuǎnyí 转移 **2** *v/i* (*when
traveling*) qiānyí 迁移; (*from one
language to another*) zhuǎnhuàn 转
换 **3** *n* (*move, of money*) diàodòng
调动; (*in travel*) diàohuàn 调换

transferable *ticket* kě diàohuàn 可
调换

transform *v/t* gǎibiàn 改变

transformation gǎibiàn 改变

transformer ELEC biànyāqì 变压
器

transfusion shūxuè 输血

transistor jīngtǐguǎn 晶体管;
(*radio*) jīngtǐguǎn shōuyīnjī 晶体
管收音机

transit: in ~ zài yùnshū zhōng 在运
输中

transition guòdù 过渡

transitional guòdù 过渡

transit lounge (*at airport*) zhuǎnjī
tīng 转机厅

translate fānyì 翻译

translation fānyì 翻译

translator fānyì 翻译

transliterate yīnyì 音译

transmission (*of news, program*)
bōfàng 播放; (*of disease*) chuánrǎn 传染; MOT biànsùqì 变速器

transmit *news, program* bōfàng 播
放; *disease* chuánrǎn 传染

transmitter (*for radio, TV*)
chuándáqì 传达器

transpacific kuàyuè Tàipíngyáng
跨越太平洋

transparency PHOT huàndēngpiān
幻灯片

transparent tòumíng 透明;
(*obvious*) míngxiǎn 明显

transplant *v/t & n* MED yízhí 遗植

transport *v/t & n* yùnshū 运输

transportation (*of goods, people*)
yùnshū 运输; **means of ~**
jiāotōng gōngjù 交通工具; **public ~** gōngzhòng jiāotōng yùnshū
gōngjù 公众交通运输工具;
Department of Transportation
Jiāotōng Bù 交通部

transvestite yì zhuāng pì zhě 易装
癖者

trap 1 *n* (*for animal*) bǔshòu jīguān
捕兽机关; (*question, set-up etc*)
quāntào 圈套; **set a ~ for X** gěi X
shè quāntào 给 X 设圈套 **2** *v/t*
animal shèlì bǔshòu jīguān 设立
捕兽机关; *person* shè quāntào 设
圈套; **be ~ped** (*by enemy, flames,
landslide etc*) xiànrù quāntào 陷入
圈套

trapdoor huóbǎnmén 活板门

trapeze diàojià 吊架

trappings (*of power*) wàizài

biāozhì 外在标志

trash (*garbage*) lājī 垃圾; (*poor product*) fèipǐn 废品; (*despicable person*) wúnéng de rén 无能的人

trashcan lājītǒng 垃圾桶

trashy *goods, novel* lièzhì 劣质

traumatic chuàngshāng xìng 创伤性

travel 1 *n* lǚxíng 旅行; **~s** lǚtú 旅途 **2** *v/i & v/t* lǚxíng 旅行

travel agency lǚxíng shè 旅行社

travel bag lǚxíng dài 旅行袋

traveler lǚxíng zhě 旅行者

traveler's check lǚxíng zhīpiào 旅行支票

travel expenses jiāotōng fèiyòng 交通 费用; **travel insurance** lǚxíng bǎoxiǎn 旅行保险; **travelsick** lǚxíng jíbìng 旅行疾病

trawler tuōwǎng yúchuán 拖网鱼船

tray tuōpán 拖盘

treacherous *person* bùzhōng 不忠; *currents, roads* àncáng wēixiǎn 暗藏危险

treachery pànnì 叛逆

tread 1 *n* zúyīn 足音; (*of staircase*) tīmiàn 梯面; (*of tire*) tāimiàn 胎面 **2** *v/i* zǒuguò 走过

♦**tread on** cǎi 踩

treason pànguó zuì 叛国罪

treasure 1 *n* cáifù 财富; (*person*) bùkě duōdé de réncái 不可多得的人材 **2** *v/t* *gift etc* zhēnxī 珍惜

treasurer sīkù 司库

Treasury Department Cáiwù Bù 财务部

treat *n* kuǎndài 款待; *it was a real ~* fēicháng lìngrén mǎnyì 非常令人满意; *I have a ~ for you* wǒ yǒu yàng hǎo dōngxi gěi nǐ 我有样好东西给你; *it's my ~* (*I'm paying*) wǒ qǐngkè 我请客 **2** *v/t* *materials* chǔlǐ 处理; *illness* zhìliáo 治疗; (*behave toward*) duìdài 对待; *~ X to Y* yòng Y kuǎndài X 用 Y 款待 X

treatment (*of materials*) chǔlǐ 处理; (*of illness*) zhìliáo 治疗; (*of people*) duìdài 对待

treaty tiáoyuē 条约

treble[1] MUS zuì gāoyīn bù 最高音部

treble[2] **1** *adv* sānbèi 三倍; **~ the price** jiàgé zhǎng sānbèi 价格涨三倍 **2** *v/i* fānle sān fān 翻了三番

tree shù 树

tremble (*of person, hand, voice*) fādǒu 发抖; (*of building*) yáohuàng 摇晃

tremendous (*very good*) juémiào 绝妙; (*enormous*) jùdà 巨大

tremendously (*very*) hěn 很; (*a lot*) hěnduō 很多

tremor (*of earth*) zhèndòng 震动

trench gōu 沟

trend qūxiàng 趋向; (*fashion*) cháoliú 潮流

trendy xīncháo 新潮

trespass fēifǎ qīnrù 非法侵入; **no ~ing** bùdé rùnèi 不得入内

♦**trespass on** *land* fēifǎ qīnrù 非法侵入; *privacy* dǎrǎo 打扰

trespasser fēifǎ qīnrù zhě 非法侵入者

trial LAW shěnpàn 审判; (*of equipment*) shìyàn 试验; *on ~* LAW shòushěn 受审; *have X on ~* *equipment etc* shìyàn X 试验 X

trial period (*for employee*) shíxí qī 实习期; (*for equipment*) shìyàn qī 试验期

triangle sānjiǎo xíng 三角形

triangular sānjiǎo xíng 三角形

tribe bùluò 部落

tribunal cáipàn yuàn 裁判院

tributary zhīliú 支流

trick 1 *n* (*to deceive*) jìmóu 计谋; (*knack*) jìqiǎo 技巧; *play a ~ on X* zhuōnòng X 捉弄 X **2** *v/t* qīpiàn 欺骗; *~ X into doing Y* piàn X zuò Y 骗 X 做 Y

trickery qīpiàn 欺骗

trickle *n & v/i* dī 滴

trickster piànzi 骗子

tricky (*difficult*) jíshǒu 棘手

tricycle sānlúnchē 三轮车

trifle (*triviality*) suǒshì 琐事

trifling suǒsuì 琐碎

trigger *n* bānjī 扳机; (*on camcorder*) qǐdòng zhuāngzhì 起

动装置

♦**trigger off** chùfā 触发

trim 1 adj (neat) zhěngqí 整齐; figure miáotiáo 苗条 **2** v/t hair, hedge xiāo 削; budget, costs xùjiǎn 削减; (decorate: dress) zhuāngshì 装饰 **3** n (light cut) xiāobiānr 削 边儿; just a ~, please (to hairdresser) qǐng zhǐ xiāobiānr 请 只削边儿; in good ~ jīngjing yǒutiáo 井井有条

trimming (on clothes) xiūshì pǐn 修 饰品; with all the ~s yǒu suǒyǒu dāpèi 有所有搭配

trinket wányìr 玩意儿

trio MUS sān chóng chàng 三重唱

trip 1 n (journey) lǚxíng 旅行 **2** v/t & v/i (~ up) bàndǎo 绊倒

♦**trip up 1** v/t (make fall) bàndǎo 绊倒; (cause to go wrong) shǐ ... fàn cuòwù 使 ... 犯错误 **2** v/i (stumble) bàndǎo 绊倒; (make a mistake) fàn cuòwù 犯错误

tripe (food) niúdǔ 牛肚

triple → **treble**

triplets sānbāotāi 三胞胎

tripod PHOT sānjiǎojià 三脚架

trite chénjiù 陈旧

triumph n shènglì de xǐyuè 胜利的 喜悦

trivial suǒsuì 琐碎

triviality suǒshì 琐事

trombone chánghào 长号

troops jūnduì 军队

trophy jiǎngbēi 奖杯

tropic huíguīxiàn 回归线

tropical rèdài 热带

tropics rèdài dìqū 热带地区

trot v/i xiǎopǎo 小跑

trouble 1 n (difficulties) kùnnan 困 难; (illness) bìngtòng 病痛; (inconvenience) máfán 麻烦; (disturbance) sāoluàn 骚乱; go to a lot of ~ to do X bùcí xīnkǔ qù zuò X 不辞辛苦去做X; no ~ méi wèntí 没问题; get into ~ zhāozhì máfán 招致麻烦 **2** v/t (worry) dānyōu 担忧; (bother, disturb) máfán 麻烦; (of back, liver etc) shǐ bù shūfu 使不舒服

trouble-free wú gùzhàng 无故障

troublemaker dǎoluàn zhě 捣乱 者

troubleshooter (mediator) tiáojiě-rén 调解人

troubleshooting páichú gùzhàng 排除故障

troublesome fánrén 烦人

trousers Br kùzi 裤子; a pair of ~ yītiáo kùzi 一条裤子

trout zūnyú 鳟鱼

truce xiūzhàn 休战

truck kǎchē 卡车

truck driver kǎchē sījī 卡车司机; **truck farm** shūcài nóngchǎng 蔬 菜农场; **truck farmer** càinóng 菜农; **truck stop** kǎchē sījī kuàicāndiàn 卡车司机快餐店

trudge v/i & n báshè 跋涉

true zhēn 真; friend gòu 够; come ~ (of hopes, dream) shíxiàn 实现

truly zhēnde 真地; Yours ~ cǐzhì 此致

trumpet lǎba 喇叭

trunk (of tree) shùgàn 树干; (of body) qūgàn 躯干; (of elephant) xiàngbí 象鼻; (large case) dà píxiāng 大皮箱; (of car) xínglǐ xiāng 行李箱

trust 1 n xìnrèn 信任; FIN shòutuō jítuán 受托集团 **2** v/t xiāngxìn 相信; I ~ you wǒ xìnrèn nǐ 我信 任你

trusted kěxìn 可信

trustee lǐshì 理事

trustful, trusting xìnrèn 信任

trustworthy zhíde xìnrèn 值得信 任

truth shìshí 事实

truthful chéngshí 诚实

try 1 v/t chángshì 尝试; LAW shěn-pàn 审判; ~ to do X chángshì qùzuò X 尝试去做X **2** v/i shìshi 试试; you must ~ harder nǐ yīdìng yào gèngjiā nǔlì 你一定要 更加努力 **3** n chángshì 尝试; can I have a ~? (of food) ràng wǒ shìshi 让我试试; (at doing sth) ràng wǒ shìshi 让我试试; give X a ~ shìzuò X 试做X

♦**try on** clothes shìchuān 试穿

♦**try out** new machine, new method

shìyòng 试用

trying (*annoying*) nányǐ róngrěn 难
以容忍

T-shirt ⇩ yuánlǐng shān 圆领衫

tub (*bath*) yùgāng 浴缸; (*of liquid*)
tǒng 桶; (*for yoghurt, ice cream*) hé
盒

tubby *adj* ǎipàng 矮胖

tube (*pipe*) guǎndào 管道; (*of
toothpaste, ointment*) guǎn 管

tubeless *tire* wú nèitāi 无内胎

tuberculosis jiéhé bìng 结核病

tuck 1 *n* (*in dress*) zhě 褶 **2** *v/t* (*put*)
sāijìn 塞进

♦**tuck away** (*put away*) shōucáng
收藏; (*eat quickly*) dàchī 大吃

♦**tuck in 1** *v/t children* gàihǎo bèizi
盖好被子; *sheets* sāihǎo guǒjǐn
塞好裹紧 **2** *v/i* (*start eating*)
kāishǐ chī 开始吃

♦**tuck up** *sleeves etc* juǎnqǐ 卷起;
tuck X up in bed gěi X gàihǎo
bèizi ānshuì 给 X 盖好被子安睡

Tuesday xīngqī èr 星期二

tuft cóng 丛

tug 1 *n* (*pull*) lā 拉; NAUT tuōchuán
拖船 **2** *v/t* (*pull*) lā 拉

tuition fǔdǎo 辅导

tulip yùjīnxiāng 郁金香

tumble *v/i* dǎo 倒

tumbledown yáoyao yùzhuì 摇摇
欲坠

tumble-dryer shuǎigān jī 甩干机

tumbler (*for drink*) wújiǎo bōlíbēi
无脚玻璃杯; (*in circus*) fān jīndǒu
zhě 翻筋斗者

tummy dùzi 肚子

tummy ache dùzi téng 肚子疼

tumor zhǒngliú 肿瘤

tumult xuānnào 喧闹

tumultuous xuānnào 喧闹

tuna jīnqiāng yú 金枪鱼

tune 1 *n* qǔdiào 曲调; *in ~* hédiào
合调; *out of ~* zǒudiào 走调 **2** *v/t
instrument* tiáo zhǔn yīndiào 调准
音调

♦**tune in** *v/i* RAD shōutīng 收听; TV
shōukàn 收看

♦**tune in to** RAD shōutīng 收听; TV
shōukàn 收看

♦**tune up 1** *v/i* (*of orchestra,*

players) tiáoyīn 调音 **2** *v/t engine*
tiáozhěng 调整

tuneful yīndiào yuè'ér 音调悦耳

tuner (*hi-fi*) tiáoxié qì 调谐器

tunic EDU duǎnpáo 短袍

tunnel *n* suìdào 隧道

turbine (*operated by air*) qìlún jī 气
轮机; (*operated by water*) wōlún jī
涡轮机; (*operated by steam*) yèlún
jī 叶轮机

turbot dàlíngpíng 大菱鲆

turbulence (*in air travel*) tuānliú 湍
流

turbulent *meeting, life, love affair*
hǔnluàn 混乱; *weather* kuángbào
狂暴

turf cǎopí 草皮

Turk Tú'ěrqí rén 土耳其人

Turkey Tú'ěrqí 土耳其

turkey huǒjī 火鸡

Turkish 1 *adj* Tú'ěrqí 土耳其 **2** *n*
(*language*) Tú'ěrqí yǔ 土耳其语

turmoil dòngluàn 动乱

turn 1 *n* (*rotation*) zhuǎndòng 转
动; (*in road*) zhuàn 转; (*in
vaudeville*) jiémù 节目; *take ~s
doing X* lúnliú zuò X 轮流做 X;
it's my ~ gāi wǒ le 该我了; *it's
not your ~ yet* méi dào nǐ ne 没到
你呢; *take a ~ at the wheel* kāi
yīhuìr chē 开一会儿车; *do X a
good ~* wèi X zuò hǎoshì 为 X 做
好事 **2** *v/t wheel* zhuàn 转; *corner*
guǎiwānr 拐弯儿; *~ one's back
on X* rēngxià X bùguǎn 扔下 X 不
管 **3** *v/i* (*of driver, car, wheel*)
zhuàn 转; *~ right / left here*
zhuànyòu / zuǒ 转右 / 左; *it has
~ed sour / cold* biànsuān / lěng le
变酸 / 冷了; *he has ~ed 40* tā
sìshí le 他四十了

♦**turn around 1** *v/t object, company*
niǔzhuǎn 扭转; (COM: *deal with*)
wánchéng 完成 **2** *v/i* (*of person*)
zhuǎnshēn 转身; (*of driver*)
diàotóu 调头

♦**turn away 1** *v/t* (*send away*) jùjué
拒绝 **2** *v/i* (*walk away*) zǒule 走
了; (*look away*) zhuǎnliǎn 转脸

♦**turn back 1** *v/t edges, sheets*
fānhuí 翻回 **2** *v/i* (*of walkers, in*

course of action) huítóu 回头

♦ **turn down** v/t offer, invitation jùjué 拒绝; volume, TV, heating guānxiǎo 关小; edge, collar fānxià 翻下

♦ **turn in 1** v/i (go to bed) shàng-chuáng 上床 **2** v/t (to police) zìshǒu 自首

♦ **turn off 1** v/t TV, faucet, heater, engine guān 关; F (sexually) shǐ shīqù xìngqù 使失去兴趣 **2** v/i (of car, driver) xià 下

♦ **turn on 1** v/t TV, faucet, heater, engine kāi 开; F (sexually) cìjī 刺激 **2** v/i (of machine) kāi 开

♦ **turn out 1** v/t lights guān 关 **2** v/i: **as it turned out** jiéguǒ shì 结果是

♦ **turn over 1** v/i (in bed) fānshēn 翻身; (of vehicle) fān guòlái 翻过来 **2** v/t (put upside down) fān guòlái 翻过来; page fān piānr 翻篇儿; FIN zhōuzhuǎn 周转

♦ **turn up 1** v/t collar fānqǐ 翻起; volume, heating kāidà 开大 **2** v/i (arrive) lòumiàn 露面

turning guǎijiǎo 拐角

turning point zhuǎnzhé diǎn 转折点

turnip luóbo 萝卜

turnout (people) cānjiā zhě 参加者

turnover FIN chéngjiāo liàng 成交量

turnpike gāosù gōnglù 高速公路

turnstile ràogān 绕杆

turntable (of record player) diànchàng pán 电唱盘

turquoise adj qīnglǜsè 青绿色

turret (of castle) jiǎolóu 角楼; (of tank) xuánzhuàn pàotǎ 旋转炮塔

turtle wūguī 乌龟

turtleneck (sweater) gāolǐng tào-shān 高领套衫

tusk xiàngyá 象牙

tutor: (**private**) ~ sīrén jiàoshī 私人教师

tuxedo lǐfú 礼服

TV diànshì 电视; **on** ~ diànshì shang 电视上

TV program diànshì jiémù 电视节目

twang 1 n (in voice) bíyīn 鼻音 **2** v/t guitar string shǐ fā xián shēng 使发弦声

tweezers nièzi 镊子

twelfth dìshí'èr 第十二

twelve shí'èr 十二

twentieth dìèrshí 第二十

twenty èrshí 二十

twice liǎngcì 两次; ~ **as much** liǎngbèi nàme duō 两倍那么多

twiddle bǎinòng 摆弄; ~ **one's thumbs** fig xiánzhe 闲着

twig n xìzhī 细枝

twilight huánghūn 黄昏

twin shuāng bāo tāi 双胞胎

twin beds liǎng zhāng chuáng 两张床

twinge (of pain) cìtòng 刺痛

twinkle v/i (of stars) shǎnyào 闪耀; (of eyes) fāguāng 发光

twin town yǒuyì shì 友谊市

twirl 1 v/t shǐ xuánzhuǎn 使旋转 **2** n (of cream etc) zhuāngshì 装饰

twist 1 v/t cuō 搓; ~ **one's ankle** niǔle jiǎohuái 扭了脚踝 **2** v/i (of road, river) pánxuán 盘旋 **3** n (in rope) nǐng 拧; (in road) guǎiwānr 拐弯儿; (in plot, story) qūzhé 曲折

twisty road wānwan qūqu 弯弯曲曲

twit bèndàn 笨蛋

twitch 1 n (nervous) chōuchù 抽搐 **2** v/i (jerk) chōuchù 抽搐

twitter v/i (of birds) zhīzhi de jiào 吱吱地叫

two èr 二; (with measure words) liǎng 俩; **the ~ of them** tāmen liǎng 他们俩

two-faced liǎngmiànpài 两面派; **two-piece** n (woman's suit) tàofú tào服; **two-stroke** adj engine èrchōngchéng 二冲程; **two-way traffic** shuāngxiàng jiāotōng 双向交通

tycoon jùtóu 巨头

type 1 n (sort) zhǒnglèi 种类; **what ~ of ...?** nǎ yīzhǒng ...? 那一种 ... ? **2** v/t & v/i (with a keyboard) dǎzì 打字

typhoid (fever) shānghán 伤寒
typhoon táifēng 台风
typhus bānzhěn shānghán 斑疹伤寒
typical diǎnxíng 典型; *that's ~ of him* tā jiù shì nàyàng 他就是那样
typically diǎnxíng 典型; ~

American diǎnxíng Měiguórén 典型美国人
typist dǎzìyuán 打字员
tyrannical bàonüè 暴虐
tyrannize shī bàonüè 施暴虐
tyranny (*behavior*) bàonüè 暴虐; (*regime*) bàozhèng 暴政
tyrant bàojūn 暴君

U

ugly chǒulòu 丑陋

UK (= **United Kingdom**) Yīngguó 英国; (*formal use*) Liánhé Wángguó 联合王国

ulcer kuìyáng 溃疡

ultimate (*best, definitive*) zuìhǎo 最好; (*final*) zuìhòu 最后; (*fundamental*) gēnběn 根本

ultimately (*in the end*) zuìzhōng 最终

ultimatum zuìhòu tōngdié 最后通牒

ultrasound MED chāoshēngbō 超声波

ultraviolet *adj* zǐwài 紫外

umbilical cord qídài 脐带

umbrella sǎn 伞

umpire *n* cáipànyuán 裁判员

umpteen F wúshù 无数

UN (= **United Nations**) Liánhéguó 联合国

un ... (*with adjs*) bù, fēi (qiánzhuì) 不，非（前缀）

unable: *be ~ to do X* (*not know how to*) bùhuì zuò X 不会做 X; (*not be in a position to*) méiyǒu nénglì zuò X 没有能力做 X

unacceptable bùnéng jiēshòu 不能接受; *it is ~ that ...* ... shì lìngrén bùnéng jiēshòu de ... 是令人不能接受的

unaccountable wúfǎ jiěshì 无法解释

unaccustomed: *be ~ to X* bù xíguànyú X 不习惯于 X

unadulterated *fig* (*absolute*) shízú 十足

un-American (*not fitting*) fēi Měiguó 非美国

unanimous *verdict* yízhì tóngyì 一致同意; *be ~ on X* duì X dáchéng yízhì 对 X 达成一致

unanimously *vote, decide* yízhì 一致

unapproachable *person* nányǐ jiējìn 难以接近

unarmed *person* wú wǔqì 无武器; *~ combat* túshǒu gédòu 徒手格斗

unassuming qiānxùn 谦逊

unattached (*without a partner*) wú gùdìng bànlǚ 无固定伴侣

unattended wúzhǔ 无主; *leave X ~* diūxià X bùguǎn 丢下 X 不管

unauthorized shànzì 擅自

unavoidable bùkě bìmiǎn 不可避免

unavoidably: *be ~ detained* chōu bù kāi shēn 抽不开身

unaware: *be ~ of* méiyǒu chájuédào 没有察觉到

unawares: *catch X ~* shǐ X chījīng 使 X 吃惊

unbalanced bù pínghéng 不平衡; PSYCH shīcháng 失常

unbearable nányǐ rěnshòu 难以忍受

unbeatable *team, quality* bùkě zhànshèng 不可战胜

unbeaten *team* wèi bèi jībài 未被击败

unbeknownst: *~ to X* X bù zhīdào X 不知道

unbelievable nányǐzhìxìn 难以置信; F *heat, value* jíduān 极端; *he's ~* F (*very good/bad*) tā zhēn búshì yìbān rén 他真不是一般人

unbias(s)ed bù piāntǎn 不偏袒

unblock *pipe* qīngchú dǔsè 清除堵塞

unborn wèi chūshēng 未出生

unbreakable *plate* dǎbúpò 打不碎; *world's record* bùkě dǎpò 不可打破

unbutton jiěkāi niǔkòu 解开纽扣

uncalled-for wú lǐyóu 无理由

uncanny *resemblance* yìhūxúncháng 异乎寻常; *skill* bùkě sīyì

不可思议; (*worrying: feeling*) líqí 离奇

unceasing búduàn 不断

uncertain *future, weather* kěnéng gǎibiàn 可能改变; *origins* bú quèdìng 不确定; ***be ~ about X*** duì X bú quèdìng 对 X 不确定

uncertainty (*of the future*) bú quèdìng 不确定; ***there is still ~ about X*** duì X háiyǒu bú quèdìngxìng 对 X 还有不确定性

unchecked: let X go ~ rèn X zìyóu fāzhǎn 任 X 自由发展

uncle (*mother's brother*) jiùjiu 舅舅; (*father's elder brother*) bóbo 伯伯; (*father's younger brother*) shūshu 叔叔; (*mother's sister's husband*) yífù 姨父; (*father's sister's husband*) gūfù 姑父; (*to older non-related men*) shūshu 叔叔

uncomfortable *chair* bù shūshì 不舒适; *sitting position* bù shūfu 不舒服; ***feel ~ about X*** (*about decision etc*) duì X yǒu zhìyí 对 X 有质疑; ***I feel ~ with him*** wǒ gēn tā zài yìqǐ gǎndào bú zìzài 我跟他在一起感到不自在

uncommon bù xúncháng 不寻常; ***it's not ~*** zhè bù hǎnjiàn 这不罕见

uncompromising bú ràngbù 不让步

unconcerned lěngmò 冷漠; ***be ~ about X*** bù bǎ X fàngzài xīn shang 不把 X 放在心上

unconditional wú tiáojiàn 无条件

unconscious MED shīqù zhījué 失去知觉; PSYCH xiàyìshí 下意识; ***knock X ~*** dǎde X bùxǐngrénshì 打得 X 不醒人事; ***be ~ of X*** (*not aware*) wèi chájué chū X 未察觉出 X

uncontrollable *anger, desire, children* kòngzhì bùliǎo 控制不了

unconventional bùxún xísú 不循习俗

uncooperative búyuàn hézuò 不愿合作

uncork *bottle* báchū ... sāizi 拔出 ... 塞子

uncover (*remove cover from*) jiēkāi 揭开; *plot* jiēlù 揭露; *ancient remains* fājué 发掘

undamaged wèishòu sǔnshāng 未受损伤

undaunted: carry on ~ yǒng wǎng zhí qián 勇往直前

undecided *question* xuán ér wèijué 悬而未决; ***be ~ about X*** duì X yóuyù bú dìng 对 X 犹豫不定

undeniable bùkě fǒurèn 不可否认

undeniably díquè 的确

under 1 *prep* (*beneath*) zài ... xiàmian 在 ... 下面; (*less than*) bú dào 不到 **2** *adv* (*anesthetized*) shīqù zhījué 失去知觉

underage *drinking etc* wèi chéngnián 未成年; ***be ~*** wèi dào fǎdìng niánlíng 未到法定年龄

undercarriage qǐluòjià 起落架

undercover *adj agent* mìmì 秘密

undercut *v/t* COM xiàjià qiǎng ... shēngyì 削价抢 ... 生意

underdog chǔyú lièshì de yìfāng 处于劣势的一方

underdone *meat* bù shútòu 不熟透

underestimate *v/t person, skills, task* guòfèn dīgū 过分低估

underexposed PHOT bàoguāng bù zú 曝光不足

underfed yíngyǎng bùliáng 营养不良

undergo *surgery, treatment* jiēshòu 接受; *experiences* jīngshòu 经受

underground 1 *adj also* POL dìxià 地下 **2** *adv work* mìmì 秘密; ***go ~*** POL zhuǎnrù dìxià 转入地下

undergrowth guànmùcóng 灌木丛

underhand *adj* (*devious*) guǐzhà 诡诈

underlie *v/t*: ***~ the theory*** gòuchéng zhè yī lǐlùn de jīchǔ 构成这一理论的基础

underline *v/t text* xià huàxiàn 下划线

underlying *causes, problems* gēnběn 根本

undermine *v/t s.o.'s position* xūruò

削弱; *theory* chèdǐ jīkuǎ 彻底击垮

underneath 1 *prep* zài ... dǐxià 在... 底下 **2** *adv* xiàngxià 向下

underpants nèikù 内裤

underpass (*for pedestrians*) dìxià tōngdào 地下通道

underprivileged dìwèi dīxià 地位低下

underrate *v/t* guòdī píngjià 过低评价

undershirt bèixīn 背心

undersized tàixiǎo 太小

underskirt chènqún 衬裙

understaffed rényuán bùzú 人员不足

understand 1 *v/t* lǐjiě 理解; *I ~ that you ...* wǒ tīngshuō nǐ ... 我听说你 ...; *they are understood to be in Canada* jù liǎojiě tāmen zài Jiānádà 据了解他们在加拿大 **2** *v/i* míngbái 明白

understandable kě lǐjiě 可理解

understandably kě lǐjiě 可理解

understanding 1 *adj person* tōngqíng dálǐ 通情达理 **2** *n* (*of problem, situation*) lǐjiě 理解; (*agreement*) xiéyì 协议; *on the ~ that ...* (*condition*) zài ... tiáojiàn xià 在 ... 条件下

understatement zhòngshì qīngshuō 重事轻说

undertake *task* chéngdān 承担; *~ to do X* (*agree to*) tóngyì zuò X 同意做 X

undertaking (*enterprise*) shìyè 事业; (*promise*) xǔnuò 许诺

undervalue *v/t* dīgū 低估

underwear nèiyī 内衣

underweight *adj* biāozhǔn zhòngliàng yǐxià 标准重量以下

underworld (*criminal*) hēi shèhuì 黑社会; (*in mythology*) yīnjiān 阴间

underwrite *v/t* FIN tóngyì zīzhù 同意资助

undeserved bú qiàdàng 不恰当

undesirable *features, changes* búshòu huānyíng 不受欢迎; *person* tǎoyàn 讨厌; *~ element* (*person*) dǎoluàn fènzǐ 捣乱分子

undisputed *champion, leader* wúkě zhēngbiàn 无可争辩

undo *parcel, wrapping* dǎkāi 打开; *buttons, shirt, shoelaces* jiěkāi 解开; *s.o. else's work* fèichú 废除; COMPUT chèxiāo 撤销

undoubtedly wúyí 无疑

undreamt-of *riches* zuòmèng yě xiǎng bú dào 做梦也想不到

undress 1 *v/t* gěi ... tuō yīfu 给 ... 脱衣服; *get ~ed* tuō yīfu 脱衣服 **2** *v/i* tuō yīfu 脱衣服

undue (*excessive*) guòdù 过度

unduly *punished, blamed* bú shìdàng 不适当; (*excessively*) guòfèn 过分

unearth *ancient remains* fājué 发掘; *fig* (*find*) fāxiàn 发现; *secret* jiěkāi 揭开

unearthly: *at this ~ hour* zài zhè gè huāngmiù de shíhòu 在这个荒谬的时候

uneasy *relationship, peace* lìngrén bù'ān 令人不安; *feel ~ about X* wèi X gǎndào bù'ān 为 X 感到不安

uneatable bùnéng chī 不能吃

uneconomic bù jīngjì 不经济

uneducated wèi shòu liánghǎo jiàoyù 未受良好教育

unemployed shīyè 失业; (*laid off from state enterprise*) xiàgǎng 下岗; *the ~* shīyèzhě 失业者; (*from state enterprise*) xiàgǎng gōngrén 下岗工人

unemployment shīyè 失业

unending wú zhǐjìng 无止境

unequal bù píngděng 不平等; *be ~ to the task* nányǐ shèngrèn zhèi xiàng gōngzuò 难以胜任这项工作

unerring *judgment, instinct* wànwúyìshī 万无一失

uneven *quality* bù yízhì 不一致; *surface, ground* bù píng 不平

unevenly *distributed, applied* bù jūnyún 不均匀; *~ matched* (*of two contestants*) bú shìjūnlìdí 不势均力敌

uneventful *day, journey* píngdàn 平淡

unexpected chūhū yìliào 出乎意料

unexpectedly yìwài 意外

unfair bù gōngpíng 不公平

unfaithful *husband, wife* bù zhōng 不忠; *be ~ to X* duì X bù zhōng 对 X 不忠

unfamiliar bù shúxī 不熟悉; *be ~ with X* bù shúxī X 不熟悉 X

unfasten *belt* jiěkāi 解开

unfavorable *report, review* fùmiàn 负面; *weather conditions* búlì 不利

unfeeling *person* wúqíng 无情

unfinished wèi wánchéng 未完成; *leave X ~* bàntú rēngxià X 半途扔下 X

unfit (*physically*) bú jiànkāng 不健康; (*not morally suited*) bú shìhé 不适合; *be ~ to eat / drink* bùyí shíyòng / yǐnyòng 不宜食用 / 饮用

unfix *part* chāixià 拆下; *screw* nǐngxià 拧下

unflappable zhèndìng zìruò 镇定自若

unfold 1 *v/t* *sheets, letter* tānkāi 摊开; *one's arms* zhāngkāi 张开 **2** *v/i* (*of story etc*) zhǎnkāi 展开; (*of view*) xiǎnxiàn 显现

unforeseen wèi yùjiàn dào 未预见到

unforgettable nánwàng 难忘

unforgivable bù kě ráoshù 不可饶恕; *that was ~ of you* bùnéng yuánliàng nǐ 不能原谅你

unfortunate *people, event* búxìng 不幸; *choice of words* bú qiàdàng 不恰当; *that's ~ for you* nǐ bù zǒuyùn 你不走运

unfortunately búxìng de shì 不幸的是

unfounded wúduān 无端

unfriendly lěngmò 冷漠; *software* bú yì shǐyòng 不易使用

unfurnished wú jiājù shèbèi 无家具设备

ungodly: *at this ~ hour* zài zhème ge huāngmiù shíhòu 在这么个荒谬时候

ungrateful bù lǐngqíng 不领情

unhappiness bù yúkuài 不愉快

unhappy bù yúkuài 不愉快; (*not content: customers etc*) bù mǎnyì 不满意; *be ~ with X* duì X bù mǎnyì 对 X 不满意

unharmed píng'ān wúyàng 平安无恙

unhealthy *person* bú jiànkāng 不健康; *conditions, food, atmosphere* yǒuhài yú jiànkāng 有害于健康; *economy, balance sheet* bù jǐngqì 不景气

unheard-of qián suǒ wèi wén 前所未闻

unhurt wèi shòu shānghài 未受伤害

unhygienic bú wèishēng 不卫生

unification tǒngyī 统一

uniform 1 *n* zhìfú 制服 **2** *adj* yízhì 一致

unify tǒngyī 统一

unilateral dān fāngmiàn 单方面

unimaginable nányǐ xiǎngxiàng 难以想象

unimaginative qùfá xiǎngxiànglì 缺乏想象力

unimportant bú zhòngyào 不重要

uninhabitable bú shìyú jūzhù 不适于居住

uninhabited *building, region* huāng wú rényān 荒无人烟

uninjured wèi shòu sǔnshāng 未受损伤

unintelligible nán lǐjiě 难理解

unintentional fēi gùyì 非故意

unintentionally wúxīn 无心

uninteresting wúliáo 无聊

uninterrupted *sleep, work* bù jiānduàn 不间断

union POL liánméng 联盟; (*labor ~*) gōnghuì 工会

unique dúyīwú'èr 独一无二; F (*very good*) biéjùyìgé 别具一格; *with his own ~ humor / style* yǐ tā dútè de yōumò / fēnggé 以他独特的幽默 / 风格

unit (*of measurement*) dānwèi 单位; (*section: of machine, structure*) bùjiàn 部件; (*part with separate function*) yuánjiàn 元件; (*department*) bù 部; MIL bùduì 部队; *work ~* dānwèi 单位; *we*

must work together as a ~
wǒmen bìxū zuòwéi yígè zhěngtǐ
yìqǐ gōngzuò 我们必须作为一
个整体一起工作

unit cost COM dānjià 单价

unite 1 *v/t* tǒngyī 统一; *family
members* tuánjù 团聚 **2** *v/i* tuánjié
团结

united tuánjié 团结

United Kingdom Yīngguó 英国;
(*formal use*) Liánhé Wángguó 联
合王国

United Nations Liánhéguó 联合
国

United States (of America)
Měiguó 美国; (*formal use*)
Měilìjiān Hézhòngguó 美利坚合
众国

unity tǒngyī 统一

universal pǔbiàn 普遍

universally yízhì 一致

universe yǔzhòu 宇宙

university 1 *n* dàxué 大学; *he is
at ~* tā zài dú dàxué 他在读大学
2 *adj* dàxué 大学

unjust bù gōngzhèng 不公正

unkempt bù zhěngjié 不整洁

unkind kèbó 刻薄

unknown 1 *adj* wèizhī 未知 **2** *n: a
journey into the ~* qiántú wèibǔ
前途未卜

unleaded *adj* wúqiān 无铅

unless chúfēi 除非

unlike *prep* búxiàng 不像; *it's ~
him to drink so much* tā hē
zhèmeduō jiǔ búxiàng tā píngshí
de yàngzi 他喝这么多酒不像
他平时的样子; *the photograph
was completely ~ her* zhàopiàn
yìdiǎnr yě bú xiàng tā běnrén 照
片一点儿也不像她本人

unlikely bú dà kěnéng 不大可能;
he is ~ to win tā bú dà kěnéng
yíng 他不大可能赢; *it is ~ that
… * … bú dà kěnéng … 不大可能

unlimited wúxiàn 无限

unload *truck, goods* xiè 卸

unlock dǎkāi 打开

unluckily yíhànde shì 遗憾的是

unlucky *day, choice* dǎoméi 倒霉;
person búxìng 不幸; *that was so*

~ for you! nà nǐ tài dǎoméi le! 那
你太倒霉了！

unmade-up *face* méi huàzhuāng
没化妆

unmanned *spacecraft* wúrén cāozòng 无人操纵

unmarried wèihūn 未婚

unmistakable juéwú jǐnyǒu 绝无
仅有

unmoved (*emotionally*) wèi bèi
gǎndòng 未被感动

unmusical *person* méiyǒu yīnyuè
tiānfù 没有音乐天赋; *sounds*
cì'ěr 刺耳

unnatural fǎncháng 反常; *it's not
~ to be annoyed* gǎndào fánnǎo
shì zhèngcháng de 感到烦恼是
正常的

unnecessary bú bìyào 不必要

unnerving lìngrén qìněi 令人气
馁

unnoticed: *it went ~* bèi hūlüè 被
忽略

unobtainable *goods* mǎi bú dào 买
不到; TELEC chábúdào 查不到

unobtrusive bù yǐnrén zhùmù 不
引人注目

unoccupied *building, house* wúrén
zhù 无人住; *room* kōngzhe 空
着; *post* wúrén chéngdān 无人承
担; *person* kòngxián 空闲

unofficial fēi zhèngshì 非正式

unofficially fēi zhèngshì 非正式

unpack 1 *v/t* dǎkāi 打开 **2** *v/i*
dǎkāi bāoguǒ 打开包裹

unpaid *work* wúcháng 无偿

unpleasant shǐ rén bù yúkuài 使
人不愉快; *he was very ~ to her*
tā dài tā hěn cūlǔ 他待她很粗
鲁

unplug *v/t TV, computer* báchū
chātóu 拔出插头

unpopular *person* bú shòu
huānyíng 不受欢迎; *decision*
bùdé rénxīn 不得人心

unprecedented kōngqián 空前; *it
was ~ for a woman to X* dāngshí,
nǚxìng X shì shǐwúqiánlì de 当
时，女性X是史无前例的

unpredictable *person, weather*
fǎnfù wúcháng 反复无常

unprincipled *pej* bú dàodé 不道德

unpretentious *person, style, hotel* bù xuānyào 不炫耀

unproductive *meeting, discussion* méiyǒu jiéguǒ 没有结果; *soil* bù féiwò 不肥沃

unprofessional *person, behavior* bú jìngyè 不敬业; *workmanship* zāogāo 糟糕

unprofitable bù yínglì 不盈利

unpronounceable nányǐ zhèng-què fāyīn 难以正确发音

unprotected *borders* wèi shèfáng 未设防; *machine* méiyǒu ānquán zhuāngzhì 没有安全装置; ~ *sex* wèi jīng bǎohù de xìng xíngwéi 未经保护的性行为

unprovoked *attack* wúduān 无端

unqualified *worker, doctor etc* bù hégé 不合格

unquestionably (*without doubt*) wúkě zhēngbiàn 无可争辩

unquestioning *attitude, loyalty* wú yìyì 无异议

unravel *v/t string, knitting* chāikāi 拆开; *mystery, complexities* chéngqīng 澄清

unreadable *book* bùzhíyìdú 不值一读

unreal bù zhēnshí 不真实; *this is ~!* F xiàng mèng yíyàng! 像梦一样!

unrealistic bú xiànshí 不现实

unreasonable *person* chāoyuè qínglǐ 超越情理; *demand, expectation* guòfèn 过分

unrelated *issues* bù xiāngguān 不相关; *people* wú qīnqī guānxi 无亲戚关系

unrelenting búxiè 不懈

unreliable bù kěkào 不可靠

unrest dòngluàn 动乱

unrestrained *emotions* wú jūshù 无拘束

unroadworthy bùyí zài gōnglù shang xíngshǐ 不宜在公路上行使

unroll *v/t carpet, scroll* zhǎnkāi 展开

unruly bù guījù 不规矩

unsafe *bridge, vehicle, wiring* wēixiǎn 危险; *district, beach* bù ānquán 不安全; ~ *to drink / eat* bùyí hē / chī 不宜喝 / 吃; *it is ~ to X* X bù ānquán X不安全

unsanitary *conditions, drains* bú wèishēng 不卫生

unsatisfactory bùnéng lìngrén mǎnyì 不能令人满意

unsavory *person, reputation* lìngrén tǎoyàn 令人讨厌; *district* lìngrén búkuài 令人不快

unscathed (*not injured*) wèi shòu sǔnshāng 未受损伤; (*not damaged*) wèi shòu sǔnhuài 未受损坏

unscrew *sth screwed on* xuánsōng 旋松; *top* nǐngkāi 拧开

unscrupulous bù jiǎng dàodé 不讲道德

unselfish wúsī 无私

unsettled *issue* wèi jiějué 未解决; *weather, stock market* yìbiàn 易变; *lifestyle* bù wěndìng 不稳定; *bills* wèi zhīfù 未支付

unshaven méi xiūmiàn 没修面

unsightly bù yǎguān 不雅观

unskilled wú tèshū jìnéng 无特殊技能

unsociable bù héqún 不合群

unsophisticated *person* zhìpǔ 质朴; *equipment* jiǎndān 简单

unstable *person* fǎnfù wúcháng 反复无常; *structure* bù jiāngù 不坚固; *area, economy* dòngdàng bù'ān 动荡不定

unsteady (*on one's feet*) bùwěn 不稳; *ladder* yáobǎi 摇摆

unstinting: *be ~ in one's efforts* búyíyúlì 不遗余力

unstuck: *come ~* (*of notice etc*) méi zhānzhù 没粘住; (*of plan etc*) shībài 失败

unsuccessful *writer, party* bù chénggōng 不成功; *candidate, attempt* shībài 失败; *he tried but was ~* tā chángshìle kěshì méi chénggōng 他尝试了可是没成功

unsuccessfully *try, apply* shībài 失败

unsuitable bù héshì 不合适

unsuspecting wú jièxīn 无戒心

unswerving *loyalty, devotion* búbiàn 不变

unthinkable bùkě sīyì 不可思议

untidy *room, desk, hair* língluàn 凌乱

untie *knot, laces, prisoner* jiěkāi 解开

until 1 *prep* zhídào 直到; *from Monday ~ Friday* cóng zhōuyī dào zhōuwǔ 从周一到周五; *I can wait ~ tomorrow* wǒ kěyǐ děngdào míngtiān 我可以等到明天; *not ~ Friday* děi zhōuwǔ 得周五; *it won't be finished ~ July* zhídào qīyuè cái néng wánchéng 直到七月才能完成 **2** *conj*: *can you wait ~ I'm ready?* nǐ kěyǐ děng wǒ zhǔnbèi hǎo ma? 你可以等我准备好吗？; *they won't do anything ~ you say so* nǐ shuōle tāmen cái néng zuò 你说了他们才能做

untimely *death* guòzǎo 过早

untiring *efforts* bújuàn 不倦

untold *riches, suffering* wúxiàn 无限; *story* wèi tòulù 未透露

untranslatable bùnéng fānyì 不能翻译

untrue bù zhēnshí 不真实

unused[1] *goods* xīn 新

unused[2]: *be ~ to X* bù xíguàn X 不习惯 X; *be ~ to doing X* bù xíguàn zuò X 不习惯做 X

unusual bùtóng xúncháng 不同寻常

unusually yìcháng 异常

unveil *memorial, statue etc* jiēmù 揭幕

unwell bù shūfu 不舒服

unwilling: *be ~ to do X* búyuàn zuò X 不愿做 X

unwind 1 *v/t tape* jiěkāi 解开 **2** *v/i* (*of tape, story*) zhǎnkāi 展开; (*relax*) fàngsōng 放松

unwise bù míngzhì 不明智

unwrap *gift* dǎkāi 打开

unwritten *law, rule* wèi chéngwén 未成文

unzip *v/t dress etc* lākāi lālián 拉开拉链; COMPUT jiě yāsuō 解压缩

up 1 *adv* xiàngshàng 向上; *look ~* xiàngshàng kàn 向上看; *~ in the sky* / *~ on the roof* zài gāokōng / zài wūdǐng shang 在高空 / 在屋顶上; *~ here* / *there* zài zhè / nà shang 在这 / 那上; *be ~* (*out of bed*) qǐchuáng 起床; (*of sun*) shēngqǐ 升起; (*be built*) jiànchéng 建成; (*of shelves*) ānhǎo 安好; (*of prices, temperature*) shàngshēng 上升; (*have expired*) dàoqī 到期; *what's ~?* zěnmele? 怎么了？; *~ to the year 1989* zhídào yījiǔbājiǔ nián 直到1989年; *he came ~ to me* tā xiàng wǒ zǒuguòlái 他向我走过来; *what are you ~ to these days?* zuìjìn zài mángxiē shénme? 最近在忙些什么？; *what are those kids ~ to?* nàxiē háizimen zài gǎo shénme guǐ? 那些孩子们在搞什么鬼？; *be ~ to something* (*bad*) méi zuò shénme hǎoshì 没做什么好事; *I don't feel ~ to it* wǒ juédé zìjǐ bùnéng shèngrèn 我觉得自己不能胜任; *it's ~ to you* nǐ lái juédìng 你来决定; *it is ~ to them to solve it* (*their duty*) jiějué zhèijiànshì shì tāmende zhízé 解决这件事是他们的职责; *be ~ and about* (*after illness*) qǐchuáng zǒudòng 起床走动 **2** *prep*: *further ~ the mountain* zài wǎng shānshàng yìxiē 再往山上一些; *he climbed ~ a tree* tā pádào shùshang qù le 他爬到树上去了; *they ran ~ the street* tāmen yánzhe jiē pǎo 他们沿着街跑; *the water goes ~ this pipe* shuǐ shùnzhe zhèitiáo guǎndào xiàngshàng xíng 水顺着这条管道向上行; *we traveled ~ to Shanghai* wǒmen lǚxíng zhì Shànghǎi 我们旅行至上海 **3** *n*: *~s and downs* gānkǔ 甘苦

upbringing jiàoyǎng 教养

upcoming *adj* (*forthcoming*) jíjiāng láilín 即将来临

update 1 *v/t file, records* xiūdìng 修订; *~ X on Y* xiàng X tígōng zuìxīn yǒuguān Y de xìnxī 向 X 提供最新有关 Y 的信息 **2** *n* (*of files,* *records*) xiūdìng 修订; (*software version*) zuìxīn bǎnběn 最新版本; *can you give me an ~ on the situation?* nǐ néng gàosù wǒ júshìde zuìxīn xìnxī ma? 你能告诉我局势的最新信息吗？

upgrade *v/t computers etc* gǎijìn 改进; (*replace with new versions*) gēngxīn 更新; *ticket* tígāo … děngjí 提高 … 等级

upheaval (*emotional*) jùbiàn 剧变; (*physical*) biàndòng 变动; (*political, social*) dòngluàn 动乱

uphill 1 *adv walk* shàngpō 上坡 **2** *adj struggle* jiānnán 艰难

uphold *traditions, rights* wéihù 维护; (*vindicate*) zhèngshí 证实

upholstery (*coverings*) jiājù zhuāngshì cáiliào 家具装饰材料; (*padding*) diànliào 垫料

upkeep *n* (*of old buildings, parks etc*) bǎoyǎng 保养

upload *v/t* COMPUT jiāzài 加载

upmarket *adj restaurant, hotel* gāojí 高级

upon → **on**

upper *part of sth* shàngbù 上部; *stretches of a river* shàngyóu 上游; *deck* shàngcéng 上层

upper atmosphere dàqì wàicéng 大气外层; **upper-class** *adj accent, family* shàngcéng shèhuì 上层社会; **upper classes** shàngděng jiēcéng 上等阶层

upright 1 *adj citizen* zhèngzhí 正直 **2** *adv sit* bǐzhí 笔直

upright (*piano*) shùshì (gāngqín) 竖式 (钢琴)

uprising qǐyì 起义

uproar (*loud noise*) xuānxiāo 喧嚣; (*protest*) kàngyì 抗议

upset 1 *v/t drink, glass* nòngfān 弄翻; (*emotionally*) shǐrén nánguò 使人难过 **2** *adj* (*emotionally*) nánguò 难过; *get ~ about X* yīn X ér nánguò 因 X 而难过; *have an ~ stomach* gǎndào chángwèi búshì 感到肠胃不适

upsetting lìngrén nánguò 令人难过

upshot (*result, outcome*) zuìhòu

jiéguǒ 最后结果

upside down *adv* dǐ cháo shàng 底朝上; *turn X ~ box etc* bǎ X shàngxià diāndǎo guòlái 把 X 上下颠倒过来

upstairs 1 *adv* zài lóushàng 在楼上 **2** *adj room* lóushàng 楼上

upstart xīnguì 新贵

upstream *adv* xiàng shàngyóu 向上游

uptight F (*nervous*) jǐnzhāng 紧张; (*inhibited*) jūjǐn 拘谨

up-to-date *information* zuìxīn 最新; *fashions* xīnshì 新式

upturn (*in economy*) hǎozhuǎn 好转

upward *adv fly, move* xiàngshàng 向上; *~ of 10,000* yíwàn duō 一万多

uranium yóuyóu 铀

urban dūshì 都市

urbanization chéngshìhuà 城市化

urchin wántóng 顽童

urge 1 *n* yùwàng 欲望 **2** *v/t: ~ X to do Y* jiélì cuīcù X zuò Y 竭力催促 X 做 Y

◆ **urge on** (*encourage*) gǔlì 鼓励

urgency (*of situation*) jǐnjí 紧急

urgent *job* jí jí 急; *letter* jǐnjí 紧急; *be in ~ need of X* jíxū X 急需 X; *is it ~?* shì jíshì ma? 是急事吗？

urinate páiniào 排尿

urine niào 尿

urn (*for ashes*) gǔhuīwèng 骨灰瓮

us wǒmen 我们

US(A) (= *United States* (*of America*)) Měiguó 美国; (*formal use*) Měilìjiān Hézhòngguó 美利坚合众国

usable kě shǐyòng 可使用

usage (*linguistic*) guànyòngfǎ 惯法

use 1 *v/t* shǐyòng 使用; *skills, knowledge* yùnyòng 运用; *car* yòng 用; *a lot of gas* xiāohào 消耗; *pej: person* lìyòng 利用; *I could ~ a drink* F wǒ zhēn xiǎng hē dōngxi 我真想喝东西 **2** *n* shǐyòng 使用; *be of great ~ to X* duì X dàyǒu yòngchù 对 X 大有

用处; *be of no ~ to X* duì X méiyǒuyòng 对 X 没有用; *is that of any ~?* nà yǒuyòng ma? 那有用吗？; *it's no ~* méiyòng 没用; *it's no ~ trying / waiting* shì / děng yě méiyòng 试 / 等也没用
♦ **use up** yòngguāng 用光
used[1] *car etc* yòngguò 用过
used[2]: *be ~ to X* duì X xíguàn 对 X 习惯; *get ~ to X* duì X zhújiàn shìyìng 对 X 逐渐适应; *be ~ to doing X* xíguàn zuò X 习惯做 X; *get ~ to doing X* zhújiàn xíguàn zuò X 逐渐习惯做 X
used[3]: *I ~ to like him* wǒ céng xǐhuānguò tā 我曾喜欢过他; *I don't work there now, but I ~ to* wǒ yǐqián zài nàlǐ gōngzuò, xiànzài bù le 我以前在那里工作，现在不了
useful *person, information, gadget* yǒuyòng 有用
usefulness yòngchù 用处
useless *information* méiyòng 没用; F *person* chàjìn 差劲; *machine, computer* bùnéng yòng 不能用; *it's ~ trying* shì yě méiyòng 试也

没用
user (*of product*) yònghù 用户
user-friendly *software, device* yònghù yǒuhǎo 用户友好
usher *n* (*at wedding*) yíngbīnyuán 迎宾员
♦ **usher in** *new era* yùshì 预示
usherette nǚ yǐnzuòyuán 女引座员
usual tōngcháng 通常; *as ~* xiàng wǎngcháng yíyàng 像往常一样; *the ~, please* gēn píngcháng yíyàng 跟平常一样
usually tōngcháng 通常
utensil yòngjù 用具
uterus zǐgōng 子宫
utility (*usefulness*) shíyòngxìng 实用性; *public utilities* gōngyòng shíyè 公用实业
utilize yìngyòng 应用
utmost 1 *adj* jídù 极度 **2** *n*: *do one's ~* jiéjìn suǒnéng 竭尽所能
utter 1 *adj* wánquán 完全 **2** *v/t sound* fāchū 发出
utterly jiǎnzhí 简直
U-turn U xíngwān U 形弯; *fig* (*in policy*) zhuǎnxiàng 转向

V

vacant *building, position* kōng 空;
look, expression mángrán 茫然

vacate *room* téngchū 腾出

vacation *n* xiūjià 休假; *be on ~*
dùjià 度假; *go to X on ~* qù X
dùjià 去 X 度假

vacationer dùjià zhě 度假者

vaccinate jiēzhòng yìmiáo 接种
疫苗; *be ~d against X* jiēzhòng X
yìmiáo 接种 X 疫苗

vaccination jiēzhòng 接种

vaccine yìmiáo 疫苗

vacuum 1 *n* PHYS zhēnkōng 真空;
leave a ~ in one's life shǐ rénde
shēnghuó biànde kōngxū 使人的
生活变得空虚 **2** *v/t floors*
xīchén 吸尘

vacuum cleaner xīchén qì 吸尘
器; **vacuum flask** bǎowēn píng
保温瓶; **vacuum-packed** zhēnkōng bāozhuāng 真空包装

vagabond *n* liúláng zhě 流浪者

vagina yīndào 阴道

vaginal yīndào 阴道

vague *answer, wording* bù mínglǎng
不明朗; *feeling, resemblance*
móhu 模糊; *taste of sth* yīdiǎndian
一点点; *he was very ~ about it*
tā hánhu qící 他含糊其辞

vaguely *answer* bù mínglǎng 不明
朗; (*slightly*) yǒudiǎn 有点; *~
possible* bú tài kěnéng 不太可能

vain 1 *adj person* zìfù 自负; *hope*
túláo 徒劳 **2** *n: in ~* bái fèilì 白费
力; *their efforts were in ~* tāmen
báigànle yīchǎng 他们白干了一
场

valet (*person*) nán púcóng 男仆从

valet service (*for clothes*) xǐyī
fúwù 洗衣服务; (*for cars*) xǐchē
fúwù 洗车服务

valiant yǒnggǎn 勇敢

valid *passport, document* yǒuxiào 有
效; *reason, argument* yǒu gēnjù 有

根据

validate (*with official stamp*) shǐ
shēngxiào 使生效; (*prove*)
quèzhèng 确证

validity (*of reason, argument*) zhèngquè xìng 正确性

valley shāngǔ 山谷

valuable 1 *adj* yǒu jiàzhí 有价值
2 *n: ~s* guìzhòng wùpǐn 贵重物
品

valuation gūjià 估价; *at his ~* jù tā
gūjià 据他估价

value 1 *n* jiàzhí 价值; *be good ~*
zhídàng 值当; *for money* qián
huāde zhídé qián huāde zhídé 钱花的值得; *rise /
fall in ~* jiàzhí shàngshēng / xiàjiàng 价值上升 / 下降 **2** *v/t s.o.'s
friendship, one's freedom* zhēnshì
珍视; *I ~ your advice* wǒ duì nǐde
quàngào shífēn zhòngshì 我对你
的劝告十分重视; *have an ob-
ject ~d* jiào rén gūjià mǒuwù 叫
人估价某物

valve fá 阀

van huòchē 货车

vandal pòhuài gōnggòng cáichǎn
zhě 破坏公共财产者

vandalism pòhuài gōnggòng
cáichǎn xíngwéi 破坏公共财产
行为

vandalize sìyì pòhuài 肆意破坏

vanilla *n & adj* xiāngcǎo 香草

vanish xiāoshī 消失

vanity (*of person*) xūróng 虚荣; (*of
hopes*) kōngxū 空虚

vanity case xiǎo shūzhuāng hé 小
梳妆盒

vantage point (*on hill etc*)
guānwàng diǎn 观望点

vapor qì qì 汽

vaporize *v/t* qìhuà 汽化

vapor trail (*of airplane*) wùhuà
wěijī 雾化尾迹

variable 1 *adj amount* kěbiàn 可

变; *moods, weather* duōbiàn 多变
2 *n* MATH, COMPUT biànliàng 变量
variation biànhuà 变化
varicose vein jìngmài qūzhāng 静脉曲张
varied *quality* bùtóng 不同; *range* gèzhǒng gèyàng 各种各样; *diet* fēngfù 丰富
variety duōyàng huà 多样化; (*type*) zhǒnglèi 种类; *a ~ of things to do* fēngfù duōcǎi de huódòng 丰富多彩的活动
various (*several*) jǐgè 几个; (*different*) bùtóng 不同
varnish 1 *n* (*for wood*) qīngqī 清漆; (*for fingernails*) zhījiǎ yóu 指甲油 **2** *v/t* tú 涂
vary 1 *v/i* biànhuà 变化; *it varies* bù yīyàng 不一样 **2** *v/t* gǎibiàn 改变
vase huāpíng 花瓶
vast *desert, city, subject* jùdà 巨大; *collection of books* dàliàng 大量; *knowledge* yuānbó 渊博
vaudeville záshuǎ 杂耍
vault[1] *n* (*in roof*) gǒngdǐng 拱顶; *~s* (*cellar*) dìjiào 地窖
vault[2] *n* (*in athletics*) chēnggān tiào 撑杆跳 **2** *v/t* beam etc yòngshǒu zhīchēng yuèguò 用手支撑跃过
VCR (= *video cassette recorder*) lùxiàng jī 录像机
veal xiǎo niúròu 小牛肉
vegan 1 *n* sùshí zhǔyì zhě 素食主义者 **2** *adj* sùshí zhǔyì 素食主义
vegetable shūcài 蔬菜
vegetarian 1 *n* sùshí zhě 素食者 **2** *adj* sùshí 素食
vehicle chēliàng 车辆; (*for information etc*) gōngjù 工具
veil 1 *n* miànshā 面纱 **2** *v/t* yǐ miànshā zhēyǎn 以面纱遮掩
vein (*in body*) jìngmài 静脉
Velcro® ⇩ zhānkòu 粘扣
velocity sùdù 速度
velvet sīróng 丝绒
vending machine zìdòng shòuhuò jī 自动售货机
vendor LAW màizhǔ 卖主
veneer (*on wood*) shìmiàn bóbǎn

饰面薄板; (*of politeness etc*) wàibiǎo 外表
venereal disease xìngbìng 性病
venetian blind bǎiyè lián 百叶帘
vengeance bàofù 报复; *with a ~* měngliè 猛烈; *raining with a ~* dàyǔ pāngtuó 大雨滂沱
venison lùròu 鹿肉
venom (*of snake*) dúyè 毒液
vent *n* (*for air*) tōngfēng kǒng 通风孔; *give ~ to feelings, emotions* fàxiè 发泄
ventilate *room, building* shǐ tōngfēng 使通风
ventilation tōngfēng 通风
ventilation shaft tōngfēng jǐng 通风井
ventilator tōngfēng shèbèi 通风设备
ventriloquist kǒujì yìrén 口技艺人
venture 1 *n* (*undertaking*) màoxiǎn 冒险; COM tóujī huódòng 投机活动 **2** *v/i* màoxiǎn 冒险
venture park chuàngyèyuán 创业园
venue (*for meeting, concert etc*) dìdiǎn 地点
veranda yóuláng 游廊
verb dòngcí 动词
verdict LAW cáijué 裁决; (*opinion, judgment*) dìnglùn 定论
verge *n* (*of road*) lùbiān 路边; *be on the ~ of ...* (*of ruin, collapse*) bīnyú ... 濒于 ...; *be on the ~ of tears* jīhū yào kūchūlái le 几乎要哭出来了
♦**verge on** jiējìn 接近
verification héshí 核实; (*confirmation*) zhèngmíng 证明
verify (*check out*) héshí 核实; (*confirm*) zhèngmíng 证明
vermicelli mǐfěn 米粉
vermin hàichóng 害虫
vermouth wèiměisī jiǔ 味美思酒
vernacular *n* fāngyán 方言
versatile *person* duōcái duōyì 多才多艺; *gadget* duō gōngnéng 多功能; *mind* fǎnfù wúcháng 反复无常
versatility (*of person*) duōcái duōyì

多才多艺; (*of gadget*) duō gōng-néng 多功能; (*of mind*) fǎnfù wúcháng 反复无常

verse (*poetry*) shī 诗; (*part of poem, song*) jié 节

versed: be well ~ in X jīngtōng X 精通 X

version (*of book*) bǎnběn 版本; (*of song, story*) gǎibiān běn 改编本; (*of events*) shuōfǎ 说法

versus: X ~ Y SP, LAW X duì Y X 对 Y

vertebra jǐzhuī 脊椎

vertebrate *n* yǒu jǐzhuī dòngwù 有脊椎动物

vertical chuízhí 垂直

vertigo xuànyùn 眩晕

very 1 *adv* hěn 很; **was it cold? – not ~** lěngbùlěng? – bù zěnme lěng 冷不冷 ? – 不怎么冷; **the ~ best** zuìhǎo 最好 **2** *adj*: **caught in the ~ act** dāngchǎng zhuāhuò 当场抓获; **that's the ~ thing I need** zhèngshì wǒ suǒ xūyào de 正是我所需要的; **the ~ thought** (*merely*) yī xiǎngdào 一想到; **right at the ~ top / bottom** zài zuì shàngmiàn / dǐxià 在最上面 / 底下

vessel NAUT chuán 船

vest bèixīn 背心

vestige (*of previous civilization etc*) yíjī 遗迹; (*of truth*) sīháo 丝毫

vet¹ *n* shòuyī 兽医

vet² *v/t applicants etc* shěnchá 审查

veteran 1 *n* tuìwǔ jūnrén 退伍军人 **2** *adj* (*old*) lǎoshì 老式; (*old and experienced*) lǎoliàn 老练

veterinarian shòuyī 兽医

veto 1 *n* fǒujué quán 否决权 **2** *v/t* fǒujué 否决

vex (*concern, worry*) shǐ shāng nǎojīn 使伤脑筋

vexed (*worried*) kǔnǎo 苦恼; **the ~ question of ...** zhēnglùn bùxiū de ... wèntí 争论不休的 ... 问题

via jīngguò 经过; (*by means of*) tōngguò 通过

viable *life form* néng yǎnghuó 能养活; *company* néng dúlì shēngcún 能独立生存; *alternative, plan*

qièshí kěxíng 切实可行

vibrate *v/i* zhèndòng 振动

vibration zhèndòng 振动

vice èxí 恶习; **the problem of ~** dàodé bàihuài de wèntí 道德败坏的问题

vice president fù zǒngtǒng 副总统

vice squad jǐngchá jiūbǔ duì 警察纠捕队

vice versa fǎnzhī yìrán 反之亦然

vicinity dìdiǎn 地点; **in the ~ of** (*the church etc*) zài ... fùjìn 在 ... 附近; **$500 etc ...** zuǒyòu ... 左右

vicious *dog* xiōnghěn 凶狠; *attack, temper, criticism* èdú 恶毒

victim shòuhài zhě 受害者

victimize shǐ shòuhài 使受害

victor shènglì zhě 胜利者

victorious zhànshèng 战胜

victory shènglì 胜利; **win a ~ over X** zhànshèng X 战胜 X

video 1 *n* lùxiàng 录像; COMPUT shìpín 视频; **have X on ~** lùle X dexiàng 录了 X 的像 **2** *v/t* lùxiàng 录像

video camera shèxiàng jī 摄像机; **video cassette** lùxiàng dài 录像带; **video conference** TELEC diànshì huìyì 电视会议; **video game** diànshì yóuxì 电视遊戏; **videophone** kěshì diànhuà 可视电话; **video recorder** lùxiàng jī 录像机; **video recording** lùxiàng 录像; **videotape** lùxiàng dài 录像带

Vietnam Yuènán 越南

Vietnamese 1 *adj* Yuènán 越南 **2** *n* (*person*) Yuènán rén 越南人; (*language*) Yuènán yǔ 越南语

view 1 *n* fēngjǐng 风景; (*of situation*) guāndiǎn 观点; **in ~ of** jiànyú 鉴于; **be on ~** (*of paintings*) zài zhǎnchū 在展出; **with a ~ to X** yǐ X wéi mùbiāo 以 X 为目标 **2** *v/t events, situation* kàndài 看待; *TV program, house for sale* shōukàn 收看 **3** *v/i* (*watch TV*) kàn 看

viewer TV guānzhòng 观众

viewfinder PHOT qǔjǐng qì 取景器

viewpoint guāndiǎn 观点

vigor (*energy*) huólì 活力

vigorous *person* jīnglì chōngpèi 精力充沛; *shake* yònglì 用力; *denial* qiángliè 强烈

vile *thing to do* èluè 恶劣; *a ~ smell* èchòu 恶臭

village cūnzhuāng 村庄

villager cūnlǐ rén 村里人

villain huàidàn 坏蛋

vindicate (*prove correct*) zhèngmíng zhèngquè 证明正确; (*prove innocent*) zhèngmíng wúgū 证明无辜; *I feel ~d* wǒ gǎndào bèi zhèngshí le 我感到被证实了

vindictive yǒu bàofù xīn 有报复心

vine pútáo 葡萄

vinegar cù 醋

vineyard pútáo yuán 葡萄园

vintage 1 *n* (*of wine*) shēngchǎn niánfèn 生产年份 **2** *adj* (*classic*) jīngdiǎn 经典

violate *rules, sanctity of a place* wéifàn 违犯; *treaty* wéibèi 违背

violation (*of rules, sanctity*) wéifàn 违犯; (*of treaty*) wéibèi 违背; *traffic ~* wéifǎn jiāotōng fǎguī 违反交通法规

violence (*of person, movie*) bàolì 暴力; (*of emotion, reaction*) kuángrè 狂热; (*of gale*) měngliè 猛烈; *outbreak of ~* bàodòng 暴动

violent *person, movie* bàolì 暴力; *emotion, reaction* kuángrè 狂热; *gale* měngliè 猛烈; *have a ~ temper* píqì bùhǎo 脾气不好

violently *react* qiángbào 强暴; *object* jīliè 激烈; *fall ~ in love with X* shēnshēn de àishàng X 深深地爱上X

violet (*color*) zǐ luólán sè 紫罗兰色; (*plant*) zǐ luólán 紫罗兰

violin xiǎo tíqín 小提琴

violinist xiǎo tíqín jiā 小提琴家

VIP (= *very important person*) yàorén 要人

viral *infection* bìngdú 病毒

virgin (*female*) chǔnǚ 处女; (*male*) chǔnán 处男

virginity zhēnjié 贞洁; *lose one's ~* shīshēn 失身

virile *man* qiángjìn 强劲; *prose* yǒulì 有力

virility nánzi qìgài 男子气概; (*sexual*) nánxìng shēngzhí lì 男性生殖力

virtual shízhì 实质

virtual reality xūnǐ xiànshí 虚拟现实

virtually (*almost*) jīhū 几乎

virtue pǐndé 品德; *in ~ of* yīnwèi 因为

virtuoso MUS yuèqì yǎnzòu míngshǒu 乐器演奏名手

virtuous dàodé gāoshàng 道德高尚

virulent *disease* èxìng 恶性

virus MED, COMPUT bìngdú 病毒

visa qiānzhèng 签证

visibility néngjiàn dù 能见度

visible *object* yìjiàn 易见; *difference* míngxiǎn 明显; *anger* yì chájué 易察觉; *not ~ to the naked eye* ròuyǎn kànbùjiàn 肉眼看不见

visibly *different* míngxiǎn 明显; *he was ~ moved* kěyǐ kànchū tā hěnshòu gǎndòng 可以看出他很受感动

vision (*eyesight*) shìlì 视力; REL *etc* yōulíng 幽灵

visit 1 *n* bàifǎng 拜访; (*to place, country*) yóulǎn 游览; *pay a ~ to the doctor / dentist* qù kàn yīshēng / yáyī 去看医生/牙医; *pay X a ~* bàifǎng X 拜访X **2** *v/t person* bàifǎng 拜访; *place, country, city* yóulǎn 游览; *doctor, dentist* kàn kàn 看看

visiting card míngpiàn 名片

visiting hours (*at hospital*) tànwàng shíjiān 探望时间

visitor (*guest*) kèrén 客人; (*to museum etc*) cānguān zhě 参观者; (*tourist*) yóukè 游客

visor màoshé 帽舌

visual shìjué 视觉; *arts* zhíguān 直观

visual aid zhíguān jiàojù 直观教具

visual display unit zhíguān xiǎnshì bùjiàn 直观显示部件

visualize xiǎngxiàng 想象; (*foresee*) shèxiǎng 设想

visually shìjué 视觉

visually impaired shìjué qùxiàn 视觉缺陷

vital (*essential*) bìbù kěshǎo 必不可少; *it is ~ that ...* ... shì hěn zhòngyào de ... 是很重要的

vitality (*of person, city etc*) huólì 活力

vitally: *~ important* fēicháng zhòngyào 非常重要

vital organs wéichí shēngmìngde zhòngyào qìguān 维持生命的重要器官

vital statistics (*of woman*) nǚzǐ sānwéi 女子三围

vitamin wéitāmìng 维他命

vitamin pill wéitāmìng yàopiàn 维他命药片

vivacious huópo 活泼

vivacity huópo 活泼

vivid *color* xiānyàn 鲜艳; *memory* qīngxī 清晰; *imagination* huóyuè 活跃

V-neck jīxīn lǐng 鸡心领

vocabulary cíhuì 词汇; (*list of words*) cíhuì biǎo 词汇表

vocal (*to do with the voice*) sǎngyīn 嗓音; (*expressing opinions*) chàngsuǒ yùyán 畅所欲言

vocal cords shēngdài 声带

vocal group MUS gēchàng tuán 歌唱团

vocalist MUS gēchàng jiā 歌唱家

vocation (*calling*) shǐmìng 使命; (*profession*) zhíyè 职业

vocational *guidance* zhíyè 职业

vodka fútèjiā 伏特加

vogue liúxíng 流行; *be in ~* zhèngzài liúxíng 正在流行

voice 1 *n* shēngyīn 声音 2 *v/t opinions* biǎodá 表达

voicemail diànhuà dálù jī 电话答录机

void 1 *n* kōngjiān 空间 2 *adj: ~ of* qùfá 缺乏

volatile *personality, moods* biànhuà wúcháng 变化无常

volcano huǒshān 火山

volley *n* (*of shots*) páiqiāng shèjī 排枪射击; (*in tennis*) jiéjī kōngzhōng qiú 截击空中球

volleyball páiqiú 排球

volt fútè 伏特

voltage diànyā 电压

volume (*of container*) róngliàng 容量; (*of work, liquid etc*) liàng 量; (*of business*) é 额; (*of book*) cè 册; (*of radio etc*) yīnliàng 音量

volume control yīnliàng tiáokòng 音量调控

voluntary *adj helper* zhìyuàn 志愿; *work* yìwù 义务

volunteer 1 *n* yìgōng 义工 2 *v/i* zhìyuàn 志愿

voluptuous *woman, figure* fēngmǎn 丰满

vomit 1 *n* ǒutù wù 呕吐物 2 *v/i* ǒutù 呕吐

♦vomit up ǒutù 呕吐

voracious *appetite* lángtūn hǔyàn 狼吞虎咽

vote 1 *n* xuǎnpiào 选票; *have the ~* (*be entitled to vote*) yǒu xuǎnjǔ quán 有选举权 2 *v/i* POL tóupiào 投票; *~ for / against ...* tóu zànchéng piào / fǎnduì piào 投赞成票 / 反对票 3 *v/t: they ~d him President* tāmen xuǎn tā dāng zǒngtǒng 他们选他当总统; *they ~d to stay behind* tāmen juédìng bùqù 他们决定不去

♦vote in *new member* xuǎnrù 选入

♦vote on *issue* tóupiào juédìng 投票决定

♦vote out (*of office*) tóupiào shǐ luòxuǎn 投票使落选

voter POL yǒu tóupiào quán zhě 有投票权者

voting POL tóupiào 投票

voting booth tóupiào jiān 投票间

♦vouch for *truth of sth* bǎozhèng 保证; *person* dānbǎo 担保

voucher piàoquàn 票券

vow 1 *n* shìyù 誓约 2 *v/t: ~ to do X* lìshì yàozuò X 立誓要做 X

vowel yuányīn 元音

voyage (*by sea*) hánghǎi 航海; (*in space*) hángkōng 航空

vulgar *person, language* cūsú 粗俗

vulnerable (*to attack*) bóruò 薄弱; (*to criticism etc*) mǐngǎn 敏感

vulture měizhōu jiù 美洲鹫

W

wad *n* (*of paper, absorbent wool etc*) tuán 团; *a ~ of $100 bills* yīdá yībǎiměiyuán de chāopiào 一沓一百美元的钞票

waddle *v/i* yáobǎide xíngzǒu 摇摆地行走

wade báshè 跋涉

♦**wade through** *book, documents* fèilìde yuèdú 费力地阅读

wafer (*cookie*) wēifú bǐnggān 威佛饼干

waffle¹ *n* (*to eat*) wǎfūbǐng 瓦夫饼

waffle² *v/i* hánhude tánhuà 含糊地谈话

wag 1 *v/t tail, finger* yáodòng 摇动 **2** *v/i* (*of tail*) bǎidòng 摆动

wage¹ *v/t war* zuòzhàn 作战

wage² *n* gōngzī 工资

wage earner yǐ gōngzī wéishēng de rén 以工资为生的人

waggle *v/t hips, ears* láihuí yáodòng 来回摇动; *loose screw, tooth etc* huàngdòng 晃动

wagon RAIL chǎngpéng huòchē 敞篷货车; *be on the ~* ┣ jièjiǔ 戒酒

wail 1 *n* (*of person, baby*) tòngkūshēng 恸哭声; (*of siren*) jiānxiàoshēng 尖啸声 **2** *v/i* (*of person, baby*) tòngkū 恸哭; (*of siren*) jiānxiào 尖啸

waist yāobù 腰部

waistline yāowéi 腰围

wait 1 *n* děngdài 等待 **2** *v/i* děng 等; *we'll ~ until he's ready* wǒmen děng tā zhǔnbèihǎo 我们等他准备好 **2** *v/t meal* zànhuǎn 暂缓; *~ table* zuò fúwùyuán 作服务员

♦**wait for** děngdài 等待; *~ me!* děng wǒ! 等我!

♦**wait on** *person* cìhou 伺候

♦**wait up** děngzhe búshuì 等着不睡

waiter nán fúwùyuán 男服务员;

~*!* fúwùyuán! 服务员!

waiting *n* děngdài 等待; *no ~ sign* bùzhǔntíngchēde biāopái 不准停车的标牌

waiting list děnghòuzhě míngdān 等候者名单

waiting room děnghòushì 等候室

waitress nǚ fúwùyuán 女服务员

wake¹ **1** *v/i*: ~ (*up*) xǐnglái 醒来 **2** *v/t* huànxǐng 唤醒

wake² (*of ship*) chuán hángguòhòu de bōlàng 船航过后的波浪; *in the ~ of* fig jǐnjiēzhe 紧接着; *follow in the ~ of X* zhuīsuí X yǐhòu 追随 X 以后

wake-up call huànxǐng diànhuà 唤醒电话

walk 1 *n* bùxíng 步行; (*path*) xiǎolù 小路; *it's a long / short ~ to the office* zǒudào bàngōngshì yào hěncháng / hěnduǎn shíjiān 走到办公室要很长/很短时间; *go for a ~* qù sànbù 去散步 **2** *v/i* zǒu 走; (*as opposed to taking the car / bus etc*) zǒulù 走路; (*hike*) chángtú túbù lǚxíng 长途徒步旅行 **3** *v/t dog* liù 遛; *~ the streets* (*walk around*) zài jiēshang zǒu 在街上走

♦**walk out** (*of spouse*) zǒule 走了; (*of room etc*) tuìchǎng 退场; (*go on strike*) bàgōng 罢工

♦**walk out on** *spouse, family* yíqì 遗弃

walker (*hiker*) túbù lǚxíngzhě 徒步旅行者; (*for baby, old person*) fúchē 扶车; *be a slow / fast ~* zǒulù màn / kuài de rén 走路慢/快的人

walkie-talkie bùhuàjī 步话机

walk-in closet dàxíng yīguì 大型衣柜

walking (*as opposed to driving*) zǒulù 走路; (*hiking*) chángtú xíngzǒu 长途行走; *be within ~ distance* zài bùxíng jùlí zhīnèi 在步行距离之内

walking stick shǒuzhàng 手杖

walking tour túbù lǚxíng dùjià 徒步旅行度假

Walkman® suíshēntīng 随身听;

walkout (*strike*) bàgōng 罢工;

walkover (*easy win*) qīngyì huòdé de shènglì 轻易获得的胜利;

walk-up n wú diàntī gōngyù 无电梯公寓

wall qiáng 墙; *fig* (*of silence etc*) sì qiángbì zhīwù 似墙壁之物; *go to the ~* (*of company*) pòchǎn 破产

wallet qiánbāo 钱包

wallop F **1** n (*blow*) zhòngjī 重击 **2** v/t měngdǎ 猛打; *opponent* dǎbài 打败

wallpaper 1 n bìzhǐ 壁纸 **2** v/t tiē bìzhǐ 贴壁纸

Wall Street Huá'ěrjiē 华尔街

walnut hétáo 核桃

waltz n huá'ěrzīwǔ 华尔兹舞

wan face cāngbái 苍白

wander v/i (*roam*) mànbù 漫步; (*stray*) zǒusàn 走散; (*of attention*) zǒushén 走神

♦**wander around** mànyóu 漫游

wane (*of interest, enthusiasm*) jiǎnruò 减弱

wangle v/t yòng guǐjì huòdé 用诡计获得

want 1 n (*need*) xūyào 需要; *for ~ of* yīn qùfá 因缺乏 **2** v/t yào 要; (*need*) xūyào 需要; *~ to do X* xiǎngzuò X 想做 X; *I ~ to stay here* wǒ xiǎng dāi zài zhèr 我想待在这儿; *do you ~ to come too? – no, I don't ~ to* nǐ yě xiǎnglái ma? – bù, wǒ bù xiǎng 你也想来吗？– 不，我不想; *you can have whatever you ~* nǐ yào shénme dōu xíng 你要什么都行; *it's not what I ~ed* zhè bùshì wǒ xiǎngyàode 这不是我想要的; *she ~s you to go back* tā yào nǐ huíqù 她要你回去; *he ~s a haircut* tā děi jiǎn tóufa 他得剪头发 **3** v/i: *~ for nothing* shénme

yě bùqù 什么也不缺

want ad suǒqiú guǎnggào 索求广告

wanted (*by police*) bèi tōngjí 被通缉

wanting: *be ~ in* qiànqù 欠缺

wanton adj zìyì 恣意

war n zhànzhēng 战争; *be at ~* chǔyú jiāozhàn zhuàngtài 处于交战状态

warble v/i (*of bird*) wǎnzhuǎnde jiào 婉转地叫

ward (*in hospital*) bìngfáng 病房; (*child*) shòu jiānhù de rén 受监护的人

♦**ward off** bìkāi 避开

warden (*of prison*) jiānguǎnrén 监管人

wardrobe (*for clothes*) yīguì 衣柜; (*clothes*) yīwù 衣物

warehouse cāngkù 仓库

warfare zhànzhēng 战争; **warhead** dàntóu 弹头; **warlord** jūnfá 军阀

warily jǐngtì 警惕

warm 1 adj nuǎnhuo 暖和; *welcome, smile* rèqíng 热情 **2** v/t shǐ nuǎnrè 使暖热

♦**warm up 1** v/t rè 热 **2** v/i (*of person*) rèshēn 热身; (*of room, soup*) rèqǐlái 热起来; (*of athlete etc*) zhǔnbèi liànxí 准备练习

warmhearted rèxīncháng 热心肠

warmly dressed nuǎnhuo 暖和; *welcome, smile* rèqíng 热情

warmth wēnnuǎn 温暖; (*of welcome, smile*) rèqíng 热情

warn jǐnggào 警告

warning n jǐnggào 警告; *without ~* méiyǒu jǐnggào 没有警告

warp 1 v/t wood shǐ wānqū 使弯曲; *character* shǐ fǎncháng 使反常 **2** v/i (*of wood*) qiáoleng 翘棱

warped fig fǎncháng 反常

warplane zhàndòujī 战斗机

warrant 1 n xǔkězhèng 许可证 **2** v/t (*deserve, call for*) shòuquán 授权

warranty (*guarantee*) bǎodān 保单; *be under ~* zài bǎoxiūqī nèi 在保修期内

warrior wǔshì 武士

warship jūnjiàn 军舰

wart yóu 疣

wartime zhànshí 战时

wary jǐnshèn 谨慎; **be ~ of** jǐnfáng 谨防

wash 1 *n* xǐdí 洗涤; **have a ~** xǐyīxǐ 洗一洗; **that jacket / shirt needs a ~** děi xǐyīxià nàjiàn jiákè / chènshān 得洗一下那件夹克 / 衬衫 2 *v/t & v/i* xǐ 洗

♦**wash up** (*wash one's hands and face*) xǐyīxǐ 洗一洗

washable kěxǐ 可洗

washbasin, **washbowl** liǎnpén 脸盆

washcloth máojīn 毛巾

washed out jīnpílìjìn 筋疲力尽

washer (*for faucet etc*) diànquān 垫圈; (*washing machine*) xǐyījī 洗衣机

washing xǐde yīwù 洗的衣物; **do the ~** xǐ yīfu 洗衣服

washing machine xǐyījī 洗衣机

Washington Huáshèngdùn 华盛顿

washroom guànxǐshì 盥洗室

wasp (*insect*) huángfēng 黄蜂

waste 1 *n* làngfèi 浪费; (*from industrial process*) fèiwù 废物; **it's a ~ of time / money** zhēnshì làngfèi shíjiān / jīnqián 真是浪费时间 / 金钱 2 *adj* fèiqì 废弃 3 *v/t* làngfèi 浪费

♦**waste away** shuāiruò 衰弱

wasteful huīhuò 挥霍

wasteland fèixū 废墟; **wastepaper** fèizhǐ 废纸; **wastepaper basket** fèizhǐlǒu 废纸篓; **waste product** fèipǐn 废品

watch 1 *n* (*timepiece*) shǒubiǎo 手表; **keep ~** fàngshào 放哨 2 *v/t* movie, TV kàn 看; (*spy on*) jiānshì 监视; (*look after*) zhàokàn 照看 3 *v/i* kàn 看

♦**watch for** shǒuhòu 守候

♦**watch out** xiǎoxīn 小心; **~!** xiǎoxīn! 小心!

♦**watch out for** (*be careful of*) dāngxīn 当心

watchful jǐngtì 警惕

watchmaker zhōngbiǎo jiàng 钟表匠

water 1 *n* shuǐ 水; **~s** NAUT lǐnghǎi 领海 2 *v/t plant* jiāo 浇 3 *v/i* (*of eyes*) liúlèi 流泪; **my mouth is ~ing** wǒ zài liú kǒushuǐ 我在流口水

♦**water down** drink xīshì 稀释

water chestnut gāncǎo lìzi 甘草栗子; **watercolor** shuǐcǎi 水彩; **waterfall** pùbù 瀑布

watering can jiāoshuǐtǒng 浇水筒

water level shuǐwèi 水位; **water-logged** jìnmǎnshuǐ 浸满水; **watermelon** xīguā 西瓜; **water-proof** *adj* fángshuǐ 防水; **water-side** *n* shuǐbiān 水边; **at the ~** zài shuǐbiān 在水边; **waterskiing** huáshuǐ 滑水; **watertight** compartment búlòushuǐ 不漏水; **waterway** shuǐlù 水路

watery duōshuǐ 多水

watt wǎtè 瓦特

wave[1] *n* (*in sea*) bōlàng 波浪

wave[2] 1 *n* (*of hand*) zhìyì 致意 2 *v/i* (*with hand*) huīshǒu 挥手; **~ to X** xiàng X huīshǒu 向 X 挥手 3 *v/t flag etc* huīwǔ 挥舞

wavelength RAD bōcháng 波长; **be on the same ~** *fig* yìqù xiāngtóu 意趣相投

waver dòngyáo 动摇

wavy hair, line bōfú 波状

wax *n* (*for floor, furniture*) là 蜡; (*in ear*) ěrgòu 耳垢

way 1 *n* (*method*) fāngfǎ 方法; (*of behaving etc*) fāngshì 方式; (*route*) lùxiàn 路线; **this ~** (*like this*) zhèyàng 这样; (*in this direction*) zhètiáolù 这条路; **by the ~** (*incidentally*) shùnbiàn wènyīxià 顺便问一下; **by ~ of** (*via*) jīngyóu 经由; (*in the form of*) zuòwéi 作为; **in a ~** (*in certain respects*) zài yīdìng chéngdùshang 在一定程度上; **be under ~** zài jìnxíngzhōng 在进行中; **give ~** MOT rànglù 让路; (*collapse*) tāntā 坍塌; **give ~ to X** (*be replaced by*) yóu X dàitì 由 X 代替; **have one's**

(*own*) ~ zìzhǔ xíngshì 自主行事; *OK, we'll do it your* ~ hǎoba, wǒmen àn nǐde fāngfǎ zuò 好吧, 我们按你的方法做; *lead the* ~ yǐnlù 引路; *lose one's* ~ mílù 迷路; *be in the* ~ (*be an obstruction*) dǎnglù 挡路; *it's on the* ~ *to the station* tā jiù zài qù chēzhàn de lùshang 它就在去车站的路上; *I was on my* ~ *to the station* wǒ zhèng zài qù chēzhàn de lù shang 我正在去车站的路上; *no* ~! juéduì bù! 绝对不!; *there's no* ~ *he can do it* tā gēnběn bùnéng zuò 他根本不能做 **2** *adv* F (*much*) yuǎnyuǎn 远远; *it's* ~ *too soon to decide* xiànzài zuò juédìng háishì tàizǎo 现在作决定还是太早; *they are* ~ *behind with their work* tāmende gōngzuò yuǎnyuǎnde làzài hòumiàn 他们的工作远远地落在后面

way in rùkǒu 入口; way of life shēnghuó fāngshì 生活方式; way out *n* chūkǒu 出口; *fig* (*from situation*) chūlù 出路

we wǒmen 我们

weak *tea, coffee* dàn 淡; *government, currency* bóruò 薄弱; (*physically*) xūruò 虚弱; (*morally*) ruǎnruò 软弱

weaken **1** *v/t* xūruò 削弱 **2** *v/i* biànruò 变弱

weakling (*morally*) ruòzhě 弱者; (*physically*) tǐruò de rén 体弱的人

weakness ruòdiǎn 弱点; *have a* ~ *for X* (*liking*) piān'ài X 偏爱 X

wealth cáifù 财富; *a* ~ *of* dàliàng 大量

wealthy fùyǒu 富有

weapon wǔqì 武器

wear **1** *n*: ~ (*and tear*) sǔnhào 损耗; *clothes for everyday / evening* ~ rìjiān / wǎnyànfú 日间 / 晚宴服 **2** *v/t* (*have on*) chuān 穿; (*damage*) yònghuài 用坏 **3** *v/i* (*of carpet, fabric: wear out*) mósǔn 磨损; (*last*) nàiyòng 耐用

♦ wear away **1** *v/i* mósǔn 磨损 **2** *v/t* chōngshí 冲蚀

♦ wear off (*of effect, feeling*) xiāoshī 消失

♦ wear out **1** *v/t* (*tire*) shǐ pífá 使疲乏; *shoes* yònghuài 用坏 **2** *v/i* (*of shoes, carpet*) yòngjiù 用旧

wearing (*tiring*) shǐrén kùnfá 使人困乏

weary kùnfá 困乏

weather **1** *n* tiānqì 天气; *be feeling under the* ~ gǎndào bùshūfu 感到不舒服 **2** *v/t crisis* jīnglì 经历

weather-beaten bǎo jīng fēngshuāng 饱经风霜; weather forecast tiānqì yùbào 天气预报; weatherman qìxiàng yùbàoyuán 气象预报员

weave **1** *v/t* biānzhī 编织 **2** *v/i* (*move*) yūhuí xíngjìn 迂回行进

web (COMPUT, *of spider*) wǎng 网

webbed feet yǒu pǔ de jiǎo 有蹼的脚

web page wǎngzhǐ 网址

web site wǎngzhǐ 网址, zhàndiǎn 站点

wedding hūnlǐ 婚礼

wedding anniversary jiéhūn zhōunián 结婚周年; wedding cake hūnlǐ dàngāo 婚礼蛋糕; wedding day hūnlǐrì 婚礼日; wedding dress hūnshā 婚纱; wedding ring jiéhūn jièzhǐ 结婚戒指

wedge *n* (*to hold sth in place*) xiēzi 楔子; (*of cheese etc*) yījiǎo 一角

Wednesday xīngqīsān 星期三

weed **1** *n* zácǎo 杂草 **2** *v/t* chúqù zácǎo 除去杂草

♦ weed out (*remove*) táotài 淘汰

weedkiller chúcǎojì 除草剂

week xīngqī 星期; *a* ~ *tomorrow* xiàyìzhōude míngtiān 下一周的明天

weekday xīngqī yī dào wǔ 星期一到五

weekend zhōumò 周末; *on the* ~ zhōumò 周末

weekly **1** *adj* měizhōu yīcì 每周一次 **2** *n* (*magazine*) zhōukān 周刊 **3** *adv* měizhōu yīcì 每周一次

weep kūqì 哭泣

weigh 1 *v/t* chēng ... de zhòngliàng 称 ... 的重量 **2** *v/i* cèchū zhòngliàng 测出重量

♦**weigh down: be weighed down with** (*with bags*) bèi ... yāwān 被 ... 压弯; (*with worries*) shǐrén jǔsàng 使人沮丧

♦**weigh up** (*assess*) gūliàng 估量

weight (*of person, object*) zhòngliàng 重量

weightlifter jǔzhòng yùndòngyuán 举重运动员

weightlifting jǔzhòng 举重

weir yàn 堰

weird guàiyì 怪异

weirdo *n* F gǔguàide rén 古怪的人

welcome 1 *adj* shòu huānyíng 受 欢迎; **you're ~!** biékèqì! 别客 气！; **you're ~ to try some** suíbiàn chángcháng 随便尝尝 **2** *n* (*for guests etc*) huānyíng 欢迎; *fig* (*to news, proposal*) yōnghù 拥护 **3** *v/t guests etc* yíngjiē 迎接; *fig: decision etc* duì ... gǎndào yúkuài 对 ... 感到愉快

weld *v/t* hànjiē 焊接

welder hànjiē gōngrén 焊接工人

welfare jiànkāng 健康; (*financial assistance*) fúlì jiùjì 福利救济; **be on ~** jiēshòu fúlì jiùjìjīn 接收福利救济金

welfare check fúlì zhīpiào 福利 支票; **welfare state** fúlì guójiā 福利国家; **welfare work** fúlì gōngzuò 福利工作; **welfare worker** fúlì gōngzuò zhě 福利工 作者

well[1] *n* (*for water, oil*) jǐng 井

well[2] **1** *adv* hǎo 好; **as ~** (*too*) yě 也; **as ~ as** (*in addition to*) hái 还; **it's just as ~ you told me** nǐ gàosù wǒ, shì jiàn hǎoshì 你告诉我, 是件好事; **very ~** (*when acknowledging an order*) shì 是; (*signifying you don't agree with sth but are doing it anyway*) hǎoba 好 吧; **~, ~!** (*surprise*) yōu, yōu! 呦, 呦！; **~ ...** (*uncertainty, thinking*) āi ... 哎 ... **2** *adj*: **be ~** jiànkāng 健 康; **feel ~** gǎndào jiànkāng 感到

健康; **get ~ soon!** zǎorì kāngfù! 早日康复！

well-balanced *person* qíngxù wěndìng 情绪稳定; *meal, diet* yíngyǎng dāpèihǎo 营养搭配好; **well-behaved** xíngwéi guījù 行 为规矩; **well-being** jiànkāng 健 康; **well-done** *meat* shútòu 熟透; **well-dressed** yīzhuó zhěngjié 衣 着整洁; **well-earned** yīngdé 应 得; **well-known** zhòngsuǒ zhōuzhī 众所周知; **well-made** zuò- gōnghǎo 做工好; **well- mannered** bīnbīn yǒu lǐ 彬彬有 礼; **well-off** fùyù 富裕; **well- read** bóxué 博学; **well-timed** shìshí 适时; **well-to-do** fùyǒu 富 有; **well-worn** yòngjiù 用旧

west 1 *n* xīmiàn 西面; **the West** (*western nations*) Xīfāng Guójiā 西 方国家; (*western part of a country*) xībù 西部 **2** *adj* xī 西 **3** *adv* xiàngxī 向西; **~ of X** X de xībù X 的西部

West Coast (*of USA*) Xī Hǎi'àn 西 海岸

westerly xīfēng 西风

western 1 *adj* zài xībù 在西部; **Western** xīfāng guójiā 西方国家 **2** *n* (*movie*) xībùpiān 西部片

Westerner Xīfāngrén 西方人

westernized xīfānghuà 西方化

Western medicine xīyī 西医; (*drugs etc*) xīyào 西药

West Lake Xīhú 西湖

westward xiàngxī 向西

wet *adj* shī 湿; (*rainy*) duōyǔ 多雨; **"~ paint"** "yóuqīwèigān" " 油漆 未干 "; **be ~ through** shītòu 湿 透

whack F **1** *n* (*blow*) zhòngjī 重击 **2** *v/t* jīdǎ 击打

whale jīng 鲸

whaling bǔjīng 捕鲸

wharf mǎtóu 码头

what 1 *pron* shénme 什么; **~ is that?** nà shì shénme? 那是什 么？; **~ is it?** (*what do you want*) zěnmele? 怎么了？; **~?** (*what do you want?*) shénme shì? 什么 事？; (*what did you say?*) shénme?

什么？; (astonishment) nǐ shuō shénme? 你说什么？; ~ about some dinner? chī diǎnr fàn zěnmeyàng? 吃点儿饭怎么样？; ~ about heading home? huíjiāba? 回家吧？; ~ for? (why?) wèishénme? 为什么？; so ~? nà yòu zěnmeyàng? 那又怎么样？2 adj shénme 什么; ~ color is the car? chē shì shénme yánsè? 车是什么颜色？; ~ university are you at? nǐ zài nǎge dàxué? 你在哪个大学？

whatever 1 pron búlùn shénme 不论什么; (regardless of) bùguǎn shénme 不管什么 2 adj rènhé 任何; you have no reason ~ to worry nǐ gēnběn búyòng dānxīn 你根本不用担心

wheat xiǎomài 小麦

wheedle: ~ X out of Y hǒng Y yǐ dédào X 哄 Y 以得到 X

wheel 1 n lúnzi 轮子; (steering ~) fāngxiàngpán 方向盘 2 v/t bicycle tuī 推 3 v/i (of birds) xuánzhuǎn 旋转

♦**wheel around** zhuǎnshēn 转身

wheelbarrow shǒutuīchē 手推车; **wheelchair** lúnyǐ 轮椅; **wheel clamp** chēlún jiájù 车轮夹具

wheeze v/i hūxīshí yǒu shēngxiǎng 呼吸时有声响

when 1 adv shénme shíhòu 什么时候; ~ do you go on vacation? nǐ shénme shíhou qù dùjià? 你什么时候去度假？; do you remember ~ you saw him last? nǐ jì bu jìde shàngcì jiàndào tā shì shénme shíhou? 你记不记得上次见到他是什么时候？2 conj dāng ... de shíhou 当 ... 的时候; ~ I was a child dāng wǒ shì ge háizi de shíhou 当我是个孩子的时候; I'll tell her ~ I see her wǒ kànjiàn tā jiù gàosu tā 我看见她就告诉她; don't interrupt ~ I'm talking wǒ shuōhuà de shíhou, bié dǎduàn wǒ 我说话的时候，别打断我

whenever wúlùn shénme shíhòu 无论什么时候

where 1 adv nǎr 哪儿; ~ should I put this? wǒ bǎ zhèige fàng nǎr? 我把这个放哪儿？; I can't remember ~ I put my glasses wǒ bújìde bǎ yǎnjìng fàng nǎr le 我不记得把眼镜放哪儿了 2 conj: the hotel ~ Chairman Mao stayed Máo Zhǔxí zhùguòde bīnguǎn 毛主席住过的宾馆; this is ~ I used to live zhè shì wǒ céngjīng zhùguò de dìfang 这是我曾经住过的地方

whereabouts adv nǎli 哪里; ~ in ... do you live? nǐjiā zài ... nǎli? 你家在 ... 哪里？

wherever 1 conj wúlùn nǎlǐ 无论哪里 2 adv dàodǐ zài nǎli 到底在哪里

whet appetite yǐnqǐ 引起

whether shìfǒu 是否

which 1 adj nǎyíge 哪一个; ~ one is yours? nǎge nǐde? 哪个是你的？2 pron (interrogative) nǎgè 哪个; (relative): the book ~ I bought wǒ mǎide nèiběn shū 我买的那本书; the flight ~ I missed wǒ méi gǎnshang de fēijī 我没赶上的飞机; take one, it doesn't matter ~ ná yígè, nǎ yígè dōu kěyǐ 拿一个，哪一个都可以

whichever 1 adj rènhé 任何 2 pron wúlùn nǎgè 无论哪个

whiff (smell) yīgǔ qìwèi 一股气味

while 1 conj: ~ ... zài ... shíqī 在 ... 时期; (although) suīrán 虽然 2 n shíjiān 时间; a long ~ hěncháng shíjiān 很长时间; for a ~ yíduàn shíjiān 一段时间; I'll wait a ~ longer wǒ zài děng yíhuìr wǒ zài děng 我再等一会儿

♦**while away** xiāoyáode dùguò 逍遥地度过

whim tūfā qíxiǎng 突发奇想

whimper 1 n wūyèshēng 呜咽声 2 v/i wūyè 呜咽

whine v/i (of dog) fāchū chángjiàoshēng 发出长叫声; F (complain) bàoyuàn 抱怨

whip 1 n biānzi 鞭子 2 v/t (beat) biāndǎ 鞭打; cream jiǎodǎ 搅打;

F (*defeat*) dǎbài 打败

♦ **whip out** F (*take out*) xùnsù náchū 迅速拿出

♦ **whip up** (*arouse*) huànqǐ 唤起

whipping (*beating*) biāndǎ 鞭打; F (*defeat*) dǎbài 打败

whirl 1 *n*: **my mind is in a ~** wǒde sīxù yípiàn hùnluàn 我的思绪一片混乱 **2** *v/i* xuánzhuǎn 旋转

whirlpool (*in river*) xuánwō 旋涡; (*for relaxation*) ànmó yùgāng 按摩浴缸

whirlwind xuànfēng 旋风

whir(r) *v/i* zuò hūhūshēng 作呼呼声

whisk 1 *n* (*kitchen implement*) jiǎodànqì 搅蛋器 **2** *v/t eggs* jiǎobàn 搅拌

♦ **whisk away** chúqù 除去

whiskers (*of man*) húzi 胡子; (*of animal*) xū 须

whiskey, whisky wēishìjìjiǔ 威士忌酒

whisper 1 *n* ěryǔ 耳语 **2** *v/i* qièqièsīyǔ 窃窃私语 **3** *v/t* dīshēng shuō 低声说

whistle 1 *n* (*sound*) kǒushàoshēng 口哨声; (*device*) shàozi 哨子 **2** *v/i* fā xūxūshēng 发嘘嘘声 **3** *v/t* yòng kǒushào chuī 用口哨吹

white 1 *n* (*color*) báisè 白色; (*of egg*) dànbái 蛋白; (*person*) báirén 白人 **2** *adj* cāngbái 苍白; *person* báirén 白人

white-collar worker báilǐng gōngrén 白领工人; **White House** Bái Gōng 白宫; **white lie** wú èyì de huǎngyán 无恶意的谎言; **white meat** báiròu 白肉; **white-out** (*for text*) túgǎiyè 涂改液; **whitewash 1** *n* bái túliào 白涂料; *fig* yǎngài zhēnxiàng 掩盖真相 **2** *v/t* fěnshuā 粉刷; **white wine** bái pútaojiǔ 白葡萄酒

whittle *wood* xuēchéngxíng 削成形

♦ **whittle down** xùjiǎn 削减

whiz(z) *n*: **be a ~ at ..** F zài ... fāngmiàn chūsè 在 ... 方面出色

♦ **whizz by, whizz past** (*of time, car*) fēiguò 飞过

whizzkid F jiāozi 骄子

who ◊ (*interrogative*) shéi 谁; **~'s that?** nà shì shéi? 那是谁？; **~ were you speaking to?** nǐ gēn shéi shuōhuà? 你跟谁说话？◊ (*relative*): **the man ~ taught me** jiāoguò wǒ de nèige rén 教过我的那个人; **those ~ can speak Chinese** huì jiǎng Zhōngwén de rén 会讲中文的人

whoever wúlùn shì shéi 无论是谁

whole 1 *adj* zhěngge 整个; **the ~ town / country** zhěngge chéngshì / guójiā 整个城市 / 国家; **it's a ~ lot easier / better** zhèyàng róngyi / hǎo duō le 这样容易 / 好多了 **2** *n* zhěngtǐ 整体; **the ~ of the United States** zhěngge Měiguó 整个美国; **on the ~** zǒngde kànlái 总的看来

whole-hearted quánxīn quányì 全心全意; **wholesale 1** *adj* pīfā 批发; *fig* dàguīmó 大规模 **2** *adv* yǐ pīfājià 以批发价; **wholesaler** pīfāshāng 批发商; **wholesome** cùjìn jiànkāng 促进健康

wholly wánquán 完全

whom: **~ did you see?** *fml* nǐ jiànde shì nǎwèi? 你见的是哪位？

whooping cough bǎirìké 百日咳

whore *n* jìnǚ 妓女

whose 1 *pron* (*interrogative*) shéide 谁的; (*relative*): **~ is this?** zhè shì shéide? 这是谁的？; **a country ~ economy is booming** yígè jīngjì zhèngzài péngbó fāzhǎn de guójiā 一个经济正在蓬勃发展的国家 **2** *adj* shéide 谁的; **~ bike is that?** nà liàng zìxíngchē shì shéide? 那辆自行车是谁的？

why wèishénme 为什么; **that's ~** nà jiùshì yuányīn 那就是原因; **~ not?** wèishénme bù? 为什么不？; **I don't know ~ I said that** wǒ bù zhīdào wèishénme nàyàng shuō 我不知道为什么那样说

wicked xié'è 邪恶

wicker téngtiáo 藤条

wicker chair téngyǐ 藤椅

wicket (*in station, bank etc*) guìtái

wide *adj* kuānkuò 宽阔; *experience* fēngfù 丰富; *range* guǎngfàn 广泛; *be 12 yards ~* shí'èr mǎ kuān 十二码宽

wide awake wánquán qīngxǐng 完全清醒

widely *used, known* guǎngfàn 广泛

widen 1 *v/t* jiākuān 加宽 2 *v/i* biànkuān 变宽

wide-open dàkāi 大开

widespread biànbù 遍布

widow guǎfu 寡妇

widower guānfū 鳏夫

width kuāndù 宽度

wield *weapon* huīdòng 挥动; *power* xíngshǐ 行使

wife ⇩ qīzi 妻子

wig jiǎfà 假发

wiggle *v/t hips* bǎidòng 摆动; *loose screw etc* niǔdòng 扭动

wild 1 *adj animal, flowers* yěshēng 野生; *teenager, party* yěxìng 野性; *(crazy: scheme)* mángmù 盲目; *applause* rèliè 热烈; *be ~ about (keen on)* rèzhōng yú 热衷于; *go ~* fēngkuáng huānhū 疯狂欢呼; *(become angry)* biàndé fènnù 变得愤怒; *run ~ (of children)* zìyóu fàngdàng 自由放荡; *(of plants)* sìchù mànyán 四处蔓延 2 *n*: **the ~s** huāngyě 荒野

wilderness *(empty place)* huāngyuán 荒原; *(garden)* zhíwù cóngshēng de dìfāng 植物丛生的地方

wildfire: **spread like ~** fēisù chuánkāi 飞速传开; **wildgoose chase** háowú xīwàng de zhuīxún 毫无希望的追寻; **wildlife** yěshēng niǎoshòu 野生鸟兽

willful *person* gùzhí 固执; *action* gùyì 故意

will¹ *n* LAW yízhǔ 遗嘱

will² *n (willpower)* yìzhì 意志

will³: *I ~ let you know tomorrow* míngtiān wǒ huì gàosù nǐ 明天我会告诉你; *~ you be there?* nǐ huì zài nàr ma? 你会在那儿吗? ; *I won't be back until late* wǒ hěn wǎn cái néng huílái 我很

晚才能回来; *you ~ call me, won't you?* nǐ huì gěi wǒ dǎ diànhuà, shì ba? 你会给我打电话, 是吧? ; *I'll pay for this – no you won't* wǒ lái fùkuǎn – nǐ bú yòng fù 我来付款 – 你不用付; *the car won't start* chē qǐdòng bù liǎo 车启动不了; *~ you tell her that ...?* nǐ kěyǐ gàosù tā ... ma? 你可以告诉她 ... 吗? ; *~ you have some more tea?* nǐ yào-búyào zài hē yìdiǎn chá? 你要不要再喝一点茶? ; *~ you stop that!* déleba! 得了吧!

willing lèyú 乐于

willingly gānxīn qíngyuàn 甘心情愿

willingness yuànyì 愿意

willow liǔshù 柳树

willpower yìzhìlì 意志力

wilt *v/i (of plant)* kūwěi 枯萎

wily jiǎohuá 狡猾

wimp F jiāoqìbāo 娇气包

win 1 *n* shènglì 胜利 2 *v/t* huòshèng 获胜 3 *v/i* yíngdé 赢得

wince *v/i* tuìsuō 退缩

wind¹ 1 *n* fēng 风; *(flatulence)* wèichángzhōng de qì 胃肠中的气; *get ~ of ...* dédào ... de fēngshēng 得到 ... 的风声 2 *v/t*: *be ~ed* qìchuǎnxūxū 气喘嘘嘘

wind² 1 *v/i (of path etc)* wānyán wānyán 蜿蜒 2 *v/t cloth etc* chánrào 缠绕

♦**wind down** 1 *v/i (of party etc)* píngjìng 平静 2 *v/t car window* yáoxià 摇下; *business* jiǎnchǎn 减产

♦**wind up** 1 *v/t clock* shàng fātiáo 上发条; *car window* yáoshàng 摇上; *speech, presentation, affairs* jiéshù 结束; *company* guānbì 关闭 2 *v/i (finish)* jiéshù 结束; *~ in hospital* zuìzhōng zhùjìn yīyuàn 最终住进医院

windfall *fig* yìwài huòdé 意外获得

winding wānyán 蜿蜒

wind instrument guǎnyuèqì 管乐器

windmill fēngchē 风车

window chuānghu 窗户; COMPUT

shìchuāng 视窗; *in the ~* (*of store*) chúchuāng 橱窗

windowpane chuāng bōlí 窗玻璃; **window-shop**: *go ~ping* liúlǎn chúchuāng 浏览橱窗; **windowsill** chuāngtái 窗台

windshield dǎngfēng bōlí 挡风玻璃; **windshield wiper** ⇩ guāshuǐqì 刮水器; **windsurfer** (*person*) fānbǎn yùndòngyuán 帆板运动员; (*board*) fānbǎn 帆板; **windsurfing** fānbǎn yùndòng 帆板运动

windy *weather, day* duōfēng 多风; *it's getting ~* qǐ fēng le 起风了

wine pútaojiǔ 葡萄酒

wine list pútaojiǔ dān 葡萄酒单

wing *n* chìbǎng 翅膀; SP biāncè 边侧

wink 1 *n* zhǎyǎn 眨眼 **2** *v/i* (*of person*) shǐ yǎnsè 使眼色; *~ at* xiàng ... zhǎyǎn 向 ... 眨眼

winner huòshèng zhě 获胜者

winning *adj* huòshèng 获胜

winning post zhōngdiǎn biāozhù 终点标柱

winnings yíngdéde qián 赢得的钱

winter *n* dōngtiān 冬天

winter sports dōngjì yùndòng 冬季运动

wintry hánlěng 寒冷

wipe *v/t* cā 擦; *tape* mǒdiào 抹掉

♦**wipe out** (*kill, destroy*) cuīhuǐ 摧毁; *debt* huánqīng 还清

wire (*made of metal*) jīnshǔsī 金属丝; ELEC diànxiàn 电线

wire netting jīnshǔwǎng 金属网

wiring ELEC xiànlù 线路

wiry *person* shòu ér jiēshí 瘦而结实

wisdom zhìhuì 智慧

wisdom tooth zhìyá 智牙

wise yīngmíng 英明

wisecrack *n* fēngliánghuà 风凉话

wise guy *pej* néngnàigěng 能耐梗

wisely *act* míngzhì 明智

wish 1 *n* yuànwàng 愿望; *best ~es* zhùhǎo 祝好 **2** *v/t* xiǎngyào 想要; *I ~ that ...* yàoshì ... jiù hǎo le 要是 ... 就好了; *~ X well* zhù

X zǒuyùn 祝 X 走运; *I ~ed him good luck* wǒ zhù tā hǎoyùn 我祝他好运 **3** *v/i*: *~ for* qídǎo 祈祷

wishful thinking zhǔguān yuànwàng 主观愿望

wishy-washy *person* kōngdòng wúwù 空洞无物; *color* dàn ér wúwèi 淡而无味

wistful kěwàng 渴望

wit (*humor*) jīzhì yōumò 机智幽默; (*person*) jīzhì yōumò de rén 机智幽默的人; *be at one's ~s' end* zhìqióngjìjìn 智穷计尽

witch nǚwū 女巫

with ◊ (*accompanied by, proximity*) hé ... yìqǐ 和 ... 一起; *she came ~ her sister* tā hé tāde mèimei yìqǐ láide 她和她的妹妹一起来的; *I work ~ some very nice people* hé wǒ yìqǐ gōngzuò de rén dōu hěn hǎo 和我一起工作的人都很好; *I live ~ my daughter* wǒ hé wǒ nǚ'ér zhù zài yìqǐ 我和我女儿住在一起; *a meeting ~ the President* yǔ zǒngtǒng huìmiàn 与总统会面; *~ no money* méiyǒu qián 没有钱; *are you ~ me?* (*do you understand?*) nǐ dǒng wǒde yìsi ma? 你懂我的意思吗? ◊ (*agency*) yòng 用; *decorated ~ flowers* yòng huā zhuāngshì 用花装饰; *write ~ a brush* yòng máobǐ xiězì 用毛笔写字 ◊ (*cause*) yóuyú 由于; *shivering ~ fear* yóuyú kǒngjù ér chàndǒu 由于恐惧而颤抖; *~ a smile / a wave* wēixiàozhe / huīzheshǒu 微笑着 / 挥着手 ◊ (*possession*) yòng yǒu; *the house ~ the red door* yǒu hóng mén de nèige fángzi 有红门的那个房子; *a girl ~ blue eyes* lán yǎnjīng de gūniang 蓝眼睛的姑娘; *we need someone ~ experience* wǒmen xūyào yǒu jīngyàn de rén 我们需要有经验的人

withdraw 1 *v/t complaint, application* chèxiāo 撤消; *money from bank* tíqǔ 提取; *troops* chèhuí 撤回 **2** *v/i* (*of competitor*) tuìchū 退出; (*of troops*) chètuì 撤退

withdrawal (*of complaint, application*) chèxiāo 撤消; (*of money*) tíkuǎn 提款; (*of troops*) chètuì 撤退; (*from drugs*) jièdú 戒毒

withdrawal symptoms jièdú shí de zhèngzhuàng 戒毒时的症状

withdrawn *adj person* gūpì 孤僻

wither diāoxiè 凋谢

withhold bù gěi 不给

within *prep* (*in expressions of distance*) bù chāoguò 不超过; (*inside*) zài ... lǐmiàn 在 ... 里面; (*in expressions of time*) zài ... zhīnèi 在 ... 之内; *we kept ~ the budget* wǒmen bǎochí zài yùsuàn zhīnèi 我们保持在预算之内; *~ my power / my capabilities* zài wǒde quánlì / nénglì zhīnèi 在我的权力 / 能力之内; *~ reach* zài shǒubiān 在手边

without méiyǒu 没有; *~ looking / asking* méi kàn / wèn 没看 / 问

withstand jīndezhù 禁得住

witness 1 *n* (*at trial*) zhèngrén 证人; (*of accident, crime*) mùjīzhě 目击者; (*to signature*) jiànzhèngrén 见证人 2 *v/t accident, crime* mùjī 目击; *signature* zuò liánshǔrén 作连署人

witness stand zhèngrénxí 证人席

witticism miàoyǔ 妙语

witty jīzhì 机智

wobble *v/i* yáohuàng 摇晃

wobbly bùwěn 不稳

wok guō 锅

wolf 1 *n* (*animal*) láng 狼; *fig* (*womanizer*) sèláng 色狼 2 *v/t*: *(down)* lángtūn hǔyàn 狼吞虎咽

wolf whistle *n* tiǎodòu hūshào 挑逗嘬哨

woman nǚrén 女人

woman doctor nǚ yīshēng 女医生

womanizer sèguǐ 色鬼

woman priest nǚ mùshī 女牧师

womb zǐgōng 子宫

Women's Day Sānbā Fùnǚjié 三八妇女节; **women's lib** fùnǚ jiěfàng 妇女解放; **women's libber** gǔchuī fùnǚ jiěfàng de rén 鼓吹妇女解放的人

wonder 1 *n* (*amazement*) jīngqí 惊奇; *no ~!* nánguài! 难怪！; *it's a ~ that ...* qíguàide shì ... 奇怪的是 ... 2 *v/i* gǎndào jīngyà 感到惊讶 3 *v/t* xiǎng zhīdào 想知道; *I ~ if you could help* wǒ xiǎng zhīdào nǐ néngbùnéng bāngmáng 我想知道你能不能帮忙

wonderful jíhǎo 极好

wood mù 木; (*forest*) shùlín 树林

wooded zhǎngmǎn shùmù 长满树木

wooden (*made of wood*) mùzhì 木制

woodwind MUS mùzhì guānyuèqì 木制管乐器

woodwork (*parts made of wood*) mùzhìpǐn 木制品; (*activity*) mùgōnghuó 木工活

wool yángmáo 羊毛

woolen 1 *adj* yángmáozhì 羊毛制 2 *n* yángmáo yīwù 羊毛衣物

word 1 *n* cí 词; (*news*) xiāoxi 消息; (*promise*) nuòyán 诺言; *is there any ~ from X?* yǒuméiyǒu X de xiāoxi? 有没有 X 的消息？; *you have my ~* wǒ xiàng nǐ bǎozhèng 我向你保证; *have ~s* (*argue*) zhēngchǎo zhēng 吵; *have a ~ with X* yǔ X sīxià tántán 与 X 私下谈谈 2 *v/t article, letter* xuǎncí 选词

wording cuòcí 措辞

word processing wénzì chǔlǐ 文字处理

word processor (*software*) wénzì chǔlǐjī 文字处理机

work 1 *n* gōngzuò 工作; *out of ~* shīyè 失业; *be at ~* shàngbān 上班; *I go to ~ by bus* wǒ zuò gōngchē qù shàngbān 我坐公车去上班 2 *v/i* (*of person*) gōngzuò 工作; (*of machine*) yùnzhuǎn 运转; (*succeed*) zòuxiào 奏效; *I used to ~ with him* wǒ céng hé tā yìqǐ gōngzuò 我曾和他一起工作; *how does it ~?* (*of device*) zhèi dōngxi zěnme yùnzhuǎn? 这东西怎么运转？ 3 *v/t employee* shǐ gōngzuò 使工作; *machine* kāidòng 开动

♦**work off** *bad mood, anger* xiāochú 消除

消除; *flab* chúqù 除去

♦ **work out 1** *v/t problem* nòng míngbái 弄明白; *solution* zhǎochū 找出 **2** *v/i (at gym)* dàliàng yùndòng 大量运动; *(of relationship etc)* qǔdé chénggōng 取得成功

♦ **work out to** *(add up to)* zǒngjìwéi 总计为

♦ **work up** *enthusiasm* jīqǐ 激起; *appetite* jīfā 激发; **get worked up** *(get angry)* shēngqì 生气; *(get nervous)* jīnghuāng 惊慌

workable *solution* kěxíng 可行

workaholic *n* F gōngzuòkuáng 工作狂

worker gōngrén 工人; **she's a good ~** *(of student)* tā hěn huì gōngzuò 她很会工作

work day *(hours of work)* gōngzuòrì 工作日; *(not a holiday)* fēi xiūxīrì 非休息日; **workforce** láodònglì 劳动力; **work hours** gōngzuò qījiān 工作期间

working class *n* gōngrén jìjí 工人阶级

working-class *adj* gōngrén jìjí 工人阶级

working knowledge jīběn zhīshí 基本知识

workload gōngzuòliàng 工作量; **workman** gōngrén 工人; **workmanlike** jìshù xiánshú 技术娴熟; **workmanship** jìyì 技艺; **work of art** jīngzhìde wùpǐn 精致的物品; **workout** duànliàn 锻炼; **work permit** gōngzuò xǔkě 工作许可; **workshop** gōngchǎng 工场; *(seminar)* jiǎngxíbān 讲习班; **work station** gōngzuòzhàn 工作站; **work unit** (gōngzuò) dānwèi (工作) 单位

world shìjiè 世界; **the ~ of computers** / **the theater** diànnǎo / xìjù lǐngyù 电脑 / 戏剧领域; **out of this ~** F hǎo dé bùdéliǎo 好得不得了

worldly shìsú 世俗; *person* lǎochéng liàndá 老成练达

world power shìjiè qiángguó 世界强国; **world war** shìjiè dàzhàn 世界大战; **worldwide 1** *adj* biànjí shìjiè 遍及世界 **2** *adv* quánshìjiè 全世界

worm *n* chóngzi 虫子

worn-out *shoes, carpet, part* pòjiù 破旧; *person* jīnpílìjìn 筋疲力尽

worried dānyōu 担忧

worry 1 *n* dānyōu 担忧 **2** *v/t* dānxīn 担心; *(upset)* shǐrén yōuchóu 使人忧愁 **3** *v/i* dānyōu 担忧; **it will be alright, don't ~!** méiyǒushì, bié dānxīn! 没有事, 别担心!

worrying lìngrén dānxīn 令人担心

worse 1 *adj* gènghuài 更坏 **2** *adv* gèng bùhǎo 更不好

worsen *v/i* biàndé gènghuài 变得更坏

worship 1 *n* chóngbài 崇拜 **2** *v/t* chóngbài 崇拜; *fig* àimù 爱慕

worst 1 *adj* zuìhuài 最坏 **2** *adv* zuìzāo 最糟 **3** *n*: **the ~** zuìhuài 最坏; **if the ~ comes to the ~** rúguǒ zuì zāogāo de shì fāshēng 如果最糟糕的事发生

worth *adj*: **$20 ~ of gas** jiàzhí wéi èrshí měiyuán de qìyóu 价值为二十美元的汽油; **be ~ ...** *(in monetary terms)* zhí ... 值 ...; **be ~ reading** / **seeing** zhídé dú / kàn 值得读 / 看; **be ~ it** hěn zhídé 很值得

worthless *object* wú jiàzhí 无价值; *person* méiyòng 没用

worthwhile *cause* zhídé zuò 值得做; **be ~** zhídé 值得

worthy kějìng 可敬; *cause* zhídé zhīchí 值得支持; **be ~ of** *(deserve)* zhídé 值得

would: **I ~ help if I could** rúguǒ wǒ néng de huà, wǒ huì bāngmángde 如果我能的话, 我会帮忙的; **I said that I ~ go** wǒ shuōguò wǒ huì qù 我说过我会去; **I told him I ~ not leave unless ...** wǒ gàosù tā, chúfēi ... bùrán wǒ búhuì zǒu 我告诉他, 除非 ... 不然我不会走; **~ you like to go to the movies?** nǐ xiǎng qù kàn diànyǐng ma? 你想去看电影

吗？；~ *you mind if I smoked?* wǒ chōuyān nǐ jièyì ma? 我抽烟你介意吗？；~ *you tell her that …?* qǐng nǐ gàosù tā … hǎoma? 请你告诉她 … 好吗？；~ *you close the door?* qǐng guānshang mén, hǎoma? 请关上门，好吗？；I ~ *have told you but …* wǒ běn yīnggāi gàosù nǐ, dànshì … 我本应该告诉你，但是…；I ~ *not have been so angry if …* rúguǒ … wǒ jiù búhuì nàme shēngqì 如果 … 我就不会那么生气

wound 1 *n* shāng 伤 **2** *v/t* (*with weapon*) dǎshāng 打伤; (*with remark*) shānghài 伤害

wow! *interj* āiya! 哎呀！

wrap *v/t parcel, gift* bāo 包; (*wind*) chánrào 缠绕; (*cover*) bāozhù 包住

♦ **wrap up** *v/i* (*against the cold*) chuān nuǎnhuo de yīwù 穿暖和的衣物

wrapper bāozhuāng zhǐdài 包装纸袋

wrapping bāozhuāng cáiliào 包装材料

wrapping paper bāozhuāngzhǐ 包装纸

wreath huāquān 花圈

wreck 1 *n* cánhái 残骸; *be a nervous ~* shìge shénjìngzhì 是个神经质 **2** *v/t* huǐhuài 毁坏; *plans, career, marriage* huǐmiè 毁灭

wreckage (*of car, plane*) cánhái 残骸; (*of marriage, career*) cánhuǐ zhuàngtài 残毁状态

wrecker tuōchē 拖车

wrecking company gùzhàng qìchē fúwù gōngsī 故障汽车服务公司

wrench 1 *n* (*tool*) bānzi 扳子; (*injury*) niǔshāng 扭伤 **2** *v/t* (*injure*) niǔshāng 扭伤; (*pull*) měnglā 猛拉

wrestle shuāijiāo 摔跤

♦ **wrestle with** *problems* nǔlì duìfù 努力对付

wrestler shuāijiāo yùndòngyuán 摔跤运动员

wrestling shuāijiāo yùndòng 摔跤运动

wrestling match shuāijiāo bǐsài 摔跤比赛

wriggle *v/i* (*squirm*) niǔdòng 扭动; (*along the ground*) wānyán xíngjìn 蜿蜒行进

♦ **wriggle out of** zhǎo jièkǒu bìmiǎn 找借口避免

♦ **wring out** *cloth* nǐngchū 拧出

wrinkle 1 *n* zhòuwén 皱纹 **2** *v/t clothes* shǐ qǐ zhòuzhě 使起皱褶 **3** *v/i* (*of clothes*) chū zhòuzhě 出皱褶

wrist shǒuwàn 手腕

wristwatch shǒubiǎo 手表

write 1 *v/t* xiě 写; *check* kāi 开 **2** *v/i* xiě 写; (*of author*) xiězuò 写作; (*send a letter*) xiěxìn 写信

♦ **write down** xiěxià 写下

♦ **write off** *debt* gōuxiāo 勾销; *car in crash* shǐ chéng fèipǐn 使成废品

writer zuòzhě 作者

write-up pínglùn 评论

writhe niǔdòng 扭动

writing (*as career*) xiězuò 写作; (*hand-writing*) zìjì 字迹; (*words*) wénzì 文字; (*script*) shūxiě tǐxì 书写体系; *in ~* yǐ shūmiàn xíngshì 以书面形式

writing brush máobǐ 毛笔

writing paper xìnzhǐ 信纸

wrong 1 *adj* cuòwù 错误; *be ~* (*of person*) cuòle 错了; (*morally*) bú duì 不对; *what's ~?* zěnmele? 怎么了？; *there is something ~ with the car* chē yǒu diǎn máobìng 车有点毛病 **2** *adv* cuòwù 错误; *go ~* (*of person*) fàn cuòwù 犯错误; (*of marriage, plan etc*) chūxiàn wèntí 出现问题 **3** *n* bù gōngzhèng de shì 不公正的事; *be in the ~* yīngshòu zébèi 应受责备

wrongful bù héfǎ 不合法

wrongly cuòwù 错误

wrong number bōcuòle hàomǎ 拨错了号码

wry: ~ smile kǔxiào 苦笑

XYZ

xenophobia kǒngwài zhèng 恐外症

X-ray 1 *n* X guāng zhàopiān X 光照片 **2** *v/t* zhào X guāng 照 X 光

yacht yóutǐng 游艇

yachting chèng yóutǐng 乘游艇

yachtsman yǒutǐng jiàshǐ yuán 游艇驾驶员

yak máoniú 牦牛

Yangtze River Chángjiāng 长江

Yank F Měiguó Lǎo 美国佬

yank *v/t* měnglā 猛拉

yap *v/i* (*of small dog*) wāngwang jiào 汪汪叫; F (*talk a lot*) guālā guālā 呱啦呱啦

yard[1] (*of prison, institution etc*) fàngfēng chǎng 放风场; (*behind house*) yuànzi 院子; (*for storage*) duīchǎng 堆场

yard[2] (*measurement*) mǎ 码

yardstick *fig* héngliáng biāozhǔn 衡量标准

yarn *n* (*thread*) shāxiàn 纱线; F (*story*) qítán 奇谈

yawn 1 *n* hēqian 呵欠 **2** *v/i* dǎ hēqian 打呵欠

year nián 年; *for ~s* F xǔduō nián 许多年; *we were in the same ~* (*at school*) wǒmén shì tóngjí de 我们是同级的; *~ of the tiger / dog* hǔ / gǒu nián 虎 / 狗年; *be born in the ~ of the ...* shǔ ... shǔ ...; *I was born in the ~ of the dragon* wǒ shǔ lóng 我属龙

yearly *adj & adv* měinián 每年

yearn *v/i* kěwàng 渴望

♦**yearn for** kěwàng 渴望

yearning *n* xiàngwǎng 向往

yeast xiàomǔ 酵母

yell 1 *n* jiàohǎn 叫喊 **2** *v/i* rāngrang 嚷嚷 **3** *v/t* dàjiào 大叫

yellow 1 *n* huángsè 黄色 **2** *adj* huáng 黄

Yellow Emperor Huángdì 黄帝; **yellow pages** huángyè 黄页; **Yellow River** Huánghé 黄河; **Yellow Sea** Huánghǎi 黄海

yelp *n & v/i* jiānjiào 尖叫

yen FIN rìyuán 日元

yes shìde 是的; *are you Mr Wang? – ~* nín shì Wáng xiānsheng ma? – shìde 您是王先生吗？– 是的 ◊ (*repetition of verb etc*): *are you cold? – ~* nǐ lěng bu lěng? – lěng 你冷不冷？– 冷; *do you like it here? – ~* nǐ xǐhuan zhèr ma? – xǐhuan 你喜欢这儿吗？– 喜欢 ◊ (*showing agreement*) duì 对; *he should go – ~* tā yīnggāi qù – duì 他应该去 – 对 ◊ (*accepting suggestion*) xíng 行; *let's go see a movie – ~* zánmen qù kàn diànyǐng ba – xíng 咱们去看电影吧 – 行

yesman *pej* zǒugǒu 走狗

yesterday zuótiān 昨天; *the day before ~* qiántián 前天

yet 1 *adv* qìjīn 迄今; *as ~* dàocǐ wéizhǐ 到此为止; *have you finished ~?* nǐ wánle méiyǒu? 你完了没有？; *he hasn't arrived ~* tā hái méidào ne 他还没到呢; *is he here ~? – not ~* tā láile ma? – méine 他来了吗？– 没呢 **2** *conj*: *~ I'm not sure* kěshì wǒ háishì bù kěndìng 可是我还是不肯定

yield 1 *n* (*from fields etc*) chǎnliàng 产量; (*from investment*) lìrùn 利润 **2** *v/t fruit, good harvest* chūchǎn 出产; *interest* shēngxī 生息 **3** *v/i* (*to enemy*) tóuxiáng 投降; (*to wish*) dāying 答应; (*of traffic*) rànglù 让路

yogurt suānnǎi 酸奶

yoke (*for carrying*) biǎndan 扁担; (*for oxen*) è 轭

yolk dànhuáng 蛋黄

you (*singular*) nǐ 你; (*plural*) nǐmen 你们; (*polite*) nín 您 (*polite plural, rare*) nínmen 您们; ~ *never know* shéi zhīdào 谁知道; *it's good for* ~ duì nǐ yǒu hǎochù 对你有好处

young *person* niánqīng 年青; *wine* wèi chéngsh óu 未成熟

youngster qīngshàonián 青少年

your (*singular*) nǐde 你的; (*plural*) nǐmen 你们的; (*polite singular*) nínde 您的; (*polite plural*) nín-mende 您们的

yours (*singular*) nǐde 你的; (*plural*) nǐmende 你们的; (*polite singular*) nínde 您的; (*polite plural*) nín-mende 您们的; (*at end of letter*) yǒngyuǎn shì nǐde 永远是你的; *a friend of* ~ nǐde péngyǒu 你的朋友

yourself nǐ zìjǐ 你自己; *by* ~ nǐ zìjǐ dúzì 你自己独自

yourselves nǐmen zìjǐ 你们自己; *by* ~ nǐmen zìjǐ 你们自己

youth (*age*) qīngchūn niándài 青春年代; (*young man*) xiǎo huǒzi 小伙子; (*young people*) qīngshào nián 青少年

youthful *fashion, ideas* shìyú qīngnián 适于青年; *person* zhāoqì péngbó 朝气蓬勃

youth hostel qīngnián zhāodàisuǒ 青年招待所

yuan (*Chinese money*) yuán 元

Yuan Dynasty Yuán Cháo 元朝

zap *v/t* COMPUT (*delete*) xiāochū 消除; F (*kill*) shāsǐ 杀死; F (*hit*) kuàijī 快击

♦**zap along** F (*move fast*) kuàisù jìnxíng 快速进行

zapped F (*exhausted*) jīngpí lìjìn 筋疲力尽

zappy F *car, pace* kuài 快; (*lively,*

energetic) jīnglì chōngpèi 精力充沛

zeal rèxīn 热心

zebra bānmǎ 斑马

Zen Chán 禅

Zen Buddhism Chánzōng Fójiào 禅宗佛教

zero líng 零; *10 below* ~ língxià shídù 零下十度

zero growth wú zēngzhǎng 无增长

♦**zero in on** (*identify*) xiàng … jízhōng zhùyì lì 向 … 集中注意力

zest rèqíng 热情

zigzag 1 *n* qūzhé xiàntiáo 曲折线条 **2** *v/i* qūzhé xíngjìn 曲折行进

zilch F yīwú suǒyǒu 一无所有

zinc xīn 锌

♦**zip up** *v/t dress, jacket* lā lāliàn 拉拉链; COMPUT yāsuō 压缩

zip code yóuzhèng biānmǎ 邮政编码

zip drive COMPUT yāsuō qūdòngqì 压缩驱动器

zipper lāliàn 拉链

zodiac huángdào dài 黄道带; *signs of the* ~ huángdào shí'èr gōngtú 黄道十二宫图

zombie F (*idiot*) mùdāidai de rén 木呆呆的人; *feel like a* ~ (*exhausted*) kuǎle kuǎ 了

zone qū 区

zoo dòngwù yuán 动物园

zoological dòngwù xué 动物学

zoology dòngwù xué 动物学

zoom F (*move fast*) jísù xíngshǐ 急速行驶

♦**zoom in** COMPUT fàngdà 放大

♦**zoom in on** PHOT lājìn 拉近

♦**zoom out** COMPUT suōxiǎo 缩小

zoom lens kěbiàn jiāojù jìngtóu 可变焦距镜头

Taiwanese equivalents

This list contains a selection of mainland Chinese words in the first Chinese column and, in the second Chinese column, equivalents which are more likely to be used in Taiwan. The Taiwanese words are written in traditional characters. It should be said that there is a good deal of linguistic interaction between the two language groups.

ace (in cards)	jiānr 尖儿	A A
adhesive plaster	chuàngkětì 创可贴	OK bèng OK绷
aerobics	zēng yǎng jiànshēn fǎ 增氧健身法	yǒuyǎng wǔdào 有氧舞蹈
afternoon: good afternoon	xiàwǔ hǎo 下午好	wǔ'ān 午安
air conditioning	kōngtiáo 空调	lěngqì 冷气
ankle	jiǎowàn 脚腕	jiǎohuái 脚踝
answerphone	lùyīn diànhuà 录音电话	diànhuà dálùjī 电话答录机
awesome F	gàilemàole 盖了帽了	kùbìle 酷毙了
ballpoint (pen)	yuánzhū bǐ 圆珠笔	yuánzǐbǐ 原子笔
Band-Aid®	chuàngkětì 创可贴	OK bèng OK绷
bar code	tiáoxíng mǎ 条形码	tiáomǎ 条码
barbecue n	shāokǎo huì 烧烤会	kǎoròu 烤肉
bicycle n	zìxíng chē 自行车	jiǎotàchē 脚踏车
blood donor	xiànxuè zhě 献血者	juānxiěrén 捐血人
burglar alarm	fángqiè jǐngbào qì	fángdàoqì 防盗器 防窃警报器
butter n	huángyóu 黄油	nǎiyóu 奶油
cell phone	shǒutí diànhuà 手提电话	xíngdòng diànhuà 行动电话
check out (of hotel)	jiézhàng 结账	tuìfáng 退房
checkout time	jiézhàng shíjiān 结账时间	tuìfáng shíjiān 退房时间
cheese	nǎilào 奶酪	rǔluò 乳酪, qǐshì 黄鹣
cheesecake	nǎilào nàngāo 奶酪蛋糕	qǐshì dàngāo 起士蛋糕
chips	shǔpiàn 薯片	yángyùpiàn 洋芋片
college exam	gāokǎo 高考	liánkǎo 联考
condom	bìyùn tào 避孕套	bǎoxiǎntào 保险套
connecting flight	liányùn fēijī 联运飞机	zhuǎnjiē bānjī 转接班机
container COM	jízhuāng xiāng 集装箱	huòguì 货柜
container ship	jízhuāng xiāng chuán 集装箱船	huòguìchuán 货柜船
corkscrew	luósī qǐzi 螺丝起子	luósī kāijiǔqì 螺丝开酒器
crosswalk	rénxíng héngdào 人行横道	xíngrén chuānyuèdào 行人穿越道
cursor	guāngbiāo 光标	yóubiāo 游标

deodorant	chúxiù jì 除臭剂	fángchòujì 防臭剂
desktop computer	táishìjī 台式机	zhuōshàngxíng diànnǎo 桌上型电脑
disco(theque) (*place*)	dítīng 迪厅	díshìkě 迪士可
disk COMPUT	cípán 磁盘	cídiépiàn 磁碟片
disk drive	cípán dàijī 磁盘带机	cídiéjī 磁碟机
diskette	ruǎn cípán 软磁盘	cídiépiàn 磁碟片
donut	zhá miànbǐngquān 炸面饼圈	tiántiánquān 甜甜圈
dress *n* (*for woman*)	liányīqún 连衣裙	yángzhuāng 洋装
driving school	jiàshǐ xuéxiào 驾驶学校	jiàxùn zhōngxīn 驾训中心
duplex (*apartment*)	èrliánshì gōngyù 二连式公寓	shuāngpīn gōngyù 双拼公寓
DVD	shùzì shìpín guāngpán 数字视频光盘	shùwèi xiǎnshì guāngdié 数位显示光碟
epicenter	zhènzhōng 震中	zhènyāng 震央
feedback	fǎnkuì xìnxī 反馈信息	huíkuì 回馈
feminism	nǚquán zhǔyì 女权主义	nǚxìngzhǔyì 女性主义
feminist	nǚquán zhǔyì zhě 女权主义者	nǚxìngzhǔyì zhě 女性主义者
floppy (**disk**)	ruǎnpán 软盘	cídiépiàn 磁碟片
folk dance	mínjiānwǔ 民间舞	mínsú wǔdào 民俗舞蹈
garbage	lājī 垃圾	lèsè 垃圾
gin and tonic	kuíníng dùsōngzǐjiǔ 奎宁杜松子酒	qínjiǔ jiā kuíníngshuǐ 琴酒加■嬡 ■
Gobi Desert	Gēbìtān 戈壁滩	Gēbì dàshāmò 戈壁大沙漠
hamburger	hànbǎobāo 汉堡包	hànbǎo 汉堡
hard currency	yìngtōnghuò 硬通货	qiángshì huòbì 强势货币
hard disk	yìngpán 硬盘	yìngdié 硬碟
highlighter (*pen*)	cǎibǐ 彩笔	yíngguāngbǐ 萤光笔
instant noodles	fāngbiànmiàn 方便面	pàomiàn 泡麵
junk food	kuàicān 快餐	lèsè shíwù 垃圾食物
Laos	Lǎowō 老挝	Liáoguó 寮国
laptop COMPUT	xiédài shì diànnǎo 携带式电脑	bǐjìxíng diànnǎo 笔计型电脑
Mandarin (*language*)	Pǔtōnghuà 普通话	Guóyǔ 国语
mayo, mayonnaise	dànhuángjiàng 蛋黄酱	měinǎizī 美奶滋
MBA	gōngshāng guǎnlǐxué shuòshì 工商管理学硕士	qìguǎn shuòshì 企管硕士
Mount Everest	Zhūmùlǎngmǎfēng 珠穆朗玛峰	Shèngmǔfēng 圣母峰
mouse COMPUT	shǔbiāo 鼠标	huáshǔ 滑鼠

New Zealand	Xīnxīlán 新西兰	Nǐuxīlán 纽西兰
North Korea	Běicháoxiān 北朝鲜	Běi Hán 北韩
orange juice	chéngzhīr 橙汁儿	lǐuchéngzhī 柳橙汁
page (*call*)	chuánhū 传呼	dǎ hūjiàoqì 打呼叫器
pager	chuánhūjī 传呼机	hūjiàoqì 呼叫器
pineapple	bōluó 菠萝	fènglí 凤梨
platform RAIL	zhàntái 站台	yuètái 月台
pool (*game*)	pǔ'ěrdànzǐxì 普尔弹子戏	zhuàngqiú 撞球
potato chips	zháshǔpiàn 炸薯片	yángyùpiàn 洋芋片
printer (*machine*)	dǎyìnjī 打印机	yìnbiǎojī 印表机
project (*housing area*)	tǒngjiàn zhùzháiqū 统建住宅区	guózhái 国宅
pump *n*	bèng 泵	(*for water*) chōushuǐjī 抽水机; (*for air*) dǎqìtǒng 打气筒
salad	sèlā 色拉	shālā 沙拉
salad dressing	sèlā tiáowèizhī 色拉调味汁	shālājiàng 沙拉酱
sauna	zhēngqìyù 蒸汽浴	sānwēnnuǎn 三温暖
scalper	piàofànzi 票贩子	mài huángniúpiàode rén 卖黄牛票的人
silicon	guī 硅	xì 矽
silicon chip	guīpiàn 硅片	xìpiàn 矽片
slot machine (*for vending*)	tóubìshòuhuòjī 投币售货机	zìdòng fànmàijī 自动贩卖机
smart card	shuākǎ 刷卡	cōngmíngkǎ 聪明卡
snooker	táiqiú 台球	sīnuòkè 斯诺克
solitaire (*card game*)	dānrén zhǐpái xì 单人纸牌戏	jiēlóng 接龙
space shuttle	hángtiān fēijī 航天飞机	tàikōngsuō 太空梭
speed limit	sùdù jíxiàn 速度极限	sùdù xiànzhì 速度限制
tampon	yuèjīng shuān 月经栓	wèishēngmiántiáo 卫生棉条
taxi	chūzūchē 出租车	jìchéngchē 计程车
teamwork	pèihé 配合	tuánduì jīngshén 团队精神
tissue paper	báozhǐ 薄纸	miànzhǐ 面纸
tonic (**water**)	tānglìshuǐ 汤力水	kuíníngshuǐ 奎宁水
tractor	tuōlājī 拖拉机	qiānyǐnjī 牵引机
T-shirt	yuánlǐng shān 圆领衫	T xuè T恤
Velcro®	zhānkòu 粘扣	móshùtiē 魔术贴
wife	qīzi 妻子	tàitai 太太, lǎopó 老婆
windshield wiper	guāshuǐqì 刮水器	yǔshuā 雨刷

Numbers

0	〇 líng		1,000,000	百万 **bǎiwàn**
1	一 yī		10,000,000	千万 **qiānwàn**
2	二 **èr** *or* **liǎng***		100,000,000	万万 **wànwàn**
3	三 sān			
4	四 sì		100,000,000	亿 **yì**
5	五 **wǔ**			
6	六 liù			

The following more complex characters are also used on bills, checks etc.

7	七 qī
8	八 bā
9	九 jiǔ
10	十 shí
11	十一 shíyī
12	十二 shí'ér
13	十三 shísān *etc*
20	二十 èrshì
30	三十 sānshí
40	四十 sìshí *etc*
21	二十一 èrshíyī
35	三十五 sānshíwǔ
99	九十九 jiǔshíjiǔ
100	百 bǎi
105	一百零五 yìbǎi líng wǔ
300	三百 sānbǎi
350	三百五十 sānbǎi wǔshí
356	三百五十六 sānbǎi wǔshíliù
1,000	千 qiān
1,005	一千零五 yìqiān líng wǔ
1,050	一千零五十 yìqiān líng wǔshí
5,300	五千三百 wǔqiān sānbǎi
10,000	万 wàn
65,300	六万五千三百 liùwàn wǔqiān sānbǎi
100,000	十万 shíwàn

0	零	**líng**
1	壹	**yī**
2	贰	**èr**
3	叁	**sān**
4	肆	**sì**
5	伍	**wǔ**
6	陆	**liù**
7	柒	**qī**
8	捌	**bā**
9	玖	**jiǔ**
10	拾	**shí**
100	佰	**bǎi**
1,000	仟	**qiān**

Ordinal numbers

Ordinal numbers are formed by putting **dì** in front of the cardinal numbers:

1	一	**yī**
1st	第一	**dìyī**
2	二	**èr**
2nd	第二	**dì'èr**
3	三	**sān**
3rd	第三	**dìsān**
etc		

* **liǎng** is used when the number two is used in combination with a measure word.